Footprint

Malaysia

The travel guide

Handbook

Joshua Eliot, Jane Bickersteth, Anna Barton
and Claire Baggaley

*To begin to understand the Malay you must
live in his country, speak his language,
respect his faith, be interested in his interests,
humour his prejudices, sympathise with him
and help him in trouble, and share his
pleasures and possibly his risks. Only thus
can you hope to win his confidence.*

Frank Swettenham, *Malay Sketches*, 1895.

Malaysia Handbook
Fourth edition
© Footprint Handbooks Ltd 2002

Published by Footprint Handbooks
6 Riverside Court
Lower Bristol Road
Bath BA2 3DZ. England
T +44 (0)1225 469141
F +44 (0)1225 469461
Email discover@footprintbooks.com
Web www.footprintbooks.com

ISBN 1 903471 27 3
CIP DATA: A catalogue record for this
book is available from the British Library

Distributed in the USA by
Publishers Group West

Credits

Series editors
Patrick Dawson and Rachel Fielding

Editorial
Editors: Ian Emery and Caroline Lascom
Maps: Sarah Sorensen and Felicity
Laughton

Production
Page layout: Leona Bailey
Proofreading: Carol Franklin and Emma
Bryers
Maps: Claire Benison and Robert Lunn
Colour maps: Kevin Feeney
Cover: Camilla Ford

Design
Mytton Williams

Photography
Front cover: Telegraph Images
Back cover: gettyone Stone
Inside colour section: Eye Ubiquitous;
Art Directors and Trip; James Davis
Worldwide; Impact, Pictures Colour
Library; Robert Harding Picture Library

Print
Manufactured in Italy by LEGOPRINT

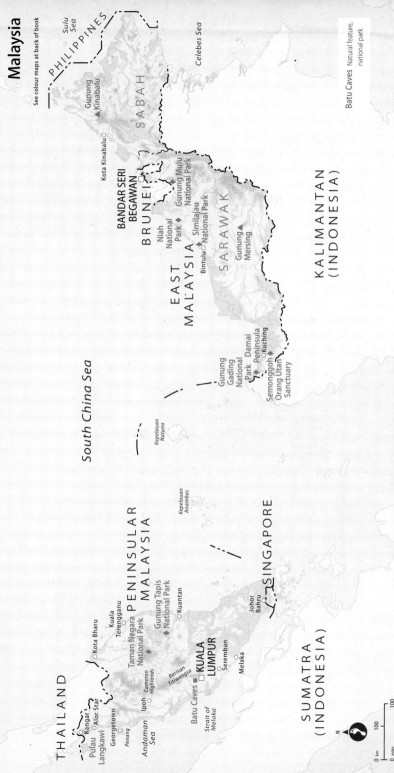

Malaysia

See colour maps at back of book

Batu Caves Natural feature, national park

Contents

Left The summer palace on the once-magnificant Pantai Kok beach

Right The Moorish architecture of the Sultan Abdul Samad building in Kuala Lumpur

A foot in the door

Below *The Dhean Hoy Temple, Kuala Lumpur*
Right *Pulau Tioman on Peninsular Malaysia's east coast, arguably one of the world's most beautiful beaches*

Above *River arteries link the sleepy fishing kampungs on Pulau Tioman*
Right *The 88-storey Petronas Towers in Kuala Lumpur are the world's tallest buildings*
Overleaf *The limestone massifs of Gunung Mulu, the second highest mountain in Sarawak*

Introduction

The 'Malay Archipelago' is a term intimately associated with the mystery of the East. It conjures up images of sultans, head-hunters and pirates; munificent jungles brimming with exotic life; clippers cutting through the warm waters of the South China Sea; and of explorers discovering new tribes while planters sit on verandahs taking tiffin and, later, a pink gin laced with quinine to keep malaria at bay.

Today's Malay Archipelago is somewhere very different. Singapore's *godowns* (warehouses) have been replaced by towering glass and steel office blocks. The rickshaw pullers, who rarely lived long enough to see middle age, have become English-speaking workers with incomes among the highest in the world and a health system that sustains them well into old age. Malaysia, thrusting and self-confident, is following where Singapore has been, with a mission to transform itself into a developed country by 2020 – and notwithstanding its brush with the Asian economic crisis.

Lord of the Rim

Malaysia divides into two different worlds. West – or Peninsular – Malaysia is the industrial, political and economic heartland of the country, while East Malaysia is a territory of forests and rivers, mountains and caves, tribes and abundant wildlife. Sandwiched between Singapore to the south and Thailand to the north, the Peninsula states support the great bulk of the country's population. And, just as Malaysia itself is a country of two halves, so the Peninsula too can be broadly divided into a vibrant western side and a bucolic east separated by the Barisan Titiwangsa, the Peninsula's jungle spine. Kuala Lumpur, the capital, and most of the country's main urban centres are to be found on the western side of the Peninsula. Tin was discovered here, so roads and railways were built which in turn favoured the growth of the rubber industry. As Malays proved reluctant to leave their *kampungs* to assist Britain to develop the Malaysian colonial economy, Chinese and Indian labourers were shipped in. So was born Malaysia's plural society. The east coast of the peninsula, in the process, became a half-forgotten backwater.

Split personality

Malaysian Borneo or East Malaysia, encompassing the states of Sabah and Sarawak, dovetails more closely with the romantic vision of 'Malaya'. While cities like Kuching and Kota Kinabalu have been colonized by the people (Malays, Chinese) and ideas of the Peninsula, the countryside remains dominated by tribal groups, collectively known as Dayaks, like the Iban, Kelabit, Kenyah, Bidayuh and Kayan, and much of it is still forested. Beyond the coast and the main towns, roads are limited and often air or river transport are the only sensible ways to travel in the interior. While the headhunters that so terrified the early colonists – and the Japanese during the Second World War – may be consigned to the history books, the territory is still mightily imposing. The country's finest national parks, indeed some of the world's finest protected areas, can be found here.

Eastern promise

Singapore is a world-class city with world-class attractions and only the barest whiff of the East. When the Orient does appear it has invariably been sequestered by New Singapore. Hundred year-old shophouses have been converted into drinking holes and edgy studios while the bumboats which used to ferry cargo from freighter to *godown* now carry tourists up and down the restaurant-lined Singapore River. Renowned for its epicurean delights, Singapore is aiming to become a regional centre for the arts too.

Singapore swing

Below *Colourful celebrations in Kuala Lumpur to commemorate Malaysian independence*
Right *Wat Chayamangkalara, the largest Thai temple in Penang*

Above *Danum Valley's virgin jungle is the lowest expanse of undisturbed lowland diptocarp forest in Sabah*
Right *With the 99 islands of Langkawi to discover, life's definitely a beach*
Overleaf *The excellence of the puppet is judged according to the fineness of the chisel-work and subtle painting*

Peninsular Malaysia

Malaysia's capital, Kuala Lumpur, is a colonial creation that owes its existence to the rich tin deposits found in the area in the 1850s. So the historical claims of Kuala Lumpur, or KL, as it is more commonly known, date back little more than a century. Chinatown, the Moorish-style railway station and one or two other notable buildings represent the old; the new is showcased in the 88-storey, 421-metre-high Petronas Twin Towers, the world's tallest building.

Capital gains

The far more venerable city of Melaka – or Malacca – has churches and trading houses reflecting its Dutch and Portuguese parentage and also a fine Chinatown. An even better array of colonial-era Chinese shophouses are to be found in Georgetown, Penang, which vied briefly with Singapore in the early 1800s for the honour of trading capital of the Melacca Straits. It lost. Today conservationists are battling to protect its architectural inheritance from rapacious developers. Ipoh is another tin-rush settlement colonised by Chinese and deserves more attention. It has a well preserved Old Town and some of the best Chinese restaurants in Malaysia.

Trading places

As the French did in Indochina and the Dutch in the East Indies, the British hunted out hill retreats where they could escape the heat and humidity of the lowlands.
The Cameron Highlands were converted into a tropical version of the home counties with beamed cottages and rose gardens in the 1920s, as was the less well-known Fraser's Hill. Despite the sprawling development of golf courses and luxury hotels it is still possible to settle down to a cream tea or roast beef and Yorkshire pudding and imagine, just for a brief moment, that the British never left.

The high life

The development of the west coast's beaches and islands had to await the invention of the bikini and suntan oil, as well as the fascination for tanned bodies. Penang Island is the west coast's best known and most developed beach resort – now linked to the mainland by one of the world's longest bridges. Langkawi and Pangkor islands are altogether more beautiful although no longer the idyllic retreats they once were.

Beyond the pale

To truly escape it is necessary to travel over the Barisan Titiwangsa to the East Coast. It is sold by Tourism Malaysia as the 'real Malaysia' using rather hackneyed PR images of a coastline fringed by coconut palms, beaches and sleepy fishing villages. While the West may be the industrial and political core of Malaysia, the East is regarded as the heartland of Malay culture and tradition. Malay sports from top-spinning to kite-flying and crafts like batik-making and silverwork remain vibrant. Islam, particularly in Kelantan and Terengganu, strongly influences public behaviour and private morals.

East of Eden

The densely forested Tioman island, once rated as one of the world's top 10 desert islands escapes by *Time* magazine, is fringed by white coral-sand beaches. East coast tropical islands such as Tioman, along with stretches of quiet (and not so quiet) coastline and beaches, offer far more diving possibilities than the west coast. While the coral around the offshore islands like Pulau Redang and the Perhentian group is not world class, this is a good area to learn to scuba dive. There is also the additional attraction of turtles, including the endangered Giant Leatherback, which come ashore to lay their eggs at numerous locations including Rantau Abang. Inland are the Peninsular's finest national parks, Endau Rompin and Taman Negara. Fishing, hiking, waterfalls, rapids and 1500 m-peaks, along with wildlife – from the Sumatran rhinoceros to civets, wild boar, hornbills and the (very) odd tiger – add to their allure.

Paradise found

Malaysian Borneo

Jungle fever The Skrang, Belaga, Rejang and Baram rivers with their trading settlements, tribal villages, rapids and terrifyingly fast river boats are the entrees into inland Sarawak and the state's magnificent natural heritage. It is an area well worth exploring by boat. There is an array of 14 protected areas from the tiny, coastal Tanjung Datu National Park to the vast and inaccessible Lanjak-Entimau National Park. Not only do these sanctuaries protect arguably the world's most diverse terrestrial ecosystem – the lowland tropical rainforest – but there is also trekking, rafting and climbing to entice the adventurous traveller.

Tribes & tributaries Of particular note are the stupendous caves of the Gunung Mulu National Park and the archaeologically significant Niah Caves. The latter have revealed evidence of early human settlement in bones and cave paintings while the former are simply part of what is one of the world's most extensive cave systems stretching over nearly 200 kilometres and including the world's largest cavern. For those who like some more human contact with their jungles, caves and wildlife, Sarawak's 1,500-odd longhouses, lining the rivers – which provide the means for getting around – are a fascinating insight into a fast-disappearing way of life. Kuching, Sarawak's capital, supports arguably Malaysia's finest museum, the Sarawak Museum, with an incomparable ethnographic collection. At the opposite extreme, is the 'living', but in reality expensively – and skilfully – contrived, Sarawak Cultural Village, on the Damai Peninsula, where well-trained 'tribal' men and women (some not tribal at all!) act out their allotted roles.

Wild at heart Like its sister state to the south, Sabah is a natural wonderland with nearly 20 protected areas. From the state capital of Kota Kinabalu it is easy to see Malaysia's highest mountain, Gunung Kinabalu, which rises to more than 4,000m. It is not the 'highest mountain in Southeast Asia', as it is continually billed, but is nonetheless a wonderful, invigorating climb. Early morning on the summit is an incomparable experience. The world's largest flower, the Rafflesia, grows here although few get to see it – the plant only flowers for a few days a year. Sandakan is Sabah's second city and within easy reach of the town is another of the state's more popular protected areas: the small Sepilok Orang Utan Rehabilitation Centre. Here domesticated and half-domesticated orang utans are weaned off their unnatural diets of pizza, beer and such like and reintroduced to the wild.

Waterworld Two of Sabah's most memorable protected areas are marine. The Turtle Islands National Park, 40 km from Sandakan, is Southeast Asia's most important turtle-breeding area. Here it is possible to see the kings of Malaysia's reptile population, Green and Hawksbill turtles, laying their eggs on three tiny islands. The second, the Sipadan Island Marine Reserve off Sabah's northeast coast, rises on a stalk 200 m from the bed of the Celebes Sea. When Jacques Couusteau visited Sipadan in 1989 he was dumfounded. "Now", he remarked, "we have found an untouched piece of art". The diving here is the best in Malaysia – indeed, some of the best in the world.

Left *Sipadan Island is a Shangri -La for serious divers with coral reefs without parallel in Malaysia*
Below *The thousands of gilded statues at the Kek Lok Si Temple in Penang, dedicated to the historic Buddha*

Above *Hindu devotees pierce their bodies with sharp skewers during the Thaipusam festival*
Left *Mount Kinabalu , the pride of Sabah and the most impressive sight in Borneo*
Overleaf *The vast karst limestone cavern at Batu Caves*

Essentials

2

Essentials

Planning your trip

Getting around Peninsular Malaysia and Singapore is not difficult and even making the trip from Kota Bharu at the northern extremity of the east coast, down to Melaka, towards the southern end of the west coast, need only take a day's travelling by road. Air links between the major towns are, self-evidently, faster still. However, many visitors with only, say, a fortnight in the area wonder whether it is possible to combine a trip to Peninsular Malaysia and the East Malaysia states of Sabah and Sarawak. This requires a little more thought. There are regular domestic air connections between the Peninsula and the major cities of East Malaysia, and from there with smaller towns in the Bornean interior. For those intending, for example, to fly to Kota Kinabalu, Sabah, stay a few days at Tanjung Aru Beach, and then return to the Peninsular, taking in East and West Malaysia should pose no difficulties. However, if intending to do more than this, such as climbing Mount Kinabalu, travelling upriver on the Baram, Rejang or Skrang rivers, or hiking through one of the national parks , then a little more leeway in terms of time is required. A minimum period to just scratch the surface would be one week; more preferable would be 10 days to two weeks. Of course some people spend many weeks in just one area and still profess to have seen only a fraction of what is on offer. (For more background on itineraries in Sarawak see page 313).

Where to go

Fraser's Hill and the Cameron Highlands offer a taste of colonial Malaya, and there are good walks around the Cameron Highlands. The Genting Highlands is more ersatz and kitsch, a favourite haunt of Kuala Lumpur's nouveau riche. Maxwell Hill is the quietest of the hill stations.

Hill stations

The national parks of the Peninsula do not compare with those of East Malaysia. Nonetheless, Taman Negara and the Endau Rompin National Park are both well worth visiting. Rantau Abang on the east coast is a stretch of shoreline where turtles come to lay their eggs. In East Malaysia, Sarawak and Sabah offer a wealth of parks and conservation areas. Some, like the Semonggoh Orang Utan Sanctuary and the Bako National Park outside Kuching, and the Sepilok Orang Utan Rehabilitation Centre and the Turtle Islands National Park outside Sandakan are accessible as day trips from the state capitals. Other parks, like the Niah and Gunung Mulu national parks, require several days to explore properly.

Wildlife & jungle

The caves at the Niah and Gunung Mulu national parks and Gunung Kinabalu, Malaysia's highest mountain, are stupendous natural features worth visiting in themselves. There are many islands you can visit off both the west and east coasts of the Peninsula, although the east coast islands come closer to popular notions of palm-fringed island idylls. Penang has a wide selection of hotels and facilities, and some may view it as over-developed. Langkawi, though more recently 'discovered', has also developed rapidly in recent years. Also off the west coast is Pulau Pangkor. Tioman, off the Peninsula's east coast, is less developed than Langkawi and Penang and there are also numerous other islands which are still less touched by the hands of humans. On the Peninsula itself, Kampung Cerating is the best known beach resort, which still has a backpacker feel to it, although it is hardly off the beaten track. There are also other groups of hotels and chalets dotted up and down the east coast. Sabah and Sarawak do not have beach 'resorts' to compare with those – at least in scale – of the Peninsula. However, there are some fine beaches and excellent snorkelling and diving, especially

Natural features

Essentials

in the Tunku Abdul Rahman National Park and the Sipadan Island Marine Reserve. Small resorts include those at Damai, north of Kuching; Tanjung Aru, outside Kota Kinabalu; and Labuan.

Historical sites   Melaka is one of Malaysia's two historic gems. There are buildings dating from the Portuguese and Dutch periods, as well as some fine Chinese shophouses. Georgetown, the capital of Penang, is Malaysia's second city of architectural and historical note, with probably the finest assembly of Sino-colonial architecture in the region. Both have come under serious development pressure over the years and this may be one reason why they have not yet made UNESCO's list of World Heritage Sites.

Culture
For information on visiting longhouses in Sarawak, see page 347
Traditional Malay culture is best preserved on the east coast of the Peninsula and especially in the Malay heartland of Kelantan (Kota Bharu), with its rural *kampongs*, or villages, and thriving craft industry. The Sarawak Cultural Village near Kuching offers an anaesthetized vision of tribal life and culture; the upriver 'tribes' and longhouses give a taste of the real thing. The Rajang, Skrang, and Kinabatanagan rivers, dotted with towns and small tribal settlements, are all worth exploring by boat.

Shopping   KL is the best place to buy the full range of handicrafts from batik to blowpipes, although prices are higher than at their source. The east coast is the centre of the Peninsula's Malay handicraft industry, particularly Kelantan (Kota Bharu). Sabah and Sarawak are the places to find tribal handicrafts. Many are on sale in the main towns, although smaller communities potentially offer the best buys.

Museums   KL's museums are less impressive than those in Singapore but are still worth visiting and are getting better all the time – the last few years has seen some extentive upgrading and renovation. Surprisingly, perhaps the best museum in East Malaysia is the Sarawak Museum in Kuching with its superb ethnographic collection (this too has been upgraded recently).

Itineraries   The above is only a selection of places of interest and is not exhaustive. It is designed to assist in planning a trip to the region. Any 'highlight' list is inevitably subjective.

Itineraries for Peninsular Malaysia and Singapore are easy to customise to meet your own needs and interests. Distances are not enormous, transport is good and the seasons rarely put particular places off-limits. (The exception to this is the east coast where the monsoon between November and February brings rough seas and heavy rains. Some islands are difficult or impossible to reach at this time, and some national parks closed too.) Most travellers arrive either in Singapore or KL, although a good number also enter Malaysia overland across its northern border with Thailand. From all these points of arrival it is possible to reach any of Malaysia's beach resorts, bar some of the islands off the east coast which require a morning boat departure from the mainland. The main question is how to combine, say, a visit to Melaka, to the south, with a few days on the beach in Penang, to the north, or east to Tioman island.

It requires a little more effort to co-ordinate and plan a visit to one of the Peninsular's national parks where two, three or four days may be necessary to explore the area to any degree. And as noted above, for those who want to combine a visit to the Peninsula with a trip to East Malaysia, and particularly if this includes river trips, trekking and longhouse stays, then even more time should be put to one side. As a rule-of-thumb, one week is the minimum length of time to get a taster of Peninsular Malaysia and Singapore, and two weeks if this is to be combined with East Malaysia.

When to go

When planning itineraries in Malaysia, always take into account the rainy seasons; the best time to visit the Peninsula's east coast is between March and September. Trips along the east coast and interior jungles are not advisable between November and February, during the northeast monsoon. The east coast suffers flooding at this time of year, and it is inadvisable and also impossible to take fishing boats to offshore islands such as Pulau Tioman as the sea can be very rough. Taman Negara National Park is closed from November to the end of January. Other parts of Peninsular Malaysia can be visited year round as the rainy season is not torrential, although it is fairly wet during the northeast monsoon period. Rainfall is worst from May to September on the west coast of the Peninsula, but it is never very heavy.

In East Malaysia, March and June are the best times to visit the interior, the worst rains are usually from November to February and some roads are impassable in these months. Conversely, in the dry season, some rivers become unnavigable. In recent years the onset of the wet and dry seasons in both Sabah and Sarawak have become less predictable; environmentalists ascribe this to deforestation and/or global warming, although there is no scientifically proven link.

Climate
For more information on climate, see page 552

Note that school holidays run from mid- to late February, mid-May to early June, mid- to late August and late November to early January. During these periods it is advisable to book hotels. Room rates also increase significantly during these holiday periods. Finally, during Ramadan (see Festivals, page 57) travel can be more difficult and many restaurants close during daylight hours, expecially in the east coast states of Kelantan and Terengganu. After dusk many Muslims break their fast at stalls which do a roaring trade, although generally Ramadan is not a period when Muslims eat out, but instead dine at home.

Holidays

Tour operators

Abercrombie & Kent Travel, Slaone Square House, Holbein Place, London SW1W 8NS, T0845-0700610, F0700607, www.abercrombiekent.com Global company with 32 offices worldwide offering a large range of tours in and around Malaysia. *Audley Travel*, 6 Willows Gate, Stratton Audley, Oxfordshire, OX27 9AU. T01869 276 200, www.audleytravel.com *Dive Worldwide*, 23 Burnham Avenue, Bognor Regis, West Sussex, PO21 2LB, T0124 3870618, info@diveworldwide.com *Eastern Oriental Express*, Sea Containers House, 20 Upper Ground, London, SE1 9PF, T0207-8055100, F8055908, www.orient-expresstrains.com Offices worldwide. Operates luxury train

In the UK

trips between Thailand, Malaysia and Singapore. *Exodus Travels*, 9 Weir Road, London SW12 0LT, T020 8675 5550, F8673 0779. www.exodus.co.uk Wide range of trips in Southeast Asia including Malaysia. The Borneo Explorer tour includes river journeys and the caves at the Niah National Park. *Explore Worldwide*, 1 Frederick Street, Aldershot, Hampshire, GU11 1LQ, T01252-760000, www.explore.co.uk Arranges small group tours (average 16 people) with any different types of trip offered including cultural excursions, adventure holidays and natural history tours. *Flightbookers*, UK, T020-77572444, sales@flightbookers.co.uk Organizes anything from airfares to self-drive trips and cruises, to jungle treks. *Gold Medal Travel*, The Trident Centre, Port Way, Ribble Docklands, Preston, Lancs, PR2 2QG, T0870-6063000, enquiries@goldmedal.co.uk *Kuoni Travel*, 5 Montpellier Street, SW7 1EX, T020-75898959, www.kuoni.co.uk Consistently high-quality service tour operator which organises trips all over Southeast Asia. *Magic of the Orient*, 2 Kingsland Court, Three Bridges Road, Crawley, West Sussex, RH10 1HL, www.magic-of-the-orient.com Specialists in tailor-made tours to Asia. *realworld-travel*, The Foundry, 156 Blackfriars Road, London, SE1 8EN, T020-759 32323, www.realworld-travel.co.uk *Silk Steps*, Tyndale House, 7 High Street, Chipping Sodbury, Bristol, BS37 6BA. www.silksteps.co.uk *Symbiosis*, 113 Bolingbroke Grove, London, SW11 1DA, T020-79245906, F020-79245907, www.symbiosis.co.uk An environmentally aware company that offers expeditions respecting traditional values and cultures. It specializes in tailor-made tours. *Thomas Cook Holidays*, PO Box 5, 12 Conigsby Road, Peterborough PE3 8XP, www.tch.thomascook.com Organized tours as well as beach holidays all over Southeast Asia. *Travelbag Adventures*, 15 Turk Street, Alton, Hampshire. GU34 1AG. T01420 541007, F541022. mail@travelbag-adventures.com

In Malaysia *Borneo Eco Tours*, Shoplot 12a, 2nd Floor, Lorong Bernam 3, Taman Soon Kiong, 88300 Kota Kinabalu, Sabah, Malaysia, www.borneoecotours.com Specializing in environmentally aware tours. *Ideal Holidays*, No 4, Ground Floor, Jalan Api-Api, Off Jalan Gaya, PO Box 21490, 88772 Luyang, Kota Kinabalu, Sabah, Malaysia, www.ideal-borneo.com Another Malaysian based tour operator. Four set tours with the option of creating your own tailormade tour. *Sarawak Tourism Board*, Level 6 & 7, Bangunan Yayasan Sarawak, Jalan Masjid, 93400, Kuching, P.O. Box 2950, 93758 Kuching, Sarawak, Malaysia. T6082 423 600, F416 700, www.sarawaktourism.com

In Australia *Intrepid Travel*, 12 Spring Street, Fitzroy, VIC, Austrailia, www.intrepidtravel.com.au Australian company with agents all over the world. Offers three different tours of Malaysia. *Coulter-Goodall Tours*, 115a Pt Cartwright Drive, Kawana Waters, Sunshine Coast, 4575 Australia, T61-7-54446500, cgtours@ozemail.com.au

Finding out more

Malaysians are pretty Internet savvy so there is a fair amount of information on the web. Tourist board websites are OK for a browse but tend to be rather generalized. The best, oddly, are those for the East Malaysian states of Sabah and Sarawak.

Useful websites

tourism.gov.my The website for *Tourism Malaysia*.
www.sarawak.gov.my The Sarawak Tourism Board's own website, with 20 pages of information, mostly commercial.
www.asiainfo-by-cj.com A good and informative non-commercial website on Malaysia and some other parts of Southeast Asia.
www.kiat.net A website set up by a young Malaysian with excellent material on things like Putrajaya, Cyberjaya, KLIA and transport systems in Malaysia.

Essentials

☞ Malaysian tourist board offices overseas

Australia, 65 York St, Sydney, NSW 2000, T92994441, mtpb.sydney@tourism.gov.my; 56 William St, Perth, WA 6000, T09-4810400, mtpb.perth@tourism.gov.my

Canada, 830 Burrard St, Vancouver, BC, V6Z 2K4, T604-6898899, mtpb.vancouver@tourism.gov.my

France, 29 Rue des Pyramides, 75001 Paris, T331-42974171, mtpb.paris@tourism.gov.my

Germany, Rossmarkt 11, 60311 Frankfurt Am Main, T069-283782, mtpb.frankfurt@tourism.gov.my)

Hong Kong, Gd Flr, Malaysia Bldg, 47-50 Gloucester Rd, T2528-5810, mtpb.hongkong@tourism.gov.my

Italy, Second Flr, Piazza San Babila 4/B, 20122 Milan, T02-796702, mtpb.milan@tourism.gov.my

Japan, 5F Chiyoda Bldg, 1-6-4 Yurakucho Chiyoda-ku, Tokyo 100, T 03 3501 8691, mtpb.tokyo@tourism.gov.my; 10th Flr, Cotton Nissay Bldg, 1-8-2 Otsubo-Honmachi, Nishi-ku, Osaka 550-004, T06-444 1220, mtpb.osaka@tourism.gov.my

Singapore, #01-01B/C/D, 80 Robinson Rd, SINGAPORE 068898, T02-5326321/5326351 mtpb.singapore@tourism.gov.my

South Africa, P.O. Box 1125, Saxonworld 2132, Johannesburg, T002711 3270400 mtpb.johannesburg@tourism.gov.my

Sweden, Klarabergsgatan 35, 2tr Box 131, 10122 Stockholm, T 0046-8-24 99 00 mtpb.stockholm@tourism.gov.my

Thailand, Unit 1001 Liberty Square, 287 Silom Rd, Bangkok 10500, T631 1994-7, mtpb.bangkok@tourism.gov.my; 183/81 Phang-Nga Road, Amphur Muang, Phuket 83000, T 076 220 192/3 mtpb.phuket@tourism.gov.my

UK, 57 Trafalgar Square, London WC2N 5DU, T020-79307932. mtpb.london@tourism.gov.my

USA, 818 Suite 804, West Seventh St, Los Angeles, CA 90017, T213 6899702, mtpb.la@tourism.gov.my; 120 East 56th Street, Suite 810, New York 10022, T001212 754 - 1113/1114/1115/1117 mtpb.ny@tourism.gov.my

---

headlines.yahoo.com/full_coverage/world/malaysia/ An excellent news site for Malaysian current affairs.
www.jaring.my/ For general information on the country.
www.malaysiaairlines.com Malaysia Airlines.
htp://members.tripod.com Homepage of *Malaysia Railways*.

Singapore www.sg/ Links to homepage with good information on events, health, sports, business and more.
www.ste.com.sg A bulletin board for businesses to post notices and adverts; also a directory of licensed travel agents in Singapore.

Note that websites on Asia are multiplying like rabbits and this makes searching a sometimes frustrating business

General www.city.net/regions/asia Pointer to information on Asian countries.
www.branch.com:80/silkroute/ Information on hotels, travel, news and business in Asia.
www.agora.stm.it/politic Information on political parties and organizations, good links, by country or by region.
www.aseansec.org Homepage of the Asean Secretariat, the Southeast Asian regional organization of which Singapore is a founder member. Lots of government statistics, acronyms etc.For websites on Malaysia and Southeast Asia, see page 23. For a list of tourist boards overseas, see box on page 24; see also box on embassies and consulates.

Malaysian embassies and consulates

Australia, High Commission, 7 Perth Ave, Yarralumla, Canberra, ACT 2600, T06-2731543

Austria, Prinz Eugenstrasse 18, A-1040 Vienna, T5051042

Belgium, 414A, Ave de Tervuren, 1150 Brussels, T7626767

Brunei, High Commission, No 473 Kg Pelambayan, Jln Kota Batu, PO Box 2826, Bandar Seri Begawan, T228410

Canada, High Commission, 60 Boteler St, Ottawa, Ontario KIN 8Y7,

France, 2 Bis Rue Benouville, Paris, T45531185

Germany, Mittelstrasse 43, 5300 Bonn 2, T0228-376803

Indonesia, 17, Jln Imam Bonjol, 10310 Jakarta Pusat, Tÿ336438; Consulate: Medan, T511233

Italy, Via Nomentana 297, Rome, T8415764

Japan, 20-16, Nanpeidai-Machi, Shibuya-ku, Tokyo 150, T34763840

Netherlands, Runtenburweg 2, 2517 KE The Hague, T070-3506506

New Zealand, High Commission, 10 Washington Ave, Brooklyn, Wellington, T852439

Singapore, 301, Jervois Rd, Singapore 1024, T2350111

Spain, Paseo de La Castellano 91-50, Centro 23, 28046 Madrid, T341-5550684

Sri Lanka, High Commission, 47/1 Jawatta Rd, Colombo 7, T94-1508973

Sweden, Engelbrektsgatan 5, PO Box 26053, 100 41 Stockholm, T08-6795990

Switzerland, Laupenstrasse 37, 3008 Berne, T252105

Thailand, 35, South Sathorn Rd, Bangkok 10120, T2861390; Consulate: Songkhla, T311062

UK, High Commission, 45, Belgrave Square, London SW1X 8QT, T020-72358033

USA, 2401, Massachusetts Ave NW, Washington, DC 200008, T202-3282700; Consulates: New York, T212-4902722; Los Angeles, T213-6212991

Vietnam, Block A-3, Van Phuc, Hanoi, T53371.

Essentials

Language

Bahasa Melayu (the Malay language, normally just shortened to *bahasa*) is the national language. It is very similar to Bahasa Indonesia, which evolved from Malay, and can be understood in southern Thailand, throughout Borneo and as far afield as the Moro areas of the southern Philippines. All communities, Malay, Chinese and Indian, as well as tribal groups in Sabah and Sarawak, speak Malay, as most are schooled in the Malay medium. Nearly everyone in Malaysia speaks some English, except in remoter rural areas, although the standard of English declined markedly during the 1980s and 1990s. Realizing this, and because of the general acceptance that good English is essential for business, the government sought to reverse the decline during the mid-1990s. The other main languages spoken in Malaysia include the Chinese dialects of Mandarin, Cantonese and Hokkien as well as Tamil and Punjabi.

For those wanting to get a better grasp of the language, it is possible to take courses in KL (enquire at *Tourism Malaysia* offices) and other big cities. The best way to take a crash course in Malay is to buy a 'teach-yourself' book; there are several on the market, but one of the best ones is *Malay in 3 Weeks*, by John Parry and Sahari bin Sulaiman (Times Books, 1989), which is widely available. A Malay/English dictionary or phrase book is a useful companion too; these are also readily available in bookshops.

Basic grammar is very simple: there are no tenses, genders or articles and the structure of sentences is straightforward. Plurals are also easy: one man, for example is *laki*, men is *laki-laki*, often denoted as *laki*. Pronunciation is not difficult as there is a close relationship between the letter as it is written and the sound. Stress is usually placed on the second syllable of a word. For example *restoran* (restaurant) is pronounced *res-TO-ran*. **Basic grammar & vowels**

For pronunciation of vowels and consonants: *a* is pronounced as *ah* in an open syllable, or as in *but* for a closed syllable; *e* is pronounced as in *open* or *bed.*; *i* is pronounced as in *feel*; *o* is pronounced as in *all*; *u* is pronounced as in *foot*. The letter *c* is pronounced as in *ch* as in *change* or *chat*. The *r*'s are rolled.

Disabled travellers

Disabled travellers are not well catered for in Malaysia (and this stands in contrast with the situation in Singapore (see page 576). Pavements are treacherous for those in wheelchairs, crossing roads is a hazard, and public transport is not well adapted for those with disabilities. This is surprising for a country which in so many other ways presents itself as cutting edge. But it is not impossible for disabled people to travel in Malaysia. For those who can afford to stay in the more expensive hotels, the assistance of hotel staff makes life a great deal easier, and there are also lifts and other amenities. And even those staying in budget accommodation will find that local people are helpful, sometimes heart-warmingly so.

Gay and lesbian travellers

Like Singapore (see page 576), Malaysia – officially at least – is not particularly accommodating of what might be regarded as alternative lifestyles and homosexuality remains a crime. (Bear in mind that even Malaysia's former deputy prime minister, Anwar Ibrahim, was charged with sodomy in 1999.) However there is a bubbling gay scene in KL and, to a lesser extent, in Johor Bahru, Melaka, KK, Kuching and Penang. The best website is http://www.utopia-asia.com/tipsmala.htm   The website's homepage states: "Gay life in Malaysia is blossoming. However, Muslims, both Malay and visitors, are subject to antiquated religious laws which punish gay or lesbian sexual activity with flogging and male transvestism with imprisonment. Police may arrest and harass any gay person (Muslim or non-Muslim) in a public place (ie cruise spots), so discretion is advised."

The Utopia website provides a listing of gay clubs, bars, discos and gyms in Malaysia (Johor Bahru, KL, KK, Kuching, Melaka and Penang) and also meeting spots for gays in those towns and cities. Other websites for gays in Malaysia include: for KL http://members.tripod.com/gaycapitalkl/ for Sarawak http://www.geocities.com/swkgayscene/ and a websites for gays in Malaysia and Singapore http://www.geocities.com-/WestHollywood/3676/

Student travellers

Anyone in full-time education is entitled to an International Student Identity Card (ISIC). These are issued by student travel offices and travel agencies across the world and offer special rates on all forms of transport and other concessions and services. The ISIC head office is: ISIC Association, Box 9048, 1000 Copenhagen, Denmark, T45-33939303.

Students can benefit from discounts on some entrance charges and special deals, for example, on trains (see page 33). However there is no institutionalised system of discounts for students.

Travelling with children

Most western baby products are now available in Malaysia

Travelling with children is a touch more difficult than in child-friendly Singapore (see page 576), but nonetheless is an awful lot easier – and safer – than in most other so-called 'developing' countries. In fact it is a good deal easier than travelling with children in the 'developed' world. Food hygiene is good, bottled water is sold amost everywhere, public transport is cheap (including taxis) and ubiquitous, most museums and other attractions provide good discounts for children, powdered milk and baby food (as well as all the other baby/child paraphernalia) are widely sold, and high chairs are available in most restaurants (even coffee shops). Furthermore, children are not viewed as problem objects to be tucked away in some corner and instructed to 'behave' and 'keep quiet'.

Many people are daunted by the prospect of taking a child to a 'developing' country, but Malaysia's level of development is high and if you are thinking of a place in the Asian tropics to travel with your child then Malaysia – and particularly the Peninsula – is one of the easiest and safest bets. Naturally, it is not something to be taken on lightly; travelling is slower and more expensive and there are additional health risks for the child or baby. But it can be a most rewarding experience. Children are excellent passports into a local culture. You will also receive the best service, and help from officials and members of the public when in difficulty.

Children in Malaysia are given 24-hour attention by parents, grandparents and siblings. They are rarely left to cry and are carried for most of the first 8 months of their lives since crawling is considered animal-like. A non-Asian child is still something of a novelty and parents may find their child frequently taken off their hands, even mobbed in more remote areas. This can either be a great relief (at mealtimes, for instance) or most alarming. Some children love the attention, others react against it; it is best simply to gauge your own child's reactions.

Disposable **nappies** can be bought in most towns in Malaysia but can be expensive. If you are staying any length of time in one place, it may be worth taking Terry's (cloth) nappies. All you need is a bucket and some double-strength nappy cleanse (simply soak and rinse). Cotton nappies dry quickly in the heat and are generally more comfortable for the baby or child.

The advice given in the health section on **food and drink** (see page 60) should be applied even more stringently where young children are concerned. Be aware that expensive hotels may have squalid cooking conditions; the cheapest street stall can be more hygienic. Where possible, try to watch food being prepared. Stir-fried vegetables and rice or noodles are the best bet; meat and fish may be pre-cooked and then left out before being re-heated. Fruit can be bought cheaply right across Southeast Asia: papaya, banana and avocado are all excellent sources of nutrition, and can be self-peeled ensuring cleanliness. Powdered milk is also available throughout Malaysia, although most brands have added sugar. But if taking a baby, breast feeding is strongly recommended. Powdered food can be bought in most towns; the quality may not be the same as equivalent foods bought in the West, but it is perfectly adequate for short periods. Bottled water and fizzy drinks are also sold widely. If your child is at the 'grab everything and put it in mouth' stage, a damp cloth and some Dettol (or equivalent) are useful. Frequent wiping of hands and tabletops can help to minimize the chance of infection.

At the hottest time of year, **air conditioning** may be essential for a baby or young child's comfort when sleeping. This rules out many of the cheaper hotels, but air conditioned accommodation is available in all but the most out-of-the-way spots. Guesthouses probably won't have cots, so it is worth bringing a travel cot, but more expensive hotels should be able to provide them (but it is worth emailing or phoning to check). When the child is bathing, be aware that the water could carry parasites, so avoid letting him or her drink it.

Public transport may be a problem; trains are fine but long bus journeys are restrictive and uncomfortable. Hiring a car is undoubtedly the most convenient way to see a country with a small child. Back-seatbelts are fitted in more recent models and it is possible to buy child-seats in capital cities and rent them from larger car hire outfits.

Essentials

Checklist
The following list provides an idea of what to take when travelling with children in Malaysia

Baby wipes; child paracetamol; disinfectant; first aid kit; flannel; immersion element for boiling water; Kalvol and/or Snuffle Babe or equivalent for colds; instant food for under-one-year-olds; mug/bottle/bowl/spoons; nappy cleanse, double-strength; ORS/ORT (Oral Rehydration Salts or Therapy) such as Dioralyte, widely available in the countries covered here, and the most effective way to alleviate diarrhoea (it is not a cure); portable baby chair, to hook onto tables – not essential but can be very useful; sarung or backpack for carrying child (and/or light weight collapsible buggy); sterilizing tablets (and an old baby-wipes container for sterilizing bottles, teats, utensils); cream for nappy rash and other skin complaints such as Sudocreme; sunblock, factor 15 or higher; sunhat; Terry's (cloth) nappies, liners, pins and plastic pants; thermometer; zip-lock bags for carrying snacks, powdered food; wet flannel.

Women travellers

Women – if not accompanied by men – usually attract unwarranted attention, particularly in more Islamic areas, such as the east coast

Most male attention is bravado and there have been few serious incidents involving foreign female tourists (or male, for that matter). However women should be sensitive to the fact that Malaysia is a predominantly Muslim country. In the east coast states of Kelantan and Terengganu particularly, where the Islamic Parti Islam is in crontrol, women should dress appropriately, avoiding short skirts and singlets. In beach resorts clothing conventions are more relaxed but topless bathing, while it occurs in some areas (eg Pulau Tioman), is beyond the pale as far as most Malaysians are concerned. If swimming outside beach resort areas bear in mind that Malay women usually bathe fully clothed so stripping off and running like a gazelle into the sea with nothing more than a bikini may raise one or two eyebrows.

When travelling it is best to keep to public transport and to travel during the day. Hitching is not advisable for women travelling on their own.

Working in the country

For a website listing jobs and working opportunities in Malaysia, as well as tips (and links) for anyone thinking of working there, see www.escapeartist.com/Malayia/Malaysia.html The Ministry of Human Resources (MOHR) provides the official view of labour law and practice in Malaysia, details of which can be found on its website, www.jaring.my/ksm/index.html

Before you travel

Getting in

Visas
Passports should be valid for six months beyond the period of intended stay

No visa is required for a stay of up to three months (provided it is not for the purpose of working) for citizens from Commonwealth countries (except India, Bangladesh, Sri Lanka and Pakistan), Albania, Algeria, Austria, Bahrain, Belgium, Britain, Czech Republic, Denmark, Egypt, Finland, Germany, Hungary, Germany, Iceland, Republic of Ireland, Italy, Japan, Jordan, South Korea, Kuwait, Lebanon, Liechtenstein, Luxembourg, the Netherlands, Norway, Morocco, Oman, Qatar, San Marino, Saudi Arabia, Republic of Slovakia, Sweden, Switzerland, Tunisia, Turkey, the United Arab Emirates, the USA and North Yemen.

Citizens of France, Greece, Poland and South Africa, as well most African and Latin American countries, are permitted to stay for one month without a visa.

On arrival visitors normally receive a one- or two-month visitor's permit (Commonwealth citizens get two-month permit). Usually, those arriving by air get two month permit, while those arriving overland, get a one-month permit. If you intend to stay longer, permits can be painlessly extended up to three months at immigration departments in KL, Penang or Johor Bahru.

Citizens of ASEAN countries (Brunei, Cambodia, Indonesia, Laos, Myanmar/Burma, Philippines, Singapore, Thailand and Vietnam), do not need advance visas for visits not exceeding one month – they are issued on arrival. Nationals of most other countries including Afghanistan, Iran, Iraq, Libya, Syria and South Yemen may stop over in Malaysia for up to 14 days without advance visas but it is preferable to have proof of outward bookings. Citizens of Bulgaria, Rumania and Russia may stay for seven days without a visa. Applications for visas should be made well in advance to the nearest Malaysian diplomatic mission, or, in countries where there are no Malaysian representatives, to the British Consular Representative.

Visitors arriving by air and who are staying less than 72 hours in the country are eligible for visa-free entry

Visit passes issued for entry into Peninsular Malaysia are not automatically valid for entry into the East Malaysian states of Sabah and Sarawak. On entry into East Malaysia from Peninsular Malaysia visitors have to go through immigration even though the flight is an internal one. You get a new stamp in your passport and it may actually reduce the time you can stay in Malaysia. A month's stamp is usual – if you want more, then you must ask the official. (The reason for this odd state of affairs is that Sabah and Sarawak maintain control over immigration and even Malaysian visitors from the 'mainland' are required to obtain a travel permit to come here.) Apply to the immigration offices in Kota Kinabalu and Kuching for an extension. There are certain areas where permits are necessary in East Malaysia – for example for upriver trips in Sarawak permits are obtained from the residents' offices (see appropriate sections). All national parks in Peninsular and East Malaysia require permits from the national or state parks offices.

Duty-free allowance 200 cigarettes, 50 cigars or 250 g of tobacco and one litre of liquor or wine. Cameras, watches, pens, lighters, cosmetics, perfumes and portable radio/cassette players are also duty-free in Malaysia. Visitors bringing in dutiable goods such as video equipment may have to pay a refundable deposit for temporary importation. It is advisable to carry receipt of purchases to avoid this problem.

Customs

Export restrictions Export permits are required for arms, ammunition, explosives, animals and plants, gold, platinum, precious stones and jewellery (except reasonable personal effects), poisons, drugs, motor vehicles. Unlike Singapore, export permits are also required for antiques (from the Director General of Museums, Muzium Negara, Kuala Lumpur).

A certificate of vaccination for yellow fever is necessary for those coming from endemic zones except for children under one year of age.

Vaccinations
See also page 60

What to take

Travellers usually take too much. Almost everything is available in the main towns and cities – and often at a lower price than in western countries. Remoter areas are inevitably less well supplied.

Suitcases are not appropriate if you are intending to travel overland by bus. A backpack, or even better a travelpack (where the straps can be zipped out of sight), is recommended. Travelpacks have the advantage of being hybrid backpacks-suitcases; they can be carried on the back for easy porterage, but they can also be taken into hotels without the owner being labelled a 'hippy'. **NB** For serious hikers, a backpack with an internal frame is still by far the best option for longer treks.

In terms of clothing, dress in Malaysia (and, but to a lesser extent, Singapore) is relatively casual – even at formal functions. Suits are not necessary except in a few of the

Essentials

most expensive restaurants. However, although formal attire may be the exception, dressing tidily is the norm. Women particularly should note that in many areas of Malaysia, they should avoid offending Muslim sensibilities and dress 'demurely' (ie keep shoulders covered and wear below-knee skirts or trousers). This is particularly true on the east coast of the Peninsula, especially in Kelantan, but does not generally apply in most beach resorts.

There is a tendency, rather than to take inappropriate articles of clothing, to take too many of the same article. Laundry services are cheap, and the turn-around rapid.

Checklist
The following lists provide an idea of what to take with you on a trip to Malaysia

Bumbag, earplugs, first aid kit, insect repellent and/or electric mosquito mats, coils, international driving licence, passports (valid for at least 6 months), photocopies of essential documents, short-wave radio, spare passport photographs, sun protection, sunglasses, Swiss Army knife, torch, umbrella, wet wipes, zip-lock bags

Those intending to stay in budget accommodation might also include: cotton sheet sleeping bag, money belt, padlock (for hotel room and pack), soap, student card, toilet paper, towel, travel wash.

For women travellers: a supply of tampons (although these are available in most towns), a wedding ring for single female travellers who might want to help ward off the attentions of amorous admirers.

There is a good smattering of camping grounds in Malaysia, both in Peninsular Malaysia and in Sabah and Sarawak. If intending to camp, then all the usual equipment is necessary: a tent, stove, cooking utensils, sleeping bag etc.

Money

Currency
For the latest exchange rates check www.oanda.com/convert/classic

The unit of currency is the Malaysian dollar, or **ringgit** (RM), which is divided into 100 cents, or **sen**. Bank notes come in denominations of RM1, 5, 10, 20, 50, 100, 500 and 1,000. Coins are issued in 1, 5, 10, 20 and 50 sen denominations. The ringgit is one of the world's few currencies still pegged to the US$ at a rate of RM3.80 = US$1. This has been the case for the last three years. However the fall in the value of the Japanese yen at the beginning of 2002 was putting pressure on the government to review the US$ peg.

Credit cards

Most of the bigger hotels, restaurants and shops accept international credit cards, including American Express, BankAmericard, Diners, MasterCard and Visa. Visa and MasterCard are the most widely accepted. Cash advances can be issued against credit cards in most banks, although some banks – notably Bank Bumiputra – limit the amount that can be drawn. A passport is usually required for over-the-counter transactions. It is also possible to draw cash from ATMs (Automatic Teller Machines) if you have a PIN number (Personal Identification Number). Maybank, with branches in most towns, will accept both Visa and MasterCard at its ATMs. Cards with the Cirrus mark will also be accepted at most banks' ATMs.

Travellers' cheques

These can be exchanged at banks and money changers and in some big hotels (often guests only). Money changers often offer the best rates, but it is worth shopping around. Banks charge commission on travellers' cheques. Those from all major issuing companies and denominated in just about any major currency are widely accepted. But, as elsewhere, US dollars are probably best. With the very wide availability of ATMs increasing numbers of visitors are finding that there is no need to arrive with travellers' cheques.

Cost of living

Prices have been relatively stable and because the ringgit has been held down at a lower-than-market exchange rate, Malaysia is cheaper for overseas visitors than a few

Essentials

Regional air connections with Kuala Lumpur

To	Connections/Week
Bangkok	numerous
Rangoon	2
Hanoi	2
Saigon	daily
Manila	twice daily
Phnom Penh	3
Singapore	numerous
Jakarta	numerous
Bali	numerous

years ago. Inflation in 2001 was 1.5% (despite robust economic growth). Except for a wild bout of consumption in 2000 the Malaysian economy has been sluggish with demand remaining relatively weak. The result is that businesses, including hotels and restaurants, have striven to keep their rates down.

Having said all this, Malaysia was no longer a cheap place to live even before the recession of 1998 and people wanting to stay in accommodation other than that pitched at the pocket of the budget traveller will find the country more expensive than neighbouring Thailand and Indonesia.

But all is not lost. It is still possible to travel on a relatively tight budget, and getting by on US$15-20 (RM60-80) per day – including accommodation, meals and transport – is certainly possible if you stay in the bottom end guesthouses, eat at stalls or in hawker centres, and travel on non-a/c public transport. Cheaper guesthouses charge around RM15-30 a night for two – which translates into a US dollar figure of about US$4-8. Dorm beds are available in many towns, and these are priced at around RM8-15, or US$2-4. It is usually possible to find a simple a/c room for RM30-70 or US$8-20. A room in a top quality, international class hotel will cost RM300-500 or US$80-130, and in a tourist class hotel (with a/c, room service, restaurant and probably a swimming pool), RM100-150 or US$26-40. Eating out is also comparatively cheap: a good curry can be had for as little as RM2-4 (US$0.50-1). Finally, overland travel is a bargain. Although private car ownership is rapidly spreading, many ordinary Malaysians still travel by bus and consequently the bus network is not only extremely good, but fares are very good value.

Getting there

Air

The new Kuala Lumpur International Airport (KLIA) is at Sepang, 72 km from the city, see page 110. Some international flights go direct to Penang, Kota Kinabalu and Kuching. Smaller airlines also run services between Singapore and island resorts such as Langkawi and Pulau Tioman. More than 25 international carriers serve KL.

Non-Malaysian passport holders are eligible for the **Discover Malaysia Pass**, if they fly into the country on *Malaysian Airlines* (*MAS*). The basic pass is US$199 for travel for up to a maximum of 5 flights within the country and is available between 1 January 2002 and 31 December 2002. The pass must be purchased within 14 days of arrival in Malaysia. It offers significant savings on domestic air travel but obviously makes most sense on longer routings. Bear in mind that holders can only cross between Peninsular Malaysia and East Malaysia (Sabah/Sarawak) once (ie a return journey across the South China Sea).

NB Flights between Singapore and Malaysia cost the same US dollar amount whether bought in Malaysia or Singapore – so it saves money buying a return ticket in Malaysia. There are flights from KL to most Asian destinations.

From Europe The approximate flying time from London to KL (non-stop) is 12½ hours. From London Heathrow *British Airways* and *MAS* (in a joint service with *Virgin*) are the two carriers. From Amsterdam: *MAS* and *KLM*. From Frankfurt: *MAS*, *Lufthansa* and *China Airlines*.

You can fly from Zurich with *MAS*, *Royal Brunei* and *China Airlines*. From Paris: *MAS*. From other cities a change of plane is often necessary *en route*.

From the USA Approximate flying time from Los Angeles International Airport (LAX) is 20 hours. *MAS*
& Canada flys from LA via Tokyo and Canada.

From You can fly direct from Sydney, Melbourne, Brisbane, Darwin, Cairns and Perth (flight
Australasia times range between five and nine hours), with *Qantas*, *British Airways*, *MAS* and many others. *MAS* also flys from Auckland.

From South From Delhi (India), *MAS* and *Air India* fly to KL. *Air Lanka* flys from Colombo (Bangla-
& Southeast desh), while *Biman Bangladesh Airlines* flys Dhaka. *Pakistan International Airlines*
Asia and *MAS* fly from Karachi. Flights via other cities available from Male and Kathmandu. There are flights to KL from all regional capitals in Southeast Asia.

From the There are numerous flights on many airlines from Hong Kong, Manila and Tokyo.
Far East

Road

It is possible to travel to and from Malaysia by bus or share-taxi from Thailand and Singapore. Direct buses and taxis are much easier than the local alternatives which stop at the borders. Singapore is six hours by taxi from KL (via Johor Bahru) and about seven hours by bus (see page 110). Taxi fares are approximately double bus fares.

There are direct buses and taxis to destinations in Thailand from most major towns in northern Malaysia (see relevant sections) and six border crossing points. For those using the north-south highway – which is most people – the crossing point is at Bukit Kayu Hitam, which links up with the Thai city of Hat Yai. On the western side of the Peninsula there are also crossings at Wang Kelian and Padang Besar. The Wang Kelian crossing (to Satun in Thailand) is convenient if driving oneself; it is quiet and usually pretty rapid. The Padang Besar crossing is easy on foot and makes sense if travelling to or from Pulau Langkawi. In Perak the crossing is at Pengkalan Hulu, and in Kelantan, on the eastern side of the Peninsula there are two more crossing points, the more important at Pengkalan Kubar, and the second from Kota Bahru to Rantau Panjang/Sungai Golok (see page 300). The more popular of these is the Rantau Panjang crossing; few people cross at Pengkalan Kubar. Local buses and taxis terminate at the border crossing points, but there are regular connections to towns and cities from each side.

It is also possible to cross overland from the East Malaysian states of Sarawak and Sabah to Kalimantan (Indonesian Borneo) and Brunei. The main crossing point is in the west, between Kuching in Sarawak and Pontianak in Kalimantan and regular buses run between these two towns.

Sea

Most passenger ships and cruise liners run between Port Klang, west of KL, Georgetown (Penang), Singapore, Kuantan, Kuching and Kota Kinabalu. Feri Malaysia connects these Malaysian ports and Singapore. Deluxe cabins are available. Schedules change annually; contact *Tourism Malaysia* for bookings, see page 34.

There are also regular ferry services from Melaka to Dumai in Sumatra and from Georgetown (Penang) to Medan, also in Sumatra (see relevant sections). Passenger boats connect Langkawi Island with Satun in South Thailand (see page 177). High-speed catamarans ply the route between Singapore and Pulau Tioman (off the

Arriving at night

KL's new international airport – KLIA – is almost 80 km from the city centre. It is one of the flashest airports around and while arriving late at night does make things a little more difficult it is nothing to get worried about. The airport is safe, well run and has oodles of facilities. As the airport management suggest – just a trifle ambitiously – it 'is a destination in itself'. But public buses to KL only run between 0530 and 0030 daily. If you arrive outside these hours you will have to either take a taxi or limo into KL or hire a care – most major rental companies have counters open 24 hours. 'Budget airport limos into the city centre cost RM66.70 with a surcharge of RM36 between midnight through to 0559. Metered taxis impose a surcharge of 50% from midnight through to 0559.

Alternatively, opt to spend the time recuperating from your flight. The Airside Transit Hotel (T603-87874848 or F87874747, airsidehotel@klia.com.my) is situated within the airport at satellite A. The 80 rooms are comfortable and there are also fitness and business centres, a bar and café. The two most convenient hotels for longer stays are the Concorde Inn Hotel (5 mins from the airport, complementary shuttle bus available) with 420 rooms, swimming pool and more, and top of the pile is the stylish Pan Pacific Hotel (T603-87873333, F87875555, panpac@pphklia.com.my) with more than 400 rooms, lots of sports facilities, restaurants and more.
For more information of KLIA see www.klia.com.my

east coast of Peninsular Malaysia), 4½ hours. Small boats also run between Johor state and Singapore's Changi Point. In East Malaysia, there are connections between Tawau and Tarakan via Nunukan (see page 474).

Train

Keretapi Tanah Melayu (KTM) run express trains daily between Singapore and the major cities on the west coast of Malaysia. There is a daily express train between Bangkok (Thailand) and Butterworth. This connects with the KL service, and from KL onwards to Singapore. Another railway line runs from Gemas (halfway between KL and Johor Bahru) to Kota Bharu, on the northeast coast.

For details on fares and schedules, see tables pages 44-45

The most luxurious way to travel by train to Malaysia is aboard the *Eastern & Oriental (E&O) Express*. This a/c train consisting of 22 carriages, including a salon car, dining car, bar and observation deck, and carrying just 132 passengers, runs once a week from Singapore to Bangkok and back. Luxurious carriages, fine wines and food designed for European rather than Asian sensibilities make this not just a mode of transport but an experience. The journey takes 43 hours with stops in Kuala Lumpur, Butterworth and Padang Besar. But such luxury is expensive. For information call Bangkok T2514862; London T020-79286000; USA T800- 5242420; and Singapore T065-2272068.

Touching down

Airport information

The new **Kual Lumpur International Airport** (**KLIA**) is at Sepang, 72 km from the city. Glitzy and high-tech, reflecting Malaysia's 2020 vision, it has loads of restaurants, shops, banks and such like. A helpful *Tourism Malaysia* desk dishes out lots of pamphlets on KL and beyond. The KLIA website is //www.klia.com.my/ The old airport at Subang (sounding confusingly similar to Sepang), 24 km southwest of KL, is still used for some domestic

Essentials

☞ **Touching down**

Emergencies *Ambulance, police or fire, T999.*
Business hours *Banks: 0930-1500 Mon-Fri and 0930-1130 Sat.* **NB** *For Kedah, Perlis, Kelantan and Terengganu banks are open 0930-1130 on Thur and closed on Fri.*
Government offices: *0800-1245, 1400-1615 Mon-Thur, 0800-1200, 1430-1615 Fri, 0800-1245 Sat. In the states of Kedah and Terengganu, 0800-1615 Sat-Wed, 0800-1245 Thur, closed Fri. In Kelantan 0800-1645 Sun-Wednesday, 0800-1245 Thursday, closed Fri and Sat.*
Shops: *0930-1900, supermarkets and department stores 1000-2200.*
In the former Federated States, which were under the British (Selangor, Melaka, Penang, Perak, Pahang and Negri Sembilan), there is a half day holiday on Sat and full day holiday on Sun. The former Unfederated States of Kelantan and Terengganu retain the traditional half day holiday on Thur and full day holiday on Fri. Sat and Sun are treated as weekdays. In the other former Un-federated States – Johor, Kedah and Perlis – the half day on Thur is often observed, but most businesses now observe the Sat/Sun weekend.
Official time *Eight hours ahead of GMT.*
Voltage *220-240 volts, 50 cycle AC. Some hotels supply adaptors.*
Weights and measures *Metric, although road distances are marked in both kilometres and miles.*

departures, by, for instance, *AirAsia*. For details of other international airports, such as Penang, Kota Kinabalu and Kuching, see the relevant regional chapters.

Public buses to KL are available one floor down from the arrivals concourse. From KLIA express coaches operate every 30 minutes to hotels in KL, RM25 (RM13 children) one-way or RM45 (RM25 children) return. From KLIA the first coach leaves at 0645 (0530 from KL) and the last departure at 0030 (and 2215 from KL). The journey takes around 1 hour. There is also an hourly service to Chan Sow Lin STAR/LRT station (RM10,children RM6) operating between 0630 and 2130. Take the clearly marked signs from the arrivals hall. Cheaper but more of a hassle is to take a bus to the Nilai train station (buses operate from 0630-2200 and leave every 20 minutes or so, RM2.50) and from there a commuter train to the KL train station (RM4.50). Bus tickets are available in the arrivals hall. For a taxi expect to pay around RM50-60. They operate on a coupon system; make sure you pick up one from the taxi counter at the exit in arrivals; touts charge more than double the official rate. Many hotels provide a pick-up service, but make sure they are aware of your arrival details; there is a hotel pick-up office just outside the terminal exit. Major car rental companies have desks in the arrivals concourse. A railway line, KL Sentral KLIA, is being built between KL and the airport, scheduled for completion in 2002. For further details on transport from KLIA to KL see the transport section of the KLIA website, www.klia.com.my/index.php

Airport tax   Airport departure tax is RM5 for domestic flights, and RM40 for all other countries.

Tourist information   *Tourism Malaysia* (headquarters), 17th Flr, Menara Dato' Onn, Putra World Trade Centre, 45, Jln Tun Ismail, 50480 Kuala Lumpur T03-2935188, F03-2935884. There is an information centre on Level two of the Putra World Trade Centre (in the convention centre). For practical advice, visitors are better advised to contact the *Malaysian Tourist Information Centre* (*MATIC*), 109 Jln Ampang, Kuala Lumpur T2423929. There are several other tourist information bureaux in KL (see page 70) and regional tourism offices in state capitals, all of which are reasonably efficient.

Tourism Malaysia has a tourist information bureau in most large towns; it is very efficient and can supply further details on tourist sights, advise on itineraries, help place

Malaysian manners – as learned from a princess

In modern, cosmopolitan Malaysia, traditional customs and cultural conventions are alive and well and rigorously adhered to. In Malaysia's multi-ethnic melting pot, Malays, Chinese, Indians, Eurasians and expatriates have discovered that cross-cultural etiquette and the art of obliging another's sense of decorum is the essence of racial harmony. The trouble is that for many visitors, committing a Malaysian-style faux pas is one of life's inevitabilities. Or it was, until Datin Noor Aini Syed Amir published her practical handbook to Malaysian customs and etiquette in 1991. As a Malay princess, Datin Noor – Malaysia's Miss Manners – should know. "While the Malays are very generous and forgiving with foreigners who make Malay faux pas, those who do not make such blunders will be highly admired and respected," the Datin says.

Her catch-all advice to visitors is to utter "a profuse apology in advance to the person you may offend". For those who forget to absolve themselves before they slip up, her social observations cover every conceivable situation mat sallehs – the local nickname for foreigners – might find themselves in. When eating with chopsticks, warns Datin Noor, avoid crossing them and never stick them vertically into your ricebowl so they resemble joss sticks. Do not be offended by enthusiastic belches and slurps around the dinner table either: Malaysians live to eat and like to share their appreciation.

Visitors must also learn to distinguish between flabby handshakes and Malay salams. "Unlike the Western handshake, which is a rather vigorous up and down movement... the Malay handshake is a simple palm-to-palm touch", she writes. The most important part of the gesture is immediately touching your hand to your heart as a signal of sincerity. And, she adds, "never use your left hand in Malay company!" Datin Noor goes on to warn newcomers not to touch people's heads, when to take their shoes off and to think before they kiss a lady's cheek – in greeting. Dazzling, long-sleeved batik shirts are what you wear to formal dinners and black is taboo for happy occasions. She explains what Tunkus, Tuns, Datuks, Dato's and Datins are and notes that the King's title 'Yang Di-Pertuan Agong' means 'He Who is Made Supreme Lord'.

Malaysian Customs & Etiquette: A Practical Handbook *by Datin Noor Aini Syed Amir. Times Books International, 1991.*

Essentials

bookings for travel and cultural events and provide updated information on hotels, restaurants and air, road, rail, sea and river transport timetables and prices. If there is no *Tourism Malaysia* office in a town, travel agents are usually helpful.

Local customs and laws

Malaysians dress for the heat. Clothes are light, cool and casual most of the time, but also fairly smart. Some establishments, mainly exclusive restaurants, require a long-sleeved shirt with tie or local batik shirt and do not allow shorts in the evening. Those visiting the Cameron Highlands or other upland areas are advised to take a light sweater. For jungle treks, a waterproof is advisable, as are canvas jungle boots, which dry faster than leather. Although many Malaysian business people have adopted the Western jacket and tie for formal occasions, the batik shirt, or *baju*, is the traditional formal wear for men, while women wear the graceful *sarung kebaya*. **Clothing**

Malaysians dress smartly, particularly in cities; tourists in vests, shorts and flip-flops look out of place in modern cosmopolitan KL. Dress codes are important to observe from the point of view of Islamic sensitivities, particularly on the Peninsula's east coast. In some places such as Marang, bikinis are banned and wearing them will cause great offence. Topless bathing is completely taboo in Malaysia; this should be remembered

Essentials

☞ ## Drugs trafficking – stiff punishment

Malaysia is well known around the world for its stringent laws against drugs. As they fill in their immigration forms, visitors cannot fail to notice the bold block capitals reading: "BE FOREWARNED – DEATH FOR DRUG TRAFFICKERS UNDER MALAYSIAN LAW". At entry points to Malaysia there are prominent posters repeating this warning, the words emblazoned over an ominous picture of a noose. World attention focuses on Malaysia whenever Westerners go to the gallows, but they represent a tiny fraction of those hanged for drug-trafficking offences. Since 1983 about 150 prisoners have been hanged and about 4,000 arrested under Section 39(B) of the Dangerous Drugs Act; about a quarter of those face execution within the next few years. Malaysia's biggest-ever mass-hanging of traffickers took place at Taiping jail in May 1990 when eight Hong Kong people were executed.

The Dadah Act - dadah is the Malay word for drugs – stipulates a mandatory death sentence upon conviction for anyone in possession of 15 or more

grams of heroin or morphine, 200g of cannabis or hashish or 40g of cocaine. Those caught with more than 10g of heroin or 100g of cannabis are deemed to be traffickers and face lengthy jail sentences and flogging with a rotan cane. Following the execution of two Australians in 1986, the then Australian Prime Minister, Bob Hawke, branded the Malaysian government 'barbaric'. A similar outcry resulted from the hanging of a Briton in 1987; the British opposition even called for a trade embargo of Malaysia. But Malaysian Prime Minister Dr Mahathir Mohamad, who is a medical doctor and as such has taken the Hippocratic Oath, has consistently refused to bow to international pleas for clemency. In a British television documentary in 1991, The prime minister, the junkie and the boys on death row, he said: "We have to carry out this death penalty because it would not be fair to those who had already been hanged and their families."

even where tourists have started doing it, such as on Pulau Tioman. Dress modestly out of respect for Muslim tradition.

Malaysia's cross-cultural differences are most apparent on the streets: many Chinese girls think nothing of wearing brief mini-skirts and shorts, while their Malay counterparts are clad from head to toe. The *tudung* (or *telukung*) veil signifies adherence to the puritanical lifestyle of the fervently Islamic *dakwah* movement; during the 1980s, this almost became a fashion among women at universities as well as among blue-collar workers in factories. Some women began to dress in the full black purdah until it was forbidden by the government. Much of this was the result of peer pressure and reflected a revival of strict Islamic values in Malaysia during and after the 1970s.

Conduct   As elsewhere in Southeast Asia, in Malaysia 'losing face' brings shame. You lose face if you lose your temper, and even in a situation like bargaining, using a loud voice or wild gesticulations will be taken to signify anger. By the same token, the person you shout at will also feel loss of face too, particularly if it happens in public. It should also be noted that in Muslim company it is impolite to touch others with the left hand and other objects – even loose change. Although men shake hands, for a man to shake a woman's hand is not the norm outside KL. Indeed excessive personal contact should be avoided: Malays, especially, do not tend to slap one another on the back!

A couple of other points of conduct should be remembered when in Malaysia. Using the index finger to point at people, even at objects, is regarded as insulting. The thumb or whole hand should be used to indicate something, or to wave down a taxi.

Before entering a private home, remember to remove your shoes; it is also usual to take a small gift for the host.

When picking up and passing food, do not use the left hand in Muslim company. It is **Eating** worth remembering that Malays do not make pork *satay* and that Hindus do not make beef curries. Chinese cooking on the other hand seems to incorporate almost anything.

Tipping is unusual in Malaysia, as a service charge of 10% is automatically added to res- **Tipping** taurant and hotel bills, plus a 5% government tax. Nor is tipping expected in smaller restaurants where a service charge is not automatically added to the bill. For personal services, porterage for example, a modest tip may be appropriate.

Remove shoes before entering mosques and Hindu and Buddhist temples; in **Religion** mosques, women should cover their heads, shoulders and legs and men should wear long trousers.

The trafficking of illegal drugs into Malaysia carries the death penalty. While **Prohibitions** alcohol is not illegal in any part of Malaysia, be aware of Muslim sensibilities, particularly in the East Coast states of Kelantan and Terengganu.

Essentials

Responsible tourism

"Tourism is like fire. It can either cook your food or burn your house down". This sums up the ambivalent attitude that many people have regarding the effects of tourism. It is one of Indonesia's largest foreign-exchange earners, and the world's largest single industry; yet many people in receiving countries would rather that tourists stayed home. Tourism is seen to be the cause of polluted beaches, rising prices, loose morals, consumerism, and much else besides.

The word 'tourist' is derived from 'travail', meaning work or torment. Travail, in turn, has its roots in the Latin word *tripalium*, which was a three-pronged instrument of torture. For many people struggling through interior Borneo this etymology should strike a chord. And yet, as *The Economist* pointed out in a survey of the industry in 1991:

"The curse of the tourist industry is that it peddles dreams: dreams of holidays where the sun always shines, the children are always occupied, and where every evening ends in the best sex you have ever had. For most of its modern life, this has been matched by a concomitant dreaminess on the part of its customers. When asked, most tourists tell whopping lies about what they want on holiday." (*The Economist*, 1991).

Most international tourists come from a handful of wealthy countries. This is why many see tourism as the new 'imperialism', imposing alien cultures and ideals on sensitive and unmodernized peoples. The problem, however, is that discussions of the effects of tourism tend to degenerate into simplifications – culminating in the drawing up of a checklist of 'positive' and 'negative' effects. Although such tables may be useful in highlighting problem areas, they also do a disservice by reducing a complex issue to a simple set of rather one dimensional 'costs' and 'benefits'. Different destinations will be affected in different ways; these effects are likely to vary over time; and different groups living in a particular destination will feel the effects of tourism in different ways and to varying degrees. At no time or place can tourism (or any other influence) be categorized as uniformly 'good' or 'bad'. Tourism can take a young Australian backpacker on US$10 a day to a guesthouse on the east coast of Peninsular Malaysia, a family to a luxury hotel in Penang where a room can cost over US$200 a night, or a young couple to the forests and longhouses of East Malaysia.

Some tourists are attracted to Malaysia, and particularly East Malaysia, because of its exotic 'tribal' peoples. When cultural erosion is identified, the tendency is to blame this

☞ How big is your footprint?

- Learn about the country you're visiting.
- Start enjoying your travels before you leave by tapping into as many sources of information as you can.
- Think about where your money goes – be fair and realistic about how cheaply you travel. Try and put money into local people's hands; drink local beer or fruit juice rather than imported brands and stay in locally-owned accommodation.
- Open your mind to new cultures and traditions. It can transform your holiday experience and you'll earn respect and be more readily welcomed by local people.
- Think about what happens to your rubbish - take biodegradable products and a water filter bottle. Be sensitive to limited resources like water, fuel and electricity.
- Help preserve local wildlife and habitats by respecting rules and regulations, such as sticking to footpaths, not standing on coral and not buying products made from endangered plants or animals.
- Use your guidebook as a starting point, not the only source of information. Talk to local people, then discover your own adventure!
- Don't treat people as part of the landscape, they may not want their picture taken. Put yourself in their shoes, ask first and respect their wishes.

NB: This is taken from the Tourism Concern website which also provides further elaboration of the points noted here. The code was developed from a Young Travellers' conference in April 2001 but is not aimed only at young travellers. As they say: "It applies to everybody who loves travelling, whether on a budget holiday or staying in a luxury community run centre".

on tourists and tourism who become the so-styled 'suntanned destroyers of culture'. The problem with views like this is that they assume that change is bad, and that indigenous cultures are unchanging. It makes local peoples victims of change, rather than masters of their own destinies. It also assumes that tourism is an external influence, when in fact it quickly becomes part of the local landscape. Cultural change is inevitable and on-going, and 'new' and 'traditional' are only judgements, not absolutes. Thus new cultural forms can quickly become key markers of tradition. Tourists searching for an 'authentic' experience are assuming that tradition is tangible, easily identifiable and unchanging. It is none of these.

Tourist art, both material (for instance, sculpture) and non-material (like dances) is another issue where views over the impacts of tourism sharply diverge. The mass of inferior 'airport' art on sale to tourists demonstrates, to some, the corrosive effects of tourism. It leads craftsmen and women to mass-produce second rate pieces for a market that appreciates neither their cultural or symbolic worth, nor their aesthetic value. Yet tourism can also give value to craft industries that would otherwise be undermined by cheap industrial goods. So, some people argue that the craft traditions of Kelantan and Teregganu, as well as those of Sabah and Sarwak have been given a new injection of vitality by the demands that tourism creates.

The environmental deterioration that is linked to tourism is due to a destination area exceeding its 'carrying capacity' as a result of overcrowding. But carrying capacity, though an attractive concept, is notoriously difficult to pin down. A second dilemma facing those trying to encourage greater environmental consciousness is the so-called 'tragedy of the commons', better described in terms of Chinese restaurants. When a group of people go to a Chinese restaurant with the intention of sharing the bill, each customer will tend to order a more expensive dish than he or she would normally do – on the logic that everyone will be doing the same, and the bill will be split. In tourism terms, it means that hotel owners will always build those few more bungalows or that extra wing, to maximize their profits, reassured in the knowledge that the environmental costs will be shared among all hotel owners. So, despite most operators appreciating that over-development may 'kill the goose that lays the golden eggs', they do so anyway. But many areas of Malaysia have few other development opportunities and those with beautiful landscapes and/or exotic cultures find it difficult not to resist the temptation to market them and attract the tourist dollar. And why shouldn't they?

One of the ironies is that the 'traveller' or 'backpacker' finds it difficult to consider him or herself as a tourist at all. This, of course, is hubris built upon the notion that the traveller is an 'independent' explorer somehow beyond the bounds of the industry. Anna Borzello in an article entitled 'The myth of the traveller' in the journal *Tourism in Focus* (no. 19, 1994) writes that, "Independent travellers cannot acknowledge – without shattering their self-image – that to many local people they are simply a good source of income … [not] inheritors of Livingstone, [but] bearers of urgently needed money." Although she does, in writing this, grossly underestimate the ability of travellers to see beyond their thongs and friendship bracelets, she does have a point when she suggests that it is important for travellers honestly to appraise their role as tourists, because, "Not only are independent travellers often frustrated by the gap between the way they see themselves and the way they are treated, but unless they acknowledge that they are part of the tourist industry they will not take responsibility for the damaging effects of their tourism."

Tourism Concern, a UK-based charity, works to resolve in a constructive manner some of the issues sketched out above. As they say on their website: "We look at the way tourism affects the people and environments in tourism destination areas. Tourism Concern raises awareness of tourism's impact with the general public, with government decision-makers and within the tourist industry itself – and we provide a unique information base for campaigners and students of tourism." It is possible to subscribe to their magazine, *In Focus* by writing to Tourism Concern, Stapleton House, 277-281 Holloway Road, London N7 8HN. Subscription rates vary between £12 and £25. Alternatively, visit their website: www.tourismconcern.org.uk

Pressure groups

Safety

Normal precautions should be taken with passports and valuables such as cameras; many hotels have safes. Pickpocketing is a problem in some cities.

Where to stay

Malaysia offers a good selection of international-standard hotels as well as simpler hotels, rest houses and hostels. Room rates are subject to 5-10% tax. Many of the major international chains have hotels in Malaysia, such as *Hilton, Regent, Holiday Inn* and *Hyatt* ,plus local and regional chains such as *Merlin, Ming Court* and *Shangri-La*; most of these are on the west coast. Room rates in the big hotels, particularly in KL, rose steeply during the early and mid-1990s but have been stable for the last few years. The number of four- and five-star hotel rooms has multiplied over the last few years and this, combined with a weak ringgit and generally depressed economy, has helped to keep prices stable. By world standards, even the most expensive hotels are good value for money. It is also possible to rent condominiums in some cities, mainly KL and Georgetown.

There are youth hostels in KL, Georgetown (Penang), Port Dickson, Fraser's Hill, Cameron Highlands, Kuantan, Kota Bahru, Kota Kinabalu and Pulau Pangkor. There are also scores of government rest houses (*rumah rehat*) around the country; these often offer well-maintained, reasonably priced rooms, although they can become heavily booked, particularly during public holidays. On the east coast of Peninsular

For our quick reference price guide to hotels, see the inside front cover of the book

☞ Hotel prices and facilities

L *RM500+* **Luxury**: *hotels in this bracket are few and far between. KL's splendid Carcosa Seri Negara is one such hotel. The Datai on Langkawi is another and the Pangkor Laut Resort on the private island of Pangkor Laut is also in the top league. Most **AL** grade hotels have luxury presidential suites.*

AL *RM260-499* **International class**: *impeccable service, beautifully appointed, offering a wide array of facilities and business services. Malaysia's AL grade hotels, most of which are grouped towards the bottom end of the price category, are regarded as among the best value in the region.*

A *RM130-259* **First class**: *good range of services and facilities. Very competitively priced, given standards of service.*

B *RM65-129* **Tourist class**: *hotels in this category will have swimming pools; most provide just a basic range of services and facilities although all will have a/c.*

C *RM40-64* **Economy**: *while there are some excellent economy hotels in this category, few provide much in the way of services. Guests will usually have the option of a/c or fan-cooled rooms and a choice of attached/shared bathrooms. Government rest houses (rumah rehat) offer the best value for money in this grade.*

D *RM20-39* **Budget**: *most hotels in this class are Chinese-run and located in town centres. They are therefore often noisy and not just because of the traffic; they also seem to be busy much later into the night because of the arrival and departure of the long distance drivers who use them. At the upper end, rooms have a/c and attached bathrooms; cheaper rooms have fans and communal bathrooms (with mandi). Some fine old tumbledown colonial relics in this range offer good value for money. Youth hostels also fall into this price range.*

E *RM10-19* **Lodging house/guesthouse/hostel**: *rooms are rarely a/c; shared mandi with squat toilet; few facilities. Lodging houses (rumah tumpangan) sometimes double as brothels. Tourist-orientated guesthouses usually offer more value and a better atmosphere; there are a few exceptionally good places in this category.*

F *under RM10: there is little accommodation in this category in Malaysia, although many guesthouses and hostels in the **D** and **E** categories provide the option of bottom-dollar, cramped dormitory accommodation. In some beach resort areas it is sometimes possible to find simple 'A'-frame accommodation in this range.*

Malaysia and in East Malaysia, it is often possible to stay with families in Malay *kampungs* (villages), the so-called Homestay programme (contact local tourist office or travel agent for more information). The most popular place to do this is at Kampung Cerating, north of Kuantan, although it has become increasingly touristy in recent years; it is also possible to stay in a kampung house in Merang. Along many of Malaysia's beaches and on the islands, there are simple *atap*-roofed 'A'-frame bungalows. Towns and cities on the tourist trail also often have guesthouses with dormitory accommodation for the seriously shallow of pocket. These are noted in the detailed comments provided for each establishment.

Accommodation in East Malaysia does not offer such value for money as hotels on the Peninsula, although, again, there are some bargains. As on the Peninsula, there are government resthouses in many of the main towns. For accommodation in national parks (see relevant chapters), it is necessary to book in advance. In Sarawak it is possible to stay in longhouses, where rates are at the discretion of the visitor (see page 347).

Reflecting Malaysia enthusiastic embrace of all things high-tech, most hotels, and even many guesthouses, have email. Many offer websites too. These are listed in the accommodation sections of the town entries along with the addresses and comments. There are also good web sources for accommodation in Malaysia. See, for example:

www.asiatravelmart.com www.aaahotels.net/malaysia-hotels/asia-ravel.com/
malaysia.html www.malaysiahoteltravel.com/ and www.malaysia- hotels.ws/

NB In the more popular holiday destinations like the Cameron Highlands, accommodation can become scarce during the school holidays – April, August and December. During these months it is worth booking ahead. It is also worth noting that many hotels in tourist resorts have two, sometimes three, room tarrifs. One for weekdays, one for weekends and, sometimes, a third for holiday periods. Room rates can vary substantially between these periods.

There are not many sites in Malaysia, but 'wild camping' is easy. In Sabah camping is a much cheaper option and you get to stay exactly where you want to be, for example at Tunkul Abdul Rahman Marine Park, Danum Valley, and the islands around Semporna.

Camping

Essentials

Getting around

Transport around the East Malaysian states of Sabah and Sarawak is not as easy as it is on the Peninsula since there are fewer roads and they are not in a good state of repair. There are excellent coastal and upriver express boat services in Sarawak and the national airline, *Malaysian Airlines* (*MAS*), has an extensive network in both states; flying is relatively inexpensive.

For recommended maps and guides, see page 567

Air

MAS operates an extensive network of flights to domestic destinations. On the Peninsula *MAS* serves:**Alor Setar**, **Ipoh**, **Johor Bahru**, **Kota Bahru**, **Kuala Lumpur**, **Kuala Terengganu**, **Kuantan**, **Langkawi** and **Penang**. In Sabah *MAS's* destinations are **Kota Kinabalu**, **Kudat**, **Labuan**, **Lahad Datu**, **Sandakan**, **Semporna**, **Tawau** and **Tomanggong**. And in Sarawak *MAS* flies to **Bario**, **Belaga**, **Bintulu**, **Kuching**, **Lawas**, **Limbang**, **Long Banga**, **Long Lelang**, **Long Seridan**, **Marudi**, **Miri**, **Mukah**, **Mulu** and **Sibu**. Local *MAS* offices are listed under each town; the head office is at Bangunan MAS (opposite *Equatorial Hotel*), Jln Sultan Ismail, 50250, Kuala Lumpur. For fares, see table. Domestic flights from KL leave either from the new international airport, KLIA, 72 km from the city, or Subang, 24 km from the city, so check your ticket. Flights get very booked up on public holidays.

For details of the MAS air pass, see page 31

A start-up airline is *AirAsia* which still has a relatively limited network (check their website – www.airasia.com/airlines/ ttable.html) offering services between KL's Subang airport and **Kuching**, **Langkawi**, **Kota Kinabalu** and and **Labuan**. For reservations T03-7457777, information T03-7077777.

For details on fares and schedules see the airlines' websites: *MAS* (www.malaysia-airlines.com.my) and *AirAsia* (www.airasia.com).

Road

Peninsular Malaysia has an excellent bus system with a network of public express buses and several privately run services. A/c express buses (and VIP buses on the more popular routes) connect the major towns; seats can be reserved and prices are reasonable. Prices quoted are for a/c buses. The a/c on Malaysian buses is, as on the trains, very cold. There are also cheaper non-a/c buses that ply between the states and provide an intra-state service. Prices vary according to whether the bus is a/c or non-a/c, express or regular, and between companies. The largest bus company is *MARA*, the government-run service. Recommended private companies are *Plusliner* (with super VIP buses) and *Transnasional*. Although these may cost a few ringgit more, it's usually money well

Bus
During the school holiday period, it can be difficult to get bus tickets and it is worth booking ahead

Essentials

Guide to domestic Mas air fares

Destination	Distance	One-way	Destination	Distance	One-way
	(km)	(RM)		(km)	(RM)
JB-Ipoh	573	430	KL-Kuching	1,035	262
JB-Kota Bharu	689	524	KL-Langkawi	-	205
JB- Langkawi	-	524	KL-Penang	283	158
JB-Penang	-	481	KL-Sandakan	-	488
Kota Kinabalu-Bintulu	-	127	KL-Sibu	-	569
Kota Kinabalu-Johor Bahru	1,502	617	Kuantan-JB	261	93
Kota Kinabalu-Kuching	811	405	Kuching-Bintulu	354	117
Kota Kinabalu-Penang	-	962	Kuching-Johor Bahru	-	300
Kota Kinabalu-Sandakan	226	148	Kuching-Labuan	-	199
Kota Kinabalu-Sibu	-	256	Kuching-Lahad Datu	-	310
KL-Alor Setar	368	307	Kuching-Miri	519	164
KL-Ipoh	178	179	Kuching-Penang	-	604
KL-JB	354	251	Kuching-Sandakan	-	505
KL-Kota Bahru	352	281	Kuching-Sibu	191	72
KL-Kota Kinabalu	1,678	777	Kuching-Tawau	-	298
KL-Kuala Terengganu	318	158	Langkawi-Penang	-	140
KL-Kuantan	224	112			

Note Specific distances were not available for certain routes.

spent. In larger towns there may be a number of bus stops; some private companies may also operate directly from their own offices. Travelling up the east coast of the Peninsula is often quicker as the roads are less congested; west coast travel is very slow but will be improved with the completion of the north-south highway.

Buses in East Malaysia are more unreliable because of the poorer road conditions. Even in East Malaysia roads are a good deal better than in Indonesian Borneo. In Sarawak, the Sibu-Bintulu and Bintulu-Miri roads are rough and often impassable in the wet season, as is the road connecting Kota Kinabalu and Sandakan in Sabah.

Car and motorcycle Car-hire companies are listed in individual towns under **Local transport**. Visitors can hire a car provided they are in possession of an international driving licence, are over 23 and not older than 65, and have at least one year's driving experience. Car hire costs from RM100 to RM250 per day approximately depending on the model and the company. Cheaper weekly and monthly rates and special deals are available.

Driving is on the left; give way to drivers on the right. Within towns the speed limit is 50 km per hour; the wearing of seat belts is compulsory for front seat passengers and the driver. Most road signs are international but *awas* means caution. Petrol costs a little over RM1 a litre. Road maps are on sale at most petrol stations; Petronas (the national oil company) produces an excellent atlas: *Touring Malaysia by Road*. Road conditions are good when compared with Indonesia and Thailand: most are kept in good repair and local drivers are generally safe. However, during the monsoon season, heavy rains may make some east coast travel difficult and the west coast roads can be congested. In Sarawak the road network is extremely limited: air or water transport are the only option in many areas. In Sabah, four-wheel-drive vehicles are *de rigeur*; they are readily available, but expensive. On some islands, such as Penang, Langkawi and Pangkor, motorbikes are available for hire, starting around RM15-25 per day. If bringing your own car into the country, no carnet or deposit is required. The vehicle is allowed to stay in the country as long as the owner has permission to stay.

Ekrwres Nasional bus fares (RM)

Depart: Kota Bharu		Kota Bharu	28.00
Singapore	46.00	**Depart: Mersing**	
Johor Bharu	32.00	Kuala Lumpur	19.50
Mersing	27.00	Kuala Terengganu	22.10
Kuantan	19.00	Kuantan	10.60
Georgetown	22.00	Ipoh	26.00
Depart: Kuala Lumpur		Johor Bharu	11.00
Ipoh	9.50	Penang	35.00
Johor Bahru	21.00	Singapore	12.60
Kota Bharu	26.00	**Depart: Singapore**	
Melaka	6.80	Melaka	15.00*
Tanah Rata	3.50	Kuala Lumpur	25.00-31.00*
Depart: Melaka			
Ipoh	17.00		
Singapore	11.50		

NB   *These prices, collected in late 2001, are indicative only; fares vary a good deal between bus companies.*
* Fare in S$

Essentials

Sea

In the Peninsula, there are regular scheduled ferry services between the main islands, Pulau Pangkor, Penang and Pulau Langkawi, and the mainland. There are services from Mersing and Singapore to Pulau Tioman. There are passenger and car ferries between Butterworth and Georgetown, Penang, every 20 minutes. For other offshore islands, mostly off the east coast, fishing boats, and sometimes regular boats, leave from the nearest fishing port.

Local water transport comes into its own in Sarawak, where lack of roads makes coastal and river transport the only viable means of communication. On the larger rivers in Sarawak, such as the Rajang and the Baram, there are specially adapted express boats (see page 351). If there is no regular boat, it is nearly always possible to charter a local longboat, although this can be expensive. In the dry season the upper reaches of many rivers are unnavigable except by smaller boats. In times of heavy rain, logs and branch debris can make rivers unsafe. Some river transport still operates on rivers on the peninsula's east coast.

Feri Malaysia runs two routes, both on a weekly schedule. (1) **Port Klang- Singapore-Kuching-Kota Kinabalu-Singapore-Kuantan-Port Klang**. (2) **Kuantan-Kota Kinabalu-Kuching-Singapore-Port Klang**. *Tourism Malaysia* offices have information on *Feri Malaysia* and can place bookings.

Train

See tables on page 44

In August 1992 the Peninsular Malaysian Railway System or Keretapi Tanah Melayu (KTM) was privatized and became the *Keretapi Tanah Melayu Berhad* or *KTMB*. Their corporate mission statement declared: "We strive to provide excellent rail and related transport services in Malaysia, utilizing our resources to optimize financial performance whilst meeting stakeholder expectations."

Notwithstanding the tendency for hyperbole in any mission statement, the *KTMB* is an economical and comfortable way to travel round the Peninsula. Privatization has pumped much needed investment into the system which, in 1981, the *New Straits Times* was predicting would "collapse into one mass heap of worthless metal".

There are two main lines. One runs up the west coast from **Singapore**, through **KL**, **Ipoh** and **Butterworth**, connecting with Thai railways at **Padang Besar** (where a half of the extra-long platform is managed by Malaysian officials and the other half by

Wau Express (RM)

Kuala Lumpur-Tumpat-Kuala Lumpur

Train No	XW/16 Dep	Arr XW/17
Kuala Lumpur	2000	0656
Kajang	2035	0611
Seremban	2119	0517
Tampin	2206	0433
Gemas	2328	0345
Bahau	0003	0248
Mentakab	0121	0128
Jerantut	0209	0011
Kuala Lipis	0305	2313
Gua Musang	0428	2143
Dabong	0530	2037
Krai	0619	1948
Tanah Merah	0649	1915
Pasir Mas	0715	1852
Wakaf Baharu	0731	1838
Tumpat	0745 Dep	Arr 1820

Timuran Express (RM)

Singapore-Tumpat-Singapore

Train No	XST/15	Arr Dep XST/14
Singapore	0850	2110
Johor Bahru	0757	2112
Kluang	0628	2233
Labis	0543	2331
Segamat	0518	2358
Gemas	0456	0040
Bahau	0411	0117
Triang	0322	0231
Mentakab	0252	0306
Jerantut	0204	0351
Kuala Lipis	0057	0446
Gua Musang	2328	0612
Krai	2131	0818
Tanah Merah	2100	0849
Pasir Mas	2036	0915
Wakaf Bahru	2023	0930
Tumpat	2005 Dep	Arr 0945

Thais) and from there continues to **Hat Yai** in Southern Thailand and north to **Bangkok**. The other line branches off from the west coast line at Gemas (halfway between KL and Singapore) and heads northeast to **Kota Bahru**. From Kota Bahru it is possible to take buses/taxis to Rantau Panjang/Sungai Golok for connections with Thai railways. The express service (Ekspres Rakyat or Ekspres Sinaran) only stops at major towns; the regular service stops at every station but is slightly cheaper. All first and second-class coaches have sleeping berths on overnight trains and all classes have a/c. Reservations can be made for both classes. Visitors should note that the a/c on Malaysian trains is very cold. First and second-class carriages are equipped with videos. In East Malaysia there is only one railway line, running from Kota Kinabalu to Tenom, via Beaufort (see page 425).

Rail passes for 10 and 30 days are available to all foreign visitors, except those from Singapore, for every class and there are no restrictions other than seat availability. Passes are available from railway stations in Singapore, KL, Johor Bahru, Butterworth, Padang Besar, Rantau Panjang, Wakaf Bahru (Kota Bahru). A 30-day pass costs US$120 (adult); US$60 (child); and a 10 day pass, US$55 (adult), US$28 (child). Students with a valid ID card (eg ISIC) can also buy an **ISSA Explorer Pass** which provide unlimited second-class travel for seven days (US$38), 14 days (US$50) or 21 days (US$60) on KTM railway services in Peninsular Malaysia, Thailand and Singapore. There are also concessions offered (including for foreigners) to family groups (4 people or more), 25%; groups of 10 or more, 25%; handicapped persons, 50%; and senior citizens (65 years+), 50%. If travelling overnight, berth charges are RM70 (lower a/c), RM50 (upper a/c) for deluxe; and RM14 (lower a/c), RM11.50 (upper a/c) for second class. There are additional charges for international express services. For a train timetable and fares see page 45.

Train information For details of KMT fares and schedules, T03-2738000. For booking and ticket delivery, T03-22743377 (0630-1630 Monday-Saturday). Alternatively, information is available on the KMT website www.ktmb.com.my or by e-mailing passener@ktmb.com.my

NB Taxis from KL's magnificent Moorish railway station run on a fixed-price coupon system; coupons must be bought in advance from the booth next to the taxi rank.

Express train fares

	Butterworth		Kuala Lumpur		Singapore	
	1	2	1	2	1	2
	RM	RM	RM	RM	$S	$S
Padang Besar			-	-	-	-
Alor Star			-	-	-	-
Sungai Petani			-	-	-	-
Butterworth	-	-	67.00	34.00	127.00	60.00
Bt Mertajam	10.00	9.00	65.00	33.00	125.00	59.00
Parit Buntar	14.00	11.00	62.00	32.00	121.00	27.00
Taiping	23.00	15.00	53.00	28.00	112.00	53.00
K Kangsar	28.00	17.00	49.00	26.00	107.00	51.00
Ipoh	36.00	21.00	40.00	22.00	100.00	48.00
Batu Gajah	38.00	21.00	38.00	21.00	97.00	47.00
Kampar	41.00	23.00	35.00	20.00	94.00	46.00
Tapah Road	44.00	24.00	32.00	19.00	92.00	45.00
Kuala Lumpur	67.00	34.00	-	-	68.00	34.00
Seremban	79.00	39.00	19.00	13.00	58.00	30.00
Tampin	85.00	42.00	27.00	17.00	50.00	27.00
Gemas	94.00	46.00	35.00	20.00	43.00	23.00
Segamat	97.00	47.00	38.00	21.00	38.00	21.00
Kluang	110.00	53.00	52.00	27.00	26.00	16.00
Johor Bahru	122.00	58.00	64.00	33.00	13.00	10.00
Singapore	127.00	60.00	68.00	34.00	-	-

Essentials

Other local transport

Bicycles are available for hire from some guesthouses and specialist hire shops, especially on islands such as Pangkor, Penang, Langkawi and Tioman, but also in some towns and hill resorts. Compared with hiring motorbikes, bike hire can seem expensive – around RM10-20 per day and substantially more (hour-for-hour) from those places that hire by the hour. Price also vary a good deal depending on the machine, locally or Chinese-made sit-up-and-beg bikes are cheaper than new mountain bikes.

Cycling

We have had a number of letters from people who have cycled through various parts of Southeast Asia. The advice below is collated from their comments, and is meant to provide a general guideline for those intending to travel by bicycle. There may be areas, however, where the advice does not hold true, and some of the letters we have received even disagree on certain points.

A good, colour map is useful in determining contours and altitude, as well as showing minor roads

Here are some points: Touring, hybrid or mountain bikes are fine for most roads and tracks in Malaysia – take an ordinary machine; nothing fancy; Mountain bikes have made a big impact in the country, so accessories and spares are widely available. Less common are components made of unusual materials – titanium and composites; As cycling is becoming more common clubs are springing up across the country. Unlike Indonesia and Thailand, a foreigner on a bike is not such an object of interest; Cars and buses rarely give way to a bicycle and so be very wary, especially on main roads; Non-a/c, cheaper buses are more accommodating of bicycles, a/c tour-buses may refuse to carry a bike; Many international airlines take bicycles free-of-charge, provided they are not boxed.Take the peddles off and deflate the tyres; In general, when cycling avoid major roads and major towns.

What to take In addition to the listing of useful things to take on page 29, bicyclists might in addition consider: pollution mask if travelling to large cities; a basic tool

Essentials

Important road signs to note

awas caution	*jalang bahaya* dangerous road ahead
beri laluan give way	*jalan licin* slippery road
berhenti stop	*jalan sehala* one way
dilarang berhenti no stopping	*kawasan kemalangan* accident area
dilarang meletak kereta no parking	*kurangkan laju* slow down
dilarang memotong no overtaking	*utara/selatan* north/south
ikut kiri keep left	*timur/barat* east/west

kit including a puncture repair kit; spare inner tubes; spare tyre; pump; a good map of the area; bungee cords; and a water filter.

Hitchhiking It is easy for foreigners to hitch in Malaysia; look reasonably presentable and it shouldn't be long before someone will stop. Hitching is not advisable for women travelling alone.

Taxi There are two types of taxi in Malaysia – local and 'out-station' – or long distance. The latter – usually Mercedes or Peugeot – connect all major towns and cities. They operate on a shared-cost basis – as soon as the full complement of four passengers turns up the taxis set off. Alternatively, it is possible to charter the whole taxi for the price of four single fares. Taxi stands are usually next door to major bus stations. Fares are fixed by the government and posted at stands, so there is no need, or point, in bargaining. If shared, taxi fares usually cost about twice as much as bus fares, but they are much faster. For groups travelling together taking a taxi makes good sense. Note that it is easier to find passengers going your way in the morning than later in the day.

Local taxi fares in Malaysia are among the cheapest in Southeast Asia. Most local taxis in major towns are now metered and a/c. Turning the a/c on costs an additional 20%. If there is no meter, or, as is more often the case, the meter is broken, fares should be negotiated in advance.

Trishaws In KL it has long been too dangerous for trishaws, apart from around Chinatown and suburban areas. In towns such as Melaka, Georgetown and Kota Bharu, as well as in many other smaller towns, they remain one of the best, and certainly most pleasant, ways of getting around, particularly for sightseeing. It is necessary to negotiate fares in advance. As Malaysia becomes more affluent, so trishaws are disappearing; before long, presumably, it will be like Singapore: an expensive way to travel for well-heeled tourists.

Keeping in touch

Communications

Internet Malaysia is one of the most gung-ho places on the planet when it comes to information technology and the internet – reflected in the prime minister's grand scheme to create Malaysia's very own Silicon Valley based on the MMSC or Multi-Media Super Corridor at, predictably, Cyberjaya. In line with this, internet cafés have sprung up all over the place and every town, however small, down-at-heel and apparently forgotten-by-the-wider-world will have, at the very least, a place offering internet services. Rates are cheap too: RM2.50 per hour at the bottom end, with most places charging around RM3-5/hour, but some hotels up to RM10/hour. Generally, internet cafés mainly geared to tourists are more expensive than those largely serving the local market.

Malaysia's post is cheap and reasonably reliable, although incoming and outgoing par-
cels should be registered. To send postcards and aerograms overseas costs RM0.50,
while letters cost RM0.90. Post-office opening hours are 0800-1700 Monday-Friday,
0800-1200 Saturday. Fax and telex services are available in most state capitals. Poste
Restante is a reliable service available at general post offices in major cities; as elsewhere, make sure your surname is capitalised and underlined. Most post offices provide a packing service for a reasonable fee (around RM5).

Post

Local There are public telephone booths in most towns; telephones take RM0.10 and
RM0.20 coins. Card phones are now widespread and they make good sense if phoning
abroad. There are two types of card: *Kadfon* and *Unicard*. *Kadfon* can only be used at
Telekom phone-booths, *Unicard* can be used at *Uniphone* phone-booths. Cards, in
denominations from RM5 to RM50, are available from airports, petrol stations and
most outlets of *7-eleven* and *Hop-In*. *Telekom* cards are sold at post offices, *Telekom*
offices, and some shops. On most public phones it is necessary to press the release but-
ton once the other person responds.

Telephone
*Operator for
'outstation' (trunk)
calls: T101
Enquiries: T102
Directory: T103
International IDD
assistance: T108*

International There is an international telephone exchange in KL and calls can be
booked to most countries in the world. Calls may be booked in advance. Collect calls
can be linked to destination countries without delay (the operator will call you back).
Direct calls can be made from telephones with IDD (international direct dialling) facility
(007 plus country code plus area code plus number). Direct international calls can be
made from most *Kedai Telekom* and telephone booths in major towns.

Media

The main English-language dailies are *The New Straits Times*, *Business Times*, *The Star*,
and *The Malay Mail* (afternoon). The main Sunday papers are *The New Sunday Times*,
The Sunday Mail and *The Sunday Star*. The English-language dailies are government-owned and this is reflected in their content which tends to be relentlessly
pro-government. *Aliran Monthly* is a high-brow but fascinating publication offering
current affairs analysis from a non-government perspective. *The Rochet* is the Democratic Action Party's opposition newspaper, and also presents an alternative perspective. Both are available at news outlets. International editions of leading foreign
newspapers and news magazines can be obtained at main news stands and book
stalls, although some of these are not cleared through customs until mid-afternoon
(notably *The Asian Wall Street Journal*). In East Malaysia the main English-language
newspapers are the *Sabah Daily News* and the *Sarawak Tribune*.

Newspapers

If you are looking for any alternative line to the government's then it would be best
to check the welter of opposition websites. A couple of years ago Prime Minister
Dr Mahathir Mohamad assured high-tech investors that he wouldn't attempt to con-
trol or censor the Web. This was all part of his attempt to create a MMSC or Multi-Media
Super Corridor, a sort of Asian Silicon Valley. The best web-based newspaper is
Malaysiakini.com to be found at malaysiakini.com/columntoday.htm.

For listings of what to do, the best sources are *Night & Day*, published weekly, and
the *What's On* section of the *Malay Mail*.

There are six government radio stations which broadcast in various languages including English. *Radio 1* broadcasts in Bahasa Melayu; *Radio 2* is a music station; *Radio 3* is
mainly Bahasa but broadcasts a special programme for tourists every day at 1800;
Radio 4 is in English; *Radio 5*, Chinese; *Radio 6*, Tamil. In KL you can tune into the Federal Capital's radio station and elsewhere in the country there are local stations. The
BBC World Service can be picked up on FM in southern Johor, from the Singapore

Radio

Essentials

Essentials

transmitter. Elsewhere it can be received on short-wave. The main frequencies are (in kHz): 11750, 9740, 6195 and 3915.

The main services that can be picke up on short-wave radio are: **British Broadcasting Corporation** (BBC, London) *Southeast Asian service* 3915, 6195, 9570, 9740, 11750, 11955, 15360; *Singapore service* 88.9MHz; *East Asian service* 5995, 6195, 7180, 9740, 11715, 11750, 11945, 11955, 15140, 15280, 15360, 17830, 21715; **Voice of America** (VoA, Washington) *Southeast Asian service* 1143, 1575, 7120, 9760, 9770, 15185, 15425; *Indonesian service* 6110, 11760, 15425; **Radio Beijing** *Southeast Asian service* (English) 11600, 11660; and **Radio Japan (Tokyo)** *Southeast Asian service* (English) 11815, 17810, 21610.

Television *RTM1* and *RTM2* are operated by **Radio Television Malaysia**, the government-run broadcasting station. Apart from locally produced programmes, some American and British series are shown. Three other channels are commercially run. There is a broad mixture of content, from Chinese kung-fu movies to Tamil musicals and English-language blockbusters and series. On the three commercial stations, all programmes are liberally interspersed with advertising, most of it for cigarettes, and leading tobacco companies sponsor film shows. Programmes for all channels are listed in daily newspapers. Singapore Broadcasting Service programmes can be received as far north as Melaka and are often listed in Malaysian papers. The government has long resisted the arrival of satellite TV, believing it to be a cultural polluter but, as they say, there's no stopping progress (or, at least, its difficult to).

Food and drink

Cuisine Malaysians, like their neighbours in Singapore, love their food, and the dishes of the three main communities, Malay, Chinese and Indian, comprise a hugely varied national menu. Even within each ethnic cuisine, there is a vast choice; every state has its own special Malay dishes and the different Chinese provincial specialities are well represented; in addition there is North Indian food, South Indian food and Indian Muslim food. Nyonya cuisine is found in the old Straits Settlements of Penang and Melaka. Malaysia also has great seafood, which the Chinese do best, and in recent years a profusion of restaurants, representing other Asian and European cuisines, have set up, mainly in the big cities. In the East Malaysian states of Sabah and Sarawak, there are tribal specialities.

For restaurant price codes, see the inside front cover. For health matters relating to food, see page 60   With a large ethnic Indian population, vegetarian food is usually available, especially on the Peninsula. In East Malaysia it can be harder to find vegetarian alternatives. There are also numerous Chinese and Malay vegetarian dishes, although it is not unusual to find slivers of meat even when a vegetable dish is specifically requested. In tourist areas and more cosmopolitan towns vegetarian restaurants are becoming popular.

Malay The best Malay food is usually found at stalls in hawker centres. The staple diet is rice and curry, which is rich and creamy due to the use of coconut milk. Herbs and spices include chillis, ginger, turmeric, coriander, lemongrass, anise, cloves, cumin, caraway and cinnamon.

Rice dishes *nasi campur* – Malay curry buffet of rice served with meat, fish, vegetables and fruit.
nasi goreng – rice, meat and vegetables fried with garlic, onions and *sambal*.
nasi lemak – a breakfast dish of rice cooked in coconut milk and served with prawn sambal, *ikan bilis*, a hard boiled egg, peanuts and cucumber.

nasi padang – plain rice served with a selection of dishes.

nasi puteh – plain boiled rice.

nasi dagang – popular on the east coast for breakfast; glutinous rice cooked in coconut milk and served with fish curry, cucumber pickle and *sambal*.

Soup *soto ayam* – popular for breakfast in Johor and Sarawak, a spicy chicken soup served with rice cubes, chicken and vegetables.

lontong – popular in the south, particularly for breakfast. Cubed compressed rice served with mixed vegetables in coconut milk. *Sambal* is the accompaniment.

Meat *satay* – chicken, beef or mutton marinated and skewered on a bamboo, barbecued over a brazier. Usually served with *ketupat*.

Noodles *kway teow* – flat noodles fried with seafood, egg, soy sauce, beansprouts and *kuchai* (chives).

laksa johor – noodles in fish curry sauce and raw vegetables.

mee goreng – fried noodles.

mee jawa – noodles in gravy, served with prawn fritters, potatoes, tofu and beancurd.

mee rebus – noodles with beef, chicken or prawn with soybean in spicy sauce.

Curries *rendang* – dry beef curry (a Sumatran dish).

longong – vegetable curry made from rice cakes cooked in coconut, beans, cabbage and bamboo shoots.

Salad *rojak* – Malaysia's answer to Indonesia's *gado gado* – mixed vegetable salad served in peanut sauce with *ketupat*.

Vegetables *sayur manis* – sweet vegetables; vegetables fried with chilli, *belacan* and mushrooms.

Sweets *(kueh)* *apam* – steamed rice cakes.

pulut inti – glutinous rice served with sweetened grated coconut.

nyonya kueh – Chinese kueh, among the most popular is *yow cha koei* – deep-fried kneaded flour.

Chinese

Cantonese and Hainanese cooking are the most prevalent Chinese cuisines in Malaysia. Some of the more common Malaysian-Chinese dishes are Hainanese chicken rice (rice cooked in chicken stock and served with steamed or roast chicken), *char kway teow* (Teochew-style fried noodles, with eggs, cockles and chilli paste), *or luak* (Hokkien oyster omelette), *dim sum* (steamed dumplings and patties) and *yong tow foo* (beancurd and vegetables stuffed with fish). Good Chinese food is available in restaurants, coffee shops and from hawker stalls.

Each province of China has its own distinct cuisine. A balanced meal should contain the five basic taste sensations: sweet, bitter, salty, spicy and acidic to balance the yin and yang

Cantonese Light and delicately flavoured dishes are often steamed with ginger and are not very spicy. Shark's fin and birds' nest soups, and *dim sum* (mostly steamed delicacies trolleyed to your table, but only served until early afternoon) are Cantonese classics. Other typical dishes include fish steamed with soya sauce, ginger, chicken stock and wine; *wan ton* soup; blanched green vegetables in oyster sauce; and suckling pig.

Hainanese Simple cuisine from the southern island of Hainan; chicken rice with sesame oil, soy and a chilli and garlic sauce is their tastiest contribution.

Hakka Uses plenty of sweet potato and dried shrimp and specializes in stewed pigs' trotters, *yong tau foo* (deep-fried beancurd), and chillis and other vegetables stuffed with fish paste.

Hokkien Being one of Singapore's biggest dialect groups means Hokkien cuisine is prominent, particularly in hawker centres, although there are very few Hokkien restaurants. Hokkien Chinese invented the spring roll and their cooking uses lots of noodles and in one or two places you can still see them being made by hand. Hokkien cuisine is also characterized by clear soups and steamed seafood, eaten with soya sauce. Fried Hokkien *mee* (yellow wheat noodles stir-fried with seafood and pork), *hay cho* (deep fried balls of prawn) and *bee hoon* (rice vermicelli cooked with prawns, squid and beansprouts with lime and chillies) are specialities.

Essentials

Distinctive fruits

Custard apple (or sugar apple) Scaly green skin, squeeze the skin to open the fruit and scoop out the flesh with a spoon. Season: June-September.

Durian (Durio zibethinus) The size of a football, this prickly fruit with yellow flesh is infamous for its pungent smell. While today regarded by many visitors as simply revolting, early Europeans (16th-18th centuries) raved about it, possibly because its taste resembled the Western delicacies of the period. Borri (1744) thought that "God himself, had produced that fruit". But by 1880 Burbridge was writing: "Its odour – one scarcely feels justified in using the word 'perfume' – is so potent, so vague, but withal so insinuating, that it can scarcely be tolerated inside the house". Banned from hotel rooms throughout the region, and beloved by most Southeast Asians, it has an alluring and some maintain addictive taste. Durian-flavoured chewing gum, ice cream and jams are all available. Season: May-August.

Jackfruit Similar in appearance to durian but not so spiky. Yellow flesh, tasting slightly like custard. Season: January-June.

Mangosteen (Garcinia mangostana) An aubergine-coloured hard shell covers this tennis ball size fruit. Cut or squeeze the shell to reach its sweet white flesh which is prized above all others by many visitors. In 1898, an American resident of Java wrote, erotically and in obvious ecstasy: "The five white segments separate easily, and they melt on the tongue with a touch of tart and a touch of sweet; one moment a memory of the juiciest, most fragrant apple, at another a remembrance of the smoothest cream ice, the most exquisite and delicately flavoured fruit-acid known – all of the delights of nature's laboratory condensed in that ball of neige parfumée". Southeast Asians believe it should be eaten as a chaser to durian. Season: April-September.

Pomelo A large round fruit the size of anything from an ostrich egg to a football, with thick, green skin and pith, and flesh similar to grapefruit, but less acidic. Season: August-November.

Rambutan (Nephelium lappaceum) Bright red and hairy (rambut is the Malay word for 'hair')with a slightly rubbery but sweet flesh this fruit is a close relative of the lychee of southern China. The Thai word for rambutan is ngoh – the nickname given by Thais to the Negrito aboriginals in the southern jungles. Season: May-September.

Salak (Salacca edulis) A small pear-shaped fruit about the size of a large plum with a rough, brown, scaly skin (somewhat like a miniature pangolin) and yellow-white, crisp flesh. It is related to the sago and rattan trees.

Tamarind (Tamarindus indicus) Brown seedpods with dry brittle skins each with a brown tart-sweet fruit which grow on a tree introduced into Southeast Asia from India. The name is Arabic for 'Indian date'. With a high tartaric acid content , the flesh is used to flavour curries, jams, jellies and chutneys as well as for cleaning brass and copper. Elephants have a predilection for tamarind balls. Season: December-February.

Hunanese Known for its glutinous rice, honeyed ham and pigeon soup.

Peking (**Beijing**) Chefs at the imperial court in Peking had a repertoire of over 8,000 recipes. Dumplings, noodles and steamed buns predominate, since wheat is the staple diet, but in Singapore, rice may accompany the meal. Peking duck, *shi choy* (deep fried bamboo shoots), and hot and sour soup are among the best Peking dishes. Peking duck (with the skin basted with syrup and cooked until crisp) is usually eaten rolled into a pancake and accompanied by hoisin sauce and spring onions. Fish dishes are usually deep-fried and served with sweet and sour sauce.

Shanghainese Seafood dominates this cuisine and many dishes are cooked in soya sauce. Braised fish-heads, braised abalone (a large shellfish) in sesame sauce, and crab and sweetcorn soup are typical dishes. Wine is often used in the preparation of meat dishes, hence drunken prawn and drunken crab.

Steamboat The Chinese answer to fondue is a popular dish in Singapore and can be found in numerous restaurants and at some hawker centres. Thinly sliced pieces of raw meat, fish, prawns, cuttlefish, fishballs and vegetables are gradually tossed into a bubbling cauldron in the centre of the table. They are then dunked into hot chilli and soya sauces and the resulting soup provides a flavoursome broth to wash it all down at the end.

Szechuan Very spicy (garlic and chilli are dominant), Szechuan is widely considered the tastiest Chinese cuisine. Szechuan food includes heaps of hot red peppers, traditionally considered to be protection against cold and disease. Among the best Szechuan dishes are smoked duck in tea leaves and camphor sawdust; minced pork with beancurd; steamed chicken in lotus leaves; and fried eels in garlic sauce.

Teochew Famous for its *muay* porridges. This is a light, clear broth consumed with side dishes of crayfish, salted eggs and vegetables.

Indian cooking can be divided into three schools: northern and southern (neither eat beef) and Muslim (no pork). Northern dishes tend to be more subtly spiced, use more meat and are served with breads. Southern dishes use fiery spices, emphasize vegetables and are served with rice. The best-known North Indian food are the *tandoori* dishes, which are served with delicious fresh *naan* breads, baked in ovens on-site. Other pancakes include roti, thosai and chapati. Malaysia's famous *mamak*-men are Indian Muslims who are highly skilled in everything from *teh tarik* (see Drink below) to *rotis*. **Indian**

Other dishes include *roti canai* – pancakes served with lentils and curry.
murtabak – a thick *roti*-pizza with minced meat, onion and egg.
nasi biriyani – rice cooked in ghee, spices and vegetable, served with beef or chicken.
nasi kandar – Mamak's version of nasi campur.
daun pisang – a Malay/South Indian *thali* – curry and rice, with poppadoms and chutneys all served on a banana leaf.

Through inter-marriage with local Malays a unique culture evolved and with it, a cuisine that has grown out of a blend of the two. Nyonya food is spicier than Chinese food, and it uses pork. Nyonya dishes in Penang have adopted flavours from neighbouring Thailand, whereas Melaka's Nyonya food has Indonesian overtones. In traditional Straits Chinese households, great emphasis was placed on presentation and the fine-chopping of ingredients.

Nyonya
See page 212 for information on the history of the Nyonyas

Typical dishes include *kapitan* – chicken cooked in coconut milk.
otak otak – minced fish, coconut milk and spices, steamed in a banana leaf.
laksa – rice noodles in spicy coconut milk and prawn-flavoured gravy blended with spices and served with shellfish, chicken, beancurd and *belacan*.
assam laksa – the specialized Penang version – rice noodles served in fish gravy with shredded cucumber, pineapple, raw onions and mint.

This is a blending of cuisines and ingredients from East and West. So far, the foodies have not agreed on a single name. It is sometimes termed 'Fusion' cuisine, sometimes Trans-ethnic, and sometimes New Asia. Perhaps this confusion over what to call the food is because people don't seem to be able to agree what constitutes the cuisine(s) in the first place. Some chefs and food critics maintain that it involves cooking Eastern ingredients using Western cooking techniques. Others see it as a combination of two styles of cooking and two sets of ingredients. One chef believes you should be able to drink wine with New Asia cuisine, something that you cannot do with Chinese food, as soy sauce kills the taste of wine. But like most things, you'll know it when you see it. Classic French and other chefs are, of course, appalled by what they see as just a confusion of tastes: the **New Asia (Fusion)**

art of good cooking is to bring out the flavour of the fish, meat or vegetables, not to anni-
hilate them with lemon grass, chillies, soy and other herbs and condiments.

Sabahan The Kadazans form the largest ethnic group in Sabah. Their food tends to use mango
and can be on the sour side.

Popular dishes include *hinava* – marinated raw fish.
sup manuk on hiing – chicken soup with rice wine.
tapai – chicken cooked in local rice wine.
pakis – ferns, which are fried with mushrooms and *belacan*. Sometimes ferns are eaten
raw, with a squeeze of lime (*sayur pakis limau*).
sup terjun – jumping soup – salted fish, mango and ginger.
hinompula – a dessert made from tapioca, sugar, coconut and the juice from
screwpine leaves.

Sarawakian *Ternbok* – fish, either grilled or steamed.
pan suh manok – chicken pieces cooked in bamboo cup and served with *bario* (Kelabit
mountain rice).

Eating out

Many restaurants charge an extra 15% service and tax

Malaysia, like Singapore, just about has it all on the restaurant front: from the swankiest
restaurants where international cuisine is served at prices that are usually rather less
than one would expect, through to stalls and hawker centres where a meal can cost
less than a Coke back home. There's also a huge range to choose from because, as
noted above, Malaysia is a plural society and home to significant Malay, Chinese and
Indian populations that have, at times, intersected in gastronomically interesting ways.
Furthermore, and again as in Singapore, good food is not confined to restaurants;
some of the best local dishes can be sampled at hawker centres, which are cheap and
often stay open late into the night.

The cheapest places to eat are in **hawker centres** and roadside **stalls** (often concentrated in or close to night markets) where it is possible to eat well for just RM2-3.
Stalls may serve Malay, Indian or Chinese dishes and, even, some food which approxi-
mates to 'Western'. Next in the sequence of sophistication and price come the ubiquitous **kedai kopi** or coffee shops which can be found in every town, and almost every
street and where a meal will cost upwards of RM5. Usually run by Chinese or Indian
families, rather than Malay, they open at around 0900 and close in the early evening.
However some open much earlier, at dawn, to serve dim sum to people making their
way to work. Chinese-run kedai kopi tend to be the last to close - sometimes as late as
midnight - and they are also the only coffee shops where it is possible to track down a
cold beer. Malay-run kedai kopi are good for lunch with their nasi campur spreads,
while Indian-run coffee shops offer what you would expect them to offer. Above the
kedai kopi come a phalanx of **restaurants** from the basic to the extremely pricey. A
special category are the restaurants geared to travellers' culinary needs which tend to
be concentrated in beach resorts. Here it is possible to live off banana pancakes, fudge
cake, smoothies, jaffles and all the other dishes that backpackers on the move seem to
need to keep body and soul together. Hotels restaurant regularly lay on **buffet
spreads**, which are good value at about RM20-30, often much cheaper than the price
of a room would suggest.

**Cookery
courses
(Malay)**

During Ramadan many Malay restaurants close during daylight hours

For those wishing to learn more about Malaysian cuisine, several state tourist boards
offer short courses in curry-making, etc. Enquire at Tourism Malaysia information centres. *Tourism Malaysia* publishes a glossy pamphlet called *Malaysian Common Recipes*
providing an introduction to spices and ingredients and easy-to-follow recipes to 16
succulent dishes, see page 34 for contact information. A wide variety of Malaysian
cookery books is available at leading bookshops.

Essentials

Soft drinks, mineral water and freshly squeezed fruit drinks are available. Anchor and
Tiger beer are widely sold, except in the more Islamic states of the east coast, especially
Kelantan, and is cheapest at the hawker stalls (RM5-7 per bottle). A beer will cost RM8-15
per bottle in coffee shops. Malaysian-brewed Guinness is popular, mainly because Chinese believe it has medicinal qualities as it has been successfully sold on the 'Guinness
Stout is good for you' line. Malaysian tea is grown in the Cameron Highlands and is very
good. One of the most interesting cultural refinements of the Indian Muslim community
is the Mamak-man, who is famed for *teh tarik* (pulled tea), which is thrown across a distance of about a metre, from one cup to another, with no spillages. The idea is to cool it
down for customers, but it has become an art form; mamak-men appear to cultivate the
nonchalant look when pouring. Malaysian satirist Kit Leee says a tea-stall mamak "could
'pull' tea in free fall without spilling a drop – while balancing a *beedi* on his lower lip and
making a statement on Economic Determinism". Most of the coffee comes from Indonesia, although some is locally produced. Malaysians like strong coffee and unless you specify *kurang manis* (less sugar), *tak mahu manis* (don't want sugar) or *kopi kosong* (empty
coffee, black, no sugar), it will come with lashings of condensed milk.

Drink

Shopping

Most big towns now have modern shopping complexes as well as shops and markets.
Department stores are fixed-price, but nearly everywhere else it is possible – and necessary – to bargain. In most places, at least 30% can be knocked off the asking price;
your first offer should be roughly half the first quote.

The islands of Langkawi and Labuan have duty-free shopping; the range of goods is
poor, however. In addition to the duty-free shops, cameras, watches, pens, lighters,
cosmetics, perfumes and portable radio/cassette players are all duty-free in Malaysia.
Film and camera equipment are still cheaper in Singapore, which offers a wider selection of most products – especially electronics and computer products.

What to buy
*For Langkawi and
Labuan see pages 186
and 439 respectively*

    Kuala Lumpur and most of the state capitals have a Chinatown which usually has a
few curio shops and nearly always a *pasar malam*, or night market. Indian quarters,
which are invariably labelled 'Little India', are only found in bigger towns; they are the
best places to buy *sarungs*, *longuis*, *dotis* and *saris* (mostly imported from India) as well
as other textiles. Malay handicrafts are usually only found in markets or government
craft centres.

The Malaysian arts and crafts industry used to enjoy much more royal patronage, but
when craftsmen went in search of more lucrative jobs, the industry began to decline.
The growth of tourism in recent years has helped to reinvigorate it, particularly in traditional handicraft-producing areas, such as the east coast states of Terengganu and
Kelantan. The Malay Arts and Crafts Society has also been instrumental in preventing
the decline of the industry. In 1981, Malaysian Handicraft and Souvenir Centres
(*Karyaneka* centres), were set up to market Malaysian arts and crafts in KL and some
state capitals. Typical Malaysian handicrafts which can be found on the Peninsula
include woodcarvings, batik, *songket* (cloth woven with gold and silver thread),
pewterware, silverware, kites, tops and *wayang kulit* (shadow puppets). For more
detail on Malaysian crafts, see page 548.

Handicrafts

    Other than the Peninsula's east coast states, Sarawak is the other place where the
traditional handicraft industry is flourishing (see page 408). The state capital, Kuching,
is full of handicraft and antique shops selling tribal pieces collected from upriver; those
going upriver themselves can often find items being sold in towns and even
longhouses *en route*. Typical Sarawakian handicrafts include woodcarvings, *pua*

kumbu (rust-coloured tie-dye blankets), beadwork and basketry (see page 333). Many handicraft shops on Peninsular Malaysia also sell Sarawakian handicrafts – particularly those in KL – although there is a considerable mark-up.

Entertainment

Most bars offer happy hours (usually 1700-1900)

Firstly, it should be said that Malaysia is most certainly not Ibiza. There has never been a really hot club and dance circuit in Malaysia, and although KL has the usual round of discos, clubs and bars with crooners, often hand-picked and flown in from the Philippines, there's not much point in gearing your entire holiday towards this. That said, there are some cool places, often because in a contrary sort of way, they are so un-cool. Karaoke is more the average Malaysians cup of *arak* than hip-hop. The main towns where there is a nightlife of sorts are KL (for obvious reasons), Johor Bahru (because Singaporeans pop down here to see whether they made the right decision leaving the Federation in the mid-1960s) and Penang (because of all the tourists). The backpacker haunts on the East Coast also have some places that live largely in the past and play Bob Marley back-numbers, while Kuching and Kota Kinabalu, the capitals of the East Coast states of Sarawak and Sabah, also have a fair sprinkling of discos and clubs, usually in the glitzier hotels (so all very sanitised).

Holidays and festivals

Tourism Malaysia has dates of movable holidays and festivals, see page 34 for contact information

Note that Islamic holidays, which are listed separately below, may vary significantly in their timing during the year. Chinese, Indian (Hindu) and some Christian holidays are also movable. To make things even more exciting, each state has its own public holidays when shops close and banks pull down their shutters. This makes calculating public holidays in advance a bit of a quagmire of lunar events, assorted kings' birthdays, and tribal festivals. But federal and state public holidays, including movable religious holidays, are listed (albeit in Malay) at www.tourism.gov.my/public_holidays2001.htm.

School holidays

Schools in Malaysia have five breaks through the year, although the actual dates vary from state to state. They generally fall in the months of January (one week), March (two weeks), May (three weeks), August (one week), and October (four weeks).

January-February

New Year's Day (**1 January**: public holiday except Johor, Kedah, Kelantan, Perlis and Terengganu). *Thaipusam* (movable: public holiday Johor, Negeri Sembilan, Perak, Penang and Selangor only, **28 January 2002**) celebrated by many Hindus throughout Malaysia in honour of their deity Lord Subramanian (also known as Lord Muruga); he represents virtue, bravery, youth and power. Held during full moon in the month of Thai, it is a day of penance and thanksgiving. Devotees pay homage to Lord Subramanian by piercing their bodies, cheeks and tongues with sharp skewers (*vel*) and hooks weighted with oranges, and carrying *kevadis* (steel structures bearing the image of Lord Muruga). There are strict rules the devotee must follow in order to purify himself before carrying the kevadi; he becomes a vegetarian and abstains from worldly pleasures. Women cannot carry *kevadis* as they are not allowed to bare their bodies in order to be pierced. Although a *kevadi* carrier can have as many as a hundred spears piercing his flesh he only loses a small amount of blood in his trance. Each participant tries to outdo the others in the severity of his torture. At certain temples fire-walking is also part of this ceremony. Many Hindus disapprove of the spectacle and believe that their bodies are a gift from Siva; they should serve as a temple for the soul and should not be abused. This festival is peculiar to Hindus in Malaysia, Singapore and Thailand and is a corruption of a Tamil ceremony from South India. The biggest gatherings are at Batu Caves just outside KL, when thousands of pilgrims congregate in a carnival-like atmosphere (see page 85); there are also festivals held in Melaka, Penang and Singapore.

Chinese New Year (movable: public holiday, two days in most states, one day in Kelantan and Terengganu) a 15-days lunar festival celebrated in late January/early February. Chinatown streets are crowded for weeks with shoppers buying traditional oranges which signify luck. Lion, unicorn or dragon dances welcome-in the New Year and, unlike in Singapore, thousands of firecrackers are ignited to ward off evil spirits. *Chap Goh Mei* is the 15th day of the Chinese New Year and brings celebrations to a close; it is marked with a final dinner, another firecracker fest, prayers and offerings. The Chinese believe that in order to find good husbands, girls should throw oranges into the river/sea on this day. In Sarawak the festival is known as *Guan Hsiao Cheih* (Lantern Festival).

Easter (movable) celebrated in Melaka with candle-lit processions and special services (see page 205). *Good Friday* is a public holiday in Sabah and Sarawak. **March-April**

Labour Day (**1 May**: public holiday). *Kurah Aran* (**1 May**) celebrated by the Bidayuh **May** tribe in Sarawak (see page 402) after the paddy harvest is over. *Wesak Day* (movable: public holiday except Labuan, **26 May 2002**) the most important day in the Buddhist calendar, celebrates the Buddha's birth, death and enlightenment. Temples throughout the country are packed with devotees offering incense, joss-sticks and prayers. Lectures on Buddhism and special exhibitions are held. In Melaka there is a procession at night with decorated floats, bands, dancers and acrobatics.

Birthday of His Majesty the King (first Saturday of the month: public holiday, **1 June** **June** **2002**) mainly celebrated in KL with processions. *Dragon Boat Festival* (movable) honours the suicide of an ancient Chinese poet hero, Qu Yuan. He tried to press for political reform by drowning himself in the Mi Luo River as a protest against corruption. In an attempt to save him fishermen played drums and threw rice dumplings to try and distract vultures. His death is commemorated with dragon boat races and the enthusiastic consumption of rice dumplings; biggest celebrations are in Penang.

Hari Kebangsaan or *National Day* (**31 August**: public holiday) commemorates Malay- **August** sian independence (*merdeka*) in 1957. Big celebration in KL with processions of floats representing all the states; best places to see it: on the Padang (Merdeka Square) or on TV. In Sarawak, Hari Kebangsaan is celebrated in a different divisional capital each year. *Mooncake* or *Lantern Festival* (movable). This Chinese festival marks the overthrow of the Mongol Dynasty in China; celebrated, as the name suggests, with the exchange and eating of mooncakes. According to Chinese legend secret messages of revolt were carried inside these cakes and led to the uprising. In the evening, children light festive lanterns while women pray to the Goddess of the Moon.

Festival of the Hungry Ghosts (movable) on the seventh moon in the Chinese lunar **August-** calendar, souls in purgatory are believed to return to earth to feast. Food is offered to **September** these wandering spirits. Altars are set up in the streets and candles with faces are burned on them.

Festival of the Nine Emperor Gods or *Kiew Ong Yeah* (movable) marks the return of the **October** spirits of the nine emperor gods to earth. The mediums whom they are to possess purify themselves by observing a vegetarian diet. The gods possess the mediums, who go into trance and are then carried on sedan chairs whose seats are comprised of razor-sharp blades or spikes. Devotees visit temples dedicated to the nine gods. A strip

Essentials

Festivals in East Malaysia

Besides those celebrated throughout the country, Sabah and Sarawak have their own festivals. Exact dates can be procured from the tourist offices in the capitals. State public holidays are listed on page 57.

Kadazan Harvest Festival or Tadau Keamatan (movable: public holiday, Sabah and Labuan only) marks the end of the rice harvest in Sabah; the magavau ritual is performed to nurse the spirit back to health in readiness for the next planting season. Traditionally, the ritual world would have been performed in the paddy fields by a bobohizan (high priestess). Celebrated with feasting, tapai (rice wine) drinking, dancing and general merry-making. There are also agricultural shows, buffalo races, cultural performances and traditional games. The traditional sumazal dance is one of the highlights of the festivities.

Gawai (movable: public holiday Sarawak only) is the major festival of the year for the Iban of Sarawak; longhouses party continuously for a week. The Gawai celebrates the end of the rice harvest and welcomes the new planting season. The main ritual is called magavau and nurses the spirit of the grain back to health in advance of the planting season. Like the Kadazan harvest festival in Sabah, visitors

are welcome to join in, but in Sarawak, the harvest festival is much more traditional. On the first day of celebrations everyone dresses up in traditional costumes, singing, dancing and drinking tuak rice wine until they drop.

Gawai Burung (Sarawak) is biggest of all the gawais and honours the war god of the Ibans. Gawai Kenyalang is one stage of Gawai Burung and is celebrated only after a tribesman has been instructed to do so after a dream.

Gawai Antu (Sarawak), also known as Gawai Nyunkup or Rugan, is an Iban tribute to departed spirits. In simple terms, it is a party to mark the end of mourning for anyone whose relative had died in the previous six months.

Gawai Batu (Sarawak) is a whetstone feast held by Iban farmers in June.

Gawai Mpijong Jaran Rantau (Sarawak) is celebrated by the Bidayuh before grass cutting in new paddy fields.

Gawai Bineh (Sarawak) is an Iban festival celebrated after harvest. It welcomes back all the spirits of the paddy from the fields.

Gawai Sawa (movable) is celebrated by the Bidayuh in Sarawak to offer thanksgiving for the last year and to make the next year a plentiful one.

of yellow cotton is often bought from the temple and worn on the right wrist as a sign of devotion. The ceremonies usually culminate with a fire-walking ritual.

October-November
Deepvali (movable: public holiday except Sarawak and Labuan, **4 November 2002**) the Hindu festival of lights commemorates the victory of light over darkness and good over evil: the triumphant return of Rama after his defeat of the evil Ravanna in the Hindu epic, the Ramayana. Every Hindu home is brightly lit and decorated for the occasion.

December
Christmas Day (**25 December**: public holiday) Christmas in Malaysia is a commercial spectacle these days with fairy lights and decorations and tropical Santa Clauses – although it does not compare with celebrations in Singapore. Mostly celebrated on the west coast and ignored on the more Muslim east coast. Midnight mass is the main Christmas service held in churches throughout Malaysia.

Islamic holidays

The timing of Islamic festivals is an art rather than a science and is calculated on the basis of local sightings of various phases of the moon. Thus dates are approximations and can vary by a day or two. Muslim festivals move forward by around 9-10 days each year. To check on dates for 2003, see the following websites: www.regit.com/malaysia/holiday/holiday.htm or www.asianinfo-by-cj.com or www.tourism.gov.my.

Hari Raya Haji (movable: public holiday; in Kedah, Kelantan, Perlis and Terengganu *Hari Raya Qurban* is also a public holiday, **23-24 February 2002**) celebrated by Muslims to mark the 10th day of Zulhijgah, the 12th month of the Islamic calendar when pilgrims celebrate their return from the Haj to Mecca. In the morning, prayers are offered and later, families hold 'open house'. Those who can afford it sacrifice goats or cows to be distributed to the poor. Many Malays have the title Haji in their name, meaning they have made the pilgrimage to Mecca; men who have been on the Haj wear a white skull-hat. The Haj is one of the five keystones of Islam. **February**

Maal Hijrah (*Awal Muharram*) (movable: public holiday, **15 March 2002**) marks the first day of the Muslim calendar, marking the Prophet Muhammad's journey from Mecca to Medina on the lunar equivalent of 16 July 622 AD. Religious discussions and lectures commemorate the day. **March**

Birthday of the Prophet Muhammad (*Maulidur Rasul*) (movable: public holiday, **25 May 2002**) to commemorate Prophet Muhammad's birthday in 571 AD. Processions and Koran recitals in most big towns. *Wesak Day* (movable, public holiday, **26 May 2002**). **May**

Hari Hol Almarhum Sultan Ismail (movable, 13 September 2002, Johor). *Israk and Mikraj* (movable, **4 October 2002**, Kedah and Negeri Sembilan). **October**

Awal Ramadan (movable: public holiday Johor and Melaka, **6 November 2002**) the first day of Ramadan, a month of fasting for all Muslims – and by implication, all Malays. During this month Muslims abstain from all food and drink (as well as smoking) from sunrise to sundown – if they are very strict, Muslims do not even swallow their own saliva during daylight hours. It is strictly adhered to in the conservative Islamic states of Kelantan and Terengganu. Every evening for 30 days before breaking of fast, stalls are set up which sell traditional Malay cakes and delicacies. The only people exempt from fasting are the elderly as well as women who are pregnant or are menstruating. *Nuzul Quran* (movable, Kelantan, Pahang, Perak, Perlis, Selangor and Terengganu, **22 November 2002**). **November**

Hari Raya Puasa or *Aidil Fitri* (movable: public holiday, **6-7 December 2002**) marks the end of the Muslim fasting month of Ramadan and is a day of prayer and celebration. In order for Hari Raya to be declared, the new moon of Syawal has to be sighted; if it is not, fasting continues for another day. It is the most important time of the year for Muslim families to get together; Malays living in towns and cities balek kampung (return home to their village), where it is 'open house' for relatives and friends, and special Malay delicacies are served. Hari Raya is also enthusiastically celebrated by Indian Muslims. **December**

State holidays

Only sultans' and governors' birthday celebrations are marked with processions and festivities; state holidays can disrupt travel itineraries – particularly in east coast states where they may run for several days.

Sultan of Kedah's birthday (**20 January 2002**, Kedah). **January**

Federal Territory Day (**1 February 2002**, KL and Labuan). **February**

March   *Installation of Sultan of Terengganu Day* (4 March 2002, Terengganu); *Sultan of Selangor's birthday* (9 March 2002, Selangor); *Sultan of Kelantan's birthday* (30-31 March 2002, Kelantan).

April   *Sultan of Johor's birthday* (8 April 2002, Johor); *Declaration of Melaka as Historic City* (15 April 2002, Melaka); *Sultan of Perak's birthday* (19 April 2002, Perak).

May   *Pahang Hol Day* (7 May 2002, Pahang); *Rajah of Perlis' birthday* (17 May 2002, Perlis); *Harvest Festival* (30-31 May 2002, Sabah and Labuan).

June   *Dayak Day* (1-2 June 2002, Sarawak).

July   *Governor of Penang's birthday* (second Saturday of the month, 13 July 2002, Penang); *Yang Di-Pertuan Besar of Negri Sembilan's birthday* (19 July 2002, Negri Sembilan); Sultan of Terengganu's birthday (20 July 2002).

September   *Governor of Sarawak's birthday* (14 September 2002, Sarawak); *Governor of Sabah's birthday* (16 September 2002, Sabah).

October   *Governor of Melaka's birthday* (second Saturday of the month, 12 October 2002, Melaka); *Sultan of Pahang's birthday* (24 October 2002, Pahang).

Sport and special interest travel

Diving   Dive sites off the Peninsula are not world class although there are some very good places to learn to scuba dive including Pulau Paya, Pulau Pangkor, Tioman, the Pulau Sibu archipelago, Pulau Redang and Pulau Perhentian. There are some world class dive sites in East Malaysia including Pulau Sipadan, Pulau Layang-Layang, the Tunku Abdul Rahman and Turtle Islands national parks, Pulau Tiga and Labuan.

West coast   Generally, the diving off the west coast of Peninsular Malaysia is the least spectacular in the country. However, as the bulk of Malaysia's population live near here, it is the most accessible from KL and other important centres. The islands of the **Paya archipelago**, to the north of Penang and south of Langkawi (see page 189), offer the best diving opportunities. It is now protected as an underwater reserve, having been gazetted in 1985. The principal islands are Paya, Kacha, Lembu and Segantan and they support a marine flora and fauna that includes 36 genera of hard corals, 92 other marine invertebrates and 45 genera of fish. On Pulau Paya itself, the waters off the rocky southwest tip have the best diving; the corals here are particularly good (with semi-precious black coral in deeper waters). Barracuda, grouper, jack and garfish are regularly seen in deeper waters. Facilities include an information centre and bathroom facilities. Camping is allowed (if the authorities are informed beforehand; see Paya, Langkawi for further information), but there is no accommodation available; the nearest hotels are on Langkawi to the north, or Penang to the south. Further expansion is planned, however.

Other west coast dive sites   Less well-known and developed dive sites off the west coast of the Peninsula include Pulau Sembilan, Pulau Pangkor and Pulau Pangkor Laut, situated not far from the town of Lumut (see page 139 139).

East coast   The waters around **Pulau Tioman** have been devastated in recent years through over-fishing and the uncontrolled activities of tourists. However, it is a convenient base to visit islands in the area including Pulau Tulai, Labas, Chebeh and Sepoi (see page 245). The **Pulau Sibu Archipelago** is a group of islands off Mersing in

Johore province and includes Pulau Rawa (see page 256), Babi Hujung, Babi Tengah, Babi Besar, Tinggi, Mentinggi and Sibu (see page 256). They are all included within a single marine park and, with the exceptions of Babi Hujung and Mentinggi, offer basic accommodation. **Pulau Tenggol** is the largest of a small group of islands, still relatively undeveloped and unspoilt. The range and number of fish here are impressive. Particularly noteworthy are the spectacular sunken cliffs. There is no accommodation available (see page 295). Like Pulau Perhentian, **Pulau Kapas** is an area suited to snorkelling and shallow dives (3-10 m). The beaches are good and there is accommodation available (see page 286).

Diving seasons in Malaysia

West coast, Peninsular Malaysia
November-May
East coast, Peninsular Malaysia
March-October
East Malaysia (Sabah & Sarawak)
March-September*
*** NB** Diving conditions at Pulau Sipadan are generally good year-round.*

Essentials

The dive sites around the protected **Pulau Redang** island group, consisting of nine islands 45 km off the Terengganu coast, are numerous and varied and are considered some of the best in Malaysia. There are an estimated 500 species of coral, 1,000 species of bivalves and some 3,000 species of fish, and the star of the show is a resident whale shark. There are also large schools of red snapper and other fish. The beaches of the islands that constitute the Pulau Redang Marine Park are nesting sites for the hawksbill turtle and rarer green turtles. A fishing village on stilts occupies one end of the island, but there is no dedicated tourist accommodation (see page 296 and box on page 285).

Shallow water snorkelling is excellent around **Pulau Perhentian**, and in July and August dolphins and pilot whales migrate through the waters fringing the island. Accommodation in 'A'-frame huts is available (see page 296).

Distant islands Pulau Aur and **Pulau Pemanggil** are situated 15 km apart about 65 km off the east coast of the Peninsula to the south of Tioman. Their remoteness has meant that they are the least disturbed diving locations in the area (see page 256).

East Malaysia The most memorable feature around **Pulau Layang-Layang** is a 2,000 m sea wall; the oceanic position means that sharks and pelagic fish are common here (see page 419). **Tunku Abdul Rahman Park** includes five pristine islands – Gaya, Sapi, Manukan, Mamutik and Sulug. The beaches are excellent and the coral and marine life, good. They are also the most easily accessible dive spots of quality from Kota Kinabalu, lying about 20 minutes by boat from the state capital. Accommodation is available on two of the islands, Mamutik and Manukan. **Pulau Mantanani** is a group of islands off Sabah's west coast of which Pulau Mantanani is the largest. Sharks and large pelagic fishes abound and the area is also a renowned fishing location. **Pulau Mengalum** is 70 km west of Kota Kinabalu and fish include marlin and sail fish along with the more common grouper, wrasse and snapper. The **Pulau Tiga** dive site comprises three islands that lie within the boundaries of a 15,864 ha park gazetted in 1978, 50 km southwest of Kota Kinabalu. Marine life includes turtles, tuna, dolphin and stingrays. The islands themselves support populations of monkeys and monitor lizards, as well as a mud volcano (see page 440). The park is primarily a research area for naturalists and so tourist facilities are intentionally kept to a minimum. Camping is allowed, but visitors need to bring their own food. The **Turtle Islands National Park** was created in 1977 and encompasses three islands: Pulau Selingaan, Gulisan and Bakkungan Kecil. As the popular name of the park suggests, it was gazetted to protect the rare green and hawksbill turtles. The peak period for egg laying is August to October for the green turtle and February to April for the hawksbill. Pulau Selingaan is the only island with accommodation (see page 460). The duty-free island of **Labuan** is a good base for visiting surrounding islands and dive spots. Because Labuan was a focus of military activity during the

Second World War, there are a number of wrecks here including Japanese and US warships (the latter includes the USS *Salute*). **Sipadan** is probably the best-known dive site in East Malaysia because of its stunning 700 m sea wall. Because Sipadan is an oceanic island, fish such as manta rays and large schools of barracuda are commonly seen here while they are rare elsewhere (see page 470).

Trekking & climbing
There are good jungle treks in Taman Negara and in the Endau Rompin National Park and hiking in the Cameron Highlands all on the Peninsula. There are numerous opportunities for climbing, especially in East Malaysia. Most of East Malaysia's parks offer hiking trails, but the best are in the Niah, Gunung Mulu and Gunung Kinabalu national parks. Climbing Mount Kinabalu in Sabah, to be at the summit for sunrise, is one of the most popular hikes.

Other activities
Other popular activities include rafting, which is becoming increasingly popular, especially in East Malaysia, and cultural tours. Again, East Malaysia offers the greatest possibilities; trips to explore longhouses in upriver settlements are your best bet.

Health

Before you go

Take out medical insurance. You should also have a dental check-up, obtain a spare glasses prescription and, if you suffer from a long-standing condition, such as diabetes, high blood pressure, heart/lung disease or a nervous disorder, arrange for a check-up with your doctor who can at the same time provide you with a letter explaining details of your medical disorder. Check the current practice for malaria prophylaxis (prevention) for the countries you intend to visit.

With the following advice and precautions, you should keep as healthy as you do at home. In Southeast Asia – and in this instance Malaysia (but not Singapore) – the health risks are different from those encountered in, say, Europe or the USA, but the region's medical practitioners have particular experience in dealing with locally occurring diseases. There is an obvious difference in health risks between the business traveller who tends to stay in international class hotels in large cities and the backpacker trekking through rural areas. There are no hard and fast rules to follow; you will often have to make your own judgements on the healthiness or otherwise of your surroundings.

Medical facilities
Malaysian health care is excellent, private clinics are found in most small towns and there are good government hospitals in major cities. All state capitals have general hospitals and every town has a district hospital. Big hotels have their own in-house doctors who are extremely expensive. Doctors are listed in the telephone directory, or consult your embassy. Most doctors speak English, but the likelihood of finding this and a good standard of care diminishes very rapidly as you move away from the big cities. On the whole it is inexpensive to visit a private doctor (about RM30-50), and a sojourn in a government hospital is cheaper than most hotels (no a/c or pool).

Pharmaceuticals are available from numerous outlets including shopping centres, supermarkets and hotels. Most pharmacists are open 0900-1800 Monday-Saturday. A number of drugs that can only be obtained on prescription in Western countries can be bought over the counter in Malaysia. Traditional Chinese pharmacies, mostly found in Chinatowns, also dispense Chinese medicines, and will advise on traditional remedies for most ailments. Facilities in East Malaysia are not as good as those on the Peninsula. There are systems and traditions of medicine wholly different from the Western model especially in rural areas and you may be confronted with less orthodox forms of treatment such as herbal medicine and acupuncture. At least you can be sure that local practitioners have a lot of experience with the particular diseases of their region.

If you are a long way away from medical help, a certain amount of self-administered medication may be necessary and you will find many of the drugs available have familiar names. However, always check the date stamping (sell-by date) and buy from reputable pharmacists because the shelf life of some items, especially vaccines and antibiotics, is markedly reduced in hot conditions. Unfortunately, many locally produced drugs are not subjected to quality control procedures and so can be unreliable. There have, in addition, been cases of substitution of inert materials for active drugs.

Visiting the Peninsula's west coast does not require any medical precautions other than some insect repellent. Those travelling to national parks, rural areas and to Sabah and Sarawak are advised to have vaccinations against cholera, typhoid and polio, hepatitis A, tetanus and Japanese encephalitis. Smallpox vaccination is no longer required. Neither is cholera vaccination, despite the fact that the disease occurs, but not at present in epidemic form. Yellow fever vaccination is not required either, although you may be asked for a certificate if you have been in a country affected by yellow fever immediately before travelling.

Infectious hepatitis This is less of a problem for travellers than it used to be because of the development of two extremely effective vaccines against the A and B form of the disease. A combined hepatitis A and B vaccine is now licensed and has been available since 1997 – one jab covers both diseases.

Typhoid (monovalent) One dose followed by a booster 1 month later. Immunity from this course lasts 2-3 years. An oral preparation is also available.

Poliomyelitis This is a live vaccine generally given orally but a full course consists of three doses with a booster in tropical regions every 3-5 years.

Tetanus One dose should be given, with a booster at 6 weeks and another at 6 months. Ten yearly boosters thereafter are recommended.

Meningitis and Japanese B encephalitis (JVE) There is an extremely small risk of these rather serious diseases; both are seasonal and vary according to region. Meningitis can occur in epidemic form; JVE is a viral disease transmitted from pigs to man by mosquitoes. For details of the vaccinations, consult a travel clinic.

Children should, in addition to the above, be properly protected against diphtheria, whooping cough, mumps and measles. Teenage girls, if they have not had the disease, should be given a rubella (German measles) vaccination. Consult your doctor for advice on BCG inoculation against tuberculosis: the disease is still common in the region.

You may find the following items useful to take with you from home: suntan cream, insect repellent, flea powder, mosquito net, coils or tablets, tampons, condoms, contraceptives, water sterilizing tablets, anti-malaria tablets, anti-infective ointment, dusting powder for feet, travel sickness pills, antiacid tablets, anti-diarrhoea tablets, sachets of rehydration salts, a first aid kit and disposable needles (also see page 65). Note, however, that you are travelling to a country where all these things, and more, are widely available and considerably more cheaply than at home. So don't bother to travel with a chemist shop in your suitcase or rucksack.

Information regarding country-by-country malaria risk can be obtained from the World Health Organization (WHO) or in Britain from the Ross Institute, London School of Hygiene and Tropical Medicine, Keppel Street, London WCIE 7HT which also publishes a highly recommended book: *The Preservation of Personal Health in Warm Climates*. The Centres for Disease Control (CDC) in Atlanta, Georgia, USA will provide equivalent information. Further information on medical problems overseas can be

Essentials

obtained from *Travellers Health: How to Stay Healthy Abroad*, edited by Richard Dawood (Oxford University Press, 1992). This revised and updated edition is highly recommended, especially to the intrepid traveller. A more general publication, with hints on health and much more besides, is John Hatt's *The Tropical Traveller* (Penguin, 1993). See also the websites listed at the end of this Essentials section.

Staying healthy

Water is clean and safe to drink in major cities on the Peninsula but in other areas it should be boiled or sterilized. Mineral water can be bought fairly easily. With food, normal precautions should be taken with shellfish; ensure stall food is properly cooked and avoid unpeeled fruits.

Intestinal upsets

Intestinal infections are common, so be prepared for them. Most of the time they are due to the insanitary preparation of food. Do not eat uncooked fish, vegetables or meat (especially pork), fruit without the skin (always peel fruit yourself), or food that is exposed to flies (particularly salads). Tap water may be unsafe, especially in the monsoon seasons and the same goes for stream water or well water. Filtered or bottled water is usually available and safe but you cannot always rely on it. If your hotel has a central hot water supply, this is safe to drink after cooling. Ice should be made from boiled water but rarely is, so stand your glass on the ice cubes instead of putting them in the drink. Dirty water should be strained through a filter bag (available from camping shops), then boiled or treated. Bringing the water to a rolling boil at sea level is sufficient. In the highlands, you have to boil the water a bit longer to ensure that all the microbes are killed (because water boils at a lower temperature at altitude). Various sterilizing methods can be used and there are proprietary preparations containing chlorine or iodine compounds. Pasteurized or heat-treated milk is now fairly widely available as is ice cream and yoghurt produced by the same methods. Unpasteurized milk products, including cheese, are sources of tuberculosis, brucellosis, listeria and food poisoning germs. You can render fresh milk safe by heating it to 62°C for 30 minutes followed by rapid cooling or by boiling. Matured or processed cheeses are safer than fresh varieties.

Fish and shellfish are popular foods throughout Malaysia but can be the source of health problems. Shellfish which are eaten raw will transmit food poisoning or hepatitis if they have been living in contaminated water. The phenomenon known as 'red tide' can also affect fish and shellfish which eat large quantities of tiny sea creatures and thereby become poisonous. Keep as well informed as possible about fish and shellfish quality in the area you are visiting. Most countries impose a ban on fishing in periods when red tide is prevalent, although this is often flouted.

Diarrhoea

There are various causes of diarrhoea – viruses, bacteria, protozoa (like amoeba), salmonella and cholera organisms. It may take one of several forms coming on suddenly or rather slowly. It may be accompanied by vomiting or severe abdominal pain, and the passage of blood or mucus (when it is called dysentery).

All kinds of diarrhoea respond favourably to the replacement of water and salts taken as frequent small sips of some kind of rehydration solution. There are proprietary preparations consisting of sachets of oral rehydration electrolyte powder, or make up your own by adding half a teaspoonful of salt (3.5 g) and 4 tbsp of sugar (40 g) to a litre of boiled water. If it is possible to time the onset of diarrhoea to the minute, then it is probably viral or bacterial and/or the onset of dysentery. The treatment in addition to rehydration is Ciprofloxacin (500 mgs every 12 hours). The drug is now widely available as are various similar ones.

If the diarrhoea has come on slowly or intermittently, then it is more likely to be protozoal, ie caused by amoeba or giardia, and antibiotics will have no effect. These cases are best treated by a doctor as should any diarrhoea continuing for more than 3 days. The drug usually used for giardia or amoeba is Metronidazole (Flagyl) or Tinidazole (Fasigyu).

The linchpins of treatment for diarrhoea are rest, fluid and salt replacement, antibiotics such as Ciprofloxacin for the bacterial types, and special diagnostic tests and medical treatment for amoeba and giardia infections. Fasting, peculiar diets and the consumption of large quantities of yoghurt have not been found useful. Salmonella infections and cholera can be devastating diseases and it would be wise to get to a hospital as soon as possible if these were suspected. Oral rehydration has, especially in children, been a lifesaving technique and as there is some evidence that alcohol and milk might prolong diarrhoea they should probably be avoided during, and immediately after, an attack. Some preventative antibiotics such as Enterovioform can have serious side effects if taken for long periods.

The burning power of the tropical sun is phenomenal, especially in highland areas. Always wear a wide-brimmed hat, and use some form of sun cream or lotion, with a protection factor between 7 and 15 or higher, on untanned skin. Avoid heatstroke by drinking lots of non-alcoholic fluid, and adding salt to your food. Full acclimatization to tropical temperatures takes about two weeks and during this period it is normal to feel relatively apathetic, especially if the humidity is high. Drink plenty of water (up to 15 litres a day are required when working physically hard in the tropics). Use salt on your food and avoid extreme exertion.

Sunburn & sunstroke

The best way of keeping mosquitos away at night is to sleep off the ground with a mosquito net and to burn mosquito coils containing Pyrethrum. Aerosol sprays or a 'flit gun' may be effective as are insecticidal tablets which are heated on a mat which is plugged into the wall socket (check voltage). In addtion, use personal insect repellent of which the best contain a high concentration of diethyltoluamide (DET). Liquid is best for arms and face; take care around eyes and make sure you do not dissolve the plastic of your spectacles. Aerosol spray on clothes and ankles deter mites and ticks. Liquid DET suspended in water can be used to impregnate cotton clothes and mosquito nets. The latter are now available in wide mesh form which are lighter to carry and less claustrophobic to sleep under.

Insects
A great nuisance and carriers of serious diseases such as malaria, dengue fever or filariasis and various worm infections

If you are bitten, itching may be relieved by cool baths and antihistamine tables (take care with alcohol or when driving), corticosteroid creams (use with great care and never use if any hint of septic poisoning) or by judicious scratching. Calamine lotion and cream have limited effectiveness and antihistamine creams have a tendency to cause skin allergies and are therefore not generally recommended. Bites which become infected (a common problem in the tropics) should be treated with a local antiseptic or antibiotic cream such as Cetrimide, as should infected scratches. Skin infestations with body lice, crabs and scabies are unfortunately easy to pick up. Use gamma benzene hexachloride for lice and benzyl benzoate for scabies. Crotamiton cream alleviates itching and also kills a number of skin parasites. Malathion lotion is good for lice but avoid the highly toxic full strength Malathion which is used as an agricultural insecticide.

If you are unlucky enough to be bitten by a venomous snake, spider, scorpion, centipede or sea creature, try (within limits) to catch or kill the animal for identification. Reactions to be expected are shock, swelling, pain and bruising around the bite, soreness of the regional lymph glands, nausea, vomiting and fever. If in addition any of the following symptoms should follow closely, get the victim to a doctor without delay: numbness, tingling of the face, muscular spasms, convulsions, shortness of breath or haemorrhage. Commercial snake-bite or scorpion-sting kits may be available but these are only useful against the specific type of snake or scorpion for which they are designed. The serum has

Bites, stings & worms
The best precaution against snake bites is not to walk in long grass with bare feet, sandals or in shorts

Essentials

Essentials

Dr Watson solves the Malayan malaria mystery

The word 'malaria' was first used in the 18th century and comes from the Italian mala aria – or 'bad air' – because it was thought to be caused by unwholesome air in swampy districts. It was not until 1899 that Dr Ronald Ross, a medical officer in Panama during the construction of the canal, discovered that the real culprit was not the air, but the swamp inhabitants themselves – mosquitos. The following year a young Scotsman, Dr Malcolm Watson, was appointed as a government medical officer in Malaya, where malaria was the biggest killer. Dr Watson was posted to Klang where a malarial epidemic was wreaking havoc.

Armed with the knowledge of the recent Panama discovery, Dr Watson set about draining the coastal swamplands, spraying them and improving the water-flow in streams. It worked, and the doctor became known as the 'White Knight of Malaria Control'. Historian Mary Turnbull writes that "it was said of Watson that 'he could probably have claimed to have saved more lives than any other physician in history', and Ronald Ross described his work in Malaya as 'the greatest sanitary achievement ever accomplished in the British Empire'". The methods used in his battle against the nyamuk – the menacing and almost onomatopoeic Malay word for mosquito – became standard practice in the colony.

to be given intravenously so is not much good unless you have had some practice in making injections into veins. If the bite is on a limb, immobilize it and apply a tight bandage between the bite and the body, releasing it for 90 seconds every 15 minutes. Reassurance of the victim is very important because death from snake bite is very rare. Do not slash the bite area and try to suck out the poison because this sort of heroism does more harm than good. Hospitals usually hold stocks of snake-bite serum.

When swimming in an area where there are poisonous fish such as stone or scorpion fish (also called by a variety of local names) or sea urchins on rocky coasts, tread carefully or wear plimsolls/trainers. The painful can be relieved by immersing the injured part of the body in water as hot as you can bear for as long as it remains painful, taking care not to scald yourself. Avoid spiders and scorpions by keeping your bed away from the wall, look under lavatory seats and inside your shoes in the morning. In the rare event of being bitten, consult a doctor. Intestinal worms are common and the more serious ones, such as hookworm, can be contracted by walking barefoot on infested earth or beaches.

Other risks and more serious diseases

Infectious hepatitis (jaundice)
The main symptoms are pains in the stomach, lack of appetite, lassitude and yellowness of the eyes and skin. The less serious but most common form is hepatitis A for which the best protection is the careful preparation of food, the avoidance of contaminated drinking water and scrupulous attention to toilet hygiene. The more serious, version is hepatitis B which is acquired usually as a sexually transmitted disease or by blood transfusion. It can less commonly be transmitted by injections with unclean needles and possibly by insect bites. The symptoms are the same as for hepatitis A but with a much longer incubation period is much longer and there are more likely to be complications.

Gamma globulin injection can be a bit painful, but it is cheaper than Havrix and may be more available in some places
Hepatitis A can be protected against with gamma globulin from a reputable source. For recommended doses always follow the manufacturer's advice. You should have a shot as close as possible before leaving and have it repeated every six months. Gamma globulin has really been superseded now by a proper vaccination against hepatitis A (Havrix), which gives immunity lasting up to 10 years. After that boosters are required. Havrix monodose is now widely available as is junior Havrix. The vaccination has negligible side effects and is extremely effective.

Hepatitis B can be effectively prevented by a specific vaccine (Engerix) – three shots over six months before travelling. If you have had jaundice in the past it would be worthwhile having a blood test to see if you are immune to either of these two types, because this might avoid the necessity and costs of vaccination or gamma globulin.

AIDS in Malaysia is not as common in Malaysia as in neighbouring countries like Thailand. Even so, it is not wholly confined to the well-known high risk sections of the population ie homosexual men, intravenous drug abusers, prostitutes and the children of infected mothers. The same precautions should be taken as when encountering any sexually transmitted disease. Supplies of blood for transfusion are supposed to be screened for HIV in all reputable hospitals so the risk should be small. The only way to be sure if you feel you have been put at risk is to have a blood test on your return to a place where there are reliable laboratory facilities. However, the test does not become positive for many months.

AIDS
Heterosexual transmission is probably now the dominant mode of infection and so the main risk to travellers is from casual sex

This is not a problem in main cities but it is advisable to take malaria pills if you are going to rural areas. Malaria is more prevalent in East Malaysia, particularly in the jungled interior of Sabah. It remains a serious disease and you are advised to protect yourself against mosquito bites as above and to take prophylactic (preventative) drugs. Start taking the tablets a few days before exposure and continue to take them 6 weeks after leaving the malarial zone. Remember to give the drugs to babies and children, pregnant women also.

Malaria
See also box

The subject of malaria prevention is becoming more complex as the malaria parasite becomes immune to some of the older drugs. In particular, there has been an increase in the proportion of cases of falciparum malaria which are resistant to the normally used drugs.

Take the advice of a reputable agency on prophylaxis but be prepared to receive conflicting advice. Chloroquine and Proguanil may still be recommended for the areas where malaria is still fully sensitive. Doxycycline, Metloquine and Quinghaosu are presently being used in resistant areas. Halofantrine Quinine and tetracycline drugs remain the mainstays of treatment.

It is still possible to catch malaria even when taking prophylactic drugs, although this is unlikely. If you do develop symptoms (high fever, shivering, severe headache, and sometimes diarrhoea) seek medical advice immediately. The risk of the disease is obviously greater the further you move from the cities into rural areas, with primitive facilities and standing water.

Dengue is a viral disease transmitted by mosquito and causes severe headaches and body pains. Complicated types of dengue known as haemorrhagic fevers occur throughout Asia but usually in persons who have caught the disease a second time. Thus, although it is a very serious type it is rarely caught by visitors.

Dengue fever
There is no treatment, you must just avoid mosquito bites

Remember that rabies is endemic in many Southeast Asian countries. If you are bitten by a domestic or wild animal seek medical assistance at once. The course of treatment depends on whether you have already been satisfactorily vaccinated against rabies. If you have (and this is worthwhile if you are spending lengths of time in developing countries) then some further doses of vaccine are all that is required. Human diploid cell vaccine is the best, but expensive: other, older kinds of vaccine such as that derived from duck embryos may be the only types available. These are effective, much cheaper and interchangeable generally with the human derived types. If not already vaccinated then anti-rabies serum (immunoglobulin) may be required in addition. It is wise to finish the course of treatment whether the animal survives or not.

Rabies

Children

Younger travellers seem to be more prone to illness abroad, but that should not put you off taking them. More preparation is necessary than for an adult and perhaps a little more care should be taken when travelling to remote areas where health services are primitive. This is because children can become more rapidly ill than adults (they often recover more quickly, however).

Diarrhoea and vomiting are the most common problems so take the usual precautions, but more intensively. The treatment of diarrhoea is the same as for adults except that it should start earlier and be continued with more persistence. Make sure all basic childhood vaccinations are up to date as well as the more exotic ones. Children should be properly protected against diphtheria, whooping cough, mumps and measles. If they have not had the disease, teenage girls should be given rubella (German measles) vaccination. Consult your doctor for advice on BCG inoculation against tuberculosis: the disease is still common in the region. Protection against mosquitos and drug prophylaxis against malaria is essential. Many children take to 'foreign' food quite happily. Milk may be unavailable outside big cities. Powdered milk may be the answer; breast feeding for babies even better.

Upper respiratory infections such as colds, catarrh and middle ear infections are common – antibiotics could be carried against the possibility. Outer ear infections after swimming are also common, antibiotic ear drops will help. Children get dehydrated very quickly in the tropics and can become drowsy and unco-operative unless cajoled to drink water or juice plus salts. Oral rehydration has been a lifesaving technique in children.

Babies and small children deteriorate very rapidly when ill. A travel insurance policy which has an air ambulance provision is strongly recommended. When planning a route, try to stay within 24 hours' travel of a hospital with good care and facilities. Many expatriats fly to Singapore for medical care, which has the best doctors and facilities in the region.

Never allow your child to be exposed to the harsh tropical sun without protection. A child can burn in a matter of minutes. Loose cotton clothing, with long sleeves and legs and a sun-hat are best. High-factor sun-protection cream is essential.

When you return home

On returning home, remember to take anti-malarial tablets for 6 weeks. If you have had attacks of diarrhoea, it is worth having a stool specimen tested in case you have picked up amoebic dysentery. If you have been living rough, a blood test may also be worthwhile to detect worms and other parasites.

Kuala Lumpur

3

In the space of a century, Kuala Lumpur grew from a trading post and tin-mining shanty town into a colonial capital. Today, it is a modern, cosmopolitan business hub and centre of government.

The economic boom that started in the late 1980s has caused a building bonanza that has rivalled Singapore's. In downtown Kuala Lumpur, old and new are juxtaposed. The jungled backdrop of the copper-topped clock tower of the Supreme Court of a century ago has been replaced by scores of stylish, high-rise office blocks, dominated by the soaring, angular-roofed **Maybank** headquarters. The Victorian, Moorish and Moghul-style buildings, the Art Deco central market and cinemas, and the Chinese shophouses stand in marked contrast to these impressive skyscrapers. The **Petronas Twin Towers** offers the most impressive recent addition to the modern skyline – part of the Kuala Lumpur City Centre (KLCC) development, this is the tallest building in the world.

Ins and outs

Getting there
See also Transport, page 109

As befitting Malaysia's capital, Kuala Lumpur (KL) is well linked both to other areas of Malaysia and to the wider world. The international airport at Sepang provides a slick point of entry to the country. It lies over 70 km to the north, but there is a rail link to the city centre. There are domestic air connections (including to Sabah and Sarawak) from Sepang and a handful from the old international airport at Subang. Visitors arriving by train or bus are deposited right in the city centre. From KL's stylish colonial railway station there are train connections with Bangkok (Thailand), Singapore and with destinations on the Malaysian peninsula. Puduraya bus station also has international connections south to Singapore and north to Bangkok, as well as to many towns on the Peninsula.

Getting around
Colour map 2, grid A2
Population:1,500,000
Phone code: 03

Kuala Lumpur is not the easiest city to navigate, with its sights spread thinly over a wide area. Until very recently, pedestrians have not been very high on the list of priorities for Malaysian urban planners, with many roads, especially outside the city centre, built without pavements, making walking both hazardous and difficult. In addition, with the exception of the area around Central Market, Chinatown and Dayabumi, distances between sights are too great to cover comfortably on foot, both because of the lack of pavements and because of heavy pollution and the hot and humid climate. Like other Southeast Asian cities, with the notable exception of Singapore, the internal combustion engine rules. The bus system is labyrinthine and congested streets means that travelling by taxi can make for a tedious wait in a traffic jam. Try to insist that taxi drivers use their meters, although do not be surprised if they simply refuse point blank. The Light Rail Transit (LRT) is undoubtedly the least hassle.

Tourist offices

Tourism Malaysia, Information Centre, Level 2, Putra World Trade Centre, 45 Jln Tun Ismail, T26935188, F26935884, www.tourismmalaysia.gov.my *Tourist Information Desks*, Terminals 1 & 2, Subang International Airport, T7465707. There is also an *Information Counter* at the Railway Station, T22746063. *Malaysian Tourist Information Complex* (*MATIC*), 109 Jln Ampang, T21643929, F21621149. Located in an opulent mansion formerly belonging to a Malaysian planter and tin miner, information on all 13 states, cultural performances and demonstrations of traditional handicrafts, it also provides money-changing facilities.

Orientation
See colour map of KL transport system at the back of the book

The streets to the **north of the Padang** – the cricket pitch in front of the old Selangor Club, next to Merdeka Sq – are central shopping streets with modern department stores and smaller shops.

The **Colonial Core** is around the Padang and down Jl Raja and Jl Tun Perak. East of the Padang, straight over the bridge on Lebuh Pasar Besar, is the main commercial area, occupied by banks and finance companies. To the southeast of Merdeka Sq is KL's vibrant Chinatown.

To find a distinctively **Malay area**, it is necessary to venture further out, along Jl Raja Muda Musa to Kampung Baru, to the northeast. To the **south of Kampung Baru**, on the opposite side of the Klang River, is Jl Ampang, once KL's 'millionaires' row', where tin magnates, or *towkays*, and sultans first built their homes. The road is now mainly occupied by embassies and high commissions. To the southeast of Jl Ampang is KL's so-called Golden Triangle, to which the modern central business district has migrated. In recent years the city's residential districts have been expanding out towards the jungled hills surrounding the KL basin, at the far end of Ampang, past the zoo to the north, and to Bangsar, to the southwest. KL has become a city of condominiums, which have sprung up everywhere from the centre of town to these outlying suburbs. Greater

Kuala Lumpur

The only legal Hash in Malaysia

At the turn of the 20th century, the annual dare in colonial KL involved swimming from the Royal Selangor Club terrace to the State Secretariat and back, when the Klang River flooded the Padang. But the 'Spotted Dog', as the club was affectionately known, was also home to another eccentric sporting event that caught on around the world. The Hash, a cross-country chase – invariably followed by a drinking bout – was started in 1938, when the Selangor Club was the preferred watering hole for colonial bachelors. A certain AS Gisbert, having drunk too much at the Long Bar, went for a jog around the Padang to sober up. In no time, Mr Gisbert's Hash had a band of disciples who took to the new sport with varying degrees of seriousness.

The run, named after the Club's dining room, the Hash House, ventured out into the countryside surrounding KL where 'hounds' chased 'hares', along a paper trail. The KL Hash, known as the 'Mother Hash' to Hash House Harriers around the world (there are now 300 clubs in more than 60 countries), normally involves a run of 3-8 km, which is usually a fairly jovial affair. Most big Malaysian towns have a Hash and there are several branches in KL – men-only, women-only and mixed. Although popular among expatriates, many locals participate these days and visitors are welcome. For details, contact Kuala Lumpur Hash House Harriers, PO Box 10182, KL; T2484846.

KL sprawls out into the Klang Valley, once plantation country and now home to the industrial satellites of Petaling Jaya and Shah Alam.

The most recent – and grandiose – development is **Putrajaya**, Malaysia's new administrative capital, which is being hacked out of plantations 35 km south of KL. It is estimated that when it is completed in 2005, Putrajaya's population will be 250,000. The city will cost a cool US$8 bn. Other developments in this area to the south of KL include the new international airport, which opened in 1998, and the Cyberjaya, the heart of Malaysia's much-vaunted Multimedia Super Corridor.

History

Kuala Lumpur means 'muddy confluence' in Malay – as apt a description today as it was in the pioneer days of the 1870s. This evocative name refers to the Klang and Gombak rivers that converge in the middle of the city – there is also some evidence that the *kopi-susu*-coloured (literally 'milky-coffee-coloured') Gombak was once known as the *Sungai Lumpur*. Kuala Lumpur, commonly known simply as KL, has grown up around the Y-shaped junction of these rivers in the area called *Ulu Klang* – the upper reaches of the Klang River.

In 1857, members of the Selangor Royal family (including Rajah Abdullah, the Bugis chief of the old state capital of Klang) mounted an expedition to speculate for tin along the upper reaches of the Klang River. Backed by money from Melakan businessmen, 87 Chinese prospectors travelled up the river by raft to the confluence of the Klang and the Gombak. After trekking through dense jungle they stumbled across rich tin deposits near what is now Ampang. On this first expedition 69 miners died of malaria within a month.

This did not stop Rajah Abdullah from organizing a second expeditionary labour force, which succeeded in mining commercial quantities of tin, taking it downriver to Klang. Until then, Malaya's tin-mining industry had been concentrated in the Kinta Valley near Ipoh, to the north. At about this time, the invention of canning as a means of preserving food led to strong world

Kuala Lumpur

To Lake Taman Tasek Titiwangsa

A

Jln Mahameru

Medical Centre

Jln Ipoh

Pekeliling

Jln Gombak

Putra World Trade Centre & Tourism Malaysia

S Batu

S Gombak

Putra

Jln Pahang

PWTC LRT

Jln Putra

Jln Chow Kit

To Ipoh & Kuantan

CHOW KIT

Sungai Gombak

Jln Tiong Nam

J Haji Taib

Sri Amar

Jln Raja Laut

Sultan Ismail LRT

Jln Tun Ismail

Jln Kuching

Jln Sultan Ismail

Jln Tun Ismail

Medan Mara

Jln Dato Onn

Bandaraya LRT

Jln Dang Wangi

Jln Setar

Singapore Airlines

Jln Tun Ismail

Jln Ampang

Jln Raja Laut

Jln Tuanku Abdul Rahman

Jln Masjid India

Jln Bukit Nanas

St John's Cathedral

ASEAN Sculpture Garden

Jln Parlimen

Masjid Jamek LRT

Benteng LRT

National Monument

Cenderawasih

Jln Bukit Aman

Padang Merdeka Square

Masjid Jamek

COLONIAL CORE

Jln Tun Perak

Jln Rajah Chulan

Panggung Anniversari

Jln Tembusi

Butterfly Park

British Council

Jln Tugu

Klang River

Jln Silang

Central Market LRT

Deer Park

Jln Tembah Perdana

Jln Kasturi

Jln Cheng Lock

Orchid Garden

Jln Cenderasari

Jln Hang Lekir

Tun Razak Memorial

Jln Perdana

Jln Sultan Hishamuddin

Pasar Seni LRT

Jln Sultan

Lake Gardens

Bird Park

CHINATOWN

Tasek Perdana

Jln Kebun Bunga

Masjid Negara

Jln Sultan Mohamed

Sikh Temple

Jln Petaling

Malay Railway Administration Building

Planetarium

National Art Gallery

Jln Kinabalu

Chan See Shu Yuen Temple

Jln Stadium

National Museum

To Temple of Goddess of Heaven, Muzium Negara & YMCA

To Airport

Jln Sulaiman

Jln Kg Attap

B

Kuala Lumpur

National Library

Jln Dr Latiff

Jln Raja Mada Abdul Aziz

Jln Haji Yaha Sheikh Ahmad

Jln Hamzah

Jln Raja Uda

Jln Tun Razak

Jln Pestaran Gurney

Jln Salteh

KAMPONG BAHRU

Jl Raja Alang

Jln Raja Muda Musa

Jln Sungai Baharu

New Zealand Embassy

Jln Raja Muda

Kampong Bahru Sunday

Jln Yap Kwan Seng

Ampang Park Shopping Complex

Australian High Commission

KLCC LRT

Jln Ampang

Jln Mayang

Jln Raja Abdullah

Klang River

Kampung Baru LRT

Jln Ampang

Angkasaraya Building

Jln Limba Kuda

To Zoo & Aquarium

Rubber Institute Building

Pakistan Embassy

Petronas Twin Towers

Dang Wangi LRT

MATIC

Jln P Ramlee

KUALA LUMPUR CITY CENTRE (KLCC)

KL Tower

Jln Puncak

Jln Sultan Ismail

Life Centre

Jln Pinang

Jln Perak

Jln Kia Peng

Jln Tengah

To Royal Selangor Golf Club

Jln Stonor

Bukit Nanas Forest Reserve

Jln Raja Chulan

Jln Conlay

Jln Ceylon

Jln Kia Peng

GOLDEN TRIANGLE

Jln Bukit Bintang

Jln Inai

Jln Kamuning

Jln Sultan Ismail

Jln W Grenier

Jln Imbi

Jln Kampong

Puduraya

Jln Pudu

Plaza Rakyat LRT

Jln Galloway

Jln Imbi

Jln Horley

Jln Barat

Tunku Abdul Rahman Park

Jln Hang Jebat

Jln etherwein

Stadium Negara

Stadium Merdeka

Hang Tuah LRT

Jln Hang Tuah

Maharajalela

To Railway Station

N

0 metres 500
0 yards 500

LRT lines
— Putra LRT line
▪▪▪ Star LRT line

Detail maps
A Colonial Core & Chow Kit, page 77
B Chinatown, page 79
C Around KLCC, page 82
D Around Golden Triangle, page 84

Kuala Lumpur

★ **24 hours in the city**

Begin the day by buying the New Straits Times *and enjoying a leisurely coffee before making a foray into town for the classic Malay breakfast:* nasi lemak *- rice cooked in coconut milk served with prawn* sembal, ikan bilis *(rather like anchovies), hard boiled egg, cucumber and peanuts.*

Make your way to Chinatown and discover two facets of Malaysia's cultural heritage: the Sri Mahamariamman Temple founded by early Tamil settlers in 1873, and the Chan See Shu Yuen Temple built in 1908. For the sake of cultural balance make your way to the Masjid Megara National Mosque.

At midday engage with a dim sum buffet lunch which you can work off with a walk in the 90 hectare Lake Gardens before looking around the National Museum near its southern tips. By mid afternoon shake off the past and witness Malaysia's tryst with modernity. Catch the LRT mass transit system to the world's tallest buildings, the Petronas Twin Towers which dominate the Kuala Lumpur City Centre (KLCC) development. For a great view of the city take a lift to the observation platform near the top of the 400 metre-plus Menara KL.

Start the evening with a mouth-tingling cold beer at the Coliseum café before heading back to Chinatown around 19.30 when the copy-watch sellers and all sorts of other hawkers emerge from their work load.

For dinner, sample another slice of this culinary melting pot in the unique Nyonya cuisine of the Straits Malays. Check listings page 641.

While KL is not Ibiza there is still a reasonably hot stock of bars and clubs on Jln Pinang, and a hipper congregation in Bangsar baru to the west of the city centre and near the university of Malaya. Still willing to continue the journey through Malaysia's gastronomic landscape? Then round off the day with a visit to the food stalls of Chow Kit for Indian and Afghan specialities – a roti canai *perhaps?*

Lie on your bed and reflect on what's in your stomach or in your head: Indian, French, Taoist, Hindu, Chinese, Malay, Muslim and Western. Quite a cultural score for one day.

demand for tin. Spotting a good business opportunity, two Chinese merchants opened a small trading-post at the confluence in 1859. One of them, Hiu Siew, was later appointed *Kapitan Cina* – the first headman of the new settlement. But secret-society rivalries between groups such as the Hai San (who controlled KL) and the Ghee Hin (who controlled a nearby settlement) retarded the township's early development. Malaria also remained a big problem and fires regularly engulfed and destroyed parts of the town.

By the mid-1860s, KL, which was still predominantly Chinese, began to prosper under the guiding hand of its sheriff, **Yap Ah Loy**. He was a Hakka gang leader from China, who arrived in Melaka in 1854, fought in Negri Sembilan's riots at Sungai Ujong (see page 201), then went to KL in 1862 where he became a tin magnate, or *towkay*, and ran gambling dens and brothels. But he emerged as a respected community leader and in 1868, at the age of 31, he was appointed *Kapitan Cina* of Kuala Lumpur by the Sultan of Selangor. He remained the headman until his death in 1885.

Frank Swettenham, the British Resident of Selangor, then took the reins, having moved the administrative centre of the Residency from Klang in 1880. The same year, KL replaced Klang as the capital of the state of Selangor; shortly after Yap's death, it became the capital of the Federated Malay States. Swettenham pulled down the ramshackle shanties and rebuilt the town with wider streets and brick houses. In the National Museum there is a remarkable photograph of the Padang area in 1884, showing a shabby line of *atap* (palm thatch) huts where the Sultan Abdul Samad Building is today. By 1887 the new national capital had 518 brick houses and a population of 4,050. By 1910, when the magnificent Moorish-style railway station was completed, the city's population had risen more than 10-fold and nearly four-fifths of the population was Chinese. The town continued to grow in the following decades, becoming increasingly multiracial in character, as the British educated the Malay nobility, then employed them as administrators. The Indian population also grew rapidly; many were brought from South India to work on the roads and railways and the plantations in the Klang Valley.

During the Second World War, the city was bombed by the Allies, but little real damage was incurred. The Japanese surrendered in KL on 13 September 1945. Three years later, there was a massive influx of squatters into the city, with the start of the Communist Emergency. The city area quickly became overcrowded, so in 1952 Petaling Jaya, KL's satellite town (see page 86), was founded to relieve the pressure. It subsequently went on to attract many of Malaysia's early manufacturing industries. Following the end of the Emergency, Malaya became the independent Federation of Malaya on 31 August 1957. Independence was declared by the first prime minister of the independent federation, Tunku Abdul Rahman ('Papa Malaysia'), in the newly built Merdeka Stadium (see page 80). Not until the almagamation of Malaya, Sarawak and Sabah, in 1963 was the name Malaysia given to the new nation.

Modern Kuala Lumpur

In 1974, the 243-sq-km area immediately surrounding the city was formerly declared the Federal Territory of Kuala Lumpur, with a separate administration from its mother state of Selangor. Today, although one of the smallest capitals in Southeast Asia, it is a rapidly growing business centre, with its industrial satellites gaining the lion's share of the country's manufacturing investment. The most recent addition to the modern skyline are the Petronas Twin Towers, the most prominent feature of the Kuala Lumpur City Centre (KLCC) complex, which on completion in 1996 became the tallest building in the world at 421 m and 88 storeys. The bridge connecting the two towers claims the title of the highest bridge in the world. When the building was under construction in 1995 and 1996 the contractors were completing a floor every four days – and were being paid around RM2.2 million per day. The structure was designed by American architect Cesar Pelli and the surrounding park by the Brazilian landscape artist Roberto Marx Burle.

There have been efforts to create a 'new Malaysian architecture', to lend the city a more integrated look and a national identity. Such buildings include the modern-Islamic Masjid Negara (the National Mosque), the National Museum and the Putra World Trade Centre (the latter two have *Minangkabau*-style roofs) and the 34-storey Dayabumi complex, by the river, with its modern-Islamic latticed arches. At the same time, KL has also been trying to cultivate a 'garden city' image like neighbouring Singapore; from the top of its skyscrapers, KL looks green and spacious, although green areas are fast being taken over by building developments. Despite all this, KL may not entirely have outgrown its pioneering tin-town mentality: rumour has it that the speculators were still looking for tin when the subterranean car park was built beneath the Padang at Merdeka Square in the mid-1980s.

Once a relatively quiet capital city KL is becoming increasingly noisy and congested, as well as suffering from serious air pollution – or 'the haze', which is widely thought to be caused by the fires that burn uncontrollably in Sumatra and Kalimantan from July to September. At the end of 1994, pollution levels at Shah Alam, a suburb of KL, reached '500' ('300' is deemed hazardous). Visibility was down to 400 m, making landings at KL's airport difficult. Locals note how convenient it is for the authorities to blame fires in another country for pollution problems at home. Environmentalists' initiatives to reduce pollution have got nowhere. Instead, while KL hospitals fill up with children suffering from bronchial problems, the health ministry feebly recommends that Malaysians wear surgical masks and give up exercising outside. "But", as S Jayasankaran wrote in 1997, "the ministry can't advise them to stop breathing."

Sights

The Colonial core

At the muddy confluence of the Klang and Gombak rivers where KL's founders stepped ashore, stands the **Masjid Jamek**, formerly the National Mosque (main entrance on Jalan Tun Perak). Built in 1909 by English architect, AB Hubbock, the design was based on that of a Moghul mosque in North India. The mosque has a walled courtyard, or *sahn*, and a three-domed prayer hall. It is striking with its striped white and salmoncoloured brickwork and domed minarets, cupolas and arches. Surrounded by coconut palms, the mosque is an oasis of peace in the middle of modern KL, as is apparent by the number of Malays who sleep through the heat of the lunchtime rush-hour on the prayer hall's cool marbled floors. ■ *Daily 0900-1100, 1400-1600. No women allowed inside the mosque at prayer time.*

Behind the mosque, from the corner of Jalan Tuanku Abdul Rahman and Jalan Raja Laut, are the colonial-built public buildings, distinguished by their grand, Moorish architecture. All were the creation of AC Norman, a colleague of Hubbock's, and were built between 1894 and 1897. The photogenic former State Secretariat, now called the **Sultan Abdul Samad (SAS) Building**, with its distinctive clock tower and bulbous copper domes, houses the Supreme Court. To the south of here is another Moorish building, the **Textile Museum**, at 26 Jalan Sultan Hishamuddin. It has excellent content, with an emphasis on weaving, as well as beadwork, batik and some embroidery. There is a video presentation and a shop. Recommended. ■ *Closed on public holidays, RM1, T2917136.*

The Sultan Abdul Samad Building faces on to the **Padang** on the opposite side of the road, next to **Merdeka Square**. The old Selangor Club cricket pitch is the venue for Independence Day celebrations. The centrepiece of Merdeka Square is the tallest flagpole in the world (100 m high) and the huge Malaysian flag that flies from the top can be seen across half the city, particularly at night when it is floodlit. The Padang was trimmed to make way for the square, which is also the venue for impromptu rock concerts, and is a popular meeting place. A shopping complex has been built underneath the square.

Non-members can only visit if accompanied by a member

The very British mock-Tudor **Royal Selangor Club** fronts the Padang and was the centre of colonial society after its construction in 1890. Much of the building was damaged by a fire in the late 1960s and the north wing was built in 1970. The Selangor Club is still a gathering place for KL's VIPs. It has one of the finest colonial saloons, filled with trophies and pictures of cricket teams. The famous Long Bar (known as 'The Dog') – which contains a fascinating collection of old photographs of KL – is still an exclusively male preserve. On the north side of the Padang is **St Mary's Church**, one of the oldest Anglican churches in Malaysia, built in 1894.

Colonial core & Chow Kit

Kuala Lumpur

To Lake Titiwangsa

To Dynasty Hotel & KFC

Pekeliling

Medical Centre

Jln Mahameru

Sungai Batu

Sungai Gombak

Jln Ipoh

& Putra World
Trade Centre

Mall

Jln Putra

PWTC

The Mall

CHOW
KIT

Federal
Cinema

Capitol
Cinema

Jln Chow Kit

Selangor
Plaza

Jln Rajah Muda

Jln Pahang

Jln Tiong Nam

Jln Raja Laut

Jln Haji Taib

Jln Raja Alang

Jln Sri Amar

Sungai Gombak

Jln Sultan Ismail

Sultan
Ismail

Medan
Mara

Pertama
Shopping
Centre

Odeon
Cinema

Jln Dang Wangi

Bandaraya

Sogo

Jln Isfahan

Campbell
Shopping
Complex

Semua
House

Jln Tuanku Abdul Rahman

Coliseum
Theatre

Little
India Night

Jln Masjid India

Jln Rajah Abdullah

To Kampung Baru & Hotel Crown Princess

Singapore
Airlines

Klang River

Jln Ampang

Bukit Nanas
Forest Reserve

To Parliament House & Lake Gardens

Gombak River

Jln Kuching

Jln Raja Laut

Jln Gombak

Jln Melayu

Benteng

Jln Parlimen

St Mary's

Supreme
Court

Masjid
Jamek

Jln Raja

Sultan Abdul
Samad Bldg

Central

Padang
Merdeka
Square

Jln Raja

Masjid
Jamek

Royal Selangor
Club

Jln Kinabalu

COLONIAL
CORE

Plaza
Putra

Museum
of National
History

Lebuh Pasar Besar

Tun H S Lee

Lebuh Ampang

KL's oldest
shophouses

Jln Tun Perak

Jln Silang

Jln Gereja

Jln Tun Tan Cheng Lock

St John's
Cathedral

Jln Raja Chulan

To Kawana Hotel

Maybank
Tower

To City Lodge & Katari Hotels

N

0 metres   400
0 yards   400

■ Sleeping

1 City	7 Elegant Inn	13 Kowloon	19 Quality
2 City Villa	8 Grand Central	14 Legend	20 Stanford
3 Chamtan	9 Grand Centrepoint	15 Noble	21 Traveller's
4 Coliseum	10 Grand Continental	16 Palace	Moon Lodge
5 De First Inn	11 Grand Pacific	17 Pan Pacific	22 Vistana
6 Drop Inn Lodge	12 Katari	18 Plaza	23 Wira

Related maps
A Chinatown,
page 79
B Around KLCC,
page 82
C Around the
Golden Triangle,
page 84

The **Bank Negara Money Museum**, on the Ground Floor of the Bank Negara Building, Jalan Dato Onn, is a must for numismatic collectors. Founded in 1989, it houses a collection of Malaysian money. ■ *0900-1630 Mon to Fri, 0900-1200 Sat.*

On the south side of Merdeka Square is a **Museum of National History**, which has only limited displays. ■ *Daily 0900-1800, T2944590.*

In 1910, Hubbock designed the fairy-tale Moorish-style **Railway Station** and, in 1917, the **Malaya Railway Administration Building** opposite (see Chinatown map, page 79). Beneath the Islamic exterior of the former, the building resembles the glass and iron railway stations constructed in England during the Victorian era – except this one was built by convict labour. The station's construction was apparently delayed because the original roof design did not meet British railway specifications; it had to be able to support snow a metre deep. The refurbished interior now includes restaurants and souvenir stalls.

Also opposite the station on Jalan Sultan Hishamuddin is the former *Majestic Hotel*, built in 1932. Saved from demolition in 1983, it has been converted into the **National Art Gallery**, housing a permanent collection of about 2,000 works by Malaysian artists as well as touring exhibitions. For a chronological tour start at the top of the building and work down. It is a diverse collection but refreshing to see that most of the work retains a distinctively Malay spirit, some of it exciting and very original. ■ *1000-1800 Mon-Sun, closed 1200-1500 Fri, T2300157. Getting there: Sri Jaya bus 30, 47, 238, 247, 251, 252, 337 (from Sultan Mohammad Bus Station) or Mini Bus 22, 33, 35, 38 (from Bangkok Bank Bus Stand, Lebuh Pasar).*

To the north of the railway station and the art gallery is the **Masjid Negara** (the National Mosque), the modern spiritual centre of KL's Malay population and the symbol of Islam for the whole country. Abstract, geometric shapes have been used in the roofing and grillwork, while the Grand Hall is decorated with verses from the Koran. Completed in 1965, it occupies a 5-ha site at the end of Jalan Hishamuddin. The prayer hall has a star-shaped dome with 18 points, representing Malaysia's 13 states and the five pillars of Islam. The 48 smaller domes emulate the great mosque in Mecca. The single minaret is 73 m tall and the grand hall can accommodate 8,000 worshippers. An annex contains the mausoleum of Tun Abdul Razak, independent Malaysia's second prime minister. ■ *0900-1800 Sat-Thu, 1445-1800 Fri. Muslims can visit the mosque from 0630-2200. Women must use a separate entrance.*

Close to the National Mosque is the **Museum of Islamic Arts**, which provides an interesting collection of textiles and metalware and is a wonderful oasis of calm in the midst of the city. It is possible to get on to the roof, at a level with the mosque's mosaic dome. ■ *Entrance to the museum is free.*

North of the mosque, back towards the Padang, is the 35-storey, marble **Dayabumi Complex** (see Chinatown map, page 79). Located on Jalan Raya, it is one of KL's most striking modern landmarks. It was designed by local architect Datuk Nik Mohamed, and introduces contemporary Islamic achitecture to the skyscraper era. The government office-cum-shopping centre used to house Petronas, the secretive national oil company, which has since moved to the even more grandiose Petronas Twin Towers. Try getting permission to stand on the 30th floor helipad where a superb, but fading (and increasingly obsolete), pictorial map of all the city's sights has been painted on the rooftop. Next door to the Dayabumi Complex is the General Post Office.

On the opposite bank to the Dayabumi Complex is the **Central Market**, a former wet market built in 1928 in Art Deco-style, tempered with 'local Baroque' trimmings. In the early 1980s it was revamped to become a focus for KL's artistic community and a handicraft centre – KL's version of London's Covent Garden or San Francisco's Fisherman's Wharf. It is a warren of boutiques, handicraft and souvenir stalls – some with their wares laid out on the wet market's original marble slabs. On the second level of the market are several restaurants and a small hawker centre.

The market is now a bit of a tourist trap, although it is definitely worth visiting for a one-stop buying spree

Chinatown

Southeast of the Central Market lies Chinatown, roughly bounded by Jalan Bandar, Jalan Petaling and Jalan Sultan. It was the core of Yap Ah Loy's KL (see page 74) and is a mixture of crumbling shophouses, market stalls, coffee shops and restaurants. This quarter wakes up during late afternoon, after about 1630, and in the evening, when its streets become the centre of frenetic trading and haggling. Jalan Petaling and parts of Jalan Sultan are transformed into an open-air night market, *pasar malam*, and food stalls selling Chinese, Indian and Malay delicacies, fruit stalls, copy watch stalls, music cassettes, leather bag stalls and all manner of impromptu boutiques line the streets. Jalan Hang Lekir,

Kuala Lumpur

Chinatown

Sleeping		
1 Backpackers' Travellers' Inn	4 Furama	9 Mandarin
2 Backpackers Travellers' Lodge	5 Impiana	10 Nan Yeang
	6 Kameleon Travellers' Lodge	11 Starlight
3 Chinatown Guesthouse	7 Lok Ann	12 Swiss Inn
	8 Malaya	

N

0 metres 200
0 yards 200

Related map
A Colonial Core &
Chow Kit, page 77

which straddles the gap between Jalan Sultan and Jalan Petaling, is full of popular Chinese restaurants and coffee shops. Off the north side of Jalan Hang Lekir, there is a lively covered fruit and vegetable market in two intersecting arcades.

South of Jalan Hang Lekir, tucked away on Jalan Tun HS Lee (Jalan Bandar) is the extravagantly decorated **Sri Mahamariamman Temple**, incorporating gold, precious stones and Spanish and Italian tiles. It was founded in 1873 by Tamils from southern India who had come to Malaya as contract labourers to work in the rubber plantations or on the roads and railways. Its construction was funded by the wealthy Chettiar money-lending caste, and it was rebuilt on its present site in 1985. It has a silver chariot dedicated to Lord Murugan (Subramaniam), which is taken in procession to the Batu Caves (see page 85) during the Thaipusam festival, when Hindu devotees converge on the temple. Large numbers flock to the temple to participate in the ritual; this is usually preceded by about half-an-hour's chanting, accompanied by music.

There are two prominent Chinese temples in the Chinatown area. The elaborate **Chan See Shu Yuen Temple**, at the southernmost end of Jalan Petaling, was built in 1906 and has a typical open courtyard and symmetrical pavilions. Paintings, woodcarvings and ceramic sculptures decorate the façade. It serves both as a place of worship and as a community centre. The older **Sze Ya Temple**, close to the central market on Lebuh Pudu, off Jalan Cheng Lock, was built in the 1880s on land donated by Yap Ah Loy. He also funded the temple's construction and a photograph of him sits on one of the altars. Ancestor worship is more usually confined to the numerous ornate clan houses (*kongsis*); a typical one is the **Chan Kongsi** on Jalan Maharajalela, near the Chan See Shu Yuen Temple.

South of Chinatown, off Jalan Stadium, is the 50,000-capacity **Merdeka Stadium**, the site of Malaysia's Declaration of Independence on 31 August 1957 (*merdeka* means 'freedom' in Malay). National and international sports events are held at the stadium (the famous boxing match between Mohammad Ali and Joe Bugner was staged here in 1975), as well as the annual international Koran reading competition, held during Ramadan. ■ *RM1*.

Lake Gardens

Overlooking Jalan Damansara, near the southern tip of the Lake Gardens, is the **Muzium Negara** (National Museum), with its traditional *Minangkabau*-style roof, and two large murals of Italian glass mosaic either side of the main entrance. They depict the main historical episodes and cultural activities of Malaysia. The museum was opened in 1963, and, set on three floors, provides an excellent introduction to Malaysia's history, geography, natural history and culture. ■ *0900-1800 Mon-Sun, closed 1200-1430 Fri, RM1, T2826255*.

Close to the museum is the south entrance to the 90-ha **Lake Gardens** (Taman Tasek Perdana). Pedal boats can be hired on the main lake, Tasek Perdana, at the weekend. The gardens also house a Hibiscus Garden (Taman Bunga Raya), with over 500 species; an Orchid Garden (Taman Bunga Orkid), which has over 800 species and is transformed into an orchid market at weekends; as well as children's playgrounds, picnic areas, restaurants and cafés, and a small deer park. At the north end of the Lake Gardens is the **National Monument**. Located at the far side of Jalan Parlimen, it provides a good view of Parliament House. The memorial, over 15 m tall, with its dramatically posed sculpted figures, is dedicated to the heroes of Malaya's 12-year Communist Emergency (see page 511). The state of emergency was

In testament to Malaysia's sometimes muddled ethnic and religious mix, it is not uncommon to find Chinese devotees joining in the Taipusam festival

The man-made park is a joggers' paradise and popular city escape

Kuala Lumpur

lifted in 1960, but members of the banned Communist Party managed to put a bomb under the memorial in 1975. Below the monument is a sculpture garden with exhibits from throughout the member countries of the Association of South East Asian Nations (ASEAN).

The showpiece of the Lake Gardens is the **Taman Burung** or **Bird Park**. Opened in 1991 in an effort to out-do neighbouring Singapore's famous Jurong Bird Park, this aviary is twice the size of Jurong, and encloses more than 2,000 birds from 200 species, ranging from ducks to hornbills. Spread out over 20 ha of landscaped gardens, most of the birds are free and very accustomed to being around people. The hornbill area is particularly exciting. It houses seven varieties of hornbill, most of which are indigenous to Malaysia. A further 25 hectares is under development and will eventually provide spacious enclosures for birds currently in cages. There is a reference centre, refreshment kiosk and binoculars for hire. ■ *0900-1800 Mon-Sun, RM3, child RM2.*

The **Butterfly Park** (Taman Rama-rama) is a five-minute drive from the main entrance of the Lake Gardens, coming in from Jalan Parlimen. It is a miniature jungle, which is home to almost 8,000 butterflies, from 150 species. There are also small mammals, amphibians and reptiles, and rare tropical insects in the park. There is an insect museum and souvenir shop on the site. ■ *Daily 0900-1800, adult RM9, child RM2, RM1 admission to film, RM2 to use a camera.*

On the southeast edge of the park is **Tun Razak Memorial**, the former residence of Malaysia's revered second prime minister, the late Tun Abdul Razak, whose great, great, great, great, great grandfather, Sultan Abdullah of Kedah, ceded Penang to the British (see page 153). In recognition of his services – he is popularly known as the father of Malaysia's development – his old home has been turned into a memorial with the aim of preserving his documents, speeches, books and awards, as well as housing his collection of walking sticks and pipes. ■ *0900-1800 Tue-Sun, closed 1200-1500 Fri, T2912111.* At the southern end of the Lake Gardens is the **National Planetarium**. The planetarium has a theatre with a 20-m-diameter domed screen where the Space Science Show (1100, 1400, 1600) and Sky movies are projected. Other facilities include an exhibition hall, an observatory, a viewing gallery and a 14-in telescope. ■ *1000-1600 every day except Fri, 1000-1900 Sat, Sun. T22735484. Space Science Show, adult RM3, child RM2, Sky movie, adult RM6, child RM4, exhibition RM1.*

The modern 18-storey **Parliament House** and its Toblerone-shaped House of Representatives is on the west fringe of the gardens. When parliament is in session, visitors may observe parliamentary proceedings (permission must be formally obtained, and visitors must be smartly dressed). In years gone by, many of the administrative arms of government were housed in the State Secretariat (now renamed the Sultan Abdul Samad Building) on the Padang.

Most of the main government ministries are now situated in scruffy 1960s suburban office blocks off Jalan Duta, to the west

■ *Getting to Lake Gardens: Take bus 244 or 250 from Sultan Mohammed Bus Station and minibus 18, 21, 46 or 48 from Jl Tun Perak. Taxis away from the park can be difficult to find – it may be worth either chartering one to wait for you or booking one in advance.*

Jalan Ampang

Jalan Ampang became the home of KL's early tin-mining millionaires and an important leafy adjunct to the colonial capital. The styles of its stately mansions range from Art Deco and mock-Palladian to Islamic. Today many of these buildings have become embassies and consulates. One of the lovelier **Art Deco-style buildings** now houses the **Rubber Research Institute**. Another of

Jalan Ampang's fine old buildings is the old **Coq d'Or restaurant**, formerly the residence of a Chinese tin mogul, and still a great place for dinner and 'stengahs' on the terrace (*setengah* is Malay for 'half', and became the colonial term for shots of whisky and water). Further into town, another renovated house is now the **Malaysian Tourist Information Complex (MATIC)**, T2643929. It was the headquarters of the Japanese Imperial Army during the Second World War, but was originally built in 1935 by Eu Tong Seng, a wealthy Chinese rubber planter and tin mogul. MATIC is a one-stop visitors' centre; as well as having a tourist information counter, it has money-changing facilities, an express bus ticketing counter, reservations for package holidays, a souvenir shop, Malay restaurant, cultural shows every Tuesday, Thursday and Sunday at 1530, and 15-minute-long audio-visual shows. The intersection of Jalan Ampang and the old circular road, Jalan Tun Razak, has become a booming shopping area in the shape of Ampang Park and City Square shopping centres.

The old Selangor Turf Club racecourse, which lies to the southeast of this intersection, has been the focus of extraordinary redevelopment in the guise of the **Kuala Lumpur City Centre** or **KLCC** – a 'city within a city'. High-rise development came late to KL but has rapidly gained a foothold; the city's offices, hotels and shopping complexes are mostly concentrated in the Golden Triangle, on the east side of the city. When completed the complex will be one of the largest real estate developments in the world, covering a 40-ha site. The first phase included the construction of the **Petronas Twin Towers** (see box, page 83). On Level 4, Suria KLCC children will enjoy Petrosains, The Discovery Centre, which is really a petroleum promotion exercise, with rides and hands-on computer games all glorifying this industry. ■ *0930-1730 Tue, Wed and Thu, 1330-1730 Fri and 0930-1830 weekends, T5818181.*

The Ampang Tower, a mere 50-storey office block, is part of phase one of the KLCC's development, as are the Suria KLCC, a crescent-shaped retail and entertainment centre on the junction of Jalan Ampang and Jalan P Ramlee, the Esso Tower, a 20-ha park with a children's playground and the *Mandarin Oriental*, a five-star hotel with over 600 rooms. Jalan Bukit Bintang and Jalan

Around KLCC

Related maps
A Around the
Golden Triangle,
page 84
B Colonial Core &
Chow Kit, page 77
C Chinatown,
page 79

0 metres   500
0 yards   500

■ **Sleeping**
1 Concorde &
  Hard Rock Café
2 Crown Princess

3 Equatorial
4 MiCasa
5 Ming Court
6 New World & Renaissance

7 Nikko
8 Shangri-La
9 Su Casa

● **Eating**
1 Le Coq d'Or

The Petronas Twin Towers: a nation's pride and joy

Malaysians take enormous pride in the fact that their capital city houses the world's tallest building . The Petronas Twin Towers building comprises two 88-storey towers soaring to 452 m above ground level, a kangaroo leap taller than the Sears Tower in Chicago, which is just 9 m shorter. However, those crucial 9 m have secured significant international coverage for Malaysia. Not only is the building, which was completed in 1997, a record breaker, but in 1999 it even featured the movie Entrapment *starring Sean Connery and Catherine Zeta Jones.*

The global attention is welcomed by Prime Minister Dr Mahatir Mohamad, who strongly believes that the towers express the nation's great ambition to become a developed country. "A country needs something to look up to and we certainly have to look up to the towers", he commented at the official opening on 30 August 1999. Displaying a lack of sensitivity to the vertically challenged, he explained that "when one is short, one should stand on a box to get a better view. The Twin Towers is to our ego what the box is to the shorty".

The RM1.8 bn towers were designed by the US-based Argentinian architect Cesar Pelli, who was also responsible for the design of Canary Wharf Tower in London. He has successfully created an imposing structure that looms spectacularly over the capital – and sometimes above the smog. On the exterior the distinctive 58-m double deck sky-bridge that links levels 41 and 42 is quite unique and makes the towers instantly recognizable. Internally the skyscraper is believed to be the only one in the world with an Islamic floor motif. The geometric patterns, common in architecture of Islamic heritage, comprise two rotated and superimposed squares with circular infills symbolizing unity, harmony, stability and rationality – all important principles in Islam. It is unfortunate that the architect forgot about the visitor: there is no top-floor restaurant, café or viewing platform.

The towers are just one of several significant building projects undertaken in Malaysia over the past few years. These include the state-of-the-art Kuala Lumpur International Airport at Sepang (KLIA), which opened in June 1998 at a cost of US$3.5bn; the new (and ongoing) federal government administrative centre in Putrajaya; and the creation of a multi-media super corridor south of KL, which will have at its heart the new 'intelligent' city of Cyberjaya. While the prime minister has always enthusiastically supported these grand projects, they have also been criticised as wasteful.

See also www.klcc.com.my The website for information on the new multi-media super corridor is www.mdc.com.my

It is possible to take a lift to the bridge level of the Twin Towers (with a free ticket that gives you 20 mins on the bridge) to experience the view of the city

Sultan Ismail was where the first modern hotels and shopping complexes went up – the *Regent*, the *Hilton*, the *Equatorial*, *Holiday Inn*, *Shangri-La* and *Concorde*. More recently the area around Jalan Ampang and Jalan Tun Razak has been transformed into a commercial centre; several towers have sprung up in the area in recent years, including the extraordinary hour-glass-shaped Pilgrims' Building, which co-ordinates the annual Haj and looks after the pilgrims' funds. There are several further developments including a *Sheraton* and *Hyatt*, both five-star tower-block hotels. One of the newest shopping plazas in the Golden Triangle is *Star Hill Plaza* on Jalan Bukit Bintang, next to the new, five-star *Marriott Hotel*.

Near the intersection of Jalan Ampang and Jalan Sultan Ismail atop Bukit Nanas stands the **KL Tower**, or **Menara KL**. This 421-m-high tower is the tallest telecommunications tower in Asia and the fourth tallest in the world (the viewing tower stands at 276 m). Characteristically, the tower is the brain-child of Prime Minister Dr Mahathir Mohammed. There are 22 levels and 2,058 stairs, so the lift is recommended! At ground level there are several shops and fast-food restaurants and a mini amphitheatre. Above the viewing platform is the *Seri Angkasa* revolving restaurant. It has excellent Malay cuisine and revolves once every 60 minutes, so diners get to see the whole city between hors d'oeuvre and ice cream. ■ *For reservations, T20205448. KL Tower is open daily 1000-2200, RM12, RM5 for children (4-12 years), free for children under 3 years, students RM6, T2085448, www.menarakl.com.my Getting there: no public transport – take a taxi or walk from one of the surrounding roads.*

The **Rumah Penghulu Abu Seman** on Jalan Stonor, otherwise known as the Heritage Centre of the Badan Warisan Malaysia, is to be found in a mock-Tudor building off Jalan Conloy, on the northern edge of the Golden Triangle. In the garden is a reconstructed headman's house made of timber – it displays detailed carvings and has been furnished in the style of a house from the 1930s. ■ *1000-1600 Mon to Fri, T2449273 for information on their exhibitions. Just to the east of the Heritage Centre is the Komplex Budaya Kraf, a local handicraft centre offering visitors the opportunity to dabble in batik or watch artists at work.*

Around the Golden Triangle

N

0 metres 100
0 yards 100

■ **Sleeping**		
1 Agora	9 Imperial	18 Swiss Garden
2 Bintang Warisan	10 Istana	19 Tai Ichi
3 Cardogan	11 Lodge	
4 Century	12 Malaysia	● **Eating**
5 Emerald	13 Marriott	1 Delaney's Irish Pub
6 Equatorial	14 Melia	2 Eden Village Seafood
7 Federal	15 Mutiara	3 Moomba
8 Fortuna	16 Nova	4 Seri Melayu
	17 Regent	5 Shark Club

Around the city area

The US$150 million **Putra World Trade Centre** (Kompleks Seni Budaya, Jalan Conlay), to the north of the city centre on Jalan Tun Ismail, took nearly 15 years to materialize, but when it opened in 1985, Malaysia proudly announced that it was finally on the international convention and trade-fair circuit. The luxurious complex of buildings includes the *Pan-Pacific Hotel*, a sleek 41-storey office block and an exhibition centre, adorned with a traditional *Minangkabau* roof. The headquarters of Prime Minister Dr Mahathir Mohamad's ruling United Malays National Organization (UMNO) occupies the top floor and there is a tourist information centre on the second floor.

The **Karyaneka Handicraft Centre** (Kompleks Seni Budaya) is on Jalan Conlay to the east of the city centre and is popular among tour groups. There is a small museum illustrating the batik, weaving and pottery processes. Craft demonstrations are held from 1000 to 1800, and there is a selection of crafts on sale from each of the 13 states of Malaysia. ■ *0900-1800 Mon-Sun. Getting there: minibus or Intrakota no 40 from Jalan Tuanku Abdul Rahman.*

East of the Karyaneka Handicraft Centre, on Jalan Bukit Bintang, is the **Jade Museum**. This small museum houses a private collection of 80 jade artefacts from China. Replicas and jade souvenirs are for sale – or so it seems. In 1997 a case of tourists visiting the museum being sold fake rubies was investigated by the police. ■ *1000-1900 Mon-Sun, RM10. Getting there: Intrakota or minibus 40 from Klang Bus Station.*

Thean Hou Temple or the **Temple of the Goddess of Heaven** is situated at Jalan Klang Lama (off Jalan Tun Sambathan, to the southwest of the city). Perched on a hill, it has a panoramic view over KL. A contemporary Buddhist pagoda and Buddha images are enshrined in the octagonal hall. It stands between a sacred Bodhi tree and a Buddhist shrine, built by Sinhalese Buddhists in 1894. ■ *Getting there: minibus 27 from Kelang bus terminal to Jalan Syed Putra.*

Excursions

North

This system of caverns set high in a massive limestone outcrop, 13 km north of KL, was 'discovered' by American naturalist William Hornaby in the 1880s. In 1891 Hindu priests set up a shrine in the main cave dedicated to Lord Subramaniam and it has now become the biggest Indian pilgrimage centre in Malaysia during the annual Thaipusam festival (see page 54), when over 800,000 Hindus congregate here.

The main cave is reached by a steep flight of 272 steps. Coloured lights provide illumination for the fantasy features and formations of the karst limestone cavern. There are a number of other, less spectacular caves in the outcrop, including the Museum Cave (at ground level) displaying elaborate sculptures of Hindu mythology. During the Second World War, the Japanese Imperial Army used some of the caves as factories for the manufacture of ammunition and as arms dumps; the concrete foundations for the machinery can be seen at the foot of the cliffs. ■ *RM1. Caves stay open until about 2100. Getting there: Intrakota or minibus 11 from Central Market. The caves are a short walk off the main road.*

Batu Caves

Templer Park
The park attracts swarms of weekend day-trippers – although most do not venture far beyond the car park and picnic area

The park, covering 500 ha and about 10 km further on up the main road from the turn-off to the Batu Caves, serves as KL's nearest jungle playground, apart from the tiny Bukit Nanas Forest Reserve in the middle of the city. It opened as a park in 1954 and is named after the last British High Commissioner of Malaya, Sir Gerald Templer, 'the Tiger of Malaya', who oversaw the tactical defeat of the Communist insurgents during the Emergency (see page 511). The park is dominated by several impressive 350-m-high limestone hills and outcrops, the biggest being **Bukit Takun** and **Bukit Anak Takun** (similar to the Batu Caves outcrop).

There are extensive networks of underground passages and cave systems within the hills, thought to have formed 400 million years ago. Unfortunately, a huge new floodlit golf course has impinged on the north boundaries of the park making access to some of these massifs more difficult – and another 180-ha golf resort is being developed. The park has a wide variety of jungle flora and fauna and is a popular venue for boy scout and youth camps. Nearby are the **Kanching Falls** (sometimes incorrectly referred to as Templer Park Falls) – dropping 300 m in several stages and a good place for swimming. ■ *Getting there: buses Len Omnibus 66, 78, 83 or 81 from Pudu Raya bus terminal (RM1.20).*

Taman Tasek Titiwangsa

Ten minutes north of KL is this man-made lake with facilities for boating, horse riding, tennis, badminton, a model car racetrack and a seafood restaurant.

Orang Asli Museum

Situated 25 km north of KL on the old Gombak Road, this museum preserves the traditions of Malaysia's indigenous Orang Asli aboriginals, who number about 60,000 on the peninsula. There are displays giving the background to the 18 different tribes and their geographical dispersal. There are also models of Orang Asli village houses and a souvenir shop attached to the museum selling Orang Asli crafts. ■ *0900-1700 Sat-Thu, closed Fri, free, T6892122. Getting there: City Liner bus 174 from Lebuh Ampang terminus (RM1.50).*

Jungle canopy walk

It is possible to do this walk through the treetops at the Forestry Research Institute of Malaysia (FRIM) at Kepong, some 30 minutes north of KL, on the Jabayan Perhutanan. However, it is important to book with the FRIM (T6342633), as it can be closed.

West and southwest

Asian Art Museum

The Asian Art Museum is housed within the university campus, about 4 km southwest of the Lake Gardens. The museum exhibits Asian art objects, sculpture, ceramics, textiles and handicrafts. ■ *0900-1600 Mon to Fri, 0900-1200 Sat. Free. To get there, take the LRT to the University and then take a taxi.*

Petaling Jaya
Bandar Utama lays claim to providing the biggest shopping mall in the country, with heaps of restaurants too

Located 15 km southwest of KL, this is a thriving industrial satellite and middle-class dormitory town for the capital and is known as PJ. Initially built to provide low-cost housing for squatter resettlement it is now a city in its own right, with shopping and administration centres. The whole town, with its streets running in semi-circles, was planned on a drawing board, but despite its unimaginative street names (or rather, numbers), is not as sterile as it might sound. In recent years it has become quite lively, with its own nightlife scene and several gourmet restaurants (particularly around Damansara Utama, where clubs stay open until 0300 or 0400), which cater for PJ's expatriate and wealthy Malaysian population. PJ is mainly frequented by business people, as Subang airport is close by. Also nearby is the Sunway Lagoon, a water theme park with a variety of watery rides on offer and some dry-land activities too. ■ *T7356000 for more information. Open 1200-1930 during the week (closed Tuesday) and 1000-1930 at the weekends. Admission: RM50 for all the park, RM18 for the waterpark and RM32 for dry-land adventures. Buses to most parts of Petaling Jaya can be boarded at Bangkok Bank stop and Kelang bus terminal (RM0.60).*

Sleeping and eating AL *Allson Sunway Lagoon Resort*, Jl Lagun Timur, Bandar Sunway, T7358886, F7365688. New and dazzling resort, the world's largest surf 'n wave pool, health and spa club, 3 tennis courts, squash, 170-m man-made beach, kiddy camp, shuttle service to KL, coffee house, Japanese restaurant, Chinese restaurant, American/Italian restaurant, poolside bar. Recommended. **AL** *Hyatt Regency Saujana Hotel & Country Club*, 2 km off Subang International Airport Highway, T7461234, F7462789. 5 mins from the airport and 2 mins from the golf course (it has 2 18-hole championship courses), low-rise hotel set in landscaped gardens, it is a particularly convenient stop-over for early morning flights, provides shuttle service to and from airport. **AL** *Pan Pacific Glenmarie Resort*, Jl Sultan, T7039090, F7032728. Resort hotel with 300 rooms set in more than 1,000 ha of grounds, 10 mins' drive from Subang Airport, with sports facilities including 2 golf courses, Olympic-sized swimming pool, squash and tennis courts. **AL** *Petaling Jaya Hilton*, 2 Jl Barat, T7559122, F7553909. A/c, restaurant, pool. **A** *Holiday Villa*, 9 Jl SS 12/1, Subang Jaya, T7338788, F7337449. A/c, restaurant, pool. **A** *Merlin Subang*, Jl 5512/1, Subang Jaya, T7335211, F7331299. A/c, restaurant, pool. **A** *Subang Airport Hotel*, Kompleks Airtel Fima, T7462122, F7461097. A/c, restaurant, pool. **B** *Shah's Village Hotel*, 3 & 5 Lorong Sultan, T79569322, F79557715, hmshah@po.jaring.my, www.shahsresorts.com A/c, restaurant, boutique-style hotel set around a garden and pool. *Grand City* is a good Indian restaurant near the University Hospital.

Shah Alam

The new state capital of Selangor, situated between KL and Port Klang, has the reputation of being Malaysia's best-planned city and is an ultra-modern showpiece town. The skyline is dominated by the State Mosque, **Masjid Sultan Salahuddin Abdul Aziz Shah**, which has a huge, blue aluminium dome, said to be the largest in the world. Completed in 1988, it is reputed to be the largest mosque in Southeast Asia and can accommodate up to 16,000 worshippers. Wet World water theme park provides some entertainment for children, including the Monsoon Buster – a watercoaster, which at one point reaches a height of 220 m. ■ *1200-2000, daily except Wed, and 1000-2000 weekend. RM7 adults, RM4 children.* There is a *Holiday Inn* (**A**) on Plaza Perangsang, Persiaran Perbandaran (T5503696, F5503913), an ugly high-rise building, but only 15 mins' drive from Subang Airport, and it has air conditioning, a restaurant and rooftop pool. ■ *Shah Alam is an hour from KL's Kelang bus station or you can take a taxi (RM20).*

Klang

The town, 30 km southwest of KL, is also known as Kelang, a name thought to derive from an old Sumatran word for tin

This royal town has a magnificent mosque and attractive royal palace, the **Istana Alam Shah**, set in well-cared-for grounds. The palace is closed to the public, but can be seen from the road. Klang had been the capital of Selangor for centuries before the tin-mining town of Kuala Lumpur assumed the mantle in 1880. Klang was the name for the whole state of Selangor when it formed one of the *Negri Sembilan* (the nine states of the Malay Federation).

Today **Port Klang** (previously known as Port Swettenham, after former British Resident Frank Swettenham) is KL's seaport and is a busy container terminal. Klang is also an important service centre for nearby rubber and palm oil plantations, which, in the early decades of the 20th century, spread the length of the Klang Valley to KL.

The **Gedung Rajah Abdullah** warehouse, built in 1857, is one of the oldest buildings in the town. Rajah Abdullah was the Bugis Chief who first dispatched the expedition to the upper reaches of the Klang River, which resulted in the founding of KL. In 1991 it was turned from a historical museum into Malaysia's first tin-mining museum. ■ *0900-1600 Mon-Sun, closed 1200-1445 Fri.* There is also a **fort** in Klang, built by Rajah Mahdi (a rival of Raja Abdullah), which guarded the entrance to the Klang valley from its strategic position overlooking the river.

The town is well known for its seafood; most of the restaurants are close to the bus terminal. Ferries leave from Klang for offshore islands such as Pulau Ketam (see below), Pulau Morib (golf course, see page 108) and Pulau Angsa. ■ *Buses 51, 58, 225, Kelang Bus Co, leave from Kelang bus terminal in KL for Klang (RM1.70), or you can take a train, departures every 30 mins; the journey takes around one-and-a-half hours.*

Pulau Ketam (Crab Island), about 10 km west of Port Klang, is like a downmarket Venice, Malaysian-style, with the whole village on stilts over the fetid water. It is a good spot for seafood. Accommodation is available on the island by way of the Homes Away from Home programme, see page 96. ■ *Bus to Port Klang (RM2) or the Komuter train and then a ferry, one hour (RM4), T3314713.*

Kuala Selangor is a coastal town on the banks of the River Sungai Selangor, 64 km northwest of KL. In the 19th century, it was a focal point of the Sultanate of Selangor. The Dutch built two fortresses here in 1784, overlooking the Sungai Selangor estuary, to blockade the Sungai Selangor in retaliation for Sultan Ibrahim of Selangor's attacks on Melaka. In 1871, British gunboats bombarded the forts – then occupied by Malays – for several hours, marking the first British intervention in the Selangor Civil War, over the possession of the tin-rich Klang Valley. The larger of the two, **Fort Altingberg**, on Bukit Melawati, serves as a royal mausoleum and museum. ■ *Open during daylight hours, Mon-Sun.* The fort overlooks the **Kuala Selangor Nature Park**, 250 ha of coastal mangrove swamp and wetland. It has several observation hides, and more than 156 bird species, including bee eaters, kingfishers and sea eagles, have been recorded here. There are also leaf monkeys. It is also one of the best places to see Malaysia's famous synchronized fireflies – the only fireflies in Southeast Asia that manage to co-ordinate their flashing (see page 564); they are best observed on a moonless night, from about one hour after sunset. The actual riverside site is around 8 km from Kuala Selangor, near a village called Kampung Kuantan. ■ *A boat trip can be taken from Kampung Kuantan (RM2 each, four people per boat), T8892403.* The Malayan Nature Society runs chalets in the park, a short walk from the last bus stop. A-frames cost RM15 and accommodate two, and chalets are RM25-30 for four people. These must be booked in advance (see below); a few days in advance for weekend visitors. There are also two small bus-station hotels (**D-E**), which have rooms with bathrooms. ■ *Getting there: There are regular direct buses from KL's Puduraya bus terminal to Kuala Selangor (RM3.50). Taxis can be chartered from Kuala Selangor to Kampung Kuantan (wait and return RM25-30; whole car). The Malayan Nature Society, which operates the park, will arrange private transport to Kampung Kuantan and back, for about the same price, when pre-arranged with their KL Office, T8892294 before 1700; T8892403 after 1700.*

South

Mines Wonderland This adventure playground, next to the site of Sepang International Airport in Sungai Besi about 20 minutes south of KL, has been constructed on a 60-ha plot, which used to be the largest tin-mining lake in the world. Attractions include a Snow House, where you can see sculptures carved out of ice by artists from China. Alternatively, take a ride on a water taxi or see the Musical Fountain or any of the other sound and light attractions. The whole 'Mines Resort City' consists of a sizeable conference centre set within a five-star hotel, a 'Beach Resort' (although there is no beach here), a shopping mall, a business park, an international-standard golf course, and a new residential development. ■ *1700-2200 weekdays and 1600-2300 weekends, RM12 adults, RM8 children. Batu 10 1/2, Jalan Sungai Besi, T9425010. Get there: KTM Komuter from KL railway station to Serdang station (walkable from here).*

Sleeping **AL** *Mines Beach Resort and Spa*, Jln Dulang, T9436688, F9435555, sales@mbr.com.my Furnished to a high standard, the resort has even managed to achieve a sandy beach. Low-rise hotel in well-landscaped gardens, a pleasant alternative to the bustle of KL. **AL** *Palace of the Golden Horses*, Jln Kuda Emas, T9436633, F9436622, pgh_reservation@signature.com.my Set on the shores of the old tin-minng lake, a hotel with 400-plus rooms hotel, luxury fittings, a range of cuisines, state-of-the-art conference centre, exquisite spa, fitness centre, free-form lagoon pool, and children's camp. The closest 5-star hotel to the new airport. **B** *Mint*, 8th Rm, KL-Seremban Highway, T9438888, F9438889. Ugly block of over 400 rooms, sizeable pool, health centre, business centre, convenient for Mines Exhibition Centre and Wonderland, and for the new airport.

East

The **Malaysian Armed Forces Museum** on Jalan Gurney exhibits pictures, paintings and weapons, including those captured from the so-called Communists Terrorists (CTs) during the Emergency (see page 511). ■ *1000-1800 Mon-Thu and Sat. Getting there: minibus 19 (RM0.60).*

Royal Selangor Complex on Jalan Pahang, in Setapak Jaya, to the north of the city, is the biggest pewter factory in the world, employing over 500 craftsmen. Royal Selangor was founded in 1885, using Straits tin (over 95%) which is alloyed with antimony and copper. Visitors can watch demonstrations of hand-casting and pewter working. Visitors can also see jewellery making and the handpainting of bonded porcelain. One of the most photographed sights at the complex is the massive pewter tankard outside the building – it is in the Guinness Book of Records as the largest in the world. As well as the Setapak Jaya Complex, there are showrooms throughout the city (see page 106). ■ *0900-1600 Mon-Sun. Getting there: Len Seng Bus from Lebuh Ampang Bus Station 12 or 10 (RM0.70).*

The **National Zoo and Aquarium** is 13 km from the centre of KL, down Jalan Ampang to Ulu Klang. The zoo encompasses a forest and a lake and houses 1,000 different species of Malaysian flora and fauna in addition to collections from elsewhere in the world. It also has an aquarium with over 80 species of marine life. ■ *0900-1700 Mon-Sun, adult RM4, child RM1. Getting there: Len Seng bus 170, Len Chee 177, Sri Jaya 255 from Jalan Ampang or minibus 17 from Chow Kit (RM0.50), T4083427.*

Tours

Many companies offer city tours, usually of around three hours, which include visits to Chinatown, Muzium Negara (the National Museum), the Railway Station, Thean Hou Temple, Masjid Negara (the National Mosque),

See also Tour operators, page 109

the Padang area and Masjid Jame – most of which cost in the region of RM25. City night tours take in Chinatown, the Sri Mahmariamman Temple and a cultural show (RM55). Other tours on offer visit sights close to the city such as Batu Caves, a batik factory and the Selangor Pewter Complex (RM25), as well as day trips to Melaka, Port Dickson, Fraser's Hill, Genting Highlands and Pulau Ketam (RM40-80). Most of these tour companies offer tours to destinations around the peninsula. Helicopter tours of the city are now run by *Mofaz Air* from Bukit Lanjan, Taman Tun Dr Ismail on weekdays and from Taman Tasik Titiwangsa on Sunday. Trips last 15 minutes and cost RM100 per person, with a maximum of six people per helicopter. Another air tour company is *Asia Tenggara Aviation Services*, T6264613, offering tours seven days per week 0800-1830. Note that aerial photography is not allowed.

For a jungle tour with a difference there is the *Utan Bara Adventure Team (UBAT)*, Unit 286-03-08, The Heritage, Jalan Pahang, T4225124, F4226125. The people who run this outfit are ex-security personnel and the names of their tours speak for themselves: 'Cross-country jungle survival course' (four-seven days, US$180-350 per person), 'Jungle wilderness medicine camp' (five days, US$250), 'Mountain trekking' (five days, US$200), '35 km Taman Negara Jungle Trail' (US$200), 'Expeditions into the jungle to locate downed US and Japanese aircraft', etc.

Essentials

Sleeping

Price codes: see inside front cover

Room rates in KL's top hotels escalated as the economy boomed in the early 1990s. However, the city's hosting of the Commonwealth Games in 1998 led to the construction of many new hotels and the number of beds available in 3, 4 and 5-star hotels more than doubled between 1997 and 2000. This, coupled with the economic crisis, the stagnation in tourism arrivals associated with the 'haze' and the political problems in the region, led in 1999 to KL (and Malaysia more generally) facing a glut of rooms, low occupancy levels, and falling room rates.

Some top hotels drastically reduce their room rates during the weekends

By international standards KL's hotels are excellent value for money, but because of the city's traffic problems, the location of a hotel has become an increasingly important consideration. Most top hotels are between Jln Sultan Ismail and Jln P Ramlee, in KL's Golden Triangle. South of Jalan Raja Chulan, in the Bukit Bintang area, there is another concentration of big hotels.

If you are staying in the larger, a/c hotels and are a non-smoker, it is possible to request a room on a non-smoking floor. Rooms with a/c generally have non-opening windows, making it difficult to freshen the air. Many of the cheaper hotels are around Jln Tunku Abdul Rahman, Jln Masjid India and Jln Raja Laut, all of which are within easy walking distance of the colonial core of KL, northeast of the Padang. There are also cheap hotels in the Chinatown area.

City centre
■ *on maps, pages 77 & 79*
Price codes: see inside front cover

A *Furama*, Komplek Selangor, Jln Sultan, T20701777, F20702110, www.furama.com.my A/c, restaurant, health centre. An uninspired hotel with the benefit of a central location in the heart of Chinatown, reasonable rates, geared, as name suggests, mainly to Japanese visitors. Includes breakfast. **A** *Impiana Hotel*, Jln Cheng Lock, situated next to the Pudu Raya bus station, T2066060, F2068332, reservation@impianakl.udanet.com New, international hotel. Well-furnished, clean a/c rooms with televisions, internet access, tea/coffee-making facilities, mini-bar and in-room safe. Restaurant and bar. Breakfast included. Walking tours of KL available. Recommended.

A *Katari*, 38 Jln Pudu, T2017777, F2017911, katari@tm.net.my A/c, restaurant, small hotel opposite Puduraya bus terminal, small, clean rooms, with showers only, price includes American breakfast, reductions available, friendly staff, safe place to leave luggage. **A** *Malaya*, Jln Hang Lekir, T20727722, F20700980 www.hotelmalaya.com.my A/c, restaurant, 1970s hotel with central location in Chinatown, pretty characterless. Staff are cold to the point of rudeness and appear unwilling to provide any information, useful or otherwise. **A** *Mandarin*, 2-8 Jln Sultan, T20703000, F20704363. A/c, restaurant, in Chinatown, used by business visitors, not as plush as its name suggests (it is not a part of the Mandarin Group), but is clean, with an interesting location and is reasonable value for money. Good à la carte menu; organised tours available. **A** *Stanford Hotel*, 449 Jln Tuanku Abdul Rahman, T26919833, F26913103, stanfordhotel@po.jaring.my Convenient business hotel close to Putra World Trade Centre, comfortable but basic rooms.

B *Heritage*, Bangunan Stesen Keretapi, Jln Sultan Hishamuddin, T22735588, F22732842. Part of the magnificent Moorish-style railway station. It has recently been redeveloped and has managed to retain some of its colonial splendour, but disappointingly the standard rooms have been furnished in a contemporary style. **B** *Lok Ann*, 113A Jln Petaling, T20789544. A/c, clean, large rooms, with televisions and telephones, well-used feel, centrally located in Chinatown. **B** *Puduraya*, 4th Flr, Puduraya Bus Station, Jln Pudu, T2321000, F2305567. A/c, restaurant, breakfast included, clean, spacious rooms, some with spectacular views overlooking the city centre. Residents have access to on-site health club. Convenient for bus station. Breakfast included. **B** *Quality Hotel*, Jln Raja Laut, T26939233, F26936332, http://asia123.com/quality/home.htm A/c, Szechuan restaurant, coffee house, pool, squash, health club, gymnasium, big enough hotel, but inside everything is rather bijou – the lobby is squashed, the swimming pool tiny and the fitness and business centres on the miniature side. **B** *Swiss Inn*, 62 Jln Sultan, T2323333, F2016699, www.swissgarden.com A/c, café, 1930s Malaya-style furnishings, in good position in the heart of Chinatown, but standard rooms are without windows. Unfriendly staff and meagre breakfast if you arrive after 0830.

C *Nan Yeang Hotel*, 83 Jln Sultan, T20787477, F20724611. Central location to Chinatown, next to the *Furama Hotel*. Clean and tidy, some rooms with balconies over road. The cheapest rooms are not good, being small and rather dirty and without a bathroom. **C** *Starlight*, 90-92 Jln Hang Kasturi, T20789811. A/c, spacious rooms with (basic) en-suite facilities. Excellent staff. Well situated for Central Market, Chinatown, bus stations, eateries, shops, places of interest. Being opposite the Kelang bus station, it can be noisy. Recommended. **C** *YWCA*, 12 Jln Hang Jebat (to the east of Chinatown and south of Jln Pudu), T2383225. Fans, hot/cold water, quiet and clean with a friendly atmosphere. Also caters for couples. Restaurant, also access to TV and fridge. Recommended. **C-D** *Backpackers' Travellers' Inn*, 2nd Flr, 60 Jln Sultan (opposite *Furama Hotel*), T2382473. Some a/c, centrally and conveniently located in Chinatown next to excellent stalls/restaurants, popular and professionally run. Rooms are small but generally clean, ranging from non-a/c dorm rooms to a/c rooms with attached showers, good facilities for the traveller including left luggage, washing and cooking facilities. Also available, book exchange, video, television and laundry. Recommended. **C-D** *Backpackers' Travellers' Lodge*, 158 Jln Tun HS Lee, T2010889. Some rooms have a/c and attached bathrooms with unpredictable hot water supply, clean and a good choice in this area, dorms. Internet access (pricey), several windowless rooms. Under same management as *Backpackers' Travellers' Inn*. **C-D** *Kawana*, 68 Jln Pudu, T2386714. Some a/c, small barrack-like rooms equipped with small TVs, but very clean, communal toilets and showers, some dorm beds.

D *Anuja's Backpacker's Inn*, 28, 1st-3rd Flrs, Toong Fong Building, Jln Pudu, T2066479, F 2013725, anujainn@tm.net.my very convenient for bus travellers, as

Most hotels are in & around Chinatown, a bustling area where KL's colonial roots have not been entirely obliterated

Kuala Lumpur

Puduraya Bus Station is only 1 min walk away. A good travellers' hangout. **D** *China-town Guesthouse*, 2nd Flr, Wisma BWT, Jln Petaling, in the centre of the *pasar malam* (night market), T20720417. Right in the middle of Chinatown, travel bulletin board, budget guesthouse, most rooms are quiet and have fans, very friendly. Run by Ron, who succeeds in creating a homely atmosphere, and maintaining a clean, efficient guest house. Don't be put off by the entrance stairs! **D** *Drop Inn Lodge*, 1 and 3 Jln Tun HS Lee, T 2386314, F 2843910. Some a/c, 13 basic and quite dirty rooms (no windows), has the advantage of being very central, but not one of the better budget places in town. **D** *Kameleon Travellers Lodge*, 37 Jln Pudu Lama, T2307770, kameleontravellerslodge@ hotmail.com Rooms with fans, large lounge area with satellite television, and book exchange. Outside bathrooms, all rooms with windows, simple but friendly and popular with backpackers. **D** *Mahligai Travel Lodge*, 2 Jln Hang Lekiu, T 2067244. About 5 mins' walk from Puduraya Bus Station and Chinatown. Some a/c, no en-suite facilities, but rooms are clean and cheap – good value for KL. **D** *Traveller's Moon Lodge*, 36B Jln Silang, T2306601. Possibly the cheapest option in KL, with dorm beds for RM8-10. **E** *Travellers Station*, right next to railway station, T2722237, station1@tm.net.my One of the few backpackers' places left, basic but friendly, some dorm rooms (small), but showers available. Good selection of recent videos. Email is RM1 for 10 mins.

Chow Kit area

■ *on map, page 77*
Price codes:
see inside front cover

AL *Pan Pacific*, Jln Putra, T40425555, F40417236, www.kualalumpur.pan-pac.com A/c, restaurant, pool, gym, spa, attached to the Putra World Trade Centre, so favoured by convention delegates, good views over the city, excellent *dim sum* restaurant, next to the WTC LRT station. **A** *Grand Continental*, Jln Belia/Jln Raja Laut, T2939333, F2939732. A/c, restaurant, pool, not really in the big league, except insofar as it has 328 unremarkable rooms, impersonal atmosphere, but reasonable facilities, similar, but much larger, to nearby *Plaza Hotel*. Breakfast included. **A** *Legend*, 100 Jln Putra, T40429888, F40411030, lengendkl@kl-hotels.com A/c, Chinese, Japanese and health food restaurants (7 in total), pool, health centre, like a monstrous Lego creation, this hotel is legendary in size, with 600 rooms and apartments, and a lobby on the ninth floor, the hotel was opened by Joan Collins and pursues a film-star image. Next to the WPTC LRT station, a very regal atmosphere. Staff are friendly and helpful. **A-B** *Wira Hotel*, 123 Jln Thamboosamy, T40423333, F40422833, www.kl-hotels.com/wira Off the main street, so slightly quieter than other typical business hotels in the area. Friendly staff, new hotel so clean, a/c, television, telephone and fridge in rooms. Coffee shop.

A good choice for business visitors using the Putra World Trade Centre. The Mall Shopping Centre next door provides a good range of shops and fast-food outlets

B *City Hotel*, 366 Jln Raja Laut, T40414466, F40415379. A/c, no restaurant, 101 rooms, refurbished in 1993, does not look much from the exterior, but rooms are clean with good hot water showers, professional management, competitively priced, most guests are Malaysians. Recommended. **B** *City Villa* (formerly *Asia*), 69 Jln Haji Hussein, T2926077, F2935143. A/c, restaurant – established and popular, karaoke bar, good value for money. Breakfast included. **B** *De First Inn*, 2 Lorong Haji Taib Lima, T40452323, F40452939. Another new hotel, standard rooms with a/c, attached bathrooms with bath, television, telephone. Small café in lobby, pleasant staff. **B** *Dynasty*, 218 Jln Ipoh, T4437777, F4436688, www.dynasty.com.my A/c, pool, Chinese or Mediterranean restaurants, business centre, a short distance from the Putra World Trade Centre, all the luxury you would expect for the price. Does 'The Ultimate Wedding Dynasty' for all religions – very tacky. Good value but inconvenient location. **B** *Elegant Inn*, 164 Jln Raja Laut, T40452288, F40456973. New hotel, situated on busy main street, standard mid-range, with a/c rooms, attached bathrooms, television and telephone. Postal and laundry services available. **B** *Grand Central*, 63 Jln Putra/Jln Raja Laut, T40413011, F40424758, http://www.grandcentral.com.sg A/c, clean but drab middle-market hotel with 138 rooms and little to recommend it but reasonable room rates, very basic restaurant. **B** *Grand Centrepoint*, 316 Jln Tuanku Abdul Rahman, T26933988, F26943688, www.ubb.com.my/hotel A/c, *Island Bar*, café, two restaurants, 100-room hotel, very clean, stylish primary colour décor, good for business people on a tight(ish) budget. Price includes breakfast. **B** *Grand Pacific*, Jln Ipoh/Jln Sultan Ismail, T4422177, F4426078. A/c, restaurant, not very grand, but delightful views of the highway (drivers have good views into hotel bedrooms), an old hotel, rather the worse for wear, very inconvenient for foot access, on the edge of the city centre, with none of the facilities one might expect from newer hotels. Not worth it given the location. **B** *Palace Hotel*, 40-46 Jln Masjid India, T26986122, F27116868, www.w3xs.com/palacehotel Slightly better quality than others in its genre, good location, offers a/c, bathroom, television, telephone, so nothing new but staff are friendly and the atmosphere less humdrum. **B** *Plaza*, Jln Raja Laut, T26982255, F2920959. A/c, restaurant, 160-room hotel offering competitive rates, price includes buffet breakfast and use of sauna. **B** *Vistana*, 9 Jln Lumut, off Jln Ipoh, T4428000, F4411400. A/c, *Thai Barn Restaurant*, coffee house, business centre, pool, classic business hotel of excellent standard but unpretentious, within easy walking distance of Putra World Trade Centre, a RM2 taxi ride from Chinatown, and close to Titwangsa STAR LRT station.

    C *Sentosa*, 316 Jln Raja Laut, T6925644. A/c, simple, Chinese-run, very good value. **C** *Hotel Putra*, 50-52 Jln Putra, T40412232, F40417889, reservation@hotelputra.com Clean, simple a/c rooms, with attached bathrooms, television and telephone. Internet café adjoining, breakfast included. A little out of town but near the PWT LRT station.

L *Istana*, 73 Jln Raja Chulan, T21419988, F21440111, www.hotelistana.com.my A/c, Chinese, Japanese and Italian restaurants, pool, this striking, almost grotesquely extravagant hotel is in the heart of KL's business district, all facilities including limousine transfer from airport to hotel. **L** *Marriott*, 183 Jln Bukit Bintang, T90259000, F90257000, jwmh@po.jaring.my Next to KL's most opulent shopping plaza *Star Hill*, has pool, fitness centre, conference facilities. Magnificent in its extravagance. **L** *Regent*, 160 Jln Bukit Bintang, T21418000, F21421441, reservations.rkl@fourseasons.com A/c, Western, Cantonese and Japanese restaurants, beautiful pool, gym with Roman baths, children's pool, a/c squash courts, health club, business centre (open until midnight), the ultimate hotel in KL – it won the 'Best Hotel in Malaysia' award the year it opened in 1990, all suites have butler service and the rooms and bathrooms are lavishly appointed, the enormous lobby is designed around a pool of cascading water. Recommended. **L-AL** *Federal*, 35 Jln Bukit Bintang, T21489166, F21482877, www.federalhotel.com.my A/c, Indian restaurant, revolving restaurant, ice-cream bar, cafés, bowling, shopping arcade, business centre, pool. When it opened in the early 1960s it was the pride of KL: its *Mandarin Palace* restaurant was once rated as the most elegant restaurant in the Far East, and is still good, but does not compare with the world-class glitz that KL has attracted of late.

    AL *Mandarin Oriental Hotel*, KLCC (next door to Petronas Twin Towers, hard to miss!), T3808888, F3808833, www.mandarinoriental.com Brand-new luxury hotel, with all that you would expect for its prestigious location. Several bars and restaurants, and function rooms named after precious stones. Health spa, swimming pool, tennis, sauna and massage rooms. **AL** *Renaissance*, corner of Jln Ismail and Jln Ampang, T21622233, F21631122, www.renaissance-kul.com A hotel with 400 rooms and an over-the-top lobby of massive black marble pillars. Furnishings in rooms are verging on the pretentious, but the lovely pool makes up for all of this. 2 tennis courts. Also a total of 9 lounges, bars and restaurants. Includes breakfast. **AL** *Shangri-La*, 11 Jln Sultan Ismail, T20322388, F20701514, www.shangri-la.com A/c, Chinese, Japanese and French restaurants, small, rather old-fashioned pool, health club, sauna, jacuzzi, tennis. With its grand marble lobby and 720 rooms, the '*Shang*' has remained KL's ritziest hotel despite the arrival of swish upstart competition. Constantly playing host to political leaders and assorted royalty for dinner, its best feature is its ground floor *Gourmet Corner* deli, which stocks a great variety of European food. Recommended.

Golden Triangle & KLCC
■ *on maps, pages 79 and 82 A big shopping and business area dominated by new high-rise hotels, shopping malls and office blocks*

Kuala Lumpur

AL *Swiss Garden*, 117 Jln Pudu, T21413333, F21415555, www.swissgarden.com A/c, Chinese restaurant, tiny pool, fitness centre with limited equipment, business centre, *Blue Chip Lounge* (a classy bar with live band and a computer terminal linked to the KL Stock Exchange), with 310 good-sized rooms and 15 storeys, but disappointing facilities. Expensive for what you get. **AL-A** *Equatorial*, Jln Sultan Ismail (opposite *MAS* building), T21617777, F21619020, www.equatorial.com A/c, restaurant (excellent Cantonese), pool, one of KL's earlier international hotels, the *Equatorial* has had several revamps over the years, its 1960s-style coffee shop has metamorphosed into one of the best hotel coffee shops in town, open 24 hrs (see below), with an international news agency in the basement, the hotel is the favoured repose of visiting journalists. Choose a room at the back to reduce disturbance by traffic noise, two no-smoking floors. **AL-A** *Bintang Warisan*, 68 Jln Bukit Bintang, T21488111, F21482333, www.bintangwarisan.com A/c, coffee house, nice little hotel, limited number of standard-price double bedrooms. Good, clean but quite basic small rooms, only facilities are two small cafés, some rooms have their own garden, prices include breakfast.

A *Agora*, 106-110 Jln Bukit Bintang, T21428133, F21427815, agorahotelkl@po.jaring.my A/c, restaurant, small 50-room hotel, located on busy intersection in shopping area of Golden Triangle, rooms on the front tend to be noisy, interesting design incorporating Greek columns and elegant furnishings. Small and past its prime but functional. **A** *Melia*, 16 Jln Imbi, T2428333, F2426623, melia@meliakl.com.my Chinese and Spanish restaurants, over 300 rooms, pool, health centre, hairdresser, florist, business centre, not quite up to the standard of many of the other big hotels charging around the same prices, but nonetheless a very reasonable place to stay. **A** *Mutiara* (formerly the *Hilton*), Jln Sultan Ismail, T21482322, F21493338, infokl@mutiarahotels.com A/c, restaurant, pool, all facilities, but not quite as good as others in this league. Under new management, with improved facilities, although is still not as good as other hotels in the area. **A** *New World*, 128 Jln Ampang, T2636888, F2631888. A total of 520 rooms in this new horror. Good-sized rooms and nice bathrooms but all a bit ostentatious. Shares its spectacular pool with the *Renaissance* (see above) next door. Includes breakfast. **A-B** *Concorde*, 2 Jln Sultan Ismail, T21442200, F21441628, www.concorde.net A/c, restaurant, decent sized pool, gym, it is the old *Merlin* (the first big modern hotel in KL) masquerading behind a face-lift and rather sterile interior décor, 4 good restaurants, coffee shop and the *Hard Rock Café* attached to it.

B *Cardogan*, 64 Jln Bukit Bintang, T21444883, F21444865, cardogan@po.jaring.my A/c, coffee house, health centre, business centre, dark wood interior. It has 61 rather bare rooms and small shower rooms attached. Price includes tax and breakfast. **B** *Fortuna*, 87 Jln Berangan, T2419111, F2418237. A/c, coffee house with live band, health centre, just off Bukit Bintang, tucked away and slightly quieter than most, behind *McDonalds*, good value for money. Recommended. **B** *Imperial*, 76-80 Jln Changkat Bukit Bintang (Jln Hicks), T2481422, F2429048. A/c, restaurant, well-priced Chinese hotel in an otherwise pricey part of town, well located for shopping centres but at this price don't expect a gem. **B** *Lodge*, Jln Sultan Ismail, T21420122, F21416819, kllodge@tm.net.my A/c, restaurant, small pool, small hotel on busy junction, surrounded by tower blocks, large rooms with 1950s fittings. **B** *Malaysia*, 67-69 Jln Bukit Bintang, T21447733, F21428579. A/c, restaurant, a rather jaded hotel amidst all the glitz, faded wallpaper, limited facilities, but a lot cheaper than many. Iron railings over windows restrict view of the street. Unsuccessful attempt at international style. **C** *Emerald*, 166 Jln Pudu, T21429233, F21445774. A/c with TV, noisy location, on edge of Golden Triangle, reasonably maintained, considering this Chinese hotel is nearly 20 years old, strong Asian feel, attached bathrooms with hot water. Basic, you get what you pay for. **C** *Tai Ichi*, 78 Jln Bukit Bintang, T21427533, F21486294. A/c. Another little hotel in this strip. Nothing in particular to recommend it.

L-AL *MiCasa Hotel Apartments*, 368b Jln Tun Razak (near junction with Jln Ampang), T2618833, F2611186, micasa@po.jaring.my A/c, restaurant, pool, shopping arcade, hair salon, dentist and doctor, children's pool, jacuzzi, tennis, squash, gym, sauna, children's playhouse, business centre, first rate, especially for longer stays, KL's only apartment hotel with 240 suites, which include fully equipped kitchen with utensils and sitting room, Italian restaurant, tapas bar. Recommended.

AL *Crown Princess*, City Square Centre, Jln Tun Razak, T21625522, F21624492, crownprincess@fhikl.com.my A/c, on the 10th floor is a pool and a restaurant, good for 'High Tea' buffet. The *Taj* Indian restaurant is on 11th floor, as is the lobby lounge with baby grand piano, cafés and Vietnamese restaurant. There is also a Szechuanese restaurant, business centre, adjacent shopping centre with 168 shops, opulent décor, and over 500 spacious rooms with panoramic views. Recommended. **AL** *Ming Court Vista Hotel*, Jln Ampang, T21618888, F21623428, minvista@tm.net.my, www.mingcourt-vista.com A/c, restaurant, good pool, room rate includes a good buffet breakfast, spacious rooms, some with a view of the Petronas Twin Towers. **AL** *Su Casa*, 222 Jln Ampang, T4513833, F4521031. A/c, restaurant, pool, business centre, store, serviced apartment suites with fully equipped kitchens for business people intending a slightly longer stay than is usual; weekly and monthly rates are negotiable. **AL** *Century*, 17-21, Jln Bukit Bintang. T21439898, F21421807, cklhres@pd.jaring.my Opened in 1998, very large, with restaurant, conference facilities and health club. **A** *Nikko*, 165 Jln Ampang, T2611111, F2611122, www.hotelnikko.com.my A/c, pool, Japanese and Chinese restaurants, near city square and Ampang shopping centres. Oriental atmosphere with very Japanese feel to it. **A-B** *Hotel Nova*, 16-22 Jln Alor (Bukit Bintang), T2431818, F2429985, novahtl@tm.net.my New hotel, quite stylish for the price range and lacking in pretention. Offers breakfast with complimentary newspaper, A/c rooms with bathroom, TV, telephone, limousine and laundry service.

B *Chamtan*, 62 Jln Masjid India, T26930144, F26932422. A/c; although clean this small establishment offers little but a good location and is clearly in decline. However, it has been recently painted, and they change the mattresses every 4 years! **B** *Kowloon*, 142-146 Jln Tuanku Abdul Rahman, T26934246, F26926548, kowloon@po.jaring.my A/c, coffee house, clean, value for money, rooms have mini-bar and TV, but those facing the main street are noisy. Residents can use health club on-site at a discounted rate. Recommended. **B** *Noble*, 4th Flr, Jln Tuanku Abdul Rahman, T27117111, F27117222, www.hotelnoble.com Modern, clean and tastefully finished. Although without much character, this hotel offers reasonable value. Rooms include TV, have standing showers and a/c. Includes breakfast and a free paper. **B** *Palace*, 40-46 Jln Masjid India, T26986122, F27116868, www.w3xs.com/palacehotel A/c, café, deli corner, shopping arcade, good lively location, but very average hotel. **C** *Coliseum*, 100 Jln Tuanku Abdul Rahman, T26926270. Fans or a/c, restaurant, colonial hotel. If arriving outside hrs, knock on one of the side doors. Large, simply furnished rooms, a famous bar and restaurant (see below) and friendly staff. No attached bathrooms. Rooms facing main street are very noisy. For those on a budget who want a taste of the 1920s, it is certainly worth a try.

L *Carcosa Seri Negara*, Taman Tasek Perdana, T2821888, F2827888. A/c, restaurant, pool, former residence of the British High Commissioner and built in 1896, it is now a luxury hotel, where Queen Elizabeth II stayed when she visited Malaysia during the Commonwealth Conference in 1989 and where other important dignitaries, presidents and prime ministers are pampered on state visits. Situated in a relatively secluded wooded hillside and overlooking the Lake Gardens, there are just 13 suites served by over 100 staff. Recommended.

AL-A *Airside Transit Hotel*, KL International Airport, T6038787, F6038787. Hotel within the Satellite Building of Sepang airport. Comfortable rooms along with gym,

Jalan Ampang
■ on map, page 82
Price codes:
see inside front cover
A relatively new commercial district, running along the northern edge of the KLCC (see box, page 82) making it a good location for anyone doing business here

Little India
■ on map, page 77
Price codes:
see inside front cover

Elsewhere

sauna and spa and business centre. The advantage for people in transit is that it is not necessary to pay the RM40 departure tax. Short stay possible at RM80 for up to 6 hrs (standard room). **AL-A** *Wenworth*, Jln Yew, T9833888, F9828088, asiatravel. com/wenworth A/c, Chinese restaurant, café, roof pool, health spa, simple but comfortable rooms, good location for North-South highway – approaching KL from the south, it is one of the first hotels in the city. The surrounding Pudu area is fast being developed with old shophouses giving way to tower blocks and 2 new shopping centres – Phoenix Plaza and the Leisure Mall. Breakfast is included in room tariff and there is a monthly food promotion. A taxi ride will get you to the city centre and Golden Triangle. Recommended. **A** *Pan Pacific Glenmarie Resort*, T7031000, F7041000. A golf resort in the suburbs of KL, close to the airport and 30 mins from the city centre, boasts two 18-hole golf courses, a pool and spa, business centre and guests are able to use the clubhouse, providing an Olympic-size pool, tennis and squash courts, fitness centre etc. Just under 300 rooms in this low-rise resort, choice of dining and a quieter atmosphere away from the city centre.

B *Concorde Inn*, Sepang, within the airport complex, T8431118, F8432118. A/c, TV, pool, tennis court, food court, restaurants, health and fitness centre, over 400 rooms and a range of sizes and prices. Good business centre. **B** *Matri Inn*, 235 Jln Tun Sambanthan, near KL-Klang Highway, 50470 Brickfields, T2731097, F2731569. A/c, café, run by an Indian family, good Indian food. Includes breakfast. **B** *Season View*, 59-61 Jln Alor, T2457577, F2433532. Renovated hotel with a/c, TV, hot water, minibar. Good-value rooms but a little far from the centre. Within walking distance of Lot 10 Shopping Centre.

C *Pan Pacific KL International Airport Hotel*, T87873333. A 450-room hotel, right next to Sepang airport, should provide all the luxury you could demand, with pool, fitness centre, tennis court, spa, business centre, several restaurants. Incredible value. **C** *YMCA*, 95 Jln Padang Belia, T22741439, F22740559. Good facilities – fitness centre, language courses, shop – neutralized by inconvenient location in Brickfields district on the southwest outskirts, off Jln Tun Sambathan, it is, however, within sniffing distance of Raju's tandoori ovens (see Eating, page 98), dormitory for men only (**D**), also private rooms. *Getting there*: minibus 12.

Homes Away   Run by the Asian Overland Service, this programme gives visitors first-hand experience
from Home   of Malaysian life by staying in fishing *kampungs*, rubber plantations, tin mines or pen-
programme   sioners' homes, RM45 per day including pick-up service, accommodation and 2 meals. Contact *Asian Overland Services*, 33M Jln Dewan Sultan Sulaiman Satu, T22925622, F22925209. *Village Home Stay*, 178 Jln Tuanku Abdul Rahman, T2920319.

Eating

Price codes: Many of KL's big hotels in the Jln Sultan Ismail/Bukit Bintang areas serve excellent value
see inside front cover   buffet lunches and offer a selection of local and international dishes. One of the best ways to sample various cuisines is to graze among the foodstalls.

Malay   **Mid-range** *Nelayan Floating Restaurant*, Titiwangsa Lake Gardens, good but expensive. *Seri Angkasa*, at the top of the KL Tower (see page 84), T22085055. A sister hotel to *Seri Melayu*. The tower revolves, achieving a full rotation in 60 mins. Good food, booking advisable for the evenings. There is also a good value buffet lunch available. *Seri Melayu*, 1 Jln Conlay, T22451833. Open 1100-1500, 1900-2300 (reservations recommended for groups of 4 or more – although it seats 500!). One of the best Malay restaurants in town in traditional Minangkabau-style building, the brain-child of Malaysian PM Dr Mahatir Mohamad, beautifully designed interior in style of Negeri Sembilan palace, don't be put off by cultural shows or the big groups – the food is superb and amazing in its variety, including regional specialities; it's very popular with locals too. Individual dishes are expensive, the buffet at RM35 (or RM70 for dinner) is the best bet (choice of more than 50 dishes), with promotions featuring cuisine from different states each month. Those arriving in shorts will be given a sarong to wear. Recommended. *Spices*, *Concorde Hotel*, 2 Jln Sultan Ismail, T22442200. Open 1130-1500, 1830-2300, closed Sun. Ironically, considering its name, the food is not overly spicy, eclectic Asian cuisine as well as traditional Malay, 4-piece band background music, a/c indoors or poolside outdoors, *setengah* (a stiff whisky drink popular in colonial times) features on the varied drinks list.

Cheap *Estana Restaurant and Garden*, Jln Sultan Ismail, opposite *The Ship*, excellent Malay and north and south Indian cuisine. *Jamal Bersaudara*, Jln Raja Abdullah, Kampung Baru. *Rasa Utara*, Bukit Bintang Plaza, Jln Bukit Bintang. *Wan Kembang* (Cik Siti), 24 Jln 14/22, Petaling Jaya (in front of the mosque), specializing in Kelantanese food. **Seriously cheap** *Malay 'buffet'*, Jln Gereja, opposite Jln Tun HS Lee. Very good-value little restaurant. *Satay Anika*, Ground Floor, Bukit Bintang Plaza, Jln Bukit Bintang, fast-food *satay*. Recommended. *Sate Ria*, 9 Jln Tuanku Abdul Rahman, fast food.

Expensive *Ampang Yong Tau Foo*, 53 Jln SS2/30, Petaling Jaya, T7753686. *Yong tau foo* (stuffed beancurd dishes) in a coffee shop. Recommended. Closed Mon. *Dynasty Garden Chinese Restaurant*, Lot M72-75, Mezzanine Flr, Plaza Yow Chuan, Jln Tun Razak. *Golden Phoenix*, *Hotel Equatorial*, Jln Sultan Ismail, T22617777. Open 1200-1430, gourmet Chinese establishment, mock Chinese courtyard setting. *Lai Ching Yuen*, *The Regent Hotel*, Jln Bukit Bintang, T2418000. Set in mock Chinese pavilion, holder of 4 Malaysian Tourism Gold Awards for consistently fine cuisine, popular with Chinese gourmets, luxury table settings, revolving solid granite table centres. *The Museum*, *The Legend Hotel*, The Mall, Putra Pl, 100 Jln Putra, T40429888. Open 1200-1500, 1830-2230, aims to look like a museum, with Chinese antiques and columns everywhere, although many display cabinets still to be filled, Teochew and Cantonese cuisine, adventurous food promotions, winner of Malaysian Tourism and Promotion best Chinese award. *Shang Palace*, *Shangri-La Hotel*, Jln Sultan Ismail, T22322388. Open 1200-1430, 1900-2300, *dim sum* lunch of over 40 varieties costs around RM50, check food promotions for evening meals. *The Blossom*, *Swiss Garden Hotel*, 117 Jln Pudu, T21413333. Open 1130-1430, 1830-2230, around 40 varieties of *dim sum*, tiger prawns a house speciality, good selection of pork dishes, abalone and birds' nests only for those on hefty expense accounts.

Mid-range *Cha Yuan Teahouse*, 5B Jln SS2/67, Petaling Jaya, traditional Chinese teahouse offering light meals and tea prepared by tea-master Paul Lim. Recommended. *Hai Tien Lo*, *Pan Pacific Hotel*, Jln Putra, T4425555. Open 1200-1500, 1900-2300, excellent *dim sum*, steamed fish with suet. Recommended. *Marco Polo*, Wisma Lim Foo Yong, 86 Jln Raja Chulan, T2412233. Open 1200-1500, 1900-2300, extensive menu, barbecue roast suckling pig recommended, 1970s-style décor, very busy lunchtimes. *Oriental Bowl*, 587 Leboh Pudu, T22025577. A/c restaurant above Chinese spice shop, convenient location for Central Market, rather formal atmosphere. *Restoran Oversea*, G2, Central Market, Jln Hang Kasturi, T2746407. Cantonese restaurant, pleasant location, very popular with locals. Good range of dishes (*dim sum* particularly recommended, served 0800-1500), excellent barbecue and roast meats, with unlikely looking 'vegetarian' dishes, which are about as vegetarian as chicken soup poured through a sieve can get. *Tsui Yuen*, 5th Flr, *Hilton Hotel*, Jln Sultan Ismail, T22482322. Open 1200-1430, 1900-2230, main attraction is the lunchtime *dim sum*, weekend 'all you can eat' promotions also worth checking and good-value set meals.

Cheap *Cameleon Vegetarian Restaurant*, 1 Jln Thamboosamy (off Jln Putra, near The Mall and *Pan Pacific*), Thai and Chinese, good *kway teow*, but vegetarians with carnivorous instincts rate the soyabean roast duck and various other ersatz meat and fish dishes whose presentation (and sometimes taste) is convincing. *Esquire Kitchen* , Level 1, Sungai Wang Plaza, Jln Sultan Ismail, T22485006.

Chinese

Kuala Lumpur

Dumplings and pork dishes good value, Shanghai dishes popular. *Halfway to Kajang*, near Sungai Besi (take Seremban highway, exit to left at Taman Sri Petaling – before toll gates, right at T-junction, over railway line and past Shell and Esso stations, turn left towards Sungai Besi tin mine, then branch right to Balakong, the restaurant is sign-posted), it is little more than a tin shed (with a fruit stall outside) but is famed among KL's epicureans for its deep-fried, paper-wrapped chicken, wild boar curry and vinegar pork shank. Recommended. *Hokkaido*, 68 Jln Lumut, off Jln Ipoh, T4411316. Open 1800-0200, located at north end of town, opposite *Vistana Hotel*, good genuine fare, not fancy, tables outside, pleasant retreat from shopping plazas and hotel complexes. Recommended. *Sin Kiew Yee*, Jln Hang Lekir (Jln Cecil, between Jln Petaling and Jln Sultan, Chinatown), mouthwatering dishes, good value for money, tables on pavement. Recommended. *Westlake*, Jln Sultan, highly rated for its Hokkien *mee* and *mee hun*, mixed with raw egg. *Yook Woo Hin*, 100 Jln Petaling, cheap *dim sum* in the middle of Chinatown, open until 1400.

Seriously cheap *Nam Heong*, 54 Jln Sultan, Hainanese chicken rice. *Seng Nam*, Lebuh Pasar Besar, Hainanese. The steamboats in the restaurant area of Chinatown are worth sampling at one of the outdoor tables.

Nyonya **Expensive** *Baluchi's*, 3 Jln SS21/60, Petaling Jaya, T7190879 (advisable to take taxi; ask for Damansara Utama Shophouse Complex), North Indian cuisine, modest décor but excellent food; chicken tikka, tandoori chicken, prawn *masala* and *palak paneer* particularly recommended; freshly baked naan. Recommended.

Mid-range *Bon Ton*, 7 Jln Kia Peng, T22413611. Open 1200-1500, 1900-2400, good Eastern Nyonya set menu, some Western dishes such as chicken pie, set in a 1930s colonial bungalow, just south of KLCC. Recommended. *Dondang Sayang*, 12 Lower Ground Floor, The Weld, Jln Raja Chulan, T22613831; also a branch at 28 Jln Telawi Lima, Bangsar Baru, T22549388. Popular and reasonably priced restaurant with big Nyonya menu. *Kapitan's Club*, 35 Jln Ampang, T22010242. Open 1100-1500, 1800-2230, spacious restaurant decorated with Straits woodwork, staff in traditional outfits, 'top hats', the house speciality is a tasty pastry and egg dish, Kapitan chicken is popular, Malay dishes also available.

Cheap *Sri Penang*, Lower Ground Flr, Menara Aik Hua, Changkat Raja Chulan (Jln Hicks), variety of Nyonya and North Malaysian dishes.

Indian & **Expensive** *The Taj*, *The Crown Princess Hotel*, 11th Flr, City Square Centre, Jln Tun Razak,
Pakistani T22625522. Open 1200-1500, 1900-2300, closed Sat lunch, stylish Anglo-Raj décor, live Indian muzak, open view kitchen, New Delhi chefs create first rate Indian cuisine, the vegetable samosas and tandooris – meat and veg – are excellent. Recommended.

Mid-range *Bangles*, 60A Jln Tuanku Abdul Rahman, T2986770. This is reckoned to be among the best North Indian tandoori restaurants in KL, often necessary to book in the evenings. Recommended. *Bombay Palace*, 388 Jln Tun Razak, next to US Embassy, T22454241. Open 1200-1500, 1830-2300, good-quality North Indian food in tasteful surroundings with staff in traditional Indian uniform, menu including vegetarian section. *Restoranua Jime*, next door to *Paradise B&B*, Jln Tunku Abdul Rahman, specializing in Moghul food and tandooris. Recommended.

Cheap *Annalakshmi*, 46 Lorong Maarof, Bangsar Baru, T22823799. Excellent Indian vegetarian restaurants run by the Temple of Fine Arts, dedicated to the preservation of Indian cultural heritage in Malaysia, the buffet is particularly recommended. *Kampung Pandan*, 1st Flr, Central Market, specialist in fish-head curry. *Sri Vani's Corner* (*Raju's*), Jln Tun Sambathan 4 (next to *YMCA* tennis courts), overgrown hawker stall rated among its dedicated clientele as the best place for tandooris and oven-baked naan in KL. Recommended. *Valentine Roti*, 6 Jln Semark (close to the National Library), this place was fortunate enough to be reviewed in the *Far Eastern Economic Review* and was billed as the best roti restaurant in town. Ilango Arokias-amy's rotis are a treat, light and flaky, and as he says "I think God wanted me to do this".

Seriously cheap *Alhmdoolilla*, 12 Jln Dang Wangi, rated for its rotis. *Lay Sin Coffee Shop*, 248 Jln Tun Sambathan, banana leaf.

Expensive *Keyaki*, Pan Pacific Hotel, Jln Putra, T4425555. Open 1200-1500, 1900-2300, good set meals, excellent sashimi and sushi made with fish flown in from Japan twice weekly, highly rated, but extremely expensive. *Nadaman*, *Shangri-La Hotel*, 11 Jln Sultan Ismail, T22322388. Shang quality and Shang prices. **Japanese**

Mid-range *Chikuyo-Tei*, Plaza See Hoy Chuan, Jln Raja Chulan, T2300729. Open 1200-1500, 1830-2230, housed in a basement, good-value set meals, quality *teppanyak*, seafood and steak. *Munakata*, 2nd Flr, Menara Promet, Jln Sultan Ismail, T2417441. *Tykoh Inagiku*, Ground Flr, Kompleks Antarabangsa, Jln Sultan Ismail (between *Equatorial* and *Hilton* hotels), T22482133.

Cheap *Sushi King*, Lower Ground Flr, The Mall, Jln Putra, T4428205 and 63 Jln Sultan Ismail, T2417312. Spotlessly clean sushi bar, prices from RM0.50 to RM3 per sushi. *Teppanyaki*, 2nd Flr, Sungai Wang Plaza, Jln Bukit Bintang and Lot 10, Jln Sultan Ismail, basement, excellent Japanese fast food, set meal for RM10.

Mid-range *Korean Restaurant*, 24 Jln Medan Imbi, T2446163. Open 1100-1500, 1800-2300, small restaurant off Jln Imbi, lashings of garlic, friendly staff. *Koryo-Won*, Kompleks Antarabangsa, Jln Sultan Ismail, T2427655. Excellent barbecues, particularly when washed down with *Jung Jong* rice wine. Recommended. **Korean**

Mid-range *Barn Thai*, 370B Jln Tun Razak (opposite *MiCasa Hotel*), T2446699. Open 1200-1430, 1900-0300, very tastefully decorated Thai style 'Jazzaurant' with excellent live music, extensive Thai menu, hot and sour sea bass and mango salad are specialities. Recommended. Also a more subdued but equally tasteful outlet in the Vistana Hotel, 9 Jln Lumut, off Jln Ipoh, T4428000. *Sawasdee Thai Restaurant*, *Holiday Inn* on the Park, Jln Pinang, T2481066. **Thai**

Cheap *Cili Padi Thai Restaurant*, 2nd Flr, The Mall, Jln Putra, T4429543. Soups and seafood are excellent, a recommended speciality is King Solomon's Treasure (chicken wrapped in *pandan* leaves). Closes at 2200 sharp. Recommended. *Johnny's Thai Steamboat*, in the basement of Bukit Bintang Plaza. Good value spicy Thai dishes.

Expensive *Mekong*, 11th Flr, *Crown Princess Hotel*, City Square Centre, Jln Tun Razak, T2625522. Well appointed, serving authentic Indo-Chinese cuisine with specialities from Vietnam and Thailand. **Mid-range** *Restoran Sri Saigon*, 53 Jln 552/30, Petaling Jaya, T7753681. Genuine Vietnamese dishes. *Vietnam House*, 6th Flr, Sogo Pernas, T2941726. Open 1200-2100, genuine Vietnamese chef and many ingredients flown from Vietnam, spring rolls and chicken with lemon grass are recommended. **Vietnamese**

Expensive *Carcosa Seri Negara*, Persiaran Mahameru, Taman Tasek Perdana (Lake Gardens), T2306766 (reservations). Built in 1896 to house the British Administrator for the Federated Malay States, Carcosa offers English-style high tea in a sumptuous, colonial setting, expensive Italian lunches and dinners are also served in the Mahsuri dining hall on fine china plates with solid silver cutlery, Continental and Malay cuisine, high tea (recommended) RM25 (1530-1800 Mon-Sun). *Ciao*, 428 Jln Tun Razak, T9854827. Open 1200-1430, 1900-2230, closed Mon, authentic tasty Italian food served in a beautifully renovated bungalow. Recommended. *Flamenco*, 1 Jln U-Thant, T4517507. Open 1100-2400, excellent South Mediterranean food, good paella, daily specialities. *Jake's*, 21 Jln Setiapuspa, Medan Damansara, off Jln Damansara, towards PJ, T2545677. Open 1200-1500, 1830-2300, Jake's steaks are highly rated in KL, served by cowboys **International**

and cowgirls. Recommended. *Lafitte*, *Shangri-La Hotel*, 11 Jln Sultan Ismail, T2322388. Open 1200-1500, 1900-2300, best French restaurant in Malaysia, but very expensive. Recommended. *Melaka Grill*, Hilton Hotel, Jln Sultan Ismail, T2482322. Open 1200-1500, 1900-2300, closed Sat and Sun lunch, well-established, popular business-lunch venue, good quality international cuisine. *Pour Toi*, 36 Jln Walter Grenier, T2455836. French cuisine, fun décor, well-balanced menu, RM15 corkage if you bring your own wine. *Sakura Café & Cuisine*, 165-169 Jln Imbi, excellent variety of Malay, Chinese and Indian dishes including fish-head curry, located in an area with many other good cheap restaurants. Recommended. *Scalini's*, 19 Jln Sultan Ishmail, just down from the Istana Hotel. Wonderful Italian food, but not cheap. Pasta dishes excellent, trendy surroundings and friendly staff. Recommended.

Mid-range *Coliseum Café*, 100 Jln Tuanku Abdul Rahman (Batu Rd), next door to the old Coliseum Theatre, long-famed for its sizzling lamb and beef steaks, Hainanese (Chinese) food and Western-style (mild) curries, all served by frantic waiters in buttoned-up white suits. During the Communist Emergency, planters were said to come here for gin and curry, handing their guns in to be kept behind the bar; it is easy to believe it. Recommended. *D'Ribeye*, Ground Flr, Central Market, Jln Hang Kasturi. Good atmosphere and steak, offering great value, full of businesspeople at lunchtime. *Hard Rock Café*, Ground Flr, Concorde Hotel, 2 Jln Sultan, Ismail, T21444062. Open 1130-0200, one of the best places for top-quality American burgers, steaks and salads, good value. Recommended. *The Jump*, Ground Flr, Wisma Inai 241, Jln Tun Razak, T2450046. Open 1100-2230, American fare prepared by US chef, good value, popular with foreigners, good cocktail band and live music venue. *Le Coq d'Or*, 121 Jln Ampang, T2429732. European/Malay, former residence of a rich mining *towkay* with a porticoed veranda and Italian marble, Western, Chinese and Malay cooking, great atmosphere of crumbling grandeur now lost and in dire need of face-lift and improved hygiene. *Sam's Curry Lunch*, Indian buffet, Sun 1230-1400, excellent à la carte selection of Malaysian dishes, including *nasi lemak* and *rendang*, open 24 hrs. Recommended. *Lot 253*, The Mall, 2nd Flr, 100 Jln Putra, T4431988. Open 1200-2200, good set menu and authentic French atmosphere. *Marble Arch*, Hotel Grand Continental, Jln Raja Laut, T2939333. Open 1100-1500, 1800-2300, good buffet lunches (RM25) and set meals during food promotions when chefs are on hand from the country being promoted. *Moomba*, Ground flr, UOA Centre, 19 Jln Pinang, T2628226. Australian bar and restaurant, selection of sandwiches, ribs, pasta, pies. Trendy lunch spot for business people, but good value. *The Ship*, 40 Jln Sultan Ismail, very dark interior, extensive menu of steaks, chicken, salads. The stone grills are particularly popular. Open from lunch until 0230. *Uno's*, corner of Jln Kia Peng, reasonable Italian pasta restaurant downstairs with disco/bar above, which is the unchallenged nocturnal playground of KL's rich and famous.

Cheap *Caleos*, 1 Jln Pinang, pastas and pizzas, Napoli-style seafood, upstairs bar and karaoke lounge. *Equatorial Coffee Shop*, Basement, Equatorial Hotel, Jln Sultan Ismail. Malay curry buffets 1230-1400, Mon-Sat. Recommended. *Federal Hotel Revolving Restaurant*, Jln Bukit Bintang. This was once one of KL's tallest buildings, now rather dwarfed but still a good spot for ice-cream sundaes with a view. *Lodge Coffee Shop*, Jln Sultan Ismail. Good value for money, particularly local dishes – *nasi goreng*, curries and buffets. Recommended. *Riverbank*, Ground Flr, Central Market. 'Hearty American Fare', which just about says it all – burgers, sandwiches etc. *Roadhouse Grill*, 42 Jln Sultan Ismail. Cheap and cheerful American fare. Open 1130-2400. **Seriously cheap** *Lakshmi Villas*, Leboh Ampang, excellent vegetarian food, try the masala dosai – pancakes stuffed with vegetables and accompanied by a lentil sauce.

Seafood
For additional seafood entries, see page 88

Mid-range *Bangsar Seafood Village*, Jln Telawi Empat, Bangsar Baru, T254555. Open 1200-1430, 1800-2300, large restaurant complex with reasonably priced seafood, fresh from tanks that line the inside of the restaurant, specialities include crab in butter sauce and Thai-style tiger prawns (and a good satay stall). *Eden Village*, 260 Jln Raja Chulan. Wide-ranging menu, but probably best known for seafood, resembles a glitzy Minangkabau palace with garden behind, cultural Malay, Chinese and Indian dances every night (less touristy outlet in PJ 25-31 Jln 5322/23, Damansara Jaya, T7193184). *Hai Peng Seafood Restaurant*, Taman Evergreen, Batu Empat, Jln Klang Lama (Old Klang Rd). The smallest and least assuming restaurant in a row of Chinese shophouses (red neon sign), but one of the very best seafood restaurants in Malaysia, where the Chinese community's seafood connoisseurs come to eat (the other seafood restaurants in the cluster include *Chian Kee*, *Pacific Sea Foods* and *Yee Kee*, most of which are good, but not as good as *Hai Peng*). Its specialities include butter crab (in clove and coconut), belacan crab, sweet and sour chilli crab and bamboo clams, the *siu yit kum* (small gold-leaf tea) – a delicious, fragrant Chinese tea, which is perfect with seafood, open until 0100. Recommended. *Studio 123*, 159 Jln Ampang. Easily missed – it's opposite the *Ming Court Hotel* – this is an unassuming place with friendly staff and excellent, good-value food. Recommended.

Cheap *MASs*, 228 Jln Dua A, Subang, Selangor, T7461200. Well out of town, past Subang Airport's Terminal 2, and strung out along the road running beside Runway One are about 10 seafood restaurants, they all do a brisk turnover, and there is not much between them; they all serve seafood and each has its own speciality, *MASs* is the one with the front end of an *MAS* jumbo jet on the roof. Recommended. *New Ocean*, 29B Medan Imbi (off Jln Imbi and Jln Hoo Teik Ee). Good seafood restaurant just round the corner from the Sungai Wang and Lot 10 shopping complexes. *Unicorn*, 1st Flr, Annex Block, Lot 10 Shopping Centre, Jln Sultan Ismail, T2441695. Open 1100-1500, 1800-0400, big, smart Chinese seafood restaurant in the Lot 10 complex, just by the footbridge to Sungai Wang, good stop for shoppers.

Teahouses Try out the traditional Chinese teahouse opposite Sungai Wang Hotel on Jln Bukit Bintang.

Foodstalls
Chow Kit is the best area for food stalls

Chow Kit On Jln Raja Muda Abdul Aziz there is a food court with great Indian and Afghan food. Jln Haji Hussien has a picturesque collection of superb food stalls, most open when the market closes at 1800 and stay open until 0200. Walk up Jln Haji Hussien and turn right and there are some good cheap (**C-D**) hotels. The food court on the top floor of The Mall, built like rows of old Chinese shophouses, is run-down but has an attractive ambience. The Indian, Malay and Chinese food is all good, but the majority of places to eat here close by 2000. It's cheap too – tandoori chicken, naan, dal and drink, all for just RM8. Jln Raja Alang and Jln Raja Bot stalls, off Jln Tuanku Abdul Rahman, are mostly Malay stalls.

East on Jln Datuk Keramat near Pasar Keramat are lots of Malay food stalls that stay open way after midnight. Next to *Keramat* supermarket there is a South Indian stall with good mutton soup. In the alleyway between *Keramat* supermarket and the Pakistani mosque there are lots of good food stalls during the day. Kampung Baharu and Kampung Datok Keramat are Malay communities. On the river front behind Jln Mesjid India are good Indian and Malay night stalls.

Opposite the *Brisdale Value Inn* on the corner of Jln Haji Hussien and Jln Raja Bot is a block of flats. In front and behind are good Indonesian restaurants but they really only function during the day.

The top floor of the Central Market has a small restaurant with amazing Thai and Nyonya cuisine. On the same floor is an excellent, but small, centre with good *nasi campur*, open at lunchtime.

Elsewhere *Ampang Park Shopping Complex*, along Jln Tun Razak, is a popular but small centre, with good variety of stalls. *Brickfields*, Jln Tun Sambathan, has a string of small outdoor restaurants. *Jln Masjid India*, Little India, has many good Indian and

Malay foodstalls. *Lorong Raja Muda Food Centre*, off Jln Raja Muda, on the edge of Kampung Baru, has mainly Malay food. *Lot 10 Shopping Complex*, Jln Sultan Ismail, there is an excellent choice of food here, if you can tolerate the high-volume music. *Medan Hang Tuah*, The Mall (Top Floor), Jln Putra (opposite the Pan Pacific Hotel). *Munshi Abdullah Food Complex*, off Lorong Tuanku Abdul Rahman (near Coliseum), for good satay. *Puduraya Bus Station*, Jln Pudu, a good variety of stalls, open at all hrs. *Sunday Market*, Kampung Baru (main market actually takes place on Sat night), has many Malay hawker stalls.

Bars

Barn Thai, 370B Jln Tun Razak, T2446699. Self-styled 'Jazzaurant', Bangkok-type wooden bar with panelled interior and tasteful Thai décor, hosts some of KL's best live acts and excellent jazz. Drinks are expensive, also serves good Thai food. Recommended. *Betelnut*, Jln Pinang, T2416455. Located in the ruins of a former colonial bungalow in a strip of bars and clubs that are not as good, disco in main house, but relaxed outdoor bar. Ladies night on Thu. Recommended. *Bier Keller*, German pub and restaurant, Ground Flr, Menara Haw Par (next to *Shangri-La Hotel*), Jln Sultan Ismail, T2013313. Authentic German draught beer served in stylish glasses, wide range of schnapps, salty German food. Recommended. *Bull's Head*, Ground Flr, Central Market, Jln Hang Kasturi, T2746428. Large bar with the darkened atmosphere of a London pub inside and with tables on the terrace outside, convenient for shopping in Central Market. *Cathy's Place*, Wisma Stephen, Jln Sultan Ismail, T2481794. Cheap beer and a regular expat crowd. *Centrepoint*, Jln Setiapuspa, Medan Damansara, off Jln Damansara, lively bar with live music every night. *Coliseum*, 100 Jln Tuanku Abdul Rahman, the bar, which has a number of long-term residents who never seem to move, is the haunt of Malaysia's star cartoonist, Lat (his Coliseum sizzling steak cartoon hangs on the wall along with his caricatures of regulars). The so-called Planters' Bar used to be the gathering point for colonial rubber planters and tin miners, then became the hangout of war correspondents during the Malayan Emergency, and is now frequented by everyone from diplomats and businesspeople to backpackers. It is a pleasant, old-time bar, which opens for business before lunch and shuts at 2200 sharp. Recommended. *Delaney's Pub*, corner of Jln Imbi and Jln Pudu, quite expensive standard Irish pub.

There is no shortage of good watering holes in KL; many have live Filipino and local cover bands, and others have discos attached. An increasing number of bars are now being taken over by karaoke

English Pub, *Shangri-La Hotel*, not as naff as it sounds, and popular with visiting business people, happy hr 1730-1930, live band 2030-2230, full-size pool table. *Hard Rock Café*, Basement and Ground Flr, Wisma Concorde, 2 Jln Sultan Ismail, T2444152. The Hard Rock, with its Harley Davidson chopper poised on the rooftop, opened in 1991 and quickly became one of the most popular and lively bars in town, good atmosphere and small disco floor. Recommended. *London Pub*, Lorong Hampshire, off Jln Ampang (behind *Ming Court Hotel*). Continuing KL's obsession with recreating English pubs, this one, part-owned by a London Cockney, is not a mock-Tudor half-timbered mess, it has a good atmosphere and a regular darts competition. *Ronnie Q's Pub*, 32 Jln Telawi Dua, Bangsar Baru. Popular with expats and locals, great sporting moments with international cricket and rugby videos. *Solutions*, City Square Centre, Jln Tun Razak, T2621689. Happy hr 1600-2200, popular after-work spot. *Tapas Bar*, *MiCasa Hotel*, 368b Jln Tun Razak (near junction with Jln Ampang), serves what are arguably the best margaritas in KL. Recommended. *Titiwangsa Bar*, *Carcosa Seri Negara Hotel*, Taman Tasek Perdana. *Traffic Lights*, 42 Jln Sultan Ismail (near Bukit Bintang junction), music (sometimes live) and attached grill.

Nightclubs and discos

Since the mid-1980s, with the rise of the KL yuppy, the city has shaken off its early-to-bed image and now has a slightly more lively club scene. Several old colonial buildings have been converted into night spots. Most nightclubs and discos in KL used to be open until 0300 during the week and until 0400 on Fri nights and weekends. But at the beginning of 1997 the government, worried at the proliferation of so-called 'social ills', introduced new regulations stipulating that nightspots must close by 0100. In the past few years, Jln Pinang, once a backstreet of crumbling bungalows, has emerged as a late-night strip of bars. There are also hundreds of karaoke lounges around KL. Bangsar Baru to the west of the city centre, not far from the University of Malaya, is probably the hippest area of town with around 20 bars and nightclubs, frequented mostly by Malaysians.

The Metro section in The Star (Malaysia's most widely read English-language daily) is devoted to what's on and where

Baze 2, Yow Chuan Plaza, Jln Tun Razak, popular for its R&B, acid jazz, and dance mixes, happy hr 2100-2300, Wed ladies night, RM30 cover charge. *Boom Boom Room*, 11 Lorong Ampang, off Jln Gereja, usually heaving by the weekend, disco plays up-to-the-minute tracks, busy upstairs bar with live show, dance and dirty jokes, RM15-20 cover. Recommended. *Betelnut*, Jln Pinang, very popular bar/disco complex, behind the disco clubhouse is a spacious outdoor bar area, Betelnut is the best in a strip of bars just down from the *Holiday Inn* on the Park, Thu ladies night. Recommended. *Cee Jay's*, Ground Flr, Menara SMI, 6 Lorong P Ramlee (behind *Shangri-La Hotel*). Good bar and a restaurant, sports bar with screens, pool, darts, but is best known for its live music, with classy local acts playing cover versions. *Club Oz*, lower lobby, *Shangri-La Hotel*, Jln Sultan Ismail, professional DJs, predominantly Chinese control, not cheap, cover RM15-30. *Club Syabas*, 1 Lorong Sultan, Petaling Jaya, the club's renowned DV8 disco is very popular with KL ravers, as is the karaoke. Recommended. Cover charge RM12-15. *Faces*, 103 Jln Ampang. Also in an old colonial house, cover RM16. *Deluxe Nite Club*, Rooftop, Ampang Park Shopping Centre, Jln Ampang. Huge hostess bar ("every inch of the way we will make you feel like an Emperor"), Chinese bands (imported from Hong Kong and Taiwan) perform every night. *Legends*, 1 Jln Kia Peng. Particularly popular with local KL crowd and again, in an old converted bungalow. *The Jump*, Ground Flr, Wisma Inai 241, Jln Tun Razak. One of the latest additions to the club scene, performance bartendering, live bands, jazz nights. Ladies night on Wed popular. RM20 cover. *Modesto's*, 1d Lorong Perak, off Jln P Ramlee. Trendy night spot, small dance floor, pizzas and Italian food. Ladies night Wed. *Tin Mine*, Basement, *KL Hilton*, Jln Sultan Ismail. One of the few old nightclubs still going strong, small dance floor and backgammon for the less energetic, has a reputation as a hostess hangout. Recommended. Cover charge RM26.

Entertainment

KL is gradually becoming a centre for local and some international artists, but the art market is not exactly flourishing, and much of the artwork around is mediocre. The following are some of the main galleries. Contemporary Malaysian art can be seen at *Art Salon*, 4 Jln Telawi Dua, Bangsar Baru, open Tue-Sun. For information on the latest show, T2822601. *Anak Alam Art Gallery*, 905 Pesiaran Tun Ismail off Jln Parliamen. *AP Art Gallery*, Ground Flr, Central Market, off Jln Hang Kasturi. *Artfolio Gallery*, 1st Flr City Sq, Jln Tun Razak, T2623339. *Art House*, 2nd Flr, Wisma Stephens, Jln Raja Chulan, T2482283. *Balai Seni*, Menara Maybank, Jln Tun Perak, T2321416. *Fine Arts Gallery*, Yow Chuan Plaza, Jln Tun Razak. *Galericitra*, 1st Flr, Shopping Arcade, *Shangri-La Hotel*, Jln Sultan Ismail. *National Art Gallery*, Jln Sultan Hishamuddin, T2300157. Open 1000-1800, closed Fri 1245-1445, admission free. *Petronas Art Gallery*, Dayabumi Complex, Lower Ground Flr, Jln Hishamudin. *Rupa Gallery*, Lot 158 Menara Dayabumi, Jln Sultan Hishamuddin.

Art galleries

Kuala Lumpur

Cinemas

Open daily from 1100. The first showing is usually a 1300 matinee with the last show at 2115 (midnight show Sat)

The *Sun* newspaper's weekly listings magazine *Time Out* publishes details of what's on at the cinemas, and screenings are also listed in *The New Straits Times* and the *Star*. Tickets cost around RM10. *Cineplex*, small cinema complexes, are increasingly popular and many are incorporated into the burgeoning shopping plazas. The main cinemas are: *Capitol*, Jln Raja Laut, T4429051; *Cathay*, Jln Bukit Bintang, T2429942; *Cathay Cineplex*, The Mall, T4426122; *Coliseum*, Jln Tuanku Abdul Rahman, T2925995; *Federal*, Jln Raja Laut, T4425014; *Odeon*, Jln Tuanku Abdul Rahman, T2920084; *Odeon Cineplex*, Central Sq, T2308548; *President*, Sungai Wang Plaza, Jln Sultan Ismail, T2480084; and *Rex*, Jln Sultan, T2383021.

Classical music

The *National Symphony Orchestra* and the *National Choir* both perform regularly at the Experimental Theatre on Jln Tun Ismail, T403252525 for information. Other orchestras are the KL Symphony Orchestra and the Malaysian Philharmonic Orchestra, which perform at the *Petronas Philharmonic Hall* (KLCC), T2077007.

Cultural shows

Performances of Bangsawan (Malay Traditional Theatre), Nadagam (Indian Traditional Theatre) and Chinese Opera all take place at the Central Market during the weekends at 1945, for further information T22746542. *Eden Village*, 260 Jln Raja Chulan, Malay, Indian and Chinese dancing every night. The *Malaysian Tourist Information Complex* (*MATIC*), 109 Jln Ampang, T2434929, has shows on Tue, Thu and Sun at 1530. Try *Seri Melayu Restaurant*, 1 Jln Conlay, for traditional Malay folk dances and singing in KL's best Malay epicurean experience (see page 96), traditional music starts at 2000, dancing at 2045, ends 2130. Also of note is the *Temple of Fine Arts*, 116 Jln Berhala, Brickfields, T2743709. This organization, set up in Malaysia to preserve and promote Indian culture, stages cultural shows every month with dinner, music and dancing. The temple organizes an annual Festival of Arts (call for details), which involves a week-long stage production featuring traditional and modern Indian dance (free, since "the Temple believes art has no price"), it also runs classes in classical and folk dancing, and in playing traditional musical instruments.

Theatre

Local theatre clubs include *Actor's Studio Theatre*, Plaza Putra, underneath Merdeka Sq, *Dramalab, Five Arts Centre* and *Instant Café* (check in local newspapers for performances by these three theatre companies), and the *National Theatre*, situated in the north of town on Jln Tun Razak, home to the National Theatre Company and a centre for drama, dance and music (T4252525 for further information).

Shopping

As recently as the early 1980s, Malaysians and KL's expatriates used to go on shopping expeditions to neighbouring Singapore as KL just was not up to it. These days, however, the city has more or less everything, with new shopping complexes springing up every year. They are not concentrated in any particular area and ordinary shopping streets and markets are also dotted all around the city.

Antiques

Oriental Spirit, 1st Flr, Central Market (northern end), T3272160. A stunning emporium of mostly mainland Southeast Asian treasures. Quite pricey but the interior is an Aladdin's Cave of goodies and is well worth a look for the imaginative way in which it's been laid out. Also renowned for its antiques is Bangsar Town Centre.

Artefacts

For a general range of Southeast Asian artefacts, the best areas are Jln Ulu Klang, Jln Pudu and Bangsar Town Centre. Try *Tibetan Treasures*, 16 Changkat Bukit Bintang, for antique Tibetan furniture and paintings.

Kuala Lumpur

Aran Novabatika Malaysia, 174 Ground Flr, Ampang Park Shopping Centre, Jln **Batik** Ampang. *Batik Bintang*, Lobby Arcade, Federal Hotel, Jln Bukit Bintang. *Batik Corner*, Lot L1.13, The Weld Shopping Centre, 76 Jln Raja Chulan, excellent selection of sarong lengths and ready-mades in batiks from all over Malaysia and Indonesia. *Batik Malaysia*, 114 Jln Bukit Bintang, Mun Loong, (also 113 Jln Tunku Abdul Rahman). *Batik Permai*, Lobby Arcade, Hilton Hotel, Jln Sultan Ismail. *Central Market*, Jln Hang Kasturi, hand-painted silk batik scarves downstairs, many shops sell batik in sarong lengths. *Evolution*, G24, Citypoint, Dayabumi Complex, Jln Sultan Hishamuddin, T2913711. Fashionable range of ready-mades and other batik gift ideas by designer Peter Hoe. *Faruzzi Weld Shopping Centre*, Jln Raja Chulan (also at 42B Jln Nirwana, just off Jln Tun Ismail), exclusive and original batiks. Recommended. *Globe Silk Store*, 185 Jln Tuanku Abdul Rahman. *Heritage*, 38 1st Flr, has a big selection of very original Kelantanese batiks (RM15-90 per m), most ordinary batiks cost about RM7 per m. *Khalid Batik*, 48 Ground Flr, Ampang Park Shopping Centre, Jln Ampang. There are several shops on Jln Masjid India; there are 2 batik factories that welcome visitors – the East Coast Batiks Factory, No 1, 8½ mile, T6891948, and No 15, Jln Cahaya 15, Taman Cahaya, Ampang, T9840205.

The following are some of the better bookshops. *Berita Book Centre* and *MPH Book-* **Books** *stores*, Bukit Bintang Plaza, 1st Flr and Ground Flr respectively, Jln Bukit Bintang. *Bookazine*, Damansara Heights, 8 Jln Batai. *Kinokuniya*, Isetan Dept Store, 2nd Flr, 50 Jln Sultan Ismail. *Minerva Book Store*, 114 Jln Tunku Abdul Rahman. *Popular Book Co*, Jln Petaling, Jln Hang Lekir, Sungai Way Plaza. *Times Books*, KLCC, Yow Chuan Plaza, 6-7 Jln Tun Razak and Weld Shopping Complex, has a good selection of English-language books. There is a second-hand bookshop on the First Floor of Central Market.

KL is a good place to buy cameras, as they are very competitively priced here. Try **Cameras** *Bukit Bintang Plaza* for a good choice. Also, *Sungai Wang Plaza*, Jln Sultan Ismail, Golden Triangle.

Ampang Park Shopping Complex, Jln Ampang. *City Square*, Jln Tun Razak, northeast **Carpets** of Golden Triangle. *KL Plaza*, Jln Bukit Bintang, Golden Triangle. **& rugs**

For designer clothing and accessories: *Starhill Shopping Centre*, Jln Bukit Bintang, **Clothing** Golden Triangle; located at Lot 10 on the corner of Jln Sultan Ismail and Jln Bukit Bintang, Golden Triangle. Also *Sogo*, Jln Tuanku Abdul Rahman. For custom-made clothing and discount fashion brands: *Sungai Wang Shopping Plaza*, Jln Sultan Ismail, Golden Triangle. Also good for discount fashion brands: the *Weld Shopping Centre*, Jln Raja Chulan, near the KL Tower, and *City Square*, Jln Tun Razak, northeast of Golden Triangle. A good place to look for custom-made shoes is along Jln Tuanku Abdul Rahman.

A good place to look for fabrics is along Jln Tuanku Abdul Rahman. Also good are: **Fabric** *Ampang Shopping Complex*, Jln Ampang; *Lot 10*, Jln Bukit Bintang; *Semua House*, Lorong Tuanku Abdul Rahman (at northern end of Jln Masjid India).

Oriental Style, 1st Flr, Central Market (southern end), and at 64 Jln Hang Kasturi, repro- **Furniture** duction Asian furniture. Pricey. *Oriental Spirit*, 1st Flr, Central Market (northern end), antique furniture. Expensive but beautiful objects. Rattan furniture is available from Bangsar Town Centre, Ampang Point and Wisma Stephens.

For gold, pearls and precious gems: Petaling St; Lot 10, Jln Bukit Bintang; City Sq, Jln **Gems** Tun Razak; *Semua House*, Lorong Tuanku Abdul Rahman (at northern end of Jln Masjid India). For semi-precious gems, jade and porcelain: *Ampang Shopping Complex*, Jln Ampang; Petaling St; Lot 10, Jln Bukit Bintang; *KL Plaza*, Jln Bukit Bintang.

Kuala Lumpur

Handicrafts   Aked Ibu Kota, Jln Tuanku Abdul Rahman, shopping centre with wide variety of goods
Many of the   including local handicrafts. *Amazing Grace*, G-3P Yow Chuan Plaza, Jln Tun Razak.
handicrafts are   *Andida Handicraft Centre*, 10 Jln Melayu. *Borneo Crafts*, 1st Flr, Central Market, mostly
imported from   wooden pieces, good selection of puppets and boxes. *Central Market*, Jln Hang
Indonesia   Kasturi, the old wetmarket is now full of handicrafts stalls, not always the cheapest but
a wide selection. *Eastern Dreams*, 101A Jln Ampang. *Oriental Style*, 1st Flr, Central
Market, selection of upmarket baskets, pots, brassware. Quite pricey but worth a look.
Golden Triangle, 1st Flr, Central Market, cornucopia of wooden figures. *Karyaneka
Handicraft Village*, Kompleks Budaya Kraf, Jln Conlay, government-run, exhibiting and
selling Malaysian handicrafts. Some batik demonstrating goes on the ground floor.
Lavanya Arts, 116A Jln Berhala Brickfields, run by the Temple of Fine Arts of
Annalakshmi vegetarian restaurant fame, which aims to preserve Malaysia's Indian
heritage. The shop sells Indian crafts: jewellery, bronzes, wood carvings, furniture,
paintings and textiles. *Lum Trading*, 123 Jln SS2/24 SEA Park, Petaling Jaya, for baskets
and bambooware. *Malaysian Arts*, 23 Jln Bukit Bintang. *South China Seas*, Level 4
Metro Jaya, Jln Bukit Bintang. The areas to look for Chinese arts and handicrafts are
along Jln Tuanku Abdul Rahman and in Bangsar Town Centre. *Jln Masjid India*, running parallel with Jln Tuanku Abdul Rahman, is an Aladdin's Cave of all things Indian,
from saris to sandalwood oil, from bangles to brassware incense burners.

Home decor   For a range of small items such as candlesticks, mirrors, table decorations, try *Peter
Hoe*, 139 Jln Tun HS Lee or 2 Jln Hang Lekir. All his products are sourced in the region.
He also sells jewellery and some locally printed clothing.

Pewter   *Dai-Ichi Arts and Crafts*, 122 Mezanine Flr, *Parkroyal Hotel*, Jln Sultan Ismail/Jln
Imbi; *KL Arts & Crafts*, 18 Ground Floor, Central Market, Jln Hang Kasturi; *Royal
Selangor Pewter Showrooms*, 231 Jln Tuanku Abdul Rahman, T2986244.

Watches   *Lot 10*, Jln Bukit Bintang; *Sungai Wang Plaza*, Jln Sultan Ismail; *KL Plaza*, Jln Bukit
Bintang. Jln Petaling is the best place to find a 'genuine copy' watch.

Markets &   *Central Market*, next to Jln Hang Kasturi, is a purpose-built area with 2 floors of bou-
shopping   tiques and stalls selling just about every conceivable craft – pewter, jewellery, jade,
streets   wood and ceramics for a start. Stalls of note include one that sells all kinds of moulds
and cutters for baking, a wonderful spice stall, another one for nuts and a third for dried
fruits. One shop worth taking a look at is *Collectibles* selling old watches, brass pieces
and birdcages. See sections on antiques and furniture for details on other shops. *Chow
Kit*, Jln Haji Hussein (just off Jln Tuanku Abdul Rahman), is a cheap place to buy almost
anything – it doubles as a red-light district, although this area is rapidly being developed and its image 'cleaned-up', the extensive wet market on Jln Haji Hussein is scheduled to be re-located to make way for building.

Jalan Melayu is another interesting area for browsing – Indian shops filled with
silk saris and brass pots and Malay shops specializing in Islamic paraphernalia such as
songkok (velvet Malay hats) and prayer rugs as well as herbal medicines and oils.
Jalan Tuanku Abdul Rahman (Batu Rd) was KL's best shopping street for decades
and is transformed into a pedestrian mall and night market every Sat between 1700
and 2200. *Kampung Baru Sunday Market (Pasar Minggu)*, off Jln Raja Muda Musa (a
large Malay enclave at the north end of KL), is an open-air market which comes alive
on Sat nights. Malays know it as the Sunday market as their Sunday starts at dusk on
Saturday (so don't go on the wrong night), when a variety of stalls selling batik
sarongs, bamboo birdcages and traditional handicrafts compete with dozens of
food stalls. However, the *Pasar Minggu* has largely been superseded by *Central Market* as a place to buy handicrafts.

Leboh Ampang, off Jln Gereja, was the first area to be settled by Indian immigrants and today remains KL's 'Little India', selling everything from samosas to silk saris. *Pasar Malam*, Jln Petaling, Chinatown is a night market full of 'copy watches', pirate cassettes and cheap clothes. *Pudu Market*, bordered by Jln Yew, Jln Pasar and Jln Pudu, is a traditional wet market selling food and produce, mainly patronized by Chinese.

For apparel, shoes, bags and textiles try Jln Sultan and Jln Tun HS Lee, close to Klang bus station. In Petaling St (Chinatown) you can barter for Chinese lanterns, paintings, incense holders, etc. The night market here is good for imitation clothes and watches.

Mid-Valley Megamall This latest addition to the shopping complex scene in KL is indeed 'mega'. It has a wide range of shops (including the French hypermarket *Carrefour*) and a choice of restaurants. There is also a multiplex cinema here. Ask any taxi driver to take you to the biggest shopping complex in KL and you'll end up here.

Shopping complexes

Jln Sultan Ismail/Bukit Bintang *Star Hill Plaza*, next to *JW Marriott Hotel*, prestigious marble-clad shopping centre housing *Tang's Department Store* (of Singapore fame) and many designer boutiques. *Kuala Lumpur Plaza*, *Tower Records* is here, also good for watches, bags, jewellery and shoes. *Lot 10*, Jln Sultan Ismail, distinctive green and blue striped façade, *Isetan Department Store*, *British India*, *Moschino*, *Knickerbox*, plus an excellent food court. *Bukit Bintang Plaza*, corner of Jln Bukit Bintang and Jln Sultan Ismail, one of KL's oldest shopping centres, houses the popular department store *Metrojaya*, *Marks & Spencer* and a labyrinth of other shops, which lead into Sungai Wang. *Sungai Wang Plaza*, Jln Sultan Ismail, one of the largest complexes in KL, houses over 500 shops and *Parkson Grand Department Store*, and a basement food court. *Imbi Plaza*, corner of Jln Sultan Ismail and Jln Imbi, good for computer hardware and software. *Low Yat Plaza Shopping Centre*, the most recent addition to the Bukit Bintang scene, it houses *BB Chinatown* and *Computer City*.

The majority of KL's shopping complexes are to be found in this area, listings are east to west

Ampang Centre for a number of complexes on the eastern edge of city: *Suria KLCC*, in the new KLCC complex, is without doubt the grooviest shopping centre in town, housing, among other things, designer fashions and jewellery shops; *Yow Chuan Plaza*, Jln Tun Razak, has antiques, curios, souvenirs and designer goods, and is linked to City Sq next door which has a *Metrojaya* department store and *Toys 'R' Us*; *Ampang Park*, Jln Tun Razak, opposite City Sq, is one of the oldest shopping complexes in town, noted for its jewellery boutiques.

Sogo Pernas Department Store, Jln Tuanku Abdul Rahman, a huge store on 10 floors. *Pertama Shopping Complex*, one of the older complexes and a great place for the bargain hunter. It has a wide range of mid-budget products from souvenirs to fashion and a basement bazaar, as well as photographic and electronic goods. KL's original department store, *Globe Silk Store*, is on Jln Tuanku Abdul Rahman.

The Mall, Jln Putra, right across from Putra World Trade Centre, is a quite trendy, large shopping mall, good for fashion, housing *Yaohan Department Store*, *Starlight Express* indoor theme park, lots of fast food outlets, *Delifrance*, *Pizza Hut* etc.

Others *The Weld*, on the corner of Jln Raja Chulan and Jln P Ramlee: a large *Times Bookstore*, *Reject Shop*, art gallery and a selection of fashion/leather shops, food outlets, etc. *Subang Parade*, Subang Jaya, houses *Parkson Grand Department Store* and *Toys 'R' Us*, an amusement park and fast-food outlets. *Kota Raya Shopping Complex*, Jln Cheng Lock, close to the Pudu Raya bus station, has cut-price goods.

Sports

Bangsar Sports Complex, Jln Terasek Tiga, Bangsar Baru, T2546065. *Jln Tun Razak Multipurpose Hall*, T4233158. *YMCA*, 95 Jln Padang Belia, off Jln Tun Sambathan, Brickfields, T2741349.

Badminton

Bowling *Federal Bowl*, *Federal Hotel*, Jln Bukit Bintang, T2489166. *Leisure Mall Bowling*, *Cheras Leisure Mall*, Jln Manis, 6 Taman Segar, T9323866. *Miramar Bowling Centre*, Wisma Miramar, Jln Wisma Putra, T2421863. *Pekeliling Bowl*, *Yow Chuan Plaza*, Jln Tun Razak, T2430953.

Golf *Plaza Putra Indoor Golf Centre*, underground complex in Dataran Merdeka, golfers can select from 7 prestigious international courses from a computerized menu, T4432541. *Kelab Golf Negara*, Subang (near Subang International Airport), 2 18-hole courses, green fees RM200, T7760388. *Royal Selangor Golf Club*, Jln Kelab Golf, off Jln Tun Razak, exclusive championship course (including 2 18-hole courses and a 9-hole course), one of the oldest in the country, non-members can only play at weekdays, green fees RM210 (without membership introduction), T9848433. *Saujana Golf & Country Resort*, Subang (near Subang International Airport), 2 18-hole championship courses, green fees RM170 weekdays, RM290 weekends, T/461466. *Sentul Golf Club*, 84 Jln Strachan, Sentul, built in 1928, recently refurbished and a swimming pool added, green fees RM30 weekdays, RM50 weekends, T4435571. *Templer Park Country Club*, 21 km north of KL, fully floodlit course for 24-hr golf, frequented by Japanese golf package tourists, developed and part-owned by Japanese company, the more environmentally minded have complained that the course has ruined the north end of Templer Park. *Kelana Jaya Sports Complex*, Lot 1772, Taman Tasek Subang, Kelana Jaya. *YMCA*, 95 Jln Padan Belia, Brickfields.

Health centres *Fitness International*, *Parkroyal Hotel*, Jln Sultan Ismail. *Good Friend Health Centre*, 33 Jln Tun Sambathan 5. *Recreation Health Centre*, 4th Flr, *Furama Hotel*, Komleks Selangor, Jln Sultan Ismail.

Roller skating *Fun World Roller Disco*, 1st Flr, Asiajaya Shopping Complex, Petaling Jaya.

Snooker *Jade Snooker Centre*, GBC Plaza, Jln Ampang, T4570345. *Snooker Paradise*, Kompleks Kotaraya.

Spectator sports Cricket, rugby and hockey are played on the *Padang*, in the centre of KL, most weekends. Football and badminton are Malaysia's most popular sports. Inter-state Malaysia Cup football matches are played at the *Merdeka Stadium* and the Stadium on Jln Stadium, off Jln Maharajalela. The (rather more successful) Selangor team play at the *Shah Alam Stadium*; Sat and Tue 2030 kick-off. RM10 entrance fee. A colourful (and safe) experience. One-way taxi costs RM15-20, but you need to ask the taxi driver to wait for you as it can be difficult getting back into town.

Squash *Bangsar Sports Complex*, Jln Terasek Tiga, Bangsar Baru, T2546065.

Swimming The KLCC park has a pleasant swimming pool, which can be used free of charge. Public pools charge a nominal fee. *Bangsar Sports Complex*, Jln Terasek Tiga, Bangsar Baru, T2546065. Open Mon-Sat 0800-1300, closed Sun. *Weld Swimming Pool*, Jln Raja Chulan. *Public pool*, next to *Chinwoo Stadium*, off Jln Hang Jebat.

Watersports *Sunway Lagoon and Adventure Park*, T7356000. Theme park, with plenty of entertainment both in and out of the water, admission RM15 (RM10 for children), open 1200-2030 Mon, Wed, Thu, 1200-2200 Fri, 1000-2000 Sat, Sun and public holidays. To get there from Klang bus station, take Sri Jaya Bus 252B USJ or Klang Bus 51. *The Mines*, Sungai Besi Tin Mine, T9487402 (admission: weekdays adult RM8, child RM4; weekends adult RM12, child RM6), 20 mins' drive from KL, before the toll booths on highway to Seremban, exit on left (at Taman Sri Petaling), turn right at T-junction, over the railway line and past *Shell* and *Esso* stations towards Serdang and Kajang, signposted to the left, located in what was the biggest tin mine in the world, in clean, turquoise water and beneath dramatic rocky cliffs. The 200-acre recreational park boasts a snow house where the temperature is regulated to create all-year-round snow. Other amusements include a roller coaster, water screen, laser show and a musical fountain.

Tour operators

Most of the big hotels have their own in-house travel agents and ticketing agencies. For domestic flights it can be cheaper to buy tickets through ticketing agencies rather than going to MAS headquarters on Jln Sultan Ismail. If you are staying in a hotel, many ticketing agencies will deliver the tickets to your room. There are plenty of travel agents in the Angkasaraya Building on the corner of Jln Ampang and Jln Ramlee. For slightly different mid-range tours, try *Dee Travel*, Central Market, T2019699. For student/cheap outbound tickets, *MSL*, near the *Grand Central Hotel*, T4424722, is recommended or *STA*, 5th Flr, Magnum Plaza, Jln Pudu, T2489800. *Ecstasy Travel*, 754 Jln Sentul, T4425688. Organizes country and city tours for about RM25 for a 3-hr trip. *Thomas Cook*, Level 18, Menara Lion, Jln Ampang (near *Nikko Hotel*), T2649252. *MATIC* (see Tourist offices, page 70) provides a telephone booking service for *Taman Negara Resort*, on T2643929, ext 113.

Transport

Butterworth 383 km, Cameron Highlands 219 km, Ipoh 217 km, Melaka 148 km, Johor Bahru 365 km, Singapore 393 km, Kuantan 274 km, Kuala Terengganu 491 km, Kota Bharu 657 km.

Distances from KL

Transport to town The *KLIA Express Coach Service* provides an efficient service from Sepang International Airport into the city centre to Hentian Duta (near the Tun Razak Hockey Stadium). The journey takes 1 hr and buses arrive at 30-min intervals from 0530 to 2400. The *Express Coach Service* also operates routes to Shah Alam, to the *Pan Pacific Glenmarie Hotel* every 1 hr between 0600 and 2430, journey time 45 mins. Bargain hard for a taxi to the city; RM110 is about the minimum. For a taxi from the city to KL Airport expect to pay around RM65. Hotels can arrange a good fare in the RM65-90 range. **NB** Make sure the taxi fare includes the motorway toll for either direction. Major car-hire firms have desks at the airport terminal. Hotel pick-up service must be arranged in advance or at the office just outside the terminal exit. A railway line, KL Sentral KLIA, being built between KL and the airport, is due for completion in 2002.

Local
See also Ins and outs, page 70

Bus An *Intrakota* bus map should be available free from the City Hall. *Intrakota* has taken over most routes now but it's not a particularly easy system to grasp. For enquiries, T7172727. Fares are in the range RM0.60-0.90.

Car hire *Apex, Budget, Hertz, Mayflower, National, SMAS, Thrifty, Tomo Express, Toyota* and *U-Drive* all have desks at Subang Airport. *Avis*, T2417144, F2429650. *Economy Car Rental (ECR)*, T2925427, F2927888. *Hakikat*, T2448404. *Hawk*, T2646455, F2646466. *Hertz*, T2486433, F2428481, enquiry@hertz-malaysia.com *Mayflower*, T6221888, F6279282. *Mansfield*, T2433333, F2426036, 225 Jln Bukit Bintang. *National*, T2480522, F2482823. *Orix*, T2423009, F2423609. *Sintat*, T2457988, F2456057. *SMAS*, T2307788, F2320077. *Thrifty*, T2488877 (T7469778 Airport), F2424907. In case of vehicle breakdowns the *Automobile Association of Malaysia (AAM)* can be contacted on T2625777.

Commuter trains The alternative to the LRT for north-south travel in the city is to hop on the *KTM KOMUTER Line*, which cuts across the LRT from north to south. Trains leave every 15-30 mins and tickets cost RM1.

LRT (Light Rail Transit) Three separate companies operate this system, which provides a good network to almost all the major landmarks in the city. The *STAR Line* is an elevated railway and the first to be completed in 1998. The *PUTRA Line* is part-elevated

Kuala Lumpur

and fully automated. The trains operate between 0600 and 2300 with a frequency of one train every 3-5 mins during peak hrs and every 8-15 mins during off-peak hrs. Fares range from RM0.75 (up to 2 stops) to RM2.95; stored-value tickets to the value of RM20 or RM50 are also available, saving hassle for those using the system regularly. To travel from Ampang to Sultan Ismail takes around 20 mins; from Ampang to Miharja, 12 mins.

It is illegal for taxis not to refuse fares within the city limits

Taxi KL is one of the cheaper cities in Southeast Asia for taxis and there are stands all over town. Most are a/c and metered: RM2 for the 1 km and RM0.10 for every 200 m thereafter. Extra charges apply between 2400 and 0600 (50% surcharge), for each extra passenger in excess of 2, as well as RM1 for luggage in the boot. Waiting charges are RM2 for the first 2 mins, RM0.10 for every subsequent 45 secs. Taxis should not be hailed; there are designated places to queue. Try and insist the driver uses the meter. For complaints, T2539044. **NB** During rush hours, shift change (around 1500) or if it's raining, it can be very difficult to persuade taxis to travel to the centre of town; negotiate a price (locals claim that waving a RM10 bill helps) or jump in and feign ignorance.

For 24-hr taxi service try the following. *Comfort*, T7330507. *Koteksi*, T7815352. *Sakti*, T4420848. *Selangor*, T2936211. *Telecab*, T2110211. *KL Taxi Drivers' Association*, T2215252. *Mesra*, T4421019. A surcharge of RM1 is made for a phone booking. If you are desperate for a taxi, go to the nearest hotel and rent a limousine (RM35 and RM60).

Long distance
See also Ins & outs, page 70

Air KL's relatively new international airport at Sepang lies 72 km south of the city. *MAS* flights to other Malaysian destinations include regular connections with **Alor Star, Ipoh, Johor Bahru, Kota Bharu, Kota Kinabalu, Kuala Terengganu, Kuantan, Kuching, Labuan, Lahad Datu, Langkawi, Miri, Penang, Tawau.** Note that some domestic flights leave from KL's old airport at **Subang**, about 25 km southwest of the city centre.

It is best to book tickets the day before leaving (although same-day departure is usually possible) and several days in advance during peak holiday periods

Bus KL's main bus terminal is **Puduraya** on Jln Pudu. Buses leave here for destinations across the Peninsula as well as to **Singapore** and **Thailand**. Most large bus companies, including the biggest, *Ekspres Nasional*, have their offices inside the terminal, above the departure hall. *Ekspres Nasional* also have a ticket counter at the *Malaysia Tourist Infomation Complex* on Jln Ampang and many hotels and guesthouses will arrange tickets too, which saves on a journey to Puduraya. There are also quite a number of bus offices opposite the terminal along Jln Pudu and, due to overcrowding within, quite a few buses drop off and pick up along that strip of road. **NB** Avoid buying tickets from touts. Inside the terminal there is an information desk, post office, tourist police booth, left luggage office (open 0800-2200 Mon-Sun, RM1.50 per item per day) and foodstalls. Puduraya serves most travellers needs – the exception being those wishing to visit **Taman Negara National Park** – KL has a number of other bus terminals. The **Pekeliling Station,** T4421256, is in the north of the city, off Jln Tun Razak. Buses to destinations in **Pahang State**, including **Jerantut** (for Taman Negara) and **Kuala Lipis**, leave from here, not from Puduraya. Other destinations include **Kuantan** and the **Genting Highlands**. The **Putra Station**, T4429530, facing the *Putra World Trade Centre*, serves the east coast and connections with destinations in **Kelantan, Terengganu** and **Pahang**, including **Kuantan, Kuala Terengganu** and **Kota Bharu**. Buses to **Penang, Ipoh** and **Johor Bahru** leave from **Medan Mara**. Regular connections with **Singapore, Johor Bahru, Melaka, Butterworth** and **Penang** (5 hrs), **Ipoh, Kuantan** and **Kota Bharu**. Finally, the small **Klang Station** in Chinatown, on Jln Hang Kasturi, serves **Port Klang** and **Shah Alam** suburb.

Train The *Central Railway Station*, Jln Hishamuddin, T2747435. There is a left-lugage office on Platform 4 and information desk at Platform 1. The desk is helpful and can advise on schedules. KL is on the main line from **Singapore** to the south and **Butterworth** (Penang) to the north; some of these trains go on through to **Bangkok**. To get on the east coastline you have to go to **Gemas**, the junction south of KL or to **Kuala**

Lipis or **Mentakab**, 150 km to the west of KL. Regular connections with **Alor Star**, **Butterworth**, **Taiping**, **Ipoh**, **Tapah Rd** (for Cameron Highlands), **Tampin**, **Gemas**, **Johor Bahru** and **Singapore**. Tourists, on production of their passport, can buy a **KTM rail pass**, which offers unlimited rail travel, although it is not valid on the Thai system. Outside the western entrance of the station is a restaurant with colonial-style décor, a small Malay menu and *laksa*. It is a good place if you need to wait for a train.

Station taxis These leave from Jln Pudu, outside the Puduraya bus station. Share taxis run to most large towns on the Peninsula; fares are about double those of the equivalent bus journeys. There are no scheduled departures, it is a case of turning up and seeing which taxis have space and where they are going.

Directory

Aeroflot, Ground Flr, Wisma Tong Ah, 1 Jln Perak, T21613331. *Air India*, Bangunan **Airline** Ankasa Raya, 123 Jln Ampang, T21420323. *Air Lanka*, UG4 Bangunan Perangasang **offices** Segemai, Jln Kampung Attap, T2323633. *Alitalia*, Plaza See Hoy Chan, Jln Raja Chulan, T2380366. *America West Airlines*, UBN Tower, 10 Jln P Ramlee, T2387057. *American Airlines*, Bangunan Angkasa Raya, 123 Jln Ampang, T21480644. *Bangladesh Biman*, Subang International Airport, T7461118. *British Airways*, 8th Flr (West Wing) Rohas Perkasa, 8 Jln Perak, T21676188. *Cathay Pacific*, UBN Tower, 10 Jln P Ramlee, T2383377. *China Airlines*, Level 3, Bangunan Amoda, 22 Jln Imbi, T21427344. *Czechoslavak Airlines*, 12th Flr, Plaza Atrium, 10 Lorong P Ramlee, T2380176. *Delta Airlines*, UBN Tower, Jln P Ramlee, T2324700. *Garuda*, Suite 3.01, Level 3, Menara Lion, Jln Ampang, T21622811. Opposite Ampang Park Shopping Mall. *Japan Airlines*, 1st Flr, Pernas International, Lot 1157, Jln Sultan Ismail, T21611728. *KLM*, Shop 7, Ground Flr, President House, Jln Sultan Ismail, T21427011. *Korean Air*, 17th Flr, MUI Plaza, Jln P Ramlee, T7465700. *Lufthansa*, 3rd Flr, Pernas International Bldg, Jln Sultan Ismail, T21614646. *MAS*, UMBC Bldg, Jln Sulaiman, T21610555. MAS Bldg, 33rd Flr, Jln Sultan Ismail, T7463000. Dayabumi Complex, T22748734. The Mall, Putra World Trade Centre, Level 3 T40426759. *Northwest Airlines*, UBN Tower, Jln P Ramlee, T21433542. *Philippine Airlines*, 104-107 Wisma Stephens, Jln Raja Chulan, T21429040. *PIA*, Ground Floor, Angkasa Raya Bldg, 123 Jln Ampang, T21425444. *Qantas*, 8th Floor (West Wing) Rohas Perkasa, 8 Jln Perak, T21676188. *Royal Brunei*, 1st Flr, Wisma Merlin, Jln Sultan Ismail, T2307166. *Royal Jordanian*, 8th Flr, Mui Plaza, Jln P Ramlee, T21487500. *Sabena*, 1st Flr, Wisma Stephens, Jln Raja Chulan, T21425820. *Saudi*, c/o Safuan Travel & Tours, 7 Jln Raja Abdullah, T26984566. *Scandinavian Airlines*, Bangunan Angkasa Raya, 123 Jln Ampang, T21426044. *Singapore Airlines*, Wisma SIA, 2 Jln Sang Wangi, T26923122. *Thai International*, Kuwasa Bldg, 5 Jln Raja Laut, T26937100. *Turkish Airlines*, Hotel *Equatorial*, 20 Jln Sultan Ismail, T21614055. *United Airlines*, Bangunan MAS, Jln Sultan Ismail, T21611433. *UTA French Airlines*, Plaza See Hoy Chan, Jln Raja Chulan, T2324179. *Virgin Atlantic*, 77 Jln Bukit Bintang (2nd Flr), T21430322/3.

There are money changers in all the big shopping centres and along the main shopping **Banks** streets. Most branches of the leading Malaysian and foreign banks have foreign exchange desks, although some (for example *Bank Bumiputra*) impose limits on charge card cash advances. The following addresses are for bank headquarters. *Bank Bumiputra*, Menara Bumiputra, Jln Melaka, T26988011. *Bank of America*, 1st Flr, Wisma Stephens, Jln Raja Chulan, T2021133. *Chase Manhattan*, 1st Flr, Bangunan Pernas International, Jln Sultan Ismail. *Hongkong & Shanghai Banking Corporation*, 2 Leboh Ampang (off Jln Gereja), T2300744. *Maybank*, 100 Jln Tun Perak, T2308833. *Public Bank*, Bangunan Public Bank, 6 Jln Sultan Sulaiman (off Jln Syed Putra), T22741788. *Standard Chartered Bank*, 2 Jln Ampang, T2326555. *United Malayan Banking Corporation*, Bangunan UMBC, Jln Sultan Sulaiman (off Jln Syed Putra), T2309866.

Communications General Post Office: Dayabumi Complex, Jln Sultan Hishamuddin (Poste Restante). **Over-seas telephone service**: *Kedai Telekom* at the airport. *Kaunter Telegraf STM*, Wisma Jothi, Jln Gereja; *Syarikat Telekom Malaysia*, Bukit Mahkamah. **Internet**: there are 2 places that offer internet access on Jln Raja Laut, Chow Kit; one on the corner of Jln Haji Taib and the other is opposite the junction with Jln Sri Amar. Both charge RM6 per hr.

Embassies & consulates Australia, 6 Jln Yap Kwan Sweng, T21423122. *Austria*, 7th Flr, MUI Plaza, Jln P. Ramlee, T21484277. *Belgium*, 4th Flr, Wisma DNP, 12 Lorong Yap Kwan Seng, T21485733. *Brunei Darussalam*, 8th Flr, Wisma Sin Heap Lee (next to the *Crown Princess Hotel*), Jln Tun Razak, T2612800. *Canada*, 7th Flr, Plaza MBS, 172 Jln Ampang, T21612000. *China*, 229 Jln Ampang, T21428495. *Czech Republic*, 32 Jln Mesra (off Jln Damai), T21427185. *Denmark*, 22nd Flr, Bangunan Angkasa Raya, 123 Jln Ampang, T2022101. *Finland*, 15th Flr, MBF Plaza, Jln Ampang, T21611088. *France*, 196 Jln Ampang, T21484318. *Germany*, 3 Jln U Thant, T21429666. *India*, 2 Jln Taman Duta, off Jln Duta, visas take 3-4 days. *Indonesia*, 233 Jln Tun Razak, T9842011. *Italy*, 99 Jln U Thant, T42565122. *Japan*, 11 Persiaran Stonor, off Jln Tun Razak, T21427044. *Laos*, 108 Jln Damai, off Jln Ampang, T21483895. *Myanmar* (Burma), 5 Jln Taman U Thant Satu, T21423863. *Netherlands*, 4 Jln Mesra (off Jln Damai), T21485151. *New Zealand*, 193 Jln Tun Razak, T2382533. *Norway*, 11th Flr, Bangunan Angkasa Raya, Jln Ampang, T21420144. *Pakistan*, Jln Ampang, in front of Tourist Centre. *Papua New Guinea High Commission*, 1 Lorong Ru Kedua (off Jln Ampang), T21455145. *Philippines*, 1 Chnagkat Kia Peng, T21484233. *Poland*, 495, 4½ mile, Jln Ampang, T42576733. *Romania*, 114 Jln Damai, T21423172. *Singapore*, 209 Jln Tun Razak, T21616277. *Spain*, 200 Jln Ampang, T21484868. *Sweden*, 6th Flr, Angkasa Raya Bldg, 123 Jln Ampang, T21485433. *Switzerland*, 16 Persiaran Madge, T21480622. *Thailand*, 206 Jln Ampang, T21488333. *Turkey*, Bangunan Citi 1, Jln Perumahan Gurney, T26986455. *UK*, 185 Jln Ampang, T21482122. *USA*, 376 Jln Tun Razak, T21489011. *USSR*, 263 Jln Ampang, T42560009. *Vietnam*, Vietnam House, 4 Persiaran Stonor, T21484036.

Language courses Available at many places (see Yellow Pages), but not cheap. *Time Spoken Language Centre*, 2nd Flr, 226-227 Campbell Complex, T26921595. Recommended but not especially, based on 'travelling *bahasa*', flexible schedules.

Libraries *National Library*, Jln Tun Razak, T26923144. *British Council Library*, Jln Bukit Aman, T26987555. *Lincoln Resource Centre*, 376 Jln Tun Razak, T21420291.

Medical facilities
Casualty wards are open 24 hrs
Hospitals: *Assunta Hospital*, Petaling Jaya, T77823433. *City Medical Centre*, 415-427 Jln Pudu, T92211255. *Damai Service Hospital*, 115-119 Jln Ipoh, T40434900. *Pudu Specialist Centre*, Jln Baba, T21429146. *Tung Shin Hospital*, 102 Jln Pudu, T2321655.

Places of worship Churches: English-language Sunday services are held at the following churches at the times stated. *Baptist Church*, 70 Cangkat Bukit Bintang, 0830, 0945. *St Andrews International Church*, 31 Jln Raja Chulan, 0900, 1100. *St John's Cathedral* (Roman Catholic), 5 Jln Bukit Nanas, 0800, 1030, 1800. *St Mary's (Anglican) Church*, Jln Raja, 0700, 0800, 0930 (family Eucharist), 1800. *Wesley Methodist Church*, 2 Jln Wesley, 0815, 1030, 1800.

Useful information *American Express*, 18th Flr, The Weld (near KL Tower), Jln Raja Chulan, T20500000 **Assisted International Calls**: T108. **Directory Enquiries**: T103. **Fire**: T994. **Immigration**: Jln Pantai Bharu, T79578155. **KL Tourist Police**: T21496593. **Police/ambulance**: T999. **Trunk Calls Assistance**: T101. **Weather Report**: T1052. **Wildlife and National Parks Department**: Km 10, Jln Cheras, T90752872, F90752873.

Northern Peninsula

4

Northern Peninsula

The north-south highway, Malaysia's equivalent of the
autobahn, which runs from KL to the Thai border,
doesn't give the traveller much of a sense of excitement
about this northern quarter of the peninsula. But there is
much more here than asphalt and Protons. North of KL
are the temperate hill resorts and tea plantations of the
Cameron Highlands and **Fraser's Hill**. The former
tin-rush town of Ipoh offers Straits Chinese architecture
and some superb food. Offshore there is the 25 km-long
island of **Penang** with its fine capital Georgetown and
an array of beachside hotels. Less developed than
Penang are the islands of **Pulau Pangkor** to the south
and **Pulau Langkawi** to the north, the latter closer to
Thailand than to mainland Malaysia, and both notable
for their jungle-clad interiors and fine beaches.

Barisan Titiwangsa and the Hill Stations

On the road north, Peninsular Malaysia's mountainous jungled backbone lies to the east. It is called the Barisan Titiwangsa or Main Range. It remains largely unsettled apart from the old British hill stations of **Fraser's Hill***, the* **Cameron Highlands** *and* **Maxwell Hill***, and some scattered Orang Asli aboriginal villages. During the Malayan Emergency in the late 1940s and early 1950s, the Communist guerrillas operated from jungle camps in the mountains and later used the network of aboriginal trails to infiltrate the peninsula from their bases in southern Thailand.*

Genting Highlands

Ins & outs
Colour map 2, grid A2
Phone code: 03
51 km NE of KL
131 km W of Kuantan

The Genting Highlands, just 51 km northeast of KL, is the city's closest hill resort and a popular source of entertainment, Las Vegas-cum-Disneyland style. The Highlands were first developed as a resort in the 1960s by a prominent Malaysian businessman, Tan Sri Lim Goh Tong. At the time, investing in construction at an altitude of 2,000 m above sea level was considered a hare-brained idea. Building the tortuous and impossibly steep road through the dense, jungle-covered hills took seven years alone. However, the idea took off, and the government conceded to allow Malaysia's only casino to operate here.

The casino attracts an estimated 30,000 clients a day and provides the main source of revenue in the Highlands

The resort's main attraction is the **Casino de Genting**, which is one of the largest casinos in the world, with endless rows of slot machines, games tables and even a computerized racetrack where it is possible to bet on Royal Ascot. The décor is glitzy; red plush and glittering chandeliers abound. Occasional grand sweeps are made: people still talk of an Indonesian who put a 4-ringgit keno token into a machine and came away with 1.5 million ringgit. Other attractions in the resort include an outdoor and indoor theme park, which is rated among the best in Malaysia and is constantly being expanded. There is a leisure zone to cater for the wet-weather days, particularly frequent in Highlands at the end of the year. It takes at least a day to get around this bonanza of entertainment and at least as long to work out how to get around. Weekends and public holidays are very busy; Chinese New Year and Hari Raya are two of the peak holiday times.

Sleeping
The accommodation at Genting Highlands comes under the umbrella of the *Genting Highlands Resorts*. Weekends and holidays have the disadvantage of visitors having to queue at check-in and check-out times. It is best to visit on a weekday if possible.

    A *Awana Golf & Country Resort*, T2113015, F2113555. The 30-storey octagonal tower dominates this resort, which is 10 km below the main resort peak, and overlooks an 18-hole golf course. All rooms have fans (a/c not needed at this altitude), bath, TV and balconies offering panoramic views. Facilities on offer include a heated pool, tennis, gymnasium, sauna, children's library, coffee house, restaurant, cocktail lounge and golf course (see Sports, page 118). Recommended. **A** *Genting Hotel*, T2111118, F2111888. Located in the heart of the action, deluxe Genting Club rooms, a heated pool and jacuzzi, restaurant, coffee house and easy access to all the resort

Northern Peninsula

★

Things to do in the Northern Peninsula

- Trekking in the Cameron Highlands. Easily accessible from KL. A small slice of the colonial past and a taste of the jungle.
- Sample Chinese food in Ipoh. Try Ipoh's legendary (well almost) chicken rice and the city's varied interpretations of *kway teow* (noodles).
- Explore Georgetown (Penang) and Taiping's colonial architectural heritage, some of the finest in Malaysia and matched only by Melaka's.
- Discover the Khoo Kongsi (Chinese clan house) in Georgetown, over a century old and arguably the finest in Malaysia.
- Luxuriate in two of Malaysia's most stylish hotels, the *Datai* and *Andaman*, on Pulau Langkawi's Datai Beach. Nice if your pocket is particularly commodious.

Northern Peninsula

facilities. **A** *Highlands Hotel*, T2112812, F2113535. Massive (900 rooms), quite new and very smart; it calls its décor London-style. **A** *Kayangan Apartments*, units designed to accommodate extensive families, the smallest unit has 3 rooms and sleeps 6, the 4-room unit sleeps 8. (Splitting the costs between a group, rates per head are in the **B-C** category.) **A** *Resort Hotel*, T2111118, F2113535. Mainly caters for tour groups and is rated as a 3-star establishment. **A** *Ria Apartments*, a 2-room unit sleeps 4 and in low season is priced at the lower end of the **A** range, a 3-room unit is even more economical and sleeps 6, either unit can take an additional 2 beds at a charge of RM20 each. **B** *Theme Park Hotel*, T2111118, F2113535. The first hotel to be built at the resort, but recently refurbished, and, as its name suggests, the rooms overlook the outdoor theme park.

Within the *Awana Golf and Country Resort* there are a number of places to eat: **Expensive** *Japanese Restaurant*. Recommended for sushi. *Sails Grill*, 2nd Flr, successfully achieves the romantic, candle-lit look combined with dark wood and ethnic masks, excellent quality, international cuisine, 5-star service. Recommended. **Mid-range** *Genting Theatre Restaurant*, 2nd Flr, tables arranged around the stage, eat while watching a show. *Korean Restaurant*. **Cheap** *Rajawali Coffee House*. Also *Restaurant Kampung*, Ground Flr, traditional Malay fare, good-value buffet and set lunch, and *Sidewalk Café*, Ground Flr, a 24-hr coffee shop.

> **Eating**
> *Eating places are all within the resort, which caters for most tastes and budgets*

The *Highlands Hotel* has a couple of places to eat: **Mid-range** *The Bistro*, continental food, pizza. **Cheap** *Good Friends Restaurant*, Chinese food. Two other hotels offer budget eateries: in the *Resort Hotel* there is *Resort Café*, offering an all-day à la carte and buffet breakfast, lunch and dinner; and *Theme Park Hotel* houses the *Happy Valley Restaurant*, a large and very popular Chinese restaurant.

Casino de Genting, part of the *Genting Hotel*. Formal dress required, a tie for men or hire a batik shirt at the door. Blackjack, baccarat, roulette, Tai-Sai are among the table games, along with slot machines, computerized racing. The International Room, for card-holders only, caters for more serious players. *Indoor Theme Park*, the usual video games as well as a Virtual Reality Dungeon, 3D Experience, Space Odyssey 2020, and their most recent simulator addition, a World Train Ride for the less techno-minded, along with plenty of rides for tots. *Leisure Zone*, 32-lane computerized bowling alley – the second largest in Malaysia – plus table-tennis and snooker. *Outdoor Theme Park*, the most recent additions are the Corkscrew Roller Coaster and the Rolling Thunder Mine Train, a monorail makes a circuit of the park and offers good views on a clear day, a cable car runs across the park – also good for views. *Big Rock Disco Café* is the main disco at the resort.

> **Entertainment**

Sports   **Golf** *Awana Golf & Country Resort*, Km 13, T2113015, F2113535. An 18-hole, interna-tional-class course featuring bunkers, ponds and streams, putting green, three-tiered driving range, open daily 0730-1730, green fees RM100 weekdays, not open to public at weekends. **Horse riding** *Awana Horse Ranch*, T2112026. Open daily 0800-1800, pony rides for children, jumps and horse trekking.

Transport   **Bus** The resort operates an a/c express bus service between the KL Puduraya bus sta-tion and Genting Highlands. The service runs every 30 mins at peak times and hourly at other times from 0800 to 1800 with an extended service on Sun and public holidays to 1900. The journey takes 1 hr, inclusive of the cable car, which runs from near the *Awana Hotel* to the resort at the peak. The ticketing office at Puduraya is at counter 43, and buses leave from platform 13. For advance reservations T2326863. A free shuttle ser-vice operates every 2 hrs between the *Awana* and the *Resort Hotel*. An hourly, 24-hr, free shuttle service connects the *Resort Hotel*, *Genting Hotel* and *Ria Apartments*.

Cable car The 'flying carpet cable car' operates between the resort at the peak and a station near *Awana*. It runs every 20 mins between 1200 and 2030 on Mon, 0830 and 2030 Tue to Fri, and 0830 to 2130 weekends and public holidays. Travelling time is 12 mins. For enquiries T2111118, ext 7751. There are plans to build a cable car from Batu caves, just outside KL, to the cable car station at the *Highlands Hotel*, which will cut travelling time considerably.

Directory   **Bank:** *Maybank*, *Genting Hotel*. **Communications** General Post Office: *Genting Hotel*.

Fraser's Hill

Colour map 2, grid A2
Phone code: 09
Altitude: 1,524m
104 km N of KL

Fraser's Hill is named after Englishman Louis James Fraser, who ran a gam-bling den, traded in tin and opium and operated a mule train in these hills at the end of the 19th century. He went on to manage a transport service between Kuala Kubu and Raub. Before Mr Fraser lent his name to it, the seven hills were known as Ulu Tras. The development of the hill station began in the early 1920s. In 1925, British High Commissioner Sir George Maxwell wrote that Fraser's Hill "would always be the most exquisite and most dainty hill station in Malaya", and although he foresaw that development would come to this hitherto remote slice of Pahang he cannot have anticipated the changes that would transform the station over the next three-quarters of a century.

Tourist offices: Fraser's
Hill Development
Corporation Office
between the golf club
and the Merlin Hotel,
maps and general
information available

It was along the road from Kuala Bubu Bharu that the British High Com-missioner, Sir Henry Gurney, was ambushed and killed by Communist insur-gents during the Malayan Emergency in 1951 (see page 512). A few years earlier British soldiers were involved in the massacre of suspected Com-munist sympathizers near Kuala Kubu. They shot dead a number of rubber tappers from a local village. There are a number of Orang Asli villages along rivers and tracks leading from the twisting road up the hill.

Fraser's Hill is close enough to KL to be a favoured weekend resort. Because it was easily accessible by train from Kuala Kubu Road, it was a popular week-end retreat long before the Cameron Highlands. Most of colonial Malaya's big companies, such as Sime Darby, Guthries' and Harrisons and Crosfield, built holiday bungalows among the hills. More and more luxury bungalows are now being built here to cater for wealthy Malaysians, but it is still more tranquil and attractive than Genting. Although it is not as varied as the Cameron Highlands by way of attractions, there is one trail (a three-hour walk), which starts just to the south of the tennis courts and ends at the *Corona Nursery Youth Hostel*, offering good opportunities for birdwatchers (260 spe-cies of migratory and local birds have been identified here) and wild flower enthusiasts, a golf course, tennis courts and gardens. Swimming at Jeriau waterfalls, 4 km from Fraser's Hill town centre, is limited as the concrete pool has all but silted up so that the water is only knee deep, but standing under the powerful waterfall is very refreshing.

AL *Ye Olde Smokehouse Hotel*, T3622226, F3622035. Small 13-room hotel in the 'olde English' style of the *Smokehouse Hotel* in the Cameron Highlands; with breakfast, a/c, TV, minibar, bath, in-house movie, tea/coffee-making facilities, restaurant and pool. Rooms are spacious, clean, with bathroom and some balconies overlooking the golf course, offering excellent views. Price includes breakfast, which makes it good value. **A** *Silverpark Holiday Resort*, Jln Lady Maxwell, T3622888, F3622185, reservations T2916633. Apartments only, no cooking facilities, associated with *De Club* golf course, pool, restaurant, children's playground. **B** *Fraser's Hill Development Corporation*, T3622311, F3622273. The organization manages the *Puncak Inn*, next to the bus stop, a nondescript 27-room hotel, and a series of 3-4 bedroom bungalows, including the **C** *Temerloh*, unusual circular but rather tatty chalets divided into 2 large rooms, very basic with shared bathroom, and the *Raub*, *Pekan*, *Jelai* and *Rompin*, for which rates are charged per room and an additional fixed rate is available for 3 daily meals; hiking and birdwatching tours can be arranged. **C** *Gap Resthouse*, 8 km before for Fraser's Hill. Restaurant serving good Chinese food, poor Western and Malay-Indian food, recently renovated large rooms but still excellent value and a very characterful place to stay. Recommended. **C** *Seri Berkat Rest House*, T8041026, book through district office at Kuala Kubu Bharu. Another colonial building with high ceilings and big rooms. **C** *Fraser Hill Travel Lodge* (YHA), MC G/5 Taman Setia (Sg Hijua), Fraser Hill, T3622443. Run by Mike Chan who will bend over backwards to help you and is very informative. Definitely the best budget option in town. Bedroom apartment with shared kitchen and bathroom with hot water. Around 15 mins' walk from town or a 5-min shuttle bus ride.

Sleeping
Many of the hotels have facilities for recreations such as tennis, squash, riding, snooker

Chinese Mid-range *Spices*, Jln Genting, 49000 Bukit Fraser, T3622510. Serves Guinness and has a small but interesting menu (Indian, Chinese and Western food). The place has a 1950s feel to it. Recommended. *Satay's Corner*, Chinese, up the hill from the main town, next to the mosque. Serves a good breakfast. **International Mid-range** *Old Smokehouse*, similar to the *Smokehouse Hotel* in the Cameron Highlands, serving English-style dishes such as beef Wellington and Devonshire cream teas. Recommended. *Restoran Puncak*, below *Puncak Inn*. **Temerloh Steak House**, Temerloh Bungalow.

Eating

Ye Olde Tavern, above the *Puncak Inn*, Fraser's answer to an English inn, with log fire. *Spices*, see Eating above.

Bars

Golf *De Club at Fraser's*, 18-hole course for members, 9-hole course for public, green fees RM30 weekdays, RM40 weekends, RM15 for club hire, T382777. **Horse riding** Available from *The Paddock* where small bajau ponies are saddled with vast Westerners. **Paddle boats** For hire on Allan's Water.

Sports

There are two routes to Fraser's Hill. Either take the KL-Karak highway and turn off at Bentong towards Raub and then left again at Tranum for The Gap. If you have more time and would like something a little more scenic, take the road to Ipoh and then turn off at Kuala Kubu Bharu for The Gap. Note the information below regarding traffic on the narrow Gap road, which is one-way at certain times of the day. A new road is under construction and may have been completed by the time this guide reaches the shelves. **Bicycle hire** From Fraser's Hill Development Corporation Office, RM4 per hr. **Bus** Regular connections from KL – the No 66 bus from platform 21 of KL's Pudu Raya station (purchase tickets on the bus) stops at Kuala Kubu Bharu. Change here to

Transport

Northern Peninsula

Fraser's Hill. The bus only runs at 0800 and 1400 from Kuala Bubu Bharu to Fraser's Hill, with return buses departing from Fraser's Hill at 1000 and 1600. **Car** A one-way traffic system operates from 0600-1940, 8 km from Fraser's Hill: uphill traffic gets right-of-way on the even hours, downhill traffic on the odd hours (with 40 mins of traffic permitted during those hours). **Taxi** Shared taxis go direct to Fraser's Hill. KL (RM10 from Kubu Bharu, or RM40 for the whole cab.

Directory **Banks** It is possible to change money at *Maybank*, in the *Merlin Hotel*, and at the *Malaysia Bank*, along from *Merlin Hotel* entrance in the same complex of shops.

Cameron Highlands

Phone code: 05
Colour map 1, grid C3
214 km N of KL
121 km E of Ipoh

The biggest and best known of Malaysia's hill stations lies on the northwest corner of Pahang, bounded by Perak to the west, and Kelantan to the north. On the jungle-clad 1,500m-high plateau the weather is reassuringly British – unpredictable, often wet and decidedly cool – but when the sun blazes out of an azure-blue sky, the Camerons are hard to beat.

Ins and outs

Getting there There are buses from KL's Puduraya terminal direct to the Cameron highlands and various tour buses make the journey too. There is a direct taxi service from Georgetown (Penang). Alternatively catch a bus to Tapah, the main way station for the Camerons. There are numerous connections from KL to Tapah, as well from Ipoh, Butterworth, Kuantan, Melaka and Singapore. From Tapah there are buses every hour to the Highlands. Alternatively, take a train to Tapah Road, Tapah's train station (outside town to the west), a bus or taxi into Tapah town, and a bus from there to the Camerons. There are rail connections with the Tapah Road from KL, Ipoh and Butterworth.

Getting around Buses from Tapah all pass through Tanah Rata and Brinchang and it is usually possible to climb aboard to travel between these centres. There are also taxis available for hire by the hour or for specific journeys.

Daytime temperatures in the Cameron Highlands average around 23°C, and in the evening, when it drops to 10°C and the hills are enveloped in swirling cloud, known as ' the white witch', pine log fires are lit in the hilltop holiday bungalows. The weather has become more unpredictable in the last 50 years – torrential downpours and landslides are no longer confined to the monsoon months of November and December. But the mountain air is still bracing enough to entice thousands of holiday makers to the Camerons from the steamy plains. Today coach-loads of Singaporeans wind their way up the mountain roads and, together with well-heeled KL businessfolk, fork out extortionate sums for weekends in timeshare apartments and endless rounds of golf.

History

In the colonial era this mountain resort was a haven for homesick, overheated planters and administrators. Its temperate climate induced an eccentric collection of them to settle and retire in their Surrey-style mansions where they could prune their roses, tend their strawberries, sip G&Ts on the lawn, stroll down to the golf course or nip over to Mr Foster's mock-Tudor *Smokehouse* for a Devonshire cream tea. The British Army also had a large presence in

Cameron Highlands tea plantations

The Cameron Highlands provide an ideal climate for tea growing. The largest and best-known estate, with 1,200 ha of mature tea plantations is the Boh Plantation. Boh tea is the standard brand in most Malaysian homes. Two estates, the Fairlie (lower Highlands) and the Sungei Palas (upper Highlands), operate free guided tours of their factories, every hour or so, daily except Monday; no tea gets plucked on a Sunday. The Sungei Palas is probably the more attractive of the two, perched high on the steep, green hills above Brinchang, and receives less visitors (see page 132 for how to get there).

Like all Cameronian tea estates, Boh Plantations, in the Lower Highlands, employ a hardcore of tea pluckers whose forebears originally came from South India. The workers live in self-contained quarters on the estates, most of which have their own shops and school. The original tea plants also came from India, mainly Darjeeling stocks, many of which are still productive. Now bonsai specimens, they can be recognized by their thick trunks and dark green leaves. Bushes planted from the 1960s onwards are mainly cloned varieties with lighter-coloured leaves.

In 1927, John Archibald Russell (known to his friends as Archie), in conjunction with Mr AB Milne, an old tea planter from Ceylon, was granted a concession of land in the Cameron Highlands. This became the Boh Estate, which was carved out of virgin jungle, an

extraordinary feat considering that the work was carried out without machinery and only with the assistance of mules.

In the 1920s, tea plucking and processing was also an all-manual process. Nowadays, machinery is used, although it is still manually intensive, with an average of 6-10 people required to look after each acre of plantation. Tea bushes are grown on slopes in places so precipitous that machinery is almost impossible to use: 45° slopes are commonplace. However, on the whole, the workers use a plucking machine, otherwise hand shears are used. Plucking takes place all-year-round every 15-25 days, depending on growth, which tends to be slower during the rainy season. Maintenance is a year-round task; the bushes need to be regularly fertilized and weeded, while pruning takes place every 3 years.

The green tea leaf is weighed (the pluckers are paid per kilogram) before being taken to the factory to be processed, where every 5 kg of green leaf produces around 1 kg of tea. The first process in the factory is to wither the leaves under artificial blowers, for 12-16 hours, depending on the moisture content. The leaves are then rolled, or broken up using a rotary blade, and graded before being put into trays for fermentation. Finally the tea is fired in an oven, the timing of which is critical, before being graded for a second time. The tea is mostly packaged in KL, from where it is distributed, mainly to local destinations as the quantity is limited.

Tanah Rata until 1971 – their imposing former military hospital (now reverted to being a Roman Catholic convent) still stands on the hill overlooking the main street. To the left of the road leading into Tanah Rata from Ringlet are a few remaining Nissen huts from the original British army camp.

While most of the old-timers – the likes of Stanley Foster, Captain Bloxham (who nursed racehorses at his bougainvillaea-fringed 'spelling station' at Ringlet) and Miss Gwenny Griffith-Jones (founder of Singapore's Tanglin School) – have now gone to rest, they bequeathed an ambience, which the Cameron Highlands has yet to shake off. Miss 'Griff' had been one of the original pioneers, trudging up through the jungle from Tapah on an oxcart, when they first cut the road, with its hairpin bends, in the 1930s.

Fifty years elapsed between the discovery of the highland plateau and the arrival of the first settlers. William Cameron, a government surveyor, first claimed to have stumbled across "a fine plateau, shut in by lofty mountains" while on a mapping expedition in 1885. In a letter in which he gave an account of this trip, he wrote: "[I saw] a sort of vortex in the mountains, while for a wide area we have gentle slopes and plateau land". The irony was that Cameron's name was bestowed on a place he never set eyes on. What he probably came across was the smaller plateau area farthest from Tanah Rata, known as Blue Valley. The highland plateau itself was discovered years later by a Malay warrior named Kulop Riau, who accompanied Cameron on his mapping expeditions.

Cameron Highlands

Sleeping

1 Arcadia
2 Bala's Holiday Chalets
3 Golf Course
4 Kea Farm & Equatorial Hotel
5 Lakehouse
6 Merlin
7 Smokehouse
8 Strawberry Park Resort

Cameron's report engendered much excitement. Sir Hugh Low, who, 34 years earlier, had made the first attempt at Sabah's Gunung Kinabalu, was by then the Resident of Perak. He wanted to develop the newly reported Highland area as "a sanitorium, health resort and open farmland". Twenty years elapsed before the first pioneers made their way up to the so-called 'Cameron's Land'.

Hot on the heels of the elderly 'gin and Jaguar' settlers (most of them insisted on solid British cars for the mountain roads) came the tea planters and vegetable farmers. The cool mountain climate was perfect for both. The forested hillsides were shaved to make way for more tea bushes and cabbages and the deforestation appears to have affected the climate. The local meteorological station reports that the average temperature has risen 2°C in the past 50 years.

The Camerons' most talked-about visitor arrived in March 1967 for a quiet sojourn in Moonlight bungalow, perched on a hilltop above the golf course. The disappearance of the US-born Thai silk emperor, art collector and military intelligence agent Jim Thompson from a lonely Cameronian backroad, propelled the hill resort into the headlines. Teams of Orang Asli trackers combed the jungle in vain, while detectives, journalists and film makers toyed with credible explanations: he had been given a new identity by the CIA; he had been kidnapped and smuggled from the Highlands in the boot of a Thai taxi; he had been eaten by a tiger. The fate of Thompson, the Lord Lucan of Southeast Asia, remains a mystery to this day.

Sights

Most of the tourist attractions in the Cameron Highlands are on and around the plateau but there are a handful of sights on the road from Tapah. These are listed in order from the bottom of the mountain up. There are three main townships in the Highlands: Ringlet, Tanah Rata (literally 'flat land') and Brinchang. The latter two are in the plateau area, either side of the golf course.

Unfortunately, the Cameron Highlands is no longer a peaceful bolt-hole in the sky. Frenetic development is turning the area, in critics' eyes, into a building site where forest is fast making way for golf courses and luxury tourist developments. When Prime Minister Dr Mahathir Mohamad's current plans for a new road from Ipoh to the Cameron Highlands are put in motion, further expansion can be expected. At present the road from Tapah is the only way up and down; this road runs through Perak until it reaches Ringlet, and the Perak state authorities are unlikely to spend much money upgrading it as Pahang state accrues all the financial returns of Cameron Highlands' tourism.

Tapah This is a centre for making the large bamboo baskets that are used to collect the tea grown in the Highlands. The town itself is very small, a single street of dilapidated shophouses with a couple of basic hotels such as **E** *Bunga Raya* (T4011436) and **E** *Hotel Utara* (T4012299), and a few eating places, including *KFC*. The bus station in Tapah is on Jalan Raja, just off the main road. There are hourly connections with Tanah Rata, as well as occasional departures for KL and Penang. Most long-distance bus departures from Tapah (including for KL, Melaka, Penang, Kuantan, and Lumut as well as connections with Hat Yai in southern Thailand) are from the *Caspian Restaurant* on the main highway. The Tapah Road Railway Station is about 10 km from the town.

Kuala Woh, a jungle park with a swimming pool, fishing and natural hot pools, is only 13 km from Tapah, on the road to the Camerons and has a basic camping area.

☞ Jungle walks: Cameron Highlands

The Cameron Highlands is great walking country, although many of the longer trails were closed in the 1970s when the army found secret food dumps for the Communist Party of Malaya (CPM), which used the Main Range as its insurgency route from its bases near Betong in South Thailand. Despite the CPM calling a halt to hostilities in 1990, the trails have not reopened. There are, however, a handful of not-so-strenuous mountains to climb and a number of jungle walks. Cameronian trails are a great place for people unfamiliar with jungle walks. They are also very beautiful.

Basic sketch maps of trails, with numbered routes, are available at the Tourist Information kiosk in Tanah Rata and from most hotels. Walkers are advised to take plenty of water with them as well as a whistle, a lighter and something warm. It is very easy to lose your way in jungle – and the district officer has had to call out Orang Asli trackers on many occasions over the years to hunt down disoriented hikers. Always make sure someone knows roughly where you are going and approximately what time you are expecting to get back.

There is a centuries-old Orang Asli trail leading from Tanjung Rambutan, near Ipoh, up the Kinta River into the Main Range. One branch of this trail goes north to the summit of Gunung Korbu (2,183 m), 16 km away. When William Cameron and his warrior companion Kulop Riau left on their elephant-back expedition into the mountains, they followed the Kinta River to its source and, from the summit of nearby Gunung Calli, saw Blue Valley 'plateau'. Cameron's view of the plateau that would later bear his name was obscured by two big mountains, Irau (the one shaped like a roller coaster) and Brinchang.

At 2,032 m, Gunung Brinchang is the Highlands' highest peak and the highest point in Malaysia accessible by road. The area around the communications centre on the summit affords a great panorama of the plateau, although it spends most of its life shrouded in cloud. The road up the mountain veers left in the middle of Boh's Sungei Palas tea estate past Km 73. From the top of Brinchang it is possible to see straight down into the Kinta valley, on the other side. Ipoh is only 15 km away, as the hornbill flies. There is an old and rarely used trail up Gunung Brinchang from the back of the old airstrip (behind the army flats) at the top end of Brinchang town.

Gunung Beremban (1,840 m) makes a pleasant hike, although its trails are well

Lata Iskandar Waterfall, 22½ km from Tapah, is a beautiful jungle waterfall, right by the roadside, which has been ruined by commercial ventures capitalizing on the picnic spot. However, it is a good place to pick up the local terracotta pottery, crafted in Kampung Kerayung. The **19th Mile**, further up the hill, is a more pleasant spot for a stop-off. To the right of the little shop, a path leads along the side of the river, up into the jungle, past Orang Asli villages, waterfalls and jungle pools. Good for birdwatching and butterflies.

Ringlet The first township on the road to the Cameron Highlands, just inside Pahang state, it was relocated to its present site in the 1960s when the original village was flooded to make way for the Sultan Abu Bakar hydroelectric scheme. *Ringlet* is the Semai aboriginal word for a jungle tree. The town itself is basically unattractive with shabby 1960s apartment blocks. There is also a cluster of hawker stalls in the town centre and a well-used temple.

After Ringlet, the road follows a wide river to a large, murky brown lake, connected to a hydroelectric dam. The lake is overlooked by the famous *Lakehouse*, a Tudor-style country house, formerly the home of Colonel Stanley Foster and now a cosy 18-room hotel, and a row of food and souvenir worn. It can be reached from Tanah Rata (trail No 7 goes up through the experimental tea in the MARDI station past the padang off Jalan Persiaran Dayang Endah), Brinchang (trail No 2 leads up from behind the Sam Poh Buddhist temple) – a more arduous route, or the golf course (follow trail No 3 past the Arcadia bungalow where the road stops) – this is the easiest. Allow about 4 hours to get up and down. There is a good view down Tanah Rata's main street from the top. It is also possible to climb Gunung Beremban from Robinson Falls (trail No 8 leads off trail No 9). The trail heading for the latter is from the very bottom of the road leading past MARDI from Tanah Rata.

Gunung Jasar (1,696 m), between the golf course and Tanah Rata, is a pleasant – but gentler – walk of about 3 hours (trail No 10). The trail goes from halfway along the old back road to Tanah Rata near the meteorological station (the road – Jalan Titiwangsa – leaves Tanah Rata from behind a hotel south of town and emerges at the golf course, on the corner next to the Golf Course Hotel). The Jasar trail also forks off to Bukit Perdah (trail No 12, which branches off the Jasar trail) 2 to 3 hours to the top and back. The path down from the summit comes out on a road leading back into the top end of Tanah Rata.

The trails to Robinson Falls (trail No 9, an hour's walk) and Parit Falls (trail No 4, 30 minutes' walk) are more frequently trampled. The trail branches off to No 9a, which leads down to the Boh tea estate road near Ringlet Lake. The walk to the Boh tea estate is a long one, but it is possible to hitch along the road or catch a bus with great views when you get there. There are tours every hour. The estate is closed on Monday, and closes at 1700 on other days; the last bus leaves the factory at 1730. The short trail to Parit Falls starts behind the Garden Hotel and mosque on the far side of Tanah Rata's padang and ends up below the Slim army camp. Parit Falls is a small waterfall in between the two, with what was once a beautiful jungle pool before it became cluttered with daytrippers and their rubbish.

There are hundreds of other trails through the Camerons, traversing ridges and leading up almost every hill and mountain. Most are Orang Asli paths, some date from the Japanese occupation in the Second World War (these are marked by barbed wire) and some aren't really trails at all – beware!

stalls. At the Habu power station, a road leads right to two of the tea growing estates of the Boh Plantations. The original Boh Estate is 6 km from the junction and the Fairlie Estate is 12 km. ■ *Free guided tours of the factory given almost every hour at the Fairlie Estate, Tue-Sun.*

Youland Flower Nursery is on the road to Gold Dollar tea estate, left off the main road to Tanah Rata from Ringlet (milestone 32). Before reaching Tanah Rata, on the right is a waterfall and picnic spot, on the left is the *Cameron Bharat* tea shop; which has a fine view over the Bharat tea estate.

Tanah Rata

A further 5 km up the mountain is Tanah Rata, the biggest of the three Cameronian towns. Having said this, it is still not very large, comprising a row of shophouses straddled along the main road where there are two or three restaurants, imitating British cafés with fish and chips on most menus. It is a friendly little town, with a resort atmosphere rather like an English seaside town. There are also several souvenir shops, including the *Yung Seng Souvenir Shop*, which is more upmarket than the others and has an interesting selection

Phone code: 05
Altitude: 1,440m
Colour map 1, grid C3

of well-priced Orang Asli crafts, ranging from blowpipes to woodcarvings. It is also worth looking in local shops for teas from surrounding estates: *Gan Seow Hooi* (seowhooigan@hotmail.com) is the only shop that will let customers sample the high-grade leaf tea grown in the area. It is worth a visit for the traditional tea ceremony as well as the tea itself. The shop also stocks traditional Chinese clay teapots and other Chinese handicrafts. ■ *There is no official* **tourist information centre** *in Tanah Rata and information is best picked up from the backpacker guesthouses and the informail stalls on the main street. However* Tourism Pahang *publish small and moderately useful guides to both Fraser's Hill and the Cameron Highlands, available free. Well-priced half-day tours of the area are organized by* Bala's Holiday Chalets *(see Sleeping, page 126), which saves on trying to negotiate the Highlands by public transport.*

Sleeping
■ *on maps, below & page 122*
Price codes: see inside front cover

It should be noted that normally during public holidays, accommodation gets fully booked and prices rise by 30-50%. It is also busy at peak school holiday periods: Apr, Aug and Dec. The most economic form of accommodation is to share a bungalow between a group of people. Most bungalows have gardens, logfires and are away from the towns.

AL *Heritage*, T4913888, F4915666, www.heritage.com.my, located just west of Tanah Rata next to the Convent School. This place has a rather bland international look, out of keeping with its surroundings, although one presumes the intention is to make it look colonial/chalet-esque in appearance. It has 170 spacious rooms, bath, TV, in-house video, mini-bar, tea/coffee-making facilities, Chinese restaurant, coffee house, sauna , health centre, squash, a bar and a chemist. **A** *Lakehouse*, T4956152, F4956213, www.cameron.concorde.net This is located a few kilometres outside Tanah Rata but has fantastic views. It is a Tudor-style country house, the final brain-child of Colonel Stanley Foster, with 18 rooms of antique furnishings, four-poster beds and en-suite bathrooms, overlooking the lake, restaurant serving English food, *Cameron Bar* and *Highlander Lounge* both have English country pub atmosphere, a great place to stay and reasonable value considering. **A** *Smokehouse Hotel*, T4911215, F4911214. This place is modelled on its namesake, the *Smokehouse* in Mildenhall (UK) and it preserves its home counties ethos and 'ye olde English' style of old-time resident Colonel Stanley Foster. Its rooms are first class, there is an original red British telephone box in the garden, restaurant serves expensive English food. **A-C** *Bala's Holiday Chalets*, T4911660, F4914500. Located 1 km outside Tanah Rata on road to Brinchang (RM3 taxi ride). Not chalets at all, but a rambling colonial house (one of the oldest in the area, formerly a British school) with some character and a pleasant garden, despite

Tanah Rata

To Ringlet

To Brinchang

CS Travel & Tours

Main Road (Jln Besar)

New Shop Houses

Jln Camellia

Foodstalls

Taxis
Toilets

Jln Masjid

N
Not to scale

■ **Sleeping**
1 BB Inn
2 Cameronian Inn
3 Cameron Highlands Resthouse
4 Cool Point
5 Daniel's Travellers Lodge
6 Downtown
7 Father's Guesthouse
8 Heritage
9 Hill View Inn
10 Kavy & Coffee House
11 Orient & Restaurant
12 Papillon Guesthouse
13 Seah Meng

● **Eating**
1 Little Grasshopper Teahouse
2 Mayflower
3 Suria
4 Thanum

renovation rooms remain dank, private bathrooms with hot-water (sporadically available) shower, great view, private cable TV. Common sitting-rooms, log fires, good atmosphere but relying on reputation, overpriced restaurant.

B *Merlin*, T4911211, F4911178. Excellent position overlooking the golf course, north of Tanah Rata, 100-room extension completed in early 1997, but there are other, more atmospheric places to stay at this price. **B** *Strawberry Park Resort*, T4911166, F4911949. Magnificent setting above Tanah Rata, dominating a hilltop with its 8 blocks of walk-up rooms and apartments, built in Tudor/Swiss-chalet style. Interior is starting to look dated, rooms are designed to hold maximum capacity, even the smallest studio rooms and 1-room apartments can sleep 4 people. All rooms with bath (inadequate water heaters), TV, in-house video, fridge, tea/coffee-making facilities. Resort facilities include indoor pool (the only one in the Cameron Highlands), tennis, squash, sauna, indoor games rooms, mini-putting green, children's play area, 7 km jogging track, *Monroe's Pub* (with the only disco in the Cameron Highlands and karaoke rooms), coffee house, *Tudor Grill* steakhouse, Chinese restaurant. Recommended. **B** *Cool Point*, Jln Dayang Indah, T4914914, F4914070. A tacky interpretation of the Tudor style and rather dated décor, recently under new management, comfortable (albeit spartan) rooms, TV, tea/coffee-making facilities, own bathroom, breakfast included in room rate, restaurant, overpriced but discounts in low season.

C *Kavy Hotel*, 44 Jln Besar, T4915652, F4915423, kavyhotel@pd.jaring.my Above the *Roselane* coffee shop, large rooms with attached bathroom and TV, a bit shabby and the block itself, ugly and compromising, will evoke images of bucolic serenity. **C** *Rumah Rehat*, Jln Dayang Endah, T4911254. Exceptionally nice little resthouse, tends to get overbooked by government employees so it pays to book in advance, tennis court. Recommended.

D *Cameron Highlands Resthouse*, T4911066. Restaurant, must book first, well run. **D** *Cameronian Inn*, 16 Jln Mentigi, T4911327, F4914966, nasan@pc.jaring.com Restaurant, garden, TV, games, sitting area, 24-hr coffee bar, laundry and internet service. Hot showers in more expensive rooms, this is one of the better mid-budget places in town (well, 300 m from town) with a large lawn and a suitably relaxing atmosphere, dorm bed also available (**F**). Quiet and back from the main road, popular. Bike, motorbike and car hire arranged. Recommended. **D** *Downtown Hotel*, 41 Jln Besar T4913159. Some rooms here come with attached bathrooms. Same quality as the *Orient* next door and similarly grubby. **D** *Hillview Inn*, 17 Jln Mentigi, T4912915, F4915212. New budget hotel, all rooms with balcony. Facilities include TV, internet service, laundry, book exchange and restaurant. **D** *Hotel BB Inn*, 79a Pesiaran Camelia 4, Tanah Rata, 39000, Cameron Highlands, T4914551, F4914552, timurcan@tm.net.my Bathroom, TV in room, good value and very friendly. **D** *Orient*, 38 Jln Besar, T4911633. Located above *The Orient* Chinese restaurant. Recommended. Price includes own bathroom. If you want to avoid the hostels, it's a great budget choice although the staff are not particularly helpful. **D** *Papillon Guesthouse*, Jln Mentigi, T4914069. Close to the *Twin Pines Chalet*, good-sized rooms (more expensive with own bathrooms) and dorm beds available, friendly and enthusiastic management. Set back from the main road among surrounding huts and houses, this is the non-tourist option. **D** *Seah Meng*, 39 Jln Besar, T4911618. On the main street but quiet. Fairly typical Chinese hotel with little atmosphere but the large rooms are kept spotless. Attentive staff. More expensive rooms have showers. Run by a friendly and hospitable family. Recommended.

D-E *Daniel's Travellers Lodge*, 9 Lorong Perdah, T4915823, F4915828, Kand@tm.net.my "Highly recommended by mouth to mouth", as they put it. Clean and friendly place to stay, although rooms are small and it can be noisy. More expensive rooms have own bathrooms. Lots of useful information available and good breakfast served (extra cost), dorm beds (**F**). Video library and book exchange and a daily walk organized around the Highlands. Enthusiastic staff. Recommended. **D-E** *Father's*

Guesthouse, Jln Gereja, T4912484, F4915484, www.fathersplace.cbj.net Near the convent, up a long flight of steps. This colonial era set of buildings is a popular backpackers' haunt, and justifiably so. The guesthouse has a very friendly atmosphere and a great communal area with grand views. There is also access to cable TV and a number of videos and DVDs are available to watch. Tours to the tea plantations and butterfly garden depart daily (RM15). *Father's* also offers internet access. Dorm beds available (**E**). **D-E** *Twin Pines Chalet*, 2 Jln Mentigi, T4912169, furhill@tm.net.my Popular guesthouse at top end of town. Small, clean rooms and dorm, more expensive rooms have own hot showers. Reasonable value. Bus tickets and tours bookable here, good source of information (good on transport around Malaysia). Its once peaceful outlook has been marred by a shopping centre development.

Bungalows Rates are for the whole bungalow, per night unless stated; most prices include resident cook. Rates may vary according to season – discounts on request. Most are dotted around the town, in the countryside, with their own gardens. There are a great many to choose from, the following gives an idea of the type of range available: **AL** *Fair Haven*; **AL** *Golf View Villa*; **A** *Highlands Villa*; **B** *Gunder Singh*; **B** *Lutheran Bungalow*; **D** *Rumah Tetamu Sri Pahang*.

Eating **Chinese Mid-range** *Little Grasshopper Tea House*, Perisan Camellia 3 (opposite *CS Tours*), specializes in steamboat and Chinese tea ceremony where the proprietor talks you through the ins and outs of the ceremony. Also serves Singaporean and Thai food (tasty *Tom Yam* soup). Popular. *Mayflower*, 22 Jln Besar, specialize in Highland steamboat, seafood, popular with locals. **Cheap** *The Orient*, 38 Jln Besar, steamboat and soups are popular, good value set lunch. Vegetarian option is packed with meat and fish.

Indian Cheap *Thanum*, 25 Jln Besar, claypot and Hainam chicken rice recommended, excellent breakfast *rotis* and *murtabak*, chairs and tables outside. *Suria*, Jln Perisan Camellia, excellent South Indian food served on a banana leaf, good range of vegetarian options. Recommended. *Kumar*, good-value food served on banana leaf, popular breakfast spot. *Restoran No 14*, on the main road, very popular place doing good *thalis* and *dosas* at good prices.

International Expensive *Lakehouse*, traditional English food, typical Sun lunch fare and cream teas. *Smokehouse*, similar to *Lakehouse*, favourites include beef Wellington, roast beef, Yorkshire pudding, steak and kidney pie, and Devonshire cream teas. **Mid-range** *Merlin*, international menu, and pleasant atmosphere but not very good value. **Cheap** *Bala's*, in *Bala's Holiday Chalets* (see Sleeping, page 126), good breakfasts and vegetarian dinners, also a popular stop for cream teas. *Roselane Coffee House*, Western and local food, set meals are good value.

Foodstalls Seriously cheap Next to the bus station, opposite the main row of shops on Jln Besar, serve good selection of Malay, Indian and Chinese food.

Entertainment The only nightlife as such takes place in the *Strawberry Park Resort* where there is the only disco in town, karaoke, and a bar. The hotel bars at the *Lakehouse* and *Smokehouse* are also popular venues for their country pub atmosphere and air of exclusivity.

Sports **Golf** *Cameron Highlands Golf Club*, T4911126. Located north of Tanah Rata, connected by a pleasant footpath, founded in 1885 by the British surveyor William Cameron, the 18-hole course is magnificently appointed, occupying pride of place in the centre of the plateau, surrounded by jungled hills. It is a favourite haunt of Malaysian royalty. Green fee and caddy fee, T4911126. Note that players are expected to wear appropriate clothing, which rules out singlets and revealing shorts. Shoe and club hire available. **Tennis** Courts across the road from golf clubhouse, rackets and balls on hire at clubhouse shop. **Treks/walks** There are a number of worthwhile forest walks/treks in the Camerons. Good walking boots and a water bottle should be taken (see box, page 124).

CS Travel & Tours, 47 Jln Besar, T4911200, F4912390. For local tours, air/train/bus tickets, and accommodation reservations. | **Tour operators**

NB Those who suffer from travel sickness are advised to take some anti-nausea medication before setting out on the mountain road. A new road to the west has been under construction for a number of years and should now be completed. | **Transport**

Local Bus/taxis: nearly all the buses from Tapah (last bus 1600) go through Ringlet, Tanah Rata and on to Brinchang and it is easy enough to climb aboard one of the buses that do this route through the day, every hr on the ½hr. *Rex* buses go from Tanah Rata to the farthest outpost on the mountain. Taxis are available for local travel – they can be chartered for individual journeys or by the hr. It is also possible just to take a seat in a taxi, going from Tanah Rata to Brinchang, for example. Taxi and local bus station (T4911485) on either side of the *Shell* station in Tanah Rata. To order a taxi: T4911234.

Car hire: because visitors pose a serious insurance problem on the mountain roads, the car rental business is not well developed in the Camerons. The only one available is semi-official: contact Ravi at *Rainbow Garden Centre* (between *The Smokehouse* and Tanah Rata), T491782. If you are driving, remember to sound your horn at bends and beware of the lorries that hurtle along. If you are wondering why there are lorries on the road it is because there is a large replantation project under way as well as construction work.

Long distance Bus: a daily bus leaves KL's Puduraya terminal, for the Cameron Highlands, at 0830 (5 hrs) , but it gets heavily booked. The *Bintang Mas* bus service operates direct a/c buses from **KL** to Tanah Rata (leaving from Jln Pudu, at the foot of the pedestrian bridge to the Puduraya bus station), departing 0900 and 1530 daily (T2324285). Most other buses for the Cameron Highlands leave from **Tapah**, 67 km from Tanah Rata, regular hourly connections with **Brinchang** and **Tanah Rata** and with **Sungai Palas** and **Kampung Raja** (in the north of the Camerons). Tickets for the return journey can be booked at travel agents or at the bus station in Tanah Rata. There are 2 daily express buses from the Camerons to **KL**, leaving at 0830 and 1530, and one express bus to **Georgetown**, Penang, 0930. Regular connections from Tapah with **Ipoh**, KL, Butterworth, Kuantan, Melaka (5 hrs), and Singapore. Tickets can be reserved at *CS Travel & Tours*, Tanah Rata. **NB** Buses coming down from the Camerons tend to be more expensive. Express buses now go from **Tanah Rata** to **Penang**, via Ipoh at 0830 and 1430 (6 hrs). **Train**: the nearest station to the Camerons is Tapah Rd in Tapah, 67 km from Tanah Rata. Regular connections with **Ipoh**, **KL**, **Butterworth** 5 a day (6 hrs).

Banks All the banks are on Jln Besar. They include: *Arab-Malaysian Finance, Hong Kong Shanghai Bank, Maybank, Sampanian National* and *Visa Finance Berhad*. It is also possible to change money at *CS Travel & Tours*, next to *Roselane Hotel* and *Coffee House* on Jln Besar. **Communications** Internet cafés There are two cafés on Jln Camelia, RM5 per hr. *Highlands Computer Centre*, 39 Main Rd, RM4 per hr. General Post Office: next to the *Orient Hotel & Restaurant*, Jln Besar. **Medical facilities** Hospitals: opposite gardens at north end of town, on Jln Besar, T4911966. **Places of worship** Anglican: *All Souls' Church*, between Kampung Taman Sedia and golf course. Converted army Nissen hut with lich-gate in memory of Miss Griffith-Jones. Services 1030 Sun. **Useful addresses** District office: T4911455, alert this office if someone you know is long overdue after a jungle walk. **Police**: T4911222, opposite gardens at north end of town. | **Directory**

Northern Peninsula

Brinchang

Phone code: 05
Colour map1, grid C3

In recent years Brinchang, 7 km beyond Tanah Rata, on the far side of the golf course, has grown fast: since the mid-1980s several new hotels have sprung up, mainly catering for mass-market Malaysian Chinese and Singaporean package tourists. It is not a very beautiful little town, although the central square with its craft centre offers a small ray of interest.

Sam Poh Buddhist Temple, a popular sight with Chinese visitors who arrive by the coach load, is located just outside Brinchang, along Jalan Pecah Batu, overlooking the golf course. It is backed by the Gunung Bereman hills and comprises both a temple and monastery, which were built here in 1971. Emphasis is on size and grandeur, with monumental double gates with dragons at either side leading into the complex. The inner chamber with its six red-tiled pillars holds a vast golden effigy of a Buddha.

Sleeping

For budget travellers Tanah Rata has a better selection of accommodation. Price codes: see inside front cover

NB As for elsewhere in the region, it should be noted that during public holidays, accommodation gets fully booked and prices rise by 30-50%. It is also busy at peak school holiday periods of Apr, Aug and Dec. The cheapest form of accommodation is a shared bungalow between a group of people. Most bungalows have gardens, log fires and are away from the towns.

A-B *Jasmine Holiday Apartments*, 40 Jln Besar, T4912408, overlooking the main square. Attractive furnished flats of varying cost and size with cooking facilities, barbecue and rooftop garden. Recommended. **A** *Rosa Passadena*, T4912288, F4912688, E-mail: rosapsch@tn.net.my Large mock-Tudor concrete block, dominates Brinchang town centre, 120 rooms, bath, TV, in-house video, mini-bar, safe, restaurant, karaoke lounge. Rooms offer superb views of the surrounding Highlands. Restaurant serves everything from steaks to Chinese steamboats.

B *Country Lodge*, T4913071, F4911396. Located on hillside above Brinchang, typical black and white Tudor-style, décor rather on the severe side, parquet floors and rattan furniture, spacious standard and deluxe rooms as well as suites, restaurant, karaoke lounge. Price is for either hotel room or apartment; great value – dinner is sometimes included free to encourage custom. **B** *Hill Garden Lodge*, 15-16 Jln Besar, T4912988, F4912226. Bath, TV, clean. Rooms facing street noisy, discounts available in off-peak season. Nothing to get excited about. **B** *Iris Hotel* 56, Jln Kuari, T4911818, F4912828, irish@tm.net.my This place opened not too many years ago and although it looks pretty hideous – a doll's house on a grand scale – it is nonetheless good value. Rather sparsely furnished rooms have hot water and TV. Average restaurant. **B** *Parkland Hotel*, T901299, F901803, Modern 30-room hotel at edge of town, bath, TV, café, restaurants (coffee shop plus a Chinese restaurant with steamboat specialities), reasonable value for money, no frills.

Brinchang

To Tringkap, Kuala Terla & Kampung Raja

Jade Shopping Centre

7 KS Mini Market & Dept Store

Balai Kraftangan (Craft Centre)

Hawker's Centre

Toilets

Titiwangsa Tours & Travel

Jade Holidays

To Tanah Rata

■ Sleeping
1 Brinchang & Restaurant
2 Country Lodge
3 Garden Lodge
4 Iris
5 Kowloon & Restaurant
6 Pines & Roses
7 Rainbow Garden
8 Rosa Passadena
9 Silverstar & Restaurant

● Eating
1 Kwan Kee

N
Not to scale

B *Rainbow Hotel*, Lot 25, T4914628, F4914668. Nearly new place with 36 good-value comfortable rooms (but don't expect Conran, more like a dentist's waiting room) all with TVs and mini-bar. Good views on one side. Recommended, although there is no restaurant. **B** *Hotel Green Garden*, Lot 13, secretary 2, Main Rd. T4915834, F4915824, Mid-size hotel, a/c, attached bathroom, television. Laundry service, room service and taxis service available. Fairly standard, central location.

   C *Brinchang Hotel*, 36 Jln Besar, T4911755, F4911246. Hot showers, TV. Enthusiastic Indian owner, but rooms are scruffy, and some are windowless. **C** *Hotel New Plastro*, 19 Jln Besar, T4911009, mediocre. **C** *Kowloon Hotel*, 34-35 Jln Besar, T4911366, F4911803. Above popular Chinese restaurant, nice rooms with shower, good value for money (under the same management as the *Parkland Hotel*).

   C-D *Pines and Roses*, T4912205, F4912203 Good value family rooms with TV and water heater although basic furnishings, dorm also available, very clean. **D** *Silverstar Hotel*, T4911387. Shower, basic but good value. Restaurant on the ground floor.

Chinese Cheap *Brinchang*, below hotel of same name on Jln Besar, popular for its steamboat, good selection of vegetable dishes. Recommended. *Coco's*, 25 Jln Besar, cheap, good choice and good portions. *Kowloon*, busy restaurant, red tablecloths and clean, tiled floors, menu priced according to size of portion, lemon chicken and steamboat are popular. Recommended.

   International Mid-range *Parkland*, Grill restaurant in *Parkland Hotel*, steaks, breakfast menu. *Ferns Restaurant*, *Rosa Passadena Hotel*, Western and oriental, good-value buffet. **Foodstalls** Hawker stalls in the central square, open after 1600, good for satay and *roti*.

Eating
*Price codes:
see inside front cover*

Apart from a couple of karaoke bars that have recently sprung up in the town, any nightlife that exists takes place in the *Rosa Passadena Hotel*.

Entertainment

Golf *Cameron Highlands Golf Club*, (see Tanah Rata, page 128).

Sports

Jade Holidays, 37a and b Jln Bandar, T4912318, F4912071, for local tours, air and bus tickets, accommodation bookings, jungle trekking; *Titiwangsa Tours & Travel*, 36 Jln Besar, T4912122, F4911246, similar services to *Jade Holidays*.

Tour operators
*See Tanah Rata,
page 129*

Local Taxis are available for local travel and can be chartered for about RM15 per hr. For travel between Tanah Rata, Brinchang and Tapah it is easy enough to climb aboard one of the buses that travels this route through the day.

Transport
*See Tanah Rata,
page 129*

Banks *Public Bank*, next to *Hill Garden Lodge*. **Communications** General Post Office: opposite the Petronas petrol station at the north end of the town. **Medical services** See Tanah Rata, page 129. **Useful addresses** Police: in central square, next to children's playground.

Directory

Around Brinchang

Up the hill from Brinchang the Cameron Highlands becomes one big market garden and the terrain becomes increasingly steep and hilly. One of the first market gardens outside Brinchang, just after the army camp on the left, is *Uncle Sam's Farm*. The farm specializes in the cultivation of the kaffir lily, as well as strawberries, oranges, apples and a selection of cacti. Beyond Uncle Sam's, 4 km up the road from Brinchang, there is a large market selling local produce to eager customers from the plains below.

Northern Peninsula

Northern Peninsula

Sights   The Cameronian climate is particularly suited to the cultivation of vegetables more usually associated with temperate climates. Cabbages, cauliflowers, carrots and tomatoes, as well as fruit such as strawberries and passion fruit, are taken by truck from the Camerons to the supermarkets of KL and Singapore. **Kea Farm**, with its neatly terraced hillsides, is down the first right turn after the market area. At the Kea turning, on the main road, Kea Farm has a small shop and café and restaurant called the *Strawberry View*. Here, perched on the hillside is the *Equatorial Hill Resort* (**AL**), T4961777, F4961333. This is a monstrosity of more than 500 rooms, very mock Tudor in style, with all the facilities of a four-star hotel – a heated pool, tennis, squash, bowling alley, Cineplex. Not exactly an intimate little place.

The **Butterfly Garden** is past the Kea Farm turning. There is a large shop attached to the garden, where everything from framed dead butterflies to Cameronian souvenirs (beetles embedded in key rings) is on sale. Outside there are fruit and vegetable stalls – all very popular with Chinese visitors. ■ *0800-1700 Mon-Sun, about RM2.50.*

The **Rose Garden** is 2 km further up the mountain. To get there, take the first left turn after the butterfly farm, on Jalan Gunung Brinchang, at what is known as the Green Cow area; a village there was burned to the ground by the Communists during the insurgency. A few kilometres beyond the Rose Garden, continue up Jalan Gunung Besar, which is a very picturesque narrow road, on the right is a turning for one of the Boh tea plantations – the **Sungai Palas**. There are guided tours of the Sungai Palas tea processing factory every 10 minutes from Tuesday-Sunday. The newly built visitors' centre has a video about tea cultivation that you can watch and a shop, as well as a charming terrace where you can order a pot of tea and enjoy the dramatic view across the steeply terraced tea plantations.

Back at the Green Cow area, the main road, the C7, continues into the mountains, finally ending at the **Blue Valley Tea Estate**, 13 km from the junction with Jalan Gunung Brinchang. Midway along the C7, at the village of Trinkap, a right turn leads to a large rose-growing establishment, **Rose Valley**. It boasts 450 varieties of rose including the thornless rose, the black rose, and the green rose, said to be the ugliest of the rose family. It also has a cactus plantation where some of the plants are 40 years old and lays claim to having the largest flower vase in Malaysia. ■ *0800-1800 daily, adults RM3, children RM1.50.*

Ipoh

Population: 500,000
Phone code: 05
Colour map 1, grid C3

The northern state of Perak is known for its tin ore (mainly in the Kinta Valley) and Ipoh, its capital, is Malaysia's third city. The city is situated in the Kinta Valley, between the Main Range and the Keledang Mountains, to the west. There are some fine examples of colonial architecture in the Old Town and outerlying areas housing among other notable sights the Perak Darul Ridzuan Museum which provides an interesting insight into Ipoh's history. Within easy reach of the city is the Sma Poh Tong, the largest cave temple in the area, and Perak Tong, one of the largest Chinese temples in Malaysia.

Ins and outs

Ipoh's airport is 15 km south of town; regular domestic connections with JB, KK, **Getting there**
Kuching, Penang, and Kota Bharu and international connections with Medan in Sumatra (Indonesia). From the train station on the edge of town there are connections with
Butterworth and KL as well as south to Singapore and north to Hat Yai in Thailand. Ipoh
is on the main N-S highway and there are regular connections with just about everywhere of any size on the Peninsular. The long-distance bus terminal is several km north
of town and requires a taxi or bus ride to reach. Share taxis are a available for journeys
to KL, Butterworth, Taiping, Alor Star and Tapah.

There are local car hire firms and taxis are also available. However, Taiping is not a large **Getting around**
place and it is perfectly possible to walk around the town. The grid layout of Taiping's
streets makes navigation a doddle.

None of Ipoh's three tourist offices offer much in the way of help and assistance, bar a **Tourist offices**
map. *Ipoh City Council Tourist Office*, Jln Abdul Adil, open 0800-1245 and 1400-1615
Mon-Thu, 0800-1212 and 1400-1615 Fri, 0800-1245 Sat. *Perak Tourist Information
Centre*, State Economic Planning Unit, Pejabat Setiausaha Kerajaan, Jln Panglima Bukit
Gantang Wahab, open 0800-1245, 1400-1615 Mon-Thu, 0800-1215, 1445-1615 Fri,
0800-1245 Sat, closed Sun, T2412957, F2418173. *Tourist Information*, Casuarina Hotel,
18 Jln Gopeng, T2532008.

Ipoh is named after the abundance of the huge, elusive ipoh (or *upas*) trees
that once grew there; the Orang Asli tribes procured the poison for their blowpipe darts from its fabled lethal sap. It was known as the deadliest poison in the
world. The city also has an abundance of imposing limestone outcrops. These
jungle-topped hills, with their precipitous white cliffs, are riddled with passages and caves, many of which have been made into cave temples.

In its early days, Ipoh's citizens became wealthy on the back of the tin- mining industry. In 1884 the Kinta Valley tin rush brought an influx of Chinese
immigrants to Ipoh; many made their fortunes and built opulent town
houses. Chinese immigrants have bequeathed what is now one of Malaysia's
best-preserved Chinatowns (the 'Old Town'). In the 1880s Ipoh vied with
Kuala Lumpur to be the capital of the Federated States of Malaya, and long
after KL took the title, Ipoh remained the commercial 'hub of Malaya'. The
city has long had an active 'flesh trade': there are frequent round-ups of Thai
and Burmese prostitutes who are smuggled across Malaysia's north border.

Few tourists spend long in Ipoh – most are en route to Penang, KL or
Pulau Pangkor. Those who do stay rarely regret it: there are excellent Chinese restaurants (a speciality is the rice noodle dish, *sar hor fun*, which literally means 'melts in your mouth'), Buddhist temples and examples of Straits
Chinese architecture. It is also a good place to pick up Chinese imported
goods, such as baskets and chinaware. The shophouses on and around Jalan
Yau Tet Shin make for good browsing. Ipoh also has a handful of very
well-established bakers. On Jalan Raja Eleram the two bakeries here have
been in the business for well over 50 years. They specialize in French bread,
buns and cakes.

Sights

The Kinta River, spanned by the Hugh Low Bridge, separates the old and new
parts of town. The **Old Town** is centred on the river between Jalan Sultan Idris

Shah and Jalan Sultan Iskander Shah, and is known for its old Chinese and British colonial architecture, particularly on Jalan Sultan Yusuf, Jalan Leech and Jalan Treacher.

Prominent landmarks include the **Birch Memorial**, a clock tower erected in memory of the first British resident of Perak, JWW Birch. His murder in 1875 was one of colonial Malaya's first anti-British incidents and the three perpetrators, after being hanged, promptly became local heroes, which they remain to this day. The four panels decorating the base of the tower depict the development of civilization; the upper part of the tower holds a bust of JWW Birch who was, local history relates, not well-liked in the area. The Moorish-style **railway station** (off Jalan Kelab), built in 1917, bears close resemblance to its Kuala Lumpur counterpart, and is known as the 'Taj Mahal' of Ipoh. The *Station Hotel* has recently reopened and is a colonial classic worth noticing. **Ipoh Town Hall**, with its Palladian façade, stands opposite. A solitary ipoh tree stands in the centre of **Taman DR Seenivasagam** (a park north of the centre). The park also contains an artificial lake and a children's playground. There are also **Japanese Gardens**, complete with a typical Japanese carp pond, nearby on Jalan Tambun. ■ *1600-2000 Mon-Fri, 0900-2000 Sat-Sun*. The **Geological Museum**, on Lorong Hariman, out of town centre, was set up in 1957. It is known for its exhibition of tin ore and collection of fossils and precious stones, as well as over 600 samples of minerals. ■ *0800-1615 Mon-Fri, 0800-1245 Sat. Free, but entry permission from the information counter is necessary*. On Jalan SP Seenivasagam there is an old colonial mission **school** with an impressive white stone façade and an Indian **mosque** next door.

Ipoh

To Perak Darul Ridzuan Museum, Perak Tong, Kuala Kangsar, Taiping & Butterworth (Rt 1)

To YMCA

Taman DR Seenivasagam

St Michael's School

Indian Mosque

Royal Ipoh Club

Ipoh Padang

Jln SP Seenivasagam

Jln Dato Onn Jaffar

Jln Sultan Yusuf

Jln Tun S Sambanthan

Jln Dato M Lela

Jln Sultan Idris Shah

Infoweb Station

Jln Raja Musa Aziz

Jln Sultan Abdul Jalil

To Japanese Gardens & Tambun

Birch Memorial Clock Tower

Ipoh Town Hall

State Mosque

Jln Pasar

Jln Laksamania

Central

Jln Mustapha Al-Bakri

Jln Dato Tahwil Azhar

Jln Raja Ekram

To Kellie's Castle, Sam Poh Tong & Kuala Lumpur

Jln Panglima Bukit Gantang Wahab

Jln Hill

Jln Leech

Jln Birch

Jln Treacher

Jln Sultan Iskander Shah

Jln Masjid

Jln Cross

Local

To Lumut

Express Long Distance

Jln Lahat

Kinta River

To Tapah Road & Kuala Lumpur

To Lumut

Jln Datoh

Jln Yang Kalsom

Jln Ali Pitchay

To Sam Poh Tong Temple

A

N

Detailed map
A Ipoh detail,
page 137

0 metres   100
0 yards   100

■ Sleeping
1 Eastern
2 French
3 Grandview & Restaurant
4 Lotte
5 Majestic (or Station)
6 New Hollywood
7 Ritz Garden

● Eating
1 Blue Window Café
2 Rahman

Heading out of town, past St Michael's School, on Jalan Panglima Bukit Gantang Wahab, after about 500m on the right is an elegant, white colonial building, which houses the **Perak Darul Ridzuan Museum**. The building, which is over 100 years old, once the home of Malay dignitaries of Kinta, now houses a collection that illustrates the history of Ipoh, and mining and forestry within the state. ■ *0900-1600 Sat-Wed, 0900-1200 Thu.*

Excursions

Down the road to Batu Gajah, just to the south of Ipoh (about a 30-minute drive), is the eccentric edifice of Scotsman William Kellie Smith, a late-19th-century rubber tycoon. He shipped in Tamil workers from South India to build his fanciful Moorish-style mansion, and, following an outbreak of fever, allowed them to build the Sri Maha Mariamman Hindu temple in the grounds, about 500 m from the castle. Another story has it that Mr Smith built the temple in 1902, when his prayers for a son and heir were answered after six years of marriage. An image of Smith is among the sculpted Hindu pantheon on the temple roof.

The castle was never completed as Smith left in the middle of its construction and died in Portugal on a business trip (local rumour has it, after inhaling the smoke of a poisoned cigar). During the Second World War the grounds of the castle were used by the Japanese as an execution area; locals say that the tall trees were used as makeshift gallows. No wonder the place is presumed to be haunted: although the wine cellar is open, the rest of the subterranean rooms are closed to visitors. A white bridge leading to the castle was completed in 1994. ■ *0830-1930 Mon-Sun, RM0.50.*

Kellie's Castle

At Gunung Rapat, 5 km south of Ipoh, is the largest of the cave temples in the area. There are Buddha statues among the stalactites and stalagmites. The temple was founded 100 years ago by a monk who lived and meditated in the cave for 20 years and it has been inhabited by monks ever since. The only break was during the Japanese occupation when the cave was turned into a Japanese ammunition and fuel dump. There is a pond at the entrance where locals release turtles to gain merit while young boys sell turtle food to earn money. ■ *0730-1800, Mon-Sun. Getting there: Kampar bus No 66. En route for KL, it is on the left side of the road, but watch out, as you need to take a sudden turn to enter the parking lot; the entrance is opposite a Mobil petrol station and the temple is named Ling Sen Tong.*

Sam Poh Tong

One of the largest Chinese temples in Malaysia is 6½ km north of Ipoh on Jalan Kuala Kangsar. Built in 1926 by a Buddhist priest from China, the temple houses over 40 Buddha statues and mystical traditional Chinese-style murals depicting legends. It is visited by thousands of pilgrims every year and is the most ornately decorated of the many cave temples at the base of the 122 m limestone hill. A path beyond the altar leads into the cave's interior and up a brick stairway to an opening 100 m above ground with a view of the surrounding countryside. Another climb leads to a painting of Kuan Yin, Goddess of Mercy, who looks out from the face of the limestone cliff. A 15-m-high reinforced concrete statue of the Buddha stands in the compound. ■ *0900-1600 Mon-Sun. Getting there: Kuala Kangsar bus or city bus No 3.*

Perak Tong

Northern Peninsula

Gua Tambun
(Tambun Cave)

Traces of a civilization dating back 10,000 years were discovered at these caves, 3 km from Ipoh near Tambun, in the 1930s. The ochre drawings on the cave walls and the limestone cliffs depict the life of prehistoric man; especially interesting is the 'Degong' fish, a drawing of a large fish that feeds on meat, rather like a piranha. **Tambun Hot Springs** nestle at the foot of this limestone hill. The Japanese were responsible for their initial development during the occupation. Two swimming pools have been built – one filled with lukewarm water and one with hot. There also saunas. ■ *Caves open 0900-1600 Mon-Sun, RM5. Hot springs open 1500-2400 Mon-Sun. Getting there: Tambun bus, a 15-min drive from Ipoh.*

Essentials

Sleeping
■ *on maps, pages 134 & 137*
Price codes: see inside front cover

A *Casuarina*, 18 Jln Gopeng, out of town, T2505555, F2508177. Over 200 rooms, a/c, restaurant, pool, Ipoh's finest but not central. **A** *Central*, 26 Jln Ali Pitchay, T2424777, F2424555. A/c, recently upgraded. Oriental atmosphere. **A** *Syuen*, 88 Jln Sultan Abdul Jalil, T2538889, F2640580, syuenht@tm.net.my A/c, 10 food and beverage outlets, central and new hotel with real style, 300 rooms, overlooking the bougainvillea park, a/c, TV, mini-bar, comfortable and well-furbished rooms, discotheque, the *Car Disco*, one of Malaysia's new night spots, pool, business centre, sauna, tennis. Recommended.

B *A-House Ipoh Station Hotel* aka *Majestic Hotel*, Bangunan Stesyen Keretapi, Jln Panglima Bukit Gantang Wahab, T2555605, F2553393. A/c, restaurant, 100 rooms, managed by the Singapore-based A-House group of hotels. Old-colonial-style décor has been retained, good range of facilities from in-house movies to a health service, well run and priced. **B** *Eastern*, 118 Jln Sultan Idris Shah, T2543936, F2501468. Small and rather grim 1970s building, a/c, restaurant and in-house videos. **B** *Excelsior*, 43 Jln Sultan Abdul Jalil, T2536666, F2536912. A/c, restaurants; with the new tower block, one of the tallest buildings in Ipoh, added in 1994, the hotel now has over 150 rooms. Hotel organizes golf trips to local courses. **B** *Grandview Hotel*, 36 Jln Horley, T2431488, F2431811. Opened Jun 1999, shower, ac, TV, restaurant. Although lacking in character, the clean and tasteful furnishings, along with the friendly and efficient service, make this one of the best value options in town. **B** *Tambun Inn*, 91 Jln Tambun, T577211. Located 4 km from city centre, most rooms are deluxe double, which are priced at upper end of **B** category but offer good value, TV, a/c, in-house video, health centre, karaoke lounge.

C *Cathay*, 90-94 Jln CM Yussuf, south of town, T2413322. Some a/c and private bathrooms, noisy and rather grubby, plenty of furniture, security poor. **C** *Fair Park*, 85 Jln Kamaruddin Isa, T2547129. The newest budget hotel in Ipoh, near DBI Sports Centre. Recommended. **C** *Fairmont*, 10 Jln Kampar, T2559999, F2556352. Bath, car park and a good-value restaurant. **C** *French*, 60-62 Jln Dato Onn Jaafar, T2533111, F2552975. Another uninspiring small concrete block, a/c, restaurant. Real 1970s atmosphere – out of date in every way. **C** *Lotte*, 97 Jln Dato Onn Jaafar, T2542215, F2551160. Its well-maintained exterior is hugely deceptive. Rooms are basic; shower, a/c. **C** *Merloon*, 92-98 Jln Mustapha al-Bakri, T2541351, F2536755. Has recently undergone an inspirational name change from *Merlin*. A/c, shower, restaurant. Clean but basic for the price – many better options. **C** *New Hollywood*, 72-76 Jln Yussuf, T2415404. Restaurant, kept clean and the room rates are reasonable but there is little to mark this place out in any way. **C** *Ritz Garden*, 78 Jln C M Yussuf, T2547777, F2545222. A/c, bath, TV, in-house video, mini-bar, coffee house, health centre, sauna, not exactly oozing character but the rooms are well priced. Restaurant recently closed. **C** *Ritz Kowloon*, 92-96 Jln Yang Kalsom, T2547778, F2533800. Run by a charming Indian owner; a/c, TV, in-house video, safe, tastefully furnished rooms.

Northern Peninsula

Recommended. **C** *Robin*, 106-110 Jln Mustapha al-Bakri, T2413755, F2541818. A/c, rooms with TV and mini-bar. Attached to a restaurant and health club. **C** *YMCA*, 211 Jln Raja Musa Aziz, take a small path along the river to get here, T2540809. Tennis courts, dorm beds available (**E**), this place is good value and the grounds as well as the rooms are spacious, but the location is inconvenient.

D *Golden Inn*, 17 Jln Che Tak, T2530866. A/c, efficiently run. Recommended. **D** *New Winner* (*Wanwah*), 32-38 Jln Ali Pitchay, T2415177. Some a/c, a bit archaic but good value and very clean. Helpful staff. The disco directly below can be a bit noisy. **D** *Shanghai*, 85 Jln Mustapha al-Bakri. Fan only, shower, restaurant, clean and central. Although in need of modernizing this is the best budget option in town.

Ipoh is well known for its Chinese food, especially Ipoh chicken rice and *kway teow* – liquid and fried versions. The pomelo and the seedless guava are both grown in the state of Perak, and the state is also known for its delicious groundnuts.

Malay Mid-range *Perwira*, Medan Gopeng, 3 km south of town centre, before Sam Poh Tong. *Sabar Menanti*, Jln Raja Musa Aziz. *Semenanjung*, Jln Sultan Idris Shah. **Cheap** *Eshan*, Jln Yang Kalsom, open 24 hrs, very popular with locals, good, cheap food and very friendly staff (though limited English spoken).

Chinese Mid-range *Central*, 51-53 Cowan St. **Cheap** *Foh San*, Jln Osbourne, *dim sum*. *Kawan*, Jln Sultan Iskandar Shah, also Malay and Indian dishes. *Kok Kee*, 272 Jln Sultan Iskandar Shah. *Ming Court*, 36 Jln Leong Sin Nam, *dim sum*. *Mung Cheong*, 511 Jln Pasir Putih, Cantonese. *Nam Thim Tong*, Mile 3.5 Gopeng Rd, Chinese, vegetarian, serves ersatz meat dishes made of soya bean. **Seriously cheap** *Chuan Fong*, 175 Jln Sultan Iskandar, speciality is curry *laksa*. *Foh San, 2 Osbourne St*, popular for Hong Kong *dim sum*, served 0600-1200. *Woh Heng Coffee Shop*, Osbourne St, good rice and noodles.

Indian Mid-range *Comfy Corner*, 61 Jln Pasar. *Gopal Corner*, Buntong. *Guru's Chapati*, *Cheong Seng Restaurant Complex*, Lebuh Raya Ipoh, Punjabi. Recommended. *Krishna Bhawan*, 8 Jln Lahat. **Cheap** *Majeedia*, Jln Dendahara/Jln Leong Boon Swee. *Rahman*, 78 Jln CM Yussuf, good food, with banana pancakes or *roti* for breakfast. Friendly, chatty owner. *Shal's Curry House*, 4 Jln Dato Maharaja Lela, a/c, excellent South Indian food and good vegetarian dishes. Recommended. **Seriously cheap** *Mohamad Ibrahim*, 786 Jln Yang Kalsom, speciality is *mee rebus*. **International Expenive** *Royal Casuarina Coffee House*, and *Il Ritrove*, Italian restaurant specializing in nouvelle cuisine, 18 Jln Gopeng. **Mid-range** *Blue Window Café*, 56 Jln Dato Onn Jaafar, Western food, aspires to 'romantic' atmosphere. *Station Hotel Coffee House*, Jln Kelab. **Cheap** *Excelsior Hotel Coffee House*, 43 Jln Clarke. *Ever Fresh Juice Station*, 21 Jln Mustapha al Bakri, good fresh juice bar. *Nam Shan Thai SeaFood Restaurant*, 29

Eating
● *on map, page 134*
Price codes:
see inside front cover

Northern Peninsula

Ipoh detail

Sleeping	
1 Casuarina	6 Merloon
2 Cathay	7 New Winner
3 Central	8 Ritz Kowloon
4 Excelsior	9 Shanghai
5 Fairmont	10 Syuen

N

0 metres 100
0 yards 100

Related map
A Ipoh, page 134

Jln Yau Tet Shin. A very friendly and helpful manager, with great command of the English language. Excellent value Thai and Chinese food.

Foodstalls Jln Clarke, Jln Dewan, Ipoh Garden, Jln Sultan Idris Shah, mainly Chinese stalls. *Railway Station*, Jln Kelab. Recommended. *Wooley Food Centre*, Canning Gardens. On Jln Ali Pitchay is *Restoran Impressive Foodstalls*, cheap (RM10), clean and new. Recommended.

Sports   **Golf** *Royal Perak Golf Club*, Jln Sultan Azlan Shah, 3 km from town centre, 18-hole course laid out over 420 ha, only open to visitors on weekdays, members only at weekends and holidays, green fees RM150, caddy fee RM20, clubhouse facilities include bowling alley, cards and billiards room, and bar. **Racing**   Races held every Sat and Sun at *Perak Turf Club*. **Swimming**   *DBI Sports Complex*, Perak Sports Centre, Lebuh Raya Thivy, T5460651. Largest swimming complex in Southeast Asia. Other facilities include: tennis, indoor badminton, table tennis, volleyball, basketball, a velodrome rugby pitch, stadium. Admission charge. Open 0900-2100 Mon-Sun.

Tour operators   *Fiyen Travels*, 1-3 Jln Che Tak, T2533455, F2506709, sightseeing tours, hotel reservations, domestic and international air ticketing. *Reliance*, Lot 1-12 1st Flr, Bangunan Sri Kinta, Jln Sultan Idris Shah, T2518711, F2538458, ticketing, travel shop, travel insurance. *HWA Yik Tour & Travel*, 23 Jln Che Tak, T2504060, F2530118, tours, hotel reservation, domestic and international air ticketing, mini-bus rental. *K & C Travel & Tours*, 250 Jln Sultan Iskandar, T2506999, F2502154, airline ticketing, hotel reservation, travel insurance, foreign exchange. *Deluxe Tours*, 58 Jln Dato Tahwil Azhar (Jln Osbourne), T2537260, F2558969, air ticketing, tours, hotel reservations. *Heris Express Travel Agency*, T2416999.

Transport
250 km to KL
161 km to Butterworth

Local   **Car hire**: *Avis*, Sultan Azian Shah Airport, T206586; *Hertz*, Royal Casuarina Hotel, 18 Jln Gopeng, T2505533, and Sultan Azlan Shah Airport, T3127109. **Taxi**: if you want to order a taxi try the *Nam Taxi Company*, 15 Jln Raja Mus Aziz, T2412189. Also *Radiocab*, T2540241.

Long distance   **Air**: Sultan Azlan Shah Airport, T3122459, approximately 15 km south of town, RM10 taxi ride. Regular connections with **Johor Bahru** (55 mins), **Kota Bharu**, **Kota Kinabalu**, **KL** (30 mins), **Penang** (25 mins) and **Kuching** on *MAS*. *MAS* provides quite a few international connections from Ipoh.

Train: Ipoh is on the main north-south line. Five daily connections with **Butterworth** and **KL**, T2540481. One train daily to **Singapore** (1100), and **Hat Yai** (0845). See page 45 for timetable. **Bus**: Ipoh is on the main north-south road and is well connected. The bus terminal is at the intersection of Jln Kelab, Kidd and Silbin (known as Medan Kidd), a short taxi trip from the town centre. Buses to **Taiping** and **Kuala Kangsar** leave from the local bus terminal. Regular connections with **Butterworth**, **KL** (3 hrs), **Alor Star**, **Kuantan**, **Sungai Petani**, **Johor Bahru**, **Kangar**, **Kuala Perlis**, **Taiping**, **Lumut** and **Tapah** (90 mins). There are also services to **Kota Bharu** and **Grik/Gerik**. An express coach company has a booking office at 2 Jln Bendahara, T535367. They operate a daily service to Singapore, Johor Bahru, KL, Butterworth, Penang, Lumut, Alor Star and Kuala Kangsar. **Taxi**: shared taxis leave from beside the bus station for KL, Butterworth, Taiping, Alor Star, Tapah.

Connections with Hat Yai in southern **Thailand** and **Singapore** (0900, 1400, 1900, 2100, RM25), T2412182.

Directory   **Airline offices**   *MAS*, Lot 108 Bangunan Seri Kinta, Jln Sultan Idris Shah, T2414155. **Banks**   *Bank Bumiputra*, *Malayan Banking*, *Hock Hua Bank* and *Maybank* are all on

Jln Sultan Idris Shah; *UMBC*, *Oriental Bank* and *Public Bank*, are on Jln Yang Kalsom; in the new town, along Jln Sultan Yussuf there is a *Southern Bank*, *Hong Kong Bank*, *Standard Chartered* and *Bank of Commerce*. *K & C Travel* (see Tour operators, page 138) also have foreign exchange facilities. **Communications** Internet cafés: *Infoweb Station*, Jln Dato Onn Jaafar, near Jln Sultan Idris Shah. There is another café on Jln Dato Onn Jaafar next to the Post Office, RM2. Avoid early afternoon, when it's full of school children. **General Post Office:** next to the railway station on Jln Panglima Bukit Gantang Wahab. There is another Post Office on Jln Dato Onn Jaafar.

Lumut

Lumut is primarily a base for the Royal Malaysian Navy, which has a population of around 25,000, compared with a populace of 1,000 in Lumut itself. The naval base houses the **Royal Malaysian Navy Museum** (closed Friday). Lumut is also a transit point for Pulau Pangkor, and in recent years it has also begun tentatively to develop as a holiday destination in its own right. The *Orient Star*, a new international-class hotel, looms large on the coast and apartment blocks are rearing their ugly heads on the hilltop of Bukit Engku Busu. The town is at its zenith during the *Pesta Laut*, a sea festival, which takes place every August at nearby Teluk Batik.

Colour map 1, grid C2
Lumut has most definitely forsaken its sleepy fishing village identity for that of a busy seaside town

Teluk Batik, 7 km south of Lumut, is a popular beach spot (often used by the naval base), with chalets, food stalls and changing rooms backing the sweeping, sandy bay. There is another good sandy beach at **Teluk Rubiah,** a further 6 km south, near the Teluk Rubia Royal Golf Club (T2619555), which has a pool and tennis courts in addition to the golf course.

AL *Swiss-Garden Resort*, 101-107 Jln Titi Panjang, T6183333. New, clinical feel, but has good facilities. **AL-A** *Orient Star*, Lot 203 and 366, Jln Iskandar Shah, T6834199, F6834223, tosrlso@po.jaring.my A hotel with 150 a/c rooms, TV, in-house video, mini fridge, free-form pool with swim-up bar, paddling pool, gymnasium, jet-ski hire, bicycle hire, coffee house, bar, palatial in size and décor, pleasantly furnished rooms with balconies and sea views but no beach. A classy place that sometimes offers excellent discounts. **A-B** *Blue Bay Resort*, T6836939, F6836239. Breakfast included in room rate. TV, tea/coffee-making facilities, complimentary newspaper, late check-out (1500), pool, a/c. Jungle and fishing treks organized, also Island cruises. Two restaurants. Great value although it looks a little spartan.

Sleeping
Price codes: see inside front cover

B *Hotel Putra*, Jln Iskandar Shah, T6838000, F6837228, dayaent@po.jaring.my New hotel, fully a/c, baths in all bedrooms, TV, telephone, tea/coffee-making facilities, some rooms with lovely view over bay towards Pangkor. Restaurant. Breakfast included in room rate. Good value. **B** *Lumut Country Resort*, 331 Jln Titi Panjang, T6835109, F6835396. A hotel with 44 a/c rooms, swimming pool, paddling pool, tennis courts, does not quite measure up to the *Orient Star*, but has some attractive features such as hand-printed batik bed covers and wooden floors. Disco, function room. Very good value; one of the best deals in town. **B/C** *Galaxy Inn*, Jln Sultan Idris Shah, T6838731, F6838732. Clean and simple rooms with attached bathrooms, a/c, apartments available for monthly rental. Seating area with television in foyer. Situated on the sea front.

C *Harbour View Hotel*, Lot 13 and 14, Jln Titi Panjang, T6837888, F6837088. Small, quiet hotel on main road along sea front, a/c, TV, mini fridge, tea/coffee-making facilities, bathroom. Recommended. Good value. **C** *Hotel Indah*, 208 Jln Iskandar Shah, T6835064, F6834220. One of the newer budget hotels on the main road along the coast, a/c, TV, hot shower, adjoining coffee house, simply furbished and very clean, with pleasant views over the esplanade. Family run with seating area and café. **C-D** *Lumut Villa Inn*, Batu 1,

Northern Peninsula

Jln Sitiawan, T6835982, F6836563. Inconveniently located outside the town if you do not have your own transport, but good value for money, rooms without a/c (**D**).

D *Phin Lum Hooi*, 93 Jln Titi Panjang, T6835641. The cheapest place around, rooms are clean (shared bathrooms) and the management friendly. Not far from the jetty, popular with local navy, so can be noisy in the restaurant downstairs, best budget option.

Eating
Price codes: see inside front cover

Chinese Mid-range *Ocean Seafood Restaurant*, 115 Jln Tit Panjang, a/c, specializes in seafood. *Sin Pinamhui*, 93-95 Jln Titi Panjang, traditional Chinese food. **Cheap** *Phin Lum Hooi*, next to Chinese Temple on Jln Titi Panjang, cheap Chinese coffee-shop fare. **Indian Cheap** *Restoran Samudera Raya*, 39 Jln Sultan Idris Shah, Indian and Malay food. **International Cheap** *Jook Joint*, Jln Sultan Idris Shah, bistro food for a change from rice and *roti*. *Kentucky Fried Chicken*, Jln Sultan Abdullah. *Makanan Laut Ocean Restaurant*, Jln Titi Panjang, fresh fish dishes available. **Malay Cheap** *Nasi Kandar*, 46 Jln Sultan Idris Shah, friendly and clean, with excellent rice and *roti*. Serves good vegetarian rice. Recommended. *Kedai Makan Sin Pinamhui* (*Green House Restaurant*), 95 Jln Titi Panjang. Another worthwhile Malay place to try; open 1030-1445 and 1715-2045, closed Thu.

Bars

New bars (and restaurants) are springing up along the sea front, possibly due to Navy influence and growing popularity of Pulau Pangkor. Bars serve beer on tap and are more often than not Western – as in Wild West – themed.

Transport
183 km to KL
170 km to Butterworth
83 km to Ipoh

Bus The bus station is in the centre of town, a few mins' walk from the jetty. Regular connections with **Ipoh**, **KL** and **Butterworth** and less regular connections with **Melaka** and **Tapah** (for the Cameron Highlands). Bus every 30 mins from Ipoh (1 hr 45 mins). Buses also run between Lumut and Singapore.

Ferry Regular crossings, at least every 30 mins from 0645 to 2000 from Lumut Jetty to **Pangkor village** on **Pangkor Island**. The crossing takes under 1 hr, half price for children. Crossings every 2 hrs from 0845 to 1830 to Pan Pacific Resort at north end of Pangkor Island. For further information contact *Lumut Ferry Station*, T935541, or *White Yellow Black Ferry*, Kompleks Kraftangan and Pusat Pemandu Pelancong, T934062. Crossings from the jetty are available every ½ hour from the companies combined.

Taxi Services available to **Ipoh**, **KL** and **Butterworth**.

International connections with Sumatra: *Kuala Perlis Langkawi Ferry Service* (*KPLFS*), T6854258, run a service between Lumut and **Belawan**, Medan's port in Sumatra, Indonesia. The service leaves Lumut at 1000 on Thu and returns from Belawan on Wed at 1100 (3½ hrs). *Indomas Express* also operates boats on this route. Both companies charge RM90 one way, RM160 return and

Lumut

Custom Office

Hilltop Development

Perak Yacht Club

Jln Titi Panjang

Jln Rajah Muda Musa

Chinese Temple

Clock Tower

Jln Dato H Ishak

Jln Pangkor

Taxi

Jln Husdsan

Jln Sultan Idris Shah

Lumut Jetty

Shops & Stalls

Jln Sultan Yusoff Izzudin

K Perlis-Langkawi Ferry Service

Jln Sultan Abdullah

Jln Iskandar Shah

Jln Sultan Aziz

To Pulau Pangkor & Medan (Sumatra)

To Kuala Lumpur, Ipoh, Penang & Sitiawan

N

0 metres 500
0 yards 500

■ **Sleeping**
1 Blue Bay Resort
2 Harbour View
3 Lumut Country Resort
4 Orient Star
5 Putra
6 Swiss Garden Resort

● **Eating**
1 Makanan Laut Ocean
2 Nasi Kandar
3 Ocean Seafood
4 Phin Lum Hooi

both include bus connections between Belawan and Medan. In Medan tickets for *Indomas* can also be booked through *Tobali Tour and Travel*, Jln Juanda Baru 52 and for *KPLFS* through *Indoma Citra Agung*, Jln Katamso 33D.

Banks *Pengurup Wang Raya*, 47 Jln Sultan Idris Shah; Bank Bumiputera Jln Sultan Idris   **Directory**
Shah. *Bank Simpanan Nasional*, Jln Sultan Idris Shah. **Communications** General Post
Office: Jln Dato JK Ishak. **Tourist offices** *Lumut Tourist Information Centre*, Jln Titi
Panjang (near petrol station), T6834057, not open on a regular basis.

Pulau Pangkor

Just 7 km across the Straits from Lumut is Pangkor, one of the most easily   *Colour map 1, grid C2*
accessible islands in Malaysia. It was on board a British ship anchored off the   *Population: 25,000*
island that the historic Treaty of Pangkor was signed in 1874, granting the   *Phone code: 05*
British entry into the Malay States for the first time.   *90 km SW of Ipoh*

Pangkor is one of the largest fish suppliers in Peninsular Malaysia. Old   *Before the Second*
Pangkor has the fishing villages of Sungai Pinang Kecil, Sungai Pinang Besar   *World War the*
and Pangkor (main village). Modern Pangkor to the north has a modern lux-   *island was used*
ury resort. To the southwest is the tiny island of Pangkor Laut. The main   *as a leper colony*
island is pretty but gets very busy, particularly at weekends and during school
holidays, as it is one of the few places on the west coast with good beaches.
Although it does not have the same heady atmosphere of some of the east
coast islands, it has a more laid-back, local feel to it, comparable to Langkawi
but on a smaller scale.

Some of the best beaches and coral can be found on nearby islands, such as
Emerald Bay on Pangkor Laut, a private island only open to guests of the resort
there (see Sleeping, page 142). Emerald Bay is the spot where F Spencer Chapman escaped from Malaya after three years fighting the Japanese behind enemy
lines, all recounted in his book *The Jungle is Neutral*. There are some hidden
beaches on the main island. North of **Pasir Bogak**, the most developed beach,
turtles lay their eggs right on **Teluk Ketapang** beach, mainly during May, June
and July. North of this are two of the best beaches **Coral Bay** (Teluk Nipah) and
Golden Sands (Teluk Belanga). The most popular beach is at Pasir Bogak. Visitors can also take boats to Pulau Mentangor and Pulau Sembilan.

There are good walks round the island: it takes nearly a day to walk all the   *For such a small place,*
way round; half a day by bicycle; and two to three hours by motorcycle. Note,   *circumnavigating the*
however, that the route is quite hilly and the parkland past the *Pan Pacific*   *island is surprisingly*
Hotel a difficult ride for all but the most determined bicyclist. The west coast is   *entertaining*
comparatively secluded with stretches of quiet beach and the occasional fish-
ing settlement, while the east coast hums with commercial activity, like boat
building and fish processing, and because the population is so ethnically
diverse, there is a lot of variety.

There is a South Indian temple, **Sri Pathirakaliaman**, at Sungai Pinang
Kecil and the **Foo Lin Kong Temple** at the foot of Sungai Pinang Besar, with a
miniature Great Wall of China in the garden. To the south at Teluk Gedung
there are ruins of a Dutch fort, **Kota Belanda**. It was built by the Dutch East
India Company in 1680 to protect Dutch interests, especially the rich tin traders, from attack by Malay pirates. It was heavily fortified and apparently its
cannon could protect the whole Strait of Dinding also known as the Manjung
Straits. The Dutch were forced to leave the fort after an assault by the Malays,
although they reoccupied it from 1745 to 1748. Little more than a shell of the
former building now remains. Pangkor village is also attractive. Its main street
is lined with stores selling dried fish packaged in pink plastic bags. There are

also souvenir shops, mostly selling T-shirts, and a handicraft centre. One or two of the coffee houses along the street still have their original marble-topped tables and Straits wooden chairs.

Excursions **Pulau Sembilan** lies 27 km south of Pulau Pangkor. There is a group of nine small islands and outcrops here, offering good diving and marine life.

Sleeping
■ *on map*
Price codes: see inside front cover. Room rates are discounted during the week – especially the more expensive hotels

Most of the mid and upper range accommodation is at Pasir Bogak and can be reached from Pangkor village by taxi. Many of the budget places are at Teluk Nipah on the west coast, which requires a rather longer taxi ride in one of the vehicles belonging to Pangkor's taxi mafia. Note that many places increase their room rates by around 50% during public holidays.

Pulau Pangkor

Teluk Nipah detail

Sleeping
1 Beach Hut
2 Coral Beach Camp
3 Flora Beach Resort
4 Hornbill Resort
5 Khoo's Holiday Resort
6 Lima Chalets
7 Nazri Nipah Camp & Joe Fisherman Village
8 Nipah Bay Villa
9 Ombak Inn Resort
10 Pan Pacific Resort
11 Pangkor Bay View Resort
12 Pangkor Coral Bay Resort
13 Pangkor Laut Resort
14 Pangkor Village Beach Resort
15 Purnama Beach Resort
16 Seagull Beach Resort
17 Seaview
18 Sri Bayu Beach Resort
19 Suria Beach Resort
20 Vikri Huts
21 Zek Pink

Eating
1 Foodstalls

N

0 metres 500
0 yards 500

Pasir Bogak **L-AL** *Sri Bayu Beach Resort*, T6851929, F6851050, www.sribayu.com.my Chalets, suites and rooms, oriental-style décor, a/c, TV, bath, coffee-making facilities, pool, tennis, karaoke, restaurant, children's club, rather overpriced but the best place to stay on Pasir Bogak. Breakfast and dinner included in the room rate. **AL-A** *Pangkor Coral Bay Resort*, T6855111, F6855666, coralbay@tm.net.my TV, a/c, pool, health club, disco/karaoke, jacuzzi, sauna. Two restaurants, and watersports are organized. Great value. **A-B** *Seaview*, T6851605, F6851970. A/c, restaurant, watersports, fishing, boat trips, pool, tennis and badminton, breakfast included in room rate. (Package for 3 or more people including all meals RM85-120.)

   B *Khoo's Holiday Resort*, T6852163, F6851164, jameskhm@hotmail.com Restaurant, newly decorated chalets on the hill and rooms in a block, with or without a/c, sea tours arranged. Breakfast included in pleasant, open roof-top café. Good views, friendly staff, bicycle and motorbike hire available. Plans to build a springwater swimming pool. **B-E** *Pangkor Village Beach Resort*, T6852227, F6853787. A/c chalet (**B**) inclusive breakfast and dinner. Also, A-frames (**D**), longhouse max 10 people (**E**), even dorms beds and a tent that sleeps 8 – all inclusive of breakfast (chalets also inclusive of dinner). The place is situated near the main cluster of foodstalls in Pasir Bogak, and it can be noisy. Tents are hot during the day. Basic, but close to sea. Not very good value.

   C *Beach Hut*, T6853426, F6851159. A/c, restaurant, watersports, one of the older hotels here and the years are beginning to show, set in a garden close to the beach. Range of rooms available from non-a/c terrace rooms through to a/c family chalets with TV. **C-D** *Vikri Huts*, T6854258. A-frames and chalets in spacious grounds. Recently placed under the management of an Indian family who have plans to introduce more cultural activities. Traditional Indian banana-leaf meals served, must be booked in the morning (staff also provide meals for an excursion organised by the *Pan Pacific Hotel*). Friendly and popular. Recommended.

Teluk Nipah **A-B** *Hornbill Resort*, T6852005, F6852006. All rooms with sea views and balcony, a/c, TV, hot shower, good breakfast menu, seafood restaurant, popular bar with local and imported brews, and recommended at sunset. **A-B** *Nipah Bay Villa*, T6852198, F6852386, www.skybusiness.com/nipahbayvilla A/c, shower, attractive wooden cottages, well equipped. Access to video library and internet (RM10 per hr), laundry service, motorbike hire, traditional massage, also has a restaurant, breakfast included in room rate. Discounts available for stays of over one night. **A-B** *Pangkor Bay View Resort*, Lot 4449, T6853540, F6851308. Wood-panelled decent rooms. A good option although staff not particularly helpful at our last visit. **B** *Flora Beach Resort*, T7762805, F6853878. Chalets similar in style to a number of other places, such as the *Lima* and *Purnama*. Breakfast included. **B-C** *Seagull Beach Resort*, T6852878, F6852857. Longhouse, mini-cabins and chalets all with bathroom and television. A/c or fan. Good location and quiet too. Clean, friendly, serves Western breakfast (not included in room rate), games and badminton available. **B-C** *Suria Beach Resort*, Lot 4441, T6853922, F6853921. A/c, shower, rooms here are clean enough but spartan and lacking in character. Overcapacity of rooms makes bargaining possible here. Restaurant serves Malay and Western food. Avoid cycle rental – not good bikes. **B-D** *Purnama Beach Resort*, T6853530, F6854269, pbr2000@tm. net.my Same style chalets as *Lima* but a larger resort with more facilities. Fan or a/c, breakfast included, some rooms with TV, restaurant, internet access and games, karaoke, mini swimming pool, motorbike hire and laundry service.

   C *Mizam Resort*, T/F6853359. A/c chalets with attached bathrooms. Restaurant serving Malay, Chinese and Western dishes. Clean and in a quiet location at the end of a row of resorts. Friendly staff, good value. Recommended. **C** *Zek Pink*, T6853529, F6889660, zek_pink@tm.net.my Curiously named but well-equipped resort popular with Malaysian tourists. Rooms with a/c or fan, attached bathroom, TV, restaurant.

Island trips available. **C-D** *Coral Beach Camp*, T6852711, F6852796. A-frame huts (**D**), with additional cost for bathroom, family rooms split between 5 (**D**), organize watersport, motorbike hire. Dorm available for 8 people sharing. Rather basic. **C-D** *Lima Chalets*, T6852494. 13 chalets with fan and bathroom. One of a number of resorts with identical chalets. Clean but nothing special. **C-D** *Ombak Inn Resort*, T6855223. Small and simple resort comprising a few a/c wood chalets some A-frames and tents. A good-value option for backpackers. **D** *Joe Fisherman Village*, T6852389. One of the most popular budget places to stay with simple A-frame chalets with 2 mattresses on the floor and a fan, bicycles for hire, meals available. Joe is (or, more accurately, was) a fisherman and will take you to fish for your dinner (RM150 for 2 people, unlimited time – you are likely to give up before he does). **D** *Nazri Nipah Camp*, T6852014, F6853730. Rather dirty rooms and we've had reports of fleas. Set in gardens, good communal area with TV and videos. Restaurant serves Thai, Malay and Western food. A-frames are larger here than other resorts on the island. Offers a variety of watersports and jungle-trekking.

If you can afford it, Pangkor Laut is not to be missed

Pangkor Laut L *Pangkor Laut Resort*, Pangkor Laut Island, T6991100, F6991200. Malaysia's top resort, officially opened in 1994 by Luciano Pavarotti who is quoted as saying: "I almost cried when I saw how beautiful God had made this paradise." Alan Whicker put the event on film, calling it 'Pavarotti in Paradise', and the Prime Minister of Malaysia chose to spend his birthday here. All this acclaim is no exaggeration; the *Pangkor Laut Resort* is idyllic. The chalets, a blend of Malay and Balinese architecture, are magnificently set, either over the sea (linked by wooden walkways) or on the jungled hillside. Each is beautifully furbished, with carved wood and rattan work. Luxurious bathrooms with recessed tubs and orchids floating on the water's surface greet you upon arrival. A/c, mini-bar (ice buckets regularly delivered), tea/coffee-making facilities, CD player (TV in lounge only), immaculate kimonos, fresh fruit. Other facilities include well-stocked library (books and CDs), 3 swimming pools, squash, watersports, health club, gymnasium, sauna, spa, jacuzzi. A steep hike, or a short shuttle ride, takes you to Emerald Bay, one of the most perfect sandy bays in Malaysia. Eating at the resort is also a delight, top-quality seafood at the *Fisherman's Cove*, steamboat at *Uncle Lim's*, or Western fare at the *Sumudra* where chimes blow in the breeze. The wildlife on Pangkor Laut is also remarkably abundant and diverse – from hornbills to macaques – and the jungle treks are recommended. Recommended.

Elsewhere AL *Pan Pacific Resort*, Teluk Belanga, T6851091, F6851852, resv@pprp.po.my Heavily discounted at present. A/c, restaurants, two pools, limited golf course, tennis courts, watersports, limited business facilities. More expensive rooms have sea views, cheaper ones look on to the garden. Excellent location on wide sandy bay, 250 rooms of varying standard and price. To get there take a ferry to the Pan Pacific Jetty from where a hotel minibus takes you the short journey to the resort.

Eating

Most hotels and chalets have their own restaurants and most guests end up eating where they are staying. Seafood is always on the menu

Chinese Cheap *Fook Heng*, Pangkor village, simple coffee shop but excellent quality Chinese food, seafood prices are high. *Guan Guan*, Pangkor village, specializes in seafood. *Wah Mooi*, Sungai Pinang Kecil, steamed carp recommended by locals. **Indonesian Cheap** *Juo*, in the same street as the Hornbill Resort, excellent food and fresh fish (including shark). **Seafood** *Ye Lin Seafood Garden*, 200 Jln Pasir Bogak, popular outdoor restaurant, prides itself on its low prices. **Foodstalls** On Pasir Bogak and Teluk Nipah.

Sports

Golf *Pan Pacific Resort*, Teluk Belanga, Golden Sands, T6851091, 9-hole, on the coast, green fees RM50; *Pangkor Yacht Club*, Teluk Gedong, T6853478, F6853480, watersports facilities, including jet skis, sailing and snorkelling, also organize fishing trips and round-island tours.

Local Bus/taxi: there are taxis, most of which are actually minibuses (*Kereta Isewa*),   **Transport**
from Pangkor village to accommodation at Pasir Bogak as well as to Teluk Nipah and
the *Pan Pacific Resort*. There is also a local bus service but this is really reserved for locals
and tourists are not expected to travel this way – nor are they particularly popular
when they take the last seats. **Motorbike/bicycle hire**: it is possible to hire motorbikes from Pangkor village for RM20-30 per day. *Soon Seng Motor* is one of several companies in the village that hire out motorbikes. They are at 12 Main Rd (near jetty),
T6851269, and also have a branch at Standard Camp, Pantai Pasir Bogak, T6851878.
Bicycles are available from many of the chalet operations, RM15 per day.

Long distance   Air: the airport is now fully operational. Currently KL is the only destination that is served. The flight takes 45 mins. T6854516. **Boat**: ferries leave from **Lumut**
jetty. Connections every hr to Pangkor Jetty (RM5 one-way, 40 mins), also regular connections with *Pan Pacific Resort* jetty close to Golden Sands (RM6 return). The first boat to
Pangkor is at 0645 and the last at 1930. From Pangkor, the first boat leaves at 0630 and
the last at 1830. For further information contact the *Pan Silver Ferry*, 1a Jln Besar, Pangkor,
T6851046, F6851782. **Ferry**: there are inter-island ferries or it is possible to hire fishing
boats from the main villages. Large hotels will organize trips to the islands.

Banks Large hotels will change money and there's a *Maybank* in Pangkor village.   **Directory**

Kuala Kangsar

Though at first glance, this royal town half-way between Ipoh and Taiping on   *Colour map 1, grid B2*
the Kangsar River seems unassuming, it is a pleasant place to stop off, with   *Phone code: 05*
plenty of atmosphere. On the east bank of the Kangsar River lies the home of   *50 km NW of Ipoh*
the Sultan of Perak. To get there, find the main roundabout in the town, which   *123 km S of*
has a distinctive clock tower at its centre, and head southeast towards the gates   *Butterworth*
marking the start of the road to the palace estate. The road twists alongside the   *270 km NW of KL*
Perak River where there is also a back walkway for those on foot. The first
monument that you come to is the **Ubudiah Mosque**, built on the slopes of
Bukit Chandan. Completed in 1917, it is one of the most beautiful mosques in
the country with its golden domes and elegant minarets. Next to it are the
graves of the Perak royal family.

Present members of the Perak royal family are resident in the beautiful
Istana Iskandariah (and south bank of the Perak), which was built in 1930
and sits on the summit of Bukit Chandan, overlooking the Perak River and
Ubudiah Mosque. It is a massive marble structure with a series of towers,
topped by golden onion domes set among trees and rolling lawns. It is not
open to the public, but the former palace, Istana Kenangan (next door to the
current Istana), is now the **Museum di Raja** and exhibits royal regalia. It is a
fine example of Malay architecture and was built by Sultan Idris of Perak
between 1913 and 1917, without recourse to any architectural plans or even a
single nail. ■ *0930-1900 Sat-Wed, 0930-1245 Thu, closed Fri.*

In the vicinity of the palaces are several grand **traditional wooden Malay
homes**, which used to house court officials. There is also another **former palace**
(not open to public) near the Ubudiah Mosque. This imposing white building
was erected in 1903 for the 28th Sultan of Perak, and is now used as a school.
Besides these buildings, in the grounds of the district office near the Agricultural
Department, is one of the first three rubber trees planted in Malaysia. HN

Ridley, also known as 'Crazy Ridley', was responsible for developing Kuala Kangsar as a rubber planting district. He obtained rubber seeds from London's Kew Gardens and brought them, first to Singapore, and then to Kuala Kangsar where the seeds were sown in 1877, when Sir Hugh Low was British President in Perak. The sole tree to remain is now marked with a memorial plaque to Ridley. Across the road from Kuala Kangsar's famed rubber tree is a charming pavilion, built in 1930 as a viewing gallery from which the sultan could watch polo on the padang. The padang is also overlooked by the attractive red-roofed building of the **Malay College**. Considered the Eton of Malaysia, the school was built in 1905 for the children of the Perak royal family. During the Japanese occupation in the Second World War, the college was turned into administration offices for the Japanese Imperial Army who interrogated and subsequently beheaded anyone found to be a traitor. A school once again in the 1950s, it attracted a celebrated crowd – Anthony Burgess taught here (see Further reading on page 567 for a listing of his novels with a Malaysian theme).

Across the Perak River (20-sen ferry ride) there is a village where **traditional pottery-making** goes on, mostly within the Handicraft Centre there. The pottery is earthenware and fired in padi husk, which gives it a rich black colour. The traditional product of the potteries is the *labu sayong*, a water pitcher, in the shape of a gourd.

Sleeping

Although Kuala Kangsar is not a popular stopover spot, due to the limited number of rooms, it is best to book in advance

There are very few places to stay in Kuala Kangsar; none is particularly desirable apart from the *Rest House*, and all are small – the largest hotel has 14 rooms.

B *Rest House (Rumah Rehat Kuala Kangsar)*, Bukit Candan, T7763872. Pleasant position just inside the gates to the palace road, old colonial mansion, huge rooms with a/c, bathroom and hot water, some rooms face the river (fabulous views), friendly, helpful staff. **C** *Seri Kangsar*, 33 Jln Daeng Selili, T7777301, F7777101, near the clock tower. Recently opened with clean a/c rooms with bathrooms. Unfriendly staff. **C-D** *Double Lion*, 74 Jln Kasa, 300 m from the bus station, T7761010, some a/c, an alternative to the *Rest House* and a pleasant enough place to stay with large rooms, some overlooking the river. **D** *Tin Heong*, 34 Jln Raja Chulan, T7762066.

Eating

Many restaurants only open at lunchtime, it can be a problem eating after dusk

The smartest restaurant seems to be the overpriced *Hotel Seri Kangsar*. In front of here is an Indian restaurant open from early morning until late evening serving good *roti canai* and chapati. The market has foodstalls serving Malay food and there's a bakery beside the Double Lion Hotel. There's a supermarket on Jln Kangsar selling most goods.

Sports

Canoeing Three-day canoe safaris depart from Kuala Kangsar and follow the Perak for almost its entire length to the Cherendoh dam. For further information contact No 3 MDKK, Jln Tebing, T7769717.

Transport

Bus: the bus terminal is in the centre of town on Jln Raja Bendahara. Regular connections with **Ipoh**, **Butterworth**, **KL**, **Lumut** and **Taiping**. There is also one morning departure a day for **Kota Bharu** on the east coast. **Taxi**: the only local transport available with average fares being in the region of RM6. Taxis leave from close to the bus station for destinations including Butterworth, KL, Ipoh and Taiping. **Train**: the station is out of town to the northeast, on Jln Sultan Idris. Trains every 2 hrs from **Ipoh** and trains on the KL-Butterworth route also stop here.

Directory

Communications **General Post Office**: Jln Taiping, near the clock tower.

Taiping

With a backdrop of the Bintang Mountains, Taiping is the old capital of Perak and one of the oldest towns in Malaysia. Around 1840, Chinese immigrants started mining tin in the area, and it is the only big Malaysian town with a Chinese name. The town is busy and friendly, with a close-knit, community-oriented atmosphere similar to that in the other Chinatowns of Terengganu and Melaka.

Colour map 1, grid B2
Phone code: 05

In the 1860s and 1870s the Larut district of Taiping, then known as Kelian Pauh, was the scene of the Perak War, caused by bloody feuding between two rival Chinese secret societies, the Hai San and Ghee Hin, over rights to the rich tin deposits. The fighting between these Hakka and Hokkien groups resulted in British armed intervention and, when it subsided, the town was renamed *thai-peng*, or 'everlasting peace'.

In the *Straits Times* in 1933, colonial administrator GL Peet wrote: "What a pleasant town Taiping is! I first saw it some years ago on a rainy, cool evening, when the air was laden with the scent of flowering angsana trees and golden light bathed the slopes of the *ijau* [green] range. Taiping has the feeling of being lived in for a long time. It was a thriving and well-appointed town when Ipoh was still a Chinese village, when Seremban was in the same state and when Kuala Lumpur was just beginning to take on some semblance of permanence and solidity."

The Japanese built a prison in Taiping during the Second World War (next to the Lake Garden), which was then converted into a rehabilitation centre for captured terrorists during the Communist Emergency. Some of the executions carried out under Malaysia's draconian drugs legislation now take place in Taiping jail (see page 36).

One of the main reasons for coming here is to visit Maxwell Hill (see page 148). There is more colonial-era architecture here than in many of Malaysia's towns; there are some fine examples on Jalan Kota, including the former District Office, and on Jalan Main and Jalan Station. Jalan Iskandar has some fine examples of Chinese shophouse architecture.

Sights

As early as 1890 the **Lake Garden** or **Taman Tasik** was set up on the site of an abandoned tin mine by Colonel ESF Walker. It is very lush due to the high rainfall and is the pride of the town. Covering 66 ha, the park lies at the foot of Bukit Larut (Maxwell Hill). At one end of the park is **Taiping Zoo**, which is one of the oldest in Malaysia and boasts over 800 animals, including Malaysian elephants, tigers and hornbills, as well as an assortment of animals from Africa. ■ *0830-1830 daily, including public holidays. RM4 (adults), RM2 (children), extra charge for camera or video camera. Animals are normally fed between 1000 and 1200.* In the early morning locals use the park for their *tai chi* exercises. Rowing boats are available for hire on lake. Built in 1883, the lovely colonial **Perak Museum** out on Jalan Taming Sari (Main Road), opposite the prison, is the oldest museum in Malaysia, dating from 1883. It contains a collection of ancient weapons, aboriginal implements, stuffed animals and archaeological finds. The bull elephant skull on show was extracted from an animal that was killed after derailing a train at Telok Anson in 1894. ■ *0930-1700 Sat-Thu, 0900-1215, 1445-1700 Fri, free.* Near the museum is **All Saints' Church**. Built of wood in 1889, it is the oldest Anglican church in Malaysia. The graveyard contains graves of early settlers and those who died in the Japanese prisoner-of-war camp nearby. Also next to the museum is the **Ling Nam Temple**, worth a visit for the Chinese antiques inside and

There is a handy pamphlet, available from the Peak Museum on Jln Taming Sari, that maps out a heritage walking tour with photographs and short descriptions of the many colonial-era buildings

Taiping's architectural heritage

A Taiping Government Offices (1898) Jalan Kota
B Temple for the Immortal Girl (1887, 1948 and 1954) Temple Street
C Police Station (1881 and later) Jalan Kota
D Taiping Market (1884-1885) Cross Street
E Old Kota Mosque (1897) Jalan Mosque
F Taiping Convent (1899) Jalan Convent
G Perak Museum (1885) Jalan Main
H King Edward VIII School (1905) Jalan Station

I St George's Institution (1915 and 1928) Jalan Station
J Ceylon Association (1901) Jalan Station
K All Saints' Church (1886) Jalan Main
L Taiping Jail (1879) Jalan Main
M Taiping Public Library (1888) Jalan Kota
Note: Taiping Tourism produce a useful and well designed heritage guide to Taiping, with a walking route and good map. See map, page 149 for letter references.

is said to be the oldest Chinese temple in Perak State. The **railway station** on Jalan Steysen, now a school, is the oldest in Malaysia.

Excursions **Kuala Sepetang** lies 16 km west of Taiping and contains a Mangrove Forest Museum, the first of its kind in Malaysia. The site lies in 40,700 ha of mangrove swamp, which is more than half the swamp area in Peninsular Malaysia. The museum aims to highlight forestry operations in Malaysia.

Malaysia's oldest hill station The foot of **Bukit Larut**, formerly known as **Maxwell Hill**, is just 12 km or so east of the Lake Gardens and most people climb the hill, whether on foot or by Land Rover, as a day excursion from Taiping. At an elevation of 1,034 m it is the wettest place in Malaysia, receiving an average of 5,029 mm of rain a year, and was once a tea plantation. Bukit Larut is a small resort with limited facilities compared to the peninsula's other hill stations. The road up was built by prisoners of war during the Japanese occupation in the Second World War. It is in such bad repair that it is virtually inaccessible in anything other than a four-wheel-drive vehicle; in any case private transport is not permitted.

On the way up you pass a **Commonwealth War Cemetery**. Many of the gravestones here are marked December 1941, which was the date a single company from the Argyle Regiment tried to hold back the Imperial Japanese 42nd Infantry on the road north of Kuala Kangsar. Another stop is the **Tea Gardens** (or what is left of them) at the Batu 3.5 mark. The administration office is at the Batu 6 marker and about 1 km on from here is the end of the road – at the *Gunung Hijau Rest House*. From here travel is on foot. On clear days, from the summit, it is possible to see for miles along the coast. The walk to the top takes about 30 minutes and is a good trail for birdwatchers. There are jungle walks near the top of the hill, but leeches can be a problem. To walk all the way down takes around two to three hours. ■ *For information phone the superintendant, T8077243.*

Sleeping and eating For bungalows it is essential to book in advance (between 0900-1200), T8077241 or write to: Officer in charge, *Bukit Larut Hill Resort*, Taiping. **B** *Cendana* and *Tempinis* both between the 6th and 7th milestones. **E** *Bukit Larut*, large bathroom, excellent value. **E** *Rumah Hijau*, also has a campsite (**F**).

Food is available at **Mid-range** *Rumah Hijau* or *Bukit Larut* guesthouses. At the bungalows, meals can be arranged with the caretaker.

Transport The steep walk from Taiping Lake Gardens takes about 2½-3½ hrs. The road is restricted and private cars are not permitted. A Land Rover service runs from the foot of the hill just above the Lake Garden in Taiping, every hr 0700-1800, T827243.

B *Lagenda Hotel*, Jln Residensi (opposite King Edward's School), T822044. Newly refurbished. Well designed with rooms set around a small outdoor pool. Good showers but poor a/c, fans are provided as well. Restaurant. Recommended. **B** *Legend Inn*, 2 Jln Long Jaafar, T8060000, F8066666. A hotel block with 88 rooms, bath, TV, video channel, coffee house, plushest place in town with well-equipped rooms. **B** *Panorama*, 61-79 Jln Kota, T834111, F8085129. A/c, TV, in-house video, bath, mini fridge, coffee-making facilities, joined to a 3-storey supermarket, the *Fajar*, restaurant. The hotel has a central location and 79 pretty ordinary rooms. **B** *Seri Malaysia*, 4 Jln Sultan Mansor, T8069502, F8069495. One of the new chain of budget hotels, located outside the town, near the Lake Gardens, spotlessly clean to the point of being sterile. **B-C** *Meridien*, 2 Jln Simpang, T8081133, F8075251. A/c, TV, shower, coffee house, restaurant.

    C *Fuliyean*, 14 Jln Barrack, T8068648, F8070648. A/c, TV, bath, quite new and good value, rooms kept very clean. **C** *Furama*, 30 Jln Peng Loong, T821077. A/c, restaurant. Recommended. **C** *New Champagne Hotel*, 17 Jln Lim Swee aqun, T8065060, opposite Cathay Cinema and a big restaurant, and round the block from *Furama Hotel*. Friendly, helpful staff, this Chinese-owned restaurant is a pleasant, clean establishment. **C-D** *Rumah Rehat Baru (New Resthouse)*, 1 Jln Sultan Mansor, Taman Tasek, T8072044. Fan or a/c, restaurant, situated a little out of town and the new block is hardly attractive but the rooms are large, with attached bathrooms, it overlooks the Lake Gardens and is good value. Recommended.

    D *Aun Chuan*, Jln Kota (above *KFC*), T8075322. A/c or fan, restaurant. **D** *Lake View*, opposite Lake Gardens at the edge of town, 1a Jln Circular, T8074941. A/c, very noisy karaoke but cheap and clean. **D** *Nanyang*, 129-131 Jln Pasar, T8074488. A/c or fan, TV.

Sleeping
Price codes: see inside front cover

Northern Peninsula

Taiping

	Sleeping		5 Legend Inn	10 Seri Malaysia
	1 Aun Chuan		6 Meridien	
	2 Fuliyean		7 Panorama	
	3 Furama		8 Peace	Ⓐ See box on Taiping's
	4 Lake View		9 Rumah Rehat Baru	architectural heritage

0 metres 100
0 yards 100

Clean, simple and friendly. **D** *Peace*, 32 Jln Iskandar, T8073379. Lots of character, basic and noisy, but good value.

Eating   **Chinese Mid-range** *Dragon Phoenix*, Jln Kota. *Malaysia Restoran*, 36 Jln Eastern. **Cheap** *Kum Loong*, 45-47 Jln Kota, good *dim sum* 0500-1000, good place to experience local 'bustle'! Recommended. *Prima Restaurant*, 21-23 Jln Kota. **Seriously cheap** *Kedai Kopi Sentosa*, Jln Kelab Cina, good Teow Chiew noodles. **Indian** There are a number of places along Jln Pasar and Jln Panggung Wayang selling the usual array of biryani dishes and *roti*. **Malay Cheap** *Restoran Bumi*, Jln Kota (next door to *Kum Loong*). Serves some western dishes. **International Mid-range** *Nagaria Steak House*, 61 Jln Pasar, dark interior, popular for beer drinking. *Panorama*, 61-79 Jln Kota, mediocre Western food and steakhouse. **Foodstalls** Large night market on Jln Panggung Wayang. *Hawker Centre* in Metro Arcade (Shopping Centre), 54 Medan Simpang (5 km from town centre, on road to Kuala Kangsar). *Malay hawker stalls* on Jln Tupai. Burger, rice and fried chicken stalls near foot of Bukit Larut (Maxwell Hill).

Sport   **Golf** *Bukit Jana Golf & Country Club*, Jln Bukit Jana, T8837500. Clubhouse has pool, paddling pool, tennis, squash, kids' playground, card room and restaurant.

Tour operators   *Poly Travels*, 53 Jln Mesjid, T820155, ticketing, currency exchange, hotel reservation, tours; *Trans Asia Pacific*, 112 Jln Barrack, T828451, ticketing, hotel reservation, car hire, package tours; *Fulham Tours*, 25 Jln Kelab Cina, T8073039, F8081330 , ticketing, hotel reservation, licensed money changers.

Transport
304 km N of KL
88 km to Butterworth
Train: the station is on the east side of town. Lying on the north-south railway line, there are regular connections with **Ipoh**, **KL** and **Butterworth** (see page 45 for timetable). **Bus**: the main long-distance bus station is 7 km out of town and getting there means either catching a town bus or a taxi. Regular connections with **Butterworth**, **Ipoh**, **Sungai Petani** and **KL**. There is also a morning bus to **Kuantan** on the east coast. For other connections, change at Ipoh. Local buses for **Ipoh**, **Grik**, **Lumut** and **Kuala Kangsar** leave from the local bus station, which is much more conveniently located in the centre of town at the intersection of Jln Mesjid and Jln Iskandar.

Directory   **Banks** *Bank Bumiputra* and *UMBC* on Jln Kota; *Standard Chartered* at crossroads of Jln Kota and Jln Sultan Abdullah. *Poly Travels*, 53 Jln Mesjid and *Fulham Tours*, 25 Jln Kelab Cina, have foreign exchange facilities. **Communications** General Post Office: Jln Barrack. **Internet**: *Discover de Internet*, 3 Jln Panggong Wayang, T8069487, RM2.50/hr. Services include printing, scanning and faxing. *Helm Computer Technology Centre*, Jln Kota, T8082454, F8086525.

Butterworth

Colour map 1, grid B2
Phone code: 04
This industrial and harbour town and base for the Royal Australian Air Force was billeted here under the terms of the Five Powers Pact. It is the main port for ferries to Penang, and most tourists head straight for the island; Butterworth is not a recommended stopping point.

Sleeping
Nearly all the hotels are located a good 20 mins' walk from the bus terminal, so a taxi ride is advisable
B *Beach Garden Hotel* 4835 Jln Pantai T3322845. No sign of the beach or a garden in this dull hotel. Located very close to the bus stop/ferry terminal, unlike all the other hotels. TV, a/c and shower, basic. **B** *Berlin*, 4802 Jln Bagan Luar, T3321701, F3323388. A/c, TV. Next to *Sayang Coffee House*, which serves meals. The best option, if you are unfortunate enough to require accommodation in Butterworth. **B** *Travel Lodge*, 1 Lorong Bagan Luar, T3333399, F3323599. A/c, TV, restaurant, shower. **C** *Hotel*

Ambassadress, 4425 Jln Bagan Luar, T3327788. A/c, bathroom. Pretty basic, and not particularly good value. **C** *Apollo*, just round corner from Capital, very clean, a/c and fan rooms, private bathroom. **D** *Capital*, 3838 Jln Bagan Luar, T331882. To be avoided. Dark and dirty, although it is very cheap.

Butterworth is the main transport hub for Penang, and buses and trains operate into Thailand, and down to KL and Singapore.

Transport
369 km to KL
386 km to Kota Bharu

Bus: the bus station is next to the ferry terminal. There are regular connections with KL, Taiping, Kuala Kangsar, Melaka, Johor Bahru, Kota Bharu, Kuala Terengganu, Kuantan and Ipoh (2 hrs). Buses leave every 30 mins from Butterworth for **Kuala Perlis** (Langkawi ferry). There are also buses to **Keroh**, on the border with Thailand, from where it is possible to get Thai taxis to Betong. **Ferry:** ferries for pedestrians and cars and leave for **Georgetown** every 15-20 mins. **Taxi:** taxis these leave from next to the ferry terminal. If you take a taxi across to Penang you must pay the taxi fare plus the toll for the bridge. **Train:** the railway station is beside the Penang ferry terminal. There are regular connections with **Alor Star**, **Taiping**, **Ipoh**, **KL** and **Johor Bahru** (see page 45 for timetable), and trains to **Bangkok**, **Thailand** (19 hrs) and **Singapore** (14 hrs). Butterworth is one of the main stopovers on the Eastern and Orient Express, which travels in style from Singapore to Bangkok. Passengers disembark here to make the 3-hr trip by ferry and rickshaw to Georgetown.

Banks *Maybank*, *UMBC* and *HSBC* on Jln Bagan Luar. **Communications** Internet Café: *Genesys*, 4922 Jln Bagan Luar, T3243710. RM6 per hr.

Directory

Penang

Penang – or, more properly, Pulau Pinang – is the northern gateway to Malaysia and is the country's oldest British settlement. It has been sold to generations of tourists as 'the Pearl of the Orient', but in shape Penang looks more like a frog than a pearl. Although the island is best known as a beach resort, it is also a cultural gem with Chinese, Malay and Indian influences. **Georgetown** *has the largest collection of pre-war houses in all Southeast Asia.*

Colour map 1, grid B1
Phone code: 04
Population: 1.2 million

Penang State includes a strip of land on the mainland opposite, Province Wellesley – named after Colonel Arthur Wellesley, later to become the Duke of Wellington, who went on to defeat Napoleon at Waterloo. Covering an area of 738 sq km, Province Wellesley is also known by its Malay name, Seberang Perai. Georgetown's founder, Captain Francis Light, originally christened Penang 'Prince of Wales Island'. In Malay, *pinang* is the word for the areca nut palm, an essential ingredient of betel nut (see page 554). The palm was incorporated into the state crest in the days of the Straits Settlements during the 19th century. Today Pulau Pinang is translated as 'betel-nut island'. Light named Georgetown after George, the Prince of Wales, who later became King George IV as it was acquired on his birthday; most Malaysians know the town by its nickname, *Tanjung*, as it is situated on a sandy headland called Tanjung Penaga.

Ins and outs

Getting there
See also Transport, page 170

Penang airport is 20 km north of Georgetown and there are regular connections with KL and several other domestic destinations, as well as international links with a handful of regional capitals. With the completion of the 13-km-long Penang Bridge to Butterworth there are now direct bus connections with KL and many other Peninsula towns, as well as international services to destinations in Thailand and Singapore. Those wishing to take the train need to alight at Butterworth and make their way across the bridge from there (or take the ferry). Ferries leave from Georgetown for Belawan, on Sumatra, Indonesia and for Langkawi and from there to Thailand.

Getting around

There are bus services around the island and in the tourist areas there are plenty of taxis. It is also possible to hire self-drive cars and motorbikes from local and international firms. In Georgetown there are city buses and taxis as well as a smattering of trishaws. There are also bicycles for rent.

Tourist offices

Penang Tourist Centre, Penang Port Commission Building, Jln Tun Syed Sheikh Barakbah (off Victoria Clocktower roundabout, opposite Fort Cornwallis), T2616663. Open weekdays 0830-1630 (closed 1300-1400), Sat 0830-1300. Closed Sun. This tourist office is known to be unreliably informed on occasions. Often your best bet for finding out information is to ask the locals. Restaurant and café owners are particularly helpful. A monthly tourist freebie newspaper is published, the *Penang Tourist Newspaper*, useful for checking out special deals, restaurants and latest fares and fees. *Tourism Malaysia Northern Regional Office*, 10 Jln Tun Syed Sheh Barakbah, round the corner from the Penang Tourist Association, T2620066; *Tourist Information Centre*, 3rd Flr, KOMTAR Tower, Jln Penang, T2614461, also branch at Batu Ferringhi, outside *Eden Seafood Village* and at Bayan Lepas Airport (T6430501), the information centre has a list of tour companies in Georgetown. Open 1000-1800. Closed Sun. You can pick up a copy of the *Penang Tourist* newspaper here. It is particularly useful for event information.

History

Before the arrival of Francis Light, who captained a ship for a British trading company, in 1786, Penang was ruled by the Sultan of Kedah. The sultanate had suffered repeated invasions by the Thais from the north and *Orang Bugis* pirates from the sea. Sultan Muhammad Jawa Mu'Azzam Shah II was also beset by a secession crisis and when this turned into a civil war he requested help from Francis Light, then based at Acheen in Sumatra, whom he met in 1771. Light was in search of a trading base on the north shore of the Strait of Melaka, which could be used by his firm, Jordain, Sulivan and De Souza, and the British East India Company. In 1771, Light sent a letter to one of his bosses, De Souza, in which he first described Penang's advantages, but before De Souza made up his mind, Light struck a private deal with the Sultan of Kedah. The Sultan installed Light in the fort at Kuala Kedah and gave him the title of Deva Rajah, ceding to him control of the Kedah coast as far south as Penang. In turn, Light promised to protect the Sultan from his many enemies.

A frisson between Sultan Muhammad and the East India Company brought developments to a standstill in 1772. Light left Kedah and sailed to Ujung Salang, which English sailors called 'Junk Ceylon' and is now known as Phuket, where he built up a trading network. Eleven years later he finally repaired relations with Kedah and the newly installed Sultan Abdullah agreed to lease Penang to the British – again, in return for military protection. On 11 August 1786, Light formally took possession of Penang. The island was covered in dense jungle and was uninhabited, apart from a handful of Malay fishermen and a few Bugis pirates.

A small township grew up around the camp by the harbour. A wooden stockade was built to defend the island on the site of the original camp and the cantonment was called Fort Cornwallis, after Marquis Cornwallis, the then Governor-General of India. Light declared Prince of Wales Island a free port to attract trade away from the Dutch, and this helped woo many immigrant traders to Penang. Penang's status as a free port was only withdrawn in 1969. Settlers were allowed to claim whatever land they could clear. The island quickly became a cultural and religious melting pot. By 1789, Georgetown had a population of 5,000, and by the end of the next decade the number had more than doubled.

The Sultan of Kedah was upset that the East India Company had not signed a written contract setting out the terms of Penang's lease. When the company began to haggle with him over the price and the military protection he had been promised, Sultan Abdullah believed the British were backing out of their agreement. In alliance with the Illanun pirates, the Sultan blockaded Penang

Penang

Detailed maps
A Georgetown,
page 156
B Penang Hill,
page 161
C Penang's
beaches, page 172

in 1790 and tried to force the Company's hand. Light went on the offensive and quickly defeated the Sultan's forces. The vanquished Sultan Abdullah agreed to an annual fee of 6,000 Spanish dollars for Penang. Francis Light remained the island's superintendent until his death, from malaria, in 1794. The disease, which struck down many early settlers, earned Penang the epithet of 'the White Man's Grave'.

Despite Georgetown's cosmopolitan atmosphere, there remained a strong British influence: the British judicial system was introduced in 1801 with the appointment of the first magistrate and judge, an uncle of novelist Charles Dickens. The previous year, Colonel Arthur Wellesley had signed a new Treaty of Peace, Friendship and Alliance with Kedah's new Sultan Diyauddin, which superseded Light's 1791 agreement and allowed for Penang's annexation of Province Wellesley, on the coast of the peninsula, in return for an annual payment of 10,000 Spanish dollars.

In 1805 Penang's colonial status was raised to that of a Residency. A young administrative secretary, Stamford Raffles, arrived to work for the governor. Georgetown became the capital of the newly established Straits Settlements, which included Melaka and Singapore (see page 506). But the glory was shortlived. Following Raffles's founding of the Singapore in 1819, Georgetown was quickly eclipsed by the upstart at the southern tip of the peninsula and by the 1830s had been reduced to a colonial backwater. From an architectural perspective, this proved a saving grace: unlike Singapore, Penang retains many of its original colonial buildings and rich cultural heritage.

In the early 19th century Penang was used as a staging post for the opium trade between India and China. The East India Company auctioned off licences to gambling dens, brothels and opium traders; the latter accounted for about 60% of colonial Penang's revenue. Vice gangs carved out territories for themselves in Georgetown and secret society feuds finally erupted on the streets in the Penang Riots of 1867. The nine days of fighting started when a member of the White Flag society (a Malay gang) threw a rambutan skin at a Toh-Peh-Kong society member whom he caught peering through his front door. Open warfare ensued and bullet holes can still be seen in the walls of the shophouses in Cannon Square. The riots were finally put down when troop reinforcements arrived from Singapore. The societies were fined RM5,000 each, which funded the construction of four new police stations in the different parts of town where the societies operated.

Colonial Penang prospered, through tin booms and rubber booms, until the outbreak of the Second World War. When the Japanese raced down the peninsula on stolen bicycles, Penang was cut off, without being formally taken. The British residents were evacuated to Singapore within days, leaving the undefended island in the hands of a State Committee, which, after three days, put down the riots that followed the British withdrawal. The Japanese administration lasted from December 1941 to July 1945; remarkably, Georgetown's buildings survived virtually unscathed, despite Allied bombing attacks.

Modern Penang Chinese make up just over half of Penang's population, while 35% are Malay and 11% Indian. Penang, along with the other two Straits settlements of Melaka and Singapore, was a centre of Peranakan culture. Peranakans, also known as Babas or Straits Chinese, evolved their own unique blend of Malay and Chinese cultures (see page 531). The Babas of Penang, however, have almost disappeared as a distinctive group – although various shops and restaurants play to the Peranakan theme.

Georgetown, the capital of Penang state, is on the northeast point of the island, nearest the mainland; Bayan Lepas Airport is on the southeast tip. The 13 km Penang Bridge, linking the island to Butterworth, is half-way down the east coast, just south of Georgetown. Batu Ferringhi, now a strip of luxury hotels, is Penang's most famous beach and is on the north coast. It is hard to believe but in 1970 just 39,454 foreign visitors were recorded as landing on the island. By 1981 this figure had risen to 249,118, and in 1990 – during Visit Malaysia Year – over 630,000 arrived. In 1998 more than five million people visited Peninsula Malaysia and it is thought that around one million chose to drop in on Penang. Nonetheless there are still a handful of small, secluded coves with good beaches on the northwest tip of the island. The west of the island is a mixture of jungle-covered hills, rubber planta-tions and a few fishing kampungs. There are more beaches and fishing vil-lages on the south coast. A short, steep mountain range forms a central spine, which includes Penang Hill, overlooking Georgetown, at 850 m above sea level.

Georgetown

The original four streets of Georgetown – Beach (now known as Lebuh Pantai), Lebuh Light, Jalan Kapitan Kling Mosque (previously Lebuh Pitt) and Lebuh Chulia – still form the main thoroughfares of modern Georgetown. Lebuh Chulia was formerly the Cantonese heartland of the Ghee Hin triad, one of the secret societies involved in the 1867 Penang Riots. The older part of town to the west of Weld Quay, in the shadow of Kapitan Kling Mosque, is predominantly Indian.

Penang's Chinatown is one of the liveliest in Malaysia; its atmosphere & most of its original architecture remain intact

Georgetown is, however, mainly Chinese; the main Chinatown area is con-tained by Jalan Kapitan Kling Mosque, Lebuh Chulia, Jalan Penang and Jalan Magazine. The shophouses were built by craftsmen from China: the rituals, burial customs, clan associations, temples and restaurants make up a self-contained Chinese community. Despite the traffic and a skyline pierced by the Kompleks Tun Abdul Razak (KOMTAR) skyscraper, the crowded streets still have plenty of charm. There are an estimated 12,000 pre-war houses still standing in Georgetown, making the town an architectural gem in Southeast Asian terms.

The Penang Heritage Trust has been established by concerned residents in the face of commercial pressures on Penang's unique heritage

How Penang has managed to preserve at least some of its heritage while that in other Malaysian towns has been torn down, is linked to a rent control cut – on the statute books for years – which has frozen rents and therefore made redevelopment unprofitable. While the houses may be mouldering, at least they aren't (usually) being demolished. But developers have brought increased pressure to bear on the federal government to abolish the Rent Control Act.

However, not all of the island is worthy of 'gem' status. Pollution and litter have spoiled parts of Penang in recent years. Some beaches are dirty and very few people swim in the sea. The coral that used to line the shore at Batu Feringghi has all gone, mainly due to the silt washed around the headland dur-ing the construction of the Penang Bridge. To dwell briefly on the 'dirt' aspect, an interesting headline in the *New Straits Times* in August 1999 read, "Penang must rid itself of refuse dump image". But the sea is not as dirty as in some of the region's other big resorts, as testified by the presence of otters on the beach at Batu Feringghi in the early morning. It has also been reported that an island-wide clean-up campaign has had some success.

Sights

Those interested in Georgetown's architectural heritage should read Khoo Su Nin's book, 'Streets of Georgetown, Penang'

Street names in Georgetown are confusing as many are now being rechristened with Malay names; streets are known by both their Malay and English names (for example Jalan Penang/Penang Rd – not to be muddled with Lebuh Penang/Penang Street). Of particular note: Lebuh Pitt (Pitt Street) has been renamed Jalan Kapitan Kling Mosque; Beach Street is now Lebuh Pantai.

The three main **tours** offered by companies are: the city tour; the Penang Hill and temple tour; and the round-the-island tour. All cost RM20-30 and most run every hour.

Georgetown

Northern Peninsula

To Wat Chayamangkalaram, Burmese Temple & Penang Buddhist Association

Singapore Airlines

Jln Sultan Ahmed Shah

Lbh Farquhar

Francis Light's Grave

Cheong Fatt Tze Mansion

Jln Sri Bahari

Jln Argyll

Jln Penang

Lbh Leith

Lbh Muntri

Jln Dato Koya

Jln Transfer

Lorong Hutton

To Sheraton Hotel & Penang Plaza

Jln Kedah

Lbh Dickens

Lbh Campbell

KG Malabak

Lbh Chulia

Bicycle Hire

Lng Madras

Jln Burmah

Jln Penang

Jalan Kuala Kangsar

Lbh Cintra

Lbh Pantai Tali

Jln Pantai

Lbh Buckingham

Taxi Stand

Lbh Kimberley

Lbh Acheh

Lrg Kinta

Jln Penang

Lbh Acheh

Lrg Carnarvon

Malay Mosque

KOMTAR

Jln Ria

Jln Maxwell

Jln Prangin

Lbh Carnarvon

Lbh Melayu

Lng Prangin

Gat Lbh Melayu

MAS Office

Shell

Jln McAlister

Lrg McAlister

Gama (Electronic Games Hall)

Lbh Tek Soon

Gat Jln Prangin

To Agora, Garden Inn, Mid Towne, Sunway Hotel & YMCA

Jln Dato Keramat

British Representative

Jln Brick Kiln (Jln Gurdwara)

Jln Magazine

Lbh Pantai

Jln Trang

Jln Timak

Lbh Noordin

1 *To Penang Bridge & Airport*

2

3 *To Penang Bridge & Butterworth*

Related maps
A Penang, page 153
B Penang Hill, page 161
C Penang's beaches, page 172

N

0 metres   100
0 yards   100

	Sleeping	
■	Sleeping	
1	Agora *C1*	
2	Blue Diamond *B3*	
3	Broadway Hostel *B4*	
4	Cathay *B3*	
5	Cititel *A3*	
6	City Bayview *A3*	
7	Continental *A3*	

8	D'Budget Hostel *C4*
9	Eastern *B2*
10	Eastern & Oriental *A3*
11	Embassy *C1*
12	Eng Aun *B3*
13	Federal *A3*
14	Golden Plaza Hostel *C4*
15	Grand Continental *D1*

16	Hang Cheow *B2*
17	Hong Ping *C4*
18	Love Lane Inn *B4*
19	Malaysia *A3*
20	Merchant *A3*
21	Mingood *A2*
22	Oasis *B4*

At the junction of Lebuh Light and Lebuh Pantai is the Penang Clock Tower, which was presented to Georgetown by a Chinese millionaire, Chen Eok, in 1897 during Queen Victoria's Diamond Jubilee celebrations. The tower is 60 ft (20 m) tall: one foot for every year she had been on the throne. Opposite the clock tower is Fort Cornwallis, on the north tip of the island. Named after Marquis Cornwallis, a Governor-General of India, it stands on the site of Francis Light's wooden stockade. It was built by convict labour between 1808 and 1810 and only its outer walls remain. The main cannon, *Serai Rambai*, which was cast in the early 17th century, is popularly regarded as a fertility symbol; offerings of flowers and joss sticks are often left at its base. It was presented to the Sultan of Johor by the Dutch in 1606 and

Clock Tower & Fort Cornwallis

The fort has had an insignificant history. It's only taste of military action came during an Allied air-strike in the Second World War

Northern Peninsula

ended up in Penang. The modern amphitheatre hosts concerts and shows. There is an example of a wooden Malay kampung house near the entrance. ■ *0830-1900 Mon-Sun.* There are many colonial buildings on Lebuh Farquhar, such as the high court, mariners' club and the town hall.

Penang Museum & Art Gallery
Behind the high court is the museum and gallery, on the junction of Lebuh Light and Lebuh Farquhar. The building was the first English-language public school in the east, established in 1816. A statue of Francis Light, cast for the 150th anniversary of the founding of Penang, stands in front of the building. As no photograph of Georgetown's founding father was available, his features were cast from a portrait of his son, Colonel William Light, founder of Adelaide in Australia. The statue was removed by the Japanese during the Second World War and later returned, minus the sword. The museum contains another sculpture – a 19th-century bust of Germany's Kaiser Wilhelm II, which turned up in Wellesley primary school. How it came to be there in the first place is a mystery.

The small museum has a fine collection of old photographs, maps and historical records charting the growth of Penang from the days of Francis Light. There are some fascinating accounts in the History Room of the Penang Riots in August 1867 (see page 154). Downstairs there is a replica of the main hall of a Chinese trader's home and, upstairs, a Straits Chinese exhibition with a marriage chamber and a room of traditional ornamental gowns. The art gallery, also upstairs, has a series of temporary exhibitions. ■ *0900-1700, closed Fri, RM1.*

St George's Church, next door to the museum on Lebuh Farquhar, was the first Anglican church in Southeast Asia. It was built in 1817 with convict labour. The building was designed by Captain Robert Smith (some of his paintings are in the State Museum). ■ *Bus No 1, 4, 7 & 10.* This church is within easy walking distant of central George Town (Jalan Chulia).

Other sights in the centre
Nearby, also on Lebuh Farquhar, is the twin-spired **Cathedral of Assumption**. This Roman Catholic church houses the only pipe-organ in Penang. The Convent of the Holy Infant Jesus – slightly further east, is the site of Francis Light's original house. Light was Adelaide's architect and planner. His grave can be found on Jalan Sultan Ahmad Shah.

The **Goddess of Mercy Temple**, also known as Kuan Yin Teng, on Jalan Kapitan Kling Mosque/Lorong Steward is a short walk from St George's, in the heart of Georgetown. It was built at the beginning of the 1800s by the island's early Chinese immigrants. Kuan Yin is probably the most worshipped of all the Chinese deities, and is revered by Buddhists, Taoists and Confucians. The goddess is a Bodhisattva, one who rejected entry into nirvana as long as there was injustice in the world. The goddess is associated with peace, good fortune and fertility, which accounts for her popularity. Kuan Yin is portrayed as a serene goddess with 18 arms; 2 arms are considered inadequate to rid the world of suffering. The roof-tops are carved to represent waves, on which stand two guardian dragons. Shops in the area sell temple-related goods: lanterns, provisions for the afterlife (such as paper Mercedes cars'), joss sticks and figurines.

Although Georgetown is mainly Chinese, it has always had a large population of Indians, living in the city centre. The Hindu **Sri Mariamann Temple**, on Lebuh Queen/Lebuh Chulia, was built in 1883. It is richly decorated and dedicated to the Hindu god Lord Subramaniam. The main statue is strung with gold, silver, diamond and emerald jewellery. It is normally used to lead a chariot procession to the Waterfall Temple during Thaipusam (see page 54). The symbols of the nine planets and the signs of the zodiac are carved into the ceiling. The surrounding area is largely Indian, with money changers and jewellery shops, as well as restaurants and tea-stalls.

There is also a Muslim community in Georgetown and the Indo-Moorish **Kapitan Kling Mosque** (on Jalan Kapitan Kling Mosque) was built by the island's first Indian Muslim settlers around 1800. It was named after the 'kapitan' or headman of the Kling – the South Indian community. As a sight it is rather disappointing.

Straight down Lebuh Chulia is the Chinese water village off Pengkalan Weld. The entrance is through the temple on the quayside. It is known as the **Clan Piers**, as each of the jetties is named after a different Chinese clan. None of the families pays tax as they are not living on land. Rows of junks belonging to the resident traders are moored at the end of the piers.

Armenian Street is worth a wander as this area of the city is being remodelled and conserved because of its historical value; you can see the house of the rich Arab merchant who constructed the mosque opposite the park and a bit further down the road can be found the traditional Chinese house where Dr Sun Yat Sen is said to have planned the Canton uprising.

Located on Jalan Acheh, off Lebuh Pitt, Khoo Kongsi is approached through an archway to Cannon Square, and is one of the most interesting sights in Georgetown. A *kongsi* is a Chinese clan house, which doubles as a temple and a meeting place. Clan institutions originated in China as associations for people with the same surname. Today they are benevolent organizations that look after the welfare of clan members and safeguard ancestral shrines. Most of the *kongsis* in Penang were established in the 19th century when clashes between rival clans were commonplace.

Khoo Kongsi

The Khoo Kongsi is the most lavishly decorated of the *kongsis* in Penang, with its ornate Dragon Mountain Hall. It was built in 1898 by the descendants of Hokkien-born Khoo Chian Eng. A fire broke out in it the day it was completed, destroying its roof. It was rebuilt by craftsmen from China and was renovated in the 1950s; the present tiled roof is said to weigh 25 tonnes. The *kongsi* contains many fine pieces of Chinese art and sculpture, including two huge carved stone guardians, which ensure the wealth, longevity and happiness of all who came under the protection of the *kongsi*. The interior hall houses an image of Tua Sai Yeah, the Khoo clan's patron saint, who was a general during the Ch'in Dynasty in the 2nd century BC. ■ *0900-1700 Mon-Fri, 0900-1300 Sat, admission pass from adjoining office.*

There are other *kongsis* in Georgetown, although none is as impressive as the Khoo Kongsi. The Chung Keng Kwee Kongsi is on Lebuh Gereja and the Tua Peh Kong Kongsi on Lebuh Armenian. The Khaw Kongsi and the modern Lee Kongsi are both on Jalan Burmah; Yap Kongsi on Lebuh Armenian and the combined *kongsi* of the Chuah, Sin and Quah clans at the junction of Jalan Burmah and Codrington Avenue. Every *kongsi* has ancestral tablets as well as a hall of fame to honour its 'sons' or clansmen who have achieved fame in various spheres of life. Today women are honoured in these halls of fame too.

Near the Khoo Kongsi, on Jalan Acheh, is the **Malay Mosque**. Its most noteworthy feature is the Egyptian-style minaret – most in Malaysia are Moorish. In the past it was better known as the meeting place for the notorious White Flag Malays, who sided with the Hokkien Chinese in street battles against the Cantonese (Red Flags) in the Penang Riots of 1867. The hole

Northern Peninsula

halfway up the minaret is said to have been made by a cannonball fired from Khoo Kongsi during the clan riots. The mosque is one of the oldest buildings in Georgetown, built in 1808.

20th-century landmarks
At 13.5 km, Penang bridge is the longest in Asia & the third longest in the world

Apart from the RM850-million **Penang Bridge** and several new hotels, one of the few visible architectural monuments of the 20th century is **Kompleks Tun Abdul Razak (KOMTAR)** on Jalan Penang. This cylindrical skyscraper, which houses the state government offices and a shopping centre, dominates Georgetown. There should be spectacular views of the island and across the straits to the mainland from the 58th floor, but unfortunately the windows are filthy and even if they were clean the smog usually prevents a clear view. The viewing gallery encircles the souvenir centre and has coin-operated telescopes. There is also a licensed money changer here. ■ *1030-2230. All buses stop at Komtar.*

Outside the town centre

On Jalan Burmah is **Wat Chayamangkalaram**, also known as Wat Buppharam, the largest Thai temple in Penang. It houses a 32-m-long reclining Buddha, Pra Chaiya Mongkol. There is a nine-storey pagoda behind the temple. The Thais and the Burmese practise Theravada Buddhism as opposed to the Mahayana school of the Chinese. Queen Victoria gave this site to Penang's Thai community in 1845. Opposite Wat Chayamangkalaram is Penang's only **Burmese temple**. It has ornate carvings and two huge white stone elephants at its gates. The original 1805 pagoda (to the right of the entrance) has been enshrined in a more modern structure. ■ *Getting there: city bus No 2 from Lebuh Victoria terminal.*

The **Penang Buddhist Association** is at 182 Jalan Burmah. The Buddha statues are carved from Carrara marble from Italy, the glass chandeliers were made in what was Czechoslovakia and there are paintings depicting the many stages of the Buddha's path to enlightenment. Next door at No 184 is a 1960s Art Deco-style building, which is a clan hall for the Lee family. Both buildings lie opposite the Chinese recreational club, which is presided over by a statue of Queen Victoria. ■ *Getting there: city bus No 202 from Lebuh Victoria terminal.*

Other sights in & around Georgetown

Cheong Fatt Tze Mansion is at 14 Lebuh Leith, T2620006, F2288246, www.cheongfatttzemansion.com Winner of the UNESCO Conservation Award 2000, and the National Architectural Award for Conservation 1995, the mansion is now a state monument. Built by Thio Thiaw Siat, a Kwangtung (Guandong) businessman who imported craftsmen from China, this Chinese equivalent of a stately home is one of only three surviving Chinese mansions in this style; the others are in Manila and Medan (Sumatra). It has become famous as 'Penang's most foremost restoration project'. ■ *Fully guided restoration tours every Mon-Fri at 1100 or 1500, and at 1100 every Sat, Sun and public holidays. RM10.*

Jalan Sultan Ahmed Shah (previously Northam Road Mansions) became known as Millionaires' Row as it was home to many wealthy rubber planters in the wake of the boom of 1911-20. Many of the palatial mansions were built by Straits Chinese in a sort of colonial baroque style, complete with turrets and castellations. Many of them have now gone to seed as they are too expensive to maintain; a few have been lavishly done up by today's generation of rich Chinese businessmen. The largest houses are the Yeap family mansion, known as the White House, and the Sultan of Kedah's palace.

Excursions

Around the Island From Georgetown, the round-island trip is a 70 km circuit. It is recommended as a day trip as there is little or no accommodation available outside Georgetown apart from the north coast beaches.

Batu Ferringhi and **Teluk Bahang** (see page 172). The **Butterfly Farm** is close enough to Georgetown to visit in one day using public transport (see page 173).

The **Nattukotai Chettiar Temple** on Waterfall Road was built by members of the Indian Chettiar money-lending fraternity and is the biggest Hindu temple on the island. It is a centre of pilgrimage during the Thaipusam festival (see page 54). ■ *Getting there: city bus No 7 from Lebuh Victoria terminal; get off at the stop before the Botanical Gardens.*

The Botanical Gardens, T2270429, also on Waterfall Road, are situated in a valley surrounded by hills 8 km from Georgetown. The gardens are well landscaped and contain many indigenous and exotic plant species. They were established in 1844. The more interesting plants are kept under lock and key and are open to visitors 0700-1900 Monday-Friday. A path leads from the gardens' Moon Gate up Penang Hill; the 8-km hike takes about 1½ hours. ■ *Daylight hrs Mon-Sun. Getting there: city bus 7 from Lebuh Victoria terminal.*

Penang Hill A short distance from Kek Lok Si is the funicular railway, which started operating in 1922. It climbs 850 m up Penang Hill and leaves every 30 minutes between 0630 and 2330. A vintage steam engine is on display at the Penang Museum. The railway was originally completed in 1899, but on its inauguration by the governor it didn't work and had to be dismantled. Penang Hill is about 5°C cooler than Georgetown and was a favoured expatriate refuge before the advent of air-conditioning. Indeed, it was the first colonial hill station developed on Peninsular Malaysia. The ridge on top of Penang Hill is known as Strawberry Hill after Francis Light's strawberry patch. On a clear day it is possible to see the mountains of Langkawi and North Kedah from the top.

The absence of a paved road up Penang Hill means that its essential qualities of seclusion & peace have been preserved on an island otherwise battered by the forces of commercialism

Bel Retiro, designed as a get-away for the governor, was the first bungalow to be built on the hill. There is a small hotel (**B**) *Bellevue: The Penang Hill Hotel*, T8299500, F8292052, penbell@tm.net.my, with spectacular views, a restaurant on the terrace serving steamboat (for RM24), some pleasant gardens, a temple, a mosque and a post office and police station on the top. There are also a few restaurants and a small hawker centre. The hill gets very crowded on weekends and public holidays. A well-marked 8-km path leads down to the Moon Gate at the Botanical Gardens (about an hour's walk) from between the post office and the police station; a steep but delightful descent, with plenty of places to sit along the way. The hill supports the last relic patch of tropical rainforest on Penang and

Penang Hill

Hindu Temple
Bel Retiro
Botanical Garden
Top Station
Viaduct Station
Claremont Station
Middle Station
Bottom Station

N

■ Sleeping
Not to scale   1 Bellevue   ⊩⊩⊩⊩ Funicular Railway

Related maps
A Penang, page 153
B Georgetown, page 156
A Penang's beaches, page 172

Northern Peninsula

as such is deemed of considerable natural value. The flora and fauna here have been protected since 1960.

In September 1990, a memorandum of understanding was signed between the Penang State Government and the company *Bukit Pinang Leisure,* which proposed to build a waterworld, two large hotels, an adventure park and 'Summit Acropolis'. Although the more extreme elements of the proposal were later dropped following sharply negative public reaction, there remain fears that future development could radically transform Penang Hill.
■ *Getting there: city bus No 130 or 101 (from Lebuh Victoria terminal), to Kek Lok Si, then bus No 8 to the railway. Most buses from Stand 3 go to Penang Hill, but if unsure the bus drivers are helpful – provided you have the right change for the fare. Funicular is RM4 return.*

The **State Mosque**, Jalan Ayer Itam/Jalan Masjid Negeri, is the largest and newest mosque in Penang and can accommodate 5,000. It was designed by a Filipino architect. There are good views from the top of the 57-m-high minaret. ■ *Getting there: city bus No 1 from Lebuh Victoria terminal.*

The **Bat Temple** at Ayer Itam, is a sanctuary for fruit bats, which hang from the cave roof. The sacred bats are zealously protected by Buddhist monks. About 60 years ago the wealthy Madam Lim Chooi Yuen, built the bat temple to protect the bats. ■ *Getting there: city bus No1 from Lebuh Victoria terminal.*

A pleasant wooded hilly area to relax in just above the town is the **Ayer Itam Dam**. There are several trails around the lake, originally shortcuts to other parts of the island. ■ *Getting there: city bus No 1 (from Lebuh Victoria terminal) then change to bus No 8.*

Kek Lok Si Temple (The Monastery of Supreme Bliss), T8283317, south of Ayer Itam, can be seen from some distance away. It took Burmese, Chinese and Thai artisans, who were shipped in specially, two decades to build it.The abbot of the Goddess of Mercy Temple on Lebuh Pitt came from China in 1885 and the landscape around Ayer Itam reminded him of his homeland. He collected money from rich Chinese merchants to fund the construction of the huge temple, modelled on Fok San Monastery in Fuchow, China. On the way up the 'ascending plane' is a pond for turtles, which are a symbol of eternity.

The temple sprawls across 12 ha and is divided into three main sections: the Hall of Bodhisattvas, the Hall of Devas and the sacred Hall of the Buddha. The seven-tier pagoda, or Ban Po, the Pagoda of a Thousand Buddhas, is built in three different styles: the lower follows a Chinese design honouring the Goddess of Mercy, Kuan Yin; the middle is Thai-Buddhist and commemorates Bee Lay Hood (the Laughing Buddha); and the upper Burmese levels are dedicated to the Gautama or historic Buddha with thousands of gilded statues. The topmost tier contains a relic of the Buddha, a statue of pure gold and other treasures, but it is closed to visitors. All pretty tacky stuff and more than half the complex has been turned into a shopping centre. All-in-all, an impressive building compromised by tack. ■ *0900-1800, free, voluntary contribution to climb the 30-m-high tower. Getting there: city bus No 1 from Lebuh Victoria terminal, or bus No 1, 91, 101 & 85, minibus No 84 & 21. The buses passengers at Ayer Itam, and then there is a stiff walk up the hill. Alternatively, bus No 8 will take you all the way.*

Penang Bird Park, on Jalan Todak, Seberang Jaya (7 km from the Penang Bridge), includes a rusty walk-in aviary. Very run down, disappointing. ■ *0900-1900 daily, adult RM10, child RM5, T39991898, F3991899, pengbird@tm.net.my Getting there: yellow bus 65 from Pengkalan Weld (Weld Quay).*

Universiti Sains Malaysia Museum and Gallery is at Minden near the Penang Bridge interchange. It has a large ethnographic and performing arts sections with a special exhibition on *wayang kulit* (shadow puppets – see Drama, page 544). There is also an art gallery with works by Malaysian artists and visiting temporary exhibitions. ■ *0900-1700 Mon-Sun. Getting there: yellow bus No 65 from Pengkalan Weld (Weld Quay).*

Snake Temple, T6437273, also known as Temple of the Azure Cloud, was built in 1850 at Bayan Lepas 12 km from Georgetown. Snakes were kept in the temple as they were believed to be the disciples of the deity Chor Soo Kong, to whom the temple is dedicated. The temple was built as the result of a donation from a Scotsman, David Brown, after he was cured by a local priest of an 'incurable disease', using local medicines. Nowadays the reptilian disciples (almost exclusively Wagler's pit vipers) are a bit thin on the ground. The number of snakes in the temple varies from day to day – there are usually more around during festivals. The incense smoke keeps them in a drugged stupor, and most of them have had their fangs extracted. Photographs with (defanged) snakes can be posed for in a new annex next door to the temple (RM4). ■ *0700-1900, RM1. Getting there: yellow bus No 66, minibus 32 from Pengkalan Weld (Weld Quay).*

Batu Maung is a Chinese fishing village near Bayan Lepas and is known for its 'floating' seafood restaurant, built out over the water. To get there, take a yellow No 69 bus. Around the south coast, there are a few beaches and a couple of unremarkable fishing kampungs. The southern beaches are more secluded than the beaches along the north coast; the drawbacks are the litter and the absence of accommodation. Veering north towards the centre of the island, however, beyond Barat, is **Balik Pulau**, a good *makan* stop with a number of restaurants and cafés. Around the town, which is known as the Durian capital of Penang, there are a number of picturesque Malay kampungs. Further up the west side of the island is the **Pantai Acheh Forest Reserve**, which also has well-marked trails into the jungle and to the bays further round; for example, to Pantai Keracut (one hour). After the Pantai Acheh junction, and on up a twisting, forested section of road, there is a waterfall with a pleasant pool, suitable for swimming, just off the road (20th milestone), called **Titi Kerawang**. ■ *Getting there: yellow buses No 11 or 66 go from Pengkalan Weld (Weld Quay) or Jln Maxwell in Georgetown to the south of the island. Change at Balik Pulau to bus No 76 for Teluk Bahang. From there blue bus No 93 to Georgetown.*

Longer fare stages cost anything up to RM1.5. As the island buses are infrequent, check departure times at each place to avoid being stranded. It is much easier to explore the kampungs and beaches around the south and west coasts – most of which are off the main road – if you have private transport.

The **Bukit Jambul Orchid** and **Hibiscus and Reptile Garden** is found along Persiaran Bukit Jambul, close to the *Hotel Equatorial* and five minutes' drive from the airport. As its name suggests, it specializes in orchids and hibiscus. There is also a reptile house here. ■ *0930-1830 daily. Snake show on Sat, Sun, public holidays at 1130 and 1530. RM5 for adults, RM2 for children.*

Essentials

Sleeping
■ on map, page 156
Price codes:
see inside front cover.
In Georgetown, most
upmarket hotels are
concentrated in the Jln
Penang area. Most
cheaper hotels are
around Lebuh Chulia
& Lebuh Leith

L *Eastern & Oriental (E&O)*, 10 Farquhar St, T2630630, F2634833. A/c, restaurant, pool, built in 1885 by the Armenian Sarkies brothers, who operated Singapore's *Raffles Hotel* (see page 598) and the *Strand Hotel* in Rangoon (Yangon), Noël Coward and Somerset Maugham figured on former guest lists. Stunning hotel, 'restored to its former glory'. Staff are friendly and efficient, atmosphere is luxurious. Endless options for varied cuisine, both international and local, from coffee houses to ballrooms. Shop, business centre, swimming pool and gymnasium. **L-AL** *City Bayview Hotel*, 25a Lebuh Farquhar, T2633161, F2634124. Recently renovated with plush new wing added. Large top-of-the-range hotel, although less formal atmosphere than others in this category. Facilities include 24-hr room service, laundry, dry cleaning, tour desk, swimming pool, health centre (at additional cost), gym and internet access. All rooms with the expected a/c, television, telephone, mini fridge, large bathroom. All rooms are pleasant, but those in the new wing are slightly more spacious and suites are available for those looking for a luxury stay. **L-AL** *Shangri-La*, Jln Magazine, T2622622, F2626526, www.shangri-la.com A/c, restaurant, 24-hr coffee garden, pool, small fitness centre, mostly used by business people rather than tourists, next to KOMTAR. Excellent conference facilities. Good central location.

AL *Agora*, 202a Jln Macalister, T2266060, F2265959, ahpsb@po.jaring.my Formerly *Ming Court*, 2 restaurants, 2 karaoke lounges, pool. Very good deal. Conference packages available. **AL** *Berjaya Georgetown Hotel*, T2277111, F2267111. One of the newest luxury hotels in Georgetown, 330 rooms, part of one-stop Midland Park Complex. All the usual amenities: swimming pool, health centre, several restaurants, business centre. **AL** *Sunway Hotel*, 11 Lebuh Tenggiri Dua, Seberang Jaya, T43707788, F43700555, sunway@swhtlpg.po.my Part of the Sunway Hotel chain, all usual services available, health and fitness centre, internet, business centre and babysitting service. **AL-A** *Cititel*, 66 Jln Penang, T3701188, F3702288, www.cititelhotel.com Breakfast included in room rate, 24-hr café, Chinese and Japanese restaurants, sports bar with electronic darts and video games. Florist, beauty salon and convenience store. Large hotel in central location. Recommended. **AL-A** *Continental*, 5 Jln Penang, T2636388, F2638718. A/c, restaurant, 18 storeys with great views from higher rooms. New wing, with more expensive rooms, renovations recently completed throughout the hotel. Swimming pool, restaurant, lounge and coffee garden. Not as grand as *Cititel*, but comfortable. **AL-A** *Sheraton*, 3 Jln Larut, T2267888, F2266615. Five-star hotel with 280 rooms. Special facilities in rooms include direct fax line, electronic safe, iron. For those who get really hungry at unpredictable hours there is a 24-hr restaurant. **AL-B** *Merchant*, 55 Jln Penang, T2632828, F2625511. A/c, restaurant, handsomely decorated, smart marble lobby, a/c, TV, in-house video, mini-bar, coffee house, trishaws for hire RM15 per hr. Friendly and helpful staff. Good value.

A *Equatorial International*, 1 Jln Bukit Jambal, T6438111, F6448000, info@pen.equatorial.com A/c, restaurant, between the airport and town, on a hill with a view over the Penang Bridge, mostly used by visiting business people as it is conveniently located for Penang's duty-free industrial zone, which lies between it and the airport. A monstrous block of 400-plus rooms with good sports facilities and adjacent 18-hole golf course. **A** *Malaysia*, 7 Jln Penang, T2633311, F2631621, hotelmal@tm.net.my A/c, restaurant, dated high-rise hotel, plush décor with coffee house, disco, health centre. **A-B** *Grand Continental*, 68 Brick Kiln Rd (Jln Gurdwara), T2636688, F2630299. A/c, restaurant, pool, health club, coffee lounge, massage centre, karaoke lounge. Good value. **A-B** *Sunway*, 33 New Lane, T2299988, F2292033, allson@po.jaring.my Pleasant décor, good facilities in rooms, a/c, TV, pulsating shower, in-house video, iron, fridge, complimentary tea/coffee, pool, jacuzzi, restaurant, tea-house, pub, tennis and squash arranged. Breakfast included. Not much character but great value for money.

B *Bellevue*, Penang Hill, T8299600. A/c, restaurant, colonial-style house, cool retreat up on the hill. Good views over Georgetown. Pleasant accommodation, small and quite isolated from the real action – other than the sites and attractions on Penang Hill. **B-C** *Cathay*, 15 Lebuh Leith, T2626271, F2639300. Some a/c, large old Chinese house, scrupulously maintained, organizes minibuses to Hat Yai and Phuket (Thailand), coffee shop, not particularly good value. Not recommended for lone females, even though the building looks well enough maintained from the exterior! Their 'health care' annex is a euphemism for their (Chinese) brothel. **B** *Mid Towne*, 101 Jln McAlister, T2269999, F2295149, www.MidtowneHotel.com New hotel, not very central but good value, actually situated out of town, does not stand out. **B** *Mingood*, 164 Argyle Rd, T2299922, F2292210, mingood@hotmail.com A/c, café, not particularly good value for money. Caters mainly for local businessmen. **B** *Oriental*, 105 Jln Penang, T2634211/6, F2635395, A/c, restaurant, dated décor, big rooms and good value, welcoming staff, well located with good views from the upper floors. Recommended. **B** *Towne House*, 70 Jln Penang, T2638621, F2623541 Chocolate-brown and cream block, features an automatic massage chair in lobby (50 sen), a/c, restaurant, TV, fridge. Better value can be found for the budget traveller.

C *Paramount*, 48F Jln Sultan Ahmad Shah, T2273649. A/c, restaurant, big rooms in run-down colonial house, right on the sea, but not central. Recommended. **C** *Peking*, 50a Jln Penang, T2636191. Once a luxury hotel, now very run-down, a/c, bath, TV. Antiquated, but large rooms. Small hotel that seems to attract mostly locals. Has own 'health centre' (frequented, spookily, mainly by male members of the population). **C** *Waldorf*, 13 Leith St, T2626140, F2637906, waldorf@pc.jaring.my A/c, bath, dated décor. **C** *YMCA*, 211 Jln Macalister, T2288211. A/c or fan-only rooms (**D**). **C-D** *Embassy*, 12 Jln Burmah, T2267515. A/c, restaurant. Some hot water showers. Spacious rooms with old décor. Friendly and clean, good budget option. **C-D** *Federal*, 39 Jln Penang, T2634170. Good location, near some excellent restaurants, recently revamped, although style is still 1920s, nothing special.

D *Blue Diamond*, 422 Lebuh Chulia, T2611089. Restaurant, fan, Chinese nationalist General Chiang Kai Shek once took refuge here, spacious rooms, bar and cheap restaurant downstairs. Pool tables and television in bar. Popular with backpackers, bar can be noisy in the evenings. Central location in China Town. **D** *Broadway Hostel*, 35f Jln Masjid Kapitan Kling, T2628550, F2619525. Clean and basic, some a/c (**D**), dorm (**F**), one of the best budget options. **D** *D'Budget Hostel*, 9 Lebuh Gereja, T2634794. Some a/c, roof terrace, laundry, money changer, tea-making, TV, hot water shower, near Medan ferry, clean but sterile, soulless place, quiet, friendly and helpful management, dorm (**E**). **D** *Eastern Hotel*, 509 Lebuh Chulia , T2614597. Fan, small rooms, reasonable budget option. **D** *Eng Aun*, 380 Lebuh Chulia, T2612333. Fan, restaurant, old house set back from the road, basic but popular with clean rooms and friendly service. **D** *Olive Tree*, 300 Chulia St, above Rainforest Restaurant, friendly staff and clean rooms makes this a very popular place to stay (so it's often hard to get a room). Dorm beds (**F**) available too. **D** *Pin Seng*, 82 Love Lane, T2619004. Original tiled floors and iron beds, fan only, run-down. Good information on local and national buses, very basic. **D** *White House Hotel*, 72 Jln Penang, T2632385, F2641409. Fan and a/c rooms available. Lovely staff, communal eating area, clean attached or common bathroom, excellent value for money. Recommended. **D** *Swiss Hotel*, 431 Lebuh Chulia, T2620133. Recent reports of rude staff and smelly toilets, next door are motorbikes for hire (quite cheap at RM15 per day), and good selection of books to rent or buy. **D** *Wan Hai*, 35 Love Lane, T2616853. Fan, restaurant, run-of-the-mill budget hotel, motorcycles for hire, visa applications for Thailand and bus tickets to Thailand organized, dorm (**F**), terrace. Not recommended by locals.

D-E *Hang Cheow*, 511 Lebuh Chulia, T2610810. Restaurant. Recommended by travellers. Rates negotiable, friendly owner! Basic budget accommodation. **D-E** *New Asia*,

Northern Peninsula

110 Jln Pintal Tali, T2613599. A/c, bar, family run. Recommended. **D-F** *Love Lane Inn*, 54 Love Lane, T4129002, ocean008@hotmail.com New establishment run by a character called Jimmy. Well travelled, he knows how to charm his guests, and offers free tea and coffee in the morning. Plenty of travel info to hand, quieter location than most, some dorms available though not as good value as the rooms. Clean and friendly with television area and some books available. Jimmy is a character, but don't expect locals to speak too highly of him! Recommended. **D-F** *Oasis Hotel*, 23 Love Lane, T2616778. Reasonable value – fan only. In a less frenetic corner of town, shared bathrooms, fan and basin in room. 'Interesting' atmosphere, set in overgrown garden, dorm beds (**F**) available. On our last visit cleanliness left a little to be desired. There are more pleasant backpacker haunts than this one. **E** *Hong Ping*, 273B, Lebuh Chulia, above *Coco Island* restaurant, T2625234. A/c, private bath, TV, bare but quiet rooms.

Eating
● *on map, page 156*
Price codes:
see inside front cover

Penang's specialities include *assam laksa* (a hot-and-sour fish soup), *nasi kandar* (curry), *mee yoke* (prawns in chilli-noodle soup) and *inche kabin* (chicken marinated in spices and then fried).

Try the foodstalls for great Malay food, see page 168

Malay Mid-range *Eliza*, 14th Flr, *City Bayview Hotel*, 25a Lorong Farquhar, sumptuous menu eaten in traditional style, seated on pandan mats, good views over the town and coast. **Cheap** *Nazir*, 4th level, KOMTAR.

Chinese Expensive *Shang Palace*, *Shangri La Hotel*, Hong Kong *dim sum* brunch, Cantonese dishes. **Mid-range** *Goh Huat Seng*, 59A Lebuh Kimberley, Teochew cuisine, best known for its steamboats. *Tower Palace*, Level 58-60 KOMTAR, good-value *dim sum*. **Cheap** *Ang Hoay Loh*, 60 Jln Brick Kiln, Hokkien food: specialities include glass noodles and pork and prawn soups. *Lum Fong*, 108 Muntri St, lively coffee shop with an arcaded front, old wooden tables and chairs, good noodles. *May Garden*, 70 Penang Rd, good food and very popular. *Sin Kheng Hooi Hong*, 350 Lebuh Pantai, Hainanese cuisine, *lor bak* (crispy deep-fried seafood rolls, with sweet-and-sour plum sauce). Recommended. *Tropics*, Sunway Hotel, 33 New Lane, good value steamboat buffet. **Seriously cheap** *Potbless*, Hutton Lane, *nasi lemak*, banana leaf, steamboat.

Penang & Melaka are the culinary centres of Nyonya cuisine (see page 51)

Nyonya Cheap *Dragon King*, 99 Lebuh Bishop, family-run business, probably the best Nyonya food in any of the old Straits Settlements, specializes in fish-head curry, good *satay*, *otak-otak* (fish marinated in lime and wrapped in banana leaf), *curry kapitan* (chicken cooked in coconut milk) and *kiam chye boey* (a meat casserole). Recommended. *Nyonya Corner*, 15 Jln Pahang, excellent *otak-otak*.

Fusion Expensive-mid-range *Thirty Two*, 32 Jln Sultan Ahmad Shah, T2622232, Chinese-owned Italian mansion built in the 1920s. Beautifully maintained. The restaurant includes a bar and lounge area with live jazz bands, a terrace by the water and a no-smoking room with a/c. Varied menu, referred to as Asian fusion cuisine. Beautiful building, friendly staff and sophisticated ambience.

Indian Penang's 'Little India' is bounded by Lebuh Bishop, Lebuh Pasar and Lebuh King, close to the quay. There is a string of good Indian restaurants along Lebuh Penang, in this area, notably: *Murugan Vilas*, *Nava India*, *Susila* and *Veloo Vilas*. They are renowned for their banana-leaf curries. **Mid-range** *Annalakshmi*, Basington Av, T2288575, 1800-2130, serves a great vegetarian curry. *Kashmir*, base of *Oriental Hotel*, 105 Jln Penang (**NB** not Lebuh Penang), north Indian food – usually very busy. Recommended. *Madras New Woodlands Vegetarian Restaurant*, 60 Penang St, north and south Indian food, newly opened and bristling clean. Looks expensive, but it's not; especially good *masala dosas*. **Cheap** *Dawood*, 63 Lebuh Queen (across from Sri Mariamman Temple), Indian Muslim restaurant known for its curries, original 1960s décor, *kari kapitan* (chicken curry) and duck are popular. Recommended. *Kaliaman's*, 43 Lebuh Penang, one of Penang's best Indian restaurants, South Indian food at lunch,

Northern Peninsula

northern Indian food in the evening, not very clean. *Kashmir*, Penang Rd, 1200-1430, 1900-2230. *The Tandoori House*, Lorong Hutton, nicer décor than *Kashmir* (above), evergreen north Indian specialities. **Seriously cheap** *Banana Leaf*, Lebuh Penang, about two blocks south of Lebuh Gereja. Serves excellent southern Indian food; an especially good place for a *thali* and the *lassis* are good. *Hameediyah*, 164A Lebuh Campbell, Indian Muslim food, *murtabak*, *rotis*, large portions. *Kassim Mustafa*, 12 Lebuh Chulia, basic coffee shop that prides itself in cooking a handful of dishes very well, most trade done between 0500 and 1200, specialities are *nasi dalcha* (rice cooked with ghee and cinnamon), *ayam negro* and mutton *kurma*. Good *roti bom* and *teh tarik*. Staff are friendly, and this is also an excellent place for breakfast. Recommended. *Kassim Nasi Kandar*, 2-1 Jln Brick Kiln, hot Indian Muslim food, open 24 hrs, recommended by locals. *Kedai Kopi Yasmeen*, 177 Jln Penang, simple open-fronted Indian coffee shop, *murtabak*, *roti* etc. Recommended.

Indonesian Cheap *Tambuah Mas*, Level 4 Komtar Tower. **Seriously cheap** *Nasi Padang*, 511 Lebuh Chulia.

Japanese *The City Bayview* and the *Bellevue* hotels both have Japanese restaurants. The latter serves a good steamboat (last orders 2000). **Expensive** *Kurumaya*, 269 Burma Rd, top quality *sushi* and *sashmi*. **Mid-range** *Kong Lung*, 11c Leith St, immaculate traditional décor, *teppenyaki* and set lunches. Recommended. *Miyabi*, 216 Jln McAlister, well-established Japanese restaurant. *Shin Miyako*, 105 Jln Penang (next to the *Oriental Hotel*), smart-looking restaurant and reasonably priced for Japanese food. *Hide No Ya*, 8 Abu Siti Lane, T2282359, small, friendly restaurant, especially good for its *tempura chauonmushi*, *karagi* and *sashimi/suishi*. Recommended.

Thai Cheap *Café D'Chiangmai*, 11 Burmah Cross, serves an interesting mixture of Thai and local dishes, renowned for its fish-head curry, popular in the evenings. *Thai Food Restaurant*, below *New Pathe Hotel*, Lebuh Light. *Yellow Light*, 1C Jln Fettis. *Coca Restaurant*, Island Plaza, 1130-2200, particularly good Thai steamboat.

International Mid-range *Beetle Nuts Fun Café*, 9-11 Leith St, in same old block as 20 Leith St, theme is American, Tex-Mex, trendy. *Bella Casa*, 105a Penang Rd, T2642030, a large choice of Italian menu, good *lasagne di carne*. **Cheap** *Brasserie*, Shangri La Hotel, Californian cuisine. *Café Tower Lounge*, 59th Flr, KOMTAR, buffet lunch, good view over the city and afterwards free entrance to viewing gallery. *Rainforest Restaurant*, 300 Chulia St, new sister company of *Green Planet*, popular with budget travellers, interesting scrapbooks of travellers' experiences, wide selection of food: nachos, sandwiches, steak, pizza, apple crumble (recommended), all home-cooked and no preservatives. Freshly baked bread. Recommended. *Coco Island Café*, Lebuh Chulia, good food, popular. *Eden Steak House*, Jln Hutton. **Seriously cheap** *Green Planet*, 63 Lebuh Cintra, a backpackers' joint serving classic travellers' food. Also provides information, ticketing services, motorbike rental, hot showers, excellent food and helpful owner. *Eng Thye Café*, 417b Lebuh Chulia. *Magnolia Snack Bar*, Jln Penang.

Seafood Expensive *Eden*, 11B Lorong Hutton, popular chain of restaurants, seafood and grills. **Mid-range** *Grand Garden Seafood*, 164 Jln Penang, seafood market restaurant, outside eating. **Cheap** *Lam Kee Seafood*, next to stalls on Esplanade (Padang Kota Lama). *Maple*, 106 Jln Penang (near *Oriental Hotel*), same management as *May Garden* and food is in the same league. *May Garden*, 70 Penang Rd (next to *Towne House*), reckoned to be among the best seafood restaurants in Georgetown, with an aquarium full of fish and shellfish to choose from. The crab is excellent and *May Garden's* speciality is frogs' legs, fried with chilli and ginger or just crispy. Recommended. *Ocean-Green*, 48F Jln Sultan Ahmad Shah (in quiet alleyway in front of *Paramount Hotel*), specialities include lobster and crab thermidor, drunken prawns and fresh frogs' legs ('paddy chicken'), lovely location, overlooking fishing boats. Recommended. *Sea Palace*, 50 Jln Penang (next to *Peking Hotel*), huge menu, popular, a/c, Chinese tableware, good value. Recommended.

Northern Peninsula

Coffee shops Most Chinese coffee shops are along Jln Burmah and Jln Penang, also some in the financial district along Lebuh Bishop, Lebuh Cina and Lebuh Union. *Khuan Kew* and *Sin Kuan Hwa*, both in Love Lane are particularly popular – the latter is well known for its Hainan chicken rice. The *Maxim Cakehouse and Bakery* on Penang Rd is also a popular stop. The oldest in Georgetown is the *Kek Seng* (382 Jln Penang), founded in 1906 and still serving *kway teow* soup and colourful *ais-kacangs*.

Penang's hawker stalls are renowned in Malaysia and serve some of the best food on the island. We have received reports though, that many have closed due to a public health drive

Foodstalls *Datuk Keramat Hawker Centre* (also called *Padang Brown*), junction of Anson and Perak roads, is one of the venues for Georgetown's roving night market – possible to check if it's on by calling tourist information centre, T2614461. Recommended. *Food Court*, base of KOMTAR. *Kota Selera Hawker Centre*, next to Fort Cornwallis, off Lebuh Light. Recommended. *Lebuh Keng Kwee*, famed locally for its *cendol* stalls – cocktails of shaved ice, palm sugar and jelly topped with *gula melaka* and coconut milk. *Lebuh Kimberley* (called noodle-maker street by the Chinese), good variety of hawker food at night. *Lorong Selamat Hawker Stalls*, highly recommended by locals. *Padang Kota Lama/Jln Tun Syed Sheh Barakbah* (Esplanade), busy in the evenings. Recommended. *Pesiaran Gurney Seawall* (Gurney Drive), long row of hawker stalls opposite the coffee shops, good range of Malay, Chinese and Indian food, very popular in the evenings. Recommended. There are also popular stalls along *Jln Burmah*, *Love Lane* and at *Ayer Itam*. Good *roti-canai* opposite *Plaza Hostel*, Lebuh Ah Quee.

Bars *Carmen's Inn*, 15th Flr, *City Bayview Hotel*, 25a Farquhar St, views over the town and coast, starts turning 1700. *20 Leith St* (next to *Waldorf Hotel*), pleasant bar, building is 150 years old and many original features have been retained, pitchers of Carlsberg, *satay* and prawn, and other light snacks. *George's*, *Sunway Hotel*, 33 New Lane, quintessentially English, live music.

Entertainment **Discos** *Celebrity*, 48H Jln Sultan Ahmad Shah; *Hotlips Disco*, next to *Continental Hotel*;

Most of the big hotels have in-house nightclubs and discos. Expect to pay cover charges if you are not a guest

Penny Lane, bottom of *City Bayview Hotel*; *Xanadu Disco*, next to *Malaysia Hotel*; *Rockworld*, 1 Drury Lane (off Campbell St), high-tech lighting and laser show; *Street One*, *Shangri La Hotel*, popular with air hostesses.

Cinemas All cinemas are now to be found in cineplexes, within the shopping centres. Best of the bunch is in the Praingin Mall, a new shopping complex opposite KOMTAR.

Festivals **February/March** *Chap Goh Meh*, celebrated on the 15th night of the first month of the Chinese lunar calendar; girls throw oranges into the sea for their suitors to catch. **June** *Penang International Dragon Boat Race*, near Penang Bridge; teams from around the region and beyond compete. *International Beach Volleyball Championship* held at the end of June on Kital Beach, Batu Ferringhi, next to *Bayview Beach Hotel*. **July** *Penang on Parade*, with three major annual events; details from Tourist Information Centre. *Floral Festival* at KOMTAR. *City parades* by Malays (at Fort Cornwallis), Chinese (at Khoo Kongsi) and Indians (at Market St). **September** *Penang Lantern Festival* held at the end of September, a parade with lanterns. **November** *Deepavali Open House*, festivities in Little India.

Shopping This requires a lot of wandering around the narrow streets & alleyways off Jln Penang. The main areas are Jln Penang, Jln Burmah and Lebuh Campbell.

Antiques An export licence is still required for non-imported goods. Shops are concentrated on and around Jln Penang with the best ones at the top end opposite *Eastern and Oriental Hotel*, such as the *Oriental Arts Co*, 3f Penang Rd. There are also

Northern Peninsula

antique shops along Rope Walk (Jln Pintal Tali). Most stock antiques from Burma, Thailand, Indonesia, Malaysia, Sabah and Sarawak, as well as a few local bargains. Another street with a number of crafty-cum-antique shops is Rope Walk or Jln Pintal Tali. *Eastern Curios*, 35 Lebuh Bishop. *Kuan Antique*, 7A Aboo Sitee Lane. *Penang Antique House*, 27 Jln Patani, showcase of Peranakan (Straits Chinese) artefacts – porcelain, rosewood with mother-of-pearl inlay, Chinese embroideries and antique jewellery.

Art galleries Georgetown's *College of Art and Music* is housed in a grand colonial building on Leith St. Exhibitions are occasionally on view in the *College Gallery*, 7 Leith St, T2618087. Other galleries in Georgetown include *The Art Gallery*, 36B Burmah Rd, T2298219; *Galerie Mai*, 54 Tung Hing Building, Jln Burmah, T377504. *Yahong Art Gallery*, Batu Ferrenghi, T8811093, open 0930-2100, has a variety of batik exhibits as well as some jewellery and other works of art.

Batik *Asia Co*, 314 Jln Penang. *Maphilindo Baru*, 217 Penang Rd, excellent range of batiks and sarongs (including songket) from Malaysia, Sumatra and Java. *Sam's Batik House*, 159 Jln Penang. *Yuyi Batik House*, Level 3, Kompleks Tun Abdul Razak (KOMTAR), Jln Penang. Factory outlet in Teluk Bahang and souvenir shops in Batu Ferringhi.

Books There are several bookshops in Lebuh Chulia near *Swiss Hotel*, which sell second-hand books. *Yasin Bookshop*, 417a Lebuh Chulia. *Parvez Book Store*, 419 Lebuh Chulia (as well as dealing in books they arrange Thai visas and trips, and car/motorbike hire). *HS Sam Bookstore*, 144 Lebuh Chulia, prides itself on being well organized and runs a sideline in travel services: Thai visas, bus ticketing, car/bike rental and has a luggage storage. *MPH Bookstore*, Island Plaza, Jln Tanjong Tokong. *Times Bookshop*, Penang Plaza, 1st Flr, 126 Burmah Rd. *Popular Bookshop*, Arked Ria 2, KOMTAR Tower and at Midland Park Complex, Jln Burmah; reasonable selection in Yaohan Department Store in KOMTAR.

Camping gear *Tye Yee Seng Canvas*, 162 Chulia St, good stock of tents, rucksacks, sleeping bags and beach umbrellas.

Cassettes, electrical and photographic equipment The best place to look for these items is in the shops along Jln Campbell

Curios and unusual bargains *Lebuh Chulia*, Bishop and Rope Walk (Jln Pintal Tali). Many of the curios are imported from China and are very well priced. There is a good selection at *Tan Embroidery Co*, 20 Lebuh Pantai.

Food shops There are a number of outlets in Georgetown, mostly Chinese-run, selling locally produced specialities. Dragon Ball biscuits, pastry balls filled with a mung bean paste, are made by *Wee Ling*, 132 Chulia St. Similar products, including *pong pneah* (pastry filled with molasses or caramel) are made at *Him Heang*, 162 Jln Burmah. For a selection of unusual pre-packaged products, such as dried mango, jackfruit, nutmeg oil and coconut cookies go to one of the large a/c outlets of *Cap Jempol Tropiks*, either at 17 Leith St (next to *Cathay Hotel*) or 50c Penang Rd (next to *Peking Hotel*). Chinese teas and ginseng in a variety of forms are the speciality of *Eu Yan Sang*, 156 Chulia St, who offer a herb-boiling service in a cauldron that bubbles inside the doorway.

Gama, behind the KOMTAR Tower, is excellent for stocking up on basics

Handicrafts Jln Penang is a good place to start with *Peking Arts & Crafts* at 3b, *Federation Arts & Crafts* at 3c, and *China Handicraft Co* at 3d. *See Koon Hoe*, 315 Lebuh Chulia, sells Chinese opera masks, jade seals and paper umbrellas; *The Mah Jong Factory* in Love Lane sells high-quality Mah Jong sets. *Arts and Culture Information Centre*, T2642273, 1200-1400 Thu to Sat.

Jewellery Lebuh Campbell and Lebuh Kapitan Klang. Reasonable quality fake wristwatches can be purchased near the Snake Temple (see page 163).

Markets The night market changes venue every night and is more often than not out of town. There are illegal street vendors selling CDs etc bargain and you might also happen to beat the odds of receiving a faulty disk. There may be plans in the future to set up a permanent night market in Chinatown but these are as yet unfulfilled. Jln Chulia and the surrounding streets do have a busy and friendly atmosphere with good late-night cafés. It is popular with westerners and most bars offer international football games on the television or a film.

Shopping complexes *Midland Park*, Jln Burmah, opposite Adventist Hospital, amusement arcades, roller skating, bowling alley, several fast-food outlets, hawker foodstalls. *Popular Bookshop* and shops. *Island Plaza*, Jln Tanjung Tokong, on road to Batu Ferringhi, upmarket shops – *East India Company*, *Guess*, *Fila*, *Coca Restaurant*, the *Forum*, a food court and a new cinema. *Bukit Jambul Shopping Complex*, close to the airport, good range of shops, food outlets and an ice-rink. *KOMTAR*, hundreds of boutiques, two department stores, fast-food restaurants, amusement arcade. *Praingin Mall*, new complex opposite KOMTAR. Far more upmarket than the others, with an ice-rink and cineplex. Also on offer is a *Starbucks* for those craving real coffee. There is an internet café on the 3rd floor called *easy-net*, restaurants, fast-food outlets and a few more upmarket shops.

Sports **Bowling alley** *Midland Park Complex*, Jln Burmah. **Golf** *Airforce Golf Club*, Butterworth, T3322632, 9-hole course, green fees weekdays RM20, weekends RM30. *Bukit Jambul Golf & Country Club*, Jln Bukit Jambul, T6442255, hilly course, green fees weekdays RM100, weekends RM150. *Indoor Golf Club*, Level 56, KOMTAR building. *Penang Turf Club*, Golf Section, Jln Batu Gantong, T2266701, 18-hole, RM84 weekdays, RM126 weekends. *Kristal Golf Resort*, Jln Valdor, Seberang Perai Selatan, T5822280, green fees weekdays RM105, weekends RM150. *Penang Golf Resort*, Lot 2462, Mk6, Jln Bertram, 13200 Kepala Bates, T5782002, F5750226. **Horse racing** *Penang Turf Club*, Jln Batu Gantung, every 2 months. **Ice -rink** *Bukit Jambul Shopping Complex*, close to the airport, RM12 for 2 hrs (skate rental extra).

Tour operators
Most of the budget travel agents are along Lebuh Chulia

Everrise Tours & Travel, Lot 323, 2nd Flr, Wisma Central, 202 Jln, T2264329; *Georgetown Tourist Service*, Jln Imigresen, T2295788 city island tours; *MSL Travel*, Ming Court Inn Lobby, Jln Macalister, T2272655 or 340 Lebuh Chulia, T2616154, student and youth travel bureau; *MS Star Travel Agencies*, 475 Lebuh Chulia, T2622906. For all your travelling needs. *Tour and Incentive Travel*, Suite 7B, 7th Flr Menara BHL, Jln Sultan Ahmad Shah, T2274522.

Transport
See also Ins & outs, page 152

NB Butterworth is the railway stop for Georgetown and Penang; taxis also tend to terminate there, with local taxis making the run across the bridge to the island; long-distance taxis will, however, cross the bridge for an extra charge.

Local **Bicycle hire**: rental from the *Eng Ann Hotel* or *Swiss Hotel*, both on Lebuh Chulia, RM20 per day.

Bus: city buses leave from Lebuh Victoria near the Butterworth ferry terminal and serve Georgetown and the surrounding districts. Green, yellow, blue and Transit Link buses leave for various points around the island from Pengkalan Weld (Weld Quay) – next to the ferry terminal or Jln Maxwell. Bus No 83 for the airport; No 101 or 130 towards Penang Hill but you will need to change to No 8 at Kek Lok Si for the final drive to the railway; No 78 for Snake Temple; No 93 to the northern beaches. Blue buses go west along the north coast to Tanjung Bungah, Batu Ferringhi and Teluk Bahang. Green buses head towards the centre of the island to Ayer Itam area. Yellow buses go south (including to Snake Temple and Bayan Lepas Airport), and then up the west side of the island to Teluk Bahang.

Car hire: *Avis*, Bayan Lepas Airport, T6439633, *Rasa Sayang Hotel* Lobby, T8811522; *Budget*, 28 Jln Penang, T6436025 and Bayan Lepas Airport; *Hawk Rent-a-car* T8813886. *Hertz*, 38 Lebuh Farquhar, T2635914 and Bayan Lepas Airport; *National Car Rental*, 17 Lebuh Leith, T2629404; *Orix*, City Bayview Hotel, 25A Lebuh Farquhar,

T2618608; *Ruhanmas*, 76 Batu Ferringhi, T8811023; *SMAS*, Bayan Lepas Airport, T6452288; *Thrifty*, Bayan Lepas Airport, T6430958; *Tomo*, 386A, 1st Flr Wayton Court, Jln Burmah, T22665636.

Motorcycle hire: in Georgetown there are several motorbike rental shops, many of them along Lebuh Chulia. It costs from around RM20 per day to hire a motorcycle depending on size; most are Honda 70s.

Taxi: there are taxi stands on Jln Dr Lim Chwee Leong, Pengkalan Weld and Jln Magazine. Fares are not calculated by meter, so agree a price before you set off; short distances within the city cost RM5-7. A trip to the airport costs RM12-14. *Radio taxis*: T2625721 (at ferry terminal); *CT Radio Taxi Service*, T2299467. **Trishaw**: bicycle rick-shaws that carry 2 people are one of the most practical and enjoyable ways to explore Georgetown. Cost RM1 per half mile or RM15 per hr; if taking an hr's trip around town, agree on the route first, bargain and set the price in advance.

Transport to Penang: for details on transport to Penang, see page 176.

Airline offices *Cathay Pacific*, AIA Building, Lebuh Farquhar, T2260411. *MAS*, Kompleks Tun Abdul Razak (KOMTAR), Jln Penang, T2620011 (the ticket office is on the ground floor, at the southern side of KOMTAR, and can only be entered from outside the complex) or at the airport, T6430811. *Singapore Airlines*, Wisma Penang Gardens, 42 Jln Sultan Ahmad Shah, T2263201. *Thai International*, Wisma Central, 202 Jln Mac-alister, T2296250. *Air Asia*, T2629882. *Cathay Pacific*, T2260411. *Emirates*, T2631100. *United Airlines*, T2636020.

Banks Most banks in Georgetown are situated in or around the GPO area and Lebuh Pantai. Most money changers are in the banking area and Jln Masjid Kapitan Keling and Lebuh Pantai, close to the Immigration Office. *Bank Bumiputra*, 37 Lebuh Pantai; *Citibank*, 42 Jln Sultan Ahmad Shah; *Hong Kong Bank*, Lebuh Pantai; *Maybank*, 9 Lebuh Union; *Standard Chartered*, 2 Lebuh Pantai. *Hong Kong Bank* issues Thomas Cook TCs and gives cash advances against Visa cards.

Communications Internet cafés: *Ginza Internet Café*, 428 Jln Chulia, T2644309; *Omegactec*, 50 Lebuh Lieth,T/F2643750, sells teaching software and internet services, friendly and helpful staff. *Easy-net*, Praingin Mall, opposite KOMTAR. There are also a number of other internet cafés along Lebuh Chulia, all offering similar rates of RM3/hr. There are also internet cafes off Jln Burma, down Jln Macalister, which cater for the more hardened computer games addict. **General Post Office:** Lebuh Pitt, efficient poste restante, also provides a parcel-wrapping service, T2618973. **Telecoms office** (international calls; fax and telex facilities): Jln Burmah.

Embassies & consulates *Denmark*, Bernam Agencies, Hong Kong Bank Cham-bers, Lebuh Downing, T2624886; *France*, 82 Bishop St, Wisma Rajab, T2629707; *Ger-many*, Bayan Lepas Free Trade Zone, T6415707; *Indonesia*, 467 Jln Burmah, T2274686; *Japan*, 2 Jln Biggs, T2268222; *Netherlands*, Algemen Bank Nederland, 9 Lebuh Pantai, T2616471; *Thailand*, 1 Jln Ayer Raja, T2268029 (visas arranged in 2 days); *UK*, Birch House, 73 Jln Datuk Keramat, T2625333.

Libraries *Penang Public Library*, Dewan Sri Pinang, Lebuh Light, T2622255. *The British Council*, T2630330.

Medical facilities Hospitals: *General Hospital* (government), Jln Residensi, T2293333; *Lam Wah Ee Hospital* (private), 141 Jln Batu Lancang, T6571888.

Places of worship *St George's Church*, Lebuh Farquhar, services in English 0830 and 1830 every Sun.

Useful addresses Immigration Office: on the corner of Lebuh Light and Lebuh Pantai, T2615122.

Directory

Northern Peninsula

Batu Ferringhi and Teluk Bahang

Batu Ferringhi
Colour map 1, grid B1

The main beach, Batu Ferringhi, whose hot, white sands were once the nirvana of Western hippies, has been transformed into an upmarket tropical version of the Costa Brava. There are now at least 10 hotels along the beach strip and graffiti are splashed across the famous Foreigner's Rock. *Ferringhi* – which is related to the Thai word *farang*, or foreigner – actually means 'Portuguese' in Malay. Portuguese Admiral Albuquerque, who captured Melaka in 1511, stopped off at Batu Ferringhi for fresh water on his way down the Straits. St Francis Xavier is said to have visited Batu Ferringhi in 1545. Towards the end of the 16th century, Captain James Lancaster, who later founded the East India Company in 1600, also came ashore at the beach.

Despite the explosion of development, Batu Ferringhi still meets most visitors' expectations

To the majority of today's tourists, Batu Ferringhi *is* Penang. The beach is just over 3 km long but it has been extended to the fishing village of Teluk Bahang at the west end. Most holidaymakers and honeymooners prefer to stick to their hotel swimming pools rather than risk bathing in the sea. Pollution, siltation and an influx of jellyfish have affected water quality, but of late, the hotels have taken much more care of the beach itself. With its palms and casuarina trees and its (almost) turquoise water, it retains at least some of its picture-postcard beauty. The hotels offer many different activities: windsurfing, water skiing, diving, sailing and fishing as well as jungle walks and sightseeing tours of the island.

Apart from the string of plush modern hotels, the Batu Ferringhi area also has many excellent restaurants, hawker stalls and handicraft shops. The **Yahong Art Gallery**, 58d Batu Ferringhi Road, T8811251, F8811093, displays batik paintings by the Teng (born in China in 1914) family. The elder Teng is regarded as the father of Malaysian batik painting. Entrance is free and the batik works are certainly worth it. Also offers packaging and transport of bought goods to any international destination.

Teluk Bahang

This small fishing kampung is situated at the westerly end of this northern stretch of beach. It is where the Malabar fishermen used to live and has now

Penang's beaches

Sleeping	6 Copthorne Orchid	11 Lone Pine
1 Ah Beng	7 Crown Prince	12 Mar Vista Resort
2 Ali's	8 ET Budget Guest House	13 Parkroyal
3 Baba's	9 Ferringhi Beach	14 Penang Mutiara Beach Resort
4 Bayview Beach Resort	10 Golden Sands	15 Rasa Sayang
5 Casuarina Beach		16 Sandy Bay Paradise

Eating
1 Eden Seafood Village
2 Happy Garden
3 Ship Steakhouse

Related maps
A Penang, page 153
A Georgetown, page 156
A Penang Hill, page 161

been dramatically changed by the *Penang Mutiara Beach Resort*. Beyond Teluk Bahang, around **Muka Head**, the coast is broken into a series of small secluded coves separated by rocky headlands; there are several tiny secluded beaches. Some of these are only accessible by boat, which can be hired either from the beach hotels, or from fishermen in Teluk Bahang, which is much cheaper. Trails also lead over the headland from the fishing kampung. One trail goes along the coast past the Universiti Malaya Marine Research Station to Mermaid Beach and Muka Head lighthouse (one-and-a-half hours); another leads straight over the headland to Pantai Keracut (two hours).

The **Teluk Bahang Recreation Forest** has several well-marked trails and a **Forestry Museum**. ■ *0900-1300, 1400-1700 Tue-Thu, Sat-Sun; 0900-1200, 1445-1700 Fri.* One kilometre up the road from the Teluk Bahang junction, the **Butterfly Farm** (Butterfly House, 830 Jln Teluk Bahang, T8851253, F8852011, tpgoh@butterfly-insects.com) claims to be the largest tropical butterfly farm in the world. It has around 4,000 butterflies at any one time, representing over 120 species of Malaysian butterflies. The best time to visit the farm is in the late morning or early afternoon when the butterflies are most active. There is a small but excellent reptile and insect museum next door. The farm is also an important research centre and breeding station. Around 20% of the butterflies are released into the wild to help secure the future of the different species. ■ *0900-1730 Mon-Fri, 0900-1800 Sat-Sun, adults RM10, children RM5.* The **Green Orchid Farm**, Jln Sungai Pinang, is situated next door to the Butterfly Farm. It is a small place with a wide range of orchids – all for sale, potted, bottled or just cut stems. The farm offers a delivery service of 25 stems to England for RM55. While it is not a garden as such it is still worth a look if you appreciate orchids. Run by Mr Cheah who is very proud, and watchful, of his crop! Open 0800-1900 daily.

Sleeping
■ *on map, page 172*
Price codes:
see inside front cover

The big international hotels all have excellent facilities, including tennis, watersports, sailing and sightseeing tours. They also offer free shuttle services at least once a day to Georgetown. With fewer European customers, many have turned their attention to the incentive travel business and the Asian market, targeting Singaporeans in particular. Hotels are still going up though. While middle-to-upmarket tourists are spoilt for choice, budget travellers' options on the north coast are rather more limited.

Batu Ferringhi L-AL *Bayview Beach*, T8812123, F8812140, www.bayiewbeach.com A/c, 2 restaurants, pool, over 400 rooms, pleasant location, away from others on the strip. Recently renovated, plush interior, sophisticated, but not strikingly different from any other 5-star hotel here. Staff are friendly. **L-AL** *Casuarina Beach*, T8811711, F8812155, caspen@tm.net.my Elegant rooms, a/c, restaurant, pool, named after the trees that line Batu Ferringhi beach, particularly nice grounds and a good beach, a variety of watersports arranged, theme parties. Tennis courts and table tennis available. Doctor on-call and laundry service. **L-AL** *Ferringhi Beach Hotel*, T8905999, F8905100, ferringhi@po.jaring.my A/c, restaurant, pool, 350 rooms, a/c, mini-bar, TV, in-house video, overhead bridge to beach, offers golf packages, caters mainly for tour groups. **L-AL** *(Shangri La's) Golden Sands Resort*, T8811911, F8811880. A/c, restaurant, pool, popular and central on the beach, arguably the best swimming pool, a *Shangri La* outfit. Restaurant and bar situated on the beach front. Well equipped and a large resort. **L-AL** *Lone Pine*, T8811511, F8811282, www.lonepinehotel.com A/c, restaurant, one of the oldest hotels along Batu Ferringhi (opened in 1948), TV, mini-bar, pool, reasonably priced, but not up to the standards of its neighbours. Wouldn't win a beauty contest but has 10 ha of landscape gardens. Nightly live band, set back from beach slightly. Quieter, less hectic atmosphere than neighbouring large resorts. **L-AL** *Mar Vista*

Resort, T8903388, F8903886, mvr@po.jaring.my All 120 suites have kitchenette (utensils extra charge), sea views, a/c, TV. Dated décor, pool, paddling pool, jacuzzi, health club, restaurant. Apartment rental ranges from weekly to yearly. Resort has all the facilities one would expect. **L-AL** *Parkroyal*, T8811133, F8812233, www.sphc.com.my A/c, 4 restaurants, attractive pool, gym, tennis court, large 300-room 5-star hotel, with excellent facilities especially for families, including children's play area, special children's programmes and babysitting. Beautiful garden area and large, airy rooms with sea views. Recommended. **L-AL** *Rasa Sayang* T8811811, F8811984, www.shangri-la.com A/c, restaurants, pool, one of the *Shangri La* group, winner of Tourism Malaysia 1995 Award for Excellence in Hotel Services. Over 500 rooms, probably the most popular along the beach strip, modern interpretation of Minangkabau-style, horse-shoe design around central pool and garden area. More sophisticated style than others on the strip, still welcoming. Recommended.

C-D *Ah Beng*, 54c Batu Ferringhi, right on the beach, T8811036. A/c, clean. At the end of the budget hotel road, rooms with a/c (**C**) or fan (**D**). Friendly, family run. Recommended. **C-D** *Ali's*, 53b Batu Ferringhi, T8811316, F8812703, alisgues@tm.net.my Alongside *Ah Beng's* (53 & 54b Batu Ferringhi), clean and good value. Full of character, some rooms with a/c and shower, bar, restaurant. A backpackers' haven, garden bar provides good place to watch the world go by – one of the best budget options. **C-D** *Baba's*, 52 Batu Ferringhi, T8811686, baba1@tm.net.my Clean, homely and relaxed. Some rooms have a/c and shower. The owner here is well informed and a good source of information. **C-D** *ET Budget Guest House*, 47 Batu Ferringhi, T8811553. Good tour and bus information, laundry service. Another good value option with travel information and tickets available.

Teluk Bahang L *Penang Mutiara Beach Resort*, Jln Teluk Bahang, T8868888, F8852829, www.mutiarahotels.com A/c, restaurant, pool, over 400 rooms, the last outpost of 5-star luxury along the beach, and a member of the 'Leading Hotels of the World' group. The *Mutiara* (Malay for 'pearl') has landscaped gardens, a great pool with a bar and every conceivable facility including a children's wonderland; a drink at the *Mutiara* bar costs the same as a huge meal in some nearby restaurants. Recommended. **E** *Madame Loh*, near the mosque (left at the roundabout), clean, good atmosphere. **E-F** *Rama's*, 365 Mukim 2, T811179. Homestay-type accommodation, dorm or rooms.

Tanjung Bungah L-AL *Copthorne Orchid Penang*, T8903333, F8903303, copresv@ po.jaring.my A/c, 2 restaurants, pool, good business facilities. A very formal atmosphere. A little dated. **L-AL** *Crown Prince*, Tanjung Bungah, T8904111, F8904777, www.crownhotel.com Over 280 rooms, not as good as *Sandy Bay Paradise* but sometimes offers good-value promotions. **L-AL** *Sandy Bay Paradise*, 527 Jln Tanjung Bungah, T8999999, F8990000, www.paradisehotel.com More than 300 rooms, all of which are suites of varying size with kitchenette, balconies, sea views, TV, in-house video, mini-bar, complimentary coffee/tea, a/c and bath. The décor is tasteful and facilities are good, free-form pool, paddling pool, watersports, tennis, squash and gym, 24-hr coffee house and lounge overlooking the sea, set around a grand open lobby. Stunning views. Recommended.

Eating
● *on map, page 172*
Price codes: see inside front cover.
Virtually every cuisine is represented along this stretch

Many of the big Batu Ferringhi hotels have excellent restaurants. They have to be good as there is plenty of good quality competition from roadside restaurants.

Malay Cheap *Papa Din's Bamboo*, 124-B Batu Ferringhi (turn left after police station and *Eden Restaurant*, 200 m up the Kampung Road by *Happy Garden Restaurant*), home-cooked Malay fish curries made by loveable *bumoh* who prides himself on being able to say 'thank you' in 30 languages, Papa Din Salat is also a renowned masseur.

Seafood Mid-range *Eden Seafood Village*, 69a Batu Ferringhi, if it swims, *Eden* cooks it – priced according to weight – not cheap, nightly cultural shows, *Eden* has now expanded to include two other big, clean red restaurants, adjacent and opposite the original, the *Ferringhi Village* at 157b and *Penang Village*. **Mid-range** *Pearl Garden*, 78 Batu Ferringhi, affiliated to *Eden*, similar set-up, open courtyard or a/c interior. *The Catch*, Jln Teluk Bahang, next to *Mutiara Hotel*, Malay, Chinese, Thai and international seafood dishes, huge fish-tanks for fresh fish, prawns, crabs, lobster etc, 1-hr-long cultural show daily, pleasant setting, one of the best seafood restaurants on the island. Recommended. **Cheap** *End of the World*, end of Teluk Bahang beach, huge quantities of fresh seafood, its chilli crabs are superb and its lobster is the best value for money on the island (about RM25 each), pleasant setting on beach, not too many tourists. Recommended. *Happy Garden*, Batu Ferringhi, left after police station and *Eden* restaurant, pretty garden, Chinese and Western dishes. *Hollywood*, Tanjung Bungah, Batu Ferringhi, great views over the beach, serves *inche kabin* chicken stews and good selection of seafood.

Chinese expensive *House of Four Seasons*, Mutiara Beach Resort, Jln Teluk Bahang, closed Tue, good old-fashioned opulence, black marble, silk and carpets, interesting menu, Cantonese and Szechuan dishes. Recommended. *Marco Polo*, Bayview Beach Resort, Batu Ferringhi, wide selection of Cantonese dishes, shark's fin is popular, bright lighting and typical Chinese décor with tables set around a courtyard. **Mid-range** *Fok Lok Sow*, Mar Vista Resort, Batu Ferringhi, good value buffet (RM22) and 7-course set dinner. **Cheap** *Sin Hai Keng*, 551 Tanjung Tokong, overlooks the sea and serves everything from noodles to pork chops, excellent *satay*.

International Expensive *Feringgi Grill*, Rasa Sayang Resort, Batu Ferringhi, popular restaurant, aims to imitate an English club, 3-piece band, specialities include prime US rib of beef served with Yorkshire pudding, expensive but memorable. *La Farfalla*, Mutiara Beach Resort, 1 Jln Teluk Bahang, closed Mon, romantic setting overlooking pool, live string band play in background, authentic Italian chef, specialities include beef carpaccio, scallops and lobster. *The Ship*, Batu Ferringhi (next to *Eden*), purpose-built wooden ship with steakhouse inside. *Tiffins*, Parkroyal Hotel, Batu Ferringhi, very popular with locals, especially business people wishing to impress clients, Nyonya décor, wood carvings and antique furniture, eclectic cooking style, many interesting items, set meal is good value. **Mid range** *Sigi's By The Sea*, Shangri La's Golden Sands Resort. New restaurant on the waterfront, includes bar, full cocktail menu and lovely atmosphere. Food is high class as you'd expect. Specialities are the quesadillas and the lamb shanks. Recommended. *Guan Guan Café*, Batu Ferringhi (opposite Yahong Art Gallery), where backpackers hang out, good-value snacks; *Kokomo*, 1c Jln Sungai Kelian, Tanjung Bungah (opposite *Novotel*), hip meeting place, light meals and snacks, happy hour 1800-2100. *Wunderbar*, 37f Jln Cantonment (near Gurney Drive), authentic German restaurant.

Japanese Expensive *Honjin*, Bayview Beach Resort, Batu Ferringhi, peaceful Japanese-style setting with a garden at centre of restaurant, good quality food, set meals are best value. *Japanese Restaurant*, Rasa Sayang Resort, Batu Ferringhi, typically spartan Japanese décor, two main areas on menu: *sushi* and *sashimi*; and *teppanyaki*.

Thai Mid-range *Dusit Thai*, 92 Batu Ferringhi (next to *Lone Pine Hotel*). **Cheap** *Thai Spices*, 62 Cantonement Rd (near Gurney Drive), good-value set lunch, good Thai chefs.

Bars *Beers*, Parkroyal, Batu Ferringhi, good selection of beers, some draught, low prices, darts and snooker nights; *Sapphire*, Ferringhi Beach Hotel, Batu Ferringhi, open 2400-0100,

30% discount on pouring brands and draught beer, Ladies' Night Tue; *Swing Pub*, *Bayview Beach Resort*, Batu Ferringhi, cross between a pub and a disco.

Entertainment **Cultural shows** *Eden Seafood Village*, Batu Ferringhi; *Penang Cultural Centre*, near the *Mutiara*, Teluk Bahang, T8851175, F8842449, daily Malay Cultural Tour for a marathon length of 2½ hrs, with Silat demonstration, handicrafts, traditional game demonstrations, a visit to a Longhouse, the Heritage Gallery and, last but not least, a 45-min Cultural Show. Theme dinners can be booked at the *Istana-Malay Theatre Restaurant*, there also facilities for business events. Most of the larger hotels also have cultural shows in evening. **Discos** The following discos all open between 2100 and 0200: *Borsalino*, *Parkroyal*, Batu Ferringhi; *Cinta*, *Rasa Sayang Resort*, Batu Ferringhi; *Ozone*, *Mar Vista Resort*, Batu Ferringhi, also karaoke and live band area.

Health & fitness **Traditional massage** *Papa Din*, 124B Batu Ferringhi (see directions for *Papa Din's Bamboo*, page 174). Health clubs, such as the *Do-Club* in the *Mar Vista Resort*, Batu Ferringhi, in all major hotels offer massage.

Shopping **Batik** *Craft Batik*, opposite the Park Royal, batik cloth sold by metre starting at RM22 and as ready-made garments for RM45 upwards, demonstrations can be seen to rear of showroom; *Deepee's Silk Shop* offers a reasonable tailoring service; *Sim Seng Lee Batik and Handicrafts*, 391 Batu Ferringhi.

Tour operators *Bonus Vista Tours*, Jln Batu Ferringhi, T8812263, F8812264, next to *Widuri Tours*. Helpful staff. Wide range of tours on offer. *E & K Travel Tours*, Jln Batu Ferringhi, next to *Casuarina Beach* hotel, T8811629. Car hire. *Widuri Tours*, T8811558, F8811419. Golf, car hire.

Transport **Local Boat**: trips can be arranged through fishermen at Teluk Bahang. Negotiate the price in advance. **Bus**: blue bus No 93 goes to Batu Ferringhi/Teluk Bahang from Pengkalan Weld (Weld Quay) or Jln Maxwell in Georgetown. **Car hire**: *Avis*, *Rasa Sayang Hotel*, Batu Ferringhi; *Hertz*, *Casuarina Beach Hotel*, Batu Ferringhi; *Kasina Baru*, 651 Mukim 2, Teluk Bahang (opposite *Mutiara Beach Resort*), T8811988; *Mayflower*, *Casuarina Beach Hotel*, Batu Ferringhi; *Ruhanmas*, 157B Batu Ferringhi, T8811576; *Sintat Rent-a-Car*, *Lone Pine Hotel*, Batu Ferringhi. **Motorbike hire**: quite a few places along Batu Ferringhi offer motorbike hire, all of them clearly signposted on the road. **Taxi**: stands on Batu Ferringhi (opposite *Golden Sands Hotel*). The big hotels along the strip are well served by taxis. Be warned though that some taxis operate on commission for certain resorts and guesthouses. Try and work out roughly where you want to stay before you get there and ring up your destination in advance to check rates. 'New' rates quoted by some taxi drivers are merely attempts to ruin honest businesses.Of course not all taxi drivers are quite so manipulative; many are friendly, honest and a good source of information.

Long distance Air: Bayan Lepas Airport is an international airport, 20 km south of Georgetown and 36 km from Batu Ferringhi, T6434411. **Transport to town**: taxis operate on a coupon system from the airport (30 mins to Georgetown, RM16) or take yellow bus No 83 for either Teluk Bahang (up the west coast) or Georgetown (up the east coast). Regular connections with **Johor Bahru**, **KL**, **Kota Bharu**, **Kota Kinabalu**, **Kuala Terengganu**, **Kuching**, **Langkawi** and **Miri**. Worldwide international connections on *MAS*, most via KL. Regular connections to **Singapore** and **Medan**, Sumatra.

Boat: boats from Georgetown for **Langkawi** Mon-Sun, depart 0800 and return from Langkawi at 1815 (3 hrs), RM35 one way, RM60 return. Tickets can be bought from travel agents all over town. Boats leave from Swettenham Pier. It is possible to take a motorcycle or bicycle aboard. *Ekspres Bahagia* offer daily boats to Langkawi at 0800 and 0845; a daily service is also provided by *Kenangan Express*. There is also a weekly overnight service to Langkawi (fortnightly during the monsoon season) from Swettenham Pier. Leaves Georgetown at 2300 and arrives Langkawi at 0700 the next morning. For schedules contact Sanren Delta Marine at *E&O Shopping Complex*, 10 Lebuh Farquhar or Kuala Perlis Ferry Service, PPC Shopping Complex, Pesara King Edward, T2625630. **Ferry**: passenger and car ferries operate from adjacent terminals, Pengkalan Raja Tun Uda, T3315780. 24-hrs ferry service between Georgetown and **Butterworth**. Ferries leave every 20 mins 0600-2400. RM0.60 return (RM0.30 for children). *Selasa Express Ferry Company* has its office by the Penang Clock Tower, next to the Penang Tourist Office, T2625630. There is now a regular ferry service from Georgetown to Langkawi and on to **Phuket**; check details at Kuala Perlis Ferry service (see below).

Bus: the bus terminal is beside the ferry terminal at Butterworth. Booking offices along Lebuh Chulia. Some coaches operate from Pengkalan Weld direct to major towns on the peninsula (see Butterworth, page 150). *Masa Mara Travel*, 54/4 Jln Burmah, is an agent for direct express buses from Penang to **Kota Bharu** and **KL** (5 hrs). Minibus companies now organize an early morning pick-up from your hotel, to **Hat Yai**, from where there are connections north to Thailand. Pick ups at 0500, 0800, 1200, 1600 and 2200 . There are also regular bus connections to Bangkok, Phuket and Surat Thani. Also some hotels (eg *New Asia* and *Cathay*) organize minibuses to destinations in Thailand. Bus and ferry to Koh Samui, Krabi and Phuket. There is an overnight bus to **Singapore**. **Taxi**: direct taxis from Penang to Thailand: overnight to Hat Yai; Surat Thani for Koh Samui, Krabi (for Phuket).

International boat connections A number of companies operate ferries to Belawan (Medan's port), **Sumatra**, from Swettenham Pier. *Ekspres Bahagia* leave Penang for Medan on Mon and Tue at 0900 and on Wed and Fri at 1000. They depart Medan/Belawan for Penang on Mon and Tue at 1330 and on Thu and Sat at 1000. The fare is RM90 one-way, RM160 return, journey time 4½ hrs. Note that the Sat departure is often full, so book a ticket beforehand if possible. Their address in Penang is *Ekspres Bahagia*, Ground Flr, Penang Port, Commission Shopping Complex, Jln Pesara King Edward, T2631943/2635255. Their agent in Medan is *Eka Sukma Wisata Tour and Travel*, Jln Sisingamangaraja 92A. *Perdana Express* is another outfit that runs high-speed ferries on the Penang-Medan route. From Penang boats leave on Tue, Thu and Sat at 0900, journey time 4 hrs ; from Medan they depart on Wed, Fri and Sun at 1000. The fares are the same as *Ekspres Bahagia*. In Penang the *Perdana Express* office is on the Ground Flr, Penang Port, Commission Shopping Complex, Jln Pesara King Edward; and in Medan, they have an office at Jln Brig Jend Katamso 35C. *Selasa Express* is yet another company operating ferries between Belawan and Penang. Their office is by the Penang Clock Tower, next to the Penang Tourist Office, T2625630, and their agent in Medan is *Tobali Tour and Travel*, Jln Juanda Baru 52. All the companies offer free transfer between Belawan and Medan.

Car: the recent completion of the north-south expressway makes the journey from Penang to KL reasonably painless, 4½ hrs and a total toll cost of RM25. There is a RM7 toll to drive across the Penang Bridge on to Penang. No payment required for the outward journey.

Taxi: long-distance taxis to all destinations on peninsula operate from the depot beside the Butterworth ferry on Pengkalan Weld.

Northern Peninsula

Train: the station is by the Butterworth ferry terminal, T2610290. Advance bookings for onward rail journeys can be made at the station or at the ferry terminal, Pengkalan Weld, Georgetown. From Butterworth: regular connections with **Alor Star**, **Taiping**, **Ipoh**, **KL** (6 hrs), **Johor Bahru** (see page 45 for timetable). See also Butterworth, page 151.

Alor Star

Colour map 1, grid A2
Phone code: 04

Alor Star is the capital of Kedah State on the road north to the Thai border. It is the home town of Prime Minister Dr Mahathir Mohamad and is the commercial centre for northwest Malaysia. Its name, which has been corrupted from Alor Setar, means 'grove of setar trees' (which produce a sour fruit). Kedah is now Malaysia's most important rice-growing state; together with neighbouring Perlis, it produces 44% of the country's rice, and is known as jelapang padi or 'rice-barn country'.

Ins and outs

Getting there Alor Star's airport is 10 km north of town. Domestic connections with KL and Kota Bharu and international connections with Beijing and Guangzhou (China). From the railway station near the town centre trains connect with KL and Singapore (and points between) and north to the border with Thailand and Hat Tai. Alor Star is also on the main N-S highway and there are bus connections with all the major destinations on the Peninsular as well as Singapore and Hat Yai. The bus terminal is several kilometres ouside town. For Kuala Kedah and the ferry to Langkawi catch bus no 106 from the local bus station. Share taxis leave from the stand near the centre of town.

Getting around Taxis are available for out of town trips from the stand on Jln Langgar and the town bus station is not far away on Jln Stesyen, also close to the train station. It's easy enough to walk around the town centre.

Tourist offices *Kedah State Tourist Office*, 2nd Flr, State Secretariat Building, Jln Sultan Badlisah. Limited selection of brochures, not much information on Alor Star or Kedah.

Kedah is the site of some of the oldest settlements on the peninsula and the state's royal family can trace its line back several centuries. The ancient Indian names for the state are Kadaram and Kathah, and archaeologists believe the site of the 5th century kingdom of Langkasuka was just to the southeast of Kedah Peak (Gunung Jerai), in the Bujang River valley, half-way between Butterworth and Alor Star.

Sights

Alor Star has some interesting buildings, most of which are clustered round the central Padang Besar (Jalan Pekan Melayu/Jalan Raja); apart from them, the town is unremarkable. The most interesting building is the State Mosque, the Moorish-style **Masjid Zahir**, completed in 1912 and designed by state architect James Gorman. Almost directly opposite is the Thai-inspired **Balai Besar**, or audience hall, built in 1898, which is still used by the Sultan of Kedah on ceremonial occasions; it houses the royal throne. In mid-2001 the Balai Besar was being refurbished but is due to re-open at the end of 2002. Close to the mosque is the **Balai Seni Negeri**, or State Art

Gallery, which contains a collection of historical paintings and antiques, including Malay handicrafts and colonial collections. The building was formerly the High Court and was built in the early 20th century. ■ *1000-1800 Sat-Thu, 1000-1200 1430-1800 Fri*. Further down Jalan Raja is the 400-year-old **Balai Nobat**, an octagonal building topped by an onion-shaped dome. This building houses Kedah's royal percussion orchestra or *nobat*; it is said to date back to the 15th century. Again, it is not open to the public.

Royal Museum Kedah, or Muzium Di Raja, is next to the Baslai Besar and gives an insight into the heritage and traditions of the Sultans of Kedah. ■ *Sat-Thu 1000-1800, Fri 1000-1200 and 1430-1800, free.*

The **State Museum**, or Muzium Negeri, situated around 2 km north of the centre, is styled on the Balai Besar and was built in 1936. The museum houses exhibits on local farming and fishing practices, a collection of early Sung Dynasty porcelain and some finds from the archaeological excavations in the Bujang Valley (see below). ■ *1000-1800 Sat-Thu, 0900-1200, 1500-1800 on Fri*. The **Pekan Rabu** or Wednesday market (which is now held all week long)

Northern Peninsula

Alor Star

To Express Bus Station
To Stadium & Airport
Swimming Pool

Sungai Anak Bukit

Jln Lebuhraya Darulaman

State Museum
Jln Telok Wan Jah

Electrik Menyinari
Hidup Anda (Radar)

Nikradharam
Buddhist Temple

Jln Perak

To Thailand

Jln Putera
7
3
4   9

Jln Istana Lama

Sungei Alor Malai Malai

Royal
Boat House

Clock
Tower

Antique
Gallery

Balai Nobat

Masjid
Zahir

Children's
Playground

Balai Besar
(Audience Hall)

Padang

Balai Seni Negeri
(State Art Gallery)

Royal
Museum Kedah

Jln Sultan Badlishah

2
8

Jln Kolam

City Plaza
Shopping Complex

Jln Tunku Ibrahim

Jln Pekan Melayu   Jln Langgar

Pekan Rabu
Shopping
Complex

Pekan Rabu

5

Jln Langgar

Jln S A Halim

Malaysian
Airlines

6

Hanka Jaya
Shopping Centre

Central

10

Jln Stesyen

Jln Pengkalan

1

Taxis

To Sungai Petani
To Rumah Kelahiran Mahathir & Penang

SKMK Buses

Limbong Kapal

N

0 metres   100
0 yards   100

■ **Sleeping**
1 Flora Inn
2 Grand Continental
3 Grand Crystal
4 Grand Jubilee
5 Holiday Villa
6 Lim Kung
7 Miramar &
   Sentosa Regency
8 Regent
9 Samila
10 Sing Tak Sing

is a good place to buy local handicrafts and try some of the traditional food of Kedah. It does not cater for tourists, and is therefore a good place to find local foods and see everyday Malay life.

Two other places of interest are the **Royal Boat House**, near the Sungai Anak Bukit, west of the clock tower. It houses boats belonging to former rulers of Kedah. For prime minister-watchers, the house where Prime Minister Dr Mahathir Mohamad was born on 20 December 1925, has been opened as a **museum**, giving an insight into his early days of 'simple' living. Photographs and various bits-and-pieces of Mahathir memorabilia including his 'favourite' bicycle are on display. It is to be found at 18 Lorong Kilang Ais, off Jalan Pegawai. ■ *0900-1800 Sat-Thu, 0900-1200, 1500-1800 Fri.*

Excursions

Bujang Valley Situated near the small town of **Sungai Petani**, to the southeast of Kedah Peak (Gunung Jerai), is this site of some of Malaysia's most exciting archaeological discoveries: finds there have prompted the establishment of the **Bujang Valley Historical Park**, under the management of the National Museum. The name Bujang is derived from a Sanskrit word, *bhujanga*, meaning serpent. It is thought to be the site of the capital of the 5th-century Hindu kingdom of Langkasuka, the hearthstone of Malay fairytale romance. While the architectural remains are a far cry from those of Cambodia's Angkor Wat, they are of enormous historical significance.

The city is thought to represent one of the very earliest Hindu settlements in Southeast Asia, several centuries before Angkor, and at least 200 years before the founding of the first Hindu city in Java. The capital of Langkasuka is thought to have been abandoned in the 6th century, probably following a pirate raid. There have been some remarkable finds at the site, including brick and marble temple and palace complexes – of both Hindu and Buddhist origin – coins, statues, Sanskrit inscriptions, weapons and jewellery. In 1925 archaeologists stumbled across "a magnificent little granite temple near a beautiful waterfall" on a hillside above the ancient city. One of them, Dr Quarith Wales, the director of the Greater-India Research Committee wrote of the temple: "It had never been robbed, except of images, although the bronze trident of Shiva was found. In each of the stone post-holes were silver caskets containing rubies and sapphires." More than 50 temples have now been unearthed in the Bujang area, most of them buried in soft mud along the river bank.

For several centuries, Indian traders used the city as an entrepôt in their dealings with China. Rather than sail through the pirate-infested Melaka Strait, the traders stopped at the natural harbour at Kuala Merbok and had their goods portered across the isthmus to be collected by ships on the east side. There is speculation that the area of the Sungai Bujang was later used as a major port of the Srivijaya Empire, whose capital was at Palembang, Sumatra. But recent findings by Malaysian archaeologists have begun to contradict some of the earlier theories that Hinduism was the earliest of the great religions to be established on the Malay peninsula. Recently excavated artefacts suggest that Buddhism was introduced to the area before Hinduism. The local archaeologists maintain that the Buddhist and Hindu phases of Bujang Valley's history are distinct, with the Hindu period following on much later, in the 10th-14th centuries. This is at odds with previous assertions by archaeologists that the remains of the temples' "laterite sanctuary towers are of the earliest type and not yet suggestive of pre-Angkorian architecture".

Many of the finds can be seen in the museum at Bukit Batu Pahat near Bedong; alongside the museum is a reconstruction of the most significant temple unearthed so far, **Candi Bukit Batu Pahat**, Temple of the Hill of Chiselled Stone. Eight sanctuaries have been restored and a museum displays statues and other finds. ■ *0900-1600 Mon-Thu, 1445-1600 Fri, 0900-1215 Sat-Sun*. There are a number of hotels in the nearest town, Sungai Petani. The plushest is the **B** *Sungai Petani Inn*, Jalan Kolam Air, T4213411, with air conditioning and pool. Among the budget places is the **D** *Hotel Duta*, 7 Jalan Petri. To get there, change buses at Bedong; it is easier to take a taxi from Alor Star.

Otherwise known as Kedah Peak, Gunung Jerai is the highest mountain in the northwest and is part of the **Sungai Teroi Forest Recreation Park**. This park is managed by the state government, and visitors to the park will be accompanied by a guide. A jeep meets visitors at the foot of the mountain and transports them to the summit. The peak has been used as a navigational aid for ships heading down the Strait of Melaka for centuries. It is between the main road and the coast, north of Sungai Petani. In 1884 the remains of a 6th- century Hindu shrine were discovered on the summit. It had been hidden under a metre-thick layer of peat, which caught fire, revealing the brick and stone construction, thought to be linked with the kingdom of Langkasuka. Archaeologists speculate that the remains may originally have been a series of fire altars. But they are destined to remain a mystery as a radio station has now been built on top. About 3 km north of Gurun, between Sungai Petani and Alor Star, a narrow road goes off to the left and leads to the top of the mountain (11 km). There is even a small hotel just below the summit and the Museum of Forestry on top. There are good views out over Kedah's paddy fields and the coast. In mid-1994 the Kedah State Government scrapped plans for a huge Disney-style theme park on the coast below the mountain. Work on the prestigious US$7bn *Jerai International Park* was to have begun in June that year. It was to have been bigger than the Disney parks in California and France. State officials pulled the plug on the project following vociferous protests from local rice farmers and fishermen.

Gunung Jerai
Altitude: 1,206m

Sleeping B *Gunung Jerai Resort*, T04414311. A 1920s resthouse, rooms and chalets, garden. **B** *Peranginan Gunung Jerai*, Sungai Teroi Forest Recreation Park, T4223345. A/c, restaurant, attached bathrooms with showers, slightly worn but reasonable.

Transport Gunung Jerai is about 4 km north of Garun. Jeeps from Gurun to the resort run 0900-1700. Gurun is 33 km south of Alor Star and 60 km north of Butterworth.

Essentials

AL *Holiday Villa*, 162/163 Jln Tunku Ibrahim (contained in the large Plaza shopping centre), T7349999, F7341199, hbas@pd.jaring.my Large luxury hotel in the centre of town, with a great swathe of facilities including IDD telephone, in-house video, and 24-hr restaurant. Guests have access to the Villa Recreational Centre with fitness centre, sauna, pool and steambath. **AL** *Sentosa Regency Hotel*, 250 Jln Putra, T7303999, F7308999, regency@po.jaring.my A new hotel with spacious rooms, some semi-suites also available. Facilities include restaurant, tea/coffee-making facilities in room, gym, laundry service, satellite TV. Pleasant and not too impersonal. **A** *Grand Continental*, Lot 134-141, Jln Sultan Badlishah, T7335917, F7335161, www.grandstay.com A/c, 138 rooms, bath, TV, in-house movies, coffee house, business centre, car rental, central location and great-value discounts from the rack rate usually available.

Sleeping
■ *on map, page 179*
Price codes:
see inside front cover

Northern Peninsula

B *Grand Crystal*, 40 Jln Kampung Perak, T7313333, F7316368, www. grandstay.com A/c, TV, bath, pool, coffee house – like the *Grand Continental* (it is part of the same chain), discounts often on offer, includes breakfast. **B** *Samila*, 27 Jln Lebuhraya Darulaman, T7318888, F7339934. A/c, restaurant, nightclub, a step down from the *Grand Crystal* in terms of price. Dark wood 1970s décor creates a stylish and rather retro interior, plus it has a friendly and comfortable atmosphere. **B** *Seri Malaysia*, Mukim Alor Malai, Daerah Kota Setar, Jln Stadium, T7308738, F7307594. A 100-room hotel, one of the 'amazingly affordable' chain, a/c, TV, shower, tea/coffee-making facilities, in-house video, café, clean, functional and good value, located between stadium and public swimming pool at north end of town.

C *Flora Inn*, 8 Kompleks Medan Raja, Jln Pengkalan Kapal, T7322375, F7308058. Overlooking the Kedah River, a/c, TV, food court, coffee-making facilities, laundry service available. Rather tired décor but spacious. Not the best-value option in town, although at the bottom end of their range of rooms they have some reasonably priced 'eco' (ie economy rather than ecological) rooms. **C** *Regent*, 1536 Jln Sultan Badlishah, T7311900, F7311291. All 25 rooms with a/c, great value for money. Recently refurbished, new TVs with cable channels and movies available, new bathrooms and entire hotel repainted to give bright, friendly atmosphere. Recommended. **C** *Rumah Rehat* (*Government Resthouse*), 75 Pumpong, T722422. Some a/c, book beforehand as it tends to fill up with government people. **C-D** *Grand Jubilee Hotel*, 429 Jln Kancut, T7330055, F7330197. Clean and well managed. Rooms with shower, some with a/c and TV. Simple but friendly.

D *Sing Tak Sing*, 2nd Flr, Jln Stesyen, T7325482. Fan only, large, dirty rooms, not a great option but cheap. Has a reputation for being less than suitable for lone females. **E** *Lim Kung*, 36A Jln Langgar, T722459. Fan only, good value. Recommended. **C** *Miramar*, 246 Jln Putra, T7338144, F7311668. Simple and clean rooms with a/c and attached bathrooms. Some cheaper fan rooms. Standard budget option.

Eating   **Chinese Mid-range** *Samila Hotel*, 27 Jln Kancut. Recommended. **Cheap** *Sri Pumpong*, Jln Pumpong, speciality: barbecued fish. **Indian Cheap** *Bunga Tanjong*, Jln Seberang, Indian Muslim food, seafood curries. **Thai Cheap** *Café de Siam*, Jln Kota, lashings of Thai-style seafood. *Kway Teow Jonid*, Jln Stadium (next to the police station), fried *kway teow*, washed down with *teh tarik*. **Malay Cheap** *Rose Restaurant*, Jln Sultan Badishah, local café serving good *roti* and *nasi*. Recommended. **Foodstalls** '*Garden*' *Hawker Centre*, Jln Stadium, good range of cuisines, next to stadium, Jln Langgar (in front of cinema); *Old Market* (*Pekan Rabu*), Jln Tunku Ibrahim.

Shopping   An extensive shopping plaza can be found in the multi-storey building at the end of Jln Tunku Ibrahim (it also houses the *Holiday Villa Hotel*). **Handicrafts** can be found in the Old Market, Pekan Rabu, on Jln Tunku Ibrahim.

Sport   **Golf** *Royal Kedah Club*, Pumpong, T7330467.

Transport   **Local Taxi**: these leave from the stand just south of Jln Langgur, near the centre of
93 km N of Butterworth   town, for Penang, Kuala Kedah (for Langkawi) and Kangar (Perlis).
462 km N of KL
409 km to Kota Bharu   **Long distance Air**: the airport is about 10 km north of town. Daily connections on MAS with **Kota Bharu** and and on *MAS* with **KL**. There are also connections with **Beijing** and **Guangzhou** in China.

Bus: Alor Star has rather a confusion of bus stations. The main bus terminal is about 2 km north of the town centre, off Jln Bakar Bata, and most long-distance buses leave from here. Destinations include **KL**, **Melaka**, **Ipoh**, **Johor Bahru**, **Kota Bharu**, **Kuantan**

and **Kuala Terengganu**. Local southbound buses, including buses to **Butterworth** and **Kuala Kedah** (for Langkawi), leave from the central bus station in front of the railway station on Jln Stesyen in the centre of town and also the express bus station. Local buses also leave from the small station by the taxi stop just off Jln Langgar; long-distance connections with **Kota Bharu** also leave from here.

International connections: the northern section of the new north-south Highway runs to the Malaysian border crossing at Bukit Kayu Hitam, from where it is easy to cross to **Sadao**, the nearest Thai town on the other side of the border. Most of the buses leave from Penang/Butterworth for **Bangkok** and other destinations on the Kra Isthmus. There are, though, two direct connections a day between Alor Star and **Hat Yai** in Thailand following the north-south highway through Changlun to Bukit Kayu Hitam – the easiest way to cross the border. These leave from the small station on Jln Sultan Badlishah, north of the town centre. Alternatively, catch a bus or taxi from Alor Star, following the north-south highway, to **Bukit Kayu Hitam**, on the border with Thailand. It is then a shortish walk past the paraphernalia of border-dom to the bus and taxi stop where there are connections with the Thai town of Sadao (a few kilometres on) and Hat Yai. A less popular alternative is to travel to Padang Besar (accessible from Kangar in Perlis), where the railway line crosses the border. From here it is an easy walk to the bus or train station for connections to Hat Yai. The other option is to take a taxi from Sungai Petani to Keroh and cross the border into Thailand's red-light outpost at Betong.

There are also bus connections with **Singapore** from the main long-distance terminal, or Express Bus Station, 1 km north of town. Share taxis are also available. A shuttle bus also goes here, from Jln Langar in the centre.

Train: station is off Jln Langgar. Regular connections with KL, Butterworth, see page 45 for timetable. There is a through-train from Alor Star to **Hat Yai** in Thailand departing daily at 0619. The international express from Singapore goes through Alor Star but does not stop to pick up passengers. See Butterworth for trains to Thailand.

Directory **Airline offices** *MAS*, 180 Kompleks Alor Star, Lebuhraya Darulaman, T711106; also next to *Flora Inn*, Jln Pengkalan. **Banks** *Bank Bumiputra*, Jln Tunku Ibrahim; *Chartered Bank*, *Overseas Union Bank* and *UMBC* are all on Jln Raja. **Communications** General Post Office: Jln Langgar, opposite the Police Station. **Internet cafés:** there is one in the Plaza shopping centre at the end of Jln Tunku Ibrahim.

Kuala Kedah
12 km W of Alor Star

Historically the town has been an important port for trade with India and there are the ruins of an old fort, built between 1771 and 1780. The fort was built for defence of the state capital from pirate attacks. It fell into the hands of the Siamese army, under the leadership of Raja Ligor in 1821 and was occupied by Siam until 1842, after which it was abandoned. Kuala Kedah is renowned for its seafood stalls. It is also a departure point for Langkawi (see page 185).

Transport **Bus**: buses leave every 30 mins from Alor Star to **Kuala Kedah**. **Boat**: regular connections with **Langkawi**. Langkawi ferry leaves 0800, 0930, 1130, 1200, 1330, 1430 and 1600. **Taxi**: from Alor Star.

Kangar
45 km from Alor Star and 138 km from Butterworth

The state of Perlis, the smallest in Malaysia, is a very picturesque area with limestone outcrops surrounded by rice paddy. The capital of Perlis is Kangar, a small and unremarkable town with a lively *pasar tani*, a farmers' market, every Saturday and a *pasar malam* (night market) which sets up at 1700 every Wednesday. The town is otherwise of little interest, with a few blocks of shabby, modern shophouses and a large concrete shopping centre being developed at its centre. The historical monuments of Perlis, the state mosque and palace, are located 12 km outside the town, in **Arau**, where a *pasar malam* takes place on a Friday.

Sleeping A *Kangar Travelodge*, 135 Jln Kangar, T9767755, F9761049. All 146 rooms have a/c, bath, TV. Also restaurant, business centre and pool. C *Federal*, 104b Jln Kangar, T9766288, F9766224. Some of the 46 rooms have a/c; shower, TV, restaurant. **D** *Malaysia*, 67 Jln Jubli Perak, T9761366. A/c, seen better days. **D-E** *Ban Cheong*, 79a Jln Besar, T9761184. Cheapest place in town, basic but serviceable.

Transport **Bus**: the bus terminal is on Jln Hospital, near the centre of town. Regular connections with **Butterworth**, **Alor Star**, **KL** (RM23.50), **Ipoh**, **Johor Bahru**, **Kuantan**. Local bus No 56 to **Kuala Perlis**, No 59 to **Padang Besar**. **Taxi**: **Alor Star**, **Kuala Perlis**, and **Butterworth**.

Kuala Perlis
14 km from Kangar

This small fishing port at the delta of the Sungai Perlis is mainly a jumping-off point for Pulau Langkawi and Phuket (in Thailand). It is noted for its local fast-food, *laksa*, and there are foodstalls by the jetty. If you miss the boat to Langkawi, the *Soon Hin Hotel* (**E**) is across from the taxi rank or *Pens Hotel* F9854131 (**B**), Jalan Kuala Perlis, T049854122. There is a night market every Tuesday. The *Putra Golf Club* is an 18-hole, par-72 course in Sungai Batu Pahat, 12 km from Kangar.

Transport **Bus and taxi**: both leave from the ferry terminal. Regular connections by bus and taxi with **Butterworth**, less-regular links with **Alor Star**, **KL** and **Padang Besar** (for connections with Thailand, see below) and local buses to **Kangar**. **High-speed ferry**: departs from Kuala Perlis jetty approximately every hr between 0900 and 1415, the journey takes 45 mins. Kuala Perlis Langkawi Ferry Service, Kuala Perlis, T9854406. Last ferry back to Kuala Perlis leaves at 1600.

Padang Besar
50 km from Kangar

This is a border town. The railway station platform is very long as half is managed by Thai officials and half by Malaysians. *Pekan Siam*, opposite the railway station, is full of Thai goods and a popular shopping spot for Malaysians.

Transport **Bus**: the station is about 1 km from the border crossing. Regular connections from Kuala Perlis and Kangar. **Taxi**: from Kuala Perlis and Kangar.

Kangar

■ **Sleeping**
1 Federal
2 Kangar Travelodge
3 Malaysia

Pulau Langkawi

The Langkawi group is an archipelago of 99 islands around 30 km off the west coast of Peninsular Malaysia, and Pulau Langkawi itself, by far the largest of the group, is a mountainous, palm-fringed island with scattered fishing kampungs, paddy fields and sandy coves. Some of the islands are nothing more than deserted limestone outcrops rearing out of the turquoise sea, cloaked in jungle, and ringed by coral.

*Phone code: 04
Colour map 1, grid A1
It is easy to get round the island at a fairly leisurely pace within a day*

The name Langkawi is the last surviving namesake of the ancient kingdom of

Northern Peninsula

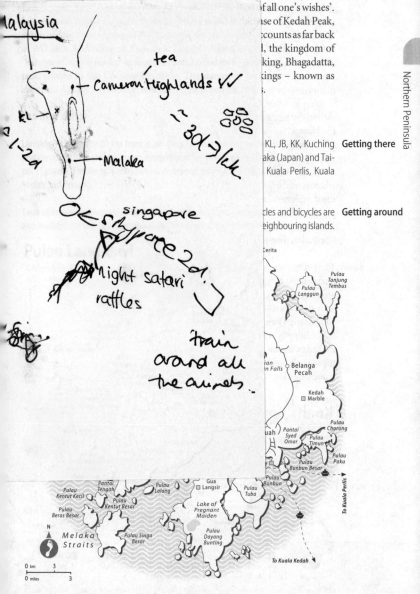

Tourist offices   *Langkawi Tourist Information Centre*, Jln Pesiaran Putra, Kuah, T9667789, F9667889. There is also an information booth at the jetty. Office and booth are open: 0900-1300, 1400-1800, daily.

In January 1987 the Malaysian government conferred duty-free status on Langkawi to promote tourism on the island. The small airport was upgraded, and the ferry service from Penang was instructed to run regularly. These efforts to turn Langkawi into one of Malaysia's big tourism money-spinners are bearing fruit as the island is attracting increasing numbers of visitors. The promotion campaign and improved transport links to the mainland means the islands can no longer be touted as 'Malaysia's best-kept secret'. New hotels, shopping centres and restaurants have sprouted with typical Southeast Asian speed and, for some former visitors at least, the Langkawi of old is just a memory. But development has been concentrated in a handful of places, so much of the island remains relatively unspoilt. Budget accommodation is still available and the construction of upmarket hotels and resorts means that a broader spectrum of tourists is being attracted. Nearby islands are just starting to develop.

Every so often, Langkawi's beautiful beaches are threatened by oil spills in the nearby Strait of Melaka. Langkawi had a close call in January 1993 when the *Maersk Navigator*, a Danish-owned supertanker carrying two million barrels of crude oil to Japan, was in collision with another vessel. One of its tanks was ruptured, the ship burst into flames and oil began gushing into the sea just north of Sumatra. The slick fortunately drifted off into the Indian Ocean where it was broken down with chemical dispersants. But Malaysia's environment minister, Law Hieng Ding, predicted that unless there was more rigid policing of the busy waterway, and adequate pollution-prevention measures were enforced, it would only be a matter of time before Malaysia was struck by a pollution disaster.

Kuah   The main town is strung out along the seafront, and is the landing point for ferries from Satun (Thailand), Kuala Perlis and Kuala Kedah. The town is growing fast and developers have reclaimed land along the shoreline to cope with the expansion. One of the largest developments on the new shores of Kuah is the *Tiara Hotel* with its pink towers and turrets, which incorporates a large shopping centre. There is also a new and rather stark park area overlooked by a giant effigy of an eagle on Dataran Lang (Eagle Square), symbol of the island's flight to prosperity. The park area itself, Chogm Park, was built to commemorate the Commonwealth Heads of Government Meeting

Kuah

Sleeping			Eating
1 Central	3 Grand Continental	6 The Gates	1 Mai
2 City Bayview	4 Nagoya City	7 Tiara Langkawi	
	5 Sheraton Perdana		

Not to scale

(CHOGM) in 1989. The old part of Kuah has several restaurants, a few grotty hotels, banks, plenty of coffee shops and a string of duty-free shops, which do a roaring trade in cheap liquor, cigarettes and electronics. There is also an attractive but historically and architecturally unimportant mosque.

The town's name *Kuah*, meaning 'gravy', is said to derive from a legend about a fight that broke out between two families who fell out over the breaking of a betrothal. Kitchen pots and pans were thrown around and a cooking pot smashed on to *Belanga Pecah* ('broken pot'); its contents splashed all over Kuah. A saucepan of boiling water landed at *Telaga Air Hangat* (the motley hot springs on the north of the island).

The road west to the golf course goes to Makam Mahsuri, the tomb of the legendary Princess Mahsuri, in the village of Mawat 12 km from Kuah. The beautiful Mahsuri was condemned to death for alleged adultery in 1355. She protested her innocence and several attempts to execute her failed. According to the legend, the sentence was finally carried out using her own *tombak* (lance) and her severed head bled white blood, thus confirming her innocence. Before Mahsuri died she cursed the island, saying it would remain barren for seven generations. Shortly afterwards, the Thais attacked, killing, plundering, looting and razing all the settlements to the ground. At the time of the Thai attacks, villagers buried their entire rice harvest on Padang Matsirat in Kampung Raja, but the Thais found it and set fire to it too, giving rise to the name Beras Terbakar, the 'field of burnt rice', nearby. The legend is more interesting than the field. ■ *0800-1700, RM1.*

Makam Mahsuri

Southwest of Mahsuri's tomb, past some beautiful paddy fields and coconut groves, are the two main beaches, Pantai Cenang and Pantai Tengah. Pantai Cenang is a strip about 2 km long, with budget and mid-range chalet operations, most of which have only a limited length of beachfront, and a few upmarket places, such as the *Pelangi Beach Resort* at the top end. At low tide between November and January a sandbar appears, and it is possible to walk across to the nearby **Pulau Rebak Kecil**. It is also possible to hire boats to the other islands off Pantai Cenang from the beach. Pantai Cenang also has a range of watersport facilities on offer and boasts the **Langkawi Underwater World**, one of the largest aquariums in Asia. It comprises more than 100 tanks with over 5,000 types of marine life. The highlight of the aquarium is the 15-m-long walk-through tunnel tank. ■ *1000-1800 daily, RM18 (RM10 for children), T9556100. www.sriwani.com.my/underwaterworld.*

Pantai Cenang & Pantai Tengah
Pantai Cenang is still one of the nicest beaches on the island and there is accommodation to suit all budgets

Most of the new beach chalet development is along the 3-km stretch of coast from Pantai Cenang to Pantai Tengah, which is at the far southern end, around a small promontory. Pantai Tengah is less developed and quieter than Pantai Cenang. The beaches can get crowded at weekends and during school and public holidays.

The road west leads past the airport to Pantai Kok, once a magnificent unspoilt bay with a dramatic backdrop of the forested Gunung Mat Cincang. However, recent years have seen considerable development all along the west coast – the backpackers have been pushed out to make way for the more favoured well-heeled travellers and accommodation has been built to house them all. There are several isolated beaches along the bay, accessible by boat from either Pantai Kok itself, Pantai Cenang (12 km away) or Kampung Kuala Teriang, a small fishing village *en route*. On the west headland, a 2-km walk from Pantai Kok, the **Telaga Tujuh** waterfalls used to be the island's so-called

Pantai Kok

'most wonderful natural attraction'. It can no longer claim to be that, as the area has been bought by *Berjaya Leisure Berhad*, 'mother' of the *Berjaya Hotels Group*. A pipeline running next to the pools, and the waterfall, goes all the way to the *Berjaya Beach and Spa Resort* on nearby Burau Bay, so water no longer cascades down a steep hillside, between huge rocks and through a series of seven (*tujuh*) pools (*telaga*); so much for development.

North coast   Right on the northwest tip of Langkawi is **Datai Bay**, which has a beautifully landscaped golf course and one of the most sophisticated resorts in Malaysia. Guests also enjoy exclusive access to one of the island's best beaches. It is accessible via a new road, which cuts up through the hills to the coast from the Pantai Kok to Pasir Hitam road. **Crocodile Adventureland Langkawi** is situated just beyond the junction, and houses more than 1,000 crocodiles. Along with the usual array of caged crocodilia that consume 1,000 kg of meat daily, this gruesome place has pythons and various other shows and delights to tantalise the discerning visitor. For those who like their crocodiles well and truly domesticated it is also possible to buy them stuffed or conveniently transformed into bags, shoes and belts. ■ *0900-1800, RM8 (RM5 for children), daily shows at 1115 and 1445, T9592559.*

Pantai Rhu (also known as Casuarina Beach) is a beautiful white-sand cove, enclosed by a jungled promontory with **Gua Cerita**, or the 'Cave of Legends', at the end of it. Within the cave, Koranic verse has been written on the walls. Beneath the sheer limestone cliff faces, there are a couple of small beaches accessible by boat. The Thai island Koh Turatao is just 4 km north. Past the *Mutiara Hotel*, there is a collection of foodstalls and small shops next to the beach. It is possible to hire boats and canoes from the beach, which is backed by a small lagoon. **Telaga Air Hangat** is another recently completed tourist attraction, a 4-acre site some 14 km northwest of Kuah centred on some hot springs. Activities include displays of traditional crafts, elephant and snake 'displays', performances of traditional dance, as well as an 18-m-long, hand-carved river stone mural. There is a restaurant and a shop here. ■ *0900-1800, RM4 (children RM2), T9591357.* At the ninth milestone, a 3-km-long path branches off to the **Durian Perangin** waterfall, on the slopes of Gunung Raya, which rises to 911 m. Not far away, on the seaward side of the road, is the **Galeria Perdana**, which houses around 2,500 gifts given to long-serving Prime Minister Dr Mahathir Mohamad (he has held the top post since 1981 and is still going strong). Not to everyone's taste but it does give the visitor an idea of what to give the PM if you are invited to his house for tea. ■ *1000-1700 Mon-Thu, 1000-1415 and 1500-1700 Fri, 0900-1800 Sat and Sun, RM3 (RM1 children), T9591498.*

Excursions to neighbouring islands

Pulau Dayang Bunting   This island, whose name means 'Island of the Pregnant Maiden', is the second-largest island in the archipelago, and lies just south of Langkawi. Separated from the sea by only a few metres of limestone is a freshwater lake renowned for its powers to enhance the fertility of women; unfortunately it is also said to be inhabited by a big white crocodile, although most people swim there unmolested. The myth surrounding this lake involves a beautiful girl named Telani, who became pregnant by the king's son. This indiscretion so angered the god Sang Kelembai that he brought a drought upon the land and turned the new-born baby into a white crocodile. Telani was turned into a rock and the king's son was transformed into an island. To the north of the lake is the intriguingly named **Gua Langsir**, or 'Cave of the Banshee'. The cave is high on a limestone cliff and is home to a large population of bats. Other nearby islands include **Pulau Bunbun**, **Pulau Beras Besar** and **Pulau Singa Besar**; there is some coral between the last two. Pulau Singa Besar is now a wildlife sanctuary, with about 90 resident bird species, wild boar and a huge population of mouse deer. A network of paths and trails are to be built around the island.

Transport Boat trips are organized to **Pulau Dayang Bunting** by many of the larger hotels and travel agents; or boats can be chartered privately from **Pantai Cenang**. Most trips also include a chance to snorkel off **Pantai Singa Besar**. Note that visibility is poor between Jul and Sep and that the sea can be rough.

This tiny island, 2 km long and 250 m wide, about an hour southeast of Langkawi, is part of a marine park. The other islands are **Segantan**, **Kala** and **Lembu**. A reef platform has been built with an underwater observation chamber and diving facilities (tank and weights RM50, full diving gear RM70, introductory dive RM100), bar and restaurant, souvenir shop. There are basic facilities on the island for day visitors, but those intending to camp on the island require the permission of the Fisheries Management and Protection Office, Wisma Tani, Jalan Mahameru, KL, T2982011, or Wisma Persekutuan, Jalan Kampung Baru, Alor Star, T725573. Trips to the islands can be arranged through many of the hotels or tour companies listed below. Several hotels and companies run day trips to Pulau Payar. These islands are also within reach of Kuala Kedah, on the mainland.

> **Pulau Paya**
> *Just to the south of Payar there is a good coral reef, reckoned to be the best off Malaysia's west coast*

> Northern Peninsula

With regard to the best time to visit, the wet season on Langkawi usually spans the months between April to October. The water clarity is poor between July and September, the months of the monsoon, and the sea can be rough.

Essentials

Langkawi is no longer a haven for backpackers. There are numerous mid- and upper-range places to stay, although people who have sampled accommodation elsewhere in Malaysia claim that prices are high. The island is particularly popular during Nov-Feb and school holidays. Outside these periods, room rates are often reduced.

> **Sleeping**
> *Price codes: see inside front cover*

Kuah **AL** *Tiara Langkawi*, Pusat Dagangan Kelana Mas, T9662566, F9662600. New waterfront hotel, 200 well-furbished rooms, French-style architecture – reputedly modelled on a castle. Rooms have a/c, shower, TV. There are also restaurants and a disco as well as an assortment of sports including fishing trips, jet skiiing and diving. Breakfast included. Clean and well equipped, but due to its grand scale feels slightly isolating. 50% discount in low season. **A-B** *City Bayview*, Jln Pandak Mayah, T9661818, F9663888. Newish block dominating Kuah village, 280 rooms with 4-star facilities, including a pool and health centre, two restaurants (Chinese and coffee house), breakfast included in the room rate. Central location. **A-B** *The Gates*, Jln Persiaran Putra, T9668466, F9668443. TV, a/c, showers, beautiful wooden chalets located in tropical gardens situated about 5 mins from the jetty. Has tennis courts and a pool, as well as 2 restaurants. Organizes tours and car rental. Hugely different prices depending on high or low season. Recommended.

> *Most of the hotels in Kuah itself tend to be rather seedy & poor value for money. Tourists are advised to head straight for the beach resorts*

B *Grand Continental*, Lot 398, Mk Kuah, T9660333, F9660288, hgcl@pd.jaring.my A/c, TV, in-house movies, tea/coffee-making facilities, restaurant, pool, gymnasium and health club. Although it is slightly out of the centre of town – and also a rather ugly block – the hotel does have good views over surrounding islands. **B** *Hotel Central*, 33 Jln Persiaran Putera, T9668585, F9667385, www.hotelcentral.com.my Over 100 rooms in this rather ugly multi-storey block (don't come here if you're looking for a slice of traditional serenity), a/c, comfortable, discounts sometimes available. Breakfast included. **B-C** *Nagoya City Hotel*, Pusat Mas, T9660700, F9660479. Located next to the *Malaysia*, this hotel offers a significant step up in quality. TV, a/c, bath, sea views available. **B-D** *Malaysia*, 30 Pusat Mas, T4895301. A/c, attached bathrooms, rooms also have a fridge and, as they put it, 'piped in music', which could be viewed as a positive or a negative attribute. Dorm beds also available. Basic.

C *Asia*, 1 Jln Persiaran Putra, T9666788. A/c, reasonable place with attached bathrooms as well as some dorm beds, 15 mins' walk from the jetty. Clean and quiet in a good location. Recommended. (On our last visit the management offered a 20% discount for visitors travelling with the *Footprint Handbook*!) **C** *Seri Pulau Motel*, 42c Jln Penarak, T9667185. Large, clean a/c rooms, with shower. **C-D** *Langkawi*, 6-8 Jln Persiaran, T9666248, F9652874. Some a/c, basic place, small and airless fan rooms without windows, one of Langkawi's first hotels. **D** *Island Motel*, 18 Dundong, T9667143. A/c and fan, small rooms, bathroom outside, hires out cars and motorcycles.

Outside Kuah L *Sheraton Perdana*, Jln Pantai Dato' Syed Omar, T9662020, F9666414, www.sheraton.com/perdana A/c, restaurant, pool, formerly the *Langkawi Island Resort*, has its own private beach with watersports facilities, and all the comforts you would expect of a *Sheraton*. **AL** *Sheraton*, Teluk Nibong, T9551901, F9551968, www.sheraton.com/langkawi Pool overlooking the islands, restaurants, children's centre, health club and spa, watersports activities, rooms arranged in individual Malay-style chalets serviced by resort bus. Total of 6 lounges and bars to choose from. Beautiful hotel, but its beach is a disappointment. **A** *Beringin Beach Resort*, round the corner from the *Sheraton Perdana*, T9666966, F9667770. A/c, restaurant, own private beach. Recommended. **A** *Twin Peaks Island Resort*, Jln Kelibang, T9668255, F9667458, new wooden chalets surrounding shadeless pool, children's playground, island tours.

The most popular of the 3 main beaches, with plenty of hotels & chalets to choose from; some are cramped a little too closely together. Despite the development, it is a picturesque beach

Pantai Cenang On Pulau Rebak Besar (dubbed Fantasy Island), opposite Pantai Cenang, there is a new resort with 150 chalets, and berthing docks for 200 leisure boats. **AL** *Pelangi Beach Resort*, T9551001, F9551122. A/c, restaurant, pool, chalet-styled 5-star resort. Guests and their baggage are whisked around in electric cars, holiday camp atmosphere, with daily activities, dirty beach. **A** *Beach Garden Resort*, T9551363, F9551221, combeer@pd.jaring.my A/c, restaurant, pool, apart from the *Pelangi* this is the nicest hotel along this stretch, with thatched roofs, a tiny swimming pool and a wonderful restaurant on the beach. Good value. Recommended. **B** *The Grand Beach Motel*, T9551457, F9553846. Some fan and some a/c chalets available. Clean and friendly, situated on the beach. **B** *Semarak Langkawi Beach Resort*, T9551377, F9551159. A/c, good restaurant, simple but attractive rooms and recently renovated chalets. All chalets set in pleasant gardens by beach, 2 recent additions housing parties of 10-13 people. **B** *Sandy Beach*, T9551308, F9551762, A/c and fan, restaurant, simple A-frame chalets with more upmarket a/c rooms, good restaurant and bar on the beach, and friendly staff. Newly furnished chalets. All chalets with bathroom attached. **B** *Lagenda Permai Chalet*, T9552806, F9552007, http://lagendapermai.tripod.com/lagenda1.html Chalets set back from beach but in pleasant plots, some with a/c, TV and fridge. Dorm rooms also available for 4 sharing. RM50 for each group of 4. Clean. Dorm rooms offer good value, although small. **B** *The Nadias Inn Comfort*, T9551401, F9551405, azlan33@ hotmail.com Clean place with 96 large and characterless rooms. The hotel has a swimming pool, restaurant and karaoke lounge. No alcohol on site. **C** *AB Motel*, T9551300, F9551466, abmotel@hotmail.com Rooms with fan or a/c, and showers. Organizes island hopping and sightseeing tours. Also has a restaurant. Popular with Thai tourists. **C** *Cenang Resthouse*, T9559928, F9559921, www.crhlangkawi.cjb.net Cramped terraced rooms, with a/c and shower. Has recently been redecorated. Good location on the beach. The place has two computers with internet access open to anyone at RM4 per hr. **C** *Suria Beach Motel*, T9551776. You get what you pay for. Also organizes a bland-looking tour. **D** *Beach View*, T/F9558513, beachvu@hotmail.com Probably the best backpackers' place in the bay. Although it is not right on the beach, it has a nice setting, and decent communal area with satellite TV and book exchange. Very friendly owner who does good Western breakfasts (included in room rate). Small wooden a/c chalets with attached shower. Dorm rooms also available. Recommended.

Pantai Cenang & Pantai Tengah

Next beach adjoining Pantai Cenang but not as nice

Pantai Tengah A *Lanai*, T9653401, F9653410. Situated at the end of the beach, with a spacious set-up. Two pools (one for kids) and a games room. Rooms have a/c, TV. Hotel organizes island tours. Good value. **A** *Langkawi Holiday Villa*, T9551701, F9551504. Over 250 rooms, 2 pools, squash, tennis, restaurants and all the amenities you would expect of a first-class resort, including a health centre and squash courts. **A** *Langkawi Village Resort*, Jln Teluk Baru, T9551511, F9551531, www.langkawi- villageresort.com A resort with 100 bunglows with sea views. A/c, bath and shower, cable TV and fridge. Tennis courts and a pool, and from 2200 onwards there is the 'Coco Jam' disco. Recommended. **A** *Sunset Beach Resort*, T/F 9551751. A/c, restaurant, some time-share apartments and 24 rooms, good restaurant and bar. Beautiful gardens surrounding well-designed chalets, with Thai-inspired interiors. Large, clean bathrooms. Honeymoon suites available. Stunning. Highly recommended. **B** *Aseania Seaview Resort*, Jln Pantai Tengah, T9552020, F9532136. This large pink and white building resembles a strawberry gateau, but with a 154-m pool complete with waterfalls it is a good option for those looking to relax. Rooms with TV, a/c, shower and fridge. Two restaurants and a business centre. Watersports organized and bikes can be hired. Breakfast included. **B** *Charlie's*, T9551200, F9551316. A/c and fan, restaurant, chalets, at the end of Pantai Tengah, so has a more private stretch of beach, one of the more established

Northern Peninsula

Map labels

- 11
- 3
- 4
- 1
- 13
- 12
- 1
- 12
- 10

Pantai Cenang

Langkawi Underwater World

- 6
- 15
- 14
- 5
- 2
- 2
- 9
- 8
- 7

Pantai Tengah

Jln Pantai Tengah

To Kuah

Jln Teluk Baru

Teluk Baru

N

0 metres (approx) 500
0 yards (approx) 500

■ **Sleeping**
1 AB Motel
2 Aseania Seaview Resort
3 Beach Garden Resort
4 Cenang Resthouse
5 Charlie's
6 Green Hill Beach Motel
7 Lanai
8 Langkawi Holiday Villa
9 Langkawi Village Resort
10 Nadias Inn Comfort
11 Pelangi Beach Resort
12 Sandy Beach
13 Semarak Langkawi Beach Resort
14 Sunset Beach Resort
15 Tanjung Mali Beach Resort

● **Eating**
1 Champor Champor
2 Sunvillage

places here and often booked up, only 15 rooms. Recommended. **B** *Green Hill Beach Motel*, T9551935. F9556935, ghmsl@hotmail.com Fan or a/c, restaurant. Comfortable and quiet, although dirty and full of cockroaches. Motorbikes available for hire, snorkelling tours arranged. Close to the beach. **B-C** *Tanjung Mali Beach Resort*, T9551891, F9556914. A/c, TV, restaurant, pretty standard but organizes vacuum-packed island tours by what its brochure calls 'hoover craft'.

Pantai Datai **L** *Andaman*, www.theandaman.com Sister hotel to the *Datai*, with less snooty clientele. This excellent hotel has a beautiful pool set among mature trees in plenty of shade (unlike *Datai*). Very friendly and helpful staff. Resident naturalist takes guests on nature walks and jungle treks. Free transport between the 2 (or 10 mins' walk along the beach). **L** *Datai*, T9592500, F9592600. Two pools, health club, 40 individual 'villas' each with private sun-bathing terrace, spacious marble bathroom, a/c, bar, minimalist décor offset by Jim Thompson silks from Bangkok, connected by walkways set in 400 ha of primary jungle where hornbills and flying squirrels remain undisturbed. There are a further 60 rooms, designed with panache, large rooms with sitting areas and cool wooden floors, own balcony with jungle (and some sea) views, private beach, fine white sand, a wealth of watersports. *Beach Restaurant* serves top-quality buffet in the evening, idyllic setting under *atap*-roofed structure, supported on trunks of original trees that were cleared to make way for resort. *Pavilion Restaurant* on stilts among treetops serves Thai food, *Dining Room*, a/c serves Malay and Western food, 18-hole golf course adjacent, attractive, very luxurious resort. Recommended.

A smaller resort than Datai, but with a more secluded beach. Has undergone a radical change since 1997

Pantai Kok Having once been the most popular place for those on a lower budget to stay, it is now largely an exclusive resort with a few top-class hotels located in absolute seclusion. All other accommodation has disappeared to make way for a planned golf course. **AL** *Berjaya Langkawi Beach Resort*, Burau Bay, T9591888, F9591886, www.berjayaresorts.com.my Malaysian-style chalets spread over 170 ha of tropical rainforest, some on stilts over water, some on jungled hillside, all serviced by minibuses. Each chalet has a/c, TV, CNN, in-house movies, mini-bar, balcony, massage shower and is very comfortably furbished with oriental carpets and classical furniture. Excellent facilities include pool, jacuzzi, Japanese restaurant, tennis, watersports, daily organized activities, white-sand beach, beach restaurant, Chinese restaurant (a/c) and good-value buffet served in Dayang café, inside vast main lobby overlooking sea. Surprisingly, this 400-room resort manages to feel friendly and not impersonal. Recommended. **AL** *Mahsuri Beach Resort*, Bukit Tekoh, Jln Pantai Kok, Km 6, T9552977. Has its own small beach. Private chalets have ac, shower, TV. **A** *Burau Bay Resort*, Jln Teluk Burau, T9591061, F9591172, sales-mktg.pbl@ meritus-hotels.com A/c, restaurant, at the far end of Pantai Kok, with Gunung Mat Cincang behind it, away from other chalets, twinned with *Pelangi* (but much more attractive), so offers same facilities, excellent value for money, quieter, cleaner beach. Recommended.

Kuala Muda A few new resorts have sprung up along and around this rather disappointing beach, which does not offer any of the more spectacular views than can be found in other areas of the island. These resorts are positioned close to the airport. **A** *De Lima Resort*, Kuala Muda, T9551801, F9551802. Restaurants, pool, large hawker centre, shopping mall, 1,200 rooms in chalet-style accommodation. **B** *Langkasuka Resort*, T9556888, F9555888. Large hotel with 214 rooms aimed primarily at the Japanese and Korean tourist market. Rooms with a/c, shower, TV. Hotel has pool and several restaurants. Little to offer. **B** *Singgahsana Kub*, Jln Kuala Muda, T9556262, F9555787. Small hotel with just 73 rooms, 5 mins' walk from the beach. Pool, restaurant, disco. Rooms with a/c, shower, TV. Popular with Malays.

Pantai Rhu L *Radisson Tanjung Rhu Resort*, Mukim Air Hangat, T9591033, F9591899, www.tanjungrhu.com.my Exquisitely laid-out resort of only 100 rooms with understated décor, beautifully presented, dining on the beach, luxurious facilities, a honeymooners' paradise. **A** *Mutiara Beach Hotel*, T9556488. A/c, restaurant, pool, smaller of the 2 hotels here.

The bay has a great view of Thailand's Koh Turatao and other islands. There are just 2 hotels

Langkawi's speciality is *mee gulong* – fried noodles cooked with shredded prawns, slices of beef, chicken, carrots, cauliflower are rolled into a pancake, served with a thick potato gravy. Langkawi is also known for its Thai cuisine. Being close to the border, Thai influences even creep into the Malay dishes with the use of hot and spicy ingredients. Thai-styled seafood is also fairly commonplace.

Eating
Price codes: see inside front cover

Kuah There are several Chinese seafood restaurants along the main street in Kuah, all quite good and reasonable value for money. **Mid range** *Sari Village*, Kompleks Pasar Lama, built out on stilts over the sea – which is now being reclaimed – vast selection of seafood. Beautifully designed restaurant with good views over bay and surrounding islands. Owned by globe-trotting architect and landscape architect Ridzuan Aziz. Menu influenced by Pakistani cuisine. Specialities include vegetable curry and fish tandoori. Recommended. **Cheap** *Fortuna*, Dekan Kuah. Recommended by locals. *Prawn Village*, Jln Persiaran Putra (near *Asia Hotel*), good seafood. New management, large open restaurant where diners can play God and choose their own fish for the chop-and-wok. *Orchid*, 3 Dundong Kuah, Chinese. Large and popular with the locals. *Naga Emas Restaurant*, 31 Pusat Bandar, Jln Pandak Mayah, Thai seafood and steamboat. *Sangkar Ikan*, Jln Pantai Penarak, seafood restaurant and fish farm where you can hire rods (RM4) and catch fish for your own dinner. *Mai*, 131 Langkawi Mall, T9660255, F9660254. Stylish restaurant serving modern Thai and Malay food. Excellent and original menu. Serves set lunch for RM10, from 1000-1500. Mai-blend fruit shake recommended. **Foodstalls** The roadside foodstalls in Kuah, just down from the *Langkasuka Hotel* are recommended. There is also a collection of stalls behind Langkawi Duty Free.

Virtually all of the beach hotels have their own restaurants, some of which are excellent; seafood is an obvious choice on Langkawi

Northern Peninsula

Pantai Cenang and Pantai Tengah Of particular note among hotel restaurants are the 2 first-class international restaurants are the **expensive** *Pelangi Beach Resort* and the **mid-range** *Beach Garden Restaurant* next door, which offers a good international selection, beautifully prepared. The latter is right on the beach and is highly recommended. Both are on Pantai Cenang. The following restaurants are all worth checking out. **Mid-range** *Orkid*, great Thai seafood restaurant on Pantai Cenang. Great variety and good value. *Champor Champor*, T9551449. International food in fantastically decorated restaurant with strong African theme. *Bon Ton*, a seafront bungalow, near the *Pelangi Beach Resort*, Nyonya and Western cuisine, different menus for lunch, afternoon tea and dinner with good home-made cakes and ice cream. Bali prawns and Nyonya noodles at lunch, and Nyonya chicken pie at dinner, good value. *Sunvillage Restaurant* and *Matahari Malay Restaurant*, Pantai Tengah, T9556200, F9551751. Two spectacular restaurants set in exquisite landscaped surroundings. The extensive menus at each offer traditionally prepared dishes. There is also a wide slection of alcoholic drinks available. Banquet hall and traditional cushioned dining area can be booked in advance. Highly recommended. *The Lighthouse*, Pantai Tengagh, T9552586, F9552633, shucor@pd.jaring.my Minimalist place, inspired by its name, right on the beach. Has a varied menu, and the *satay* is particularly recommended. All-in-all, a beautiful restaurant and bar.

Pantai Datai **Expensive** *Pavillion*, *The Datai*, Datai Bay, stunning setting on a high terrace in jungle tree-tops, top-class Thai chefs, papaya salad, excellent seafood. *The*

Dining Room, *The Datai*, Datai Bay, quintessentially tasteful in the style of the resort, overlooking turquoise pool and spotlit jungle, French chef combines Malay and Western cuisine, interesting menu.

Pantai Kok Expensive *Oriental Pearl*, *Berjaya Langkawi Beach Resort*, Buran Bay, upmarket Chinese restaurant, simple a/c restaurant with ocean views, steamboat recommended.

Elsewhere Mid-range *Barn Thai*, Kampung Belanga Pecah, Mukim Kisap, T9666699, F9666669, barntlgk@tm.net.my Around 9 km from Kuah on the road to Padang Lalang, this is a unique restaurant set in mangrove swamp, reached along a 450-m wooden walkway, housed in a fine wooden building that blends with its natural surroundings. Moreover it has excellent Thai food, complemented by jazz music.

Nightlife Nightlife in Langkawi mainly centres on the larger hotels, which offer bars, discos, karaoke and live music. Otherwise there are a few discos including *Top Ten*, in Kuah, *Beach Disco*, Kelibang, and *Dallas*, Jln Penarak, outside Kuah. On Pantai Cenang there is the *Reggae Bar*, which stays open until around 0200. In Pantai Tengah there is the *Coco Jam Disco* at the *Langkawi Village Resort*.

Shopping Duty free shops line the main street in Kuah, and alcohol is especially good value. There is a duty free shopping complex at the jetty. The only shop selling alcohol here, *Sime Duty Free*, is on the first floor. Although Langkawi enjoys duty free status there is not much reason to come here for the shopping. At least on a cursory appraisal, the range seems to be limited and the prices hardly bargain basement. There is also: *Cenang Duty Free* next to Underwater World; the *Langkawi Fair Shopping Centre*, Persiaran Putra, Kuah (near the jetty); *Langkawi Mall*; the *Saga Shopping Centre*; and *Zone Shopping Paradise*. The *Oriental Village* is a new shopping development overlooking Burau Bay. Lots of themed restaurants to go with the duty free shopping. Open 1000-2200, daily. All-in-all, lots of shopping – although for visitors from outside Malaysia and Singapore it seems a long way to come to hole up in some surreal tropical shopping paradise. **Fishing tackle** There is a fishing shop opposite the *Langasuka Hotel* in Kuah. **Handicrafts** Many small shops in Kuah sell textiles. The best-stocked handicraft shop is in front of the *Sari Restaurant* in Kuah, *Batik Jawa Store*, 58 Pekan Pokok Asam. Also recommended is *Sunshine Handicraft*, Jln Pandak Mayah (left turning before the Duty Free) stocks a range of *songket* products, particularly *songket* sarongs; open daily. *Flint Stones Handicraft*, Jln Pandak Mayah, offers a good range of Asian handicrafts. Both these places offer 30% discount during the low season.

Sports **Golf** *Datai Bay Golf Club*, Teluk Datai, T9592620, F9592216, green fees RM140, 18-hole course, magnificent fairways, sea views. Tee-off times, 0730-1630 daily. *Gunung Raya*, Jln Air Hangat, Kisap, T9668148. Designed by Max Wexler on a 750-ha former rubber plantation, this is an 18-hole course. There is also a driving range. Open 0700-1700 daily. *Langkawi Golf Club*, Jln Bukit Malut, T9667195. **Watersports** The big resorts and hotels all offer watersports facilities. *Cabana Watersports*, T0124705325, which opened in 1998, offers the most extensive range of watersports activities on the island, including scuba diving and snorkelling, jet and water skiing, parasailing, banana boat rides and island hopping. Friendly staff. Café attached.

Tour operators Organized tours around Langkawi and neighbouring islands can be booked through the larger hotels like the *Pelangi Beach Resort* and *Sheraton Perdana*. *Langkawi Coral* operate a regular Catamaran trip from Kuah (departing at 1030) to Pulau Payar (returning at 1530). The journey each way takes 45 mins and the package costs RM 220 adult, RM140 child, T9667318, F9667308; *Indra Travel & Tours*, 17 Jln Psn Mutiara, T9660163, organizes island tours, car and motorbike hire; *Le Bumbon Island Resort*, T3332797, organizes a variety of tours including island hopping (3 days, 2 nights, RM258, day trip RM45). Many hotels run boat trips and fishing trips round the islands. *Sheraton Perdana* runs fishing trips (RM39-180, depending on duration) and diving trips to Pulau Payar (RM220). *Suaska Kristal*, 5 Telok Baru, Pantai Tengah, T9555295. Island-hopping and tours available. *Mahamas Tours*, Jetty Point, Kuah, T9667797, F9666189, Car, van, motorcycle rental, hotel reservations, island-hopping and tours. *Rangsajaya Holidays*, 83 Jln Teluk Baru, Pantai Tengah, T9555598, F9557594. Watersports tours, scuba diving and snorkelling. *The Shop*, Pantai Cenang, T9555551. Offers island hopping with snorkelling, diving, and free canoe and paddle boat included. Also hires out bicycles and motorbikes.

Transport
112 km N of Penang
30 km to Kuala Perlis

Northern Peninsula

Local Bicycle hire: on the main beaches, RM10-15 per day. **Boats**: it is well worth hiring a boat if you can get a large group of people together, otherwise it tends to be expensive – approximately RM150 per day. Many of the beach hotels run boat trips to the islands as well as one or two places in Kuah (see **Tour operators** above). Trips to Fantasy Island (opposite Pantai Cenang) leave from the beach next to *Pelangi Resort* (signposted from the road). **Bus**: tourist Information advise that there are no local buses. **Car hire**: *Mayflower Acme*, *Pelangi Beach Resort*, Pantai Cenang, T911001; *Tomo Express*, 14 Jln Pandak Maya 4, Pekan Kuah, T9669252; *Langkawi Island Resort* and *Island Motel* in Kuah. Expect to pay about RM80 per day. **Motorcycle hire**: motorbikes, usually Honda 70s, are reasonably cheap to hire (RM35 per day) and are far-and-away the best way to scoot around the island. There are rental shops in Kuah and on all the main beaches, including: Kuah – *Island Motel*, 18 Dundong, T9669143; Pantai Cenang – *MBO*, opposite Semarak Langkawi; and *ASK*, opposite *Green Hill Beach Motel*; Pantai Kok – *Mila Beach Motel*; T9551049. *Tropica Beach Motel*, T9551049. **Taxi**: fares around the island are very reasonable (for example from the jetty to Kuah RM2, Kuah to Pantai Cenang RM14, jetty to Datai Bay RM25-30), readily available and are often minibuses, which are no more expensive, T9551800.

Long distance Air: the international airport is the other side of Pantai Cenang, about 20 km from Kuah and 8 km from Pentai Cenang, at Padang Mat Sirat. Transport to town: a taxi to Kuah is RM12 and around RM10 to Pantai Kok. Prices are fixed – coupons on sale in the airport building. Daily connections with **Johor Bahru**, **Kota Kinabalu**, **KL**, **Kuching**, and **Penang** on *MAS*, and on *Air Asia* five times a week. The runway has been extended to cater for larger planes. *MAS* and *Silk Air* operate daily connections with **Singapore**, and there are also connections with **Osaka** (Japan) and **Taipei** (Taiwan).

Boat: ferries to Langkawi leave from both Kuala Perlis and Kuala Kedah. Timetables subject to seasonal change (fewer boats during the monsoon months, Apr-Sep), journey time from Kuala Perlis is 45 mins and from Kuala Kedah 1¼ hrs. *Lada Ferry Service*, Kuah jetty, T9668820; *Kuala Perlis-Langkawi Ferry Service*, Kuah jetty, T9666950. Regular connections with **Kuala Perlis** every hr from 0600-1800, 45 mins. From **Kuala Kedah** there are boats every 90 mins or so, 0800-1830, 1 hr. Cheaper for the slow boats. The **Kuala Perlis-Langkawi** Ferry Service operates daily boats to **Penang**, leaving at 1730, 2½-3 hrs. From Penang, the boat leaves at 0800. *Nautica Ferries*, T9666929 (Penang), T9666950 (Kuala Kedah & Kuala Perlis). Regular express boat connections with **Pak Bara** (port 8 km from Satun, Thailand); departures 0930, 1200, 1600, 1700 Mon-Sun. Boats leave Satun at 0900, 1300 and 1600. Private yachts also make the journey during the high season. *Ekspres Bahagia (Langkawi)* offer daily departures for Penang at 1400 and 1730 (departures from Penang to Langkawi leave at 0800 and 0845).

Road (and boat): it is a 6-7-hr journey from KL to Kuala Perlis; from there catch the boat to Langkawi (see below).

Train (and boat): take a train to Alor Star (see page 45 for timetable), T7314025, from there a bus to Kuala Perlis and then the boat to Langkawi.

Directory   **Airline offices** *MAS*, Ground Floor, Langkawi Fair Shopping Mall, Persiaran Putra, Kuah, T7463000; *Silk Air*, c/o *MAS*, T2923122; *Air Asia*, T2027777. **Banks** *Maybank* and *United Malayan Banking Corporation* are just off the main street in Kuah in the modern shophouse block. Note that banks are open all day Mon-Thu and Sun, but only in the morning on Fri and Sat. There are several money changers along the main street, mainly in textile shops. There is also a money changer at Pantai Cenang (across the road from *Sandy Beach* and 100 m north), open all day Mon-Thu, Sat and Sun 1500-2100. **Communications** General Post Office: at the jetty end of the main street in Kuah. **Internet cafés**: a number of places in Kuah, including *Langkawi Online Café*, 79 Langkawi Mall. **Useful addresses** Customs office T9666227, **Immigration Office** T9694005.

Southern Peninsula

5

Southern Peninsula

The drive south from KL through **Seremban** to **Melaka** runs on the first stretch to be completed of the much-vaunted north-south Highway, and is an easy, pleasant drive through rubber and oil palm plantations. Like the route north from KL, the towns are predominantly Chinese, while the rural kampungs are almost exclusively Malay. **Negri Sembilan**, a confederacy of nine small states, is renowned for its Minangkabau-style architecture. This is characterized by buffalo-horn shaped roof peaks, reflecting the influence of the state's first inhabitants who came from Sumatra.

On the coast, southwest of Seremban, off the main highway, is the seaside resort town of **Port Dickson** (PD), which serves as a popular weekend retreat from KL but is not generally frequented by tourists from abroad. The drive southeast from PD to Melaka (Malacca) is much more interesting along the coastal backroads that run through open countryside and Malay kampungs. Melaka is one of the Malaysian tourism industry's trump cards, thanks to its Portuguese, Dutch and British colonial history, its rich Peranakan (Straits Chinese) cultural heritage and its picturesque hinterland of rural Malay kampongs. The route south from Melaka is a pleasant but unremarkable drive through plantation country to **Johor Bahru** (JB), on the southernmost tip of the peninsula. It is a short hop across the causeway from JB to Singapore, and Malaysia's east coast islands and resorts are within easy reach.

Things to do in the Southern Peninsula

- Wander through the streets of historic Melaka, a city on the verge of UNESCO World Heritage status – if only the authorities would stop people fiddling with it.
- Taste Malaysia's unique contribution to global gastronomy and forerunner of fusion cuisine – the spicy food of the Nyonyas.

Seremban

Colour map 2, grid B2
Phone code: 06

*Seremban is the capital of the state of Negri Sembilan, which translates from Bahasa as 'nine states', and was historically a loose federation of districts, lorded over by four territorial chiefs. Seremban (formerly known as Sungei Ujong) started life as another rough and ready tin-mining centre with a large population of Chinese. A lively town, its major sight is the **Teman Seni Budaya** (Cultural Complex) which offers an intersting insight into the Minangkabau culture. The town can easily be visited in a day from either KL or Melaka.*

History Tin mining flourished in the early years of the 19th century – one of the reasons Melaka continued as a thriving trading port. The control of the river, Sungei Linggi, which was the route Sungei Ujong's tin took to the sea, became a great source of contention between the 1820s and 1860s. The *Dato Klana*, or territorial chief of the Sungei Ujong district, frequenty clashed with other members of the council of chiefs over the highly profitable river taxes and port dues. All wanted a share of the river tolls and erected illegal forts along the river to levy tolls from the Chinese merchants from Melaka and the Chinese miners. In 1857 the British sent an expedition up the river to destroy these fortified toll booths, but in no time they were back in business. In 1860 the confrontation came to a head when the tin miners in Sungei Ujong rebelled against the chiefs; hundreds were killed in the subsequent riots. One of the Chinese ring-leaders was a ruthless young Hakka ruffian name a **Yap Ah Loy**, who went on to become headman of a new tin boomtown called Kuala Lumpur in 1862.

Sights

Tourist office: State Economic Planning Unit, 5th floor Wisma Negeri, T7622311

Along the fringe of the outstanding **Taman Bunga** (Lake Gardens) is the **State Mosque**, with its nine pillars representing the nine old mine-states of Negri Sembilan. The **Teman Seni Budaya** (Cultural Complex) is on 4-ha site at the junction of Jalan Sungai Ujong and the KL-Seremban road, 2 km from the centre of town. The main building is the **Terak Perpatih**, originally constructed as the pavilion for an international Koran-reading competition in 1984 and now a museum. On the ground floor are handicraft displays and upstairs there is an exhibition of historical artefacts. Also within the complex is a beautifully carved traditional Minangkabau wooden house, **Rumah Contoh Minangkabau**, built in 1898 (originally at Kampung Air Garam). In 1924 it was shipped to England and exhibited as an example of Malay architecture. On its return it was reassembled near the Lake Gardens in Seremban before being moved to Taman Seni Budaya.

The **State Museum** is also part of the complex and is itself a good example of Minangkabau architecture; it is a reconstructed 19th-century palace (Istana Ampang Tinggi), a high stilt building with an *atap* roof. The museum houses a small collection of ceremonial weapons and tableaux depicting a

Minangkabau: the 'buffalo-horn' people from across the water

Negri Sembilan's early inhabitants were immigrants from Minangkabau in Sumatra. They started to settle in the hinterland of Melaka and around Sungai Ujong (modern Seremban) during the 16th and 17th centuries, and were skilled irrigated paddy farmers. Minangkabau roughly translates as 'buffalo horns' and the traditional houses of rural Negri Sembilan and Melaka have magnificent roofs that sweep up from the centre into two peaks. The Minangkabau architectural style has been the inspiration behind many modern Malaysian buildings, notably the Muzium Negara (National Museum) and the Putra World Trade Centre in Kuala Lumpur.

The Minangkabau introduced Islam, a sophisticated legal system and their matrilineal society to the interior of the Malay peninsula. In 1773 they appealed to the Minangkabau court at Pagar Ruyong in Sumatra to appoint a ruler over them and a Sumatran prince – Raja Melewar – was installed as the first king, or Yang di-Pertuan Besar, of the confederacy of mini-states, with his capital at Sri Menanti. But Negri Sembilan's four undang, or territorial chiefs, saw to it that he wielded no real power. In all there were four kings from Sumatra, all of them ineffectual, and the link with Sumatra finally ended in 1824 with the establishment of an indigenous hereditary royal family. The current Sultan of Seremban, educated at Oxford, continues to reside in his palace outside the town.

royal wedding and some photographs and other memorabilia from the time of the Malayan Emergency. ■ *1000-1800 Tue-Wed, 0815-1300 Thu, 1000-1215, 1445-1800 Fri, 1000-1800 Sat-Sun, closed Mon.*

Sri Menanti, the old Minangkabau capital of Negri Sembilan, is 30 km east of Seremban, about 10 km before Kuala Pilah. This area is the Minangkabau heartland. *Sri* is the Minangkabau word for 'ripe paddy', and *Menanti* means 'awaiting' – although it is colloquially translated as 'beautiful resting place'. It was also common for early kings to add the Sanskrit honorific 'Sri' to their titles and palaces. The former royal capital is on the upper reaches of Sungai Muar, which meanders through the valley that was known as Londar Naga, or the tail of the dragon. The Istana Lama Sri Menanti is a beautifully carved wooden palace built in Minangkabau style in 1908. It has 99 pillars depicting the 99 warriors of the various *luak-luak* (clans). It was, until 1931, the official residence of the Yang di-Pertuan Besar, the state ruler. On the fourth floor is a display of royal treasures. It is not officially a museum but is open to visitors. ■ *1000-1800 Sat-Wed, 0815-1300 Thu, closed Fri.* This royal town also has a large mosque. Most people come here on a day trip from Seremban, but there is a reasonable resort hotel next to the Istana Lama, the **B** *Sri Menanti Resort*, T4976200, with air conditioning, pool and restaurant, and good, well-equipped rooms. *United Bus* goes to Kuala Pilah every 15 minutes.

Seremban has only a handful of hotels, one of which is among the best of Malaysia's resort hotels, the *Allson Klana*. There are 3 mid-range hotels; the rest are basic, Chinese-run establishments of an almost uniformly poor quality.

AL *Allson Klana Resort*, PT4388 Jln Penghulu Cantik, Taman Tasik Seremban, T7629600, F7639218. Now that the new KL airport is open at Sepang, the *Allson* is a good alternative to staying in KL, the airport being only 20 mins from the new site, set in 18 acres of landscaped gardens. The *Allson Klana* is a luxurious and well-established

Sleeping
■ *on map, page 202*

Brand-name Satay from the source

Kajang, about 20 km south of KL on the Seremban road, is named after the palm-leaf canopy of a bullock cart, once ubiquitous and still occasionally seen in Negri Sembilan. At hawker centres all over Malaysia, there are stalls called 'Satay Kajang': the town long ago gained the reputation for the best satay in the country. There are many satay stalls in Kajang today. Selamat makan!

resort hotel, overlooking one of the largest lagoon-shaped pools in Malaysia and has over 200 very comfortable and spacious rooms with a/c, in-house video, shower and bath, mini-bar, other facilities include tennis, health club, sauna, business centre, delicatessen and boutique, outstanding food outlets include *Yuri Japanese Restaurant*, *Blossom Court Chinese Restaurant* as well as a coffee house.

B *Carlton Star*, 47 Jln Dato Sheikh Ahmad, T7625336, F7620040. Good central position, a/c, coffee house, fitness centre, karaoke lounge, recently refurbished but with a lack of flair and an excess of kitsch. **B** *Seri Malaysia*, Jln Sungai Ugung, T7644181, F7644179. One of the 'ey polivalue for money' chain, good and in reasonably good nick, but not central. **B** *Tasik*, Jln Tetamu, T7630994, F7635355. Located next to the Lake Gardens, a/c, TV, shower, restaurant, pool, business centre, seen better days but has a good central position and outlook over the Lake Gardens.

D *Golden Hill*, 42 Jln Tuan Sheikh, T7613760. Basic. **D** *Happy*, 35 Jln Tunku Hassan, T7630172. Probably the best of the budget places to stay, although that is not saying much. The rooms may be dark but at least they are reasonably clean. **D** *New International*, 126 Jln Tan Sri Manickavasagam, T7634957. Fan only. **D** *Oriental*, 11 Jln Lemon,

Seremban

Sleeping
1 Carlton Star
2 Century
3 Golden Hill
4 Nam Yong
5 Oriental
6 Seri Malaysia
7 Tasik

Southern Peninsula

T7630119. Restaurant, just about tolerable. **D-E** *Nam Yong*, 5 Jln Tuanku Munawir, T7620155. Restaurant, grotty hotel, the only plus being the price of the rooms. **D-E** *Century*, 25-29 Jln Tuanku Munawir, T7626261.

Malay *Anira*, Kompleks Negeri Sembilan; *Bilal*, 100 Jln Dato Bandar Tunggal; *Fatimah*, 419 Jln Tuanku Manawir; *Flamingo Inn*, 1a Jln Za'aba.   **Chinese Expensive** *Blossom Court*, *Allson Klann Resort*, classy Chinese restaurant, expensive-looking décor, popular for extensive range of *dim sum*, good Peking duck and Cantonese dishes. *Happy*, 1 Jln Dato Bandar Tunggal; *Regent*, 2391-2 Taman Bukit Labu; *Seafood*, 2017-8 Blossom Heights, Jln Tok Ungku; *Suntori*, 10-11 Jln Dato Sheikh Ahmad. **Indian   Seriously cheap** *Samy*, 120 Jln Yam Tuan, banana leaf. *Anura*, 97 Jln Tuanku Antah. **Japanese   Expensive** *Yuri*, *Allson Klana Resort*, excellent quality, traditional Japanese, good, private Tatami rooms, sushi bar, Teppanyaki counter, good-value set meals. **Foodstalls** *Jalan Tuanku Antah*, near the post office; *Jalan Dr Murugesu*, opposite Masjid Janek mosque.

Eating
Price codes: see inside front cover

Train Connections every 2 hrs with KL, express service to Singapore, see page 45 for timetable. **Bus** Newish, brightly coloured station on Jln Sungai Ujong. Connections with JB, Melaka, KL, Kota Bharu and Port Dixon. **Taxi** Port Dickson, KL, Melaka, T7610764.

Transport
62 km S of KL
83 km N of Melaka

Banks *Bumiputra*, Wisma Dewan Permagaa Melayu; *Maybank*, 10-11 Jln Dato Abdul Rahman; *OCBC*, 63-65 Jln Dato Bandar Tunggal; *Public Bank*, 46 Jln Dato Lee Fong Yee; *Standard & Chartered*, 128 Jln Dato Bandar Tunggal; *UMBC*, 39 Jln Tuanku Munawir. **Communications Post Office:** Jln Tuanka Antah.

Directory

Port Dickson

Port Dickson, typically shortened to PD, is 32 km from Seremban and is one of the most popular seaside resorts in Malaysia, as testified by all the modern condominium developments. The pace of development has given the little fishing port a pollution problem in recent years and many people regard the sea as so toxic that it is best not to swim at all. This is a narrow point of the Melaka Strait and large ships use the deep-water channel, which cuts close to the Malaysian coast. Rarely a month goes by when the Malaysian authorities aren't giving chase to tankers, which have an increasingly alarming tendency to dump thousands of tonnes of sludge, oil and effluent into the strait. Although for KL's residents it may be a convenient destination for a day trip or weekend, it is, frankly, hard to imagine why those with more time on their hands would wish to come here.

Colour map 2, grid B2
Phone code: 02

The port town, originally called Tanjung Kamuning, was renamed after Sir Frederick Dickson, British Colonial Secretary and acting Governor in 1890. Port Dickson itself is quiet and undistinguished but to the south is a long, sandy beach, stretching 18 km down to the **Cape Rachado** lighthouse, although there are cleaner places to swim in Malaysia. Built by the British on the site of a 16th-century Portuguese lighthouse, Cape Rachado has panoramic views along the coast (it is necessary to acquire permission from the Marine Department in Melaka to climb to the top). At **Kota Lukut**, 7 km from Port Dickson, is Raja Jamaat fort, built in 1847 to control the tin trade in the area.

Because PD is a favourite family getaway for KL's weekenders, beach hotels are often quite full – and rates are comparatively high. During the week, discounts are often on offer. There is not much selection for the budget-minded traveller, who may be wise to give Port Dickson a miss.

Sleeping
Price codes:
see inside front cover

AL *Ilham Resort* Tanjung Biru, T6626800, F6625646. Resort comprising 59 apartments. All rooms have a/c and phones. Facilities include a pool, tennis court, squash court and spa on site. A babysitting service is available. **A** *Bayu Beach Resort*, Batu 4½, Jln Pantai, T6473703, F6474362. Pool, luxury 300-room beach resort, good watersports facilities, all rooms with a/c, kitchenette, TV, minibar, Chinese restaurant, coffee house, karaoke lounge. **A** *Corus Paradise Resort Port Dickson* (formerly the *Delta Paradise Lagoon*), 3½ km Jln Pantai, T6477600, F6477630. Luxury hotel, the best on the strip, over 200 rooms, all with ocean views, bath, TV, in-house video, mini-bar, tea/coffee-making facilities, other amenities include pool, children's playground, tennis, squash, watersports, business centre, coffee house. **A** *Regency*, Batu 5, T6474090, F6474792. Minangkabau-style architecture, tennis, squash, children's pool, two restaurants, business centre. **A** *Tanjung Tuan Beach Resort*, Batu 5, Jln Pantai, T662013. A/c, restaurant, pool, good sports facilities and weekday discounts.

B *Seri Malaysia*, Batu 4, Jln Pantai, T6476070, F6476028. One of newer additions to this budget chain of hotels, good views across beach and good value. Recommended. **B** *Travers Hotel*, Batu 9, T6625273. Quiet location facing the sea, charges include breakfast, clean. **B-C** *Golden Resort*, Batu 10, Jln Pantai, T6625176. Rooms have a/c, mini-fridge and TV. Facilities include restaurant and pool.

C *Beach Point Motel*, Batu 9, Jln Pantai, T6625889. Located down a track off main road, a/c, shower, basic but spotlessly clean. **C** *Lido*, Batu 8, Jln Pantai, T6625273. Restaurant, quiet location, set in large grounds. **D** *Kong Meng*, Batu 8, Teluk Kemang, T6625683. restaurant, on the beachfront, reasonable for the price. **E** *Port Dickson Youth Hostel*, Km 6 Jln Pantai, T6472188. YHA card holders only (although some non-members seem to land a room), separate dorm for men and women, dining/cooking area, large compound, camping facilities.

Eating
Price codes:
see inside front cover

Malay Cheap *Santan Berlada*, Batu 1, Jln Pantai. **Chinese Cheap** *Pantai Ria*, Batu 7½, Jln Pantai, seafood. **Seafood Mid-range** *Blue Lagoon*, Cape Rachado (on the way to the lighthouse). **Cheap** *Haw Wah Seafood*, Teluk Kamang, simple but clean coffee shop at end of row of modern shophouses on main road, good seafood. *Kemang Seafood*, Batu 7, Malay seafood, crab sold by weight (1 kg RM25). **Western Cheap** *Kentucky Fried Chicken*, PD centre. **Foodstalls** Scattered around town and along Jln Pantai.

Transport
94 km to KL
32 km to Seremban
90 km to Melaka

Bus The station is on Jln Pantai, just outside the main centre, but buses will normally stop on request anywhere along the beach. Regular connections with **KL** and **Melaka**. **Taxi** T7610764, shared taxis to Melaka, KL and Seremban.

Directory

Banks *Bumiputra*, 745 Jln Bharu; *Public*, 866 Jln Pantai; *Standard Chartered*, 61 Jln Bharu. **Communications** General Post Office: opposite bus station in PD. **Medical facilities** Hospital: on the waterfront by the bus station, Jln Pantai.

Port Dickson

Not to scale

■ Sleeping
1 Bayu Beach Resort
2 Regency
3 Seri Malaysia
4 Tanjung Tuan Resort
5 Travers

● Eating
1 Haw Wah Seafood
2 Kemang Seafood
3 Pantai Ria
4 Santan Belada

Melaka (Malacca)

Thanks to its strategic location on the strait that bears its name, Melaka was a rich, cosmopolitan port city long before it fell victim to successive colonial invasions. Its wealth and influence are now a thing of the past, and the old city's colourful history is itself a major money-spinner for Malaysia's modern tourism industry. The **Jerak Warison Heritage Trail** *is a great introduction to historical Melaka with its striking* **Dutch colonial core** *and bustling, although somewhat manufactured,* **Chinatown** *which houses the most unusual shoe shop,* **Wah Aik Shoemaker Shop**, *and the oldest* **Chinese temple** *in Malaysia.*

Colour map 2, grid B3
Phone code: 06

Ins and outs

There is an airport 10 km from town but few people arrive here by air. It is a comparatively painless overland journey either south from KL (150 km) or north from Singapore (250 km). There are numerous express buses plying the KL-Melaka and Singapore-Melaka routes and there are also connections with numerous other towns on the peninsula including Seremban, Port Dickson, Ipoh, Lumut, Klang, Penang, Butterworth, Alor Star, JB, Muar, Kuantan, Kuala Terengganu and Kota Bahru. Travelling directly from KL Airport, take the bus to Nilai, then through to Seremban and from there board a coach direct to Melaka. On arrival at the bus station you will be assailed by touts offering places to stay. Although this is a bit intimidating after a hot coach ride, they may be worth paying attention to if you are planning on staying in a guest house or hostel as these are often hard to find without a little help. The railway line does not run through Melaka – the nearest stops is at Tampin some 40 km north of town. There are daily express international ferry connections with Dumai on Sumatra.

Getting there
See also Transport, page 226

While Melaka is a largish town it is still possible to enjoy many of the sights on foot; bicycles are also available for hire from some of the guesthouses and shops in town. There is a town bus service; the No 17 bus runs from the bus station to historical Melaka and on to the Portuguese area while the No 19 runs from the bus station out to Ayer Keroh (where the butterfly farm, reptile park and 'Mini Malaysia' are situated). Metered taxis are plentiful. While trishaws are available for rent these are not part of Melaka's public transport system: they survive by providing a service to tourists who are willing to shell out for the enjoyment of being pedalled around town.

Getting around

Tourism Malaysia, Jln Kota (opposite *Christ Church*), T2814803, F2849022. Open 0845-1700 Sat-Thu, 0845-1215 and 1445-1700 Fri. Also tourist information desk at Ayer Keroh, T3125811. www.melaka.gov.my

Tourist offices

History

The city was founded by Parameswara, a fugitive prince from Palembang in Sumatra. According to the 16th-century *Sejara Melayu* (the Malay Annals), he was a descendant of the royal house of Srivijaya, whose lineage could be traced back to Alexander the Great. Historians, however, suspect that he was really a Javanese refugee who, during the 1390s, invaded and took Temasek (Singapore), before he himself was ousted by the invading Siamese. He fled up the west coast of the peninsula and, with a few followers, settled in a fishing kampung.

The Malay Annals relate how Parameswara was out hunting one day, and while resting in the shade of a tree watched a tiny mouse deer turn and kick one of his hunting dogs and drive it into the sea. He liked its style and named

Southern Peninsula

The Flor de la Mar: sunken treasure beyond measure

From the early years of the first millennium, Chinese junks were plying the Nanyang, or South Seas, and by the 1400s a sophisticated trade network had built up, linking Asia to India, the Middle East and Europe. For three centuries, Melaka was at the fulcrum of the China trade route and even before the Europeans arrived, hundreds of merchants came each year from Arabia, Persia, India, China, Champa, Cambodia, Siam, Java, Sumatra and the eastern Isles. By the early 1500s, more than 100 large ships were anchoring at Melaka every year. It was known as the emporium of the east.

But this trade was not without its casualties and the sunken wrecks littering the coastal waters of the South China Sea and the Strait of Melaka have given rise to a new, highly profitable industry: treasure-hunting. Divers, in league with marine archaeologists and maritime historians, have flocked to the region in recent years. The most publicized find was the 1987 salvage of a cargo of Chinese porcelain from a vessel that sank off the Riau Islands in 1752; the booty was auctioned by Christie's in Amsterdam two years later for US$16 million. But treasure hunting carries with it political sensitivities over the ownership of wrecks. Salvage operators have been jailed in Indonesia and salvaged antiquities have been confiscated in Thailand.

The ultimate sunken treasure trove lies in

what remains of the wreck of the Flor de la Mar, at the bottom of the Strait of Melaka. The Portuguese vessel, commanded by Admiral Alfonso d'Albuquerque, is thought to be the richest ship ever lost. Having left Lisbon in 1503, Albuquerque plundered his way from Mozambique, the Red Sea and India to the coastal regions of Burma and Thailand. By July 1511, when he anchored off Melaka, he had amassed untold riches. After capturing the city, he plundered it.

In his book The Search for Sunken Treasure, the treasure hunter Robert F Marx writes: "The spoils the Portuguese took from Malacca stagger the imagination." They included more than 60 tonnes of gold booty in the form of solid gold statues of elephants, tigers, birds and monkeys, all studded with gemstones. There was gilded furniture, gold ingots, gold coins, gold-plated royal litters, chests full of diamonds, rubies and sapphires and several tonnes of Chinese and Arabic coins. And this was just the loot from Sultan Ahmad's palace". In London, Sotheby's auction house tentatively valued the treasure at US$9 billion; by far the world's richest wreck. Albuquerque stole so much gold that Melaka was left without any coinage. Tin coins were minted instead, for the first time.

Two days after setting off for Portugal, his fleet of four ships ran into a storm at the northeastern tip of Sumatra. Two ships went down, then the Flor de la Mar itself hit a reef.

his nearby settlement after the *malaka* tree he was sitting under. Sadly it seems more likely that the name Melaka is derived from the Arabic word *malakat*, or market, and from its earliest days the settlement, with its sheltered harbour, was an entrepôt. Melaka was sheltered from the monsoons by the island of Sumatra, and perfectly located for merchants to take advantage of the trade winds. Because the Strait's deep-water channel lay close to the Malayan coast, Melaka had command over shipping passing through it.

In 1405 a Chinese Muslim Admiral, the eunuch Cheng Ho, arrived in Melaka bearing gifts from the Ming Emperor (including a yellow parasol, which has been the emblem of Malay royalty ever since) and the promise of protection from the Siamese. Cheng Ho (Zheng Ho) made seven voyages to the Indian Ocean over the next three decades and used Melaka as his supply base. The Chinese gained a vassal state and Melaka gained a sense of security: Parameswara was wary of possible Siamese encroachment. Court rituals, ceremony and etiquette were formalized and an exclusive royal court language

Albuquerque survived the shipwreck and managed to salvage a gold sword, a jewel-encrusted crown, a ruby bracelet and a ring, which today are on display in a Lisbon museum. The rest was lost in 37 m of water. The admiral returned to Portugal on his one remaining ship. With his pilot, who also survived, he drew up a chart indicating where the ship went down – 8 km off Tanjung Jambu Air in Aceh.

It lay there, forgotten, for nearly 500 years. In 1988 an Italian specialist in underwater wrecks and an Australian marine historian claimed to have located the Flor de la Mar, hidden under several metres of mud, using satellite imaging. The Indonesian government , in whose territorial waters the wreck lay, then awarded a salvage contract to PT Jayatama Istikacipta, a company linked to the family of President Suharto, which sub-contracted the diving operation to an Australian, arrested in Indonesia the previous year for illegal treasure-hunting. He hired former divers from the British Navy's Special Boat Squadron to join the search. In 1989 they found a couple of wrecked Chinese junks but no Flor de la Mar and, in frustration, the operation was called off.

The same year, the Indonesians granted a search permit to a Singapore salvage firm. After a year's fruitless exploration, they hired Robert Marx, who, with the aid of a facsimile of Albuquerque's chart, located the reef that the ship had struck. Numerous artefacts were recovered, but, he writes, "a thorough sonar and magnetometer survey revealed that the main section of the wreck lies in an area the size of five football fields at a depth of 37 m under 15 m of concrete-like mud."

The discovery sparked a political row. Malaysia and Portugal contested Indonesia's claim to the booty and the matter was passed to the International Court in The Hague for adjudication. Meanwhile, an endless stream of conspiracy stories – none of them confirmed – surrounds the fate of the Flor de la Mar. In 1991, it was reported that "powerful interests linked to President Suharto" had harassed other treasure-hunters researching the location of the wreck and had privately tried to force them to help mount a covert salvage operation. In late 1991, following further reports that Indonesian Navy divers had tried again, Jakarta and Kuala Lumpur reportedly entered a joint-venture agreement. Under it, Malaysia agreed to bear the entire cost of the operation and split the booty 50/50. There are constant rumours about secret salvage operations circulating among Singapore's commercial diving community, but the matter is so sensitive and the stakes potentially so high that lips are firmly sealed.

Southern Peninsula

evolved. In 1411, three years before his death, Parameswara sailed with Cheng Ho to China with a large retinue and was received by the third Ming Emperor, Chu Ti. Melaka's next two rulers continued this tradition, making at least two visits each to China.

But China began to withdraw its patronage in the 1430s, and to make sure Melaka retained at least one powerful friend, the third ruler, Sri Maharaja, married the daughter of the sultan of the flourishing maritime state of Samudra-Pasai in Sumatra. Historian Mary Turnbull says "he embraced Islam and hitched Melaka's fortunes to the rising star of the Muslim trading fraternity". He adopted the name Mohamed Shah, but retained the court's long-standing Hindu rituals and ceremonies. He died without a child from his marriage to the Pasai princess and a succession crisis followed. The rightful royal heir, the young Rajah Ibrahim, was murdered in a palace coup after a year on the throne and Kasim, one of Mohamed's sons by a non-royal marriage, declared himself Sultan Muzaffar Shah. Melaka's first proper sultan made Islam the state religion and beat off two Siamese invasions during his reign. Islam was also spreading through the merchant community. In the latter half of the 15th century the faith was taken from Melaka to other states on the peninsula as well as to Brunei and Javanese port cities that were breaking away from the Hindu kingdom of Majapahit.

In the late 15th century, Malay power reached its pinnacle. Muzaffar's successor, Sultan Mansur Shah, extended Melaka's sway over Pahang, Johor and Perak, the Riau archipelago and Sumatra. Contemporary European maps label the entire peninsula 'Malacca'. According to the Malay Annals, the sultan married a Chinese princess in 1460. This marriage and the arrival of the princess and her followers marked the formal beginning of the unique and prosperous Straits Chinese *Peranakan* culture (see page 212).

Another cultural blend that had its roots in medieval Melaka was the Chitty Indian community, the result of Indian merchants inter-marrying with local women, including the Malay nobility. Because foreign traders had to wait several months before the winds changed to allow them to return home, many put down roots and Melaka, 'the city where the winds met', had hundreds of permanent foreign residents. There were no taboos concerning cross-cultural marriage: the polygamous Muslim Sultan Mansur Shah even visited the crumbling Majapahit court in East Java where he cemented relations by his second royal marriage, to the Hindu ruler's daughter.

By the beginning of the 16th century Melaka was the most important port in the region. Foreign merchants traded in Indian and Persian textiles, spices from the Moluccas (Maluku), silk and porcelain from China as well as gold, pepper, camphor, sandalwood and tin. The Malay language became the *lingua franca* throughout the region.

Tales of luxuriance and prosperity attracted the Portuguese who came in search of trading opportunities, with the aim of breaking the Arab merchants' stranglehold on trade between Europe and Asia. Spices from the Moluccas came through the Strait and whoever controlled the waterway determined the price of cloves in Europe. The Portuguese – known to Melakans as 'the white Bengalis' – combined their quest for riches with a fervent anti-Muslim crusade, spurred by their hatred of their former Moorish overlords on the Iberian peninsula. They arrived in 1509, received a royal welcome and then fled for their lives when Gujerati (Indian) traders turned the sultan against them. Alfonso d'Albuquerque, the viceroy of Portuguese India, returned two years later with 18 ships and 1,400 men. After an initial attempt at reconciliation, he too was beaten off. D'Albuquerque then stormed and conquered the city in July 1511, the year after he seized Goa on India's west coast. The Melakan court fled to Johor where Sultan Ahmad re-established his kingdom.

The foreign merchants quickly adapted to the new rulers and under the Portuguese the city continued to thrive. Tomé Pires, a Portuguese apothecary who arrived with d'Albuquerque's fleet and stayed two years, wrote in his account, *Suma Oriental*: "Whoever is lord of Melaka has his hand on the throat of Venice," adding that "the trade and commerce between different nations for a thousand leagues on every hand must come to Melaka". The port became known as the 'Babylon of the Orient'. Despite the two-year sojourn of Spanish Jesuit priest St Francis Xavier, Christianity had little impact on the Muslim Malays or the hedonistic merchant community. A large Eurasian population grew up, adding to Melaka's cosmopolitan character; there are still many Pereiras, D'Cruzes, de Silvas, da Costas, Martinezes and Fernandezes in the Melaka phone book.

Back in Lisbon in the early 17th century, the Portuguese monarchy was on the decline, the government in serious debt and successive expeditions failed to acquire anything more than a tenuous hold over the Spice Islands, to the east. The Portuguese never managed to subdue the Sumatran pirates, the real rulers of the Strait of Melaka. As Dutch influence increased in Indonesia, Batavia (Jakarta) developed as the principal port of the region and Melaka declined. The Dutch entered an alliance with the Sultanate of Johor and foreign traders began to move there. This paved the way for a Dutch blockade of Melaka and in 1641, after a six-month seige of the city, Dutch forces, together with troops from Johor, forced the surrender of the last Portuguese governor.

Over the next 150 years the Dutch carried out an extensive building programme; some of these still stand in Dutch Square. Melaka was the collecting point for Dutch produce from Sumatra and the Malay peninsula, where the new administration attempted to enforce a monopoly on the tin trade. They built forts on Pulau Pangkor and at Kuala Selangor, north of Klang, to block Acehnese efforts to muscle in on the trade, but the Dutch, like the Portuguese before them, were more interested in trade than territory. Apart from their buildings, the Dutch impact on Melaka was minimal. Their tenure of the town was periodically threatened by the rise of the Bugis, Minangkabaus and Makassarese, who migrated to the Malay peninsula, having been displaced by the activities of the Dutch East India Company in Sulawesi and Sumatra. In 1784 Melaka was only saved from a joint Bugis and Minangkabau invasion by the arrival of the Dutch fleet from Europe.

By the late 18th century, the Dutch hold on the China trade route was bothering the English East India Company. In 1795 France conquered The

Southern Peninsula

Melaka

To Ayer Keroh & Post Office

To Fort St John, Lotus Inn & Johor Bahru

Jln Grahau Maju
Jln Tun Ali
Villa Sentosa
Jln Tun Mamet
Melaka
Taxis
Express
Jln Tan Chay Yan
Immigration Department
Footbridge
Jln Kubu
Jln Bunga Raya
Jln Bendahara
Jln Sri Lanang
St Peter's
Jln Munshi Abdullah
Jln Puteri Hang Li Po
Bukit Cina
Sam Poh Kong Temple
Jln Laksamana Cheng Ho
To Fort St John, Lotus Inn & Johor Bahru
A
CHINA TOWN
Bukit China
Lorong
Jln Temenggung
Sultan's Well
Sikh Temple
St John's Hill
Jln Tamby Abdullah
Jln Tun Tan Cheng Lock
To Pulau Upah
To Pulau Besar
Melaka River
Jln Chan Koon Cheng
St Paul's
St Paul's Hill
Maritime Museum
Light & Sound Show
Padang Pahlawan
Meden Portugis
Jln Bandar Hilir
Jln Parameswara
To Portugese Settlement
Customs
Jln Merdeka
Mahkota Shopping Centre
To Century Mahkota
To Dumai (Sumatra)
Jln Melaka Raya
Jln Taman Melaka
Robin's Nest

N

0 metres 200
0 yards 200

■ Sleeping			
1 Accordian	6 Equatorial	11 Mimosa	17 Sunny's Inn
2 Baba House	7 Grand Continental	12 Ng Fook	
3 City Bayview	8 Kancil	13 Orkid	● Eating
4 Eastern Heritage	9 Melaka Town	14 Palace	1 Bayonya
5 Emperor	Holiday Lodge	15 Renaissance Melaka	2 Foodcourt
	10 Melaka Youth Hostel	16 Robin's Nest	

*Detail map
A Melaka detail,
page 211*

Netherlands and the British made an agreement with the exiled Dutch government, allowing them to become the caretaker of Dutch colonies. Four years later the Dutch East India Company went bankrupt, but just to make sure that they would not be tempted to make a comeback in Melaka, the British started to demolish the fortress in 1807. The timely arrival of Stamford Raffles, the founder of modern Singapore, prevented the destruction from going further, and in 1824, under the Treaty of London, Melaka was surrendered to the British in exchange for the Sumatran port of Bencoolen (Bengkulu).

In 1826 Melaka became a part of the British Straits Settlements, along with Penang and Singapore. But by then, its harbour had silted up and it was a town of little commercial importance. In 1826 it had a population of 31,000 and was the biggest of the settlements; by 1860, although its population had doubled, it was the smallest and least significant of the three. In 1866, a correspondent for the *Illustrated London News* described Melaka (which the British spelled *Malacca*) as "a land where it is 'always afternoon' – hot, still, dreamy. Existence stagnates. Trade pursues its operations invisibly. It has no politics, little crime, rarely gets even two lines in an English newspaper and does nothing towards making contemporary history". In 1867 the Straits Settlements were transferred to direct colonial rule and Melaka faded into obscurity. Strangely, it was the town's infertile agricultural hinterland that helped reinvigorate the local economy at the turn of the 20th-century. The first rubber estate in Malaya was started by Melakan planter Tan Chay Yan, who accepted some seedlings from 'Mad' Henry Ridley, director of Singapore's Botanic Gardens, and planted out 1,200 ha in 1896. The idea caught on among other Chinese and European planters and Melaka soon became one of the country's leading rubber producers.

Sights

Arriving in Melaka by road it is not immediately apparent that the city is Malaysia's historical treasure-trove

Jalan Munshi Abdullah, which runs through the middle of the more recent commercial district, is like any Malaysian main street. The taxi station and express bus terminal are away from the central core of old Melaka, and while the old city is quite compact, the town itself is neither as small or medieval-looking as visitors are led to suppose. The historical sights from the Portuguese and Dutch periods are interesting because they are in Malaysia – not because they are stunning architectural wonders. That said, the old red Dutch buildings on the east bank of the river and the magnificent Peranakan architecture and stuccoed shophouses on the west side, lend Melaka an atmosphere unlike any other Malaysian town. It also lays claim to many of the country's oldest Buddhist and Hindu temples, mosques and churches.

Exploring historical Melaka

It is possible to walk around Melaka's historical sights. There is now an interesting 'trail' – called the **Jerak Warisan Heritage Trail**, which starts at the Tourist Office on Jalan Kota, near the quayside; by following this trail the visitor gets to see all the major cultural sights of interest. The route crosses the bridge, to the Baba Nyonya Heritage Museum, takes in all the temples on Jonkers Street and then back across the bridge to Stadthuys, St Paul's Church, St Paul's Hill and the Porta de Santiago Independence Monument. For a 'handout' on the trail, ask at the Tourist Office. A more leisurely way to get around is by trishaw. There are also many places around town that rent bicycles.

There are boat tours (see below) down the river through the original port area and past some of the old Dutch houses. However, the river is a little pungent, but the 16th-century sanitation adds to the realism. On the west bank is **Kampung Morten**, a village of traditional Melakan houses. It was named after a man who built Melaka's wet market and donated the land to the Malays. The main attraction here is Kassim Mahmood's hand-crafted house.

The most interesting parts of the old town are close to the waterfront

The Dutch colonial architecture in the **town square** is the most striking feature of the riverfront. The buildings are painted a bright terracotta red and are characterized by their massive walls, chunky doors with wrought-iron hinges and louvred windows. The most prominent of these is the imposing **Stadthuys**. Completed in 1660, it is said to be the oldest-surviving Dutch building in the East, and served as the official residence of the Dutch governors. The recently renovated building now houses a good **history museum** detailing in maps, prints and photographs the history and development of Malacca/Melaka. Also here are a cultural museum and a literature museum, which are of less obvious interest to the average visitor. ■ *0900-1800 Sat-Thu 0900-1245, 1445-1800 Fri, RM2.* Just southwest from Stadthuys, on the river is a half-size replica of the galley that the viceroy of Portuguese India arrived in. The **Tang Beng Swee Clock Tower** looks Dutch but was built by a wealthy Straits Chinese family in 1886. **Christ Church** was built between 1741 and 1753 to replace an earlier Portuguese church, which was by then a ruin (church records date back to 1641). Its red bricks were shipped out from Zeeland in Holland. It is Malaysia's oldest Protestant church and the floor is still studded with Dutch tombstones. The original pews are intact – as are its ceiling beams, each hewn from a single tree trunk more than 15 m long. On the altar there is a collection of

Southern Peninsula

Melaka detail

N

| 0 metres | 20 |
| 0 yards | 20 |

■ **Sleeping**
1 Heeren House

● **Eating**
1 Discovery Café

- - -◄ Jerak Warisan Heritage Trail

Related map
A Melaka, page 209

The Nyonyas and the Babas

By the early 1400s Melaka was one of the most important ports of call for Chinese trade missions. They arrived between November and March on the northeast monsoon winds and left again in late June on the southwest monsoon; giving them plenty of time to settle down and start families. Melaka's early sultans made several visits to China, paying obeisance to the Ming emperors to ensure Chinese imperial protection for the sultanate. When Sultan Mansur Shah married the Ming Chinese princess Hang Li Poh in 1460, she brought with her a retinue of 500 'youths of noble birth' and handmaidens who settled around Bukit Cina – or Chinese Hill.

Subsequent generations of Straits Chinese came to be known as Peranakans – from the Bahasa word anak, or offspring, and means 'born here'. Peranakan women were called Nyonyas and the men, Babas. Sultan Mansur's marriage set a precedent and Peranakans combined the best of Chinese and Malay cultures. They created a unique, sophisticated and influential society and were known for their shrewd business acumen and opulent lifestyles. When the Dutch colonists moved out in the early 1800s, more Chinese moved in, continuing the tradition of intermarriage while clinging to the ancient customs brought with them from China.

Peranakan culture reached its zenith in the 19th century. Although Melaka was the Peranakan hearthstone, there were also large Straits Chinese communities in Penang and Singapore. The Nyonyas adopted Malay dress and were known for their fastidiousness when it came to clothes. The women were renowned for their intricate jewellery and glass beadwork – which are now prized antiques. The Nyonyas imported colourful porcelain from China for ceremonial occasions, which became known as Nyonya-ware and was typically emblazoned with phoenix and peony-flower motifs. They also imported craftsmen from China to make their intricate silver jewellery, including elaborate belts, hairpins and pillow end plates.

Peranakan weddings were elaborate affairs; couples were paired off by marriage-brokers, contracted by the groom's parents to consult horoscopes and judge the suitability of the match. If a match proved auspicious, there was a lengthy present-exchanging ritual for the young couple, who were not permitted to see each other until they finally got to the nuptial chamber. Wedding rituals often went on for 12 days and ended in a lavish feast before the couple went upstairs and the heavily veiled bride first showed her face to her new husband. As was the custom, he would then say: "Lady, I have perforce to be rude with you", whether he liked what he saw or not, for the marriage had to be consummated immediately.

Peranakan architecture is exemplified

sacramental silverware bearing the Dutch coat-of-arms and there is a beautiful altar carving of the Last Supper. ■ *Thu-Tue.*

On Jalan Kota, which runs in a curve round **St Paul's Hill** from the square, is the **Porta de Santiago**, the remains of the great Portuguese fort **A Famosa**, said to have been built in four months flat under Admiral Alfonso d'Albuquerque's supervision in 1511. What remains is largely a Dutch reconstruction, the result of repair work carried out following the siege in 1641; it prominently displays the Dutch East India Company's coat-of-arms. The fort originally sprawled across the whole hill and housed the entire Portuguese administration, including their hospitals and five churches. It was flattened by the British between 1806 and 1808 when they occupied Melaka during the Napoleonic Wars. They wanted to ensure that the fort was not reclaimed by the Dutch. Stamford Raffles arrived for a holiday in Melaka just in time to forestall the destruction of its last remaining edifice.

in the Chinese Palladian townhouses – the best examples of which are in Melaka – with their open courtyards and lavish interiors, dominated by heavy dark furniture, inlaid with marble and mother-of-pearl. Aside from their magnificent homes, one of the Peranakans' most enduring endowments is their cuisine, the result of the melding of cultures. The food is spicy but uses lots of coconut milk and is painstakingly prepared – Nyonya-Baba restaurants are difficult business propositions. For details of particular dishes, see page 48).

The cliquey Peranakan upper-class assimilated easily into British colonial society, following the formation of the Straits Settlements in 1826. The billiard-playing, brandy-swilling Babas, in their Mandarin dresses, conical hats, pigtails and thick-soled shoes successfully penetrated the commercial sector and entered public office. Many became professionals, such as lawyers, doctors and teachers, although they were barred from entering government above the clerical level. "Strange to say," wrote Vaughan, "that although the Babas adhere so loyally to the customs of their progenitors they despise the real Chinamen and are exclusive fellows indeed; [there is] nothing they rejoice in more than being British subjects...". In Penang they were dubbed 'the Queen's Chinese'. Over the years they evolved their own Malay patois, and, in the

19th century, English was also thrown into their linguistic cocktail. They even devised a secret form of slang by speaking Baba Malay backwards.

Although they chose not to mix with immigrant Chinese, they retained a strong interest in events in China. The Straits Settlements provided a refuge for exiled reformers from the motherland – most notably Dr Sun Yat-sen, who lived in both Singapore and Penang in the early 1900s and became the first president of the Republic of China in 1911.

The Baba community's most famous son was Tan Cheng Lock, who was born into a distinguished Melakan Baba family in 1883. He lent his name to the Peranakans' architectural treasure, Jalan Tun Tan Chen Lock (formerly Heeren Street) in Melaka's Chinatown. Tan served in local government in colonial Melaka from 1912-1935 and vociferously fought British discrimination against the Straits and Malayan Chinese. He charged that the British had done nothing to "foster and strengthen their spirit of patriotism and natural love for the country of their birth and adoption". Tan was the spokesman for Malaya's Chinese community and fought for equality among the races; he founded the Overseas Chinese Association and became a prominent reformist politician in the years leading up to Malaysian independence.

From behind the gate, a path leads up to the ruins of **St Paul's Church**, built on the site of the last Melakan sultan's *istana*. The small chapel was originally built by the Portuguese in 1521 and called *Nossa Senhora da Annunciada*, Our Lady of the Annunciation. The body of St Francis Xavier (the 16th-century Jesuit missionary who translated the catechism into Malay and visited the church regularly), was temporarily interred in the church vault following his death off the coast of China in 1552. His remains were later sent to Portuguese Goa on the west coast of India. An armless marble statue, erected in 1953, now commemorates Malaysia's best-known missionary. The Portuguese added gun turrets and a tower to the church and it became a fortress between 1567 and 1596. During the Dutch seige of Melaka in 1641, it was badly damaged but the invaders repaired it and renamed it St Paul's. It became a Protestant church and remained so until Christ Church was completed in 1753. St Paul's ended its life as a cemetery; it was used as a special burial ground for Dutch nobles, whose tombs line the walls. There are good views of the city and out over the sea from the top of Saint Paul's Hill.

A wooden replica of Sultan Mansur Shah's 15th-century *istana* now houses the **Muzium Budaya** (Melaka Cultural Museum) below St Paul's. The palace has been painstakingly reconstructed from a description in the 16th-century *Serjarah Melayu* (Malay Annals) and was built in 1985 using traditional construction techniques and materials. Mansur – who came to the throne in 1459 – inherited what was reputed to be the finest royal palace in the world, with a roof of copper and zinc in seven tiers, supported by wooden carved pillars. According to the Annals, his magnificent *istana* was destroyed by fire after being struck by lightning the year after his accession. Exhibits in the museum focus on Melakan culture, including clothes, games, weapons, musical instruments, stone inscriptions and photographs. It also features a diorama of the Sultan's court. **Note**: The museum was closed for renovation for much of 2001 and was due to re-open towards the end of the year; this should have improved the display. ■ *0900-1800, closed Tue, closed Fri 1215-1445, RM1.50.*

The **Proclamation of Independence Memorial**, opposite the Cultural Museum, was built in 1912 and formerly housed the Malacca Club. The old Dutch colonial building was the social centre of British colonial Melaka. Perhaps appropriately, it now houses an extensive timeline exhibition covering Malaysia's journey to independence. There are lots of photographs – interesting to those who like that sort of thing – and it also represents a fine example of nation-building. ■ *0900-1800 Sat-Thu, 0900-1200 and 1500-1800 Fri, free.*

A concrete bridge from the south end of Dutch Square leads to **Chinatown**, the old trading section of Melaka. **Jalan Hang Jebat**, formerly known as **Jonker Street**, was once famous for its antique shops: Nyonya porcelain, Melakan-style 'red and gold' carved furniture, wooden opium beds, Victorian mirrors, antique fans and Peranakan blackwood furniture inlaid with mother-of-pearl. There are some good examples of Peranakan architecture along the street – notably the renowned Jonkers Melaka Restoran. But none of these Peranakan houses compare with the picturesque **Jalan Tun Tan Cheng Lock**. Named after a leading Melakan Baba, instrumental in pre- independence politics (see box, page 212), it is lined with the Straits Chinese community's ancestral homes and is Melaka's 'Millionaires' Row'. Many of the houses have intricately carved doors that were often specially built by immigrant craftsmen from China. Today tour buses exacerbate the local traffic problem, which clogs the narrow one-way street, but many of its Peranakan mansions are still lived in by the same families that built them in the 19th century.

One of the most opulent of these houses has been converted into the **Baba-Nyonya Heritage Museum**, 48-50 Jalan Tun Tan Cheng Lock. It is in a well-preserved traditional Peranakan town house, built in 1896 by millionaire rubber planter Chan Cheng Siew. Today it is owned by William Chan and his family, who conduct tours of their ancestral home. The interior is that of a typical 19th-century residence and all the rooms are still as they would have been 100 years ago. The house contains family heirlooms and antiques, including Nyonyaware porcelain and blackwood furniture with marble or mother-of-pearl inlay, and silverware. There is also a collection of traditional wedding costumes, photographs and kitchen utensils. The kitchen sink has the name of William Chan's great grandfather carved on it. The information-packed tours are run regularly throughout the day. ■ *1000-1230 and 1400-1600, closed all day Tue; RM8, children RM4.*

Although at first glance, tourists may be impressed by the streets around **Chinatown**, the sad truth is that the desire to attract mass tourism to this 'heritage' town has probably destroyed more heritage than it has protected. Over the past 18 months over 20 buildings have been demolished and many traditional trades evicted in the interests of bigger business. False 'heritage' façades and trinket shops have taken the place of the authentic article. A new project, 'Jonker Walk' – a renaming of Jonker Street (Jalan Hang Jebat) – has led to the pedestrianization of the street over the weekends. There are two ways of looking at Jonker Walk. Most visitors come away thinking that the night market here is fun and zingy, they like the shophouse architecture, the hawkers sell tasty snacks, and the pedestrianization of the street makes it all more human, The alternative view is that the street has been transformed from a place with real people running traditional businesses to a contrived and ersatz place geared to the needs of foreigners. No local residents were consulted about the project, the original traders and guilds have been displaced, and an accumulation of rubbish and associated rats and cockroaches has created health problems. Take your pick!

One of Melaka's most significant cultural assets was removed from 92 Jonker Street this year, to make way for a new hotel. Eighty-year-old Mr Yeo, the proprietor, was given three days to move out. For two generations the Yeo family, at **Wah Aik Shoemaker Shop**, have been the only cobblers catering for the country's dwindling population of ageing Chinese women with bound feet. The practice, which was considered *de rigeur* for women of noble stock during the Ch'ing Dynasty (1644-1912), was rekindled among the families of nouveau riche Chinese tin towkays during the days of the British Straits Settlements. The process involved binding the feet firmly with bandages before they were fully formed; it was supposed to add to a woman's sensuality, but in reality it just caused a lot of pain. In China, the practice was outlawed in 1912. There are only a handful of women in Malaysia with bound feet, most of them in Melaka and all of them in their 80s or 90s. Mr Yeo Sing Guat makes these *san choon chin lian* (3-in golden lotus feet) shoes – with brocade on authentic Shanghai Hang Chong silk – for them and as tourist souvenirs; he also makes the Peranakan *kasut manik* 'pearl shoes', sewn with miniature pearl beads. Today, the shoemaker can be found at 103 Jalan Kubu.

Malaysia's most unusual shoe shop

The **Cheng Hoon Teng Temple**, on Jalan Tokong, was built in 1645, although there were later additions in 1704 and 1804. The name literally means 'Temple of the Evergreen Clouds' and was founded by Melaka's Kapitan Cina, Lee Wi King from Amoy, a political refugee who fled from China. All the materials used in the original building were imported from China, as were the craftsmen who built it in typical South Chinese style. The elaborate tiled roofs are decorated with mythological figures, flowers and birds, and inside there are wood carvings and lacquer work. The main altar houses an image of Kuan Yin, the Goddess of Mercy (cast in solid bronze and bought from India in the 19th century), who is associated with peace, good fortune and fertility. On her left sits Ma Cho Po, the guardian of fishermen and on her right, Kuan Ti, the god of war, literature and justice. The halls to the rear of the main temple are dedicated to Confucius and contain ancestral tablets.

The oldest Chinese temple in Malaysia

Nearby, on Jalan Tukang Emas, is the **Sri Poyyatha Vinayagar Moorthi Temple**, built in 1781 and the oldest Hindu temple in use in Malaysia. It is dedicated to the elephant-headed god Vinayagar (more usually known as Ganesh). Near to this Hindu temple on Jalan Tukang Emas is the **Masjid Kampung Kling**, a mosque built in 1748 in Sumatran style, with a square base surmounted by a three-tiered roof and pagoda-like minaret. Another 18th-century mosque in the same style is the **Masjid Tranquerah**, 2 km out of town on the road to Port Dickson. Next door is an unusual free-standing octagonal minaret with Chinese-style embellishments, in marked contrast to Malaysia's traditional Moorish-style mosques. In the graveyard is the tomb of Sultan Hussein Shah of Johor who, in 1819, signed the cession of Singapore to Stamford Raffles.

St Peter's Church on Jalan Taun Sri Lanang was built in 1710 by descendants of the early Portuguese settlers when the Dutch became more tolerant of different faiths. Iberian design is incorporated in the interior, where Corinthian pillars support a curved ceiling above the aisle, similar to churches in Goa and Macau. It is the centre of the Catholic faith in Malaysia. Easter candlelit processions to St Peter's seem strangely out of context in Malaysia. ■ *Open until 1900 Mon-Sun.*

In 1460 when Sultan Mansur Shah married Li Poh, a Ming princess, she took up residence on Melaka's highest hill, **Bukit Cina**, which became the Chinese quarter. The Malay Annals do not record what became of the princess's palace but the hill, off Jalan Munshi Abdullah/Jalan Laksamana Cheng Ho, remained in the possession of the Chinese community and because of its good *feng shui* – its harmony with the supernatural forces and the elements - it was made into a graveyard. The cemetery now sprawls across the adjoining hills of Bukit Gedona and Bukit Tempurong and is the largest traditional Chinese burial ground outside China, containing more than 12,000 graves. Chinese graveyards are often built on hillsides because the hill is said to protect the graves from evil winds; this hill has the added advantage of overlooking water and the ancestral spirits are said to enjoy the panoramic view over the city and across the Strait of Melaka. Some of the graves date back to the Ming Dynasty, but most of these are overgrown or disintegrating.

The hill was ceded in perpetuity to the Chinese by successive colonial governments, but in mid-1991 the city burghers, backed by the Lands and Mining Department, demanded RM10m in rent arrears, going back 500 years, from the general manager of Cheng Hoon Teng temple, who is responsible for the upkeep of Bukit Cina. Unless the Chinese community paid up in full, the city threatened to repossess the 42 ha of prime-site real estate it sits on. An impasse ensued, which was still unresolved at the time of writing.

At the foot of the hill is an old Chinese temple called **Sam Poh Kong**, built in 1795 and dedicated to the famous Chinese seafarer, Admiral Cheng Ho (see page 206). It was originally built to cater for those whose relatives were buried on Bukit Cina. This temple has a peaceful and relaxed atmosphere and is interesting to explore. Next to the temple is the **Sultan's Well** (*Perigi Rajah*), also called the **Hang Li Poh Well**, said to have been sunk in the 15th century. It is believed that drinking from this well ensures a visitor's return to Melaka – but anyone foolhardy enough to try this today is liable to contract dysentery and instead stay rather longer than they anticipated. However, while the water may be off-limits to all but the most foolhardy, there is a small market situated beside the well where the visitor can sample the local fruits.

The ruined **Fort St John**, another relic of the Dutch occupation, is to the west of Bukit Cina on Jalan Bendahara (Air Keroh road, off Jalan Munshi Abdullah at *Renaissance Melaka*). Its hilltop location affords some excellent views although its aspect has been spoiled by the water treatment plant and high-rise apartment block on either side of it.

The **Maritime Museum** is housed in a full-scale reconstruction of the Portuguese trading vessel *Flor de la Mar*, on the riverbank, 200 m downstream from the river boat embarkation point. Of all the museums in Melaka, this is one of the better ones – many of the other museums are rather repetitive, but as Melaka's history is the history of sea-trade, this is a more interesting option. It has a collection of models of foreign ships that docked at Melaka during its maritime supremacy from the 14th century to the Portuguese era. The *Flor de la Mar* itself ended its days on the sea bed just off-shore, laden with treasure that was bound for Portugal (see box, page 206). ■ *0900-1800, closed Tue all day, closed Fri 1215-1445, RM2.* Entry to the Maritime Museum also gives access to the **Royal Malaysian Navy Museum**, across the road, which displays the salvaged remains of 19th-century vessels that have foundered or been sunk in the Melaka Strait, as well as more contemporary bits and pieces.

About 3 km from the town centre is the Portuguese Settlement (Medan **Portuguese** Portugis) at Ujong Pasir, where the descendants of the Portuguese occupiers **Settlement** settled. A Portuguese community (of sorts) has managed to survive here for nearly five centuries; unlike the subsequent Dutch and British colonial régimes, the Portuguese garrison was encouraged to intermarry and generally treat the Malays as social equals. Today these Malaysians of Portuguese descent number around 4,500 (although other estimates are much lower). In the country as a whole, there are thought to be some 20,000. The process of integration was so successful that when the Dutch, after capturing the city in 1641, offered Portuguese settlers a choice between amnesty and deportation to their nearest colony, many chose to stay. In the 1920s, as their distinctive culture was threatened with extinction, the leaders of the community pleaded with the British to allot them a piece of land on which they could settle. A small area of swampland was duly allocated and the neat and well-planned settlement visible today was built, its street named after Portuguese heroes largely unrecognized in Malaysia. The main square, built only in 1985, is a concrete replica of a square in Lisbon – and is visibly ersatz. The descendants of the original settlers still speak a medieval Portuguese dialect called *Cristao* (pronounced 'Cristang'), spoken nowhere else in the world.

Today there are just a few tourist-oriented restaurants and shops in the modern Portuguese Square, and cultural shows are staged on Saturday nights (see **Eating** page 223). Other than tourism, the residents of the Portuguese settlement earn their livelihoods by fishing and through a small number of cottage industries including shrimp paste production. The central role that the sea plays in the community's coherence and identity is threatened by a land reclamation project that will cut off its access to the sea. This will destroy the settlement's fishing industry, its fish-based cottage industries and also undermine its attraction to tourists. As Gerard Fernandis remarked in August 1995, "Our history, our culture, songs, dances and food are all linked to the sea", adding that without the sea the "settlement will become an island in a sea of concrete." To get there, take a No 17 bus.

Boat tours of Melaka's docks, go-downs, old Dutch trading houses, wharves **Tours** and seafront markets run from the quay close to the *Tourism Malaysia* office. Predictably this area is known as Melaka's 'Little Venice', but it does not live up to the description. However, the guides are generally informative, pointing out settlements and wildlife. There are views of the giant lizards on the banks and plenty of rubbish floating downstream. Boats leave when full and usually there is a departure every hour or so between 1000 and 1400, although departures do vary according to the tides. Tickets for the river boat can be purchased from the tourist office (45 minutes, RM8). For reservations, T062865468 (RM6; RM3 for children).

Southern Peninsula

Excursions

Tanjung Kling
Tanjung Kling is a much more relaxing place to stay than Melaka itself

About 9 km northwest of Melaka, it is a pleasant drive past beachside kampungs despite the muddy sea and dirty beach from passing tankers that have a habit of swilling out their tanks. This does not seem to affect the taste of the seafood – or perhaps it improves it – and there are several restaurants and hawker stalls along the roadside at **Pantai Kundur**, where there are a number of hotels. Kampung Kling is thought to have got its name from Tamils who originally settled there, having come from Kalingapatam, north of Madras. For the less geographically confident, local tour companies offer organized tours on foot or by car, including visits to the plantation and to Ayer Keroh. Ask at the tourist office for details.

Sleeping A *Klebang Beach Resort*, 92-1, km 9, Batang Tiga, Tanjung Kling, T3155888, F3151713. Small hotel that opened a few years back, clean and comfortable, but unimaginative décor, small free-form pool, paddling pool, children's playground, 2 restaurants. A *Mutiara Malacca Beach Resort*, Pantai Kundur, Tanjung Kling, T3517419, F3517517. Over 218 all-suite units, a/c, TV, mini-bar, kitchenette, spacious but not stylish, 2 restaurants (limited menu), Bubbles Fun Pub, tennis, pool, mountain bikes, watersports, sauna, gymnasium, 20 mins' taxi ride from the centre of Melaka, with views over the Straits and the oil refinery, awful beach and a spartan resort but friendly staff. A *Riviera Bay Resort*, 10 km Jln Tanjung Kling, T3151111, F3153333. Opened late 1995, classical architecture on a palatial scale, takes the form of a U-shaped building on 14 floors with 450 spacious suites, tastefully decorated in shades of green and all sea-facing, with a/c, TV, in-house movies, tea and coffee-making facilities, mini-bar, other amenities include 3 restaurants under a top Swiss chef, the Buccaneer pub, hair salon, children's playground, watersports, tennis, pool with swim-up bar, paddling pool. Just 15 mins' drive from Melaka's town centre. Recent reports have been of rather slap-dash service and levels of cleanliness. B *Shah's Beach Resort*, 9 km, Tanjung Kling, T3152120. A/c, restaurant, pool, 1950s front with two lines of a/c chalets behind, tennis court and pool can be used by non-guests for a fee. Breakfast included. C *Motel Tanjung Kling*, 5855C Pantai Pangkalan Perigi, Tanjung Kling, T515749. A/c, restaurant. C *Straits View Lodge*, C-7886, Pantai Kundur, Batu 9, Tanjung Kling, T514627, F325788. Simple chalets, friendly atmosphere, boat, bike and fishing equipment for hire.

Eating Cheap *Yashika Traveller Hostel*, Batu 8, Pantai Kundur, beach restaurant, international. **Seriously cheap** *Roti John*, Pantai Kundur, on the seafront, Melaka's Roti John specialist.

Transport *Patt Hup* buses 51, 18, 42 and 47 buses can be caught from Jln Tengkera (at the north end of Jln Tun Tan Cheng Lock, in Melaka); there are also taxis.

Tanjung Bidara

Further up the road towards Port Dickson, about 20 km northwest of Melaka, is Tanjung Bidara. It has a long beach and plenty of hawker stalls but the sea is generally rather dirty. There is the upmarket chalet-style A *Tanjung Bidara Beach Resort*, T3842990, with air conditioning, a restaurant and pool. Take a *Patt Hup* bus to get there, see **Transport**, above.

Ayer Keroh

Situated just off the highway to KL, 11 km northeast of Melaka, Ayer Keroh has a lake, jungle, a golf course and a country club. It is also the site of **Melaka Zoo** (RM3, RM1 for children), **reptile park** (RM3, children RM1) and **Mini-Malaysia Complex**, where the various states of Malaysia are represented by 13 traditional houses containing works of art and culture (similar to the Karyaneka Handicraft Centre in KL) as well as an Orang Asli village. All the houses look remarkably alike, except the Borneo one. It also stages cultural shows. It is, however, overstaffed and badly managed. Mini-ASEAN is next door and is more varied (and included in the ticket price). ■ *All the above sights are open 0900-1800 Mon-Sun, RM4, children RM2.* The Ayer Keroh Golf and Country Club is the longest golf course in Malaysia, with green fees at RM70 for weekdays and RM100 for weekends, T320822, handicap cards must be produced. To get there, take bus 19 (known as Townbus 19), every 30 minutes.

Sleeping A *Malacca Village Paradise Resort*, T2323600, F2325955. Formerly the *Park Plaza*, this is a recent addition to the Paradise chain, popular with Singaporeans at weekends, but reduced rates often available during week, over 500 rooms in imposing Malaccan-red buildings, 2 swimming pools, 2 tennis courts, gymnasium, 2 squash courts, recreation centre, health club (good value shiatsu massage), beauty salon, jogging track, children's playground and sand-pit, 2 restaurants, all rooms with a/c, bath, mini-bar, tea and coffee-making facilities, TV, in-house video. Breakfast included, great value. Recommended. **B-C** *Air Keroh Country Resort*, T2325211, F2320422. Motel-like atmosphere, a/c, restaurant, pool. **Camping** Only at Ayer Keroh Recreational Forest and at Durian Tunggal Recreational Lake (on the way to Selandar).

(margin: Southern Peninsula)

Pulau Besar Contrary to its name, Pulau Besar is a small, quiet island, about 8 km southeast of Melaka, which is popular at weekends. According to local legend, a princess became pregnant by a Melakan commoner and was banished to the island to die. There is a shrine on the island dedicated to an early Muslim missionary, who is said to have come to Melaka in the 1400s. The island has good beaches (although the sea is not clean and most of the coral is dead) and there are jungle walks. Located on 22 ha of the 133-ha island is the **B** *Panda Nusa Resort*, at 37 Jalan Chan Koon Cheng, T2818007, a deluxe beach resort designed to look like a traditional Melakan village. It has air conditioning, a restaurant, and a pool complex complete with open-air jacuzzi.

Gunung Ledang
Altitude: 1,276 m
This is one of the peninsula's best-known mountains, also called Mount Ophir, located on the east side of the North-South Highway, equidistant from Melaka and Muar and just inside Johor state. It is isolated from the mountains of the Main Range and is sacred to the Orang Asli of Melaka. A Straits Chinese and Malay rumour has it that the mountain is the domain of a beautiful fairy endowed with the local version of the Midas Touch: she has a habit of turning Gunung Ledang's plant-life into gold. The mountain is said to be guarded by a sacred tiger, which is possessed by the fairy.

Ayer Keroh

Would-be climbers are strongly recommended to refer to the detailed trail-guide in John Briggs', 'Mountains of Malaysia', available in Singapore and KL bookshops

Gunung Ledang is a strenuous climb involving some very steep scrambles, particularly towards the top. In 1884 an expedition reached the summit while trying to demarcate the boundary between Johor and Melaka. Most climbers choose to camp overnight on the summit, although, at a push, it can be done in a day, from dawn to dusk. The mountain is surrounded by and covered in virgin jungle, and rises through mossy forest (where there are several varieties of pitcher plant, see page 563) to the rocky summit. Climbers are strongly advised to stick closely to the trails: since 1987, two separate parties of Singaporeans have become lost for several days after straying off the trail. The trail is complex in places and the climb should be carefully planned. There are two main trails up the mountain; the best route starts 15 km from Tangkak, just beyond Sagil. Waterfalls (*Air Terjun*) are signposted off the road that leads to Air Penas, an over-popular local picnic spot. The trail begins just beyond the rubber factory. Those attempting the climb without a trail-guide can hire a local guide from Tangkak.

If you want to stay overnight, **A** *Gunung Ledang Resort*, 91-a, Jln Sutera, Taman Sentosa, T3347061, F3344270 (Sales office: 28, Jln Segamat, 84020 Sagil, T9772888, ledang@tm.net.my, www.ledang.com/index21.html) This place has 60 chalets and 30 jungle huts set in the jungle, facilities and activities include a swimming pool, gym, health centre, restaurant and convention centre. The resort is about 2 hrs' drive on the North-South Express through Tangkak Town to Sagil; from there drive up the mountain.

Essentials

Sleeping
■ *on map, page 209*
Price codes: see inside front cover

There's plenty of choice in Melaka but the cheaper hotels tend to be further out of town. There are several good hotels around Tanjung Kling (see **Excursions**, above). There are several good budget hotels at Taman Melaka Raya.

L *Century Mahkota*, Jln Merdeka, T2812828, F2812323, http://www.centuryotel.com On the waterfront next to the Mahkota Parade Shopping and Entertainment Complex, this is one of Melaka's first resort hotels. Two pools, health centre, tennis court, two squash courts, mini golf, children's playground, spread out over several towers, the 20 'rooms' are actually suites and apartments, with the usual facilities plus kitchen. **L** *Renaissance Melaka*, Jln Bendahara, T2848888, F2849269, enquiries@renaissance-melaka.com The only 5-star hotel in Melaka, 24 storeys high, it is the tallest building in the town, with 300 rooms all of which are spacious and elegantly appointed with Malaccan wood furniture, a/c, mini-fridge, TV, in-house video and grand views either over the town or to the sea, other amenities include coffee shop, restaurants, fitness centre, pool on the 9th floor. Recommended. **AL** *City Bayview*, Jln Bendahara, T2839888, F2836699, cbviewmk@tm.net.my A/c, restaurant, pool, the rooms visitors are shown are not always like the ones they will end up with. Directly opposite the hospital and with a good location in historic Melaka. The most hideous crystal chandelier greets you as you enter the hotel. This poor taste is in keeping with much of the hotel. Overpriced. **AL** *Golden Legacy Malacca*, 146 Jln Hang Tuah, T2816868, F2819898, pplhm@plegacy.po.my New and sophisticated hotel with 250 plus rooms (although billed as 'boutique'), business facilities, gymnasium, pool and more. Well designed and popular with business visitors. **A** *Equatorial*, Jln Parameswara, T2828333, F3089333, info@mel.equatorial.com A monstrous 500-room block, pools, gym, several restaurants including Chinese, Nyonya and Japanese. Conference facilities. Towers over the south side of town, includes 'Churchill's cigar and wine bar', good-sized rooms, but dirty and prone to traffic noise. **A-B** *Heeren*

House, 1 Jln Tun Tan Cheng Lock, T2814241, F2814239. A/c, restaurant, rates include breakfast, 5 a/c nicely furnished rooms in colonial and Peranakan style, with canopied 4-poster beds (booking recommended) co-owned by a British lecturer from Singapore and his Chinese partner, afternoon tea, pleasant position in front of the river. Timber floors and 4-poster beds add to the charm of this riverside hotel. Expensive for what you get (rooms are small), but it's a quiet, family-run establishment. Breakfast included. Recommended. **A-B** *Mimosa Hotel*, 108 Jln Buya Raya, T2821113, F2819122, www.mimosahotel.com Newish hotel located in Chinatown – decent, fully carpeted rooms with a/c, TV and shower. Its restaurant is curiously only open between 0700-1400. Popular with Japanese tours.

B *Accordian Hotel*, 114 Jln Bendahara, T2821911, F2821333, accordian_hotel @asia1.com 47 a/c rooms, shower, TV. Rooms in this rather gloomy hotel are a bit cramped. Price includes breakfast. **B** *Emperor*, 123 Jln Munshi Abdullah, T2840777, F2838989, www.angelfire.com/biz2/emperorhotel/index.html A/c, restaurant, pool, health centre, reasonably clean. Great sea views and excellent value at present prices. Breakfast included and special offers on meals. Renovation of a large portion of this hotel was begun in late 2001 with no definite completion date or future plans. **B** *Grand Continental*, 20 Jln Tun Sri Lanang, T2840088, F2848125. Consists of 150 a/c rooms, restaurant, large rooms, good service, buffet for all meals, at a good price. Recommended. Breakfast included. **B** *Hotel Orkid*, 138 Jln Bendahara, T2825555, F2827777. Smart hotel at an affordable price. A/c, shower, TV. Facilities include a spa, restaurant and bar. Primarily a business visitor's stopover but good value for tourists. **B** *Lucky Inn*, 116 Jln Bendahara, T2810070, F2810071. New hotel. Rooms carpeted and newly furnished with TV and shower. **B** *Palace*, 201 Jln Munshi Abdullah, T2825355, F2848833. A/c restaurant, 48 rooms and 7 storeys; rooms are rather lacklustre and on the small side. Steer clear. **B** *Straits Meridian*, 1 Jln Malinja, Taman Malinja, towards Ayer Keroh, T2841166, F2830030, www.sherwoodhotels.com All suite accommodation. Many special deals on both meals and accommodation available here so worth checking it out. **B-C** *Baba House,* 125-127 Jln Tun Tan Cheng Lock, T2811216, F2811217. In the centre of Chinatown, 60 a/c rooms, no restaurant, TV, attractive traditional Baba house, beautiful design, rooms quite plain and some overly small but clean, mostly without windows. **C** *Lotus Inn*, 2846 Jln Semabok, T2837211, F2837213. East of town and inconveniently situated, with 50 a/c rooms and restaurant.

D *Chong Hoe*, Jln Tukang Emas, T2826102. A/c, good location near all the central sights and temples and reasonable value. **D** *Eastern Heritage*, 8 Jln Bukit Cina, T233026. Great old Chinese building with carved wood and gold inlay, spacious rooms on 2nd floor, dorm on 3rd floor, small pool on 1st floor, batik lessons available, closer to the heart of the city than other low budget places. Extremely popular, with an authentic feel. **D** *Kancil*, 177 Jln Parameswara (Bandar Hillir), T2814044, kancil@ machuita.com.sg Cool and quiet, quiet backyard/garden, bicycles for hire. Inconveniently situated on a narrow main road with no pavement. Basic rooms, some without windows, reasonable. **D** *Melaka Town Holiday Lodge*, 148b Taman Melaka Raya, T2848830. Limited breakfast included, hot showers, bikes for hire, laundry service, clean and well looked after, dormitory or rooms, friendly. Recommended. City tours and postal service available. **D** *Melaka Town Holiday Lodge*, 52 A-B-C, Kampung Empat. Same name as the *Holiday Lodge* on Taman Melaka, but slightly more upmarket and in a quieter residential area. A little more expensive, but services include bus ticket reservation and bicycle hire; worth the few extra ringgit if you can afford it. **D** *Ng Fook*, 154 Jln Bunga Raya, T2828055. Some a/c, clean but simple rooms, all with bathrooms, some with television. Good value at this price. **D** *Robin's Nest 2*, 202 Jln Taman Melaka Raya, T6026022. This new addition to Robin's expanding empire is located around the corner from the original (see below). Virtually identical and a/c is available. Most rooms with shared shower/toilet, but some en-suite. Cheap, simple meals available to guests at both hostels, served at Robin's Nest 1. Very friendly owners. **D** *Sunny's Inn*, 253B Jln Taman Melaka Raya, T2275446, sunnysinn@hotmail.com A couple of single and double rooms and a dorm (**F**), kitchen, bikes for hire, nightly video, good information, friendly staff, bus tickets. Very similar to most budget hotels in this area – in other words, pretty basic. **D** *Grand Star Hotel*, 256b & 257b, Taman Melaka Raya Jalan 3, T2818199. An extensive guesthouse, a little grubby but with friendly staff and good facilities. Internet access, TV, video, kitchen, open 24 hours. Smokers welcome. **D** *Travellers Guest House*, 151 Jln Bunga Raya, T2824962. With a/c but without windows. Rabbit hutches with basin and shower head in room, together with drain (and the smells from all the other rooms and toilets). Overpriced.

E *Melaka Youth Hostel*, 341 Taman Melaka Raya, T2827915, F2741115. Clean and well run with 56 dorm beds (including an a/c dorm), laundry service available but no kitchen. Spacious common room with TV. Midnight curfew. **E-F** *Robin's Nest*, 205B Jln Taman Melaka Raya, T2829142. Clean and comfortable, helpful proprietor, dorm and fan rooms. Nightly video, shared washing facilities.

Eating
Price codes: see inside front cover

Malay Cheap *Anda*, 8b Jln Hang Tuah, popular modern coffee shop, specialities include *ikan bakar* (grilled fish), *sayur masak lemak* (deep-fried marinated prawns) and *rendang*. **Seriously cheap** *Mini*, 35 Jln Merdeka, good for *ikan panggang* (grilled fish with spicy sauce) and *nasi campur*. *Sederhana*, 18A Jln Hang Tuah, near the bus station, good selection of Malay dishes. *Taman*, 10 Jln Merdeka, on the sea front, known for its *ikan assam pedas* – hot (chilli-hot) fish curry. *Cendol* can be drunk all over Malaysia – sample it at the Clock Tower, near Bukit St Paul. It is made up of crushed ice, coconut milk, *gula melaka* – glutinous rice beads and strips of green jelly – delicious!

Chinese Mid-range *Good New World Restoran*, Taman Melaka Raya, T2842528, large and modern, specializes in Cantonese dishes. Locally recommended. **Cheap** *Dragon Village Restaurant*, 1 Jln Kubu Melaka, T2815678, in charming old building, popular, although out of the hub of things at the edge of Chinatown. *Chop Teo Soon Leng*, 55 Jln Hang Tuah, Teochew cuisine. *Keng Dom*, 148 Taman Melaka Raya, T2826409, locally renowned for its steamboats. **Seriously cheap** *Bee Bee Hiong*, City Park, Jln Bunga Raya, for fish-ball fans. *Hoe Kee Chicken Rice*, Jln Hang Jebat, Hainanese chicken rice in Chinatown coffee shop, incredibly popular with workers at lunchtime. Recommended. *Kim Swee Huat*, 38 Jln Laksamana, big menu with staple western fillers (include travellers' food) as well as local food. *New Oriental Satay and Mee*, 82 Jln Tengkera (road to Tanjung Kling), being a Chinese stall, serves pork satay and other variations such as cuttlefish (*sotong*) satay, also well known for its *yee kiow mee*. *UE Teahouse*, 20 Lorong Bukit Cina, *dim sum* from early morning until 1200. Recommended. *Famosa Chicken Rice Ball*, 29 Jln Hang Kasturi, is to be avoided, not only for its food that has apparently caused food poisoning on more than one occasion, but also for the way in which it has destroyed a beautiful old shophouse, which not so long ago housed one of Melaka's oldest goldsmiths.

Nyonya Mid-range *Jonkers*, 17 Jln Hang Jebat. Old Nyonya house, with restaurant in the old ancestral hall. Good atmosphere and excellent food – Nyonya and international, set menu good value at RM20 (changes regularly), worth a visit for the house alone but the food is also excellent. Recommended. *Nam Hoe Villa* (*Restoran Peranakan*), 317c Klebang Besar (6 km towards Port Dickson), T3154436. Open 1100-1500, 1830-2300; cultural show at 2000 (except Sat). Originally the house of a Chinese rubber tycoon, now a restaurant and Peranakan showpiece, all the best-known Nyonya dishes are served; buffet. *Restoran Peranakan Town House*, 107 Jln Tun Tan Cheng Lock, T245001, same management and concept as *Nam Hoe*

Villa. *Ole Sayang*, 1988199 Taman Melaka Raya, T2831966, serves all the favourites, including chicken *pongteh* (in sweet and sour spicy sauce). Recommended. *Restoran Manis Sayang*, 617-618 Taman Melaka Raya, T2813393, traditional Nyonya chicken and fish dishes. **Cheap** *Bayonya*, 164 Taman Malaka Raya, bayonyarest@hot-mail.com Excellent Peranakan cuisine. The establishment is owned by a real enthusi-ast who will provide a culture lesson with your meal. Recommended. *Heeren House*, 1 Jln Tun Tan Cheng Lock, good value set lunch, cakes, appeals to western tastes, some Peranakan and Portuguese dishes, a/c, attractive Peranakan furniture. *Nyonya Makko*, 124 Taman Melaka Raya, T2840737, located near the bottom of St Paul's Hill, good selection, cheap and friendly. Recommended. **Seriously cheap** *Nancy's Kitchen*, 15 Jln Hang Lekir, housed in the *Old China Cafe*. Excellent, authentic Nonya food clas-sics such as 'chicken candlenut curry'. Small range of local cakes and biscuits available to take out. Open lunchtimes, closed Wednesdays. Robert and his family are great hosts and Nancy, the chef, occasionally emerges from the kitchen. Recommended.

Indian **Cheap** *Mitchell Raaju Nivaas*, Jln Laksamana, aside from its good curries, this restaurant also offers cooking lessons, RM2, for those who want to make Indian breads and basic curries. *Veni*, 34 Jln Temenggong, banana leaf restaurant with good selection of meat curries and vegetarian dishes, *roti canai* breakfasts. **Seriously cheap** *Banana Leaf*, 42 Jln Munshi Abdullah, South Indian meat curries and vegetar-ian dishes, biriyani specials on Wed and Sat evenings. *Kerala*, Jln Melaka Raya, good value. *Sri Lakshmi Villas*, intersection of Bendahara and Temenggong, fabulous *dosai masalas* and other good value Indian dishes.

Thai **Mid-range** *My Place*, 357 Jln Melaka, also some Malay, Chinese and Indian dishes.

Portuguese Most restaurants in the *Medan Portugis* are expensive tourist traps but some of the spicy seafood dishes are worth trying. **Mid-range** *Restaurante d'Nolasco*, 18b Medan Portugis, specializes in Portuguese cuisine. *Restoran de Lisbon*, Portuguese Square, run by Senhor Alcantra, this places comes recommended with its dishes that blend Malaysian and Portuguese cuisines – including devil chicken curry and sea bass roasted in a banana leaf, all washed down with ice-cold Portuguese lager or wines, cultural shows Sat evenings. *San Pedro*, Portuguese Settlement (just off the square), family run and probably the best at the Portuguese settlement, specialities include spicy baked fish, wrapped in banana leaf.

International **Expensive** *Taming Sari Grill*, *Renaissance Melaka Hotel*, Jln Bendahara, T2848888, seafood and meat cooked on marble with a little olive oil, served with bread, baked potato and salad. **Cheap** *Pandan*, Jln Kota, T2836858 (behind tourist information office), western and local dishes, claypot noodle a special-ity, pleasant location by roadside, friendly staff but over-salted food. Good for juices. *Café Sixties*, 12 Jln Melaka Raya 23, Taman Melaka Raya, T2819507, rock 'n' roll interior, fish 'n' chips, steak, curry and others. *Coconut House*, 128 Heeren St, a townhouse that now serves excellent woodfire pizzas, houses an art gallery and bookshop and is also a venue for art films. The restaurant also serves fresh fruit juices, beers, a selection of cof-fees and fresh cakes. Patrons can choose music from the owners' CD collection. Friendly welcoming staff, recommended. Closed Thur. *Discovery Café*, 3 Jln Bunga Raya, discovery-café@hotmail.com Opened in December 1999, this new addition is a haven for backpackers. A small friendly café and bar situated just along from the tourist office it has a terrace, pool table, darts board, television, internet access and a library of travel guides (this one included!). Plans to develop into a guest house. Recommended *Loony Planet*, Jln Laksamana. The philosophy of this place is similar to the *Discovery Café* but it specializes in Portuguese food. Internet access available. **Seriously cheap** *Bunga Raya Square*, 96 Jln Bunga Raya. Another addition for the Millennium, a large, outdoor complex offering Japanese, Malay, Chinese, Italian and vegetarian food from different counters, live entertainment, entertaining and you can indulge in a

👉 ## Peranakan Table Manners

Local food is served with local superstition. The heritage of the Babas and the Nyonyas includes a detailed etiquette of what to do and what to avoid at mealtimes. Food is considered a symbol of jerki, meaning luck or fortune. For this reason food should not be squashed, dropped or trodden upon and anything spilt must be picked up. If food is not treated with due respect this is known as sway, and brings bad fortune. Meals should be eaten at a circular table; sitting at a corner is to be avoided. Once seated diners should not sit with their chin in their hand, nor should they move from seat to seat as this will lead to a restless life. Other acts of sway include farting or crying at the dinner table, discussing depressing topics while eating, breaking or using chipped crockery, and piling plates one on top of one another. If cutlery is clashed together, sibling squabbles will follow.

For women there are yet further complications. If a woman drinks too much soup it will rain on her wedding day; if she leaves food on her plate she will marry an ugly husband; and if she sings at the table her husband will be old.

These traditions reach out to a wider belief system that sees inanimate objects as potential habitats for spirits. Thankfully they are not followed to the letter by Perankan restaurants in Melaka, although the proprietors are often happy to offer further insights into this culture.

range of foods. *Geographer Café*, 83 Jonkers St, geocafe@mystall.com The little sister of *Bunga Raya Square*, this is mostly patronized by tourists but is nonetheless a friendly establishment with a good choice of local and western food. Internet access. Recommended if only for Mr Burns, Malaysia's answer to Frank Sinatra, singing live.

Seafood Pengkalan Pernu (Pernu Jetty), 10 km south on the way to Muar, has several fish restaurants and stalls where you can pick your own fish and have it grilled. North of Melaka, towards Tanjung Kling, there are a few Chinese seafood restaurants along the beach. **Exspensive** *Bunga Raya Restaurant*, 39-40 Jln Taman, T2836456, crab, prawn and lobster are house specialities.

Foodstalls Seriously cheap *Glutton's Corner*, along the old esplanade on Jln Merdeka/Jln Taman: excellent choice of food, although the stalls now face a painted wall rather than the sea, thanks to a land reclamation project. *Prince Satay Celup*, at No 16. Recommended. *Jalan Bendahara*, several noodle stalls and a Mamak man (Indian Muslim) who serves *sup kambing* (mutton soup) and the bits – for marrow suckers (opposite the *Capitol*), Chinese food. *Jalan Bukit Baru*, just off the main road past the state mosque, mostly Chinese food. *Jalan Bunga Raya*, stalls (next to Rex Cinema), seafood recommended. *Jalan Semabok* (after Bukit Cina on road to JB), Malay-run fish-head curry stall, which is a local favourite. *Klebang Beach*, off Jln Klebang Besar, Tanjung Kling – stalls, with several *ikan panggang* (grilled fish) specialists.

Bakery and *Softee* ice cream In basement of *Parkson Grand Department Store & Supermarket*, two more outlets in *Mahkota Parade Shopping Mall*; *Renaissance Melaka Hotel* has a good bakery shop in lobby.

Entertainment **Cinemas** Jln Bunga Raya for English-language films. **Cultural shows** At the Portuguese Settlement every Sat at 2030. Songs and dances including the famous *beranyo*, an excuse for a sing-along and knees-up. *Nam Hoe Villa* (Restoran Peranakan), 317c Klebang Besar (6 km towards Port Dickson), T3154436, 2000 Sun-Fri, *Taman Mini Malaysia*, Ayer Keroh, 1120 and 1430 Sat, Sun and public hols. **Son et Lumière** *Melaka Light and Sound Show*, on the Padang, opposite St Paul's Hill,

T011-664166, chronological history of Melaka, an hour-long show with a distinctly Malay nationalist perspective, 5 mins' mention of European rule and no mention of the contribution by the Chinese and Indian ethnic communities, not expertly presented. Mon-Sun 2000 (Malay), 2030 (English), RM 10. **Cosmopolitan Club** 14 Hang Lekir is the site of a club, which was formerly the Malayan Chinese Literary Association, exclusively for the Babas of Heeren St. Today, it is patronized by locals playing mah-jong and snooker. Non-members may participate in the games for a small fee. The club is run by a friendly, English-speaking family with insiders' knowledge of their home town.

March/April *Easter Procession* (movable), on Good Friday and Easter Sunday, starts **Festivals** from St Peter's Church.

May *Saint Sohan Singh's Prayer Anniversary* (movable) thousands of Sikhs from all over Malaysia and Singapore congregate at the Melaka Sikh temple, Jalan Temenggong, to join in the memorial prayers.

June *Pesta San Pedro (Feast of St Peter)* (movable) celebrated at the Portuguese Settlement by fishermen. The brightly decorated fishing boats are blessed and prayers offered for a good season. *Mandi Safar* (movable) bathing festival at Tanjung Kling. *Kite Festival* (movable) on the sea front.

Antiques *Jalan Hang Jebat* (formerly Jonker St) is the best place for antiques, from **Shopping** shadow puppets to Melakan furniture inlaid with mother-of-pearl. **Books** *Boon* *Melaka is best known* *Hoong Sports and Bookstore*, 13 Jln Bunga Raya; *Times Bookshop*, Jaya Jusco Stores, *for its antique shops,* Mukim Bukit Baru. **Book exchange** Jln Taman Melaka Raya for a good number of *which mainly sell* English language books. **Clothing** Artist Charles Cham sells very original T-shirts from *European and* his shop the *Orang Utan House*, 59 Lorong Hang Jebat. His place is hard to miss – a *Chinese items* huge orange orang utan is painted on the outside of the building. **Food** *Tan Kim* *Hock Product Centre*, 153 Jln Laksamana Cheng Ho, T2835322, distinguishable by its colour (pink), this shop is near the *Ramada Renaissance Hotel*, and is a delight for the eye and stomach: cookies and sweets in a great many varieties. Just ask for the 'Dodol Man'; everybody knows who he (Tan Kim Hock) is, a self-made man who became a billionaire with his business. A hotel in town has been named after him.

General Main shopping centres on Jln Hang Tuah and Jln Munshi Abdullah. *Mahkota Parade Shopping and Entertainment Complex*, including *Parkson Grand* *Department Store and Supermarket*, 1 Jln Merdeka, just south of the river mouth, a good choice of shops – the centre won an award for the best shopping centre in the country. Has a very western feel with many international chain stores and the intriguingly named *Kenny Rogers Café*. **Handicrafts** *Karyaneka* (handicraft) centres at *1 Jalan Laksamana* and *Mini Malaysia Complex*, Ayer Keroh. Also *Crystal D'beaute*, 18 Medan Portugis. Dulukala, Jln Laksamana. A varied collection including prints and batiks. **Paintings** *Orang Utan House*, 59 Lorong Hang Jebat, paintings by local artist Charles Cham. *Jonker Art Collection*, 76 Jalan Hang Jebat T2836578, a small shop selling prints by local artists, in particular the work of Titi Kwok, son of the well-known Macau-based artist Kwok Se and owner of the Cheng Hoon Art Gallery situated a couple of streets away on Jln Tokong. He is often in the shop selling his own beautiful Chinese-style ink paintings and has plenty of time for his customers. Recommended. **Shoes** *Wah Aik Shoemaker Shop*, formerly of Jln Hang Jebat, but now to be found at 103 Jln Kubu, outside the conservation area. Shoes are still made here for Chinese grannies with bound feet (see page 215) and tourists. One pair of bound shoes costs US$100-150. Mr Yeo, the owner of the shop, proudly displays the shoes, which cost so much because "the silk is very expensive and comes from China". **Woodwork** *Malacca Woodwork*, 312c Klebang Besar, T3154468, specialist in authentic reproduction antique furniture including camphor wood chests.

Southern Peninsula

Sports **Golf** *Ayer Keroh Golf & Country Club*, 14 km from Melaka, green fees RM70 weekdays, RM100 weekends, T2320822; *"A" Famosa Golf Resort*, Jln Kemus, Pulan Sebang, T5520888, near the Alor Gajah interchange of the north-south expressway, 18-hole course, green fees RM100 weekdays, RM150 weekends, RM40 buggy, RM20 caddy.

Tour operators *Annah (Melaka) Tours & Travel*, 27 Jln Laksamana, T2835626; *AR Tours*, 302a Jln Tun Ali, T2831977; *Satik Tour & Travel*, 143 Jln Bendahara, T2835712. *Stadthuys Tours & Travel*, T2846373.

Transport
149 km to KL
90 km to Port Dickson
216 km to Johor Bahru

Local Bicycle hire: many of the cheaper hotels/hostels rent out bikes, as do one or two shops in town, RM5-8 per day. **Buses**: local buses leave from Jln Hang Tuah, right next to the long distance bus station. Less than RM1 round town. There is also an historical shuttle bus that takes tourists through the main historical areas and out to Ayer Keroh. A day pass costs RM5 and this allows three journeys. Hourly departures, 0930-1630. **Car hire**: *Avis*, 124 Jln Bendahara, T2846710. *Hawk*, T2837878. *Sintat*, *Renaissance Melaka Hotel*, Jln Bendahara, T2848888. *Thrifty*, G-5 Pasar Pelancong, Jln Tun Sri Lanang, T2849471. **Taxi**: all taxis now have meters. When directing a taxi be careful not to confuse street names with general district areas; use the former whenever possible. There are stands outside major hotels and shopping centres, or T2823630. Between 0100 and 0600, there is a 50% surcharge. **Trishaws**: mostly for the tourist trade, they congregate at several points in town (there are usually a number near the the tourist information centre on the town square) – RM2 for single destination or RM10-15 per hour.

It is necessary to secure a visa from the Indonesian Embassy in KL (see page 171) before departing for Sumatra from Melaka

Long distance Air: airport is at Batu Berendam, 10 km out of town. Town bus 65 runs to the airport from the local bus station. **Bus**: long distance buses leave from the terminal on Jln Hang Tuah. Regular connections with **KL**, **Seremban**, **Port Dickson**, **Ipoh**, **Butterworth**, **Lumut** (Pulau Pangkor), **Kuantan**, **Kuala Terengganu**, **Kota Bharu**, **Johor Bahru** and **Singapore** (direct, 4 hrs). **Train**: nearest station is at Tampin, 40 km north; Tampin railway station, T411034. See page 45 for timetable. **Taxi**: station opposite the local bus terminal on Jln Gaha Maju, just off Jln Hang Tuah. Vehicles leave for **KL**, **Seremban**, **Penang**, **Mersing**, **Johor Bahru**. Passengers for Singapore must change taxis at the long distance terminal in JB. Ferry: express ferries to **Dumai** (Sumatra), leave daily from the public jetty on Melaka River, 2 hrs (RM80). Tickets from **Atlas Travel Service**, Jln Hang Jebat, T2820777; **Madai Shipping**, Jln Tun Ali, T2840671 – service leaves Malacca at 0900, one-way adult fare RM 80; return RM 150. Other ferry companies include: *Tunas Rupat Utama Express*, 17A Jln Merdeka, T2832506; *Maharani* (Ferry Malaysia Sdn Bhd), T-472, Jetty Quayside, T2844344.

Directory **Airline offices** MAS, 1st Flr, Hotel Shopping Arcade, *City Bayview Hotel*, Jln Bendahara, T2835722 (confirmations), T2829597 (enquiries). **Banks** *Bumiputra*, Jln Kota. *Hong Kong & Shanghai*, Jln Kota. Several banks on Jln Hang Tuah near the bus station and Jln Munshi Abdullah. *Spak Sdn*, 29 Jln Laksamana, T282674, authorized money changer. *Islah Enterprise*, G79 Spice Route 27, Mahkota Parade, Jln Merdeka, T2811488, authorized money changers. **Communications** **General Post Office:** just off Jln Kota next to Christ Church. Sells a range of cards, in addition to stamps the PO . **Internet cafes** These are many in number, easy to come across and very inexpensive. The most central ones are as follows. Internet café, beside the Youth Museum in Historical Melaka, RM3 per hour; Red House, 16 Jln Laksamana, T2926080. RM3 per hour, credits can also be bought for international phone calls (RM1.50 per minute). Stream, 203F&F1, Jln Kenanga, RM10 per hour, student discount, reduced rates after 1800, food and drink available. Other popular places with internet access include: The Geographer Café, The Discovery Café, Loony Planet and Grand Star Hotel (also see Hotels and Restaurants). **Medical facilities** Hospitals: *Straits Hospital*, 37 Jln Parameswara, T2835336. **Useful addresses** Central Police Station: Jln Kota, T2825522. **Immigration office:** Bangunan Persekutaan, Jln Hang Tuah, T2824958/2824955 (for visa extensions). **Tourist Police:** Jln Kota, T2703238 (close to the Tourism Malaysia office).

Johor Bahru

Modern Johor Bahru – more commonly called JB – is not a pretty town. It lies on the southernmost tip of the peninsula and is the gateway to Malaysia from Singapore. JB is short on tourist attractions but has for many years served either as a tacky red-light reprieve for Singaporeans and/or as a large retail outlet. But Johor's paucity of cultural features belies its pivotal role in Malay history.

Colour map 2, grid C5
Phone code: 07

Ins and outs

JB has grown in size and stature over the last 5 years or so and is now a very important industrial centre. Senai airport is 20 km from town and there are connections with KL and several other destinations in East and Peninsular Malaysia. There are international air links with several destinations in Indonesia. A shuttle bus service runs from the ariport to town. There is a regular bus service between Singapore and KL, and links with most other towns on the Peninsula. Outstation taxis provide a service to KL, Melaka, Kuantan and Kota Bharu. The KL-Singapore railway line runs through JB and there are trains to both destinations including commuter trains to Singapore. There is a FerryLink service between Changi Point in Singapore and Tanjung Belungkor, as well as ferries from JB's new jetty to Mersing on the East Coast.

Getting there
See also Transport, page 235

Cheap metered taxis and a comprehensive town bus service provides the main form of transport for most visitors. For exploring further afield, there is a good range of local and international car hire firms to choose from.

Getting around
Hiring cars in JB is considerably cheaper than in Singapore

Johor Tourist Information Centre (JOTIC), T2249960, and *Malaysian Tourism Promotion Board*, T2223591, both located at 2 Jln Air Molek. Open: 0900-1700 Mon-Sat, 1000-1600 Sun. *Southern Region Tourism Office*, 4th flr, KOMTAR, T2223591.

Tourist offices

Background

During the 1980s JB became an industrial adjunct to Singapore, attracting land and labour-intensive manufacturing industries. Johor's manufacturing boom has brought a measure of prosperity to the state capital and its dingy streets have begun to get a much-needed face-lift. Foreign investors have embarked on property buying sprees and new hotels, shopping plazas and office complexes have been springing up.

The state government's intention is to emulate the development process of neighbouring Singapore

At weekends JB is jammed with Singaporeans, here, it would seem, largely for sex and/or shopping – and, perhaps, the chance to escape for a few hours from the stultifying atmosphere of their own clean and green country. During 1997, JB became the subject of a bitter spat between Malaysia and Singapore. In March, Singapore's Senior Minister Lee Kuan Yew suggested that the city was "notorious for shootings, muggings and car-jackings". The Malaysian press and some politicians reacted with fury – The Youth Head of the ruling United Malays National Party (UMNO) going so far as to accuse Lee of being "senile and uncouth". Lee later apologized "unreservedly".

Southern Peninsula

Southern Peninsula

Modern Johor: riding on the merlion's tail

Johor is still a predominantly agricultural state, and is Malaysia's leading producer of palm oil, rubber, cocoa and coconuts. But in recent years, Singapore's prosperity has spilled across the 1.2-km causeway linking the island republic with JB. An explosion in foreign manufacturing investment led by Singapore has turned Johor into an industrial oasis.

In the past few years Johor has attracted about a quarter of total foreign investment in Malaysia. The industrial estates surrounding JB produce everything from typewriters and televisions to condoms and Kentucky Fried Chicken. Almost everything is immediately exported from JB's Pasir Gudang port. Recently, big Japanese and Taiwanese petrochemicals plants have set up in the state too, one of them near Johor Lama, the site of the old royal capital.

Johor is now the northern point of the so-called 'Growth Triangle', which also incorporates Singapore and parts of Indonesia's Riau Archipelago. The state government, now facing a labour shortage, wants its industries to be increasingly hi-tech. Tourism is big in Johor too. Nearly three-quarters of all tourists visiting Malaysia come from Singapore: each day about 50,000 people cross the causeway to JB to take a break from city life.

The old causeway across the *Selat Tebrau* (Strait of Johor), built in 1924, is still the only land-link to Singapore. It is overburdened with road traffic and also carries the railway and water pipelines: Singapore relies on Johor for most of its water supply. A new link between JB and Singapore has finally been completed and is known, perhaps inevitably, as the Second Link. But it is not very popular. It is situated 30 km out of town to the west at Gelang Patah and the toll is actually higher than the causeway.

History

Following his trouncing by the Portuguese invaders in 1511, Melaka's young Sultan Ahmad fled south with what remained of the royal court, eventually arriving at Bintan in the Riau Archipelago. Ahmad was promptly executed by his father, Mahmud, for gross ineptitude and there then followed 15 years of attrition between the Portuguese and Mahmud, before the Portuguese destroyed his capital at Bintan in 1526. Mahmud died two years later and his remaining son became the first Sultan of Perak, while his stepson established the Sultanate of Johor near Kota Tinggi, to the east of modern JB.

At the same time, the Sultanate of Aceh, on the north tip of Sumatra, was enjoying a meteoric rise to prominence. Rivalry between Johor and Aceh overshadowed their hatred of the Portuguese and the Acehnese terrorized Johor for another 60 years, frequently sacking the capital and twice carrying the royal family back to Sumatra as prisoners.

The Johor court was re-established on the Johor River in 1641 and the sultanate grew powerful again as an entrepôt, until the capital was destroyed by the rival Sumatran kingdom of Jambi in 1673. The sultanate moved to Bintan, then back to Kota Tinggi in 1685. But Sultan Mahmud was a tyrant who frightened off foreign traders; he was also a murderer and sexual pervert and was finally assassinated by his own people, thus ending the centuries-old Melaka Dynasty. Switching its capitals between the Johor River and Riau, the sultanate declined and remained weak throughout the 18th century; the Malay rulers, wracked by in-fighting, were by then firmly under the thumb of the ascendant Buginese and constantly squabbling over trade issues with the Dutch.

In 1818, with the Dutch temporarily absent due to the Napoleonic Wars, the British resident of Melaka, Colonel William Farquhar, signed a trade pact with the sultan in Riau. Thomas Stamford Raffles was meanwhile looking to set up a British trading post on the south end of the peninsula, and after casting around the Riau Archipelago, settled on Singapore. There, in 1819, he signed a deal with Temenggong Abdur Rahman, the sultan's minister on the island, and later with one of two blue-blooded Malays claiming to be Sultan of Johor, allowing the English East India Company to establish a trading post in Singapore.

Johor Bahru

The 1824 Treaty of London between the British and the Dutch put an end to the Johor-Riau Empire, partitioning it between the two European powers. The Riau side became known as the Sultanate of Lingga, while the Temenggong was left to wield Malay power. Abu Bakar, the grandson of Singapore's Temenggong Abdur Rahman, moved his headquarters to the small settlement of Tanjong Putri in Johor, which he renamed Johor Bahru in 1866. The Anglophile Abu Bakar was known as the Maharajah of Johor until 1877, and in 1885, was recognized as Sultan by Queen Victoria. He developed the state's agricultural economy and, in the early 20th century, Johor attracted many European rubber planters. Sultan Abu Bakar is known as the father of modern Johor, which became the last state to join the colonial Malay Federation, in 1914.

Sights

The Royal Museum is one of Malaysia's best museums and makes a stay in otherwise unexciting JB worth while

While it is possible to write at considerable length about JB's past it is rather more difficult to raise sufficient enthusiasm to write about the present (I can feel JB's army of supporters already reaching for their pens and paper). One of the most prominent buildings in JB is the recently renovated **Istana Besar**, the Sultan's former residence on Jalan Tun Dr Ismail (built by Sultan Abu Bakar in 1866). It is now a royal museum, the **Royal Abu Bakar Museum**. Today the Sultan lives in the Istana Bukit Serene, which is on the west outskirts of town (it is not open to the public). The Istana Besar is a slice of Victorian England set in beautiful gardens, overlooking the strait. In the north wing is the throne room and museum containing a superb collection of royal treasures, including hunting trophies, as well as Chinese and Japanese ceramics. ■ *0900-1800 Mon-Sun, US$7 (payable in ringgit at a very poor exchange rate), children under 12 US$3.*

Not far away, on Jalan Abu Bakar, is the **Sultan Abu Bakar Mosque**, which faces the Strait of Johor. It was finished in 1900 and clearly reflects the Victorian climate of the period. The mosque can accommodate 2,500 worshippers.

The 32-m-high tower of the 1930s **Istana Bukit Serene** on Jalan Skudai – the home of the Sultan of Johore and not open to the public – is only outdone by the 64-m tower of the State Secretariat, on Bukit Timbalan, which dominates the town.

As JB is hardly bursting with sights that aren't immediately forgettable the itinerant **pasar malam** (night market) stands out as something of note. The market shifts from day to day (but doesn't operate on Thursdays) and stallholders sell a range of fresh and dry goods from traditional medicines to frog meat.

Excursions

Kukup On the Strait of Melaka 40 km southwest of Johor, this small Chinese fishing kampung renowned throughout the country, and in Singapore, for its seafood, especially prawns and chilli crab. Most of the restaurants, known as *kelong*, are built on stilts over the water. The kampung has become so popular with Singaporeans that coach tours are laid on, and some of the restaurants – notably *Restoran Kukup* – are geared to cater for big groups. Weekend visits are not recommended for this reason. The kampung is also now dominated by a 36-hole golf course, ■ *Kukup Golf Resort, Pekan Penorok, T6960952, F6960961, green fees weekdays RM120, weekends RM165.* Next to the resort is a new dolphin learning centre where dolphin shows are held. To get there, take bus No 3 to Pontian Kecil, and from there take a taxi to Kukup;

alternatively take a taxi the whole way. A pier has been built at Kukup and direct ferry connections with Tuas in Singapore are likely.

At Lombong, 56 km northeast of JB below Gunung Muntahak, a series of **Lombong** waterfalls have cut natural swimming pools. Lombong is 13 km from **Kota Tinggi**, a former royal capital of Johor. Many of the mausoleums of the former sultans of Johor – including that of Mahmud Shah, the last sultan of the Melaka Dynasty – are nearby. The mausoleum of Sultan Mahmud, the feared ruler who was finally assassinated by one of his courtesans (see page 228) is at Kampung Makam (turn right 1 km north of Kota Tinggi, before Desaru sign).

The site of the old royal capital of **Johor Lama** ('Old Johor' – as opposed to Johor Bahru, or 'New Johor') is on the east bank of the Johor River, south of Kota Tinggi. Because it was twice burned to the ground there are no impressive ruins. The site is, however, clearly signposted off the Kota Tinggi-Desaru road (12 km). Just before Telok Sengat, turn right down a laterite track through an oil palm estate. Johor Lama, most of which lies under a rubber tappers' kampung, is 6 km down the track. There is no public transport to the site or to Telok Sengat so it is necessary to charter a taxi.

Sleeping and eating C *Waterfall Chalet*, Kota Tinggi Waterfall, T8331146 (must be booked in advance). A/c, reasonably well maintained. C *Sri Bayn Resort*, near Telok Sengat (5 km up laterite track through oil palm estate opposite turn-off to Johor Lama), only accessible for those with own transport. This is possibly the most tranquil and certainly the most remote chalet resort on the peninsula, set on steep hillside overlooking Johor estuary among coconut palms in neat gardens, chalets have balconies and fantastic views. **Kota Tinggi**: there are a number of places to stay including the **D** *Sin May Chun Hotel*, 36 Jln Tambatan, T8333573. Spacious, good value rooms. C *Nasha Hotel*, 40 Jln Tambatan, T78338000.

The seafood restaurant and coffee shops in nearby Telok Sengat are recommended

Transport From JB take bus 41 to **Kota Tinggi** (many departures), and from Kota Tinggi bus 43 to the waterfall. Or a taxi the whole way.

Northwest of Johor, a new venture in agritourism is emerging. Situated on the **Agritourism** coastal road from Ayer Hitam viat Batu Pahat to Muar, look for a signpost to the right, to Sungai Sarang Buaya village. Visitors stay with local people and visit fruit gardens, sample the produce, take a walk in a forest, or go on a river trip. ■ *Kadmin Bin HS Ahma, 60B Kampong Sarang Buaya, Batu Pahat, T4162388*. Another such venture is taking place nearer to Johor at the Kluang Veterinary Institute, 8km from Air Hitam and 13 km from Kluang, T(07)7596810. Here, you can visit a working farm and can kayak, fish or picnic. Accommodation is in (**B**) bungalows overlooking the Semberong dam. Price includes breakfast.

This holiday resort, set on a 20-km-long beach at Tanjung Penawar, 90 km **Desaru** east of JB, has been aggressively marketed in Singapore and as a result it gets *By the mid-1990s* invaded on weekends and public holidays. Although the beach is picturesque, *around ½ million* the sea can get very rough, and there is a strong undertow; most holiday-mak- *tourists were visiting* ers stick to their hotel pools. The most popular pursuit here is golf on its beau- *this busy resort each* tifully landscaped seaside course. In 1991, in a fit of dollar-driven madness, a *year* consortium of American and Japanese investors proposed transforming Desaru into a resort of obscene proportions at a projected cost of US$1.4bn. Incredibly, they even planned to build a Winter Wonderland complete with snow. Fortunately, it died soon after birth. However, in 1995 a new investor

Southern Peninsula

proposed a slightly more modest plan, worth just US$200 million, to build hotels, more golf courses, a shopping complex et al.

Designed with golf-crazed Singaporeans in mind, although on weekdays chalet accommodation is reasonable. Budget travellers are better advised to head for Mersing and the offshore islands

Sleeping and eating **AL** *Desaru Golf Inn*, T8221106, F8221408. A/c, restaurant, pool. **A** *Desaru Perdana Beach Resort* (PO Box 29, Bandar Penawar). Good beach location with reasonable pool, suitable for families. **A** *Desaru View* (PO Box 71, Kota Tinggi), Tanjung Penawar, T8238221. A/c, restaurant, pool. **A-C** *Desaru Golden Beach Resort*, PO Box 50, Tanjung Penawar, T8221101, F8221480. A/c, restaurant, pool, former *Merlin Inn* with standard 4-star facilities, fills up with golfers on weekends, chalets next door are part of same resort (guests can use hotel pool) and are good value during the week. **C** *Tanjung Balau Fishing Village*, T8221201, F8221600. Dormitory-only accommodation in fishing village just outside Desaru, for those wanting to experience a fisherman's life.

Transport Bus No 41; regular connections with **JB** via **Kota Tinggi**; taxi from JB. Two daily shuttles from most major hotels in Singapore. Regular boats connect **Desaru** with **Changi Point**, **Singapore** to **Tanjung Pengileh**, where taxis are available to **Desaru**.

Teluk Mahkota

Those taking the road north from Kota Tinggi may be tempted by countless roadside signs to *Jason's Bay Beach Resort* at Teluk Mahkota (25 km off main east coast road from turning 15 km northeast of Kota Tinggi). Despite its privacy, it is not really worth the bother. The once-lovely beach is muddy and disappointing; the resort is grimy and rooms smell musty. To get there, take bus No 300 from Kota Tinggi.

Essentials

Sleeping
■ *on map, page 229*
Price codes: see inside front cover

JB's recent expansion has led to a number of new business hotels. Middle-market and cheaper hotels are as tacky as ever though: the 'hostess girl industry' is big business in JB. Many hotels rent out rooms by the hour. As such facilities are usually prominently advertised, patrons should know what to expect. Though many of these hotels are brothels to locals, for a tourist they are reasonably priced hotels in an otherwise expensive city. Room rates also increase on Fri and weekends.

JB's top hotels cater for businesspeople and have all the 5-star facilities. Most budget travellers don't stop in JB so there really isn't much choice at the bottom end, except for seedy short-stay hotels

A *Holiday Inn Crowne Plaza*, Jln Dato Sulaiman, Century Garden, T3323800, F318884, Admin@holinn.po.my A/c, restaurant, pool, 24-hr coffee house, unhelpfully located on suburban one-way system, frequented by the rich and the royal because of its recently renovated Szechuan restaurant. **A** *Hyatt Regency*, Jln Sungai Chat, T2221234, F2232718, www.hyatt.com/Malaysia/ Over 2 km west of town centre, all the comforts you would expect of the *Hyatt* chain including pool, tennis and an internet room. 10 mins from downtown JB close to the Sultan's Palace. **A** *Merlin Inn*, 10 Jln Bukit Meldrum, T2237400, F2248919. A/c, restaurant, pool, comfortable hotel that looks like a truncated Toblerone, with another wing added a few years ago, good value but cut off from centre of town by railway and flyovers. **A** *Puteri Pan Pacific Johor Bahru*, Jln Abdullah Ibrahim, T2233333, F2236622, www.panpac.com/Malaysia/ A/c, 3 restaurants, pool, sauna, fitness and business centres, good city centre location for those on business, 500 rooms, tennis and squash courts, babysitting arranged, room rate includes airport transfer, fruit basket and welcome drink. Situated in the government and commercial heart of JB and just 5 mins from the causeway to Singapore. Recommended.

B *Causeway Inn*, 6b Jln Meldrum, T2248811, F2248820. A/c, unlike neighbouring premises, this is a clean, quiet, well-run hotel that looks smart and does not overcharge with TV, excellent bathroom (bath). Check the room though because some have no view. Recommended. **B** *Crystal Crown*, 117 Jln Harimau, 117 Jln Tebrau, T3334422, F3343582, www.crystalcrown.com.my A/c, restaurants, TV, business centre, tea and coffee-making facilities, minibar, pool, organizes car hire. Breakfast included. A tourist-class hotel geared to business visitors that opened in 1993 with a location in the commercial heart of JB. **B** *Grand Continental*, 799 Jln Tebrau, T3323999, F3321999. Part of the *Grand Continental Chain*, 4-star hotel geared to the business visitor, rates include breakfast, rooms with a/c, TV, mini-bar and tea and coffee-making facilities, pool, health centre and business centre. Breakfast included. **B** *Rasa Sayang Baru*, 10 Jln Dato Dalam, T2248600. A/c, restaurant, inconveniently situated on the outskirts of town, discounts available in off-peak season. **B** *Straits View*, 1d Jln Scudai, T2241400, F2242698. A/c, restaurant (next door to *Jaws 5*), not much of a Straits view from downstairs rooms but the hotel is clean and the management friendly. **B** *Surf Pacific Hotel*, Jln Pelanduk, Century Garden, T3333300, F3333385. Three-star boutique hotel, 80 comfortable rooms with a/c, TV, in-house video, mini-fridge, tea/coffee-making facilities. Breakfast included. **B** *Top Hotel*, 12 Jln Meldrum, T2244755. Much better value than most of the mid-range hotels in this area. Large rooms with huge beds. Bathrooms of a very good standard. Recommended. **B** *Tropical Inn*, 15 Jln Gereja, T2247888, F2241544. A/c, restaurant, pool. Slightly reminiscent of an airport lounge but this offers very good value for JB. Breakfast included.

C *Gateway Hotel*, 61 Jln Meldrum, T2235029, F2235248. Colourful hotel exterior, a/c, shower, TV, central location. Good value. **C** *Hawaii*, 23 Jln Meldrum, T2240633, F2240631. Average Chinese-run hotel; much better value on weekdays when rates are slashed. Cheaper than most but by no means outstanding. **C** *JB Hotel*, 80a Jln Wong Ah Fook, T2234788. Some a/c, clean, reasonably spacious rooms and at this price. **C** *Le Tian*, 2 A-D Jln Sin Nam (just off Jln Meldrum), T2248151. Beyond the absolutely terrifying Chinese receptionist, the rooms are run down and the bathrooms resemble a public convenience. A/c. Better options are available elsewhere. **C** *Meyah Hotel*, 22 Jln Jaya, T3328789, F3325789. Clean, well managed, quiet place. Simple rooms with TV, a/c, shower. Inconvenient location for this mid-range hotel.

D *Cosy Inn*, 38a Jln Jaya, T3353388. Poorly maintained Chinese hotel with very basic amenities, avoid. **E** *Footloose Homestay*, 4H Jln Ismail, T2242881. In a quiet area of town outside the city centre, just 1 double room along with some dorm beds, friendly and well maintained, room rate includes breakfast. Recommended. **E** *Wadi Hassan Traveller's Home*, 52E Jln Wadi Hassan. Restaurant, dorm rooms, family rooms with fan, breakfast included, laundry service, tours organized, good local information. Recommended.

Malay Mid-range *Dapur Rembia*, 1A-2 Jln Mohd Amin (close to *Jaws 5* restaurant), old bungalow with tables outside. **Cheap** *Sedap Corner*, 11 Jln Abdul Samad, Chinese as well as Malay dishes, a good line in fish-head curries. **Seriously cheap** *Wadi Hassan Travellers Home*, good traditional food.

Chinese Expensive *Grand Court Restaurant*, Hotel Grand Continental, 3rd flr, T3345578, good selection including some Cantonese and Nyonya dishes. **Mid-range** *Eastern Dragon Restoran*, 49851 Jln Serigala, Century Garden, T3319600. Very popular. *Ming Dragon*, G12-14 *Holiday Plaza*. Recommended. **Cheap** *Teoyuan*, 21 Jln Maju, T331278. A/c, very clean. **Indian** There are some good Indian restaurants in town including the **Cheap** *Restoran Nilla* at 3 Jln Ungku Puan.

Thai Expensive *Manhattan Grill*, Plaza Kotaraya, Jln Trus (opposite Pan Pac), haunt of JB's rich and relatively famous, grill room with excellent food at half the price of the equivalents across the causeway. *Meisan*, Holiday Inn JB, Jln Dato Sulaiman, Century Garden, superb but expensive spicy Szechuan restaurant. *Selashi*, Puteri Pan Pacific, The Kotaraya, top quality Malay cuisine in tastefully decorated, expensive restaurant. **Mid-range** *134 Jalan Serampang*, Taman Pelangi, tables in the garden. *Jaws 5 Seafood*, 1d Jln Skudai, very popular, next to *Straits View Hotel* and Machinta

Eating
Price codes:
see inside front cover

JB is best known for its seafood, which is considerably cheaper than in Singapore

Southern Peninsula

strip club, the food is very good, but not cheap, specialities include drunken prawns, frogs' legs and chilli crabs, diners may find flashing neons and revolving stage unsettling. Recommended. *Newsroom Café*, Puteri Pan Pacific, The Kotaraya, offering reasonably priced local/continental dishes (enclosed brasserie area called *Editor's Corner*). **Cheap** *Medina*, corner of Jln Meldrum and Jln Siew Niam, cheap and delicious *murtabak*, rotis, fish-head curries etc, open 24 hrs.

Bakeries Seriously cheap *Hiap Joo Bakery*, intersection of Jln Tan Hiok Nee and Jln Trus. A traditional bakery producing cakes and buns in a wood-fired oven (said to be 70 years old) with ingredients including *ikan bilis sambal*, grated coconut and custard. *Shamsul Hak*, Jln Dhoby (about 75 m from *Hiap Joo Bakery*). Another great traditional bakery, this one Indian. Delicious mutton curry puffs and other Indian breads.

The night market on Jln Wong Ah Fook is also a great place to sample the full array of stall dishes

Foodstalls Seriously cheap *Tepian Tebrau*, Jln Skudai (facing the sea beside the General Hospital) good for Malay food – satay and grilled fish. There is also good stall food at the long distance bus terminal and outside the railway station. There is a sprawling outdoor hawker centre right in the centre of town, adjacent to the Plaza Kotaraya on Jln Trus. *Pantai Lido* is another well-known hawker centre and there is a 'food court' in the *Kompleks Tun Abdul Razak*, Jln Wong Ah Fook as well as the *Plaza Kotaraya* on Jln Trus.

Entertainment **Discos** *Caesar's Palace*, *Holiday Plaza*; *Millennium*, *Holiday Inn*, Jln Dato Sulaiman.

Shopping **Books** *Johore Central Store*, Plaza Kota Raya, Jln Abdullah Ibrahim; *MPH Bookstore*, Holiday Plaza, Jln Dato Sulaiman; *Times Bookshop*, Plaza Pelangi, 4th Flr, in Kerry's Department Store, 2 Jln Kuning.

It is worth pointing out that one of JB's raisons d'etre is as a shopping outlet for cash-rich Singaporeans

General Large shopping complexes include *Holiday Plaza*, Jln Datuk Sulaiman, 3 floors of retails outlets as well as a cinema, night club, hawker centre and various fast food outlets; *Kompleks Tun Abdul Razak* (KOMTAR), Jln Wong Ah Fook; *Plaza Pelangi*, Jln Tebrau, billed as JB's 'most exciting mall'; shops include fashion goods, souvenirs, handicrafts and there is also the usual range of food and beverage outlets; *Sentosa Complex*, Jln Sutera; *Kotaraya*, off Jln Trus, a pink building situated in the centre of the city, opposite the night market – possibly the best place to shop with a hawker centre upstairs; *Johor Bahru Duty Free Complex*, this place is next to the International Ferry Terminal and is said to be one of the largest such complexes in the world (ugh!) – better known as ZON; *Kompleks Lien Hoe*, Jln Tebrau (around 5 km north of JB), budget shopping plaza with some of the best deals in JB as well as a good food court.

Handicrafts *Craftown Handicraft Centre*, Jln Skudai; *Jaro*, Jln Sungai Chat; *Johorcraft*, Kompleks Kotaraya and Kompleks Tun Abdul Razak, Jln Trus; *Karyaneka Centre* at Kompleks Mawar, 562 Jln Sungeai Chat; *Mawar*, Jln Sultanah Rogayah, Istana Besar. There is also a big *Johorcraft* complex 1 km before Kota Tinggi on the road from JB selling rather downmarket arts and crafts from all over Malaysia. It is aimed at big coach tours from Singapore, has a large restaurant and provides demonstrations of pottery, batik and songkhet production. Open Mon-Sun 0800-1800.

Sports **Bowling** *Holiday Bowl*, 2nd flr *Holiday Plaza*, Jln Dato Sulaiman. **Horse riding** *Pasir Pelangi Horse riding school*, opposite the JB polo ground and 5 mins' drive from the causeway. 30 horses and 10 acres, the school has a small café. Open: 0700-1800 Mon-Sun (closed on public holidays), but riding only between 0700-1000 and 1430-1800. Boots and helmets available for hire. **Golf** *Royal Johor Country Club*, Jln Larkin, T2233322, green fees RM100 weekdays, RM200 weekends. *Palm Resort Golf* and Country Club, Jln Persiaran Golf, off Jln Jumbo (near airport), Senai, T5996222, F5996001, course is part of a 5-star resort, which includes tennis, squash, bowls, pool, fitness centre, sauna, Japanese baths and luxury hotel and bungalows, green fees RM135 weekdays, RM250 weekends, RM25 caddy fee, RM20 buggy.

Local Bus: local buses leave from the main bus terminal on Jln Wong Ah Fook. **Car hire**: it is much cheaper to hire a car in JB than it is in neighbouring Singapore but check whether the car hire company allows the car to go to Singapore. *Avis*, *Tropical Inn Hotel*, 15 Jln Gereja, T2244824; *Budget*, Suite 216, 2nd flr Orchid Plaza, T2243951; *Calio*, *Tropical Inn*, Jln Gereja, T2233325; *Halaju Selatan*, 4M-1 Larkin Complex, Jln Larkin; *Hertz*, Room 646, Puteri Pan Pacific Hotel, Jln Salim, T2237520; *National*, 50-B ground flr Bangunan Felda, Jln Sengget, T2230503 (and at the airport); *Thrifty*, *Holiday Inn*, Jln Dato Sulaiman, T3332313; *Sintat*, 2nd Flr, Kompleks Tun Abdul Razak (KOMTAR), Jln Wong Ah Fook, T2227110. **Taxis**: all urban taxis are now metered and plentiful.

Transport

134 km to Mersing
224 km to Melaka

Long distance Air: *MAS* fly into Senai, JB's airport, 20 km north of the city. Transport to town: buses every hour and taxis. For passengers flying *MAS* to Singapore, there is a shuttle service from the airport to *Novotel Orchid Inn*, Singapore with express immigration clearance. *MAS* operates an a/c shuttle bus from *Puteri Pan Pacific Hotel* to the airport. Regular connections on *MAS* with **Ipoh**, **Kota Kinabalu**, **KL**, **Kuala Terengganu**, **Kuantan**, **Kuching**, **Labuan**, **Lahad Datu**, **Miri**, **Penang** and **Tawau**.

MAS also operates international connections with **Denpasar** (Bali), **Jakarta**, **Surabaya**, **Sandakan** and **Ujung Pandang**, all in Indonesia as well as other worldwide destinations.

Road Bus: the Larkin bus terminal is inconveniently located 4 km north of the town centre. Book opposite railway station on Jln Tun Abdul Razak. Regular connections with **Melaka**, **KL** (RM20), **Lumut**, **Ipoh** (RM25.80), **Butterworth** (RM33.50), **Mersing**, **Kuantan**, **Kuala Terengganu**, **Alor Star** (RM37.70), **Kota Bharu**. The *Singapore Bus Service* between **Singapore** and JB runs every 10 mins from 0630 to 2400. The Ban San Terminal in Singapore is between Queen St and Rochor Canal Rd. From Singapore, it costs twice as much as from JB, and from JB the Singapore Bus Service takes almost double the time to do the journey. The 170 Singapore bus and the SBS Johor/Singapore Express only leave from the JB Larkin terminal. To save time at the border, get entry forms for Singapore at the terminal.

The causeway between JB and Singapore should be avoided at all costs during public holidays. It gets particularly jammed at rush hours although a Special Priority Lane is now open for speedier clearance of tourists

Taxi: The main long-distance taxi station is attached to the Larkin bus terminal 4 km north of town. However the old terminal, on Jln Wong Ah Fook, is also still operating and much more convenient. Taxis from here to destinations including KL, Melaka, Mersing and Kuantan.

Malaysian taxis leave, when full, for **Singapore** from the taxi rank on the 1st flr of the car park near the KOMTAR building on Jln Wong Ah Fook and go to the JB taxi rank on Rochor Canal Rd in Singapore. Drivers provide immigration forms and take care of formalities, making this a painless way of crossing the causeway. Touts also hang around JB's taxi rank offering the trip to Singapore in a private car. They will take you directly to your address in Singapore, although their geography of the island is not always expert. This is also a fairly cost-effective way to travel and is reliable.

Sea JB's ferry terminal to the east of the causeway is operating ferry services to **Mersing** and **Tanjung Belungkor**. Bumboats leave from various points along Johor's ragged coastline for **Singapore**; most go to **Changi Point** (Changi Village), on the northeast of the island, where there is an immigration and customs post. The bumboat routes from **Tanjung Surat** and **Tanjung Pengileh** to **Changi Point** make sense for those coming from the east coast, **Teluk Makhota** (Jason's Bay) or **Desaru** (taxis to the jetty from Desaru cost RM28). The boats run from 0700-1600 and depart when full (12

Southern Peninsula

passengers). There is now a vehicle ferry from **Tanjung Belungkor** (JB) to **Changi Point** 3 times a day, T653236088. JB's ferry terminal east of the causeway ferry connnections with **Changi Point** and the World Trade Centre in **Singapore**, and **Batam** in Indonesia.

Train the station is on Jln Campbell, near the causeway, off Jln Tun Abdul Razak. Regular connections with **KL** and all destinations on the west coast, see page 45 for timetable. Malaysian and Singapore immigration desks are actually in the Singapore railway station, so for those wanting to avoid delays on the causeway, this is a quick way to get across the border; there are regular commuter trains across to the island, see page 45 for details of timetable.

Directory **Airline offices** *MAS*, 1st flr, Plaza Pelangi, Menara Pelangi, Jln Kuning, Taman Pelangi, T3341003/3341001 – a little over 2 km from the town centre. **Banks** *Bumiputra*, *Hong Kong and Shanghai* and *United Asia* are on Bukit Timbalan. Other big banks are on Jln Wong Ah Fook, several rnoney changers in the big shopping centres and on/around Jln Ibrahim/Jln Meldrum. **Communications** Post Office: Jln Tun Dr Ismail. **Telephone office:** Jln Trus (opposite the *Puteri Pan Pacific Hotel*). **Medical facilities** Hospitals: *Sultanah Aminah General Hospital*, Jln Skudai. **Useful addresses** Immigration office: 1st flr, Block B, Wisma Persektuan, Jln Air Molek, T2244253.

East Coast Peninsula

6

East Coast Peninsula

It might just be on the other side of the peninsula, but Malaysia's east coast could as well be on a different planet than the populous, hectic and industrialized west coast. Its coastline, made up of the states of **Johor**, **Pahang**, **Terengganu** and **Kelantan**, is lined with coconut palms, dotted with sleepy fishing kampungs and interspersed with rubber and oil palm plantations, paddy fields, beaches and mangroves.

With its jungle, beaches and islands and its strong Malay cultural traditions, it holds many attractions for tourists. The only problem is that during the Western world's winter holiday period, the east coast is awash with monsoon flood water, which confines the tourist season to between March and October. Many beach resorts completely close down during these monsoon months as do the offshore islands. The best-known tourist attraction on the east coast is the grimy village of **Rantau Abang** in Terengganu, where leatherback turtles lumber up the beach to lay their eggs between May and October.

Background

Until the 19th century, the narrow coastal plain between the jungled mountains and the sea was largely bypassed by trade and commerce and its 60-odd coral-fringed (and largely uninhabited) offshore islands were known only to local fishermen. The mountainous interior effectively cut the east coast off from the west coast, physically, commercially and culturally. The east coast did not have the tin deposits which attracted Chinese speculators and miners to the towns on the other side of the Main Range in the 19th century; and in more recent decades it was left behind as Malaysia joined the development race. The rural parts have been buffered from Western influence; traditional kampung lifestyles have been tempered only by the arrival of the electric lightbulb, the outboard motor and the Honda 70. The east coast's fishermen and paddy farmers are Malaysia's most conservative Muslims. In the 1990 general election, the people of Kelantan voted a hardline Islamic opposition party into power. In the 1995 general election they made the same choice once more and in the general election of 1999 they managed to add the state of Terengganu to their growing mini-fiefdom on the East Coast. Parti Islam now runs two state governments and represents their constituencies in federal parliament. The rural Malays of the east coast have not enjoyed much in the way of 'trickledown' from Malaysia's new-found economic prosperity. Although they are *bumiputras* – or 'sons of the soil' (see page 524) – few have reaped the benefits of more than two decades of pro-Malay policies.

The September 11 atrocities in the US and the war in Afghanistan would seem, however, to have stopped the PAS's expansion in its tracks, for the time being at least (see page 515). Party leaders rather short-sightedly called for a jihad in support of the Taliban, they organised a rather bad-tempered demonstration outside the US embassy in KL, and also refused to rule out violence. Prime Minister Mahathir played all this to his advantage. In reality, however, while some members of the PAS are pretty extreme in the main the party has managed Kelant and, more latterly, Terengganu, pretty sensibly.

During the Second World War, the Japanese Imperial Army landed at Kota Bharu and sped the length of the peninsula within six weeks on stolen bicycles (see page 508). The east coast did not figure prominently during the war, except in the realm of literary fiction, starring in Neville Shute's *A Town Like Alice*.

Before and after the war, rubber and oil palm plantations sprang up – particularly in the south state of Johor – which changed the shape of the agricultural economy. But the most dramatic change followed the discovery of large quantities of high-grade crude oil and natural gas off the northeast coast in the 1970s. By the mid-1980s, huge storage depots, gas processing plants and refineries had been built in Terengganu, and the battered old coast road was upgraded to cater for Esso and Petronas tankers. The town of Kerteh, halfway between Kuantan and Kuala Terengganu, is a refinery town, built along one of the best beaches on the peninsula. The construction boom and the rig work helped boost the local economy and provide employment, but the east coast states (bar Johor, which straddles the entire south tip of the peninsula) have singularly failed to attract much industrial investment in the way their west coast neighbours have. Oil money has, however, helped transform the fortunes of Terengganu.

On the whole, the east coast has been less sullied by industrial pollution; the South China Sea is a lot cleaner than the Strait of Melaka. Despite the oil the East Coast is still the rural backwater of the peninsula (95% of state revenues from oil go straight into federal coffers in KL).

East Coast Peninsula

Islam on the east coast: fundamental pointers

Because the east-coast states are a bastion of Islamic conservatism, which was reinforced by the victory of Parti Islam in Kelantan in the 1995 general election, visitors should be particularly sensitive to the strictures of Islam. Those determined to get an all-over tan should not attempt to acquire it on the east coast's beaches, and women should dress 'respectfully' in public. Many Malay women choose to wear the tudung:, the veil which signifies adherence to the puritanical lifestyle of the fervently Islamic dakwah reformist movement. The east coast stands in contrast to other parts of the peninsula, where this garb is more often a fashion accessory than representative of a lifestyle. In 1988 cultural purists on the east coast began voicing concern about the 'cultural and moral pollution' that tourism brought in its wake. But any resentment that the arrival of Western tourists may have sparked seems to have evaporated in the face of the economic opportunities generated.

Malaysia's Islamic powerhouse in the states of Kelantan and Terengganu poses one possible occupational hazard for tourists, particularly if they travel north-to-south. In these two states, the weekend starts on Thursday lunchtime and everyone drifts back to work on Saturday. By and large, even the Chinese businesses observe the Muslim weekend. This means

banks are shut and those unfortunate to mistime their travels can find themselves arriving in Kuantan just in time for the banks there to close down too. Pahang state observes the Saturday/Sunday weekend. Be warned. In common with other strict Islamic states, there have also been moves in Kelantan to restrict the sale of alcohol, although at present it is still available in Chinese-run shops. Malay-run establishments in Terengganu and Kelantan are barred from serving alcohol. The bars and discos which contribute to a lively nightlife scene on the west coast are conspicuously absent on the east coast. In Kota Bharu even the large hotels do not serve alcohol, and recently there was a petition to form separate queues in supermarkets for men and women. In 1997 the state government in Kelantan went so far as to issue an edict that cinemas keep their lights on when showing films – just in case movie-goers have any amorous intentions. During Ramadan, which is strictly observed, Malay food and beverage outlets remain closed until Muslims break puasa (fast) after sundown. Although this means that it is impossible to find a good rendang or satay until the evening, travellers can feast on the amazing variety of colourful kueh – or cakes – which are sold at roadside stalls.

East Coast Peninsula

Getting there The east coast can be reached from various points on the west coast. Routes from Butterworth (Penang) and Kuala Kangsar in the north, lead across to Kota Bharu on the northeast coast. The highway from KL goes to Kuantan (halfway down the east coast) and the railway cuts north from Gemas (south of KL) to Kota Bharu. There are also road routes from KL to the southeast coast. Another common route is to follow the trunk road north from Johor Bahru which hits the east coast at Mersing, the launch-pad for Pulau Tioman and the islands of the Seribuat group. **Ins & outs**

Mersing

This small fishing port is a pleasant little town distinguished only by the Masjid Janek, a green-tiled mosque, half a kilometre out of town on the top of a hill. Most people are in a hurry to get to the islands, namely **Pulau Tioman**, the best known of the East Coast's islands, and spend as little time as possible in the town. There are 64 islands which can be reached from Mersing *Colour map 2, grid B5* *Phone code: 07* including: Pulau Rawa, Pulau Sibu, Pulau Tinggi, Pulau Tengah, Pulau Aur and Pulau Pemanggil (see page 256).

Taxis run from KL, JB, Melaka, Kuala Terengganu and Kuantan. See page 245 for more information

As fishing boats can only make it out to sea at high tide, some people will inevitably get stuck here for the night. In recent years a number of good little restaurants have sprung up and Mersing is not an unpleasant place to spend a day or two. The town is evidently prospering, thanks to the flow of tourists to the islands. There is a plethora of tour and ticketing agencies as well as a shiny shopping plaza. ■ *Mersing Tourist Information Centre, Jln Abu Bakar (about 1 km from the jetty walking into town), T7995212. Friendly and useful source of information. Mon-Thu 1400-1600, Fri 1445-1630. There's an office at the jetty: weekdays 0800-1300.*

For details of Endau Rompin National Park, see page 258

Pantai Air Papan, 9 km north of Mersing, is the best mainland beach in the area. Formerly, the most popular beach was **Sri Pantai**, but it is now stony and unpleasant. Pantai Air Papan is 5 km off the main road north and the beach is about 2 km long, between two headlands. The beach is quite exposed but is backed by lines of casuarina and coconut palms. There is a liberal scattering of rubbish among the trees. There are a number of places at the end of the road offering budget accommodation within the **C-E** range. These include *Teluk Godek Chalet (Lani's Place)*, T7994469, which looks the newest and best; *Mersing Chalet and Restaurant (Seri Mersing)*, T7994194; *Air Papan Chalets*, T7992384. More secluded is *Nusantara Chalet*, 1½ km north through the kampung which stretches along the beach. There are a few beach shelters dotted along the beach. Boats for fishing trips can be chartered by groups of 12 or more from the jetty. Owners may be reluctant to take the long journey out to the far off shore islands. ■ *Getting there: Mersing-Endau bus (No 5) to Simpang Air Papan (turn-off); there is no bus service connecting with the beach, although it is possible to hitch-hike. Chartered taxi available. Arrangements can be made for pick-ups later in the day.*

Sleeping

B *Mersing Inn*, 38 Jln Ismail, T7991919, F7991919. Fairly new, so discounts are available (10% off all rooms on weekdays), clean and bright, a/c, with telephones and televisions in every room, all rooms en suite, with a bath in the triple and deluxe rooms B *Seri Malaysia*, Jln Ismail, T7991876, F7991886, gwicro@ rpb.com.my A/c, tea and coffee-making facilities, pool, restaurant, no charge for children under 12, situated just out of the centre. B *Timotel*, 839 Jln Endau, T79995898, F7995333. Looks like a set of offices from the outside but offers huge, luxurious rooms. Just out of the centre of town. C *Kali's Guesthouse*, No 12E Kampung Sri Lalang, T7993613. Fan only, restaurant, arguably the best-kept,

Mersing

To Mosque

Jetty □ Plaza R & R

Dr Ismail

Parkson Supermarket

Jln Pasar

Taxis □

To Air Papan

To Kuantan

Island Connection Travel

To Johor

N

Not to scale

■ **Sleeping**
1 Country
2 Embassy
3 Golden City
4 Kali's Guesthouse
5 Mersing

6 Mersing Inn
7 New Merdeka
8 Omar's Backpacker's Dorm
9 Seri Malaysia
10 Sheikh Guesthouse
11 Syuan Koong
12 Timotel

● **Eating**
1 Kedai Kek Kile Bakery

East Coast Peninsula

Things to do on the East Coast Peninsula ★

- Go turtle watching at one of several spots along the east coast, including Kuala Abang, and watch giant leatherbacks claw their way up the beach to lay their eggs.
- Get a taste of tropical jungle in Peninsula Malaysia's best equipped park, Taman Negara in the hills of Kelantan, Terengganu and Pahang. Treks, hides, fishing and river trips beckon.
- Chill out in the laid-back atmosphere of Kampung Cherating where sarongs and smoothies offer a tempting blend.
- Venture further still to one of the east coast's off shore islands, the most popular being Tioman but the most serene Pulau Rawa or one of the Perhentians.
- Dive in the waters off Pulau Redang, a marine park and possible the best dive site in Peninsula Malaysia.
- Witness the arts and crafts of Kelantan from silver-making to kite-flying.

friendliest and most relaxed place to stay in Mersing area, rooms range from longhouse dorm to 'A'-frames and bungalows, atap-roofed bar and small Italian restaurant in garden next to beach, managed by Kali (a qualified diving instructor) and two Italians. Highly recommended. To get there take a bus heading for Endau. **D** *Country Hotel*, 11 Jln Sulaiman, T7991799. A/c or fan, formerly the *Mandarin Hotel*, clean and has a convenient location near the market and the bus and taxi stands. **C-D** *Embassy*, 2 Jln Ismail, T7993545/7991301, F7995279 Some a/c, restaurant, very well-kept hotel – scrupulously clean, rooms without TVs considerably cheaper. Recommended. **D** *Golden City*, 23 Jln Abu Bakar, T7995028, F7991723. Bathroom (shower), near the bus station, some cheaper rooms with outside shower (RM10), free mineral water and a bike/motorcycle storage facility (RM1.50), friendly. **D** *Mersing Hotel*, 1 Jln Dato Mohammed Ali, T7991004. A/c, restaurant, spartan rooms now a bit tatty, clean enough but *Embassy* a better bet. Some a/c. **D** *New Merdeka Hotel*, 27 Jln Ismail, T7993506. Some a/c, slightly run down but a possible mid-range place. **D** *Omar Backpackers' Dorm*, Jln Abu Bakar, T7995096, F7744268. Clean and well looked-after but only 10 beds, excellent information on Sibu and other less visited islands, treks and river cruises. Relaxed place where the owner seems to let the guests run things. Very basic rooms (2 doubles and 1 dorm). Recommended. **E** *Comfort Inn*, 60-62 Jln Abu Bakar. Dormitory sleeping 12 with boarding school-style partitions and individual lockers, limited kitchen facilities, fan only, well-kept. The staff here are helpful and also represent the Endau Rompin National Park, providing tickets and information for boats, buses and tours. **E** *Mersing Guest House*, 3 Jln Ismail, T7993545. This place is owned by the *Embassy Hotel*. Rooms are basic and fan only, shared bath rooms but with same good standard of cleanliness **F** *Sheikh Guesthouse*, 1B Jln Abu Bakar, T7993767. Dorms only, clean and friendly, efficient tourist agency attached with information on all the islands, the *Sheikh Tourist Agency* downstairs offers ticketing, tours, accommodation booking and up-to-date information on Tioman and other islands. Ask here for details on other accommodation up the coast. **E** *Syuan Koong*, 44A Jln Abu Bakar, T7991498. Fan only, lockers available, clean but dated.

Eating **Malay Cheap** *Golden Dragon Restaurant*, 2 Jln Ismail, big Chinese seafood menu, reasonably priced, chilli crabs, drunken prawns, wild boar and *kang-kong belacan*. Excellent banana/pineapple pancakes for breakfast. Recommended. *Mersing* (Ground Floor, *Mersing Hotel*), Jln Dato Mohammed Ali, excellent seafood. *Mersing Seafood*, 56 Jln Ismail, a/c restaurant with spicy Szechuan or Cantonese seafood dishes, try squid with salted egg yoke, spicy coconut butter prawns. Big menu, reasonable prices. *Sin*

Nam Kee Seafood, 387 Jln Jemaluang (1 km out of town on Kota Tinggi road), huge seafood menu and reckoned by locals to be the best restaurant in Mersing, occasional karaoke nights can be noisy. **Seriously cheap** *Malaysia*, opposite the bus stop, open all night. *Restoran Al-Arif*, 44 Jln Ismail (opposite *Parkson* supermarket), cheap Muslim restaurant with good rotis and curries as well as local dishes. If this is your first stop after the west coast or Singapore Al-Arif is a good place to get into the east coast groove. *Sri Mersing Café*, opposite *Restoran Malaysia*.

Chinese Mid-range *New I came also*, 181 Jln Jemalang, excellent Chinese food, very friendly service. **Seriously cheap** *Yung Chuan Seafood*, 51 Jln Ismail, big open coffee shop with vast selection, speciality: seafood steamboat.

Bakeries *Kedai Kek Kile*, Jln Abu Bakar. A good selection of cakes and pastries cooked on the premises. European-style coffee available.

Foodstalls There are a number of upmarket stalls and coffee shops in the new *Plaza R & R* next to the river. There are also a smattering of more traditional stalls alongside the fresh fruit and vegetables in the market on Jln Ismail

Cafés **Internet café** *Mersing Café*, Jln Endau, below the *Timotel Hotel*, T7995888, open 1800-0000, MTV, live football, internet. *Cyberworld*, Jln Abu Bakar, below the *Backpackers Hostel*, cyberworld99@xoommail.com Open 0930-1830, 2030-2330. RM4 /hr. *Nas@nets* Jln Abu Bakar. Open 1030-2230. RM3/hr.

Shopping *Arts Souvenir*, 1, Gerai MDM, Jln Tun Dr Ismail, next to Malay restaurants on the corner after *R & R Plaza*. Artist Sulaiman Aziz specializes in colourful t-shirts, shorts and beachware and hand-painted batiks. There are some knick-knack souvenir shops in the *R & R Plaza*. The market on Jln Ismail offers more authentic batiks and is worth wandering around.

Tour operators
Competition is intense at peak season and tourists can be hassled for custom

Ticketing and travel agents all over town are much of a muchness and visitors are unlikely to be ripped off – although use licensed agents (usually displayed on the door). Agencies tend to promote their own business so expect the truth to be warped, bent and generally polished to a high and unlikely sheen. Many agents are now located in the new *Plaza R & R* on Jln Tun Dr Ismail, next to the river. They also promote package deals to specific chalet resorts; sometimes they are good value, but buying a boat ticket puts you under no obligation to stay at a particular place. Among the better agents are: *Golden Mal Tours*, 9 Jln Sulaiman, T7991463; *Island Connection Travel & Tours*, 2 Jln Jemaluang, T7992535; *Omar's*, opposite the Post Office, T7995096; *Island Connection* 2 Jln Jemaluang (owns *Mukut Village Chalets* on Tioman), T7994033; *Sheikh Tourist Agency*, 1B Jln Abu Bakar, T7994990. *Kebina*, Jln Abu Bakar, T7993123, F7995118.

Transport **Local Bus**: the local bus station is on Jln Sulaiman opposite the *Country Hotel*.

133 km N of Johor Bahru
189 km S of Kuantan
353 km to KL

Long distance Boat: the jetty is a 5-min walk from the bus stop. Most of the ticket offices are by the jetty but boat tickets are also sold from booths near the bus stop. (See transport to individual islands.) The boat trip to the islands from Mersing can be extremely rough during the monsoon season; boats will sometimes leave Mersing in the late afternoon, on the high tide, but rough seas can delay the voyage considerably. During peak monsoon all ferry services are cancelled and the ferry companies move to the west coast to find work there. It is advisable only to travel during daylight hrs. Mersing Island Ferry Information, Jln Abu Bakar, T7993606/0107734496.

Bus: long-distance buses leave from two locations: the roundabout by the *Restoran Malaysia* and Jln Abu Bakar, not far from the jetty. Tickets can be bought from *Plaza R&R*. Regular connections with **KL** (1130, 1230, 1830 and 2200, RM19.50 adults RM9.80

children), **JB** (1230 express; RM11, 0815 and 1400 local; RM5.10), **Kuala Terengganu** (1200, 1300, 1400 and 2200, RM22.10)), **Kuantan** (1200, 1300, 1400 and 2200, RM10.60), **Ipoh** (1200, 2200; RM26), **Penang** (1700; RM35), and **Singapore** (1200, 1330, 1400 and 1600, RM 12.60), **KB** (2130; RM25.10). Passengers have reported having their bags stolen *en route* between Mersing and Singapore while stored in the luggage compartment of the coach; eg on buses of the *Johora Express*.

Taxi: taxis leave from Jln Sulaiman opposite the *Country Hotel*, next to the local bus station; **KL**, **JB** (RM80) (for Singapore, change at JB), **Melaka** (RM25), **Kuala Terengganu** and **Kuantan**.

Banks *Maybank*, Jln Ismail; *UMBC*, Jln Ismail, no exchange on Sat. Money changer on Jln Abu Bakar and *Giamso Safari*, 23 Jln Abu Bakar also changes TCs. **Communications** Post Office: Jln Abu Bakar. **Internet**: see **Cafés**, above. **Medical facilities** Dentists: Dr Logesh, Klinik Pergigian, 28 Jln Mohd, Ali, T7993135. **Doctors**: Dr Lai Chin Lai, Klinik Grace, 48 Jln Abu Bakar, T7992399.   **Directory**

Pulau Tioman

*Tioman, 56 km off Mersing, is the largest island in the volcanic Seribuat Archipelago at 20 km by 12 km. The island is dominated by several jagged peaks, notably the twin peaks of **Nenek Semukut** and **Bau Sirau** towards the southern end of the island, and in Malay legend its distinctive profile is the back of a dragon whose feet got stuck in the coral. It is densely forested and is fringed by white coral-sand beaches; with kampungs around the coast.*

Colour map 2, grid B6
Phone code: 07

East Coast Peninsula

Getting there   **Air**: The airport is in the centre of Tekek. The runway is being extended to take larger aircraft. The *Berjaya Tioman Beach Resort* (see page 248) sends a bus to meet each plane and various touts approach likely looking passengers. The jetty is just 100 m or so away. Daily connections with KL. Multiple daily connections with Johor Bahru on *Tiram Air* and daily with Mersing. International connections with Singapore. **Boat**: Most people arrive on Tioman by ferry from Mersing. The jetty at Mersing is 5 mins' walk out of Mersing next to the blue-roofed *R & R Plaza*. Tickets can be bought from one of the many ticket offices at the R & R Plaza. The variety can be confusing and slightly concerning but in fact all licensed vendors comply with the regulation price and all ferry tickets can be used on all ferries. Open return tickets are now available and these offer the best value and flexibility; the ferry timetable is only drawn up a month in advance because it depends on tides.

Ins & outs
See page 255 for further details

Getting around   There are very few trails around the island and only one road, a 2 km stretch from the airstrip at Tekek to the *Berjaya Tioman Beach Resort*. The west side of the island is connected to the east by a beautiful jungle trail. To get from one kampung to another, the best way is to go by boat and a 'sea bus' service works its way around the island.

Best time to visit   Many guesthouses and resorts close down between November and February when it is wet and can be windy and rough. Chinese New Year seems to be a popular time for places to open, cashing in on the Singapore market, but as Chinese New Year is a moveable feast the date can vary considerably from year to year. Transport from Mersing also becomes more difficult during the off season; ferries will only leave if there is sufficient demand to make it worth their while.

The highest peak is Gunung Kajang (1,049 m) or Palm Frond Mountain. It has been used as a navigational aid for centuries and is mentioned in early Arab and Chinese sailing charts. In the mid-1970s, 12th-century Sung Dynasty porcelain was unearthed on the island.

The Tioman website, www4.jaring.my/ spsj/island/tioman/ tio_main.htm has lots of local information and pictures of many guesthouses and resorts

Despite the growth in hotels and guesthouses, Tioman – some years ago rated one of the world's 10 best 'desert island escapes' by *Time* magazine – remains a beautiful island. In the 1950s it was discovered by Hollywood and selected as the location for the musical *South Pacific* where it starred as the mythical island of Bali Hai. All this attention put Tioman on the map; tourism accelerated during the 1970s and 1980s as facilities were expanded. However, over the last decade business has not been quite so brisk and prices, which for some establishments during the 1980s were absurdly high, given the level of amenities on offer, have now levelled out. Indeed most hotels have not increased their rates for five years or so. Even so there are various new hotels under construction and guesthouses still seem to be building new chalets or upgrading existing ones.

The cheaper beach-hut accommodation is mostly to be found on the northwest side of the panhandle, and despite a growth in the number of places to stay, these little kampungs have retained their charm and are still very laid back, making them an idyllic retreat for anyone who is looking for a deserted beach, a touch of snorkelling or diving and some great seafood. Thankfully, as yet, there are no nightclubs or fast-food restaurants and the tourist trinket shops are very low key. But the emergence of a condotel – even the name must be one of the ugliest in the English language – to the south of the *Berjaya Tioman Beach Resort* (and owned by them) is, perhaps, a sign of things to come.

Treks
See cross section below

The **cross-island trail**, from the mosque in Kampung Tekek to Kampung Juara, on the east coast, is a two to three-hour hike (around 4 km), which is quite steep in places. The trail is reasonably well marked: follow the path past the airport and then turn inland towards the mosque. From Juara, the trail begins opposite the pier. It is a great walk, although for those planning to stay at Juara, it is a tough climb with a full pack. The section from Tekek is part natural path, part concrete steps. Three-quarters of the way up from Tekek there is a small waterfall, really just a jumble of rocks and water, just off the path to the right. It can be wonderfully refreshing after the arduous climb, but check for leeches when you emerge. Shortly after the waterfall the route levels out and works it way through an upland plateau. This is the most enchanting part of the walk: massive trees and dense forest, strangling figs – a real taste of jungle. It is not unusual to see squirrels, monkeys and various tropical insects.

Tekek to Juara

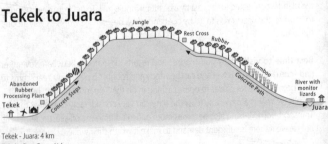

Tekek - Juara: 4 km
Tekek - Rest Cross: ½ hr
Rest Cross - Juara: 1 hr

Some enterprising Livingstones have even carved 'Jane' and 'Tarzan' on one of the trees. Just as the path begins to descend towards Juara there is a small drinks stop, the *Rest Cross*, incongruously located amongst the giant trees. This marks the beginning of the concrete trail which winds down to Juara. A motorcycle taxi service is available for the truly exhausted as well as fruit juices and soft drinks. The section down to Juara is less dramatic and more culti-vated with rubber trees and banana groves, but even here it is common to see some wildlife, including monkeys and squirrels. To return to the west coast, there is a daily sea bus service from Juara leaving at 1500.

There are also many easier jungle and coastal walks along the west coast: south from Tekek, past the resort to kampungs **Paya** and **Genting** and north to **Salang**. **Mount Kajang** can be climbed from the east or west sides of the island; an unmarked trail leads from the Tioman Island golf course (advisable to take a guide). It is also possible to trek to **Bukit Nenek Semukut** (Twin Peaks) and **Bukit Seperok**. The trail up Semukut starts from Pasir Burong, the beach at Kampung Pasir. Guides available from *Berjaya Tioman Beach Resort* and *Happy Café, Juara* and *Zaha's Information Service* (near the jetty at Tekek) and Kampung Tekek. The trail from Kampung Juara, on the east coast, is longer and more arduous.

Diving Tioman's coral reefs are mainly on the western side of the island, although sadly large areas have been killed off. This is in part due to fishing boats drag-ging anchor, partly through nimble-fingered snorkellers pilfering coral stalks (this kills neighbouring corals), partly because all the boat activity kicks up sand and retards the growth or kills the coral, and partly because of the crown-of-thorns starfish (see page 285). Wholesale coral 'harvesting' has also been going on, to feed the increasingly lucrative trade in salt-water aquaria. Live coral specimens are loaded into water-filled bags, having been hacked off reefs with pick axes. This practice has more or less ended around Tioman now, but is still reported to be going on off other east coast islands. Pollution is also said to be a coral-killer. Both sewerage and effluent from building sites can alter water salinity levels, killing coral and resulting in the proliferation of harmful algae.

There are still some magnificent coral beds within easy reach of the island. Pulau Renggis, just off the *Berjaya Tioman Beach Resort*, is the most easily accessible coral from the shore, with a depth of up to 12 m and a good place for new divers to find their flippers. For more adventurous dives, the islands off the northwest coast are a better bet. There is cave diving off Pulau Chebeh, 20 minutes from the *Berjaya* (up to 25 m), and varied marine life off the cliff-like rocks of Golden Reef (25 minutes from the *Berjaya* and up to 20 m) and nearby Tiger Reef (20 minutes from *Berjaya* with 9 to 24 m dives). Off the northeastern tip of the island is Magicienne Rock (30 minutes from *Berjaya* and 20-24 m dives) – where bigger fish have been sighted. Off the southwest-ern coast is Bahara Rock (30 minutes from *Berjaya* and 20 m), considered one of the best spots on the island. Best time to dive: mid-March to May, when vis-ibility is at its best, but it is possible to dive through to the end of October. There are dive shops based in most of the kampung: at Salang, Tekek, Genting, Paya, Ayer Batang and at the *Berjaya Tioman Beach Resort* (see the listings under each kampung).

Boat tours Boats leave from Kampung Tekek: to Pulau Tulai (or Coral Island) Turtle Island; to a waterfall at Mukut, or an around-island trip. All boats must be full otherwise prices increase. Boat trips can also be arranged to other nearby islands. Boats can be booked through *Zaha's Information Service*, near the jetty, Kampung Tekek and from many of the guesthouses.

Essentials

Sleeping
Sandflies can be a problem on Tioman and mosquito coils are recommended

The *Berjaya Tioman Beach Resort* and most of the cheaper places to stay are scattered along the west coast (the island is virtually uninhabited on the southeast and south-west sides and north of Juara Beach on the east coast, apart from a few fishing kampungs). Most of the accommodation on the island is simple: they are often individually owned by locals who may offer home-cooked meals and it is often hard to distinguish between them in terms of facilities and quality: atap or tin-roofed chalets/huts (**C-E** categories), 'A'-frames (**E-F**) or dorms (**F**). Chalets with attached bathrooms fall into our **C-D** categories and upwards. Not all have electricity. Rooms are fairly spartan, expect to pay more for mosquito nets and electricity. Inevitably, beachfront chalets cost more. Due to stiff competition, many prices are negotiable depending on the season.

Pulau Tioman

Sleeping
1 Berjaya Tioman Beach Resort

Kampung Lalang AL *Berjaya Tioman Beach Resort*, Lalang, T4191000, F4145718. A hotel with 400 rooms set in 200 acres of land, built on the site of the old Kampung Lalang. Bought by Tan Sri Vincent Tan in 1993, when it was dramatically expanded, this tourist class hotel is by far the biggest and most expensive resort on Tioman, with a good range of facilities and a lovely stretch of beach. This is not the place to come if you are hoping for a quiet retreat; during holiday periods, the whole place is heaving with activity. Rooms are adequately equipped but furnishings are a little dated. Choice of rooms; the cheapest have garden views and are the older 1-storey chalets. The deluxe and superior 2-storey chalets are bigger and are more suitable for families, some overlook the sea (if you crane your neck). All rooms have wooden floors and balconies, a/c, TV and mini-bar. Rather shabby bathrooms, with hot water shower only (bath tubs in deluxe rooms only). The suites are very forgettable. Several restaurants (see Eating below). Rather cramped area for the freeform pool with children's slides and jacuzzi. Watersports centre (including scuba diving facilities, RM800 for a 6-7 day PADI certification course) with boats for diving and snorkelling parties to nearby islands (it is possible to snorkel 100 m out from the northern end of the bay and at the very southern end, near the beach), jet skis, windsurfers, 18-hole golf course (see Sports below), gym – with good range of (underused) equipment, donkey and horse riding, tennis courts.

Kampung Lalang is not really a kampung at all but a beach devoted solely to the Berjaya Tioman Beach Resort and its sister condotel

The *Condotel* is a very ugly 4-storey block perched on a rocky promontory to the south of the *Berjaya*, which opened in March 1997. All the rooms are suites, with a sitting area looking onto balconies. The drawback here is that there are no eating outlets (just a small shop with ready to eat food and pantries in all the suites). A shuttle bus service runs to the hotel at meal times. There is a large lengths pool with no shade. The best rooms face south. The *Condotel* is largely a time share affair but will also be used as an overflow place for the *Berjaya*.

Kampung Tekek is the kampung-capital of Tioman and, frankly, is nothing special. However because boats from Mersing first call at Tekek's large concrete jetty, and the airport is also here, many visitors decide to stay put rather than face another journey. Others find they have to stay a night here 'in transit'. Tekek has the longest beach on the island, but for a large stretch north of the jetty it is rather

East Coast Peninsula

Kampung Tekek

■ Sleeping
1 Babura Sea View, Chinese Restaurant & Dive Shop
2 Coral Reef Seaview
3 Faira
4 Mastura
5 Peladang
6 Persona Island Resort
7 Ramli's House
8 Seroja Inn II
9 Sri Tioman Beach Resort
10 Tekek Inn
11 Tioman Enterprise
12 Tioman Sea View

● Eating
1 Liza
2 Malay No Name
3 Peladang

Sleeping
■ on map
Price codes: see inside front cover

dirty and with an ugly concrete breakwater. Almost all the coral is dead and broken, the river is polluted and there are rusting oil drums and other paraphernalia littering the town. There are many places to stay at Tekek, mostly south of the jetty or towards the northern end of the bay. However, much of the accommodation is run down and the place doesn't have much of a tropical island resort atmosphere. It feels like a small service centre, which is what it is. Tekek has a small post office, a police post, a clinic, a couple of money changers, the administrative HQ for the island, a few mini-marts, and an immigration post. There are two main areas of accommodation. One group of guesthouses is south of the jetty within 5-10 mins' walk of the jetty and airport. A second group begins 500 m north of the jetty and airport and stretches towards the National Park office at the far end of the bay. These are quieter, cheaper, but in general do not seem to be so well run. The 'road' here is just a 1 m-wide concrete path.

A-C *Babura Sea View*, T4191139. Some a/c, restaurant, the last place at the south end of the beach with 23 varied rooms. It consists of 3 separately owned businesses – the resort, a good Chinese restaurant, and *Tioman Reef Divers*, a PADI/NAUI dive shop. The rooms are clean and well maintained although some can be dark; the best are in the new block on the beach front. Recommended. **B** *Persona Island Resort*, T/F41911213 . Some a/c, restaurant, turn right at jetty and this place is a 10 min walk. It is the flashest place to stay in Tekek with 24 clean and functional rooms in 2-storey buildings but it is not on the beach. Large restaurant. **B-C** *Peladang*, T4191249, F011950852. Some a/c, a well-kept little place with clean and comfortable chalets. Its big drawback is that it is on the opposite side of the road some distance from the beach so it is neither possible to watch the sun go down over the horizon nor dash headlong from your chalet into the water. **B-D** *Coral Reef Seaview*, T4191137. Some a/c, restaurant, a group of chalets all looking rather jaded and dusty, some facing onto the sea, others set back and facing one another. **B-D** *Sri Tioman Beach Resort*, T4191189. Some a/c, restaurant, a popular place and one of the better places to stay in this price range in Tekek. Sea-facing chalets shaded beneath casuarina trees, good restaurant with prawn, squid and fish dishes as well as the usual range of pancakes etc. **C** *Mastura*, T0133412266. Restaurant (American breakfast included in room rate) on the beach and run by Zuki. Much the same as *Tekek Inn* and *Sri Tioman Beach Resort* (the three actually share guests when they are full) although *Mastura* suffers from being next to what looks like an oil storage depot. **D** *Seroja Inn II*, T7995209. Restaurant, 24 undistinguished chalets in front of beach, bicycles for hire. The following are all around RM25 (**D**) and there is little to mark them out from one another: *Faira*, *Ramli's House*, and *Tioman Sea View*. **D** *Tekek Inn*, T011358395. This is perhaps the best of the cheaper places to stay. It is on the beach, rooms are OK with attached showers, the management is suitably relaxed and there are snorkels and canoes for hire. No restaurant here, just a drinks station. Recommended. **D** *Tioman Enterprise*, T011952856. Lovingly cared for but very small chalets – more like Wendy Houses. The guesthouse is right at the end of the runway.

Kampung Penuba **C-D** *Penuba Paradise Inn*, situated just to the north of Kampung Ayer Batang, on the next promontory, and has its own jetty. Attractively laid out chalets built on stilts on the hillside, many with seaviews. Rocky beach, snorkelling in front of resort, restaurant, rather idyllic being so secluded, homely atmosphere, **F** for dorms.

Sleeping
■ *on map*
Price codes: see inside front cover
Accommodation at Ayer Batang is better than at Tekek

Kampung Ayer Batang This lies just north of Tekek. Accommodation here is spread out around the bay and is generally quite good. The beach is rocky at low tide and the sandy area quite small. The better portion of the beach is south of the jetty. There are said to be some monitor lizards here and the tall coconut palms are home to scores of bickering fruit bats during the day. Mini market next to *Sri Nelayan's* for basic supplies and souvenirs.

East Coast Peninsula

B-C *Johan's House*, T4191359. Big plot with small chalets on the beach and some newer and bigger rooms with a/c on the hill. Extensive travellers' food menu, snorkelling equipment for hire, library, speedboat available. **B-D** *Nazri's*, T4191329. The most southerly of the guesthouses in Ayer Batang. This has a range of accommodation. The complex is set around a mangrove swamp (so bring your mosquito coils), reputedly home to large monitor lizards. Some rooms in rows with a running verandah (5 with a seaview), some simple 'A' frames at the back of the plot, amongst the mango trees. Spartan but clean rooms, restaurant on seafront, friendly management, good discounts available during low season. Recommended.

C *Nazri 11* (also called *Air Batang Beach Cabanas*), the most expensive on this beach and by far the nicest, with decent, clean and not too cramped rooms with wooden floors and seaviews. A raised restaurant provides a spectacular view of the bay. Laundry service, jet ski, fishing and snorkelling available. Recommended. **C-E** *Mokhtar's*, T011719950. Huts look onto an attractive little garden, fan and mosquito nets provided, basic restaurant, unfriendly owner. **D-E** *South Pacific*, T4191176. 19 basic but adequate and clean rooms with fans and mosquito nets in choice of setting, some have seaview, 2 restaurants with good fish, notably the owner's fresh water catfish which he rears in ponds behind the guesthouse. Plenty of fruit available from trees on plot in the right season. Friendly owner from Kuantan will happily negotiate a good price for room. Recommended. **D-E** *TC*, 12 'A' frames, very basic, mosquito nets provided, no food here.

E *ABC*, T4191154. Last place to stay at northern end of beach, good beach here, small 'A'-frames, attractive rather intimate little plot with family atmosphere, good cheap food, hammocks, volleyball, friendly service. Recommended. **E** *Double Ace*, small rooms in 'A'-frames on a cramped plot. **E** *Mawar*, basic rather gloomy 'A' frames all with balconies right on the beach. Restaurant with lots of seafood, hammocks. **E** *My Friend Place*, very small rooms, fan and mosquito net. **E** *Rinda House*, small rooms with mosquito nets set around a very attractive little garden with outside café. **E** *Sri Nelayan*, row of 10 small chalets. **E** *Tioman House*, T4191196. 20 small huts built at right angles to the beach, a bit cramped, basic with fans. Seaside restaurant.

East Coast Peninsula

Kampung Ayer Batang

N

Not to scale

■ **Sleeping**
1 ABC
2 Double Ace
3 Johan's House
4 Mawar
5 Mokhtar's
6 My Friend Place
7 Nazri II
8 Nazri's
9 Rinda House
10 South Pacific
11 Sri Nelayan
12 TC
13 Tioman House

● **Eating**
1 Eziza's Café

B & J Diving Centre

Kampung Salang The northernmost development on the island and is set in a sheltered cove with a beautiful beach. The mangrove swamp to the south of the jetty, though dirty, still holds plenty of monitor lizards which cruise around like primeval monsters. Some are getting on for 2 m in length. There are minimarts at *Salang Indah* and at *Khalid's Place* for basic supplies such as drinks, toilet paper, nibbles, fruit, etc. A 150-room resort, the unattractively named *Nadia Inn Comfort*, has been under construction for a number of years at the south end of the Bay, past *Zaid's Place*, despite a supposed ban on new developments. Salang's laidback atmosphere is already falling prey to European backpackers.

B-D *Khalid's Place*, T011953421. 36 rooms in relatively new compound, a pleasant garden setting with fairly basic rooms. Family room available. If Khalid's

Sleeping
■ *on map*
Price codes:
see inside front cover
Development here
is quite ramshackle,
with a scattering of
beachside restaurants
and a relaxed
atmosphere

girth is anything to go by, the restaurant must be good. **B-D** *Salang Beach Resort*, T4195015, F4192024. Chinese restaurant, spacious chalets with verandahs set in well-kept grounds, some with a/c. This is the northernmost development so it is quiet and the beach is virtually a private one. The management can be brusque. **B-D** *Salang Indah*. Large, rather garish, restaurant with some delicious seafood specialities. Variety of chalets in all price brackets, some with attached bathrooms right on the sea, others with a/c and private stairs down to the sea, plus the original rather drab rooms in a U-shaped barrack of a building. The guesthouse is owned by the Orang Kayah and expansion is still underway with a number of new Minang-style chalets built in 1997, provides a minimart and various other services. It is hard to avoid the conclusion that it has over-expanded. **C** *Zaid's Place*, a popular place, with fairly switched-on management. There's a choice of rooms, some with seaview, others which face onto a little garden, all are clean and have fans. Money changer, library, good restaurant. Recommended. **D** *Paklong*, 5 rooms with fan, no sea view, but friendly family management, rather fetid swamp close by.

A quiet place with a small surau (prayer hall) and a couple of restaurants

Kampung Paya is south of Tekek. The jetty here has now been upgraded and the ferries from Mersing stop here. The beach is attractive enough but at low tide a belt of dead and broken coral makes swimming difficult.

A *Paya Resort* (booking office Jln Sulaiman 11, Mersing, T077991432. Or in Singapore at 101 Upper Cross St, 01-36 People's Park Centre, T5341010), T01762534. Restaurant, small resort with 30 a/c rooms, which is clean and well looked-after but perhaps a little over-priced given the standard of the rooms. There is a PADI dive school attached to the hotel, the resort is owned by the director of *Giamso Safari* tour agency in Mersing. The resort is closed Nov-Jan. **B-D** *Sri Paya Tioman Enterprise*, T011765774, T02(Singapore) 3656974. Ten a/c bungalows with twin double beds so that four can share and attached bathrooms, 8 small fan rooms. Clean but not a place to induce that tropical island paradise feeling. **D** *Sri Paya Holiday*, T011716196. 26 small bungalows in the middle of the village by the pier, little character.

Kampung Salang

Sleeping
1 Khalid's Place
2 Pakong
3 Salang Beach Resort
4 Salang Indah
5 Zaid's Place

Eating
1 Amin's Café
2 Salang Dreams
3 Sunset Boulevard

N
Not to scale

Kampung Genting lies to the south of Kampung Paya and is the second largest village on the island. However it is not as popular as some of the other kampungs and has the feeling of a locals' resort; tourists are mainly from the mainland and Singapore. The extensive jetty gives an impression that the village had hoped for greater things. The beach here is poor; rocks are exposed at low tide and the coral is largely broken and dead. There is, though, an incredibly modest sight: the graves of Tun Mohamad bin Tun Adbul Majid, the sixth Bendahara of Pahang, and his wife, also of royal blood being the daughter of Sultan Mahmud of Johore-Riau-Lingga-Pahang. In 1803 the Bendahara (who had assumed the position the year before) and his wife were at sea between Tioman and the mainland when their boat foundered in a thunderstorm. With their cabin locked the couple were unable to escape and both drowned. Their bodies, though, were recovered and buried here after having been washed in fresh water from the local river – which is now known as the Sungai Air Rajah. Another version has it that the bodies were never found and the graves are purely symbolic. There is a *surau*, or prayer hall, by the jetty.

B *Tropical Coral Inn*, T011713465. This place is owned by *Sany Travel and Tour*, 545 Orchard Rd (Far East Shopping Centre), Singapore, T4661360, F7328137 and 70% of guests come from Singapore on package deals. The chalets are adequate, there is a/c, a good restaurant and *Sharkey's Dive Shop* is attached. **D** *Bayu*, at the north end of the beach, quiet and secluded. **D** *Damai*, bookable in Mersing at Jln Abu Bakar, T4197055. About 80 rather grotty looking double chalets with balconies, restaurant, minimarket and 24-hr electricity, speedboat to Mersing. **D** *Island Reef Resort*, set back on hillside behind jetty, with chalets side on to beach, so no views except in the restaurant. **D** *Sun Beach Resort*, about 50 rambling bungalows built too close together, some on the seafront, others piled up the hill behind. Monstrous restaurant on stilts.

Kampung Nipah (south of Kampung Genting). **B-D** *Beach Chalet Nipah*, beachside chalets with attached bathrooms. Because this is the only accommodation available, Kampung Nipah is one of the most secluded and tranquil spots on the island.

Kampung Mukut on south side of island. **C** *Mukut Coral Resort*, T7992535, restaurant, traditional-style atap-roofed chalets with balconies, a/c, owned by Island Connection (see above), secluded and beautiful location with magnificent backdrop. **D** *Asah Resort* and **D** *Mukut Waterfall Backpacker Resort*.

Kampung Juara

Sleeping
1 Atan's Place
2 Bushman
3 Busong
4 Juara Bay Resort
5 Juara Mutiara
6 Musni Chalet
7 Paradise Point
8 Saujana Bay Resort
9 Sunrise

Eating
1 Beach Café
2 Mini Café

Kampung Juara This is the only kampung on the east coast with accommodation. It has beautiful long white beaches which sometimes have good breakers. The snorkelling though, is poor. Being on the seaward side, Juara has a completely different atmosphere from the west coast kampungs; it is quieter, friendlier, more laid-back and bucolic, thanks mainly to its seclusion. However, because of its reputation, it is occasionally subject to waves of tourists who pass through on coach tours and unfortunately building activity indicates that its relative seclusion is soon to be shattered. There is a path from Kampung Tekek, through the jungle, to Juara (see **Treks** above). Alternatively, it is possible to take a boat from Tekek. Accommodation is cheaper at Juara. The Sungai Baru which flows into the sea here is home to some monitor lizards. **Getting to Kampung Juara**: being on the east

Sleeping
■ *on map*
Price codes:
see inside front cover

East Coast Peninsula

side of the island, the ferries from Mersing rarely call here and it is necessary to catch one of the sea buses that circle the island, RM18 from Tekek to Juara, 2 hrs. To walk from Tekek to Juara is a tough 3-hr walk.

D *Juara Bay Resort*, restaurant, rather ugly series of new hillside chalets at the southern end of the main beach. This is the most sophisticated place to stay and there have even been murmurings of a/c. Though it is quiet and the chalets have attractive views over the bay they do not have the beach front position of the other places. **D** *Saujana Bay Resort*, the last place to stay at the southern end of the bay. It is quite a walk from the jetty over the headland. **D-E** *Juara Mutiara*, organizes diving trips or island tours, booking office in Mersing, 6 Jln Abu Bakar, near *Plaza R & R*. The more expensive rooms sleep 4, all have attached showers, clean and popular, some chalets right on the beach, can be noisy (for Juara) as there are other chalet operations on both sides.

E *Bushman*, near the southern end of the beach, simple 'A'-frame huts. **E** *Paradise Point*, restaurant with extensive menu, one of only two places to stay on the northern side of the beach. Simple rooms, attached showers, the chalets siding onto the beach get the breeze, a quiet place with a relaxed atmosphere. Recommended. **E-F** *Atan's Place*, T7992309. Same management as *Juara Mutiara*, restaurant (*Turtle Café* – but you don't go there for the food), 'A'-frames and chalets with small verandahs. **E-F** *Busong*, same ownership as *Paradise Point* and close to the northern end of the beach, near a mangrove fringed lagoon which, after heavy rain, discharges into the sea. There are some simple 'A'-frame huts as well as more recently built chalets. Very quiet and right on the beach. **E-F** *Musni Chalet*, over the headland at the southern end of the beach, isolated and quiet. **E-F** *Sunrise*, restaurant, simple and small 'A' frame huts that become airless and stuffy on still days. Good water activities: canoes, windsurfers and boats for hire.

Eating
Not all restaurants sell beer

Most restaurants are small family-run kitchens attached to groups of beach huts. All provide Western staples such as omelettes and French toast, as well as Malay dishes. On the whole, the food is of a high standard. Understandably it makes most sense to eat seafood: superb barbecued shark, barracuda, squid, stingray and other fish.

Kampung Lalang *Berjaya Tioman Beach Resort Restaurant* offers a choice of restaurants, none of which are outstanding. The best bet is the buffet meal, which is quite good value and a huge spread is on offer. The other restaurants offer barbecue and steamboat. Service for à la carte meals is painfully slow and pretty inefficient. The golf club offers a snack bar with good pizzas and sandwiches.

Kampung Tekek This has a good range of restaurants. The *Babura Sea View Chinese Restaurant* (separate ownership from the guesthouse) is recommended and so too is the *Liza Restaurant*, which is the most sophisticated place to have a meal and serves delicious Malay food. Of the guesthouse restaurants the one at the *Sri Tioman Beach Resort* is worth trying, especially the squid and chilli prawns, while the small *Malay No Name Restaurant* north of the *Babura* and before the bridge is also recommended, as are the food stalls just north of the pier. There are a number of minimarts in the Kampung; *Pak Ali Nasir's* stall is the best place for fruit; and there is a very small market area next to the *Peladang Restaurant*.

Kampung Ayer Batang *Eziza's Café* near the jetty offer simple dishes.

Kampung Salang This is a sizeable hamlet, so there are a number of restaurants independent of the guesthouses. *Sunset Boulevard* is built over the sea north of the *Salang Indah*. Good seafood and the best spot for a cold beer. Among the best of the warungs is the place just north of the *Sunset Boulevard* – simple dishes, breakfast served. Another good option is *Amin's Café* right by the jetty; it provides breakfast, lunch and dinner, simple, low key place. *Salang Dreams* next to the *Salang Indah Minimart* has good Malay food and a good evening seafood barbecue.

Kampung Paya The *Mekong Restaurant* at the south end of the bay produces good Chinese seafood dishes.

Kampung Juara All the guesthouses serve roughly the same dishes: curries, noodle and rice dishes, pancakes, fish, omelettes etc. There are also a couple of independent restaurants – the *Mini Café* and the *Beach Café*, both near the pier. Inevitably fish is good: chilli fish, sweet and sour, or simply grilled.

Souvenirs Tioman is not a place to come shopping. However, there are a handful of souvenir shops in Tekek selling the usual range of sea-derived knick-knacks including shells fashioned into improbable scenes and jewellery which most people discard immediately upon their return home. **Shopping**

Diving Most beaches have dive centres attached to at least one guesthouse. PADI, NAUI and SSI (Scuba Schools International) certification available. **Sports**

  Kampung Tekek: the best dive shop is reputedly *Tioman Reef Divers* attached to *Babura Sea View*. It offers PADI and NAUI certification courses. Other dive shops include *Scuba Point* (PADI) next to *Coral Reef Holidays*, and a new dive shop (PADI) attached to the *Tekek Inn*.

  Kampung Ayer Batang: *B&J Diving Centre* next to *Johan's House* has a small pool for diving practice and can provide PADI certification.

  Kampung Salang: Salang is sold as a snorkellers' haven but, sadly, that is history – the coral is disappointing. It does, however, get better further out, and where the coral cliff drops off to deeper water, there is a more interesting variety of marine life including the odd reef shark. *Ben's Diving Centre*, next to *Salang Indah* hires out equipment and can organize PADI certification and diving trips to nearby islands. A 4-day PADI course costs RM625, two dives RM110, which include equipment and boat. *Dive Asia* by the *Salang Beach Resort* also offers PADI certification; one dive with a full set is costed at RM70, night dives also arranged. *Fishermen Dive Centre* near the *Salang Indah* offer SSI (Scuba Schools International) certification, a full course costs RM750, a full day's diving, RM140. There is also *B&J* another PADI outfit, T011717014, F011954247. Snorkels and fins can be hired just about everywhere, about RM7-10 per day.

  Kampung Paya: dive shop at the *Paya Resort* with PADI certification courses.

  Kampung Genting: *Sharkeys*, the *Tropical Coral Inn*, runs SSI certificated courses.

  Kampung Juara: snorkelling and fishing gear can be hired from most guest-houses. *Beruntan Dive Centre*, T01377720690, reef, wreck and night dives, RM80 (also water-skiing, jungle-trekking and rock-climbing).

Golf *Tioman Island Golf Club*, T445445, F445716, most club-members are weekend trippers from KL and Singapore, beautiful 18-hole course, green fees RM80 weekdays, RM100 weekends. Equipment including clubs (full set RM50), golf shoes (RM10), and buggy (RM40 weekdays, RM50 weekends) all available for hire.

Zaha's, Tekek Pier, sells boat tickets to Mersing and round-the-island excursions. **Tour operators**

Local Boat: beaches and kampungs are connected by an erratic sea-bus service, which runs roughly every hr or so from 0800 to 1800. The early-morning sea-bus goes right round the island; otherwise it is necessary to charter a boat to get to the waterfalls (on the south coast) and Kampung Juara. All the boats from Mersing take passengers **Transport** *60 km to Mersing*

East Coast Peninsula

to the kampungs on the west side; the first port of call is Kampung Tekek. Sea-bus fares (per person, children half price) from Kampung Tekek to: Kampung Ayer Batang/ABC (RM4), Penuba (RM6), Salang (RM9), Lalang (*Berjaya Tioman Beach Resort*) (RM6), Juara (RM20). Note that there is a slightly different schedule on Fri. The east coast is accessible by (very slow) boat or by the jungle trail. Fast boats leave at hourly intervals when the tide is high.

Baggage allowance is 10 kg

Long distance Air Several connections a day with Seletar Airport (on north side of Singapore Island, see page 582) with *SilkAir*. A bus from the *Berjaya Tioman Resort* meets each arrival and transports guests to the hotel. Alternatively walk to the pier and catch one of the sea-buses to the other beaches.

It is inadvisable to leave Mersing after 1500 as it can be difficult to find accommodation after nightfall and most restaurants close early

Boat Fast boats from **Mersing** to **Tioman** leave at hourly intervals when the tide is high. A/c fast boats (eg *Seagull Express*, T7994297), RM30, take 1½hrs to **Selang**; catamarans (RM30) take 2 hrs to **Selang**; and the ferry (RM25) takes 3hrs. During the monsoon season (Nov-Feb) departures can be erratic; boats may not run if there are insufficient passengers and the sea can get quite rough. All boats land on the west coast of Tioman and call at each of the main kampungs; occasionally they may cross to the east side of the island and call at **Juara**, but it is usually necessary to catch one of the 'sea-buses' that circle the island. If intending to stay at Juara leave enough time to catch a sea-bus; it takes around 2 hrs from Kampung Tekek to Juara. The *Auto Tioman* leaves from **Tanah Merah**, Singapore 0830 and returns 1430, 4½ hrs (S$85 one way, children S$55). Reservations at *Auto Batam*, 1 Maritime Square, World Trade Centre, Singapore T2714866, www.sembcorp.com.sg/autobatam

Directory **Airline offices** *Silk Air* operates out of *Berjaya Resort*, T4145445, F4145718. **Banks** There are 2 money changers at Tioman Airport in the new blue-roofed shopping plaza. Some shops in Salang will also change money. TCs can be changed at the *Berjaya Tioman Beach Resort* (large surcharge). Recently, some smaller resorts have begun to accept them. **Communications** Public phones in all villages, IDD calling from *Berjaya* and some guesthouses. Phones to be installed in guesthouses sometime in the near future. **Post Office:** mini-post office in Kampung Tekek. **Card phones:** in Tekek next to the Mini Pos (cards available at Post Office). **Medical facilities** There is a small clinic in Tekek.

Other islands

*There are a total of 64 islands off Mersing; many are inaccessible and uninhabited. There is accommodation available and boats to **Pulau Rawa**, **Pulau Babi Besar** (Big Pig Island), **Pulau Tinggi**, **Pulau (Babi) Tengah**, **Pulau Sibu**, **Pulau Aur** (Bamboo Island) and **Pulau Pemanggil**.*

Pulau Rawa
For pictures of Pulau Rawa and resort rates, check www4.jaring.my/spsj/ island/rawa/rawa

A small island 16 km off Mersing, Pulau Rawa is owned by a nephew of the Sultan of Johor and was one of the first resorts built in the area; it remains highly rated by lots of travellers. The island has a fantastic beach and for those in need of a desert island break Rawa is perfect, for there is absolutely nothing to do except mellow out. Unfortunately the coral reef is disappointing, but more active visitors can windsurf, canoe, and fish. The island gets busy at weekends as it is close enough for day visitors; it is also a popular getaway for Singaporeans.

Pulau Babi Besar is larger and closer to the mainland than Rawa. It is a very peaceful island and is particularly well known for its beaches and coral. Pulau Tinggi is probably the most dramatic-looking island in the Seribuat group, with its 650-m volcanic peak but is less popular than neighbouring Sibuh Tengah. Pulau Sibuh Tengah, formerly a refugee camp for Vietnamese boat people, is an hour away from Mersing. The government has declared it a marine park because of its reef and the fact that giant leatherback turtles (see page 284) lay their eggs there between June and August.

Pulau Babi Besar, Pulau Tinggi & Pulau Subuh

Pulau Sibu, otherwise known as the Island of Perilous Passage because it used to be a pirate haunt, has been recommended by many travellers for its beaches and watersports. Sibu is frequented more by Singaporeans and expatriates than by Western tourists. It is popular for fishing and diving and because it is larger than the other islands there is more of a sense of space and there are also some good walks. The best beaches on Pulau Pemanggil are at kampungs Buan and Pa Kaleh, which is fortunately where the accommodation is sited. Landmarks include the Harimo (Tiger) Caves which is a good location for snorkelling.

Pulau Sibu & Pulau Pemanggil

In addition to these more established islands, there are also other places being developed. It is worth asking around in Mersing for more information and enquiring from people on the jetty who have just returned. Islands currently under development include **Pulau Hujung** and **Pulau Aur**. The latter is the most remote. **Note** The islands listed here are not the only islands in the group; there are many which can be visited on island-hopping tours but which do not have resorts or accommodation.

Developing islands

East Coast Peninsula

Essentials

All resorts have their own restaurants. Most of the accommodation on these islands is run by small operators, who organize packages from Mersing. Resort bookings must be made in either Mersing or Johor Bahru.

Sleeping & eating
Price codes:
see inside front cover
Rawa has no kampungs on it and, as yet, only one resort

Pulau Rawa A-B *Rawa Safaris Island Resort*, Tourist Centre, Jln Abu Bakar, Mersing T7991204. Some a/c, restaurant (Malay and international dishes), bungalows, chalets and 'A'-frames, watersports, Sahid mixes some powerful cocktails in the bar; drink more than two Rawa specials and you'll be on the island for good.

Pulau (Babi) Besar A *Harlequin*, (aka *D'Coconut Island Resort*), built on the land of an old coconut plantation, with chalets, a large restaurant, pool and watersports. **A** *Radin Island Resort*, 9 Tourist Information Centre, Jln Abu Bakar, Mersing, T7994152. Restaurant (some a/c) stylish traditional chalets with jungle hillside backdrop. **A-C** *Nirwana Beach Resort*, choice of chalets, some with a/c, restaurant attached, dorms available. **A-C** *White Sand Beach Resort*, 98 Jln Harimau Tarum, Century Garden, Johor Bahru, T077994995. Runs diving packages, 4 days for 2 people. **B** *Besar Marina Resort*, 10 Tourist Information Centre, Jln Abu Bakar, Mersing, T7993606. **B** *Hillside Beach Resort*, 5B Jln Abu Bakar, Mersing or book through Suite 125, 1st Flr, Johor Tower, 15 Jln Gereja, Johor Bahru, T077994831, F2244329. Restaurant, very attractively designed Kampung-style resort, nestling on jungled slopes above beach, watersports. **C** *Besar Beach Chalet*, new resort with government-style chalets backed by Irish jungle. **C** *Perfect Life Resort*, range of rooms from chalets to honeymoon suites. **C-E** *Batu Kembar*, 18 large chalets on a hillside, for 4 people each in bunks, a/c, hot showers and balconies. **E** *Atlantis Bay*, basic with outdoor showers, non-a/c. **E** *Bluewater Resort*, chalet or longhouse accommodation in this place in Aur village.

Pulau Tinggi A *Nadia Comfort Inn*, c/o 17 Tingkat 2, Tun Abdul Razak, Kompleks (KOMTAR), Jln Wong Ah Fook, Johor Bahru, T072231694. Booking office in Mersing opposite *Plaza R & R*, Jln Abu Bakar, restaurant, pool, luxurious Malay-style wooden chalets. Also 'A'-frames (**F**), chalets (**D**) and bungalows (**C**) on the island; **A-B** *Tinggi Island Resort*, bookings from *Sheikh Tourist Agency*, 1B Jln Abu Bakar, Mersing, T7993767/7994451. Attractive chalets balanced precariously on steep hillside and next to beach, excellent range of indoor and outdoor facilities, boat trips arranged to nearby islands (Pulau Lima and Pulau Simbang) for diving.

Pulau (Babi) Tengah More accommodation is planned on the island. **B** *Pirate Bay Island Resort*, restaurant, spacious cottages built in traditional style with full selection of amenities, watersports.

Pulau Sibu Besar A *Twin Beach Resort*, 40 chalets, no a/c or hot water but good sports facilities. **A-D** *Sibu Island Cabanas* (c/o G105 *Holiday Plaza*, Century Garden JB), T073317216. Restaurant, chalets and deluxe bungalows. **C-D** *O & H Kampung Huts* (c/o 9 Tourist Information Centre, Jln Abu Bakar, Mersing), T7993124/7993125. Good restaurant, chalets, some with attached bathrooms, clean and friendly, trekking and snorkelling. Recommended. **C-D** *Sea Gypsy Village Resort*, 9 Tourist Information Centre, Jln Abu Bakar, Mersing, T7993124. Restaurant, chalets and bungalows. Recommended.

Pulau Sibu Tengah **C** *Sibu Island Resorts*, Suite 2, 14th Flr, KOMTAR, Jln Wong Ah Fook, Johor Bahru, T072231188. Recently renovated.

Pulau Aur **F** *Longhouse* provides basic accommodation.

Pulau Pemanggil Package deals for *Wira Chalets and longhouse* (also has dive shop). There is a small agent at the very front of Mersing's *Plaza R & R* dealing exclusively with Pemanggil travel and accommodation. **C-E** *Dagang Chalets and Longhouse*, Kampung Buau (1 longhouse room sleeps 8 at RM10 per person), restaurant serving local food, *Mara Chalet* at Kampung Pa Kaleh, on southwest side. Contact *Tioman Accommodation & Boat Services*, 3 Jln Abu Bakar, Mersing, T7993048.

Boats to the islands leave daily from Mersing, usually around 1100 and return 1530 (all slow boats): **Rawa** (1½ hrs, RM25 return), **Tengah** (RM18 return), **Babi Besar** (RM30 return), **Sibu** (RM25 return), **Tinggi** (RM50 return). No regular boats to **Pulau Aur** or **Pulau Pemanggil** – though this may change as the islands develop. Getting to **Pulau Aur** takes 4 hrs or more. Also boats to **Sibu** from **Tanjung Sedili Besar** at **Teluk Mahkota** (23 km off the Kota Tinggi-Mersing road), south of Mersing (RM22 return).

Endau Rompin National Park

Colour map 2, grid B5
Phone code: 09

This park straddles the border of Johor and Pahang states and is one of the biggest remaining tracts of virgin rainforest on the peninsula; about 80,000 ha. In the late 1980s Endau Rompin was upgraded to the status of a national park to protect the area from the logging companies who ravaged the park through the 1970s. Within the park, it may be possible to see a diverse range of flora and fauna, namely the endangered Sumatran rhino, tigers, wild boars, tapir, elephant, deer and mousedeer. Birdlife includes hornbills and the argus pheasant. Amongst the flora there are fan palms (Endau ensis), walking stick palm (Phychorapis singaporensis) and climbing bamboo (Rhopa loblaste), pitcher plants and orchids.

Ins and outs

There are two ways of getting to the Park; either via Rompin, Pahang, (paved road to Selanding and then a rough track for 25 km to the park boundary at Kinchin). The other route is from Johor in the south, on route 50 from Kahang; its 48 km on a logging route to Kampung Peta (the visitors' centre and entry point to the Park). From the visitors' centre it's another 15 km to base camp at Kuala Jasin (3 hrs on foot or 45 mins by boat [RM10/person upon request]). For arrivals to the Park by boat, travel to Endau, 33 km up the coast from Mersing, and from there, take a 6-hr motorboat ride upstream to Kampung Peta (RM200 one way).

Visitors who take the Johor route into the park will be stung for a multitude of costs (park permit, guide hire, use of camera, etc). For visitors arriving via Pahang, none of these charges apply. Both Johor and Pahang state authorities recommend that visitors come on an organised tour (see listings below), given the convoluted travel instructions and excessive fees, this is a sensible option.

Due to the extended travel time required to reach the park, visitors should consider a visit of around three nights

The park is managed by the Johor National Parks Association, a private body set up by local government which has made access to the park easier and has allowed some new accommodation. Because of privatisation, prices for entry and accommodation are relatively high. Unlike Taman Negara National Park, trips to Endau require careful planning and are best organized by tour agents who usually end up cheaper than trying to arrange it independently, (see below). Some guides do offer one-day treks (see *Omah's tours* in the Mersing section) but this should not be attempted alone.

If arriving via Endau by boat, at the junction of the Endau and Jasin rivers (9 hrs from Endau) is a good campsite and base for trekking and fishing expeditions. Boats go further upstream, but it is advisable to take a guide from Endau or the Orang Asli kampungs (RM20-30 per day). At present it is necessary to take all provisions and camping equipment with you.

Most package trips involve a 70-km jeep trip from Mersing to Kampung Peta followed by a 1½-hr longboat ride to the first campsite. Visitors to the park can trek around the Asli trails and visit spectacular waterfalls, the biggest of which is the Buaya Sangkut waterfall on Sungai Jasin. Fishing trips are best organized between February and August.

Entrance fees must be paid at the Park Headquarters in Kampung Peta where the officer on duty will provide a briefing of rules and regulations that apply in the park. Two websites with information on the park are www.kwikxs.com.my/NPC/index2.html and www.johortourism.com.my/html/eco/e.end.fac.html

Essentials

Kuala Rompin A *Lanjut Golden Beach Resort*, 20 km north of Kuala Rompin. A golf resort with a/c, 2 restaurants, pool, rooms and bungalows. **B** *Seri Malaysia Rompin*, Tg Gemok, T7944724, F7944732. Located 55 km from the national park, organizes tours, clean and comfortable rooms in new government chain hotel. **B-D** *Hotel Sri Rompin*, T4146236. A gem of a place, built 1998, clean and very comfortable, 2 mins from the bus station. **C** *Government Resthouse*, clean-looking. **C** *Rumah Rehat* (Rest House), 122.5 Milestone, T565245. Restaurant, 2-storey resthouse, all rooms with attached bathroom. **D-E** *Watering Hole Bungalows* (closed during wet season), 3 km south of Kuala Rompin and then 2 km or so towards the coast, T011411894. Quiet and clean, price including breakfast and dinner, we have had reports the Swiss-Malaysian couple who run this place could be friendlier and more welcoming but it is still a relaxing hideaway and well run.

Sleeping
*Price codes:
see inside front cover*
There is no accommodation available in the park; camping only

Camping At the moment the only facilities for overnight stays in Endau Rompin are campsites at Kuala Jasin, Batu Hampar, Upih Guling and Kuala Marong, which have

Pahang: the land of the sacred tree

A Malay legend tells of a huge, majestic Mahang (softwood) tree that once stood on the bank of the Pahang River, not far from Pekan, towering over everything else in the jungle. The tree was said to resemble the thigh of a giant and considered sacred by the Orang Asli and the Jakun tribespeople. The Malays adopted the name, which, in time, became Pahang. Perhaps not coincidentally, pahang also happens to be the Khmer word for 'tin'; there are ancient tin workings at Sungai Lembing near Kuantan, where traces of early human habitation have been found.

Until the end of the 19th century, Pahang, the peninsula's largest but least populous state, had always been a vassal. It paid tribute to Siam, Melaka and then Johor. In 1607 the Dutch set up a trading post in Pahang, but the state found itself caught in the middle of protracted rivalries between Johor and Aceh, the Dutch and the Portuguese. Pekan was sacked repeatedly by Johor and Aceh in the early

17th century, before coming under the direct rule of the Sultan of Johor in 1641; it stayed that way for two centuries.

In 1858, the death of the chief minister of Pahang, resulted in a five-year civil war. The dispute between his two sons was finally settled when the younger, Wan Ahmad, declared himself Chief Minister and then became the Pahang's first sultan in 1863. Sultan Wan Ahmad was autocratic and unpopular, so the British entered the fray, declaring the state a protectorate in 1887. An anti-British revolt ensued, supported by the sultan, but Wan Ahmad's power was whittled away. In 1895 the state's administrative capital was moved from Pekan to Kuala Lipis, 300 km up the Pahang River and later to Kuantan. Pahang became part of the federated Malay states in 1896. It was completely cut off from the west coast states, except for a couple of jungle trails, until a road was built from Kuala Lumpur to Kuantan in 1901. Pahang remains a predominantly Malay state.

a combined capacity of 250-300 visitors. The long-awaited chalets, dorms, barbecue pits, restaurants and sanitation facilities are under construction but not expected to be completed until 2002.

Tour operators Organized expeditions, which cost anything from RH90-200 per person per day, includes return vehicle and boat transfer, camping equipment, cooking utensils and permits, can be booked through: *Eureka Travel*, 277A Holland Ave, Holland Village, Singapore, T654625077, F4622853. Offers ecologically orientated tours to Endau Rompin National Park. Recommended. *Giamso Travel*, 23 Jln Abu Bakar, Mersing, T077992253. Approximately RM190 per person for 3 days/2 nights, RM210 per person for 4 days, 3 nights. The company can supply camping equipment, or through *Shah Alam Tours*, 138 Mezz Flr, Jln Tun Sambanthan, Kuala Lumpur T032307161, F032745739. *Sheikh Tourist Agency*, 1B Jln Abu Bakar, Mersing, T793767. Trips of 4 days/3 nights RM380 per person, all in RM100 deposit payable on booking; *Wilderness Experience*, 6B Jln SS 21/39, Damansara Utama, Petaling Jaya, T037178221. Hotels and guesthouses in Kuala Rompin also usually organize trips into the park.

Transport **Road** **Bus**: Connections with **Johor Bahru**, **Terengganu** and **Kuantan**. Buses from
130 km S of Kuantan Johor Bahru and Kuantan stop on demand at **Endau**, or regular local buses from
37 km N of Mersing Mersing to Endau. There is a 56-km jungle road from Kahang town to Kampung Peta where there is a visitors' centre and the entry point to the park. **Taxi**: from Mersing. **Boat** Speed boats to first Orang Asli village (Kampung Punan). This can cost anything from RM200-400 for a 2-day trip. It is possible to charter longboats (carrying up to 6 passengers) from Kampung Punan to go further upstream.

Pekan

The old royal capital of Pahang, Pekan has a languid feel to it. It has a reason-   *Colour map 2, grid A5*
ably picturesque row of older wooden shophouses on the busy street along the
river, but is otherwise not a particularly photogenic town. Aside from its
mosques, Pekan's most distinguishing feature is its bridge, which straddles
the Pahang River, the longest river on the peninsula.

Pekan means 'town' in Malay. It used to be known as Pekan Pahang, the
town of Pahang. Even before the Melakan sultanate was established in the late
14th century, it was known by the Sanskrit name for town: *Pura*. It is divided
into Old Pekan (Pekan Lama) and New Pekan (Pekan Bharu); the former was
the exclusive abode of the Malay nobility for centuries.

There are two mosques in the centre of Pekan: the **Abdullah Mosque**, Jalan
Sultan Ahmad (beyond the museum), and the more modern **Abu Bakar
Mosque** next door. On the north outskirts of the town is the **Istana Abu
Bakar**, the royal palace, just off Jalan Istana Abu Bakar. Its opulent trimmings
are visible from the road, but it is closed to the public. The small but interesting **Sultan Abu Bakar Museum**, on Jalan Sultan Ahmad, is housed in a splendid colonial building and has a jet-fighter mounted Airfix-style in the front
garden. The museum includes a collection of brass and copperware, royal
regalia, porcelain from a wrecked Chinese junk and an exhibition of local arts
and crafts. In the back garden there is a depressing mini-zoo which rarely gets
visited. It is home to Malayan honey bears, a tapir, a collection of monkeys, a
black panther and a fish eagle, all squeezed into tiny cages. A good map of
Pekan is provided. ■ *0930-1700 Tue-Thu, Sat-Sun; 0930-1215, 1445-1700
Fri, RM1.*

D *Pekan*, 60 Jln Tengku Ariff Bendahara, T71378. A/c, restaurant, badly run, but quite   **Sleeping**
friendly people. **D** *Rumah Rehat* (rest house), beside the football field (*padang*), off Jln   *There is a poor*
Sultan Abu Bakar, T421240. A big, low-slung colonial building in need of a lick of paint   *selection of hotels in*
with a cool, spacious interior and big, clean rooms, restaurant. It is advisable to try to   *Pekan; the*
book accommodation in advance if visiting during the Sultan's birthday celebrations.   *government rest
house is the best bet*

Cheap *Pekan Hotel Restaurant*, 60 Jln Tengku Ariff Bendahara, nothing special.   **Eating**
There are a couple of reasonable coffee shops in the new town. The foodstalls on Jln
Sultan Ahmad, near the bus/taxi stands, are the best Pekan has to offer.

October *Sultan's Birthday* (24th: state holiday) celebrated with processions, dancing   **Festivals**
and an international polo championship which the sultan hosts on his manicured polo
ground at the istana.

Polo Matches are held in season; Prince Charles is said to have played here. The polo   **Sports**
field is surrounded by traditional Malay houses.

Bus Bus stop on Jln Sultan Ahmad in the centre of town. Regular connections with   **Transport**
Kuantan and from there onward although there are direct buses to **Mersing**.   *47 km S of Kuantan*
Taxi Taxis for **Kuantan** and elsewhere stand between Jln Sultan Ahmad and the
waterfront, opposite the indoor market.

Banks *Bumiputra*, 117 Jln Engku Muda Mansur. **Communications** Post Office: in   **Directory**
the middle of town.

East Coast Peninsula

Kuantan

Colour map 2, grid A5
Phone code: 09

*The modern capital of Pahang has a population of around 100,000 and is a bustling, largely Chinese, town at the mouth of the Kuantan River. Kuantan is the main transport and business hub for the east coast; most visitors spend at least a night here as a base to explore the mystical lake of **Tasek Cini**, the Semelai aboriginal kampungs of lake **Tasek Bera**, the **Caras Caves** and the adventure sports of the **Gunung Tapis Park**.*

Ins & outs

Getting there Kuantan's airport is 20 km from town. There are connections with KL, Kota Bahru and Kuala Terengganu as well as with Tioman. There are bus connections with all towns up and down the east coast as well as with key destinations on the west, including KL. Outstation taxis travel to Kuala Terengganu, KL and Mersing.

Getting around Kuantan is not a large town, despite its importance as a centre for transport connections to regions across the country. City buses provide a regular service to the beach and hotels at Teluk Cempedak and there are also a number of car hire firms in town.

Tourist offices *LKNP Tourist Information Centre* Jalan Mahkota, 25000 Kuantan, Pahang Darul Makmur, T 609- 516 1007, email: pkbf@tm.net.my Pleasant staff, very helpful, up-to-date information covers a large proportion of Malaysia, specifically Pahang states.

Sights While many tourists pass through Kuantan not many seem to stay longer than it takes to wipe their feet and take a couple of breaths before moving on, and wandering around the centre you are unlikely to meet many Westerners. It is noticeable, for example, that local people, while not unfriendly, do not speak very good English. When people do remain in the Kuantan area for any length of time they seem to stay in the fishing villages to the north and south of town.

East Coast Peninsula

Kuantan

Sleeping
1 Annex Rest House
2 Bersatu
3 Chusan
4 Cityview
5 Classic
6 Deluxe
7 Embassy & Suraya
8 Grand Continental
9 Kuantan
10 Makmur
11 Mega View

Kuantan's brand new **Sultan Ahmad Shah** mosque (also known as the Masjid Negeri), in the centre of town, is worth wandering around. Visitors are asked to don oversized hooded cloaks. These enormous cloaks, the time limits given to non-Muslim visitors by the stern yet surprisingly amused guards, and the restrictions placed on females, do not detract from the cool and calming beauty of the building. Freshly decorated in blue, green and white, with a cool marbled interior, the mosque can be seen across the town. It has blue and yellow stained-glass windows and the morning sun projects their coloured patterns on the interior walls. Kuantan has several streets of old shophouses which date from the 1920s. Most of the oldest buildings are opposite the padang on **Jalan Mahkota**. The **Kuantan River** might also qualify as a sight, such is the dearth of obvious things to see. The 300-km stretch of coast between Kuantan and Kota Bharu is comprised of long beaches, interspersed with fishing kampungs and the occasional natural gas processing plant and oil refinery.

Excursions

Just 4 km east of Kuantan is Teluk Cempedak, see page 268. There are regular connections on bus no 39 from the local bus station. A short walk north of Teluk Cempedak are Methodist Bay and Teluk Pelindong, which are beyond the range of most picknickers.

Teluk Cempedak

This is an amalgam of 13 freshwater lakes about 100 km southwest of Kuantan, see page 269. Getting there is not easy on public transport. See page 269 for details.

Tasek Cini

Temerloh is one of the best access points for Tasek Bera, or the lake of changing colours. There are several Jakun, so-called proto-Malays, and Semelai aboriginal kampungs (including the largest Kota Iskandar) around the lake, once a major centre for the export of jelutong resin, used as a sealant on boats and as jungle chewing gum. Similar to Tasek Cini (see page 269), Tasek Bera is

Lake Tasek Bera
The biggest natural lake in Malaysia

12 MS Garden	16 Pacific	20 Top One	● **Eating**
13 New Meriah	17 Shahzan Inn		1 Foodstalls
14 Orchid	18 Sin Nam Fong		2 Tiki's
15 Oriental Evergreen	19 Tong Nam Ah		

East Coast Peninsula

Dateline Kuantan: Churchill's Malayan nightmare

"In all the war, I never received a more direct shock," wrote former British wartime Prime Minister Winston Churchill in his memoirs. "As I turned and twisted in bed, the full horror of the news sank in upon me." On 10 December 1941 Churchill got the news that a Japanese air strike force operating from Saigon (South Vietnam) had destroyed and sunk two of the most powerful warships in the Royal Navy. HMS Prince of Wales, a 35,000-ton battleship, and HMS Repulse, a 32,000-ton battle cruiser, sank within an hour of each other, with the loss of 1,196 lives, 95 km off Kuantan.

A few days earlier the ships had arrived in Singapore, then the biggest naval operations base in the world, to underscore Britain's commitment to protecting its colonies in the East. They were soon speeding north in an effort to pre-empt and disrupt Japan's amphibious invasion of Malaya, but the flotilla, which had no air cover, was spotted by a Japanese submarine. The first wave of Japanese fighter-bombers arrived at 1100; by 1233, the Repulse, its thick armour-plated hull holed by five torpedoes, was sunk. The Prince of Wales went down 47 minutes later in about 60m of water. Accompanying destroyers rescued 1,900 men from the two vessels before retreating to Singapore, which fell to the Japanese Imperial Army eight weeks later. The wrecks of the two ships were declared war graves and in 1991, on the 50th anniversary of the Japanese attack, a team of British Navy divers laid white ensign flags on both ships to commemorate the dead.

a maze of shallow channels connecting smaller lakes, in all about 5 km wide and 27 km long. During the dry season it is little more than a swamp, but in the wet it becomes an interconnected array of shallow lakes. The Semelai traditionally exploited the expansion and contraction of the lake(s), fishing during the wet season and collecting non-timber forest products during the dry. When the waters reached their peak, and wild pigs became stranded on the many islands that dot the lake, the Semelai would hunt. One of the lake's resident species is the rare fish-eating 'false' gharial crocodile (*Tomistoma schlegeli*). Asli boatmen on the lake can be hired for about RM10 per day.

Do not attempt this trip without taking adequate supplies and provisions, including basic cooking utensils

■ *Getting there: there is no scheduled public transport to the lake. It is possible to take a bus or share taxi to Triang, due south of Temerloh, and then charter a taxi to the lake. Or take a taxi from Temerloh, an expensive option which may make sense in a group. Alternatively, bus from Kemayan to Bahau, 45 mins; bus from Bahau to Ladang Geddes, 30 mins; hitch or taxi to Kota Iskandar on the south side of the lake (where there are bungalows with cooking facilities, bookable through the Department of Aboriginal Affairs in Temerloh). Kota Iskandar is one of the best places on the peninsula to visit Orang Asli villages. Boats can be hired to explore the lake but requires enthusiastic negotiation.*

Caras Caves   These lie 25 km northwest of town; take a right fork at the 24 km mark. In 1954, the Sultan of Pahang gave a Thai Buddhist monk permission to build a temple in a limestone cave at Pancing, known as the 'yawning skull' cave. A steep climb up 200 stone steps leads into the cave which contains shrines and religious icons cut into the rock. The collection is dominated by a 9 m-long reclining Buddha, set among the limestone formations. There is always a monk in residence in the cave. ■ *Catch bus 48 running towards Sungai Lembing from the local bus station and get off at Pancing, from here it is 5 km to the caves, although it may be possible to catch a lift on the back of a motorbike.*

Beyond the caves is **Sungai Lembing**, an old tin mine and the site of some of the oldest tin workings on the peninsula. It claims to be the deepest tin mine in the world. It has now opened to visitors. To get there, take bus 48, every hour.

This is a new state park, 49 km from Kuantan, offering rafting, fishing (the local fish, ikankelah, is said to be delicious) and trekking. The park is centred on Gunung Tapis which rises to 1,500 metres and can be climbed in three days. However facilities are still poorly developed although there are camp sites. Permits can be obtained from the Sungai LambingTapis Resort (T 09-5411339) or made through the Tourist Information Centre in Kuantan or the local Outward Bound Society. It is only accessible by jeep via Sungai Lembing; from here accessible via a 12 km track. **Gunung Tapis Park**

Once a picturesque fishing kampung, 10 km north of Kuantan, Beserah has now become a rather touristy suburb of the town. But like Teluk Cempedak to the south it does provide a slightly quieter place to stay. To get there, take bus nos 27, 28, 30 from the main bus terminal in Kuantan, which all run through Beserah. Departures are every 30 minutes. **Beserah**

Essentials

The upmarket hotels are mostly at Teluk Cempedak (4 km north of Kuantan, see page 268). There are plenty of cheap Chinese hotels in Kuantan itself, mostly on and around Jln Teluk Sisek and Jln Besar. Several smart new hotels have sprung up in the **B-C** range which offer excellent value for money. **Sleeping**
■ *on map, page 262*
Price codes:
see inside front cover

AL *Golden Tulip Swiss Garden Resort*, Lot 2656 & 2657, Mukim Sungai Karang, Berserah, 8 km north of Kuantan town, T5447333, F5449555. An international class hotel on the beach with over 300 rooms, gardens and a good pool, business facilities, health club and sauna, and much more. **A** *Le Village Beach Resort*, Lot 1260 Sungai Karang, 8 km north of town, T5447900, F5447899, fal@tm.net.my Indian management, a pleasant enough place with a pool and tennis, getting popular with tour groups. **A** *Mega View Hotel*, 567 Jalan Besar, T5551888, F5553999/5553999. Large (150 rooms) and recently built multi-storey hotel on the banks of the Kuantan River. Conveniently situated, offering comfortable rooms with telephones and televisions, some with views over the river. Services include restaurant, coffee shop, drinks lounge and karaoke. Aimed at businessmen, it offers a health centre to help unwind. **A** *MS Garden Hotel*, Jln Lorong Garnbut T5555899, F5554558. An enormous hotel, which is very elegant inside, at the business end of town. Restaurant and coffee garden. Includes breakfast. Promotional offers available.
   B *Cityview Hotel*, Jln Haji Abdul, T5553888, F5552999, cityview@ pd.jaring.my Quite bare, with few extras but comfortable rooms. Good value. Breafast included. **B** *Hotel Grand Continental*, Jln Gambut, T5158888, F5159999, hgcktm@ pd.jaring.my, www.grandcentral.com.sg New addition to the *Grand Continental* chain, not much character but comfortable and smart, over 200 rooms all with a/c, TV, in-house movie, tea and coffee-making facility, other facilities include pool, coffee house, Chinese restaurant, health centre, business centre. Promotional rates available. **B-C** *Bersatu*, 2-4 Jln Darat Makbar (off Jln Wong Ah Jang), T5142328. A/c, TV, Cramped and run down, though the staff are friendly. Aimed at Malaysian businessmen.
   C *Classic*, 7 Bangunan LKNP, Jln Besar, T5554999, F5134141. A/c, extremely clean, big rooms and spacious attached bathrooms, certainly represents good value – Recommended. **C** *Shahzan Inn*, Lot 240 Jln Bukit Ubi, T5136688, F5135588. A/c, shower, TV. Hotel also has a pool, bar and restaurant in opulent environment. Complimentary

East Coast Peninsula

paper and breakfast included. **C-D** *Hotel Makmur* Lorong Pasar Baru 1, T5141363. A/c, clean and cheap. Decent size rooms, although not all have windows. More expensive rooms have bathrooms attached. **C** *Hotel Orchid* 11 Jalan Merdeka, T5555570. Family-run hotel, very clean, rooms are large with attached bathrooms. Friendly and helpful owners, a/c, special group rates and 24 hrs service. Although small, highly recommended. **C** *Pacific*, 60-62 Jln Bukit Ubi, T5141980, hpacifik@tm.net.my +A/c, the sixth floor has recently been renovated and upgraded, tasteful and recommended, good hotel in central location. But better value can be found elsewhere. **C** *Suraya*, 55-57 Jln Haji Abdul Aziz, T5154266, F5126728. A/c, coffee area, simple, well-appointed rooms, attached bathrooms, video, catering mainly for business people and domestic tourist market, good value.

D *Chusan*, 37-39 Jln Dato Wong Ah Jang, T5134422, F5130728. Friendly staff who deliver an English language paper to your room in the morning. However, the place is dirty and noisy. **D** *Deluxe*, 1st Flr, 53 Jln Wong Ah Jang (next to *Chusan Hotel*), T5131410. A/c, above all-night restaurant, small rooms, dirty, some rooms with no windows or inside toilets. The whole place has not seen any renovations in about the last 20 years and certainly does not live up to its name. **D** *Embassy*, 60 Jln Teluk Sisek, T5127486. Ac, well looked after, all rooms have attached bathroom, good value, above *Tanjung Ria* coffee shop, some rooms rather noisy because of main road. **D** *Hotel Top One*, 8-10 Jln Pasar Baru, T5139573. Some a/c, bathroom with hot water but dark and slightly dirty. **D** *New Meriah*, 142 Jln Telok Sisek, T5125433. A/c, TV, some rooms with attached bathrooms and hot water, very large and clean rooms but the exterior is grotty, there is a stairway and the whole ambience is run-down. **D** *Oriental Evergreen*, 157 Jln Haji Abdul Rahman, T5130168. A/c, Chinese restaurant, prominently advertised hotel. The décor leaves a bit to be desired, but it is clean and comfortable, great value. Slightly out of the way. Recommended.

E *Sin Nam Fong*, 44 Jln Teluk Sisek, T5121561. Restaurant, friendly management but when the traffic is heavy you might as well be camped on the central reservation. **E** *Tong Nam Ah*, 98 Jln Besar, T5144204. Fan, conveniently located for bus station and hawker stalls. Rooms are very basic (with a fan and basin), but what you would expect from the cheapest place in town.

Eating

Eating out may present difficulties due to the language barrier and the apparent reluctance of locals to accommodate the uninitiated

Mid-range *Cheun Kee*, Jln Mahkota, large open-air Chinese restaurant, good selection of seafood. **Cheap** *Cantina*, 16 Lorong Tun Ismail 1 (off Jln Bukit Ubi), smart a/c restaurant with waiters in batik bajus, Indonesian-style seafood and curries. Recommended by locals. *Kuantan Seafood*, Jln Wong Ah Jong, opposite *BKT* (*Restoran Malam*), hawker-style stalls in big open restaurant, very popular. **Seriously cheap** *Choo Kong*, Jln Mahkota, Chinese noodles, cold beer, marble top tables, basic but good. Recommended. *Kheng Hup*, 17 Jln Mahkota (on corner), opposite *Taman Salera Hawker Centre*, big, lively old coffee shop with marble-top tables and good *nasi lemak* and *nasi daggang* in the mornings, unchanged for 50 years. *Sri Patani*, 79 Bangunan Udarulaman, Jln Tun Ismail, excellent Malay/South Thai food. Recommended. *Z & Z*, 60 Jln Teluk Sisek (below *Embassy Hotel*), good breakfasts (especially *nasi lemak*), bright, sunny and friendly. *Tiki's*, Jln Mahkota (opposite Maybank), cheap Western fare and local dishes, good for Western-style breakfast. *Zul Satay*, junction of Jln Teluk Sisek and Jln Beserah (known as Kuantan Garden, between Kuantan and Teluk Cempedak), upmarket satay joint. All the usual plus rabbit and offal. Recommended. *Art Café*, Jln Besar (opposite *Classic Hotel*), new, surprisingly stylish coffee house.

Foodstalls Malay cafés and foodstalls along the river bank, behind the long distance bus station, busy and popular. Recommended, especially for seafood. There are more hawker stalls on junction of Jln Mahkota and Jln Masjid (Taman Salera), next to local bus station. *Kuantan Garden*, junction of Jln Teluk Sisek and Jln Beserah (between Kuantan and Teluk Cempedak), large number of Chinese stalls.

The Sampan Bar, on the *Hyatt Hotel* beachfront, is in the atap-roofed shell of a junk which beached in 1978 with 162 Vietnamese refugees aboard. The bar capitalizes on this slightly perverse novelty by charging more. *Boom Boom Bar* Jln Besar. Pool, bands and restaurant. Also on site, *Mini Boom Boom*, outdoor café.

Bars
The best bars and nightlife are along the beachfront at Teluk Cempedak

Books *Hamid Brothers*, 23 Jln Mahkota (this place is also a money changer, recommended locally for efficiency and reasonable rates). *Syarikat Ganesh*, 18C Jln Besar; *Teruntum Enterprise*, Wakil Dewan Bahasa, Jln Mahkota. Several craft shops along Jln Besar, expensive and touristy.

Shopping plaza *Kuantan Parade*, corner of Jalan Penjara and Jalan Haji Abdul Rahman. Brand new shopping plaza. Fully air conditioned, offers western chain stores to those experiencing consumer cold turkey.

Shopping

Golf *Royal Pahang Golf Club*, green fees RM100 weekdays, RM1500 weekends.

Sports

Kuantan River Cruise. For information and booking, Jabatan Perhubugan Awam, Majilis Perbandaran Kuantan, Jalan Tanah Putih, T5121555/5121666, amjpa2@mpk.gov.my Leaving from the jetty at the IBU Pejabat MPK, this cruise takes in the mangrove swamps and jungle surrounding the Kuantan River. Boats leave at 1100 and 1430 and the excursion takes between 1-2 hrs. RM10, (RM 5 for children).

Tour operators

Tours including trips around the Kuantan area, river tours and trips to Lake Kenyir (see page 294). *East Coast Holidays*, 13 Telok Cempedak, T 5665228. *Kenyir Lake Tourist*, 01-83 Jln Tun Ismail, T5105687; *Reliance*, 66 Jln Teluk Sisek, T5102566. *SMAS Travels*, 1st Flr, Kompleks Teruntum, Jln Mahkota, T5113888. *Syarikat Perusahaan*, 38, 2nd Flr, Bangunan DPMP, Jln Wong Ah Jang. *Taz Ben Travel & Tours*, 2nd Flr, Kompleks Teruntum, Jln Mahkota, T5102255.

Local Bus: local bus station is on junction of Jln Haji and Jln Abdul Rahman. Regular connections with Teluk Cempedak; for Cherating take bus no. 27. **Car hire**: *Budget*, 59 Jln Haji Abdul Aziz, T5126370 or *Coral Beach Resort*, 152 Sungai Karang, Beserah, T5447544. *Hertz*, *Samudra River View Hotel*, Jln Besar, T5122688. *National*, 49 Jln Teluk Sisek, T5127303.

Transport
219 km to Kuala Terengganu
229 km to KL
325 km to Johor Bahru

Long distance Air: Sultan Ahmad Shah Airport is 20 km south of town. Regular connections with **Johor Bahru**, **KL** and **Kuala Terengganu**. Taxis available for the journey to town (RM20). **Bus**: there is a new long distance bus station on Jln Stadium and companies have their offices on the second floor. Regular connections with **KL**, **Mersing**, **JB**, **Singapore**, **Melaka**, **Penang**, **Kuala Terengganu** and **Kota Bharu**. To get to **Cherating** take bus no. 27 from the local bus station on Jln Haji. **Taxi**: taxi station on Jln Besar, near intersection with Jln Abdul Rahman. **KL**, **Mersing** (RM100-150 for 4 people) and **Kuala Terengganu**.

Airline offices *MAS*, Ground Floor, Wisma Bolasepak Pahang, Jln Gambut, T5157055, F5157870; *Silk Air*, c/o MAS, T5157055, F5157870. **Banks** Along Jln Mahkota and Jln Besar, between GPO and bus station. **Communications** General Post Office: Jln Mahkota (east end). **Medical facilities** Hospitals: Jln Mat Kilau. **Useful addresses** Immigration Office: Wisma Persektuan, Jln Gambut, T5142155.

Directory

East Coast Peninsula

Teluk Cempedak

Colour map 2, grid A5
Phone code: 09

This beach resort is just 4 km east of Kuantan and marks the beginning of the beaches. The Pahang state government has reserved the 30 km stretch of coast from Teluk Cempedak beach north to the Terengganu state border exclusively for tourism-related projects, so there is likely to be much more development in the next few years. Teluk Cempedak was once the site of a quiet kampung, and is now a beach strip with a range of hotels, a string of bars and restaurants. There is a government-run handicraft shop (*Kedai Kraf*) beside the beach, specializing in batik.

Sleeping

Teluk Cempedak provides a more relaxed alternative to the noisier hotels in Kuantan

AL *Hyatt Regency Kuantan*, Telok Chempedak,T5661234, am@hrktn.com.my, www.hyatt.com A/c, several restaurants and bars, 2 pools, fitness centre, low-rise hotel in landscaped gardens and a beautiful setting on the beach, good sports (including watersports) facilities, well-stocked craft shop, well-managed with good views, Sampan Bar (formerly a Vietnamese refugee boat), an extension with new rooms was added recently. Friendly and efficient staff.. Recommended. **B-C** *Annex Rest House*, Jln Teluk Sisek, 2 km before Teluk Cempedak. Restaurant (rather inadequate), newly renovated, though we have had reports of bad service and broken down facilities, spacious grassy grounds. **B-C** *Kuantan*, opposite *Hyatt*, T5680026. A/c, restaurant, very clean, cheaper rooms fan only but all have attached bathroom, noisy television lounge, very pleasant terrace for sundowners, although it now faces the new Hyatt extension. The manager here is very helpful and friendly, and the place has a relaxed atmosphere. Recommended. **C** *Hill View*, a/c, restaurant in block of karaoke lounges, bars and restaurants, not good value for money.

Eating

Mid-range *Taj Mahal Curry House*, 13 Teluk Cempedak, North Indian cuisine plus fish-head curry. **Cheap** *Cempedak Seafood*, A-1122, Jln Teluk Sisek, big Chinese restaurant at the crossroads on the way to Teluk Cempedak, specialities: chilli crab and freshwater fish. *Pattaya*, on the beach front, good views of the beach, serves crab priced by weight, good food and good value. *Selera Warisan*, next door to the *Pattaya*. Good sea food and pleasant situation overlooking the beach. **Fastfood**: A sizeable McDonald's has, tragically, recently openednext to the *Pattaya Restaurant*. **Foodstalls**: group of *gerai makan* in newish brick kiosks, next to the beach alongside the Handicraft centre. They serve Malay,Thai, Chinese and Western food.

Bars

There are a number of bars along the seashore. One pub which comes recommended is the *Ranch Pub* (formerly the Country Ranch), not far from the *Hyatt Hotel*. New karaoke bars and pubs have sprouted up in town, most with a distinctly Western theme. *Lips* and *Urban Beach*, situated on the main road into Cempedak, opposite the Hyatt carpark, both offer beer and karaoke, possibly a bad combination, but they are friendly enough, and make up for the general absence of night life in Kuantan where many restaurants close early in the evening.

Tour operators

East Coast Holidays, 13 Teluk Cempedak, T5665228/5676839, helpful staff; they offer tours to Lake Cini, the Panching caves and waterfall, Kapas Island, Kuala Trengganu and a Turtle watching tour. Rates range from RM35 to RM130. The company also offers services such as flight reconfirmation, hotel reservation and car rental. *Mayflower Acme Tours*, Hyatt Kuantan, Teluk Cempedak, T5121469; *Morahols Travel*, 11 Teluk Cempedak, T5100851.

Transport

4 km E of Kuantan

Car hire *Avis*, Hyatt Hotel, Teluk Cempedak, T5661234, and Ground Floor, Loo Bros Bldg, 59 Jln Haji Abdul Aziz, T5123666; *Mayflower*, Hyatt Kuantan, Teluk Cempedak,

T5131234; *Sinat*, Lot 3, *Merlin Inn*, Teluk Cempedak, T5141388; *Thrifty*. **Bus** Regular
connections from Kuantan: bus 39 from the its local bus station. A short walk north of
Teluk Cempedak are Methodist Bay and Teluk Pelindong, which are beyond the range
of most picknickers.

Tasek Cini

Tasek Cini is an amalgam of 13 freshwater lakes, whose fingers reach deep into *Colour map 2, grid A4*
the surrounding forested hills, 100 km southwest of Kuantan. The lake and *Phone code: 09*
the adjoining mountain are sacred to the Malays; legend has it that Lake Cini is
the home of a huge white crocodile. The Jakun proto-Malay aboriginals, who
live around Tasek Cini, believe a *naga*, or serpent, personifying the spirit of
the lake, inhabits and guards its depths. Some commentators think that as
tourism picks up there, Tasek Cini will acquire the status of Scotland's Loch
Ness, although Lake Cini's monster has not been spotted now for 12 years.
Locals call their monster 'Chinnie'.

  More intriguing still are tales that the lake covers a 12th-14th century
Khmer walled city. The rather unlikely story maintains that a series of
aquaducts were used as the city's defence and that when under attack, the city
would be submerged. In late-1992, however, the *Far Eastern Economic Review*
reported that recent archaeological expeditions had uncovered submerged
stones a few metres underwater at various points around the lake. But the
Orang Asli fishermen do not need archaeologists to support their convictions
that the lost city exists. Between June and September the lake is carpeted with
red and white lotus flowers.

C *Lake Cini Resort*, T4086308/4567897. Ten chalets, some with attached bathrooms, **Sleeping**
camping (**F**), small restaurant attached to the resort serving simple dishes. **E** *Rajan
Jones Guest House*, this is the cheapest place to stay situated 30 mins' walk from the
Lake Cini Resort, room rate includes all meals but the accommodation is very basic, no
running water or electricity, tours and treks arranged.

There are a few tour companies which run package tours to the lake. Recom- **Tour operators**
mended is *Malaysian Overland Adventures*, Lot 1.23, 1st Flr, Bangunan
Angkasaraya, Jalan Ampang, Kuala Lumpur, T03-2413569.

Bus and boat Take the KL highway (Rt 2) from **Kuantan** towards **Maran**; 56 km down **Transport**
the road, Tasek Cini is signposted to the left. From here there used to be buses to *Getting to Tasek Cini*
Kampung Belimbing, a trip of 12 km, but there are reports that this service has been sus- *is difficult by public*
pended. If so, hitch or walk to Belimbing. At Belimbing it is possible to hire a boat across *transport; by far the*
the Pahang River and onto the waterways of Tasek Cini. It is also possible to be dropped *easiest way to visit*
off at the resort and picked up at an arranged time. An alternative way to get to Tasek Cini *the lake is on an*
is by catching a bus from **Kuantan** or **Pekan** for **Kampung Cini** (12 km from the resort). *organized tour*
From here there is a sealed road to the resort but, again, no public transport – although *(RM60). Contact the*
people have managed to persuade local motorcyclists to take them pillion. *Tourist Information*
Centre

Beserah

Once a picturesque fishing kampung, 10 km north of Kuantan, Beserah now *Colour map 2, grid A5*
sprawls and is not much more than a suburb of Kuantan. Beserah is a *Phone code: 09*
friendly place but aesthetically it bears little comparison with villages further
north. There is, however, a local handicraft industry still; there is a batik factory to the north of the village. The village's speciality is   *ikan bilis*, or

anchovies, which are boiled, dried and chillied on the beach and end up on Malaysian breakfast tables, gracing *nasi lemak* (rice cooked in coconut milk). Beserah's fishermen use water buffalo to cart their catch directly from their boats to the kampung, across the middle of the shallow lagoon. The kampung has become rather touristy in recent years, but there is a good beach, just to the north, at Batu Hitam.

Excursions **Kampung Sungai Ular** (Snake River Village), 31 km north of Kuantan, is a typical laid-back and very photogenic Malay fishing village. There is a small island, Pulau Ular, just offshore. The beach is usually deserted, is backed by coconut palms and has fine white sand. The Kampung is signposted to the right, just off the main road. Catch a bus running up the east coast road and asked to be dropped off at Kampung Sungai Ular.

Sleeping **A** *Coral Beach Resort* (formerly *Ramada*), 152 Sungai Karang (about 6 km north of
Most of the resort Beserah), T5447544, F5447543. A/c, restaurants, pool, paddling pool, playground,
hotels are around good range of facilities including tennis, squash, badminton, gymnasium, jacuzzi and
Sungai Karang, 3-6 watersports. Adjacent to fine white-sand beach, popular stop-over for cruises, hence
km N of Beserah its amphitheatre which can seat 800 people for cultural shows, all rooms spacious, a/c,
village itself TV, in-house video, mini-bar, tea and coffee-making facilities, non-smoking rooms available; *Reliance tour agency* in arcade. **A-B** *Le Village Beach Resort*, Sungai Karang, T5447900, F5447899. Restaurants, pool, beach front with watersport facilities, tennis, playground and paddling pool, neatly landscaped grounds with well-spaced chalets and a new 66-room extension, good atmosphere and attractive décor. **B** *Blue Horizon Beach Resort*, Kampung Balok (5 km north of Beserah), T5448119, F5448117. North of Beserah on good beach, pool, clean and spruce with big wooden chalet rooms, built around central area, garden a bit of a wilderness, discounts often available. **B** *Gloria Maris Resort* (1 km north of Beserah), T5447788, F5447619. A/c, restaurant, watersports, very small pool, sandwiched between road and Pasir Hitam (not such a good stretch of beach), small chalets and friendly management. **B** *Tiara Beserah Beach Resort*, 812 Jln Beserah, T5448101, F5141979. Thirty-two rooms in new atap-roofed chalets, a/c, TV, pool, café. **E** *La Chaumiere*, T5447662. This is the most popular of the budget places to stay, under French management it is well run and pleasant, to get here ask to be let off at Kampung Pantai Beserah and walk towards Kampung Pelidong and the sea, about 1 km. **E-F** *Jaffar's Place*, very rudimentary kampung accommodation, room rate includes all meals, away from the beach.

Eating **Mid-range** *Pak Su Seafood Restaurant*, popular Chinese restaurant on terrace next to the beach. Recommended. *Beserah Seafood*, Malay/Chinese, speciality: buttered prawns. *Gloria Maris Golden Cowrie Restaurant*, near the chalets, Malay/Indian/Thai and traditional Sun lunch at fixed price, seafood salad by weight.

Transport **Bus** Bus nos 27, 28 and 30 from Kuantan's main bus terminal all pass through Beserah, departures every 30 mins.

Temerloh Situated on the Pahang River, Temerloh is the halfway point on the
Phone code: 09 KL-Kuantan road and a popular makan stop. The Karak Highway tunnels through the Genting Pass, to the northeast of KL and the road then runs east through Mentakab (where there is a railway station) to Temerloh. From Temerloh it is possible to take a river trip to **Pekan**, the old royal capital of Pahang (see page 261) and to **Tasek Bera** (page 263). Frankly, there's not much to bring people to Temerloh, although it is emerging as an important administrative and service centre.

Sleeping and eating B *Hotel Green Park*, Lot 373, Jln Serendit, T2963055, F2962517. *The accommodation*
A/c, complimentary tea/coffee, TV, newly opened and smartly furbished. Recom- *in Temerloh is basic*
mended. **B** *Seri Malaysia Temerloh*, Lot 370/6/92, Jln Hamzah, T2965788, F2965711.
One of the new budget chain, a/c, TV, coffee/tea-making facilities, money changer,
restaurant, good value. Recommended. **C** *Kam San*, C-67 Jln Datuk Ngau Ken Lock,
T2965606. **C** *Rumah Rehat* (*Rest House*), Jln Datuk Hamzah, T2963254, F2963431.
Some a/c, restaurant, great position on the river, large rooms. Recommended. **C-D** *Ban*
Hin, 40 Jln Tangku, T2962331. Some a/c, better rooms with attached bathrooms, rea-
sonable. **D** *Kwai Pan*, 66 Jln Datuk Ngau Ken Lock, T2961431. **D-E** *Isis*, 12 Jln Tengku
Babar, T2963136. Some a/c, the best of the cheaper places to stay, more expensive
rooms with attached bathrooms.

Bus and taxi The bus terminal is close to the centre of town. Daily connections with **Transport**
KL's Pekeliling terminal, **Melaka**, **Penang**, **Kota Bharu**, **Kuantan**, **Alor Setar**,
Seremban, **Kuala Lipis**, **Kangar** and **Ipoh**. Taxis run to **KL**, **Kuantan**, **Mentakab** and
Jerantut. **Train** The nearest railway station is at **Mentakab**, 12 km west of Temerloh.
Connections south with **Singapore** and north to **Kota Bharu**, see page 45 for details of
timetabling.

Taman Negara National Park

Once known as King George V Park, Taman Negara was gazetted as a national *Colour map 1, grid C5*
park in 1938 when the Sultans of Pahang, Terengganu and Kelantan agreed to *Phone code: 09*
set aside a 43,000 ha tract of virgin jungle where all three states meet. Taman
*Negara is in a mountainous area (it includes **Gunung Tahan**, the highest moun-*
tain on the peninsula) and lays claim to some of the oldest rainforest in the world.
This area was left untouched by successive ice ages and has been covered in jungle
for about 130 million years which makes it older than the rainforests in the Congo
or Amazon basins.

Getting there Taman Negara straddles the mountainous interior of three states. **Ins & outs**
Because it is one of the most popular destinations on the peninsular there are lots of *Altitude: 2,187 m*
ways to get here. Most visitors get a bus or taxi to Kuala Tembeling jetty (there is a shuttle service from KL) where there are boats to the Park HQ at Kuala Tahan, a 2½-hr
upriver trip. It is also possible to take a train to Tembeling Halt (but tell the guard as it is
an unscheduled stop!); from here it is a 30-min walk to the jetty.

Best time to visit Between March and September, during the dry season. The park
may be closed during the height of the monsoon season from the beginning of
November to the end of December, when the rivers are in flood, although this isn't
always the case.

Gunung Tahan is the highest of three peaks on the east side of the park, and
marks the Pahang-Kelantan border. Its name means 'the forbidden mountain': according to local Asli folklore the summit is the domain of a giant monkey, who guards two pots of magic stones. The first expeditions to Gunung
Tahan were despatched by the Sultan of Pahang in 1863 but were defeated by
the near-vertical-sided Teku Gorge, the most obvious approach to the mountain, from the Tahan River. The 1,000 m-high gorge ended in a series of waterfalls which came crashing 600 m down the mountain. Several other ill-fated
European-led expeditions followed, before the summit was finally reached by
four Malays on another British expedition in 1905.

East Coast Peninsula

Until the park was set up, **Kampung Kuala Tahan**, now the site of the park headquarters, was one of the most remote Orang Asli villages in North Pahang, at the confluence of the Tembeling and Tahan rivers. This area of the peninsula remained unmapped and mostly unexplored well into the 20th century. These days, Kuala Tahan is sometimes over-run with visitors; park accommodation has expanded rapidly under private sector management. But most visitors do not venture more than a day or two's walk from headquarters, and huge swaths of jungle in the north and east sections of the park remain virtually untouched and unvisited. Taman Negara now has scores of trails, requiring varying amounts of physical exertion; the toughest walk is the nine-day Gunung Tahan summit trek.

The range of vegetation in the park includes riverine species and lowland forest to upland dwarf forest on the summit of Gunung Tahan. Over 250 species of bird have been recorded in Taman Negara, and wildlife includes wild ox, sambar, barking deer, tapir, civet cat, wild boar and even the occasional tiger and elephant herd. However, the more exotic mammals rarely put in an appearance, particularly in the areas closer to Kuala Tahan.

Hides Some hides or *bumbun* are close to the park headquarters, as close as a five-minute walk, and nearly all are within a day's walk or boat ride. Visitors can stay overnight, but there are no facilities other than a sleeping space (sheets can be borrowed from Kuala Tahan for RM5 per night) and a pit latrine. Take a powerful torch to spotlight any animals that visit the salt-licks. You are more likely to see wildlife at the hides further from the Park HQ, as the numbers of people now visiting Taman Negara have begun to frighten the animals away. Rats are not frightened: food bags must be tied securely at night. During popular periods and on weekends it is best to book your spot at a salt-lick.

Permits The Department of Wildlife has a bureau at the Kuala Tembeling jetty (see below) and issues permits and licences. Park permit RM1; fishing licence RM10; camera licence RM5; camping fee RM2, canopy walk RM5.

Fishing Fishing is better further from Kuala Tahan; there are game-fishing lodges near the confluence of the Tenor and Tahan rivers, at Kuala Terenggan (up the Tembeling from Kuala Tahan) and at Kuala Kenyam, at the confluence of the Kenyam and the Tembeling. The best months to fish are February-March and July-August; during the monsoon season. At the height of the monsoon, in November and December travel can be difficult and the park sometimes closed. The rivers Tahan, Kenyam and the more remote Sepia (all tributaries of the Tembeling) are reckoned to be the best waters. There are more than 200 species of fish in the park's rivers including the *kelasa* which is a renowned sport fish. A permit costs RM10, rods for hire (see also Booking, Equipment and Sleeping, below).

River trips Boat trips can be arranged from Park HQ to the Lata Berkoh rapids on Sungai Tahan (near Kuala Tahan), Kuala Terengganu (several sets of rapids to be negotiated), and to Kuala Kenyam (from where a trail leads to the top of a limestone outcrop). A trip to the rapids, misleadingly called a waterfall, by park authorities, on a boat that accommodates four passengers will cost RM80. Although this is a comparatively expensive way to see the park it is probably the most enchanting and when split between a number of people (boats carrying up to 12 people can be booked) is worthwhile.

Treks

Trails are signposted from Park HQ. Tours are conducted twice daily by park officials and these include night walks (RM15 per person), cave treks (RM35) and other treks and walks. Because most visitors tend to stick to the trails immediately around the Park HQ, even a modest day's outing will take you away from the crowds. A full listing and details on various routes can be obtained at Park HQ. Independent day treks/walks can be taken to caves, swimming holes, waterfalls, along rivers (again with swimming areas), to salt-licks and hides, and, of course, through forest. Longer overnight treks are also possible although guides must be taken on all these longer forays. The most demanding is climbing Gunung Tahan.

This is a nine-day trek to the summit and back. It is best climbed in February and March, the driest months. **Day 1**: Kuala Tahan to Kuala Melantai (four to five hours). **Day 2**: Kuala Melantai to Kuala Puteh (eight hours). No streams en route; succession of tough climbs along the ridge, final one is Gunung Rajah; 1½ hours descent to campsite by Sungai Tahan. **Day 3**: Kuala Puteh to Kuala Teku (2½-4½ hours). Route follows Sungai Tahan, which must be crossed several times. The campsite is at the Sungai Teku confluence and was the base camp for the first successful Gunung Tahan expedition in 1905. **Day 4**: Kuala Teku to Gunung Tangga Lima Belas (seven hours). Long uphill slog (4½ hours) to Wray's Camp (named after 1905 expedition member). This is a good campsite; alternatively climb through mossy forest to Gunung Tangga Lima Belas campsite, which has magnificent views, but is very exposed. **Day 5**: Gunung Tangga Lima Belas to summit, returning to the Padang. After a scramble up the side of a rockface on Gunung Gedong, the trail leads to the Padang – a plateau area (three to four hours). Set up tents and leave equipment at campsite; route to summit follows ridge and takes 2½ hours. Essential to take raincoat; summit often shrouded in mist. Begin descent to the Padang by 1600. **Days 6-9**: Padang to Kuala Tahan, following the same route. **Hiring a guide** A guide is necessary for this climb (around RM400 per week, RM50 for each additional day); maximum of 12 people with one guide. **NB** A sleeping bag and a tent are vital, all of the camps have water and firewood.

Another mountain in Taman Negara that is less frequently climbed is **Gunung Gagau** (1,377 m), far to the northeast of Kuala Tahan. It is a six to seven day trek of which one day is spent travelling up river on Sungai Sat. This area of the park is rarely visited and it is advisable to take a guide.

The Canopy Walk, half an hour from headquarters, is worth a visit in order to take in jungle life at close proximity. The walkway is suspended about 30 m above the forest floor and stretches for over 400 m. ■ *1100-1500 Sat-Thu and 0900-1200 Fri, RM5.*

For trekking it is worth having walking boots for even the shortest of excursions as rain turns mud paths into skid patches, a thick pair of socks and long (loose) trousers. Leeches are common in the park after rain, spraying clothes and boots with insect repellent and wearing leech socks helps. Having said this, minimal clothing is needed, as it's hot work. A good torch is essential equipment for those going to hides and a water bottle is also essential on longer walks and treks. A raincover may be useful. Visitors are not permitted to carry glass into the park. The shop at Park HQ hires out torches, tents, water bottles, cooking equipment and fishing tackle - even jungle boots. Camera permit RM5.

Gunung Tahan
Altitude: 2,187 m

East Coast Peninsula

Equipment

Booking

Those who risk turning up at the Kuala Tembeling jetty without booking may be turned away if boats are full

Visits to the national park can be arranged individually or be pre-arranged at *River Park Sdn Bhd*, 260 h, 2nd Mile Jalan Ipoh, KL, T032915299 or *Malaysian Tourist Information Centre* (MATIC), Jalan Ampang, KL, T032643929 ext 25. Visitors are required to pay a RM30 deposit to confirm bookings for the park boat and accommodation at Kuala Tahan (Park HQ). The boat to headquarters costs RM15 per person (one way).

Park headquarters

At Kuala Tahan, on the south boundary of the park, accessible by boat from Kuala Tembeling, a two-to three-hour beautiful journey. At Kuala Tahan all visitors are required to check in at the reception desk. ■ *0800-2200, Mon-Sun. Park headquarters provide a range of facilities, although prices tend to be steep, including shop, restaurant, money changing facilities (poor rates), telephone service, equipment hire, etc.*

Tours

Various companies run tours to Taman Negara. It is a more expensive way to visit the park, but permits, itineraries, etc are well organized in advance. Many visitors, particularly those unfamiliar with travelling in Malaysia, have recommended tours for their logistical advantages. Since the park has been run privately, however, it has become much more user-friendly and it is easy to visit independently. The disadvantage of independent travel is that tour groups tend to book up the hides. *Asia Overland Services*, 35M Jalan Dewan Sultan

Taman Negara

Sleeping

1 Taman Negara Resort & Park HQ

Sulaiman Satu (off Jalan Tunku Abdul Rahman), Kuala Lumpur, T2925622, three-day safari US$245. *Malaysia Overland Adventures*, Lot 1.23, 1st Flr, Bangunan Angkasaraya, Jalan Ampang, Kuala Lumpur, T032413659. *NKS Hotel & Travel SDN BHD*, in Sri Emas Hotel, Jln Besar, Jerantut, T2664499, F2664801. *Overland Discovery Tours*, Unit 5, 1st Podium Flr, *Shangri-La Hotel*, 11 Jalan Sultan Ismail, Kuala Lumpur, T2302942. *Scenic Holidays and Travel*, Lot SO64, 2nd Flr Sungai Wang Plaza, Jalan Sultan Ismail, Kuala Lumpur, T2424522. *SPKG Tours*, 16th Flr LKNP Building, Bandar Baru, Jerantut, T262369, F2664369. *Tuah Travel & Tours*, 12 Jalan Lipis, Kuala Lipis, T312144. *Camp Nusa*, 16 LKNP Building, New Town Jerantut, T262369, F264369. Packages can also be organized by Kuala Tahan Office, Taman Negara Resort, Kuala Tahan, T263500, F261500.

Essentials

Kuala Tahan and Kampung Kuala Tahan The management of *Taman Negara* was handed over to the private sector in 1990. All accommodation for the *Taman Negara Resort* must be booked in advance, either direct to Taman Negara Resort, Kuala Tahan, 27000 Jerantut, Pahang T09-2663500, F092661500 or through the sales office: 2nd Floor, *Hotel Istana*, no. 73 Jln Raja Chulan, T032455585, F032455430. The resort encompasses a range of rooms and types of accommodation (some with self-catering facilities): starting at the bottom of the range are bunk beds in the hostel (8 people per dorm) with communal facilities at RM40 per person including breakfast. Moving up, rooms in the original accommodation centre cost RM110. Self-contained chalets and bungalows range from the standard wooden chalet at RM216, to RM300 for the deluxe chalet, to RM600 for 2-bedroom suite bungalows. Note that it is also possible to camp (see below).

    An alternative to the park is to stay in **Kampung Kuala Tahan**, on the other side of the river (which can be crossed by a small boat for 50c throughout the day – last boat 2300), where accommodation is much cheaper – albeit slightly less convenient. **B** *Teresek Hill View*, T2663065, range of places to stay including dorm beds, basic chalets and more sophisticated bungalows with attached bathrooms. **E** *Argoh Chalets*, basic doubles with fan and shower RM 35, dorm beds also available. **E** *Liana Hostel*, T2669322, basic with 4 beds per room. **D-F** *Nusa Camp*, T2662369, F2664369, restaurant, across the river from Park HQ and then 15 mins upriver, Offers a range of accommodation including dorms with two bunk beds per room, bungalows with attached bathrooms, and also tents for hire, the owner 'Byoing' is keen to help and will organize trips to the rapids (not particularly exciting), various hikes and trips to an Orang Asli village. To get to *Nusa Camp* take one of the longboats from Park HQ (there is a shuttle boat every 2 hrs); they also run a direct service from Kuala Tembeling with boats leaving at 0900 and 1400 every day (Fri 1430). **E-F** *Tembeling Hostel*, much like *Liang* in price and standard, but 2 beds per room.

    Accommodation elsewhere in the Park In addition, there are a number of fishing lodges in the park, in which beds and mattresses are provided; there is no bedding or cooking equipment however. These can be booked at Kuala Tahan HQ (RM8 per night). Visitor Lodges (**B**) for hides at **Kuala Terenggan** and **Kuala Kenyam** can also be booked from Kuala Tahan HQ. These are right away from the crowds but are surprisingly comfortable with attached bathrooms and restaurant. There is no charge for staying in the hides themselves.

Sleeping

Camping

The landscaped campsite can accommodate up to 200, but fortunately never does. *Taman Negara Resort* rents out tents (2/3/4-person) for RM6-12 per night. There is an additional RM1 fee for use of the campsite. Tents, once hired, can be taken with you on

East Coast Peninsula

treks. There are communal toilet facilities and lockers are available. **Hides** It is possible to spend a night in one of the wildlife observation hides. These are raised up among the trees at Tabang, Belau, Yong, Cegar Anjing and Kumbang.

Eating

Because of the cost of food at the resort, many tourists prefer to bring their own

The resort operates two restaurants and a bar – the rotan and bamboo *Tembeling Lounge* which even gets daily newspapers, it is open 1100-2400, Mon-Sun. The *Tahan Restaurant* and *Teresek Cafeteria* serve both local and Western cuisine; the former is more expensive, both are open 0700-2300 Mon-Sun. On the other side of the river at **Kampung Kuala Tahan** are a number of floating restaurants which serve unremarkable food but at prices considerably lower than those in the park complex. Beer, though, tends to be expensive.

Useful services

The *Taman Negara Resort* include an overpriced mini market (selling provisions for trekking and camping, open 0800-2230), a clinic (open 0800-1615 Mon-Sun; hospital attendant on call 24 hrs, for emergencies), a mini-post office and a library. There is also a jungle laundry service. In the 'Interpretative Room', there is a thrice daily film and slide-show on the park's flora and fauna (2045 Mon-Sun).

Transport

All access to Taman Negara – other than for those who fly in – is by longboat from Kuala Tembeling

Air There is an airstrip at Sungai Tiong (30-mins boat ride from Kuala Tahan). Over the years both *Pelangi Air* and *Kris Air* have operated irregular flights from KL.

Boat It is a 59-km journey from **Kuala Tembeling** jetty, up the **Sungai Tembeling** to **Kuala Tahan** (Park HQ), 2½ hrs, depending on river level; departures at 0900 and 1400 (1430 on Fri). The return trip takes 2 hrs; departures at 0900 and 1400. *Nusa Camp* also operates a boat service from Kuala Tembeling to their own resort (see **Sleeping**, above). Although it is now possible to go by road all the way to Kampung Kuala Tahan the boat journey is far more interesting and enjoyable.

Bus/taxi The easiest way into the park is to catch one of the direct tourist mini-buses from **KL** to **Kuala Tembeling**, where the jetty for boats to the park is situated. Most guesthouses in KL can arrange tickets and also some tour companies. The nearest town to Kuala Tembeling is **Jerantut** where there is a range of accommodation. For those who want to use regular public transport or who are travelling from elsewhere, there are regular connections from **KL** via **Temerloh** (see Jerantut entry below for details). There is now a road all the way from **Jerantut** to **Kampung Kuala Tahan** but it is rough and requires 4WD – transport is provided by guesthouses in Jerantut but it means missing out on the river journey.

Train **Tembeling Halt**, the nearest stop for **Kuala Tembeling**, is accessible from **Kuala Lumpur**, **Kota Bharu** and **Singapore**. It is necessary to inform the guard/conductor if you want to alight at Tembeling Halt, as it is still an unscheduled stop. From there it is a 30-min walk to the jetty at **Kuala Tembeling**. From **Kota Bharu**: to **Tembeling Halt**; departures from Wakaf Bharu station (outside KB) at 1150 on Sun, Tue, Wed and Fri. From **KL**: trains to **Tembeling Halt**, via **Gemas** (on KL-Singapore line). The overnight sleeper departs 2200, arrives Tembeling Halt 0630. From **Singapore**: change at **Gemas**; connections to **Tembeling Halt** at 0530 Mon-Sun. Note that trains rarely pick up at Tembeling Halt and the nearest regular station is at **Mela**, a short bus journey away from the jetty.

Jerantut

Phone code: 09

The nearest town to Kuala Tembeling, the most popular entry point into Taman Negara, is Jerantut some 16 km away; a trip that costs RM15 by taxi. For those travelling to the park on public transport it may be necessary to spend a night here and there is a range of accommodation on offer.

Sleeping and eating **B** *Sri Mas Hotel*, T2664499, F2664801, howann@tm.Net.my *There are a number of* Some a/c, shower, the most sophisticated hotel in town, excellent source of informa- *Malay-style coffee* tion on the park, free transport to and from bus/rail station. *NKS Tour* who run the hotel *shops in town as well* will also organize trips to the park and will book your accommodation there, dorm *as the usual stalls in* beds available – as well as a storeroom to leave your luggage while you are in the park. *the market area* (**F**). Internet cafe, movies and a (poor) restaurant here. Recommended. **C-D** *Jerantut Resthouse*, T2666200, nkstour@hotmail.com (also run by *NKS*). Some a/c, restaurant, popular place with range of options including a/c rooms with attached bathrooms, simple fan rooms, and dorm beds (**F**), they organize daily trips to the park. **E** *Chet Fatt Hotel*, T2665805 adequate. **E** *Hotel Piccadilly*, T2662895 312 Sungai Jan.

Transport   Bus and taxi   The bus and taxi station in **Jerantut** is in the centre of *16 km to Kuala* town. Regular connections from **KL**'s Pekeliling terminal via **Temerloh**. Taxis direct to *Tembeling* **Jerantut** from **KL** leave from the Puduraya bus terminal. From the east coast, there are hourly buses from **Kuantan** to **Jerantut** as well as taxis. For **Kuala Tembeling** (and Taman Negara) there are buses and taxis; some of the guesthouses also lay on mini-buses. There is now a road all the way from **Jerantut** to **Kampung Kuala Tahan** but it is rough and requires 4WD. Transport is provided by guesthouses in Jerantut but it means missing out on the river journey.

   Train   Jerantut is accessible from **KL**, **Kota Bharu** and **Singapore**. From **Kota Bharu**: to **Jerantut**; departures from Wakaf Bharu station (outside KB). There are two options: the slow, but scenic jungle train, departs 0615 and arrives Jerantut at 1630; or the express train, departs Wakaf Bharu 2020 arrives Jerantut at 1340. From **KL**: trains to **Jerantut**, via **Gemas** (KL-Singapore line) including overnight sleeper. From **Singapore**: change at **Gemas** for connections to Jerantut.

Kuala Lipis and the Kenong Rimba National Park

Kuala Lipis is a pleasant and relaxed town on the Jelai and Lipis rivers, 100 km *Colour map 1, grid C4* north east of Fraser's Hill. Unlike other Malay towns it has not been thought- *Phone code: 09* lessly redeveloped and many colonial buildings still survive. This is probably because Malaysia's development has passed Kuala Lipis by. At the end of the 19th century it grew to prominence as a gold mining town and, for a short period, was the area's administrative capital. However, gold fever has passed (although the mines have recently been re-opened) and the town's adminis-trative role passed to Kuantan in 1955. Today, as well as being a good base from which to trek to Kenong Rimba, it has not inconsiderable charms.

Kenong Rimba Park is 1½ hours east of Kuala Lipis by boat down the Jelai **Excursions** River to Kampung Kuala Kenong. The park, which encompasses the Kenong River valley and encompasses some 120 sq km, is the home of the *Batik Orang Asli* tribe, who are shifting cultivators. There is a network of Asli trails around the park and several caves and waterfalls. There are two campsites along the river; the first, *Kesong Campsite*, has three atap huts which serve as basic accommodation. There are also some simple huts, the *Persona Chalets*, at Gunung Kesong. The park is a good alternative to Taman Negara. Though it may not have the same variety of animal life (and especially large mammals) it is less touristed and trekking here is cheaper. Note that a registered guide is required. For tours and treks to Kenong Rimba, see **Tours** below. Entrance to the park is to Batu Sembilan (accessible on the jungle train), and from there by boat to Jeti Tanjung Kiara.

East Coast Peninsula

Tours Mr Appu Annandaraja who runs the *Kuala Lipis Hotel* (see **Sleeping** below) comes highly recommended as a trek organizer. He organizes a four-day trek including food and boat transport in and out of Kenong Rimba for approximately US$65. Another guesthouse which organizes trips to the park for much the same price is the *Gin Loke Hotel*, 64 Jalan Besar. Organized treks into Kenong Rimba are also run by *Tuah Travel & Tours*, 12 Jalan Lipis, Kuala Lipis, T312144. There are other registered freelance guides who can be hired from Kuala Lipis.

Sleeping **B** *Taipan*, Jln Lipis Bentar, T3122555. A/c, new hotel on the outskirts of town and the most expensive place to stay. **C-D** *Rumah Rehat* (*Rest House*), T3122599. Some a/c, this place was formerly the home of the British Resident in Pahang, large rooms with attached bathrooms, certainly the most atmospheric of places to stay in Kuala Lipis, outside town on a hill. **D** *Hotel Kuala Lipis* (aka *Appu's Guesthouse*), 63 Jln Besar, T3121388. Some a/c, shared bathrooms run by Mr Appu who runs highly recommended tours to Kenong Rimba (see tours), good source of information. Recommended. **D** *Hotel Jelai*, 44 Jln Jelai, T3121192. Near the Jelai River, small, clean rooms, shared bathrooms with hot water and reasonable value. **D** *Hotel Sri Pahang*, T3122445, some a/c, clean and well-run place. **E** *Gin Loke*, 64 Jln Besar, T3121388. Simple rooms, shared facilities, organizes treks into Kenong Rimba. **E** *Hotel Tongkok*, Jln Besar, T3121027. Clean, good value.

Transport **Bus** Regular bus connections with **Kuala Lumpur** leave from the Pekeliling bus terminal in KL. Daily connections from **Kuala Lipis** with **Kota Bharu** and **Kuantan**. There are also connections with **Fraser's Hill**. **Train** The *Golden Blowpipe* train, travels from **Kuala Lumpur** through **Kuala Lipis**. There are also slow jungle trains and connections with **Kota Bharu** and **Jerantut/Tembeling Halt** (for Taman Negara). Connections with **Singapore**, either direct or via **Gemas**.

Kampung Cherating

Colour map 1, grid C6
Phone code: 09

A quiet seaside village, set among coconut palms, a short walk from the beach, Kampung Cherating has become a haven for those who want to sample kampung life or just hang out in a simple chalet-style budget resort. Over the years it has metamorphosised into something a little more sophisticated and more upmarket.

Ins & outs **Getting there** The nearest airport is at Kerteh, 40 km to the north; connections with KL. Bus stop on the main road around 500 m from the kampung itself, down two lanes. Connections with most destinations on the east coast as well as with Singapore and KL.

Sights Cherating never was much of a kampung until the tourists arrived – there was a small charcoal 'factory', using *bakau* mangrove wood, but the local economy is now entirely dependent on sarong-clad Westerners and, more recently, growing numbers of Malaysian and Singaporean tourists. The beach at Cherating is big, but not brilliant for swimming because the sea is so shallow. However while it was dirty and rather unkempt at our visit before last, when we most recently visited the beach is was clean and well cared for.

Cherating is named after the sand-crabs which are very common along the beach. They may look like heavily armoured tanks, but they are not dangerous. There are a couple of very private and beautiful little beaches tucked into the rocky headland dividing Cherating beach and the *Club Med* next door. These are more easily accessible from the sea (boats can be hired from the kampung) than from the steep trail leading over the promontory. This path goes right over to the *Club Med* Beach which is private. Bathers and sun-bathers should be prepared for periodic low-level fly-pasts by the Royal Malaysian Army whose helicopters swoop over the beaches.

Cherating has grown explosively in recent years. Big, modern resort complexes have sprung up 3-km south of the original kampung; it is known as Cherating Bharu, or New Cherating. The old roadside village (together with the string of atap-roofed chalet resorts) is called Cherating Lama, or Old Cherating. Although the old kampung atmosphere has been irreversibly tempered by the arrival of *Anchor* Beer and the population explosion, Cherating is still a peaceful haunt with some excellent places to stay and one or two of the best bars in Malaysia. Cherating's Malay residents have taken the boom stoically – although their obvious prosperity has helped them tolerate the 'cultural pollution'.

It is possible to hire boats to paddle through the mangroves of the Cherating River, to the south side of the kampung, where there is a good variety of birdlife as well as monkeys, monitor lizards and otters. For a price there are also demonstrations of silat, the Malay martial art, top-spinning, kite-flying and batik-printing in the village. There are some monkeys in the kampung which are trained to pluck coconuts. A couple of kilometres up the road, on Cendor Beach, green turtles come ashore to lay their eggs; they are much smaller than the leatherbacks which lay their eggs at Rantau Abang, further north. Cherating is also a good base to visit some of the sights in this part of the east coast including Tasek Cini (see page 269) and the Caras Caves (see page 264), for example.

Boat trips These are organized from The River Sports Centre and the two other tourist information centres (see below) and by several beach hotels/chalets, six people are needed to fill a boat, with a full boat approximately RM8 per person, depending on distance up river.

East Coast Peninsula

Kampung Cherating

Sleeping			Eating
1 Cherating Bay Resort	4 Cherating Cottage	11 Kampung Inn	1 Driftwood
2 Cherating Bayview Resort	5 Cherating Holiday Villa	12 Legend	2 Intan
3 Cherating Beach Mini Motel	6 Cherating Inn & Restaurant	13 Mak De's House	3 Mimi's
	7 Cherating Palm Resort	14 Mak Long Teh's Guesthouse	4 Seaside Seafood
	8 Cherating Ria Garden	15 Moon	5 Sunrise Seafood
	9 Coconut Inn	16 Ranting Resort	
	10 Duyong Beach Resort & Restaurant	17 Residence Inn	
		18 Riverside	
		19 Tanjung Inn	

Essentials

Sleeping Many new bungalows and chalets have sprung up along the beach in the past decade; larger developments including the *Impiana* resort which has gone up about 2 km north of Cherating Lama. There is a good range of accommodation available, from simple kampung-style stilt-houses and 'A'-frame huts to upmarket chalets. Some of the accommodation in the kampung proper is family run; 'A'-frame and chalet accommodation is along the beach. The smarter, plusher hotels 3 km down the road at Cherating Bharu are much closer to the sea –and have a much nicer stretch of beach. 'A'-frame huts start at about RM10-15 while the more salubrious chalets cost from RM30-60. Note that the mid- and upper-range places whose guests are predominantly Malaysians and Singaporeans on weekend breaks, usually offer discounts during the week.

L-A *Cherating Holiday Villa*, Lot 1303, Mukim Sungai Karang, T5819500. A/c, restaurant, disco (boasts to be largest in town), pool, 2 rooms and 13 Malaysian chalets – corny but nice inside. Recommended. **AL** *Impiana Resort Cherating*, Km 32, Jln Kuantan, T5819000, F5819090. A hotel with 250 rooms in spacious buildings elegantly decorated with wood and rattan, good range facilities including pool, kid's pool, outdoor jacuzzi, tennis, children's playground and playhouse with caretaker. Two restaurants, pub with happy hour, all rooms have balconies facing sea, a/c, fan, TV, in-house movies, CNN, minibar, tea/coffee-making facilities, four-poster wooden beds with nets. Recommended. **AL** *Legend*, Lot 1290, Mukim Sungai Karang (Cherating Bharu), T5819818. A/c, Italian and Thai restaurant, huge pool, villas near the beach with smartly appointed rooms, sports centre, tennis courts, watersports facilities, disco, rooms, which overlook big garden and beach, are pleasant and bright. Recommended.

A *Canoona Beach Resort* (just north of *Holiday Villa*, Cherating Bharu), pleasant hotel with chalet blocks in grounds next to beach. **A** *Club Med* (round the headland from Kampung Cherating), T439131/591131. A/c, restaurant, totally self contained resort designed to resemble a Malay village – private beach, watersports facilities, body-building classes and evening entertainment, minimum stay: two nights. Closed Nov-Jan. The 'Circus Village' teaches children and adults to juggle, walk a tightrope or fly a trapeze – will be familiar to those who know Club Meds elsewhere. **A-B** *Cherating Bay Resort*, T0193523836. Large new place with pool and children's play area, all rooms a/c. Five minute walk from the beach.

B *Cherating Bayview Resort*, Cherating Lama, T6095819248, F5819415, www.cheating.homstead.com Modern chalets on beach front, some with a/c and TV, restaurant, a good mid-range place to stay. Slightly overpriced for the fan rooms, shower and breakfast included in the room rate (although the owner warns that breakfast is not always guaranteed!). **B** *Residence Inn Cherating*, T5819333, F5819252, richotel@tm.net.my, www.ric.com.my Located on the same lane as *The Moon*, at the northern end of the village, between the main road and the 'village street'. Pool, kid's pool, jacuzzi, restaurant, disco, karaoke, comfortable rooms with a/c, minibar, TV, tea/coffee-making facilities. Breakfast included, attractive hotel which is also host to various cultural events.

C *Cherating Palm Resort*, T5819378 F5819328. Hotel apartments have recently closed down but clean modern chalets with TV, a/c, bathroom all set in an immaculately maintained garden are still available. Good value. **C** *Duyong Beach Resort*, Batu 28, T5819189 (left at end of lane from main road, at far end). A large number of modern chalets on the beach next to jungled hillside, mainly attracts Malaysian and Singaporean tourists, some rooms with a/c and TV. **C** *Ranting Resort*, T5819068 (turn left at bottom of lane from main road bridge). Popular restaurant (Western and local dishes), extra for a/c and 2-room chalets on stilts, no TV, quite smart. **C** *Tanjung Inn*, turn right at bottom of lane down from main road, after *Coconut Inn*, T5819081, tanjunginn@jaring.my, www.tanjunginn.com.my Attractive choice of accommodation ranging from first class big bungalows for families to budget chalets (with communal shower and toilet), restaurant, set in carefully tended and landscaped grounds with palms and two ponds, has a good restaurant which serves excellent breakfasts. This is a charming place to stay and has won the second prize for best-kept accommodation in the state of Pahang. Recommended.

D *Kampung Inn*, right at end of lane from main road, at far end on left, T5819344. Fan, shower – nothing too special with very average chalet accommodation and 'A'-frames and not much atmosphere, but advantageously located near *Boathouse Bar* and close to beach. Hugely overpriced. **D** *Cherating Cottage*, T5819273. A range of accommodation, from dorms to large a/c chalets all set in spacious gardens. Better value can be found elsewherealthough the place does have the advantage of a central location; the restaurant is slightly expensive. **D** *Cherating Beach Mini Motel*, T5819335. Under same management as neighbouring *Duyong Beach Resort*. Decent chalets on the beach, which is a pretty unique set up in Cherating, rooms have fan and bathroom. **D** *Cherating Inn*, T5819266. Fan, shower – Shabby looking chalets in poorly maintained garden. The restaurant is good value (see below). **D** *Cherating Ria Garden* (opposite the *Coconut Inn*), T5819263. A small number of chalets and A-frames attached to a picturesque restaurant (see below), some with a/c, new bar and reception gives the impression that there has been some investment. **D** *Mak De's House*, in the old village, next to police station, T5819316. *Mak De* has been offering kampung accommodation since the late-1970s but his chalets are now only available for long-stays so are not recommended for the average visitor. The proprietor has a long-standing reputation for hospitality and good food, quiet chalets in good condition. **D** *Mak Long Teh Guesthouse*, T503290. Restaurant, like *Mak De*, this family-run operation was up-and-running long before Cherating was discovered by main-stream tourists, friendly, with excellent Malay home cooking – again, and like *Mak De's*, it can be noisy. Unfortunately the garden is messy and full of rubbish and the place is increasingly run-down. **D** *Matahari Chalets*, T5819835. On the southern of the two lanes from the main Juantan-Kemaman road, no phone. Two rows of attractive bungalows facing each other, with a lawn of about 30 m in between. Some bungalows (with spacious verandahs) have fridges. One of the more pleasant places to stay here. Recommended.

D *Moon*, T5819186 or T0109877564 (the northernmost chalet resort on the loop off the main road). 'Come up, be welcome but beware, we are different, even a bit peculiar'. Fan and bathroom, attractive, more rustic chalets in spacious leafy grounds, up a hillside, excellent bar (see below) and restaurant, chalets and longhouse (**E**), much more tranquil surroundings than chalet resorts along the beach. Recommended. **D** *Riverside*, some a/c, popular place with some more sophisticated rooms. The owners are not particularly helpful. **E** *Coconut Inn*, T5819299, coconutinn@yahoo.com Run by Ilal, one of the kampung's best-known characters, and his Dutch wife. 'A'-frames with rusting roofs, badly in need of some maintenance, but very cheap.

Mid-range *Sunrise Seafood Restaurant*, one of the new restaurants on main road, pleasant terrace set back from road, Western and local dishes. **Cheap** *Seaside Seafood*, opposite *Cherating Cottages*, on the beach. Good Chinese/Malay seafood restaurant where you can choose your own fish and itwill be grilled on banana leaves. One of the most popular restaurants in Cerating. Recommended. *Intan Restaurant*, along from the Cerating Bayview. A Malay seafood restaurant with local touches and an extensive menu. *Restoran Duyong*, T5819578 (inside the *Duyong Beach Resort*), lovely setting on raised wooden terrace at edge of beach, lobster and prawns sold by weight, good selection of Western and local dishes. *The Deadly Nightshade* (part of *The Moon* chalet resort at northwest end of loop off main road), also known as 'the restaurant at the end of the universe', enchantingly vague menu, mainly Western with some

Eating
A few new restaurants have sprung up along the main road. Since most chalet hotels have restaurants there's few outside food outlets, but there are plenty of foodstalls

East Coast Peninsula

concessions to local tastes, great atmosphere. *Mimi's Restaurant, Services and Tours* (left at end of lane from main road, on left), restaurant inefficient, and tours par for the course, but *Mimi's* offers useful laundry service. **Seriously cheap** *Cerating Inn Restaurant*, a small place that produces unusually good roti and the Cerating Inn Pancake (made with coconut).

Bars *The Moon* (part of chalet resort of same name at northwest end of loop off main road), great bar amid atap and leafy foliage, second only to the *Boathouse*. Recommended. *The Driftwood*, at southern end of beach, very laid back, serves Western food.

Entertainment *Kampung Budaya Cerating (Cerating Cultural Centre)*, western end of the village street, before the *Cerating Bay View Resort*, pavilion-style attraction, in landscaped garden with a big rather uncosy restaurant, where shows take place. Batik painting, top spinning, songkhet weaving and other typical east coast activities can be seen. The work of artist Ayam is particularly worth a look.

Shopping **Batik** There are 3 batik shops in Cerating; all the artists offer classes; prices (which include tuition) T-shirt RM30-35, sarong RM35, singlet RM18. *Limbang Art* (left at bottom of lane down from main road bridge), mainly shirts, t-shirts painted by *Munif Ayu Art* (on lane down from main road bridge); *Cerating Collection* (in old village, next to main road and *Mak De's*), designs more colourful and abstract than its two local competitors; *Matahari Chalets* local artist Ayu sells his batik t-shirts here and does batik painting classes. **Handicrafts** Next to Cerating Cottages is a large new craft superstore endorsed by Club Med. Endorsement of this type, of course, may do more harm than good and some visitors will want to keep the place at a sarong arm's length. Certainly, a fair proportion of the products do have that mass-produced look, but it does stock some unusual woodwork and good batik.

Sports **Golf** *Kelab Golf Desa Dungun*, T8441041, Dungun, 18 holes, green fees RM40. **AL** *Awana Kijal Beach and Golf Resort*, Kijal, just south of Kerteh Airport, opened in 1996, same management as Genting Highlands, 5-star resort and 18-hole golf course, T603262 3555, F603261 6611, rather monstrous design, with extensive facilities, surrounded by golf course and the beach. **Watersports** *Cerating Beach Recreation Centre*, arranges water skiing and windsurfing, RM10 hire, RM15 lesson; *Club Med*, watersports facilities and body-building classes open to non-guests 0900-1100 and 1400-1600 Mon-Sun (RM60 for half day).

Transport See Checkpoint Cherating, under **Useful addresses**, below. **Air** Kerteh Airport is *50 km to Kuantan* about 40 km north of Cherating. **Bus** Regular buses from Kuantan (Kemaman bus). Bus stops at both ends of the kampung. Regular connections with **Rantau Abang**, **Kuala Terengganu**, **Marang**, **Kota Bharu**. Minibuses leave Checkpoint Cherating for **Kuantan** at 0730 Mon-Sun and to **Kemaman**, to change to northbound express buses. Buses also depart for KL and Singapore. **Taxi** Rantau Abang, Kuantan, Kuantan airport.

Directory **Banks** See *Cerating Travel Post*, under **Useful addresses**, below. The nearest bank is at Kemaman, 12 km north. **Communications** Internet cafés: Available at *Cerating Travel Post* (next to *Mimis*, see below); *Cerating Library and Cyber Café* ('Capacity.com'), opposite *Duyong Resort*, T095819330, closed Wed. **Useful addresses** *Badgerlines Information Services* (about 20 m down on left from lane leading from main road bridge), an additional source of local info, which is independently run. Open 0900-1700 and 2000-2200. *Cerating Travel Post* (next to *Mimis*), ticketing (buses, taxis, minibuses), vehicle hire: car, motorbike, mountain bike, boats, foreign exchange (including TCs, poor rate), mobile phone, book rental, newspapers and tourist information; also organizes tours to Tasek Cini, night market, turtle hatching Terengganu National Park, batik factories and night-time jungle trek. Internet access, overseas telephone calls and flight confirmation. Phew! *Cerating River Sports Centre*, T0199653591, opposite Tanjung Inn. Organises kayaking (RM40, half day), river trips, Snake Island trip, fishing, snorkelling and turtle watching.

On the road north from Cherating there are several stretches of beach, among the best of which is Kemasik. It is off the main road to the right (85 km north of Kuantan, 28 km north of Cherating), just before the oil and gas belt of Kerteh. Ask buses to stop shortly after windy stretch through hills. At Kemasik, the beach is deserted; there is a lagoon, some rocky headlands and safe bathing. There are no facilities.

Kemasik

Turtles also come ashore at Kuala Abang, a few kilometres north of Dungun, which is much quieter than Rantau Abang, although there are still a few hotels. There are also several places to stay, although not right on the beach, at the small port of **Kuala Dungun**, famed for its *kuini*, a local mango. There is a weekly night market (*pasar malam*) in Dungun on Thursdays. From there it is possible to hire a boat to Pulau Tenggol, 29 km out, popular with snorkellers.

Kuala Abang
Phone code: 09

Sleeping B *Merantau Inn*, T8441131. At the south end of the turtle beach, some a/c, restaurant, big, clean chalets above old fish ponds, past its prime, but 3 decent chalets on the beach. Not outstanding but reasonable value. **C-D** *Kasanya*, 225-227 Jln Tambun, T9841704. A/c. **C-D** *Sri Dungun*, K135 Jln Tambun, T9841881. A/c, restaurant. **D** *Mido*, 145-6 Jln Tambun, a/c, T9841246. **D** *Sri Gate*, 5025 Jln Sura Gate, a/c. **D** *Sun Chew*, 10 Jln Besar Sura Gate, T9841412. A/c, restaurant.

 Tanjung Jara: AL-A *Tanjung Jara Beach Hotel*, 6 km north of Dungun, T8441801, F8442653. A/c, restaurant, pool, the best known 5-star beach resort on the east coast, its Malay-inspired design won it the Aga Khan award for outstanding Islamic architecture, tour excursions, windsurfing, golf and tennis facilities, also offers local tours.

Transport Bus: express buses leave for Kuantan, Mersing, KL and JB/Singapore. **Taxi**: Kuala Terrenganu, Kota Bharu, Dungun, and Kuantan.

Rantau Abang

This strung-out beachside settlement owes its existence to turtles. Every year between May and September, five different species of turtle (penyuin Malay) come to this long stretch of beach to lay their eggs, including the endangered giant leatherbacks.

Colour map 1, grid B6
Phone code: 09

 Every year, tens of thousands of tourists also make the pilgrimage. During the peak egg-laying season, in August (which coincides with Malaysia's school holidays), the beach gets very crowded. Up until the mid-1980s the egg-laying 'industry' was poorly controlled; tourists and locals played guitars around bonfires on the beach and scrambled onto turtles' backs for photographs as they laid. Conservationists became increasingly concerned about the declining number of giant leatherbacks that chose to nest on the beach and began to press for stricter policing and management.

 Parts of the beach have now been set aside by the government, and access is prohibited; there are also sections of beach with restricted access, where a small admission charge is levied by guides. The Fisheries Department does not charge. Local guides, who trawl the beach at night for leatherbacks

East Coast Peninsula

☞ ## The giant leatherback turtle (Dermochelys coriacea)

The symbol of the old Malaysian Tourist Development Corporation, the giant leatherback turtle is so-called for its leathery carapace, or shell. It is the biggest sea turtle and one of the biggest reptiles in the world. The largest grow to 3m in length and most of the females who lumber up Rantau Abang's beach to lay their eggs are over 1½m long. On average they weigh more than 350 kg, but are sometimes more than double that. Giant leatherbacks are also said to live for hundreds of years. They spend most of their lives in the mid-Pacific Ocean, although they have been sighted as far afield as the Atlantic, and return to this stretch of beach around Rantau Abang each year to lay their eggs, in the way salmon return to the same river. The beach shelves steeply into deeper water, allowing turtles to reach the beach easily.

They are not well designed for the land. It requires huge effort to struggle up the beach, to above the high-tide mark. After selecting a nesting site, the turtle first digs a dummy hole before carefully scooping out the actual nest pit, in which she lays up to 150 soft white eggs between the size of a golf ball and a tennis ball. The digging and egg-laying procedure, punctuated by much groaning and heaving and several rest-stops, takes up to two hours, after which she covers the hole and returns to the sea. During the egg-laying period, the turtle's eyes secrete a lubricant to protect them from the sand, making it appear as if it is crying. In the course of the egg-laying season (from May to September) this exhausting slog up the beach might be repeated up to nine times.

The gestation period for the eggs is 52-70 days. During this period the eggs are in danger from predators, so the Fisheries Department collects up to 50,000 eggs each season for controlled hatching in fenced-off sections of beach. The eggs are also believed to be an aphrodisiac and can be bought in wet markets along the east coast for about RM1 each (a small quota is set aside for public consumption). Young hatchlings are regularly released into the sea from the government hatchery. Many are picked off by predators, such as gulls and fish, and few reach adulthood. The turtles have been endangered by drift-net fishing and pollution. It is also prized for its shell which is thought to have the most beautiful markings of any sea turtle. In nature it is used to camouflage, it is thought, the turtle against a dappled coral background. The 'tortoiseshell' is fashioned into combs and cigarette boxes. In 1990 the Malaysian government started fitting radio transmitters to leatherbacks to enable satellites to monitor their movements in international waters. French satellite information is providing a stronger database on turtle populations and movements allowing the formulation of a more effective conservation strategy.

Even so, the leatherback turtle appears to be fighting a losing battle against extinction. There are just five main places in the world where these behemoths lay their eggs: South Africa's east coast, Surinam, Costa Rica, the Pacific coast of Mexico, and Rantau Abang. In the mid-1950s 10,000 turtles were arriving at Rantau Abang alone; in 1996 it was a mere 68. When one considers the odds against an egg turning into a mature adult leatherback – around one in a 1,000 (some say, 10,000) – and couple that with all the new threats that the leatherback has to contend with from drift nets to pollution, it is small wonder that some marine biologists believe this magnificent creature could, by the end of the millennium, be on the verge of extinction.

Green turtles come ashore to lay their eggs later in the season. For more details on these, see page 471.

coming ashore, charge tourists RM2 a head for a wake-up call. Turtle-watching is free along the stretch around the Turtle Information Centre. The Fisheries Department also runs three hatcheries to protect the eggs from

The crown-of-thorns – the terminator on the reef

The crown-of-thorns starfish (Acanthaster planci) – a ruthlessly efficient, cold-blooded killing machine – launched an invasion of the Pulau Redang Marine Park in the early 1990s. The destructive starfish, which did serious damage to Australia's Great Barrier Reef in the 1980s, can regenerate and multiply rapidly leading to sudden infestations on coral reefs. The crown-of-thorns grazes on staghorn coral (Acropora) in particular and if population explosions are left unchecked, the starfish can reduce rich coral colonies into blanched skeletal debris. One crown-of-thorns can suck the living tissues from a coral in a matter of hours and, if present in large numbers, they can eat their way across a reef, devastating it in a matter of weeks or months.

The crown-of-thorns is aptly named. It measures about 50 cm across and is covered in thousands of poisonous spines, each 3-5 cm long. The spines are extremely sharp and toxic – if they puncture human skin, they cause a severe reaction, including nausea, vomiting and swelling. These short spines grow on the starfish's legs, of which it has more than 20. But

marine conservationists, concerned about the threat to the coral and fish breeding grounds, face a daunting task in ridding reefs of the unwelcome echinoderms. Because of their amoeba-like regenerative abilities, the crown-of-thorns cannot simply be chopped in half in situ, because this would create two of them. Instead, each one has to be prised off the coral, taken to the surface and buried on land.

The Malaysian Fisheries Department, with private sector backing, mounted a reef-rescue expedition to Redang in 1992 to do exactly this. The department's marine biologists were unsure as to what had triggered the infestation of crown-of-thorns starfish; it could be that they invade in natural cycles or human interference could have something to do with it. The last major infestation was in the early 1970s. Following their difficult task of picking the starfish off the reef, the divers buried them on shore, as instructed. Perhaps they should have driven wooden stakes through their hearts too: the starfish can go for as long as nine months without food.

predators and egg-hunters: they are a local delicacy. The closest is five minutes' walk from *Awang's*. Officers from the department patrol the beach in three-wheeler beach buggies.

NB Do not interfere with the turtles while they are laying. There is now a ban on flash photography and unruly behaviour is punishable by a RM1,000 fine or six months' imprisonment. Camp fires, loud music, excessive noise and littering are all illegal, although the latter is not well enforced.

Rantau Abang Turtle Information Centre, 13th Mile Jalan Dungun, T8441533, F8442653, opposite the big *Plaza R & R*, has an excellent exhibition and film presentation about sea turtles, focusing on the giant leatherback. A slide-show also opened in 1993. The Fisheries Department at the centre is very helpful and friendly. ■ *Sat-Thu 0900-1300, 1400-1900, 2000-2300, Fri 0900-1200, 1500-2300 (Jun-Aug); 0800-1245, 1400-1600 Sat-Wed, 0800-1245 Thu, closed Fri (Sep-Apr).*

Kuala Abang, south of Rantau Abang, is easily accessible. See page 283.

Excursions

Rantau Abang's accommodation is strung-out along the main road; there are many overpriced, unpleasant little hovels. New places are opening and old ones closing all the time. Security is a problem here: it is inadvisable to leave valuables in rooms. The only upmarket place to stay near here (unless new outfits have opened) is the beautiful

Sleeping
Most hotels have their own restaurants

Tanjung Jara Beach Hotel which is roughly halfway between Rantau Abang and Kuala Dungun, see Kuala Abang above for details.

B-E *Ismail's*, T8441054. Next to *Awang's*, good restaurant (only open in peak season), south of the Visitor's Centre, average beach-side set-up, similar to *Awang's*. **C-D** *Awang's*, T8443500. Restaurant, some a/c, some rooms are very poor, the best are only average. Not good value for money. **C-D** *Dahimah's*, T8452483. 1 km south of Visitor's Centre, restaurant, clean rooms in Malay wooden chalets. Some a/c.

Eating

There are roadside stalls and coffee shops near the bus stop

Cheap *Awang's*, right on the beach, Awang was formerly the chef at the *Tanjung Jara Beach Hotel*. *Ismail's* also has a restaurant and there are some stalls in the *Plaza R & R; Mikinias*, just down from *Awang's*. Big menu but service is slow if it gets busy.

Transport

22 km north of Kuala Dungun, 58 km south of Kuala Terengganu, 160 km north of Kuantan. **Bus** Regular connections with **Kuala Terengganu** and **Kuala Dungun** from opposite *Turtle Information Centre*. From Kuala Dungun connections with Kuantan and other destinations.

Marang

Colour map 1, grid B6
Phone code: 09

This is a colourful Malay fishing kampung at the mouth of the Marang River, although it is not as idyllic as the tourist literature suggests. To get into the town from the main road, follow signs to LKIM Komplex from the north end of the bridge. Marang has been buffeted by the vagaries of the tourist industry over the last couple of decades. In the 1980s and 1990s there was a rush to put up budget accommodation, placing it firmly on the tourist map for the first time. Then, by the mid- to late-1990s the kampung began to acquire a bit of a run-down look as the early developments lost their sheen. With the new Millennium, a number of new, plusher developments along the shorefront in Marang Town have instilled a slightly more chi-chi atmosphere to the place. Notwithstanding all these twists and turns, it is still a very lovely village, with its shallow lagoon full of fishing boats. The best beach is opposite Pulau Kepas at Kampung Ru Muda. It was the centre of a mini-gold-rush in 1988 when gold was found 6 km up the road at Rusila. On the road north of Marang there are a number of batik workshops, all of which welcome visitors.

Excursions

Pulau Kapas is 6 km (30 minutes) off the coast, with some good beaches. Those wanting a quiet beach holiday should avoid weekends and public holidays when it is packed. The coral here has been degraded somewhat and there is much better snorkelling at **Pulau Raja**, just off Kapas, which has been declared a marine park. All the guesthouses organize snorkelling and the *Kapas Garden Resort* also has scuba equipment. Many hotels in Marang offer day trips to the islands and it is easy enough to grab a ride. The *Abdul Tourist Boat Service* is helpful and will pick up even at low tide. They have fast boats.

Sleeping A *Primula Kapas Island Village Resort*, T/F6236110. Malay-style chalets, pool. Since a change of management this place seems to have gone downhill: service is poor, the beach dirty, bathrooms poorly maintained, food ghastly and therefore significantly overpriced. **B-C** *Tenggol Aqua Resort*, Pulau Tenggol, T9861807. The only accommodation on the island. **C** *Tuty Purri Island Resort*, T0192151938. **C** *Kapas Garden Resort*, T0109841686. Fourteen rooms. **C-D** *Makcik Gemok Chalet*, T6181221. Largest outfit on the island with a range of rooms from simple huts with shared facilities through to larger chalets with attached bathrooms. **C** *Pulau Kapas Resort*,

T6236110. Restaurant, snorkelling, forest tours, fishing trips (RM150 per day). **D** *Cadten Lighthouse*, T0102155338. **D** *Kapas Garden Resort*, T0119871305. Friendly place with well maintained rooms, some with attached bathrooms. **D-E** *Zaki Beach Resort*, T6120258. Restaurant, chalets.

River and island tours Half-day river tours organized by *Rapas Travel and Tours (Primula Hotel)*, T6235915. The same people also offer efficiently run tours to nearby islands; most hotels in town can arrange trips to Pulau Kapas. The Marang Guest House Information Centre (office by the jetty), offers boat transfers, snorkelling trips (RM42 for a day trip), squid fishing trips, and a river safari. Open 0900-1700, Mon-Sun, T6181976, F6181976.

A *Marang Resort and Safaris*, 1 Jln Dungan, T6182588, F6182334. A/c, 60 rooms, one of the few upmarket options in the area. **A** *Buai Beach Resort* before the road bridge to Marang Town, (if approaching from the south), follow the signs from the road. T6183888, T6183999, F6183388. Secluded chalets, connected by raised boardwalks. Private beach to the rear of reception area, stunning views of Pulau Kapas. Swimming pool, restaurant, watersports, island tours and turtle watching trips available. Beautiful resort, not too big, staff are friendly and the atmosphere is luxurious yet relaxed. Recommended. **B** *Seri Malaysia Marang*, Lot 3964, Kampung Paya, T6182889, F6181289. One of the *Seri Malaysia* chain, opened in 1995, good value, views of Pulau Kapas, a/c, TV, coffee/tea-making facility, restaurant, launderette, organize island trips, the best option along this row of accommodation although not extravagant, breakfast included. However the restaurant is overpriced , the variety of food available limited, and the service slap-dash. **B-D** *Angullia Beach House*, 12¼ milestone, Kampung Rhu Muda, T6181322, F6181322. Some a/c, restaurant (with good set meal), extremely friendly, family-run chalet resort on lovely stretch of beach opposite Pulau Kapas (therefore sheltered), leafy, well-kept grounds and very clean chalets (no alcohol served), some visitors reckon it is overpriced. Recommended.

Sleeping
■ *on map,*
Price codes:
see inside front cover

East Coast Peninsula

Marang

■ Sleeping
1 Angullia Beach House
2 Buai Beach Resort
3 Mare Nostrum Holiday Resort
4 Zakaria Guesthouse

There are hotels and guesthouses in Marang itself and in Kampung Rhu Muda, about 2 km before the bridge over the Marang River

C *Island View*, opposite the lagoon, T6182006. Some a/c, free bicycles, chalets with attached bathrooms and some simpler rooms, popular. Very attractive setting with a central bougainvilia garden to relax in. However be prepared to share your room with various visitors from the animal kingdom. A little run down now. **C** *C.R. Marang Resort* (aka *Marang Riverview Hotel*), next to the market and jetty), T6185250. 29 rooms, some with fan, some a/c. Simple but spacious rooms with large clean bathrooms. This hotel opened in 2000 and in 2001 were still contemplating whether to open a restaurant. Staff are friendly and helpful, and the hotel has good sea views at the rear. Good value. **C** *Rumah Rehat Semarak* (*Rest House*), Taman Rehat Semarak, Km 17, Jln Kuala Terengganu (4 km south of Marang), T6227631. Chalets on the beach, formerly government-owned, past its prime, but pleasant rooms with balconies, the best ones facing the sea, small restaurant and stalls next door. **C-E** *Mare Nostrum Holiday Resort*, Kampung Rhu Muda, T6182417. A/c, restaurant, clean and hospitable, boat trips, pleasant little resort next door to *Angullia*, well-kept compound (if a little cramped) and clean chalets. Recommended. **C-D** *Travellers Check Point*, (aka *Marang Guest House and Restaurant*). On the hill top above Kamal. Scenic views of the lagoon and sea beyond. Clean and friendly, good restaurant, with TV lounge and seating area with games. Well-built chalets with a/c or fan, excellent value for money. Connected to MGH Travel Centre (see above).

E *Green Mango Inn*, A-71 Bandar Marang, T6182040. Fan, small, bare A-frame chalets but cheap. Dorm rooms available. Excellent atmosphere, good views over the bay, a small garden, and sitting area with library and games. Free tea and coffee. **E** *Marang Inn & Garden Café*, 132 Bandar Marang, T6182132. Restaurant, in decorated blue-and-orange shophouse overlooking lagoon, helpful, organizes tours around Terengganu and trips to islands. **E** *Zakaria Guesthouse*, Kampung Rhu Muda, T6182328. Basic and further out of the village, dorm or rooms. **E-F** *Kamal's*, T6182181. Opposite the lagoon, very popular, dormitory and chalets, now very rundown but still popular with friendly staff. Tours and activities organized. **E-F** *Marang Inn*, Batu 22 Rhu Muda, T6182288. Dorm and chalets.

Eating   Most hotels have good restaurants serving Malay and international dishes. There are cheap food stalls along the waterfront next to the market. Stalls at Taman Selera, Kampung Rhu Muda, along the roadside are well known, particularly by long-distance bus and taxi drivers, for their Malay and Thai-style seafood (closed Fri).

Shopping   **Handicrafts** Market in Marang has a craft market upstairs and there are several handicraft shops along the main street.

Northwest Marang

To Kuala Terengganu

Carving Hall

Marang Handicrafts

Kg Paya

Jln Paya Hulu Banang

Jln Kastam Lama

Lookout Point

Children's Playground

Food Stalls

Bus kiosk
Laundry

Jln Hakaf Tapai   Jln Tg Sulong Musa

Shopping Complex (Under construction)

Small Jetty

To Pulau Kapas

Express Bus Stop

Jln Panjan Lot

Bandar Marang

Large Jetty

Jln Kumia Jaya

Not to scale

To Kuantan & Rantau Abang

■ Sleeping
1 Green Mango Inn
2 Island View
3 Kamal's
4 Marang Inn & Garden Café
5 Marang Resort & Safaris
6 Seri Malaysia Marang
7 Travellers Check Point

Balai Ukiran Terengganu (Terengganu Woodcarving Centre), Kampung Rhu Rendang, near Marang, master-carver Abdul Malek Ariffin runs the east coast's best-known woodcarving workshop, makes wide range of intricately carved furniture from cengal wood, carved with traditional floral geometric and Islamic calligraphic patterns, the varnished cengal wood is not to everyone's taste, but everything from mirrors to beds can be ordered for export, because most pieces are made to order there is little on show in Abdul's chaotic workshop, but carvers can be seen at work during the day. Good **batik** in Marang.

Bus Bus stop on the main road up the hill from Marang. Tickets can be bought from the kiosk nearby on Jln Tg Sulong Musa, however, this runs very unpredictable hours so book in advance. Connections with **Kuala Terengganu** every hour, and with **Kuala Dungun** via **Kuala Abang**.

Transport
18 km to Kuala Terengganu

Communications There is an internet café next to the bus kiosk on Jln Tg Sulong Musa. Next door to this there is a laundry service.

Directory

Kuala Terengganu

*The royal capital of Terengganu state was a small fishing port (the state accounts for about a quarter of all Malaysia's fishermen) until oil and gas money started pumping into development projects in the 1980s. The town has long been a centre for arts and crafts, and is known for its kain songket, batik, brass and silverware. The focal point of the town is the **Pasar Besar Kedai Payang** market place. The town's colourful history is revealed in the chinese shophouses and temple, in the **Zainal Abdin** Mosque and the ceremonial house of **Istana Maziah**, once home to the Terengganu royal family.*

Colour map 1, grid B6
Phone code: 09

East Coast Peninsula

Like neighbouring Pahang, Terengganu state was settled at least as far back as the 14th century, and over the years has paid tribute to Siam and, in the 15th century, to the sultanate of Melaka. When the Portuguese forced the Melaka royal house to flee to Johor, Terengganu became a vassal of the new sultanate. In the 18th century, Terengganu is recorded as having a thriving textile industry; it also traded in pepper and gold with Siam, Cambodia, Brunei and China. A Chinese merchant community grew up in Kuala Terengganu. In 1724, the youngest brother of a former sultan of Johor, Zainal Abidin, established Terengganu as an independent state and declared himself its first sultan. Today's sultan is a direct descendant. The state has always been known for its ultra-conservative Islamic traditions.

Background

Tourism Malaysia, 5th Flr, Menara Yayasan Islam Terengganu, Jln Sultan Omar, T6221433, F6221791. *State Tourist Information Centre* (TIC), Jln Sultan Zainal Abidin, near the Istana Maziah on the jetty, T6221891. Impressive looking place bursting with information. Open: 0900-1700, Sat-Thu.

Tourist offices

Sights

The **Pasar Besar Kedai Payang**, the main market place on Jalan Sultan Zainal Abidin, is the busiest spot in town – particularly in the early morning, when the fishing fleet comes in. The market sells batik, brocade, songket, brassware, and basketware as well as fruit and vegetables (open 0700-1800). **Jalan Bandar**, leading off from the market, is a street of old Chinese shophouses and there is also a busy and colourfully painted Chinese temple. Nearby is the imposing **Zainal Abdin Mosque**, on Jln Masjid. Not far from the mosque (on the other side of Jalan Kota) is the apricot-coloured **Istana Maziah**, the old home of Terengganu's royal family, built in French style. It is now only used on ceremonial occasions and is not open to the public.

Some of Kuala Terengganu's older buildings have fine examples of traditional Malay carvings. Another of these traditional houses was taken apart and reassembled in Kuala Lumpur in the grounds of the National Museum as an example of classical Malay architecture.

The **State Museum**, one of the largest in the country, is situated in Losong, a town 5 km southwest of the city. The museum is at the end of Jalan Losong Feri, facing Pulau Sekati. It exhibits rare Islamic porcelain, silver jewellery, musical instruments and weaponry – including a fine selection of *parangs* and *krises*. It is an eclectic collection, erratically labelled. ■ *Admission: RM5, open 0900-1700 all week (closed Fri 1200-1400). Take bus no. 10 from MPKT bus station (15 minute journey).* **Bukit Puteri**, near the Istana, has fortress remains on it and provides excellent views of the town.

Excursions

A number of tour agents offer tours to the offshore islands and trekking tours to the Kenyir Lake area (see page 294)

There is a thriving cottage industry in and around Kuala Terengganu and many of Malaysia's best-known handicrafts are made locally. Surrounding kampungs practise silverwork, batik-printing, songket-weaving and *wau* kite-building, but the best way to see these under one roof is in the Cendering handicraft centres (see below).

Pulau Duyung Besar
This is the largest island in the Terengganu Estuary and famed for its boat-building. It mainly survives by custom-building yachts. Take minibus no. 20, and then a boat (50c). If you want to stay overnight, the **F** *Awi's Yellow*

Kuala Terengganu

Sleeping
1 Bunga Raya
2 Grand Paradise
3 Kenangan & KT Mutiara
4 KT Travellers' Inn
5 Midtown
6 Primula Parkroyal
7 Ping Anchorage
8 Seaview
9 Seri Hoover
10 Seri Malaysia
11 Terengganu

House, T017-8829564. Is built out over the river on stilts and is very popular with budget travellers. Dorm and atap-roofed huts, some with balconies over river, pleasant location with cool breezes, there are some stalls at the bus stop near the bridge, but most travellers bring their own food from KT and have use of kitchen facilities, *Awi's Yellow House* is not yellow and can be hard to find but is well enough known to sniff out. ■ *Getting there: boat from jetty on Jln Bandar – last boat around 2200 – or by road, via the new Sultan Mahmud bridge (taxis or bus from KT). The river is navigable for quite a distance upstream and it is possible to hire boats from the jetty for river trips.*

This is situated on the estuary of the Ibai River. Its name is a slight misnomer; it has been built in such a way that it gives the illusion of floating. Located 6 km from town; take bus either 13 or 13c (70c). **Floating Mosque**

This songket-weaving and batik centre, 6 km upriver, is known for its traditional Petani-Terengganu wooden houses. Take a boat from the jetty on Jalan Sultan Zainal Abidin. The village can also be reached by bus from the bus station on Jalan Syed Hussin. **Kampung Pulau Rusa**

Home to several handicraft centres, Cendering lies 7 km south of Kuala Terengganu. *Kraftangan Malaysia*, with a beautifully displayed selection of silver, woodwork, silk, batik, brass and basketware as well as handicrafts from elsewhere in Malaysia, is very classy compared with *Rusila* (below). To get there, take Marang-bound buses from Jalan Syed Hussin – 13, or 13c. The turning is clearly signposted off the main road. ■ *0800-1630 Sat-Wed, 0830-1200 Thu.* Next door to *Kraftangan Malaysia* is the huge *Nor Arfa Batik Factory*, producing modern and traditional designs and readymades (T6175700). Behind *Kraftangan Malaysia* is the *Sutera Semai* silk factory. **Cendering**

The Planetarium, at Kompleks Planetarium Megeri, Padang Hiliran, T6248934, has an impressive array of information including shows at the following times: Sunday-Thursday, every hour, 0930-1230, 1430, and 1530; Saturday every hour 0900-2100. Take minibus 20 or 16 (70c). ■ *RM3.* **Planetarium**

Batu Buruk beach, running down the northeast side of KT, is not safe for swimming. But there are some good beaches near Kuala Terengganu: Merang 30 km (see page 295) and Batu Rakit 20 km north. There is a (**D**) guesthouse at the latter. There are regular buses to both beaches from Jalan Syed Hussin. **Beaches & islands**

Numerous **islands** lie off shore from Kuala Terengganu including **Pulau Redang** (see page 296) . Boats leave for the islands from Merang and from the Jalan Bandar jetty in Kuala Terengganu, from which there are now scheduled departures.

Set in the midst of tropical forest, the **Peladang Resort** offers a 280-ha plot, complete with lakes, arboretum, mini bird park, swimming pool and, for the enthusiast - an obstacle course. Popular with groups, if also provides a campsite. Situated 83 km west of Kuala Terengganu, T(609)6977136, F6977135, agro_setiu@hotmail.com **Peladang Setiu Agro Resort**

Essentials

There are only a couple of hotels at the top end of the market but there are several cheaper hotels scattered round town, mainly at the jetty end of Jln Sultan Ismail and on **Sleeping**

Jln Banggol, but the selection is not great. For budget travellers it is worth considering staying at Awi's Yellow House on Pulau Duyung (see **Excursions**, above).

A *Primula Parkroyal*, Jln Persinggahan, T6222100, F6233360. A new name, but not a new look unfortunately, a/c, restaurant (good Malay-food buffet for RM25), good pool, highrise hotel with all mod-cons but rooms are shabby and not soundproofed, they do have a sea view though, also organizes island excursions. Great value for money. **B** *Permai Park Inn*, Jln Sultan Mahmud, T6222122, F6222121, ppilplai@tm.net.my Good quality hotel offering value for money, just under 150 rooms, friendly staff, very comfortable, carpeted rooms with a/c, TV, in-house movies, mini fridge, tea/coffee-making facilities, pleasant pool and children's pool, restaurant, *SI Travel Services* organize local packages, eg Lake Kenyir. Breakfast included. Recommended. **B** *Kenangan*, 65 Jln Sultan Ismail, T6222342, F6222688. A/c, restaurant, bathroom. Slightly cheaper than the *KT Mutiara* next door and not nearly as nice. **B** *KT Mutiara*, 67 Jln Sultan Ismail, T6222655, F6236895. A/c, shower (hot water), TV, recently redecorated and extremely good value. Recommended. **B** *Midtown* (aka Yen Tin Midtown or sometimes, YT Midtown), Jln Tok Lam, T6235288, F6234399, ythotel@po.jaring.my A/c, laundry, business centre, tea/coffee-making facilities, fridge, restaurant, serves good breakfast to non-residents for RM8. In the centre of town with good facilities and a variety of information on transport and sights. **B** *Seri Malaysia*, Lot 1640, Jln Hiliran, T6236454, F6238344. A/c, restaurant (good, inexpensive), another in the well-run modern *Seri Malaysian* chain, a/c, TV, minibar, light airy rooms overlooking the river. Recommended.

C *Bunga Raya*, 105-111 Jln Banggol, T6221911, F6223084. Bit run-down and noisy, on road. **C** *KT Travellers Inn*, 201, 1st Flr, Jln Sultan Zainal Abidin, T6223666, F6232692. Convenient location downtown, a/c, TV, clean rooms. Quite expensive for what you get. **C** *Motel Desa*, Bukit Pak Api, T6223033, F6223863. A/c, TV, in-house video, minibar, restaurant, pool, set in gardens on a small hill overlooking the town, a possibility for those with own transport. **C** *Qurata Riverside*, Lot 175K Kuala Ibai, T6175500, F6175511. Small and friendly hotel, 7 km south of Kuala Terengganu, 21 rooms in individual wooden chalets on stilts near the Kuala Ibai River. Designed by a nephew of the local royal family to resemble a Malay village, set in meticulous garden, only marred by proximity of main road, comfortable rooms with wood floors, a/c, ceiling fans, TV and shower room. At low tide it is possible to walk across the river mouth to nearby sand beach. Recommended. **C** *Seaview Hotel*, 18a Jln Masjid Abidin, T6221911, F6223048. Slightly overpriced but near the jetty with clean, comfortable rooms, a/c, centrally located opposite Istana Maziah, good mid-range place to stay. **C** *Seri Hoover*, 49 Jln Sultan Ismail, T6233833, F6225975 A/c, restaurant, large, rather ugly hotel with 71 rooms but they are big andclean, bathrooms with hot water, although slightly musty smell.

C-D *Grand Paradise*, 28 Jln Tok Lam, T6228888, F6238899, www.paradisegroup.com.my A/c, shower (hot water), TV. Quite good value although the bathrooms are matchbox size and not all rooms have windows. Breakfast included in room rate. **C-D** *Terengganu*, 12 Jln Sultan Ismail, T/F6222906 A/c (with fan D), rooms could do with lick of paint but clean and reasonable value. Staff not particularly friendly or helpful. **D** *Batu Burok Chalet*, 906-A, Pantai Batu Burok, T6221410, F6232904. Some a/c, restaurant, the only chalet-style accommodation in town, not bad, pleasant open restaurant overlooking the beach (which is dangerous for swimming).

E *Ping Anchorage*, 77A Jln Dato' Isaac, T6220851. Roof-top café, free breakfast, helpful with travel information, organizes trekking trips to Kenyir Lake area and offshore islands, dorm beds available. Extremely bare rooms and thin cardboard walls so noise can be a problem but competitive prices. There is also a café under the same management (see below), and tour information available in their travel centre (again, see below).

Nasi dagang – known as 'fishermen's breakfast' – is a speciality of the area. It is made **Eating**
with aromatic or glutinous rice, served with *gulai ikan tongkol* (tuna fish with tamarind
and coconut gravy). *Keropok* – or prawn crackers – are another Terengganu speciality.

Malay Mid-range *Rhusila Coffee House*, *Primula Beach Resort*. **Permai Park Inn**, Jln
Sultan Mahmud, good value buffet. **Cheap** *Keluarga IQ*, 74 Jln Banggol, good place
for *nasi dagang* breakfast, also excellent *nasi campur* (curry buffet), open 0630-0300,
closed Fri. **Restoran Terapung Puteri**, Jln Sultan Zainal Abidin, T6235396, New floating
restaurant opposite the tourist information centre, serving a wide range of Malay and
western food, good fresh fruit drinks available. Friendly service, good location near Chinatown. Recommended. **Mali**, 77 Jln Banggol, near the bus station, popular, cheap
coffee shop – *nasi lemak*, *nasi campur*, satay and good rotis. **Nik**, 104 Jln Sultan Ismail,
standard curries. **Zainuddin**, Jln Tok Lam; **Sri Intan**, 14 Taman Sri Intan, Jln Sultan Omar,
well-appointed restaurant serving standard Malay dishes.

   Chinese Expensive *KT Wok*, 1081 Block W, Jln Sultan Sulaiman, T6243825, ultra
modern décor, black and pink colour scheme, specialize in *dim sum*. **Cheap** *Awana*,
near public swimming pool, Jln Pantai Batu Buruk. Recommended by locals. **Golden
Dragon Restaurant**, 198 Jln Bandar, good pork, interesting vegetable dishes, some
tables on street. Recommended. **One-Two-Six**, 102 Jln Kampung Tiong 2 (off Jln Sultan
Ismail), big open-air restaurant with hawker stalls, good seafood menu, special: fire
chicken wings (comes to table in flames). Recommended. Restaurants **Good Luck**, **Kui
Ping** and **Lee Kee** all along Jln Engku Sar, standard Chinese fare.

   Indian Cheap *Taufik*, 18 Jln Masjid Abidin (opposite Istana Maziah), North and
South Indian dishes, well-known for its rotis; **Kari Asha**, 1-H Jln Air Jermh, good range
of curries (including fish heads, dosai and rotis).

   International Mid-range *Husni*, 954 Jln Sultan Mohammed, Thai, Malay and
Western dishes, vast menu. **Chef's Steak House**, attached to *The Grand Paradise Hotel*,
T6230899, F6238899. The chef here recommends the ternderloin steak and crème caramel. **Cheap** *Midtown Café*, Jln Tok Lam, a broad selection of Western and Eastern
cuisine, should suit all tastes. **Ping Anchorage Traveller's Café**, Jln Dato'Isaac. Friendly,
pleasant atmosphere, good breakfast menu, small souvenir shop with some items less
tacky than found elsewhere.

   Seafood *Nil*, Jln Pantai Batu Buruk (near the *Pantai Primula Hotel*), view of the
beach, good selection of seafood and renowned for its butter crabs in batter; **Taz**, Jln
Sultan Zainal Abidin (below *Seri Pantai Hotel*).

Foodstalls *Gerai Makanan* (foodstalls) opposite the bus station; Malay; **Kampung
Tiong** (off Jln Bandar), excellent hawker centre with Malay food on one side, Chinese and
Indian on the other, open 8 till late; *Jalan Batu Buruk*, near the Cultural Centre, some
excellent Malay food and seafood stalls. Recommended. Also **Warung Pak Maidin**,
nearby on Jln Haji Busu, which is good on seafood; **Kompleks Taman Selera Tanjung** (1st
Flr), huge area of stalls with good variety of dishes, open-air terrace; **Majlis Perbandaran**
stalls, Jln Tok Lam; **Pasar Besar Kedai Payang** (Central Market), 1st Flr, Malay snacks,
good views over the river. There are also some stalls next to *Stadium Negeri*.

Batik Some of the best batik in Malaysia can be found in the central market (*Pasar* **Shopping**
Besar Kedai Payang). **Wan Ismail Tembaga & Batik**, near turtle roundabout, off Jln Sultan Zainal Abidin – a small, old-fashioned batik factory. There are a number of small
craft and batik factories in Kampung Ladang – the area around Jln Sultan Zainal Abidin;
Desa Craft, 73 Jln Sultan Ismail, in the centre of town, has a good selection of silk and
batik readymades and sarongs. The Central Market sells batik, silk, songket etc. Other
shops selling batik can be found on Jln Bandar, including the **Batik Gallery** at number
194 and **Yuleza** (Chinese for batik) at number 208. **Noor Arfa**, A3 Jln Sultan Zainal

East Coast Peninsula

Abidin, T6235173, an established producer of batik for many years. Cloth and ready made clothes available and will take orders. *Teratai Arts and Crafts Shop*, 151 Jln Bandar, T6252157. High quality craft shop, with batik, woodwork, metalwork and jewellery. Also sells numerous prints and postcards my Malaysian artist Chang Fee Ming. He depicts the colourful nature of local life with stunning watercolours, well worth a visit just to see his work.

Handicrafts The **Central Market** is touristy, but offers a range of handicrafts, textiles, brassware etc. *Desa Craft*, on Jln Sultan Ismail, is another good centre. Out of town, there are centres in Cendering (see **Excursions**, page 291).

Sports **Diving** *Merlin Enterprise*, 1-E, 1st Flr, Wisma Guru, Jln Hiliran, T636200, manager David Chua has a reputation as one of the country's leading divers and is well known for his scuba expeditions. **Golf** *Badariah Golf Club*, south of town, 9 holes, requires special permission from the Sultan's private secretary's office, T632456. *Berjaya Redang Golf Club*, T6233369.

Tour operators Hedaco Travel, Ground Floor, Terengganu Foundation Bldg, Jln Sultan Ismail, T631744; *Uncle John's Hotel Travel* (aka *The Little Traveller*), PO Box 117, T673218, F671527, trips to islands, equipped with comfortable houseboats on Lake Kenyir; *WLO Travel & Air Cargo*, Ground Floor, *Hotel Pantai Primula*, Jln Persinggahan, T635844. *Hubungan Travel and Tours*, Terminal Feri Shah Bandar, Jln Sultan Zainal Abidin, T6263501, F6263502. *Turtleliner* (a Reliance franchise), Jln Sultan Masjid Abidin, T6237000, F6231122, services include flight booking and confirmation, individual and group tours. Helpful staff.

Transport
455 km to KL
168 km to Kota Bharu
209 km to Kuantan

Local Bus: from the main bus terminal on Jln Masjid. **Car hire**: *South China Sea*, Permai Park Inn, T6224903. **Taxi**: T621581. **Trishaw**: RM2-3 for short trips around town.

Long distance Air: the Sultan Mahmud airport lies 18 km northwest of town, T6664204 for information. Regular connections with **KL**, **Kuantan**, **Penang** and **Johor Bahru**. Transport to town: RM15 by taxi. *MAS* T621415. **Bus**: Kuala Terengganu has two bus stations. The express, long distance bus terminal is at Medan Selera, on the northern edge of the city centre. Local and intra-provincial buses leave from the MPKT station on Jln Syed Hussin which runs off Jln Masjid. Connections every 2 hrs to **KL**, **JB**, **Kota Bharu**, **Kuantan**, **Rantau Abang**, **Mersing**, **Singapore**, **Melaka**, **Butterworth**, **Alor Star** and **Marang**. **Taxi**: taxis operate from next to the bus station on Jln Masjid and from the waterfront. Destinations include Kota Bharu, Rantau Abang, Marang, Kuantan, KL, JB and Penang.

Directory **Airline offices** *MAS*, 13 Jln Sultan Omar, T6222266/6221415. **Banks** There are several banks along Jln Sultan Ismail. *Bumiputra*, UMNO Jln Masjid Zainal Abidin; *Hong Kong Bank*, 57 Jln Sultan Ismail; *Maybank*, 69 Jln Paya Bunga; *Public*, 1 Jln Balas Baru; *Standard Chartered*, 31 Jln Sultan Ismail; *UMBC*, 59 Jln Sultan Ismail. There are virtually no money changers in Kuala Terengganu. **Communications** General Post Office: Jln Sultan Zainal Abidin. **Telekom**: Jln Sultan Ismail. **Internet cafés**: *Golden Wood Internel Café*, 59 Jln Tok Lam. **Medical facilities** Hospitals: Jln Peranginan (just off Jln Sultan Mahmud), T6233333.

Kenyir Lake

See also the very informative website www.tourism.gov. my/terengganu/ kenyir.html

This man-made 370-km sq lake, 55 km south of Kuala Terengganu, is Kuala Terengganu's latest holiday destination. Having completed the Kenyir Dam in 1985, the state economic development board has built a 2½-km access road, a jetty and a tourist information centre at a place called Pengkalan Gawi. There are facilities for fishing, canoeing and boating. Major hotel and resort developments have gone up over the last few years, as well as luxury chalets – some of them 'floating chalets', built over the lake – and the inevitable 18-hole golf course. Most are centred on Pengkalan Gawi or at Pengkalan Utama, 5 km away.

The lake is surrounded by jungled hills although the lake edge itself is still rather bare and devastated. There are plans to use Kenyir Lake as a back-door to the remote east side of Taman Negara. The lake itself has more than 300 islands. In parts swimming can be as hazardous as navigation thanks to the millions of submerged and semi-submerged trees. It has been stocked with fish and tour operators from Kuala Terengganu, some of which have houseboats on the lake, offer fishing tackle, canoeing and water-skiing as part of the package. The **Sekayu waterfalls**, with natural water-cut pools for swimming, are also 15 km from Kuala Berang.

Mosquitoes are a problem around the lake

AL-A *Musang Kenyir Resort,* Sungai Tembat, T9837886. **AL-A** *Tasik Lenir Golf Resort*, T6668888, F6668316. **AL-B** *Tasik Kenyir Golf Resort*, Pengkalan Gawi, T6249150, **A** *Uncle John's Resort*, T6262020 12 rooms. **A-B** *Primula Kenyir Lake Resort,* Poh Island, T095146002/T011950609. Restaurant, 73 rooms, children's play area, pool, Malay-style chalets (and 8 floating chalets), no a/c, mosquito nets at windows, tiny shower room, no fridge or tea/coffee-making facilities, organizes activities on the lake. Other developments about 30 mins by boat from Pengkalan Gawi are the sales@glenmarie.com A Glenmarie Resort. **C** *Rumah Rehat Kerajaan Persekutuan*, Pulau Sah Besar, T010-9130381.

Sleeping
There are plans to provide camping facilities in the Kenyir Lake area although currently there is no budget accommodation

Bus to **Kuala Berang**, off the inland road south at **Ajil**, and then taxi to the lake, or by taxi from **Kuala Terengganu** (RM 60). From KL), buses depart at 0900 and 2100 from Putra Station. Many tour companies in **Kuala Terengganu** run inclusive packages to the lake.

Transport

Merang

Merang is a small fishing kampung with a long white sandy beach; it is also the departure point for the many offshore islands, the biggest and best-known of which is Pulau Redang. Recently, Pulau Bidong has opened to tourists (Bidong's coral is said to be superb); throughout the 1980s it served as a Vietnamese refugee camp. The only island with accommodation is Pulau Redang.

Colour map 1, grid B6
Phone code: 09

A number of islands are accessible from Merang, notably **Pulau Redang** (see below). Other islands, most of which are uninhabited and all of which are endowed with good coral, include Pulau Pinang, Pulau Lima, Pulau Lang Tengah, Pulau Tenggol and Pulau Ekor Tebu; fishing boats are usually happy to stop off on request. Tenggol is notable for its diving opportunities, with a sandy bay on the west coast, and good diving on the east. Tours can be organized to this island and surrounding islands.

Excursions

L-AL *Dhe Aryani Resort*, Jln Rhu Tapai-Merang, Pantai Peranginan Merang, 21010 Setiu, T6532111 F6531007. The original heritage timber suites have private courtyards with outdoor bath (but are in the **L** price bracket), elevated restaurant, pool, luxurious. **A-B** *Sutra Beach Resort*, Kampung Rhu Tapai, T6531111, F6696410. A/c, restaurants, pool, 124 chalets, good sports facilities, 20 mins from Kuala Terengganu's airport. **C** *Stingray Beach Chalet*, T019-3278855, F6532018. Built in 1997, directly on the beach, fan, bathroom, immaculately run and offers a dive service. Recommended. **D** *Kembara Resort*, 474 Pantai Peranginan Merang, 21010 Setiu, T6238771, F6248772. Situated on an endless palm-fringed deserted white beach, running south from the jetty, set in a beautiful garden compound, relaxed atmosphere, just 8 bungalows and 8

Sleeping

East Coast Peninsula

rooms all with attached shower and toilet, and fans. Cheap dorm accommodation. No restaurant but there's a large kitchen in the court which is well equiped and can be used freely, a little-known paradise. Recommended. **E** *Sugi Man's Homestay*, 500 m beyond junction, on road to Penarek (signposted from the road). Restaurant, basic kampung farm house, quite a walk from the beach, cooking lessons and kite making, including meals.

Transport

38 km N of KT, on the coast road

Bus Two buses a day from **Kuala Terengganu** to Merang (RM2.50), and then on to **Penarek**. Minibus connections also available from **Kuala Terengganu**, from Jln Masjid. **Taxi** Taxis from **Merang** to **Penarek**. An a/c taxi from **Kuala Terengganu** to **Merang** should cost RM20-30.

Pulau Redang

Colour map 1, grid B6
Phone code: 09

Twenty-seven kilometres off Merang is this archipelago, a marine park of nine islands with some of Malaysia's best reefs, making it one of the most desirable locations for divers. In the months after the monsoon, visibility increases to at least 20 m but during the monsoon the island is usually inaccessible. Line-fishing is permitted and squid fishing, using bright lights, is popular between June and September; the fishermen use a special hook called a *candat sotong*. The lamps light the surrounding waters, attracting the squid. *Scuba Quest* (T/F032636032) organize diving trips to the islands.

Sleeping

Resorts on Redang offer competitive and flexible package deals – check with *Tourism Malaysia*. **A** *Berjaya Redang Island Resort*, T6973988, F6973899. **A** *Berjaya Redang Golf and Spa Resort*, T6971111, F6971000. A hotel with 152 rooms with a/c, TV, minibar, pool, restaurants, health spa, gym, 18-hole golf course, popular destination for business visitors wishing to combine work and golf (limited business facilities), dive centre, gym, tennis courts, health spa. Not popular with locals or environmentalists. **A** *Redang Beach Resort*, T6223352,F6250225 (contact office: 36E, 1st Flr, Jln Dato' Isaac). Full range of facilities, package deals available. **A** *Redang Pelangi Resort*, T6223158, F6235282. **D** *Pulau Redang Resort*, book in Kuala Terengganu, T6227050. Bungalows, 'A'-frames slightly cheaper.

Transport

Boat These leave for the islands from Merang as well as from the jetty in Kuala Terengganu. It has, however, become very expensive to charter boats from Merang. *Tourism Malaysia* in Kuala Terengganu recommends that tourists take advantage of the package deals offered by the island's resorts; further details can be obtained from the *Tourism Malaysia* office. There are now scheduled departures to Redang from Kuala Terengganu. From Merang: RM80 return for boat (takes 8 people) A typical 2-day/2-night trip costs around RM230 per person; all food, camping and snorkelling equipment included. As always, if you value a measure of privacy and seclusion, avoid weekends and public holidays. For further information contact *Coral Redang*, Jln Kampung Cina.

Pulau Perhentian

Colour map 1, grid A5
Travellers should be wary of risking the boat trip too close to the beginning or end of the Dec-Feb monsoon season

Two more beautiful east coast islands, Pulau Perhentian Besar (big) and Pulau Perhentian Kecil (small), just over 20 km off the coast are separated by a narrow sound with a strong current. Despite considerable development in recent years, with more hotels, restaurants, bars, diving outfits and much more noise, the Perhentian islands still remain a paradise, with excellent diving and snorkelling, magnificent beaches and some of the best places for swimming on the east coast. There is a fishing village and a turtle hatchery in the middle of Long Beach (Pasir Panjang) on Perhentian Kecil. There are jungle trails across Perhentian Besar; all are well marked.

All the resorts and chalets now have their own generators; and all have fresh water from wells. Competition for accommodation is fierce due to the ever increasing popularity of the Perhentians; this must be one of the few places in the world where demand regularly outstrips availability – strict planning laws ensure development is restricted. As the islands are not on the main phone system many of the numbers provided are mobile numbers which are liable to change. Bookings are therefore difficult to make, but worth trying as in the peak season many hotels will only accept people who have reservations. Upmarket resorts employ booking agents on the mainland. For those that don't it's advisable to take the earliest boat possible (particularly Kecil) and accept the first accommodation offer (see Transport page 299).

Sleeping

It is not uncommon for some travellers to end up sleeping on restaurant floors on their first night

Perhentian Besar There are a number of bays with accommodation on the larger island. The majority of it is located on the west coast, which is divided into 3 small beaches by outcrops of rock. There is more accommodation in the secluded bay of Telok Dalam. **A** *Coral View Island Resort*, T6974943 or T0109030943. A/c, shower. Quite an exlusive resort with 72 chalets at northern end of beach, rooms close together, bathroom attached. Sea views more expensive. **AL-A** *Perhentian Island Resort* (bookings c/o 25 Menara Promet, Jln Sultan Ismail, KL, T03 2448530, F2434984), T09030100 or T6974900, www.jaring.my/perhentian Some of the 103 rooms have a/c, licensed but expensive restaurant, some watersports facilities, tennis, swimming pool, diving equipment and courses available. **A-C** *Flora Bay Chalet*, Telok Dalam, T6977266 or 011977266. Provides a range of accommodation in the south of the island. **C** *ABC*, T0196977568. Eight cheap and basic huts, on the beach. **C** *Coco Hut Chalets*,T696977982 or T0199105019. Restaurant, unspecial 'A'-frames, although new ones with showers are being constructed. **B-C** *Fauna Beach Chalets*, T6977607 also on Telok Dalam. Reasonable chalets. **B-C** *Mama's*, T0109813359. Fan, shower. Selection of chalets for families or couples. Like every other hostel a daily snorkelling trip is organized. We have received some less than positive reports of this place. **B-D** *Abdul's*, T6977058. Decent looking chalets on the beach, fan and shower, with popular restaurant. Good local reputation. **B-D** *Cozy Chalet*, T0199595646 or T0123715234. Located at the end of the main beach on Besar. Chalets are perched elegantly on rocks over the sea. However this places does not have a good reputation. **B-D** *Tuna Bay Chalet* (formerly *Ibi's Chalet*), T0906974719. Fan, shower. Run down chalets on the beach. **C-D** *Perhentian Paradise Resort*, T0109810930 or T0199125151. Family or doubles available. Nice location set slightly back from the beach. Electricity from 1900-0700. **D** with seaview. **E** *Seahorse Chalets*, T0109841181. Affiliated to a dive centre, also offers internet access. Run-down 'A'-frames; cheap.

    Camping: RM5 at *Perhentian Island Resort*; camping is not restricted on the island. Restaurant and dive shop floors go for RM10; anybody found sleeping on the beach will be moved on.

Perhentian Kecil While there is more budget accommodation on Kecil it has gradually lost its reputation as a destination solely for backpackers and is becoming as popular as Besar. However Coral Bay is still fairly secluded. Accommodation is split, with some huts on the beautiful white sandy beach of Pasir Panjang, on the east side of the island, and some on Coral Bay, on the west. There are a couple of places at the southern tip, not far from Perhentian village and an isolated spot at Teluk Kerma.

    Long Beach There is a hotel complex being built at the end of Long Beach to cater, apparently, to the growing domestic tourist market. **A-B** *D'Lahar*, T0109853589. Significantly more expensive than any other accommodation on Long Beach although

East Coast Peninsula

not noticeably better than some, a/c, **B** with fan. **C** *Mohsin*, T0103338897. Elevated position behind *Cempaka*, steep stairs to get to the restaurant where there are great views. 30 rooms, mostly in rows. Considered one of the best places on the island, with attached bathrooms and 24-hr electricity. Good restaurant and daily snorkelling tour. One of the only places on the island to take bookings. **C-D** *Cempaka*,T6877604. Southern end, pleasantly uncramped site with sea views for all the 10 chalets, no electricity, but lamps are provided, charcoal for cooking is provided, shared bathroom. Run down but functional. **C-D** *Matahari*,T0199568726. Excellent restaurant, the best place to stay on the island, often full, proof of its popularity. Set back slightly from the beach but central. **C-D** *Panorama*, T0109122518. Attractive chalets with attached showers and toilets, fans and mosquito nets, a reasonable option. **C-D** *Moonlight Chalets*, T01998582222. No fan, shared bathroom, some less than glittering repots regarding some of the employees here. **D** *Simfony*, T0199104236. Simple chalets with common showers and toilets, with fan and 24 hr electricity, no bathroom. **D-E** *Rock Garden*, below *Mohsin's*. Shared bathroom, very basic, but cheap.

Coral Bay B-C *Maya Beach Resort*, T0199379136. New chalets with fan and attached bathrooms in the centre of the beach. Restaurant. **B-C** *Sunset View Chalets*, T0199631961. Elevated restaurant with good sea views, with 24 hr electricity. **C** *Butterfly Chalets*, built on the rocks at the end of the beach. Fan. **C** *Coral Bay*, T0123707676. Modern, clean chalets and good restaurant. **B-D** *Rajiwali's*,T6977906. At the end of the bay with elevated views, dirty and old, but extremely friendly and helpful staff. **C-D** *DJ's*, another reasonable option on the beach. Separate bathroom, fan. **D** *Aur Beach*, and nicer than *DJ's* next door. Cheaper rooms available without bathroom.

Pulau Perhentian

N

Not to scale

■ **Sleeping**
1 ABC
2 Abdul's
3 Coco Hut Chalets
4 Cempaka
5 Coral View Island Resort
6 Cozy Chalet
7 D'Lagoon
8 D'Lahar
9 Flora Bay Chalet
10 Mama's Chalets
11 Matahari
12 Maya Beach Resort
13 Mohsin
14 Moonlight Chalets
15 Panorama

Other B-E *D'Lagoon*, Teluk Kerma, T010/0199857089, www.geocities.com/d_lagoon_my Very remote position at the northern end of the island, some rooms in a longhouse, chalets have attached bathrooms, restaurant, a secluded, quiet spot with excellent snorkelling. **C** *Pasir Petani Resort*, T0199571624. At the southern end of the island, chalets with fans and attached bathrooms. **C-E** *Mira Beach Chalets*, T0199640582, Mira beach, south of Coral Bay (accessible on foot). Cheap chalets on this small but beautiful beach.

Eating

There are a couple of restaurants on Perhentian Besar serving simple food – banana pancakes, etc. Particularly popular are the restaurants attatched to *Coral View Island Resort*, *Coco Hut Chalets* and *Abdul's*. There are also coffee shops in the kampung on Perhentian Kecil and almost all the chalets here have restaurants at very similar prices (RM8). Milkshakes, fruit juices and pancakes are particularly recommended. On Coral Bay *Barracuda's* is good. In order to compete with restaurants on the beach, resorts further back have increased the price of their accommodation to include meals. Although this is not bad value it does limit choice at mealtimes.

Sports

Diving and snorkelling The coral around the Perhentian islands is some of the best off the east coast. Most guesthouses arrange snorkelling trips and provide masks, snorkels and fins. There are also dive shops (PADI) on Pulau Perhentian Besar which run courses and arrange dives for beginners to old hands, including night dives. *Turtle Bay Divers* (Long Beach, Perhentian Kecil) T0103319624. It is advisable to shop around for the best deal, and seek other tourists' advice to get an idea about the quality of the instructors who tend to vary from season to season.

Transport
20 km offshore

As it is important to get to the islands as early as possible on the day of arrival due to high demand for accommodation, it is a good idea to spend the previous night in **Kuala Besut**. This small fishing village has one main place to stay: *Nan's Guest House*, which is situated around the corner from the Perhentian Ferry Travel and Tours, and offers simple rooms with a/c or fan and attached bathroom.(Recommended). Business in this little fishing village has expanded to cater for those tourists passing through and good food can be found at a series of small restaurants along the waterfront.

Road Bus: From **Kuala Terengganu** (Jln Masjid): Kota Bharu-bound bus to Jerteh. Regular connections between **Jerteh** and **Kuala Besut**. From **Kota Bharu**: Bus 3, south-bound to **Pasir Puteh** (36 km south). Regular connections between **Pasir Puteh** and **Kuala Besut**. From **Kuala Lumpur**: *Rangkalan Mewah* bus company leaves at 0900 and 2130, T4432805. Boats leave from here to **Perhentian**. **Taxi**: Kuala Terengganu;

Pulau
Perhentian
Besar

East Coast Peninsula

16 Pasir Petani Resort
17 Perhentian Island Resort
18 Perhentian Paradise
    Resort
19 Seahorse Chalets
20 Simfony Chalets,
    Watercolour Divers &
    Turtle Bay Divers
21 Sunset View Chalets
22 Tuna Bay Chalet

Kota Bharu. Taxis from **Pasir Puteh** or **Jerteh** to **Kuala Besut**. Boats leave from here to **Perhentian**. Locals warn of a taxi scam which involves one particular firm running taxis from Kota Bharu to where they claim is Kuala Besut but in fact is Tok Bali. From here tourists can only buy return tickets valid on one type of ferry. – inconvenient to the traveller; double check your destination.

Boat We list set times of boats, but believe that there are now more options than listed, so it is worth taking a visit to the ferry company to enquire. Fast boats leave **Kuala Besut** at 0930, 1030, 1430, and take 30 mins, boats carry 8-10 people. The same boats leave **Pulau Perhentian** for **Kuala Besut** between 1130-1200 and 1530-1600. Slow boats leave Kuala Besut at approximately 0900 and 1630, take 1½-2 hrs and carry 12 people. They return from the islands at 0800, 1200 and 1600. For further information, call *Perhentian Ferry Travel & Tours*, T6919679. Those staying at the more remote *Pasir Petani Resort* on Perhentian Kecil should pre-arrange a pick-up time. Travellers should be wary of risking the boat trip too close to the beginning or end of the Dec-Feb monsoon season. The fishing boats are not best equipped for rough seas and life jackets are rarely available.

Directory **Banks** Note that there are no banks or ATM machines on the islands or in Besut and very few of the hotels accept credit cards. If you arrive in Besut short on cash, the nearest bank is a half-hour bus journey away, in Jerteh; buses leave every half hour. **Communications** Internet cafés: there are only two cafés on the islands, both located on Besar. They are very expensive compared to the mainland: 30 mins will set you back around RM12. The locations are: *Checkpoint*, which doubles as a shop and tour organizer, and the *Seahorse Dive Centre and Chalets*.

Kota Bharu

Colour map 1, grid A5
Phone code: 09

*Kota Bharu is the royal capital of Kelantan, 'the land of lightning', and is situated near the mouth of the Kelantan River. The city is one of Malaysia's Malay strongholds, despite its proximity to the Thai border. This was reinforced during the latest general elections when the opposition PAS once again managed to secure KB and Kelantan. While some people react against the state government's enthusiastic support for an Islamic interpretation of public (and private) morals, KB is one of Malaysia's more culturally interesting and colourful towns with many eclectic museums, mosques and grandiose royal palaces, including the Istana Batu, Istana Balai and Istana Jahar. The city's **wet market** is an unmissable experience and an architectural delight, and the **Kampung Kraftangan** handicraft village forms part of the impressive **Kelantan cultural zone**.*

Ins and outs

Getting there KB's airport is 8 km from town. There are links on *MAS* with KL, Penang and Ipoh. Unusually, the train station is 5 km from town at Wakaf Bharu. The line runs south to KL and Singapore. There is a confusion of 3 bus terminals in KB but the majority of express buses depart from the most central. There are connections with all major destinations on the Peninsula. Buses also run to Rantau Panjang and Pengkalan Kubor, both on the Thai border. Outstation taxis also offer a service to many larger towns.

Getting around The trishaw used to be the backbone of the town's public transport system, but taxis have just about elbowed them out of the scene. There is also a city bus service and a number of local and international car hire firms.

Tourist Information Centre, Jln Sultan Ibrahim, T7485534, F7482120. A helpful office, which will arrange taxis and ferries to the islands, as well as booking accommodation on the islands.

History

Kelantan may have been part of the second-century kingdom of Langkasuka (see page 180), but from early in the first millennium AD, it was an established agricultural state which adopted the farming practices of the kingdom of Funan on the lower Mekong River. Because it was effectively cut off from the west coast states of the peninsula, Kelantan always looked north: it traded with Funan, the Khmer Empire and the Siamese kingdom of Ayutthaya.

The fertile alluvial soils of the Kelantan River valley and the coastal plain have supported mixed farming and a thriving peasant economy for centuries

Kota Bharu

East Coast Peninsula

```
N
0 metres    200
0 yards     200
```

■ Sleeping
1 Aman
2 Ansar
3 City
4 Crystal Lodge
5 Dynasty Inn
6 Hostel Pantai Timor
7 Ideal Travellers' House
8 Indah
9 Johnty's Malay Guesthouse
10 Juita Inn
11 KB Backpackers Lodge
12 Kencana Lodge
13 Maryland
14 Menora
15 New Tokyo Baru
16 Perdana
17 Prince
18 Sabriena Court
19 Safar Inn
20 Sentosa
21 Yee
22 Zeck Traveller's Inn

● Eating
1 Mubihah Vegetarian Cake House

By the 14th century, Kelantan was under Siamese suzerainty, although at that time it also fell under the influence of the Javanese Majapahit Empire. For a while, during the 15th and 16th centuries, Kelantan joined other peninsular states in sending tribute to the Sultanate of Melaka, and its successor, Johor. By then the state had splintered into a number of small chiefdoms; one local chief, Long Mohammed, proclaimed himself Kelantan's first sultan in 1800.

When a succession dispute erupted on the death of the heirless Sultan Mohammed, Siam supported his nephew, Senik the 'Red-Mouth' who reigned for 40 peaceful years. On the next succession crisis, in 1900, Bangkok installed its own nominee as sultan. But in 1909, a treaty between Siam and Britain pushed Bangkok to cede its suzerainty over Kelantan to the British. This severed the state from its Islamic neighbour, the former sultanate of Petani, in Southeast Thailand. British interference caused much resentment and provoked a brief revolt in 1912. After using Kota Bharu as one of their beachheads for the invasion of Malaya in December 1941, the Japanese Imperial Army won support for restoring Kelantan to Thailand. In October 1945 however, Kelantan reluctantly joined the Malayan Union, under the British colonial administration.

Modern Kelantan Today Kelantan is Malaysia's most conservative and traditional state and since October 1990 it has been ruled by the hard-line Parti Islam – or *PAS*, its Malay acronym. In 1993 the PAS-led state government voted to introduce strict Islamic – or Syariat – law. Non-Muslims in the state – mainly in Kota Bharu, where one-third of the population is Chinese or Indian – were alarmed by the prospect of the '*hudud*' criminal code being implemented. It dictates that for crimes such as theft, fornication, intoxication and apostasy, 'criminals' should have their hands and/or legs severed or should be lashed until death if unrepentant. When Islamic officials broke up a rowdy Chinese New Year party in Kota Bharu in 1994, the local Chinese community thought their fears had been realized and that this was a taste of things to come.

Hudud can't become law until it's passed by a two-thirds majority in Federal Parliament, but the whole matter has become a conundrum for Muslim politicians in KL. Dr Mahathir's government does not want to be seen as un-Islamic by opposing Kelantan's move, so the Prime Minister has been busily polishing his own Islamic credentials by building new mosques and sponsoring Koran-reading competitions. For Dr Mahathir, the idea of having a mini-Iran as part of his Malaysian Federation is anathema. It totally conflicts with the vision of Islamic moderates and modernists. The battle between Kelantan and the government in KL continues. In the most recent general elections the opposition PAS once again managed to hold onto Kelantan despite the most fervent efforts by UMNO to secure a victory here and the promise of massive development funds. The state is a hotbed of opposition politics. PAS's newspaper is effectively the country's only opposition publication (or it was until its publishing license was withdrawn at the beginning of 2000). Tunku Razaleigh Hamzah, a prince of the Kelantan royal family, is a long term thorn in Mahathir's side. In 1987 when Razaleigh again faced up against Mahathir by trying to establish a breakaway mainstream Malay party (in which he failed), he said: "We don't have the problems that exist elsewhere. In Malaysia's quest for industrialization, those in power accept any development, whatever the cost to the environment. In Kelantan we resist."

This highly charged political and religious atmosphere contrasts with the Kelantanese people's laid-back, gentle manner. Tourists visiting the state should be particularly aware of Islamic sensitivities (see page 241), but the trappings of Islam rarely impinge on the enjoyment of the state's rich cultural heritage. But don't expect to find much in the way of funfairs: it was reported at the end of 1995 that the state government had banned bumper cars and Ferris wheels on the pretext that they allow teenagers too much body contact.

The crafts for which Kelantan is renowned – such as silverware, weaving and metal-working – were in part the result of the state's close relations with the Siamese kingdom of Ayutthaya in the 17th century. The *makyung*, a traditional Malay court dance, is still performed in Kelantan and *wayang kulit* (shadow puppet plays) still provide entertainment on special occasions in the kampungs. Kota Bharu is the centre for Malay arts and crafts, although batik printing, woodcarving, songket-weaving and silver working are more often confined to the villages.

Sights

The heart of Kota Bharu is the **central market** off Jalan Temenggong, which is one of the most vibrant and colourful wet markets in the country. It operates daily from 0900 to 2000. It is housed in a three-storey octagonal concrete complex painted green which has a glass roof and, because it's so bright, is a photographer's paradise. In the modern Buluh Kubu complex across the road on Jalan Tengku Petra Semerak, there are many shops selling Kelantanese batik and other handicrafts. Nearby is the **Istana Balai Besar**, the 'palace with the big audience hall', built in Patani-style in 1844 by Sultan Mohammed II. The *istana*, with its decorative panels and wood-carvings is still used on ceremonial occasions. The palace contains the throne-room and the elaborate royal barge, which the sultan only ever used once for a joy ride on the Kelantan River in 1900. It is not usually open to the public. Beside the old istana is the single-storey **Istana Jahar**, constructed in 1889 by Sultan Mohammed IV; it is now the 'centre for royal customs' and is part of the new cultural complex (see below). It exemplifies the skilled craftsmanship of the Kelantanese woodcarvers in its intricately carved beams and panels. There is a small craft collection including songket and silverware. ■ *0830-1645 except Fri, RM3.*

Kampung Kraftangan or Handicraft Village is close to the central market. It aims to give visitors a taste of Kelantan's arts and crafts all under one roof. The large enclosure, in which *merbuk* birds (doves) sing in their bamboo cages, contains four buildings, all wooden and built in traditional Malay style. They are part of the Kelantan cultural zone area which will include several museums, including the Istana Jahar. The complex is quite impressive, but visitors appear few and far between, giving the sprawling place a slightly empty, lackadaisical feel. The Handicraft Museum contains exhibits and dioramas of traditional Kelantanese crafts and customs. There is also a batik workshop and demonstration centre where local artists produce hand-painted batiks. There are several stalls, stocked with handicrafts such as batik, silverware and *songket*, for sale. At ground level there is a pleasant restaurant serving Kelantanese delicacies. ■ *Kampung Kraftangan free; Handicraft Museum RM1.* Opposite the new complex is the **Istana Batu**, the sky-blue Stone Palace, which was built in 1939 and was one of the first concrete buildings in the state. The former royal palace was presented to the state by the Sultan for use as a royal museum and contains many personal possessions of the royal family.

A little north of the commercial centre is **Padang Merdeka**, built after the First World War as a memorial. Merdeka Square is also where the British hanged Tok Janggut, 'Father Long-beard', who led the short-lived revolt against British land taxes in 1915. Opposite, on Jalan Sultan Zainab, is the **State Mosque**, which was completed in 1926. Next door is the State Religious Council building, dating from 1914. Next to the mosque on Jalan Merdeka is a magnificent two-storey green-and-white mansion with traditional Islamic latticework carving on eaves, which houses the **Islamic Museum**. The building itself is more noteworthy than its eclectic contents. ■ *0830-1645 Sat-Thu; donations only.* The **War Museum** next to the Islamic Museum gives visitors an informative account of the Second World War in Southeast Asia. Beginning with Pearl Harbor, it tells the story of the Japanese invasion of Kelantan in December 1941 and the subsequent conquest of Malaya. It includes many pictures and items from the period. ■ *0830-1645 except Fri, RM2 adult, RM1 child.*

Directly west of the mosque, running north-south along the riverbank is **Jalan Pasar Lama**, off Jalan Post Office Lama. This is an interesting area for a gentle stroll; there are many beautiful but rapidly decaying old Chinese shophouses (there's a large Chinese community in this part of town). Most of the buildings date to the early 1900s. Some have been rendered completely uninhabitable because vast trees have taken root inside them.

At the **Gelanggang Seni** (Cultural Centre), on Jalan Mahmud, opposite the stadium and close to *Perdana Hotel*, many traditional arts are regularly performed. The centre tends to get rather touristy but it is the best place to see a variety of cultural performances in one place. For more detail on each of these traditional forms of entertainment, see page 491. These include:

Demonstrations of *silat* (the Malay art of self-defence).

Drumming competitions (Sat and Mon, 1530-1730) using the *rebana ubi* Kelantan drums, made from hollowed-out logs.

Wayang kulit (shadow-puppet) performances (Wednesday nights, 2100-2300).

Kite-flying competitions (Saturday afternoons) with the famous paper-and-bamboo *wau bulan* – or Kelantan moon-kites, the symbol of *MAS*. This has been a Kelantanese sport for centuries; the aim is to fly your kite higher than anyone else's and, once up there, to defend your superiority by being as aggressive as possible towards other competitors' kites. Kite-flying, according to the Malay Annals, was a favourite hobby in the heyday of the Melaka sultanate in the 15th century. *Top-spinning* competitions (Saturday and Monday afternoons).

Other cultural performances include traditional dance routines such as the royal *Mak Yong* dance and the *Menora*, both of which relate local legends. A set programme of shows, available from the Tourist Promotion Board, usually Saturdays 2100-2300. Coconut-Husk Percussion is on Wednesday 1530-1730. All shows only March to October and the schedule is subject to change; check with the Tourist Information. One-off shows also happen at specific dates throughout the year (some outside Kota Bharu). These include, for example, traditional food and handicraft competitions. The organiser of many of these shows, Roselan Hanafiah Al-Idrus is also the manager of the local Tourist Information office and runs his own in-house cookery workshop followed by a five-course meal of traditional Malay food (RM55). Booking should be made a day in advance (T7485534, or home 7748130, roselanhanafiah@hotmail.com). This colourful tourism mogul also runs his own river cruise, see below.

The **State Museum** is situated on Jalan Sultan Ibrahim near the clock tower and next to the Tourism Malaysia office. ■ *0830-1645, Sat-Thu, T7482266. RM2.*

Excursions

Also known as Tin Heng Keong, this Chinese temple is 1 km out of town, on **Kong Mek** the road to PCB (see below). It is about 100 years old and is particularly colourful; best time to visit is 0900-1000 each day when the temple is particularly lively. There is another smaller temple with a grotesque laughing Buddha and a grotto on the riverbank, closer to town. From KB follow road to PCB; after 500 m, on sharp right bend, turn left at vegetable market; go down dirt track and turn right through Chinese gateway at bottom.

This is KB's most famous beach, now renamed **Pantai Cahaya Bulan**, but still **Pantai Cinta** known as **PCB**, 10 km north of the city. It is really only famous for its name, **Berahi** meaning the 'Beach of Passionate Love'. In 1994 the Islamic state government, which takes a dim view of passionate love, rechristened it the Beach of the Shining Moon, which conveniently retains the old acronym, PCB. In comparison with some other east coast beaches, it is an unromantic dump. In Malay, the word *berahi* is, according to one scholar, "loaded with sexual dynamite ... a love madness". Local Malays, alluding to this heated innuendo, used to euphemistically call it *pantai semut api* – the beach of the fire ants. Today, young Malay lovers do not even dare to hold hands on the beach, for fear of being caught by the religious police and charged with *khalwat*, the crime of 'close proximity', under *Syariat* Islamic law. The origin of the name *cinta berahi* is lost. One theory is that it was used as a code word by Malay and British commandos during the Japanese wartime occupation: the site of the Imperial Army's invasion, in 1941, is nearby, on Pantai Dasar Sabak (see page 305). Despite being rather over-rated, there are several resorts along the beach. It gets crowded on weekends and room rates rise accordingly. To get there take a minibus 10, which leaves every 20 minutes from Bazaar Buluh Kubu, off Jalan Tengku Chik or from Jalan Padang Garong, or take a taxi.

Sleeping **A** *Perdana Resort* (also known as *PCB Resort*), Jln Kuala Pa'Amat, T7744000, F7744980. A/c, restaurant, pool, watersports, pleasanter stretch of beach, dotted with white chalets colour schemed blue, green and pink according to room type, not very well maintained, popular with business conventions and meetings. **C-D** *Long House Beach Motel*, T7731090. Some a/c, restaurant (Thai food), not bad value really but it doesn't have a great deal of charm. **D-E** *HB Village*, T7734993. Very clean, very friendly and very big crocodiles in attached farm.

Pantai Dalam Rhu, also known as Pantai Bisikan Bayu, or the 'Beach of the **Other beaches** Whispering Breeze', lies 40 km southeast of KB: There is **E** *Dalam Rhu Homestay*, which has simple kampung-style accommodation and is well looked after. Take bus 3, southbound, and change at Pasir Puteh. **Pantai Irama**, the 'Beach of Melody', 25 km south of KB, is the best of the nearby beaches for swimming. The **B-C** *Motel Irama Bachok*, Bachok, T7788462, is clean and reasonable value. To get there, take a bus 2A or 2B to Bachok, which leaves every 30 minutes. **Pantai Dasar Sabak**, 13 km northeast of KB, is where the Japanese troops landed on 7 December 1941, 90 minutes before they bombed Pearl Harbor. Nearby Kampung Sabak is a good place to watch fishing boats come in in the morning. To get there, take a bus 8 or 9 from old market terminal.

Waterfalls In the area round Pasir Puteh there are several waterfalls: Jeram **Other** Pasu, Jeram Tapeh and Cherang Tuli. **Jeram Pasu** is the most popular, 35 km **excursions**

from Kota Bharu. It is most easily accessible by taxi or bus 3 to Padang Pak Amat (RM1.70) and taxi to the waterfalls.

Tumpat Around Tumpat, next to the border, are small Thai communities where there are a few Thai-style buildings and wats; they do not, however, compare with the Thai architecture on the other side of the border. **Wat Phothivian** at Kampung Berok 12 km east of KB, on the Malaysian side of Sungai Golok, has a 41 m reclining Buddha statue, built in 1973 by chief abbot Phra Kruprasapia Chakorn, which attracts thousands of Thai pilgrims every year. Take bus 27 or 19 to Chabang Empat and then a taxi the last 3-4 km to Kampung Jambu. This last part of the journey also makes for a pleasant enough rural stroll.

Masjid Kampung Laut at Kampung Nilam Puri, 10 km south of KB, was built 300 years ago by Javanese Muslims as an offering of thanks for being saved from pirates. Having been damaged once too often by monsoon floods, it was dismantled and moved inland to Kampung Nilam Puri, which is an Islamic scholastic centre. It was built entirely of cengal, a prized hardwood, and constructed without the use of nails. It vies with Masjid Kampung Kling (in Melaka) for the title of Malaysia's oldest mosque. Bus 44 or express bus 5 leaves every 30 minutes.

River trips From Kuala Kerai (a 1½-hour bus trip south from Kota Bharu, bus 5) departs 0745 Monday-Sunday, it is possible to take a boat upriver to Dabong, a small kampung nestled among the jungled foothills of the Main Range (two hours, departs 1000 but not on Friday), where there is a resthouse and restaurant. Dabong, in the centre of Kelantan state, is on the north-south railway, so it is possible to catch the train back to Wakaf Bharu (across the river from KB), the journey takes two hours 45 minutes (third class only). Alternatively, take a taxi.

Tours

KTIC (Kelantan State Tourist Information Centre) organizes a number of tours – river and jungle-safari trips, staying in kampungs and learning local crafts. They also organize three-day 'Kampung Experience' tours which are not as contrived as their name suggests. Full board and lodging provided by host families which can be selected from list including potters, fishermen, batik-makers, kite-makers, silversmiths, dance instructors, top-makers and shadow puppet-makers. All only available by request. Cost from RM285 (all in); minimum two people. They also run short Kelantanese cooking courses.

For an insider's view of the town and surrounding areas, Mr Al-Idrus offers his own tour in which he promises a unique view of Kelantan life, taking visitors into the home of shadow-puppet makers and to out-of-the-way temples. T7485534, or home 7748130, roselanhanafiah@hotmail.com

Essentials

Sleeping
None of the hotels except for the Murni serves alcohol so minibars are usually a bleak sight

Budget travellers are spoilt for choice in KB; there are some very pleasant cheaper hostels and guesthouses (most of them in secluded alleyways with gardens) and they are locked in fearsome competition. As a result, new ones start up all the time as old ones fold; the State Tourist Information Centre has a list of budget accommodation and is happy to make recommendations. Until recently, the selection of top-bracket and mid-range hotels was poor – however, a number of new **A-B** bracket hotels have recently opened.

A *Perdana*, Jln Mahmud, T7485000, F7447621. A/c, restaurant, pool, tennis and squash courts, bowling alley, best in town, central location, babysitting, gym, sauna, traditional massage. Broad spectrum of tour information available and also a travel agent on site. **A-B** *Mawar*, Jln Doktor, T7448888, F7476666. New and well located. **A-B** *Crystal Lodge*, 124 Jln Che Su, T7470888, F7470088, crystlod.tm.net.my A/c and attached bathroom, breakfast with morning newspaper provided. Attractive and good open-air roof restaurant. Karaoke and mini-cinema. **A-B** *Dynasty Inn*, 2865 D and E Jln Sultan Zainab, T7473000, F7473111, dynasty@hotmail.com A hotel with 47 rooms, a/c, TV, hot shower, good views, rooftop coffee house, Chinese seafood restaurant. Extra bed available for RM18.

B *Ansar*, Jln Maju, T7474000, F7461150. New, clean hotel, conveniently located near the night market, it is an Islamic hotel, so no shoes, prayers in the hallways and signs mentioning Allah in the elevators, basic breakfast included, overpriced. Very comfortable with decent rooms and business centre. **B** *Juita Inn*, Jln Pintu Pong, T7446888, F7445777, Hotel@tm.net.my Attractive hotel with 70 rooms, a/c, TV, minibar, restaurant, room rates include breakfast. Rooms are small but clean and well furnished – note that the superior rooms have no windows, not particularly good value. **B** *Safar Inn*, Jln Hilir Kota, T7478000, F7479000. A hotel with 31 rooms, a/c, TV, carefully furnished rooms with wall-to-wall carpets. Undergoing rennovations in 2001. Good location, in the heart of town. **B** *Sentosa*, 3180-A Jln Sultan Ibrahim, T7443200/7443292. A/c, restaurant (formerly *Irama Baru & Apollo Hotel*), all spruced up, very clean and car rental organized. Great value.

B-C *Suria Hotel*, Jln Padan Garong, T7432255, F7432555, suriakb@tm.net.my 49 rooms all with a/c, television, telephone and fridge, semi-suite rooms also available. **B-C** *New Tokyo Baru*, 3945 Jln Tok Hakim, T7449488/7444511. A/c, well-maintained place, friendly. Recommended. **B-D** *Sabriena Court*, Jln Padang Garong, T7447944, F7447955, SabrienaCourt@hotmail.com A/c, restaurant, reasonable value for money, also offers some backpacker accommodation; do not confuse with sister hotel, *Hotel Sri Kencana*.

C *Hotel Indah*, Jln Tengku Besar, T7485081, F7482788. A/c, shower. Another average hostel, not particularly good value. **C** *Hotel Sri Kencana* (City Centre), Jln Doktor, T7440944, F7440181. A/c, shower, slightly dingier but large rooms. **C** *Kencana Lodge*, Jln Sn Cemerang, T74772222, F7477111. A/c, shower, TV. Pretty average with an inconvenient location. **C** *Maryland*, 2726-2727 Jln Tok Hakim, T7482811. A/c, reasonably priced, clean with big, airy rooms but no atmosphere. **C** *Prince*, 2953 Jln Temenggong, T7482066. Run by a very friendly man named Fendi (who also guides groups in the national park and takes trips to Pulau Perhentian), a/c, clean, with large communal area, good value. **C-E** *Johnty's Malay Guesthouse*, 7 Jln Buluh Kubu, Tingkat 2, (off Jln Dusun Raja), T7432600/, tekjohntys@hotmail.com Some a/c, popular but past its peak, rooms and dorm, offers excursions, bike hire, traditional massage and free breakfast to keep up with the Joneses, in a quiet corner on the outskirts of town.

D *Aman*, 23C/D Jln Tengku Besar, T7443049. A/c, restaurant, not particularly good value, but no extra charge for regular alarm calls courtesy of mosque next door. Desperately in need of refurbishment. **D** *Hostel Pantai Timor*, Lot 391 Jln Pengkalan Chepa, behind Safra Jaya supermarket, T7483753. Well kept, friendly, also dorms. **D** *Ideal Travellers' House*, 5504a Jln Padang Garong, T7442246, idealtrahouse@hotmail.com Quiet, friendly, pleasant verandah, rooms and dormitory. This family-run, popular hostel also helps with onward transport to Thailand and the Perhentians. However, we have received a report of unpleasant behaviour on the part of the owner, who attempts to offer 'chinese treatments' to single women – avoid succumbing to his persuasive ways. **D** *KB Backpackers Lodge*, T7432125. Opposite *KB Inn* on Jln Padang Garong, fan, separate bathroom (tepid water), very small rooms with no windows, bored staff and generally run down. **D** *KB Inn*, 1872 Jln Padang Garong, T7441786. Very close to bus station and night market, breakfast and hot drinks free,

East Coast Peninsula

small sitting area, typical of centre of town budget accommodation. **D** *Sri Cemerlang Hostel*, 5640 U-X Jln Sri Cemerlang, T7449648. A/c, good value, clean. **D-F** *Town*,286 Jln Pengkalan Chepa, T 7461858, F2053803, www.tghkb. ourfamily.com Some rooms with a/c and own bathroom, travel information and booking available here. Friendly, helpful management.

E *Floating Homestay*, Raft House 70, Jln Tengku Chik, T010-906252/011-977252 (both mobile). Close to centre of town, off Jln Post Office Lama; unlicensed with tourist board but very well run and river cruises. A new boat has recently been built, rooms are clean and simple, mosquito nets provided; unique and recommended. **E** *Menora*, Wisma Chua Tong Boon, (1st Flr) Jln Sultanah Zainab, T7481669. Well kept, facilities include TV and powerful showers, dorm (**F**). Recommended. **E** *Rainbow*, 4423 Jln Pengkalan Chepa. Helpful, attractive garden but near noisy road, breakfast included. **E** *Zeck Traveller's Inn*, 7088-G Jln Sri Cemerlang, T7431613, ztraveller_Inn@ hotmail.com Some rooms with private shower, dorm rooms, verandah, light meals available, free pick-up from bus station, one of the most popular places to stay. **E** *Zee Hostel*, 696-a Lorong Hj. Sufian, Jln Sultanah Zainab, T7445376. Dormitory accommodation.

E-F *City*, 2nd Flr, 35 Jln Pintu Pong (next to *Kentucky Fried Chicken*), clean and helpful on local information, price including breakfast, dorm (**F**), email facility, cramped but acceptable. **E-F** *Wann's*, Jln Sultanah Zainab, T7485381 (behind silversmith). Clean, good value. Recommended. **E-F** *Yee*, Jln Padang Garong, 2nd Flr, T7441944. Everything you need: laundry, breakfast, showers, travel information, bicycles for hire, dorm (**F**), unfortunately, the rooms are dirty. **F** *DE999*, next to *Rebana*, Jln Sultanah Zainab, T7481955. Cheap and clean rooms, close to the Cultural Centre, price including breakfast, free bicycles, dorm and rooms.Popular with Japanese tourists.

Eating
Beer and other alcoholic beverages are only available in certain Chinese coffee shops, notably along Jln Kebun Sultan

The Kelantan speciality is *ayam percik* – roast chicken, marinated in spices and served with a coconut-milk gravy. *Nasi tumpang* is a typical Kelantanese breakfast; banana-leaf funnel of rice layers interspersed with prawn and fish curries and salad. **Mid-range** *Kuchino Italiano*, 147 Jln Pengkalau Chepa, on main road between city centre and the airport, family run restaurant, a poor attempt at Italian cuisine; *Ambassador*, 7003 Jln Kebun Sultan, big Chinese coffee shop next to *Kow Lun* (below), Chinese dishes including pork satay and other iniquitous substances – like beer; *Kow Lun*, 7005 and 7006 Jln Kebun Sultan, good lively Chinese coffee shop with large variety of dishes and lots of beer; *Malaysia*, 2527 Jln Kebun Sultan, Chinese cuisine, speciality: steamboat, this is the place to sample turtle eggs – legally; **Cheap** *Meena Curry House*, 3377 Jln Gajah Mati, Indian curry house, banana leaf restaurant. Recommended. *Neelavathy*, Jln Tengku Maharani (behind *Kencana Inn*), South Indian banana-leaf curries. Recommended. *Qing Liang*, Jln Zainal Abidin, excellent Chinese vegetarian, also Malay and Western dishes. Recommended. *Satay Taman Indraputra*, Jln Pekeliling/Jln Hospital garden; *Syam*, Jln Hospital, Thai-influenced.

Indian Food can be found on Jln Gajah Mati. **Chinese** food is available on Jln Kebun Sultan.

Foodstalls *Night market* (in car park opposite local bus station, in front of Central Market), exclusively Malay food, satays and exquisite array of curries; for a delectable sweet dish to round off the evening, try the banana *murtabak*. Colour-coded tables – if you eat from a certain stall and sit at a blue table, you are obliged to buy your drink from a stall in the blue area; excellent fruit juices, no alcohol. Open every night from 1800, but closes from 1900-2000 for evening prayers. More choice and atmosphere at the weekends. Recommended. *Nasi Padang Osman Larin* (otherwise known as *Nasi Hoover* as it is outside *Hotel Hoover*) is a stall on Jln Datuk Pati (between the Tourist Information Centre and the bus station) famed locally for its curries. By the stadium in Jln Muhamud.

Bakery *Mubihah Vegetarian Restaurant and Cake House*, opposite *Kentucky Fried Chicken*, 157 Jln Pintu Pong. Eat in or takeaway; excellent breads, pastries, cakes etc – one of the best '*kek and roti*' shops in Malaysia.

Cultural shows Regular cultural shows at the *Gelanggang Seni* (cultural centre), Jln Mahmud (see above). **Entertainment**

May/Jun: *Malaysia International Kite Festival*, Pantai Seri Tujuh (Beach of the Seven Lagoons), Turnport (adjacent to Thai border), 7 km from KB. To get there take bus 43. **Festivals**
Jul: *Drum festival* (movable) a traditional east coast pastime. *Sultan's birthday celebrations* (10th-12th).
Aug: *Bird Singing Contest* (movable) when the prized *merbuk* (doves) or *burong ketitir* birds compete on top of 8 m-high poles. Bird singing contests are also held on Fri mornings around Kota Bharu.
Sep: Top-spinning contest (movable) another traditional east coast sport which is taken very seriously.

Antiques *Lam's*, Jln Post Office Lama (in contrast to the modern town walk there are several old bamboo raft houses along this street). **Shopping**
Batik *Astaka Fesyer*, 782K (3rd floor). Recommended. *Bazaar Buluh Kubu*, Jln Tengku Petra Semerak, just across the road from the Central Market, houses scores of batik boutiques; also in the building are tailors' shops which can turn out very cheap shirts, blouses and dresses within 24 hrs.
Handicrafts The Central Market is cheapest for handicrafts. There are numerous handicraft stalls, silver-workers, kite-makers and wood-carvers scattered along the road north to Pantai Cinta Berahi. At Kampung Penambang, on this road, just outside KB, there is a batik and songket centre.
Silverware On Jln Sultanah Zainab (near *Rabana Guest House*), before junction with Jln Hamzah, there are 3 shops selling Kelantan silver including *KB Permai*, a family business which works the silver on the premises. The new *Kampung Kraftangan* (Handicraft Village) contains many stalls with a huge range of batik sarongs and ready-mades, silverware, songket, basketry and various Kelantanese knick-knacks.

Golf *Royal Kelantan Golf Club*, 5488 Jln Hospital, green fees weekdays RM80, weekends RM120, 18-hole course. **Sports**

Batuta Travel & Tour, 1st Flr, Bangunan PKDK, Jln Dato' Pati, T7442652; *Boustead Travel*, 2833 Jln Temenggong, T7449952; *Kelmark Travel*, Kelmark House, 5220 Jln Telipot, T7444211; *Pelancongan Bumi Mars*, Tingkat Bawah, Kompleks Yakin, Jln Gajah Mati, T7431189. The *Tourist Information Centre* also arrange tours as do several of the guesthouses in town. **Tour operators**

Local Bus: city buses and many long-distance express buses leave from the Central Bus Station, Jln Hilir Pasar, so there is no need to go to the inconveniently located long distance bus stations in the south of the city. Regional buses to places like **Gua Musang** and **Pasir Puteh** also depart from this station. **Car hire**: *Avis, Hotel Perdana*, Jln Sultan Mahmud, T7484457, South China Sea, airport, T7744288, F7736288; from *Perdana Hotel*. *Pacific*, T7447610. **Trishaw:** short journeys RM2-4; RM12-15 per hr; recommended way of touring town but they are gradually disappearing as salaries rise and people opt for motorized transport. **Transport**
474 km to KL
168 km to Terengganu
371 km to Kuantan

East Coast Peninsula

Long distance Air: airport is 8 km from town; RM12 per taxi. Regular connections with **Ipoh**, **KL**, **Penang** on *MAS*. Transport to town: by taxi RM10 per person or town bus No 9.

Bus: KB has 3 long-distance bus stations although many express buses leave from the central terminal on Jln Hilir Pasar, saving on a trip to one of the two out of town stations. The main intercity express bus company is the state-owned *SKMK* and its buses leave both from the central station on Jln Hilir Pasar and from the Langgar bus station south of town on Jln Pasir Puteh. The second out of town bus terminal is also south of town on Jln Hamzah and all bus companies other than *SKMK* operate vehicles from here. Regular connections with: **Grik**, **Kuala Terengganu**, **Jerantut**, **Kuantan**, **KL**, **JB**, **Penang**, **Alor Star**, **Kuala Lipis**, **Butterworth**, **Melaka**, **Mersing**, **Temerloh**, and many other destinations. Buses from Kuala Lumpur leave at 0900 and 2100 from Putra Station (*Mutiara Express*, T4433655, *PPMP*, T4445699, *Naela Express*, T4439155). **Taxi**: taxi station next to the Central Bus Station, Jln Hilir Pasar. Destinations include **Kuala Terengganu**, **Kuantan**, **KL**, **JB**, **Butterworth**, **Grik**. Also taxis to **Rantau Panjang** (for **Sungai Golok, Thailand**).

International connections The Thai border is at the Malaysian town of Rantau Panjang; on the other side is the Thai settlement of Sungai Golok. Bus no 29 for **Rantau Panjang** leaves on the hr through the day from the central bus station, off Jln Hilir Pasar (1½ hrs). From here it is a shortish 1-km walk across the border to **Sungai Golok's** train and bus stations where there are connections to other destinations in Thailand including Hat Yai, Surat Thani (for Koh Samui) and Bangkok. Trishaws and motorbike taxis wait to assist people making the crossing. Another route into Thailand is via **Pengkalan Kubor**, a quieter and much more interesting crossing to **Ta Ba** (Tak Bai). Bus nos. 27, 27a and 43 go to **Pengkalan Kubor**. Small boats cross the river regularly and there is also a car ferry. Long-tails cater for the clientele of the cross-border prostitution industry only. There are also regular bus connections with **Singapore**.

Train: Wakaf Bharu station is 5 km out of town, across the Kelantan River. Bus 19 or 27. Daily connections with **Singapore** and **KL** via **Gua Musang**, **Kuala Lipis**, **Jerantut** and **Gemas**. The jungle railway is slow but the scenery makes the journey worthwhile. *Golden Blowpipe* departs Wakaf Bharu in the early afternoon and arrives Gemas at around midnight (connections arrive Singapore/KL early next morning). Second class a/c connections with Jerantut-Taman Negara, KL and Singapore.

Directory **Airline offices** *MAS*, Ground Floor, Komplek Yakin, Jln Gajah Mati (opposite the clock tower), T7447000 and T7440557 at the airport; **Banks** Money changers in main shopping area. *Bumiputra*, Jln Maju; *D & C*, Jln Gajah Mati; *Hongkong & Shanghai*, Jln Sultan. **Communications** General Post Office: Jln Sultan Ibrahim. **Telegraph Office:** Jln Doktor. **Embassies and consulates** *Royal Thai Consulate*, Jln Pengkalan Chepa, T7440867 (open 0900-1200, 1330-1530, Mon-Thu and Sat). **Medical facilities** Hospitals: Jln Hospital. T7485533. **Useful addresses** Immigration Office: 3rd Flr, Federal Bldg, Jln Bayam. T7482120.

Gua Musang Gua Musang is the largest town on Route 8, the road through the interior, and lies in Kelantan state close to the border with Pahang. It began life as little more than a logging camp but has now expanded into a thriving administrative centre. The jungle is studded with limestone outcrops in this area of the Peninsula and a particularly impressive one overshadows Gua Musang. There have been reports of large mammals including wild elephants, tigers and tapirs along the roads near here and this is about as wild as Peninsular Malaysia gets outside the national parks and wildlife reserves.

C *Kesedar Inn*, T099121229. On the edge of town, attractive lawn, clean rooms, friendly. **E** *Rest House*, rather run down but an attractive place to stay, shared facilities.

Bus: daily buses from Kuala Lipis to Gua Musang (0800 and 1300) and Kuala Krai (1430) with onward connections to Kota Bharu.

Grik

Also spelt Gerik, Grik was once a remote logging town just a few kilometres south of the Thai border. It is now on an important junction, and the beginning of the east-west highway. Few people stay the night there, but it is a good staging post and midday *makan* stop. The huge Temenggor and Lenering man-made reservoirs are nearby.

Grik can be reached from Kuala Kangsar in Perak (see page 147) or from Butterworth via either Kulim (directly east of the town) or Sungai Petani (35 km north of town) which lead first to Keroh, on the Thai border, then on to Grik. The Kuala Kangsar route is a particularly scenic drive along a 111 km road which winds its way up the Perak River valley, enclosed by the Bintang mountains to the west and the Main Range to the east. En route, the road passes Tasek Chenderoh, a beautiful reservoir, surrounded by jungled hills. At **Kota Tampan**, just north of the lake, archaeologists have unearthed the remains of a Stone Age workshop, with roughly chiselled stone tools dating back 35,000 years. The road cuts through the jungle and there are some spectacular viewpoints. There are landslides along this stretch of road during the wet season.

Sleeping **A** *Banding Island Resort*, PO Box 69, Banding, T7912273. Restaurant situated on an island on Lake Temengor and 15 years old. It went through a bad patch but has recently been renovated and expanded with new facilites and bungalows. The only shame is that the previously beautiful views of the inlet and headland have been reportedly partially obscured. Popular with tour groups. **D** *Diamond*, 40A Jln Sultan Iskander, T892388. **D** *Kong Seng*, 32 Jln Sultan Iskander, T892180. **D** *Rumah Rehat Grik*, Jln Meor Yahaya, T891211. **D-E** *Bee Hoon*, Jln Tan Sabah, T892201.

Because Grik is not on the main tourist track, accommodation is basic

Transport **Bus**: Connections with **Butterworth**, **KL**, **Taiping** and **Ipoh**. For **Kota Bharu** change at **Tanah Merah**. It is possible to cross the border into Thailand from **Keroh**, 50 km north of Grik. There are regular taxis from **Keroh** to the border post and Thai taxis and *saamlors* (trishaws) on the other side. There are Thai taxis to **Betong** which is 8 km from the border.

Coast to coast

*The East-West highway makes for a memorable journey. It runs from **Kota Bharu** to **Penang**, straight across the forested backbone of the peninsula and was one of the biggest civil engineering projects ever undertaken in Malaysia. During its 11-year construction, contractors had to push their way through densely jungled mountains, coping with frequent landslides and even hit-and-run attacks by Communist insurgents.*

To the east of **Grik**, the highway runs close to the former bases of the Communist Party of Malaya, which, until 1989, operated out of their jungle headquarters near Betong, just across the Thai border. The area was known as 'Target One' by the Malaysian security forces. The construction of the road opened

East Coast Peninsula

the previously inaccessible area up to timber companies; there has been much illegal logging – and cross-border drug-smuggling – in this 'cowboy country' of North Perak and Kelantan. The 200 km-long highway opened in 1982, and for the first few years was closed to traffic after 1600 because of the security threat posed by Communist insurgents; this threat has now ended. However, road maintenance is something of a hazard, and the journey is slow going with a whole series of road works and places where the road has subsided.

The *Golden Blowpipe* trundles along the railway line which cuts a diagonal through the peninsula, running due north from Gemas (south of KL on the KL-Singapore line) to **Kota Bharu**. Much of the route is through the jungle, and the track skirts the west boundary of **Taman Negara**, the national park (see page 271). Those heading into Taman Negara must disembark at **Tembeling Halt**, to the southeast of **Kuala Lipis**, or at **Jerantut**. The train is slow, but it is an interesting journey. From **Gemas** the line goes through Jeranut, Kuala Lipis, **Gua Musang**, **Kuala Krai** and on to Kota Bharu. It is possible to catch the train at **Mentakab** (along the Karak Highway, east of KL) or at Kuala Lipis, which can be reached by road via **Fraser's Hill** and **Raub**. It is also possible to drive from Kuala Lipis via Gua Musang to Kota Bharu. There are buses from Kuala Lipis to Gua Musang and Kuala Krai.

Sarawak

7

Sarawak

The 'land of the hornbill', Sarawak is the largest state in Malaysia covering an area of nearly 125,000 sq km in Northwest Borneo and with a population of only a little more than two million. Sarawak has a swampy coastal plane, a hinterland of undulting foothills and an interior of steep-sided, jungle-covered mountains. The lowlands and plain are dissected by a network of broad rivers that are the main arteries of communication and where the majority of the population are settled.

In the mid-19th century, Charles Darwin described Sarawak as "one great wild, untidy, luxuriant hothouse, made by nature for herself". Sarawak is Malaysia's great natural storehouse, where little more than half a century ago great swathes of forest were largely unexplored and where tribal groups, collectively known as the Dayaks, would venture downriver from the heartlands of the state to exchange forest products of hornbill ivory and precious woods. Today, admittedly, much has changed; the Dayaks have been gradually incorporated into the mainstream and the market economy has infiltrated the lives of the great majority of the population. But much remains unchanged. The grandeur of the forests, although much reduced by a rapacious logging industry, are still some of the most species-rich on the globe; more than two-thirds of Sarawak's land area, roughly equivalent to that of England and Scotland combined, is still covered in jungle.

Kuching

Colour map 3, grid C1
Population: 460,000
Phone code: 082

Because of Kuching's relative isolation, and the fact that it was not bombed during the Second World War, Sarawak's state capital has retained much of its 19th-century dignity and charm, despite the increasing number of modern high-rise buildings. Chinese shophouses still line many of the narrow streets. Covered sampans, or perahu tambang, paddle back and forth across the river from the riverfront esplanade to the kampongs and the Astana on the north bank. Kuching is a great starting point to explore the state and there are many sights within it's compact centre, including the renowned **Sarawak Museum** *and the* **Petra Jaya State Mosque***. Within easy reach is the* **Semenggoh Orang Utan Sanctuary** *and the* **national parks** *of* **Gunung Gading** *and* **Kubah***.*

Sarawak's capital is divided by the Sarawak River; the south is a commercial and residential area, dominated by Chinese while the north shore is predominantly Malay in character with the old kampong houses lining the river. The **Astana**, **Fort Margherita** and the **Petra Jaya area**, with its modern government offices, are also on the north side of the river. The two parts of the city are very different in character and even have separate mayors. Kuching's cosmopolitan make-up is immediately evident from its religious architecture: Chinese and Hindu temples, the imposing state mosque and Protestant and Roman Catholic churches.

Of all the cities in Malaysia, Kuching has been the worst affected by the 'smog' - euphemistically known as the 'haze' - that periodically engulfs large areas of Borneo and the Indonesian island of Sumatra. This was most severe in mid-1997 (see page 566), but it has also occurred since, in 1998 and 2000, for example. At the peak of the 'emergency' in late September 1997 – for that is what it became – Kuching came to a stop. It was too dangerous to drive and, seemingly, too dangerous to breathe. People were urged to remain indoors. Schools, government offices and factories closed. The port and aiport were also closed. Tourism traffic dropped to virtually zero and for 10 days the city stopped. At one point there was even discussion of evacuating the population of the State of Sarawak. People began to buy up necessities and the prices of some commodities rose 500%.

Ins and outs

Getting there
See also Transport page 335
There are daily connections with KL and also regular flights to other destinations in Peninsular and East Malaysia. International connections are limited to Bandar Seri Begawan (Brunei), Singapore, Hong Kong, Taipei, Manila, Seoul, Tokyo, Perth and Pontianak (Kalimantan, Indonesia). There are several out-of-town bus companies and they provide services to destinations along the main coastal road north to Miri, close to the border with Brunei, and south to Sematan. Interior towns are sometimes difficult to access by road. There is also a bus service to Pontianak in Kalimantan (Indonesia) and to Brunei, via Miri. Express boats serve Sibu and Sarikei.

Getting around
The central portion of the city, which is the most interesting, can be negotiated on foot. Sampans, known locally as *tambangs*, provide cross-river transport and operate as river taxis. There are 2 city bus companies that provide a cheap and fairly efficient service. Taxis are found outside many of the larger hotels and at designated taxi stands. There are also several international as well as local self-drive car hire firms in Sarawak.

Things to do in Sarawak ★

- One day: A visit to Sarawak Cultural Village and perhaps the Matang Wildlife Centre along with the sights of Kuching itself.
- Two days: Spend a night in one of the close Bidayuk longhouses and take a short trek in the jungle. Organise this through one of the tour companies in Kuching to make sure you are back in time.
- Five days: Travel to Miri and from there to the Mulu National Park, for example. A couple of nights or three in a longhouse and some more strenuous treks and river journeys. Flying means more can be crammed in to what is still a tight schedule.
- Seven days: A week or more in Sarawak makes easier to undertake some D-I-Y exploration, visit the more out-of-the-way towns like Belaga and venture up river from there to longhouses and national parks.

National Parks and Wildlife Office, Visitors Information Centre, Lot 31, Jln Masjid, (T248088, F256301) for information on national parks and advance bookings for the Bako, Gunung Gading, Kubah and Matang Wildlife Centres. (Note that it is also possible to use the National Park Booking Office in the Sarawak Tourist Information Centre). *Sarawak Tourism Board's Visitors' Information Centre*, 31 Jln Masjid, Padang Merdeka, T410944, F256301, stb@po.jaring.my (beside the new wing of the Sarawak Museum), open 0800-1800 Mon-Fri, 0800-1600 Sat (excluding the first Sat of the month), and 0900-1500 Sun (and first Sat of the month). The centre provides daily videoshows at 1000 and 1500 on the variety of attractions in the state and has a good stock of maps and pamphlets. *Sarawak Tourism Centre*, waterfront, Main Bazaar, T240620, F427151. Open: 0800-1245 and 1400-1615 Mon-Thu, 0800-1130 and 1430-1645 Fri, and 0800-1245 Sat. There is also a desk at Kuching International Airport, T456266; good for information on bus routes, approved travel agents and itineraries. *Sarawak Tourism Board*, Level 6 and 7, Bangunan Yayasan Sarawak, Jln Masjid, 93400 Kuching, T423600, F416700, www.sarawaktourism.com It is possible to call the STB toll-free from Kuala Lumpur (T8009291) or from Singapore (T8006011043) from 0800-1245, 1400-1615 Mon-Thu, 0800-1130, 1415-1615 Fri and 0800-1245 Sat. *Tourism Malaysia*, Bangunan Rugayah, Jln Song Thian Cheok, T246775, F246442, information on Sarawak and rest of Malaysia – good stock of brochures.

Tourist offices The state and national tourism organizations are both well informed and helpful; they can offer advice on itineraries, travel agents and up-to-date information on facilities in national parks

Sarawak

History

The Sarawak Tourism Board, like all such organizations worth their salt, does a pretty good job in making Kuching seem like a gem: "Kuching…is simply unique. No other city in Malaysia has such an unlikely and romantic history. And no other city in Malaysia displays its charms with such an easy grace". Certainly the city's history is pretty remarkable; and it also has its charm. But don't go under the impression that this is going to be the Sienna of Sarawak.

Shortly after dawn on 15 August 1839 James Brooke sailed round a bend in the Sarawak River and, from the deck of his schooner, *The Royalist*, had his first view of Kuching. According to the historian Robert Payne, he saw "…a very small town of brown huts and longhouses made of wood or the hard stems of the nipah palm, sitting in brown squalor on the edge of mudflats." The settlement, 32 km upriver from the sea, had been established less than a decade earlier by Brunei chiefs who had come to oversee the mining of antimony in the Sarawak River valley. The antimony – used as an alloy to harden other metals, particularly pewter – was exported to Singapore where the tin-plate industry was developing.

By the time James Brooke had become Rajah in 1841, the town had a population of local Malays and Dayaks and Cantonese, Hokkien and Teochew traders. Chinatown dominated the south side of the river while the Malay kampongs were strung out along the riverbanks to the west. A few Indian traders also set up in the bazaar, among the Chinese shophouses. Under Charles Brooke, the second of the White Rajahs, Kuching began to flourish; he commissioned most of the town's main public buildings. Brooke's wife, Ranee Margaret, wrote: "The little town looked so neat and fresh and prosperous under the careful jurisdiction of the Rajah and his officers, that it reminded me of a box of painted toys kept scrupulously clean by a child."

Like other cities in East Malaysia, Kuching's population is predominantly Chinese and Malay and they easily outnumbered the Dayaks who live here.

Sights

Sarawak Museum Kuching's biggest attraction is this internationally renowned museum, housed in two sections on both sides of Jalan Tun Haji Openg. The old building to the east of the main road is a copy of a Normandy town hall, designed by Charles Brooke's French valet. The Rajah was encouraged to build the museum by the naturalist Alfred Russel Wallace, who spent over two years in

Kuching

	Sleeping	5	Fata	10	Merdeka Palace
1	Anglican Guesthouse	6	Hilton	11	Supreme
2	B & B Inn	7	Holiday Inn	12	Telang Usan
3	Borneo	8	Longhouse		
4	Crown Plaza Riverside	9	Mandarin & Orchid Inn		

0 metres 200
0 yards 200

Sarawak, where he wrote his first paper on natural selection. The museum was opened in 1891, extended in 1911, and the 'new' wing built in 1983. Its best known curators have been naturalist Eric Mjoberg, who made the first ascent of Sarawak's highest peak – Gunung Murud (see page 374) – in 1922, and ethnologist and explorer Tom Harrisson, whose archaeological work at Niah made world headlines in 1957. The museum overlooks pleasant botanical gardens and the Heroes Memorial, built to commemorate the dead of the Second World War, the Communist insurgency and the confrontation with Indonesia. Across the road, and linked by an overhead bridge, is the Dewan Tun Abdul Razak building, a newer extension of the museum.

The museum has a strong ethnographic section, although some of its displays have been superseded by the Cultural Village (see page 339), Sarawak's 'living museum'. The old museum's ethnographic section includes a full-scale model of an Iban longhouse, a reproduction of a Penan hut and a selection of Kayan and Kenyah woodcarvings. There is also an impressive collection of Iban war totems (*kenyalang*) and carved Melanau sickness images (*blum*), used in healing ceremonies. The museum's assortment of traditional daggers (or *kris*, see page 504) is the best in Malaysia. The Chinese and Islamic ceramics include 17th-20th century Chinese jars, which are treasured heirlooms in Sarawak (see page 322).

The natural science collection, covering the flora and fauna of Sarawak, is also noteworthy. The new Tun Abdul Razak ethnological and historical collection includes prehistoric artefacts from the Niah Caves, Asia's most important archaeological site (see page 367); there is even a replica of Niah's Painted Cave – without the smell of guano.

There is a library attached to the museum as well as a giftshop, the Curio Shoppe, all proceeds of which go to charity, and a bookshop. Permits to visit the Niah's Painted Cave can be obtained, free of charge, from the curator's office. In 2001 yet another new wing of the museum opened. ■ *Daily 0900-1800. Audio-visual showings: 1015, 1215, 1430, 1445, 1530. Museum open 0800-1800 Mon-Sun, closed on first day of public holidays. Admission: free (but there has been talk of introducing an entrance fee for this and other museums in the city).*

Check the website www.museum.sarawak .gov.my for information on Sarawak's museums

Sarawak

Not far from the Sarawak Museum is this museum, located on Jalan P Ramlee in the restored Maderasah Melayu Building, an elegant, single-storey colonial edifice. As its name suggests, the museum is

Sarawak Islamic Museum

Tom Harrisson: life in the fast lane

Reputed to be one of the most important figures in the development of archaeology in Southeast Asia, Tom Harrisson, the charismatic 'egomaniac', put Borneo and Sarawak on the map.

Tom Harrisson loved Sarawak and, it would seem, Sarawak loved him. It was only appropriate that when he was killed in a traffic accident in 1976 it was in Thailand and not in Malaysia. He first visited Sarawak in 1932 as part of a Royal Geographical Expedition sent, along with around 150 kg of Cadbury's chocolate, to collect flora and fauna from one of the world's great natural treasure stores. Instead Harrisson found himself entranced by the territory's human populations and so the love affair began.

By all accounts, Harrisson was a difficult fellow – the sort that Imperial Britain produced in very large numbers indeed. He was a womaniser with a particular penchant for other people's spouses, he could be horribly abusive to his fellow workers, and he apparently revelled in putting down uppity academics (nothing very wrong in that). But he was also instrumental in putting Sarawak, and Borneo more generally, on the map and in raising awareness of the ways in which economic and social change was impacting on Sarawak's tribal peoples. Before taking up the curatorship of the Sarawak Museum in 1947 Harrisson also distinguished himself as a war hero, parachuting into the jungle and organising around 1,000 headhunters to terrorize the Japanese. All-in-all, Tom Harrisson led life in the fast lane.

(For those wanting to read a good biography of Harrisson get hold of the recently published The most offending soul alive *by Judith M Heimann, Honolulu: Hawaii University Press.)*

devoted to Islamic artefacts from all the ASEAN countries, with the collection of manuscripts, costumes, jewellery, weaponry, furniture, coinage, textiles and ceramics spread over seven galleries, each with a different theme, and set around a central courtyard. ■ *Sat-Thu 0900-1800.*

Astana Apart from the Sarawak Museum, the White Rajahs bequeathed several other architectural monuments to Kuching. The Astana, a variant of the usual spelling *istana*, or palace, was built in 1870, two years after Charles Brooke took over from his uncle. It stands on the north bank of the river almost opposite the market on Jalan Gambier. The Astana was hurriedly completed for the arrival of Charles' new bride (and cousin), Margaret. It was originally three colonial-style bungalows, with wooden shingle roofs, the largest being the central bungalow with the reception room, dining and drawing rooms. "How I delighted in those many hours spent on the broad verandah of our house, watching the life going on in the little town on the other side of the river", Ranee Margaret later reminisced in her book *My Life in Sarawak*. The crenellated tower on the east end was added in the 1880s at her request. Charles Brooke is said to have cultivated betel nut in a small plantation behind the Astana, so that he could offer fresh betel nut to visiting Dayak chiefs. Today it is the official residence of the governor, Yang Di Pertuan Negeri, of Sarawak and is only open to the public on Hari Raya Puasa, a day of prayer and celebration to mark the end of Ramadan (see page 57). To the west of the Astana, in the traditionally Malay area, are many old wooden kampong houses.

Fort Margherita Not far away from the Astana, past the Kubu jetty, (and also on the north shore) is this fort, now the **Police Museum**, on Jalan Sapi. It was also built by Rajah Charles Brooke in 1879 and named after Ranee Margaret, although

A town called Cat

There are a number of explanations as to how Sarawak's capital acquired the name 'Cat'. (Kuching means 'cat' in Malay – although today it is more commonly spelt kucing *as in modern Bahasa 'c' is pronounced 'ch'.) Local legend has it that James Brooke, pointing towards the settlement across the river, inquired what it was called. Whoever he asked, mistakenly thought he was pointing at a passing cat. If that seems a little far-fetched, the Sarawak museum offers a*

*few more plausible alternatives. Kuching may have been named after the wild cats (*kucing hutan*) which, in the 19th century, were commonly seen along jungled banks of the Sarawak River. Another theory is that it was called after the fruit* buah mata kucing *('cat's eyes'), which grows locally. Most likely, however, is the theory that the town may originally have been known as* Cochin – *or* port – *a word commonly used across India and Indochina.*

there was a fort on the site from 1841 when James Brooke became Rajah. It commanded the river approach to Kuching, but was never used defensively, although its construction was prompted by a near-disastrous river-borne attack on Kuching by the Ibans of the Rejang in 1878. Even so, until the Second World War a sentry was always stationed on the lookout post on top of the fort; his job was to pace up and down all night and shout 'All's well' on the hour every hour until 0800. The news that nothing was awry was heard at the Astana and the government offices.

After 1946, Fort Margherita was first occupied by the Sarawak Rangers and was finally converted into a police museum in 1971, which is a lot more interesting than it sounds. There is a large collection of armour and weaponry on the ground floor, including weapons captured during the Indonesian *konfrontasi* from 1963-65 (see page 398). The museum has recently been renovated and upgraded and was only reopened in 2001. Up the spiral staircase, on the second floor, there is a display of police uniforms and communications equipment used by jungle patrols. The third floor houses an exhibition on drugs, counterfeit currency and documents, supplies and weapons captured from Communist insurgents in the 1960s and 1970s. From the top, there are good views across the city and up and down the Sarawak River. En route to the courtyard at the bottom, former prison cells have been set up to recreate an opium den – complete with emaciated dummy – and to reinforce the dangers of *dadah,* (drugs) the courtyard itself contains the old town gallows complete with hanging dummy. During the rule of the White Rajahs, however, death sentences were carried out by a slash of the kris (traditional Malay sword) through the heart. ■ *1000-1800 Tue-Sun, closed public holidays, free. Getting there: sampan across the river from the Pangkalan Batu next to Square Tower on Main Bazaar to the Istana and Fort (RM0.30 one way; the boats can be hired quite cheaply at an hourly rate, around RM20-25 per hour).*

The **Malay kampungs** along the riverside next to Fort Margherita are seldom visited by tourists – however, they have some beautiful examples of traditional and modern Malay architecture. The **Kuching Orchid Garden** has been redeveloped close by to Fort Margherita, completed in October 2000, the park is divided into two; the Orchid Nursery and and a garden, with 112 species of orchids. ■ *Tues-Sun 1000-1800. Free. To get there take* Matang *transport No 3, or a river taxi from the waterfront. T446688, dbkuqrc@po.jaring*

Sarawak

Sarawak

🐾 A ceramic inheritance

Family wealth and status in Sarawak was traditionally measured in ceramics. In the tribal longhouses upriver, treasured heirlooms include ancient glass beads, brass gongs and cannons and Chinese ceramic pots and beads (such as those displayed in the Sarawak Museum). They were often used as currency and dowries. Spencer St John, the British consul in Brunei, mentions using beads as currency on his 1858 expedition to Gunung Mulu. Jars, or pesaka, had more practical applications; they were (and still are) used for storing rice, brewing tuak (rice wine) or for keeping medicines. Their value was dependent on their rarity: brown jars, emblazoned with dragon motifs, are more recent and quite common while olive-glazed dusun jars, dating from the 15th-17th centuries are rare. The Kelabit people, who live in the highlands around Bario, treasure the dragon jars in particular. Although some of the more valuable antique jars have found their way to the Sarawak Museum, many magnificent jars remain in the Iban and other tribal longhouses along the Skrang, Rejang and

Baram rivers. Many are covered by decoratively carved wooden lids.

Chinese contact and trade with the north coast of Borneo has gone on for at least a millennium, possibly two. Chinese Han pottery fragments and coins have been discovered near the estuary of the Sarawak River and from the 7th century, China is known to have been importing birds' nests and jungle produce from Brunei (which then encompassed all of North Borneo), in exchange for ceramic wares. Chinese traders arrived in the Nanyang (South Seas) in force from the 11th century, particularly during the Sung and Yuan dynasties. Some Chinese pottery and porcelain even bore Arabic and Koranic inscriptions – the earliest such dish is thought to have been produced in the mid-14th century. In the 1500s, as China's trade with the Middle East grew, many such Islamic wares were traded and the Chinese emperors presented them as gifts to seal friendships with the Muslim world, including Malay and Indonesian kingdoms.

South side of the river Around Main Bazaar are some other important buildings dating from the Brooke era; most of them are closed to the public. The **Supreme Court** on Main Bazaar was built in 1871 as an administrative centre. State council meetings were held here from the 1870s until 1973, when it was converted to law courts. In front of the grand entrance is a memorial to Rajah Charles Brooke (1924) and on each corner there is a bronze relief representing the four main ethnic groups in Sarawak – Iban, Orang Ulu, Malay and Chinese. The clock tower was built in 1883. The **Square Tower**, also on Main Bazaar, was built as an annex to Fort Margherita in 1879 and was used as a prison. Later in the Brooke era it was used as a ballroom and is now a one-stop information centre for tourists, with a video wall and an interactive video on Sarawak past and present and a Waterfront Information Counter, providing details of forthcoming events. The square tower marks one end of Kuching's waterfront esplanade which runs alongside the river for almost 900 m to the *Hilton*.
■ *The information centre no longer opens on a regular basis; if you want to be sure of getting in T426093.*

The **Waterfront** has recently been transformed into a landscaped esplanade through restoration and a land reclamation project. It has become a popular meeting place, with foodstalls, restaurants and entertainment facilities including an open-air theatre. There is a restored Chinese pavilion, an observation tower, a tea terrace and musical fountains, as well as a number of modern sculptures. During the day, the waterfront offers excellent views of the Astana, Fort Margherita and the Malay kampungs which line the north bank of the river. At night, the area comes alive as younger members of Kuching's growing middle class make their way down here to relax.

The **General Post Office**, with its majestic Corinthian columns, stands in the centre of town, on Jalan Tun Haji Openg. It was built in 1931 and was one of the few buildings built by Vyner Brooke, the last Rajah. It has recently been renovated and has been earmarked to become the home of the **Sarawak Art Museum**.

The **Court House** complex was built in 1871 as the seat of Sarawak's government and was used as such until 1973. It remains one of Kuching's grandest structures. The buildings have belian (ironwood) roofs and beautiful detailing inside and out, reflecting local art forms. It continues to house the state's high court and magistrate's court as well as several other local government departments. The colonial-baroque **clock tower** was added in 1883 and the **Charles Brooke Memorial** in 1924. The complex also includes the **Pavilion Building** which was built in 1907 as a hospital. During the Japanese occupation it was used as an information and propaganda centre and it is now undergoing renovation with a view to making it the home of a new **textile museum**. The **Round Tower** on Jalan Tun Abang Haji Openg (formerly Rock Road) was originally planned as a fort (1886) but was never fully completed. The whole area is undergoing restoration for future art galleries and cultural exhibits. The **Steamship Building** was built in 1930 and was previously the offices and warehouse of the Sarawak Steamship Company. It has been extensively restored and now houses a restaurant, souvenir stalls, a handicrafts gallery and an exhibition area.

The **Bishop's House**, off Jalan McDougall, near the Anglican Cathedral, is the oldest surviving residence in Sarawak. It was built in 1849, entirely of wood, for the first Anglican Bishop of Borneo, Dr McDougall. The first mission school was started in the attic – developed into St Thomas's and St Mary's School, which is now across the road on Jalan McDougall.

Kuching's Chinese population, part of the town's community since its foundation, live in the shophouses lining the narrow streets around **Main Bazaar**. This street, opposite the waterfront, is the oldest in the city, dating from 1864. The Chinese families who live here still pursue traditional occupations such as tin smithing and woodworking. Kuching's highest concentration of antique and handicraft shops is to be found here. **Jalan Carpenter**, parallel to Main Bazaar, has a similar selection of small traders and coffee shops, as well as foodstalls and two small Chinese temples. Off **Leboh China** (Upper China Street), there is a row of perfectly preserved 19th-century Chinese houses. The oldest Chinese temple in Kuching, **Tua Pek Kong** (also known as Siew San Teng), in the shadow of the *Hilton* on Jalan Tunku Abdul Rahman, was built in 1876, although it is now much modernized. There is evidence that the site has been in use since 1740 and a Chinese temple was certainly here as early as 1770. The first structure was erected by a group of Chinese immigrants thankful for their safe journey across the hazardous South China Sea. New immigrants still come here to give thanks for their safe arrival. The Wang Kang festival to commemorate the dead is also held here. Just to the east of here, **Jln Padungan** has some of Kuching's finest Chinese shophouses. Most were built during the rubber boom of the 1920s and have been restored. There are also some great coffee shops in this quarter of town. Further east still, the kitsch statue of the **Great Cat of Kuching** – the sort of thing to induce nightmares in the aesthetically inclined – mews at the junction of Jln Padungan and Jln Central.

Sarawak

The **Chinese History Museum** stands on the Waterfront, opposite Tua Pek Kong Temple. The building itself is of interest: it was completed in 1912 and became the court for the Chinese population of Kuching. The Third Rajah was keen that the Chinese, like other ethnic groups, should settle disputes within their community in their own way and he encouraged its establishment. From 1912 until 1921, when the Chinese court was dissolved, all cases pertaining to the Chinese were heard here in front of six judges elected from the local Chinese population. The building itself is a simple cella with a flat roof and shows English colonial influences. In 1993 it was handed over to the Sarawak Museum and was turned into the Chinese History Museum. The museum documents the history of the Chinese in Sarawak, from the early traders of the 10th century to the waves of Chinese immigration in the 19th century. The museum building was constructed in the early 20th century as the Chinese court, officially established in 1911 by Rajah Charles Brooke. ■ *Sat-Thu 0900-1800, T231520.* Admission free.

Hian Tien Shian Tee (Hong San) temple, at the junction of Jalan Carpenter and Jalan Wayang, was built in 1897. The **Indian Mosque**, or **Mesjid India** on Lebuh India, originally had an atap roof and *kajang* (thatch) walls; in 1876 belian-wood walls were erected. The mosque was built by South Indians and is in the middle of an Indian quarter where spices are sold along the Main Bazaar. When the mosque was first built only Muslims from South India were permitted to worship here; even Indian Muslims from other areas of the subcontinent were excluded. In time, as Kuching's Muslim population expanded and grew more diversified, so this rigid system was relaxed. It is hard to get to the mosque as it is surrounded by buildings. However a narrow passage leads from Lubuh India – between shop numbers 37 and 39.

The Moorish, gilt-domed **Masjid Bandaraya** (Old State Mosque) is near the market, on the east side of town; it was built in 1968 on the site of an old wooden mosque dating from 1852.

Petra Jaya The new **State Mosque**, is situated across the river at Petra Jaya and was completed in 1968. It stands on the site of an older mosque dating from the mid-19th century. Its interior is of Italian marble.

Kuching's architectural heritage did not end with the White Rajahs; the town's modern buildings are often based on local styles. The new administration centre is in Petra Jaya, on the north side of the river. The **Bapak** (father) **Malaysia** building is named after the first Prime Minister of Malaysia and houses government offices; the **Dewan Undangan Negeri**, next door, is based on the Minangkabau style. Kuching's latest building is the ostentatious **Masjid Jamek**. Also in Petra Jaya, like a space launch overlooking the road to Damai Peninsula, is the **Cat Museum** which houses everything you ever wanted to know about cats. ■ *Mon-Sun 0900-1700 (closed public holidays). Getting there: Petra Jaya Transport No 2B or 2C.*

The **Timber Museum** nearby, on Wisma Sumber Alam (next to the stadium), is meant to look like a log. It was built in the mid-1980s to try to engender a bit more understanding about Sarawak's timber industry (see page 384). The museum, which has many excellent exhibits and displays, toes the official line about forest management and presents facts and figures on the timber trade, along with a detailed history of its development in Sarawak. The exhibition provides an insight into all the different forest types. It has background information on and examples of important commercial tree species, jungle produce as well as many traditional wooden implements. The final touch is an air-conditioned forest and wildlife diorama, complete with leaf-litter; all the trees come from the Rejang River area. While the museum sidesteps the more delicate moral issues involved in the modern logging business, its detractors might do worse than to brush up on some of the less emotive aspects of Sarawak's most important industry. The museum has a research library attached to it. ■ *Mon-Thu 0830-1600, Fri 0830-1130, 1430-1630, Sat 0830-1230, closed Sun and public holidays. Getting there: Matang Transport bus No 8.*

On the south side of the river the extraordinary-looking **Civic Centre** on Jalan Taman Budaya, is Kuching's stab at the avant garde. It has a viewing platform for panoramas of Kuching. ■ *0800-0930, 1030-1200, 1400-1530, 1630-1800.* The Civic Centre complex houses an art gallery with temporary exhibits, mainly of Sarawakian art, there is also a restaurant and a pub-cum-karaoke bar one floor down, together with a public library. ■ *Mon-Thu 0915-1730, Sat and Sun 0915-1800.* Malaysia's first planetarium is also within the complex: **Sultan Iskandar Planetarium** opened in 1989 and has a 15-m dome and a 170-seat auditorium. ■ *Shows: Tue only. RM2. Getting there: bus from Lebuh Market, south along Jalan Tun Haji Openg.*

Civic Centre & Planetarium

Excursions

Permits for national parks and the orang utan sanctuary are available from the Sarawak Tourist Information Centre on Padang Merdeka, T410944, F256301 or the National Parks office in Petra Jaya, Wisma Sumber Alam, T442180.

Semenggoh, 32 km from Kuching, on the road to Serian, became the first forest reserve in Sarawak when the 800 ha of jungle was set aside by Rajah Vyner Brooke in 1920. It was turned into a wildlife rehabilitation centre for monkeys, orang utans, honey bears and hornbills in 1975. All were either orphaned as a result of logging or were confiscated having been kept illegally as pets. The aim has been to reintroduce as many of the animals as possible to their natural habitat. In late 1998 many of the functions which previously attracted visitors to Semenggoh were transferred to the Matang Wildlife Centre (see page 328). However, there are a few trails around the park including a plankwalk and a botanical research centre, dedicated to jungle plants with medicinal applications. Even when Semenggoh was operating as an orang utan rehabilitation centre, it did not compare with Sepilok in Sabah (see page 462), which is an altogether more sophisticated affair. Visitors need a permit (free) to visit the sanctuary, available from Visitors' Information Centre on Padang Merdeka. ■ *Mon-Sun 0800-1245, 1400-1615. Getting there: Sarawak Transport Co bus 6 from Ban Hock Wharf, Jawa St (RM1.50). From there, hitch a lift to the centre which is another 3 km away. Tour operators also run trips to the centre.*

Semenggoh Orang Utan Sanctuary

Jong's Crocodile Farm, Mile 18.5 Kuching (29 km from Kuching), Jalan Endap, off the Serian Highway, T242790 (Kuching) or T863570, has several types of crocodile – albino, saltwater, and the freshwater Malayan gharial (*Tomistoma schlegeli*) – all bred for their skins. These are 'harvested' at about 10 years of age and 2 sq cm of skin fetches about RM60; younger crocodiles are also killed for their valuable tender belly skin. In the entrance area, there is a ghoulish collection of photographs of people who have been mauled by crocodile; one depicts the contents of a maneater's stomach – not for the faint-hearted. There have been eight fatal attacks from crocodiles in Sarawak since the mid-1970s; so far none of these has been at Jong's which is a squalid affair and does not inspire

Sarawak

much confidence in terms of security. ■ *Daily 0900-1700, Feeding times every Sun at 1000. RM8 adult, RM2 child. Take bus 3, 3A, 9A, 9B from STC bus station to Siburan village. 40 mins. Several departures daily.*

Taman Nor Badia Wildlife & Reptile Park

Apart from crocodiles there are also numerous species of birds and animals only found in Borneo at this park: monkeys, leopard-cats, sunbears, bearcats, pheasants, civets, barking deer, sambar deer, turtles, fruit bats, monitor lizards, pythons and hornbills. ■ *Daily 1000-1800, RM5 adults, RM2 children. Getting there: Sarawak Transport Co bus 3, 3A and 9A and 9B from Ban Hock Wharf, every 15 mins.*

Gunung Penrissen
Altitude: 1,329 m

This is the highest peak in the mountain range south of Kuching running along the Kalimantan border. The mountain was visited by naturalist Alfred Wallace in 1855. Just over 100 years later the mountain assumed a strategic role in Malaysia's *konfrontasi* with Indonesia (see page 398) – there is a Malaysian military post on the summit. Gunung Penrissen is accessible from Kampung Padawan; it lies a few kilometres south of Anna Rais, right on the border with Kalimentan. It is a difficult mountain to climb requiring two long days, but affords views over Kalimantan to the south and Kuching and the South China Sea to the north. Guides – most of whom were former border scouts during *konfrontasi* – can be hired through the headman at Kampung Padawan; prospective climbers are advised to consult the detailed trail-guide in John Briggs' *Mountains of Malaysia*. The book is usually obtainable in the Sarawak Museum bookshop. ■ *Getting there: it's 100 km from Kuching to Anna Rais; take an STC bus No 9 from Kuching's Lebuh Jawa. Buses leave every 30 mins and take 2 hrs.*

Around Kuching

■ Sleeping

1 Camp Permai
2 Holiday Inn Resort Damai Beach
3 Holiday Inn Resort Damai Lagoon
4 Santubong Kuching Resort

Sleeping The *Borneo Highlands Resort* is under construction on Gunung Penrissen plateau at an altitude of between 600 and 1,000 m. The vision is a grand one: several hotels, golf, jungle trekking and various other eco-activities. The first phase of the resort is now open, T234266 for details.

Gunung Gading National Park was constituted in 1983 and covers 411,1060 ha either side of Sungai Lundu, 65 km north-west of Kuching. There are some marked trails, the shortest of which takes about two hours and leads to a series of waterfalls on the Sungai Lundu. Gunung Gading and Gunung Perigi summit treks take seven to eight hours; it is possible to camp at the summit. The park is made up of a complex of mountains with several dominant peaks including Gunung Gading (906 m). The Rafflesia, the largest flower in the world, is found in the park but if you are keen to see one in bloom, it might be worth phoning the Park HQ first, since it has a very short flowering period. ■ *T735714. Park fees: RM3, guide fees: RM5/hr. 2, 3-bedroom chalets (RM120) and a hostel (RM10/person) are available. Bookings taken through the Visitor Information Centre, Kuching. T410942. Getting there: 5-mins' drive from Lundu. From Kuching take STC Bus 2B to Lundu, from there, take a Pandan bus 17c and ask to be dropped off at the park.*

Gunung Gading National Park

Park essentials Upon arrival in the park, visitors must register at the headquarters, which is small, consisting of an information centre, toilet blocks, and accommodation. Park fees are RM10 for adults, RM5 for children, with additional fees for cameras and videos. There are 2 3-room chalets (**B**), washrooms, toilets, electricity and a *hostel* (**D**), with 4 beds per room, bookable through the Visitors' Information Centre in Kuching. Gunung Gading National Park is between Lundu and Semantan, with regular bus connections with Kuching (see below).

About 60 km from Kuching is **Bau**, which had its five minutes of fame during the 19th century as a small-scale mining town. Nowadays, it is a market town and administrative centre. There are several caves close by; the **Wind Cave** is a popular picnic spot. The **Fairy Cave**, about 10 km from Bau, is larger and more impressive, with a small Chinese shrine in the main chamber and varied vegetation at the entrance. A torch is essential. Another reason to travel to Bau is to see the Bindayuh celebrating their *gawai padi*, a festival with animistic roots that thanks the gods for an abundant rice harvest. Singing, dancing, massive consumption of *tuak* (rice wine) and colourful shamans make this a cultural highlight. Ask at the tourist office in Kuching for details of times. ■ *Tour companies organize trips. By public transport, take STC bus No 2 (RM3) which leaves every 40 mins and takes around 1 hr (first bus 0600, last bus 1800); or take a taxi.*

Bau

These villages have beautiful, lonely beaches and there is a collection of deserted islands off Sematan. One of the islands, **Talang Talang**, is a turtle sanctuary and permission to visit it must be obtained from the local district officer. ■ *Sarawak Transport Co bus 2B goes to Lundu via Bau (two hours, RM7.80 with departures at 0800, 1045, 1345 and 1545); from there take a Pandan bus and ask to be dropped off at the park.*

Lundu & Sematan

Sleeping In **Lundu** are **C** *Lundu Gadung Hotel*, Lot 174 Lundu Town District, T735199, (a/c but shared bathroom) and **D** *Cheng Hat Boarding House*, 1094 Lundu Bazaar, T735018 (some a/c). The plushest place to stay in Semantan is **A** *Ocean Resort*, 176 Siar Beach. Jln Pandan, T452245 (Kuching office) or 011-225001 (resort), some

Sarawak

rooms in hostel, 2 bedroom chalets with attached kitchen also available. In the centre of Semantan is **C-D** Sematan Hotel, T731162, with some a/c rooms.

Kubah National Park This is a mainly sandstone, siltstone and shale area, 20 km west of Kuching, covering some 2,230 ha with three mountains: Gunung Serapi, Gunung Selang and Gunung Sendok; there are at least seven waterfalls and bathing pools. Flora include mixed dipterocarp and *kerangas* (heath) forest; the park is also rich in palms (93 species) and wild orchids. Wildlife includes bearded pig, mouse deer and hornbills and numerous species of amphibians and reptiles. Unfortunately for visitors, Kubah's wildlife tends to stay hidden; it's not really a park for 'wildlife encounters'. There are four marked trails, ranging from 30 minutes to three hours; one, the **Rayu Trail**, passes through rainforest that contains a number of bintangor trees (believed to contain two chemicals which have showed some evidence of being effective against AIDS). Visitors may be able to see some trees which have been tapped for this potential rainforest remedy. ■ *Getting there: take the* Matang Transport Company *bus No 11 or 18 that departs from outside the Saujana Car Park (RM1.70, 50 mins, first bus departs at 0630 and last return bus at 1640). Buses no longer drop off at the Matang Wildlife Centre; ask to be dropped of at the Park HQ. Travel agents also arrange tours to the park.*

Park essentials Permits can be obtained through the National Parks Booking Office, Kuching, T082248088; day visitors can pay and register at the Park HQ (T225003) or at the gate of the Matang Wildlife Centre, RM10/RM5. There are 5 huge bungalows at the park HQ at RM180 per night with full kitchen facilities, 4 beds (2 rooms), a/c, hot water, TV and verandah. Book through the Visitors' Information Centre, Jln Masjid, in Kuching, T410942, or through the National Park's Booking Office.

The **Matang Wildlife Centre** (T225012) is part of the Kubah National Park. It houses endangered wildlife in spacious enclosures which are purposefully placed in the rainforest. The key attraction are the orang utans which are rehabilitated for release back into the wild. (This function used to be carried out at the Semenggoh Orang Utan Rehabilitation Centre which closed towards the end of 1998.) Other animals include sambar deer, sun bears, civets and bear cats. Animal feeding times: orang utans, 0900 and 1500 daily; hornbills, 0830 and 1500 daily; sambar deer, 0900 and 1500 daily; and crocodiles, 1430 Sun only. There is an Information Centre and education programmes, which enable visitors to learn more about the conservation of Sarawak's wildlife. The Centre has also established a series of trails. There are chalets at RM120 and an eight-room hostel block (**F**) bookable through the Visitors' Information Centre in Kuching, Jln Masjid, T410942. ■ *Matang Transport Company bus No 11 or 18 departs from outside the Saujana car park (see Kubah National Park, above, for details). However this bus does not go all the way to the Matang Wildlife Centre; ask to be deposited at the turning for the Polytechnic and wait for a lift. (Some visitors say that the service to the Centre has stopped. Alternatively, take a taxi from Kuching (RM30-35, one-way) and ask the taxi to wait. Travel agents also arrange tours to the park.*

Tanjung Datu National Park This is the newest and smallest park in the state of Sarawak, first gazetted in 1994, at the westernmost tip, 100 km from Kuching. The land is covered with mixed dipterocarp forest, rich flora and fauna, and beautiful beaches with crystal clear seas and coral reefs. Facilities for visitors are currently being developed and it may be worth checking with the tourist office in Kuching whether it is open to visitors. ■ *Take a bus to Lundu (see Gunung Gading National Park page 327) and on to Sematan and Teluk Melano. Boats to the park leave when full, RM20, 10 mins.*

Tours

Most tour companies offer city tours as well as trips around Sarawak: to Semenggoh, Bako, Niah, Lambir Hills, Miri, Mulu and Bario. There are also competitively priced packages to longhouses (mostly up the Skrang River – see page 346). It is cheaper and easier to take organized tours to Mulu, but these should be arranged in Miri (see page 371) as they are much more expensive if arranged from Kuching. Other areas are easy enough to get to independently.

Essentials

There is a good choice of international standard hotels in Kuching. Most of them are along Jln Tunku Abdul Rahman with views of the river and the Astana and Fort Margherita on the opposite bank. For a listing of hotels and resorts with websites see the listing on the Sarawak Tourism Board site (www.sarawaktourism.com). The choice at the lower end of the market is limited, except for the *Anglican Guesthouse*; the cheaper hotels and lodging houses are concentrated around Jln Green Hill, near the Tua Pek Kong temple. Some newer, mid-range accommodation has grown up in the area around Jln Ban Hock. For an alternative to the usual hotels and guesthouses, you could try the **Homestay Programme**. These cover not just fishing villages in the vicinity of Kuching but also a number of up-country communities. The host families are chosen so that at least one member speaks English and they are also suitable for families. For further information contact the Sarawak Tourism Board (T60 82 423600 or stb@sarawaktourism.com).

Sleeping
■ *on map, page 318*
Price codes:
see inside front cover
It is possible to negotiate over room rates and many of the hotels seem to have special deals

Sarawak

L-AL *Crowne Plaza Riverside*, Jln Tunku Abdul Rahman, PO Box 2928, T247777, F425858, cprk@tm.net.my 5-star, high-rise glitz hotel now owned by *Holiday Inn*, with an adjoining, 5-storey shopping complex complete with bowling alley and cineplex. All 250 rooms have a/c, mini-bar, tea and coffee-making facilities, personal safe, TV, in-house movies, en suite bathroom with marble vanity and good shower, plush carpets, wood furnishings carved with Sarawak designs. Facilities include pool, fitness centre, squash court, pâtisserie, 3 restaurants including the *Sri Sarawak* on the 18th floor which has panoramic views and serves Malay and international food, regular shuttle (RM10) to sister hotel, *Damai Lagoon*, on the Damai Peninsula. Recommended.
L-AL *Harbour View Hotel*, Lorong Temple, T274666, F274777, harview@po.jasing.my Good position overlooking the Waterfront next to Tua Pek Kong Temple. Business centre and in-room internet port, café and bar with live entertainment. **L-AL** *Holiday Inn*, Jln Tunku Abdul Rahman, PO Box 2362, T423111, F426169, www.holidayinn-sarawak. com The first international hotel to open in Kuching and the only one right on the river front. Popular with families, plenty of organized activities, 305 rooms with a/c, tea and coffee-making facilities, TV with movies and satellite channels, mini-bar, pool, fitness centre, 3 restaurants, souvenir and bookshop.
AL *Hilton*, Jln Tunku Abdul Rahman, PO Box 2396, T248200, F428984, www.hilton.com White modern block commanding superb views of river and town. Lives up to its name in providing quality and exclusive atmosphere. All 322 rooms have a/c, TV, in-room movies, mini-bar, tea and coffee making facilities. Very pleasant pool with swim-up bar, shaded by palms, and separate children's pool and playground, tennis, fitness centre. Four restaurants including good steak house (air-freighted meat from Australia), boutique, hair salon, travel agent. Recommended.

AL-A *Grand Continental*, Lot 42, Section 46, Jln Ban Hock, T230399, F230339, www.grandstay.com Small pool and business centre. Rooms have TV, IDD, minibar, and tea and coffee-making facilities. **A** *Kingwood Inn*, Jln Padungan, T330888, F332888, kingwd@po.jaring.my Rooms have TV. Facilities include a pool, coffee house and bar. Late checkout available. Out of town but pleasant. **A** *Merdeka Palace* Jln Tun Abang Haji Openg, T258000, F425400, www.jaring.my/mpalace Newish place with central location. Pool, health-club and business facilities. The 214 rooms have mini-bar, satellite TV and coffee/tea-making facilities. Six bars, restaurants on site. Great value. Recommended. **A-B** *Borneo*, 30 Jln Tabuan, T244122, F254848. Chinese atmosphere in this hotel located about a 10 min walk from the centre of town. Rooms with a/c and bath. Good value restaurant, breakfast included. **A-B** *Telang Usan*, Jln Ban Hock (next to *Supreme*), T415588, F425316, tusan@po.jaring.my The best of these 2 hotels located in an untidy area of town. A/C, TV, bath, restaurant, in-house travel agent, *orang ulu* owned and managed hotel, friendly with traditional *kenyah* décor, karaoke and bar, conference rooms, smart and comfortable, quiet location, excellent value.

B *Rajah Court*, Jln Tun Razak, T484799, F482750, rajcourt@tm.net.my Pleasant budget hotel slightly out of town with good facilities for conferences, variety of rooms, chalets and apartments, pool, squash court, good atmosphere. **B-C** *Supreme*, Jln Ban Hock, T255155, F252522, supremehotel@hotmail.com 74 rooms, a/c, en suite bath or shower, mini-bar, TV, in-house videos. Evening entertainment; bands or karaoke. A little run down. **B-C** *Fata*, Jln McDougall, T248111, F428987. Clean hotel with a 1970s feel. A/c, restaurant, rooms in the older part are cheaper and better value for money. **C** *Goodwood Inn*, 16-17 Jln Green Hill, T244862, F235690. A/c, TV, very similar to the other hotels around it. **C** *Longhouse*, Jln Abell, T419333, F421563. A/c, restaurant, good value but a bit out of town (past the *Holiday Inn*). **C** *River View Inn*, 22-23 Jln Green Hill, T412551, F256302. A/c, TV. Large rooms but quite tatty. Friendly management but more expensive than most in this price range. Don't expect it to live up to its name.

C-D *Mandarin* , 6 Jln Green Hill, T418269, F410139. The best and cleanest of the groups of hotels located in the Jln Green Hill area. Rooms have a/c, TVs, and are fairly small, but with good bathrooms and reasonably well furnished. **C-D** *New Furama House*, 4 Jln Green Hill, T413561. A/c, TV, smelly and slightly damp, has bath but no shower. Run down. **C-D** *Orchid Inn*, 2 Jln Green Hill, T411417, F241635. A/c. Very similar to the *Mandarin*, but a little more run down. **C-E** *B&B Inn*, Tabuan Rd, T237366, F239189, gohyp@pb.jaring.my Although popular and central, not particularly cheap. Tours organized, clean and safe, dorms beds available.

D-E *Anglican Guesthouse*, back of St Thomas' Cathedral (path from Jln Carpenter), T414027. Fan, old building set in beautiful gardens on top of the hill, spacious, pleasantly furnished rooms, with basic facilities, far and away the best of the cheaper accommodation in town. More expensive family rooms are big with sitting room and attached bathroom, recent visitors warn of a spate of thefts from the guesthouse, so take precautions. Recommended. **D-E** *Kuching*, Lebuh Temple, T413985. Adequate Chinese-run hotel, reasonable rates for rooms with fan and wash-hand basin, shared bathrooms.

Eating
● *on map, page 318*

Kuching, with all its old buildings and *godowns* along the river, seems made for open-air restaurants and cafés – but good ones are notably absent. However, the town is not short of hawker centres. Local dishes worth looking out for include *Umai* – a spicy salad of raw marinated fish with limes and shallots. Other distinctive Sarawakian ingredients are *midin* and *paku* – jungle fern shoots.

Price codes:
see inside front cover
For information on
local specialities see
Essentials page 48

Malay Malay food here seems to be less spicy than on the Peninsula. Sarawak specialities available include *laksa* (spicy noodles – a Malaysia wide dish, but especially good here), and *umai*. *Rex Café*, Main Bazaar, good mixed rice, rojak and laksa. *National Islamic Café*, Jln Carpenter. *Sri Sarawak*, *Riverside Majestic Hotel*, gourmet food, good views. *Glutton's Corner*, Lorong Rubber 12, wide selection, closed 1900 and on Sun. *Home Cook*, Jln Song Thian Cheok, clean and good value, speciality Assam fish. *Suan Chicken Rice*, Jln Tunku Abdul Rahman, next to Sarawak Plaza, steamed or curried chicken. There are a handful of Malay/Indian coffee shops on India St including *Madinah Café*, *Jubilee* and *Malaysia Restaurant*.

Chinese Mid-range *City Tower*, top of Civic Centre, T234396. Wonderful views and gourmet food. *Hornbill Corner Café*, 85 Jln Ban Hock. All-you-can-eat steamboat and barbecue, popular. *Red Eastern Café*, Jln Ban Hock, specializes in steamboat. *River Palace*, *Riverside Majestic Hotel*, first-class Chinese restaurant, offers regular food promotions. **Cheap** *Beijing Riverbank*, enjoys good location on riverfront, opposite *Riverside Majestic*, in a circular pavilion-style building, serves Chinese Muslim food and coffee-shop fare. Recommended. *Hot and Spicy House*, Lot 303, Section 10, Rubber Rd, T250873. Closed Tue, Chinese cooking with West Malaysian influence. Speciality is Ipoh-style *yong tau hoo* (vegetables stuffed with beancurd), just outside the city centre. *Lan Ya Keng,* Jln Carpenter, opposite old temple, specializes in pepperfish steak. *Lok Thian*, 1st floor, Bangunan Beesan, Jln Padungan, T331310. Good food, pleasant surroundings and excellent service, booking advisable, especially at the weekends. *Min Kong Kee*, 157 Jln Pandungan. A good selection of dishes with authentic Chinese and Malay breakfasts. *Meisan,* *Holiday Inn*, Jln Tunku Abdul Rahman, *dim sum*, RM12.50 set lunch; Sun eat-as-much-as-you-can *dim sum* special (RM13), also Schezuan cuisine. Recommended. *Minsion Canteen*, end of Jln Chan Chin Ann, on right, speciality is *daud special* (thick noodles in herbal soup with chunks of chicken). *Tsui Hua Lau*, Lot 321-324, Jln Ban Hock, T414560. Shanghai-style dishes.

All the major hotels have Chinese restaurants; most open for lunch and dinner, closing in between

Indonesian Mid-range *Minangkabau Nasi Padang*, 168 Chan Chin Ann Rd, spicy Padang food including such classics as beef *rendang*, lunch time only.

Indian Mid-range *Bismillah*, Leboh Khoo Hun Reang (near Central Police Station), North Indian Muslim food, good tandoori chicken. *Banana Leaf*, 7G Lorong Rubber 1, T239404. Open all day, specializes in Indian banana leaf meals. *Pots 'n' Buns*, Taman Sri Sarawak Mall, opposite rear store entrance, good *roti canai*, *murtabak*, plus usual hawker stall food. *Rahamath Café*, 19 Jln Padungan, good roti canai. *Lyn's Restaurant*, Lot 62, 10G Lg 4, Jln Nanas, a worthwhile taxi-ride from the centre – genuine North Indian tandoori cuisine, excellent naan, locals recommend it, closed Sun evenings. *Serapi*, *Holiday Inn*, specializes in North Indian tandoori, good vegetable dishes, also serves air-freighted steak. Recommended.

There are several cheap Indian Muslim restaurants along Lebuh India

Japanese Expensive *Ten-Ichi*, Bangunan Bee San, Jln Pandungan, T331310. Elegant surroundings. Mid-range *Kikyo-Tei*, Jln Crookshank, in front of Government Resthouse, also some Chinese and western dishes, large main room with separate Teppanyaki and Tatami rooms. The set lunch is a good deal. Recommended by locals. *Minoru*, Lot 493, Section 10, Rubber Rd, T251021. Set lunch and dinner as well as an extensive menu and good service.

Thai Mid-range *Steamship Restaurant*, Kuching Waterfront, wide selection of Thai-Chinese and Singaporean dishes in former building of the Steamship Company, trendy. **Cheap** *Bangkok Thai Restaurant*, Jln Pending, maybe not up to Bangkok standards, but not bad for Sarawak, pleasant surroundings, good service, advisable to book. Recommended by locals.

Mid-range Seafood *Benson Seafood*, Lot 122/3, Section 49, Jln Abell, T255262. Full range of Sarawak seafood. *Ah Leong*, Lot 72, Jln Pandungan, near *Kingwood Inn*, good choice of seafood. *KTS Seafood Canteen*, 157, Jln Chan Chin Ann, excellent butter prawns and grilled stingray. *Pending Seafood Centre*, behind Kuching Port, in industrial area, range of stalls selling fabulous choice of seafood, if you go by taxi, arrange a pick-up time to avoid getting stranded. *See Good*, Jln Bukit Mata Kuching, behind *MAS* office, extensive range of seafood. Recommended by locals. Strong flavoured sauces, lots of herbs, extensive and exotic menu, unlimited free bananas,

Excellent seafood is to be found in Kuching

Sarawak

closed 4th and 18th of every month. On Kampung Buntal are several seafood restaurants on stilts over the sea, 25 km north of Kuching, very popular with Kuchingites.

International Expensive *Serapi*, *Holiday Inn*, imported steaks, excellent selection of grills and seafood, North Indian tandoori, elegant surroundings, open lunch and dinner but not between times. **Mid-range** *Orchid Garden*, *Holiday Inn*, Jln Tunku Abdul Rahman, good breakfast and evening buffets, international and local cuisine. Recommended. *San Francisco Grill*, 76 Jln Ban Hock, steak house, cosy atmosphere, live piano, largely Chinese clientele which means steak is seasoned with 5 spices, meat is air-freighted, chips mediocre but nice atmosphere. *Waterfront*, *Hilton Hotel*, Jln Tunku Abdul Rahman, reasonably priced for the venue, the best pizzas and a family brunch buffet on Sun which is very popular. **Cheap** *Dulit Coffee House*, *Telang Usan Hotel*, Jln Ban Hock, pleasant terrace café, mix of western and eastern food, specializes in French oxtail stew and the only genuine chicken kebabs in Kuching. *Hani's Bistro*, Jln Chan Chin Ann (near *Holiday Inn*), reasonably priced café, good mix of eastern and western cuisine, generous helpings, tasty haricot oxtail, good background music. Recommended.

Many Chinese coffee shops serve excellent laksa (breakfast) of curried coconut milk with a side plate of sambal belacan (chillied prawn paste)

Coffee shops *Fook Hoi*, Jln Padungan, old-fashioned coffee shop, famous for its *sio bee* and *ha kau* (pork dumpling). **Seriously cheap** *Life Café*, 108 Ewe Hai St (near Carpenter St, behind Main Bazaar), T411954. Closed Tue, attractive café serving mostly vegetarian food plus a good range of teas and coffees (including Sarawak tea), friendly staff and pleasant atmosphere. *Borneo Deli*, *Borneo Hotel*, Jln Tabuan, selection of coffees, teas, cakes and pastries in a relaxing atmosphere. *Chang Choon Café*, Jln Abell, opposite *City Inn*. *Choon Hui Café*, Jln Ban Hock. *Green Hill Corner*, Lebuh Temple; *Tiger Garden*, opposite Rex Cinema, Lebuh Temple. *Wonderful Café*, opposite Miramar Theatre, Jln Palm.

Foodstalls and food centres *Hock Hong Garden*, Jln Ban Hock, opposite *Grand Continental*, finest hawker stall food in Kuching, little English spoken but definitely worth trying to be understood. *Chinese Food Centre*, Jln Carpenter (opposite temple), Chinese foodstalls offering hot and sour soups, fish balls and more. *King's Centre*, Jln Simpang Tiga (bus No 11 to get there), large range of foodstalls, busy and not many tourists. *Kubah Ria Hawker stalls*, Jln Tunku Abdul Rahman (on the road out of town towards Damai Beach, next to Satok Suspension Bridge), specialities *sop kambling* (mutton soup). *Petanak Central Market*, Jln Petanak, above Kuching's early morning wet market, light snacks, full seafood selection, good atmosphere, especially early in the morning. *Satok Bridge*, under the suspension bridge, very good barbecued chicken and seafood. *Saujana Food Centre*, 5th floor of the car park near the mosque (take the lift), mostly Malay food but also seafood. *Song Thieng Hai Food Centre*, between Jln Padungan and Jln Ban Hock, every type of noodle available. *Third Mile (Central Park)*, opposite Timberland Medical Centre, difficult to get to, mainly hawker stalls.

Some of the best food centres are located in the suburbs; a taxi is essential

Permata Food Centre, behind *MAS* office, purpose-built alternative to the central market, prices are higher but the choice is better, bird-singing contests (mainly red-whiskered bulbuls and white-rumped sharmas) every Sun morning, excellent range of fresh seafood. Recommended. *Batu Lintang Open-Air Market*, Jln Rock (to the south of town, past the hospital). *Capital Cinema Hawker Centre*, Jln Padungan. *Jln Palm Open-Air Market*. *Lau Ya Keng*, Jln Carpenter, opposite temple, specializes in Chinese dishes. *Rex Cinema Hawker Centre*, Jln Wayang/Jln Temple, squashed down an alleyway, satay. Recommended. *Thompson's Corner*, Jln Palm/Jln Nanas. *Top Spot Food Court*, Jln Bukit Mata Kuching, top floor of a car park, wide range of stalls, popular. *Tower Market*, Lebuh Market.

Casablanca Lounge, *Riverside Majestic Hotel*, cocktail lounge and karaoke. *Cat City*, Jln Chan Chin Ann (turn left at *Pizza Hut*), happy hour 2030-2215, followed by live bands (usually Filipino) playing a mixture of Western rock covers and Malay and Chinese ballads, open late. *The Club*, *Riverside Majestic Hotel*, large video screen and private karaoke rooms. *De Tavern*, Taman Sri Sarawak Mall (facing *Hilton* car park), friendly kayan-run corner pub, serves good rice wine, open 1630-0130, happy hour until 2030. *The Fisherman's Pub*, 1st floor, Taman Sri Sarawak Mall, karaoke, friendly staff and a pleasant crowd of regulars. *Hornbill's Corner Café*, Jln Ban Hock, breezy open air pub. *Margerita Lounge*, *Hilton Hotel*, the best cocktails and good live music. *Rejang Lobby Lounge*, *Holiday Inn*, small but popular. *Tribes*, downstairs at *Holiday Inn*, ethnic food, tribal décor and a variety of live music, open 1600-0100.

Bars
Expect to pay around RM8-10 for a beer, slightly more in the swisher hotel bars. Most places have happy hours, and two-for-one offers. Bars tend to close around 0100-0200, a little later in hotels

Don't expect Kuching to be another Ibiza. However there are enough clubs, pubs and bars to keep most people reasonably happy. Clubs and discos usually have a cover charge although there is usually a drink or 2 thrown in with the price. Expect to pay around RM10-15 for a beer, and RM20-25 for a spirit.

Entertainment
The main centres of evening entertainment are: Jln Tunku Abdul Rahman, Jln Mendu, Jln Padungan, and Jln Borneo

Cinemas *Riverside Cineplex*, Riverside Complex, T427061, check local press for details of programme. *Miramar*, on the corner of Jln Satok and Jln Tun Ahmad Zaidi Adruce (Palm Rd), T411488, highest tech of the cinemas, with a ground floor karaoke lounge, a food court and a rooftop beer garden. *Star Cineplex*, Level 9, Medan Pelita, top floor of car park on Temple St. *Laserdisc centres*, all around town, where you can watch a scheduled film in a small cinema or rent a private room to see the film of your choice.

Cultural shows *Cultural Village*, Damai Beach, cultural shows, with stylized and expertly choreographed tribal dance routines, 1130 and 1630, Mon-Sun.

Discos *Peppers*, *Hilton Hotel* (downstairs), top 40 hits and pool table, very busy on ladies nights (Wed and Fri). *Marina Fun Pub and Disco*, Jln Ban Hock, live band until 0200, then a DJ until 0330, crowded at weekends. *Tropical Pub & Bar*, Jln Abell. The place to go for a lively local disco (Malaysian music). *Jupiters*, Jln Ban Hock. Only open on Fri, Sat and eve of public holidays – top 40 hits.

Exhibitions The *Society Atelier* holds regular exhibitions at various venues in the city. Its HQ is an old government house near to the Civic Centre, 10 mins' walk from Main Bazaar. Phone for details of current and forthcoming events, Jln Taman Budaya, T243222.

Karaoke Karaoke lounges abound, with songs in Chinese, English, Iban, Malay, Japanese and Korean. *City Tower*, top of the Civic Centre, good views and well priced drinks. *Palm Super Lounge*, Jln Tun Ahmad Zaidi Adruce (Palm Rd), in Miramar Cinema Building. Some private rooms, smart bar and wide range of songs, good service. *Dai Ichi Karaoke*, Jln Tunku Abdul Rahman (above *Pizza Hut*), for connoisseurs, large choice of songs, friendly and good service.

Gifts from Sarawak: a quick primer

Basketry, especially from the Bidayuh
Beadwork from one of the upriver tribal groups
Betel boxes
Blowpipes and bracelets made by the Penan
Carved hornbill casques
Edible birds' nests
Hand-woven Iban textiles (umbu)
Headdresses
Local pottery
Sarawak pepper
Silver belts

When it comes to choice, Kuching is the best place in Malaysia to buy tribal handicrafts, textiles and other artifacts, but they are not cheap. In some of Sarawak's smaller coastal and upriver towns, you are more likely to find a better bargain, although the selection is not as good. If buying several items, it is a good idea to find one shop which sells the lot, as good discounts can be negotiated. It is essential to shop around: the best-stocked handicraft and antique shops in and near the big

Shopping

Sarawak

hotels are usually the most expensive. It is possible to bargain everywhere. **NB** It is illegal to export any antiquity without a licence from the curator of the Sarawak Museum. An antiquity is defined as any object made before 1850. Most things sold as antiquities are not; some very convincing weathering and ageing processes are employed.

Antiques and curios Most of these shops are scattered along Main Bazaar, with a few in the Padungan area. **Artwork** *Galleri M*, *Hilton* Lobby, paintings from a wide range of Sarawakian artists. **Birds' nests** Mostly exported to China. *Teo Hoe Hin Enterprise* (next to *McDonalds*) is worth visiting to view the delicacies.

Books and maps *Berita Book Centre*, Jln Haji Taha, has a good selection English-language books. *HN Mohd Yahia & Son*, *Holiday Inn*, Jln Tunku Abdul Rahman, and in the basement of the Sarawak Shopping Plaza, sells a 1:500,000 map of Sarawak. It is also possible to get good maps from the State Government offices (2nd floor) near the end of Jln Simpang Tiga. It is necessary to obtain police clearance for the purchase of more detailed sectional maps. *Times Books*, 1st floor, Riverside Shopping Complex, Jln Tunku Abdul Rahman, best and biggest bookshop for foreign language books. *Pasara Bookstore*, Jln Haji Taha.

Most shops are closed Sun

Handicrafts Most handicraft and antique shops are along Main Bazaar, Lebuh Temple and Lebuh Wayang. *Telang Usan Hotel*, some Orang Ulu and Penan crafts, including good modern beadwork and traditional headgear. *Sarakraf*, Upper Ground Floor, *Sarawak Plaza Shopping Complex*, sarakraf@tm.net.my Wide range of souvenirs and handicrafts with outlets in major hotels in Kuching, Damai, Sarawak Cultural Village and Miri airport (chain set up by the Sarawak Economic Development Corporation). *Gallerie M*, *Hilton* Lobby, 26 Main Bazaar. Exclusive jewellery, bead necklaces and antiques, best available Iban hornbill carvings. *Bong & Co*, 78 Main Bazaar. *Borneo Art Gallery*, Sarawak Plaza, Jln Tunku Abdul Rahman. *Borneo Arts & Crafts*, 56 Main Bazaar. *The Curio Shoppe* is attached to the Sarawak Museum, prices are high but profits go to charity. There is a Sunday market (which starts on Sat afternoon) on Jln Satok, to the southwest of town, with a few handicraft stalls. Sat evening or Sun early morning are the best times to visit. *Eeze Trading*, Lot 250, Section 49, Ground floor, Jln Tunku Abdul Rahman. *Karyaneka (handicrafts) Centre* at Cawangan Kuching, Lot 324 Bangunan Bina, Jln Satok. *Loo Pan Arts*, 83 Jln Ban Hock. *Native Arts*, 94 Main Bazaar. *Sarawak Batik Art Shop*, 1 Lebuh Temple. *Sarawak House*, 67 Main Bazaar (more expensive). *Atelier Gallery*, 104 Main Bazaar. *Syarikat Pemasarah Karyaneka*, Lot 87, Jln Rubber. *Tan & Sons*, 54 Jln Padungan. *Thian Seng*, 48 Main Bazaar (good for *pua kumbu*); *Art Gallery*, 5 Wayang St, designer T-shirts with Sarawak motifs amongst other crafts. *Fabriko*, Main Bazaar in beautifully restored Chinese shophouse, interesting souvenirs and gallery.

Markets The *Vegetable* and *Wet market* are on the riverside on Jln Gambier; further up is the *Ban Hock Wharf market*, now full of cheap imported clothes. The *Sunday Market* on Jln Satok sells jungle produce, fruit and vegetables (there are a few handicraft stalls) and all sorts of intriguing merchandise; it starts on Sat night and runs through Sun morning and is well worth visiting. There is a jungle produce market, Pasar Tani, on Fri and Sat at Kampong Pinang Jawa in Petra Jaya.

Postcards *Adventure Images showroom*, 55 Main Bazaar, good range of both colour and black and white postcards, also sell greetings cards and posters. **Pottery** Rows of pottery stalls along Jln Penrissen, out of town, take a bus (STC 3, 3A, 9A or 9B) or taxi to Ng Hua Seng Pottery bus stop. Antique shops sell this pottery too. **Shopping complexes**: *Sarawak Plaza*, next to the *Holiday Inn*, Jln Tunku Abdul Rahman; *Riverside Shopping Complex*, next to *Riverside Majestic Hotel*, best complex in Kuching, has Parkson Department Store and good supermarket in basement.

Sports **Bowling** Riverside Complex, Jln Tunku Abdul Rahman, 24-lane bowling alley. **Fishing** Offshore from Santubong or deep sea game fishing at Tanjung Datu (near

Indonesian border), contact Mr Johnson, Fui Lip Marketing, 15 Ground floor, Wisma Phoenix, Jln Song Thian Cheok. **Golf** *Damai Golf Course* , Jln Santubong, T846088, F846044. Green fees RM150 weekdays, RM180 weekends. Due to its popularity bookings should be made 3 days in advance, designed by Arnold Palmer, right on the sea, a very long 18 holes - with electric buggies (the only ones in Sarawak) to prevent your expiring through perspiring. Swimming, tennis and squash courts are among the other facilities available here. *Kelab Golf Course*, Petra Jaya, 18 holes, green fee RM84 (weekdays), RM126 (weekends), T440966. *Prison Golf Club*, Jln Penrissen, T613544, 9-hole, green fees RM30, RM50 at weekends. *Sarawak Golf and Country Club*, Petra Jaya, T440966, green fees RM105 weekdays, RM157.50 weekends. **Golf Driving Range** *City North Driving Range*, Kuching's only dedicated driving range, open 0700-2300 Mon-Sun, RM7 for a tray of 50 balls. **Hash house harriers** Men only harriers on Tue at 1730, ladies harriettes on Wed at 1730, mixed city hash on Sat at 1630. Contact Tom Leng (T416778) or Jennifer Yap (T411694, F413700). **Jogging** Track at Reservoir Park. **Mountain biking** Good trails from Kamppung Singgai, about 30 mins from Kuching (across the Batu Kawa bridge). Beginners to intermediate – good trail near Kampung Apar. Advanced trail – Batang Ai. *Borneo Adventure* (T245175) on Main Bazaar rent mountain bikes and can arrange specialized tours. Alternatively, hire a bike from Kuching and tour the Malay villages adjacent to the Astana and Fort Margherita. Cross the Sarawak River by sampan (RM1 for you and your bike) and then follow the small road that runs parallel to the river. The *Rainforest Cup* mountain bike race is open to enthusiasts. Details at www.rainforestcup.com **Outward bound** *Camp Permai Sarawak*, PO Box 891, Satok Post Office, T321497, F321500. **Rock Climbing** 'Batman Wall' at the Fairy Caves outside Bau has 20 routes and rises to 40 m. Contact *Best Systems*, T019-8570488, www.bestsystems.com.my **Spectator sports** Malaysia Cup football matches held in the *Stadium Negeri Sarawak*, Petra Jaya. The *Turf Club* on Serian Rd is the biggest in Borneo (see newspapers for details of meetings). **Swimming** *Kuching Municipal Swimming Pool*, next to Kuching Turf Club, Serian Rd, admission RM1, open mornings only. Another public pool is on Jln Pandungan, just past the Kuching City South Council office complex. **Watersports** Damai Beach.

Borneo Adventure, No 55 Main Bazaar, T245175, F422626, www.borneoadventure.com Known for its environmentally friendly approach to tourism. Offers tours all over Sarawak. Recommended. *Borneo Exploration,* 76 Jln Wayang, T252137, F252526, ckkc@tm.net.my *Borneo Transverse*, Ground floor, 16 Jln Green Hill, T257784, F421419, bttt@po.jaring.my *Harrisons Travel*, 28 Jln Green Hill, T240977, F244542. Advice on tours as well as air, bus and boat tickets. *Ibanika Expeditions*, Lot 435, Ground floor, Jln Ang Cheng Ho, T424022, F424021, ibanika@po.jaring.my Long-established company offering longhouse and more general tours, also offers French and German-speaking guides. *Journey Travel Agency*, Lobby Floor, *Kuching Hilton Hotel*, Jln. Borneo, T424934, dolores@pd.jaring.my   *Interworld*, 1st floor, 161/162 Jln Temple, T252344, F424515. *Gaya Holidays*, 37 Main Bazaar, T415476, for river cruises (RM30/person/hr), sales@interworld-borneo.com *Jollytours*, T412194, F252909, www.jollytravelsarawak.com *Pan Asia Travel*, 2nd floor, Unit 217-218, Sarawak Plaza, Jln Tunku Abdul Rahman, T419754, half-day excursions from Kuching. *Saga Travel*, Level 1, Taman Sri Sarawak Mall, Jln Tunku Abdur Rahman, T418705, F426299. *Tropical Adventure*, 1st floor, 17 Main Bazaar, T413088, F413104.

Tour operators

Local Boat: sampans, or *tambangs*, cross the Sarawak River from next to the Square Tower on Main Bazaar to Fort Margherita and the Astana on the north bank (RM0.30). Small boats and some express boats connect with outlying kampungs on the river. Sampans can also be hired by the hour (RM20-25 per hour) for a tour up and down the river.

Transport
See also Ins & outs, page 316

Sarawak

Bus: there are 2 bus companies around town: blue and white *Chin Lian Long* buses serve the city and its suburbs. Major bus stops are at Jln Mosque, the Post Office and Gambier St. The green and yellow *Sarawak Transport Company* (STC) buses leave from the end of Lebuh Jawa, next to Ban Hock Wharf and the market. STC buses operate on regional routes; bus 12A (RM0.80) airport service starts at 0630, departs every 40 mins until 1915. Chin Lian Long blue buses 19 or 17 to the Bintawa Express Wharf for Sibu (RM0.40).

Car hire: *Cet City Holidays*, Lot 2537, 1st flr, Central Park, Commercial Centre, T412500, leelan@pc.jaring.my *Pronto Car Rental*, 1st floor, 98 Jln Padungan, T/F236889, also at Kuching International Airport; *Mayflower Car Rental*, Lot 4.24A, 4th floor, Bangunan Satok, Jln Satok, T410110, F410115, Kuching International Airport booth, T575233; *Wah Tung Travel Service*, counter at Kuching International Airport, T616900, for city office T248888.

Taxi: local taxis congregate at the taxi stand on Jln Market, or outside the big hotels, they do not use meters (but there are plans to introduce them), so agree a price before setting off. 24-hr radio taxi service T343343, 342255. Short distances around town should cost RM5-7. 'Midnight' surcharge of RM50 2400-0600.

Long distance Air: the airport is 10 km south of Kuching. Regular connections with **KL** (8-10 flights daily, both from KLIA and Subang, RM262), **JB**, **KK**, **Bintulu**, **Miri** (RM164), **Sibu** (RM77), **Penang**, **Labuan** (RM199), **Mukah**, **Bandar Seri Begawan**, **Brunei**. **NB** *MAS* has advance purchase fares and 50% group discounts on certain flights (bookable only in Malaysia). *MAS* offers connections between **Kuching** and **Kuala Lumpur**, **Johor Baru** and **Kota Kinabalu**, as well as many interior towns in East Malaysia. *Air Asia* has daily flights to Kuala Lumpur's old Subang airport. *MAS Rural Air Service* operate Twin Otters to a large number of airfields across the state including Miri-Bario (for the **Kelabit highlands**), Miri-Mulu (for **Gunung Mulu**) and Sibu-Kapit-Belaga (for the **Rejang River**). Transport to town: Green bus *Sarawak Transport Co*, 12A (1.00) to **Lebuh Jawa** (45-min journey, departing every 50 min) which operate between 0710 (0630 from Kuching) and 2000, or taxi to town (RM16.50 – buy a coupon from the counter in the arivals lounge).

Airport information: T457373

MAS has flights to **Bandar Seri Begawan** (Brunei), **Singapore** (2 connections daily), **Hong Kong** (via Kota Kinabalu), **Taipei**, **Manila**, **Seoul**, **Tokyo**, **Perth** and **Pontianak** (Indonesia). *SIA* offers daily connections with **Singapore** (RM267), *Royal Brunei Airlines* with **Bandar Sri Begawan**, and *Dragon Air* a twice weekly direct service to **Hong Kong**.

See box on page 45 for details of fares and destinations

Bus: There are a cornucopia of companies each serving different areas and operating out of several stations; The *Sarawak Transport Company* (T242967) operates green and yellow buses. They leave from Lebuh Jawa, next to Ban Hock Wharf, and serve the Kuching area and southwest Sarawak. *Petra Jaya Transport* (T429418) serves Bako, Damai and Santubong. Their buses (yellow with black and red stripes) depart from the open-air market near *Electra House*. *Matang Transport Company*'s yellow and orange buses depart from outside the Saujana Car Park and go to Matang and Kubah. Additional city services are provided by the blue and white *Chin Lian Long* buses and *Regas Transport*'s rather naff beige machines.

Long distance buses depart from the Regional Express Bus Terminal on Jln Penrissen. The most convenient place to buy tickets is at the *Biaramas Express* office on Jln Khoo Hun Yeang (near Electra House), T429418. *Biaramas* also has a 24-hr office at the terminal (T452139). Buses to **Sibu**, **Bintulu** and **Miri** often involve a change of bus in Sarikei. Other long-distance services are provided by *Borneo Highway Express* (T619689, tickets available from 63 Main Bazaar) and *PB Ekpres* (T461277).

International connections: there are 2 express bus departures a day to Pontianak in Kalimantan, Indonesia, 10 hrs (depart 0700-1230, RM34.50). It is necessary to have a valid Indonesian visa (see **Embassies and consulates** below). Buses leave from Khoo Hun Yeang St. Booking office: Mile 3.5, Penrissen Rd, T454548, 454668 or through Kedai Jam Ban Poh, 130 Jln Padungan or *Borneo Interland Travel*, 63 Main Bazaar. There are now several bus companies, providing a/c, reclining seats, wc. *SJS Executive Bus Co*, leaves from 3½ mile. Bus Terminal, Jln Penrissen – daily service to Pontianak, morning departure, 10 hrs (so long as there is no delay at the border). Other companies include *Biaramas* and *Tebakong*. For a more adventurous route take *Sarawak Transport Company* buses 3 or 3A to **Serian**, 1 hr; *Mara Transport Company* bus from Serian to Tebedu, 1½ hrs, and from Tebedu it is possible to trek across the border to Balai Kerangan in **Kalimantan**. There are 5 departures daily from Kuching via Miri and Kuala Belait to **Bandar Seri Begawan** (Brunei).

It is possible to enter Sarawak from Indonesia driving a private vehicle (including rental vehicles) so long as it has international insurance cover

Boat: express boats leave from the Marine Base, Jln Pending, 4 km east of town. Take a blue bus 19 or 17 from Lebuh Jawa or a taxi from Lebuh Market. Tickets for Kuching-Sibu are no longer on sale in town; try and get to the jetty in Pending around 30 mins before departure to be sure of a seat. Regular connections with Sibu (involving a change to a river express boat at Sarikei); 4 hrs (RM35, or RM38 for first class). There are also cargo boats going to Sibu and **Miri** 18 hrs: further information from Sarawak Tourist Association (see Tourist Offices below).

Airline offices *British Airways*, 92 Jln Green Hill, T242367. *Hornbill Skyways*, North Pan Hangar, International Airport, PO Box 1387, T455737, F455736. *MAS*, Lot 215, Jln Song Thian Cheok, T246622, F244563. *Merpati* ticket agent, *Sin Hwa Travel Service*, 8 Lebuh Temple, T246688. *Singapore Airlines*, Jln Tunku Abdul Rahman, T240266, F238487. *Royal Brunei*, 1st floor, Rugayah Building, Jln Song Thian Cheok, T243344, F244563. *Dragonair*, 1st floor, Wisma Bukit Mata Kuching, Jln Tunku Abdul Rahman, T233322, F238819. *Saega Airlines*, Level 16, Wisma Ting Pek Khing, 1 Jln Pandungan, T236905, F236922. *Qantas*, 41 Jln P Ramli, T231832. *SIA*, Ground floor, Wisma Bukit Mata Kuching, Jln Tunku Abdul Rahman, T240266, F238487.

Directory

Sarawak

Banks Money changers in the main shopping complexes usually give a much better rate for cash than the banks – although if changing TCs the rates are much the same. ATMs are two-a-penny. Note that the first Sat of every month is a bank holiday. *Standard Chartered*, Wisma Bukit Mata Kuching (opposite *Holiday Inn*), Jln Tunku Abdul Rahman. *Hongkong*, 2-4 Jln Tun Haji Openg (Main Bazaar end). *American Express*, 70 Jln Padungan (assistance with Amex traveller's cheques) T252600. *Majid & Sons Money Changer*, 45 Jln India. *Mohamed Yahia & Sons* (money changer), GF3, Sarawak Plaza.

Communications Internet: *Cyber City*, Taman Sri Sarawak (opposite the *Hilton*), T419016, , open 1000-2200 (RM10 per hr). *Net@Café* T234008, Lot 352, Lorong 12, Rubber Rd 0900-2100 (RM6 per hr). *Cyber Borneo* Upper Ground floor, Star Car Park Complex, Temple/Wayang Street (RM6 per hr). *Stargate Cyber* T259072, Lot 291, Abell Rd, Mon-Thu 0930-2400, Fri-Sun 0930-0200 (RM5 per hr). **Telekom:** (for international telephone calls) Jln Batu Lintang (open 0800-1800 Mon-Fri; 0800-1200 Sat and Sun). International calls can also be made from most public cardphones. Major hotels all have cardphones in their lobbies. **General Post Office:** Jln Tun Haji Openg, open Mon-Sat 0800-1800, Sun 1000-1300. Operates a *poste restante* service.

Embassies and consulates *Indonesian Consulate*, 111 Jln Tun Abang Haji Openg, T241734 or T234241. *Australian Honorary Consul*, T245661. *British Consulate*, Rugayah Building, Jln Song Thian Cheok, T231320. *Canadian Consulate*, 1 Jln

Padungan, T237000. *Chinese Consulate*, Lot 3719 Dogan Garden, Jln Dogan (off Jln Batu Kawa), T453344. *French Consul*, c/o *Telong Usan Hotel*, T415588. **New Zealand** **Consulate**, T482177.

Medical facilities Dentist: Taman Sri Sarawak (behind *De Tavern*). **Hospitals:** *Kuching General Hospital*, Jln Tan Sri Ong Kee Hui, off Jln Tun Haji Openg, T257555. *Normah Medical Centre*, across the river on Jln Tun Datuk Patinggi Hj. Abdul Rahman Yakub, T440055, private hospital with good reputation. *Doctor's Clinic*, Main Bazaar, opposite Chinese History Museum is said to be excellent and is used to treating travellers' more minor ailments (RM20 for consultation). *Poliklinik*, 11 Jln P Ramlee, T240741. *Timberland Medical Centre*, Rock Rd, T234991. Recommended. **Pharmacies:** *Apex Pharmacy*, 125 1st floor, Sarawak Plaza, open 1000-2100; *YK Farmasi*, 22 Main Bazaar, open 0830-1700; *UMH*, Ban Hock Rd, open 0900-2030, Sat 0900-1800.

Places of worship Christian churches conduct services in a number of languages. The Muslim Council of Sarawak provides details of Muslim prayer times throughout the state, T429811. **Anglican:** St Thomas' Cathedral, Jln McDougall, T240187 for times of services. **Baptist:** Sarawak Baptist Church, Setampak, Stampin, T413462. **Evangelical services:** Lot 1863 Block 10, 26 Iris Gardens, T425212. **Methodist:** Trinity Methodist Church, 57 Jln Ellis, T411044. **Roman Catholic:** St Joseph's Cathedral, Jln Tun Abang Hj, T423424.

Useful addresses Immigration: 1st floor, Bangunan Sultan Iskandar (Federal Complex) Jln Simpang Tiga, T245661. **Police:** T241222. Office located opposite Padang Merdeka. **Resident's Office:** T243301.

Damai Peninsula

Colour map 3, grid C1   *The peninsula, 35 km north of Kuching, is located at the west mouth of the Sarawak River and extends northwards as far as Mount Santubong, a majestic peak of 810 m. Its attractions include the **Sarawak Cultural Village**, trekking up **Mount Santubong**, sandy beaches, a golf course, adventure camp and three resorts which are particularly good value off season when promotional rates are available. It has been developed over recent years by the Sarawak Economic Development Corporation, partly to create local employment and partly to open up the area to tourism.*

Ins & outs   **Getting there**   : It's a 40-minute bus journey to Buntal, on the eastern side of the peninsular. Take bus No 26 from the Petra Jaya terminal. Buses depart every 40 mins throughout the day. From here, buses continue to Santubong, winding through the foothills.

Santubong The village of **Santubong** itself, located at the mouth of the Sarawak River, **& Buntal** is small and quiet. Formerly a fishing village, most of the villagers now work in one of the nearby resorts. However, some fishing still goes on, and the daily catch is still sold every morning at the quayside. Near the quayside are two or three Chinese-run grocery stores and a simple coffee shop. The rest of the village is made up of small houses strung out along the road, built in the Malay tradition on stilts – many are wooden and painted in bright colours. The only other village on the peninsula is **Buntal** which lies just off the Kuching-Santubong road. Popular with local Kuchingites who come here at the weekends for the seafood restaurants, the resort that was built here never really took off and it is planned to be turned into a hotel training centre.

The Sarawak Cultural Village (Kampong Budaya Sarawak) was the brainchild of the Sarawak Development Corporation which built Sarawak's 'living museum' at a cost of RM9.5m to promote and preserve Sarawak's cultural heritage. With increasing numbers of young tribal people being tempted from their longhouses into the modern sectors of the economy, many of Sarawak's traditional crafts have begun to die out. The Cultural Village set out to teach the old arts and crafts to new generations. For the state development corporation, the concept had the added appeal of creating a money-spinning 'Instant Sarawak' for the benefit of tourists lacking the time or inclination to head into the jungle. As with any such artificial scheme, it is rather contrived, but the Cultural Village has been a resounding success and contains some superb examples of traditional architecture. In 2000 it received more than 100,000 visitors. It should be on the sightseeing agenda of every visitor to Kuching, if only to provide an introduction to the cultural traditions of all the main ethnic groups in Sarawak.

Sarawak Cultural Village

Each tribal group is represented by craftsmen and women who produce handicrafts and practise traditional skills in houses built to carefully researched design specifications. Many authentic everyday articles have been collected from longhouses all over Sarawak. In one case the village has served to preserve a culture – pickled – that is already effectively dead: today the Melanau people all live in Malay-style kampongs, but a magnificent traditional wooden Melanau house has been built at the Cultural Village and is now the only such building in Sarawak. Alongside it there is a demonstration of traditional sago processing. A resident Melanau craftsman makes sickness

Sarawak

Sarawak Cultural Village

☞ The Penan – museum pieces for the 21st century?

Economic progress has altered many Sarawakians' lifestyles in recent years; the oil and natural gas sector now offers many employment prospects and upriver tribespeople have been drawn into the logging industry (see page 384). But it is logging that has directly threatened the 9,000-strong Penan tribe's traditional way of life. Sarawak's nomadic hunter-gatherers have emerged as 'the noble savages' of the late 20th century, as their blockades of logging roads drew world attention to their plight. In 1990, Britain's Prince Charles' remarks about Malaysia's "collective genocide" against the Penan prompted an angry letter of protest from Prime Minister Dr Mahathir Mohamad. He is particularly irked by western environmentalists – especially Bruno Manser, who lived with the Penan in the late 1980s. "We don't need any more Europeans who think they have a white man's burden to shoulder," Dr Mahathir said.

Malaysia wants to integrate the Penan into mainstream society, on the grounds that it is morally wrong to condemn them to a life expectancy of 40 years, when the average Malaysian lives to well over 60. "There is nothing romantic about these helpless, half-starved, disease-ridden people," the Prime Minister said. The government has launched resettlement programmes to transform the Penan from hunters into fishermen and farmers. One of these new longhouses can be visited in Mulu (see page 379); it has failed to engender much enthusiasm from the Penan, although 4,000-5,000 Penan have now been resettled. Environmentalists countered that the Penan should be given the choice, but, the government asks, what choice do they have if they have only lived in the jungle?

The Cultural Village, opened by Dr Mahathir in 1990, offered a compromise of sorts – but the Penan had the last laugh. One tribal elder, called Apau Madang, and his grandson were paid to parade in loincloths and make blowpipes at the Penan hut while tourists took their snapshots. The arrangement did not last long as they did not like posing as artefacts in Sarawak's 'living museum'. They soon complained of boredom and within months had wandered back to the jungle where they could at least wear jeans and T-shirts. Today, the Penan hut is staffed by other Orang Ulu. There are thought to be only 400 Penan still following their traditional nomadic way of life.

images (*blum*) – each representing the spirit of an illness, which were floated downriver in tiny boats as part of the healing ritual.

There are also Bidayuh, Iban and Orang Ulu longhouses, depicting the life-styles of each group. In each there are textile or basket-weavers, wood-carvers or sword-makers. There are exhibits of beadwork, bark clothing, and *tuak* (rice wine) brewing. At the Penan hut there is a demonstration of blowpipe making and visitors are invited to test their hunting skills. There is a Malay house and even a Chinese farmhouse with a pepper garden alongside. The tour of the houses, seven in all (you can collect a stamp from each one for your passport!) is capped by an Andrew Lloyd Webber-style cultural show which is expertly choreographed, if rather ersatz. It is held in the on-site theatre which is fully air conditioned.

The Cultural Village employs 140 people, including dancers, who earn around RM300 a month and take home the profits from handicraft and tuak sales. Special application must be made to attend heritage centre workshops where courses can be requested in various crafts such as wood-carving, mat-weaving, batik-painting; also intensive day and three to four day courses. There is a restaurant and craft shop, *Sarakraf*. ■ *Mon-Sun 0900-1730, cultural show 1130-1215 and 1630-1715, adult RM45, child*

(6-12 years) RM22.50, including cultural show, T846411, F846988
www.sarawakculturalvillage.com

Excursions

Situated on the Santubong Peninsula, Gunung Santubong's precipitous southern side provides a moody backdrop to Damai Beach. The distinctive mountain is most accessible from the east side, where there is a clear ridge trail to the top. There are two trails to the summit, one begins opposite the *Palm Beach Seafood Restaurant and Resort*, about 2½ km before the *Holiday Inn Damai Beach*. The conical peak – from which there are spectacular views – can be reached in seven to nine hours (the last stretch is a tough scramble), guides are not necessary (but can be provided), check with the hotel recreation counters or at the Santubong Mountain Trek Canteen. ■ *T846153. The official Damai guide provides a more detailed description of the trek. Take supplies of food and water. There is a bus to Damai Beach or (more regularly) to Santubong from Petra Jaya terminal, take No 2b (40-min journey).*

Gunung Santubong
Altitude: 810m

North of Kampung Telaga Air, Pulau Satang Besar has been designated a Turtle Sanctuary to protect the green turtles which come ashore here to lay their eggs. Inquire at the Visitor Information Centre, overlooking the Padang (T410942), in Kuching for departures from Santubong or Kampung Telaga Air.

Pulau Satang Besar

Trips up the Salak River depart from the terminal at Santubong village, a 10-minute drive from the resort hotels. River tours last about three hours. The journey ventures into smaller rivers and a creek and it is a good introduction to the mangrove forest ecosystem. Contact hotel recreation counters or tour operators for details (see Directory below 335).

Salak River

Essentials

L-AL *Holiday Inn Resort Damai Lagoon*, Teluk Penyuk, Santubong, PO Box 3159, T846900, F846901. Managed by *A&A Hotels*, it is the sister of the *River Majestic* in Kuching. Superbly located at the foot of Mount Santubong, on a small, well-kept, sandy beach, its 256 rooms and 30 chalets are in stylish buildings with steep, wood-shingled roofs. There are polished wood floors and decorative woodcarving throughout; a monumental, timber-roofed lobby open to the sea, and pleasant gardens dotted with tribal wooden effigies surrounding a lagoon-style pool (the largest in Sarawak) which has a sandy slope for kids at one end and a man-made cave, complete with cascade and stage for shows, at the other. The lagoon also has a circular, swim-up bar, shaded by colonial, wood-shingled roof, all rooms have a/c, TV, in-house movies, mini-bar, tea and coffee-making facilities, balcony and personal safe. Other facilities include restaurant, tea-house (excellent for sunset views), bar, health club (with spa), tennis, boutique, bicycle hire, canoe hire, watersports and children's playground. Sterling competition for the *Holiday Inn* and definitely better in terms of access to beach and general tranquillity. Recommended.

Sleeping
■ *on map, page 326*
Price codes:
see inside front cover

　　AL-A *Holiday Inn Resort Damai Beach*, Teluk Bandung, Santubong, PO Box 2870, T846999, F846777, hirdb02@po.jaring.my Taken over from the *Sheraton* in 1987, the resort calls itself the 'Crown Jewel of Sarawak', although the real jewel in the crown is the large, private, wooden mansion at the top of the resort which belongs to the Sultan of Brunei. The new hill-top extension, directly below the Sultan's mansion, has chalets modelled on ethnic designs, such as the circular Bidayuh buildings which make this a better than average *Holiday Inn*. The beach is bigger than that at *Damai Lagoon Resort*,

Sarawak

but less accessible if you are staying at the hill-top site. All 302 rooms, including 179 chalets, have a/c, colour TV, in-house movie, coffee and tea-making facilities. Other facilities including 2 pools, tennis, spa pool, watersports, kids' club, bicycle/scooter hire, games room, restaurant (good value buffet), PV Fun Pub (a popular night spot for Kuchingites), children's playground and lobby shops.

A-B *Damai Rainforest Resort (Camp Permai)*, Pantai Damai, Santubong, PO Box B91, Satok Post Office, T321498, F321500. Located at the foot of Mount Santubong, near the *Damai Lagoon Resort*, this is an outward-bound centre which offers a number of courses including adventure training and leadership development. Other facilities include artificial climbing wall, obstacle course, abseiling, sailing, canoeing, paintball competitions. Sleeping in 10 a/c tree houses or log cabins, cafeteria, tents and camping equipment for hire. **A** *Santubong Kuching Resort*, Jln Santubong, PO Box 2364, T846888, F846666. Surrounded by the *Damai Golf Course*, 380 rooms all with a/c, restaurant, large pool, chalets with jacuzzis, tennis, basketball, volleyball, gym, mountain biking, etc. Nestling beneath Mount Santubong, a low-rise resort popular with golfers, it also has the largest conference and banquet facilities in Sarawak. Price includes breakfast.

Eating *Santubong Mountain Trek Canteen*, T846153, 5 mins' walk from hotels, rice and noodle dishes, in nearby *Buntal village* there are excellent seafood restaurants. *New Dolphin Seafood Restaurant*, Kampung Buntal, T846441, great position on the coast, good food, above average prices.

Bars *PV The Fun Pub* at *Holiday Inn Damai Beach* is Damai's main night spot and very popular – an open-air pub with pool and karaoke and live bands.

Entertainment **Cultural shows** *Sarawak Cultural Village*, Damai Beach, cultural shows, with stylized and expertly choreographed tribal dance routines, 1130 and 1630, Mon-Sun. See page 339.

Sports **Golf** *Damai Golf Course*, Jln Santubong, PO Box 400, T846088, F846044, international standard, 18-hole golf course designed by Arnold Palmer, laid out over approximately 6½ km, 10-bay driving range, green fees weekdays (RM150), weekends (RM180). Caddies, clubs and shoes for hire, spacious club house, restaurant, bar, pro shop, tennis, squash, pool. **Mountain biking** Close to the *Damai Rainforest Resort* is the purpose-built *Damai Cross Country Track* where visitors can get very hot, sweaty and dirty as they career around the 3.5-km track; bikes can be hired from hotels. **Watersports** *Holiday Inn Resort Damai Beach* and the *Holiday Inn Resort Damai Lagoon* both offer a range of watersports from jetskiing through to sailing. Snorkelling trips also arranged. The *Damai Rainforest Resort* has a slightly more restricted range of watersports on offer.

Transport **Bus** There are shuttle buses from the *Holiday Inn* and *Riverside Majestic* in Kuching *Santubong is 31 km* (RM10, RM5 for children, 40 mins, first bus at 0730 from Kuching, last return bus at *from Kuching and* 2200) or take the public bus No 2B, operated by Petra Jaya Transport (yellow buses *Damai Beach, 35 km* with black and red stripes) to Santubong at a fraction of the price (RM2.80) from the market place at the end of Jln Gambier. Tour companies offer packages for US$60, for transport on shuttle bus, entrance to the Sarawak Cultural Village and lunch. **Taxi** From Kuching costs RM35, from the airport RM46.50.

Sarawak

Bako National Park

*Bako is situated on the beautiful Muara Tebas Peninsula, a former river delta which has been thrust above sea level. Its sandstone cliffs, which are patterned and streaked with iron deposits, have been eroded to produce a dramatic coastline with secluded coves and beaches and rocky headlands. Millions of years of erosion by the sea has resulted in the formation of wave-cut platforms, 'honeycomb' weathering, solution pans, arches and sea stacks. Bako's most distinctive feature is the westernmost headland – **Tanjung Sapi** – a 100-m high sandstone plateau, which is unique in Borneo.*

Established in 1957, Bako was Sarawak's first national park. It is a very small park (2,742 ha) but it has an exceptional variety of flora and guaranteed wildlife spotting! Its beaches and accessible trails make it a wonderful place to chill out for a few days.

Getting there Bako lies 37 km north of Kuching, a 2-hour bus journey from Petra Jaya Terminal; a longboat needs to be rented to reach Park HQ. Travelling by car, the drive from Kuching takes about 40 mins, parking is safe at Kampong Bako (from where you rent a boat). **Getting around** It is possible to hire boats around the park: speed boats RM85 (can accommodate 5-6). **Ins & outs**

There are seven separate types of vegetation in Bako. These include mangroves (*bakau* is the most common stilt-rooted mangrove species), swamp forest and heath forest – known as *kerangas*, an Iban word meaning 'land on which rice cannot grow'. Pitcher plants (*Nepenthes ampullaria*) do however grow in profusion on the sandy soil (see page 563). There is also mixed dipterocarp rainforest (the most widespread forest type in Sarawak, characterized by its 30-40m-high canopy), beach forest, and *padang* vegetation, comprising scrub and bare rock from which there are magnificent views of the coast. The rare *daun payang* (umbrella palm) is also found in Bako Park; it is a litter-trapping plant as its large fronds catch falling leaves from the trees above and funnel them downwards where they eventually form a thick organic mulch enabling the plant to survive on otherwise infertile soil. There are also wild durian trees in the forest, which can take up to 60 years to bear fruit. **Flora & fauna**

Bako is one of the few areas in Sarawak inhabited by the proboscis monkey (*Nasalis larvatus*), known by Malays as 'Orang Belanda', or Dutchmen, or even 'Pinocchio of the jungle', because of their long noses (see page 559). Bako is home to approximately 150 rare proboscis monkeys. They are most often seen in the early morning or at dusk in the Teluk Assam, Teluk Paku and Teluk Delima areas (at the far west side of the park, closest to the headquarters) or around Teluk Paku, a 45-minute walk from the Park HQ. The park also has resident populations of squirrels, mousedeer, sambar deer, wild pigs, long-tailed macaques, flying lemur, silver leaf monkeys and palm civet cats. Teluk Assam, in the area around the Park HQ, is one of the best places for birdwatching: over 150 species have been recorded in the park, including pied and black hornbills. Large numbers of migratory birds come to Bako between September and November. Other inhabitants of the park are the blue fiddler crab, which has one big claw, and is forever challenging others to a fight and mudskippers, evolutionary throw-backs (half-fish, half-frog), which are common in mangrove areas. Also in the park there are two species of otter: the oriental small-clawed otter and the hairy-nosed otter (the best area to see them is at Teluk Assam). The Bornean bearded pig is the largest mammal

Sarawak

found Bako and is usually seen snuffling around the Park HQ. There are many lizards too, the largest being the water monitor which is often found near the accommodation. The only poisonous snake occasionally seen is the Wagler's pit viper. Nocturnal animals include flying lemur, pangolin, mousedeer, bats, tarsier, slow loris and palm civet (the beach by the Park HQ is a great place for a night time stroll).

Treks

On arrival visitors are required to register at the Park HQ

There is a good range of well-marked trails throughout the park – over 30 km in total; all paths are colour coded, corresponding to the map available from Park HQ. The shortest trek is the steep climb to the top of **Tanjong Sapi**, overlooking Teluk Assam, with good views of Gunung Santubong, on the opposite peninsula, across Tanjong Sipang, to the west. The 3.5-km trek to Tajor waterfall is amongst the most popular with varied walking – some steep climbs – spectacular views and a chance of a refreshing swim at the waterfall. The longest trek is to Telok Limau; a five- to seven-hour walk through a variety of terrain. You can arrange with Park HQ to lay on a boat to bring you back (around RM200). Some trails are temporarily closed – check with Park HQ. Full-day treks and overnight camping expeditions can be arranged. There are plank walkways with shelters at intervals to provide quiet watching spots particularly required for viewing the proboscis monkey in the early morning.

Beaches

There are seven beaches around the park, but some are rather inaccessible, with steep paths down to the cliffs. The best swimming beach is at **Teluk Pandan Kecil**, about 1½ hours' walk, northeast from the Park HQ. It is also possible to swim at **Teluk Assam** and **Teluk Paku**. Enquire about jellyfish at the Park HQ before swimming in the sea; it is advisable not to swim in March and April.

Park essentials

Permits Available from the Visitors Information Centre in Kuching overlooking the Padang, T410942, or the National Parks Office, Jln Masjid, T248088.

Bako National Park trails

1 Tanjung Sapi	6 Telok Pandan Besar &	10 Bukit Keruing	15 Telok Limau
2 Telok Paku	Telok Pandan Kecil	11 Paya Jelutong	16 Telok Keruing
3 Ulu Assam	7 Lintang	12 Bukit Gondol	17 Pulau Lakei
4 Telok Delima	8 Tajor	13 Ulu Serait	18 Wildlife
5 Serait	9 Tanjung Rhu	14 Telok Sibur	Observation Post

Information Centre Next to Park HQ, with a small exhibition on geology, flora and fauna within the park. Visitors can request to see an introductory video to Bako National Park, duration 42 mins. Open 0800-1245 (0800-1100 on Fri) 1400-1615 Mon-Sun. **Entrance to Park** RM10 per adult, RM5 per child or student. Photography permit RM5, video camera RM10, professional camera RM200. The Park HQ has a canteen.

All bookings to be made at the National Parks and Wildlife Booking Office, c/o Visitors' Information Centre, Lot 31, Jln Masjid, Kuching, T248088, F256301. The hostels are equipped with mattresses, kerosene stoves and cutlery. Resthouses have refrigerators and electricity until 2400. Unless a researcher, the recommended length of stay is 2 days/1 night. Resthouses and the hostel have fans, *Lodge*, RM84 per house or RM42 per room. *Hostel*, RM50 per room, RM10.50 per bed, check-out time 1200.

Sleeping

    Camping For those not intending to trek to the other side of the park, it is not worth camping as monkeys steal anything left lying around and macaques can be aggressive. In addition, the smallest amount of rain turns the campsite into a swimming pool. It is however necessary to camp if you go to the beaches on the northeast peninsula. Tents can be hired for RM8 (sleeps 4); campsite RM4.

The canteen is open 0700-2100. It serves local food at reasonable prices and sells tinned foods and drinks. No need to take food, there is a and a good seafood restaurant near the jetty.

Eating

Bus and boat *Petra Jaya* (yellow/red/black stripes) bus 6 or bus company *Chin Lian Long*, *Regas Transport* or *Sarawak Transport* every 15 mins from Electra House on Lebuh Market to **Kampong Bako**, 45 mins (RM3.80) every hr; also minibuses from Lebuh Market. From Kampong Bako, charter a private boat to **Sungai Assam** (30 mins) which is a short walk from park HQ, RM30 per boat each way – ask price before boarding (up to 6 people). **NB** In the monsoon season, between Nov and Feb, the sea can be rough.

Transport
37 km to Kuching

Sarawak

Bandar Sri Aman

Previously called Simmanggang, Bandar Sri Aman lies on the Batang Lupar, a three- to four-hour journey from Kuching, and is the administrative capital of the Second Division. The river is famous for its tidal bore; several times a year, a wall of water rushes upstream wreaking havoc with boats, small and large alike, and divides into several tributaries: the Skrang River is one of these (see below). The Batang Lupar provided Somerset Maugham with the inspiration for his short story 'Yellow Streak' in 'Borneo Tales'. It was one of the few stories he wrote from personal experience: he nearly drowned after being caught by the bore in 1929.

Colour map 3, grid C2

The major sight in Bander is the defensive **Fort Alice**. Most tourists do not stop in Bandar but pass through on day trips from Kuching to visit the traditional **Iban longhouses** sited along the Skrang River. The route to Bandar goes through pepper plantations and many 'new' villages. During Communist guerrilla activity in the 1960s (see page 397), whole settlements were uprooted in this area and placed in guarded camps.

Sights

Fort Alice was constructed in 1864. It has small turrets, a central courtyard, a medieval-looking drawbridge, and is surrounded by a fence of iron spikes. Rajah Charles Brooke lived in the Batang Lupar district for about 10 years, using this fort – and another downriver at Lingga – as bases for his punitive expeditions against pirates and Ibans in the interior. The fort is the only one of its type in Sarawak and was built commanding this stretch of the Batang Lupar River as protection against Iban raids. The original fort here was built in 1849 and named Fort James; the current fort was constructed using much of the original material. It was renamed Alice in honour of Ranee Margaret Brooke (it was her second name). It is said that every evening at 2000, until the practice was ended in 1964, a policeman would call from the fort (in Iban): "Oh ha! Oh ha! The time is now 2000. The steps have been drawn up. The door is closed. People from upriver, people from downriver are not allowed to come to the fort anymore." (It probably sounded better in Iban.)

Excursions

Skrang longhouses The Skrang River, the second longest river in Sarawak, was one of the first areas settled by Iban immigrants in the 16th-18th centuries. The slash-and-burn agriculturalists originally came from the Kapual River basin in Kalimantan. They later joined forces with Malay chiefs in the coastal areas and terrorized the Borneo coasts; the first Europeans to encounter these pirates called them 'Sea Dayaks' (see page 400). The Ibans took many heads. Blackened skulls – which local headmen say date back to those days – hang in some of the Skrang longhouses. In 1849, more than 800 Iban pirates from the Batang Lupar and Skrang River were massacred by Rajah James Brooke's forces in the notorious Battle of Beting Marau. Four years later the Sultan of Brunei agreed to cede these troublesome districts to Brooke; they became the Second Division of Sarawak.

There are many traditional Iban longhouses along the Skrang River, although those closer to Pias and Lamanak (the embarkation points on the Skrang) tend to be very touristy – they are visited by tour groups almost every day. Long Mujang, the first Iban longhouse, is an hour upriver. Pias and Lamanak are within five hours' drive of Kuching. Jungle trekking is available (approximately two hours), RM20. The guide provides an educational tour of the flora and fauna.

Sleeping All longhouses along the Skrang River are controlled by the Ministry of Tourism so all rates are the same – RM40 inclusive of all meals. Resthouses at most of the longhouses can accommodate 20-40 people, mattresses and mosquito nets are provided in a communal sleeping area with few partitions, basic conditions, with flush toilet, shower, local food (visitors are sometimes allowed to sleep on the communal area), phone available and clinic nearby. If the stay is 3 days/2 nights, on the second night it is possible to camp in the jungle and then get a return boatride to the longhouse.

Transport Buses 14 and 19 to Pias and bus 9 to **Lemanak**. Self-drive car rental (return) or minibus (8-10 people, return) from **Kuching** to **Entaban**. From these points it is necessary to charter a boat to reach the nearest longhouses. Many of the Kuching-based tour agencies offer cut-price deals for 1 to 2-day excursions to Skrang (see page 335). Unless you are already part of a small group, these tours work out cheaper because of the boat costs.

Batang Ai The Batang Ai River, a tributary of the Batang Lupar, has been dammed to form Sarawak's first hydro-electric plant which came into service in 1985; it provides 60% of Sarawak's electricity supply, transmitting as far as Limbang. The area was slowly flooded over a period of six months to give animals and wildlife a chance to escape, but it has affected no less than 29

Visiting longhouses: house rules

There are more than 1,500 longhouses in Sarawak, and as the state's varied tribal culture is one of its biggest attractions, trips to longhouses are on most visitors' itineraries. Longhouses are usually situated along the big rivers and their tributaries, notably the Skrang (the most easily accessible to Kuching, see page 346), the Rejang (see page 356) and the Baram (see page 371). The Iban, who are characteristically extrovert and hospitable to visitors, live on the lower reaches of the rivers. The Orang Ulu tribes – mainly Kayan and Kenyah – live further upriver, and are generally less outgoing than the Iban. The Bidayuh (formerly known as the Land Dayaks) live mainly around Bau and Serian, near Kuching. Their longhouses are usually more modern than those of the Iban and Orang Ulu, and are less often visited for that reason. The Kelabit people live in the remote plateau country near the Kalimantan border around Bareo (see page 388).

The most important ground rule is not to visit a longhouse without an invitation. People who arrive unannounced may get an embarrassingly frosty reception. Tour companies offer the only exception to this rule, as most have tribal connections. Upriver, particularly at Kapit, on the Rejang (see page 356), such 'invitations' are not hard to come by; it is good to ensure that your host actually comes from the longhouse he is inviting you to. The best time to visit Iban longhouses is during the gawai harvest festival at the beginning of June, when communities throw an open house and everyone is invited to join the drinking, storytelling and dancing sessions, which continue for several days.

On arrival, visitors should pay an immediate courtesy call on the headman (known as the tuai rumah in Iban longhouses). It is normal to bring him gifts; those staying overnight should offer the headman between RM10 and RM20/head. The money is kept in a central fund and saved for use by the whole community during festivals. Small gifts such as beer, coffee, tea, biscuits, whisky, batik and food (especially rice or chicken) go down well. It is best to arrive at a longhouse during late afternoon after people have returned from the fields. Visitors who have time to stay the night generally have a much more enjoyable experience than those who pay fleeting visits. They can share the evening meal and have time to talk and drink. Visitors should note the following:

- On entering a longhouse, take off your shoes.
- It is usual to accept food and drink with both hands. If you do not want to eat or drink, the accepted custom is to touch the brim of the glass or the plate and then touch your lips as a symbolic gesture; sit cross-legged when eating.
- When washing in the river, women should wear a sarong and men, shorts.
- Ask permission to take photographs. It is not uncommon to be asked for a small fee.
- Do not enter a longhouse during pantang (taboo), a period of misfortune – usually following a death. There is normally a white (leaf) flag hanging near the longhouse as a warning to visitors. During this period (normally one week) there is no singing, dancing or music, and no jewellery is worn.
- Bow your head when walking past people older than you. It is rude to stride confidently past with head held high.
- Try not to shout or be loud and noisy.

Trips upriver are not cheap. If you go beyond the limits of the express boats, it is necessary to charter a longboat. Petrol costs RM2-4/litre, depending on how far upriver you are. Guides charge approx RM40-80 a day and sometimes it is necessary to hire a boatman or front-man as well. Prices increase in the dry season when boats have to be lifted over shallow rapids. Permits are required for most upriver areas; these can be obtained at the resident's or district office in the nearest town.

Sarawak

longhouses, 10 of which are now completely submerged. The re-housing of the longhouse community has been the topic of controversial debate over the last 10 years. The communities were moved into modern longhouses and given work opportunities in local palmeries. However, it now seems that the housing loans that were initially given are not commensurate with local wages and will be very difficult for the longhouse communities ever to pay off. In addition, the modern longhouses were not provided with farmland, so many local people have returned to settle on the banks of the reservoir. Near the dam there is a freshwater fish nursery. These fish are exported to Korea, Japan and Europe. Those families displaced by the flooding of the dam largely work here and many of the longhouses surrounding the dam depend upon this fishery for their own fish supply.

The Batang Ai dam has created a vast and very picturesque man-made lake which covers an area of some 90 sq km, stretching up the Engkari and Ai rivers. Beyond the lake, more than an hour's boat ride upriver from the dam, it is possible to see beautiful lowland mixed dipterocarp forest.

The **Batang Ai National Park** covers an area of over 24,040 ha and was inaugurated in 1991. It protects the much endangered orang utan, and is home to a wide variety of other wildlife, including hornbills and gibbons. As yet there are no visitor facilities, but four walking trails have been created, one of which takes in an ancient burial ground. Trips to one of the 29 longhouses surrounding the dam and to Batang Ai National Park are organized by *Borneo Adventure Travel Company* who are based in Kuching (55 Main Bazaar, T410569, F422626) and have a counter in the *Hilton Batang Ai Longhouse Resort*. Many of the restaurant staff in the resort are locals and discreet enquiries may get you a trip to a longhouse and/or Batang Ai National Park for considerably less than the *Borneo Adventure Travel Company* charge. The park is 250 km from Kuching and takes two hours from the jetty by boat.

Sleeping A *Hilton International Batang Ai Longhouse Resort*, T083-584388, F083-584399 or c/o *Kuching Hilton International*, T248200, F428984. On the eastern shore of the lake, the *Hilton* have built a luxury longhouse resort. Opened in 1995, the resort is made up of 11 longhouses, built of the local belian (ironwood) to traditional designs; despite its lakeside location there are no views, except from the walkways, as longhouses are built, for purposes of defence, to face landwards – in this case over the buggy track. However, compromises to modern comforts have been made; the rooms are cluttered with furniture and TV sets. One hundred rooms all with a/c, fan, TV, shower room, tea and coffee-making facilities, mini-bar, other facilities include a pool and paddling pool, restaurant, 18-km jogging track, shuttle from *Kuching Hilton International*, tour desk. If the *Hilton* is not your style (or your pocket cannot stretch to it), there is, unfortunately, not much else. Although, the park does not supply rooms private tour companies provide accommodation in the longhouses here, in a much more central location within the park than the *Hilton*.

Essentials

Sleeping &
eating
There is only a limited
selection of hotels

B *Bukit Saban Resort* is located on the rarely visited Paku River, just north of the Skrang and Lemnak rivers, about 4½ hrs from Kuching. Sales office T423167 or T258795, F245551, resort T083-477246. 50 rooms in longhouse style with traditional sago palm thatch, RM92, restaurant, a/c, TV, hot water, seminar facilities. **B** *Champion*, 1248 Main Bazaar, T320140. A small but central establishment. **B-C** *Taiwan*, 1 Jln Council, T322493. A/c. **C** *Sum Sun*, 62 Jln Club, T322191, a/c. **Seriously**

cheap **Alison Café & Restaurant**, 4 Jln Council, Chinese cuisine. **Chuan Hong**, 1 Jln Council, Chinese coffee shop, also serves Muslim food. **Melody**, 432 Jln Hospital, Chinese and Muslim food.

135 km to Kuching. **Bus** Regular connections with **Kuching** (RM12) and **Sibu** (via Sarikei).   **Transport**

Useful addresses Residents' Office: T322004.   **Directory**

The Rejang River and Sibu

*The Batang Rejang is an important thoroughfare and Malaysia's longest river at 563 km (it is, however, 12 times shorter than the Nile). Tours to upriver longhouses can be organized from **Sibu**, or more cheaply from Kapit and Belaga. The second largest town in Sarawak, Sibu is sited at the confluence of the Rejang and the Igan rivers 60 km upstream from the sea. It is the starting point for trips up the Rejang to the towns of **Kapit** and **Belaga**.*

Colour map 3, grid B3
Population: 150,000
Phone code: 084

Getting there The airport is 25 km from town; flights to Kuching, Bintulu, Miri, Marudi, Kapit and Belaga and the odd connection with KK. The bus station is just a few hundred metres from the centre of town, close to the river, and there are daily connections with Bintulu and Miri, and Kapit and Kuching via Sarikei, and also buses to Kalimantan (Indonesia). Boats for Kuching and Sarikei dock at 2 wharfs close to the centre of town.

Ins & outs
See also Transport, page 354

Getting around Although Sarawak's second largest town, it is still possible to see most of Sibu's sights on foot.

Tourist offices *Visitors' Information Centre*, Ground floor, 32 Cross Rd, T340980, F341280, stbsibu@tm.net.my

Thanks to the discovery of the Kuala Paloh channel in 1961, Sibu is accessible to boats with a sizeable draft. Sibu is a busy Chinese trading town – the majority of the population came originally from China's Foochow Province – and is the main port on the Batang Rejang (also spelt 'Rajang'). In 1899, Rajah Charles Brooke agreed with Wong Nai Siong, a Chinese scholar from Fukien, to allow settlers to Sibu. Brooke had reportedly been impressed with the industriousness of the Chinese: he saw the women toiling in the paddy fields from dawn to dusk and commented to an aide: "If the women work like that, what on earth must the men be like?"

Background

The Kuching administration provided these early agricultural pioneers with temporary housing on arrival, a steamer between Sibu and Kuching, rice rations for the first year and tuition in Malay and Iban. The town grew rapidly, (its expansion is documented in a photographic exhibition in the Civic Centre) but was razed to the ground in 'the great fire' of 1828. The first shophouses to be constructed after the fire are the three-storey ones still standing on Jalan Channel. At the beginning of the 20th century, Sibu became the springboard for Foochow migration to the rest of Sarawak. Today it is an industrial and trading centre for timber, pepper and rubber, and home to some of Sarawak's wealthiest families, mostly timber *towkays* (merchants).

Sarawak

Sarawak

👉 The Rajahs' fortresses – war and peace in the Rejang

The lower reaches of the Batang Rejang are inhabited by the Iban and the upper reaches by the Kenyah and Kayan tribes, the traditional enemies of the Iban (for details on tribes, see page 399). During the days of the White Rajahs, a number of forts were built along the river in an effort to keep the peace and prevent head-hunting (see page 355). All the forts in Sarawak had chambers where confiscated heads were stored, each with a tag detailing the name of the tribe which took it and the name of the victim. Head-hunting proved a difficult practice to stamp out. In 1904, when Vyner Brooke was based at Kapit Fort as Resident of the Third Division (before he succeeded Charles as Rajah) he reported an attack on one longhouse in which head-hunters severed the heads of 80 women and children while their men were working in the fields. Tribal head-hunting raids were regular occurrences until 1924, when wild boars were exchanged between the Iban and Orang Ulu tribes at a peace-making ceremony in Kapit, presided over by the Rajah. (There are photographs of this ceremony in the Kapit Museum.)

The river fortresses were also used as bases for punitive raids against tribal rebels in the interior. One of the first stops on the

route upriver from Sibu is Kanowit, where Charles Brooke built Fort Emma. In 1859 the Rejang Resident and the fort commander were murdered there by local tribespeople. Charles Brooke swore to bathe his hands in the blood of the murderers. With 15,000 'friendly' Ibans, he went upriver in 1862, and led his expedition past the Pelagus Rapids and Belaga to the Kayan and Kenyah strongholds. Brooke then led the Ibans into a lengthy pitched battle in which hundreds died that finally broke the power of the Orang Ulu.

While the Brookes successfully forged alliances with the Rejang's Ibans, some individual groups rebelled from time to time. In her book My Life in Sarawak, Ranee Margaret (Charles Brooke's wife) relates the story of one Iban chief's dawn attack on the Rajah's fort at Sibu. Inside were several other 'friendly' Dayak chiefs. "The manner in which the friendly Dyak chiefs behaved during the skirmish amused me very much," she wrote, "for they did nothing but peer through the lattice-work, and shout Dyak insults at the attacking party, most of whom they knew very well. They made unpleasant remarks about the enemy's mothers, and inquired whether the men themselves belonged to the female sex, as their efforts were so feeble."

Sights The old trading port has now been graced with a pagoda, a couple of big hotels and a smart **esplanade**, completed in 1987. The 1929 shophouses along the river are virtually all that remains of the old town. The seven-storey **pagoda**, adjacent to Tua Pek Kong Temple, cost RM1.5m to build; there are good views over the town from the top. In the **Sibu Civic Centre**, 2½ km out of town on Jalan Tun Abang Haji Openg, there is an exhibition of old photographs of Sibu and a mediocre tribal display. This serves as Sibu's municipal museum. Five aerial photographs of the town, taken every five years or so between 1947 and 1987, chart the town's explosive growth. ■ *1030-1730 Tue- Sun. To get there, take bus No 3 from the bus terminal and ask for the Civic Centre.*

Essentials

Sleeping
■ *on map*
Price codes:
see inside front cover

A *Kingwood*, 12 Lorong Lanang 4, PO Box 1201, T335888, F334559. Largest hotel in Sibu with 168 rooms, more expensive ones have views of Rejang River. All rooms with a/c, TV, mini-bar, *Riverfront Cage*, Chinese restaurant, pool, health centre. **A** *Premier*, Jln Kampung Nyabor, T323222, F323399. Restaurant, clean rooms with a/c, TV, own bath,

Sarawak's river express boats – smoke on the water

Sarawak's Ekspres boats, powered by turbo-charged V-12 engines, are the closest most upriver tribespeople come to experiencing supersonic flight. They look like floating aircraft fuselages, are piloted from a cockpit and have aircraft-style cabins below, complete with reclining seats and head rests. Journeying downriver, these sleek Chinese-run bullet-boats reach speeds of 70 km/hour, and in their wake, longhouse landing rafts are left rocking in metre-high swell. On straighter stretches of river, pilots like to race each other, while the 'front-man', perched on the bows, keeps a lookout for semi-submerged logs – or 'floaters' – which regularly damage propellers. Incapsulated in the air-conditioned cabins, passengers (everyone from Chinese businessmen to tattooed Orang Ulu) are oblivious to the hazards. Most of them remain gripped, throughout the trip, by the deafening kung-fu films continuously screened on video.

Express boats are used on most of the major rivers in Sarawak; ocean-going versions also ply the coastal waters. They have reduced travelling time dramatically: when Ranee Margaret Brooke made the most exciting trip of her life, from Kapit to Belaga and back in the 1880s, the journey upriver took six days. Today it can be done in five hours. But navigating the coffee-coloured waters of the Rejang and Baram rivers is a dangerous occupation. Free-floating logs pose an ever-present threat. Log rafts, huge chevrons of timber, up to 500 m long, which are towed downstream by tugs, swing wide on meanders, leaving narrow gaps for the express boats. But a pilot can only claim to have cut his teeth once he has shot the Rejang's famous Pelagus Rapids, 45 minutes upriver from Kapit.

Over this 2.5 km-long stretch of white water, he has to contend with logs, rocks, whirlpools and cataracts while keeping a look-out for express boats from the opposite direction. When Ranee Margaret Brooke shot these rapids over a century ago, she wrote: "As I stood looking at the whirlpool, Hovering Hawk [her Iban steersman], who was standing near me, pointed with his thumb to the swirling water, all flecked with foam. 'See there', he said, 'who knows how many eyes lie buried beneath that foam!'" More eyes have been buried beneath the foam in recent years with the loss of 10 lives in June 1991 when an express boat capsized.

But accidents happen even without the rapids. In 1990, two express boats collided head-on in early morning fog just downriver from Kapit. One boat rolled and sank within seconds. Older boats have just one emergency exit, at the back, which is said to be impossible to open underwater as it opens outwards; windows are sealed. Newer boats have more exits, fitted under a more rigid safety code introduced in 1990. On the older boats it is possible to ride the gauntlet on the roof-top (tourists are strongly advised to take adequate precautions against sunburn). Other points to bear in mind when contemplating travel by express boat: first, given the number of express boat trips made daily, the actual accident rate is low; and second, flying from Kapit to Belaga is only marginally more expensive.

Sarawak

some with river view. Helpful staff, adjoins the *Sarawak House Shopping Centre*, discounts often available. Recommended. **A *Tanah Mas***, Jln Kampung Nyabor, T333188, F333288. A/c, very high-standard restaurant, well-appointed modern hotel with swimming pool and conference facilities. Recommended.

A couple of the top hotels are good, but those at the lower end of the market are very mediocre

B *Bahagia*, 11 Jln Central, T320303. A/c, restaurant, reasonable value for money. **B** *Capitol 88*, 19 Jln Wong Nai Siong, T336444, F311706. A/c, restaurant, rooms are clean and reasonable value. **B** *Garden*, 1 Jln Hua Ping, T317888, F330999. A/c, restaurant, well-kept and efficiently run with a good central location and a serviceable coffee shop. **B** *Li Hua*, Long Bridge Commercial Centre, T324000, F326272. Slightly out of town, but located along the river. TV, a/c, restaurant, coffee house and roof-top swimming pool. Good value.

C *Centre Point Inn*, Jing Hwa Building, off Jln Central, T320222, F320496. A/c, often offers sizeable discounts. **C** *Phoenix*, 1 & 3 Jln Kai Peng (off Jln Kampung Nyabor), T313877, F320392. TV, a/c. A very well-run hotel with spacious rooms and decent bathrooms. **C** *Sarawak*, 34 Cross Rd, T333455, F320536. A/c, attached bathroom, TV. Centrally located and a well-furnished place, good value. **C** *Sentosa Inn*, 12 Jln Pulau, T349875, F311706. A/c, TV, simple but good value. **C** *Wen Ya*, 1st floor, 39 High St (Teboh Tinggi), T321288. Big, clean rooms, one of the better in this price bracket. Good option.

Cheaper hotels tend to be around the nightmarket in Chinatown but there is also a selection within each walk of the jetty

D *Mandarin*, 183 Jln Kampung Nyabor, T339177, F333425. A/c, popular with travellers, great value. **D** *New World*, 1 Jln Wong Nai Siong, T310311. A/c, clean rooms with attached bathrooms. **D** *Ria* 21 Jln Channel, T326622. A/c, reasonable value. **D** *Emas*, 3A Foochow Lane, T310877, F320848. Some a/c, clean. **D** *Rejang*, 40 Jln Blacksmith (opposite *Standard Chartered Bank*), T315590. Some a/c and with attached bathrooms.

Sibu

Sleeping

1 Bahagia	4 Emas	7 Li Hua	10 Phoenix
2 Capitol 88	5 Garden	8 Mandarin	11 Premier & Sarawak
3 Centre Point Inn	6 Kingwood	9 New World	House Shopping Centre

0 metres 100
0 yards 100

Malay **Cheap** *Sheraton*, Delta Estate (out of town), Malay (and some Chinese), fish head curries recommended by locals. **Seriously cheap** *Metropol*, 1st floor, 20 Jln Morshidi Sidek, also serves Melanau curries. **Chinese Mid-range** *Jhong Kuo*, 13 Jln Wong Nai Siong, Foochow. **Cheap** *Blue Splendour*, 1st floor, 60-62 Jln Kampung Nyabor (opposite *Premier Hotel*), recommended by locals. *Golden Palace*, *Tanahmas Hotel*, Jln Kampung Nyabor, Cantonese and Schezuan. *Hock Chu Leu*, 28 Jln Black-smith, Foochow dishes only. **International** *Peppers Café*, *Tanahmas Hotel*, Jln Kampung Nyabor, western and local food, curries particularly recommended, popular. *Villa by the Grand*, Grand Meridien Building, 2nd floor, 131 Jln Kampung Nyabor, run by a group of Canadian graduates.

Eating
Price codes: see inside front cover

   Foodstalls There is a hawker centre on Jln Market, in the centre of town. *Rex Food Court*, 28 Jln Cross, is new and clean, one correspondent recommends it, saying it serves an excellent selection of foods.

Handicrafts Stalls along express boat wharves at Jln Channel, mainly selling basketware. One shop on Jln Central for a variety of handicrafts. **Markets** Pasar Malam, along High St, Jln Market and Lembangan Lane (Chinatown). Native mar-ket (Lembangan market), on Lembangan River between Jln Mission and Jln Chan-nel, sells jungle produce. **Pottery** Two potteries at Km 7 and 12 Ulu Oya Rd. **Supermarket** Sarawak House Shopping Complex, Jln Kg Nyabor, has Premier Department Store.

Shopping

To Sunday Market

Jln Foochow La

Jln Pedada

5

Jln Bukit Assek

Foodstalls

Catholic

Jln Lanang

Jln Mission

Jln Tan Sri

Jln Maju

Lorong Lanang 4

7

Rejang Esplanade

6

Upriver Express
Boat Wharf (Kapit)

Rejang River

Golf *Sibu Golf Club*, Km 17 Ulu Oya Rd, green fees RM15. **Bowling** *Sibu Superbowl*, 2 Lorong Perpati (off Jln Wong King Huo), T331111, F318980. Open Mon-Sat 1000-0000, Sun 0900-0000.

Sports

Sibu Superbowl

Sarawak

Hornbill, 1, 1st floor, Jln Bengkel, T321005, F318987. *Equatorial Tour & Travel Centre*, 11 Raminway, T331599, F330250. *Golden Horse Travel*, 20B-21B Sarawak House Complex, T323288, F310600. *Hornbill Holiday*, No 1, 1st floor, Jln Bengkel, Lorong 1, T321005, F318987. *Hunda Holiday Tours*, 11 Tingkat Bawah, Lorong 1, Brooke Drive, T326869, F310396. *Kiew Kwong Travel*, 175B Jln Kampung Nyabor, T315994, F318236. *Metropolitan Travel*, 72-4 Jln Pasar, T322251, F310831; ylwong8@tm.net.my *RH Tours & Travel*, 32 Blacksmith Rd, T316767, F316185. *Sazhong Trading & Travel*, 4 Jln Central, T336017, F338031, very efficient and courteous. Recom-mended. *Sibu Golden Tours*, 15 1st floor, Jln Workshop, T316861, F318680. *Sitt Travel*, 146 ground floor, Jln Kampung Nyabor, T320168. *Travel Consortium*, 14 Jln Central, T334455, F330589. *WTK Travel*, Ground floor, Bangunan Hung Ann, T319393, F319933.

Tour operators
Most companies run city tours plus tours of longhouses, Mulu National Park and Niah Caves. It is cheaper to organize upriver trips from Kapit or Belaga than from Sibu

12 Ria	**15** Tanah Mas	● Eating
13 Sarawak		**1** Metropol
14 Sentosa Inn		

Transport

Air The airport is 25 km north of town, bus 1 or taxi. Regular connections with **Kuching** (RM72), **Bintulu**, **Miri**, **Marudi**, **Kapit** and **Belaga**. There are also some connections with **Kota Kinabalu**. Sibu airport information centre, T307072.

The express bus station is a 10-min drive out of town

Bus These leave from Jln Khoo Peng Loong. Regular connections with **Bintulu**, 3 hrs and **Miri** along a surfaced road. Best to purchase tickets the day before departure. The early morning buses to Bintulu connect with the buses direct to Batu Niah (see Bintulu). There are also daily connections with **Kapit** and **Kuching** via Sarikei (2 hrs to Sarikei, 5-6 hrs Sarikei to Kuching).

Boat These leave from the wharf in front of the pagoda. Ticket agents Sibu-Kuching: *Ekspress Bahagia* 20 Jln Tukang Besi and *Capitol Hotel 88*; 1 Bank Rd and 14 Jln Khoo Peng Loong. There are 3 express boats a day between Sibu and Kuching. These boats stop off at **Sarekei**. It is necessary to change to an ocean-going boat at Sarikei for Sibu. Boats to **Kapit** leave from the Kapit wharf, a little further upriver. Regular express boats to Kapit 2-3 hrs and in the wet season, when the river is high enough, they continue to **Belaga**, 5-6 hrs. If travelling from Sibu through Kapit to Belaga, take one of the early morning boats (the first leaves at 0545) which connects all the way through. The last Sibu-Kapit boat departs at around 1300. In the dry season passengers change on to smaller launches to get up-river to Belaga (see below). The Sibu-Kapit boats stop off at **Kanowit** and **Song** on their journey up-river.

Directory

Airline offices *MAS*, 61 Jln Tunku Osman, T326166. *Singapore Airlines*, T332203. **Banks** *Standard Chartered*, Jln Cross. *Hong Kong* 17 Jln Wong Nai Siong Hock Hua, Jln Pulau. **Communications** General Post Office: Jln Kampung Nyabor. **Useful addresses** Police: Jln Kampung Nyabor, T322222. Residents' Office: T321963.

Sarawak

Kapit

Colour map 3, grid C4
Population: 70,000
Phone code: 084

Kapit is the 'capital' of Sarawak's Seventh Division, through which flows the Batang Rejang and its main tributaries, the Batang Balleh, Batang Katibas, Batang Balui and Sungai Belaga. In a treaty with the Sultan of Brunei, Rajah James Brooke acquired the Rejang Basin for Sarawak in 1853. Kapit is the last 'big' town on the Rejang and styles itself as the gateway to 'the heart of Borneo' – after Redmond O'Hanlon's book (Into the Heart of Borneo) which describes his adventure up the Batang Balleh in the 1980s. Kapit is full of people who claim to be characters in this book. The main sights in the town are Fort Sylvia and the Kapit Museum but, like O'Hanlon and his journalist companion James Fenton, most visitors coming to Belaga venture into the interior to explore the upper Rejang and its tributaries, where there are many Iban and Orang Ulu longhouses.

There are only a few tens of kilometres of metalled road in and around Kapit, but the little town has a disproportionate number of cars. It is a trading centre for the tribespeople upriver and has grown enormously in recent years with the expansion of the logging industry upstream (see page 565). Logs come in two varieties – 'floaters' and 'sinkers'. Floaters are pulled downstream by tugs in huge chevron formations. Sinkers – like belian (ironwood) – are transported in the Chinese-owned dry bulk carriers which line up along the wharves at Kapit. When the river is high these timber ships are able to go upstream, past the Pelagus Rapids. The Batang Rejang at Kapit is normally 500 m wide and in the dry season, the riverbank slopes steeply down to the water. When it floods, however, the water level rises more than 10 m, as is testified by the high water marks on Fort Sylvia. The highest recorded level was in 1983 when the water reached halfway up the fort's walls.

Sights

Fort Sylvia near the wharves was built of belian (ironwood) by Rajah Charles Brooke in 1880, and is now occupied by government offices. It was originally called Kapit Fort but was renamed in 1925 after Rajah Vyner Brooke's wife. Most of the forts built during this time were designed to prevent the Orang Ulu going downriver; Fort Sylvia was built to stop the belligerent Iban head-hunters from attacking Kenyah and Kayan settlements upstream.

The other main sight is the **Kapit Museum**, enlarged in the 1990s, and moved to Fort Sylvia. It exhibits on Rejang tribes and the local economy. Set up by the Sarawak Museum in Kuching it includes a section of an Iban longhouse and several Iban artifacts including a wooden hornbill (see page 561). The Orang Ulu section has a reconstruction of a longhouse and mural, painted by local tribespeople. An Orang Ulu *salong* (burial hut), totem pole and other wood-carvings are also on display. The museum also has representative exhibits from the small Malay community and the Chinese. Hokkien traders settled at Kapit and Belaga and traded salt, sugar and ceramics for pepper, rotan and rubber; they were followed by Foochow traders. Appropriately, the Chinese exhibit is a shop. There are also displays on the natural history of the upper Rejang and modern industries such as mining, logging and tourism. All exhibits are labelled in English. The museum's energetic and erudite curator, Wilfred Billy Panyau, is very knowledgeable on the area. ■ *0900-1200, 1400-1600 Mon-Fri, 0900-1200 Sat and Sun. The museum is often closed during opening hours and it may be necessary to actively search for the curator to open it.*

Kapit has a particularly colourful daily **market** in the centre of town. Tribeswomen bring in fruit, vegetables and animals to sell; it is quite normal to see everything from turtles, frogs, birds and catfish to monkeys, wild boar and even pangolin and pythons.

Sarawak

Kapit

Rejang River

- **Sleeping**
- 1 Ark Hill Inn
- 2 Dragon Inn
- 3 Dung Fang
- 4 Greenland Inn
- 5 Hiap Chong
- 6 Meligai
- 7 Methodist Guesthouse
- 8 New Rejang
- 9 Orchard Inn
- 10 Rejang
- 11 Well Inn

- **Eating**
- 1 Foodstalls

Excursions

Pelagus Rapids These are 45 minutes upstream from Kapit on the Batang Rejang. The 2.5-km long series of cataracts and whirlpools are the result of a sudden drop in the riverbed, caused by a geological fault-line. Express boats can make it up the Pelagus to Belaga in the wet season (September-April), but the rapids are still regarded with some trepidation by the pilots (see page 351). When the water is low (May-August), the rapids can only be negotiated by the smallest longboats. There are seven rapids in total, each with local names such as 'The Python', 'The Knife' and one, more ominously, called 'The Grave'.

Sleeping A-B *Pelagus Resort*, set on the banks of the Rejang overlooking the rapids, T082-233982, F245551. 40 longhouse-style rooms, with restaurant, pool, bar and sun-deck, deluxe rooms have a/c, otherwise there are fans. Trips organized from resort to longhouses, nature treks and river safaris, whitewater rafting on the rapids. Regular express boats pass through the rapids upstream.

Longhouses around Kapit
Those planning to visit longhouses should refer to the guidelines, see page 347

Some longhouses are accessible by road and several others are within an hour's longboat ride from town. In Kapit you are likely to be invited to visit one of these. Some hotels will help organize trips, or inquire at the police station. There are guides in Kapit who charge too much for very unsatisfactory tours. Visitors are strongly advised not to visit a longhouse without an invitation, ideally from someone who lives in it. As a general rule, the further from town a longhouse is, the more likely it is to conform with the image of what a traditional longhouse should be like. That said, there are some beautiful traditional longhouses nearby, mainly Iban. One of the most accessible, for example, is **Rumah Seligi**, about 30 minutes' drive from Kapit. Cars or vans can be hired by the half-day; RM10. Only a handful of longhouses are more than 500 m from the riverbanks of the Rejang and its tributaries. Most longhouses still practise shifting cultivation (see page 400); rice is the main crop but under government aid programmes many are now growing cash crops such as cocoa. Longhouses are also referred to as *Uma* (Sumah) and the name of the headman, ie Long Segaham is known locally as *Uma Lasah*, *Lasah* being the chief.

On our last visit, Belaga was temporarily closed

Longhouse tours To go upriver beyond Kapit it is necessary to get a permit (no charge) from the offices in the State Government Complex. The permit is valid for travel up the Rejang as far as Belaga and for an unspecified distance up the Balleh. For upriver trips beyond Belaga another permit must be obtained there; however, these trips tend to be expensive and dangerous.

The vast majority of the population, about 72%, in Sarawak's Seventh Division is Iban. They inhabit the Rejang up to, and a little beyond, Kapit as well as the lower reaches of the Balleh and its tributaries. The Iban people are traditionally the most hospitable to visitors, but as a result, their longhouses are the most frequently visited by tourists. Malays and Chinese account for 5% and 3% of the population respectively. The Orang Ulu live further upriver; the main tribes are the Kayan and the Kenyah (12%) and a long list of sub-groups such as the Kejaman, Beketan, Sekapan, Lahanan, Seping, and Tanjong. In addition there are the nomadic and semi-nomadic Penan, Punan and Ukit. Many tribal people are employed in the logging industry, and with their paid jobs, have brought the trappings of modernity to even the remotest longhouses.

The longhouse – prime-site apartments with river view

Most longhouses are built on stilts, high on the riverbank, on prime real estate. They are 'prestigious properties' with 'lots of character', and with their 'commanding views of the river', they are the condominiums of the jungle. They are long-rise rather than high-rise, however, and the average longhouse has 20-25 'doors' (although there can be as many as 60). Each represents one family. The word long in a settlement's name – as in Long Liput or Long Terawan – means 'confluence' (the equivalent of kuala in Malay), and does not refer to the length of the longhouse.

Behind each of the doors – which even today, are rarely locked – is a bilik, or apartment, which includes the family living room and a loft, where paddy and tools are stored. In Kenyah and Kayan longhouses, paddy (which can be stored for years until it is milled) is kept in

elaborate barns, built on stilts away from the longhouse, in case of fire. In traditional longhouses, the living rooms are simple atap roofed, bamboo-floored rooms; in modern longhouses – which are designed on exactly the same principles – the living rooms are commonly furnished with sofas, lino floors, a television and an en suite bathroom. At the front of the bilik is the dapur, where the cooking takes place. All biliks face out onto the ruai, or gallery, which is the focus of communal life, and is where visitors are usually entertained. The width of the wall which faces onto the ruai indicates the status of that family. Attached to the ruai there is usually a tanju – an open verandah, running the full length of the house – where rice and other agricultural products are dried. Long ladders – notched hardwood trunks – lead up to the tanju; they can get very slippery and do not always come with handrails.

Longhouses between Kapit and Belaga are accessible by the normal passenger boats but these boats only go as far as Sungai Bena on the Balleh River (2½ hours). To go further upriver it is necessary to take a tour or organize your own guides and boatmen. The sort of trip taken by Redmond O'Hanlon and James Fenton (as described in O'Hanlon's book *Into the Heart of Borneo*) would cost more than RM1,500 a head. ■ *Longhouse tours along the Rejang and Balleh rivers can be organized by the following: Ark Hill Inn, Lot 451, Shop Lot 10, Jalan Airport, T794168, F796337, manager David Tan (who is very helpful) can organize upriver trips and tours of longhouses around Kapit. If contacted in advance, they can arrange full itinerary from Kuching or Sibu; Dinnel Nuing, PBDS office, Kapit, T796494; Rejang*

Hotel, *28 New Bazaar, T796709. Recommended. Tan Seng Hi, Jln Tan Sit Leong. The Residents' office also has some official tourist guides on its books.*

Rumah Tuan Lepong Balleh Only enter this longhouse with the local policeman called Selvat Anu who lives there; ask for him at Kapit Police Station. During the day Selvat and some members of the longhouse can take visitors on various adventure tours: river trips, visiting longhouses, jungle treks, fishing, pig-hunting, camping in the jungle, trips up to logging areas, swimming in rivers, mountain trekking. Selvat is very knowledgeable and has good relations with the longhouse communities. Visitors can eat with the family and occasionally have the chance to experience a traditional Iban ceremony.
■ *You can stay in his longhouse, RM20-25, inclusive of meals, generator until 2300, basic. It is about one hour's drive from Kapit; take a minibus and ask for 'Selvat and Friends Traditional Hostel and Longhouse'.*

Essentials

Sleeping
■ *on map*
Price codes:
see inside front cover
All hotels are within walking distance of the wharf

B *Greenland Inn*, 463 Jln Teo Chow Beng, T796388, F797989. A/c, well-maintained small hotel with good rooms. Recommended. Although it charges an inflated rate for what is offered, it is comfortably the smartest hotel in town. **B-C** *New Rejang Hotel*, clean rooms in a modern mid-range hotel. Rooms with a/c, bathroom with fantastic showers, desk and satellite TV. **C** *Meligai*, 334 Jln Airport, T796817/796611. Full range of accommodation from VIP suite to dingy standard rooms, has some of the trappings of a city hotel but rooms are generally poor. Also home to a cheap restaurant and the *Meligai* pub. **C** *Orchard Inn*, 64 Jln Airport, T796325. A/c, restaurant, clean rooms and helpful staff, although problematic communication with the Chinese management. Deluxe rooms with a/c, TV, bath to economy rooms (cheapest rooms have no window).

D *Ark Hill Inn*, 451 Jln Airport, T796168, F796337. A/c, bathroom, friendly, clean rooms. It is also situated on the river and there are great views from some of the rooms. Recommended. **D** *Dragon Inn*, Lot 467, Jln Teo Chow Beng, T796105. Central, near Express wharves, clean and well kept. **D** *Dung Fang Hotel*, 116 Jln Temenggong. T797779. A/c, own bathroom, fully carpeted. Great value. **D** *Hiap Chong*, 33 Jln Temenggong Jugah, T796314. Some a/c, no attached bath, top floor best bet. **D** *Rejang*, 28 New Bazaar, T796709. Some a/c, basic but clean – if you can afford the extra cash its slightly newer sister hotel is a better option. **D** *Well Inn*, 40 Jln Court, T796009. A/c, variable rooms but ask to look at the range. **E** *Methodist Guesthouse*. Sometimes budget rooms available here.

Eating
Price codes:
see inside front cover
Kapit's cuisine is predominantly Chinese

Malay *MI*, Jln Pedral, Malay Muslim food. **Chinese Seriously cheap** *Hua Hua*, Jln Airport/Jln Court, Chinese food. *Lily Pond*, in the middle of the lily pond, off Jln Hospital, pleasant setting, plenty of mosquitoes and an unimaginative menu. *S'ng Ee Ho Restaurant*, next to *Metox* supermarket, happy to cook anything you ask for. *Jade Garden*, Jln Pedral, local and Chinese food, smart. *99*, Jln Pedral, fresh air, clean local and Chinese food. *Seafood Restaurant*, Jln Pedral. **International Mid-range** *Orchard Inn*, 64 Jln Airport, T796325. The most upmarket restaurant in Kapit, food well presented but the coffee shops taste just as good, disco from 2200-0100.

Bakeries and breakfast *Ung Tong Bakery*, opposite the market, bakery and café, good continental-style breakfasts – big selection of rolls and good coffee, fresh bread baked twice daily (0600 and 1100). Recommended. *Chuong Hin*, opposite the Sibu wharf, best-stocked coffee shop in town.

Foodstalls Stalls at the top end of the road opposite the market (dead-end road; brightly painted on the outside). Good satay stall on Jln Hospital, next to the lily pond.

Handicrafts *Lai Lai Antique Shop*, next road along on the right from the *Putena Jaya* (see below), small selection of woven rugs/sarongs, prices are high but they are similar to the starting prices at the longhouses. *Din Chu Café*, next to *Methodist Resthouse*, sells antiques and handicrafts.

Shopping

Air The airport is 4 km south of town. There is a weekly connection with **Sibu** and **Belaga** leaving on a Sun morning. Book in advance. Low cloud at Kapit often prevents landing and the plane goes straight to Belaga. **Boat** All 3 wharves are close together. Regular connections with **Sibu** from 0600-1530, 2-3 hrs. **Belaga** is not accessible by large express boats during the dry season. Prices for the express boats start at RM15. For the smaller boats going upriver in the dry season prices are higher and start at RM60.

Transport
160 km to Sibu

Airline offices *MAS* in block opposite Sibu jetty. **Banks** There are 2 banks which will accept TCs, one in the New Bazaar and the other on Jln Airport, but it is easier to change money in Sibu. **Libraries** On the other side of the road from first floor State Government Complex. Good selection of books on history and natural history of Borneo. Open 1615-2030 Mon-Sat, 0900-1115, 1400-1630 Sat, 0900-1100, 1400-1830 Sun. **Useful addresses** Maps: Land Survey Department, Jln Beletik on Jln Airport. Maps of Kapit Division and other parts of Sarawak. **Resident's Office:** 1st floor State Government Complex (opposite the lily pond), T796963. Permits for upriver trips. Tourists going to Baleh or Upper Rejang areas must sign a form saying they fully understand they are travelling at their own risk.

Directory

Belaga

This is the archetypal sleepy little town; most people while their lifetime in coffee shops. They are the best place to watch life go by, and there are always interesting visitors in town, from itinerant wild honey-collectors from Kalimantan to Orang Ulu who have brought their jungle produce downriver to the Belaga bazaar or those who are heading to the metropolis of Kapit for medical treatment. At night, when the neon lights flicker on, Belaga's coffee shops are invaded by thousands of cicadas, beetles and moths.

Colour map 3, grid B5
Phone code: 084

A few Chinese traders set up shop in Belaga in the early 1900s, and traded with the tribespeople upriver, supplying essentials such as kerosene, cooking oil and shotgun cartridges. The Orang Ulu brought their beadwork and mats as well as jungle produce such as beeswax, ebony, *gutta-percha* (rubbery tree gum) and, most prized of all, bezoar stones. These are gall-stones found in certain monkeys (the *wah-wahs*, *jelu-merahs* and *jelu-jankits*) and porcupines. To the Chinese, they have much the same properties as rhinoceros horn (mainly aphrodisiacal) and even today, they are exported from Sarawak to Singapore where they fetch S$300 per kg.

Belaga serves as a small government administration centre for the remoter parts of the Seventh Division as it is the last settlement of any size as you venture up the Rejang. It is also a good place to arrange visits to the Kayan and Kenyah longhouses on the Linnau River. There is a very pretty **Malay kampung** (Kampung Bharu) along the esplanade downriver from the Belaga Bazaar. The Kejaman burial pole on display outside the Sarawak Museum in Kuching was brought from the Belaga area in 1902.

Excursions To go upriver beyond Belaga it is necessary to obtain a permit from the Resident's office and permission from the police station. There is an informed and enthusiatic tour guide based in Belaga called Daniel, he might not be able to bring the resources of a multinational to bear in his small operation, but he does have knowledge and good links with upriver longhouses. Contact him through the *Belaga Hotel*.

When the river is high, express boats go upstream as far as **Rumah Belor** on the Batang Balui, but for the purpose of visiting longhouses in the Belaga area, it is best to hire a boat in Belaga. Many of the longhouses around Belaga are quite modern, although several of the Kenyah and Kayan settlements have beautifully carved wooden tombstones, or *salongs*, nearby. All the longhouses beyond Belaga are Orang Ulu. Even longhouses which, on the map, appear very remote (such as Long Busang), are now connected by logging roads from Kapit, only four hours' drive away. To get well off the beaten track, into Penan country, it is possible to organize treks from Belaga towards the Kalimantan border, staying in longhouses *en route*.

About 2 km up the Batang Balui from Belaga are the **Pasang Rapids** rapids, which are certainly the biggest in Sarawak. It appears that no one has purposely tried to shoot them as they are too dangerous. Boats can get reasonably close, however, and in the dry season, it is possible to climb up to a picnic area, overlooking the white water. To get there, hire a boat from Belaga.

Tours The *Belaga Hotel* will contact guides for upriver trips and the District Office can also recommend a handful of experienced guides. In this part of Sarawak, guides are particularly expensive – sometimes up to RM80 a day,

Upper Rejang

mainly because there are not enough tourists to justify full-time work. It is necessary to hire experienced boatmen too, because of the numerous rapids. The best guide for longer trips (to jungle areas northeast of Belaga and to Penan areas along the Kalimantan border) is Ronald Bete. Such trips require at least five or six days. Prices for trips to longhouses upriver vary according to distance and the water level, but are similar to those in Kapit. As a rough guideline, a litre of petrol costs about RM10-15; a 40 hp boat uses nearly 20 litres to go 10 km. English is not widely spoken upriver, basic *Bahasa* comes in handy. (See page 25.)

D *Bakun Puri Hotel*, Lot 57 Belaga Bazaar, T461371. Fan only, marginally overpriced in comparison to its two competitors. **D** *Bee Lian Hotel*, 11 Belaga Bazaar, T461439. A/c, rooms are fine. **D** *Belaga Hotel*, 14 Belaga Bazaar, T461244. Some a/c, restaurant, no hot water, particularly friendly proprietor, good coffee shop downstairs, in-house video and cicadas. Best option.

Sleeping & eating
Several small, cheap coffee shops along Belaga Bazaar and Main Bazaar

Handicrafts *Chop Teck Hua*, Belaga Bazaar, has an intriguing selection of tribal jewellery, old coins, beads, feathers, woodcarvings, blowpipes, *parangs*, tattoo boards and other curios buried under cobwebs and gekko droppings at the back of the shop, although the owner is noticeably uninformed about the objects he sells.

Shopping

It is possible to travel by road and river to Bintulu (see below), but it is drawn out and expensive. It is likely that road links will improve, particularly after the decision taken at the end of Feb 2001 that the controversial Bakun Dam project would go ahead (shelved after the Asian financial crisis hit Malaysia in 1998). The road between Bakun and Bintulu has been gradually upgraded and is now surfaced along almost its full length. Journeys take about 3 hrs and you have to arrange travel yourself or hitch.

Transport
At the moment Belaga is comparatively isolated and overland links are poor

Air Connections on Sun with **Kapit** and on to **Sibu**. **Boat** There is a daily boat from **Kapit** leaving early in the morning, which costs RM60, for a trip that takes approximately 6 hrs depending on the season. In the dry season passengers disembark at the rapids and walk this distance, while the pilot picks a route through these potentially dangerous obstacles. When the river is very low the only option is to fly to Belaga.

To **Tabau** and on to **Bintulu**: it is possible to hire a boat from Belaga to Kestima Kem (logging camp) near Rumah Lahanan Laseh (RM60 per person in a group or RM260 for 2-3 people); from there logging trucks go to Tabau on the Kemena River. Logging trucks leave irregularly and you can get stuck in logging camps. It is a 3-hr drive to Tabau; this trip is not possible in the wet season. There are regular express boats from Tabau to Bintulu (RM20). This is the fastest and cheapest route to Bintulu, but not the most reliable. It is necessary to obtain permission from the Resident's office and the police station in Belaga to take this route.

To **Kalimantan**: it is not legal to cross the border by way of Kapit, Belaga and up the Batang Balui to Long Nawang, although it has been done. You may be turned back.

Airline offices *MAS*, c/o Lau Chun Kiat, Main Bazaar. **Communications** Internet: next to the MAS counter on the main street (RM5 per 30 mins). **Post Office:** In the District Office building. **Useful addresses** **District Office:** (for upriver permits) on the far side of the basketball courts.

Directory

Sarawak

The Bakun hydroelectric project: dam time bomb

The Bakun Dam, upriver from Belaga on the Upper Rejang and 400 km east of Kuching, has had more twists and turns than the river on which it (may be) built. The RM6 billion project (US$2.4 bn), one of the largest infrastructure projects in all of Southeast Asia, will flood a tract of virgin rainforest that supports 43 species of endangered mammals and birds. It will also displace around 8,000 tribespeople living in at least 14 longhouses. The dam is going to be twice the height of the Aswan Dam in Egypt and will flood 69,000 hectares – an area bigger than Singapore. Mahathir has described it as "a project whose time has come". Environmentalists say it will be an ecological time bomb in the heart of Borneo.

If one didn't know better it would be easy to count Prime Minister Dr Mahathir Mohamad a ditherer. In 1990 the Prime Minister said that the project had been scrapped for environmental reasons. In January 1993 he gave the green light to the project. In late 1997, in the midst of Malaysia's economic crisis, when money was scarce, he declared that the project had been shelved. And, most recently on 28

February 2001, he once again gave the controversial project the go-ahead. But projects like these have their own momentum and it seems that when the project was shelved in late 1997 preparations for the dam, including resettlement of displaced tribespeoples, continued. In 1998 3,000 local people were relocated from the dam site, and in 1999 another 10,000 were moved.

It is planned that Bakun will generate 2,400 MW of electricity. The power will be consumed within Sabah and Sarawak, and possibly Brunei and Kalimantan, and involve the construction of 800 km of high voltage power lines (plans for a 600+ km undersea cable have been shelved). The project will require the construction of roads through dense jungle to bring building materials and engineering equipment to the remote site, above the Bakun Rapids. Malaysian lobby groups such as the Environmental Protection Society predict that the project will cause severe soil erosion in an area already suffering from the effects of logging. In the early 1990s the riverwater was clear and fish abundant; now the river is a muddy

Bintulu and Similaju National Park

Bintulu

Colour map 3, grid B4
Population: 50,000
Phone code: 086

The word Bintulu is thought to be a corruption of *Mentu Ulau*, which translates as 'the place for gathering heads'. Bintulu, on the Kemena River, is in the heart of Melinau country and was traditionally a fishing and farming centre until the largest natural gas reserve in Malaysia was discovered just offshore in the late 1970s, turning Bintulu into a boomtown overnight. *Shell, Petronas* and *Mitsubishi* moved to the town in force. In 1978 the town's population was 14,000; it is now over 50,000. More than RM11 bn was invested in Bintulu's development between 1980 and 1990.

www.forest.gov.my
for the Sarawak
Forestry
Department's (rose
tinted) view of it all

Few tourists stay long in Bintulu, although it is the jump-off point to the **Similajau National Park** (which opened in 1991) and **Niah Caves**. The longhouses on the Kemena River are accessible, but tend not to be as interesting as those further up the Rejang and Baram rivers. The Penan and Kayan tribes are very hospitable and eager to show off their longhouses and traditions to tourists.

brown and water levels fluctuate wildly. Nor is the project a long-term one: even the government admits its productive life is likely to be in the region of 25 years before it silts up.

Two of Ekran's main shareholders are the sons of Sarawak's Chief Minister, Abdul Taib Mahmud, who is widely believed to own a third of the state's timber concessions through nominees and political allies. Another leading shareholder is James Wong, Sarawak's environment minister who doubles as a big timber concessionaire in Limbang (the district adjacent to Mulu). In May 1994 a group of longhouse dwellers from the Long Murum area were prevented from delivering a petition opposing the Bakun project to the Sarawak state parliament. They allege that members of the government-appointed committee on Bakun do not defend their interests because, like Wong and Taib's sons, they are the very people responsible for selling tribal land they don't own to loggers.

Over recent years, 17 technical studies – including environmental impact analyses – have been carried out on Bakun. Most,

though, have not been released to the public. In 1995 one study carried out by a team from Sarawak University concluded that severe environmental effects were unavoidable. Friends of the Earth Malaysia says: "This project is going to have a tremendous effect on the lives of natives, plants and animals and bio-diversity of the pristine forests where it is going to be built". The local tribespeople, whose ancestors battled for decades against the White Rajahs, have, it seems, finally met their match, in Malaysia's relentless thrust towards modernity.

For web links see:
www.irn.org/index.html – Homepage of the International Rivers Network, with a Bakun related page and map.

vcn.bc.ca/spc/bakun.html – Sarawak's peoples' campaign. Activist site fighting for the rights of tribal peoples and the forest against the Malaysian government and commercial interests.

www.edf.org/programs/International/ Dams/AsiaOceania/a_Bakun.html – home page of Environmental Defense, another global site with a Bakun entry.

Sarawak

The remnants of the old fishing village at Kampong Jepak are on the opposite bank of the Kemena River. During the Brooke era the town was a small administrative centre. The **clock tower** commemorates the meeting of five representatives from the Brooke government and 16 local chieftains, the birth of Council Negeri, the state legislative body.

Background

The first project to break ground in Bintulu was the RM100 m crude oil terminal at Tanjong Kidurong from which 45,000 barrels of petroleum are exported daily. A deep-water port was built and the liquefied natural gas (LNG) plant started operating in 1982. It is one of the Malaysian government's biggest investment projects. The abundant supply of natural gas also created investment in related downstream projects. The main industrial area at Tanjong Kidurong is 20 km from Bintulu. The **viewing tower** at Tanjong Kidurong gives a panoramic view of the new-look Bintulu, out to the timber ships on the horizon. They anchor 15 km offshore to avoid port duties and the timber is taken out on barges.

Bintulu has a modern **Moorish-style mosque**, completed in 1988, called the **Masjid Assyakirin**; visitors may be allowed in when it is not prayer time. There is a new, colourful, centrally-located Chinese temple called **Tua Pek Kong**. **Pasar Bintulu** is also an impressive recently-constructed building in the centre of town, built to house local jungle produce market, foodstalls and

Sights

The massacre at Long Nawang

The Japanese Imperial Army invaded the country 100 years and three months after James Brooke was proclaimed Rajah of Sarawak. On Christmas Day 1941, when Rajah Vyner Brooke was visiting Australia, they took Kuching; a few days earlier they had occupied the Miri oilfields. Japanese troops, dressed for jungle warfare, headed upriver. They did not expect to encounter such stiff resistance from the tribespeople. The Allies had the brainwave of rekindling an old tribal pastime – head-hunting, which successive Brooke administrations had tried to stamp out. Iban and Orang Ulu warriors were offered 'ten-bob-a-knob' for Japanese heads, and many of the skulls still hanging in longhouses are said to date from this time. The years of occupation were marked by terrible brutality, and many people fled across the border into Dutch Borneo – now Kalimantan. The most notorious massacre in occupied

Sarawak involved refugees from Kapit.

Just a month after the Japanese invasion, a forestry officer stationed on the Rejang heard that a group of women and children from Kapit were planning to escape across the Iran Range into Dutch territory. He organized the evacuation, and led the refugees up the rivers and over the mountains to the Dutch military outpost at Long Nawang. The forester returned to Kapit to help organize resistance to the Japanese. But when the invading forces heard of the escape they dispatched a raiding party upriver, captured the Dutch fort, lined up the fifty women and ordered the children to climb into nearby trees. According to historian Robert Payne: "They machine-gunned the women and amused themselves by picking off the children one by one... Of all those who had taken part in the expedition only two Europeans survived."

limited handicrafts stalls. A landscaped **wildlife park** has been developed on the outskirts of town, on the way to Tanjong Batu. It is a local recreational area and contains a small zoo and a botanic garden (the only one in Sarawak). ■ *0800-1900 Mon-Sun, RM2.*

Excursions **Similajau National Park**, see below. **Niah Caves and National Park**, see page 367. The Niah Caves are just off the Miri-Bintulu road and are easily accessible from both towns. Trips to Similajau National Park and longhouses on the Kemena River (rarely visited) can be organized from Bintulu. More than 20 Kemena River longhouses can be reached by road or river within 30 minutes of Bintulu. Iban longhouses are the closest; further upriver are the more traditional Kayan and Kenyah longhouses. Overpriced tours are organized by *Similajau Adventure Tours* (see tour companies) or hire a boat from the wharf. A two-hour river cruise, five-hour Iban longhouse tour, four-hour Iban longhouse tour (by boat), two-hour longhouse tour (by boat).

Sleeping **B** *Hoover*, 92 Jln Keppel, T337166. Restaurant, cable TV, coffee house, smallish rooms, but well-kept place. A great deal better than the slightly cheaper hotels nearby. **B** *Plaza*, Jln Abang Galau, 116 Taman Sri Dagang, T335111, F332742. A/c, restaurant, pool, very smart hotel, and, compared with other upmarket hotels in Sarawak, excellent value for money. Recommended. Very popular, so definitely worth booking. **B** *Regent*, Kemena Commercial Complex, Jln Tanjong Batu, T335511, F333770. 47 rooms with a/c, TV, mini-bar, restaurant, coffee house. **B** *River Front Inn*, 256 Jln Sri Dagang, T333111, F339577. Smart place with good restaurant. Set slightly back from the main road, overlooking the river. **B** *Royal Inn*, 10-12 Jln Pedada, T315888, F334028. Overpriced.

C *Fata Inn*, 113 Taman Sri Dagang, Jln Masjid, T332998. A/c, TV, bathroom. Reasonable. **C** *Kemena*, 78 Jln Keppel, T331533. A/c, refurbished and on a quiet street, good quality room with TV, fridge. Recommended. **C** *King's Inn*, 162 Taman Sri Dagang, Jln Masjid, T337337, F332570. **C** *National*, 2nd floor, 5 Jln Temple, T337222, F334304. A/c, clean and well kept. Recommended. **C** *Queen's Inn*, 238 Taman Sri Dagang, T338922. This hotel and its sister, the King's Inn, are carbon copies from the receptions to the rooms. Both charge a reasonable rate and have small, clean, carpeted a/c rooms with cramped bathroom. OK for a night. **C** *Sea View*, 254 Jln Masjid, Taman Sri Dagang, T339118. A/c, shower, TV, spacious rooms with views over the river. Good value for Bintulu. **C** *Sunlight Inn*, 7 Jln Pedada, T332577, F334075. A/c, TV. **D** *AA Inn*, 1st floor, 167 Taman Sri Dagang, T335733. One of the cheapest options in town but dirty and run down. Watch out for the cockroaches. **D** *Dragon Inn*, Jln Abang Galau. Some a/c, a reasonable place to stay and the a/c rooms are good value.

There are several cheap options (RM20) on Jln Sri Dagang; they are extremely run down and dirty with a few dodgy characters hanging around. Only if desperate

Bintulu

Umai, raw fish pickled with lime or the fruit of wild palms (*assam*) and mixed with salted vegetables, onions and chillies is a Melanau speciality. Bintulu is famed for its *belacan* – prawn paste – and in the local dialect, prawns are *urang*, not *udang*. Locals quip that they are 'man-eaters' because they *makan urang*.

Eating

Mid-range *Marco Polo*, on the waterfront on the edge of town, locals recommend pepper steak. **Cheap** *Fook Lu Shou*, *Plaza Hotel*, Jln Abang Galau, Taman Sri Dagang, seafood and Chinese cuisine, including birds' nest soup, boiled in rock sugar (RM45). *River Inn*, opposite wharf, Western and local food. **Seriously cheap** *Popular Corner*, opposite Hospital, Chinese. *Kemena Coffee House*, Western, Malay and Chinese, open 24 hrs. *Sarawak*, 160 Taman Sri Dagang (near *Plaza Hotel*), cheap Malay food.

Foodstalls *Pantai Ria*, near Tanjong Batu, mainly seafood, only open in the evenings. Recommended. *Chinese stalls* behind the Chinese temple on Jln Temple. Stalls at both markets.

Handicrafts *Dyang Enterprise*, Lobby floor, *Plaza Hotel*, Jln Abang Dalau, Taman Sri Dagang. The latter is rather overpriced because of the *Plaza*'s more upmarket clientele; the best handicrafts are to be found at *Li Hua Plaza*, near the *Plaza Hotel*, in a 4-storey building.

Shopping

Golf *Tanjong Kidurong*, 18-hole course, north of Bintulu, by the sea (regular buses from town centre), green fees RM15. *Bintulu Golf Club*, green fees RM105

Sports

Sarawak

Sleeping
1 AA Inn
2 Dragon Inn
3 Hoover
4 Fata
5 Kemena
6 King's Inn
7 National
8 Plaza
9 Queen's Inn
10 River Front Inn
11 Royal Inn
12 Sea View
13 Sunlight Inn

Eating
1 Foodstalls
2 Popular Corner

weekdays, RM157.50 weekends. **Sports complex** Swimming pool (RM2), tennis, football. To get there, fork right from the Miri road at the Chinese temple, about 1 km from town centre.

Tour operators *Deluxe Travel*, 30 Jln Law Gek Soon, T331293, F334995; *Similajau Travel and Tours*, *Plaza Hotel*, Jln Abang Dalau offers tours around the city, to the Niah caves, longhouses and Similajau National Park. *Hunda Travel Services*, 8 Jln Somerville, T331339, F330445. There are half a dozen other agents in town.

Transport **Air** The airport is in the centre of town. Regular connections with Kuching, Miri, Sibu. There are also some connections with Kota Kinabalu.

  Road **Bus**: There are two stations in town. The terminal for local buses is in the centre of town. The long-distance Medan Jaya station is 10 mins by taxi from the centre, on the road towards Miri (RM8). Regular connections with **Miri** (RM18), **Sarikei** (RM32), **Batu**, **Niah** (RM10) and **Sibu** (RM16). There are several bus companies but the main one is the *Syarikat Bas Suria* T334914. **Taxi**: For **Miri** and **Sibu**, taxis leave from Jln Masjid. Because of the regular bus services and the poor state of the roads, most taxis are for local use only and chartering them is expensive.

Enquire at the wharf for times and prices **Sea** Regular connections with **Tabau**, 2½-3 hrs, last boat at 1400 (RM18). Connections with **Belaga**, via logging road, see page 361; this route is popular with people in Belaga as it is much cheaper than going from Sibu. Direct boat connections with Sibu, Miri, Kuching, Song, Kapit and Belaga.

Directory **Airline offices** *MAS*, Jln Masjid, T331554. **Banks** *Bank Bumiputra* and *Bank Utama* on Jln Somerville; *Standard Chartered*, Jln Keppel. **Communications** General Post Office: Far side of the airport near the Resident's office, 2 km from town centre – called Pos Laju. **Useful addresses** National Parks Booking Office: T331117, ext 50, F331923.

Similajau National Park

Colour map 3, grid B4 It is Sarawak's most unusually shaped national park being more than 32 km long and only 1.5 km wide. Similajau was demarcated in 1978, but has only really been open to tourists since the construction of decent facilities in 1991. Lying 20 km northeast of Bintulu, Similajau is a coastal park with sandy beaches, broken by rocky headlands. **Pasir Mas**, or Golden Sands, is a beautiful 3½ km long stretch of coarse beach, to the north of the Likau River, where green turtles (see page 471) come ashore to lay their eggs between July and September. A few kilometres from the Park HQ at **Kuala Likau** is a small coral reef, known as **Batu Mandi**. The area is renowned for birdwatching. Because it has only been gazetted for a few years, and because Bintulu is not on the main tourist track, the park is very quiet. Its seclusion makes it a perfect escape.

  The **beaches** are backed by primary rainforest: peat swamp, *kerangas* (heath forest), mixed dipterocarp and mangrove (along Sungai Likau and Sungai Sebubong). There are small rapids on the Sebulong River. The rivers, particularly the beautiful **Sungai Likau**, have sadly been polluted by indiscriminate logging activities upstream.

Flora & fauna One of the first things a visitor notices on arrival at Kuala Likau is the prominent sign advising against swimming in the river, and to watch your feet in the headquarters' area: Similajau is well known for its saltwater crocodiles (*Crocodylus perosus*). Similajau also has 24 resident species of mammals (including gibbons, Hose's langurs, banded langurs, long-tailed macaques, civets, wild boar, porcupines, squirrels) and 185 species of birds, including many migratory species. Marine life includes dolphins, porpoises and turtles; there are some good coral reefs to the north. Pitcher plants grow in the *kerangas* forest and along the beach.

Several trails have been cut by park rangers from the Park HQ; longish but not too difficult. One path follows undulating terrain, parallel to the coast. It is possible to cut to the left, through the jungle, to the coast, and walk back to Kuala Likau along the beach. The main trail to **Golden Beach** is a three- to four-hour walk crossing several streams and rivers where estuarine crocodiles are reputed to lurk. Most of these crossings are on 'bridges', which are usually just felled trees with no attempt made to assist walkers (some 'bridges' have drops of around 5 m) – a good sense of balance is required. Another enjoyable and rewarding walk is the trail to **Selansur Rapids**, around two-and-a-half hours in total. Start off by following the trail to the Golden Beach; after about an hour a marked trail leads off into the forest. The walk ends at the rapids where it is possible to take a dip and cool off.

Treks
For additional trails ask for information at the Park HQ

Permits are available from the Bintulu Development Authority. The information centre at is at Park HQ, T085737450, F085737454, at the mouth of Sungai Likau, across the river from the park. Entrance fee: RM10, RM5 for children. A boat is needed to cross the 5m of crocodile-infested river. Because the facilities to the park are actually outside the park, visitors do not need a permit to stay there. This has led to the 'park' becoming very popular with Bintulites at the weekend.

Park essentials

   Sleeping C Two chalets, 2 hostels and a 'mega' hostel – with 27 4-bed rooms. The latter has attractive polished hardwood décor. It can get block-booked. There is 24-hour electricity. The canteen at Park HQ serves basic food. Picnic shelters at park HQ.

   Transport   A new road from Bintulu has been completed. There is no regular bus service to the park. **Taxis** travel the route (30 mins). Rm 40 Bintulu-Similajau trip. RM 60 for a return trip. *Bintulu taxi station*, T086-332009. Boats are available from the wharf or arrange through *Similajau Tours* in Bintulu.

Niah National Park

*Niah's famous caves, tucked into a limestone massif called **Gunung Sabis**, made world headlines in 1959, when they were confirmed as the most important archaeological site in Asia. The park is one of the most popular tourist attractions in Sarawak and attracts more than 15,000 visitors every year. The caves were declared a national historic monument in 1958, but it was not until 1974 that the 3,000 ha of jungle surrounding the caves were turned into a national park to protect the area from logging.*

Colour map 3, grid A5

Getting there   The nearest town to the park is Batu Niah. There are regular bus connections with Miri, Bintulu and Sibu. From Batu Niah it is around 4 km to the Park HQ and the caves. Either walk through the forest (45 mins), take a longboat, or catch a taxi.

Ins & outs
see page 245 for further details

Getting around   From Park HQ there are well-marked trails to the caves. Longboats can be chartered for upriver trips.

About 40,000 years ago, when the Gulf of Thailand and the Sunda Shelf were still dry ground, and a land-bridge connected the Philippines and Borneo,

Background

Niah was home to Homo sapiens. It was the most exciting archaeological discovery since Java man (Homo erectus).

Scientist and explorer A Hart Everett led expeditions to Niah Caves in 1873 and 1879, after which he pronounced that they justified no further work. Seventy-nine years later, Tom Harrisson, ethnologist, explorer and conservationist and curator of the Sarawak Museum, confirmed the most important archaeological find in Southeast Asia at Niah. He unearthed fragments of a 37,000-year-old human skull – the earliest evidence of *Homo sapiens* in the region – at the west mouth of the Niah Great Cave itself. The skull was buried under 2.4 m of guano. His find debunked and prompted a radical reappraisal of popular theories about where modern man's ancestors had sprung from. A wide range of Palaeolithic and Neolithic tools, pottery, ornaments and beads were also found at the site. Anthropologists believe Niah's caves may have been permanently inhabited until around 1400 AD. Harrisson's excavation site, office and house have been left intact in the mouth of the Great Cave. A total of 166 burial sites have been excavated, 38 of which are Mesolithic (up to 20,000 years before present) and the remainder Neolithic (4,000 years before present). Some of the finds are now in the Sarawak Museum in Kuching.

To reach the caves, take a longboat across the river from Park HQ at Palangkalan Lubang to the start of the 4 km belian (ironwood) plankwalk to the entrance of the **Great Cave**. Take the right fork 1 km from the entrance. The remains of a small kampong, formerly inhabited by birds' nest collectors (see below) and guano collectors, is just before the entrance, in the shelter of overhanging rocks. It is known as **Traders' Cave**. Beware of voracious insects; wear long trousers and plenty of repellent. There are no lights in the Great Cave (see below), so torches are needed.

The **Painted Cave** is beyond the Great Cave. Prehistoric wall paintings – the only ones in Borneo – stretch for about 32 m along the cave wall. Most of the drawings are of dancing human figures and boats, thought to be associated with a death ritual. On the floor of the cave, several 'death-ships' were found with some Chinese stoneware, shell ornaments and ancient glass beads. These death-ships served as coffins and have been carbon-dated to between 1 and 780 AD. By around 700 AD there is thought to have been a

Niah National Park

Niah's guano collectors: scraping the bottom

Eight bat species live in the Niah Caves, some are quite common such as the horseshoe bat and fruit bats. Other more exotic varieties include the bearded tomb bat, Cantor's roundleaf horseshoe bat and the lesser bent-winged bat. The ammonia-stench of bat guano permeates the humid air. People began collecting guano in 1929 and it is used as a fertilizer and to prevent pepper vines from rotting. Guano collectors pay a licence fee for the privilege of sweeping up tahi sapu *(fresh guano) and digging up* tahi timbang *(mature guano) which they sell to the Bat Guano Co-operative at the end of the plankwalk.*

flourishing community based in the caves, trading hornbill ivory and birds' nests with the Chinese in exchange for porcelain and beads. But then it seems the caves were suddenly deserted in about 1400. In Penan folklore there are references to 'the ancestors who lived in the big caves' and tribal elders are said to be able to recall funeral rites using death boats similar to those found at Niah.

Flora & fauna The Niah National Park primarily comprises of alluvial or peat swamp as well as some mixed dipterocarp forest. Long-tailed macaques, hornbills, squirrels, flying lizards and crocodiles have all been recorded in the park. There are also bat hawks which provide an impressive spectacle when they home in on one of the millions of bats which pour out of the caves at dusk.

Treks A lowland trail called **Jalan Madu** (Honey Road), traverses the peat swamp forest and up Gunung Subis; it is not well marked. Return trips need a full day. The trail leads off the plankwalk to the right, about 1 km from Pangkalan Lubang (Park HQ). The left fork on the plankwalk, before the gate to the caves, goes to an Iban longhouse, Rumah Chang (40 minutes' walk), where cold drinks can be bought.

Park Information Centre At the Park HQ is this centre, with displays on birds' nests and flora and fauna. The exhibition includes the 37,000-year-old human skull which drew world attention to Niah in 1958. Also on display are 35,000-year-old oyster shells, as well as palaeolithic pig bones, monkey bones, turtle-shells and crabs which were found littering the cave floor. There are also burial vessels dating from 1600 BC and carved seashell jewellery from around 400 BC. ■ *0800-1230, 1400-1615 Mon-Fri; 0800-1245 Sat; 0800-1200 Sun.*

Park essentials

The park HQ are at Pangkalan Lubang next to Sungai Subis. You must apply for an entry permit here before proceeding into the park. You will need your passport and pay an RM10 entry fee for each person (RM5 for children) and RM5 for camera, RM10 for video and RM200 for professional photography. The park and caves are open daily, the park 0800-1700, with the caves closing 30 mins earlier. A guide is not essential but they provide information and can relate legends about the paintings. But even with a guide, visitors cannot cross the barrier 3 m in front of the cave wall. A guide will cost RM35 for groups of up to 20 and can be hired from the Park HQ. From Park HQ, longboats can be hired for upriver trips (maximum of eight people per boat). Visitors are advised to bring a powerful torch for the caves. Walking boots are advisable during the wet season as the plankwalk can get very slippery.

For more information on the park, contact Deputy Park Warden, Niah National Park, PO Box 81, Miri Post Office, Batu Niah, T085 737450, F085 737918

Sarawak

How to make a swift buck

The Malay name for Niah's Painted Cave is Kain Hitam – or 'black cloth' – because the profitable rights to the birds' nests were traditionally exchanged for bolts of black cloth. The Chinese have had a taste for swiftlets' nests for well over 1,000 years, and the business of collecting them from 60 m up in the cavernous chamber of the Great Cave is as lucrative – and as hazardous – a profession now as it was then. The nests are used to prepare birds' nest soup – blended with chicken stock and rock salt – which is a famous Chinese delicacy, prized as an aphrodisiac and for its supposed remedial properties for asthma and rheumatism. Birds' nests are one of the most expensive foods in the world: they sell for up to US$500/kilo in Hong Kong, where about 100 tonnes of them (worth US$40m) are consumed annually. The Chinese communities of North America import 30 tonnes of birds' nests a year. Locally, they fetch RM150-600/kg, depending on the grade.

Hundreds of thousands – possibly millions – of swiftlets (of the Collocalia swift family) live in the caves. Unlike other parts of Southeast Asia, where collectors use rotan ladders to reach the nests (see Gomontong Caves, Sabah, page 457), Niah's collectors scale belian (ironwood) poles to heights of more than 60 m. They use bamboo sticks with a scraper attached to one end (called penyulok) to pick the nests off the cave-roof. The nests are harvested three times each season (which run from August to December and January to March). On the first two occasions, the nests are removed before the eggs are laid and a third left until the nestlings are fledged. Nest collectors are now all supposed to have licences, but in reality, no one does. Although the birds' nests are supposed to be protected by the national park in the off-season, wardens turn a blind eye to illegal harvesting – the collectors also know many secret entrances to the caves. Officially, people caught harvesting out of season can be fined RM2,000 or sent to jail for a year, but no one's ever caught. Despite being a dangerous operation (there are usually several fatal accidents at Niah each year), collecting has become so popular that harvesters have to reserve their spot with a lamp. Nest collecting is run on a first-come, first-served basis.

Nests of the white nest swiftlets and the black nest swiftlets are collected – the nests of the mossy-nest and white-bellied swiftlets require too much effort to clean. The nests are built by the male swiftlets using a glutinous substance produced by the salivary glands under the tongue which is regurgitated in long threads; the saliva sets like cement producing a rounded cup which sticks to the cave wall. In the swifts' nest market, price is dictated by colour: the best are the white nests which are without any plant material or feathers. Most of the uncleaned nests are bought up by middlemen, agents of traders in Kuching, but locals at Batu Niah also do some of the cleaning. The nests are first soaked in water for about three hours, and when softened, feathers and dirt are laboriously removed with tweezers. The 'cakes' of nests are dried overnight: if left in the sun they turn yellow.

On 1 December 1993, a two-year ban on the collection of nests in Niah's Great Cave was introduced. The authorities were swayed by evidence that the number of birds nesting there had declined to fewer than 100,000 from the estimated four million in 1962. Environmentalists say the aerodramus species is now endangered. Reports on the ground suggested, however, that illegal collecting continued during the ban. The authorities blamed Indonesian immigrants.

Family Chalet, similar to hostel but with cooker and a/c, 2 rooms with 4 beds in each, RM65 per room. *5 Hostels*, each with 4 rooms of 4 beds each, all rooms have private bathrooms, clean and western-style with shower, toilet, electric fans, fridges, large sitting area and kitchen. No cooking facilities but kettle, crockery and cutlery can be provided on request. Booking advisable during holiday season (Jun, Aug, Dec), RM50 for 1 room, 4 beds, or RM10.50 for 1 bed. *VIP Resthouse*, RM250 per room, a/c, TV, hi-fi.

Sleeping
Call Miri, at the Old Forestry Building, Jln Angkasa, T085436637. All accommodation has 24-hr electricity and treated water

Batu Niah There are also 4 small hotels in Batu Niah (4 km from Park HQ). **C** *Park View Hotel*, T085737023. Range of comfortable rooms with TV, a/c, bath but no shower. Some rooms face inwards, discounts often available. **C** *Niah Caves Inn*, T(085) 737333, F737332. A/c, shower, spacious, fully-carpeted rooms. Reasonable value. **D** *Niah Caves Hotel*, T085737726. Some a/c, shared facilities, 6 rooms (singles, doubles and triples available). Basic, but light and clean, next to the river. A fair budget option. **Camping** Tents can be hired from Park HQ (RM8) or from the site (RM4).

The Guano Collectors' Co-operative shop at the beginning of the plankwalk sells basic food and cold drinks and camera film. There is another basic shop/restaurant just outside the park gates. There is a canteen at Park HQ, which serves good local food and full western breakfast, good value, barbecue site provided, the canteen is supposed to be open from 0700-2300, but is a little erratic.

Eating
Emergency rations recommended

Road Boat From Batu Niah (near the market) to Park HQ at Pengkalan Lubang, Niah National Park (RM10 per person or if more than 5 people, RM2 per person) or 45 mins' walk to Park HQ. **Bus**: Hourly connections with Miri, 2 hrs, 7 buses a day to **Bintulu**, 2 hrs and **Sibu** via Bintulu to **Batu Niah**. **Taxi**: From **Miri** to Park HQ, will only leave when there are 4 passengers. From Bintulu to Batu Niah (RM30). RM10 to Park HQ, however the river boat is far more scenic.

Transport
109 km from Miri to Batu Niah

Sarawak

Miri and the Baram River

Miri

Miri is the starting point for adventurous trips up the Barani River to **Marudi**, **Bario** and the **Kelabit Highlands**. Also accessible from Miri and Marudi is the incomparable **Gunung Mulu National Park** with the biggest limestone cave system in the world and one of the richest assemblages of plants and animals.

Colour map 3, grid A5
Phone code: 085

The capital of Sarawak's Fourth Division is a busy, prosperous town, with more than half its population Chinese. Many new buildings were constructed in the 1990s including two big new hotels, the *Mega* and the *Grand Palace* each of which has an adjoining shopping mall. One of the newer projects is a waterfront development with a marina – there is a pleasant walk on the peninsula here across the Miri River, and some good fishing. Another project recently completed is the *Bintang Plaza*, a large shopping complex on the edge of town on the road to the Baram River which contains *Parkson*, one of Malaysia'a largest department store chains. ■ *Tourist Information Centre: Lot 452, Jln Malay (next to bus station), T434181, F434179.* Permits and accommodation bookings for Niah, Mulu and Lambir. Stb@po.jaring.my Accommodation booking, T434184.

In the latter years of the 19th century, a small trading company set up in Sarawak, to import kerosene and export polished shells and pepper. In 1910, when 'earth oil' was first struck on the hill overlooking Miri, the little trading

History

company took the plunge and diversified into the new commodity – making, in the process, Sarawak's first oil town. The company's name was Shell. Together with the Malaysian national oil company, *Petronas*, *Shell* has been responsible for discovering, producing and refining Sarawak's offshore oil deposits. Oil is a key contributor to Malaysia's export earnings and Miri has been a beneficiary of the boom. There is a big refinery at Lutong to the north, which is connected by pipeline with Seria in Brunei. Lutong is the next town on the Miri River and the main headquarters for *Shell*.

The oil boom in this area began on Canada Hill, behind the town (where, incidentally, this limestone ridge provides excellent views of the town). **Oil Well No 1** was built by *Shell* and was the first oil well in Malaysia, spudded on 10 August 1910. The well was still yielding oil 62 years later, but its productivity began to slump. It is estimated that a total of 600,000 barrels were extracted from Well No 1 during its operational life. It was shut off in 1972. There are now 624 oil wells in the Miri Field, producing 80 million barrels of oil a year.

Sights Juxtaposed against Miri's modern boom-town image is **Tamu Muhibba** (the native jungle produce market, open 24 hours), opposite the *Park Hotel* in a purpose-built concrete structure with pointed roofs on the roundabout connecting Jalan Malay and Jalan Padang. The Orang Ulu come downriver to sell their produce, and a walk around the market provides an illuminating lesson

Miri

Sleeping	4 Gloria	7 Mega	Eating
1 Cosy Inn	5 Grand Palace	8 Park	1 Apollo
2 Dynasty	& Miri Plaza	9 Tai Tong	2 Aseanika
3 Fairland Inn	6 Kingwood Inn	Lodging House	3 Bilal

in jungle nutrition. Colourful characters run impromptu 'stalls' from rattan mats, selling yellow cucumbers that look like mangoes, mangoes that look like turnips, huge crimson durians, tiny loofah sponges, sackfuls of fragrant Bario rice (brown and white), every shape, size and hue of banana, *tuak* (rice wine) in old Heineken bottles and a menagerie of jungle fauna – including mouse-deer, falcons, pangolins and the apparently delicious long-snouted *tupai*, or jungle squirrel. There is a large selection of dried and fresh seafood – fish and *bubok* (tiny prawns), and big buckets boiling with catfish or stacked with turtles, there are also some handicrafts.

Taman Bulatan is a scenic centrally-located park with foodstalls and boats for hire on the manmade lake.

Permits are required to go anywhere upriver. Apply at the Resident's office, Jalan Kwantung, T433205 – with passport photocopy. Permits are also available from Marudi. After acquiring a permit, the police station will need to stamp it. If travelling with a tour company it will take care of the bureaucracy.

Excursions
Miri is the main centre for organizing tours up the Baram River, to Mulu National Park

Niah Caves and National Park, see page 367. **Gunung Mulu National Park**, see page 379. **Hawaii Beach** is a pristine palm fringed beach, popular for picnics and barbecues. There are chalets to stay in. It is 15 minutes' taxi ride from Miri.

Lambir Hills is a park mainly consisting of a chain of sandstone hills bounded by rugged cliffs, 19 km south of Miri and just visible from the town; the main attractions are the beautiful waterfalls. *Kerangas* (heath forest) covers the higher ridges and hills while the lowland areas are mixed dipterocarp forest. Bornean gibbons, bearded pigs, barking deer and over 100 species of bird have been recorded in the park. There is only one path across a rickety suspension bridge at present, but there are numerous waterfalls and tree towers for birdwatching, and several trails which lead to enticing pools for swimming. The park attracts hordes of daytrippers from Miri at weekends. If you want to stay overnight there are chalets, one with 2 rooms, 3 beds, 4 units with 2 rooms, 2 beds, RM50 per room or RM80 per house; a/c chalet, 2 rooms with 3 beds, RM60 per room or RM120 per house. **Campsite** Rental RM4. A canteen is provided, no cooking allowed in chalet, you can cook at campsite or take food into canteen.
■ *Park entrance: RM10 (RM5 for children), photography RM5, video camera RM10, professional camera RM100. The Park HQ is close to the*

Malay Kampung
Jl Bendahara
Jln Permaisuri
To Lutong
Jln Yu Seng Utara
Imperial Shopping Mall
Jln Unus
Public Swimming Pool
Jln Pata
Immigration Office
Jln Gartak
Jln Bintang
Civic Centre
Jln Merdu
Gilbert Park
Bintang Plaza
Jln Miri-Pujut
To Kuala Baram & Express Boats
5
Canada Hill

Sarawak

Miri-Niah road, there is an audio visual room with seating for 30 here. Getting there: from Park Hotel *take Bintulu or Bakong bus.*

Loagan Bunut National Park is located in the upper reaches of the Sungai Bunut and contains Sarawak's largest natural lake. At approximately 650 ha, Loagan Bunut may not be large but it is no ordinary lake since the water level in the lake is totally dependent on the water level of the rivers Bunut, Tinjar and Baram. The level is at its lowest in the months of February, May and June and sometimes, for a period of about two to three weeks, the lake becomes an expanse of dry cracked mud. The main cultural attraction at the lake is the traditional method of fishing (*selambau*), which has been retained by the Berawan fishermen. The surrounding area is covered with peat swamp forest. The common larger birds found here are the darters, egrets, herons, bittern, hornbill and kites. Gibbons are also common. At present, there are no visitor facilities.

Trips can be organized through tour operators in Miri. For details of dive spots, see www.borneo. com.au/diving/

Luconia Island is surrounded by a pristine coral reef. The Luconia Shoals are approximately 150 nautical miles north of Miri and it is only possible to dive here from a live-aboard boat. The reef covers around more than 300 sq km and is said to be untouched with large pelagics from mantas and tuna to black-tip sharks. The best months for diving are between April and August. Some dive sites are easy while others, with strong currents and deep walls, require experience and care. The better known sites are Hayes Reef (excellent wall diving) and Atken Reef (very good drift diving with large pelagics). Night diving, with many large morays, is reported to be excellent.

Tours

The National Parks Office and Visitor Information Centre are closed on the 1st and 3rd Saturday of the month

Although most tour companies specialize in trips up the Baram River to Mulu National Park, some are much better than others – in terms of facilities and services offered. The best agents are *Alo Doda* and *Tropical Adventure* which have private accommodation in the park and run an interesting selection of more off-beat treks to remote destinations; they are also the most expensive. *Alo Doda*, for example, organizes treks to the Penan areas and Kenyah longhouses of Ulu Baram – on the upper stretches of the river. Every agency in Miri has a Mulu National Park itinerary covering the caves, pinnacles and summits. It is also possible to trek to Bario and Mount Murud, as well as to Limbang from Mulu. Most of the agencies employ experienced guides who will be able to advise on longer, more ambitious treks. The Mulu National Park is one destination where it is usually cheaper to go through a tour company than to try to do it independently. Costs vary considerably according to the number of people in a group. For the three-day Mulu trip, a single tourist can expect to pay RM500; this drops to RM400 a head for a group of four and about RM350 each for a group of 10, all accommodation, food, travel and guide costs included. An eight day tour of Ulu Baram longhouses would cost RM1,800 for one person and RM1,200 per person in a group of 10. A 20-day trek will cost two people (minimum number) around RM2,000 each, and a group of 6-10, RM1,300 a head. For those who want to visit remote longhouses, tour companies present by far the best option. Tour fees cover 'gifts' and all payments to longhouse headmen for food, accommodation and entertainment.

Sleeping

■ on map
Price codes: see inside front cover

Most people going to Mulu will have to spend at least a night in Miri. The town has a growing selection of mid-to-upmarket hotels with discounts of 30-40% off quoted prices as a matter of course. Many of the mid-range hotels are around Jln Yu Seng Selatan.

A *Dynasty*, Lot 683, Block 9, Jln Pujut-Lutong, T421111, F422222, dyhlmyy@ po.jaring.my A/c, restaurants, pool, health centre, next to Oil Town Shopping Complex. **A** *Grand Palace*, 2 km Jln Miri-Pujut, Pelita Commercial Centre, T428888, F427777, jrobson@pc.jaring.my Imposing peach and pastel building on town outskirts next to Miri Plaza Shopping Centre, 125 comfortable, carpeted rooms with a/c, TV, bathroom, mini-bar, tea and coffee-making facilities, pool, fitness centre, karaoke, restaurant. **A** *Holiday Inn*, Jln Temenggong Datuk Oyong Lawai, T418888, F419999, www.holiday-inn.com.my/hi-swak Situated 2 km from town centre, at mouth of the Miri River, this 5-storey, modern, white block, curves around the South China Sea, very popular with families at weekends (check for special weekend rates (**B**) price category), 168 rooms all with a/c, TV (no less than 11 channels), bathroom, tea and coffee-making facilities, mini-bar, balcony, thick carpets and comfy beds, sunsets over sea, colourful but noisy river traffic, free-form pool, pleasantly surrounded by plants and palms with swim-up bar in form of traditional boat (popular with kids), jacuzzi and baby pool, sandy area for kids to play, beach too near town to be clean and sea not safe for swimming but pleasant for sunset strolls, coffee house, Chinese restaurant, bar and bakery/delicatessen, fitness centre, sauna. Recommended. **A** *Mega*, Lot 907, Jln Merbau, T432432, F433433, www.megahotel.net The tallest and largest hotel in Miri town centre, 228 rooms with a/c, TV, bathroom, Chinese restaurant, coffee house, pool with jacuzzi, health centre, business centre, internet, shopping mall attached. **A** *Rihga Royal*, Lot 799, Jln Temenggong Datuk Oyong Lawai, T421121, F421099. Japanese-managed hotel on coast south of Miri, 5-star comforts, 225 rooms, all rooms with a/c, mini-bar, TV, tea and coffee-making facilities, Japanese restaurant (the only one in Miri), Chinese restaurant and coffee house, pool, tennis, health centre. **B** *Gloria*, 27 Jln Brooke, T416699, F418866. A/c, restaurant, 42 rooms, better than it looks from outside, although the economy rooms are windowless, comparatively expensive. **B** *Kingwood Inn*, Jln Yu Seng Utara, T415888, F415009. A/c, restaurant, one of the smaller mid-range places to stay.

Being an oil town, and close to Brunei, Miri has a booming prostitution industry

C *Cosy Inn*, 545-547 Jln Yu Seng Selatan, T415522, F415155. A/c, restaurant. Looks better from the outside than it is, nevertheless better than others in its class. **C** *Park*, Jln Raja, T414555, F414488. A/c, Chinese restaurant. Until the *Holiday Inn* opened, the *Park* was the best hotel in town. Ranked a 3-star hotel, although now rather run down, it is good value for money and convenient for the bus station. People, though, seem to have rather mixed experiences – some report things being pilfered from their rooms, other have been propositioned, however more recommend it without reservation. **C-D** *Tai Tong Lodging House*, 26 Jln China, T411498. Some a/c, Chinese guesthouse-cum-hotel with range of rooms from a/c with attached bathrooms to fan-cooled with shared facilities, dorm beds also available (**F**), although possessions left here are reputedly not very secure. **D** *Fairland Inn*, Jln Raja, T413981. A/c, small, dirty rooms, bathroom with minuscule toilet but the best of a bad bunch.

Many of the cheaper lodgings, particularly around Jln China, are sleazy brothels. Those listed here represent the more respectable end of the market

Malay Cheap *Aseanika*, Jln China, also serves good Indian and Indonesian food. **Seriously cheap** *Nabila's*, 1st floor, 441 DUBS Building, Jln Bendahara, also serves Indonesian and Oriental, curries, good rendang. **Chinese Mid-range** *Kok Chee*, 1st floor *Park Hotel*, Jln Kingsway. **Cheap** *Apollo*, Lot 394 Jln Yu Seng Selatan (close to *Gloria Hotel*), good seafood, popular. *Sea View Café*, Jln China. **Indian Cheap** *Bilal*, Jln Persiaran Kabor, excellent curries and rotis, coffee house. **International Mid-range** *Golden Steak Garden*, *Gloria Hotel*, 27 Jln Brooke, steak. *Park View Restaurant* (coffee house of *Park Hotel*), Jln Malay, most sophisticated menu in town, jellyfish, good selection of seafood and grill. **Cheap** *Bonzer Garden Steak House*, Jln Yu Seng Utara, local dishes much cheaper than burgers. **Seriously cheap** *Sugar Bun*, Ground floor, Wisma Pelita Tunku, burgers, pastries, cakes etc. *Cosy Garden* (and in *Mega Hotel* block), pleasant restaurant, but the a/c inhibits any cosiness, limited menu but reasonable prices, steak.

Eating
● *on map, page 372*
Price codes:
see inside front cover

Sarawak

Bakeries *Appletree*, Ground floor, Wisma Pelita Tunku. *Deli Corner*, *Holiday Inn*.

Foodstalls   *Taman Seroja*, Jln Brooke, Malay food, best in the evenings. *Tamu Muhibba* (Native Market), opposite *Park Hotel* on roundabout connecting Jln Malay and Jln Padang, best during the day. *Tanjong Seafood stalls*, Tanjung Lobung (south of Miri), best in evening. *Gerai Makan*, near Chinese temple at end of Jln Oleander, Malay food.

Entertainment Miri has scores of karaoke lounges and discos, mostly along Jln Yu Seng. Check local paper for information on films and cultural events. The *Holiday Inn* stages regular performances of Western music and theatre. *Rig* disco in *Regal Hotel*, very popular.

Shopping **Books** *Pelita Book Centre*, 1st floor, Wisma Pelita Tunku; *Parksons Department Store*, Bintang Plaza.

Handicrafts *Longhouse*, 2nd floor, Imperial Mall, the best in town. *Kong Hong*, Wisma Pelita, 1st floor. *Sarawak Handicrafts*, 2nd floor, Soon Hup Centre. *Joy art and fashion House*, M floor, Wisma Pelita Tunju. *Syarikat Unique arts and handicrafts centre*, Lot 2994. *Morsjaya Commercial Centre*, Jln Miri. *Royal Selangor*, 28F, High St. *Swet Love Gift Shop*, Lot 219, 2nd floor, Wisma Pelita Tunku. Roadside stalls at Nakat, 18 km down the southbound road to Niah (1 km before Lambir Hills National Park) also sell baskets.

Shopping malls *Boulevard*(BSC), Jln Pujut Lutong, Miri's largest shopping complex, foodcourt on the top floor, supermarket, department store and boutiques. *Bintang Plaza*, Jln Miri. *Imperial Mall*, Jln Parry. *Soon Hup Tower*, next to *Mega Hotel* with Parkwell's supermarket and department store. *Wisma Pelita Tunku*, near bus station, department store.

Supermarket *Pelita*, Ground floor, Wisma Pelita Tunku, useful for supplies for upriver expeditions; *Sing Liang Supermarket* on Jln Nakhoda Gampar – Chinese store; *Parkson Grand*, Bintang Plaza; *Ngiukee*, moving from Pelita to Imperial Mall.

Sports **Golf** *Miri Golf Club*, Jln Datuk Patinggi, T416787, F417848, by the sea, green fees RM84 weekdays, RM126 weekends. Because this is the only golf course in this area of Sarawak, with a large membership, it is worth phoning beforehand to book a tea-off slot. **Swimming** Public pool off Jln Bintang, close to the Civic Centre, RM1. **Fitness centres** *Holiday Inn* and *Rihga Hotels* both have centres where non-residents can become short-term members.

Tour operators *Borneo Adventure*, *Pacific Orient Hotel*, 49 Jln Brooke, T414935, F419543, has been recommended over the years by a number of readers; they may be expensive by comparison with other outfits, but it appears to be worth it. *Borneo Leisure*, Lot 227, Ground floor, Jln Maju, Beautiful Jade Centre, T413011. *Borneo Overland*, 37 Ground floor, Bangunan Raghavan, Jln Brooke, T4302255, F416424. *East-West*, 792 Jln Bintang, T410717, F411297. *Hornbill Travel*, G26 Park Arcade, Jln Raja, T417385, F412751. *JJ Tour Service*, Lot 231, Jln Maju Taman, Jade Centre, T418690, F413308. *JJM Tours & Travel*, Lot 3002, Ground floor, Morsjaya Commercial Centre, 2.5 miles, Miri-Bintulu Rd, T416051, F414390, young company with some very experienced guides. Recommended. *KKM Travel & Tours*, 236 Jln Maju, T417899, F414629. *Malang Sisters Agency*, 248 Jln Bendahara, T417770, F417123. *Robert Ding*, Lot 556, 1st floor, Royal Snooker Centre, Jln Permaisuri, T416051, F414390, recommended by National Parks Office. *Seridan Mulu*, Lot 351, 2nd floor, Jln Brooke, T422277, F415277, private accommodation within park, recommended by National Parks Office. *Transworld Travel Service*, 9th floor Wisma Pelita Tunku, T422226, F410057, simtw@pc.jaring.my *Tropical Adventure*, Ground floor, *Mega Hotel*, Jln Merbau, Soon

Hup Tower, PO Box 2197, T419337, F414503, hthee@pc.jaring.my   private accommodation within Mulu Park. Recommended.

Local Car hire: *Mega*, No 3, Lorong 1, Sungai Krokop, T431885. Fleet of Proton Sagas   **Transport** available. RM120-150 per day. *Kimoto*, T411007. *Jasara Service*, T870980. **Ferry**: operates every 15 mins from 0630-2000. **Taxi**: T432277.

Long distance Air: regular connections on *MAS* with Kuching (RM164), Sibu, Marudi, Bario via Marudi, Bintulu, Limbang, Lawas, Mulu and Labuan. Also connections with Kota Kinabalu. For transport information, T33433. Fare by taxi to town from Padang Kirbua Terminal is RM20, or RM12 to the old bus station. Bus no 7 runs between town and the airport from early morning to early evening. *Royal Brunei* operate twice daily flights to BSB (RM111 including tax).

Bus: a new bus terminal opened at Pujuk Padang Kerbau, Jln Padang a few years back, around 4 km from the town centre. A taxi to the terminal should cost around RM10 – watch out for inflated pricing! Regular connections from early morning to early/mid-afternoon with **Batu Niah** 2-3 hrs, **Bintulu** 3 hrs, **Sibu** 6 hrs, and **Kuching**. Tickets can be booked at following agents: *Lanang Road Bus Co*, next to *Park Hotel*, T435336, *Syarikat Bas Express*, next to *Park Hotel*, T439325. Express buses to **Marudi**, depart from Kuala Baram, the port area, 2 hrs, RM18.

To **Kuala Baram** and the express boat upriver to **Marudi** Regular bus connections with Kuala Baram; there are also taxis to Kuala Baram, either private or shared. Express boats upriver to Marudi from Kuala Baram, 3 hrs. Roughly 1 boat every hr from 0715. Last boat 1430. This is the first leg of the journey to Mulu and the interior.

Five departures a day (*Miri-Belait Transport Company*, T419129) to Kuala Belait in **Brunei**, 1½ hrs, RM12, with onward connections to Bandar Seri Begawan. There is also a direct minibus service between Miri and Brunei's capital (4 hrs). Travelling by your own means of transport from Miri it is necessary to take the car ferry across the Baram River, then pass through immigration, before another ferry across the Belait River. At weekends and public holidays there are long queues for the ferries as well as at immigration – so be prepared for a long, hot wait. Be warned also that the ferry across the Belait River takes an unscheduled 1-hr break for lunch. Distance itself is nothing – the ferry crossings take no more than 10 mins each and Miri to Kuala Belait is just 27 km. Bus passengers bypass the queues because they board the ferry as foot passengers and then hop on another bus the other side of the river. From Kuala Belait regular connections with Seria, 1 hr and from Seria regular connections with Bandar Seri Begawan ($1 Brunei), 1-2 hrs. It takes minimum 5 hrs to reach Bandar Seri Begawan.

Airline offices *MAS*, 239 Halaman Kabor, off Jln Yu Seng Selatan, T414144. *Royal*   **Directory** *Brunei*, Lot 263, South Yu Send Rd (Halaman Kabor), T426322. *Seagga*, Jln Sim Cheng Kay, near mosque, T439954. **Banks** All major banks are represented in Miri. **Communications** General Post Office: just off Jln Gartak. **Telecom Office:** Jln Gartak, open Mon-Sun 0730-2200. **Internet**: *Direct Response Television Shop*, 3rd floor, Imperial Mall, Jln Parry (RM6/hour). **Medical facilities** Hospital: opposite Ferry Point, T420033. **Useful addresses** Immigration Office: Jln Unus, T442100. **National Parks and Wildlife Office:** Jln Puchong, T436637, F431975 (note that it is closed every first and third Sat of the month). **Police Station:** Jln Kingsway, T432533. **Resident's Office:** Jln Kwantung, T43320

Sarawak

Marudi

Four major tribal groups – Iban, Kelabit, Kayan and Penan – come to Marudi to do business with the Chinese, Indian and Malay merchants. Marudi is the furthest upriver trading post on the Baram and services all the longhouses in the Tutoh, Tinjar and Baram river basins. Most tourists only stop long enough in Marudi to down a cold drink before catching the next express boat upriver; as the trip to Mulu National Park can now be done in a day, not many have to spend the night here. Because it is a major trading post, however, there are a lot of hotels, and the standards are reasonably good.

Sights   Fort Hose was built in 1901, when Marudi was still called Claudetown, and has good views of the river. It is named after the last of the Rajah's residents, the anthropologist, geographer and natural historian Dr Charles Hose. The fort is now used as administrative offices. Also of note is the intricately carved Thaw Peh Kong Chinese Temple (diagonally opposite the express boat jetty), also known as Siew San Teen. It was shipped from China and erected in Sarawak in the early 1900s, although it was probably already 100 years old by the time the temple began life in its new location.

Excursions   Gunung Mulu National Park, see below. The Marudi-Kampong Teraja log walk is normally done from the Brunei end, as the return trek, across the Sarawak/Brunei border takes a full day, dawn to dusk. It is, however, possible to reach an Iban longhouse inside Brunei without going the full distance to Kampong Teraja. The longhouse is on the Sungai Ridan, about 2½ hours down the jungle trail. The trail starts 3 km from Marudi, on the airport road. A local Chinese man, who runs an unofficial taxi service to and from the trail head, may spot you before you find the trail (ask at the houses along the road). There is no customs post on the border; the trail is not an official route into Brunei. Trekkers are advised to take their passports in the unlikely event of being stopped by police, who will probably turn a blind eye. Kampong Teraja in Brunei is the furthest accessible point which can be reached by road from Labi.

Permits are necessary to go upriver from Marudi. Permits for Mulu and Bario are issued by the district officer in Fort Hose

Three longhouses, *Long Seleban*, *Long Moh* and *Leo Mato*, are accessible by four-wheel drive vehicle from Marudi.

Sleeping   A-C *Grand*, Lot 350 Backlane, T755711, F775293. Some a/c, large but good hotel, restaurant, 30 clean rooms with cable TV, close to jetty and plenty of information on upriver trips. B *Mount Mulu Hotel*, Lot 80 & Lot 90, Marudi Town District, T756671, F756670. A/c, discounts are available making this place very good value. C *Victoria*, Lot 961-963 Jln Merdeka, T756067, T7556864. All 21 rooms have cable TV. D *Mayland*, 347 Mayland Building, T755106, F755333. A/c, 41 rooms, slightly rundown but a good range of accommodation.

Eating   There are several coffee shops dotted around town. Seriously cheap *Rose Garden*, opposite *Alisan Hotel*, a/c coffee shop serving mainly Chinese dishes.

Transport   Air The airport is 5 km from town. Connections with Miri (RM29) Bario (RM55), Sibu (RM100). Boat These leave from opposite the Chinese temple. Connections with Kuala Baram; 8 boats a day from 0700-1430 (RM18), Tutoh, for longboats to Long Terawan and Mulu National Park, 1 boat at 1200, (RM20), Long Lama, for longboats to Bario, 1 boat every hr 0730-1400.

Banks There are 2 local banks with foreign exchange facilities. **Communications** Post Office: Airport Rd. **Useful addresses** Police station: On Airport Rd.

Gunung Mulu National Park

*Tucked in behind Brunei, this 52,866 ha park lays claim to **Gunung Mulu**,
which at 2,376 m is the second highest mountain in Sarawak, and the biggest
limestone cave system in the world. In short, Mulu is essentially a huge hollow
mountain range, sitting on top of 180-million-year-old rainforest. Its primary
jungle contains astonishing biological diversity.*

Colour map 3, grid A6

In Robin Hanbury-Tenison's book *The Rain Forest*, he says of Mulu: "All
sense of time and direction is lost." Every scientific expedition that has visited
Mulu's forests has encountered plant and animal species unknown to science.
In 1990, five years after it was officially opened to the public, the park was han-
dling an average 400 visitors a month. Numbers have increased markedly
since then – the area is now attracting about 12,000 tourists a year – and as the
eco-tourism industry has extended its foothold, local tribespeople have been
drawn into confrontation with the authorities. A series of sabotage incidents
in 1993 have been blamed on the Berawan tribe, who claim the caves and the
surrounding jungle are a sacred site.

In 1974, three years after Mulu was gazetted as a national park, the first of a
succession of joint expeditions led by the British Royal Geographical Society
(RGS) and the Sarawak government began to make the discoveries that put
Mulu on the map. In 1980 a cave passage over 50 km long was surveyed for the
first time. Since then, a further 137 km of passages have been discovered. Altogether 27 major caves have now been found – speleologists believe they probably represent a tiny fraction of what is actually there. The world's biggest
cave, the **Sarawak Chamber**, was not discovered until 1984.

The first attempt on Gunung Mulu was made by Spencer St John, the British consul in Brunei, in 1856 (see also his attempts on Gunung Kinabalu,
Sabah, page 444). His efforts were thwarted by "limestone cliffs, dense jungle
and sharp pinnacles of rock". Dr Charles Hose, Resident of Marudi, led a
25-day expedition to Gunung Mulu in 1893, but also found his path blocked
by 600-m high cliffs. Nearly 50 years later, in 1932, a Berawan rhinoceros
hunter called Tama Nilong guided Edward Shackleton's Oxford University
expedition to the summit. One of the young Oxford undergraduates on that
expedition was Tom Harrisson, who later made the Niah archaeological discoveries, see page 368. Tama Nilong, the hunter from Long Terawan, had previously reached the main southwest ridge of Mulu while tracking a
rhinoceros.

The limestone massifs of Gunung Api and Gunung Benarat were originally
at the same elevation as Gunung Mulu, but their limestone outcrops were
more prone to erosion than the Mulu's sandstone. Northwest of the gorge lies
a large, undisturbed alluvial plain which is rich in flora and fauna. Penan
tribespeople (see page 340) are permitted to maintain their lifestyle of fishing,
hunting and gathering in the park. At no small expense, the Malaysian government has encouraged them to settle at a purpose-built longhouse at **Batu
Bungan**, just a few minutes upriver from the Park HQ, but its efforts have met
with limited success because of the desire of many Penan to maintain their
peripatectic lifestyle. Penan shelters can often be found by river banks.

Reeling from international criticism, the Sarawak state government

*The cliffs of the
Melinau Gorge rise a
sheer 600 m, and are
the highest limestone
rockfaces between
North Thailand and
Papua New Guinea*

announced in 1994 that it had set aside 66,000 ha of rainforest as what it called 'biosphere', a reserve where indigenous people could practise their traditional lifestyle. Part of this lies in the park. In Baram and Limbang districts, the remaining 300 Penan will have a reserve in which they can continue their nomadic way of life. A further 23,000 ha has reportedly been set aside for 'semi-nomadic' Penan.

Flora & fauna In the 1960s and 1970s, botanical expeditions were beginning to shed more light on the Mulu area's flora and fauna: 100 new plant species were discovered between 1960 and 1973 alone. Mulu park encompasses an area of diverse altitudes and soil types – it includes all the forest types found in Borneo except mangrove. About 20,000 animal species have been recorded in Mulu Park, as well as 3,500 plant species and 8,000 varieties of fungi (more than 100 of these are endemic to the Mulu area). Mulu's ecological statistics are astounding: it is home to 1,500 species of flowering plant, 170 species of orchid and 109 varieties of palm. More than 280 butterfly species have been recorded. Within the park boundaries, 262 species of birds (including all eight varieties of hornbill), 67 mammalian species, 50 species of reptile and 75 amphibian species have been recorded.

Mulu's caves contain an unusual array of flora and fauna too. There are three species of swiftlet, 12 species of bat, and nine species of fish, including the cave flying fish (*Nemaaramis everetti*) and blind catfish (*Silurus furnessi*). Cave scorpions (*Chaerilus chapmani*) – which are poisonous but not deadly – are not uncommon. Other subterranean species include albino crabs, huntsman spiders, cave crickets, centipedes and snakes (which dine on swiftlets and bats). These creatures have been described as "living fossils...[which are] isolated survivors of ancient groups long since disappeared from Southeast Asia."

Treks

Trails around headquarters are well marked but it is illegal to go anywhere without hiring a guide.

Gunung Mulu The minimum time to allow for the climb is four days, three nights; tents are not
The views from the required if you stay at Camps 1 and 2. The main summit route starts from the
summit are best plankwalk at Park HQ heading towards Deer Cave. The Mulu walkway forks
during April and May left after about 1 km. From the headquarters it is an easy four- to five-hour trek to Camp 1 at 150 m, where there is a shelter, built by the RGS/Sarawak government expedition in 1978. The second day is a long uphill slog (eight to 10 hours) to Camp 4 (1,800 m), where there is also a shelter. Past Camp 3, the trail climbs steeply up Bukit Tumau, which affords good views over the park, and above which the last wild rhinoceros in Sarawak was shot in the mid-1940s. There are many pitcher plants (*Nepenthes lowii*) along this stretch of trail (see page 563). From Camp 4, known as 'The Summit Camp', the path passes the helicopter pad, from where there are magnificent views of Gunung Benarat, the Melinau Gorge and Gunung Api. The final haul to the summit is steep; there are fixed ropes. Around the summit area, the *Nepenthes muluensis* pitcher plant is common – it is endemic to Mulu. From Camp 4 it takes 1½ hours to reach the summit, and a further seven hours back down the mountain to Camp 1.

Equipment Camp 1 has water, as does Camp 4 if it has been raining. Water should be boiled before drinking. It is necessary to bring your own food; in the rainy season it is wise to bring a gas cooking stove. A sleeping bag and waterproofs are also necessary and spare clothes, wrapped in a plastic bag, are a good idea.

Mulu can also be climbed from the south ridge of Melinau Gorge (see below) – three hours to Camp 1, five hours to Camp 3, steep four to five hour climb to Camp 4, two hours to the top. Forest changes from alluvial/swamp forest through mixed dipterocarp to mossy sub-montane and summit scrub.

Treks from Camp 5, which is located in the Melinau Gorge, facing Gunung Benarat, take about four to six hours upstream from the Park HQ. From the

Gunung Mulu National Park

BRUNEI

Beachcomber's Cave

Terikan
Rivers Cave

Blue
Moonlight
Cave

Menagerie Cave

Cobweb Cave

Tiger Cave

Sakai's Cave

Lutut River

Melinau Trail

Pinacles Trail

Imperial
Cave

Melinau
Camp

Melinau River

Black
Rock Cave

Melinau Gorge

Gunung Api
(1,750m)

Wonder Cave

Cobra Cave

Good Luck Cave

Melinau Paku River

Clearwater Cave

Cave of the Winds

Paku
Camp

Simon's
Cave

Mulu Airstrip

Green
Cave

Nipa River

Gunung Mulu Trail

Gunung
Mulu
(2,376m)

National Park HQ

Snake Cave

Giam Camp

Lumut
Camp

Deer Cave

Tapin River

Ubung River

N

0 km   2
0 miles   2

camp it is possible to trek up the gorge as well as to the Pinnacles, on Gunung Api. It is advisable to hire a longboat for the duration of your time at and around Camp 5. The boat has to be abandoned at Kuala Berar, at the confluence of the Melinau and Berar rivers. It is only used for the first and last hours of the trip, but in the event of an emergency, there are no trails leading back to the Park HQ and there are grim stories of fever-stricken people being stranded in the jungle. For a three-day trip, a longboat will cost about RM350 (bargain hard) to hire – as opposed to RM350 if you just arrange to be collected three days later. It takes two to three hours, depending on the river level, from Park HQ to Kuala Berar; it is then a two- to three-hour trek (8 km) to Camp 5. Visitors to the Camp 5 area are also advised to plan their itinerary carefully as it is necessary to calculate how much food will be required and to carry it up there. There is a basic shelter (built by the RGS/Sarawak government expedition in 1978), which can house about 30 people. The camp is next to the Melinau River; river water should be boiled before drinking.

Melinau Gorge   Camp 5 nestles at the south end of the gorge, across a fast-flowing section of the Melinau River and opposite the unclimbed 1,580 m Gunung Benarat's stark, sheer limestone cliffs. The steep limestone ridges, that lead eventually to Gunung Api, comprise the east wall of the gorge. Heading north from Camp 5, the trail fizzles out after a few minutes. It takes an arduous two to three hours of endless river crossings and scrambles to reach a narrow chute of white water, under which is a large, deep and clear jungle pool with a convenient sandbank and plenty of large boulders to perch on. Alfred Russel Wallace's *Troides brookiana* – the majestic Rajah Brooke's birdwing – is particularly common at this little oasis, deep in undisturbed jungle. The walk involves criss-crossing through waist-deep, fast-flowing water and over stones that have been smoothed to a high polish over centuries: strong shoes are recommended – as is a walking stick. Only occasionally in the walk upstream is it possible to glimpse the towering 600 m cliffs.

   The Pinnacles are a forest of sharp limestone needles three-quarters of the way up Gunung Api. Some of the pinnacles rise above tree-tops to heights of 45m. The trail leaves from Camp 5, at the base of the Melinau Gorge. It is a very steep climb all the way and a maximum time of three to four hours is allowed to reach the pinnacles (1200 m); otherwise you must return. There is no source of water *en route*. It is not possible to reach Gunung Api from the pinnacles. It is strongly recommended that climbers wear gloves as well as long-sleeved shirts, trousers and strong boots to protect themselves against cuts from the razor-sharp rocks. Explorers on Spenser St John's expedition to Mulu in 1856 were cut to shreds on the pinnacles: "three of our men had already been sent back with severe wounds, whilst several of those left were much injured," he wrote, concluding that it was "the world's most nightmarish surface to travel over".

Gunung Api (Fire Mountain)   The vegetation is so dry at the summit that it is often set ablaze by lightning in the dry season. The story goes that the fires were so big that locals once thought the mountains were volcanoes. Some of the fires could be seen as far away as the Brunei coast. The summit trek takes a minimum of three days. At 1,710 m, it is the tallest limestone outcrop in Borneo and, other than Gunung Benarat (on the other side of the gorge), is probably the most difficult mountain to climb in Borneo. Many attempts to climb it ended in failure; two Berawans from Long Terawan finally made it to the top in 1978, one of them the grandson of Tama Nilong, the rhinoceros-hunter who had climbed Gunung Mulu in 1932. It is impossible to proceed upwards beyond the Pinnacles.

Kerangas forest From Camp 5, cross the Melinau River and head down the Limbang trail towards Lubang Cina. Less than 30 minutes down the trail, fork left along a new trail which leads along a ridge to the south of Gunung Benarat. Climbing higher, after about 40 minutes, the trail passes into an area of leached sandy soils called *kerangas* (heath) forest. This little patch of thinner jungle is a tangle of many varieties of pitcher plants.

Limbang It is possible to trek from Camp 5 to Limbang, although it is easier to do it the other way. (See page 389.)

Caves

In 1961 geologist Dr G Wilford first surveyed Deer Cave and parts of the Cave of the Winds. But Mulu's biggest subterranean secrets were not revealed until the 1980s.

This part of the Clearwater System, on a small tributary of the Melinau River, is 107 km long. The cave passage – 75 km of which has been explored – links Clearwater Cave (Gua Ayer Jernih) with the **Cave of the Winds** (*Lubang Angin*), to the south. It was discovered in 1988. Clearwater is named after the jungle pool at the foot of the steps leading up to the cave mouth, where the longboats moor. Two species of monophytes – single-leafed plants – grow in the sunlight at the mouth of the cave. They only grow on limestone. A lighting system has been installed down the path to Young Lady's Cave, which ends in a 60 m-deep pot hole.

Clearwater Cave
The longest underground cavity in SE Asia and the 7th longest in the world

Sarawak

On the cave walls are some helictites – coral-like lateral formations – and, even more dramatic, are the photokarsts, tiny needles of rock, all pointing towards the light. These are formed in much the same way as their monstrous cousins, the pinnacles (see above), by vegetation, in this case algae, eating into and eroding the softer rock, leaving sharp points of harder rock which 'grow' at about half a millimetre a year. Inside Clearwater it is possible to hire a rowing boat for RM10 – the river can be followed for about 1½ km upstream, although the current is strong. It is illegal to fish at Clearwater, although it is possible to fish anywhere else in park waters with a hook and line. Clearwater can be reached by a 30-minute longboat ride from the Park HQ. Individual travellers must charter a boat for a return trip. Tour agents build the cost of this trip into their package, which works out considerably cheaper.

This is another of Mulu's record-breakers: it has the world's biggest cave mouth and the biggest cave passage, which is 2.2 km long and 220 m high at its highest point. Before its inclusion in the park, the cave had been a well-known hunting ground for deer attracted to the pools of salty water running off the guano. The silhouettes of some of the cave's limestone formations have been creatively interpreted; notably the profile of Abraham Lincoln. Adam's and Eve's Showers, at the east end of the cave, are hollow stalactites; water pressure increases when it rains. This darker section at the east end of Deer Cave is the preferred habitat of the naked bat. Albino earwigs live on the bats' oily skin and regularly drop off. The cave's east entrance opens onto 'The Garden of Eden' – a luxuriant patch of jungle, which was once part of the cave system until the roof collapsed. This separated Deer Cave and Green Cave, which lies adjacent to the east mouth; it is open only to caving expeditions.

Deer Cave

☞ **A land where money grows on trees**

Ever since Sarawak's riverbanks were first settled, the Iban and Orang Ulu tribespeople have practised shifting cultivation, growing crops in their clearings. Today, most of the clearing is done by commercial loggers and the cash-crop is the jungle itself. No one can travel up the Baram without feeling alarmed at the volume of logs, stockpiled like giant matchsticks, on either side of the river for mile after mile. In July 1991 members of two European environmental protest groups chained themselves to logs at Kuala Baram; they were promptly arrested and deported. In March 1992, James Barclay, author of A stroll through Borneo, a book about logging on the Baram, was also deported from Sarawak after a month in jail. The government says environmentalists are ill-informed and are presenting a false picture to the world. Sarawak's forests, it maintains, will be there in perpetuity.

The Borneo Company first tried logging on the Baram in the early 1900s, and built Sarawak's first timber mill at Kuala Baram in 1904 but early logging operations were not successful as the timber was attacked by pests. Commercial logging only really began in the 1950s with the arrival of the tractor and the chainsaw. During the 1980s and early 1990s, Sarawak's 130-million-year-old forests were being felled at an unprecedented rate. In the first eight months of 1999 Sarawak exported 3.6 mn m^3 of logs or a total of more than 6 mn m^3 of wood products - with a value of RM4bn. While logging has slowed down considerably over the last five years or so, this is partly, it seems, because the more accessible and valuable forests have been logged out.

Who derives the benefits from the lucrative logging industry is a sensitive political issue – in Sarawak, politics is timber. Logging licences are tickets to get rich quick and the state's chief minister can award timber concessions to whoever they want. In 1987 a rival politician disclosed that the Chief Minister and his allies held about a third of the state's logging concessions alone. The previous Chief Minister had held nearly as much. Sarawak's Minister for Tourism and the Environment, James Wong, is himself a partner in a 180,000-ha logging concession in Limbang. Environmentalists say these politicians, together with Chinese timber tycoons, are amassing fortunes at the expense of forest tribes. The rush to extract what they can before environmental pressure puts them out of business has fuelled allegations of political manoeuvring, corruption and malpractice.

Although logging companies have provided jobs for upriver tribespeople (a total of 150,000 people are employed in Sarawak's timber industry), logging has wreaked ecological havoc and impinged on tribal lands. The traditional lifestyles of the Penan hunter-gatherers and other Orang Ulu tribes have been threatened as loggers push deeper into the jungle. In the past, Kayan tribesmen would simply have decapitated anyone caught trespassing on their tribal lands; these days the Orang Ulu protest against the encroachment by blockading logging access roads. Many have been jailed for such protests. The government argues that the jungle tribes are a sideshow and says they have been hijacked by Western environmental groups

The west end of the cave is home to several million wrinkle-lipped and horseshoe bats. Hundreds of thousands of these bats pour out of the cave at dusk. Bat hawks can often be seen swooping in for spectacular kills. The helipad, about 500 m south of the cave mouth, provides excellent vantage points. VIPs' helicopters, arriving for the show, are said to have disturbed the bats in recent years. From the analysis of the three tonnes of saline guano the bats excrete every day, scientists conclude that they make an 80 km dash to the coast for meals of insects washed down with seawater. Cave *in a bid to give their campaigns a human face. Environmentalist groups counter that the livelihoods of the forest tribes are as important in the sustainability stakes as the trees themselves.*

Since the early 1980s, the water in Sarawak's main rivers has turned brown due to the sediment which is washed into it from the timber camps upstream. Water supplies have been contaminated by chemical pollutants and fish stocks have been depleted – few can survive in the turgid waters. In Belaga, on the upper Rejang, the price of fish has risen 10-fold in a decade. In Orang Ulu longhouses, tribespeople complain that logging operations have chased their game away, turning hunting trips for wild boar into major expeditions.

The state government is eager to allay fears that it is logging without regard to the forest ecology and the indigenous tribes. But while the state's forestry policy looks good on paper, the Enforcement Division of the Forest Department cannot cope with the vast territory it has to police; it is now using satellites to detect areas where illegal logging has occurred. The government dismisses warnings that Sarawak's logging rates (which are the highest in the world) cannot be sustained as scaremongering. But in 1991, the Japan-based International Tropical Timber Organization said that if logging rates were not halved, the state could be 'logged-out' within the decade.

While so-called sustainable logging is now being practised (many environmentalists scoff at the idea), the state remains dependent on the revenue it derives from logging concessions and

taxes. The great bulk of income from oil and gas is diverted to federal coffers in Kuala Lumpur. Without logging Sarawak would be left high and dry. The irony is that it may be the value of Borneo's rain forests which saves them from total destruction. Increasingly, the rain forest is being seen as a reservoir of valuable medicinal compounds that might form the bases for new drugs. Calanolide A, for example, is undergoing testing in the US as a potential Aids palliative. It seems to reduce blood levels of human immunodeficiency virus and may also be effective against tuberculosis. If so then its value could be several hundred million US$. The reason why companies are taking such a long, hard look at the tropical forest is because of their staggering species richness – biodiversity, in the jargon. Kuching is already home to the Sarawak Biodiversity Centre. In the past, drug companies would just swan into countries and pillage forests for anything that might be of value; now it is increasingly accepted that profits and benefits should be shared with local people and their local and national governments. If it is recognised that there could be more economic value in keeping the tropical forests where it is, rather than cutting it down, parts of Sarawak at least may remain green.

Useful websites *www.forest.gov.my/ www.ran.org/ www.wcmc.org.uk/forest/data/ vcn.bc.ca/spc/ www.spotimage.fr/home/appli/forest/bor neo/welcome.htm*

Sarawak

cockroaches eat the guano, ensuring that the cavern does not become choked with what locals call 'black snow'. ■ *Getting there: an hour's trek along a plank walk from Park HQ.*

Part of the same hollow mountain as Deer Cave, Lang's Cave is less well **Lang's Cave** known but its formations are more beautiful, and contains impressive curtain stalactites and intricate coral-like helictites. The cave is well illuminated and protected by bus stop-style plastic tunnels.

The Sarawak Chamber
The largest natural chamber in the world

Discovered in 1984, this chamber is 600 m long, 450 m wide and 100 m high – big enough, it is said, to accommodate 40 jumbo jets wing-tip to wing-tip and eight nose-to-tail. Unfortunately it is not open to the public as it is considered too dangerous.

For cavers wishing to explore caves not open to the public (those open to visitors are known as 'show' caves) there are designated 'adventure caves' within an hour of Park HQ. Experienced cave guides can be organized from headquarters. The most accessible of these is the one-hour trek following the river course through Clearwater Cave. Cavers should bring their own equipment.

Rapids

Just outside the national park boundary on the Tutoh River there are rapids which are possible to shoot; this can be arranged through tour agencies.

Park essentials

Entrance fee & permits
It is best to avoid visiting the park during school and public holidays. In December the park is closed to locals, but remains open to tourists

Admission is RM10 (RM5 for children), RM5 for camera, RM10 for video, RM200 for professional filming. Permits can be obtained from the National Parks and Wildlife Office c/o Visitors' Information Centre, Lot 452, Jln Melayu, Miri, T434184, F434179. Open Mon-Thu 0800-1245 and 1400-1645, Fri 0800-1130 and 1430-1615, Sat 0800-1245. It is necessary to book and pay a deposit for accommodation at the same time. Permits can also be picked up from the National Parks and Wildlife Office, 1st floor, Wisma Sumber Alam, Kuching, T248088. Accommodation can be booked through Kuching too. It is also necessary to get a permit from the police and the Miri or Marudi Residents. In Marudi, both the resident's office (Fort Hose) and the police station are on the airport road. This bureaucratic mess can be avoided if travel arrangements are left to a Miri travel agent. For further information www.sarawaktourism.com

Equipment

There is a small store at the Park HQ that sells basic necessities; there is also a small shop just outside the park boundary, at Long Pala. A sleeping bag is essential for Gunung Mulu trips; other essential equipment includes good insect repellent, wet weather gear and a powerful torch.

Guides
It is usual to tip guides and porters

No visitors are permitted to travel in the park without an authorized guide which can be arranged from Park HQ or booked in advance from the national parks office in Miri (see above). Most of the Mulu Park guides are very well informed about flora and fauna, geology and tribal customs. Tour agencies organize guides as part of their fee. **Guide fees**: RM20 per cave (or per day) and an extra RM10 per night. Mulu summit trips: around RM280 for 4 days, 3 nights; Melinau Gorge and Pinnacles: minimum RM110 (3 days, 2 nights). Ornithological guides cost an additional RM10 a day. Porterage: max 10 kg and RM30 per day. RM1 for each extra kilo. Mulu summit: minimum RM90; Melinau Gorge (Camp 5): minimum RM65.

Sleeping

Sleeping in the park must be booked in advance at the National Parks and Wildlife Office Forest Department in Miri or Kuching. Booking fee is RM20 per party and the maximum party size is 10 people. Bookings must be confirmed 5 days before visit. Two Miri-based travel agents have private accommodation in the park: *Seridan Mulu Tour* (RM10 per night) and *Tropical Adventure* (RM10 per night).

Park HQ *Annexe* (hostel) (1 room, 10 per room) RM10 per person; *Annexe* (8 rooms, 5 per room) RM75 per room; *Chalet class 3* (4 rooms, 4 per room) RM63 per room; *Chalet class 2* (2 rooms, 3 per room) RM94 per room or RM180 per house; *VIP Chalet* (3 per room), RM200, *Rumah Rehat Jenis 2*, RM210 per room; *Rumah Rehat Jenis 3*, RM157 per room. For accommodation bookings contact the National Parks and Wildlife Office.

There is also a privately owned hostel, the **Melinau Canteen**, T011291641 or T085657884, with dorm beds about 5 mins' walk downstream from the Park HQ, on the other bank of the river, RM10 per person.

Long Pala AL *Royal Mulu Resort*, Sungai Melinau, Muku, Miri, T085421122, F085421088. A/c, restaurants, owned by Japan's Royal Hotel Group *Rihga* the resort currently has 50 chalets and plans more, also proposes to carve an 18-hole golf-course out of rainforest adjacent to parks, 35 mins from Miri, has sparked much resentment among local tribespeople. In Aug 1993, Berawan tour guides, boat-operators and labourers in the park went on strike for 2 weeks because they say the resort was built on land which is theirs by customary right. A 20-min (RM5) boat ride downstream from Park HQ. Two hostels, run and owned by tour companies but with rooms available for drop-ins if not already booked, kitchen and bathrooms, crockery and bed linen provided. Private guesthouses are run by tour companies (RM10-15 plus meals). Tour agents offer private accommodation of a high standard, just outside the national park boundary. There is 12-hr electricity supply; the water supply is treated but it is advised to boil the water before drinking.

Camping You can only use tents provided, RM8.

Eating

There are stoves and cooking utensils available and the small store at Park HQ also sells basic supplies. There is a small canteen at Park HQ but the menu is limited and the food rather boring. As an alternative, cross the suspension bridge and walk alongside the road to the first house on the left; down the bank from here is the **Mulu Canteen**, which fronts onto the river (so there is no sign on the road). There is also the **Melinau Canteen**, just downriver from the Park HQ. There is a small shop with basic supplies at Long Pala. All tour companies with their own accommodation offer food.

Transport

Visitors are recommended to go through one of the Miri-based travel agents (see page 376). The average cost of a Mulu package (per person) is RM350-400 (4 days/3 nights) or RM500 (6 days/5 nights).

Around the park Independent travellers will find it more expensive arranging the trip on their own. Longboats can be chartered privately from Park HQ, if required (maximum 10 people per boat). The cost is calculated on a rather complicated system which includes a rate for the boat, a charge for the engine based on its horsepower, a separate payment for the driver and front-man, and then fuel on top of that. The total cost can be RM100+. How far these boats can actually get upriver depends on the season. They often have to be hauled over rapids, whatever the time of year.

Air Daily flights from Miri to Marudi, 15 mins. A new airstrip has been constructed just downriver from Park HQ and is now able to accommodate larger 50 seater planes. Currently 3 flights per day from **Miri**, and 2 daily from **Marudi** and **Limbang**. Telephone *MAS* for more information, T082 246622. The price of a flight is only marginally more expensive than taking the bus and boat from Miri.

Bus/taxi/boat Bus or taxi from **Miri** to **Marudi** express boat jetty near **Kuala Baram** at mouth of the Baram River (see page 377). Regular express boats from **Kuala Baram** to **Marudi**, 3 hrs (RM15) from early morning until about 1500. One express boat per day (leaves around noon) from Marudi to **Long Tarawan** on the Tutoh River (tributary of the Baram), via **Long Apoh**. During the dry season express boats cannot reach Long Terawan and terminate at Long Panai, on the Tutoh River, where longboats continue to Long Terawan (RM20). Longboats leave Long Tarawan for Mulu Park HQ: this used to be regular and comparatively cheap; now that most people travel to Mulu by air, longboats are less frequent and sometimes need to be privately chartered – an expensive business. Mulu Park HQ is 1½ hrs up the Melinau River (a tributary of the

Tutoh) (RM35). As you approach the park from Long Tarawan the Tutoh River narrows and becomes shallower; there are 14 rapids before the Melinau River, which forms the park boundary. When the water is low, the trip can be very slow and involve pulling the boat over the shallows, this accounts for high charter rates. For a group of 9 or 10 it is cheaper to charter a boat (RM250 one-way). The first jetty on the Melinau River is **Long Pala**, where most of the tour companies have accommodation. The Park HQ is another 15 mins upriver. Longboats returning to Long Terawan leave the headquarters at dawn each day, calling at jetties *en route*.

Bario and the Kelabit Highlands

Colour map 4, grid C2

Bario (Bareo) lies in the Kelabit Highlands, a plateau 1,000m above sea level close to the Kalimantan border (Indonesia). The highlands are Sarawak's answer to the hill stations on the peninsula. The undulating Bario valley is surrounded by mountains and fed by countless small streams which in turn feed into a maze of irrigation canals.

The best time to visit Bario is between March and October

The local Kelabits' skill in harnessing water has allowed them to practise wet rice cultivation rather than the more common slash-and-burn hill rice techniques. Fragrant Bario rice is prized in Sarawak and commands a premium in the coastal markets. The Kelabit Highlands' more temperate climate also allows the cultivation of a wide range of fruit and vegetables.

The plateau's near-impregnable ring of mountains effectively cut the Kelabit off from the outside world: it is the only area in Borneo which was never penetrated by Islam. In 1911 the Resident of Baram mounted an expedition which ventured into the mountains to ask the Kelabit to stop raiding the Brooke Government's subjects. It took the expedition 17 days to cross the Tamu Abu mountain range, to the west of Bario. The Kelabit were then brought under the control of the Sarawak government.

The most impressive mountain in the Bario area is the distinctive twin peak of the sheer-faced 2,043 m **Bukit Batu Lawi** to the northwest of Bario. The Kelabit traditionally believed the mountain had an evil spirit and so never went near it. Today such superstitions are a thing of the past since locals are mostly evangelical Christians.

In 1945, the plateau was selected as the only possible parachute drop zone in North Borneo not captured by the Japanese. The Allied Special Forces which parachuted into Bario were led by Tom Harrisson, who later became curator of the Sarawak Museum and made the famous archaeological discoveries at Niah Caves (see page 367). His expedition formed an irregular tribal army against the Japanese, which gained control over large areas of North Borneo in the following months.

Treks around Bario

It is necessary to have a permit to visit the Bario area, obtainable from the Resident's offices in Miri or Marudi

Because of the rugged terrain surrounding the plateau, the area mainly attracts serious mountaineers. There are many trails to the longhouses around the plateau area, however. Treks to Bario can be organized through travel agents in Miri, see page 371. Guides can also be hired in Bario and surrounding longhouses for RM30-40 per day. It is best to go through the Penghulu, Ngiap Ayu, the Kelabit chief. He goes round visiting many of the longhouses in the area once a month. It is recommended that visitors to Bario come equipped with sleeping bags and camping equipment. There are **no formal facilities** for tourists and provisions should be brought from Miri or Marudi. There are no banks or money changers in Bario.

Several of the surrounding mountains can be climbed from Bario, but they are, without exception, difficult climbs. Even on walks just around the Bario area, guides are essential as trails are poorly marked. The lower ('female') peak of **Bukit Batu Lawi** can be climbed without equipment, but the sheer sided 'male' peak requires proper rock-climbing equipment – it was first scaled in 1986. **Gunung Murudi** (2,423 m) is the highest mountain in Sarawak; it is a very tough climb.

Bario Lodging House, above the shop, or with the Penghulu in his kampong house, at Bario Bharu, 10 mins from the airstrip. There is also another recommended place to stay, *Tarawe's* (**D**), which is a good source of information and well run. Most visitors camp. **Sleeping**

Air The only access to Bario is by air on *MAS*. Bario's airstrip is very small and because of its position, flights are often cancelled because of mist and clouds. During school holidays flights are also often booked up. Connections with **Miri** and **Marudi**. **Foot** It is a 7-day trek from Marudi to Bario, sleeping in longhouses *en route*. This trip should be organized through a Miri travel agent (see page 374). *Alo Doda* is recommended. **Transport**

Limbang

Limbang is the administrative centre for the Fifth Division, and was ceded to the Brooke government by the Sultan of Brunei in 1890. The Trusan Valley, to the east of the wedge of Brunei, had been ceded to Sarawak in 1884. Very few tourists reach Limbang or Lawas but they are good stopping-off points for more adventurous routes to **Sabah** *and* **Brunei**. *Limbang is the finger of Sarawak territory which splits Brunei in two.* **Sights**
Colour map 4, grid B2

Limbang's **Old Fort** was built in 1897, renovated 1966, and was used as the administrative centre. During the Brooke era half the ground floor was used as a jail. It is now a centre of religious instruction, *Majlis Islam*. Limbang is famous for its **Pasar Tamu** every Friday, where jungle and native produce is sold. Limbang also has an attractive small museum, **Muzium Wilayah**, 400 m south of the centre along Jalan Kubu. Housed in a wooden villa, painted beige and white, the museum has a collection of ethnic artefacts from the region, including basketry, musical instruments and weapons. ■ *0900-1800, Tue-Sun*. To the right of the museum, a small road climbs the hill to a park with a man-made lake.

Trek to Gunung Mulu National Park Take a car south to Medamit; from there hire a longboat upriver to Mulu Madang, an Iban longhouse (three hours, depending on water level). Alternatively, go further upriver to Kuala Terikan (six to seven hours at low-water, four hours at high-water) where there is a simple zinc-roofed camp. From there take a longboat one hour up the Terikan River to Lubang China, which is the start of a two-hour trek along a well used trail to Camp 5. There is a park rangers' camp about 20 minutes out of Kuala Terikan where it is possible to obtain permits and arrange for a guide to meet you at Camp 5. The longboats are cheaper to hire in the wet season. **Excursions**
Sitt Travel, T085-420567, specializes in treks in this area and is the ticketing agent for Miri tour operators

Essentials

Limbang has become a sex stop for Bruneians whose government takes a more hard-line attitude to such moral transgressions and consequently many hotels and guesthouses have a fair share of short-time guests. **Sleeping**

Sarawak

B *Centre Point Hotel*, T212922. Newish place with a/c and restaurant which tops Limbang's limited bill of hotels. **B-C** *Muhibbah*, Lot T790, Bank St, T213705, F212153. Located in town centre, has seen better days, but rooms are fairly clean with a/c, TV and bathroom. **B-C** *Metro*, Lot 781, Jln Bangkita, T211133, F211051. A fairly new addition to Limbang's mid-range accommodation, under 30 rooms, all with a/c, TV, fridge, tea and coffee-making facilities, good quality beds, small but clean rooms. Recommended. **B-C** *National Inn*, 62a Jln Buangsiol, T212922, F212282. Probably the best of the 3 hotels along the river here, comfortable a/c rooms with TV, mini-bar, tea and coffee-making facilities, higher rates for river view.

Eating **Mid-range** *Tong Lok*, a/c Chinese restaurant next to *National Inn*, gruesome pink table cloths and fluorescent lighting, but good quality Chinese food. **Cheap** *Maggie's Café* on the riverside near *National Inn*, Chinese coffee shop, pleasant location, tables outside next to river in evening – braziers set up in evening for good grilled fish on banana leaf. Recommended. **Seriously cheap** *Hai Hong*, 1 block south of *Maggie's*, a simple coffee shop – good for breakfast with fried egg and chips on the menu.

Festivals **May** The movable *Buffalo Racing* festival marks the end of the harvesting season.

Transport **Air** Daily connections with **Miri**, **Mulu** and **Lawas**; weekly flights to **Labuan**; and twice weekly connections with KK. The airport is about 5 km from town and taxis ferry passengers in. **Boat** Regular connections with Lawas, departs early in the morning (2 hrs, RM15). There is also an early morning express departure to Labuan. **International connections with Brunei** Regular boat connections with Bandar Seri Begawan, Brunei (30 mins, RM15).

Directory **Useful addresses** Residents' Office: T21960.

Lawas

Lawas District was ceded to Sarawak in 1905. The Limbang River, which cuts through the town, is the main transport route. It is possible to travel from Miri to Bandar Seri Begawan (Brunei) by road, then on to Limbang and Lawas. From Lawas there are direct buses to Kota Kinabalu in Sabah.

Sleeping **A-B** *Country Park Hotel*, Lot 235, Jln Trusan, T85522, A/c, restaurant. **C** *Lawas Federal*, 8 Jln Masjid Baru, T85115. A/c, restaurant. **D** *Hup Guan Lodging House*, T85362. Some a/c, above a pool hall so can be noisy but the rooms are clean and spacious and reasonable value for money.

Transport **Air** Connections with **Miri**, **Limbang**, **Kuching**, **Labuan** and **Kota Kinabalu**. **Bus** Connections with **Merapok** on the Sarwak/Sabah border (RM5). From here there are connections to **Beaufort** in Sabah. Twice-daily connections with **Kota Kinabalu**, 4 hrs (RM20). **Boat** Regular connections to **Limbang**, 2 hrs. Daily morning boat departures for **Brunei**.

Background

About a third of the population is made up of Iban tribespeople – who used to be known as the 'Sea Dayaks' – former headhunters, who live in longhouses on the lower reaches of the rivers. Chinese immigrants, whose forebears arrived during the 19th century, make up another third. A fifth of the population is Malay; most are native Sarawakians, but some came from the peninsula after the state joined the Malaysian Federation in 1963. The rest of Sarawak's inhabitants are indigenous tribal groups, of which the main ones are the Melanau, the Bidayuh and upriver Orang Ulu such as the Kenyah, Kayan and Kelabits; the Penan are among Southeast Asia's few remaining hunter-gatherers.

For general background on Borneo, see page 502. For information on Sarawak's geography, climate, flora and fauna, page 553

For over 150 years, Sarawak was under the rule of the 'White Rajahs' who tried to keep the peace between warring tribes of headhunters. The Brooke family ran Sarawak as their private country and their most obvious legacies are the public buildings in Kuching, the state capital, and the forts along the rivers. Outside Kuching, the towns have little to offer; most are predominantly Chinese and are mainly modern, without much grace or character. One or two are boom-towns, having grown rich on the back of the logging and oil and gas industries. From a tourist's point of view, the towns are just launching-pads for the longhouses and jungle upriver.

History

Sarawak earned its place in the archaeological textbooks when a 40,000-year-old human skull belonging to a boy of about 15 was unearthed in the Niah Caves in 1958 (see page 368), predating the earliest relics found on the Malay peninsula by about 30,000 years. The caves were continuously inhabited for tens of thousands of years and many shards of Palaeolithic and Neolithic pottery, tools and jewellery as well as carved burial boats have been excavated at the site. There are also pre-historic cave paintings. In the first millennium AD, the Niah Caves were home to a prosperous community, which traded birds' nests, hornbill ivory, bezoar stones, rhinoceros horns and other jungle produce with Chinese traders in exchange for porcelain and beads.

Some of Sarawak's tribes may be descended from these cave people, although others, notably the Iban shifting cultivators, migrated from Kalimantan's Kapuas River valley from the 16th-19th centuries. Malay *Orang Laut*, sea people, migrated to Sarawak's coasts and made a living from fishing, trading and piracy. At the height of Sumatra's Srivijayan Empire in the 11th and 12th centuries, many Sumatran Malays migrated to North Borneo. Chinese traders were active along the Sarawak coast from as early as the seventh century: Chinese coins and Han pottery have been discovered at the mouth of the Sarawak River. Most of the coins and ceramics, however, date from the Chinese Song and Yuan periods in the 11th-14th centuries.

From the 14th century right up to the 20th century, Sarawak's history was inextricably intertwined with that of the neighbouring Sultanate of Brunei, which, until the arrival of the White Rajahs of Sarawak, held sway over the coastal areas of North Borneo. For a more detailed account of how Sarawak's White Rajahs came to whittle away the sultan's territory and expand into the vacuum of his receding empire.

As the Sultanate of Brunei began to decline around the beginning of the 18th century, the Malays of coastal Sarawak attempted to break free from their tributary overlord. They claimed an independent ancestry from Brunei and exercised firm control over the Dayak tribes inland and upriver. But in the early 19th century Brunei started to reassert its power over them, dispatching Pangiran Mahkota from the Brunei court

Enter James Brooke

Sarawak

to govern Sarawak in 1827 and supervise the mining of high-grade antimony ore, which was exported to Singapore to be used in medicine and as an alloy. The name 'Sarawak' comes from the Malay word *serawak*, meaning 'antimony'.

Mahkota founded Kuching, but relations with the local Malays became strained and Mahkota's problems were compounded by the marauding Ibans of the Saribas and Skrang rivers who raided coastal communities. In 1836 the local Malay chiefs, led by Datu Patinggi Ali, rebelled against Governor Mahkota, prompting the Sultan of Brunei to send his uncle, Rajah Muda Hashim to suppress the uprising. But Hashim failed to quell the disturbances and the situation deteriorated when the rebels approached the Sultan of Sambas, now in Northwest Kalimantan, for help from the Dutch. Then, in 1839, James Brooke sailed up the Sarawak River to Kuching.

Hashim was desperate to regain control and Brooke, in the knowledge that the British would support any action that countered the threat of Dutch influence, struck a deal with him. He pressed Hashim to grant him the governorship of Sarawak in exchange for suppressing the rebellion, which he duly did. In 1842 Brooke became Rajah of Sarawak. Pangiran Mahkota – the now disenfranchised former governor of Sarawak – formed an alliance with an Iban pirate chief on the Skrang River, while another Brunei prince, Pangiran Usop, joined Illanun pirates. Malaysian historian J Kathirithamby-Wells writes: "… piracy and politics became irrevocably linked and Brooke's battle against his political opponents became advertised as a morally justified war against the pirate communities of the coast."

The suppression of piracy in the 19th century became a full-time occupation for the rulers of Sarawak and Brunei – although the court of Brunei was well known to have derived a substantial chunk of its income from piracy. Rajah James Brooke believed that as long as pirates remained free to pillage the coasts, commerce would not pick up and his kingdom would never develop; ridding Sarawak's estuaries of pirates – both Iban ('Sea Dayaks') and Illanun – became an act of political survival. In his history of the White Rajahs, Robert Payne writes:

"Nearly every day people came to Kuching with tales about the pirates: how they had landed in a small creek, spread out, made their way to a village, looted everything in sight, murdered everyone they could lay their hands on, and then vanished as swiftly as they came. The Sultan of Brunei was begging for help against them."

Anti-piracy missions afforded James Brooke an excuse to extend his kingdom, as he worked his way up the coasts, 'pacifying' the Sea Dayak pirates. Brooke declared war on them and with the help of Royal Naval Captain Henry Keppel (of latter-day Singapore's Keppel Shipyard fame), he led a number of punitive raids against the Iban 'Sea Dayaks' in 1833, 1834 and 1849. "The assaults", writes DJM Tate in *Rajah Brooke's Borneo*, "largely achieved their purpose, and were applauded in the Straits, but the appalling loss of life incurred upset many drawing-room humanitarians in Britain." There were an estimated 25,000 pirates living along the North Borneo coast when Brooke became Rajah. He led many punitive expeditions against them, culminating in his notorious battle against the Saribas pirate fleet in 1849.

In that incident, Brooke ambushed and killed hundreds of Saribas Dayaks at Batang Maru. The barbarity of the ambush (which was reported in the *Illustrated London News*) outraged public opinion in Britain and in Singapore – a commission of inquiry in Singapore acquitted Brooke, but badly damaged his prestige. In the British parliament, he was cast as a 'mad despot' who had to be prevented from committing further massacres. But the action led the Sultan of Brunei to grant him the Saribas and Skrang districts (now Sarawak's Second Division) in 1853, marking the beginning of the Brookes' relentless expansionist drive. Eight years later, James Brooke persuaded the sultan to give him what became Sarawak's Third Division, after he drove out the Illanun pirates who had disrupted the sago trade from Mukah and Oya, around Bintulu.

In 1857, James Brooke ran into more trouble. Chinese Hakka goldminers, who had been in Bau (further up the Sarawak River) longer than he had been in Kuching, had grown resentful of his attempts to stamp out the opium trade and their secret societies. They attacked Kuching, set the Malay kampongs ablaze and killed several European officials; Brooke escaped by swimming across the river from his *astana*. His nephew, Charles, led a group of Skrang Dayaks to chase after the Hakka invaders, who fled across the border into Dutch Borneo; about 1,000 were killed by the Ibans on the way; 2,500 survived. Historian Robert Payne writes: "The fighting lasted for more than a month. From time to time Dayaks would return with strings of heads, which they cleaned and smoked over slow fires, especially happy when they could do this in full view of the Chinese in the bazaars who sometimes recognized people they had known." Payne says Brooke was plagued by guilt over how he handled the Chinese rebellion, for so many deaths could not easily be explained away. Neither James nor Charles ever fully trusted the Chinese again, although the Teochew, Cantonese and Hokkien merchants in Kuching never caused them any trouble.

Charles Johnson (who changed his name to Brooke after his elder brother, Brooke Johnson, had been disinherited by James for insubordination) became the second Rajah of Sarawak in 1863. He ruled for nearly 50 years. Charles did not have James Brooke's forceful personality, and was much more reclusive – probably as a result of working in remote jungle outposts for 10 years in government service. Historian Robert Payne notes that "in James Brooke there was something of the knight errant at the mercy of his dream. Charles was the pure professional, a stern soldier who thought dreaming was the occupation of fools. There was no nonsense about him." He engendered great loyalty, however, in his administrators, who he worked hard for little reward.

The second generation: Rajah Charles Brooke

Charles maintained his uncle's consultative system of government and formed a Council Negeri, or national council, comprised of his top government officials, Malay leaders and tribal headmen, which met every couple of years to hammer out policy changes. His frugal financial management meant that by 1877 Sarawak was no longer in debt and the economy gradually expanded. The country was not a wealthy one, however, and had very few natural resources – its soils proved unsuitable for agriculture. In the 1880s, Charles' faith in the Chinese community was sufficiently restored to allow Chinese immigration, and the government subsidized the new settlers. By using 'friendly' downriver Dayak groups to subdue belligerent tribes upriver, Charles managed to pacify the interior by 1880.

When Charles took over from his ailing uncle in 1863 he proved to be even more of an expansionist. In 1868 he tried to take control of the Baram River vall2ey, but London did not approve secession of the territory until 1882. It became the Fourth Division; in 1884, Charles acquired the Trusan Valley from the Sultan of Brunei, and in 1890, he annexed Limbang ending a six-year rebellion by local chiefs against the sultan. The two territories were united to form the Fifth Division, after which Sarawak completely surrounded Brunei. In 1905, the British North Borneo Chartered Company gave up the Lawas Valley to Sarawak too. "By 1890," writes Robert Payne, "Charles was ruling over a country as large as England and Scotland with the help of about 20 European officers." When the First World War broke out in 1914, Charles was in England and he ruled Sarawak from Cirencester.

At the age of 86, Charles handed the reins to his eldest son, Charles Vyner Brooke, in 1916 and died the following year. Vyner was 42 when he became Rajah and had already served his father's government for nearly 20 years. "Vyner was a man of peace, who took no delight in bloodshed and ruled with humanity and compassion," writes Robert Payne. He was a delegator by nature, and under him the old

The third generation: Charles Vyner Brooke

Sarawak

☞ James Brooke: the white knight errant

James Brooke lived the life of a Boy's Own comic-book hero. To the socialites of London, many of whom idolized him, he was the king of an exotic far-away country, on a mysterious jungled island, inhabited by roving tribes of headhunters. It was a romantic image, but while it was also a tough life, it was not far from the truth. The Brookes were a family of benevolent despots, characterized by historian Robert Payne as "tempestuous and dedicated men, who sometimes quarrelled violently among themselves, but closed ranks whenever the fortunes of their people were at stake. They were proud and possessive, but also humble." There were three White Rajahs, who ruled for over a century, but it was James Brooke, with his forceful personality, violent temper, vengeful instincts but compassion for his people, that set the tone and created the legend.

James was born in India in 1803, the son of a High Court judge in Benares. He joined the Indian army, and fought in the First Anglo-Burmese War as a cavalry officer, where he was mentioned in dispatches for "most conspicuous gallantry." But in 1825 he was hit in the chest by a bullet and almost left for dead on the battlefield. He was forced to return to England where any military ambitions he might have had were dashed by the severity of his injury. He recovered enough to make two trips to the East in the

1830s, on one of which he visited Penang and Singapore where he became an admirer of Sir Thomas Stamford Raffles, Singapore's founding father. Back in England, he bought a schooner, The Royalist, and drew up plans to sail to Maurdu Bay (North Sabah), to explore the fabled lake at Kini Ballu (see page 441). His trip did not work out as planned.

The Royalist arrived in Singapore in 1839 and the governor asked Brooke to deliver a letter of thanks to Rajah Muda Hashim, the ruler in Kuching, who had rescued some shipwrecked British sailors. He called in briefly, as promised, was intrigued with what he found, but sailed on. When he returned a year later, the Rajah Muda was still struggling to contain the rebellion of local Malay chiefs. Hashim said that if Brooke helped suppress the rebellion, he could have the Sarawak River area as his and the title of Rajah. Brooke took him up on the offer, quelled the revolt and after leaning heavily on Hashim to keep his word, became acting Rajah of Sarawak on 24 September 1841. His title was confirmed by the Sultan of Brunei the following year.

The style of Brooke's government – which also characterized that of his successors – is described by historian Mary Turnbull as "a paternal, informal government based upon consultation with local community chiefs". Brooke realized the

paternalistic style of government gave way to a more professional bureaucracy. On the centenary of the Brooke administration in September 1941, Vyner promulgated a written constitution, and renounced his autocratic powers in favour of working in co-operation with a Supreme Council. This was opposed by his nephew and heir, Anthony Brooke, who saw it as a move to undermine his succession. To protest against this, and his uncle's decision to appoint a mentally deranged Muslim English-man as his Chief Secretary, Anthony left for Singapore. The Rajah dismissed him from the service in September 1941. Three months later the Japanese Imperial Army invaded; Vyner Brooke was in Australia at the time, and his younger brother, Bertram, was ill in London.

Japanese troops took Kuching on Christmas Day 1941 having captured the Miri oilfield a few days earlier. European administrators were interned and many later died. A Kuching-born Chinese, Albert Kwok, led an armed resistance against the Jap-anese in neighbouring British North Borneo (Sabah) – see page 489 – but in Sarawak, there was no organized guerrilla movement. Iban tribespeople instilled fear into the occupying forces, however, by roaming the jungle taking Japanese heads, importance of maintaining tribal laws and observing local customs; he also recognized that without his protection, the people of Sarawak would be open to exploitation by Europeans and Chinese. He determined to keep such influences out. In 1842, shortly after he was confirmed as Rajah, he wrote: "I hate the idea of a Utopian government, with laws cut and dried ready for the natives... I am going on slowly and surely basing everything on their own laws, consulting all the headmen at every stage, instilling what I think is right – separating the abuses from the customs." Like his successors, James Brooke had great respect for the Dayaks and the Malays, whom he treated as equals. In the 1840s he wrote: "Sarawak belongs to the Malays, Sea Dayaks, Land Dayaks, Kenyahs, Milanos, Muruts, Kadayans, Bisayahs, and other tribes, and not to us. It is for them we labour, not for ourselves."

Unlike most colonial adventurers of the time, Brooke was not in it for the money. He had a hopeless head for figures and his country was constantly in debt; it would have gone bankrupt if it were not for an eccentric English spinster, Angela Burdett-Coutts, who lent him large amounts of money. In his history of The White Rajahs of Sarawak, Robert Payne wrote that "he was incapable of drawing up a balance sheet [and] could never concentrate upon details. He had the large view always and large views incline dangerously towards absolute power, and he had seized power with all the strength and cunning that was in him. He possessed the Elizabethan love for power, believing that some Englishmen are granted a special dispensation by God to wield power to the uttermost."

By pacifying pirate-infested coastal districts, Brooke persuaded the Sultan of Brunei to cede him more and more territory, so that towards the end of his reign, Sarawak was a sizeable country. An attack of smallpox, combined with the emotional traumas of a Chinese rebellion in 1857 and the public inquiry into his punitive ambush on the Saribas pirates, seems to have broken his spirit, however. His illness aged him, although an old Malay man, who knew him well, said his eyes remained "fierce like those of a crocodile". Rajah Sir James Brooke (he was knighted by Queen Victoria) visited Sarawak for the last time in 1863 following a succession dispute in which he disinherited his heir, Brooke Johnson. He retired to Dorset in England a disillusioned and embittered man. On Christmas Eve 1867 he had a stroke, and died six months later. When news of his death reached Sarawak, guns sounded a thunderous salute across the Sarawak River.

which were proudly added to much older longhouse head galleries. Despite the Brooke régime's century-long effort to stamp out head-hunting, the practice was encouraged by Tom Harrisson (one of Sarawak's most famous 'adopted' sons) who parachuted into the Kelabit Highlands towards the end of the Second World War and put together an irregular army of upriver tribesmen to fight the Japanese. He offered them 'ten-bob-a-nob' for Japanese heads. Australian forces liberated Kuching on September 11 1945 and Sarawak was placed under Australian Military Administration for seven months.

After the war, the Colonial Office in London decided the time had come to bring Sarawak into the modern era, replacing the anachronous White Rajahs, introducing an education system and building a rudimentary infrastructure. The Brookes had become an embarrassment to the British government as they continued to squabble among themselves. Anthony Brooke desperately wanted to claim what he felt was his, while the Colonial Office wanted Sarawak to become a crown colony or revert to Malay rule. No one was sure whether Sarawak wanted the Brookes back or not.

Piracy: the resurgence of an ancient scourge

The straits of Melaka and its many islands, one of the world's busiest waterways, have always had a murderous reputation. During 2000 the International Maritime Bureau *recorded a total of 220 pirate attacks on shipping in the Melaka Straits and the waters surrounding the Straits, far more than anywhere else in the world. In October/November 2001 the IMB released yet another general warning to ships negotiating the Straits recommending that they avoid anchoring along the Indonesian coast and to be extra vigilant when transiting the waters off Aceh (at the northern end of the Straits).*

Some ships just suffer hit-and-run attacks; other pirates hijack entire vessels, whose cargo is removed and the ship resold under another name. In autumn 1998 the Japanese-owned Tenyu, carrying a cargo worth US$2m, left an Indonesian port – and a day later, radio contact was lost. In December 1998 the ship, renamed and with a new crew, was discovered in a Chinese port, the original crew presumed murdered and thrown overboard. The original owners of the vessels had to pay the equivalent of nearly US$200,000 to get their ship back.

Many modern pirates use high-speed boats to escape into international waters and avoid capture by racing from one country's waters into another's.

Co-operative international action offers the only way to successfully patrol the shipping lanes. Following the IMB conference, a Regional Piracy Centre was set up in Kuala Lumpur.

But, while modern shipping companies might consider the rise in piracy a new and dangerous threat, there is nothing new about piracy in Southeast Asian waters. For centuries, pirates have murdered and pillaged their way along the region's coasts, taking hundreds of slaves as part of their booty. As far back as the 6th century, pirates are thought to have been responsible for the destruction and abandonment of the ancient Hindu capital of Langkasuka, in the northwest Malaysian state of Kedah. Piracy grew as trade flourished: the Strait of Melaka and the South China Sea were perfect haunts, being on the busy trade routes between China, India, the Middle East and Europe. Most of the pirates were the Malay Orang Laut (sea gypsies) and Bugis who lived in the Riau Archipelago, the Acehnese of North Sumatra, the Ibans of the Sarawak estuaries and – most feared of all – the Illanun and Balinini pirates of Sulu and Mindanao in the Philippines. The Illanuns were particularly ferocious pirates, sailing in huge perahus with up to 150 slaves as oarsmen, in as many as three tiers. The name lanun means pirate in Malay.

The end of empire In February 1946 the ageing Vyner shocked his brother Bertram and his nephew Anthony, the Rajah Muda (or heir apparent), by issuing a proclamation urging the people of Sarawak to accept the King of England as their ruler. In doing so he effectively handed the country over to Britain. Vyner thought the continued existence of Sarawak as the private domain of the Brooke family an anachronism; but Anthony thought it a betrayal. The British government sent a commission to Sarawak to ascertain what the people wanted. In May 1946, the Council Negri agreed – by a 19-16 majority – to transfer power to Britain, provoking protests and demonstrations and resulting in the assassination of the British governor by a Malay in Sibu in 1949. He and three other anti-cessionists were sentenced to death. Two years later, Anthony Brooke, who remained deeply resentful about the demise of the Brooke Dynasty, abandoned his claim and urged his supporters to end their campaign.

As a British colony, Sarawak's economy expanded and oil and timber production increased which funded the much-needed expansion of education and health services. As with British North Borneo (Sabah), Britain was keen to give Sarawak political independence and, following Malaysian independence in 1957, saw the best means to this end as being through the proposal of Malaysian Prime Minister Tunku Abdul Rahman, who suggested the formation of a federation to include Singapore, Sarawak, Sabah and Brunei as well as the peninsula. In the end, Brunei opted out, Singapore left after two years, but Sarawak and Sabah joined the federation, having accepted the recommendations of the British government. Indonesia's President Sukarno denounced the move, claiming it was all part of a neo-colonialist conspiracy. He declared a policy of confrontation – *Konfrontasi*. A United Nations commission which was sent to ensure that the people of Sabah and Sarawak wanted to be part of Malaysia reported that Indonesia's objections were unfounded.

Communists had been active in Sarawak since the 1930s. The *Konfrontasi* afforded the Sarawak Communist Organization (SCO) Jakarta's support against the Malaysian government. The SCO joined forces with the North Kalimantan Communist Party (NKCO) and were trained and equipped by Indonesia's President Sukarno. But following Jakarta's brutal suppression of the Indonesian Communists, the Partai Komunis Indonesia (PKI), in the wake of the attempted coup in 1965, Sarawak's Communists fled back across the Indonesian border, along with their Kalimantan comrades. There they continued to wage guerrilla war against the Malaysian government throughout the 1970s. The Sarawak state government offered amnesties to guerrillas wanting to come out of hiding. In 1973 the NKCP leader surrendered along with 482 other guerrillas. A handful remained in the jungle, most of them in the hills around Kuching. The last surrendered in 1990.

Politics and modern Malaysia

In 1957 Kuala Lumpur was keen to have Sarawak and Sabah in the Federation of Malaysia and offered the two states a degree of autonomy, allowing their local governments control over state finances, agriculture and forestry. Sarawak's racial mix was reflected in its chaotic state politics. The Ibans dominated the Sarawak National Party (SNAP), which provided the first Chief Minister, Datuk Stephen Kalong Ningkan. He raised a storm over Kuala Lumpur's introduction of Bahasa Malaysia in schools and complained bitterly about the federal government's policy of filling the Sarawakian civil service with Malays from the peninsula. An 'us' and 'them' mentality developed: in Sarawak, the Malay word *semenanjung* – peninsula – was used to label the newcomers. To many, semenanjung was Malaysia, Sarawak was Sarawak.

In 1966 the federal government ousted the SNAP, and a new Muslim-dominated government led by the Sarawak Alliance took over in Kuching. But there was still strong political opposition to federal encroachment. Throughout the 1970s, as in Sabah, Sarawak's strongly Muslim government drew the state closer and closer to the peninsula: it supported *Rukunegara* – the policy of Islamization – and promoted the use of Bahasa Malaysia. Muslims make up less than one-third of the population of Sarawak. The Malays, Melanaus and Chinese communities grew rich from the timber industry; the Ibans and the Orang Ulu (the upriver tribespeople) saw little in the way of development. They did not reap the benefits of the expansion of education and social services, they were unable to get public sector jobs and to make matters worse, logging firms were encroaching on their native lands and threatening their traditional lifestyles.

It has only been in more recent years that the tribespeoples' political voice has been heard at all. In 1983, Iban members of SNAP – which was a part of Prime Minister Dr Mahathir Mohamad's ruling Barisan Nasional (National Front) coalition – split to form the Party Bansa Dayak Sarawak (PBDS), which, although it initially remained in the coalition, became more outspoken on native affairs. At about the same time, international outrage was sparked over the exploitation of Sarawak's tribespeople by politicians and businessmen involved in the logging industry. The plight of the

Politics

Sarawak

☞ Konfrontasi

The birth of the Federation of Malaysia on August 31 1963 was not helped by the presence of heckling spectators. The Philippines was opposed to British North Borneo (Sabah) joining the federation because the territory had been a dependency of the Sultan of Sulu for over 170 years until he had agreed to lease it to the North Borneo Chartered Company in 1877. But Indonesia's objection to the formation of the federation was even more vociferous. In Jakarta, crowds were chanting 'Crush Malaysia!' at President Sukarno's bidding. He launched an undeclared war against Malaysia, which became known as konfrontasi, or confrontation.

Indonesian armed forces made numerous incursions across the jungled frontier between Kalimantan and the two new East Malaysian states; it also landed commandos on the Malaysian peninsula and despatched 300 saboteurs who infiltrated Singapore and launched a bombing campaign. Sarawakian Communists fought alongside Indonesians in the Konfrontasi and there were countless skirmishes with Malaysian and British counter-terrorist forces in which many were killed. Sukarno even managed to secure Soviet weapons, dispatched by Moscow "to help Indonesia crush Malaysia". Konfrontasi fizzled out in 1965 following the Communist-inspired coup attempt in Indonesia, which finally dislodged Sukarno from power.

Penan hunter-gatherers came to world attention due to their blockades of logging roads (see page 384) and the resulting publicity highlighted the rampant corruption and greed that characterized modern Sarawak's political economy.

The National Front remain firmly in control in Sarawak. But unlike neighbouring Sabah, or indeed any other state in the country with the exception of the PAS-ruled states on the Peninsula's east coast, Sarawak's politicians are not dominated by the centre. The chief minister of Sarawak is Taib Mahmud, a Melanau, and his Parti Pesaka Bumiputra Bersatu is a member of the UMNO-dominated National Front. But in Sarawak itself UMNO wields little power.

While the Anwar case dominated political debate on the Peninsula in the months leading up to the elections in 1999 and led many voters – especially the young – to vote against UMNO, this was not the case in Sarawak which, even in political terms, can sometimes seem a world apart. Furthermore, Sarawak survived the economic crisis relatively unscathed, so even this did not carry much influence in the campaign. The ruling National Front won the election in Sarawak with much to spare, successfully playing on voters' local concerns and grievances. The opposition DAP, which in the last election won just one seat, was hamstrung by a long-running and acrimonious dispute between the DAP national leader, Lim Kit Siang, and local strongman Sim Kwang Yang which led the latter to join the Parti Keadilan Nasional. The problem for the opposition was that local people think that it is the state legislature which can make a difference, not the federal parliament in KL which seems distant and ineffective. For this reason, UMNO does not have a presence and it is the Parti Pesaka Bumiputra Bersatu which represents Sarawak in the National Front. The most recent indication of political inclinations in Sarwak came in a legislative assembly election held on September 27th 2001: the National Front won 60 out of 62 seats and the opposition PAS and Keadilan ended the night empty handed.

The challenge of getting the voters out in some of the most remote areas of the country was clearly illustrated in Long Lidom. There it cost the government RM65,000 to provide a helicopter to poll just seven Punan Busang in a longhouse on the Upper Kajang, close to the border with Indonesia. Datuk Omar of the election

Commission said that mounting the general election in Sarawak, with its 28 parliamentary seats, was a "logistical nightmare". Along with a small air force of helicopters, the Commission used 1,032 long boats, 15 speed boats and 3,054 land cruisers. The Commission's workforce numbered a cool 13,788 workers in a state with a population of just two million.

Today there are many in Sarawak as well as in Sabah, who wish their governments had opted out of the Federation like Brunei. Sarawak is of great economic importance to Malaysia, thanks to its oil, gas and timber. The state now accounts for more than one-third of Malaysia's petroleum production (worth more than US$800m per year) and more than half of its natural gas. As with neighbouring Sabah however, 95% of Sarawak's oil and gas revenues go directly into federal coffers.

A famous cartoon in a Sarawak newspaper once depicted a cow grazing in Sarawak and being milked on the peninsula. While Sarawak has traditionally been closer to federal government than Sabah (there has never been any hint of a secessionist movement), discontent surfaces from time to time. In late 1989, all it took was a quarrel over a football match between Sarawak and Selangor state to touch off deep-seated resentments in Kuching.

Culture

About 30% of Sarawak's population is Iban, another 30% Chinese, 20% is Malay and the remaining 20% is divided into other tribal groups. The total population of the state in 1999 was a shade over 2 million – 2,027,100 – less than one tenth of the total population of Malaysia. The people of the interior are classified as Proto-Malays and Deutero-Malays and are divided into at least 12 distinct tribal groups including Iban, Murut (see page 481), Melanau, Bidayuh, Kenyah, Kayan, Kelabit and Penan. In upriver Dayak communities, both men and women traditionally distend their earlobes with brass weights – long earlobes are considered a beauty feature – and practise extensive body tattooing. For the longhouse communities, the staple diet is hill rice, which is cultivated with slash-and-burn farming techniques.

People

For those intending to visit any of Sarawak's tribal peoples, see page 347

Malay About half of Sarawak's 300,000-strong Malay community lives around the state capital; most of the other half lives in the Limbang Division, near Brunei. The Malays traditionally live near the coast, although today there are small communities far upriver. There are some old wooden Malay houses, with carved façades, in the kampongs along the banks of the Sarawak River in Kuching; other traditional Malay houses still stand on Ha Datus in Kuching. In all Malay communities, the mosque is the centre of the village, but while their faith is important to them, the strictures of Islam are generally less rigorously enforced in Sarawak than on the peninsula. Of all the Malays in Malaysia, the Sarawak Malays are probably the most easy-going. During the days of the White Rajahs, the Malays were recruited into government service, as they were on the Malay peninsula. They were renowned as good administrators and the men were mostly literate in Jawi script. Over the years there has been much intermarriage between the Malay and Melanau communities. Traditionally, the Malays were fishermen and farmers.

Chinese Hakka goldminers had already settled at Bau, upriver from Kuching, long before James Brooke arrived in 1839. Cantonese, Teochew and Hokkien merchants also set up in Kuching, but the Brookes did not warm to the Chinese community, believing the traders would exploit the Dayak communities if they were allowed to venture upriver. In the 1880s, however, Rajah Charles Brooke allowed the immigration of large numbers of Chinese – mainly Foochow – who settled in coastal towns like Sibu (see page 349). Many became farmers and ran rubber

Shifting cultivation – how to grow hill rice

Winding upriver on Sarawak's express boats, it is hard not to notice that the hillsides on either bank have been shaved of their jungle: evidence of shifting cultivation (see page 556). The Iban, who live in the middle reaches of Sarawak's big rivers, have always been shifting cultivators; the deep peat soils meant it was impossible to farm wet-rice. Any secondary forest (belukar) seen growing on the riverside slopes is really just fallow land, and in 8-15 years' time, it will be cut again and the ladang will be replanted. The Malaysian government claims there are three million hectares of land like this in Sarawak, left idle, through slash-and-burn cultivation. In defence of its environmental record, it says shifting cultivators are more destructive than logging firms and cause serious soil erosion.

What the government tends to overlook, however, is that the rivers were clear before the loggers arrived and that the swidden farmers, in labour terms, managed highly productive agricultural systems. As long as the land is allowed to lie fallow for long enough, the Iban can produce rice with far less effort than lowland wet rice farmers. The Iban clear their designated hillsides in the middle of the year and burn them off in August. In September, planting starts: holes are made in the soot-blackened soil with sharp-pointed dibble-sticks called tugal. Women drop a few grains into each hole and the rice is interplanted with maize. Harvesting is done by the women, who use special knives called ketap.

smallholdings. The Sarawak government subsidized the immigrants for the first year. During the Brooke era, the only government-funded schools were for Malays and few tribal people ever received a formal education. The Chinese, however, set up and funded their own private schools and many attended Christian missionary schools, so they formed a relatively prosperous, educated élite. Now the Chinese comprise nearly a third of the state's population and are almost as numerous as the Iban; they are the middlemen, traders, shopkeepers, timber *towkays* (magnates) and express-boat owners. At the last census on 30 June 1990, the Chinese population numbered 483,301 with similar numbers of Foochow and Hakka (each representing 32% of the total), being the largest groups. Hokkien constitute 13% of the Chinese population, and Teochew, 9%.

Iban Sarawak's best known erstwhile head-hunters make up nearly a third of the state's population and while some have moved to coastal towns for work, many remain in their traditional longhouses. But with Iban men now earning good money in the timber and oil industries, it is increasingly common to see longhouses bristling with television aerials, equipped with fridges, self-cleaning ovens and flush-toilets, and with Land Cruisers in the car park. Even modern longhouses retain the traditional features of gallery, verandah and doors. The Iban are an outgoing people and usually extend a warm welcome to visitors. Iban women are skilled weavers; even today a girl is not considered eligible until she has proven her skills at the loom by weaving a ceremonial textile, the *pua kumbu* (see page 407). The Ibans love to party, and during the harvest festival in June, visitors are particularly welcome to drink copious amounts of *tuak* (rice wine) and dance through the night.

The Iban are shifting cultivators who originated in the Kapuas River basin of West Kalimantan and migrated into Sarawak's Second Division in the early 16th century, settling along the Batang Lupar, Skrang and Saribas rivers. By the early 19th century, they had begun to spill into the Rejang River valley. It was this growing pressure on land as more and more migrants settled in the river valleys that

Tribal tattoos

Tattooing is practised by many indigenous groups in Borneo, but the most intricate designs are those of the upriver Orang Ulu tribes. Designs vary from group to group and for different parts of the body. Circular designs are mostly used for the shoulder, chest or wrists, while stylized dragon-dogs (aso), scorpions and dragons are used on the thigh and, for the Iban, on the throat. Tattoos can mean different things; for the man it is a symbol of bravery and for women, a good tattoo is a beauty feature. More elaborate designs often denote high social status in Orang Ulu communities – the Kayans, for example, reserved the aso design for the upper classes and slaves were barred from tattooing themselves at all. In these Orang Ulu groups, the women have the most impressive tattoos; the headman's daughter has her hands, arms and legs completely covered in a finely patterned tattoo. Designs are first carved on a block of wood, which is then smeared with ink. The design is printed on the body and then punctured into the skin with needles dipped in ink, usually made from a mixture of sugar, water and soot. Rice is smeared over the inflamed area to prevent infection, but it usually swells up for some time.

Tattooed Kenowit, with pendulous earlobes
Illustrated London News, 10 November 1849

led to fighting and headhunting (see page 404). Probably because they were shifting cultivators, the Iban remained in closely bonded family groups and were a classless society. Historian Mary Turnbull says "they retained their pioneer social organization of nuclear family groups living together in longhouses and did not evolve more sophisticated political institutions. Long-settled families acquired prestige, but the Ibans did not merge into tribes and had neither chiefs, *rakyat* class, nor slaves."

The Ibans joined local Malay chiefs and turned to piracy – which is how Europeans first came into contact with them. They were dubbed Sea Dayaks as a result – which is really a misnomer as they are an inland people. The name stuck, however, and in the eyes of Westerners, it distinguished them from Land Dayaks, who were the Bidayuh people from the Sarawak River area (see page 402). While Rajah James Brooke only won the Ibans' loyalty after he had crushed them in battle (see page 392), he had great admiration for them, and they bore no bitterness towards him. He once described them as "good-looking a set of men, or devils, as one could cast eye on. Their wiry and supple limbs might have been compared to the troops of wild horses that followed Mazeppa in his perilous flight." The Iban have a very easygoing attitude to love and sex, which is best explained in Redmond O'Hanlon's book *Into the Heart of Borneo*. Free love is the general rule among Iban communities which have not become evangelical Christians, although once married, the Iban divorce rate is low and they are monogamous.

Melanau The Melanau are a relaxed and humorous people. Rajah James Brooke, like generations of men before and after him, thought the Melanau girls particularly pretty. He said that they had "agreeable countenances, with the dark, rolling,

The palang – the stimulant that makes a vas diferens

One of the more exotic features of upriver sexuality is the palang, or penis pin, which is the versatile jungle version of the French tickler. Traditionally, women suffer heavy weights being attached to their earlobes to enhance their sex appeal. In turn, men are expected to enhance their physical attributes and entertain their womenfolk by drilling a hole in their organs, into which they insert a range of items, aimed at heightening their partner's pleasure on the rattan mat. Tom Harrisson, a former curator of the Sarawak Museum, was intrigued by the palang; some suspect his authority on the subject stemmed from first-hand experience. He wrote: "When the device is put into use, the owner adds whatever he prefers to elaborate and accentuate its intention. A lively range of objects can so be employed – from pigs' bristles and bamboo shavings to pieces of metal, seeds, beads and broken glass. The effect, of course, is to enlarge the diameter of the male organ inside the female." It is said that many Dayak men, even today, have the tattoo man come and drill a hole in them as they stand in the river. As the practice has gone on for centuries, one can only assume that its continued popularity proves it is worth the agony.

open eye of the Italians, and nearly as fair as most of that race". The Melanau live along the coast between the Baram and Rejang rivers; originally they lived in magnificent communal houses built high off the ground, like the one that has been reconstructed at the Cultural Village in Kuching, but these have long since disappeared. The houses were designed to afford protection from incessant pirate raids (see page 392), for the Melanau were easy pickings, being coastal people. Their stilt-houses were often up to 12m off the ground. Today most Melanau live in Malay-style pile-houses facing the river. Hedda Morrison, in her classic 1957 book *Sarawak*, says: "As a result of living along the rivers in swamp country, the Melanaus are an exceptionally amphibious people. The children learn to swim almost before they can walk. Nearly all progress is by canoe, sometimes even to visit the house next door."

The traditional Melanau fishing boat is called a *barong*. Melanau fishermen employed a unique fishing technique. They would anchor palm leaves at sea as they discovered that shoals of fish would seek refuge under them. After rowing out to the leaves, one fisherman would dive off his barong and chase the fish into the nets which his colleague hung over the side. The Melanaus were also noted for their sago production – which they ate instead of rice. At Kuching's Cultural Village there is a demonstration of traditional sago production, showing how the starch-bearing pith is removed, mashed, dried and ground into flour. Most Melanau are now Muslim and have assimilated with the Malays through intermarriage. Originally, however, they were animists (animist Melanau are called *Likaus*) and were particularly famed for their elaborately carved 'sickness images', which represented the form of spirits which caused specific illnesses (see page 409).

Bidayuh In the 19th century, Sarawak's European community called the Bidayuh Land Dayaks, mainly to distinguish them from the Iban Sea Dayak pirates. The Bidayuh make up 8.4% of the population and are concentrated to the west of the Kuching area, towards the Kalimantan border. There are also related groups living in West Kalimantan. They were virtually saved from extinction by the White Rajahs. Because the Bidayuh were quiet, mild-mannered people, they were at the mercy of the Iban head-hunters and the Brunei Malays who taxed and enslaved them. The Brookes afforded them protection from both groups.

Most live in modern longhouses and are dry rice farmers. Their traditional

Green pen pals: Mahathir versus Manser

Few people infuriate Prime Minister Datuk Seri Mahathir Mohamad more than Bruno Manser, green activist and self-styled defender of the tribal peoples of Borneo, and particularly the Penan. The Swiss Manser spent six years living with the Penan and now fights for their rights. Mahathir's views on Manser, 'green imperialism' in general, and the 'plight' of the tribals comes through nowhere clearer than in a letter he wrote to Manser in March 1992:

Herr Manser,
If any Penan or policeman gets killed or wounded in the course of restoring law and order in Sarawak, you will have to take the blame. It is you and your kind who instigated the Penans to take the law into their own hands and to use poison darts, bows, arrows and parangs to fight against the Government.

As a Swiss living in the laps of luxury with the world's highest standard of living, it is the height of arrogance for you to advocate that the Penans live on maggots and monkeys in their miserable huts, subjected to all kinds of diseases. It is fine for you to spend a short holiday tasting the Penan way of life and then returning to the heated comfort of your Swiss chalet. But do you really expect the Penans to subsist on monkeys until the year 2500 or 3000 or forever? Have they no right to a better way of life? What right have you to condemn them to a primitive life forever?

Your Swiss ancestors were hunters also. But you are now one of the most 'advanced' people living in beautiful Alpine villages, with plenty of leisure and very high income. But you want to deny even a slight rise in the standard of living for the Penans and other Malaysians.

The Penans may tell you that their primitive life is what they like. That is because they are not given a chance to live a better life like the other tribes in Sarawak. Those of the Penans who have left the jungle are educated and are earning a better living have no wish to return to their primitive ways. You are trying to deny them their chance for a better life so that you can enjoy studying primitive peoples the way you study animals. Penans are people and they should be respected as people. If you had a chance to be educated and live a better life, they too deserve that chance.

Stop being arrogant and thinking that it is the white man's burden to decide the fate of the peoples in this world. Malaysians, the Penans included, are an independent people and are quite capable of looking after themselves. Swiss imperialism is as disgusting as other European imperialism. It is about time that you stop your arrogance and your intolerable European superiority. You are no better than the Penans. If you have a right to decide for yourself, why can't you leave the Penans to decide for themselves after they have been given a chance to improve their living standards.
Dr Mahathir Mohamad
Reproduced in Far Eastern Economic Review, 27 August 1992

longhouses are exactly like Iban ones, but without the *tanju* verandah. The Bidayuh tribe comprises five sub-groups: the Jagoi, Biatah, Bukar-Sadong, Selakau and Lara, all of whom live in far West Sarawak. They are the state's best traditional plumbers, and are known for their ingenious gravity-fed bamboo water-supply systems. They are bamboo-specialists, making everything from cooking pots and utensils to finely carved musical instruments (see page 408) from it. Among other tribal groups, the Bidayuh are renowned for their rice wine and sugar cane toddy. Henry Keppel, who with Rajah James Brooke fought the Bidayuhs' dreaded enemies, the Sea Dayaks, described an evening spent with the Land Dayaks thus: "They ate and drank, and asked for everything, but stole nothing."

👉 ## Skulls in the longhouse: heads you win

Although head-hunting has been largely stamped out in Borneo, there is still the odd reported case, once every few years. But until the early 20th century, head hunting was commonplace among many Dayak tribes and the Iban were the most fearsome of all. Following a head-hunting expedition, the freshly taken heads were skinned, placed in rattan nets and smoked over a fire, or sometimes boiled. The skulls were then hung from the rafters of the longhouse and they possessed the most powerful form of magic.

The skulls were considered trophies of manhood (they increased a young bachelor's eligibility), symbols of bravery and they testified to the unity of a longhouse. The longhouse had to hold festivals – or gawai – to appease the spirits of the skulls. Once placated, the heads were believed to bring great blessing – they could ward off evil spirits, save villages from epidemics, produce rain and increase the yield of rice harvests. Heads that were insulted or ignored were capable of wreaking havoc in the form of bad dreams, plagues, floods and fires. To keep the spirits of the skulls happy, they would be offered food and cigarettes and made to feel welcome in their new home. Because the magical powers of a skull faded with time, fresh heads were always in demand. Tribes without heads were considered spiritually weak.

Today, young Dayak men no longer have to take heads to gain respect. They are, however, expected to go on long journeys (the equivalent of the Australian aborigines' Walkabout), or bejalai in Iban. The one unspoken rule is that they should come back with plenty of good stories, and, these days, as most bejalai expeditions translate into stints at timber camps or on oil rigs, they are expected to come home bearing video recorders, TV sets and motorbikes. Many Dayak tribes continue to celebrate their head-hunting ceremonies. In Kalimantan, for example, the Adat Ngayau ceremony uses coconut shells, wrapped in leaves, as substitutes for freshly cut heads.

Dayak decorated human skull
Adapted from Hersey, Irwin (1991) Indonesian Primitive Art, OUP: Singapore

Orang Ulu The jungle, or upriver, people encompass a swathe of different small tribal groups. Orang Ulu longhouses are usually made of belian (ironwood) and are built to last. They are well known swordsmiths, forging lethal *parangs* from any piece of scrap metal they can lay their hands on. They are also very artistic people, are skilled carvers and painters and are famed for their beadwork – taking great care decorating even simple household utensils. Most Orang Ulu are plastered with traditional tattoos (see box, page 401).

Kenyah and Kayan These two closely related groups were the traditional rivals of the Ibans and were notorious for their warlike ways. Historian Robert Payne, in his history *The White Rajahs of Sarawak* described the Kayans of the upper Rejang as "a treacherous tribe, [who] like nothing better than putting out the eyes and cutting the throats of prisoners, or burning them alive". They probably originally migrated into Sarawak from the Apo Kayan district in East Kalimantan. Kenyah and Kayan raids on downriver people were greatly feared, but their power was broken by Charles Brooke, just before he became the second White Rajah, in 1863. The Kayans had retreated upstream above the Pelagus Rapids on the Rejang River (see page 356), to an area they considered out of reach from their Iban enemies. In 1862 they killed two government officers at Kanowit and went on a killing spree. Charles Brooke led 15,000 Ibans past the Pelagus Rapids, beyond Belaga and attacked the Kayans in their heartland. Many hundreds were killed. In November 1924, Rajah Vyner Brooke presided over a peace-making ceremony between the Orang Ulu and the Iban in Kapit (there is a photograph of the ceremony on display in the Kapit Museum).

The Kenyahs and Kayans in Sarawak live in pleasant upriver valleys and are settled rice farmers. They are very different from other tribal groups, have a completely different language (which has ancient Malayo-Polynesian roots) and are class-conscious, with a well-defined social hierarchy. Traditionally their society was composed of aristocrats, noblemen, commoners and slaves (who were snatched during raids on other tribes). One of the few things the Kayan and Kenyah have in common with other Dayak groups is the fact that they live in longhouses, although even these are of a different design, and are much more carefully constructed, in ironwood. Subgroups include the Kejamans, Skapans, Berawans and Sebops. Many have now been converted to Christianity.

In contrast to their belligerent history, the Kenyahs and Kayans are much more introverted than the Ibans; they are slow and deliberate in their ways, and are very artistic and musical. They are also renowned for their parties; visitors recovering from drinking *borak* rice beer have their faces covered in soot before being thrown in the river. This is to test the strength of the newly forged friendship with visitors, who are ill-advised to lose their sense of humour on such occasions.

Penan Perhaps Southeast Asia's only remaining true hunter-gatherers live mainly in the upper Rejang area and Limbang. They are nomads and are related, linguistically at least, to the Punan, former nomadic forest-dwellers who are now settled in longhouses along the upper Rejang. The Malaysian government has long wanted the Penan to sedentarise too, but has had limited success in attracting them to expensive new longhouses. Groups of Penan hunter-gatherers still wander through the forest in groups to hunt wild pigs, birds and monkeys and search for sago palms from which they make their staple food, sago flour. The Penan are considered to be the jungle experts by all the other inland tribes. Because they live in the shade of the forest, their skin is relatively fair. They have a great affection for the coolness of the forest and until the 1960s were rarely seen by the outside world. For them sunlight is extremely unpleasant. They are broad and much more stocky than other river people and are extremely shy, having had little contact with the outside world. Most of their trade is conducted with remote Kayan, Kenyah and Kelabit longhouse communities on the edge of the forest.

In the eyes of the West, the Penan have emerged as the 'noble savages' of the late 20th century for their spirited defence of their lands against encroachment by logging companies. But it is not just recently that they have been cheated: they have long been the victims of other upriver tribes. A Penan, bringing baskets full of rotan to a Kenyah or Kayan longhouse to sell may end up exchanging his produce for one bullet or shotgun cartridge. In his way of thinking, a bullet will kill one wild boar which will last his family 10 days. In turn, the buyer knows he can sell the same rotan downstream for RM50-100. Penan still use the blowpipe for small game, but shotguns for wild pig. If they buy the shotgun cartridges for themselves, they have to exchange empties first. Some of their shotguns date back to the Second World War, when the British supplied them to upriver tribespeople to fight the Japanese. During the Brooke era, a large annual market would be held which both Chinese traders and Orang Ulu (including Penan) used to attend; the district officer would have to act as judge to ensure the Penan did not get cheated.

👉 ## Festivals in Sarawak

Most of Malaysia's mainstream festivals are celebrated in Sarawak, including Chinese New Year, Christmas and Hari Raya. But there are also some festivals that are peculiarly Sarawakian:

- Gawai Dayak *(31st May – 1st June);* Sarawak's major home-grown festival, marking the end of the rice harvest. Vast quantities of food are prepared and tuak brewed. Urban residents return to their rural roots for a major binge.
- Kaul *(moveable, mid-March – early April): celebrated by the Melanau community. Although the Melanu are now largely Muslim and Christian, this animist festival continues to be celebrated – most enthusiatically in the coastal town of Mukah. Fishermen appease the spirits of the sea before the onset of the fishing season by launching miniature wooden boats. Young men compete in a game known as tibou where they see how many can swing from a single rope.*

Those wishing to learn more about the Penan should refer to Denis Lau's *The Vanishing Nomads of Borneo* (Interstate Publishing, 1987). Lau has lived among the Penan and has photographed them for many years; some of his recent photographs appear in the photographic collection entitled *Malaysia – Heart of Southeast Asia* (published by Archipelago Press, 1991).

Kelabit The Kelabits, who live in the highlands at the headwaters of the Baram River, are closely related to the Murut (see page 481) and the Lun Dayeh of Kalimantan. It was into Kelabit territory that Tom Harrisson parachuted with Allied Special Forces towards the end of the Second World War. The Kelabit Highlands around Bario were chosen because they were so remote. Of all the tribes in Sarawak, the Kelabits have the sturdiest, strongest builds, which is usually ascribed to the cool and invigorating mountain climate. They are skilled hill-rice farmers and their fragrant Bario rice is prized throughout Sarawak. The highland climate also allows them to cultivate vegetables. Kelabit parties are also famed as boisterous occasions, and large quantities of *borak* rice beer are consumed – despite the fact that the majority of Kelabits have converted to Christianity. They are regarded as among the most hospitable people in Borneo. For information on religion, see page 539.

Dance, drama and music

Dance Dayak tribes are renowned for their singing and dancing, and the most famous is the hornbill dance. In her book *Sarawak*, Hedda Morrison writes: "The Kayans are probably the originators of the stylized war dance which is now common among the Ibans but the girls are also extremely talented and graceful dancers. One of their most delightful dances is the hornbill dance, when they tie hornbill feathers to the ends of their fingers which accentuate their slow and graceful movements. For party purposes everyone in the longhouse joins in and parades up and down the communal room led by one or two musicians and a group of girls who sing." On these occasions, drink flows freely. With the Ibans, it is *tuak* (rice wine), with the Kayan and Kenyah it is *borak*, a bitter rice beer. After being entertained by dancers, a visitor is under compunction to drink a large glassful, before bursting into song and doing a dance routine themselves. The best guideline for visitors on how to handle such occasions is provided by Redmond O'Hanlon in his book *Into the Heart of Borneo*. The general rule of thumb is to be prepared to make an absolute fool of yourself, throwing all inhibition to the wind. This will immediately endear you to your hosts.

Sarawak

The most common dances in Sarawak are: *Kanjet Ngeleput* (Orang Ulu) dance performed in full warrior regalia, traditionally celebrating the return of a hunter or head-hunters. *Mengarang Menyak* (Melanau) dance depicting the processing of sago from the cutting of the tree to the production of the sago pearls or pellets. *Ngajat Bebunuh* (Iban) war dance, performed in full battle dress and armed with sword and shield. *Ngajat Induk* (Iban) performed as a welcome dance for those visiting longhouses. *Ngajat Lesong* (Iban) dance of the *lesong* or mortar, performed during gawai. *Tarian Kris* (Malay) dance of the *kris*, the Malay dagger, which symbolizes power, courage and strength. *Tarian Rajang Beuh* (Bidayuh) dance performed after the harvesting season as entertainment for guests to the longhouse. *Tarian Saga Lupa* (Orang Ulu) performed by women to welcome guests to the longhouse, accompanied by the *sape* (see below). *Ule Nugan* (Orang Ulu) dance to the sound of the *kerebo bulo*, or bamboo slates. The music is designed to inspire the spirit of the paddy seeds to flourish. The male dancers hold a dibbling stick used in the planting of hill rice.

Music

Gongs range from the single large gong, the tawak, to the engkerumong, a set of small gongs, arranged on a horizontal rack, with five players. An engkerumong ensemble usually involves between five and seven drums, which include two suspended gongs (tawak and bendai) and five hour-glass drums (ketebong). They are used to celebrate victory in battle or to welcome home a successful head-hunting expedition. Sarawak's Bidayuh also make a bamboo gong called a pirunchong. The jatang uton is a wooden xylophone which can be rolled up like a rope ladder; the keys are struck with hardwood sticks.

The Bidayuh, Sarawak's bamboo-specialists, make two main stringed instruments: a three-stringed cylindrical bamboo harp called a tinton and the rabup, a rotan-stringed fiddle with a bamboo cup. The Orang Ulu (Kenyah and Kayan tribes) play a four-stringed guitar called a sape, which is also common on the Kalimantan side of the border. It is the most common and popular lute-type instrument, whose body, neck and board are cut from one piece of softwood. It is used in Orang Ulu dances and by witch doctors. It is usually played by two musicians, one keeping the rhythm, the other the melody. Traditional sapes had rotan strings, today they use wire guitar strings and electric pick-ups. Another stringed instrument, more usually found in Kalimantan, or deep in Sarawak's interior, is the *satang*, a bamboo tube with strings around the outside, cut from the bamboo and tightened with pegs.

One of the best known instruments in Sarawak is the engkerurai (or *keluri*), the bagpipes of Borneo, which is usually associated with the Kenyahs and Kayans, but is also found in Sabah (where it is called a *sompoton*). It is a hand-held organ in which four vertical bamboo pan-pipes of different lengths are fixed to a gourd, which acts as the wind chamber. Simple engkerurai can only manage one chord; more sophisticated ones allow the player to use two pipes for the melody, while the others provide an harmonic drone. The Bidayuh are specialists in bamboo instruments and make flutes of various sizes; big thick ones are called branchi, long ones with five holes are kroto and small ones are called nchiyo.

Crafts

The weaving of cotton *pua kumbu* is one of the oldest Iban traditions, and literally means 'blanket' or 'cover'. Iban legend recounts that 24 generations ago the God of War, Singalang Burong, taught his son how to weave the most precious of all *pua*, the *lebor api*. Dyed deep red, this cloth was traditionally used to wrap heads taken in battle.

Textiles

Sarawak

The weaving of *pua kumbu* is done by the women and is a vital skill for a would-be bride to acquire. There are two main methods employed in making and decorating pua kumbu: the more common is the *ikat* tie-dyeing technique, known as *ngebat* by the Iban. The other method is the *pileh*, or floating weft. The Ibans use a warp-beam loom which is tied to two posts, to which the threads are attached. There is a breast-beam at the weaving end, secured by a back strap to the weaver. A pedal, beneath the threads, lowers and raises the alternate threads which are separated by rods. The woven material is tightly packed by a beater. The material is tie-dyed in the warp.

Because the pua kumbu is made by the warp-tie-dyeing method, the number of colours is limited. The most common are a rich browny-brick-red colour and black, as well as the undyed white sections; blues and greens are used in more modern materials. Traditionally, pua kumbu were hung in longhouses during ceremonies and were used to cover images during rituals. The designs and patterns are representations of deities which figure in Iban myths and are believed to protect individuals from harm; they are passed down from generation to generation. Such designs, with deep spiritual significance, can only be woven by wives and daughters of chiefs. Other designs and patterns are representations of birds and animals, including hornbills, crocodiles, monitor lizards and shrimps, which are either associated with worship or are sources of food. Symbolic representations of trees, plants and fruits are also included in the designs as well as the events of everyday life. A typical example is the zigzag pattern which represents the act of crossing a river – the zigzag course is explained by the canoe's attempts to avoid strong currents. Many of the symbolic representations are highly stylized and can be difficult to pick out.

Malay women in Sarawak are traditionally renowned for their *kain songket*, sarongs woven with silver and gold thread.

Woodcarvings Many of Sarawak's tribal groups are skilled carvers, producing everything from huge burial poles (like the Kejaman pole outside the Sarawak museum in Kuching) to small statues, masks and other decorative items and utensils. The Kenyah's traditional masks, which are used during festivals, are elaborately carved and often have large protruding eyes. Eyes are always emphasized, as they are to frighten the enemy. Other typical items carved by tribal groups include spoons, stools, doors, walking sticks, *sapes* (guitars), ceremonial shields, tops of water containers, tattoo plaques, and the hilts of *parang ilang* (ceremonial knives). The most popular Iban motif is the hornbill, which holds an honoured place in Iban folklore (see page 561), being the messenger for the sacred Brahminy kite, the ancestor of the Iban. Another famous Iban carving is the sacred measuring stick called the *tuntun peti*, used to trap deer and wild boar; it is carved to represent a forest spirit. The Kayan and Kenyahs' most common motif is the *aso*, a dragon-like dog with a long snout. It also has religious and mythical significance. The Kenyah and Kayan carve huge burial structures, or *salong*, as well as small ear pendants made of hornbill ivory. The elaborately carved masks used for their harvest ceremony are unique.

Bamboo The Bidayuh ('Land Dayaks') are best known for their bamboo carving. The bamboo
carving is usually carved in shallow relief and then stained with dye, which leaves a pattern in the areas which have been scraped out. The Bidayuh carve utilitarian objects as well as ceremonial shields, musical instruments and spirit images used to guard the longhouse. The Cultural Village (Kampong Budaya) in Kuching is one of the best places to see demonstrations of Bidayuh carving.

Blowpipes

Blowpipes are made by several Orang Ulu tribes in Sarawak and are usually carved from hardwood – normally belian (ironwood). The first step is to make a rough cylinder about 10 cm wide and 2.5m long. This rod is tied to a platform, from which a hole is bored through the rod. The bore is skilfully chiselled by an iron rod with a pointed end. The rod is then sanded down to about 5cm in diameter. Traditionally, the sanding was done using the rough underside of *macaranga* leaves. The darts are made from the *nibong* and wild sago palms and the poison itself is the sap of the *upas* (Ipoh) tree (*Antiaris toxicari*) into which the point is dipped.

Beadwork

Among many Kenyah, Kayan, Bidayuh, and Kelabit groups, beads have long been symbols of status and wealth; necklaces, skull caps and girdles are handed down from generation to generation. Smaller glass or plastic beads, usually imported from Europe, are used to decorate baby carriers, baskets, headbands, jackets, hats, sheaths for knives, tobacco boxes and handbags. Beaded baby carriers are mainly used by the Kelabit, Kenyah and Kayan and often have shells and animals' teeth attached which make a rattling sound to frighten away evil spirits. Rounded patterns require more skill than geometric patterns, the quality of the pattern used to reflect the status of the owner. Only upper-classes are permitted to have beadwork depicting 'high-class' motifs such as human faces or figures. Early beads were made from clay, metal, glass, bone or shell (the earliest have been found in the Niah Caves). Later on, many of the beads that found their way upriver were from Venice, Greece, India and China – even Roman and Alexandrian beads have made their way into Borneo's jungle. Orang Ulu traded them for jungle produce. Tribes attach different values to particular types of beads.

Sickness images

The coastal Melanau, who have now converted to Islam, but used to be animists, have a tradition of carving sickness images (*blum*). They are usually carved from sago or other soft woods. The image is believed to take the form of the evil spirit causing a specific illness. They are carved in different forms according to the ailment. The Melanau developed elaborate healing ceremonies; if someone was struck down by a serious illness, the spirit medium would perform the *berayun* ceremony, using the blum to extract the illness from the victim's body. Usually, the image is in a half-seated position, with the hands crossed across the part of the body which was affected. During the ceremony, the medium attempts to draw the spirit out of the sick person and into the image, after which it is set adrift on a river in a tiny purpose-made boat or it is hidden in the jungle. These images are roughly carved and can, from time to time, be found in antique shops.

Basketry A wide variety of household items are woven from rotan, bamboo, bemban reed as well as nipah and pandanus palms. Malaysia supplies 30% of the world's demand for *manau rotan* (rattan). Basketry is practised by nearly all the ethnic groups in Sarawak and they are among the most popular handicrafts in the state. A variety of baskets are made for harvesting, storing and winnowing paddy as well as for collecting and storing other items. The Penan are reputed to produce the finest rattan sleeping mats – closely plaited and pliable – as well as the *ajat* and *ambong* baskets (all-purpose jungle rucksacks, also produced by the Kayan and Kenyah). Many of the native patterns used in basketry are derived from Chinese patterns and take the form of geometrical shapes and stylized birds. The Bidayuh also make baskets from either rotan or sago bark strips. The most common Bidayuh basket is the *tambok*, which is simply patterned and has bands of colour; it also has thin wooden supports on each side.

Hats

The Melanau people living around Bintulu make a big colourful conical hat from nipah leaves called a *terindak*. Orang Ulu hats are wide-brimmed and are often

Sarawak

decorated with beadwork or cloth *appliqué*. Kelabit and Lun Bawan women wear skull-caps made entirely of beads, which are heavy and extremely valuable.

Pottery Malaysia's most distinctive ceramic designs are found in Sarawak where Iban potters reproduce shapes and patterns of Chinese porcelain which was originally brought to Borneo by traders centuries ago (see page 322). Copies of these old Chinese jars are mostly used for brewing *tuak* rice wine.

Sabah

8

Sabah

*Sabah may not have the colourful history of neighbouring Sarawak, but there is still a great deal to entice the visitor. It is second largest Malaysian state after Sarawak, covering 72,500 sq km, making it about the size of Ireland. Occupying the northeast corner of Borneo it is shaped like a dog's head, the jaws reaching out in the Sul and Celebes seas, and the back of the head facing onto the South China Sea. The highlights of Sabah are natural and cultural, from caves, reefs, forests and mountains to tribal peoples. The **Gununa Kinabulu National Park** is named after Sabah's (and Malaysia's) highest peak and is one of the state's most popular destinations. Also popular is the **Sepilok Orang-utan Rehabilitation Sanctuary** outside Sandakan. Marine sights include the **Turtle Islands National Park** and **Sipadan Island**, one of Asia's finest dive sites. While Sabah's indigenous tribes were not cossetted in the way that they were in Sarawak by the White Rajahs, areas around towns such as **Kudat**, **Tenom**, **Keningau** and **Kota Belud** still provide memorable insights in the peoples of the area.*

Kota Kinabalu

Colour map 4, grid B3
Population: 180,000
Phone code: 088

KK is most people's introduction to Sabah for the simple reason that it is the only town with extensive air links to other parts of the country as well as with a handful of regional destinations. KK is a modern state capital with little that can be dated back more than 50 years. Highlights include the State Museum and the town's markets. Out of town, within a day's excursion, are attractive beaches such as Tanjung Aru Beach and those near Tuaran, as well as a number of Kadazan and Bajau districts, with their distinctive markets. While it is necessary to go rather further afield to get a real glimpse of tribal life, this is better than nothing.

The city is strung out along the coast, with jungle-clad hills as a backdrop. Two-thirds of the town is built on land reclaimed from the shallow Gaya Bay; and during the spring tides it is possible to walk across to Gaya Island. Jalan Pantai, or Beach Rd, is now in the centre of town. Successive land reclamation projects have meant that many of the original stilt villages, such as Kampung Ayer, have been cut off from the sea and some now stand in stinking, stagnant lagoons. The government is cleaning up and reclaiming these areas and the inhabitants of the water villages are being rehoused.

Ins and outs

Getting there
See transport, page 427 for further details

KK's airport is 5 km from town. There are connections with other towns in East Malaysia and the Peninsula as well as with various destinations in the Asian region. For buses into town, there is a bus stop 10-mins walk from the airport, RM1 to city centre. Taxis from the airport cost about RM12 to the city centre and RM10 to the *Shangri-La Tanjung Aru Resort* (see page 422). There is a limited railway line with trains to Beaufort and Tenom and an extensive network of bus, minibus and taxi links to destinations in Sabah. Ferries throughout the day for Labuan. Getting to Brunei overland takes around 5 hrs and 2 ferry crossings at Temburong and Terusan (in Brunei).

Getting around
Most companies run city tours

City buses and minibuses provide a service around town and to destinations in the vicinity of KK. The bus station is behind the *Centre Point* Complex. Taxis are unmetered. There is a good number of international and local car hire firms.

Tourist offices

Sabah Tourist Promotion Corporation, 51 Jln Gaya, T212121, F212075, www.sabahtourism.com *Malaysia Tourism Promotion Board*, Ground Flr, Wing On Life Building, Jln Sagunting, T211732, mtpbki@tourism.gov.my Both offices have a wealth of information although the Tourism Malaysia office is of little use for Sabah. The *Sabah Tourist Promotion Corporation* is excellent and very helpful.

History

Kota Kinabalu started life as a trading post in 1881 by the British North Borneo Charter Company under the directorship of William C Cowie, see page 462; not on the mainland, but on Gaya Island, opposite the present town, where a Filipino shanty town is today. On 9 July 1897 rebel leader Mat Salleh (see box on page 433), who engaged in a series of hit-and-run raids against the British North Borneo Chartered Company's administration, landed on Pulau Gaya. His men looted and sacked the settlement and Gaya township was abandoned.

Things to do in Sabah ★

- Experience Malaysia's finest diving at the Sipadan Island Marine Reserve.
- Climb Malaysia's tallest peak, Gunung Kinabalu, and you may be lucky to arrive at the summit on a clear morning – simply mesmerising.
- Get up close and personal with the world's most lovable apes in the Sepilok Orang Utan Santuary, outside Sandakan.
- Watch green turtles lay their eggs on the beaches of the Turtle Islands National Park north of Sandakan.
- Experience the jungle in style at the Danum Valley and Borneo Rainforest Lodge, possibly the best designed 'eco lodge' in Malaysia.

Two years later the Europeans established another township but this time located on the mainland, opposite Pulau Gaya, adjacent to a Bajau stilt village. The kampung was called '*Api Api*' – meaning 'Fire! Fire!' – because it had been repeatedly torched by pirates over the years. After the Gaya experience, it was an inauspicious name. The Chartered Company rechristened it Jesselton, after Sir Charles Jessel, one of the company directors. However, for years, only the Europeans called it Jesselton; locals preferred the old name, and even today Sabahans sometimes refer to their state capital as 'Api'.

Jesselton owed its raison d'être to a plan that backfired. William C Cowie, formerly a gun-runner for the Sultan of Sulu, became managing director of the Chartered Company in 1894. He wanted to build a trans-Borneo railway and the narrow strip of land just north of Tanjung Aru and opposite Pulau Gaya, with its sheltered anchorage, was selected as a terminus.

Photographs in the Sabah State Museum chart the town's development from 1899, when work on the North Borneo Railway terminus began in earnest. By 1905, Jesselton was linked to Beaufort by a 92-km narrow-gauge track. By 1911 it had a population of 2,686, half of whom were Chinese and the remainder Kadazans and Dusuns; there were 33 European residents. Jesselton was of little importance in comparison to Sandakan, the capital of North Borneo.

When the Japanese Imperial Army invaded Borneo in 1942, Jesselton's harbour gave the town strategic significance and it was consequently completely flattened by the Allies during the Second World War. Jesselton followed Kudat and Sandakan as the administrative centre of North Borneo, at the end of the Second World War and the city was rebuilt from scratch. In September 1967 Jesselton was renamed Kota Kinabalu after the mountain; its name is usually shortened to KK.

Sights

Only three buildings remain of the old town: the old **General Post Office** on Jalan Gaya, **Atkinson's Clock Tower** (built in 1905 and named after Jesselton's first district officer) and the old red-roofed **Lands and Surveys building**. The renovated post office now houses the **Sabah Tourist Promotion Corporation.**

Masjid Sabah & Sabah State Museum

The golden dome of Masjid Sabah, on Jalan Tunku Abdul Rahman, is visible from most areas of town, although it is actually about 3 km out of town. Regular minibuses connect it with the town centre. Completed in 1975, it is the second biggest mosque in Malaysia and, like the Federal Mosque in Kuala Lumpur, a fine example of contemporary Islamic architecture. It can accommodate 5,000 worshippers.

Perched on a small hill overlooking the mosque is the relatively new (opened 1985) purpose-built Sabah State Museum (and State Archives) on Jalan Mat Salleh/Bukit Istana Lama (Old Palace Hill), designed to resemble a Rungut longhouse. The museum is divided into ethnography, natural history, ceramics, history and archaeology. The ethnographic section includes an excellent exhibition on the uses of bamboo. Tribal brassware, silverware, musical instruments, basketry and pottery are also on display. On the same floor is a collection of costumes and artefacts from Sabah tribes like the Kadazan/Dusun, Bajau, Murut and Rungus.

One of the most interesting items in this collection is a *sininggazanak* – a sort of totem pole. If a Kadazan man died without an heir, it was the custom to erect a *sininggazanak* – a wooden statue supposedly resembling the deceased – on his land. There is also a collection of human skulls – called a *bangkaran* – which before the tribe's wholesale conversion to Christianity, would have been suspended from the rafters of Kadazan longhouses. Every five years a *magang* feast was held to appease the spirits of the skulls.

The museum's archaeological section contains a magnificently carved coffin found in a limestone cave in the Madai area. Upstairs, the natural history section, provides a good introduction to Sabah's flora and fauna. Next door is a collection of jars, called *pusaka*, which are tribal heirlooms. They were originally exchanged by the Chinese for jungle produce, such as beeswax, camphor and birds' nests.

Next door is the **Science Museum**, containing an exhibition on Shell's offshore activities. The **Art Gallery and Multivision Theatre**, within the same

Kota Kinabalu

South China Sea

Sabah Port

A

City Bird Sanctuary

Likas Stadium

Jln Tuaran

Jln Damai

Sutera Harbour Marina

Sutera Harbour Golf Club

1

2

Jln Kolam

Masjid Sabah

State Museum

Sabah Golf & Country Club

Tanjung Aru Marina

Jln Mat Salleh

Queen Elizabeth

Sikh Temple

Pek Nam Thong Temple

Jln Bunda Ulam Raya

Kinabalu Golf Club

Jln Penampang

Tanjung Aru Beach

Jln Putatan

Sabah Railway Station

International Airport

To Monsopiad Cultural Village

N

0 metres 800

0 yards 800

■ Sleeping

1 Magellan

2 Pacific Sutera

complex, are also worth a browse. The art gallery is small and mainly exhibits works by local artists; among the more interesting works on display are those of Suzie Mojikol, a Kadazan artist, Bakri Dani, who adapts Bajau designs and Philip Biji who specializes in burning Murut designs onto chunks of wood with a soldering iron. The ethnobotanical gardens are on the hillside below the museum complex. There is a cafeteria at the base of the main building.
■ *1000-1800 Mon-Thu, 0900-1800 Sat-Sun. RM5. www.mzm.sabah.gov.my Guided tours available. Minibuses stop near Wisma Kewangan on the Kota Kinabalu - Tanjung Aru road and near Queen Elizabeth Hospital on the Kota Kinabalu – Penampang road.*

Sabah has a large Christian population and the **Sacred Heart Cathedral** has a striking pyramidal roof which is clearly visible from the Sabah State Museum complex.

Further into town and nearer the coast are a series of water villages, including **Viewpoints**
Kampung Ayer, although its size has shrunk in recent years. **Signal Hill** (Bukit Bendera), just southeast of the central area, gives a panoramic view of the town and islands. In the past, the hill was used as a vantage point for signalling to ships approaching the harbour. There is an even better view of the coastline from the top of the **Sabah Foundation (Yayasan Sabah) Complex**, 4 km out of town, overlooking Likas Bay. This surreal glass sculpture has circular floors suspended on high-tensile steel rods and houses the Chief Minister's office. The Sabah Foundation was set up in 1966 to help improve Sabahans' quality of life. The foundation has a 972,800 ha timber concession, which it claims to manage on a sustainable-yield basis (achievement of a high level annual output without impairing the long-term productivity of the land). Two-thirds of this concession has already been logged. Profits from the timber go towards loans and scholarships for Sabahan students, funding the construction of hospitals and schools and supplying milk, textbooks and uniforms to school children. The Foundation also operates a 24-hour flying ambulance service to remote parts of the interior. See also www.ysnet.org.my

The fact that between the Yayasan Sabah and the core of the city is one of Borneo's largest squatter communities visibly demonstrates that not everyone is sharing equally in the timber boom.

Gaya street market is held every Sunday from 0800, selling a vast range of **Markets**
goods from jungle produce and handicrafts to pots and pans. The market almost opposite the main minibus station on Jalan Tun Fuad Stephens is known as the **Filipino market**, as most of the stalls are run by Filipino immigrants. A variety of Filipino and local handicrafts are sold in the hundreds of cramped stalls, along winding alleyways which are strung with low-slung curtains of shells, baskets and bags. The Filipino market is a good place to buy cultured pearls (about RM5 each) and has everything from fake gemstones to camagong-wood salad bowls, fibre shirts and traditional Indonesian medicines. Further into town, on the waterfront, is the **central market** selling mainly fish, fruit and vegetables. The daily fishing catch is unloaded on the wharf near the market.

Excursions

Tours that are widely available include: Kota Belud *tamu* (Sunday market), *For Tunku Abdul*
Mount Kinabalu Park (including Poring Hot Springs), Sandakan's Sepilok *Rahman Park, see*
Orang-utan Rehabilitation Centre, train trips to Tenom through the Padas *page 429*

Gorge and tours of the islands in the Tunku Abdul Rahman National Park. Several companies specialize in scuba-diving tours, see page 426.

Tanjung Aru Beach

This is the best beach near KK, after those in Tunku Abdul Rahman National Park, and is close to *Tanjung Aru Resort*, 5 km south of KK (see page 422). It is particularly popular at weekends and there is a good hawker centre. ■ *Getting there Minibuses leave frequently from the terminus in front of the market on Jln Tun Fuad Stephens; red and white buses to Tanjung Aru leave from outside the MPKK building, next to the State Library, or take a red bus marked 'beach' from Jln Tunku Abdul Rahman.*

Penampang
on map
This Kadazan district is 13 km southeast of KK

The old town of Donggongon was demolished in the early 1980s and the new township built in 1982. The population is mainly Kadazan or Sino-Kadazan and about 90% Christian. The oldest church in Sabah, **St Michael's** Roman Catholic church, is on a steep hill on the far side of the new town. Turn left just before bridge – and after turn-off to the new town – through kampung and turn left again after school. It's a 20-minute walk; a granite building with a red roof. It was originally built in 1897 but is not dramatic to look at and has been much renovated over the years. Services are conducted in Kadazan but are fascinating to attend and visitors are warmly welcomed; hymns are sung in Kadazan and Malay. The social focus of the week is the **market** every Sunday.

There are many **megaliths** in the Penampang area which are thought to be associated with property claims, particularly when a landowner died without

Around Kota Kinabalu

Source: Periplus

Layang-Layang Atoll: OK coral

Malaysia is just one of five claimants to the countless reefs and atolls in the Spratly group. While Vietnam and China are more interested in the prospective riches from what are thought to be oil-bearing strata beneath the seabed, Malaysia is the only country to have cashed in on tourism on the reefs themselves. Layang-Layang (or 'Kite') atoll is about 250 km northwest of Kota Kinabalu – a 16-hour boat ride – and has recently been added to other coral reefs such as Sipadan Island, off Sabah's east coast (see page 481) as part of the state's growing list of fabulous dive sites. Layang-Layang – formerly known as

Swallow Reef – is 7-km long and 5 km wide, with a lagoon in the middle. There is a Malaysian navy base at one end and basic tourist accommodation (in concrete and breeze block houses) next to it. The island attracts migratory birds, but is best-known as a scuba paradise. Divers visiting Layang-Layang usually stay aboard the MV Coral Topaz and make trips to other nearby reefs. There are reportedly several wrecks in the area, but most diving focuses on the coral walls on the outer edges of the reefs which drop sheer to the seabed 2,000 m below. This area also has some of Southeast Asia's finest game fishing.

a direct heir. Some solitary stones, which can be seen standing in the middle of paddy fields, are more than 2 m tall. The age of the megaliths has not been determined. Wooden figures, called *sininggazanak* can also be seen in the ricefields (see page 416). *Yun Chuan*, Penampang New Town (also known as Donggongon Township), specializes in Kadazan dishes, such as *hinava* – or raw fish, the Kadazan equivalent of sushi. Tapai chicken is also recommended. See page 52 for details on Kadazan cuisine. ■ *Getting there: Take a green and white Union Transport bus from in front of the MPKK building next to the State Library.*

The Monosopiad Cultural Village

This is in Kampung Monsopiad (named after a fearsome Kadazan warrior-cum-headhunter – Siou do Mohoing, the so-called Hercules of Sabah) just outside Penampang. There are 42 fragile human skulls in the collection, some of which are said to be 300 years old and possess spiritual powers. They are laced together with leaves of the *hisad* palm, which represents the hair of the victims. For those who have already visited longhouses in Sarawak, this collection of skulls, in the rafters of an ordinary little kampung house overlooking the village and the Penampang River, is a bit of an anti-climax. But Dousia Moujing and his son Wennedy are very hospitable and know much about local history and culture. They preside over their ancestor's dreaded sword (although Wennedy reckons it's not the original, even though there are strands of human hair hanging off it). A three-day, three-night long feast is held at the house in May, in the run-up to the harvest festival. Visitors should remove footwear and not touch the skulls or disturb the rituals or ceremonies in progress. A reconstruction of the original Monosopiad main house allows the visitor an insight into the life and times of the warrior and his descendants. There is a good restaurant here serving traditional dishes; the *kadazandusun hinara* is recommended. It consists of fresh, sliced, raw fish marinated in lime juice and mixed with finely sliced chilli, garlic, gourd and shallots. ■ *From 0900-1700, Mon to Fri. For more information, Borneo Legends and Myths, 5 km Ramaya/Putaton Rd, Penampang, T761336, mcv@tm.net.my The house is hard to find; from new town take the main road east, past Shell station and turn right at sign to Jabatan Air; past St Aloysus Church, house on left about 1½ km*

Sabah

from turn-off; minibus from Donggongon Township, 10 km south of KK, to Kampung Monsopaid. Regular minibuses travel between KK and Donggongon from Jalan Tun Fuad Stephens. A taxi costs RM30 from KK.

Riding at Kinarut

For Kinarut Riding School, 21 km south of KK, call Dale Sinidal, an Australian who has run this school for over 10 years. There are trail rides of approximately two hours through villages and padi fields or along the beach and across to an island at low tide. The surroundings are stunning and the horses are well kept and good tempered. ■ *It is RM60 for 2 hrs, RM50 for 1½ hrs. Call Ms Sinidal, T225525, 0108100233 mob, and she will organize transport from KK. For places to stay near Kinarut, see the Papar entry on page 445.*

Tampuruli

This popular stop for tour buses is 32 km north of KK at the junction of the roads north and east. It has a suspension bridge straddling the Tuaran River which was built by the British Army in 1922. There is a good handicraft shopping centre here. ■ *Minibuses leave from the terminus in front of the market on Jln Tun Fuad Stephens. Regular green buses leave for Tuaran from the padang at the foot of Signal Hill.*

Mengkabong Water Village

Because the Mengkabong is so accessible it tends to get rather crowded; don't expect a bucolic experience

This *Baja*, or sea gypsy, fishing stilt village is within easy reach of KK (see page 414) and is likened to an Asian Venice. The village is particularly photogenic in the early morning, before Mount Kinabalu – which serves as a dramatic backdrop, is obscured by cloud. The fishermen leave Mengkabong at high tide and arrive back with their catch at the next high tide. They use sampan canoes, hollowed out of a single tree-trunk, which are crafted in huts around the village. Some of the waterways and fields around Menkabong are choked by water hyacinth, an ornamental plant that was originally introduced by Chinese farmers as pig-fodder from South America. ■ *Getting there: take a minibus to Tuaran, from where there are taxis to Menkabong. Alternatively, book onto one of the many tours.*

For visitors wanting to escape the popular beaches close to KK, **Tuaran**, 45 minutes north of KK, offers a quieter alternative and is a good access point for several different destinations including Mengkabong.

Further north

The nearby **Karam Bunai Beach** has a good picnic area, clean beach and sea. Close by is the *Club Sabah Golf & Beach Resort* (**A-B**), No 1 Kuala Matinggi, Kampung Pulau, Simpangan, T787799, F787775, clubsabah@hotmail.com It has chalets, a private beach, watersports, fishing, mini zoo, karaoke bar, horseriding, volleyball, children's playground, Malay/Chinese and Western food. **Surusup** is another 10-15 minutes beyond Tuaran. Ask at the store in Surusup for Haji Abdul Saman, who will take visitors by boat to the lesser known Bajau fishing village, **Kampung Penambawan**, also likened to an Asian Venice, on the north bank of the river. Nearby there is a suspension bridge and rapids where it is possible to swim. There is the *Pantai Palit Resthouse*. ■ *Getting there: take a boat from Surusup, around RM15 return.*

Essentials

Sleeping
■ *on map, page 421*
Price codes:
see inside front cover

The scenic Karambunai Peninsula 30 km north of KK has been transformed by a sprawling multi-million dollar golf and beach resort complex. *The Nexus Golf Resort Karambunai*, P. O. Box 270, 88450 Menggatal, T411222, F411020 www.borneo-online.com.my the complex is built on 45 acres of land sprawling along the coast and has 490 ocean-view rooms, along with all the usual facilities including an 18-hole golf course and a host of other sporting activities. It is popular for conferences and is patronised by businessmen from the region. South of KK, the *Borneo Golf and Beach Resort*, including two 18-hole courses – one designed by Jack Nicklaus, the other by his

Kota Kinabalu centre

Sabah

Sleeping	5 City Inn *B2*	14 Promenade *E1*	22 Wah May *B2*
	6 Diamond *C2*	15 Ruby Inn *D2*	23 Winner *D2*
1 Ang's *B2*	7 High Street Inn *B2*	16 Shangri-La *D3*	
2 Berjaya Palace *E2*	8 Holiday/Gunung Emas *C2*	17 Sinsuran Inn *C2*	**Eating**
3 Capital *B2*	9 Hyatt Regency *B1*	18 Suang Hee *B2*	1 Bilal *B2*
4 Century *D3*	10 Jesselton *B2*	19 Town Inn *B2*	2 Nishiki *B2*
	11 Kinabalu Daya *B2*	20 Trekker's Lodge, Pantai *B2*	3 Port View *A1*
	12 Mandarin *C2*	21 Trekker's Lodge,	
	13 New Sabah *B2*	Sinsuran *C1*	

0 metres 100
0 yards 100

son – is up-and-running. The *Shangri-La* group, which now owns the *Tanjung Aru*, has built the *Rasa Ria Resort* at Pantai Dalit, near Tuaran (see below). Well-heeled tourists will seek the more refined out-of-town resorts; but in KK itself, mid-range hotels have improved immeasurably in recent years. The best bets, offering good value for money, are those catering for itinerant Malaysian businessmen, such as the *Mandarin Palace* and *Shangri-La*.

AL *Rasa Ria Resort*, overlooking Pantai Dalit Beach, PO Box 600, T792888, F792777, rrr@shangri-la.com Top-class *Shangri-La* resort with 330 rooms, free-form pool, watersports, 18-hole golf course, driving range, spacious gardens, conference facilities, cultural events, several restaurants including an Italian and a seafood beach-front restaurant, torch lighting ceremony, 30 ha of forest nature reserve nearby means that orang-utans are frequent visitors. To get there, take a local bus to Tuaran. Recommended.

AL *Shangri-La Tanjung Aru Resort*, Tanjung Aru, T225800, F214155, www.shangri-la.com A/c, 500 rooms, pool, one of the best hotels in Sabah, although it is now in competition with its sister hotel the *Rasa Ria* at Tuaran (see above). Tanjung Aru is a public beach, frequented by kite-flyers, swimmers, joggers, and lovers, the hotel is noticeably on the European honeymoon circuit. Recommended. **AL** *Sutera Harbour Resort*, www.suteraharbour.com/ 384-acre resort created out of reclaimed land which was previously the South China Sea, it lies to the south of the city centre. Opened in July 2000, the Harbour consists of 2 hotels, the **AL** *Magellan Sutera*, and the **AL** *Pacific Sutera*, 1 Sutera Harbour Boulevard, Sutera Harbour Resort, 88100 Kota Kinabalu, T318888, F317777. The *Magellan Sutera* offers the more relaxed resort, with much in the way of sporting activities, including 27 holes of golf and a spa. The *Pacific Sutera* is more focused towards businessmen, providing excellent conference facilities. Together, they offer almost 1,000 rooms. A *Berjaya Palace*, 1 Jln Tangki, Karamunsing, T211911, F211600, www.berjayaresorts.com.my 160 rooms, pool, sauna and gym, conference rooms. This distinctive castellated hotel stands on a hill south of KK. The proprietor James Sheng has a small resort, with chalets, on Pulau Gaya, at Maluham Bay, east of Police Bay, enquire at hotel. A *Jesselton*, 64 Jln Gaya, T223333, F240401, www.jaring.my/jess The first hotel to open in KK, this classic hotel dates from 1954. With just 32 rooms, it was upgraded in mid-1990's and is now considered KK's premier 'boutique'-style hotel. Old establishment, with everything from a London taxi to shoe-shining at your service. A *Langkah Syabas Beach Resort*, PO Box 451, Kinarut, T752000, F752111, lsr@po.jaring.my A resort with 14 detached and semi-detached chalets encircling the swimming pool, a/c, fans, TVs, tennis and riding centre close by, attractive garden setting. A *Promenade*, 4 Lorong Api-Api 3, Api-Api Centre, T265555, F246666, www.promenade.com.my/ Attractive seafront position. Several restaurants, business facilities, gym with good range of equipment, pool. A *Sabandah Bay Resort*, off Jln Pantai Dalit, Jln Sabandar, T787722, F787575.

B *Borneo Resthouse*, Mile 3.5, Jln Penampang, Taman Fraser, T718855, F718955. A/c, 2 star hotel with 50 rooms, restaurant, pool, garden. B *Capital*, 23 Jln Haji Saman, T231999, F237222. www.borneo-online.com.my/hotel/capital/ A/c, TV, 102 rooms, coffee shop, central position. B *Century*, Lot 12, Jln Masjid Lama, T242222, F242929. www.borneo-online.com.my/hotel/century/ A/c, 54 rooms, good seafood restaurant. B *Holiday/Gunung Emas*, Lot 1 & 2, Block F, Segama Shopping Complex, off Jln Tun Razak, T213116, F215576. A/c, quite good with central location, but overpriced. B *Hotel Shangri-La*, 75 Bandaran Berjaya, T212800, F212078, kkshang@po.jaring.my A/c, restaurant, not in the international *Shangri-La* group; reasonable hotel though and the haunt of business visitors. B *Hyatt Regency*, Jln Datuk Salleh Sulong, T221134, F218909, www.hyatt.com/malaysia/sabah/hotels/hotel_bkiki A/c, 288 rooms, 3 restaurants, pool and children's small pool, good central location, rooms vary in standard, business centre, live entertainment (*Shenanigan's Fun Pub*). Tours and treks organized.

Good value. **B** *Kinabalu Daya*, Lot 3 & 4, Jln Pantai, T240000, F263909. 68 rooms, a/c, the top flr restaurant serves Asian and western food, seminar room. Breakfast included. **B** *Mandarin*, 138 Jln Gaya, T225222, F225481. A/c, restaurant, very swish, marble floors, well-fitted rooms, excellent central location, friendly staff, 6th flr rooms with good view over town; deluxe and super-deluxe particularly spacious. Recommended.

C *Ang's*, 28 Jln Pantai, T234999, F217867. A/c, 35 rather threadbare rooms. **C** *Bilal*, 2nd Flr, Block B, Lot 1 & 2 Segama Complex, T256709, F263220, chapsel@pc.jaring.my Some a/c, above the Indian Muslim restaurant *Bilal*, this centrally-located basic hotel is spotless and bright with friendly management, rooms have hot water showers and TV, tourist information. Recommended. **C** *City Inn*, 41 Jln Pantai, T218933, F218937. A/c, bathroom and TV; good for the price, often full. **C** *Diamond*, Jln Haji Yaakub, T261222, F231198. Very adequate 32 rooms. **C** *Golden Inn*, Sinsuran Complex, T211551. **C** *High Street Inn*, 38 Jln Pantai, T218111, F219111. A/c, TV, in-house films, hot water, small but comfortable rooms – very typical of the characterless hotels in this price range. **C** *New Sabah*, Block A, Lot 394 Segama Complex, No 9-11 Jln Padas, T224590, F224648. A/c, TV, bathroom, average hotel, very noisy. **C** *Pantai Inn*, 57 Jln Pantai, T219221, F216839. A/c, good central location, well-appointed rooms, small but very clean. **C** *Ruby Inn*, Jln Laiman Diki, Kampung Ayer, T213222, F231198. 90 rooms, in a rather drab block. Better off elsewhere. **C** *Sinsuran Inn*, Block 1, Lot 1, 1st Flr, Sinsuran Complex, T 271263, F262818, alexander@trekkerslodge.com Newly renovated and centrally located, clean rooms have attached bathroom and hot water. Good tour information and free baggage storage and a big cat named Ronnie. **C** *Suang Hee*, Block F, 7 Segama Shopping Centre, T254168, F217234. A/c, restaurant, 24 rooms, clean Chinese hotel, reasonable value for money, a/c, TV and bathroom. **C** *Town Inn*, 31-33 Jln Pantai, T225823, F217762. A/c, 24 rooms, clean with excellent facilities, central location, good for the price. Recommended. **C** *Wah May*, 36 Jln Haji Saman, T266118, F266122. Modern Chinese hotel, 36 clean rooms kitted out with a/c, TV, fridge. Tight security with CCTV in operation. **C** *Winner*, 9 & 10 Jln Pasar Baru, Kampung Ayer, T243222, F217345. A/c, 36 rooms, restaurant, pleasant, central hotel, friendly staff, good restaurant.

C-D *Trekkers Lodge*, 46 Jln Pantai, T213888, www.trekkerslodge.com Also has dorm rooms for RM17-20 (for a/c). Breakfast included. Centrally located, managed by USA-trained Alex Yee, who is extremely helpful. All the staff have been well trained and the place is spotlessly clean. Laundry and storage facilities available. Recommended. **C-D** *Trekkers Lodge, Sinsuran*, Block L, Lot 5, 2nd Flr, Sinsuran Complex, T252263, F258263, www.trekkerslodge.com Also has dorm rooms for RM17-20. Used to be the *Travellers Rest Hostel*, but is now under *Trekkers Lodge* management. It calls itself 'KK's original hostel', rates include breakfast, like its sister establishment, it is clean and bright, provides internet access, free baggage storage and safe facility and is a good source of tour and travel information. Hot water showers and a pleasant sitting area make this a popular spot with backpackers.

D *Islamic Hotel*, Kampung Ayer, T254325, cheap accommodation with fan only rooms and separate mandis. Excellent restaurant downstairs sells very good roti. **D** *Jack's B&B*, 17, 1st Flr, Block B, Karamunsing Warehouse, Jln Karamunsing, T232367, bbjack@tm.net.my A/c, including breakfast, clean and friendly, jungle tours organized. Recommended. **E** *Backpacker Lodge*, Australia Pl, 25 Lorong Dewan, T261495. Friendly, clean dorms with a good breakfast included in the room rate.

Malay Cheap *Copelia*, Jln Gaya, *nasi lemak* for breakfast, also does takeaway. **Seriously cheap** *Restoran Ali*, Segama Complex, opposite *Hyatt Hotel*, best in a string of coffee shops, all of which are good value for money. **Chinese Mid-range** *Hyatt Poolside Hawker Centre*, *Hyatt*, Jln Datuk Saleh Sulong, steamboat (minimum 2 people). **Cheap** *Avasi Cafeteria & Garden Restaurant*, EG 11 Kompleks Kuwasa, steamboat and seafood. *Nan Xing*, opposite the *Hyatt* and emporium, *dim sum* and Cantonese

Eating
Jalan Gaya, or 'Gaya Walk', is a popular place to wander and stop for a drink or a bite to eat

Sabah

specialities. *Phoenix Court*, *Hyatt*, Jln Datuk Saleh Sulong, *dim sum* 0700-1400. *Tioman*, Lot 56 Bandaran Berjaya, good claypot and lemon chicken. **Seriously cheap** *Chuan Hin*, Jln Kolam (next to the *Cottage Pub*), excellent *ikan panggang*. *Friendly*, Tuaran Rd, Mile 2, Likas, cheap. **Nyonya Cheap** *Sri Melaka Restoran*, 9 Jln Laiman Diki, Kampung Ayer (Sedco Complex, near *Shiraz*).

Found in most areas of KK, hot and cold drinks are served as well as a variety of local noodle and rice dishes

Other Asian cuisine Mid-range *Nagisa*, *Hyatt*, Jln Datuk Salleh Sulong, Japanese, T221234. *Azuma*, 3rd Flr, Wisma Merdeka, Japanese. *Jaws*, 4th Flr, Gaya Centre, Jln Tun Fuad Stephens, Thai/Chinese cuisine, such as *tom yam* steamboat. *Nishiki*, Jln Gaya (opposite Wing On Life Building), Japanese. **Cheap Korean**, Jln Bandaran Berjaya, next to *Asia Hotel*, large selection, barbecues are a speciality. *Shiraz*, Lot 5, Block B, Sedco Square, Kampung Ayer, Indian. Recommended. **Seriously cheap** *Bilal*, Block B, Lot 1 Segama Complex, Indian Muslim food, *rotis*, chapatis, curries. Recommended. *Islamic Restoran*, Kampung Ayer, the best roti in town. *Sri Sakthi*, Mile 4.5, Jln Penampeng (opposite Towering Heights Industrial Estate), South Indian banana-leaf – good value. *Jothy's Curry Restaurant*, Api Api Centre.

International Mid-range *Gardenia Grill Room*, *Jesselton Hotel*, 69 Jln Gaya, T223333. *Peppino*, *Tanjung Aru Beach Resort*, T225800, tasty but expensive, Italian, good Filipino cover band. *Brass Monkey Cafe and Bar*, No 1 Lorong Lintas Plaza 4, T0178878717. **Cheap** *Sri Kapitol*, Ground Flr, *Hotel Capital*, 23 Jln Haji Saman, T219688, European breakfasts. **Seriously cheap** *Fat Cat*, Jln Haji Saman, cheap slap-up breakfasts.

This is seasonally prone to red tide. Locals will know when it's prevalent. Avoid all shellfish if there is any suspicion

Seafood Mid-range *Kampung Nelayan Floating Seafood Market*, Taman Tun Fuad, Bukit Padang, T269991. *Garden Restaurant*, *Tanjung Aru Beach Resort*, tables outside. *Merdeka*, 11th Flr, Wisma Merdeka, reasonably good seafood, but the view is better in this restaurant which offers 'karaoke at no extra charge'. *Seafood Market*, Tanjung Aru Beach, T238313, pick your own fresh seafood and get advice on how to have it cooked. **Cheap** *Golf Field Seafood*, 0858 Jln Ranca-Ranca (better known by taxi-drivers as *Ahban's Place*), excellent marine cuisine, local favourite. Recommended. **Seriously cheap** *Port View*, Jln Haji Saman (opposite old customs wharf), T252813, huge selection of fresh seafood and delicious chilli crab, open until 0200 weekdays and 0300 on Sat, very popular with locals. *Golf View*, Jln Swamp (near Sabah Golf and Country Club), recommended by locals.

Bakeries KK bakers abound and are particularly good.

Foodstalls Cheap Stalls above central market. *Sedco Square*, Kampung Ayer, large square filled with stalls, great atmosphere in the evenings, ubiquitous *ikan panggang* and satay. Night market on Jln Tugu, on the waterfront at the Sinsuran Food Centre and at the *Merdeka Foodstall Centre*, Wisma Merdeka. *Tanjung Aru Beach*, mainly seafood – recommended for *ikan panggang* – and satay stalls: very busy at weekends, but on weekdays it is rather quiet, with only a few stalls to choose from.

Bars *Hard Rock Café*, Sutera Harbour. *The Cottage*, Jln Bukit Padang.

Entertainment Cinemas *Poring* and *Capital* cinemas, near Sedco Complex. **Cultural shows** *Kadazan-Dusun Cultural Centre* (Hongkod Koisaan), KDCA Building, Mile 4.5, Jln Penampang, restaurant open year-round, but at the end of May, during the harvest festival, the cultural association comes into its own, with dances, feasts and shows and lots of *tapai* (RM15). *Tanjung Aru Beach Hotel* on Wed and Sat, 2000. **Discos** *Shennanigan's*, *Hyatt Hotel*, the smartest in town. *Next Door*, *Tanjung Aru Beach Hotel*. *Tiffiny*, Tanjung Aru, opposite Sacred Heart Church. *LA Rock*, along the left side of *Tong Hing Supermarket*. *Rockies*, Promenade Hotel. **Karaoke** Very popular in KK; found in Damai, Foh Sang and KK centre. **MTV** *Popeye's MTV* in Bandaran.

Sabah

May *Magavau* (see page 56), a post-harvest celebration, carried out at Hongkod Koisaan (cultural centre). Mile 4.5, Jalan Penampang. To get there, take a green and white bus from the MPKK Building, next to state library.

Festivals

Antiques Good antiques shop at the bottom of the Chun Eng Building on Jln Tun Razak, a couple also on Jln Gaya. **Merdeka Complex** and **Wisma Wawasan 2020** hold a number of antique shops. It is necessary to have an export licence from the Sabah State Museum if you intend to export rare antiques.

Shopping

For markets, see page 417

    Books *Arena Book Centre*, Lot 2, Ground Floor, Block 1, Sinsuran Kompleks. *Rahmant Bookstore*, *Hyatt Hotel*, Jln Datuk Salleh Sulong. *Iwase Bookshop*, Ground Floor, Wisma Merdeka, T233757, selection of English language books and magazines. Wisma Merdeka is the best place to go for the widest range of books.

    Clothes *The House of Borneo Vou'tique* Lot 12A, First Flr, Lorong Bernam 3, Taman Saon Kiong, Jln Kolam, T268398, F263398, for that ethnic, exotic and exclusive look for men and women – corporate uniforms, souvenir items, tablecloths, cushion covers etc. **Centrepoint Mall** provides the biggest selection of designer clothing.

    Electronic goods VCDs, DVDs and stereo equipment is considered the cheapest in the country here. Both **Karamunsing Complex** and **Centrepoint** are the places to go.

    Handicrafts Mainly baskets, mats, tribal clothing, beadwork and pottery. *Borneo Gifts*, Ground Floor, Wisma Sabah. *Borneo Handicraft*, 1st Flr, Wisma Merdeka, local pottery and material made up into clothes. *Elegance Souvenir*, 1st Flr, Wisma Merdeka, lots of beads of local interest (another branch on Ground Floor of Centre Point). *Malaysian Handicraft*, Cawangan Sabah, No 1, Lorong 14, Kg Sembulau, T234471, F223444, open Mon-Sat 0815-1230 and Fri 0815-1600. *The Crafts*, Lot AG10, Ground Floor, Wisma Merdeka, T252413. *Filipino Market*, Jln Tun Fuad Stephens (see page 417). *Kaandaman Handicraft Centre* below *Seafood Market Restaurant*, Tanjung Aru Beach. *Kampung Air Night Market*, mainly Filipino handicrafts. *Sabah Art and Handicraft Centre*, 1st Flr, Block B, Segama Complex (opposite *New Sabah Hotel*). *Sabah Handicraft Centre*, Lot 49 Bandaran Berjaya (next to *Shangri-La*) good selection (also has branches at the museum and the airport). There are also several handicraft shops in the arcade at the *Tanjung Aru Beach Hotel* and one at the airport. *Api Tours*, Lot 49, Bandaran Berjaya also has a small selection of handicrafts.

    Jewellery Most shops in Wisma Merdeka.

    Shopping complexes *Segama*, Jln Tun Fuad Stephens and *Sinsuran*. Beware of pickpocketing during the day and more particularly at night. *Kinabalu Emporium*, Wisma Yakim, Jln Daruk Salleh Sulong is the main department store. *Likas Square*, Likas, pink monstrosity with 2 floors of shopping malls, foodstalls and restaurants. Cultural shows in central lobby.

The sports complex at Likas is open to the general public. It provides volleyball, tennis, basketball, a gym, badminton, squash, aerobics and a swimming pool. To get there take a Likas-bound minibus from town. *Likas Square*, the monstrous pink shopping complex north of Likas Sports Complex, has a Recreation Club within it providing tennis, squash, jogging, golf, driving range, a pool and a children's playground.

Sports

Bowling *Merdeka Bowl*, 11th Flr, Wisma Merdeka. **Diving** Snorkelling and scuba-diving in Tunku Abdul Rahman National Park. Tour operators specializing in dive trips also organize dives all over Sabah. **Golf** Green fees are considerably higher over the weekend – as much as double the weekday rate. Fees range from about RM50 during the week at the cheaper courses, to as much as RM200 or more over the weekend at flasher clubs. *Golf Booking Centre Malaysia* provides escorted golf tours, email: nbtt@tm.net.my Courses around KK include the *Sabah Golf and Country Club* at Bukit Padang, T247533, the oldest course in the state, this18-hole championship course

Sabah

affords magnificent views of Mt Kinabalu on clear days, green fees RM150 (weekdays), RM200 (weekends). *Sutera Harbour Golf & Country Club*, a 27 hole layout on reclaimed land just to the south of the city. Glorious views across the water to the islands of Tunku Abdul Rahman Park. **Hashing** There are 3 hashes in KK. **1**: *K2 H4* (KK Hash House Harriers) – men only, T428535, Mon, 1715. **2** *K2 H2* (KK Hash House Bunnies) – women (but not exclusively), T244333, ext 389. **3** *K2 H4* (KK Hash House Harriers and Harriets) – mixed, T217541, Fri, 1715. **Roller blading** Centre Point, 3rd Floor, Jln Gaya. **Sailing** Yacht club at Tanjung Aru, next to the hotel. **Watersports** *Tanjung Aru Marina*, snorkelling RM10 per day, water skiing RM120 per hr, fishing RM12-25 per day, sailing RM20-40 per hr, water scooter RM60 per hr. Snorkelling equipment for rent at good prices from the *Travellers Resthouse*. **Whitewater rafting** Papar River (Grades I & II), Kadamaian River (Grades II & III), Padas River (Grade IV). Usually requires a minimum of 3 people. Main operators including *Api Tours*, *Borneo Expeditions* and *Discovery Tours*.

Tour operators

The Sabah Tourism Promotion Corporation has a full list of tour and travel agents operating in the state

Adventure Journey World Travel, Ground Floor, Lot 5, Block A, Taman Fortuna Shoplots, Jln Penampang, T88223918, F248331, jworld@po.jaring.my *Airworld Travel & Tours*, 15, Ground Floor, Jln Pasar Baru, Kampong Air, T242996, F230998, airworld@tm.net.my *AIS Travel & Tours Sdn Bhd*, Lot 5, Block A, 1st Floor, Lorong Singgah Mata 1, Asia City, T223022, F238954, ais2506@tm.net.my *Api Tours (Borneo)*, No 13 Jln Punai Dekut, Mile 5, Jln Tuaran, PO Box 12851, T424156, F424174, www.jaring.my/apitours Offers a wide variety of tours, including some more unusual ones such as overnight stays in longhouses. Recommended. *Borneo Divers & Sea Sports*, 9th Floor, Menara Jubili, 53 Jln Gaya, T222226, F221550, www.jaring.my/bdivers (there is another branch in the *Tanjung Aru Beach Hotel*), operates exotic scuba diving trips and runs a dive station on Pulau Sipadan (see page 481), *Borneo Divers* also runs an excellent dive store and operates 5-days training courses with classes tailored for beginners or advanced divers (RM575-875 depending on group size), the company also has an office in Tawau T089761214, F089761691, and in Labuan, T087415867, F087413454 (see page 439) which organizes 2-day dives to shipwrecks off the island, trips are seamlessly organized, but very expensive. *Borneo Eco Tours*, Lot 12A, 2nd Floor, Lorong Bernam 3, T234002, F233688, www.borneoecotours.com Adventure and culture tours, ecotourist specialists – their *Sukau Rainforest Lodge* on the Kinabatangan River is highly recommended. *Borneo Sea Adventures*, 1st Flr, 8a Karamunsing Warehouse, T230000, F221106, bornsea@pop1.jaring.my Also conducts scuba diving courses and runs diving and fishing trips all around Sabah. It specializes in the 'Wall Dive' off Pulau Sipadan (see page 481). *Borneo Wildlife Adventures*, Lot F, 1st Floor, General Post Office Building, T213668, F219089, bwa@tm.net.my Specializing in nature tours, wildlife and cultural activities. *Coral Island Cruises*, 10th Floor, Wisma Merdeka, Jln Tun Razak, T223490, F223404, miao@po.jaring.my Specializes in boat cruises, mostly around Tunku Abdul Rahman National Park, and offers night fishing trips. *Coral Island Cruises* has teamed up with the Labuan-based dive company *Ocean Sports* to run 6-day scuba-diving trips to Layang Layang, an atoll in the disputed Spratly group, 6-16 days dive packages, costing RM1,000+, leave 2-3 times a month in peak season (Jun-Aug) (see box, page 419). Also operates dive voyages aboard *MV Coral Topaz* to Sipadan/Ligitan islands (see page 481). Recommended. *Diethelm Borneo Expeditions*, Suite 303, 2nd Floor, EON-CMG Life Building, 1 Jln Sagunting, T266353, T260353, dbex@tm.net.my *Discovery Tours*, Lot G22, Wisma Sabah, Jln Haji Saman, T221244, F221600, distour@po.jaring.my. Run by experienced tour operator Terry Lim. Recommended. *Exotic Borneo* , PO Box 470, Likas Post Office, Likas, T245920, F245902, exotic@po.jaring.my Organize well-run theme tours including culture, adventure and nature, at a price. *North Borneo Tours*, Lot 7, Ground Floor, Lorong Angsa 1, off Jln Kolam, Luyang, T, T268339, F268893, nbtt@tm.net.my Specializes in arranging golf days and tours. ***Pan Borneo Tours & Travel***, 1st Floor, Lot 127, Wisma Sabah, T221221, F219233, panborn@po.jaring.my Sightseeing, diving, wildlife tours. ***Sipadan Dive Centre***, 11th Flr, Wisma Merdeka, Jln Tun Razak, T240584, F240415, www.jaring.my/sipadan PADI dive courses taught and accommodation on Sipadan organized. Diving at Tunku Abdul Rahman Park also arranged. ***Tanjung Aru Tours***, The Marina, *Tanjung Aru Beach Hotel*, T214215, F240966, Fishing and island tours – particularly to Tunku Abdul Rahman National Park. ***Transworld***, 2nd Flr, Bangunan Dewan Perniagaan, Bumiputera Sabah, Jln Gaya, T211044, F225444 (also an office at *Tanjung Aru Beach Resort*). Glass-bottom boat trips to Tunku Abdul Rahman National Park.

Local Buses: city buses leave from the area between Jln Tun Razak and Jln Tugu. Buses from behind the *Centre Point Shopping Complex* go to Kapayan, Queen Elizabeth Hospital, Sembulan, Putatan, Jln Baru and Penampang. Red and white buses go to Penampang and Tanjung Aru and leave from the bus station in front of the MPKK Building, next to the state library. Green buses go to areas north of KK (Tuaran, Likas etc) and leave from the padang at the bottom of Signal Hill. *Luen Thong* white a/c buses go from in front of the *Shangri-La Hotel*, they go to Tuaran, Telipok, Dayavila and Kampung Likas. From MPKK building, *Luen Thong* a/c buses go to Tanjung Aru and Kapayan. **Minibuses**: all minibuses have their destinations on the windscreen, most rides in town are RM0.40-0.60 and they will leave when full. You can get off wherever you like.

Car hire: not all roads in the interior of Sabah are paved and a 4WD vehicle is advisable. However, car hire is expensive and ranges between RM30-80/hour. Rates often increase for use outside a 50 km radius of KK. All vehicles have to be returned to KK as there are no agency offices outside KK, although local car-hire is usually available. drivers must be between the ages of 22 and 60 and be in possession of an international driving licence. ***Adaras Rent-a-Car***, Lot G03, Ground Floor, Wisma Sabah, T2166671, F216010. ***Avis***, *Hyatt Kinabalu Hotel*, Jln Datuk Salleh Sullong, T428577. ***ABAN-D Rent a Car***, Lot 22, 1st Flr, Taman Victory, Mile 4.5, Jln Penampang, T 722300, F721959. ***Kinabalu Rent-a-Car***, Lot 3.61, 3rd Flr, Kompleks Karamunsing, T232602, F242512, www.kinabalurac.com/ ***Sabah Holidays Travel Rent-A-Car***, Lot 20 Ground Floor, Wisma Sabah, T222708, F 221751. ***Samzain Rent a Car***, Lot 10, Tingkat 2 Putatan Point, putatan 88200, Penampang, T765805.

Taxis: there are taxi stands outside most of the bigger hotels and outside the General Post Office, the Segama complex, the Sunsuran complex, next to the MPKK building, the Milemewah supermarket, the Capitol cinema and in front of the clocktower (for taxis to Ranau, Keningau and Kudat). Approximate fares from town: RM10 to *Tanjung Aru Beach Resort*, RM10 Sabah Foundation, RM8 to the museum, RM12 airport.

Long distance Air: the airport is 6 km from town, T238555. Air is the most widely-used form of transportation between the major towns of Sabah (**KK**, **Sandakan**, **Tawau**, **Lahad Datu**). Taxi RM17 to town centre; coupon can be purchased in advance from the booths outside the arrivals hall. Regular connections with KL, cheaper flights if in a group of 3 or more, late-night flights, or book 14 days in advance (RM311, 2 hrs 30 mins). There are also connections from **KK** with **Bintulu**, **Johor Bharu**, **Kuching** (RM233, 1 hr 20 mins), **Kudat**, **Lahad Datu**, **Labuan**, **Miri** (RM100, 40 mins), **Penang**, **Sandakan** (RM88, 40 mins), **Sibu** and **Tawau** (RM101, 45 mins). International connections are with **Singapore**, **Brunei**, **Hong Kong**, **Philippines**, **Korea**, **Japan** and **Taiwan**.

Road Bus: buses around the state are cheaper than minibuses but not as regular or efficient. The large buses go mainly to destinations in and around KK itself. **Minibus and taxi**: there is no central bus station in KK. Taxis and minibuses bound north for **Kota Belud**, **Tamparuli** and **Kudat** and those going south to **Papar**, **Beaufort**, **Keningau** and

Transport
77 km to Kota Belud
128 km to Keningau
386 km to Sandakan

Sabah

Most taxis are not metered

Advanced booking is suggested for minibus and taxi journeys

Tenom leave from Bandar Berjaya opposite the Padang and clocktower. Taxis and minibuses going west to **Kinabalu National Park**, **Ranau** and **Sandakan** leave from Jln Tunku Abdul Rahman, next to the Padang and opposite the State Library. **Tamparuli**, a few kilometres east of Tuaran, serves as a mini-terminus for minibuses heading to **Kinabalu National Park**. Minibuses leave when full and those for long-distance destinations leave in the early morning. Long-distance taxis also leave when full from in front of the clocktower on Jln Tunku Abdul Rahman. Minibus services from KK to **Tuaran** 45 mins, **Kota Belud** 2 hrs, **Kudat** 4-5 hrs, **Beaufort** 2-3 hrs, **Keningau** 2-3 hrs, **Tenom** 4 hrs, **Kinabalu National Park** 1½ hrs, **Ranau** 2 hrs, **Sandakan** 8-10 hrs.

Sea: There is a ferry service between **KK** and **Labuan** every day between 0710 and 1500. Ferries to **Brunei** leave from the Labuan jetty.

Train The station is 5 km out of town in Tanjung Aru. There is only one train line on Sabah, and rolling stock dates from the colonial era. Diesel trains run 3 times daily to **Beaufort**, 2 hrs and on to **Tenom**, a further 3 hrs. Departure times are subject to change, T254611. There is also a steam train which operates along this same line. For transport from the railway station to town: long distance buses stop near the station.

Directory **Airline offices** *British Airways*, Jln Haji Saman, T428057/428292. *Cathay Pacific*, Ground Floor, Block C, Lot CG, Kompleks Kuwasa, 49 Jln Karamunsing, T428733. *dragonair*, T 254733. *Garuda Airways*, Wisma Sabah. *MAS*, Ground Flr, Karamunsing Kompleks (off Jln Tunku Abdul Rahman, south of Kampung Ayer), Jln Kemajuan, T213555, F240135, also have an office at the airport. *Philippine Airlines*, 3rd Flr, Karamunsing Complex, Jln Kemajuan, T239600. *Royal Brunei Airlines*, Ground Flr, Kompleks Kowasa, T242193, *Sabah Air*, KK Airport, T256733. *Singapore Airlines*, Ground Flr, Block C, Kompleks Kowasa, T255444. *Thai Airways*, T232896, Lot CG14, Block C, Ground Flr, Kompleks Kowasa. *Qantas*, T216998.

Banks There are money changers in main shopping complexes. *Hong Kong & Shanghai*, 56 Jln Gaya. *Sabah Bank*, Wisma Tun Fuad Stephens, Jln Tuaran. *Standard Chartered*, 20 Jln Haji Saman. *Maybank*, Jln Kemajuan/ Jln Pantai.

Communications **General Post Office**: Jln Tun Razak, Segama Quarter (poste restante facilities). **Telekom**: Block C, Kompleks Kuwaus, Jln Tunku Abdul Rahman, international calls as well as local, fax service. **Internet cafés**: *Cybercafé*, Lot 95, Jln Gaya, T231089. Open 1000-0100. *Cybermaster*, Ground and 1st Flr, Api-Api Centre, T239868. Open 0900-0100.

Embassies and consulates *British Consul*, Hong Kong Bank Building, 56 Jln Gaya. *Indonesian Consulate*, Jln Karamunsing, T428100. *Japanese Consulate*, Wisma Yakim, T428169.

Medical facilities Health Care: one of the better private clinics is the Damai Specialist Centre.

Parks offices *Forestry Division*, Sabah Foundation, Sabah Foundation Building, Likas, T34596. *Innoprise Corporation Building*, Sadong Jaya, T243251 for the Danum Valley Field Centre (see page 478). *Sabah National Parks Office Headquarters*, 1st Flr, Lot 1-3, Block K, Sinsuran Kompleks, Jln Tun Fuad Stephens, T211652, F211585, necessary to book accommodation for the national parks (T211881), particularly Mount Kinabalu National Park or Poring Hot Springs. Also has general information on the parks, the office has a good library with reports on wildlife in the parks and natural history surveys which can be used with the permission of the office, open 0800-1600 Mon-Fri, 0830-1230 Sat.

Places of worship English: *St Simon's Catholic Church*, Likas, Sun 1700. *Stella Maris* (Tanjung Aru) Sun 0700. *SIB*, Likas (Baptist), Sun 0800.

Useful addresses **British Council:** Wing On Life Building, Jln Sagunting, 1st Flr, not very helpful. **Business centres:** at the *Hyatt Hotel* and *Shangri-La Tanjung Aru Resort* and *Shangri-La Rasa Ria*. **Immigration:** 4th Flr Government Building, Jln Haji Yaakub. Visas can be renewed at this office, without having to leave the country.

Tunku Abdul Rahman Park

The five islands in Gaya Bay, which make up Tunku Abdul Rahman Park (TAR), lie 3-8 km offshore. Named after Malaysia's first Prime Minister, they became Sabah's first national park in 1923 and were gazetted in 1974 in an effort to protect their coral reefs and sandy beaches. Geologically, the islands are part of the Crocker Range formation, but as sea levels rose after the last ice age, they became isolated from the massif. Coral reefs fringe all the islands in the park. The best reefs are between **Pulau Sapi** *and* **Pulau Gaya**, *although there is also reasonable coral around* **Manukan**, **Mamutik** *and* **Sulug***. The islands can be visited all year round.* Colour map 4, grid A3

Getting there Boats for the park leave from the jetty in central KK near the Hyatt Hotel (see map page 421). There are also frequent boats from the *Tanjung Arv Beach Resort*. Ins & outs

Some of the only undisturbed coastal dipterocarp forest left in Sabah is on Pulau Gaya. On the other islands most of the original vegetation has been destroyed and established secondary vegetation predominates, such as ferns, orchids, palms, casuarina, coconut trees and tropical fruit trees. Mangrove forests can be found at two locations on Pulau Gaya. Animal and bird life includes long-tailed macaques, bearded pig and pangolin (on Pulau Gaya), white-bellied sea eagle, pied hornbill, green heron, sandpipers, flycatchers and sunbirds. Flora & fauna

There is a magnificent range of marine life because of the variety of the reefs surrounding the islands. The coral reefs are teeming with fish-tank exotica such as butterfly fish, Moorish idols, parrot fish, bat fish, razor fish, lion fish and stone fish, in stark contrast to the areas which have been depth-charged by Gaya's notorious dynamite fishermen.

By far the largest island, **Pulau Gaya**, was the site of the first British North Borneo Chartered Company settlement in the area in 1882. The settlement lasted only 15 years before being destroyed in a pirate attack. There is still a large settlement on the island on the promontory facing KK – but today it is a shanty town, populated mainly by Filipino immigrants (see page 496). On Pulau Gaya there are 20 km of marked trails including a plank-walk across a mangrove swamp and many beautiful, little, secluded bays. Police Bay is a popular shaded beach. No facilities here, so bring own drink, food and snorkel gear. **Pulau Sapi**, the most popular of the island group for weekenders, also has good beaches and trails. It is connected to Pulau Gaya at low tide by a sandbar. Good day-use facilities but no accommodation available here. Beware of leaving your clothing unattended at the edge of the forest, as monkeys have been known to run off with it! **Pulau Mamutik** is the smallest island but closer to the mainland and has a well-preserved reef off the northeast tip, there is no The islands

Sabah

longer any accommodation here but there are diving facilities on the island and meals are provided for *Borneo Divers* clients. **Pulau Manukan** is the site of the Park HQ and most of the park accommodation. It has good snorkelling to the south and east and a particularly good beach on the east tip. It is probably the best of all the islands but is heavily frequented by day trippers and rubbish is sometimes a problem. Marine sports facilities stretch to the hire of mask, snorkel and fins (RM15 plus RM50 deposit for the day), no sub-aqua gear available, swimming pool, watersports centre for sailing, banana boat, windsurfing etc. Glass-bottom boat trips available. Fish feeding off the jetty attracts large shoales of fish - it is possible to snorkel amongst them when this is going on. The best reefs are off **Pulau Sulug**, which is less developed being a little bit further away. This small island has a sand spit, making it good for swimming. There are dive facilities and a restaurant here now.

Essentials

It is necessary to hire snorkel, mask and fins from boatmen at the KK jetty beforehand. Fishing with a hook and line is permitted but the use of spearguns and nets is not. Permits are not necessary. **Park HQ** is on Pulau Manukan; ranger stations on Gaya, Sapi and Mamutik.

Sleeping
Rooms are significantly discounted during the week

A *Gayana Island EcoResort* , Lot 16, Ground Floor, Wisma Sabah, Jln Tun Razak, T245158, F245168, www.gayana-ecoresort.com for more information. Set on the east coast of the island, 44 a/c chalets, restaurant (serves Asian and Western food, T245158), barbecue site, private beach, activities include diving, snorkelling, windsurfing, trekking in the jungle, fishing, yachting and a reef rehabilitation research centre.

Gaya and Manukan A (weekends)**–B** (weekdays) *Chalets*, Pulau Manukan, restaurant, pool, facilities including tennis and squash courts, football field, 1,500-m jogging track and a diving centre. *Chalets at Maluham Bay*, east of Police Bay, Pulau Gaya. **Camping** It is possible to camp on any of the islands (obtain permission from the Sabah Parks Office in KK). *Borneo Divers* provide 2 and 4 person tents for hire on Pulau Mamutik (RM35/pax/night).

Eating
Excellent restaurant on Pulau Manukan. Pulau Mamutik and Pulau Sapi each have a small shop selling a limited range of very expensive food and drink, and Sapi has some hawker-style food. For Pulau Sulug, Sapi and Mamutik take all the water you need – there is no drinkable water supply here, shower and toilet water is only provided if there has been sufficient rain.

Diving
There are at least ten popular dive sites around the TAR islands, with reef depths ranging from 3-21 m, providing a great variety of dive experiences. It is possible to dive throughout the year with an average visibility of about 12 m. The water is cooler from Nov to Feb, when visibility is not as good. For extensive information on the various coral/fish/dive sites, contact *Borneo Divers* at www1.jaring.my/bdivers/ Established in 1984, they remain the only professional full service dive company on Borneo.

Transport
3-8 km offshore

Boat Most boats leave from the jetty opposite the *Hyatt Hotel* throughout the day, fares ranges from RM10-16 and you can bargain. All passengers should wear a life-jacket. If you want to visit more than 1 island, a boat needs to be chartered, at a cost of about RM280 for a 3 island tour or RM360 for a 5 island tour, taking 12 passengers. Contact *Sutima Express*, 1st Flr, Lot 5, Sinsuran Complex. It is possible to negotiate trips with local fishermen. Boats also leave from *Tanjung Aru Beach Hotel*.

Directory

Useful addresses The following tour operators organise a variety of tours to the park, *Adventure JourneyWorld Travel*, Ground Floor, Lot 5, Block A, Taman Fortuna Shoplots, Jln Penampang, T88223918, F248331, jworld@po.jaring.my *Beringgis Marina and Tours*, 1st Floor, Lot 3, Block B, Bundusan Plaza, Jln Bundusan, T710395, F726395, bmteah@tm.net.my *Coral Island Cruises*, 10th Floor, Wisma Merdeka, Jln Tun Razak T223490, F223404, miaovo@pc.jaring.my *Tanjung Aru Tours*, *Tanjung Aru Beach Hotel*, T214215, F240966.

South of Kota Kinabalu

*Travelling south from KK, the route crosses the Crocker Range to **Tambunan**. Continuing south the road passes through the logging town of **Keningan** and on to **Tenom**, where it is possible to take the North Borneo railway, which snakes down the **Padas Gorge** to **Beaufort**. The **Padas River** is the best place to go whitewater rafting in Sabah. Few towns are worth staying in for long on this route but it is a scenic journey.*

Tambunan

The twisting mountain road that cuts across the **Crocker Range National Park** (see page 432) and over the Sinsuran Pass at 1,649 m is very beautiful. There are dramatic views down over Kota Kinabalu and the islands beyond and glimpses of Mount Kinabalu to the northeast. The road itself, from KK to Tambunan, was the old bridle way that linked the west coast to the interior. Inland communities traded their tobacco, rattan and other jungle produce for salt and iron at the coastal markets. The road passes through Penampang. Scattered farming communities raise hill rice, pineapples, bananas, mushrooms and other vegetables which are sold at road-side stalls, where wild and cultivated orchids can also be found. After descending from the hills the road enters the sprawling flood plain of Tambunan – the Pegalam River runs through the plain – which, at the height of the paddy season, is a magnificent patchwork of greens.

Colour map 4, grid B3
Population: 24,000

The Tambunan area is largely Kadazan/Dusun, Sabah's largest ethnic group, and the whole area explodes into life each May during the harvest festival when copious quantities of *lihing*, the famed local rice wine, are consumed and the *Bobolians* or high priestesses are still called upon to conduct various rituals (see page 491). There is a lihing (rice wine) brewery inside the *Tambunan Village Resort Centre*. The Tambunan District covers an area of 134,540 ha. At an altitude of 650 m to 900 m, it enjoys a spring-like climate during much of the year.

Tambunan, or 'Valley of the Bamboo', so-called as there are at least 12 varieties of bamboo to be found here, also lays claim to the Kitingan family. Joseph was Sabah's first Christian Chief Minister until deposed in March 1994. His brother, Jeffrey, was formerly head of the Sabah Foundation. He entered politics in 1994 on his release from detention on the peninsula. He had been charged under Malaysia's Internal Security Act of being a secessionist conspirator.

A concrete structure at Tibabar, just outside Tambunan, situated amongst the ricefields and surrounded by peaceful kampung houses, commemorates the site of **Mat Salleh's fort** and the place of his death. Mat Salleh, now a nationalist folk-hero, led a rebellion for six years against the Chartered

Rafflesia: the largest flower in the world

The rafflesia (Rafflesia arnoldi), named after Stamford Raffles, the founder of modern Singapore, is the largest flower in the world. The Swedish naturalist Eric Mjoberg wrote in 1930 on seeing the flower: "The whole phenomenon seems so amazing, so unfamiliar, so fantastic, that we are tempted to explain: such flowers cannot be real!" Stamford Raffles, who discovered the flower for Western science one hundred years earlier during his first sojourn at Bengkulu on the west coast of Sumatra, noted that it was "a full yard across, weighs 15 pounds, and contains in the nectary no less than eight pints [of nectar]...". The problem is that the rafflesia does not flower for very long – only for a couple of weeks, usually between August and December. Out of these months there is usually nothing to see. The plant is in fact parasitic, so appropriately its scent is more akin to rotting meat than any perfume. Its natural habitat is moist, shaded areas.

Company administration until he was killed in 1900 (see box). The memorial has been set up by the Sabah State Museum and houses some exhibits including weapons, Salleh paraphernalia and a photo of the man himself.

The Rafflesia Information Centre, located at the roadside on the edge of a Forest Reserve that has been set aside to conserve this remarkable flower (see box). The Information Centre has a comprehensive and attractive display on the Rafflesia and its habitat and provides information on flowers in bloom. If trail maps are temporarily unavailable, ask the ranger to point out the site blooms seen on the large relief model of the Forest Reserve at the back of the Information Centre. The blooming period of the flower is very short so to avoid disappointment, it may be worth phoning the centre first. ■ *Mon-Fri 0845-1245, 1400-1700, Sat-Sun 0800-1700, T087774691.*

Ahir Terjan Sensuron is a waterfall 4 km from Rafflesia Information Centre on the Tambunan-KK road (heading towards KK). From the road, it is a 45- minute walk to the waterfall. A large **market** is held here every Thursday morning – on sale are tobacco, local musical instruments, clothing, strange edible jungle ferns and yeast used to make fermented rice wine. There are also bundles of a fragrant herb known as *tuhau*, a member of the ginger family that is made into a spicy condiment or *sambal* redolent of the jungle. A smaller market is held every Sunday in Kampung Toboh, north of Tambunan.

Excursions **Crocker Range National Park** incorporates 139,919 ha of hill and montane forest, which includes many species endemic to Borneo. It is the largest single totally protected area in Sabah. No visitors' facilities have yet been developed. But private development is taking place along the narrow strips of land each side of the KK-Tambunan road, which were unfortunately overlooked when the park was gazetted. A decrepit motel – complete with a horrifying menagerie – has sprung up at Sinsuran Pass and an outward bound school also has its headquarters here. ■ *Getting there: see Transport below, as for Tambunan.* The **Mawah Waterfall** is reached by following the road north towards Ranau to Kampung Patau, where a sign beside the school on the left indicates a gravel road leading almost to the waterfall (*Mawah Airterjun*). It is 15 mins down road by car and five-ten minutes' walk along the trail.

Mat Salleh – fort-builder and folk hero

Mat Salleh was a Bajau, and son of a Sulu Chief, born in the court of the Sultan of Sulu. He was the only native leader to stand up against the increasingly autocratic whims of the North Borneo government as it sequestrated land traditionally belonging to tribal chiefs. Under the British North Borneo Chartered Company and the subsequent colonial administration, generations of school children were taught that Mat Salleh was a deplorable rabble-rouser and trouble-maker. Now Sabahans regard him as a nationalist hero.

In the British North Borneo Herald of 16 February 1899, it was reported that when he spoke, flames leapt from his mouth; lightening flashed with each stroke of his parang (cutlass) and when he scattered rice, the grains became wasps. He was said to have been endowed with 'special knowledge' by the spirits of his ancestors and was also reported to have been able to throw a buffalo by its horns.

In 1897 Mat Salleh raided and set fire to the first British settlement on Pulau Gaya (off modern-day Kota Kinabalu). For this, and other acts of sabotage, he was declared an outlaw by the Governor. A price tag of 700 Straits dollars was put on his head and an administrative officer, Raffles Flint, was assigned the unenviable task of tracking him down. Flint failed to catch him and Mat Salleh gained a reputation as a military genius.

Finally, the managing director of the Chartered Company, Scottish adventurer and former gun-runner William C Cowie, struck a deal with Mat Salleh and promised that his people would be allowed to settle peacefully in Tambunan, which at that time was not under Chartered Company control. After the negotiations Cowie wrote: "His manner and appearance made me aware that I was face to face with the Rob Roy of British North Borneo, the notorious Mat Salleh, whom I at once saluted with a takek [a greeting from an inferior]."

Half the North Borneo administration resigned as they considered Cowie's concessions outrageous. With it looking less and less likely that the terms of his agreement with Cowie would be respected, Mat Salleh retreated to Tambunan where he started building his fort; he had already gained a fearsome reputation for these stockades. West Coast Resident G Hewett described it as "the most extraordinary place and without [our] guns it would have been absolutely impregnable". Rifle fire could not penetrate it and Hewett blasted 200 shells into the fort with no noticeable effect. The stone walls were 2.5 m thick and were surrounded by three bamboo fences, the ground in front of which was studded with row upon row of sharpened bamboo spikes. Hewett wrote: "...had we been able to form any idea of the external strength of the place we should never have attempted to rush in as we did." His party retreated having suffered four dead and nine wounded.

Mat Salleh had built similar forts all over Sabah, and the hearts of the protectorate's administrators must have sunk when they heard he was building one at Tambunan. A government expedition arrived in the Tambunan Valley on the last day of 1899. There was intensive fighting throughout January, with the government taking village after village, until at last, the North Borneo Constabulary came within 50 m of Mat Salleh's fort. Its water supply had been cut off and the fort had been shelled incessantly for 10 days. Mat Salleh was trapped. On 31 January 1900 he was killed by a stray bullet which hit him in the left temple.

Sabah

Altitude: 2,642 m
The best time to climb is in March and it is advisable to take guides and porters for the tough climb (ask the District Officer in Tambunan)

Gunung Trusmadi, 70 km southeast of KK, is the second highest mountain in Malaysia, but very few people climb it: the climb is difficult and facilities, compared with Gunung Kinabalu, few. There are two main routes to the top: the north route, which takes four days to the summit (and three days down) and the south route, which is harder but shorter; two days to the summit. Trusmadi is famous for its huge, and very rare, pitcher plant *Nepethes trusmadiensis*, which is only found on one spot on the summit ridge (see page 563). It is also known for its fantastic view north, towards Gunung Kinabalu, which rises above the Tambunan Valley. There is a wide variety of vegetation on the mountain as it rises from dipterocarp primary jungle through oak montane forest with mossy forest near the summit and heath-like vegetation on top. An expedition to Trusmadi requires careful planning – it should not be undertaken casually. A more detailed account of the two routes can be found in *Mountains of Malaysia – A Practical Guide and Manual*, by John Briggs.

Sleeping & eating
The area is renowned for its rice wine (lihing) – watch it being brewed at the TVRC factory

C *Tambunan Village Resort Centre (TVRC)*, signposted off the main road before the town located on both sides of the Pegalam River, T774076, F774205. Collection of chalets and a 'longhouse' dormitory made of split bamboo. Restaurant, motel and entertainment centre (with karaoke and slot machines), hall and sports field. There are also a couple of retreat centres located about 10 mins' walk away. **C** *Gunung Emas Highlands Resort*, Km 52 (about 7 km from the Rafflesia Centre) some dorm rooms (**E**), some very basic tree houses, a fresh climate and good views. Mini zoo and restaurant serving local food. To get there take the Rabunan or the Keningau minibus and then another bus from Tambunan. **C-D** *Government Resthouse*, T774339. All hotels are out of town.

Shopping

Handicrafts *Handicraft Centre*, just before the Shell petrol station, for traditional weaving and basketry from the area. **Market** *Tamu* on Thu.

Transport
90 km to KK

Minibus: minibuses for **Tambunan** leave from the corner of Australia Pl/Jln Tunku Abdul Rahman in KK. Those leaving **Tambunan** go from the centre of town by the mosque. Regular connections to **KK**, 1½ hrs (RM10) and **Ranau** (RM10). **Taxi**: to KK for RM100.

Keningau

Colour map 4, grid B3
Phone code 087

The Japanese built fortifications around their base in Keningau during the Second World War. It is now rather a depressing, shabby lumber town, smothered in smoke from the sawmills. The timber business in this area turned Keningau into a boom town in the 1980s and the population virtually doubled within a decade. The felling continues, but there is not much primary forest left these days. There are huge logging camps all around the town and the hills to the west. Logging roads lead into these hills off the Keningau-Tenom road which are accessible by four-wheel drive vehicles. It is just possible to drive across them to Papar, which is a magnificent route. Anyone attempting the drive should be warned to steer well clear of log-laden trucks on their way down the mountain.

Excursions

Murut villages Sapulut is deep in Murut country and is accessible from Keningau by a rough road via Kampung Nabawan (four-wheel drive required). At Sapulut, follow the river of the same name east through Bigor and Kampung Labang to Kampung Batu Punggul at the confluence of Sungai Palangan, a two-and-a-half-hour journey. **Batu Punggul** is a limestone outcrop protruding 200 m above the surrounding forest, 30-minutes' walk from the kampung; it can be climbed without any equipment, but with care. It is quite a dangerous climb, but there are plenty of handholds, and the view of the surrounding forest from the top is spectacular. Both the forest and the caves in and around Batu Punggul are worth exploring. Nearby is the recently discovered, but less impressive, limestone outcrop, **Batu Tinahas**, which has huge caves with many unexplored passages. It is thought to have at least three levels of caves and tunnels.

From Sapulut, it is a fairly painless exercise to cross the border into Kalimantan. A short stretch of road leads from Sapulut to Agis which is just a four-hour boat ride from the border. There is even an immigration checkpoint at Pegalungan, a settlement en route. One particular longhouse is **Kampung Selungai**, only 30 minutes from Pegalungan. Here it is possible to see traditional boat builders at work, as well as weaving, mat making and beadwork. There are many rivers and longhouses in the area worth exploring. Given the luxury of time, it is a fascinating area where traditional lifestyles have not been much eroded. It is possible to charter a minibus along the Nabawan road to Sapulut, where you can hire boats upriver. At Sapulut, ask for Lantir (the headman, or *kepala*). He will arrange the boat trip upriver, which could take up to two days depending on the river, and accommodation in Murut longhouses, through the gloriously named *Sapulut Adventurism Tourism Travel Company*, run by Lantir and his mate. As in neighbouring Sarawak, these long upriver trips can be prohibitively expensive unless you are in a decent-sized group.

Leeches can be a problem here, so take salt with you

A-L *Juta*, T337888, F332888. **B** *Hillview Garden Resort*, PO Box 210, T333678 F331757, hillview@ tm.net.my Newer place with 25 rooms. Good option. **B** *Perkasa*, Jln Kampung Keningau, T331045, F334800. On the edge of town, a/c, Chinese restaurant, coffee house, health centre, comfortable rooms. **C** *Kristal Hotel*, Pegalan Shopping Complex, T338888, F736134. Reasonable place, void of any real character, but a relatively cheap option in a town short on decent cheap accommodation. **D-E** *Government Rest House*, T331525, dorms (**F**), book through Rural Development Corporation, T088428910.

Sleeping & eating
Seri Wah Coffee Shop, on the corner of the central square and a selection of foodstalls

Air Connections with **KK**. **Minibus** Minibuses leave from centre of town, by the market. Regular connections with **KK** and **Tenom**. **Taxi** KK costs around RM180.

Transport
40 km to Tenom
128 km to KK

Tenom

Situated at the end of the North Borneo Railway, southwest of Kenigau on the banks of the Sungei Lapas, Tenom is a hilly inland town, with a population of about 4,000, predominantly Chinese. Although it was the centre of an administrative district under the Chartered Company from the turn of the century, most of the modern town was built during the Japanese occupation in the Second World War. It is in the heart of Murut country, but do not expect to see longhouses and Murut in traditional costume; many Murut have moved into individual houses, except in the remoter parts of the interior, and their modernized bamboo houses are often well equipped.

Colour map 4, grid B3
Phone code 087

The surrounding area is very fertile and the main crops here are soya beans, maize and a variety of vegetables. Cocoa is also widely grown. The cocoa trees are often obscured under shade trees called *pokok belindujan*, which have bright pink flowers. The durians (see page 50) from Tenom (and Beaufort) are reckoned to be the best in Sabah. *Tamu* (market) on Sunday.

Excursions **Murut villages** There are many Murut villages surrounding Tenom all with their own churches. In some villages there is also an over-sized mosque or *surau*. The federal government has viewed the spread of Christianity in Sabah with some displeasure and there are financial incentives for anyone converting back to Islam. The Murut Cultural Centre lies 10 km out of town. Run by the Sabah Museum, it displays something of the material culture of the Murut people including basketry, cloth and the famous Murut trampolines of *lansaran*. The best local longhouses are along the Padas River towards Sarawak at Kampung Marais and Kampung Kalibatang where blowpipes are still made. At Kemabong, about 25 km south of Tenom, the Murut community, who are keen dancers, have a *lansaran* dancing trampoline; a wooden platform sprung with bamboo which can support about 10 Murut doing a jig. ■ *Getting there: there are irregular minibuses to the Murut villages; catch a bus from Tenom heading for Kuela Tomani.*

Sabah Agricultural Park, 15 km northeast of Tenom, is an initiative developed by the Sabah State Government for research. This is also the site of Tenom's orchid farm, which has been developed into an agrotourism park. ■ *0800-1300, Mon-Fri. Rumah Rehat Lagud Sebren (Orchid Research Station Resthouse, **E**) is 5 km from the centre and has a/c. Take a minibus from the main road and if driving, take the road over the railway tracks next to the station and head down the valley.*

Batu Bunatikan Lumuyu (rock carvings) are at Kuala Tomani near Kampung Tomani, 40 km south of Tenom. A huge boulder, now protected from the elements by a corrugated tin roof, is carved with mysterious, distorted faces. Swirling lines, etched into the rock, depict various facial features as well as feet, a bird and a snake. The rock was discovered by villagers clearing land for agriculture around the River Lumuyu in April 1971. The Sabah State Museum in KK has no idea what the patterns represent or how old they are. The local explanation is an absurd story about seven brothers, one of whom is killed, the other six doodle on a rock in their bereaved depression as they head into the mountains to bury him. Disappointing. ■ *Getting there You need a four-wheel drive vehicle to get there: from Tenom, head south, crossing the Padas River at Tomani. After 2 km, turn right, follow this track for 20 km, through Kampung Kungkular to Kampung Ulu Tomani. Outside Kampung Ulu Tomani, turn right just before the river. Follow the track for 1½ km. At the point*

Tenom

Not to scale

■ **Sleeping**   ● **Eating**
1 Orchid   2 Perkasa   1 Chi Hin   2 Restaurant   3 Yong Lee

Sabah

The railway which ran out of steam

In the last years of the 19th century, William Cowie, the managing director of the North Borneo Chartered Company, had a vision. With Governor Beaufort, he outlined his ambitious plans for a Trans-Borneo Railway, cutting through 200 km of dense jungle, from Brunei Bay to Sandakan, straight through the interior of North Borneo. Work started at Weston on Brunei Bay in 1896 and two years later, the stretch of line linking the new township and Beaufort triumphantly opened.

But AJ West, the railway engineer who humbly named the new town after himself, somehow overlooked the fact that Weston was surrounded by an impenetrable mangrove swamp, not an ideal location for a railway terminus or port. Two alternative sites were toyed with before the stretch of narrow land opposite Pulau Gaya was finally selected as the site for the new terminus in 1899. It was thought to be a promising site for a town as it had a sheltered harbour. They called it Jesselton.

But Cowie's visionary railway project, and the innovative telegraph line that was to run alongside the track, was to be a costly undertaking. The administration, headed by Governor Beaufort, levied a new tax on rice to pay for it: a move which proved disastrously unpopular. Chinese retailers and tribal chiefs petitioned London to intervene, but to no avail. Historians believe the North Borneo Railway indirectly sparked the six-year Mat Salleh rebellion (see page 433).

The 92-km line between Jesselton and Beaufort started operating in 1905. The track was pushed into the interior at the same time, and on 5 April 1905 the first train steamed into Tenom. The line went on to the railhead at Melalap, 16 km further up the valley. But that was as far as the 186-km 'trans-Borneo railway' ever got – it seems that after struggling up the Padas Gorge from Beaufort, the prospect of building another 200 km of track was too much to bear. The idea was abandoned. The towns of Papar, Beaufort and Tenom however, became totally dependent on the railway. The Chartered Company administration refused to build roads in an effort to force people to use it.

Oscar Cook, a former District Officer in the North Borneo Civil Service, served in Tenom in 1912, and recorded his journey from Beaufort in his 1923 book, Borneo: the Stealer of Hearts. "Normally the journey of about 30 miles took three hours, but one always considered it lucky to reach one's destination only an hour late. The route twisted and turned to such an extent, as the line followed its precarious course along the river bank, that passengers in the front portion could almost put their hands out of the windows and shake those of passengers in the rear. On wet days up certain grades passengers have even been known to descend and help push the train over the most slippery and steepest gradients, while at one watering place chocks of wood were invariably put under the engine wheels to prevent the train from slowly slipping backwards!"

The train, now pulled by a diesel engine, still creeps along the 45 km narrow-gauge track, and the 2½ hour trip is well worth it.

where a stream crosses the track, take the footpath to the rock carvings (20 mins). An HEP station was built on the Tenom River about 15 years ago. The power it generates supplies Tenom and all the surrounding districts.

AL-B *Perkasa*, top of the hill above the town (RM3 taxi ride), PO Box 225, T735811, F736134. A/c, restaurant, the *Tenom Perkasa* (one of a chain of three – the others are at Keningau and Kundasang) is a large, modern hotel, 7 storeys high, commanding superb views over Tenom and surrounding countryside. Rooms are spacious, carpeted, attractively furnished, with a/c, en suite bathroom, TV. As guests are few and far between, the restaurant has a limited but well-priced selection of Chinese and Western dishes. Staff are

Sleeping
Orchid Hotel and Sri Jaya Hotel are both within walking distance of the bus stop

friendly and helpful in organizing local sightseeing. Recommended. **C** *Orchid Hotel*, Block K, Jln Tun Mustapha, T737600, F736058, excelng@tm.net.my Small but friendly with clean, well-maintained rooms. **D** *Hotel Kim Sun*, 1 street north of Jln Tun Mustapha, T735485, friendly. **D** *Hotel Sri Jaya*, PO Box 47, T735007. The cheapest option, with 12 a/c rooms, shared bathroom, basic but clean.

Eating **Cheap** *Jolly*, near the station, serves Western food (including lamb chops) and karaoke. *Restaurant Curry Emas*, specializes in monitor lizard claypot curries, dog meat and wild cat. *Sabah*, Jln Datuk Yaseen, Muslim Indian food, clean and friendly. *Sapong*, Perkasa Hotel, local and Western. *Y&L (Young & Lovely) Food & Entertainment*, Jln Sapong (2 km out of town), noisy but easily the best restaurant in Tenom. It serves mainly Chinese food: freshwater fish (steamed *sun hok* – also known as *ikan hantu*) and venison, these can be washed down with the local version of *air limau* (or *kitchai*) which comes with dried plums, there is a giant screen which was shipped in to allow Tenomese to enjoy the 1990 Football World Cup. Recommended. **Seriously cheap** *Yong Lee Restaurant*, coffee shop serving cheap Chinese fare in town centre. *Restoran Chi Hin*, another Chinese coffee shop.

Foodstalls are at Gerai Makanan, above the market

Transport **Minibus** Minibuses leave from centre of town on Jln Padas. Regular connections with **Keningau** and KK 4 hrs. Minibuses to **Keningau** leave from rail station after a train has arrived. **Taxi** To **KK** costs around RM200 or shared taxis are available for a fraction of the price; they leave from the main street (Jln Padas). **Train** The journey through the **Padas River** gorge is particularly spectacular. Leaves 4 times a day and takes about 3 hrs to **Beaufort** and another 2½ hrs to **Tanjung Aru**, T735514.

140 km to KK
45 km to Beaufort

Sipitang Located on the coast, is a sleepy town with little to offer the traveller apart from a supermarket and the **B-C** *Shangsan Hotel*, T821800, which has fairly comfortable rooms with a/c and TV. The **B-C** *Hotel Asanol*, T821506, offers value for money rooms with bathrooms. There is the ubiquitous coffee shop in the same street as the *Shangsan* and a line of minibuses and taxis along the waterfront. The jetty for ferries to Labuan (daily departures) is a 10-minute walk from the centre.

Beaufort

Colour map 4, grid B3
Phone code: 087

This small, sleepy, unexciting town is named after British Governor P Beaufort of the North Borneo Company, who was a lawyer and was appointed to the post despite having no experience of the East or of administration. He was savaged by Sabahan historian KG Tregonning as "the most impotent Governor North Borneo ever acquired and who, in the manner of nonentities, had a town named after him." Beaufort is a quaint town, with riverside houses built on stilts to escape the constant flooding of the Padas River. The *Tamu* (market) is on Saturday.

Beaufort

■ **Sleeping**
1 Beaufort

● **Eating**
1 Ching Chin

Not to scale

To Sarawak Sipitang is south of Beaufort and the closest town in Sabah to the Sarawak border. It is possible to take minibuses from Beaufort to Sipitang and on to Sindumin, where you can connect with buses bound for Lawas in Sarawak by walking across the border to Merapok. There is an immigration checkpoint here and month-long permits are given for visitors to Sarawak.

C *Beaufort Hotel*, Lot 19-20, Lochung Park, T211911 F212590. Centre of town, a/c, 25 rooms. **D** *Mandarin*, Lot 38, Jln Beaufort Jaya, T212800. A/c. **D** *Padas*, riverfront by the bridge (opposite the fish market), T211441. A/c, restaurant, not as nice as the *Beaufort*.
   Cheap *Jin Jin Restaurant*, behind *Beaufort Hotel*, Chinese, popular with locals. *Beaufort Bakery*, behind *Beaufort Hotel*, "freshness with every bite". **Seriously cheap** *Ching Chin Restaurant*, Chinese coffee shop in town centre.

Sleeping & eating
A poor selection of hotels, all roughly the same and slightly overpriced. Rooms are a/c and have bathrooms

Minibus Minibuses meet the train, otherwise leave from centre of town. Regular connections with **KK**, 2 hrs. **Train** The KK-Tenom line passes through Beaufort: **Tenom**, 2½ hrs, KK, 3 hrs.

Transport
90 km to KK

Banks *Hongkong Bank & Standard Chartered* in centre of town. **Communications** General Post Office & Telekom: next to *Hongkong* Bank.

Directory

Pulau Labuan

Labuan is one of the historically stranger pieces of the Malaysian jigsaw, and so it remains such. Originally part of the Sultanate of Brunei, the 92 sq km island, 8 km off the coast of Sabah, was ceded to the British in 1846 – who were enticed to take it on because of the discovery of rich coal deposits. It joined the Malaysian Federation in 1963, along with Sabah and Sarawak. In 1984 it was declared a tax-free haven – or an 'International Offshore Financial Centre' – and hence this small tropical island with just 75,000-odd inhabitants has a plethora of name plate banks and investment companies. For the casual visitor – rather than someone wanting to salt away their million but in somewhere other than Switzerland – it offers some attractions, but not many. There are good hotels, lots of duty-free shopping, a golf course, sport fishing and diving plus a handful of historic and cultural sights.

Colour map 4, grid B2
Population: 75,000
Phone code: 087

Getting there From the airport 5 km from town there are flights to KK, Miri, Kuching and KL. By boat there are regular speedboats to Menumbok (2 hrs by bus from KK) and daily boat connections with Lawas and Limbang (Sarawak) and Sipitang. Ferries link Labuan with Brunei. **Getting around** There is a reasonable island bus network, a few car hire frims and a small number of taxis. **Tourist offices** Tourist Information, Lot 4260, Jln Dewan/Jln Berjaya, T423455, mtpblbu@tourism.gov.my

Ins & outs

History

With a superb, deep water harbour, Labuan promised an excellent location from which the British could engage the pirates which were terrorizing the Northwest Borneo coast. Labuan also had coal, which could be used to service steamships. Sarawak's Rajah James Brooke became the island's first governor in 1846. Two years later it was declared a free port. It also became a penal colony: long-sentence convicts from Hong Kong were put to work on the coal face and in the jungle, clearing roads. The island was little more than a malarial swamp and its inept colonial administration was perpetually plagued by fever and liver disorders. Its nine drunken civil servants provided a gold mine of eccentricity for the novelists Joseph Conrad and Somerset Maugham. In 'The Outstation', Maugham describes the desperate attempt by the resident Mr Warburton to keep a grip on civilization in the wilds of Malaysia: "The only concession he made to the climate was to wear a white dinner jacket; but otherwise, in a boiled shirt and high collar, silk socks and patent leather shoes, he dressed as formally as though he was dining at his club in Pall Mall. A careful host, he went into the dining room to see that the table was properly laid. It was gay with orchids, and the silver shone brightly... Mr Warbuton smiled his approval....".

By the 1880s ships were already bypassing the island and the tiny colony began to disintegrate. In 1881 William Hood Treacher moved the capital of the new territory of British North Borneo from Labuan to Kudat. And eight years later, the Chartered Company was asked to take over the administration of the island. In 1907 it became part of the Straits Settlements, along with Singapore, Malacca (Melaka) and Penang.

Modern Labuan

In 1946 Labuan became a part of British North Borneo and was later incorporated into Sabah as part of the Federation of Malaysia in 1963. Datuk Harris is thought to own half the island (including the *Hotel Labuan*). As Chief Minister, he offered the island as a gift to the federal government in 1984 in exchange for a government undertaking to bail out his industrial projects and build up the island's flagging economy. The election of a Christian government in Sabah in 1986 proved an embarrassment to the Malaysian Prime Minister Doctor Mahathir Mohamad: making it Malaysia's only non-Muslim-ruled state. As a result, Labuan has assumed strategic importance as a Federal Territory, wedged between Sabah and Sarawak. It is used as a staging post for large garrisons of the Malaysian army, navy and air force.

Bandar Labuan

South China Sea

Sleeping
1 Federal
2 Federal Inn
3 Global
4 Labuan
5 Mariner
6 Oriental

To Menumbok Ferry Terminal

Customs & Excise

Labuan Supermarket

Labuan Duty Free

Taxi Stand

Ferry Terminal

Labuan Fisheries

0 metres 100
0 yards 100

In declaring Labuan a tax haven – or, more properly, an International Off-shore Financial Centre – the Malaysian government set out its vision of Labuan becoming the Bermuda of the Asia-Pacific for the 21st century; more than 250 off-shore banks, insurance firms and trust companies had set up operations on the island by mid-1994. The island has attracted loans and deposits of more than US$1.6 billion. Critics and sceptics have long pointed to the fact that the standard trimmings of a tax haven are still hundreds of millions of dollars away, but the Financial Park complex with four 17-floor office towers was built to attract more business to the island. This, together with several five star hotels such as the *Sheraton* and the *Waterfront*, makes it seem that Labuan's days of being a sleepy rural backwater are over.

Included in the island's population of about 75,000 are 10,000 Filipino refugees, with about 21 different ethnic groups. The island is the centre of a booming 'barter' trade with the South Philippines; the island is home to a clutch of so-called string vest millionaires, who have grown rich on the trade. In Labuan, 'barter' is the name given to smuggling. The Filipino traders leaving the Philippines simply over-declare their exports (usually copra, hardwood, rotan and San Miguel beer) and under-declare the imports (Shogun jeeps, Japanese hi-fi and motorbikes), all ordered through duty-free Labuan. With such valuable cargoes, the traders are at the mercy of pirates in the South China Sea. To get round this, they arm themselves with M-16s, bazookas and shoulder-launched missiles. This ammunition is confiscated on their arrival in Labuan, stored in a marine police warehouse, and given back to them for the return trip.

Sights

Away from the busy barter jetty, Labuan Town, a name largely superseded by its name of Port Victoria, is a dozy, unremarkable Chinese-Malaysian mix of

Sabah

7 Pantai View	9 Pulau Labuan Inn	11 Victoria	● Eating
8 Pulau Labuan	10 Sheraton		1 Foodstalls
			2 Wong Kee

shophouses, coffee shops and karaoke bars. The **Labuan An'Nur Jamek State Mosque** is an impressive site, whilst the manicured **golf course** provides some light relief for tired businessmen. Illegal cockfights are staged every Sunday afternoon. There is an old brick **chimney** at Tanjung Kubong, believed to have been built as a ventilation shaft for the short-lived coal mining industry which was established by the British in 1947 to provide fuel for their steamships on the Far Eastern trade route. Remnants of the industry, which had petered out by 1911, are to be found in the shape of a maze of **tunnels** in this area. Near to Tanjung Kubong is a **Bird Park**.

On the west coast there are pleasant beaches, mostly lined with kampungs. There is a large Japanese war memorial on the east coast and a vast, and well tended, Allied war cemetery between the town and the airport with over 3,000 graves, most of which are unknown soldiers. In 1995 a commemoration service was held at the cemetery to mark the 50th anniversary of Allied Forces landing in Labuan. It was attended by veterans from the US, Australia and Britain. The Peace Park at Layang Layangan marks the Japanese surrender point on 9 September, 1945, which brought the Second World War to an end in Borneo.

Excursions

Boat trips can be made to the small islands around Labuan, although only by chartering a fishing vessel. The main islands are Pulau Papan (a boring island between Labuan and the mainland), Pulau Kuraman, Pulau Rusukan Kecil (known locally as '*the floating lady*' for obvious reasons) and Pulau Rusukan Besar ('*floating man*'). The latter three have good beaches and coral reefs but none has any facilities.

Off the south coast of the island is the **Marine Park**; a great place to dive, especially as there are four shipwrecks scattered in these waters. The park boasts 20 dive sites. See *Diving* below.

Essentials

Sleeping
■ *on map, page 440*
Price codes:
see inside front cover

There is plenty of choice here, but very little at budget level. **AL** *Sheraton Labuan*, Lot TL 462, Jln Merdeka, T422000, F422222, www.sheraton.com Situated opposite the Financial Park complex, this deluxe city hotel has 183 rooms and suites all with spacious bathrooms, and all the trimmings you would expect. Other facilities include pool with whirlpool and swim-up bar, business centre (in-room personal computer and faxes also available). Décor has all the opulence of a *Sheraton* with a vast lobby, clad in marble and dripping with chandeliers, and classy food outlets including *Victoria's Brasserie* for European fare and *The Emperor Chinese Restaurant* which specializes in Cantonese food. Staff are professional and offer top service with a smile. Recommended.

A *Labuan*, Jln Merdeka, T412502, F415355. A/c, restaurant, large concrete block on edge of town, grand lobby with an arcade of shops, rooms have seen better days but have a/c, in-house video and attached bathroom, Chinese and Japanese restaurants, coffee house and the *Rock Café Fun Pub*, pool. **A** *Manikar Beach Resort*, Jln Batu Manikar, T418700, F418732. On the northwest tip of Labuan, 20 mins from town centre (complimentary shuttle), although local ex-pats like to comment that things have slipped since it was taken over by the *Sheraton*, it is a stylish resort built with polished wood (the owner is a timber tycoon), set in 15 ha of gardens, dotted with tall palms which reach down to the beach. The 250 rooms, all sea-facing with generous balconies, are very spacious, paved with stone, tastefully furnished, complete with a/c, mini-bar, TV, in-house video, tea and coffee-making facilities. Large pool set at sea level with swim-up bar, separate children's pool, fitness centre, tennis, play-room, business centre, duty-free shop. The beach is regularly cleaned and sprayed so sandflies are not a problem, but the sea is not recommended for swimming due to jellyfish. Restaurant with indoor and outdoor dining areas, excellent quality food, good value theme buffet nights. Enquire about discounts offered – 50% discount for bookings and payment 14 days in advance. **A** *Tiara Labuan*, Jln Tanjung Batu, PO Box 80537, T414300, F410195. On the west coast next to the golf course, 5-min taxi ride from town centre, beautiful hotel and serviced apartments surrounding a large lotus pond and deep blue pool complete with jacuzzi. Built onto Adnan Kashoggi's old mansion, the property has an Italian feel with terracotta tiles, putty pink stone, a glorious gilt fountain, and long shady arcades. The original mansion now holds the reception, restaurant (food mediocre), and acres of opulent lounge including an Arab lounge which has low sofas, hubbly-bubbly pipes and a marble fountain. All 25 rooms, and also the 48 serviced apartments (1 or 2 bedroom) are complete with a/c, TV, mini-bar, ring electric hob, cooker hood and sink, and a living room. The Tanjung Batu beach, just across the road, is rather muddy, but good for walks when the tide is out. The *Labuan Beach Restaurant* is here too. On the whole, holiday-makers opt for the larger hotels, especially families, as the *Tiara* has no organized activities or kiddy pool, but this is partly what makes it a haven of tranquillity. Recommended. **A** *Water-front Labuan Financial Hotel*, 1 Jln Wawasan, T418111, F413468. This property, overlooking the new yacht marina (and also an industrial seascape) has cultivated a marina-look combined with the atmosphere of being on a luxury cruise. It has over 200 rooms, all with a/c, mini-bar, TV, tea and coffee-making facilities and opulent fittings. The main restaurant, in seafaring spirit, called the *Clipper*, serves Western and local food, there is also a bar, the *Anchorage*, which has live entertainment every evening except Mon. Other facilities include pool, tennis and health centre. The hotel also manages the marina with its total of 50 berthing spaces each of which has internationally rated facilities. The Harbour Master also organizes yacht charters and luxury cruises. Recommended.

B *Federal Inn*, Jln Dewan, T417811, F417996. Smart hotel, clean and reasonable, 39 rooms with a/c, attached bathroom, TV, in-house video and mini-bar. **B** *Global*, U0017, Jln OKK Awang Besar (near market), T425201, F425180. Best value for money in town, a/c, mini-bar, tea and coffee, TV, in-house video, complimentary shuttle to ferry and airport. Recommended. **B** *Mariner*, Jln Tg Purun (on crossroads opposite police HQ), T418822, F418811. A/c, restaurant, rooms well-equipped (including mini fridge, a/c, TV, in-house video and attached bathroom), good coffee house. Generous discounts available on request. **B** *Oriental*, U0123-4, Lot 33 and 34, Jln Bunga Mawar, T419019, F419408. Reception on first floor, clean, tiled rooms with a/c, TV, private bathroom. **B** *Pulau Labuan*, 27-28 Jln Muhibbah, T416288, F416255. A/c, restaurant (*Golden Palace Restaurant* downstairs). **B-C** *Pantai View*, Lot 119 and 120, Jln OKK Awang Besar, T411339, F419408. A/c, basic, not very clean and not much of a view of the *pantai*. **B-C** *Pulau Labuan Inn*, Lot 8, Jln Bunga Dahlia, T416833, F441750. The downmarket sister of the *Pulau Labuan*, spotlessly clean but small a/c rooms.

C *Federal Hotel*, Jln Bunga Kesuma, T411711, F411337. A/c, restaurant, all rooms have a/c, TV, in-house video, mini-bar fridge, complimentary tea and coffee maker, pink and pastels colour scheme, Chinese-run catering mainly for business people, clean, good value, run by same management as *Federal Inn*. **C** *Kelab Golf*, Jln Tanjung Batu, a/c, restaurant, 6 simple but pleasant rooms in the clubhouse, 3 have a view down the manicured fairways. **C** *Pertama*, Hujong Pasir, Jln OKK Awang Besar (next to fish market), T413311. A/c. **C** *Victoria Hotel*, Jln Tun Mustapha, T218511, F218077. One of the oldest hotels in Labuan, pale pink exterior with white stucco decorated lobby, 46 rooms, a/c, private bath. Recommended.

Sabah

Eating

Price codes: see inside front cover

Malay Cheap *Restoran Zainab*, Jln Merdeka (opposite duty-free shop), Indian/Muslim. *Seri Malindo*, next to *Federal Inn*, mixture of Malay and Western food. **Chinese** Several basic places to be found along Jln Merdeka and Jln OKK Awang Besar. **Expensive** *The Emperor Chinese Restaurant*, *Sheraton Labuan*, top-class Chinese cuisine, Cantonese specialities, fresh seafood, special *dim sum* on Sun and public holidays. Recommended. **Mid-range** *Golden Palace*, 27 Jln Muhibbah. *Wong Kee*, Lot 5 and 6, Jln Kemuning, large, brightly lit restaurant with a/c, good steamboat. Recommended. **Seriously cheap** *Café Imperial*, Chinese coffee shop behind *Federal Hotel*, better than average coffee shop fare.

International Mid-range *Country Deli Restaurant and Wine Bar*, Lot 25, Block D, Jati Commercial Centre, T410410. Malaysian pizza, take-aways possible. *Labuan Beach*, Jln Tanjung Batu, T415611. International and local cuisine, breezy location on sea shore, food not special but ambience makes up for it, as does very well chilled draft Carlsberg. Recommended. *Victoria's Brasserie*, *Sheraton Labuan*, European brasserie-style, good theme buffets as well as á la carte, prides itself on its 'show kitchen concept'. Recommended. *The Clipper*, *Waterfront Labuan Financial Hotel*, 24-hour up-market coffee shop with local and Western cuisine. Recommended.

Seafood Mid-range *Restaurant Pulau Labuan*, Lot 27-28, Jln Muhibbah, smart interior complete with chandeliers, a/c, fresh fish sold by weight – good tiger prawn). Recommended. *Sung Hwa Restaurant*, 2nd Flr, Ujong Pasir, Jln OKK Awang Besar (across from fish market and above Kedai Kopi South Sea. Recommended. **Cheap** *New Sung Hwa Seafood*, Jln Ujong Pasir, PCK Building, amongst best value seafood restaurants in Malaysia, chilli prawns, grilled stingray steak recommended, no menu. Recommended.

Foodstalls Above wet market and at the other end of town, along the beach next to the *Island Club*. There is an area of stalls on Jln Muhibbah opposite the end of Jln Bahasa, west of the cinema and there are a few hawker stalls behind *Hotel Labuan*.

Shopping

If you plan to take duty-free goods into Sabah or Sarawak, you have to stay on Labuan for a minimum of 72 hrs

Labuan Duty-free, Bangunan Terminal, Jln Merdeka, T411573. This opened in Oct 1990, 142 years after Rajah James Brooke first declared Labuan a free port. The island's original duty-free concession did not include alcohol or cigarettes, but the new shop was given special dispensation to sell them. Two months later the government extended the privilege to all shops on the island, which explains the absurd existence of a duty-free shop on a duty-free island. The shop claims to be the cheapest duty-free in the world, however, you will find competitively priced shops in town too, including *Monegain*. It can undercut most other outlets on the island due to the volume of merchandise it turns over: more than RM1mn a month. The shop owes its success to Filipino 'barter traders' who place bulk purchase orders for VCRs or hundreds of thousands of dollars' worth of *Champion* cigarettes. These are smuggled back to Zamboanga and Jolo and find their way onto Manila's streets within a week. Brunei's alcohol-free citizens also keep the shop in business – they brought nearly RM 2m worth of liquor from Labuan into Brunei within the first 3 months of the shop opening. Behind Jln Merdeka and before the fish market, there is a congregation of corrugated tin-roofed shacks which houses a small Filipino textile and handicraft market and an interesting Wet market.

Supermarkets *Milimewah*, Lot 22-27, Lazenda Commercial Centre, Phase II, Jln Tun Mustapha, department store with supermarket on ground floor. *Financial Park*, Jln Merdeka, shopping complex with Milimewah supermarket. *Thye Ann Supermarket*, central position below *Federal Inn*. *Labuan Supermarket*, Jln Bunga Kenanga, centre of town.

Sabah

Diving *Borneo Divers*, Lot 28, Lazenda Commercial Centre, Phase II (next to water-front), T415867, F413454. Specializes in 2-day packages diving on shipwrecks off Labuan for certified scuba divers, there are 4 wrecks in total, each wreck costs about RM100, 2-day packages with accommodation at the Manikar are possible. *Ocean Sports*, 134 Jln OKK Awang Besar, T415389, F411911/415844. Offers 5-day full-time scuba courses for RM700 and reef dives on the nearby islands of Pulau Kuraman, Pulau Rusukan Kecil and Pulau Rusukan Besar. These islands have good beaches but no facili-ties. Diving around Pulau Papan is not very exciting and the water is often cloudy because of river silt. The reefs around Labuan suffer from the after-effects of the Allied bombing during the Second World War and from Filipino dynamite fishermen. *Ocean Sports*, in association with *Coral Island Cruises* in KK takes groups of divers 18 hrs into the South China Sea to Terumba Layang Layang, an atoll on the edge of the disputed Spratly group, reputed to be "even better than Sipadan" (see also page 419).
Golf *Kelab Golf*, Jln Tanjung Batu. Magnificent 9-hole golf course. Visitors may be asked to see proof of handicap or a membership card from your own club. Non-mem-bers pay RM30 a round on weekdays, RM50 on weekends. There are also tennis courts at the golf club and a swimming pool which can be used by visitors for a modest fee.
Horse riding *Labuan Horse Riding Centre*, for a different way to sightsee.

Sports

Local Bus: local buses around the island leave from Jln Bunga Raya. **Car hire**: *Adaras Rent-a-Car*, T422630. *Travel Rent-a-Car*, T423600. **Taxi**: old Singapore NTUC cabs are not in abundant supply, but easy enough to get at the airport and from outside *Hotel Labuan*. It is impossible to get a taxi after 1900 but minibuses abound.

Transport
70 km to mainland

Long distance Air: airport 5 km from town. Regular connections with **KK**, **Miri**, **Kuching** and **Kuala Lumpur**. The MAS office is on Jln Bunga Kesuma, T412263. **Boat**: from the Bangunan Terminal Feri Penumpang next to the duty-free shop on Jln Merdeka. All times are subject to change, tickets are sold at arrival points at the ferry terminal, but can be bought in town at *Duta Muhibbah Agency* T413827. Regular connections with **Menumbok** (the nearest mainland point) by speedboat (30 minutes) or car ferry. It's a 2-hr bus ride from here to **KK**. At present there are 5 boats a day to **Kota Kinabalu**, 2½ hrs. There is a daily boat to **Limbang** at 1230 and one to **Lawas** (both Sarawak), at 1300. There's also a boat to **Sipitang**, on the border with Sarawak.
   To Brunei: on weekends and public holidays in Brunei the ferries are packed out and it is a scramble to get a ticket. It is possible to reserve tickets to Brunei at the follow-ing agents: *Victoria Agency House*, T412332, (next to the *Federal Hotel* in Wisma Kee Chia), *Borneo Leisure Travel*, T410251, F419989 (opposite *Standard Chartered*) and the booking office at the back of the *Sports Toto* on Jln Merdeka all deal with advanced bookings to Brunei. 4 boats leave Labuan for Brunei (Bandar Seri Begawan) at 0830, 1100, 1200 and 1500, 1½ hrs.

Airline offices *MAS*, Wisma Kee Chia, Jln Bunga Kesuma, T412263.
Banks *Hongkong*, Jln Merdeka. *Standard Chartered*, Jln Tanjung Kubang (next to *Victoria Hotel*). *Syarikat K Abdul Kader*, money changer. **Communications** General Post Office: Jln Merdeka.

Directory

Papar

Formerly a sleepy Kadazan village, about 40 km south of KK, Papar is devel-oping fast. In *bandar lama* (the old town) there are several rows of quaint wooden shophouses, painted blue and laid out along spacious boulevards lined with travellers' palms. There is a large market in the centre of town. The Papar area is famous for its fruit and there is a good *tamu* every Sunday.

Colour map 4, grid B3
Phone code: 088

There is a scenic drive between Papar and KK, with paddy fields and jungle lining the roadside. The nearby beach at Pantai Manis is good for swimming and can be reached easily from Papar. It is also possible to make boat trips up the Papar River, which offers gentle rapids for less-energetic whitewater-rafters. Whitewater rafting trips can be organized through tour agents in KK (see page 426).

Excursions **Pulau Tiga National Park** is 48 km south of KK. Declared a forest reserve in 1933, the 15,864 ha park is made up of three islands: Pulau Tiga, Kalampunian Damit and Kalampunian Besar. Pulau Tiga has achieved notoriety as being the location for the reality TV series 'Survivor', chosen for its unspoilt natural landscape. Pulau Tiga's three low hills were all formed by mud volcanoes. The last big eruption was in 1941, which was heard 160 km away and covered the island in a layer of boiling mud. The dipterocarp forest on the islands is virtually untouched and they contain species not found on other west coast islands, such as a poisonous amphibious sea snake (*Laticauda colubrina*), which comes ashore on Pulau Kalampunian Damit to lay its eggs. Rare birds such as the pied hornbill (*Anthracoceros convexus*) and the megapode (*Megapodus freycinet*) are found here, as well as flying foxes, monitor lizards, wild fruit trees and mangrove forest. A network of trails, marked at 50 m intervals leads to various points of interest. The best time to visit is between February and April, when it is slightly drier and the seas are calmer. The Park HQ, on the south side of Pulau Tiga, is mainly used as a botanical and marine research centre and tourism is not vigorously promoted, as a result there are no special facilities for tourists. ■ *Getting there: either drive 140 km to Kuala Penyu, at the tip of the Klias Peninsula and then take a 30- minute boat-ride, or charter a speedboat from KK; call the Parks Office to organize transport to the island, T011 810636. RM30/person with a minimum of five passengers.*

Sleeping *Pulau Tiga Resort*, T(088)240584, F240415, sipadan@po.jaring.my Wholly owned by *Sipadan Dive Centre*. There is also a hostel that can accommodate 32 people. Accommodation must be booked in advance through the Sabah Parks Office in KK; no food is provided. It is possible to camp.

The **Klias Wetlands** is a 'new' destination being promoted by Sabah Tourism Promotion Corporation, popular with visitors who do not have time to visit the east coast of Sabah. It provides the experience of taking a boat through a mangrove swamp. As boats take visitors down the Klias River, wildlife on offer include the hideous proboscis monkey, long-tailed macaques, silver languor monkeys and an abundance of birdlife. ■ *To get there, the Klias Peninsula lies 120 km south of KK. Trips down the Klias River depart from the Kota Klias jetty. Engaging a tour operator is recommended* (Beringgis Marina *and* Tours, Comfort Paradise, Diethelm Borneo Expeditions *or* Suniland Travel and Tours, *all in KK*).

Pantai Manis, just outside Papar, is a 3-km long stretch of golden sand, with a deep lagoon.

Sleeping **A** *KRK 'Mai Aman Country Rest House*, KM 35, off Old Papar Rd, Kinarut. T912580, F256717, verus@pc.jaring.my 6-room country resthouse and 12 room bush hostel. Luxurious place, with fishing on site in spacious grounds with an orchard. **B** *Beringgis Beach Resort*, Km 26, Jln Papar, Kampung Beringgis, Kinarut, T752333, F752999, ketlee@bigfoot.com A/c, hot baths, car rental, conference halls, private beach, pool, watersports, tours and sports facilities. **B** *Walai Sabah (Borneo Paradise Beach Hotel)*, Km 22.5, Papar-KK Highway, Kinarut, T 752693, F752692, walai@po.jaring.my **B-E** *Sea Side Travellers Inn*, Km 20 Papar-KK Highway, Kinarut, T750555, F750479, www.infosabah.com.my/seaside Restaurant, range of a/c or fan accommodation from dorm to detached bungalows, breakfast included, pleasant location off the beach. Tennis court, pool. Horse-riding and tours can be organized.

There are several run-of-the-mill coffee shops and restaurants in the old town. **Seriously cheap** *Seri Takis*, Papar New Town (below the lodging house), Padang food; *Sugar Buns Bakery*, old town.

Eating

Minibus: leave from Bandar Lama area. Regular connections with **KK**, 1 hr and Beaufort, 1 hr.

Transport
40 km S of KK

North of Kota Kinabalu

*From KK, the route heads north to the sleepy Bajau town of **Kota Belud** which wakes up on Sunday for its colourful tamu market (open air-trade fair). Near the northernmost tip of the state is **Kudat**, the former state capital. The region north of KK is a more interesting area with **Gunung Kinabalu** always in sight. From Kota Belud, the mountain looks completely different. It is possible to see its tail, sweeping away to the east and its western flanks, which rise out of the rolling coastal lowlands.*

Kota Belud

This busy little town is in a beautiful location, nestling in the foothills of Mount Kinabalu on the banks of the Tempasuk River, but has little to recommend it save its *tamu*. It is the heart of Bajau country – the so-called 'cowboys of the East' but is of little obvious interest to most tourists.

Colour map 4, grid A3

The first Bajau to migrate to Sabah were pushed into the interior, around Kota Belud. They were originally a seafaring people but then settled as farmers in this area. The famed Bajau horsemen wear jewelled costumes, carry spears and ride bareback on ceremonial occasions. The ceremonial headdresses worn by the horsemen, called *dastars*, are woven on backstrap looms by the womenfolk of Kota Belud. Each piece takes four to six weeks to complete. Traditionally, the points of the headdress were stiffened using wax; these days, strips of cardboard are inserted into the points.

The largest *tamu*, in Sabah is held every Sunday in Kota Belud behind the mosque, starting at 0600. A mix of races, Bajau, Kadazan/Dusun, Rungus, Chinese, Indian and Malay, come to sell their goods and it is a social occasion as much as it is a market. Aside from the wide variety of food and fresh produce on sale, there is a weekly water buffalo auction at the entrance to the *tamu*. However the 'tamu besar', or big market, is held in November, when cultural performances take place and handicrafts are on sale.

Visitors are strongly recommended to get there early, but don't expect to find souvenirs at these markets

This is the account of a civil servant, posted to the KB district office in 1915: "The tamu itself is a babel and buzz of excitement; in little groups the natives sit and spread their wares out on the ground before them; bananas, *langsats*, pines and bread-fruit; and, in season, that much beloved but foul-smelling fruit the Durian. Mats and straw-hats and ropes; fowls, ducks,

Sabah

Tamus in Kota Belud District

Tuesday: Pandasan (along the Kota Belud to Kudat road).
Wednesday: Keelawat (along the Kota Belud to KK road).
Thursday: Pekan Nabalu (along the Kota Belud to Ranau road).

Friday: Taginambur (along the Kota Belud to Ranau road, 16 km from Kota Belud).
Monday and Saturday: Kota Belud.
Market time: 0600-1200. All tamus provide many places to eat.

goats and buffaloes; pepper, *gambia sirih* and vegetables; rice (padi), sweet potatoes, *ubi kayu* and indian-corn; dastars and handkerchiefs, silver and brassware. In little booths, made of wood, with open sides and floors of split bamboos and roofs of atap (sago palm-leaf) squat the Chinese traders along one side of the Tamu. For cash or barter they will sell; and many a wrangle, haggle and bargain is driven and fought before the goods change hands, or money parted with."

Excursions   **Tempasuk River** has a wide variety of migrating birds and is a proposed conservation area. More than 127 species of birds have been recorded along this area of the coastal plain and over half a million birds flock to the area every year, many migrating from north latitudes in winter. These include 300,000 swallows, 50,000 yellow longtails and 5,000 water birds. The best period for birdwatching is from October to March.

Between Kota Belud and the sea, there are **mangrove swamps** with colonies of proboscis monkeys. It is possible to hire small fishing boats in town to go down the Tempasuk River (RM10 per hour).

Sleeping   **C** *Kota Belud*, 21 Lebuh Francis (just off the central square), T976576. A/c, noisy. **C** *Tai Seng*, also on Central Square, some a/c, minimalist but adequate. **D** *Impian Siu Motel*, Kg Sempirai, Jln Kuala Abai, T976617. Just 5 rooms in this reasonable place. You get what you pay for. **E** *Government Resthouse*, Jln Ranau (on hill north of town, signed from the main road), T967532. Some a/c, often full of officials.

Homestay programme in Kota Belud village: there is no limit to your length of stay. Live with and be treated as part of the family, getting invited to celebrations such as weddings, etc. Activities include buffalo riding, jungle trekking, river swimming, cultural dancing, visits to local *tamus*, padi planting. The basic price is RM10 per week. Arrange through *Borneo Expedition and Exotic Borneo*, for more information contact Terisah Yapin, PO Box 13337, T242433, F223443. Very affordable for young travellers and an excellent way to learn the language and gain an in-depth knowledge of the culture.

Eating   There are several Indian coffee shops around the main square. **Cheap** *Bismillah Restoran*, 35 Jln Keruak (main square), excellent *roti telur*. *Indonesia Restoran*, next to the car park behind the *Kota Belud Hotel*.

Entertainment   The annual *Tamu Besar* includes a parade and equestrian games by the Bajau Horsemen, a very colourful event, held in Nov (contact the tourist office in KK for more details, 52 Jln Gaye, T212121, info@sabatourism.com).

Shopping   Market in main square every day, fish market to the south of the main market. Large *tamu* every Sun and an annual Tamu Besar, both provide a wide variety of local handicrafts amongst the day-to-day items. **Handicraft centre** Just outside town.

The **'Longhouse Experience'** is possibly the most memorable thing to do in Kudat. A stay at a longhouse enables visitors to observe, enjoy and take part in the Rungus' unique lifestyle. There are two Baranggaxo longhouses with 10 units. Nearby there are the village's only modern amenities, toilets and showers. During the day, the longhouse corridor is busy with Rungus womenfolk at work stringing elaborate beadworks, weaving baskets and their traditional cloth. Visitors can experience and participate in these activities. Longhouse meals are homegrown, fish and seafood come from nearby fishing villages, drinks consist of young coconuts and local rice wine. Evening festivities consist of the playing of gongs with dancers dressed in traditional Rungus costume. Tour companies organize trips.

Look at Longhouse rules for advice on visiting longhouses (see page 347)

For those wanting a less touristy visit to a longhouse, **Matunggong** is an area found on the road south of Kudat best known for its longhouses, though they are rather dilapidated now. For more information in visiting longhouses, enquire at the Sabah Tourist Promotion Corporation (STPC), T212121, www.sabahtourism.com

At **Kampung Gombizau**, visitors get to see bee-keeping and the process of harvesting beeswax, honey and royal jelly; while **Kampung Sumangkap**, an enterprising little village, offers visitors traditional gong-making and handicraft-making by the villagers.

C *Greenland*, Lot 9/10, Block E, Sedco Shophouse (new town), T613211, F611854. A/c, standard rooms, shared bath. **C** *Kinabalu*, Kudat Old Town, T613888. A/c, clean enough, average value. **C** *Sunrise*, 21 Jln Lo Thien Hock, T611517. A/c, restaurant (*Silver Inn*). **D** *Southern Hotel*, Kudat Old Town, T613133. Only 10 rooms, but quite cheap and represents reasonable value in comparison to its competitors. **E** *Government Resthouse*, T61304. **E** *Oriental*, Jln Lo Thien Chock, T61677/61045. A/c, big, clean rooms, some shared bathrooms.

Sleeping & eating
The Sunrise and Oriental hotels are within walking distance of the bus stop

Malay Seriously cheap *Restoran Rakyat*, Jln Lo Thien Hock. *Cahaya Timur*, Jln Lo Thien Hock (next to *Kudat Hotel*). **Chinese Cheap** *Silver Inn*, Jln Lo Thien Hock (below *Sunrise*).

Air Connections with **KK**, **Sandakan**. **Minibus** Minibuses leave from Jln Lo Thien Hock. Regular connections with **KK**, 4 hrs.

Transport
122 km N of KK

Banks *Standard Chartered*, Jln Lo Thien Hock.

Directory

Gunung Kinabalu Park

Gunung Kinabalu is the pride of Sabah, the focal point of the national park and probably the most magnificent sight in Borneo. In recognition of this, in 2000 the park was declared a World Heritage Site by UNESCO – a first for Malaysia. Although Gunung Kinabalu has foothills, its dramatic rockfaces, with cloud swirling around them, loom starkly out of the jungle. The view from the top is unsurpassed and on a clear day you can see the shadow of the mountain in the South China Sea, over 50 km away.

Colour map 4, grid A3
Phone code 088

In the first written mention of the mountain, in 1769, Captain Alexander Dalrymple of the East India Company, observing the mountain from his ship in the South China Sea, wrote: "Though perhaps not the highest mountain in the world, it is of *immense* height." During the Second World War Kinabalu was used as a navigational aid by Allied bombers – one of whom

Sabah

was quoted as saying "That thing must be near as high as Mount Everest". It's not, but at 4,101 m, Gunung Kinabalu is the highest peak between the Himalayas and New Guinea. It is not the highest mountain in Southeast Asia: peaks in Northern Burma and the Indonesian province of Irian Jaya are higher.

Gunung Kinabalu is an important watershed with eight major rivers originating on the mountain. It has been gazetted to protect the mountain and its remarkably diverse flora and fauna

There are a number of theories about the derivation of its name. The most convincing is the corruption of the Kadazan *Aki Nabulu* – 'the revered place of the spirits'. For the Kadazan, the mountain is sacred as they consider it to be the last resting place of the dead, and the summit was believed to be inhabited by their ghosts. In the past the Kadazan are said to have carried out human sacrifices on Mount Kinabalu, carrying their captives to the summit in bamboo cages, where they would be speared to death. The Kadazan guides still perform an annual sacrifice to appease the spirits. Today they make do with chickens, eggs, cigars, betel nuts and rice, on the rock plateau below the Panar Laban Rockface.

The Chinese also lay claim to a theory. According to this legend, a Chinese prince arrived on the shores of Northern Borneo and went in search of a huge pearl on the top of the mountain, which was guarded by a dragon. He duly slew the dragon, grabbed the pearl and married a beautiful Kadazan girl. After a while he grew homesick, and took the boat back to China, promising his wife that he would return. She climbed the mountain every day for years on end to watch for her husband's boat. He never came and in desperation and depression, she lay down and died and was turned to stone. The mountain was then christened *China Balu* – or Chinaman's widow.

In 1851, Sir Hugh Low, the British colonial secretary in Labuan made the first unsuccessful attempt at the summit. Seven years later he returned with Spencer St John, the British Consul in Brunei. Low's feet were in bad shape after the long walk to the base of the mountain, so St John went on without him, with a handful of reluctant Kadazan porters. He made it to the top of the conical southern peak, but was "mortified to find that the most westerly [peak] and another to the east appeared higher than where I sat." He retreated, and returned three months later with Low, but again failed to reach the summit, now called Low's Peak (standing at 4,095 m above sea level). It remained unconquered for another 30 years. The first to reach the summit was John Whitehead, a zoologist, in 1888. Whitehead spent several months on the mountain collecting birds and mammals and many of the more spectacular species bear either Low's or Whitehead's name. More scientists followed and then a trickle of tourists but it was not until 1964, when Kinabalu Park (encompassing 75,000 ha) was gazetted, that the 8½ km trail to the summit was opened. Today the mountain lures around 200,000 visitors a year. Although the majority are day visitors who do not climb the peak, the number of climbers is steadily increasing, with around 30,000 making the attempt each year.

In plan, the top of the mountain is U-shaped, with bare rock plateaux. Several peaks stand proud of these plateaux, around the edge of the U; the space between the western and eastern arms is the spectacular gully known as Low's Gully. No one has ever scaled its precipitous walls, nor has anyone climbed the Northern Ridge (an extension of the eastern arm) from the back of the mountain. From Low's Peak, the eastern peaks, just 1½ km away, look within easy reach. As John Briggs points out in his book *Mountains of Malaysia*, "It seems so close, yet it is one of the most difficult places to get to in the whole of Borneo."

Flora and fauna

The range of climatic zones on the mountain has led to the incredible diversity of plant and animal life. Kinabalu Park is the meeting point of plants from Asia and Australasia. There are thought to be over 1,200 species of orchid alone, and this does not include the innumerable mosses, ferns and fungi. These flowering plants of Kinabalu are said to represent more than half the families of flowering plants in the world. Within the space of 3 km, the vegetation changes from lowland tropical rainforest to alpine meadow and cloud forest. The jungle reaches up to 1,300 m; above that, to a height of 1,800 m, is the lower montane zone, dominated by 60 species of oak and chestnut; above 2,000 m is the upper montane zone with true cloud forest, orchids, rhododendrons and pitcher plants. Above 2,600 m, growing among the crags and crevices of the summit rock plateau are gnarled tea trees (*Leptospermums*) and stunted rhododendrons. Above 3,300 m, the soil disappears, leaving only club mosses, sedges and Low's buttercups (*Ranunculus lowii*), which are alpine meadow flowers.

It has one of the richest assemblages of flora in the world, with over 2,000 species of flowering plants

Among the most unusual of Kinabalu's flora is the world's largest flower, the rust-coloured Rafflesia (see box on page 432). They can usually only be found in the section of the park closest to Poring Hot Springs. Rafflesia are hard to find as they only flower for a couple of days; the main flowering season is from May to July.

Kinabalu is also famous for the carnivorous pitcher plants, which grow to varying sizes on the mountain. A detailed guide to the pitcher plants of Kinabalu can be bought in the shop at Park HQ. Nine different species have been recorded on Kinabalu. The largest is the giant Rajah Brooke's pitcher plant; Spencer St John claimed to have found one of these containing a drowned rat floating in four litres of water. Insects are attracted by the scent and when they settle on the lip of the plant, they cannot maintain a foothold on the waxy, ribbed surface. At the base of the pitcher is an enzymic fluid which digests the 'catch' (see box, page 563).

Rhododendrons line the trail throughout the mossy forest (there are 29 species in the park), especially above the Paka Cave area. One of the most beautiful is the copper leafed rhododendron, with orange flowers and leaves with coppery scales underneath. There are an estimated 1000 species of orchid in the park, along with 621 species of fern and 52 palm species.

It is difficult to see wildlife on the climb to the summit as the trail is well used, although tree shrews and squirrels are common on the lower trails. There are, however, more than 100 species of mammal living in the park. The Kinabalu summit rats, which are always on cue to welcome climbers to Low's Peak at dawn, and nocturnal ferret badgers are the only true montane mammals in Sabah. As the trees thin with altitude, it is often possible to see tree-shrews and squirrels, of which there are over 28 species in the park. Large mammals, such as flying lemurs, redleaf monkeys, wild pigs, orang-utan and deer, are lowland forest dwellers. Nocturnal species include the slow loris (*Nycticebus coucang*) and the mischievous-looking bug-eyed tarsier (*Tarsius bancanus*).

Over half of Borneo's 518 species of bird have also been recorded in Kinabalu Park, but the variety of species decreases with height. Two of the species living above 2,500 m are endemic to the mountain: the Kinabalu friendly warbler and the Kinabalu mountain blackbird.

More than 61 species of frogs and toads and 100 species of reptile live in the park. Perhaps the most interesting frog in residence is the horned frog,

Sabah

which is virtually impossible to spot thanks to its mastery of the art of camouflage. The giant toad is common at lower altitudes; he is covered with warts, which are poisonous glands. When disturbed, these squirt a stinking, toxic liquid. Other frogs found in the park include the big-headed leaf-litter frog, whose head is bigger than the rest of its body, and the green stream shrub frog, who has a magnificent metallic green body, but is deadly if swallowed by any predator.

The famous flying tree snake (the subject of an early film by the British nature documentary-maker David Attenborough) has been seen in the park. It spreads its skin flaps, which act as a parachute when the snake leaps blindly from one tree to another.

There are nearly 30 species of fish in the park's rivers, including the unusual Borneo sucker fish (*Gastomyzon borneensis*), which attaches itself to rocks in

Gunung Kinabalu Trail

Sleeping
1 Laban Rata
Resthouse & Restaurant

fast-flowing streams. One Sabah Parks publication likens them to 'underwater cows', grazing on algae as they move slowly over the rocks.

Walkers and climbers are more likely to come across the park's abundant insect life than anything else. Examples include pill millipedes, rhinoceros beetles, the emerald green and turquoise jewel beetles, stick insects, 'flying peapods', cicadas, and a vast array of moths (including the giant atlas moth) and butterflies (including the magnificent emerald green and black Rajah Brooke's birdwing).

The climb

The climb to the summit and back should take two days; four to six hours from park HQ at 1,585 m to the *Laban Rata Resthouse* (3,550 m) on the first day and then three hours to the summit for dawn, returning to the Park HQ at around 1300 hours on the second day. Gurkha soldiers and others have made it to the summit and back in well under three hours. For the really keen, or the really foolhardy, depending on one's perspective and inclination, there is also the annual Kinabalu Climbathon which is held in early October. Having said that the climb to the top 'requires no special skills', the death of an English student on the mountain in 2001 highlights the hazards of climbing an unfamiliar mountain where changes in the weather can be sudden and dramatic. Keep to the trails and avoid parting company with your group.

Mount Kinabalu is a tough, steep climb but requires no special skills or equipment

A jeep for 12 people can take groups from headquarters to the power station at 1,829 m where the trail starts (RM10-20). A minibus also makes the 5½ km run to the power station from Park HQ on a regular basis (RM2). It is a 25-minute walk from the power station to the first shelter, Pondok Lowi. The trail splits in two soon afterwards, the left goes to the radio station and the helipad and the right towards the summit. The next stop is Layang Layang staff headquarters (drinking water, cooking facilities, accommodation) – also known as *Carson's Camp* (2,621 m), named after the first warden of the park. There is one more shelter, Ponkok Villosa (2,942 m, and about 45 minutes from Carson's Camp) before the stop at the path to Paka Caves – really an overhanging rock on the side of a stream. Paka is a 10-minute detour to the left, where Low and St John made their camps.

From the cave/fifth shelter the vegetation thins out and it is a steep climb to Panar Laban huts – which includes the well-equipped *Laban Rata Resthouse*, affording magnificent views at sunset and in the early morning. The name *Panar Laban* is derived from Kadazan words meaning 'place of sacrifice': early explorers had to make a sacrifice here to appease the spirits and this ritual is still performed by the Kadazan once a year. Sayat Sayat (3,810 m) hut – named after the ubiquitous shrubby tea tree – is an hour further on, above the Panar Laban Rockface. Most climbers reach Panar Laban (or the other huts) in the early afternoon in order to rest up for a 0300 start the next morning in order to reach the summit by sunrise. This second part of the trail – 3-km long – is more demanding technically, but the trail is well laid out with regular half mile resting points. Ladders, hand-rails and ropes are provided for the steeper parts (essential in the wet, as the granite slabs can be very slippery). The final 1 km has no hand rails or ropes but is less sleep. The first two hours after dawn are the most likely to be cloud-free. For enthusiasts interested in alternative routes to the summit, John Briggs's *Mountains of Malaysia* provides a detailed guide to the climb.

Sabah

👈 ## Mountain rescue: five soldiers and seven white chickens

Anyone who has peered from Kinabalu's summit into the seemingly bottomless depths of Low's Gully will appreciate the special sort of lunacy exhibited by two groups of British and Hong Kong soldiers who decided to abseil down it. One group emerged traumatised and exhausted a week later than they said they would. The other team got lost in the jungle below and were not found for three weeks. The dramatic jungle mountain rescue story, which took place in March 1994, catapulted the name Kinabalu into the British media, where it was mispronounced with gay abandon.

For the five soldiers who tackled the precipitous walls of the Gully which plunge a sheer 1,600 m from Kinabalu's summit, Sabah's much-touted "paradise" turned into a living hell. Having abseiled down the rock faces (which have yet to be scaled) they disappeared. More than 300 troops, rangers and mountain rescue specialists were involved in the search. When they were finally discovered, it emerged that they had been unable to move from their little jungle encampment at the foot of the

gully; the terrain was too hostile even for them. Although their rations had run out, the soldiers recovered quickly after spending a night in hospital in Kota Kinabalu.

They were lucky men. Irene Charuruks, the head of Sabah's Tourism Promotion Corporation, was quick to point out that "Aki Nabalu means the resting place of the dead in Kadazan". She said that because the five soldiers had been entering an area of the mountain never trodden before, they would have been well advised to have sacrificed seven white chickens so as to avoid offending the spirits of the mountain. Whether or not the spirits were involved, the men owe their lives to a Malaysian helicopter rescue team. The rescue effort was a successful story of co-operation between Malaysia and Britain, who at the time were still embroiled in an acrimonious trade dispute over British press allegations that Malaysian politicians are corrupt. Sadly the happy ending at the resting place of the dead was not enough to prompt the resurrection of Anglo-Malaysian relations.

Equipment   A thick jacket is recommended, but at the very least you should have a light waterproof or windcheater to beat the windchill on the summit. Remarkably, no one appears to have set up rental facilities; contrary to rumour, it is not possible to hire jackets or windcheaters from Park HQ. It is also necessary to bring a sweater or some thick shirts. Walking boots are recommended, but not essential – many people climb the mountain in trainers. Sleeping bags are provided free of charge in both the **Laban Rata Resthouse** and the **Sayat Sayat**; they are crucial for a good night's sleep. Carry food and a few sweets as a precaution. Essential items include: torch, toilet paper, water bottle, plasters, headache tablets and suntan lotion. A hat is also a good idea – as protection against the sun and the cold. Gloves, balaclavas and torches can be bought at the shop at Park HQ, which also sells a range of food and drinks suitable for the climb. Lockers are available, RM1 per item, at the Park HQ reception office. The *Laban Rata Resthouse* has welcome hot water showers, but soap and towels are not provided. The hostel is well heated and bedding is provided.

Guides   Hiring a guide is compulsory: RM60 for the round trip (one to six people). Porters available at a charge of RM6 for every kilogram carried, maximum load 11 kg. Guides and porters should be reserved at least a day in advance at the Park HQ or at the parks office in KK. On the morning of your climb, go to the HQ and a guide will be assigned to you. A guide is not compulsory if you

The Borneo Death March

The four years of Japanese occupation ended when the Australian ninth division liberated British North Borneo. Sandakan was chosen by the Japanese as a regional centre for holding Allied prisoners. In 1942 the Japanese shipped 2,750 prisoners of war (2,000 of whom were Australian and 750 British) to Sandakan from Changi Prison, Singapore. A further 800 British and 500 Australian POWs arrived in 1944. They were ordered to build an airfield (on the site of the present airport) and were forced to work from dawn to dusk. Many died, but in September 1944 2,400 POWs were force-marched to Ranau, a 240-km trek through the jungle which only six Australians survived. This 'Death March', although not widely reported in Second World War literature, claimed more Australian lives than any other single event during the war in Asia, including the notorious Burma-Siam railway.

The power of the Sulu sultanate was already on the wane when Cowie set up. In its early trading days, there were many nationalities living in Sandakan: Europeans, Africans, Arabs, Chinese, Indians, Javanese, Dusun and Japanese. It was an important gateway to the interior and used to be a trading centre for forest produce like rhinoceros horn, beeswax, and hornbill ivory along with marine products like pearls and sea cucumbers (*tripang*, valued for their medicinal properties). In 1812, an English visitor, John Hunt, estimated that the Sandakan/Kinabatangan area produced an astonishing 37,000 kg of wild beeswax and 23,000 kg of bird's nests each year.

The modern town of Sandakan was founded by an Englishman, William Pryer, in 1879. Baron von Overbeck, the Austrian consul from Hong Kong who founded the Chartered Company with businessman Alfred Dent, had signed a leasing agreement for the territory with the Sultan of Brunei, only to discover that large tracts on the east side of modern-day Sabah actually belonged to the Sultan of Sulu. Overbeck sailed to Sulu in January 1878 and on obtaining the cession rights from the Sultan, dropped William Pryer off at Kampung German to make the British presence felt. Pryer's wife Ada later described the scene: "He had with him a West Indian black named Anderson, a half-cast Hindoo named Abdul, a couple of China boys. For food they had a barrel of flour and 17 fowls and the artillery was half a dozen sinder rifles.". Pryer set about organizing the three existing villages in the area, cultivating friendly relations with the local tribespeople and fending off pirates. He raised the Union Jack on 11 February 1878.

Cowie tried to do a deal with the Sultan of Sulu to wrest control of Sandakan back from Pryer, but Dent and Overbeck finally bought him off. A few months later Cowie's Kampung German burned to the ground, so Pryer went in search of a new site, which he found at Buli Sim Sim. He called his new settlement Elopura, meaning 'beautiful city', but the name did not catch on. By the mid-1880s it was recalled Sandakan and, in 1884, became the capital of North Borneo when the title was transferred from Kudat. In 1891 the town had 20 Chinese-run brothels and 71 Japanese prostitutes; according to the 1891 census there were three men for every one woman. The town quickly established itself as the source of birds' nests harvested from the caves at Gomontong (see page 465) and shipped directly to Hong Kong, as they are today.

Timber was first exported from this area in 1885 and was used to construct Beijing's Temple of Heaven. Sandakan was, until the 1980s, the main east coast port for timber and it became a very wealthy town. In its heyday, the

Agnes Keith's house

American authoress Agnes Keith lived with her English husband in Sandakan from 1934 to 1952. He was the Conservator of Forests in North Borneo and she wrote three books about her time in the colony. The Land Below the Wind *relates tales of dinner parties and tiffins in pre-war days;* Three Came Home *is about her three years in a Japanese internment camp during the war on Pulau Berhala, off Sandakan, and in Kuching and was made* into a film White Man Returns *tells the story of their time in British North Borneo. The Keiths' rambling wooden house on the hill above the town was destroyed during the war but was rebuilt by the government to exactly the same design when Harry Keith returned to his job after the war. The house, near Sandakan Viewpoint and Ramada Renaissance Hotel, has been unoccupied for a number of years and its garden neglected.*

town is said to have boasted one of the greatest concentrations of millionaires in the world. The timber-boom days are over: the primary jungle has gone, and so has the big money. In the mid-1990s the state government adopted a strict policy restricting the export of raw, unprocessed timber. The hinterland is now dominated by cocoa and oil palm plantations.

Following the Japanese invasion in 1942, Sandakan was devastated by Allied bombing. In 1946 North Borneo became a British colony and the new colonial government moved the capital to Jesselton (later to become Kota Kinabalu).

Sights

Sandakan is strung out along the coast but in the centre of town is the riotous **daily fish market**, which is the biggest and best in Sabah. The best time to visit is at 0600 when the boats unload their catch. The **Central Market** along the waterfront, near the local bus station, sells such things as fruit, vegetables, sarongs, seashells, spices and sticky rice cakes.

The **Australian war memorial**, near the government building at Mile Seven on Labuk Rd, between Sandakan and Sepilok, stands on the site of a Japanese prison camp and commemorates Allied soldiers who lost their lives during the Japanese occupation. The Japanese invaded North Borneo in 1942 and many Japanese also died in the area. In 1989 a new **Japanese war memorial** was built in the Japanese cemetery, on Red Hill (Bukit Berenda), financed by the families of the deceased soldiers. ■ *Getting there: take Labuk bus service nos 19, 30 and 32.*

St Michael's Anglican church is one of the very few stone churches in Sabah and is an attractive building, designed by a New Zealander in 1893. Most of Sandakan's stone churches were levelled in the war and, indeed, St Michael's is one of the few colonial-era buildings still standing. It is just off Jalan Singapura, on the hill at the south end of town. In 1988 a big new **mosque** was built for the burgeoning Muslim population at the mouth of Sandakan Bay. The main Filipino settlements are in this area of town. The mosque is outside Sandakan, on Jalan Buli Sim Sim where the town began in 1879, just after the jetty for Turtle Islands National Park and is an imposing landmark. There is also a large water village here, offering a glimpse of traditional culture and life.

Pertubuhan Ugama Buddhist (Puu Jih Shih Buddhist temple) overlooks Tanah Merah town. The US$2 mn temple was completed in 1987 and stands at the top of the hill, accessible by a twisting road which hairpins its way up the hillside. The temple is very gaudy, contains three large Buddha images and is nothing special, although the 34 teakwood supporting pillars, made in Macau, are quite a feature. There is a good view of Sandakan from the top, with Tanah Merah and the log ponds directly below, in Sandakan Bay. The names of local donors are inscribed on the walls of the walkway.

There are a couple of other notable Chinese temples in Sandakan. The oldest one, the **Goddess of Mercy Temple** is just off Jalan Singapura, on the hillside. Originally built in the early 1880s, it has been expanded over the years. Nearby is **Sam Sing Kung Temple** which becomes a particular focus of devotion during exam periods since one of its deities is reputed to assist those attempting examinations. The **Three Saints Temple**, further down the hill at the end of the padang, was completed in 1887. The three saints are Kwan Woon Cheung, a Kwan clan ancestor, the goddess Tien Hou (or Tin Hou, worshipped by seafarers) and the Min Cheong Emperor.

The only **Crocodile Farm** in Sabah is a commercial licensed enterprise, set up in 1982 when the government made the estuarine crocodile a protected species. The original stock was drawn from a population of wild crocodiles found in the Kinabatangan River. Visitors can see around 2,000 crocs at all stages of maturity waiting in concrete pools for the day when their skins are turned into bags and wallets and their meat is sold to local butchers. The farm, at Mile 8, Labuk Road, is open to the public and has about 200 residents. Feeding time and the only active time is at 1000. ■ *0800-1700 Mon-Sun, RM2, Labuk Rd bus.*

The **Forest Headquarters** (*Ibu Pejabat Jabatan Perkutanan*) is on Labuk Road next to the Sandakan Golf Course and contains an exhibition centre and a well laid out and interesting mini-museum showing past and present forestry practice.

Excursions

Most tour companies operate tours to Turtle Islands, Sepilok, the Gomontong Caves, Sukau and the Kinabatangan River. See **Tour operators**, page 469. **Sepilok Orang-utan Sanctuary**, see page 473. **Turtle Islands National Park**, see page 470. **Kinabatangan River**, see page 475. For accommodation at Turtle Islands, contact *Crystal Quest*.

Gomontong Caves

These are 32 km south of Sandakan Bay, between the road to Sukau and the Kinabatangan River, or 110 km overland on the Sandakan-Sukau road. The name Gomontong means 'tie it up tightly' in the local language and the caves represent the largest system in Sabah. They are contained within the 3,924 ha Gomontong Forest Reserve. There are sometimes orang-utan, many deer, mouse deer, wild boar and wild buffalo in the reserve, which was logged in the 1950s. There are several cave chambers. The main limestone cave is called Simud Hitam, or the *Black Cave*. This cave, with its ceiling soaring up to 90 m overhead, is just a five-minute walk from the registration centre and picnic area. The smaller and more complex *White Cave* (or Simud Putih) is above. It is quite dangerous climbing up as there is no ladder to reach the caves and the rocks are slippery. Two to three hundred thousand bats of two different species are thought to live in the caves: at sunset they swarm out to feed. Sixty-four species of bat have been recorded in Sabah, most in these caves are fruit and wrinkled-lipped bats whose guano is a breeding ground for cockroaches. The squirming larvae make the floor of the cave seethe. The guano

Edible nests

The edible nests of black and white swiftlets are collected from the cave chambers, but the trade is now strictly controlled by Wildlife Department wardens. The white nests (of pure saliva) fetch more than US$500 per kg in Hong Kong; black nests go for around US$40 per kg. The nest-collectors pick about 250 kg a day in the lower chamber and about 50 kg a day in the upper chamber. They earn about M$25 a day. The collectors use 60 m-long rotan ladders. Heavy bundles of wood are lashed to the ladders to minimize swaying – but fatal accidents do occur. On average, a collector is killed once every four or five years in a fall. Bat guano is not collected from the floor of the cave so that it can act as a sponge mattress in the event of a serious fall.

The nests, which are relished as a delicacy by the Chinese are harvested for periods of 10 days, twice a year. The nests are first harvested just after the birds have made them (between February and April). The birds then build new nests, which are left undisturbed until after the eggs have been laid and hatched; these nests are then gathered, sometime between July and September. Harvesting contracts are auctioned to wholesalers who export the nests to Hong Kong, where their impurities are taken out and they are sold at a huge mark-up. Of the profits, about half go to the state government, and more than a third to the contractor. Less than a fifth goes to the collectors. It is possible to buy the birds' nests in Sandakan restaurants, although they are all re-imported from Hong Kong.

can cause an itchy skin irritation. The bats are preyed upon by birds like the bat hawk, peregrine falcon and buffy fish owl.

There are also an estimated one million swiftlets which swarm into the cave to roost at sunset, the birds of birds' nest soup fame (see box). The swiftlets of Gomontong have been a focus of commercial enterprise for perhaps 400 or 500 years. However it was not until 1870 that harvesting birds' nests became a serious industry here. The caves are divided into five pitches and each is allocated to a team of 10-15 people. Harvesting periods last 15 days and there are three each year (February-April, July-September, and December). Collecting the nests from hundreds of feet above the ground is a dangerous business and deaths are not uncommon. Before each harvesting period a chicken or goat is sacrificed to the cave spirit; it is thought that deaths are not the result of human error, but an angry spirit. The birdlife around the caves is particularly rich, with crested serpent eagles, kingfishers, Asian fairy bluebirds, and leadbirds often sighted. Large groups of richly coloured butterflies are also frequently sighted drinking from pools along the track leading from the forest into the caves. The Niah Caves are on an even larger scale and yet more interesting. At the Park HQ there is an information centre, a small cafeteria where drinks and simple dishes are sold, and a pit latrine. If you arrive independently then one of the nest workers, a person from the information centre, or a ranger will show you around. ■ *0800-1600, Mon-Sun. The bats can be seen exiting from the caves between 1800 and 1830; to request to see this it is necessary to ask at the information centre (Wildlife Department).*

Sleeping and eating A *Gomontong Rainforest Chalet*, this place is owned by *Sabah Travel*, chalets are clean, with shared bathrooms and guides are provided. **A-B** *Proboscis Lodge*, Sukau (T240584 or F240415, Kota Kinabalu), 2 hrs by road from Sandakan, wooden stilt cabins set in the heart of the jungle, restaurant.

Transport It is easiest on a tour (see page 469). The caves are accessible by an old logging road, which can be reached by bus from the main Sandakan-Sukau Rd. The timing of the bus is inconvenient for those wishing to visit the caves, although an alternative is to charter a Labuk/Leila bus from Pryer St, opposite the bus station. It is much easier to take the 1100 boat from Sandakan's fish market to Suad Lamba, 1½ hrs. From there it is possible to take a minibus to Gomontong (quite cheap, if there are a reasonable number of passengers). Visitors can stay overnight in the resthouse at nearby Sukau (see below). Plans to build a chalet and restaurant at Gomontong should be completed by now. Minibuses will pick up passengers for the return trip to Suad Lamba by arrangement. The daily boat back to Sandakan leaves Suad Lamba at 0530.

This island is ideal for picnicking and swimming. It has 200-m rust-coloured **Pulau Berhala** sandstone cliffs on the south end of the island, with a beach at the foot, within easy reach by boat. The island was used as a leper colony before the Second World War and as a prisoner of war camp by the Japanese. Agnes Keith was interned on the island during the war. Boats to the island leave from the fish market.

Essentials

AL-A *Sanbay*, Mile 1.25, Jln Leila, T275000, F275575, www.sabahnet.com.my/sanbay a more recent addition to Sandakan, spacious rooms with bathrooms. **A** *Renaissance Sandakan* Km 1, Jln Utara, T213299, F271271, www.renaissance-intl.com With a/c, restaurants, attractive pool, Sandakan's only 5-star hotel, with 120 rooms, fitness centre, tennis, pool and squash courts. **A** *Hotel Sandakan*, 4th Ave, T221122, F221100, tengis@tm.net.my A/c, coffee house, 2 restaurants (Japanese and Cantonese), bar with live music, business centre. Centrally located, this is not cheap but provides excellent service.

Sleeping
■ *on map, page 468*
Price codes:
see inside front cover

   B *City View*, Lot 1, Block 23, 3rd Ave, T271123, F273115. Restaurant, bath and shower, TV, fridge, a/c. For a little more than the standard guesthouses this is a considerable step up. Recommended. **B** *Hsiang Garden*, Km 1, T273122, F273127. A/c, restaurant, all facilities, good bar. **B** *Ramai*, Km 1.5, Jln Leila, T273222, F271884. A/c, restaurant, all 44 rooms are a good size, with bathrooms. Recommended. **B** *Sepilok Inn*, Block 46, Lot 9, Tingkat 1,2,3, Jln Sekolah T271222, F273831. A/c, clean rooms with attached bathrooms and TVs, good value.

   C *Hung Wing*, Lot 4, Block 13, Jln Tiga, T218855, F271240. Some a/c, shower, a wide variety of rooms and prices available. Rooms are spacious, clean and light with bathrooms. The owner is very helpful and speaks excellent English. Probably the best of the mid-range hotels. **C** *London*, Lot D1, Block 10, Jln Empat, T216366. A/c, shower and bath, TV, light rooms although not large. **C** *Mayfair*, 24 Jln Pryer. A/c, shower, communal TV. The décor leaves something to be desired but there's a very friendly atmosphere and is in a central location with views of the market and the sea, good value. **C** *New Sabah*, 18 Jln Singapura, T218711, F273725. A/c, TV, hot shower, well kept.

   D *Uncle Tan's*, Mile 17.5 (Km 29), Labuk Rd (5 km beyond Sepilok junction), T531917, F271215, tansulim@tm.net.my Set in a fruit plantation; bicycle hire RM3 per day, all meals included, tours arranged to Kinabatangan (see **Tour operators** below), very cheap but not very clean and being on the main road, it's noisy from the logging trucks which continue to thunder past all night long. One redeeming feature is Uncle Tan himself who is a great raconteur, the other is Susie, a Filipino who runs the place and provides excellent food. A popular stop for travellers. **D-E** *Travellers Rest Hostel*, 2nd Flr, Apt 2, Block E, Jln Leila, Bandar Ramai-Ramai, T221460. Some a/c, no attached bathrooms and limited toilet facilities, friendly with lots of travel information. Cooking and washing facilities.

Sabah

Eating

Sandakan is justifiably renowned for its inexpensive and delicious seafood

Malay Cheap *Jiaman*, 1st Flr, Wisma Khoo Siak Chiew, serves interesting selection of Malay and Bajau dishes, no alcohol. *Perwira*, *Hotel Ramai*, Jln Leila, Malay and Indonesian, good value. Recommended. **Chinese** Two Chinese seafood restaurants on Trig Hill overlooking the harbour, namely **Mid-range** *Golden Palace*, Trig Hill (2 km out of town), fresh seafood, specializes in drunken prawns, crab and lobster, and steamboats (owners will provide transport back to Sandakan if there are no taxis available). Recommended. *Trig Hill*, *Ming Restaurant*, *Renaissance Sandakan Hotel*, T213299. Km 1, Jln Utara. Cantonese and Szechuan cuisine, particularly renowned for *dim sum* (breakfast). *Japanese Corner*, *Hsiang Garden Hotel*, Jln Leila, Hsiang Garden Estate, T273122. Lobster and tiger prawns, good value and a popular local lunch venue. *See Lok Yum*, next door to *Sea View Garden*, also very popular with locals.

Seafood In the semi-outdoor restaurants situated at the top of Trig (Trigonometry) Hill (see entries under 'Chinese' cuisine). Great views of Sandakan and good food, *Pesah Putih Baru*, on the coast, nearly at the end of Sandakan Bay, about 5 km from the port, recommended. **Korean Mid-range** *Korean Restaurant*, Hsiang Garden Estate, 1½ km, Jln Leila, T43891.

Malay foodstalls next to minibus station, just before the community centre on the road to Ramai Ramai, also at summit of Trig Hill

International Mid-range *XO Steak House*, Lot 16, Hsiang Garden Estate (opposite the *Hsiang Garden Hotel*), Mile 1.5, Jln Leila, lobster and tiger prawns and a good choice of fresh fish as well as Australian steaks, buffet barbecue on Fri nights. Recommended. **Cheap** *Hawaii*, *City View Hotel*, Lot 1, Block 23, 3rd Ave, Western and local food, set lunch. Recommended. *Sandakan Recreation Club*, just off the Padang. *Seoul Garden*, Hsiang Garden Estate, Mile 1.5, Leila Rd, Korean. **Seriously cheap** *Apple Fast Food*, Lorong Edinburgh, good spot for breakfasts. *Fat Cat*, 206 Wisma Sandakan, 18 Jln Haji Saman, several branches around town, breakfasts recommended. **Vegetarian Cheap** *Supreme Garden Vegetarian Restaurant*, Block 30, Bandar Ramai Ramai, Jln Leila (west of town), well priced and excellent range of dishes, open for lunch and dinner.

Sabah

Sandakan

To Goddess of Mercy Temple · To Trig Hill

St Michael's

Sam Sing Kung Temple

Three Saints Temple

Jln Puncak · Jalan Utara · Jalan Tokong

BUKIT ELTON

Jln Singapura

Padang

To Ramai Hotel, Hsiang Garden Hotel, Travellers' Rest Hostel, Sanbay Hotel, XO Steakhouse, Long Distance Bus Station, Tanah Merah Town & Buddhist Temple

Night

Jln Leila

Tun Razak Park

Community Centre

Lebuh Tiga (3rd Av)

Fountain

Jln Dua

Jln Europa

(2nd Av)

Jln Pelabuhan

MAS

Bus Terminal (Local)

Boats to Suad Lamba (Kinabatangan, Gomotong & Batu Tulug) & Berhala Isle

Fisherman's

N

0 metres (approx) 100
0 yards (approx) 100

Sleeping
1 City View
2 Hung Wing
3 London
4 Mayfair
5 New Sabah
6 Sandakan
7 Sepilok Inn

Fast food Cheap *Fairwood Restaurant*, Jln Tiga, an inexpensive, a/c fast-food place with all the local favourites, situated in the centre of town.

Coffee shops *New Bangsawan*, next to New Bangsawan cinema, just off Jln Leila, Tanah Merah, no great shakes, but best restaurant in Tanah Merah (where there are stacks of coffee shops). *Silver Star Ice Cream and Café*, 3rd Ave, popular coffee shop with on-site satay stall in the evenings, particularly friendly and helpful management. Recommended. *Union Coffee Shop*, 2nd Flr Hakka Association Building, Third Ave, budget.

Cinemas *Cathay Cinema*, next to Wisma Sabah and town mosque. **Discos and** **Entertainment**
karaoke There is a karaoke parlour on just about every street. *Tiffany Discotheatre and Karaoke*, Block C, 7-10, Ground and first floors, Jln Leila, Bandar Ramai-Ramai.

Almost everything in Sandakan is imported. There are some inexpensive batik shops **Shopping**
and some good tailors. *Wisma Sandakan*, next to the town mosque and the *Cathay*, trendiest place in town and offers 3 Flrs of a/c Singapore-style shopping.

Bowling *Champion Bowl*, Jln Leila, Bandar Ramai Ramai. **Golf** *Sandakan Golf Club*, **Sports**
10 km out of town, open to non-members. **Recreation clubs** *Sepilok Recreation Club*, Bandar Ramai Ramai, with snooker, sauna and darts as well as karaoke.

Alexander Ng Sandakan Adventure Tours, Pejabat Pos Jln Utara, Batu 1.5, T212225, **Tour operators**
F219959, caters for specialist interests and offers individually tailored tours. *Borneo Ecotours*, c/o Hotel Hsiang Garden, PO Box 82, Jln Leila, T220210, F213614. *Crystal Quest*, 12th Flr Wisma Khoo Siak Chiew, T 212711, the only company running accommodation on Pulau Selingaan, Turtle Islands National Park. *Discovery Tours*, Room 908 10th Flr, Wisma Khoo Siak Chiew, T274106, F274107. *Megan Travel Services*, Jln Tiga, T223377. *Tay Travel Services*, Jln Tiga, T215584, F271240. Ticketing, tour and hotel services. *Uncle Tan's*, Mile 17.5 (Km 29), Labuk Rd (5 km beyond Sepilok junction), T531917, inexpensive tours to his 'Utan Wildlife Camp' on the Kinabatangan (see page 475) (max 20 people), there are guides and a cook at the camp, daily departures during peak season (meals included in price), also runs reasonably priced tours to Turtle Islands and Gomontong Caves, advance bookings can be addressed to PO Box 620, 90007 Sandakan. Recommended. *Unique Tours*, Lot 6, Block 1, Bandar Kim Fung, Batu 4, Jln Utara, T212150. *Wildlife Expeditions*, Room 903, 9th Flr, Wisma Khoo Siak Chiew, Lebuh Tiga, Jln Buli Sim-Sim, T219616, F214570 (branches in Renaissance Sandakan Hotel), the most expensive, but also the most efficient, with the best facilities and the best guides. Recommended.

To Airport, Australian & Japanese War
Memorials, Crocodile Farm, Labuk Road, Sepilok,
& Renaissance Sandakan Hotel (500m)

Agnes
Keith's House

Rotary
Observation Pavilion

Sabah
Parks
Office

Town
Mosque

Jalan Empat
Cathay Cinema

Lebuh Empat

To Jln Buli Sim-Sim & Wisma Khoo Siak Chiew

Lebuh Tiga

Office

Jln Dua

Jln Empat (4th St)

Jln Tiga (3rd St)

Jln Lima (5th St)

Jln Pryer

Scheduled
Buses

Central

Fish

Open

Wharf

To Turtle Islands

Sabah

160 k

sand. The egg-laying process can take about an hour or two to complete. Some say the temperature of the sand effects the sex of the young, if it is warm the batch will be mostly female and if cold, mostly male. After laying her eggs, a tag reading "If found, return to Turtle Island Park, Sabah, East Malaysia" is attached to each turtle by the rangers, who are stationed on each island. Over 27,000 have been tagged since 1970; the measurements of each turtle are recorded and the clutches of eggs are removed and transplanted to the hatchery where they are protected from natural predators – such as monitor lizards, birds and snakes.

The golf ball-sized eggs are placed by hand into 80 cm-deep pits, covered in sand and surrounded by wire. They take up to 60 days to hatch. The hatchlings mostly emerge at night when the temperature is cooler, breaking their shells with their one sharp tooth. There are hatcheries on all three islands and nearly every night a batch is released into the sea. More than 2.6 million hatchlings were released between 1977 and 1988. They are released at different points on the island to protect them from predators: they are a favoured snack for white-bellied gulls and sadly only a fraction, about 1%, survive to become teenage turtles.

Permits These are required by all visitors, RM30 from the Sabah Parks Office in Sandakan: Room 906, 9th Floor, Wisma Khoo, Lebuh Tiga (3rd Avenue), T273453. It is necessary to acquire special permits to visit Pulau Bakkungan Kecil and Pulau Gulisaan. Unofficially, however, it is possible to make the five-minute boat trip to Pulau Bakkungan Kecil where there is some excellent coral. Visitors are advised to wait in their chalets for the park ranger, who will tell them when their turtle is laying eggs.

Visitors should not walk on the beach after dark unaccompanied

Sabah
Sabah
Col

Tours The average cost of a one night tour is RM150-250. Most tour companies (see page 469) operate tours to Turtle Islands and have their own boats, which makes the trip a bit cheaper. An expedition to the islands needs to be well planned; vagaries such as bad weather, which can prevent you from leaving the islands as planned, can mess up itineraries. Most visitors book their trips in advance.

Best time to visit The driest months and the calmest seas are between March and July. The egg laying season is July-October. Seas are rough between October and February.

Sleeping & eating The number of visitors to the islands is restricted, even at peak season. There are 3 cabins (one with 2 double bedrooms, two with 6 double bedrooms) on Pulau Selingaan (RM150 per night per room). It is necessary to book in advance through the Sabah Parks office, Room 906, 9th Flr, Wisma Khoo, Lebuh Tiga (Third Ave),

Sandakan Bay

Small and hairy: the Sumatran rhinoceros

Although not as rare as its Javan brother, the Sumatran, or lesser two-horned rhino (Didermoceros sumatrensis) is severely endangered. It was once widespread through mainland and island Southeast Asia but has now been hunted to the point of extinction; there are probably less than 1,000 in the wild, mostly in Sumatra but with small populations in Borneo, Peninsular Malaysia and Vietnam. It is now a protected species. Only on Sumatra does it seem to have a chance of surviving. The situation has become so serious that naturalists have established a captive breeding programme as a precaution against extinction in the wild. Unfortunately this has been spectacularly unsuccessful. Around one-third of animals have died during capture or shortly thereafter and, according to naturalists

Tony and Jane Whitten, the only recorded birth was in captivity in Calcutta in 1872. The species has suffered from the destruction of its natural habitat, and the price placed on its head by the value that the Chinese attach to its grated horn as a cure-all. Should the Sumatran rhino disappear so too, it is thought, will a number of plants whose seeds will only germinate after passing through the animal's intestines.

The Sumatran rhino is the smallest of all the family, and is a shy, retiring creature, inhabiting thick forest. Tracks have been discovered as high as 3,300 m in the Mount Leuser National Park in Sumatra. It lacks the 'armoured' skin of other species and has a soft, hairy hide. It also has an acute sense of smell and hearing, but poor eyesight.

Sandakan, T273453, F274718. Chalets are equipped with cooking facilities and visitors can bring their own food. Restaurant in the Information Centre building.

Ferries Daily 50-60 seater ferry, 2-3 hrs. The National Parks office in Sandakan can recommend speedboats of licensed tour companies.

Transport
40 km NE of
Sandakan

Sabah

Sepilok Orang-utan Sanctuary and Rehabilitation Centre

Sepilok, a reserve of 43 sq km of lowland primary rainforest and mangrove, was set up in 1964 to protect the orang-utan, *Pongo pygmaeus*, from extinction. It is the first and largest of only three orang-utan sanctuaries in the world and now welcomes around 40,000 visitors a year. Logging has seriously threatened Sabah's population of wild orang-utan, as has their capture for zoos and as pets. The orang-utan (see page 558) lives on the islands of Borneo and Sumatra and there are estimated to be perhaps as few as 10,000 still in the wild. In Sabah there are populations of orang-utan in the Kinabatangan basin region (see page 475) and in the Danum Valley Conservation Area as well as in a few other isolated tracts of jungle.

Colour map 4, grid B5

Sepilok is an old forest reserve, that was gazetted as a forestry experimentation centre as long ago as 1931, and by 1957 logging had been phased out. Orphaned or captured orang-utans which have become too dependent on humans through captivity are rehabilitated and protected under the Fauna Conservation Ordinance and eventually returned to their natural home. Many, for example, may have been captured by the oil palm planters, because they eat the young oil palm trees. Initially, the animals at the Centre and in the surrounding area are fed every day but as they acclimatize, they are sent further and further away or are re-released into the Tabin Wildlife Reserve near Lahad Datu. In 1996, researchers placed microchip collars on the orang-utans enabling them to be tracked over a distance of up to 150 km so that a better understanding of their migratory habits and other behaviour could be acquired.

After an initial period of quarantine at Sepilok, newly arrived orang-utans are moved to Platform A and taught necessary survival skills by the rangers. At the age of seven they are moved deeper into the forest to Platform B, about half an hour's walk from Platform A and now not open to the public. At Platform B, they are encouraged to forage for themselves. Other animals brought to Sepilok include Malay sun bears, wild cats and baby elephants. ■ *Feeding times: Platform A, 1000 and 1500.*

Sepilok also has a rare Sumatran rhinoceros, *Didermoceros sumatrensis*, also known as the Asian two-horned rhinoceros, see box above. This enclosure is closed to the public.

The **Mangrove Forest Trail** takes two to three hours one way. The walk takes in transitional forest, pristine lowland rainforest, a boardwalk into a mangrove forest, water holes and a wildlife track. All enquiries at the Visitors' Reception Centre. The **Information Centre**, next to the Park HQ, runs a nature education exhibition with replicas of jungle mammals and educational videos. Video viewing times are at 1130 and 1530. ■ *The park is open from 0900-1130, 1400-1530, RM10, video camera RM10. It is worth getting to the park early.*

Excursions The **Rainforest Interpretation Centre** on the road to Sepilok provides detailed and informative displays about the vegetation in the area. It is run by the Forest Research Centre, which is also found on this road. Great emphasis is given to participation, with questionnaires, games and so on; it offers a wide range of information about all aspects of tropical rainforests and the need for their conservation. The centre is located in the Forest Research Centre's arboretum and in addition to the exhibits there is a 800-m rainforest walk around the lake. ■ *Mon-Thu 0815-1215, 1400-1600, Fri 0815-1135, 1400-1600, Sat 0815-1215, free. A free booklet is available. For more information contact the Forest Research Centre, PO Box 14-07, T531522, F531068.*

Sleeping & eating

Price codes: see inside front cover

There is a good restaurant at the Centre

B *Wildlife Lodge*, Mile 14, Labuk Rd, Sepilok Orang-Utan Sanctuary, PO Box 2082, 100 m behind the *Government Resthouse*, T089533031, F089533029. Office in Sandakan: Ground Flr, Lots 1 and 2, Block C, Taman Grandview, Sim Sim Highway, T089273711, F089273010. Some a/c, some dorm beds for RM20, cheaper rooms have shared bathrooms, with hot water showers, cafeteria. The *Lodge* is the realization of a dream for John and Judy Lim, who have gradually purchased all the land on the edge of the forest and have landscaped the area surrounding three manmade lakes and cleared the fruit orchards they inherited. They have planted lots of flowering and fruiting trees, attracting butterflies and birds in the process. Pleasant restaurant, great setting, clean and comfortable, boats for fishing available. Recommended. **B-C** *Sepilok Jungle Resort* Labuk Rd, Sandakan T089533031 F533029 sepilokjr@yahoo.com Wooden chalets, well furnished with a good range of accommodation, price includes breakfast. Some a/c and some cheaper dorm beds. **C** *Orang-Utan Rehabilitation Centre Rest House (Government Resthouse)*, Mile 14 Labuk Rd, T089531180. Basic and characterless The *Sepilok B&B* is preferable. **C** *Sepilok B&B*, Jln Sepilok, of Mile 14, PO Box 155, T089535288, F089217668. Breakfast included. Around 1 km from the Orang-Utan sanctuary. Better than the Centre accommodation and good value although there is no hot water. **Camping** Campsite at *Sepilok Wildife Lodge*.

Bus 8 daily public buses from **Sandakan**, from the central mini-bus terminal in front of *Nak Hotel*. Ask for the Sepilok Batu 14 line. From the airport, the most convenient way to reach Sepilok is by **taxi**. Sepilok is 1.9 km from the main road.

Transport
23 km to Sandakan

Useful information Further information about Sepilok can be obtained from: Co-ordinator, Sepilok Orang-Utan Rehabilitation Centre, Sabah Wildlife Department, WDT 200, 95000 Sandakan, T089-531180, F531189.

Directory

Kinabatangan River

At 560 km, this river is Sabah's longest. Much of the lower basin is gazetted under the Kinabatangan Wildlife Sanctuary and meanders through a flood plain, creating numerous ox-bow lakes and an ideal environment for some of the best wildlife in Malaysia. One of the principal reasons why the Kinabatangan has remained relatively unscathed by Sabah's rapacious logging is because much of the land is permanently waterlogged and the forest contains only a small number of commercially valuable trees. Just some of the animals include: tree snake, crocodile, civet cat, otter, monitor lizard, long-tailed and pig-tailed macaque, silver-, red- and grey-leaf monkey and proboscis monkey. It is the most accessible area in Borneo to see the proboscis monkeys which are best viewed from a boat in the late afternoon, when they converge on tree tops by the river banks to settle for the night. Sumatran rhinoceros have also been spotted (see box page 473) and herds of wild elephant often pass through the park. The birdlife is particularly good and includes oriental darter, egret, storm's stork, osprey, coucal owl, frogmouth, bulbul, spiderhunter, oriole, flowerpecker and several species of hornbill, see page 561.

Because of the diversity of its wildlife, the Kinabatangan riverine forest area has been proposed as a forest reserve. In addition, there has been little disturbance from human settlements: the Kinabatangan basin has always been sparsely inhabited because of flooding and the threat posed by pirates. The inhabitants of the Kinabatangan region are mostly Orang Sungai or people of mixed ancestry including Tambanua, Idahan, Dusun, Suluk, Bugis, Brunei and Chinese. The best destination for a jungle river safari is not on the Kinabatangan itself, but on the narrow, winding Sungai Menanggol tributary, about 6 km from Sukau. The Kinabatangan estuary, largely mangrove, is also rich in wildlife, and is a haven for migratory birds. Boats can be chartered from Sandakan to Abai (at the mouth of the river).

Batu Tulug, also known as Batu Putih, or White Stone, on the Kinabatangan River 100 km upstream from Sukau, is a cave containing wooden coffins dating back several hundred years. Some of the better examples have been removed to the Sabah State Museum in KK. The caves are about 1 km north of the Kinabatangan Bridge, on the east side of the Sandakan-Lahad Datu road. ■ *Take the Sukau bus from Sandakan, 1400.*

Visitors who prefer an in-depth look at the area's wildlife can stay overnight at Sukau, two hours by road from Sandakan, where accommodation is provided by local tour operators. Tour operators take visitors by boat in the late afternoon through the freshwater swamp forest to see proboscis monkeys and other wildlife. There are also walks through the jungle. Because of the lack of public transport to Sukau, the only way to visit the area is with a tour; all tours must be booked in Sandakan or KK (see below).

Sabah

Sleeping Most companies running tours to the Kinabatangan put their guests up in Sukau. The one exception is *Borneo Eco Tours* (see below). **A** *Sukau Rainforest Lodge (SRL)*, accessible by boat from Sukau, provides eco-friendly accommodation for 40 visitors, in traditional Malaysian-style chalets, on stilts. All 20 rooms have solar-powered fans, twin beds, mosquito netting, and attached tiled bathroom with hot water. Other facilities include an open dining and lounge area (good restaurant), garden and sundeck overlooking the rainforest, and gift shop. Friendly and efficient service. All in all, a shining example of eco-tourism at its best, highly recommended.

Tour operators *Borneo Eco Tours*, c/o *Hotel Hsiang Garden*, Jln Leila, PO Box 82, Sandakan, T220210,
All Sandakan F213614. *Discovery Tours*, 1008, 10th Flr, Wisma Khoo Siak Chiew, Sandakan,
telephone numbers T274106, F274107. *S.I. Tours*, Lot 3B, 3rd Floor, Yeng Ho Hong Building, Sandakan,
are prefixed with 089 T213502, F271513. *Wildlife Expeditions*, Room 903, 9th Floor, Wisma Khoo Siak Chiew, Sandakan and Ground Floor, *Ramada Renaissance Hotel*, Jln Utara, Sandakan, T219616, F214570. *Sukau Rainforest Lodge (SRL)*, owned and managed by *Borneo Eco Tours*, Shoplot 12A, 2nd Flr, Lorong Bernam 3, Taman Soon Kiong, Kota Kinabalu, T234009, F233688, betsbl@po.jaring.my This last establishment is the most expensive tour operator but is worth it, as it can provide much more than the others and has won several awards for excellence. It is situated at the edge of the sanctuary in a secluded spot on the Kinabatangan River. Qualified guides use wooden boats built by local orang sungai craftsmen, powered by electric engines to minimize disturbance to wildlife.

Transport **Road** It is possible to charter a minibus to take you from **Suad Lamba** to **Gomontong** and on to **Sukau**. It will pick passengers up again at a set time, by arrangement (RM70-100 return). A bus leaves from **Sandakan** to **Sukau** (via Gomontong turn-off) at 1100 and 1400, 115 km 3½ hrs (RM20). The return bus leaves Sukau for Sandakan at 0600. **Boat** To **Suad Lamba**, on the far side of **Sandakan Bay** leaves from the rear of Sandakan's wet market at 1100 every day, 1½ hrs, RM3. The return boat leaves Suad Lamba at 0530.

Lahad Datu

Colour map 4, grid B5 Lahad Datu is Malaysia's 'wild East' at its wildest, and its recent history testi-
Phone code 089 fies to its reputation as the capital of cowboy country. The population is an
The town itself is intriguing mixture of Filipinos, Sulu islanders, migrants from Kalimantan,
grubby and Orang Bugis, Timorese and a few Malays. Most came to work on the oil palm
uninteresting plantations. Nowadays there are so many migrants few can find employment. There are reckoned to be more illegal Filipino immigrants in Lahad Datu than the whole official population put together. Piracy in the Sulu Sea and the off-shore islands in Kennedy Bay is rife; local fishermen live in terror.

During the Second World War, the Japanese made Lahad Datu their naval headquarters for East Borneo. After the war, the timber companies moved in: the British Kennedy Bay Timber Company built Lahad Datu's first plywood mill in the early 1950s. Oil palm plantations grew up in the hinterland after the timber boom finished in the 1970s. As for the town, what it lacks in aesthetic appeal is made up for by its colourful recent history.

Kampung Panji is a water village with a small market at the end of Jalan Teratai, where many of the poorer immigrant families live.

Excursions The only good **beaches** are on the road to Tungku; Pantai Perkapi and Pantai Tungku. They can be reached by minibus from Lahad Datu or by boat from the old wharf. It is possible to get to the nearby **islands** from the old wharf behind the *Mido Hotel*, but because of lawlessness in the area, particularly at sea, a trip is not advisable. In April 2000, the Philippines-based radical Islamic group *Abv* kidnapped 21 people from Sipadan (see page 481).

Madai Caves are about 2 km off the Tawau-Lahad Datu road, near Kunak. The caves are an important archaeological site; there is evidence they were inhabited over 15,500 years ago. The birds' nests are harvested three times a year by local Idahan people whose lean-to kampung goes right up to the cave mouth. ■ *Getting there Your own transport is required for this trip as it doesn't really cater for tourists.*

Another 15 km west of Madai is **Baturong**, another limestone massif and cave system in the middle of what was originally Tingkayu Lake. The route is not obvious, so it is advisable to take a local guide. Stone tools, wooden coffins and rock paintings have been found there. Evidence of humans dating from 16,000 years ago, after the lake drained away, can be found at the huge rock overhang. Take a torch. ■ *It is possible to camp here, take a minibus from Lahad Datu.*

Gunung Silam, 8 km from Lahad Datu on the Tawau road, a track leads up the mountain to a Telekom station at 620 m and from there, a jungle trail to the summit. There are good views over the bay, when it isn't misty, and out to the islands beyond. It is advisable to take a guide. There is the *Silam Lodge* (**B**), Silam, T088243245, F088254227, which is owned by the *Borneo Rainforest Lodge* and is mostly used by people in transfer to the Danum Valley. ■ *Getting there   Minibuses run from Lahad Datu.*

B *Executive*, Jln Teratai, T881333, F881777. A smart 53-room hotel that is easily the priciest in town. An uninspiring place and overpriced. **B-C** *Jagokota*, Jln Kampung Panji, T882000, F881526, well-furnished establishment. **C** *Mido*, 94 Jln Main, T881800, F881487. A/c, restaurant, the façade (facing the *Standard Chartered Bank*) is pock-marked with M-16 bullet holes, the result of over-curious residents watching the 1986 pirate raid on the bank; the *Mido* comes with all the sleaze of the 'wild East' and fails miserably to live up to its reputation as the best hotel in town. **C** *Ocean*, Jln Teratai (just past the Esso Station), T881700. A/c, shower attached. **C** *Permaisaba*, Block 1, Lot 3, 1/4 Jln Tengah Nipah, T883800, F883681. 5 mins' drive from the airport and town, seafood restaurant, Malaysian and Indian food, conference hall, free transfers to/from the airport and town. Big rooms with bathroom attached and hot water, information on the Danum Valley, characterless but convenient.

Sleeping
Lahad Datu is not a popular tourist spot and accommodation is poor and expensive. Avoid the Perdana and Venus hotels on Jln Seroja

Seafood   Mid-range *Melawar*, 2nd Flr, Block 47, off Jln Teratai (around the corner from the *Mido Hotel*), seafood restaurant, popular with locals. *Ping Foong*, 1½ km out of Lahad Datu, on Sandakan Rd, open-air seafood restaurant, highly recommended by locals. **Cheap** *Evergreen Snack Bar and Pub*, on 2nd Flr, Jln Teratai, opposite the Hap Seng Building, a/c, excellent fish and chips and best-known for its tuna steaks. Recommended. *Golden Key*, on stilts over the sea opposite the end of Jln Teratai, it is really just a tumble-down wooden coffee shop, but is well known for its seafood. *Good View*, just over 500 m out of town on Tengku Rd. Recommended by locals. *Seng Kee*, Block 39, opposite *Mido Hotel* and next to *Standard Chartered Bank*, cheap and good. *Restoran Ali*, opposite *Hotel New Sabah*, Indian, good *roti*. **Foodstalls   Seriously cheap** *Pasar Malam* behind *Mido Hotel* on Jln Kastam Lama. Spicy barbecued fish (*ikan panggang*) and skewered chicken wings recommended. The new market has foodstalls upstairs with attractive views out to sea.

Eating

The *Lacin Cinema*, which usually screens violent kung-fu movies, is next to the post office on Jln Kenanga.

Entertainment

Shopping There is a new *Central Market* on Jln Bungaraya and a spice market off Jln Teratai where Indonesian smugglers tout Gudang Garam cigarettes and itinerant dentists and *bumohs*, or witchdoctors, draw large crowds.

Tour operators *Borneo Nature Tours*, Block 3, Fajar Centre, T880207, F885051.

Transport **Air** Connections with **Tawau**, **Sandakan**, **Semporna**, **KK** and **Kudat**. **Minibus** Minibuses and what are locally known as wagons (basically 7-seater, 4WD Mitsubishis) leave from the bus station on Jln Bunga Raya (behind Bangunan Hap Seng at the mosque end of Jln Teratai) and from opposite the Shell station. Regular connections with **Tawau**, 2½ hrs, **Semporna** (RM10), **Sandakan** (RM17), **Madai**. **Boat** Fishing boats take paying passengers from the old wharf (end of Jln Kastam Lama) to the **Kennedy Bay islands**, **Tawau** and **Semporna**, although time-wise (and, more to the point, safety-wise) it makes much more sense to go by road or air.

Directory **Airline offices** *MAS*, Ground Flr, *Mido Hotel*, Jln Main, T881707. **Banks** *Standard Chartered*, in front of *Mido Hotel*. **Communications** Post Office: Jln Kenanga, next to the Lacin cinema. **Useful addresses** *Sabah Foundation* 2nd Flr, Hap Seng Building, Jln Main, T881092. Bookings for Danum Valley. Bookings can also be made at the Sabah Foundation headquarters in Kota Kinabalu (T354496).

Danum Valley Conservation Area

Colour map 4, grid B5 Danum Valley's 438 sq km of virgin jungle is the largest expanse of undisturbed lowland dipterocarp forest in Sabah. The field centre, which is 65 km west of Lahad Datu and 40 km from the nearest habitation, was set up by the Sabah Foundation (Yayasan) in 1985 for forest research, nature education and recreation; when we last visited the centre, it was only open to Malaysian school trips. Tourists are allowed to visit **only** through the *Borneo Rainforest Lodge*. The Segama River runs through the conservation area, and past the field centre. The Danum River is a tributary of the Segama joining it 9 km downstream of the Field Centre. Gunung Danum (1,093 m) is the highest peak, 13 km southwest of the Field Centre. Within the area is a Yayasan Sabah timber concession, which is tightly controlled.

This area has never really been inhabited, although there is evidence of a burial site which is thought to be for the Dusun people who lived here about 300 years ago. There is also growing evidence of pre-historic cave dwellers in the Segama River area. Not far downstream from the field centre, in a riverside cave, two wooden coffins have been found, together with a copper bracelet and a tapai jar, all of uncertain date. There is evidence of some settlement during the Japanese occupation; townspeople came upstream to escape from the Japanese troops. The area was first recommended as a national park by the World Wide Fund for Nature's Malaysia Expedition in 1975 and designated a conservation area in 1981. The field centre was officially opened in 1986.

The main reason for this large conservation area is to undertake research into the impact of logging on flora and fauna and to try and improve forest management, to understand processes which maintain tropical rainforest and to provide wildlife management and training opportunities for Sabahans. Many are collaborative projects between Malaysian and foreign scientists. The Sabah state tourism promotion board has recently thought to capitalize on this remote tract of jungle though. Following the opening of the *Borneo Rainforest Lodge*, Danum Valley will be promoted as an exclusive expedition centre.

Because of its size and remoteness, Danum Valley is home to some of Sabah's **Flora & fauna**
rarest animals and plants. The dipterocarp forest is some of the oldest, tallest
and most diverse in the world, with 200 species of tree per ha; there are over
300 labelled trees in the conservation area. The conservation area is teeming
with wildlife: Sumatran rhinoceroses have been recorded, as have elephants,
clouded leopards, orang-utans, proboscis monkeys, crimson langur,
pig-tailed macaques, sambar deer, bearded pigs, western tarsier, sunbears and
275 species of bird including hornbills, rufous picolet, flowerpeckers and
kingfishers. A species of monkey, which looks like an albino version of the
red-leaf monkey, was first seen on the road to Danum in 1988, and appears to
be unique to this area. There are guided nature walks on an extensive trail system. Features include a canopy walkway, ancient Dusun burial site, waterfalls
and a self-guided trail. ■ *RM30 per person. Leech socks are essential here.*

AL *Borneo Rainforest Lodge*, c/o *Borneo Nature Tours*, Block 3, Ground Floor, Fajar **Sleeping**
Centre, Lahad Datu, T089880207, F089885051. KK office: Block D, Lot 10, 3rd Floor,
Sadong Jaya Complex, T243245, F254227, ijl@po.jaring.my One of the finest tourism
developments in Sabah. 18 bungalows in a magnificent setting beside the Danum
River, built on stilts from belian (ironwood) and based on traditional Kadazan design
with connecting wooden walkways. There are 28 rooms, each with private bathroom
and balcony overlooking the Danum River, good restaurant, jacuzzi (solar-heated
water). Based on *Tiger Tops* in Nepal and designed by naturalists, the centre aims to
combine a wildlife experience in a remote primary rainforest with comfort and privacy
and provide high quality natural history information. There is a conference hall, excellent guides, who pre-plan their routes so that visitors don't bump into each other while
thinking they are latter day Indiana Jones's; day visits to a forest management centre,
an adequate library of resource books, after dinner slide shows, a gift shop, rafting is
available and night drives can be organized. Mountain bikes, fishing rods and river
tubes all available for hire. Electricity available all day; the lodge is being marketed
internationally in association with *Tiger Tops*. Expensive but well worth it. Price
includes meals and guided jungle excursions.

From Lahad Datu, turn left along the logging road at Km 15 on the Lahad Datu-Tawau **Transport**
road to Taliwas and then left again to field centre. The *Borneo Rainforest Lodge* is 97 km *85 km west of Lahad*
(not an easy trip) from **Lahad Datu**; they provide a transfer service (2 hrs), telephone *Datu*
the *Lodge* for details. **Air** 2 flights daily with *MAS* from **Kota Kinabalu** to Lahad Datu.
Bus Lahad Datu is 7 hrs from KK, 3 hrs from **Sandakan**, 3 hrs from **Semporna**, 2 hrs
from **Tawau**.

Semporna

Semporna is a small fishing town at the end of the peninsula and is the main *Colour map 4, grid B6*
departure point for Sipidan Island, see below. Semporna has a lively and very *Phone code: 089*
photogenic market, spilling out onto piers over the water. It is a Bajau town
and is known for its seafood. There are scores of small fishing boats, many
with outriggers and square sails. There is a regatta of these traditional boats
every March. The town is built on an old coral reef, said to be 35,000 years old,
that was exposed by the uplift of the seabed. Many illegal Filipino immigrants
pass through Semporna, as it is only two hours from the nearest Philippine
island, which gives the place quite a different feel to other Malay towns.

Sabah

Excursions The islands off Semporna stand along the edge of the continental shelf, which
For Sipadan, drops away to a depth of 200 m to the south and east of Pulau Ligitan, the out-
see below ermost island in the group. Darvel Bay, and the adjacent waters, are dotted
with small, mainly volcanic islands all part of the 73,000 acre Semporna
Marine Park. The bigger ones are Pulau Mabol, Pulau Kapalai, Pulau Si Amil,
Pulau Danawan and Pulau Sipadan. The coral reefs surrounding these islands
have around 70 genera of coral, placing them, in terms of their diversity, on a
par with Australia's Great Barrier Reef. More than 200 species of fish have also
been recorded in these waters.

Locals live in traditional boats called *lipa-lipa* or in pilehouses at the water's
edge and survive by fishing. In the shallow channels off Semporna, there are
three fishing villages, built on stilts: Kampung Potok Satu, Kampung Potok
Dua and Kampung Larus. There are many more islands than are marked on
the map; most are hilly, uninhabited and have beautiful white sandy beaches.

Reefs in Semporna Marine Park include Bohey Dulang, Sibuan Ulaiga,
Tetugan, Mantabuan Bodgaya, Sibuan, Maigu, Selakan and Sebangkat. Pulau
Bohey Dulang is a volcanic island with a Japanese-run pearl culture station.
Visitors can only visit if there is a boat from the pearl culture station going out.
The Kaya Pearl company leases part of the lagoon and Japanese pearl oysters
are artificially implanted with a core material to induce the growth of pearls.
The oysters are attached to rafts moored in the lagoon. The pearls are later
harvested and exported directly to Japan. The islands can be reached by local
fishing boats from the main jetty by the market, including Sibun, Sibankat,
Myga and Selakan.

Sleeping **B** *Dragon Inn (Semporna)*, T781088, F781008. Stands out as the hotel built on stilts
over the sea, a/c, restaurant, quite a novel setting but not great value. **C** *Lee's
Resthouse and Cafe*, Pekau Baru, Semporna New Town, T/F784491,
www.geocities.com/leesresthouse/lees Restaurant, a/c, TV, hot shower, very helpful
staff. Recommended. **C-D** *Seafest Inn*, Jln Kaslam, T782399, F781282,
seafestinn@hotmail.com A/c, hot shower, cable TV, overlooking the sea. Owned by a
slightly overbearing Australian who has spent time making this the best place in town.
Email facilities. Cheaper price is for a 3-bed dorm. Recommended.

Eating **Cheap** *Floating Restoran dan Bar*, attached to *Dragon Inn*, pilehouse with good seafood, verify prices before ordering. *Seafest Restaurant*, next to the *Seafest Inn*, Malay
food predominantly with some excellent fish dishes. Good standard for very reasonable prices. There is an excellent Muslim restaurant at the top end of town, furthest
from the market, and a number of coffee shops.

Shopping Cultured pearls are sold by traders in town. Filipino handicrafts.

Sport The *Semporna Ocean Tourism Centre* has recently been built, with a marina from
where watersports and marine expeditions can be organized.

Transport **Air** Regular connections with **Sandakan**. **Boat** To charter a boat costs RM200 to
106 km North of **Sipadan**. There are day trips from **Tawau** to **Sipadan** with bigger boats, cutting the
Tawau price down to RM50 (weekends only); the local papers supply information. **Minibus** Minibus station in front of USNO headquarters. Regular connections with **Tawau**
and **Lahad Datu**.

Directory **Communications** General Post Office: next to minibus station.

Sipadan Island Marine Reserve

The venerable French marine biologist Jacques Cousteau 'discovered'   *Colour map 4, grid C6*
Sipadan in 1989 and after spending three months diving around the island
from his research vessel *Calypso* had this to say: "I have seen other places like
Sipadan 45 years ago, but now no more. Now we have found an untouched
piece of art." Since then Sipadan has become a sub-aqua *shangri-la* for serious divers. In September 1990 Australia's *Sport Diving* magazine called the
island "one of the most exciting dive spots imaginable; an absolutely bewil-
dering underwater experience." More recently, Sipadan landed 6,000 votes
for Top Dive Destination in the World by a leading dive magazine, *Rodale's
Scuba Diving*. The reef is without parallel in Malaysia. But Sipadan Island is
not just for scuba divers: it is a magnificent, tiny tropical island with pristine
beaches and crystal clear water and its coral can be enjoyed by even the most
amateur of snorkellers.

But while Sipidan may win lots of points from dive enthusiasts, it has also
been in the news for less savoury reasons. In April 2000 Abu Sayyaf, a separatist group in the Philippines, kidnapped 21, people including 10 foreign tourists, from the island. Abu Sayyaf, linked to the Moro Islamic Liberation Front,
and probably bankrolled and supported by Osama bin Laden, spirited the
hostages to the Philippine island of Jolo. Here they remained under guard and
threat of execution while the Armed forces of the Philippines tried, sometimes
incompetently, to rescue them. The hostages were freed in dribs and drabs
with the final batch being released in September 2000, but it wasn't the sort of
publicity that Sipadan was looking for.

Pulau Sipadan is the only oceanic island in Malaysia; it is not attached to the
continental shelf, and stands on a limestone and coral stalk, rising 200 m from
the bed of the Celebes Sea. The limestone pinnacle mushrooms out near the
surface, but a few metres offshore drops off in a sheer underwater cliff to the
seabed. The reef comes right into the island's small pier, allowing snorkellers
to swim along the edge of the coral cliff, while remaining close to the
coral-sand beach. The edge is much further out around the rest of the island.
The tiny island has a cool forested interior and it is common to see flying foxes
and monitor lizards. It is also a stop-over point for migratory birds, and was
originally declared a bird sanctuary in 1933. It has been a marine reserve since
1981 and three Wildlife Department officials are permanently stationed on
the island. The island is also a breeding ground for the green turtle; August
and September are the main egg-laying months (see page 471).

Sipadan is known for its underwater overhangs and caverns, funnels and
ledges, all covered in coral. 5 m down from the edge of the precipice there is a
coral overhang known as the Hanging Gardens, where coral dangles from the
underside of the reef. The cavern is located on the cliff right in front of the
island's accommodation area. Its mouth is 24-m wide and the cave, which has
fine formations of stalactites and stalagmites, goes back almost 100 m, sometimes less than 4 m below the surface. Visibility blurs where fresh water mixes
with sea water. Inside, there are catacombs of underwater passages.

The island is disputed between the Indonesian and Malaysian governments. Indonesia has asked Malaysia to stop developing marine tourism
facilities on Sipadan. Malaysia's claim to the island rests on historical documents signed by the British and Dutch colonial administrations. Periodically the two sides get around the negotiating table, but it appears that
neither is prepared to make a big issue of Sipadan. Occasionally guests on
the island see Indonesian or Malaysian warships just offshore and in 1994

Sabah

☞ **Lines on the map: sensitive territory**

There's a new distraction on the horizon for scuba divers and sun-worshippers on Sipadan Island: warships. Sipadan, along with the neighbouring island of Ligitan, is disputed by the Indonesian and Malaysian governments, frigates from the alternate navies regularly make their presence felt by prowling around the turquoise waters like cats sniffing out their territorial boundaries. The issue of the overlapping claims lay dormant for decades but things changed with the discovery of Sipadan's incomparable underwater charms. With Malaysia giving the go-ahead to the construction of resorts on Sipadan, the government in Jakarta has been pressing harder for an urgent diplomatic solution to the dispute.

An agreement signed in 1969 allowed Malaysia to retain control of the islands until a solution was found. But Indonesia now says that agreement is being flouted. The two sides agreed to halt any developments until the dispute is settled by negotiation, but even the presence of the Indonesian frigates does not appear to have discouraged Malaysian developers. A joint commission has recently been studying the competing claims; both sides have reportedly produced further evidence to substantiate their claims. But a successful resolution of the dispute – which, thanks to good neighbourly relations, is extremely unlikely to escalate – could pave the way to the resolution of other similar disputes in the region.

Another long-standing dispute is the Philippine claim to the whole of Sabah, which Manila has never officially recognized as a legal part of the Malaysian Federation, formed in 1963. The Philippines' historic claim to the territory rests on Sabah's original status as a dependency of the Sultanate of Sulu, in the Philippine islands, southwest of Mindanao. The sultan leased the land to the British North Borneo Chartered Company in 1877 and the British government inherited the lease when Sabah became a crown colony after the Second World War. Manila maintains that London had no right to then cede that lease to Kuala Lumpur and has never relinquished its claim, to the chagrin of Malaysia's federal government.

The very existence of the Association of Southeast Asian Nations (ASEAN) puts the brakes on the escalation of such disputes. Today, trade and investment deals have helped paper over cracks in bilateral relations, formalizing the characteristically non-confrontational Asian way of doing things. But there is one outstanding territorial quarrel which is yet to really raise its ugly head: the Spratly Islands – an archipelago of 250 atolls dispersed over 800,000 sq km in the middle of the South China Sea. They are claimed by China, Vietnam, The Philippines, Malaysia and Taiwan; Indonesia and Brunei also stake claims to various islands but have not yet occupied them. Because the atolls straddle shipping lanes to Japan and lie on top of what are thought to be oil and mineral-rich strata, the Spratlys represent Southeast Asia's hottest potential flashpoint.

rumours were circulating in Sabah that the Governor of the neighbouring Indonesian province of Kaltim wanted to send settlers to the island. A third party also contests ownership of Sipadan: a Malaysian who claims his grandfather, Abdul Hamid Haji, was given the island by the Sultan of Sulu. He has the customary rights to collect turtles eggs on the island, although the Malaysian government disputes this.

The island's tourist facilities are run by three tour companies, who control everything. They are required to restrict the number of visitors allowed on the island at any one time to about 40 and on arrival visitors have to sign a guarantee that they will do nothing to spoil the island. One of the directors of the

Sipadan Dive Centre, a lawyer from Kota Kinabalu, has presented proposals to the state government concerning future environmental safeguards for the island. These have the support of the other resort owners on Sipadan who have agreed to bear the costs together. The proposals recommend that human activity be carefully controlled by further restricting the number of visitors (particularly day-trippers and weekenders), limiting the size and speed of boats using the jetty, the introduction of a bio-digester to dispose of all waste and a scale-down of all diving and snorkelling activities during the height of the northeast and southwest monsoons, to allow the island a recovery period.

Tours Each operator rents out equipment (RM75-100 per day) and provides all food and accommodation. Pre-arranged packages operated by the companies include air transfer to and from Kota Kinabalu. 'Walk-in' rates marginally cheaper. *Borneo Divers*, Rooms 401-412, fourth floor, Wisma Sabah, Kota Kinabalu, T222226, F221550, bdivers@po.jaring.my Runs monthly trips, eight to 20 divers for any trip, packages (all in) cost around US$1,065 (five days per four nights). *Pulau Sipadan Resort*, 484, Block P, Bandar Sabindo, T765200, F763575, www.sipadan-resort.com Organizes dive tours, food and lodging and diving instruction, snorkelling equipment is also available, maximum of 30 divers at any one time; *Sipadan Dive Centre*, A1103, 10th Flr, Wisma Merdeka, Jalan Tun Razak, Kota Kinabalu, T240584, F240415, sipadan@po.jaring.my Packages (all in) approx: US$740 (5D/4N). Recommended. *Borneo Divers* and *Sipadan Dive Centre* both provide four-day PADI training courses. The PADI Divemaster Scuba courses – conducted off KK's TAR Park islands – cost US$250-330. The *Coral Island Cruises tour company* (based in KK) also operates a small ship, the MV *Coral Topaz*, which makes special diving voyages to the Sipadan/Ligitan island group. The 'live-on-board' dive vessel features a/c accommodation, bars, lounges and buffet meals. Five days/four nights cruises cost US$760 per person (diving equipment included).

Best time to visit The best diving season is from mid-February to mid-December when visibility is greater (20-60 m); mostly drift diving; night diving is said to be spectacular.

Sleeping & eating **A** *Sipadan Longhouse Resort*, fan rooms with shower, buffet Western food, RM390 for 2 days and nights, full board. **A** *Sipadan Lodge*, a/c, hot water, local, Chinese and Western food, private boats available. The island's drinking water is brought in from Semporna. *Sipadan Dive Centre*'s facilities are marginally better; its chalets have attached bathrooms and hot water.

Sport **Deep sea fishing** For tuna, marlin, barracuda and bonito, fishing can be organized from Sipadan. Trawler operated by *Pulau Sipadan Resort* is charged per person and per hr. Early mornings and evenings are best. Because the island and the reef are protected, line fishing from the shore is illegal.

Transport
22 km from Semporna in the Celebes Sea

Boat Organized by the 2 tour companies from Semporna, included in price of trip. Also boats from **Tawau** once a week from the main dock (much rougher journey as have to go more on the open sea). **Speedboat**: hired, 1½ hrs from **Semporna**.

Mabul Island Located between Semporna and Sipadan, this island of 21 ha is considerably larger than Sipadan and is partly home to Bajau fishermen who live in traditional palm-thatched houses. In contrast to Sipadan's untouched forest, the island is predominantly planted with coconut trees. Diving has been the most recent discovery; an Australian diver claims it is "one of the richest single destinations for exotic small marine life anywhere in the world". It has already become known as the world's best 'muck diving' – so called because of the silt-filled waters and poor visibility (for this area, though still reasonable, at least 12 m usually, compared with many other places). The island is surrounded by gentle sloping reefs with depths from 3-35 m and a wall housing numerous species of hard corals.

Sleeping and eating Mabul was chosen to provide more upmarket accommodation than that found on Sipadan, offering exclusive private chalets. For people diving off Sipadan, Mabul is a convenient place to stay and considerably less crowded. There are 2 resorts on the island. **AL***Sipadan Water Village*, for reservation PO Box 62156, T089751777, F089752997, swvill@tm.net.my General sales agent: *Pan Borneo Tours and Travel*, constructed on several wharves in Bajau water village-style on ironwood stilts over the water. 35 chalets with private balconies, hot water showers, restaurant serving good range of cuisine, dive shop and centre, deep sea fishing tours available. Budget or student travellers are sometimes given large discounts. Prices range from RM470 for divers, including equipment, to RM370 for non-divers. **L** *Sipadan Mabul Resort*, located at the southern tip of the island, overlooking Sipadan, PO Box 14125, T08823000, F088242003, mabul@po.jaring.my 25 beach chalets with a/c, hot water showers, balcony, pool and jacuzzi, restaurant serving Chinese and Western food in buffet style, all-inclusive price, padi diving courses, snorkelling, windsurfing, deep sea fishing, volleyball, private diving boats.

Transport Air and sea: flight to **Tawau**, met upon arrival and then taken to **Semporna** (1½ hrs), from where it is a 30-min boat ride to **Mabul Island**.

Tawau

Colour map 4, grid C5
Phone code 089

Tawau is a timber port in Sabah's southeastern corner. It is a busy commercial centre and the main channel for the entry of Indonesian workers into Sabah. Kalimantan is visible, just across the bay.

The town was developed in the early 19th century by the British who planted hemp. The British also developed the logging industry in Sabah, using elephants from Burma. The Bombay Burma Timber Company became the North Borneo Timber Company in 1950; a joint British and Sabah government venture.

Tawau is surrounded by plantations and smallholdings of rubber, copra, cocoa and palm oil. The local soils are volcanic and very fertile and palm oil has recently taken over from cocoa as the predominant crop; Malaysian cocoa prices dropped when its quality proved to be 20% poorer than cocoa produced in Nigeria and the Ivory Coast. In addition, the cocoa plants became diseased. As a result of the decline, many of the cocoa growers emigrated to the Ivory Coast. KL is now an established research centre for palm oil and recently it has been discovered that palm oil can be used as a fuel.

Now that the Sandakan area has been almost completely logged, Tawau has taken over as the main logging centre on the east coast. The forest is disappearing fast but there are ongoing reforestation programmes. At Kalabakan west of Tawau there is a well established, large-scale reforestation project with experiments on fast-growing trees such as *Albizzia falcataria*, which is said to grow 30 m in five years. There are now large plantation areas. The tree is processed into, among other things, paper for paper money.

Sabah

Tawau Hills State Park lies 24 km northwest of Tawau; it protects Tawau's water catchment area. The Tawau River flows through the middle of the 27,972-ha park and forms a natural deep water pool, at Table Waterfall, which is good for swimming. There is a trail from there to some hot water springs and another to the top of Bombalai Hill, an extinct volcano. Most of the forest in the park below 500 m has been logged. Only the forest on the central hills and ridges is untouched. The park is popular with locals at weekends. **Camping** is possible but bring your own equipment. ■ *RM2, for more information, contact Ranger Office, Tawau Hills Park, T810676, F011-884917. Access to the park is via a maze of rough roads through the* Borneo Abaca Limited *agricultural estates. It is advisable to hire a taxi.*

Excursions

A *Belmont Marco Polo*, Jln Abaca/Jln Clinic, T777988, F763739. A/c, restaurant, best hotel in Tawau although considerably more expensive than the competition. **B** *Emas*, Jln Utara, T762000, F763569. A/c, restaurant. **B** *Merdeka*, Jln Masjid, T776655, F761743. A/c, restaurant. **B** *Millennium*, 561 Jln Bakau, T771155, F755511. A/c, spacious rooms. Considerably cheaper than the *Marco Polo* and very acceptable. **B** *North Borneo*, 52-53 Dunlop St, T763060, F773066. A/c, TV, hot shower, reasonable but expensive for Tawau. **C** *Loong*, Jln Abaca, T765308. A/c, fully carpeted, clean and light. **C** *Pan Sabah*, Jln Stephen Tan, behind local minibus station, T762488. A/c, TV, attached bathrooms, clean rooms and very good value compared to other options in town. **C** *Sanctuary*, Jln Chester, T751155. A/c, clean, central and spacious, but sterile and characterless. **C** *Tawau*, 72-3 Jln Chester, T771100. Cheaper rooms without attached bathroom and smelly and dirty. Best avoided.

Sleeping
Hotels here are not great value for money. Avoid the cheaper lodging houses around Jln Stephen Tan, Jln Chester and Jln Cole Adams

Malay Cheap *Asnur*, 325B, Block 41, Fajar Complex. Thai and Malay, large choice. *Venice Coffee House*, *Marco Polo Hotel*, Jln Abaca/Jln Clinic, 'hawker centre' for late night eating, Malay and Chinese. *Yun Lo*, Jln Abaca (below the *Hotel Loong*), good Malay and Chinese. A popular spot with the locals, this has a good atmosphere. Recommended.

Chinese Cheap *Dragon Court*, 1st Flr, Lot 15, Block 37 Jln Haji Karim, Chinese, popular with locals, lots of seafood. **International Cheap** *Dreamland*, 541 Jln Haji Karim. Good local selection. *The Hut*, Block 29, Lot 5, Fajar Complex, Town Extension II, Western, Malay and Chinese, large menu. *Kublai Khan*, *Marco Polo Hotel*, Jln Abaca/Jln Clinic. **Seafood Mid-range** *May Garden*, 1 km outside town on road to Semporna, outside seating. **Cheap** *Maxims*, Block 30, Lot 6 Jln Haji Karim. **Foodstalls** along the seafront.

Eating

Cinema is on Jln Stephen Tan, next to central market. There are **karaoke** bars on every street corner. Several of the hotels have nightclubs and bars.

Entertainment

General and fish market at the west end of Jln Dunlop, near the Customs Wharf.

Shopping

Diving *Borneo Divers*, 46 1st Flr, Jln Dunlop, T762259, F761691. **Golf** 9-hole golf course, modest green fees, even cheaper during the week.

Sport

GSU, T772531, booking agent for Kalimantan; *Pulau Sipadan Resort Tours*, 1st Flr, no 484, Bandar Sabindo, T242262, F213036.

Tour operators

Air The airport is 2 km from town centre. Regular connections with **KK, Lahad Datu** and **Sandakan**. **Boat** Packed boats leave Tawau's Customs Wharf (behind Pasar Ikan) twice daily at 0800 and 1600 for **Pulau Nunukan Timur**, in Kalimantan, Indonesia, 2 hrs, RM25 per 16,000Rp. It is possible to get a direct boat from **Tawau** to **Tarakan** at 0800 (RM45). Tickets available from the offices opposite Pasar Ikan. From there it is possible to get a boat to Tarakan the next day, or a direct boat to **Pare Pare** (Sulawesi), 48

Transport
110 km to Semporna

Sabah

however, and Overbeck was forced to sell out. The first managing director of the company was the Scottish adventurer and former gun-runner William C Cowie. He was in charge of the day-to-day running of the territory, while the British government supplied a governor.

The new chartered company, with its headquarters in the City of London, was given sovereignty over Sabah and a free hand to develop it. The British administrators soon began to collect taxes from local people and quickly clashed with members of the Brunei nobility. John Whitehead, a British administrator, wrote: "I must say, it seemed rather hard on these people that they should be allowed to surrender up their goods and chattels to swell even indirectly the revenue of the company". The administration levied poll-tax, boat tax, land tax, fishing tax, rice tax, *tapai* (rice wine) tax and a 10% tax on proceeds from the sale of birds' nests. Resentment against these taxes sparked the six-year Mat Salleh rebellion (see page 433) and the Rundum Rebellion, which peaked in 1915, during which hundreds of Muruts were killed by the British.

Relations were not helped by colonial attitudes towards the local Malays and tribal people. One particularly arrogant district officer, Charles Bruce, wrote: "The mind of the average native is equivalent to that of a child of four. So long as one remembers that the native is essentially a child and treats him accordingly he is really tractable." Most recruits to the chartered company administration were fresh-faced graduates from British universities, mainly Oxford and Cambridge. For much of the time there were only 40-50 officials running the country. Besides the government officials, there were planters and businessmen: tobacco, rubber and timber became the most important exports. There were also Anglican and Roman Catholic missionaries. British North Borneo was never much of a money-spinner – the economy suffered badly whenever commodity prices slumped – but it managed to pay for itself for most of the time up until the Second World War.

The Japanese interregnum Sabah became part of *Dai Nippon*, or Greater Japan, on New Year's Day 1942, when the Japanese took Labuan. On the mainland, the Japanese Imperial Army and *Kempetai* (military police) were faced with the might of the North Borneo Armed Constabulary, about 650 men. Jesselton (Kota Kinabalu) was occupied on 9 January and Sandakan, 10 days later. All Europeans were interned and when Singapore fell in 1942, 2,740 prisoners of war were moved to Sandakan, most of whom were Australian, where they were forced to build an airstrip. On its completion, the POWs were ordered to march to Ranau, 240 km through the jungle. This became known as 'The Borneo Death March' and only six men survived (see page 463).

The Japanese were hated in Sabah and the Chinese mounted a resistance movement which was led by the Kuching-born Albert Kwok Hing Nam. He also recruited Bajaus and Sulus to join his guerrilla force which launched the 'Double Tenth Rebellion' (the attacks took place on 10 October 1943). The guerrillas took Tuaran, Jesselton and Kota Belud, killing many Japanese and sending others fleeing into the jungle. But the following day the Japanese bombed the towns and troops quickly retook the towns and captured the rebels. There followed a mass execution in which 175 rebels were decapitated. On 10 June 1945 Australian forces landed at Labuan, under the command of American General MacArthur. Allied planes bombed the main towns and virtually obliterated Jesselton and Sandakan. Sabah was liberated on 9 September, and thousands of the remaining 21,000 Japanese troops were killed in retaliation, many by Muruts.

A British Military Administration governed Sabah in the immediate aftermath of the war, and the cash-strapped chartered company sold the territory to the British crown for £1.4 mn in mid-1946. The new crown colony was modelled on the chartered company's administration and set about rebuilding the main towns and war-shattered infrastructure. In May 1961, following Malaysian independence, Prime Minister Tunku Abdul Rahman proposed the formation of a federation incorporating Malaya (ie Peninsular Malaysia), Singapore, Brunei, Sabah and Sarawak (see page 514). Later that same year, Tun Fuad Stephens, a timber magnate and newspaper publisher formed Sabah's first-ever political party, the United National Kadazan Organisation (UNKO). Two other parties were founded shortly afterwards – the Sabah Chinese Association and the United Sabah National Organization (USNO). The British were keen to leave the colony and the Sabahan parties thrashed out the pros and cons of joining the proposed federation. Elections were held in late-1962 in which a UNKA-USNO alliance (the Sabah Alliance) swept to power and the following August, Sabah became an independent country...for 16 days. Like Singapore and Sarawak, Sabah opted to join the federation, to the indignation of the Philippines and Indonesia which both had claims on the territory. Jakarta's objections resulted in the *konfrontasi* – an undeclared war with Malaysia (see page 398) which was not settled until 1966.

Modern Sabah

Politics

Sabah's political scene has always been lively and never more so than in 1994 when the Malaysian Prime Minister, Doctor Mahathir Mohamad, pulled off what commentators described as a democratic *coup d'état*. With great political dexterity, he out-manoeuvered his rebellious rivals and managed to dislodge the opposition state government, despite the fact that it had just won a state election. The reasons why Doctor Mahathir was motivated to bulldoze his own party into power there go back more than 10 years and the roots of Sabah's political instability go back even further.

Following Sabah's first state election in 1967, the Sabah Alliance ruled until 1975 when the newly formed multi-racial party, Berjaya, swept the polls. Berjaya had been set up with the financial backing of the United Malays National Organization (UMNO), the mainstay of the ruling Barisan Nasional (National Front) coalition on the Peninsula. Over the following decade that corrupt administration crumbled and in 1985 the opposition Sabah United Party (PBS), led by the Christian Kadazan Datuk Joseph Pairin Kitingan, won a landslide victory and became the only state government in Malaysia that did not belong to the UMNO-led coalition. It became an obvious embarrassment to Prime Minister Doctor Mahathir Mohamad to have a rebel Christian state in his predominantly Muslim federation. Nonetheless, the PBS eventually joined Barisan Nasional, believing its partnership in the coalition would help iron things out. It did not.

When the PBS came to power, the federal government and Sabahan opposition parties openly courted Filipino and Indonesian immigrants in the state, almost all of whom are Muslim, and secured identity cards for many of them, enabling them to vote. Doctor Mahathir has made no secret of his preference for a Muslim government in Sabah. Nothing, however, was able to dislodge the PBS, which was resoundingly returned to power in 1990. The federal government had long been suspicious of Sabahan politicians, particularly following the PBS's defection from Doctor Mahathir's coalition in the run-up to the 1990 general election, a move which bolstered the opposition alliance. Doctor Mahathir described this as "a stab in the back", and referred to Sabah as "a thorn in the flesh of the Malaysian federation". But in the event, the Prime Minister won that national election convincingly without PBS help, prompting fears, in Sabah, of political retaliation. Those fears proved justified in the wake of the election.

Sabah paid a heavy price for its 'disloyalty'; several prominent Sabahans were arrested as secessionist conspirators under Malaysia's Internal Security Act, which provides for indefinite detention without trial. Among them was Jeffrey Kitingan,

Sabah

brother of the Chief Minister head of the influential Yayasan Sabah, or Sabah Foundation (see page 417). At the same time, Joseph Pairin Kitingan himself was charged with corruption. There was a feeling in Sabah that the two Kitingans were bearing the brunt of Doctor Mahathir's personal political vendetta.

As the political feud grew more venomous, the federal government added to the fray by failing to promote Sabah to foreign investors. As investment money dried up, so did federal development funds; big road and housing projects were left unfinished for years. Many in Sabah felt that their state was being short-changed by the federal government. The political instability had a detrimental effect on the state economy and the business community began to feel that continued feuding would be economic lunacy. Politicians in the Christian-led PBS, however, continued to claim that Sabah wasn't getting its fair share of Malaysia's economic boom. They said the agreement which enshrined a measure of autonomy for Sabah when it joined the Malaysian federation had been eroded.

The main bone of contention was the state's oil revenues, worth around US$852 mn a year, of which 95% disappeared into federal coffers. There were many other sore points too and as the list of grievances grew longer, the state government exploited them to the full. By 1994, anti-federal feelings were running high. The PBS continued to promote the idea of 'Sabah for Sabahans', a defiant slogan in a country where the federal government was working to centralize power. Because Doctor Mahathir likes to be in control, the idea of granting greater autonomy to a distant, opposition-held state was not on his agenda. A showdown was inevitable.

It began in January 1994. As Datuk Pairin's corruption trial drew to a close, he dissolved the state assembly, paving the way for fresh elections. He did this to cover the eventuality of his being disqualified from office through a 'guilty' verdict: he wanted to have his own team in place to take over from him. He was convicted of corruption. But the fine imposed on him was just under the disqualifying threshold, and, to the Prime Minister's fury, he led the PBS into the election. Doctor Mahathir put his newly appointed deputy, Anwar Ibrahim, in charge of the National Front alliance campaign.

Datuk Pairin won the election, but by a much narrower margin than before. He alleged vote-buying and ballot rigging. He accused Doctor Mahathir's allies of whipping up the issue of religion. He spoke of financial inducements being offered to Sabah's Muslim voters, some of whom are Malay, but most of whom are Bajau tribes people and Filipino immigrants. His swearing-in ceremony was delayed for 36 hours: the governor said he was sick; Datuk Parin said his political enemies were trying to woo defectors from the ranks of the PBS, to overturn his slender majority. He was proved right.

Three weeks later, he was forced to resign; his fractious party had virtually collapsed in disarray and a stream of defections robbed him of his majority. Datuk Parin's protestations that his assemblymen had been bribed to switch sides were ignored. The local leader of Doctor Mahathir's ruling party, Tan Sri Sakaran Dandai, was swiftly sworn in as the new Chief Minister.

Following this 'constitutional coup', Mahathir might reasonably have hoped that the people of Sabah would come to realize that Datuk Pairin's head was the price they had to pay for political reconciliation with Kuala Lumpur and the financial inducements that would follow. However, in the 1995 general election the PBS did remarkably well, holding onto eight seats and defeating a number of Front candidates who had defected from the PBS the previous year. Sabah was one area, along with the East Coast state of Kelantan, which resisted the Mahathir/BN electoral steamroller.

The March 1999 state elections once again pitted UMNO against Pairin's PBS. And once again the issues were local autonomy, vote rigging, the role of national politics and political parties in state elections, and money. A new element was the role that Anwar Ibrahim's trial might play in the campaign (see page 517) but otherwise it was old wine in mostly old bottles.

The outcome was a convincing win for Mahathir and the ruling National Front who gathered 31 of the 48 state assembly seats – three more than the Prime Minister forecast. Mahathir once again used the lure of development funds from KL to convince local Sabahans where their best interests might lie. Mahathir is a politician who does not mince his words, and is quite happy to pork barrel when needs call: "We are not being unfair" he said. "We are more than fair, but we cannot be generous to the opposition. We can be generous to a National Front government in Sabah. That I can promise." As a *Straits Times* journalist put it: 'Sabahans got the point'. While the elections were marred by allegations of vote buying there can be little doubt that this was an impressive victory for Mahathir and the NF machine.

But worryingly for the National Front, the opposition Parti Bersatu Sabah (PBS) still managed to garner the great bulk of the Kadazan vote and in so doing won 17 seats. That the Kadazan electorate were voting for the party and not for influential local politicians was clear in what happened to those PBS politicians who had crossed over to the National Front in the months leading up to the elections: they lost their seats. In other words, the large Kadazan population still don't believe, whatever Mahathir's rhetoric, that the NF represents their interests. As in Sarawak, the election, in the end, was more about local politics than about the economic crisis and the Anwar trial.

Nine months later when it came to the general elections the PBS won only three out of 20 seats. But while the National Front may have won that state it did so on a share of less than 50 per cent of the vote.

The latest twist in this long-running saga is the possibility that the PBS might rejoin the National Front. In November 2001 PBS president Joseph Pairin Kitingan, at the party's annual congress, asked the delegates for guidance in the matter. It seems that the National Front would welcome the PBS notwithstanding Mahathir's fury at the manner in which the party left the fold back in 1990, just before a general election. It would seem that both sides in this long-running and often acrimonious dispute see advantages in patching up their differences.

Culture

Sabah's main tribal communities comprise the Kadazan, who mostly live on the west coast, the Murut, who inhabit the interior, to the south, and the Bajau, who are mainly settled around Gunung Kinabalu. There are more than 30 tribes, more than 50 different languages and about 100 dialects. Sabah also has a large Chinese population and many illegal Filipino immigrants.

People

Kadazans The Kadazans are the largest ethnic group in Sabah comprising about a third of the population and are a peaceful agrarian people with a strong cultural identity. Until Sabah joined the Malaysian Federation in 1963, they were known as 'Dusuns', meaning 'peasants' or 'orchard people'. This name was given to them by outsiders, and picked up by the British. It became, in effect, a residual category including all those people who were not Muslim or Chinese. Most Kadazans call themselves after their tribal place names. They can be broken into several tribes including the Lotud of Tuaran, the Rungus of the Kudat and Bengkoka Peninsula, the Tempasuk, the Tambanuo, Kimarangan and the Sanayo. Minokok and Tengara Kadazans live in the upper Kinabatangan River basin while those living near other big rivers are just known as *Orang Sungai*, or 'river people'. Most Kadazans used to

Sabah

Sabah's ethnic breakdown

	Population	%
Kadazan/Dusun	340,060	19.6
[Kadazan	110,866	6.4]
[Dusun	229,194	13.2]
Murut	50,315	2.9
Bajau	202,995	11.7
Malay	107,570	6.2
Other Muslim	235,960	13.6
Chinese	199,525	11.5
Indonesia	421,605	24.3
Filipino	142,270	8.2
Others	34,700	2.0
Total population	1,735,000	100

Source: 1991 census

live in longhouses; these are virtually all gone now. The greatest likelihood of a visitor coming across a longhouse in Sabah is in the Rungus area of the Kudat Peninsula; even there, former longhouse residents are moving into detached, kampung-style houses while one or two remain for the use of tourists.

But Kadazan identity is not that simple. The 1991 census lists both Kadazans (110,866) and Dusuns (229,194). In the 1970 census all were listed as Kadazan, while in the 1960 census they were all Dusun. In 1995 the Malaysian government agreed to add the common language of these people(s) to the national repertoire to be taught in schools. This they named Kadazandusun. The other four are Malay, Chinese, Tamil and Iban.

All the Kadazan groups had similar customs and modes of dress (see below). Up to the Second World War, many Kadazan men wore the *chawat* loin cloth. The Kadazans used to hunt with blowpipes, and in the 19th century, were still head-hunting. Today, however, they are known for their gentleness and honesty; their produce can often be seen sitting unattended at roadside stalls, and passing motorists are expected to pay what they think fair. The Kadazans traditionally traded their agricultural produce at large markets, held at meeting points, called *tamus* (see box). The Kadazan are farmers, and the main rice-producers of Sabah. They used to be animists, and were said to live in great fear of evil spirits; most of their ceremonies were rituals aimed at driving out these spirits. The job of communicating with the spirits of the dead, the *tombiivo*, was done by priestesses, called *bobohizan*. They are the only ones who can speak the ancient Kadazan language, using a completely different vocabulary from modern Kadazan. Most Kadazans converted to Christianity, mainly Roman Catholicism, during the 1930s, although there are also some Muslim Kadazan.

The big cultural event in the Kadazan year is the **Harvest Festival** which takes place in May. The ceremony, known as the *Magavau* ritual, is officiated by a high priestess, or *Bobohizan*. These elderly women, who wear traditional black costumes and colourful headgear with feathers and beads, are now few and far between. The ceremony culminates with offerings to the *Bambaazon*, or rice spirit. After the ceremonies Catholic, Muslim and animist Kadazans all come together to play traditional sports such as wrestling and buffalo racing. This is about the only occasion when visitors are likely to see Kadazan in their traditional costumes. In the Penampang area a woman's costume consists of a fitted, sleeveless tunic and ankle-length skirt of black velvet. Belts of silver coins (*himpogot*) and brass rings are worn round the waist; a colourful sash is also worn. Men dress in a black, long-sleeved jacket over black trousers; they also wear a *siga*, colourful woven head gear. These costumes have become more decorative in recent years, with colourful embroidery. Villages send the finalists of local beauty contests to the grand final of the Unduk Ngadau harvest festival queen competition in Penampang, near Kota Kinabalu.

It is the Kadazans who dominate the Pasti Bersatu Sabah (PBS), the critical piece in Sabah's political jigsaw.

Bajau The Bajau, the famous 'cowboys' of the 'wild East', came from the South Philippines during the 18th and 19th centuries and settled in the coastal area around Kota

Tamus – Sabah's markets and trade fairs

In Sabah, an open trade fair is called a tamu. Locals gather to buy and sell jungle produce, handicrafts and traditional wares. Tamu comes from the Malay word 'tetamu', to meet, and the biggest and most famous is held at Kota Belud, north of Kota Kinabalu in Bajau country. Tamus were fostered by the pre-war British North Borneo Chartered Company, when district officers would encourage villagers from miles around to trade among themselves. It was also a convenient opportunity for officials to meet with village headmen. They used to be strictly Kadazan affairs, but today tamus are multiracial events.

Sometimes public auction of water buffalo and cattle are held. Some of the biggest tamus around the state are:

Monday:	*Tandek*
Tuesday:	*Kiulu, Topokan*
Wednesday:	*Tamparuli*
Thursday:	*Keningau, Tambunan, Sipitang, Telipok, Simpangan*
Friday:	*Sinsuran, Weston*
Saturday:	*Penampang, Beaufort, Sindumin, Matunggong, Kinarut*
Sunday:	*Tambunan, Tenom, Kota Belud, Papar, Gaya Street (KK)*

Belud, Papar and Kudat, where they made a handsome living from piracy. The Bajau who came to Sabah joined forces with the notorious Illanun and Balinini pirates. They are natural seafarers and were dubbed 'the sea gypsies'; today they form the second largest indigenous group in Sabah and are divided into subgroups, notably the Binadan, Suluk and Obian. They call themselves 'Samah'; it was the Brunei Malays who first called them Bajau. They are strict Muslims and the famous Sabahan folk hero, Mat Salleh, who led a rebellion in the 1890s against British Chartered Company rule, was a Bajau (see page 433). Despite their seafaring credentials, they are also renowned horsemen and (very occasionally) still put in an appearance at Kota Belud's *tamu* (see page 448). Bajau women are known for their brightly coloured basketry – *tudong saji*. The Bajau build their atap houses on stilts over the water and these are interconnected by a network of narrow wooden planks. The price of a Bajau bride was traditionally assessed in stilts, shaped from the trunks of bakau mangrove trees. A father erected one under his house on the day a daughter was born and replaced it whenever it wore out. The longer the daughter remained at home, the more stilts he got through and the more water buffalo he demanded from a prospective husband.

Murut

The Murut live around Tenom and Pensiangan in the lowland and hilly parts of the interior, in the southwest of Sabah and in the Trusan Valley of North Sarawak. Some of those living in more remote jungle areas retain their traditional longhouse way of life, but many Murut have now opted for detached kampung-style houses. *Murut* means 'hill people' and is not the term used by the people themselves. They refer to themselves by their individual tribal names. The Nabai, Bokan and Timogun Murut live in the lowlands and are wet-rice farmers, while the Peluan, Bokan and Tagul Murut live in the hills and are mainly shifting cultivators. They are thought to be related to Sarawak's Kelabit and Kalimantan's Lun Dayeh people, although some of the tribes in the South Philippines have similar characteristics. The Murut staples are rice and tapioca, they are known for their weaving and basketry and have a penchant for drinking *tapai* (rice wine – see page 496). They are also enthusiastic dancers and devised the *lansaran*, a sprung dance floor like a trapeze. The Murut are a mixture of animists, Christians and Muslims and were the last tribe in Sabah to give up head-hunting, a practice finally stopped by British North Borneo Chartered Company administrators.

👉 **Dance**

Name of dance	Tribe	District
Sumazau Penampang	Kadan/Dusun	Penampang, west coast
Angalang	Murut	Pensiangan and Tenom interior and south
Mangiluk	Suluk	East coast
Magunatip	Murut and Kwijau Dusun	Interior and south
Adai Adai	Brunei Malay	Sipitang and Membakut, southwest of Sabah
Mongigol Sumundai	Rungus	Kudat and Pitas, north of Sabah
Limbai	Bajau	Kota Belud, west coast is called bertitik.
Dansa	Cocos	Lahad Datu, east coast
Bolak Bolak	Bajau	Semporna, east coast
Mongigol Sumayan	Lotud	Tuaran, west coast
Umang-Umang Ting-Ting	Brunei Malay	Bongawan, west coast
Daling-Daling	Suluk	East coast
Sumazau Papar	Kadazan, Dusun	Paper, west coast
Titikas	Orang Sungai	Kinabatangan, east coast
Liliput	Bisaya	Beaufort, west coast
Kuda Pasu	Bajau	Kota Belud, west coast

Sabah

Chinese The Chinese accounted for nearly a third of Sabah's population in 1960; today they make up just a fifth. Unlike Sarawak, however, where the Chinese were a well-established community in the early 1800s, Sabah's Chinese came as a result of the British North Borneo Chartered Company's immigration policy, designed to ease a labour shortage. About 70% of Sabah's Chinese are Christian Hakkas, who first began arriving at the end of the 19th century, under the supervision of the Company. They were

Description

Performed during Annual harvest Pemanpang Festival (Pesta Kaamatan) *to honour the rice spirit* (Bambaazon). Sumazau *means dancing.*

*A solo warrior dance, accompanied by a group of women dancers (*angalong). *Originally performed after a victorious battle or head-hunting trip.*

Performed at weddings and social events.

These dancers need skill and agility to dance among bamboo poles which are hit together to produce the rhythm of the dance.

Evolved from a song; it tells of the activities of the local fishermen and farmers

Can be performed as part of certain ritual festivals. For instance, Thanksgiving to rice spirit for a bountiful harvest or moving into a new house.

Performed at weddings, characterized by graceful wrist rotations. Accompanying music

Performed at weddings. It features energetic foot stomping.

Bolak Bolak is Malay for castanets. The dancers hold the castanets and create the rhythm of the music.

Ritual dance performed during Rumaha *ceremony to honour spirits of skulls, or the* Mangahau *ceremony for the spirits of sacred jars.*

Celebrates the birth of a newborn child

A 'courting' dance said to be derived from the English 'darling'. Usually accompanied by a love song.

Performed at similar occasions to Sumazau Penampang. Distinctive foot work.

Titikas is based on the Ingki-Ingki *game, similar to hopscotch.*

Liliput means 'go around'. It is a dance to cast away evil spirits in a possessed person.

Originally performed by horsemen or escort a bridegroom and his entourage to the bride's home. The female dancers hold handkerchieves as a sign of welcome.

given free passage from China and most settled in the Jesselton and Kudat areas; today most Hakka are farmers. There are also large Teochew and Hokkien communities in Tawau, Kota Kinabalu and Labuan while Sandakan is mainly Cantonese, who originally came from Hong Kong.

Sabah

Tapai – Sabah's rice wine

Tapai, the fiery Sabahan rice wine, is much loved by the Kadazan and the Murut. It was even more popular before the two tribal groups' wholesale conversion to Christianity in the 1930s. Writer Hedda Morrison noted in 1957 that: "The squalor and wretchedness arising from [their] continual drunkenness made the Murut a particularly useful object of missionary endeavour. In the 1930s missionaries succeeded in converting nearly all the Murut to Christianity. The Murut grasped at this new faith much as the drowning man is said to grasp at a straw. From being the most drunken people in Borneo, they became the most sober." In the Sabah State Museum (see page 415) there is a recipe for tapai, also known as buffalos' blood, which was taken down by an administrator during chartered company days:

"Boil 12lbs of the best glutinous rice until well done. In a wide-mouthed jar, lay the rice in layers of no more than two fingers deep, and between layers, place a total of about 20½-oz yeast cakes. Add two cups of water, tinctured with the juice of six beetroots. Cover jar with muslin and leave to ferment. Each day, uncover it and remove dew which forms on the muslin. On the fifth day, stir the mixture vigorously and leave for four weeks. Store for one full year, after which it shall be full of virtue and potence and most smooth upon the palate."

Tapai is drunk from communal jars, which were also used as burial urns, through bamboo straws. The jar is filled nearly to its brim with tapai. Large leaves are placed on the top just under the lower edge of the rim. These leaves are pierced with straws for sucking up the liquid and the intervening space between the leaves and the top of the jar is filled with water.

Etiquette demands that one drinks till the water has been drained off the leaves. They are then flooded again and the process is repeated. There is also the distilled form of tapai, called montaku, which is even more potent. When North Borneo became a British crown colony after the Second World War, the administration was concerned about the scourge of tapai drinking on three counts. First, it was said to consume a large portion of the natives' potential food crop, second, it usually caused a crime wave whenever it was drunk, and thirdly, it was blamed for the high rate of infant mortality as mothers frequently gave their babies a suck at the straw.

Oscar Cook, a former district officer in the North Borneo Civil Service, noted in his 1923 book Borneo: the Stealer of Hearts, that tapai was not to everyone's fancy and certainly not to his. "As an alternative occupation to head-hunting, the Murut possess a fondness for getting drunk, indulged in on every possible occasion. Tapai, or pengasai, as the Murut calls it, is not a nice drink. In fact, to my thinking it is the very reverse, for it is chiefly made from fermented rice... is very potent, and generally sour and possessed of a pungent and nauseating odour. Births, marriages, deaths, sowing, harvesting and any occasion that comes to mind is made the excuse for a debauch. It is customary for Murut to show respect to the white man by producing their very best tapai, and pitting the oldest and ugliest women of the village against him in a drinking competition." Cook admits that all this proved too much for him and when he was transferred to Keningau, he had to employ an 'official drinker'. "The applicants to the post were many," he noted.

Filipinos Immigration from the Philippines started in the 1950s and refugees began flooding into Sabah when the separatist war erupted in Mindanao in the 1970s. Today there are believed to be upwards of 700,000 illegal Filipino immigrants in Sabah (although their migration has been undocumented for so long that no one is certain), and the state government fears they could soon outnumber locals. There are many in Kota Kinabalu, the state capital and a large community – mainly women and children – in Labuan, but the bulk of the Filipino population is in Semporna, Lahad Datu, Tawau and Kunak (on the east coast) where they already outnumber locals 3:1. One Sabah government minister, referring to the long-running territorial dispute between Malaysia and the Philippines, was quoted as saying "We do not require a strong military presence at the border any more: the aliens have already landed".

Although the federal government has talked of its intention to deport illegal aliens, it is also mindful of the political reality: the majority of the Filipinos are Muslim, and making them legal Malaysian citizens could ruin Sabah's predominantly Christian, Kadazan-led state government. The Filipino community is also a thorn in Sabah's flesh because of the crime wave associated with their arrival: the Sabah police claims 65% of all crimes in the state are committed by Filipinos. The police do not ask many questions when dealing with Filipino criminal suspects; about 40-50 are shot every year. Another local politician was quoted as saying: "The immigrants take away our jobs, cause political instability and pose a health hazard because of the appalling conditions in which some of them live".

There are six different Filipino groups in Sabah: the Visayas and Ilocano are Christian as are the Ilongo (Ilo Ilo), from Zamboanga. The Suluks are Muslim; they come from South Mindanao and have the advantage of speaking a dialect of Bahasa Malaysia. Many Filipinos were born in Sabah and all second generation immigrants are fluent in Bahasa. Migration first accelerated in the 1950s during the logging boom, and continued when the oil palm plantation economy took off; the biggest oil palm plantation is at Tungku, east of Lahad Datu. Many migrants have settled along the roadsides on the way to Danum Valley; it is easy to claim land since all they have to do is simply clear a plot and plant a few fruit trees.

Crafts

Compared with neighbouring Sarawak and Kalimantan, Sabah's handicraft industry is rather impoverished. Sabah's tribal groups were less protected from Western influences than Sarawak's, and traditional skills quickly began to die out as the state modernized and the economy grew. In Kota Kinabalu today, the markets are full of Filipino handicrafts and shell products; local arts and crafts are largely confined to basketry, mats, hats, beadwork, musical instruments and pottery.

The elongated Kadazan backpack baskets found around Mount Kinabalu National Park are called *wakids* and are made from bamboo, rattan and bark. Woven food covers, or *tudong saji*, are often mistaken for hats, and are made by the Bajau of Kota Belud. Hats, made from nipah palm or rattan, and whose shape varies markedly from place to place, are decorated with traditional motifs. One of the most common motifs is the *nantuapan*, or 'meeting', which represents four people all drinking out of the same tapai (rice wine) jar. The Rungus people from the Kudat peninsula also make *linago* basketware from a strong wild grass; it is tightly woven and not decorated (see page 450 for more detail on the Rungus). At *tamus*, Sabah's big open-air markets (see page 493), there are usually some handicrafts for sale. The Kota Belud *tamu* is the best place to find the Bajau horseman's embroidered turban, the *destar* (see page 492). Traditionally, the Rungus people, who live on the Kudat Peninsula, were renowned as fine weavers, and detailed patterns were woven into their ceremonial skirts, or *tinugupan*. These patterns all had different names, but, like the ingredients of the traditional dyes, many have now been forgotten.

Sabah

Background

Introduction

Over the four decades since independence the country has been transformed from a poor, undeveloped British colony, reliant on the export of primary products like rubber and tin, to a self-confident industrializing nation with a burgeoning middle class and an increasingly sophisticated economy. The figures, as they say, speak for themselves: between 1970 and 2000 per capita income rose thirteen-fold to RM13,418, the number of children dying before the age of one was cut from 40/1,000 live births to 8 and, most striking of all, the number of people living in poverty in Peninsular Malaysia was reduced from one in two to less than one in 10. Malaysia has become a country where people – and especially the prime minister, Mahathir Mohamad – think big. He has set out a vision which will bring Malaysia developed country status by 2020, and he is forever cajoling his people to join him in the effort.

During 1997 and 1998 many Western pundits – long annoyed by Mahathir's abrasive and anti-Western manner – predicted that the economy was set for a period of slow growth, brought on by the Asian economic crisis (see page 527 for more details). They also speculated that Mahathir himself would fall because his political legitimacy was so closely tied to the country's economic vitality. As it turned out they were wrong on both counts. The economy has since recovered and Mahathir convincingly won a general election at the end of 1999. But they were not completely wrong.

Malaysia is sometimes called 'the lucky country of Asia' because it is so richly endowed with natural resources. It has the world's largest tin deposits, extensive oil and gas reserves and is cloaked in rainforest containing valuable tropical hardwoods. Until the 1980s, the economy was heavily dependent on these resources and plantation crops such as palm oil, natural rubber, pepper and cocoa. But in the late 1980s and early 1990s, a sudden explosion of industrial growth, spearheaded by a surge in manufacturing, changed the complexion of Malaysia's economy beyond recognition. In 1992, Michael Vatikiotis, Kuala Lumpur correspondent for *The Far Eastern Economic Review*, wrote: "Malaysia in many ways forms the leading edge of social change in Southeast Asia. ... Prime Minister Dr Mahathir Mohamad has captivated his people with a vision of a developed Malaysia by 2020. Deploying this distant vision of the future has allowed Malaysians to think of themselves as becoming a nation of airline pilots and nuclear physicists by 2020."

Malaysia is a young country; until the end of the last century there was just a collection of divided coastal sultanates around the peninsula and three colonial trading settlements. The British grouped the different states into a federation, but Malaysia did not emerge in its present form until 1965, eight years after independence from the British. Today the Federation of Malaysia includes the 11 peninsular states together with Sabah and Sarawak on the island of Borneo (East Malaysia). Singapore left the federation in 1965 social after an unsuccessful two year experiment. The politically dominant Malays of the peninsula had felt uncomfortable with the destabilizing effect of Singapore's mainly Chinese population on the country's racial equation and the uncomfortable marriage of convenience came to an end.

A favourite Malaysian dish is *rojak* – a tossed salad with many different ingredients. It is not uncommon to hear the rojak analogy applied to Malaysia's exotic ethnic mix of Malays, Chinese, Indians and indigenous tribes. The country's cultural blend makes Malaysia interesting, but it is also a potentially volatile mixture. Yet only once since independence in 1957 has the communal melting pot boiled over. Today, most Malaysians are too young to remember the 1969 race riots, although they have lived with their consequences ever since. The government's affirmative action policies have attempted to lessen the economic disparities between the races and have

Background

☞ ## Biggest = best: Malaysia's race for the skies

Malaysia, one of the world's fastest growing and most self-confident nations, seems intent on dominating the Guinness Book of Records. The country now boasts:

The world's tallest flagpole at 100m in Merdeka Square, Kuala Lumpur.

The Petronas Twin Towers in Kuala Lumpur, rising through 88 storeys to 450m. On their completion in 1996 the towers claimed the title of the tallest building(s) in the world. The Petronas Twin Towers are part of the Kuala Lumpur City Centre project which, when completed, will have no fewer than 22 office blocks.

Asia's tallest tower, the KL Tower, at 421m which opened on 1 October 1996.

The Bakun Hydroelectric Dam in the East Malaysian state of Sarawak. Preparatory work began in 1995 and when it is completed (there is still a chance it won't be) it will be the highest HEP dam in the world and the largest such project in

Southeast Asia, generating 2,400 megawatts. The cost? A paltry US$6bn and 10,000 people uprooted.

In 1995 Prime Minister Mahathir laid the foundation stone for Putrajaya, Malaysia's new capital city 35 km south of Kuala Lumpur. It is due for completion in 2005, will support a population of 250,000, and has a price tag of a cool US$8bn. Along with the new international airport and Cyberjaya, both under construction near Putrajaya, the total cost is projected at US$20bn.

Standard Chartered Securities in Kuala Lumpur drew up a list of the 31 largest projects Malaysia had embarked upon or had announced it was undertaking. Totting up the cost, the bill came to RM163bn or US$65bn. NB With the weakening of the Malaysian economy during 1997 some of these projects were delayed or shelved.

given the Malays – the economic underdogs – a helping hand. Over the years, non-Malays have complained bitterly about discrimination against them by the Malay-led government, but somehow, tensions have been kept below boiling point. Today, there is much more inter-mixing between Malaysians from all ethnic backgrounds; many of them are more interested in cashing in on the economic boom than worrying about race. When Malaysia celebrated 35 years of nationhood in August 1992, Dr Mahathir said that on independence, many had predicted that its multiracial, multicultural and multireligious society would collapse. "Malaysia has proven to the world", he said, "that its multiracial nature has not prevented it from achieving progress and success. We must continue to co-operate and be united."

The tourism industry plays a crucial role in Malaysia's economy. The country is endowed with good beaches, coral reefs, jungle, mountains and hill resorts, islands and, these days, hundreds of golf courses. It also has a handful of urban attractions: notably Penang's beautifully preserved Chinatown and Melaka's architectural heritage. As the world's largest exporter of sawn timber Malaysia's logging industry has earned the country notoriety among environmentalists. The industry is riddled with corruption and the Malaysian government admits to problems enforcing its surprisingly stringent forestry policies. But a substantial part of Malaysia's land area is forested (especially in the states of East Malaysia) and the government has been enthusiastically promoting ecotourism; there are several magnificent national parks, both on the peninsula and in the East Malaysian states of Sarawak and Sabah. In Sarawak there are also many jungle tribes, whose culture has remained remarkably intact.

Borneo

The East Malaysian states of Sarawak and Sabah, and the Sultanate of Brunei, occupy the northern third of the island of Borneo. Sabah and Sarawak represented the

translated as 'River of
Martapura in the south

History

Precolonial Mala

With the arrival of suc
the earliest settlers – tl
interior. The Malays est
and in riverine areas ar
thanks to the peninsul
China. Although the or
they were not entirely
'upriver' tribal groups e
metal implements with
551). Malay culture on
cultural traditions, Hind
power shifted from Sun
page 205). In 1430, the
sultan; the city quickly
was the most importan
attention of the Portug
sacked the town and se
established (see page 2
with the powerful tradir
guese, Johor never gain
its capital between Johc

The colonials arriv

The Portuguese were th
Malay peninsula. They w
page 205 for a history of
troops at the end of the
colonial era began. Histc
control were, firstly, to b
the trade system upon w
spheres of influence and
states which are heirs to
ment and establish the ir
development required; n
consequence of econom
During the 17th centu
the fearsome master-sea
homeland in South Sulav
Sumatra, the Bugis nearly
by the arrival of Dutch wa
Selangor on the west coa
influence on the Johor-Ri
By then however, offshoc
ates of Pahang and Perak

Putting Malaya on the map

The names of most of Malaysia's states are older than the name Malaya; until the 1870s the scattered coastal sultanates were independent of each other. Many of the Malay areas were colonized by Sumatrans long ago and it is possible that the word 'Melayu' – or 'Malay' – derives from the Sungai Melayu (Melayu River) in Sumatra. The name in turn is derived from the Dravidian (Tamil) word malai, or 'hill'. As the Malays are coastal people, the paradox is explained by their pre-Islamic religion, which is thought to have been based on a cult in which a sacred mountain took pride of place.

The Graeco-Roman geographer Ptolemy called the Malay peninsula Aurea Chersonesus, or the 'The Golden Chersonese': it was the fabled land of gold. By the early 1500s, European maps were already marking Melaka and Pulau Tioman, which were well known to Chinese mariners. During the Portuguese and Dutch colonial periods, the whole peninsula was simply labelled 'Malacca', and the town was the only significant European outpost until the British took possession of Penang in 1786. There was very little mapping of the peninsula until the early 19th century, and the names of states only gradually appeared on maps over the course of the 17th and 18th centuries.

According to cartographic historian RT Fell, the first maps of the interior of the peninsula, beyond the bounds of the British Straits Settlements, did not appear until the late 19th century. In 1885 the Survey Department was founded and charged with mapping the interior – one of the tasks William Cameron was undertaking when he stumbled across the highland plateau named after him that same year. But right into the 20th century, large tracts of mountainous jungle were still unexplored.

'other' Malaysia, divided by much more than 500 km of sea from the states of the 'Mainland'. Here, in East Malaysia, 'tribal' Dayaks dominate the human landscape and the local economy is sustained not by manufacturing but by the exploitation of natural resources, particularly timber and oil and gas. Sabah and Sarawak were only integrated into the Federation of Malay States in 1963 and visitors from the mainland are still required to obtain a travel permit to come here and a work permit if they want a job. The states maintain control over immigration, education and language issues because of the fear that without these controls the indigenous peoples of Sabah and Sarawak would be elbowed out by their more sophisticated brethren from across the South China Sea.

The name Borneo is thought to be a European mispronunciation of 'Burni' or Brunei. Early Western books variously spelt Borneo 'Burni', 'Burney', 'Burny', 'Borny', 'Borney', 'Burneo', 'Bornei', 'Bruneo', 'Porne' and 'Borneu'. This was not entirely the Europeans' fault, for as John Crawfurd points out in A Descriptive Dictionary of the Indian Isles (1856), the name is "indifferently pronounced by the Malays, according to the dialect they happen to speak – Brune, Brunai, Burne or Burnai". The Chinese, for good measure, referred to the island from the early ninth century as P'o-ni, or P'o-li, or Fo-ni. The sultanate itself became known as 'Borneo Proper', and its capital as Brunei Town. Crawfurd concluded that "the name of the town was not extended to the island by European writers, but by the Mohamedan navigators who conducted the carrying trade of the archipelago before the advent of Europeans". Borneo Proper was first visited by Europeans in the early 16th century, most notably by Antonio Pigafetta, the official chronicler on the Portuguese explorer Ferdinand Magellan's expedition, which called in on the Sultan of Brunei in 1521. The Ibans of Sarawak maintain that the name Borneo derives from the Malay buah nyior, meaning 'coconut', while the Malays had another, less well-known name

The k
Malay
short
mean
either
100 b
edges
these
as far
attrib
repute
family
in Tai
reput
dark,
clean
displa
power
comp
they b
or inh

The
been
assum
were
more
pre-M
magic
were
histori
proces
of iron
blade
paralle
which
the go

The
the 14
reliefs
also at
Howev
introdu
during

Kris
nickelif
in a co

for the
wild m
chosen

Malaysia's monarchs – the public swings against the sultans

Malaysia's nine hereditary rulers, who take it in turn to be king, represent the greatest concentration of monarchs in the world. In 1993 they were at the forefront of the most heated political controversy that Malaysia has seen in years. The battle royal ended in mid-March 1993 with the opposition Democratic Action Party voting with the government to remove the sultans' personal immunity from prosecution. For Prime Minister Dr Mahathir Mohamad, the 1993 Constitutional Amendment Bill was a personal victory. He had long made it known that he regarded the country's nine traditional rulers as a residual anachronism in modern Malaysia. A further constitutional amendment in May 1994 drove that victory home. It makes clear that from now on, the king can only act on the advice of the government. And even if the king does not approve of legislation passed by the government, it becomes law anyway after 30 days.

Malaysia's sultans emerged in the 14th and 15th centuries as the rulers of the small rivermouth states – or negeri – that grew up around the peninsula's coasts. The word 'sultan' is a Turkish term for the Malay Yang di-Pertuan – literally, 'He who is made Lord'. Sultans wielded more than temporal authority (kuasa); they were vested with an aura of sanctity and magical authority, or dualat. Malaya's sultans came through the British colonial period and the Japanese interregnum with their status and powers surprisingly intact.

On independence in 1957, Malaysia became a constitutional monarchy, with the king elected for a five-year term from among the ranks of the sultans. In 1969, following race riots, the government amended the Sedition Act to make it an offence to question the position or prerogatives of traditional rulers. But in 1983, Prime Minister Mahathir provoked a constitutional crisis when he curtailed the power of the king by removing the monarch's right to veto legislation.

Most of Malaysia's rulers have expensive tastes and some live jet-setting playboy lifestyles. Many have used their position to amass prodigious wealth. Traditional Malays considered such behaviour unacceptable in light of the sultans' traditional position as the upholders of Islamic values. One or two sultans added to their unsavoury reputation by committing acts of violence, safe in the knowledge that they would not be prosecuted. Resentment over such acts could never be articulated without falling foul of the Sedition Act. Such activities are not without precedent. In the 17th century, Sultan Mahmud of Johor was notorious for his cruelty; on one occasion he ordered a pregnant woman to be ripped apart because she had eaten a jackfruit from his garden. The woman's husband ran the sultan through with a kris with the full support of palace officials.

Until very recently it has not been possible to print the alleged crimes of Sultan Mahmud's modern successors in the

(KMT), although it was eventually banned by the British, as it was becoming an obvious focus of anti-colonial sentiment. The KMT allowed Communists to join the movement until 1927, but in 1930 they split off to form the Malayan Communist Party (MCP) which drew its support from the working class.

Japanese occupation

Under cover of darkness on the night of 8 December 1941, the Japanese army invaded Malaya, landing in South Thailand and pushing into Kedah, and at Kota Bharu in Kelantan (see page 305). The invasion, which took place an hour before the attack on Pearl Harbor, took the Allies in Malaya and 'Fortress' Singapore completely by surprise. The Japanese forces had air, land and sea superiority and quickly overwhelmed the Commonwealth troops on the peninsula. Militarily, it was a brilliant

Background

Background

House of Johor. But in early 1993 a government MP referred in parliament to 23 incidents since 1972 involving today's Sultan Mahmud of Johor and his son, the Rajah Muda Abdul Majid Idris. The most notorious of these concerned the death of a caddie on the Cameron Highlands golf course. Sultan Mahmood allegedly killed him by smashing his head with a club after the caddie sniggered at a duffed shot.

Other sultans' disregard for various facets of the law of the land was highlighted by His Royal Highness Tuanku Ismail Petra Ibni Al-Marhum Sultan Tahya Petra of Kelantan. He managed to import 30 luxury cars duty free. In March 1992, he eluded customs officials by claiming he was taking his new Lamborghini Diablo for a test drive. Following that incident, the government took full advantage of its ownership of most national newspapers by devoting pages and pages to exposés of the sultans' flamboyant lifestyles. The RM200m it cost Malaysian taxpayers each year to maintain them was broken down in detail. It emerged that entire hospital wards were reserved for their exclusive use. More than RM9m was spent on new cutlery and bedsheets for the King – a sum which the New Straits Times said would have built two new hospitals or 46 rural clinics or 46 primary schools.

The Prime Minister had long lost patience with the sultans over their interference in politics and business and gambled that the unveiling of such royal scams would swing public opinion in favour of constitutional amendments. In July 1992 his government agreed a 'code of conduct' with the sultans, but they refused to accept constitutional amendments undermining their powers. Mahathir responded by withdrawing royal privileges such as their generous financial stipends. In January 1993, parliament passed amendments removing their legal immunity. Deadlock ensued as Malaysian law said the sultans had to approve legislation affecting their position. Finally, after a tense stand-off, the government and the sultans agreed to a compromise. The sultans secured an undertaking that no ruler would be taken to court without the Attorney General's approval.

Mahathir emerged from the fray with his executive powers strengthened and his no-nonsense reputation enhanced. The sultans' reputation, by contrast, has been severely dented.

This contretemps between the King and the Prime Minister is history because Malaysia must be the only country where a prime minister has outlasted not one king but four – he is now onto his fifth. Malaysia's current monarch is the extravagantly titled Yang di-Pertuan Agong, Sultan Salahuddin Abdul Aziz Shah, who was named as the country's eleventh constitutional monarch in February 1999. He took on his five-year term from the outgoing Sultan of Negri Sembilan, the urbane, Oxford-educated Ja'afar ibni Abdul Rahman.

Background

campaign, made speedier by the fact that the Japanese troops stole bicycles in every town they took, thus making it possible for them to outpace all Allied estimates of their likely rate of advance.

By 28 December they had taken Ipoh and all of northern Malaya. Kuantan fell on the 31st, the Japanese having sunk the British warships *Prince of Wales* and *Repulse* (see page 264) and Kuala Lumpur on 11 January 1942. They advanced down the east coast, centre and west coast simultaneously and by the end of the month had taken Johor Bahru and were massed across the strait from Singapore. By 15 February they had forced the capitulation of the Allies in Singapore. This was a crushing blow, and, according to Malaysian historian Zainal Abidin bin Abudul Wahid, "the speed with which the Japanese managed to achieve victory, however temporary that might have been, shattered the image of the British, and generally the 'whiteman', as a superior people". Right up until the beginning of the Second World War, the British had managed to placate the aristocratic leaders of the Malay community and the wealthy Chinese merchants and there was little real threat to the status quo. The Japanese defeat of the British changed all that by altering the balance between conservatism and change. Because Britain had failed so miserably to defend Malaya, its credentials as a protector were irrevocably tarnished.

For administrative purposes, the Japanese linked the peninsula with Sumatra as part of the Greater East Asia Co-prosperity Sphere. All British officials were interned and the legislative and municipal councils swept aside. But because the Japanese had lost their command of the seas by the end of 1942, nothing could be imported and there was a shortage of food supplies. The 'banana' currency introduced by the Japanese became worthless as inflation soared. Japan merely regarded Malaya as a source of raw materials, yet the rubber and tin industries stagnated and nothing was done to develop the economy.

After initially severing sultans' pensions and reducing their powers, the Japanese realized that their co-operation was necessary if the Malay bureaucracy was to be put to work for the occupation government (see page 508). The Indians were treated well since they were seen as a key to fighting the British colonial régime in India. But Malaya's Chinese, while they were not rounded up and executed as they were in Singapore, were not trusted. The Japanese, however, came to recognize the importance of the Chinese community in oiling the wheels of the economy. The Chinese Dalforce militia (set up by the Allies as the Japanese advanced southwards) joined the Communists and other minor underground dissident groups in forming the Malayan People's Anti-Japanese Army. British army officers and arms were parachuted into the jungle to support the guerrillas. It was during this period that the Malayan Communist Party (MCP) broadened its membership and appeal, under the guise of a nationwide anti-Japanese alliance.

The brutality of the Japanese régime eased with time; as the war began to go against them, they increasingly courted the different communities, giving them more say in the run of things in an effort to undermine any return to colonial rule. But the Japanese's favourable treatment of Malays and their general mistrust of the Chinese did not foster good race relations between the two. A Malay paramilitary police force was put to work to root out Chinese who were anti-Japanese, which exacerbated inter-communal hostility. The Japanese never offered Malaya independence but allowed Malay nationalist sentiments to develop in an effort to deflect attention from the fact they had ceded the North Malay states of Kedah, Perlis, Kelantan and Terengganu to Thailand.

The British return

During the war, the British drew up secret plans for a revised administrative structure in Malaya. The plan was to create a Malayan Union by combining the federated and unfederated states as well as Melaka and Penang, leaving Singapore as a crown colony. Plans were also drawn up to buy North Borneo from the Chartered Company (see page 489) and to replace the anachronous White Rajahs of Sarawak (see page 394) with a view to eventually grouping all the territories together as a federation. As soon as the Japanese surrendered in September 1945, the plan was put into action. Historian Mary Turnbull notes that "Malaya was unique [among Western colonies] because the returning British were initially welcomed with enthusiasm and were themselves unwilling to put the clock back. But they were soon overwhelmed by the reaction against their schemes for streamlining the administration and assimilating the different immigrant communities."

A unitary state was formed on the peninsula and everyone, regardless of race or origin, who called Malaya 'home', was accorded equal status. But the resentment

Harold Briggs, was later adopted (rather less successfully) by the Americans in South Vietnam.

In much the same way as they had been caught unprepared by the Japanese invasion in 1941, the British were taken by surprise and in the first few years the MCP (whose guerrillas were labelled 'CTs' – or Communist Terrorists) gained the upper hand. In 1951 British morale all but crumbled when the High Commissioner, Sir Henry Gurney, was ambushed and assassinated on the road to Fraser's Hill (see page 118). His successor, General Sir Gerald Templer, took the initiative, however, with his campaign to 'win the hearts and minds of the people'. Templer's biographer, John Cloake, gave him Japanese General Tomoyuki Yamashita's old sobriquet 'Tiger of Malaya', and there is little doubt that his tough policies won the war. In his book *Emergency Years*, former mine-manager Leonard Rayner says the chain-smoking Templer "exuded nervous energy like an overcharged human battery". Within two years the Communists were on the retreat. They had also begun to lose popular support due to the climate of fear they introduced, although the Emergency did not officially end until 1960.

Historians believe the Communist rebellion failed because it was too slow to take advantage of the economic hardships in the immediate aftermath of the Second World War and because it was almost exclusively Chinese. It also only really appealed to the Chinese working class and alienated and shunned the Chinese merchant community and Straits-born Chinese.

The road to Merdeka

The British had countered the MCP's claim to be a multi-racial nationalist movement by accelerating moves towards Malayan independence, which Britain promised, once the Emergency was over. The only nationalist party with any political credibility was UMNO. Its founder, Dato' Onn bin Jaafar wanted to allow non-Malays to become members, and when his proposal was rejected, he resigned to form the Independence of Malaya Party. The brother of the Sultan of Kedah, Tunku Abdul Rahman, took over as head of UMNO and to counter Onn's new party, he made an electoral pact with the Malayan Chinese Association (MCA) and the Malayan Indian Congress (MIC). With the MCP out of the picture, the Chinese community had hesitantly grouped itself around the MCA. The Alliance (which trounced Onn's party in the election) is still in place today, in the form of the ruling *Barisan Nasional* (National Front). After sweeping the polls in 1955, the Alliance called immediately for *merdeka*, or independence, which the British guaranteed within two years.

With independence promised by non-violent means, Tunku Abdul Rahman offered an amnesty to the Communists. Together with Singapore's Chief Minister, David Marshall and Straits-Chinese leader Tan Cheng Lock (see page 212), he met Chin Peng in 1956. But they failed to reach agreement and the MCP fled through the jungle into the mountains in southern Thailand around Betong. While the Emergency was declared 'over' in 1960, the MCP only finally agreed to lay down its arms in 1989, in a peace agreement brokered by Thailand. The party had been riven by factionalism and its membership had dwindled to under 1,000. In 1991, the legendary Chin Peng struck a deal with the Malaysian government allowing the former guerrillas to return home.

Historian Mary Turnbull writes: "When Malaya attained independence in 1957 it was a prosperous country with stable political institutions, a sound administrative system and a good infrastructure of education and communications – a country with excellent resources and a thriving economy based on export agriculture and mining". Under the new constitution, a king was to be chosen from one of the nine sultans, and the monarchy was to be rotated every five years. A two-tier parliament was

Background

set up, with a *Dewan Rakyat* (People's House) of elected representatives and a *Dewan Negara* (Senate) to represent the state assemblies. Each of the 11 states had its own elected government and a sultan or governor.

Politicians in Singapore made it clear that they also wanted to be part of an independent Malaya, but in Kuala Lumpur, UMNO leaders were opposed to a merger because the island had a Chinese majority. (A straight merger would have resulted in a small Chinese majority in Malaya.) Increasing nationalist militancy in Singapore was of particular concern to UMNO and the radical wing of the People's Action Party, which was swept to power with Lee Kuan Yew at its head in 1959, was dominated by Communists. Fearing the emergence of 'a second Cuba' on Malaysia's doorstep, Tunku Abdul Rahman proposed that Singapore join a greater Malaysian Federation, in which a racial balance would be maintained by the inclusion of Sarawak, Brunei and British North Borneo (Sabah). Britain supported the move, as did all the states involved. Kuala Lumpur was particularly keen on Brunei joining the Federation on two scores: it had Malays and it had oil. But at the eleventh hour, Brunei's Sultan Omar backed out, mistrustful of Kuala Lumpur's obvious designs on his sultanate's oil revenues and unhappy at the prospect of becoming just another sultan in Malaya's collection of nine monarchs (see page 508).

Prime Minister Tunku Abdul Rahman was disheartened, but the Malaysia Agreement was signed in July 1963 with Singapore, Sarawak and Sabah. Without Brunei, there was a small Chinese majority in the new Malaysia. The Tunku did not have time to dwell on racial arithmetic, however, because almost immediately the new federation was plunged into an undeclared war with Indonesia – which became known as *Konfrontasi*, or Confrontation (see page 398) – due to President Sukarno's objection to the participation of Sabah and Sarawak. Indonesian saboteurs were landed on the peninsula and in Singapore and there were Indonesian military incursions along the borders of Sabah and Sarawak with Kalimantan. Konfrontasi was finally ended in 1966 after Sukarno fell from power. But relations with Singapore – which had been granted a greater measure of autonomy than other states – were far from smooth. Communal riots in Singapore in 1964 and Lee Kuan Yew's efforts to forge a nation-wide opposition alliance which called for 'a democratic Malaysian Malaysia' further opened the rift with Kuala Lumpur. Feeling unnerved by calls for racial equality while the Malays did not form a majority of the population, Tunku Abdul Rahman expelled Singapore from the federation in August 1965 against Lee Kuan Yew's wishes.

Racial politics in the 1960s

The expulsion of Singapore did not solve the racial problem on the peninsula, however. Because the Malay and Chinese communities felt threatened by each other - one wielded political power, the other economic power - racial tensions built up. Resentment focused on the enforcement of Malay as the medium of instruction in all schools and as the national language and on the privileged educational and employment opportunities afforded to Malays. The tensions finally exploded on 13 May 1969, in the wake of the general election.

The UMNO-led Alliance faced opposition from the Democratic Action Party (DAP) which was built from the ashes of Lee Kuan Yew's People's Action Party. The DAP was a radical Chinese-dominated party and called for racial equality. Also in opposition was *Gerakan* (the People's Movement), supported by Chinese and Indians, and the Pan-Malayan Islamic Party, which was exclusively Malay and very conservative. In the election, the opposition parties - which were not in alliance – deprived the Alliance of its two-thirds majority in parliament; it required this margin to amend the constitution unimpeded. Gerakan and DAP celebrations provoked counter-demonstrations from Malays and in the ensuing mayhem hundreds were killed in Kuala Lumpur.

The government suspended the constitution for over a year and declared a **State of Emergency**. A new national ideology was drawn up – the controversial New Economic Policy (see page 523), which was an ambitious experiment in social and economic engineering aimed at ironing out discrepancies between ethnic communities. The *Rukunegara*, a written national ideology aimed at fostering nation-building, was introduced in August 1970. It demanded loyalty to the king and the constitution, respect for Islam and observance of the law and morally acceptable behaviour. All discussion of the Malays' 'special position' was banned as was discussion about the national language and the sovereignty of the sultans. In the words of historian John Gullick, "Tunku Abdul Rahman, whose anguish at the disaster had impeded his ability to deal with it effectively," resigned the following month and handed over to Tun Abdul Razak. Tun Razak was an able administrator, but lacked the dynamism of his predecessor. He did, however, unify UMNO and patched up the old Alliance, breathing new life into the coalition by incorporating every political party except the DAP and one or two other small parties into the newly named *Barisan Nasional* (BN), or National Front. In 1974 the Barisan won a landslide majority.

Tun Razak shifted Malaysia's foreign policy from a pro-Western stance to non-alignment and established diplomatic relations with both Moscow and Beijing. But within Malaysia, Communist paranoia was rife: as Indochina fell to Communists in the mid-1970s, many Malaysians became increasingly convinced that Malaysia was just another 'domino' waiting to topple. There were even several arrests of prominent Malays (including two newspaper editors and five top UMNO politicians). But when Chin Peng's revolutionaries joined forces with secessionist Muslims in South Thailand, the Thai and Malaysian governments launched a joint clean-out operation in the jungle along the frontier. By the late 1970s the North Kalimantan Communist Party had also been beaten into virtual submission too (see page 397). In 1976 Tun Razak died and was succeeded by his brother-in-law, Dato' Hussein Onn (the son of Umno's founding father). He inherited an economy which was in good shape, thanks to strong commodity prices, and in the general election of 1978, the BN won another comfortable parliamentary majority. Three years later he handed over to Dr Mahathir Mohamad (see profile, page 518) who in April 1995 secured yet another term in office having won a massive majority in Parliament, see below.

Modern Malaysia

Politics

On the face of it, Malaysia's political landscape is remarkably unchanging. Dr Mahathir Mohamad, as leader of the United Malays National Organization (UMNO), heads the *Barisan Nasional* (BN), or National Front coalition, and has won every one of five elections since coming to power in 1981. There is no question who leads and dominates the coalition: UMNO. It is notable that Mahathir's hold on power is only really challenged from within UMNO; the other members of the BN would not risk speaking out against the premier and it sometimes seems as though they are only along for the ride. Since the first general election was held back in 1959 the largest number of parliamentary seats won by an opposition party has been 27 – by the PAS in the most recent poll in 1999. But that 27 seats represents just 14% of the total. By contrast the BN garnered 148 seats. As in

Prime Minister Mahathir & UMNO

Background

neighbouring Singapore where the PAP dominates political proceedings, the ruling coalition are very much in control and have been over all 10 general elections held since 1959.

With the rapid expansion in Malaysia's economy, and notwithstanding the recession associated with the Asian economic crisis of 1997-99, there has emerged a substantial *nouveau riche* middle class. There has, in turn, been the expectation in some quarters that a more open political system might evolve as prosperous, and increasingly well educated, people demand more of a political say. But the government does not readily tolerate dissent and during the premiership of Dr Mahathir power has, in fact, become increasingly concentrated in the hands of the government.

The 1999 The 1999 general election was fought against the background of the trial of former
general deputy prime minister Anwar Ibrahim (see below) and an economic recession. Both
election injected elements of uncertainty into the contest. There is no doubt that many Malaysians, and especially younger ones, were appalled at the treatment of Anwar Ibrahim and the apparent vindictiveness of the premier's campaign against his former right-hand man. In addition, Mahathir was fighting against the backdrop of a shrinking economy. In 1998 GDP declined by 7.5 percent as Malaysia battled with the Asian economic crisis. Furthermore there was criticism of the grandiose projects with which the prime minister is closely associated, from the world's tallest buildings to a new federal capital, and with the nepotism that seems to be such a part of the Malaysian political economy. With all this, one might wonder how on earth Mahathir, 74 years old in 1999 and with rumours of ill-health, could win another term of office. But he did; and did so convincingly. The government won 148 seats in the 193-seat parliament. Understanding why Mahathir and UMNO won sheds light on the peculiarities of the Malaysian political system.

To begin with, the media is effectively government-controlled. It is extremely hard for opposition groups to get their voices heard. The only area where the government does not have a stranglehold is the internet and, while Malaysia may view itself as cyber-savvy, there aren't that many people who habitually trawl for news on the web. On 3 May 1999 during World Press Freedom Day the New York-based Committee to Protect Journalists voted Mahathir one of the world's top 10 'enemies of the press'. Even the World Bank classifies the Malaysian press as 'not free'.

There is also no doubt that Mahathir is an extremely astute political operator. He called the election in November so that 680,000 young Malaysians who came onto the electoral role in February 2000 could not vote. Most, he no doubt reasoned, would have voted for the opposition. He is also very adept at playing to his domestic audience. Indeed, it could be argued that most of his anti-Western invective is just for domestic consumption. So when he cautioned, in 1999, his people to watch out for "ethnic Europeans [many of whom] are of the opinion that Muslim people cannot succeed, more so when their skin colour is brown" he was not intending that it should be digested by an overseas audience.

But perhaps most convincing as an explanation as to why Mahathir won the election despite this plethora of problems and concerns is what is termed 'ethnic politics'. The Malays make up a bare majority of the population, about 55 percent. The closely fought general election of 1969 (in which the Alliance won just 74 seats out of 144) brought Malay and Chinese into conflict with hundreds of deaths. The fear that this could happen again scares many people into voting for continuity rather than change. This applies mainly to the Chinese who, one might have thought, would naturally vote for a Chinese opposition party. Thus there is a paradox: many people who are disenchanted with Mahathir, UMNO and the BN are also afraid that should the opposition win another bout of communal unrest could follow.

Finally, and linked to the last reason, there is an enduring sense that the opposition in Malaysia is not a credible one, a view no doubt accentuated by the government's hold over the media. To try and present a united front in the run-up to the November 1999 elections the opposition parties formed their own alliance, the Alternative Front. This linked the Muslim PAS which is strongly represented in the east coast states of Kelantan and Terengganu, and also in Perlis and Kedah with the Chinese-dominated DAP which usually produces a strong showing in urban centres. These two well-established opposition parties were joined by the multi-ethnic Malaysia People's Party and by the Justice Party (Keadilan), led by Anwar Ibrahim's wife, Wan Azizah Ismail. The four parties agreed on a common platform and also agreed not to challenge one another on their home turfs. (Of Malaysia's 192 constituencies, 134 have a *bumiputra* [Malay] majority, 32 a Chinese majority, while 26 have neither a Chinese nor a *bumi* majority.)

While Mahathir won, and did so handsomely, there were also signs that support was beginning to fall away. The opposition managed to more than double their number of seats, from 16 in the 1995 elections to 42 in 1999, and increase their share of the vote from 35 percent in 1995 to 44 percent in 1999. Furthermore, and significantly, it was mainly Malays who deserted the National Front, not Chinese. It was the PAS and the Justice Party which did best, gathering 27 and 5 seats respectively. The DAP (a 'Chinese' party) did not significantly increase its share of seats in parliament, gaining 10 seats as opposed to 8 in the previous election in 1995. Ironically, it could be argued that it was the Chinese, more than any other group, who won the election for Mahathir.

Mahathir's leadership has been challenged several times over the last decade, but no one has got close to ousting him. However now that he is well into his 70s – he was 77 in 2001 – there is a sense that his days as Prime Minister are numbered. Mahathir has even said that he wishes to step down before the next election – although that would seem to have been quietly forgotten.

Who can follow Mahathir?

The poor showing of UMNO in the last elections seemed to emphasise the need for a change at the helm. There was some talk of democratising the selection process (currently voting is limited to the 2,000 delegates to the annual general assembly), but this came to little. In 2000 Datuk Seri Abdullah Badawi was anointed as Mahathir's likely successor (something of a poisoned chalice). On May 10th 2000 he gave his maiden speech to the faithful at the UMNO general assembly warning that the party was at risk of losing its core vote. He urged UMNO party members and officials to "Return to them. Win over their hearts. Share your wealth with them. Respect, appreciate and love them. They are our staunch supporters who may now feel alienated. Umno is not an elitist party." Badawi may be the son of a famous religious scholar but he is seen as a pragmatic politician who, like Mahathir, will fight the trend towards extremism.

While Mahathir has expressly said that he wants to stand down no one has ruled out the possibility that he might find a reason to fight just one more election. After all, the PAS are in turmoil. In late 2000 reporters in Hong Kong asked him when he would stand down. He replied, characteristically cryptically: 'It's only fair for me to stay on until he [Badawi] is competent enough.'

It may have become commonplace in Malaysia for opposition politicians, free-thinking jurists, environmentalists and other assorted annoyances to be hounded, arrested, tried and jailed, but not mainstream Malay politicians. It is this which rocked Malaysia's political establishment when Anwar Ibrahim, former deputy prime minister and Mahathir's successor in waiting, was arrested in late 1998.

Anwar Ibrahim: Malaysia's trial of the century

Anwar was sacked by Mahathir on 2 September 1998. This was preceded by a

Mahathir Mohamad – recalcitrance rules OK

He's blunt; he's abrasive and he's headstrong. His detractors regularly accuse him of autocratic tendencies. His supporters talk of a man of conviction. Over the past decade, Prime Minister Dr Mahathir Mohamad has curtailed the power of the judiciary, clamped down on the press, jailed his critics and removed the privileges enjoyed by Malaysia's nine hereditary monarchs. In the international arena, Mahathir has emerged as the self-appointed champion and spokesman for the developing world. He made a name for himself in 1992 by vociferously defending Malaysia's environmental record at the Earth Summit in Rio de Janeiro (see page 565). And Dr M has a virulent dislike of the western media.

The papers may have dubbed him "the Prickliest Premier in the East", but Mahathir has put Malaysia firmly on the world map. "If you can't be famous," he said "then at least be notorious!"

For all the notoriety born of his possibly Machiavellian manoeuvering, the Malaysian premier is also sensitive to criticism. A home-grown, made-in-Malaysia product, he is quick to seize on any opportunity to lash out at what he sees as the condescending, neo-colonialist attitudes of the West. For Mahathir has become the CEO for Malaysia Inc. He has continued to win elections

because with him has come the political stability and prosperity which has kept most Malaysians happy. He's also imbued them with a new self-confidence – particularly the Malays. Britain got its first taste of Mahathir's wrath a decade ago after the British government raised fees for foreign students. His no-nonsense response was to instruct Malaysians to "Buy British Last". In November 1993, the Australian Prime Minister, Paul Keating nearly provoked a trade war when he branded Mahathir "recalcitrant" for his refusal to attend a regional summit. Keating was forced to apologize.

During Malaysia's race riots of May 1969, Mahathir gained notoriety as a rabble-rouser and outspoken critic of Tunku Abdul Rahman, Malaysia's first Prime Minister. He outlined his extreme pro-Malay views in a book, The Malay Dilemma, *which was promptly banned. Ironically, Mahathir himself is not fully Malay: his father was an Indian Muslim. But his pro-Malay views struck a chord and through the early 1970s, he fought his way into the upper echelons of the political hierarchy. Mahathir entered the cabinet as education minister and by 1976 had become deputy prime minister. Over the next five years, he gained a reputation as a dynamic Malay leader with a sense of purpose. In 1981 Mahathir*

series of murky allegations impugning Anwar's morals. In particular, there were whispers that he was bisexual. Not only is this beyond the pale in a largely Muslim country like Malaysia, but homosexuality remains a crime. Anwar's supporters saw this whispering campaign as politically motivated and the result of a widening gulf between Mahathir and his deputy over how to manage the economy.

A few days after he was sacked, Anwar was arrested and charged with five counts of sodomy and five charges of abuse of power. But before his second appearance in court Anwar appeared with bruised arms and a black eye, and accused the police of beating him. Mahathir seemed to imply that the injuries were self-inflicted. Anwar's treatment at the hands of the police as well as the crude and one-sided coverage in the government-controlled press angered many Malaysians. They did not believe the charges, and as the trial continued they became less and less credible. Nonetheless, on 14 April 1999, Anwar was convicted of corruption and jailed for six years. More to the point, even when he is released he won't be able to hold political office for a further five years. For Anwar, the verdict, as he put it "stinks to high heaven". At the end of the trial, Anwar read from a prepared statement and said: "I have no hope

(see page 565)

was elected President of the politically dominant United Malays National Organization (UMNO); the President automatically becomes Prime Minister.

Unlike his predecessors, Mahathir climbed the political ladder without the help of aristocratic connections. He was the first Malaysian leader not to have been educated in the West – he trained as a medical doctor at the University of Singapore. And he had humble origins; he was born in a small Malay kampung house on the outskirts of Alor Star in Kedah. In his school days, during the Japanese occupation, the young Mahathir worked as a stallholder at the local market. His first stall was torn down by Japanese soldiers. He revealed all this in 1991, while attempting to convince stallholders in the same market of the wisdom of turning it into a modern shopping complex.

From his first day in office, Mahathir gained respect for his determination to root out corruption, although the rise of money-politics – a consequence of his policy to promote Malay businesses – undermined this. One of his first actions was to loosen Malaysia's ties with the Commonwealth – particularly with Britain, through the 'Buy British Last' campaign, in which he instructed Malaysians to 'Look East' to the booming economies of Japan, South Korea and Taiwan. One of Mahathir's enduring legacies will be the Proton Saga, the national car and ultimate symbol of the new high-tech 'Made-in-Malaysia' image the Prime Minister has been so keen to promote.

Mahathir has won a string of impressive election victories – most recently in 1999 – and has weathered both economic recession and criticism of his sometimes abrasive and often autocratic style. His health is the one wild card: he suffered a big heart attack in 1989 and in 1997 celebrated his 71st birthday. But so far at least, whenever there has been the merest glimpse of a threat Mahathir has outmanoeuvred his opponent with consummate skill and not a little ruthlessness.

More than anything, Mahathir has changed the way Malaysian's, and especially Malays, think about themselves. When he came to power, Malays were all to ready to put themselves down, to admit defeat to the more assiduous Chinese. Now Malaysians are self-confident and willing not just to compete with the Chinese on a level playing field but to take their new-found confidence into the international arena and to play – and win.

Background

of justice… The charges are part of a political conspiracy to destroy me and ensure Mahathir Mohamad's continued hold on power at whatever cost". Certainly Mahathir would seem to have succeeded in taking Anwar out of the political equation for at least 11 years.

In the immediate aftermath of the Anwar affair it seemed as though it might, in retrospect, prove to be a turning point in Malaysia's political fortunes. It brought demonstrators onto the streets of Kuala Lumpur. It created demands for *reformasi*. It led to the creation of a new opposition party, the Justice Party (Keadilan), led by Anwar's wife Wan Azizah. It even brought the US ambassador to remark that Anwar was the world's "newest and most famous political prisoner". But following the September 11th attacks in the US and the failure of the PAS to produce a measured response to those event (see below) the Anwar affair was pushed very much into the background.

With Anwar sacked and now in jail, Mahathir appointed a new deputy prime minister, Adbullah Badawi. No doubt aware of what happened to Anwar when he got a little bit uppity, Abdullah will, one imagines, be playing the loyal deputy. But with

Calling names

Soros on Mahathir	*Mahathir on Soros and currency speculators*
Mahathir is 'a menace to his own country' and a 'loose cannon'	Currency trading is 'unnecessary, unproductive and immoral'
Mahathir was using Soros 'as a scapegoat to cover up his own failure'	Foreign investors are 'ferocious beasts'
	Soros is 'a moron'

Mahathir in his mid-70s, time is not on the premier's side. Mahathir has publicly said that this will be his last term as prime minister.

Money, politics & corruption

The entrenched position of UMNO and the BN has, in the eyes of the government's critics, allowed money politics and political patronage to flourish. It is argued that the use of political power to dispense favours and make money has become endemic, so much so that it is accepted as just another part of the political land-scape. In 1995 Datuk Rafidah Aziz, the highly respected minister of International Trade and Industry, revealed in court that her son-in-law, a son of Prime Minister Mahathir, and a brother of Anwar Ibrahim had all benefited from share allocations which fell under her largesse. Such allocations are permitted – indeed encouraged – as part of the effort to increase bumiputra representation in the economy. But the scale to which relatives and political supporters benefit is questioned. Mahathir announced a new code of conduct for senior officials and politicians in early 1995 in an attempt to foster greater probity.

Nonetheless, the years since have seen a gradual drip, drip of scandal which has threatened to take the shine off Malaysia's glossy image. This so incensed Prime Minister Mahathir that in an UMNO address in October 1996 he wept as he warned party members that money politics and corruption 'would destroy the country'. Critics have suggested that UMNO's unquestioned political supremacy has created the con-ditions where corruption and money politics can flourish. In 1996 it was alleged that people in positions of power had managed to manipulate the legal system. The United Nations Centre for Human Rights released a press statement saying: "Com-plaints are rife that certain highly placed personalities in Malaysia ... are manipulating the Malaysian system of justice and thereby undermining the due administration of independent and impartial justice by courts." The statement referred to a series of allegations that litigants had managed to select judges of their own choice. In an address to the UMNO Supreme Council in May 1997 shortly after two senior UMNO leaders had been sacked in connection with missing funds, Mahathir pointedly said "We will not defend anyone who's corrupt". A few months earlier on 22 December 1996, to the intense embarrassment of the Prime Minister, Muhammad Muhammad Taib, Chief Minister of Selangor, was detained trying to leave Brisbane, Australia with close to US$1m in cash stashed into a suitcase; an offence under Australian law. Muhammad rather feebly explained to a packed and incredulous press conference that the money had been entrusted to him by his brothers to buy property on Aus-tralia's Gold Coast. He continued: "I do not feel any sense of wrongdoing in this mat-ter and if it is an offence, it is a technical one ..."

The anti-corruption drive continued through the year and by the middle of 1997 a chief minister (the above Muhammad Muhammad Taib), a deputy minister and a host of government officials and UMNO party stalwarts had been sacked or had resigned. Anwar Ibrahim, the Prime Minister's number two, responded to Mahathir's fears by heading an anti-corruption drive to root out the guilty and announced that the powers of the Anti-Corruption Agency would be strengthened. By all accounts there are more than a few unusually wealthy politicians pacing the deep shag pile of their luxury apartments considering their futures. Although no one considers Mahathir himself to be among the guilty, there are those who suggest that the Prime Minister's style and his emphasis on wealth creation has helped to promote corruption. Chandra Muzaffar, a political scientist at the Science University of Malaysia in Penang, for example, argues that "He's created a culture that places undue emphasis on wealth accumulation for its own sake. The new heroes are all corporate barons."

Another challenge for the government is how to curb the growth of what Prime Minister Mahathir has termed 'social ills'. For a country which has argued that 'Asian values' have permitted it to modernize without the social and moral degradation evident in the West, this is a sensitive subject. Research has revealed a surge in drug taking (particularly recreational drugs like Ecstasy), illegitimate pregnancies, wife abuse, gangsterism and incest. Moreover, this research seems to show that the problem is predominantly concentrated among Malays. Never one to shy away from a problem, however embarrassing, Mahathir has bluntly pointed out: "In terms of population breakdown, the Malays form 55 percent while the Chinese make up about 25 percent and Indians, 10 percent. But when comparing social problems, the Malays account for 67 percent, while Chinese involvement is only 16 percent." State and national government rushed to introduce legislation to control this rash of so-called ills.

Social ills

Since the race riots of 1969 relations between Malaysia's Malay and Chinese populations have dominated political affairs. Now that Malaysia is fast attaining economic maturity a debate is beginning to emerge about whether it is time to consign racial politics, and racial quotas, to the dust heap. Prime Minister Mahathir's Vision 2020 (see page 526), which sets out a path to developed country status by 2020, significantly talks of a 'Malaysian race working in full and equal partnership'. There is no mention here of 'bumiputras' and 'Chinese Malaysians', but of a single Malaysian identity which transcends race.

Racial relations in the New Malaysia

Not everyone agrees with this vision. There are those who note that the communal peace which has descended on the nation since 1969 has been based on a fast-growing economy in which everyone has gained even while the portions of the cake allotted to each group have changed. They worry that a slowing economy could bring racial conflicts to the fore again, although this did not happen to any significant degree during 1998 when the economy contracted by 7.5 percent. Others, like Sarawak's state minister for tourism James Masing, would like to see a plural society where difference is respected and accepted. "To say I'm Iban", Masing explains, "doesn't mean I'm any less Malaysian."

Background

In foreign affairs Malaysia follows a non-aligned stance and is fiercely anti-Communist. This, however, has not stopped its enthusiastic investment in Indochina and Myanmar (Burma). Malaysia is a leading light in the Association of Southeast Asian Nations (ASEAN), and Mahathir has made his mark as an outspoken champion of the developing world. As such, he has frequently clashed with the West. Malaysia needs continued foreign investment from industrialized countries, but Dr Mahathir remains deeply suspicious of Western motives and intentions.

Foreign relations

Malaysia's most delicate relations are with neighbouring Singapore, a country with which it is connected by history and also by water pipelines and a causeway. For a few years Singapore was part of the Malaysian Federation, until it was ejected in 1965, and Singapore's status as a largely Chinese city state makes for an uneasy relationship with Malay-dominated Malaysia. In 1997 mutual sensitivities were made all too clear in a spat which threatened to escalate into a major diplomatic conflict. The cause? A dispute over whether Johor Bahru was a safe place or not.

Malaysia,
Islam &
September 11

Like neighbouring Indonesia, the events of September 11 and, more significantly, the reaction by the US, has caused Malaysia to tread a fine line between slavishly supporting the US government on the one hand, and appearing to side with the Osama bin Laden and the Taliban on the other. Prime Minister Mahathir has long warned against the dangers posed by Muslim extremists but he is also aware that 60% of Malaysians are Muslim and that there has been something of an Islamic resurgence in recent years.

Prime Minister Mahathir immediately condemned the attacks in New York and Washington. Furthermore, he expressed his concern that the US should respond in a measured manner. But the events also offered Mahathir an opportunity to paint the country's Islamic opposition party, the PAS, as extreme. And it would seem to have worked. The ruling BN was way ahead In the polls towards the end of 2001 and the PAS, on a wave after its success in the 1999 general elections (see above), was in danger of finding those gains snuffed out. While Mahathir doesn't have to hold an election until 2004 there are some who believe he will call a poll in 2002.

In September 2001 the DAP left the Alternative Front – which links the PAS, DAP and Keadilan – because of the PAS's desire to make Malaysia an Islamic state. As DAP member Chen Man Hin said at the time, "We are alarmed by the calls of those who preach martyrdom and those who are prepared to die for an Islamic state". Mahathir, as usual, appeared to be ahead of events. In August, 10 people were arrested under the Internal Security Act and accused of belonging members to the Mujahideen Group of Malaysia, intent on overthrowing the government. One of the ten, Nik Adli, is the eldest son of the PAS chief Nik Abdul Aziz Nik Mat and was said to have received training in Afghanistan and from Muslim militants in the Philippines. He – along with eight others – was gaoled for two years. Certainly some moderate Muslim voices in Malaysia believe that the PAS has overstepped the mark and revealed its true colours. Following the September 11 atrocities an editorial in the PAS mouthpiece *Harakah* was titled 'The coming war is a crusade against Islam'.

Economy

Malaysia has an abundance of natural resources. Today, though, tin mining, rubber and palm oil are declining in importance, and while the country's oil, gas and timber wealth are valuable sources of revenue, the manufacturing sector has become the powerhouse of the economy. At the same time, the service sector is booming, and tourism is now the third largest foreign exchange earner. Over recent years, Malaysia has been one of the fastest-growing economies in the world. The World Bank defines Malaysia as an upper-middle-income country. There is a Malay saying which goes: *ada gula, ada semut* ('where there's sugar, there's ants') and from the late 1980s foreign investors swarmed to Malaysia, thanks to its sugar-coated investment incentives as well as its cheap land and labour, its good infrastructure and political stability.

Until 1997, and despite one banker likening Malaysia's economic policies to 'Noddyomics', the country's economy grew extraordinarily rapidly. It was this, of course, which played a large part in the World Bank including Malaysia in its list of 'Miracle Economies' (rather more prosaically called High Performing Asian Economies by the World Bank). But the Asian economic crisis, which began in Thailand in mid-1997 and then spread to Malaysia and other Asian countries, put a spanner in the spokes of Malaysia's fast moving economy.

In the late 1800s, as the British colonial government developed the infrastructure of the Federated Malay States, they built a network of roads, railways, telephones and telegraphs which served as the backbone of the export economy. In the 50 years following 1880, export earnings rose 30-fold. Most of the tin mines and plantations were in the hands of British-owned companies and remained foreign-owned until the Malaysian government restructured foreign equity holdings in the 1970s.

On independence in 1957, resource-rich Malaysia's future looked bright and foreign investment was encouraged, the capitalist system maintained and there was no threat to nationalize industry. The first national development plan aimed to expand the agricultural sector and begin to reduce dependence on rubber, which, even then, was beginning to encounter competition from synthetic alternatives. But rubber and tin remained the main economic props. In 1963, when the Federation of Malaysia was formed, only six percent of the workforce was employed in industry and 80 percent of exports were contributed by tin, rubber, oil palm, timber, and oil and gas.

The structure of Malaysia's economy has been radically altered since independence, and particularly since the 1980s. Commodity exports such as rubber and palm oil, which were the mainstay of the post-colonial economy, have declined in significance and, within 30 years, this sector is unlikely to contribute more than six percent of Malaysia's export earnings. A turning point was 1987, when agriculture was overtaken by the manufacturing sector in terms of contribution to GDP. Manufacturing output has almost tripled in 25 years, thanks mainly to the fact that Malaysia has been the darling of foreign investors. The value of manufactured exports is growing even faster; today they are approaching three-quarters of Malaysia's export earnings. The country that used to be the world's biggest producer of rubber and tin is now the world's leading producer of semiconductors and air-conditioning units. In May 1993, another landmark was created in Malaysia's economic history: the *Malaysia Mining Corporation*, one of the country's biggest remaining tin producers, pulled out of tin mining. Tin production costs have increased while the price of tin has slumped. In 1990 there were still 141 tin mines in Malaysia; by 1993 there were only 50.

But the type of products Malaysia manufactures is also undergoing rapid change. One of the main reasons for this is Malaysia's labour squeeze. The main industrial boom zones (the Klang Valley around Kuala Lumpur, Johor and Penang) are already suffering shortages, and while infrastructural developments have just about kept pace with the flood of foreign manufacturing investment, the labour pool is drying up. In 1996 the unemployment rate was, in practical terms, zero and the government was forced to recruit blue-collar migrant labourers from Thailand, Bangladesh, Myanmar (Burma) and Indonesia. But even with this flow of legal migrant labour it was not sufficient to fill the labour void and there has been a much larger flow of illegal migrant labour. It was estimated that there were 1.75 million migrant workers - in a country with a workforce of eight million – of whom just 750,000 were working legally in the country.

The **New Development Policy** (NDP), unveiled in 1991 (see box, page 524) promotes hi-tech industries, higher value-added production, skills development and increased productivity and is the basis of the government's economic development strategy. It is a much more economically and socially liberal document than its predecessor, the New Economic Policy. Through it, the government tacitly concedes that without continued inflows of foreign capital, Malaysia's ambitious targets will not be realized. The NDP envisages a fourfold increase in the value of private-sector investment by 2000 and the private sector – both local and foreign – has been charged with spearheading economic growth and enhancing the country's industrial profile. The Ministry of International Trade and Industry has energetically promoted the concept of 'Malaysia Incorporated' in its effort to foster consultation and dialogue with the private sector and the all-important foreign investors. This has helped cut the red tape. Since Mahathir adopted his 'Look East' policy in the 1980s

The evolution of the Malaysian economy

Background

The new economic policy – Malaysia's recipe for racial harmony

Just over two decades ago Malaysia's Malay-led government woke up to the fact that Malays and indigenous groups – collectively called bumiputras, or 'sons of the soil' – made up more than half the country's population but owned just two percent of corporate equity. Their average income was also less than half that of non-Malays. The Malay élite worked in the civil service, but most Malays were poor farmers. Economic power was concentrated in the hands of foreigners and urban Chinese while rural Malays lived on, or under, the breadline. The Chinese virtually ran the economy – they were the bankers, brokers and businessmen. In 1970, in the wake of the bloody race riots in which hundreds died (see page 514), the controversial New Economic Policy, or NEP, was introduced. The NEP aimed to wipe out poverty irrespective of race and completely restructure society by putting the Malay, Chinese and Indian communities on an equal footing. The idea was to abolish racial stereotyping, making it more difficult to associate a person's job with the colour of his or her skin.

The NEP was designed to prevent a recurrence of the bloodletting by keeping multiracial Malaysia intact. It offered

Malays, the economic underdogs, a chance to catch up and encouraged them to move to the cities. Racial quotas were introduced to raise their stake in the economy to at least 30 percent. They were granted scholarships and directorships, they were pushed into managerial jobs, subsidized, goaded and given a ticket to get rich quick – which many did. But because the NEP favoured the Malays, it antagonized almost everyone else. For 20 years, the NEP was denounced as racist by its critics and flagrantly abused by many of those it tried to help. The policy was an invitation to bribery and corruption and the hijacking and exploitation of the NEP by wealthy bumiputras alienated non-Malays and fanned resentment.

But the NEP's targets were not met. Although poverty has been markedly reduced since 1970, the bumiputras' stake in the economy was a fraction over 20 percent in 1995 instead of the targeted 30 percent. While the jump from two percent to 20 percent is enormous, only seven percent of that is in the hands of individuals – most is owned by big bumiputra investment companies, institutions and government trust agencies. A sizeable chunk of the remainder is concentrated in the hands of

(instead of relying solely on trade links with the West), most of Malaysia's foreign investment has come from the East.

Evidence of the growing maturity of the Malaysian economy can be seen in the degree to which the country – Malaysia Inc. – is pursuing its industrial ambitions in the global arena. Between 1991 and mid-1996 US$7.1bn was invested in enterprises off-shore. This ranged from the acquisition of Lotus sports cars in Britain, to timber operations in New Zealand, Guyana and Canada, and construction in Albania and Uruguay.

Transforming the economy

A key element in Malaysia's development strategy is how to manage the transition from a production centre where comparative advantage is based on labour cost to an economy where high levels of education and skills provide the industrial impetus. Malaysia invariably looks across to Singapore as both a role model in this regard and as a competitor.

Among Prime Minister Mahathir's favourite programmes is the so-called MSC or 'Multimedia Super Corridor' – an attempt to build an Oriental Silicon Valley on a 15 km-by-50 km stretch of land south of KL. This is linked to the new administrative capital of Putrajaya and the associated international airport at Sepang. When you

pumping money into the domestic economy, pushing through infrastructure projects, raising civil servants' salaries, offering bonuses, and cutting taxes. Not all commentators believe this will work. There were some bright spots in an otherwise
murky picture: demand for latex gloves, of which Malaysia is the world's largest producer, was up by 50 percent in response to the anthrax scare.

Malaysia's economic crisis came quick on the heels of Thailand's fall from economic
grace in July 1997, which led to the devaluation of the baht and a US$15bn IMF rescue
package. Though Thailand's problems were uniquely serious there were enough com-
monalities to cause concern in KL's financial district: a high current account deficit; a
currency linked to the US$; a booming property sector; and a lack of transparency in
some aspects of financial management. It was these similarities with Thailand – and
perhaps also a sense that the economies of Asean, having boomed together would
also fall together – which led currency speculators to attack the ringgit.

Falling tigers

Prime Minister Mahathir, predictably, blamed perfidious currency speculators and
in particular George Soros, the Hungarian-born billionaire. Mahathir allegedly compared speculators to drug dealers, labelling them anarchists, saboteurs and rogues
(*The Economist*, 2 August 1997). In July 1997 at their annual meeting, the nine Asean
foreign ministers released a joint communiqué stating that the currency crisis was
due to the "well co-ordinated efforts [by speculators] to destabilize ASEAN currencies
for self-serving purposes". *The Economist* opined that blaming Soros for Thailand's
plight was "rather like condemning an undertaker for burying a suicide".

Unlike the other countries of the region, Mahathir did not stick with the IMF's
medicine. Instead he imposed tight currency controls in September 1998. While
his actions were widely condemned in the international press, the recovery of the
Malaysian economy by mid-1999, in Mahathir's eyes at least, vindicated his
actions. Of course, opponents of the controls maintained that the country's economic recovery had little to do with the controls *per se*. Indeed, they say that of all
the countries of the region Malaysia was best placed to deal with the crisis and
that the currency controls were an irrelevance in the broader economic context.
The danger, these critics of Malaysian economic policies maintain, is that because
the country was affected least by the crisis it also did the least to confront the
structural problems that created the conditions for the crisis in the first place. In
other words they wonder whether it could all happen again.

Culture

People

Visitors sometimes get confused over the different races that make up Malaysia's
population. All citizens of Malaysia are 'Malaysians'; they are comprised of Malays,
Chinese and Indians as well as other 'tribal' groups, most of whom live in the East
Malaysian states of Sabah and Sarawak.

Malaysia had a total population in 1999 of 22,710,000, of whom more than 8 in 10
live on the peninsula, eight percent in Sabah and nine percent in Sarawak. Statistics
on the ethnic breakdown of Malaysia's multi-racial population tend to differ and
because politics is divided along racial lines, they are sensitive figures. For Malaysia as
a whole, Malays and other indigenous groups make up roughly 58 percent of the
population, Chinese 27 percent, Indians eight percent and 'others', seven percent.
The Malays and indigenous groups are usually lumped together under the umbrella
term *bumiputra* – or 'sons of the soil'. This includes both Malays and tribal groups
such as the assorted Dayaks of East Malaysia. On the peninsula the Chinese make up

The new breed: farewell to the old Malaise

In recent years, the easy-going Malay kampung world of old wooden houses, water buffalo and coconut curries has clashed head-on with modern Malaysia and its hi-tech office towers, six-lane highways and polypropylene refineries.

For the past 30 years, the government has done just about everything in its power to coax Malays out of the villages in an effort to catapult them into the modern economy. The New Economic Policy formalized this attempt to increase the Malays' stake of national wealth, see page 524. But because life was made easy for them, many massaged the system to their advantage, and arrived on top of the heap having expended comparatively little effort. This engendered much resentment.

The racial quotas introduced by the NEP still have not been met – even with all the scholarships and free directorships, Malays do not comprise a third of the corporate workforce. But today, in Kuala Lumpur's penthouse boardrooms and behind the terminals in dealing rooms, a new breed of Malay professional has begun to appear. At last, they are there not because they are Malay but because they are good.

There is a Malay phase associated with this phenomenon: kurang ajar. It is coarse language – if you accuse someone of being kurang ajar, it means they are

extremely rude, ignorant and ill-bred. Not long ago, the phrase was actually banned in the Malaysian parliament after one opposition MP used it to describe a member of the government. But with a little good-humoured antiseptic, the quality of kurang ajar has come to represent the new assertiveness of the 1990s Malay. A Malay who is more critical, more analytical, more willing to stand up for his – or her – rights and a Malay who is more able. Enter bumiputras with attitude: the New Malay. Anwar Ibrahim, the relatively youthful, confident, clean-cut, urbane deputy Prime Minister, has emerged as a role model for the aspiring New Malay.

Although immersed in the wheeling and dealing of modern progressive Malaysia, the boomtown bumiputra has not entirely forsaken his kampung roots. Lat, Malaysia's favourite cartoonist, has a series of books on the theme of the rural Malay struggling to keep pace with the times. His opinion is that every mobile-phone-wielding, Rayban-clad, BMW-driving KL yuppy is really a kampung kid at heart. And to be sure, every weekend and public holiday, the highways and airports become clogged as the new city species – balek kampung – head back to their villages.

a rather large share of the population, amounting to some 31 percent, while bumis comprise 58 percent and Indians nine percent.

In theory being a *bumi* bestows certain advantages. The New Economic Policy or NEP (see page 524), introduced after the race riots in 1969, discriminates in favour of the indigenous population – mostly the Malays, but also the non-Malay tribal peoples of East Malaysia and the Orang Asli of the peninsula. They receive preferential treatment when it comes to university places, bumi entrepreneurs have an inside track securing government contracts, and they also benefit from discounts on houses. However there have been stories of non-Malay bumiputras not being accorded the affirmative action rights of Malay bumis. In 1997, for example, it was revealed that an Iban ('tribal' Dayak from East Malaysia) man was refused the five to seven percent discount which bumis are entitled to when he tried to buy a house in Melaka. The federal government was appalled but many commentators were not altogether surprised. What it means to qualify as a bumi has never been adequately defined. It appears that for some people being a bumi not only means being indigenous, it also means being Muslim, and many of the non-Malay bumis are Christian.

CULTURE **529**

Tikus Rahmat: Malaysian racial relations in rat form

Tikus Rahmat *or Blessed Rat written by Hassan Ibrahim and first published in 1963 is the only Malay novel in satire form and it is modelled closely on George Orwell's Animal Farm. The novel is based on relations between various groups of rats in Tikusia Raya (Ratland), each of which is symbolic of the different races in Malaysia. The similarities between the inhabitants of Tikusia Raya and the stereotypical view of the races of Malaysia are clear. The farm rats or tikus ladang symbolize the Chinese: they are the newcomers; they play the role of the middleman; and they are hard-working and diligent. The novelist also writes that they are: "... capable in the art of cheating as it is their way of life, taught by their parents since birth."*

The valley rats *or tikus lembah are the Malays. They are the poorest rats, whose interests are continually sacrificed in the interests of the rest of the population. But they are also very religious and humble. Needless to say, the other rats view them as lazy good-for-nothings.*

The farm rats insist that their own language – cok cak *– be used as the lingua franca of Tikusia Raya and in an election the farm rats win a majority. The valley rats rebel against the results of the election and attack and kill the rich white rats (symbolizing white people) and farm rats. The few that survive this epic rat battle agree to settle their differences and follow the Prophet Solomon (Muhammad). Although the novel was written before the 1969 race riots, parts of the story coincidentally mirror the tragic events of that year.*

Malaysia's population is growing by just under 2 percent per annum and the total fertility rate – the number of children born to each woman – stands at 3.24. This fertility rate, however, is not equally distributed between the ethnic groups. Since 1970, the bumiputra population has grown fastest, and, on the peninsula, their proportion of the total population has increased from 53 percent. In the same period, the proportion of the Chinese population has declined from 36 percent while the proportion of Indians has remained roughly the same. Mahathir announced at the beginning of the 1990s that for Malaysia to become an industrialized country, it would need a strong domestic market, so he encouraged Malaysians to procreate – his once suggested target was a population of 70 million by 2010, up from 17 million in 1990 and 20 million in 2000. The target date has subsequently been revised to 2095. The higher average fertility rate of the Malay compared with the Chinese population means that the delicate racial balance that was such a potential source of instability at independence is becoming less of a worry. It has been estimated that by 2020 the bumiputra population will comprise 70 percent of the total population of the country. The fear that the Chinese might represent a political threat to Malay domination is receding as each year passes.

The Malay people probably first migrated to the peninsula from Sumatra. Anthropologists speculate that the race originally evolved from the blending of a Mongoloid people from Central Asia with an island race living between the Indian and Pacific oceans. They are lowland people and originally settled around the coasts. These 'Coastal Malays' are also known as 'Deutero-Malays'. They are ethnically similar to the Malays of Indonesia and are the result of intermarriage with many other racial groups, including Indians, Chinese, Arabs and Thais. They are a very relaxed, warm-hearted people who had the good fortune to settle in a land where growing food was easy. For centuries they have been renowned for their hospitality and generosity as well as their well-honed sense of humour. When Malays converted to Islam in the early 15th century, the language was written in Sanskrit script which evolved into the Arabic-looking *Jawi*.

Malays

🖙 Running amok

The word amok is one of the few Malay words to have been embraced by the English language, most obviously used in the expression 'to run amuck'. Amok refers to aberrant behaviour which, at least until the early 20th century, was prevalent among the Malay peoples. There are two forms of amok – martial amok, where it is used as an honourable tactic of warfare (martial amok was also common in India), and solitary amok. It is the latter which has attracted the most attention, as it appears to occur suddenly, without warning, and with little apparent reason. The earliest reference to solitary amok occurs in the work of Nicolo Conti dating from the early 15th century. All references agree that it is a frenzied, murderous and usually unselective attack on all and everyone that an amok-runner or pengamok might meet, and that it almost always ended in the death of the attacker, such is the madness of the violence. Some authorities have attributed amok to social alienation (amok-runners are usually new arrivals in an area); others to the disgrace of penury that might force a person into slavery; some to the effects of drugs (this was the usual colonial explanation, as the cause is clear and easily understood); others to some deep-seated grief (for example following the death of a man's wife or child); while still others have maintained that it is religiously motivated. Within the Malay social context, the amok-runner was viewed as a person with a certain honour: the act itself, although it might well lead to the death of innocent bystanders, was seen as an honourable escape from some dire situation.

The British in Malaya tended to view pengamok in Western terms, and to moralize about their crimes. On 8 July 1846, Sunan, a respectable Malay house-builder ran amok in Penang. According to the judicial disposition at his trial:

"... before he [Sunan] was arrested [he] killed an old Hindu woman, a Kling, a Chinese boy, and a Kling girl about three years old in the arms of its father, and wounded two Hindus, three Klings, and two Chinese, of whom only two survived." He had, apparently, been devastated by the death of his wife and only child. Nonetheless, the magistrate sentenced the man with the words:

"The sentence of the Court therefore is, that you, Sunan, be remanded to the place from whence you came, and that on the morning of Wednesday next you be drawn from thence on a hurdle to the place of execution, and there hanged by the neck until you are dead. Your body will then be handed over to the surgeons for dissection, and your mangled limbs, instead of being restored to your friends for decent interment, will be cast into the sea, thrown into a ditch, or scattered on the earth at the discretion of the Sheriff. And may God Almighty have mercy on your miserable soul!"

Source of quote: Spores, John C (1988) Running amok: an historical inquiry, Ohio University Center for International Studies: Athens, Ohio.

Because Malays were traditionally farmers and were tied to rural kampungs, they remained insulated from the expansion of colonial Malaya's export economy. Few of them worked as wage labourers and only the aristocracy, which had been educated in English, were intimately involved in the British system of government, as administrators. "... In return for the right to develop a modern extractive economy within the negeri [states] by means of alien immigrant labor," writes historian William R Roff, "the British undertook to maintain intact the position and prestige of the ruling class and to refrain from catapulting the Malay people into the modern world". Rural Malays only began to enter the cash economy when they started to take up rubber cultivation on their smallholdings – but this was not until after 1910. In 1921, less than five percent of Malays lived in towns.

On attaining independence in 1957, the new constitution allowed Malays to be given special rights for 10 years, enabling them to become as prosperous as the Chinese 'immigrants'. To this end, they were afforded extra help in education and in securing jobs. The first economic development plan focused on the rural economy, with the aim of improving the lot of the rural Malays. It was the Malay community's sense of its own weakness in comparison with the commercial might of the Chinese that led to ethnic tensions erupting onto the streets in May 1969. Following the race riots, the Malays were extended special privileges in an effort to increase their participation in the modern economy (see box, page 524). Along with indigenous groups, they were classed as bumiputras, usually shortened to 'bumis' – a label many were able to use as a passport to a better life.

The Chinese community accounts for about a third of Malaysia's population. In 1794, just eight years after he had founded Georgetown in Penang, Sir Francis Light wrote: "The Chinese constitute the most valuable part of our inhabitants: ... they possess the different trades of carpenters, masons, smiths, traders, shopkeepers and planters; they employ small vessels. They are the only people from whom a revenue may be raised without expense and extraordinary effort by the government. They are a valuable acquisition ..." Chinese immigrants went on to become invaluable members of the British Straits Settlements – from the early 1820s they began to flood into Singapore from China's southern provinces. At the same time they arrived in droves on the Malay peninsula, most of them working as tin prospectors, shopkeepers and small traders.

Chinese

Although the great bulk of Chinese in Malaysia arrived during the massive immigration between the late 19th and early 20th centuries, there has been a settled community of Chinese in Melaka since the 15th century. Many arrived as members of the retinue of the Chinese princess Li Poh who married Melaka's Sultan Mansur Shah in 1460 (see page 216). Over the centuries their descendants evolved into a wealthy and influential community with its own unique, sophisticated culture (see page 212). These **Straits Chinese** became known as **Peranakans** (which means 'born here'); men were called **Babas** and women, **Nyonyas**. When Peranakans began to be known as such is not known. Baba came into common usage during the 19th century and it is thought that Peranakan was already a well-established label at that time. 'Baba' does not seem to be of Chinese origin but is probably derived from Arabic, or perhaps Turkish, roots. To begin with Baba was used to refer to all local-born foreigners in Malaya, whether they were ethnic Chinese, Indians or Europeans. However, before long it became solely associated with the Straits Chinese.

The centres of Peranakan Chinese culture were the Straits Settlements of Melaka, Penang and Singapore. There were, however, significant differences between the communities in the three settlements. For example, Nyonya food in Penang shows culinary influences from Thailand, while food in Melaka and Singapore does not.

The Peranakans of Malaysia and Singapore saw their futures being intimately associated with the British. They learnt English, established close links with the colonial administration system and colonial businesses, and even their newspapers were written in English rather than Chinese. With the massive infusion of new Chinese blood from the mainland beginning at the end of the 19th century there emerged a two-tier Chinese community. The Peranakans were concentrated in the commercial and professional sectors, and the 'pure' Chinese in the manual sectors. But as the 20th century progressed so the influence of the Peranakans declined. Competition from non-Baba Chinese became stronger as their businesses expanded and as sheer weight of numbers began to tell. The Straits Chinese British Association (SCBA) was eclipsed by the Malaysian Chinese Association (MCA) as a political force and the Peranakans found themselves marginalized. As this occurred, so the Babas found

Background

themselves the object, increasingly, of derision by non-Baba Chinese. They were regarded as having 'sold out' their Chinese roots and become ridiculous in the process. Today the Straits Chinese, in terms of political and economic power, have become – to a large extent – an irrelevance.

Today Peranakan culture is disappearing. Few Baba Chinese identify themselves as Baba; they have become Chinese Malaysians. Only in Melaka (and to some extent in Singapore) does the Baba cultural tradition remain strong. In Penang the numbers of people who see their Baba roots as anything but historical are dwindling. But although Peranakan culture is gradually disappearing, it has left an imprint on mainstream Malaysian culture. For example the custom among Peranakan women of wearing the *sarong* and *kebaya* has become subsumed within Malay tradition and has, in the process, become inter-ethnic. Baba cuisine has also been incorporated within Malay/Chinese cuisine.

The Peranakans may be the most colourful piece in Malaysia's Chinese mosaic, but the vast majority of modern Malaysia's prosperous Chinese population arrived from China rather later, as penniless immigrants. They left China because of poverty, over-population and religious persecution – and were attracted by the lure of gold. In the mid-19th century, these newly arrived immigrants came under the jurisdiction of secret societies and *kongsis* – or clan associations. Some of the most striking examples of the latter are in Penang (see, for example the Khoo Kongsi, page 159). The secret societies sometimes engaged in open warfare with each other as rival groups fought over rights to tin mining areas.

The overseas Chinese have been described as possessing these common traits: the ability to smell profits and make quick business decisions; a penchant for good food (they prefer to sit at round tables to facilitate quicker exchange of information); and a general avoidance of politics in favour of money-making pursuits. Like most stereotypes, these characteristics break down when put to the detailed test but at a certain level of generalization, hold true. It is also true to say – broadly speaking – that the Chinese population felt little loyalty to their host society. At least, that is, until the 1949 Communist take-over in China, which effectively barred their return. Despite the community's political and economic gripes and traumas in the intervening years, Chinese culture has survived intact and the community enjoys religious freedom; Chinese cuisine is enthusiastically devoured by all races and the mahjong tiles are still clacking in upstairs rooms. Today about 80 percent of Chinese schoolchildren attend private Chinese primary schools – although all secondary and tertiary education is in Malay.

Indians   Indian traders first arrived on the shores of the Malay peninsula more than 2,000 years ago in search of Suvarnadvipa, the fabled Land of Gold. There was a well established community of Indian traders in Melaka when the first sultanate grew up in the 1400s – there was even Tamil blood in the royal lineage. But most of the 1½ million Indians in modern Malaysia – who make up nearly nine percent of the population – are descendants of indentured Tamil labourers shipped to Malaya from South India by the British in the 19th century. They were nicknamed 'Klings' – a name which today has a deeply derogatory connotation. Most were put to work as coolies on the roads and railways or as rubber tappers.

About 100 years on, four out of five Indians are still manual labourers on plantations or in the cities. This has long been explained as a colonial legacy, but as modern Malaysia has grown more prosperous, the Tamils have remained at the bottom of the heap. Other Indian groups – the Keralans (Malayalis), Gujeratis, Bengalis, Sikhs and other North Indians, who came to colonial Malaya under their own volition, are now well represented in the professional classes. The South Indian Chettiar money-lending caste, which was once far more numerous than it is today, left the country in droves in the 1930s. Their confidence in British colonial rule was shaken by events in Burma, where anti-Indian riots prompted tens of thousands of Chettiars to return to India. While most of Malaysia's Indian community are Hindus, there are also Indian Muslims, Christians and Sikhs. In Melaka there is a small group of Indians with Portuguese names – known as Chitties.

Today the chanted names of the Hindu pantheon echo around the cool interior of the Sri Mariamman Temple in the heart of Kuala Lumpur as they have since its construction in 1873. But large numbers of Tamils still live in the countryside, where they still make up more than half the plantation workforce. Because the estates are on private land, they fall outside the ambit of national development policies and Malaysia's economic boom has passed them by. The controversial New Economic Policy (see page 524) gave Malays a helping hand, and although it was aimed at eradicating poverty generally, it did not help Indians much – who often, and justifiably, feel that they are the group who have missed out most. They lack the economic clout of the Chinese, and the political might of the Malays, and can, it seems, conveniently be forgotten.

Tribes of Borneo

Tribes

1	Banjarese	10	Kenyah/Kayan	18	Modang
2	Bugis	11	Land Dayak	19	Murut
3	Chinese	12	Lun Dayeh	20	Ngaju
4	Desa	13	Limbai	21	Ot Danum
5	Iban	14	Malays	22	Taman
6	Kadazan	15	Maloh	23	Tebidah
7	Kantu	16	Ma'anyan &	24	Tunjung
8	Kedayan		Lawangan		
9	Kelabit	17	Melanau	—	Approx tribal limits

N

Not to scale

Background

The new policy document which replaced the NEP in 1991 officially recognizes that Indians have lagged behind in the development stakes. Education is seen as the key to broadening the entrepreneurial horizons of Tamils, getting them off the plantations, out of the urban squatter settlements and into decent jobs. But in the privately run Tamil shanty schools on the estates, the drop-out rate is double the national average. Critics accuse the Malaysian Indian Congress (MIC), which is part of the ruling coalition, of perpetuating this system in an effort to garner support. Because Indians are spread throughout the country and do not form the majority in any constituency, the plantations have been the MIC's traditional support base. It is not in the MIC's interests to see them move off the estates.

But things are beginning to change on the plantations – an unprecedented national strike in 1990 guaranteed plantation workers a minimum wage for the first time. Workers are becoming more assertive and aware of their individual and political rights. A new party, the Indian Progressive Front, has drawn its support from working class Indians. It seems that these stirrings of new assertiveness represent rising aspirations on the estates – which will have to continue to rise if the Tamils are ever going to escape from their plantation poverty trap, which one prominent Indian leader refers to as 'the green ghetto'. In 1970 ethnic Indians controlled about 1.1 percent of the country's wealth. By 1992, at the end of the 20-year NEP, this figure had declined to one percent. It has been estimated that two-thirds of Indians still live in poverty and for the Indians the NEP has been largely irrelevant. While Malays have enjoyed cumulative gains from the NEP and the Chinese have seen their slice of the cake grow in size if not in proportion, the Indian community have been left trailing and marginalized – a classic 'excluded' community.

Orang Asli (Aboriginals) While the Malay population originally settled on the coasts of the peninsula, the mountainous, jungled interior was the domain of the oldest indigenous groups – the aboriginals. They are a sinewy, dark-skinned race, characterized by their curly hair and are probably of Melanesian origin – possibly related to Australian aborigines. During the Pleistocene ice age, when a land-bridge linked the Philippines to Borneo and mainland Southeast Asia, these people spread throughout the continent. Today they are confined to the mountains of the Malay peninsula, Northeast India, North Sumatra, the Andaman Islands and the Philippines. The Negrito aboriginals – who in Malay are known as *Orang Asli*, or 'Indigenous People' – were mainly hunter-gatherers. As the Malays spread inland, the Orang Asli were pushed further and further into the mountainous interior. Traditionally, the Negritos did not build permanent houses – preferring makeshift shelters – and depend on the jungle and the rivers for their food.

A second group of Orang Asli, the *Senoi* – who are also known as the *Sakai* – arrived later than the Negritos. They practised shifting cultivation to supplement their hunting and gathering and built sturdier houses. The third aboriginal group to come to the peninsula were the Jakuns – or proto-Malays – who were mainly of Mongoloid stock. They were comprised of several subgroups, the main ones being the Mantera and Biduanda of Negeri Sembilan and Melaka and the Orang Ulu, Orang Kanak and Orang Laut ('Sea People') of Johor. Their culture and language became closely linked to that of the coastal Malays, and over the centuries many of them assimilated into Malay society. Most practised shifting cultivation; the Orang Laut were fishermen.

Malaysia's aborigines have increasingly been drawn into the modern economy. Along with the Malays, they are classified as *bumiputras* and as such, became eligible, as with other tribal groups in East Malaysia, for the privileges extended to all bumiputras following the introduction of the New Economic Policy (NEP) in 1970 (see page 524). In reality, however, the NEP offered few tangible benefits to the

Orang Asli, and while the government has sought to integrate them – there is a Department of Aboriginal Affairs in Kuala Lumpur – there is no separate mechanism to encourage entrepreneurism among the group.

Religion

Malays are invariably Muslims and there is also a small population of Indian Muslims in Malaysia. The earliest recorded evidence of Islam on the Malay peninsula is an inscription in Terengganu dating from 1303, which prescribed penalties for those who did not observe the moral codes of the faith. Islam did not really gain a foothold on the peninsula, however, until Sri Maharaja of Melaka – the third ruler – converted in 1430 and changed his name to Mohamed Shah (see page 207). He retained many of the ingrained Hindu traditions of the royal court and did not attempt to enforce Islam as the state religion. The Arab merchant ships which made regular calls at Melaka probably brought Muslim missionaries to the city. Many of them were Sufis – belonging to a mystical order of Islam which was tolerant of local customs and readily synthesized with existing animist and Hindu beliefs. The adoption of this form of Islam is one reason why animism and the Muslim faith still go hand in hand in Malaysia (see below). Mohamad Shah's son, Rajah Kasim, was the first ruler to adopt the title 'Sultan', and he became Sultan Muzaffar; all subsequent rulers have continued to preserve and uphold the Islamic faith. The Portuguese and Dutch colonialists, while making a few local converts to Christianity, were more interested in trade than proselytizing.

Islam

The British colonial system of government was more 'progressive' than most colonial régimes in that it barred the British residents from interfering in 'Malay religion and custom'. So-called Councils of Muslim Religion and Malay Custom were set up in each state answerable to the sultans. These emerged as bastions of Malay conservatism and served to make Islam the rallying point of nascent nationalism. The Islamic reform movement was imported from the Middle East at the turn of the 19th century and Malays determined that the unity afforded by Islam transcended any colonial authority and the economic dominance of immigrant groups. The ideas spread as increasing numbers of Malays made the Haj to Mecca, made possible by the advent of regular steamer services. But gradually the sultans and the Malay aristocracy – who had done well out of British rule – began to see the Islamic renaissance as a threat.

On Fridays, the Muslim day of prayer, Malaysian Muslims congregate at mosques in their 'Friday best'. The 'lunch hour' starts at 1130 and runs through to about 1430 to allow Muslims to attend the mosque; in big towns and cities, Friday lunchtimes are marked by traffic jams. In the fervently Islamic east coast states, Friday is the start of the weekend. Men traditionally wear *songkoks* – black velvet hats – to the mosque and often wear their best sarung (sometimes *songket*) over their trousers. Those who have performed the Haj pilgrimage to Mecca wear a white skullcap. However, at least until recently (see below), Malaysia's Islam has been moderate by Middle Eastern standards. Traditionally, for example, women were not required to wear the head scarf or *tudung*.

But Malaysia has emerged as an outspoken defender of Muslims and Islamic values around the world. On occasions, Dr Mahathir has made outspoken attacks on Western attitudes towards Islam, in which, he says, Muslims are cast as pariahs and bogeymen. Partly this can be viewed as part of the Prime Minister's efforts to polish his own Islamic credentials. At home, Dr Mahathir's government feels threatened by the rise of fundamentalist sentiments – particularly in the northeastern state of Kelantan, where the Islamic government has approved a bill calling for the introduction of a strict Islamic penal code (see page 302). Hard-line Islam is perceived as a threat to secular society in Malaysia. The former deputy Prime Minister, Anwar

Background

The practice of Islam: living by the Prophet

Islam is an Arabic word meaning 'submission to God'. As Muslims often point out, it is not just a religion but a total way of life. The main Islamic scripture is the Koran or Quran, the name being taken from the Arabic al-qur'an or 'the recitation'. The Koran is divided into 114 sura, or 'units'. Most scholars are agreed that the Koran was partially written by the Prophet Mohammad. In addition to the Koran there are the hadiths, from the Arabic word hadith meaning 'story', which tell of the Prophet's life and works. These represent the second most important body of scriptures.

The practice of Islam is based upon five central tenets, known as the Pillars of Islam: Shahada (profession of faith), Salat (worship), Zakat (charity), saum (fasting) and Haj (pilgrimage). The mosque is the centre of religious activity. The two most important mosque officials are the imam – or leader – and the khatib or preacher – who delivers the Friday sermon.

The **Shahada** is the confession, and lies at the core of any Muslim's faith. It involves reciting, sincerely, two statements: 'There is no god, but God', and 'Mohammad is the Messenger [Prophet] of God'. A Muslim will do this at every **Salat**. This is the daily prayer ritual which is performed five times a day, at sunrise, midday, mid-afternoon, sunset and at night. There is also the important Friday noon worship. The Salat is performed by a Muslim bowing and then prostrating himself in the direction of Mecca (in Malaysian kiblat, in Arabic qibla). In hotel rooms throughout there is nearly always a little arrow, painted on the ceiling – or sometimes inside a wardrobe – indicating the direction of Mecca and labelled kiblat. The faithful are called to worship by a mosque official. Beforehand, a worshipper must wash to ensure ritual purity. The Friday midday service is performed in the mosque and includes a sermon given by the khatib.

A third essential element of Islam is **Zakat** – charity or alms-giving. A Muslim is supposed to give up his 'surplus' (according to the Koran); through time this took on the form of a tax levied according to the wealth of the family. In Malaysia there is no official Zakat as there is in Saudi Arabia, but good Muslims are expected to contribute a tithe to the Muslim community.

The fourth pillar of Islam is **saum** or fasting. The daytime month-long fast of Ramadan is a time of contemplation, worship and piety – the Islamic equivalent of Lent. Muslims are expected to read one-thirtieth of the Koran each night. Muslims who are ill or on a journey have dispensation from fasting, but otherwise they are only permitted to eat during the night until "so much of the dawn appears that a white thread can be distinguished from a black one".

The **Haj** or Pilgrimage to the holy city of Mecca in Saudi Arabia is required of all Muslims once in their lifetime if they can afford to make the journey and are physically able to. It is restricted to a certain time of the year, beginning on the eighth day of the Muslim month of Dhu-l-Hijja. Men who have been on the Haj are given the title Haji, and women hajjah.

The Koran also advises on a number of other practices and customs, in particular the prohibitions on usury, the eating of pork, the taking of alcohol, and gambling. There is quite a powerful Islamic revival in Malaysia and Brunei. The use of the veil is becoming de rigeur in Brunei and increasingly in Malaysia. The Koran says nothing about the need for women to veil, although it does stress the necessity of women dressing modestly. In Indonesia, the practices and customs are not strictly interpreted.

Ibrahim – once a young Islamic firebrand himself – became during his time in office an eloquent proponent of Islamic moderation. He appealed in articles submitted to international newspapers for less rhetoric in the name of political expediency from Muslim leaders around the world and for greater understanding of Islam in the West.

Malay magic and the spirits behind the prophet

Despite the fact that all Malays are Muslims, some traditional, pre-Islamic beliefs are still practised by Malays – particularly in the northeast of the peninsula, the conservative Islamic heartland. The bomoh – witch doctor and magic-man – is alive and well in modern Malaysia. The use of ilmu (the malay name for magic), which is akin to voodoo, is still widely practised and bomohs are highly respected and important members of kampong communities. They are often called in to perform their ancient rituals – to bring rain or to determine the site of a new house; on other occasions to make fields (or married couples) fertile or to heal sickness. The healing ceremony is called the main puteri: there are certain illnesses which are believed to be caused by spirits or hantu – who have been offended and must be placated.

The bomoh's job is to get the protective, friendly spirits on his side, in the belief that they can influence the evil ones. He knows many different spirits by name; some are the spirits of nature, others are spirits of ancestors. Many bomohs are specialists in particular fields. Some, known as pewangs, traditionally concentrated on performing spells to ensure fruitful harvests or safe fishing expeditions. Bomohs are still consulted and contracted to formulate herbal remedies, charms, love potions and perform traditional massage (urut). The belian – or shaman –

specializes in more extreme forms of magic conducting exorcisms and spirit-raising seances, or berhantu. In Kelantan, a bomoh who acts as a spirit medium is known as a Tok Peteri and once a spirit has entered him, during a seance, his assistant, called the Tok Mindok, is required to question the spirit, present offerings and address the spirit in a secret language of magic formulae. Seances are always held in front of the whole village after evening prayers.

Manipulation of the weather is one area where the magic is still widely used. In 1991 actors from Kuala Lumpur's Instant Café Theatre Company called on a bomoh to ensure their open-air production of A Midsummer Night's Dream was not washed out. The only occasion on which rain interrupted the play was during an extra performance, not covered in the bomoh's contract.

All natural and inanimate objects are also capable of having spirits and Malays often refer to them using the respectful title Datuk. Other spirits, like the pontianak (the vampire ghost of a woman who dies in childbirth) are greatly feared. Any suspicion of the presence of a pontianak calls for the immediate intervention of a belian, who is believed to inherit his powers from a hantu raya – great spirit – which attaches itself to a bloodline and is subsequently passed from generation to generation.

Background

All of this, of course, has taken on even greater significance in the light of the events of September 11 (see the discussion above, under Politics). But it is worth remembering that the debate over the role and place of Islam in modern Malaysia dates back before the attacks in New York and Washington.

In 1994, Dr Mahathir was forced to clamp down on a fundamentalist Islamic sect known as **Al Arqam** with 10,000 followers, an estimated 200,000 sympathizers, and assets of RM15mn in businesses ranging from property firms to textile factories. Ashaari Muhammed, the leader of the sect, was arrested after being deported from Thailand and then held in detention under the Internal Security Act. Unlikely liberals leapt to defend Mr Ashaari who taught that women should be kept in their place, and operated his sect almost like a secret society. Why the Prime Minister should have issued an order for Mr Ashaari's arrest was a point of dispute. The Prime Minister's office maintained that the sect's teachings were 'deviationist' – as also argued by the National Fatwah Council – and that he

In Siddhartha's footsteps: a short history of Buddhism

Buddhism was founded by Siddhartha Gautama, a prince of the Sakya tribe of Nepal, who probably lived between 563 and 483 BC. He achieved enlightenment and the word buddha means 'fully enlightened one', or 'one who has woken up'. Siddhartha Gautama is known by a number of titles. In the West, he is usually referred to as The Buddha, ie the historic Buddha (but not just Buddha); more common in Southeast Asia is the title Sakyamuni, or Sage of the Sakyas (referring to his tribal origins).

Over the centuries, the life of the Buddha has become part legend, and the Jataka tales which recount his various lives are colourful and convoluted. But, central to any Buddhist's belief is that he was born under a sal tree (Shorea robusta), that he achieved enlightenment under a bodhi tree (Ficus religiosa) in the Bodh Gaya Gardens, that he preached the First Sermon at Sarnath, and that he died at Kusinagara (all in India or Nepal).

The Budda was born at Lumbini (in present-day Nepal), as Queen Maya was on her way to her parents' home. She had had a very auspicious dream before the child's birth of being impregnated by an elephant, whereupon a sage prophesied that Siddhartha would become either a great king or a great spiritual leader. His father, being keen that the first option of the prophecy be fulfilled, brought him up in all the princely skills (at which Siddhartha excelled) and ensured that he only saw beautiful things, not the harsher elements of life.

Despite his father's efforts Siddhartha saw four things while travelling between palaces – a helpless old man, a very sick man, a corpse being carried by lamenting relatives, and an ascetic, calm and serene as he begged for food. These episodes made an enormous impact on the young prince, and he renounced his princely origins and left home to study under a series of spiritual teachers. He finally discovered the path to enlightenment at the Bodh Gaya Gardens in India. He then proclaimed his thoughts to a small group of disciples at Sarnath, near Benares, and continued to preach and attract followers until he died at the age of 81 at Kusinagara.

threatened state security. To begin with the government even suggested that the sect had a 313-man 'death squad'. Opponents maintained that his arrest was more to do with domestic politics: Al Arqam was attracting middle class Malays, just the sort of people who are the bedrock of UMNO's support. The arrest was not, in their view, anything to do with religion, but a great deal to do with politics. Nonetheless the government were able to get Ashaari Muhammed to renounce his teachings on television, thereby preventing him becoming a martyr.

Mahathir has been concerned for more than a decade that radical Islam might destabilize Malaysia's delicate racial and religious cocktail. Sects like Al Arqam, and the spread of Shia theology, are closely watched by a government that wishes to maintain its secular credentials and to control what has been termed 'creeping Islamization'. In mid-1997, Mahathir showed his displeasure at the enforcement of a fatwa in the state of Selangor banning all beauty contests. In June, three Malay contestants were arrested and handcuffed on stage after they had competed in the Miss Malaysia Petite contest. The prime minister rebuked the religious officials who had exceeded their 'little powers'. Earlier he had set in motion a wide-ranging review of Islamic jurisprudence or fiqh. In confronting the clerics and their supporters Mahathir took on a powerful conservative group closely allied with the opposition PAS and, until September 11th, there were those who wondered whether the ulamas (Muslim theologians) might successfully challenge the Prime Minister for the hearts and minds of ordinary Malaysians. But events since then have played into Mahathir's hands (again, see above).

In the First Sermon at the deer park in Sarnath, the Buddha preached the Four Truths, which are still considered the root of Buddhist belief and practical experience. These are the 'Noble Truth' that suffering exists, the 'Noble Truth' that there is a cause of suffering, the 'Noble Truth' that suffering can be ended, and the 'Noble Truth' that to end suffering it is necessary to follow the 'Noble Eightfold Path' – namely, right speech, livelihood, action, effort, mindfulness, concentration, opinion and intention.

Soon after the Buddha began preaching, a monastic order – the Sangha – was established. As the monkhood evolved in India, it also began to fragment as different sects developed different interpretations of the life of the Buddha. An important change was the belief that the Buddha was transcendent: he had never been born, nor had he died; he had always existed and his life on earth had been mere illusion. The emergence of these new concepts helped to turn what up until then was an ethical code of conduct, into a religion. It eventually led to the appearance of a new Buddhist movement, Mahayana Buddhism which split from the more traditional Theravada 'sect'.

Despite the division of Buddhism into two sects, the central tenets of the religion are common to both. Specifically, the principles pertaining to the Four Noble Truths, the Noble Eightfold Path, the Dependent Origination, the Law of Karma and nirvana. In addition, the principles of non-violence and tolerance are also embraced by both sects. In essence, the differences between the two are of emphasis and interpretation. Theravada Buddhism is strictly based on the original Pali Canon, while the Mahayana tradition stems from later Sanskrit texts. Mahayana Buddhism also allows a broader and more varied interpretation of the doctrine. Other important differences are that while the Thervada tradition is more 'intellectual' and self-obsessed, with an emphasis upon the attaining of wisdom and insight for oneself, Mahayana Buddhism stresses devotion and compassion towards others.

Buddhism

While Buddhism is the formal religion of most of Malaysia's Chinese population, many are Taoists, who follow the teachings of the three sages – Confucius, Mencius and Lao Tse. Taoism is characterized by ancestor worship and many deities. As with Islam, this has been mixed with animist beliefs and spirit worship forms a central part of the faith.

Hinduism

Hindu (and Buddhist) religions were established on the Malay peninsula long before Islam arrived. Remains of ancient Hindu-Buddhist temples dating from the kingdom of Langkasuka in the early years of the first millennium have been found in the Bujang Valley, at the foot of Gunung Jerai (Kedah Peak) in Kedah (see page 180). The majority of Malaysia's Indian population is Hindu, although there are also many Indian Muslims.

Borneo

In Sabah and Sarawak, apart from the Malays, Bajaus, Illanuns and Suluks, who accepted Islam, all the inland tribes were originally animists. The religion of all the Dayak tribes in Borneo boiled down to placating spirits, and the purpose of tribal totems, images, icons and statues was to chase bad spirits away and attract good ones, which were believed to be capable of bringing fortune and prosperity. Head-hunting (see page 404) was central to this belief, and most Dayak tribes practised it, in the belief that freshly severed heads would bring blessing to their longhouses. Virtually everything had a spirit, and complex rituals and ceremonies were devised to keep them happy. Motifs associated with the spirit world – such as the hornbill (see page 561) – dominate artwork and textiles and many of the

The Ramayana and Mahabharata

Across much of Southeast Asia, the Indian epics of the Ramayana and Mahabharata have been translated and adapted. The stories of the **Mahabharata** are the more popular. These centre on a long-standing feud between two family clans: the Pandawas and the Korawas. The feud culminates in an epic battle during which the five Pandawa brothers come face to face with their 100 first cousins from the Korawa clan. After 18 days of fighting, the Pandawas emerge victorious and the eldest brother becomes king. The plays usually focus on one or other of the five Pandawa brothers, each of whom is a hero.

The **Ramayana** was written by the poet Valmiki about 2,000 years ago. The 48,000 line story tells of the abduction of the beautiful Sita by the evil king, Ravana. Sita's husband Rama, King of Ayodhia, sets out on an odyssey to retrieve his wife from Ravana's clutches, finally succeeding with the help of Hanuman the monkey god and his army of monkeys. Today it is rare to see the Ramayana performed; the orchestra needs to be large (and is therefore expensive), and in the case of wayang few puppet masters have a sufficiently large collection of puppets to cover all the characters.

woodcarvings for sale in art and antique shops had religious significance. Islam began to spread to the tribes of the interior from the late 15th century, but mostly it was confined to coastal districts or those areas close to rivers like the Kapuas and Barito where Malays penetrated into the interior to trade. Christian missionaries arrived with the Europeans but did not proselytize seriously until the mid-19th century. The Dutch, particularly, saw missionaries fulfilling an administrative function, drawing the tribal peoples close to the Dutch and, by implication, away from the Muslim Malays of the coast: it was a policy of divide and rule by religious means. Both Christianity and Islam had enormous influence on the animist tribes, and many converted en masse to one or the other. Despite this, many of the old superstitions and ceremonial traditions, which are deeply ingrained, remain a part of Dayak culture today. (The traditional beliefs of Kalimantan's Dayaks is formalized in the *Kaharingan* faith, which, despite the in-roads made by Christianity and Islam, is still practised by some Mahakam and Barito river groups. The Indonesian government recognizes it as an official religion.)

Art and architecture

Unlike the countries of mainland Southeast Asia and its neighbour, Indonesia, Malaysia is not known for its art and architecture. Arriving at Kuala Lumpur's Sabang International Airport and driving into town, there is apparently scarcely anything worth an aesthetic second glance. Many of Malaysia's artistic treasures have either been torn down to make way for modern buildings with scarcely a concrete ounce of artistic merit, or have simply rotted away through sheer neglect. However, the country is far from being the artistic desert that a cursory glance might suppose. The sadness, though, is that much of what is deemed to be 'worth seeing' (ie a 'sight') is not Malaysian *per se*, but colonial. The most attractive towns – notably Georgetown (Penang) and Melaka – are notable mainly for their Chinese shophouses, and Dutch, Portuguese and English colonial buildings. Vernacular Malay houses must be sought out more carefully; few are preserved, and most are being demolished to make way for structures perceived to be more fitting of a thrusting young country on the verge of developed nation status.

In his book *The Malay House*, architect Lim Jee Yuan writes that traditional houses, which are built without architects, "reflect good housing solutions, as manifested by

The Malay istana – royals on the riverside

The Malay word istana derives from the Sanskrit for 'sleeping place' – but the Malay sultans adopted it as the term for their royal palaces. Because Malay sultanates were usually focused on the mouths of rivers, the istanas were normally sited on a prominent point on the riverbank, along which the sultan's powerbase extended. This meant they were prone to flooding, however, and over the centuries, a number slipped into the river – notably in Perak. The 16th century Sejarah Melayu (Malay Annals) provide a description of Sultan Mansur Shah's palace in Melaka (see page 214). The building has been reconstructed from notes and historical data and now serves as Melaka's Muzium Budaya (Cultural Museum). The original palace was said to have had a seven-tiered roof and 12 halls; it was razed to the ground by the invading Portuguese in 1511.

Traditionally, istanas included everything from the sultan's private quarters (at the rear) to the state administrative and cultural centre. They also doubled as forts in time of war. The sultan's concubines lived in outhouses, dotted around the compound, which also included the mosque and the rumah wakaf – the lodging house for commoners (such as the Istana Jahar in Kota Bharu, which is now the Kelantan State Museum). There are several other istanas in Kelantan and Terengganu states, all dating from the 19th century. The most impressive of the surviving istanas are the Istana Lama Sri Menanti and the Istana Ampang Tinggi in Negri Sembilan (see page 200), the Istana Balai Besar in Kedah – one of the grandest and best-preserved on the peninsula, and now the state museum – and the Istana Kenangan at Kuala Kangsar in Perak, which is now the Royal Museum (see page 145). There are only 11 wooden palaces remaining in Malaysia, and none of them houses a royal family any longer.

the display of a good fit to the culture, lifestyle and socio-economic needs of the users; the honest and efficient use of materials; and appropriate climatic design". Classic Malay houses are built of timber and raised on stilts with wooden or bamboo walls and an *atap* roof – made from the leaves of the nipah palm. It should have plenty of windows and good ventilation – the interior is usually airy and bright. It is also built on a prefabricated system and can be expanded to fit the needs of a grow-ing family. Malay houses are usually simple, functional and unostentatious, and even those embellished by woodcarvings blend into their environment. Lim Jee Yuan says "the Malay house cannot be fully appreciated without its setting – the house com-pound and the kampung". Kampung folk, he says, prefer "community intimacy over personal privacy" which means villages are closely knit communities.

Most Malays on the peninsula traditionally lived in pile houses built on stilts along the rivers. The basic design is called the bumbung panjang ('long roof'), although there are many variations and hybrids; these are influenced both by the Minangkabau house-forms (of West Sumatra) and by Thai-Khmer designs. The dif-ferences in house-styles between regions is mainly in the shape of the roof. The bumbung panjang is the oldest, commonest, simplest and most graceful, with a long gable roof, thatched with atap. There are ventilation grills at either end, allowing a throughflow of air. From the high apex, the eaves slope down steeply, then, towards the bottom, the angle lessens, extending out over the walls. Bumbung panjang are most commonly found in Melaka, but the design is used widely throughout the peninsula.

These days it is more usual to find the atap replaced with corrugated zinc roofs which require less maintenance and are a measure of status in the community. But zinc turns houses into ovens during the day, makes them cold at night and makes a deafen-ing noise in rainstorms. On the east coast of the peninsula, the use of tiled roofs is more

Background

World Heritage List potential

Malaysia has proposed six sites for inclusion on the UNESCO World Heritage List. The list currently comprises 582 cultural and natural sites around the world, including such renowned locations as the pyramids of Egypt and the Taj Mahal in India. However, Malaysia is not currently represented. In an attempt to remedy this situation the Government plans to forward six candidates to be considered for inclusion. Sarawak's Gunung Mulu National Park, Sabah's Kinabalu National Park, and Pahang's Taman Negara will be proposed as natural heritage sites, while listing is also being sought for the Niah Caves in Sarawak, Penang's Georgetown and the historic city of Melaka as cultural sites.

The authorities will be hoping that the World Heritage Committee which operates as part of UNESCO will approve its submissions and add the first Malaysian site at one of its annual meetings over the next 10 years. Any of the 157 states that signed the 'Convention Concerning the Protection of the World Cultural and Natural Heritage' that was conceived in 1972 is eligible for inclusion. To date 114 states parties are included on the list and the absence of a country as rich in natural and cultural wonders as Malaysia is surely only temporary. There are clear incentives for the Malaysian authorities to gain inclusion on the list. It would provide a boost to the tourist industry. Statistics have shown a five-fold increase in tourist arrivals once a country gets a site included on the World Heritage List. It would also open the way for possible funding for projects.

But while the government may be trying to get these sites listed as part of the world's heritage it is, at the same time, creating the conditions where some, at least, can have their integrity undermined. In particular, there is serious concern that Melaka and Georgetown are being gradually eroded. Georgetown has more than 10,000 buildings of heritage value showing Malay, Chinese and Indian influences, while Melaka has around 4,000 pre-war buildings which particularly reflect the Dutch colonial influence. UNESCO's regional adviser for culture in Asia and the Pacific, Richard A. Engelhardt, believes that the two towns risk losing their heritage value if efforts are not taken to preserve and revitalize their traditional and commercial aspects. Melaka has recently lost its connection to the sea through a series of insensitive land reclamation projects. There are even more serious concerns about Georgetown's historic enclave which was included in the 1999/2000 edition of the 'World Monuments Watch List of 100 Endangered Sites' published by the New York based World Monuments Fund. It is threatened by severe development pressure, heavy traffic and developers eager to demolish old buildings.

For more information see:
www.unesco.org/whc
(website of World Heritage List)
www.worldmonuments.org/
(website of World Monuments Fund).

common. Towards the north, Thai and Khmer influences are more pronounced in roof style. As in Thai houses, walls are panelled; there are also fewer windows and elaborate carving is more common. Because Islam proscribes the use of the human figure in art, ornamental woodcarvings depict floral and geometric designs as well as Koranic calligraphy. Most are relief-carvings on wood panels or grilles. In Melaka, colourful ceramic tiles are also commonly used as exterior decoration.

The oldest surviving Malay houses date from only the 19th century. The traditional design is the rumah berpanggung, which is built high off the ground on stilts with an A-shaped roof. The basic features include: Anjung: covered porch at the top of entranceway stairs where formal visitors are entertained; Serambi gantung: verandah, where most guests are entertained; Rumah ibu ('the domain of the mother of the house'): private central core of the house, with raised floor level, where the family talks, sleeps, prays, studies and eats (particularly during festivals); *Dapur*: kitchen, always at the back, and below the level of the rest of the house; most meals are taken here. The dapur is connected to the rumah ibu by the *selang*, a closed walkway. Near the dapur, there is usually a *pelantar*, with a washing area for clothes, a mandi and a toilet.

The best places to see traditional Malay houses are Melaka and Negeri Sembilan, on the west coast, and Terengganu and Kelantan states to the northeast. Minangkabau influence is most pronounced in Negeri Sembilan state, between Kuala Lumpur and Melaka. There, houses have a distinctive, elegant, curved roofline, where the gable sweeps up into 'wings' at each end – the so-called Minangkabau 'buffalo horns'.

Today the traditional Malay house has lost its status in the kampung – now everyone wants to build in concrete and brick. Many planned modern kampungs have been built throughout Malaysia, with little regard for traditional building materials or for the traditional houseforms. Many like-minded architects despair of the 'vulgarization' of the Malay houseform, which has been used as an inspiration for many modern buildings (notably in Kuala Lumpur, see page 75). The curved Minangkabau roof, for example, which has been borrowed for everything from modern bank buildings to toll-booths, has merely become a cultural symbol, and has been deprived of its deeper significance.

Peranakan

The Straits Chinese (Peranakan) communities of Melaka, Penang and Singapore developed their own architectural style to match their unique cultural traditions (see page 212). The finest Peranakan houses can be seen along Jalan Tun Tan Cheng Lock in Melaka (see page 214), notably the Baba-Nyonya Heritage Museum. Typical Peranakan houses were long and narrow, and built around a central courtyard. Their interiors are characterized by dark, heavy wood and marble-topped furniture, often highly decorated, and made by Chinese craftsmen who were brought over from China.

Language and literature

Bahasa Melayu (literally, 'Malay Language') – or to give the language its official title, *Bahasa Kebangsaan* ('National Language') – is an Austronesian language which has been the language of trade and commerce throughout the archipelago for centuries. It is the parent language of – and is closely related to – modern Indonesian. In 1972, Indonesia and Malaysia came to an agreement to standardize spelling – although many differences still remain.

Modern Malay has been affected by a succession of external influences – Sanskrit from the seventh century, Arabic from the 14th and English from the 19th century. These influences are reflected in a number of words, most of them of a religious or technical nature. All scientific terminology is directly borrowed from the English or Latin. However, there are many common everyday words borrowed from Arabic or English: *pasar*, for example, comes from the Arabic *bazaar* (market) and there are countless examples of English words used in Malay – particularly when it comes to modern modes of transport – *teksi*, *bas* and *tren*. Where a Malay term has been devised for a 20th century phenomenon, it is usually a fairly straightforward description. An alternative word for train, for example is *keretapi* (literally 'fire car') and the word for aeroplane is *kapalterbang* (flying ship).

From the seventh century, the Indian Pallava script was in restricted use, although few examples survive. The *Jawi* script, adapted from Arabic, was adopted in the 14th century, with the arrival of Muslim traders and Sufi missionaries in Melaka. To account for sounds in the Malay language which have no equivalent in Arabic, five

Background

additional letters had to be invented, giving 33 letters in all. Jawi script was used for almost all Malay writings until the 19th century, and romanized script only began to supplant Jawi after the Second World War. Many older Malays still read and write the script and it is not uncommon to see it along the streets. Some Chinese-owned banks, for example, have transliterated their names into Jawi script so as to make Malays feel a little more at home in them.

Malay literature is thought to date from the 14th century – although surviving manuscripts written in Jawi only date from the beginning of the 15th century. The first printed books in Malay were produced by European missionaries in the 17th century. The best known of Malay literary works are the 16th-century *Sejara Melayu* or Malay Annals; others include the romantic *Hikayat Hang Tuah* and the 19th-century *Tuhfat al-Nafis*.

The first of Malaysia's 'modern' authors was the 19th century writer Munshi Abdullah – who has lent his name to a few streets around the country. Although he kept to many of the classical strictures, Abdullah articulated a personal view and challenged many of the traditional assumptions underlying Malay society. His best known work was his autobiography, *Hikayat Abdullah*. However, it was not until the 1920s that Malayan authors began to write modern novels and short stories. Among the best known writers are Ahmad bin Mohd. Rashid Talu, Ishak Hj. Muhammad and Harun Aminurrashid. Their work laid the foundations for an expansion of Malaysian literature from the 1950s and today there is a prodigious Malay-language publishing industry.

Since independence, the government has promoted Bahasa Melayu at the expense of Chinese dialects and English. However in 1994 Prime Minister Mahathir signalled a switch in strategy when he declared that university courses in the sciences and technology would be taught in English rather than Bahasa. The emphasis on Bahasa is regarded to some extent as yesterday's battle – the battle to build a national, Malaysian identity. Today's battle is to produce an educated workforce conversant and at home in the world of international business – in other words, people who can use English. When comparisons are made between Malaysian and other overseas students, Malaysian students come out poorly. This is one reason why so many wealthy Malays and Chinese send their children to private English language schools. Now the government appears to have realized the necessity for state schools and universities to reintroduce English. The announcement that a London University campus in Kuala Lumpur would be built is perhaps indicative of this liberalization in education policies. (Not that the process is necessarily one-way: in mid-1997 the government ruled that Islamic civilization would become a mandatory course for all university students – they would need to take and pass it in order to graduate. Needless to say, non-Muslim Malaysians, and some Muslim Malaysians, thought this a step backwards and going against the trend towards a modern, outward-looking, and inclusive Malaysia. Later it was announced that the course would also include study of other Asian civilizations.)

Drama, dance and music

Drama **Wayang Kulit** *Wayang* means 'shadow', and the art form is best translated as 'shadow theatre' or 'shadow play'. Shadow plays were the traditional form of entertainment in Malay kampungs. Although film and television have replaced the *wayang* in many people's lives – especially the young – they are still performed in some rural parts of the peninsula's east coast and are regular fixtures at cultural events. Some people believe that the wayang is Indian in origin, pointing to the fact that most of the characters are from Indian epic tales such as the Ramayana and Mahabharata (see page 540).

By the 11th century *wayang* was well-established in Java. A court poet of the Javanese King Airlangga (1020-1049), referred to wayang in *The meditation of
King Ardjuna*: There are people who weep, are sad and aroused watching the puppets,
though they know they are merely carved pieces of leather manipulated and made to
speak. These people are like men, thirsting for sensual pleasures, who live in a world of
illusion; they do not realize the magic hallucinations they see are not real.

It seems that by the 14th century the art form had made the crossing from the Javanese Majapahit Empire to the courts of the Malay Peninsula and from there spread to
kampungs across the country.

There are many forms of wayang – and not all of them are, strictly speaking,
shadow plays – but the commonest and oldest form is the wayang kulit. Kulits are
finely carved and painted leather, two-dimensional puppets, jointed at the elbows
and shoulders and manipulated using horn rods. In order to enact the entire repertoire of 179 plays, 200 puppets are needed. A single performance can last as long as
nine hours. The plays have various origins. Some are animistic, others are adapted
from the epic poems. The latter are known as 'trunk' tales or *pondok* and include the
Ramayana. Others have been developed over the years by influential puppet masters. They feature heroic deeds, romantic encounters, court intrigues, bloody battles,
and mystical observations, and are known as *carangan* or 'branch' tales.

The gunungan or Tree of Life, is an important element of wayang theatre. It represents all aspects of life, and is always the same in design: shaped like a stupa, the tree
has painted red flames on one side and a complex design on the other (this is the
side which faces the audience). At the base of the tree are a pair of closed doors,
flanked by two fierce demons or *yaksas*. Above the demons are two garudas and
within the branches of the tree there are monkeys, snakes and two animals – usually
an ox and a tiger. The gunungan is placed in the middle of the screen at the beginning and end of the performance – and sometimes between major scene changes.
During the performance it stands at one side, and flutters across the screen to indicate minor scene changes.

Traditionally, performances were requested by individuals to celebrate particular
occasions – for example the seventh month of pregnancy (*tingkep*) – or to accompany village festivities. Admission was free, as the individual commissioning the performance would meet the costs. Of course, this has changed now and tourists
invariably have to pay an entrance charge.

In the past, the shadows of the puppets were reflected onto a white cotton cloth
stretched across a wooden frame using the light from a bronze coconut oil lamp.
Today, electric light is more common – a change which, in many people's minds, has
meant the unfortunate substitution of the flickering, mysterious shadows of the oil
lamp, with the constant harsh light of the electric bulb. There are both day and night
wayang performances. The latter, for obvious reasons, are the more dramatic,
although the former are regarded as artistically superior.

The audience sits on both sides of the screen. Those sitting with the puppet master
see a puppet play; those on the far side, out of view of the puppet master and the
accompanying gamelan orchestra, see a shadow play. It is possible that in the past, the
audience was segregated according to sex: men on the to' dalang's side of the screen,
women on the shadow side.

The puppet-master is known as the *to' dalang*; he narrates each story in lyrical classical Malay and is accompanied by a traditional gamelan orchestra of gongs, drums,
rebab (violins) and woodwind instruments. He slips in and out of different characters,
using many different voices throughout the performances, which lasts as long as three
to four hours. The words *to' dalang* are said to be derived from *galang*, meaning bright
or clear, the implication being that the to' dalang makes the sacred texts

Making a wayang kulit puppet

Wayang kulit puppets are made of buffalo hide, preferably taken from a female animal of about four years of age. The skin is dried and scraped, and then left to mature for as long as 10 years to achieve the stiffness required for carving. After carving, the puppet is painted in traditional pigments. In carving the puppet, the artist is constrained by convention. The excellence of the puppet is judged according to the fineness of the chisel-work and the subtlety of painting. If the puppet is well made it may have guna – a magical quality which is supposed to make the audience suspend its disbelief during the performance. Puppets

accumulate guna with age; this is why old puppets are preferred to new ones.

Each major character has a particular iconography, and even the angle of the head and the slant of the eyes and mouth are important in determining the character. Some puppets may be called on to perform a number of minor parts, but in the main a knowledgeable wayang-goer will be able to recognize each character immediately.

The cempurit or rods used to manipulate the puppet are made of buffalo horn while the studs used to attach the limbs are made of metal, bone or bamboo. Court puppets might even be made of gold, studded with precious stones.

understandable. He sits on a plinth, an arm's length away from the cloth screen. From this position he manipulates the puppets, while also narrating the story. Although any male can become a to' dalang, it is usual for sons to follow their fathers into the profession. The to' dalang is the key to a successful performance: he must be multi-skilled, have strength and stamina, be able to manipulate numerous puppets simultaneously, narrate the story, and give the lead to the accompanying gamelan orchestra. No wonder that an adept to' dalang is a man with considerable status.

Chinese classical street operas (wayang) date back to the seventh century. They are performed in Malaysia by troupes of roving actors during Chinese festivals, particularly during the seventh lunar month, following the Festival of the Hungry Ghosts. For more details on the wayang, see box, page 546.

Dance
Malaysia's best-known silat gurus live along the east coast

Silat (or, more properly, *bersilat*) is a traditional Malay martial art, but is so highly stylized that it has become a dance form and is often performed with the backing of a percussion orchestra. *Pencak silat* is the more formal martial art of self-defence; *seni silat* is the graceful aesthetic equivalent. A variety of the latter is commonly performed at ceremonial occasions – such as Malay weddings – it is called *silat pulut*. Silat comprises a fluid combination of movements and is designed to be as much a comprehensive and disciplined form of physical exercise as it is a martial art. It promotes good blood circulation and deep-breathing, which are considered essential for strength and stamina. The fluidity of the body movements require great suppleness, flexibility and poise.

The ***Mak Yong*** was traditionally a Kelantanese court dance-drama, performed only in the presence of the sultan and territorial chiefs. Performed mainly by women (the mak yong being the 'queen' and lead dancer), it is accompanied by an orchestra of gongs, drums and the *rebab* (violin). There are only ever two or three male dancers who provide the comic interludes. The dance is traditionally performed during the Sultan of Kelantan's birthday celebrations. Unlike the wayang kulit shadow puppet theatre (above), the stories are not connected to the Hindu epics; they are thought to be of Malay origin. Other Kelantanese court dances include: the *garong*, a lively up-tempo dance by five pairs of men and women, in a round (a *garong* is a bamboo cow bell). The *payang*, a folk dance, is named after the distinctive east coast fishing boats; traditionally it was danced on the beach while waiting for the kampung fishing fleet to return.

The **joget** dance is another Malay art form which is the result of foreign cultural influence – in this case, Portuguese. It has gone by a variety of other names, notably the *ronggeng* and the *branyo*. It is traditionally accompanied by the gamelan orchestra. Arab traders were responsible for importing the **zapin** dance and Indonesians introduced the **inang**. Immigrants from Banjarmasin (South Kalimantan), who arrived in Johor in the early 1900s, brought with them the so-called Hobbyhorse Dance – the **Kuda Kepang** – which is performed at weddings and on ceremonial occasions in Johor. The hobbyhorses are made of goat or buffalo skin, stretched over a rotan frame. There are countless other local folk dances around Malaysia, usually associated with festivals – such as the **wau bulan** kite dance in Kelantan.

The **Lion Dance** is performed in Chinese communities, particularly around Chinese New Year, and is accompanied by loud drums and cymbals – hard to miss. The lion dance originated in India, where tamed lions were led around public fairs and festivals as entertainment, but because lions were in short supply, dancers with lion masks took their place. The dance was introduced to China during the Tang Dynasty. The lion changed its image from that of a clown to a symbol of the Buddha and is now regarded as 'the protector of Buddhism'. The lion dance developed into a ceremony in which demons and evil spirits are expelled (hence the deafening cymbals and drums).

Bharata Natyam (Indian classical dance) is performed by Malaysia's Indian community and is accompanied by Indian instruments such as the *tambura* (which has four strings), the *talam* (cymbals), *mridanga* (double-headed drum), *vina* (single stringed instrument) and flute. In Malaysia, the Temple of Fine Arts in Kuala Lumpur is an Indian cultural organization which promotes Indian dance forms. The Temple organizes an annual Festival of Arts (see page 104).

Music

Traditional Malay music, which accompanies the various traditional dances, offers a taste of all the peninsula's different cultural influences. The most prominent of these were Indian, Arab, Portuguese, Chinese, Siamese and Javanese – and finally, Western musical influence which gave birth to the all-pervasive genre 'Pop Melayu' – typically melancholic heavy rock. Traditional musical instruments reflect similar cultural influences, notably the *gambus* or lute (which has Middle Eastern origins and is used to accompany the *zapin* dance), the Indian harmonium, the Chinese *serunai* (clarinet) and gongs, the *rebana* drums, also of Middle Eastern origin, and the Javanese *gamelan* orchestra. Because Malays have traditionally been so willing to absorb new cultural elements, traditional art forms have been in danger of extinction. Most traditional Malay instruments are percussion instruments; there are very few stringed or wind instruments. There are six main Malay drums, the most common of which is the cylindrical, double-headed *gendang*, which is used to accompany wayang kulit performances and silat. Other drums include the *geduk* and the *gedombak*; all three are played in orchestras.

Rebana, another traditional Malay drum, is used on ceremonial occasions as well as being a musical instrument. Traditionally, drumming competitions would be held following the rice-harvesting season (in May) and judges award points for timing, tone and rhythm. The best place to see the rebana in action is during Kelantan's giant drum festivals at the end of June. The drums are made from metre-long hollowed-out logs and are brightly painted. In competitions, drummers from different kampungs compete against each other in teams of up to 12 men. Traditionally the rebana was used as a means of communication between villages, and different rhythms were devised as a sort of morse code to invite distant kampungs to weddings or as warnings of war. *Kertok* are drums made from coconuts whose tops are

Background

sliced off and replaced with a block of *nibong* wood (from the sago palm) as a sounding board; these are then struck with padded drumsticks.

There are three main gongs; the biggest and most common, the *tawak* or *tetawak* is used to accompany wayang kulit shadow puppet theatre and Mak Yong dance dramas. The other smaller gongs are called *canang* and also accompany wayang kulit performances. The only Malay stringed instrument is the *rebab*, a violin-type instrument found throughout the region. The main wind instrument is the *serunai*, or oboe, which is of Persian origin and traditionally accompanies wayang kulit and dance performances. Its reed is cut from a palm leaf.

The **Nobat** is the ancient royal orchestra which traditionally plays at the installation of sultans in Kedah, Perak, Selangor, Terangganu and Brunei. It is thought to have been introduced at the royal court of Melaka in the 15th century. The instruments include two types of drums (*negara* and *gendang*), a trumpet (*nafiri*), a flute (*serunai*) and a gong. The Nobat also plays at the coronation of each new king, every five years.

Crafts

The Malay heartland, on the east coast of Peninsular Malaysia, is the centre of the handicraft industry – particularly Kelantan. An extensive variety of traditional handicrafts, as well as batiks, are widely available in this area, although they are also sold throughout the country, notably in Kuala Lumpur and other main towns (see individual town entries). In East Malaysia, Sarawak has an especially active handicraft industry (see page 408).

Most kite-flying competitions take place after the rice harvest in May, when kampungs compete against each other

Kites Kite-making and kite-flying (or *main wau*) are traditional pursuits in the northern Malaysian states of Perlis, Kedah, Kelantan and Terengganu. Malaysia's most famous kite is the crescent-shaped Kelantanese *wau bulan* (moon kite) which has a wingspan of up to 3 m and a length of more than 3 m; they can reach altitudes of nearly 500 m. Bow-shaped pieces of bamboo are often secured underneath, which make a melodious humming noise (*dengung*) in the wind. Wau come in all shapes and sizes however, and scaled-down versions of wau bulan and other kites can be bought. It is even possible to find batik-covered *wau cantik* or *wau sobek*, which are popular wall-hangings but make for awkward hand-luggage. There are often kite-flying competitions on the east coast, where competitors gain points for height and manoeuvering skills. Kites are also judged for their physical attributes, their ability to stay in the air and their sound. On the east coast, all kites are known as *wau*, a word which, it is said, is derived from the arabic letter of the same sound, which is shaped like a kite. Perhaps the most recognizable one is Terengganu's *wau kucing* (cat kite), which Malaysia Airlines adopted as its logo. There are also *wau daun* (leaf kites) and *wau jala budi* (which literally means 'the net of good deeds kite'). Elsewhere in Malaysia, kites are known as *layang-layang* (literally, 'floating objects').

Tops Top spinning (*main gasing*) is another traditional form of entertainment, still popular in rural Malay kampungs – particularly on the east coast of the peninsula. There are two basic forms of tops. The heart-shaped *gasing jantung* and the flattened top, *gasing uri*. The biggest tops have diameters as big as frisbees and can weigh more than 5 kg; the skill required in launching a top is considerable. Top-making is a precision-craft, and each one can take up to three days to make; they are carved from the upper roots and stem-bases of merbau and afzelia trees.

Woodcarving Originally craftsmen were commissioned by sultans and the Malay nobility to decorate the interiors, railings, doorways, shutters and stilts of palaces and public buildings. In Malay woodcarving, only floral and animal motifs are used as Islam prohibits depiction of the human form. But most widely acclaimed are the carved statues of malevolent spirits of the Mah Meris, an Orang Asli tribe.

Batik (*Batek*) The word *batik* may be derived from the Malay word *tik*, meaning 'to drip'. It is believed that batik replaced tatooing as a mark of status in the Malay archipelago. (In eastern Indonesia the common word for batik and tattoo are the same.) Although batik-technology was actually imported from Indonesia several centuries ago, this coloured and patterned cloth is now a mainstay of Malaysian cultural identity. Traditionally, the wax was painted onto the woven cloth using a *canting* (pronounced 'janting'), a small copper cup with a spout, mounted on a bamboo handle. The cup is filled with melted wax, which flows from the spout like ink from a fountain pen – although the canting never touches the surface of the cloth. Batik artists have a number of canting with various widths of spout, some even with several spouts, to give varied thicknesses of line and differences of effect.

In the mid-19th century the 'modern' batik industry was born with the invention (in Java, but quickly adopted in Malaysia) of the *cap* (pronounced 'jap'). This is a copper, sometimes a wooden stamp which looks something like a domestic iron, except that it has an artistically patterned bottom, usually made from twisted copper and strips of soldered tin. Dripping with molten wax, the jap stamps the same pattern across the length and breadth of the cloth, which is then put into a vat of dye. The waxed areas resist the dye and after drying, the process is repeated several times for the different colours. The cracking effect is produced by crumpling the waxed material, which allows the dye to penetrate the cracks. The cloth is traditionally printed in 12 m lengths.

The cap speeded-up production, but it also took the artistry out of waxing: waxers merely stamp the design onto the cloth

Recent years have seen a revival of hand-painted batiks (*batik tulis*), particularly on silk. Price depends on the type of material, design, number of colours used and method employed: factory-printed materials are cheaper than those made by hand. Batik is sold by the *sarung*-length or made up into shirts – and other items of clothing.

Kain songket is Malaysia's 'cloth of gold', although it is also woven in other parts of the region, particularly coastal southern Sumatra. Originally cloth made from a mix of cotton and silk was inter-woven with supplementary gold or silver thread. Today imitation thread is generally used although the metallic thread from old pieces is also removed to provide yarn for new lengths.

The songket evolved when the Malay sultanates first began trading with China (where the silk came from) and India (where the gold and silver thread derived). Designs are reproduced from Islamic motifs and Arabic calligraphy. It was once exclusive to royalty, but is used today during formal occasions and ceremonies (such as weddings). In Kelantan, Terengganu and Pahang the cloth can be purchased directly from workshops. Prices increase with the intricacy of the design and the number of threads used. Each piece is woven by hand and different weavers specialize in particular patterns – one length of cloth may be the work of several weavers.

Background

Pewterware Pewter-making was introduced from China in the mid-19th century; it was the perfect alloy for Malaysia, which until recently, was the world's largest tin-producer: pewter is 95 percent tin. Straits tin is alloyed with antimony and copper. The high proportion of tin lends to the fineness of the surface. It is made mainly into vases, tankards, water jugs, trays and dressing table ornaments. The dimpling effect is made by tapping the surface with a small hammer.

Selangor Pewter is the world's biggest and best pewter manufacturer, there are factories in KL and Singapore

Wayang kulit (shadow puppets – see box, page 546) are crafted from buffalo-hide and represent figures from the Indian epic tales. They are popular handicrafts as they are light and portable.

Silverware Silverwork is a traditional craft and is now a thriving cottage industry in Kelantan. It is crafted into brooches, pendants, belts, bowls and rings. Design patterns incorporate traditional motifs such as *wayang kulit* (see above) and hibiscus flowers (the national flower). The Iban of Sarawak also use silver for ceremonial headdresses and girdles, and some Iban silvercraft can be found for sale on the peninsula.

Land and environment

Geography

Malaysia covers a total land area of 329,054 sq km and includes Peninsular Malaysia (131,587 sq km) and the Borneo states of Sarawak (124,967 sq km) and Sabah (72,500 sq km). Geologically, both the peninsula and Borneo are part of the Sunda shelf, although the mountains of the peninsula were formed longer ago than those in Borneo. This 'shelf', which during the Pleistocene ice age was exposed forming a land bridge between the two halves of the country, was inundated as the glaciers of the north retreated and sea levels rose.

The Malay peninsula is about 800 km north-south, has a long narrow neck, a tapered tail and a bulging, mountainous, middle. The neck is called the **Kra Isthmus**, which links the peninsula to the Southeast Asian mainland. The isthmus itself is in southern Thailand – Peninsular Malaysia comprises only the lower portion of the peninsula and covers an area larger than England and a little smaller than Florida. Nestled into the southernmost end of the peninsula is the island of Singapore, separated from the peninsula by the narrow Strait of Johor. The thin western coastal plain drains into the Strait of Melaka, which separates the peninsula from Sumatra (Indonesia) and is one of the oldest shipping lanes in the world. The eastern coastal lowlands drain into the South China Sea.

The **Barisan Titiwangsa** (Main Range) comprises the curved jungle-clad spine of Peninsular Malaysia. It is the most prominent of several, roughly parallel ranges running down the peninsula. These subsidiary ranges include the Kedah-Singgora Range in the northwest; the Bintang Range (stretching northeast from Taiping), the Tahan Range (which includes the peninsula's highest mountain, Gunung Tahan, 2,187m). In the northern half of the peninsula, the mountainous belt is very wide, leaving only a narrow coastal strip on either side.

The Main Range – or Barisan Titiwangsa – runs south from the Thai border for nearly 500 km, gradually receding as it approaches the coastal plain, near Melaka. The average elevation is about 1,000m and there are several peaks of more than 2,000m. The southern end of the range is much narrower and the mountains, lower; the most prominent southern 'outlier' is Gunung Ledang (Mount Ophir) in Johor. Until just over a century ago, when William Cameron first ventured into the mountains of the Main Range, this was uncharted territory – British colonial Malaya was, in fact, little more than the west coastal strip. Not only was the west coast adjacent to the important trade routes (and therefore had most of the big towns), its alluvial deposits were also rich in tin. Because roads and railways were built along this western side of the peninsula during the colonial period, it also became the heart of the plantation economy.

In addition to the mountain ranges, the Malay peninsula also has many spectacular limestone outcrops. These distinctive outcrops are mainly in the Kuala Lumpur area, such as Batu Caves and those in and around Templer Park, and in the Kampar Valley near Ipoh, to the north. The erosion of the limestone has produced intricate solution-cave systems, some with dramatic formations. The vegetation on these hills is completely different to the surrounding lowland rainforest.

River roads

In Borneo, rivers are often the main arteries of communication. Although roads are being built, linking most main towns, many Dayak (tribal) longhouse communities are only accessible by river. Rivers are the mediators that divide forest dwellers from coastal settlers and this is usually expressed in terms of upriver, or hulu and downstream, or hilir. The two terms are not just geographical; they also reflect different lifestyles and economies, different religions and cultures. In Borneo, to be hulu is to set oneself apart from the Malay peoples of the lowlands and coasts.

Contrary to many assumptions, the tribal hulu peoples were never entirely isolated and self reliant. From early times, there was a flourishing trade between the coasts and the interior. Upriver tribal peoples would exchange exotic jungle products like rattan, benzoin, camphor, skins, hornbill 'ivory', precious stones and rare dyes for products that they could not obtain in the forest – like iron, salt, dried fish (now, tinned fish), betel and gambier. They also bartered for prestige objects like brass gongs, large ceramic Chinese pots, and Dutch silver coins. Many of these prestige objects can still be seen in the longhouses of Borneo and have become precious heirlooms or pusaka.

Malaysia's year-round rainfall has resulted in a dense network of rivers. The peninsula's longest river is the Sungai Pahang, which runs for just over 400 km. Most rivers flood regularly, particularly during the northeast monsoon season, and during the heavy rain the volume of water can more than double in the space of a few hours. It is thought that the flooding of Malaysian rivers has become more pronounced due to logging and mining. Waterfalls are very common features in Peninsular Malaysia; these occur where rivers, with their headwaters in the hills, encounter resistant (usually igneous) rocks as they cut their valleys.

Three countries have territory on Borneo, but only one of them, the once all-powerful and now tiny but oil-rich sultanate of Brunei, is an independent sovereign state in itself. It is flanked to the west by the Malaysian state of Sarawak and to the east by Sabah. Sarawak severs and completely surrounds Brunei. Sabah, formerly British North Borneo, and now a Malaysian state, occupies the northeast portion of Borneo. The huge area to the south is Kalimantan, Indonesian Borneo, which occupies about three-quarters of the island.

Borneo

Borneo is the third largest island in the world after Greenland and New Guinea covering almost 750,000 sq km. During the Pleistocene period, Borneo was joined to mainland Southeast Asia, forming a continent which geologists know as Sundaland. The land bridge to mainland Asia meant that many species, both flora and fauna, arrived in what is now Borneo before it was cut off by rising sea levels. Borneo is part of the Sunda shelf. Its interior is rugged and mountainous and is dissected by many large rivers, navigable deep into the interior. The two biggest rivers, the Kapuas and Mahakam, are both in Kalimantan, but there are also extensive river systems in the East Malaysian states of Sabah and Sarawak. About half of Borneo's land area is under 150m, particularly the swampy south coastal region.

Borneo's highest mountain, Gunung Kinabalu in Sabah (4,101m) is often declared the highest mountain in Southeast Asia (see page 451). Despite this claim being repeated so many times that it has taken on the status of a truth, it isn't: there are higher peaks in Indonesia's province of Irian Jaya and in Myanmar (Burma). Kinabalu is a granite mound called a pluton, which was forced up through the sandstone strata during the Pliocene period, about 15 million years ago. The mountain ranges in the west and centre of the island run east-to-west and curve round to the north-east. Borneo's coal, oil and gas-bearing strata are Tertiary deposits which are heavily folded; most of the oil and gas is found off the northwest and east coasts. The island is much more geologically stable than neighbouring Sulawesi or Java – islands in the so-called 'ring of fire'. Borneo only experiences about four mild earthquakes a year compared with 40-50 on other nearby islands. But because there are no active volcanoes, Borneo's soils are not particularly rich.

Climate

The Malay peninsula has an equatorial monsoon climate. Temperatures are uniformly high throughout the year, as is humidity, and rainfall is abundant and well distributed, although it peaks during the northeast monsoon period from November to February.

Mean annual temperature on the coastal lowlands is around 26°C. The mean daily minima in the lowlands is between 21.7°C and 24.4°C; the mean daily maxima is between 29.4°C and 32.8°C. The maxima are higher and the minima, lower, towards the interior. In the Cameron Highlands, the mean annual temperature is 18°C. Temperatures dip slightly during the northeast monsoon period. The highest recorded temperature, 39.4°C, was taken on Pulau Langkawi in March 1931. The lowest absolute minimum temperature ever recorded on the peninsula was in the Cameron Highlands in January 1937 when the temperature fell to 2.2°C. The Cameron Highlands also claims the most extreme range in temperature – the absolute maximum recorded there is 26.7°C.

The developed west coast of the peninsula is sheltered from the northeast monsoon which strikes the east coast with full force between November and February. The east coast's climatic vagaries have reinforced its remoteness: it is particularly wet and the area north of Kuantan receives between 3,300mm and 4,300mm a year. About half of this falls in the northeast monsoon period. The northwest coast of the peninsula is also wet and parts receive more than 3,000mm of rain a year. Bukit Larut (Maxwell Hill), next to Taiping has an annual rainfall of more than 5,000mm. The west coast receives its heaviest rainfall in March and April. October and April are the transitional months between the southwest and northeast monsoons.

Thunderstorms provide most of Malaysia's rainfall. In the most torrential downpour ever recorded in Kuala Lumpur 51mm of rain fell in 15 minutes. Heavy rain like this causes serious soil erosion in areas which have been cleared of vegetation.

In the more heavily populated coastal districts of the peninsula, the temperature is ameliorated by sea breezes which set in about 1000 and gather force until early afternoon. In the evenings, a land breeze picks up. These winds are only felt for distances up to 15 km inland. Another typical weather feature on the Malay peninsula is the squall, which is a sudden, violent storm characterized by sharp gusts of wind. These can be very localized in their effect, very unpredictable and, from time to time, very hazardous to light fishing vessels. Squalls are caused by cool air either from sea breezes in the late morning or land breezes in the evening undercutting warmer air; squall lines are marked by stacks of cumulo-nimbus clouds. Most squalls occur between May and August; the ones that develop along the west coast between Port Klang and Singapore during this period are called 'Sumatras' and produce particularly violent cloudbursts. Most Sumatras occur at night or in the early morning, while squalls between November and February usually occur in the afternoon.

Borneo   Borneo has a typical equatorial monsoon climate: the weather usually follows predictable patterns, although in recent years it has been less predictable, a phenomenon

Climatic variations: yes, we have no monsoons

One of the problems frustrating Peninsular Malaysia's east coast states in their efforts to promote tourism is the weather. The northeast monsoon starts to blow just as the northern hemisphere's Christmas holidays get underway and antipodeans start thinking about their summer getaways.

Tourism Malaysia says too much is made of the word 'monsoon' and points the finger at Club Med, which owns an idyllic private beach at Cerating in Pahang, for reinforcing the problem by shutting down during the northeast monsoon season. The tourism committee in Northeast Terengganu state has gone as far as to ban the use of the word altogether because they believe it has created a stigma among tourists and investors. They say 'rainy weather' is a perfectly adequate description. Others might consider this an understatement: more than 600 mm of rain has fallen on parts of the east coast within a single day. It also ignores the fact that there are also dry monsoons.

On the other side of the peninsula, however, states occasionally suffer from

too little rain. In 1991, for example, there was a water crisis in Melaka – the worst for 30 years – and on behalf of the state government, the Chief Minister contracted an American company, TJC-Atmos Engineers, to help resolve the problem. The company was promised more than RM3m if it created enough rain to fill the local reservoir. But after claiming to have produced rain on 30 separate occasions over a two month period, Kuala Lumpur's Meteorological Services Department (MSD) dismissed the company's techniques as 'unscientific' and said any rain was a natural consequence of the south-west monsoon.

The director of TJC-Atmos claimed to use 'etheric engineering techniques' to attract clouds, by "manipulating the qi [or subtle life-force] in the atmosphere". He had developed the techniques while investigating Unidentified Flying Objects in the 1950s and described himself as 'a hi-tech bomoh' (Malay witch doctor). The director of the MSD took a dim view of his 'metaphysical' techniques however and TJC-Atmos Engineering left Malaysia empty handed.

some environmentalists attribute to deforestation and others to periodic changes to the El Nino Southern Oscillation. Temperatures are fairly uniform, averaging 23-33°C during the day and rarely dropping below 20°C at night, except in the mountains, where they can drop to below 10°C. Most rainfall occurs between November and January during the northeast monsoon; this causes rivers to burst their banks, and there are many short, sharp cloudbursts. The dry season runs from May to September. It is characterized by dry south-easterly winds and is the best time to visit. Rainfall generally increases towards the interior; most of Borneo receives about 2,000-3,000 mm a year, although some upland areas get more than 4,000 mm.

Flora and fauna

Originally 97 percent of Malaysia's land area was covered in closed-canopy forest. According to the government, about 56 percent of Malaysia is still forested – although it is difficult to ascertain exactly how much of this is primary rainforest. Only five percent of the remaining jungle is under conservation restrictions. The Malaysian jungle, which, at about 130 million years old, is believed to be among the oldest forests in the world, supports more than 145,000 species of flowering plant (well over 1,000 of which are already known to have pharmaceutical value), 200 mammal species, 600 bird species and countless thousands of insect species. The rainforest is modified by underlying rock-type (impervious rocks and soils result in swamp forest)

The universal stimulant – the betel nut

Throughout the countryside in Southeast Asia, and in more remote towns, it is common to meet men and women whose teeth are stained black, and gums red, by continuous chewing of the 'betel nut'. This, though, is a misnomer. The betel 'nut' is not chewed at all: the three crucial ingredients that make up a betel 'wad' are the nut of the areca palm (Areca catechu), the leaf or catkin of the betel vine (Piper betel), and lime. When these three ingredients are combined with saliva they act as a mild stimulant. Other ingredients (people have their own recipes) are tobacco, gambier, various spices and the gum of Acacia catechu. The habit, though also common in South Asia and parts of China, seems to have evolved in Southeast Asia and it is mentioned in the very earliest chronicles. The lacquer betel boxes of Burma and Thailand, and the brass and silver ones of Indonesia and Malaysia, illustrate the importance of chewing betel in social intercourse. Galvao in his journal of 1544 noted: "They use it so continuously that they never take it from their mouths; therefore these people can be said to go around always ruminating". Among Westernized Southeast Asians the habit is frowned upon: the disfigurement and ageing that it causes, and the stained walls and floors that result from the constant spitting, are regarded as distasteful products of an earlier age. But beyond the élite it is still widely practised.

and by altitude (lowland rainforest gives way to thinner montane forest on higher slopes). All the main forest types are represented on the peninsula; these include mangrove swamp forest, peat swamp forest, heath forest, lowland and hill mixed *Dipterocarp* forest and montane forest. Where primary forest has been logged, burned or cleared by shifting cultivators or miners, secondary forest grows up quickly. The fields cultivated by shifting cultivators are known as swiddens – a word which is derived from an old English term meaning 'burnt field'. In Malaysia, the secondary regrowth is known as *belukar*. It can take up to 250 years before climax rainforest is re-established. The pioneer plant species colonizing abandoned *ladang* (sites cleared by shifting cultivators) is called *lalang* (elephant grass).

Borneo's ancient rainforests are rich in flora and fauna, including over 9,000-15,000 species of seed plants (of which almost half may be endemic), 200 species of mammals, 570 species of birds, 100 species of snake, 250 species of freshwater fish and 1,000 species of butterfly. The theory of natural selection enunciated by Victorian naturalist Alfred Russel Wallace – while that other great Victorian scientist Charles Darwin was coming to similar conclusions several thousand miles away – was influenced by Wallace's observations in Borneo. He travelled widely in Sarawak between 1854 and 1862.

Despite years of research the gaps in scientists' knowledge of the island's flora and fauna are becoming ever more yawning

Flora As late as the middle of the 19th century, the great bulk – perhaps as much as 95 percent – of the land area of Borneo was forested. Alfred Russel Wallace, like other Western travellers, was enchanted by the island's natural wealth and diversity: "ranges of hill and valley everywhere", he wrote, "everywhere covered with interminable forest". But Borneo's jungle is disappearing fast and since the mid-1980s there has been a mounting international environmental campaign against deforestation. The campaign has been particularly vocal in Sarawak (see page 384) but other parts of the island are also suffering rapid deforestation, notably Sabah and also Indonesia's province of East Kalimantan. Harold Brookfield, Lesley Potter and Byron state in their hard-headed book *In place of the forest* (1995): Concerning those large areas of forest that have been totally cleared and converted to other uses or that lie waste [in Borneo] A great resource has been squandered, and the

Durian: king of fruits

In Southeast Asia, the durian is widely regarded as the most delicious of fruits – to the horror of many foreign visitors. In his book The Malay Archipelago *(1869), Alfred Russel Wallace describes it in almost orgiastic terms:*

"*The consistence and flavour are indescribable. A rich butter-like custard highly flavoured with almonds gives the best general idea of it, but intermingled with it come wafts of flavour that call to mind cream-cheese, onion sauce, brown sherry and other incongruities. Then there is a rich glutinous smoothness in the pulp which nothing else possesses, but which adds to its delicacy. It is neither acid, or sweet, nor juicy, yet one feels the want of none of these qualities, for it is perfect as it is. It produces no nausea or other bad effect, and the more you eat of it the less you feel inclined to stop. In fact to eat Durian is a new sensation, worth a voyage to the East to experience.*"

major part of the habitat of a great range of plant and animal species has been destroyed. Moreover, this has been done with far less than adequate economic return to the two nations [Malaysia and Indonesia] concerned.

How extensive has been the loss of species as a result of the logging of Borneo's forests is a topic of heated debate. Brookfield *et al* in the volume noted above suggest that there "is very little basis in firm research for the spectacular figures of species loss rates that appear not infrequently in sections of the conservationist literature and that readily attract media attention." But they do admit that the flora and fauna of Borneo is especially diverse with a high degree of endemism and that there has been a significant loss of biodiversity as a result of extensive logging. It has been estimated that 32 percent of terrestrial mammals, 70 percent of leaf beetles, and 50 percent of flowering plants are endemic to Borneo; in other words, they are found nowhere else.

The best-known timber trees fall into three categories, all of them hardwoods. Heavy hardwoods include *selangan batu* and *resak*; medium hardwoods include *kapur*, *keruing* and *keruntum*; light hardwoods include *madang tabak*, *ramin* and *meranti*. There are both peat-swamp and hill varieties of meranti, which is one of the most valuable export logs. *Belian*, or Bornean iron wood (*Eusideroxylon zwageri*) is one of the hardest and densest timbers in the world. It is thought that the largest belian may be 1,000 years or more old. They are so tough that when they die they continue to stand for centuries before the wood rots to the extent that the trunk falls. On average, there are about 25 commercial tree species per ha, but because they are hard to extract, 'selective logging' invariably results in the destruction of many unselected trees.

The main types of forest include: **lowland rainforest** (mixed dipterocarp) predominates up to 600m. Dipterocarp forest is stratified into three main layers, the top one rising to heights of 45m. In the top layer, trees' crowns interlock to form a closed canopy of foliage. The word 'dipterocarp' comes from the Greek and means 'two-winged fruit' or 'two [di]-winged [ptero] seed [carp]'. The leaf-like appendages of the mature dipterocarp fruits have 'wings' which makes them spin as they fall to the ground, like giant sycamore seeds. Some species have more than two wings but are all members of the dipterocarp family. It is the lowland rainforest which comes closest to the Western ideal of a tropical 'jungle'. It is also probably the most species rich forest in Borneo. A recent study of a dipterocarp forest in Malaysia found that an area of just 50 ha supported no less than 835 species of tree. In Europe or North America a similar area of forest would support less than

Background

Fields in the forest – shifting cultivation

Shifting cultivation, also known as slash-and-burn agriculture or swiddening, is one of the characteristic farming systems of Southeast Asia. It is a low-intensity form of agriculture, in which land is cleared from the forest through burning, cultivated for a few years and then left to regenerate over 10-30 years. It takes many forms, but an important distinction can be made between shifting field systems where fields are rotated but the settlement remains permanently sited, and migratory systems where the shifting cultivators shift both field (swidden) and settlement. The land is usually only rudimentarily cleared, tree stumps being left in the ground, and seeds sown in holes made by punching the soil with a dibble stick.

For many years, shifting cultivators were regarded as 'primitives' and their methods were contrasted unfavourably with 'advanced' settled rice farmers. Many government officials in Southeast Asia continue to adhere to this mistaken belief, arguing that shifting cultivators are the principal cause of forest loss and soil erosion.

Shifting cultivators have an intimate knowledge of the land, plants and animals on which they depend. One study of a Dayak tribe, the Kantu' of Kalimantan (Borneo), discovered that households were cultivating an average of 17 rice varieties and 21 other food crops each year in a highly complex system. Even more remarkably, Harold Conklin's classic 1957 study of the Hanunóo of the Philippines – a study which is a benchmark for such work even today – found that the Hanunóo identified 40 types and subtypes of rocks and minerals when classifying different soils. The shifting agricultural systems are usually also highly productive in labour terms, allowing far more leisure time than farmers using permanent field systems.

But shifting cultivation contains the seeds of its own extinction. Extensive, and geared to low population densities and abundant land, it is coming under pressure in a region where land is becoming an increasingly scarce resource, where patterns of life are dictated by an urban-based élite, and where populations are pressing on the means of subsistence.

100 tree species. The red resin produced by many species of dipterocarp, and which can often be seen staining the trunk, is known as *damar* and was traditionally used as a lamp 'oil'. Another characteristic feature of the trees found in lowland dipterocarp rainforest is buttressing, the flanges of wood that protrude from the base of the trunk. For some time the purpose of these massive buttresses perplexed botanists who arrived at a whole range of ingenious explanations. Now they are thought, sensibly, to provide structural support. Two final characteristics of this type of forest are that it is very dark on the forest floor (explaining why trees take so long to grow) and that it is not the impenetrable jungle of Tarzan fantasy. The first characteristic explains the second. Only when a gap appears in the forest canopy, after a tree falls, do light-loving pioneer plants get the chance to grow. When the gap in the canopy is filled by another tree, these grasses, shrubs and smaller trees die back once more.

Many of the rainforest trees are an important resource for Dayak communities. The jelutong tree, for example, is tapped like a rubber tree for its sap ('jungle chewing gum') which is used to make tar for waterproof sealants – used in boat-building. It also hardens into a tough but brittle black plastic-like substance used for *parang* (machete) handles.

Montane forest occurs at altitudes above 600m, although in some areas it does not replace lowland rainforest until considerably higher than this. Above 1,200m mossy forest predominates. Montane forest is denser than lowland forest with smaller trees of narrower girth. Moreover, dipterocarps are generally not found while flowering shrubs like magnolias and rhododendrons appear. In place of dipterocarps, tropical latitude oaks as well as other trees that are more characteristic of temperate areas, like myrtle and laurel, make an appearance. Other familiar flora of lowland forest, like lianas, also disappear while the distinctive pitcher plant (Nepenthes) become common.

The low-lying river valleys are characterized by **peat swamp** forest, where the peat is up to 9m thick, which makes wet-rice agriculture impossible.

Heath forest or *kerangas* – the Iban word meaning 'land on which rice cannot grow' – is found on poor, sandy soils. Although it mostly occurs near the coast, it is also sometimes found in mountain ranges, but almost always on level ground. Here trees are stunted and only the hardiest of plants can survive. Some trees have struck up symbiotic relationships with animals – like ants – so as to secure essential nutrients. Pitcher plants (Nepenthes) have also successfully colonized heath forest. The absence of bird calls and other animal noises make heath forest rather eerie, and it also indicates their general biological poverty.

Along beaches there are often stretches of **casuarina forest**; the casuarina grows up to 27m, and looks like a conifer, with needle-shaped leaves. **Mangrove** occupies tidal mud flats around sheltered bays and estuaries. The most common mangrove tree is the *bakau* (*Rhizophora*) which grows to heights of about 9m and has stilt roots to trap sediment. Bakau wood is used for pile-house stilts and for charcoal. Further upstream, but still associated with mangrove, is the *nipah* palm (*Nipa fruticans*), whose light-green leaves come from a squat stalk; it was traditionally of great importance as it provided roofing and wickerwork materials.

Mammals The continual development of forested areas has destroyed many habitats in recent years. The biggest mammal in Malaysia and Asia is the Asiatic elephant. Adult elephants weigh up to three to four tonnes; they are rarely seen, although the carnage caused by a passing herd can sometimes be seen in Taman Negara National Park. For more detail on elephants. Borneo's wild elephants pose a zoological mystery. They occur only at the far northeast tip of the island, at the furthest possible point from their Sumatran and mainland Southeast Asian relatives. No elephant remains have been found in Sabah, Sarawak or Kalimantan. It is known that some animals were introduced into Sabah – then British North Borneo – by early colonial logging concerns and certainly that there were already populations established in the area. Another theory has it that one of the sultans of Sulu released a small number of animals several centuries ago. The difficulty with this explanation is that experts find it difficult to believe that just a handful of elephants could have grown to the 2,000 or so that existed by the end of the last century. Some zoologists speculate that they were originally introduced at the time of the Javan Majapahit Empire, in the 13th and 14th centuries. Antonio Pigafetta, an Italian historian who visited the Sultanate of Brunei as part of Portuguese explorer Ferdinand Magellan's expedition in July 1521, tells of being taken to visit the sultan on two domesticated elephants, which may have been gifts from another ruler.

It is possible, however, that elephants are native to Borneo and migrated from the Southeast Asian mainland during the Pleistocene when sea levels were lower and land-bridges would have existed between Borneo and the mainland. Their concentration in northeast Borneo could be explained by the presence of numerous salt-licks between the Sandakan and Lahad Datu areas of Sabah. This would make the present population a relic of a much larger group of elephants. Borneo's male elephants are up to 2.6m tall; females are usually less than 2.2m. Males' tusks can grow up to 1.7m in length and weigh up to 15 kg each. Mature males are solitary creatures, only joining herds to mate. The most likely places to see elephants

Fauna

Background

in the wild are the Danum Valley Conservation Area (see page 478) and the lower Kinabatangan basin (see page 475), both in Sabah.

Orang utan (*Pongo pygmaeus*): Walt Disney's film of Rudyard Kipling's *Jungle Book* made the orang utan a big-screen celebrity, dubbing him "the king of the swingers" and "the jungle VIP". Borneo's great red-haired ape is also known as 'man of the jungle', after the translation from the Malay: orang (man), utan (jungle). The orang utan is endemic to the tropical forests of Sumatra and Borneo although at the beginning of the historic period it was distributed from tropical China to Java. The Sumatran animals tend to keep the reddish tinge to their fur, while the Bornean ones go darker as they mature. It is Asia's only great ape; it has four hands, rather than feet, bow-legs and has no tail. The orang utan moves slowly and deliberately, sometimes swinging under branches, although it seldom travels far by arm-swinging. Males of over 15 years old stand up to 1.6m tall and their arms span 2.4 m. Adult males (which make loud roars) weigh 50-100 kg – about twice that of adult females (whose call sounds like a long, unattractive belch). Orang utans are said to have the strength of seven men but they are not aggressive. They are peaceful, gentle animals, particularly with each other. Orang utans have bluey-grey skin and their eyes are close together, giving them an almost human look. Males develop cheek pouches when they reach maturity, which they fill with several litres of air; this is exhaled noisily when they demarcate territory.

Orang utans mainly inhabit riverine swamp forests or lowland dipterocarp forests. Their presence is easily detected by their nests of bent and broken twigs woven in much the same fashion as a sun bear's, in the fork of a tree. They are solitary animals and always sleep alone. Orang utans have a largely vegetarian diet consisting of fruit and young leaves, supplemented by termites, bark and birds' eggs. They are usually solitary but the young remain with their mothers until they are five or six years old. Two adults will occupy an area of about 2 sq km and are territorial, protecting their territory against intruders. They can live up to 30 years and a female will have an average of three to four young during her lifetime. Females reach sexual maturity between seven and nine years, and the gestation period is nine months. Female orang utans usually have only one young at a time although twins and even triplets have been recorded. After giving birth, they do not mate for around another seven years.

THE ORAN = OOTAN

The 'Oran-ootan' as remembered by an early European visitor

Source: Beeckman, David (1718) A Voyage to and from the island of Borneo

Estimates of the numbers of orang utan vary considerably. One puts the figure at 10,000-20,000 animals; another at between 70-100,000 in the wild in Borneo and Sumatra. Part of the difficulty is that many are thought to live in inaccessible and little researched areas of peat swamp. But this is just a very rough estimate, based on one ape for each 1½ sq km of forest. No one, so far, has attempted an accurate census. What is certain is that the forest is disappearing fast, and with it the orang utan's natural habitat. Orang utans' favoured habitat is lowland rainforest and this is particularly under threat from logging. The black market in young apes in countries like Taiwan means that they fetch relatively high returns to local hunters. At the

Background

village level an orang utan might command US$100; in local markets, around US$350; and at their international destination, along with all the necessary forged export permits, travel costs and so on, from US$5,000 to as much as US$60,000.

Monkeys: the five species of monkeys found in Malaysia are the long-tailed macaque, pig-tailed macaque, and three species of leaf monkey (langur) – the banded, dusky and silvered varieties. Malaysia's cutest animal is the little slow loris, with its huge sad eyes and lethargic manner; among the most exotic is the flying lemur, whose legs and tail are joined together by a skin membrane. It parachutes and glides from tree to tree, climbing each one to find a new launch-pad.

Little research has been done on proboscis monkeys; they are notoriously difficult to study as they are so shy

The proboscis monkey (*Nasalis larvatus*) is an extraordinary-looking animal, endemic to Borneo, which lives in lowland forests and mangrove swamps all around the island. Their fur is reddish-brown and they have white legs, arms, tail and a ruff on the neck, which gives the appearance of a pyjama-suit. Their facial skin is red and the males have grotesquely enlarged, droopy noses; females' noses are shorter and upturned. The male's nose is the subject of some debate among zoologists: what ever else it does, it apparently increases their sex-appeal. To ward off intruders, the nose is straightened out, "like a party whoopee whistle", according to one description. Recently a theory has been advanced that the nose acts as a thermostat, helping to regulate body temperature. But it also tends to get in the way: old males often have to resort to holding their noses up with one hand while stuffing leaves into their mouths with the other.

Proboscises' penises are almost as obvious as their noses – the proboscis male glories in a permanent erection, which is probably why they are rarely displayed in zoos. The other way the males attract females is by violently shaking branches and making spectacular – and sometimes near-suicidal – leaps into the water, in which they attempt to hit as many dead branches as they can on the way down, so as to make the loudest noise possible. The monkeys organize themselves into harems, with one male and several females and young – there are sometimes up to 20 in a group. Young males leave the harem they are born into when the adult male becomes aggressive towards them and they rove around in bachelor groups until they are in a position to form their own harem.

Proboscis monkeys belong to the leaf monkey family, and have large, pouched stomachs to help digest bulky food – they feed almost entirely on the leaves of one tree – the *Sonneratia*. The proboscis is a diurnal animal, but keeps to the shade during the heat of the day. The best time to see them is very early in the morning or around dusk. They can normally be heard before they are seen: they make loud honks, rather like geese; they also groan, squeal and roar. Proboscis monkeys are good swimmers; they even swim underwater for up to 20m – thanks to their partially webbed feet. Males are about twice the size and weight of females. They are known fairly ubiquitously (in both Malaysian and Indonesian Borneo) as 'Orang Belanda', or Dutchmen – which is not entirely complimentary. In Kalimantan they also have other local names including *Bekantan*, *Bekara*, *Kahau*, *Rasong*, *Pika* and *Batangan*.

Other monkeys found in Borneo include various species of leaf monkey – including the grey leaf monkey, the white-fronted leaf monkey, and the red leaf monkey. One of the non-timber forest products formerly much prized was bezoar stone which was a valued cure-all. Bezoars are green coloured 'stones' which form in the stomachs of some herbivores, and in particular in the stomachs of leaf monkeys. Fortunately for the leaf monkeys of Southeast Asia though, these stones – unlike rhino horn – are no longer prized for their medicinal properties. One of the most attractive members of the primate family found in Borneo is the tubby slow loris or *kongkang*. And perhaps the most difficult to pronounce – at least in Dusun – is the tarsier which is locally known as the *tindukutrukut*.

The ape family includes the white-handed gibbon (known locally as *wak-wak*), the dark-handed gibbon (which is rarer) and *siamang*, which are found in more mountainous areas.

Background

Rhinoceros: the two-horned Sumatran rhinoceros, also known as the hairy rhinoceros, is the smallest of all rhinos and was once widespread throughout Sumatra and Borneo. The population has been greatly reduced by excessive hunting. The horn is worth more than its weight in gold in Chinese apothecaries, and that of the Sumatran rhino is reputedly the most prized of all. But the ravages of over-hunting have been exacerbated by the destruction of the rhino's habitat. Indeed, until quite recently it was thought to be extinct on Borneo. Most of Borneo's remaining wild population is in Sabah, and the Malaysian government is attempting to capture some of the thinly dispersed animals to breed them in captivity, for they remain in serious danger of extinction (see page 473).

Other mammals: one of the strangest Malayan mammals is the tapir, with its curled snout – or trunk – and white bottom. The starkly contrasting black and white is good camouflage in the jungle, where it is effectively concealed by light and shade. Young tapirs are dark brown with light brown spots, simulating the effect of sun-dappled leaf-litter.

Other large mammals include the common wild pig and the bearded pig, and the *seladang* (or gaur) wild cattle; the latter live in herds in deep jungle. There are two species of deer on the Malay peninsula: the *sambar* (or *rusa*) and the *kijang* (barking deer); the latter gets its English name from its dog-like call. The mouse deer (*kanchil* and *napoh*) are not really deer; they are hoofed animals, standing just 20 cm high. The mouse deer has legendary status in Malay lore – for example, the Malay Annals tell of Prince Parameswara's decision to found Melaka on the spot where he saw a mouse deer beat off one of his hunting dogs (see page 205). Despite their reputation for cunning, they are also a favoured source of protein.

Malaysia's most famous carnivore is the tiger – *harimau* in Malay. Tigers still roam the jungle in the centre of the peninsula, and on several occasions have made appearances in the Cameron Highlands, particularly during the dry season, when they move into the mountains to find food. Other members of the cat family are the clouded leopard and four species of wild cat: the leopard cat, the golden cat, the flat-headed cat and the marbled cat. Other jungle animals include the Malayan sun bear (which have a penchant for honey), the *serigala* (wild dog), civet cats (of which there are many different varieties), mongooses, weasels and otters.

Malaysia has several species of fruit bats and insect-eating bats, but the best-known insect-eater is the pangolin (scaly anteater), the animal world's answer to the armoured car. Its scales are formed of matted hair (like rhinoceros horn) and it has a long thin tongue which it flicks into termite nests. More common jungle mammals include rodents, among which are five varieties of giant flying squirrels. Like the flying lemur, these glide spectacularly from tree to tree and can cover up to about 500m in one 'flight'.

Other large mammals include the **banteng**, a wild cattle known as the *tembadau* in Sabah. These are smaller than the *seladang* of Peninsular Malaysia, and are most numerous in lowland areas of eastern Sabah where herds are encountered on country roads. The **bearded pig** is the only member of the pig family found in Borneo and is a major source of meat for many Dayak groups. Of the **deer family**, Borneo supports two species of barking deer or *kijang*, and the Greater (*npau*) and Lesser mouse deer. The latter barely stands 30 cm tall.

Birds   In ornithological circles, Malaysia is famed for its varied bird-life. The country is visited by many migratory water birds, and there are several wetland areas where the Malayan Nature Society has set up birdwatching hides; the most accessible to Kuala Lumpur is the Kuala Selangor Nature Park (see page 88). Migratory birds winter on Selangor's mangrove-fringed mudflats from September to May. There are also

The Iban Hornbill Festival

One of the main Iban festivals is Gawai Kenyalang, *or the Hornbill Festival. The* kenyalang – *a carved wooden hornbill – traditionally played an important part in the ceremony which preceded head-hunting expeditions, and the often ornate, brightly painted images also made appearances at other gawais, or festivals. The kenyalang is carved from green wood and the design varies from area to area. A carved hornbill can be about 2 m long and 1 m high and is stored until a few days before the festival, when it is painted, bringing the carving to life. It is carried in procession and offered* tuak *(rice wine), before being mounted on a carved base on the tanju, the longhouse's open verandah. As the singing gets underway, the*

kenyalang is adorned with specially woven pua kumbu *(see page 407) and then raised off the ground to face enemy territory. Its soul is supposed to attack the village's enemies, destroying their houses and crops.*

Kenyalong, hornbill image
From Roth, Henry (1896) The Natives of Sarawak and British North Borneo, *Truslove & Hansen: London*

spectacular birds of prey, the most common of which are the hawk eagles and brahminy kites. Among the most fascinating and beautiful jungle species are the crested firebacks, a kind of pheasant; the kingfisher family, with their brilliantly coloured plumage; the hornbills (see below); greater racquet-tailed drongos – dark blue with long, sweeping tails; and black-naped orioles, saffron-coloured lowland residents. There are also wagtails, mynas, sunbirds, humming birds (flower-peckers), bulbuls, barbets, woodpeckers and weaver-birds.

Hornbill There are nine types of hornbill on Borneo, the most striking and biggest of which is the rhinoceros hornbill (*Buceros rhinoceros*) – or *kenyalang*. They can grow up to 1.5m long and are mainly black, with a white belly. The long tail feathers are white too, crossed with a thick black bar near the end. They make a remarkable, resonant "GERONK" call in flight, which can be heard over long distances; they honk when resting. Hornbills are usually seen in pairs – they are believed to be monogamous. After mating, the female imprisons herself in a hole in a tree, building a sturdy wall with her own droppings. The male bird fortifies the wall from the outside, using a mulch of mud, grass, sticks and saliva, leaving only a vertical slit for her beak. She remains incarcerated in her cell for about three months, during which the male supplies her and the nestlings with food – mainly fruit, lizards, snakes and mice. Usually, only one bird is hatched and reared in the hole and when it is old enough to fly, the female breaks out of the nest hole. Both emerge looking fat and dirty.

The 'bill' itself has no known function, but the males have been seen duelling in mid-air during the courting season. They fly straight at each other and collide head-on. The double-storeyed yellow bill has a projection, called a casque, on top, which has a bright red tip. In some species the bill develops wrinkles as the bird matures: one wrinkle for each year of its life. For this reason they are known in Dutch, and in some eastern Indonesian languages as 'year birds'.

Most Dayak groups consider the hornbill to have magical powers and the feathers are worn as symbols of heroism. In tribal mythology the bird is associated with the creation of mankind, and is a symbol of the upper world. The best place to see hornbills is near wild fig trees – they love the fruit and play an important role in seed

The hornbill is the official state emblem of Sarawak

Background

dispersal. The helmeted hornbill's bill is heavy and solid and can be carved, like ivory. These bills were highly valued by the Dayaks, and have been traded for centuries. The third largest hornbill is the wreathed hornbill which makes a yelping call and a loud – almost mechanical – noise when it beats its wings. Others species on Borneo include the wrinkled, black, bushy-crested, white-crowned and pied hornbills.

Reptiles   The kings of Malaysia's reptile population are the giant leatherback turtles (see page 284), hawksbill and green turtles (see page 471); there are several other species of turtle and three species of land tortoise. The most notorious reptile is the estuarine crocodile (*Crocodilus porosus*) – which can grow up to 8 m long. The largest population of estuarine crocodiles are found in the lower reaches of Borneo's rivers. However, they have been so extensively hunted that they are rarely a threat, although people do very occasionally still get taken. The Malayan gharial (*Tomistoma schlegeli*) is a fish-eating, freshwater crocodile which grows to just under 3m. Lizards include common house geckos (*Hemidactylus frenatus* – or *cikcak* in Malay), green-crested lizards (*Calotes cristatellus*), which change colour like chameleons, and flying lizards (*Draco*), which have an extendable undercarriage allowing the lizard to glide from tree to tree. Monitors are the largest of Malaysian lizards, the most widespread of which is the common water monitor (*Varanus salvator*), which can grow to about 2½ m.

The Malaysian jungles also have 140 species of frogs and toads, which are more often heard than seen. Some are dramatically coloured, such as the appropriately named green-backed frog (*Rana erythraea*) and others have particular skills, such as Wallace's flying frog (*Rana migropalmatus*) which parachutes around on its webbed feet.

Of Malaysia's 100-odd land snakes, only 16 are poisonous; all 20 species of sea snake are poisonous. There are two species of python, the reticulated python (*Python reticulatus*) – which can grow to nearly 10m in length and has iridescent black and yellow scales – and the short python (*Python curtus*), which rarely grows more than 2.5m and has a very thick, rusty-brown body. Most feared are the venomous snakes, but the constrictors can also pose a threat to humans.

Among the most common non-poisonous snakes is the dark brown house snake (*Lycodon aulicus*) which likes to eat geckos, and the common Malayan racer (*Elaphe flavolineata*), which grows to about 2 m and is black with a pale underbelly. The most beautiful non-poisonous snakes are the paradise tree snake (*Chrysopelea paradisi*), which is black with an iridescent green spot on every scale and the mangrove snake (*Boiga dendrophilia*) which grows to about 2 m long and is black with yellow stripes. The former is famed for its gliding skills: it can leap from tree-to-tree in a controlled glide by hollowing its underbelly, trapping a cushion of air below it. In the jungle it is quite common to see the dull brown river snake which goes by the unfortunate name of the dog-faced water snake (*Cerberus rhynchops*); it has a healthy appetite for fish and frogs.

The most feared venomous snake is the king cobra (*Naja hannah*) which grows to well over 4m long and is olive-green with an orange throat-patch. They are often confused with non-poisonous rat snakes and racers. The king cobra eats snakes and lizards – including monitor lizards. Its reputation as an aggressive snake is unfounded but its venom is deadly. Both the king cobra and the common cobra (*Naja naja*) are hooded; the hood is formed by loose skin around the neck and is pushed outwards on elongated ribs when the snake rears to its strike posture.

Other poisonous snakes are the banded krait (*Bungarus fasciatus*) with its distinctive black and yellow stripes and the Malayan krait (*Bungarus candidus*) with black and white stripes. Kraits are not fast movers and are said to bite only under extreme provocation. Coral snakes (of the genus *Maticora*) have extremely poisonous venom,

Nepenthes – the jungle's poisoned chalice

There are about 30 species of insectivorous pitcher plants in Malaysia; they come in all shapes and sizes – some are bulbous and squat, some are small and elegant, others are huge and fat. All are killers, and are among the handful of insect-eating plants in the world. Pitcher plants grow on poor soils, either in the mountains or in heath (kerangas) forest. The Malay name for the Nepenthes family is periuk kera – or 'monkey cups'. The Chinese call them after the tall wicker baskets used to take pigs to market – shu long cao. The plants remain sealed until they have begun to secrete the fluids which help them supplement their meagre diet. One of these liquids is sweet and sticky and attracts insects; the other, which builds up at the bottom, digests

each victim which ventures in. The 'lid' opens invitingly when the plant is ready for business and it is virtually impossible for insects to escape – the pitcher plant's waxed interior offers little traction for the uphill climb and the upper lips, past the overhanging ridge, are serated and very slippery. This plant amazed the first Europeans to visit the Malay archipelago. George Rumphius, the German naturalist, thought it one of nature's freaks when he travelled through the region at the end of the 17th century. Two centuries later, the British naturalist, Frederick Burbridge, wrote that seeing the plants "was a sensation I shall never forget – one of those which we experience but rarely in a whole lifetime".

but because the snake virtually has to chew its victim before the venom can enter the bite (its poison glands are located at the very back of its mouth), there have been no recorded fatalities. Pit vipers have a thermo-sensitive groove between the eye and the nostril which can detect warm-blooded prey even in complete darkness. The bite of the common, bright green Wagler's pit viper (*Trimeresurus wagleri*) is said to be extremely painful, but is never fatal. They have broad, flattened heads; adults have yellow bars and a bright red tip to the tail.

Insects

Malaysia has a literally countless population of insect species; new ones are constantly being discovered and named. There are 120 species of butterfly in Malaysia. The king of them is the male Rajah Brooke's birdwing (*Troides brookiana*) – the national butterfly – with its iridescent, emerald zig-zag markings on jet-black velvety wings. It was named by Victorian naturalist Alfred Russel Wallace after his friend James Brooke, the first White Rajah of Sarawak (see page 394). The males can be found along rivers while the much rarer females (which are less spectacularly coloured), remain out of sight among the treetops.

There are more than 100 other magnificently coloured butterflies, including the black and yellow common birdwing, the swallowtails and swordtails, the leaf butterflies (which are camouflaged as leaves when their wings are folded) such as the blue and brown saturn and the rust, white and brown tawny rajah. Among the most beautiful of all is the delicately patterned Malayan lacewing (*Cethosia hypsea*) with its jagged markings of red, orange, brown and white. There are several butterfly farms around the country, including in Kuala Lumpur (see page 89), Penang (see page 173) and the butterfly capital of Malaysia, the Cameron Highlands (see page 132).

The most spectacular moths are the huge atlas moth (*Attacus atlas*) and the swallow-tailed moth (*Nyctalemon patroclus*); these can be found on exterior walls illuminated by strip-lights late at night, particularly in remoter parts of the country.

The Malaysian beetle population is among the most varied in the world. The best known is the rhinoceros beetle (*Oryctes rhinoceros*), which can grow to nearly 6cm in length and is characterized by its dramatic horns. The empress cicada (*Pomponia imperatoria*) is the biggest species in Malaysia and can have a wingspan of more than

Background

👉 Fireflies – flashers in the forest

There are plenty of fireflies (Lampyridae) in Malaysia. But the ones which sit in the trees along the Selangor River, to the west of Kuala Lumpur, are special. They flash in synch – thousands of them go on and off like Christmas-tree lights. Although there are a few reported instances of this happening elsewhere in Southeast Asia, Kampong Kuantan, near Kuala Selangor (see page 88), is the best place to witness the phenomenon, which many visitors suspect is a clever electric hoax. The Lampyrid beetle which exhibits the synchrony is the Pteroptyx malaccae, which grows to about 9mm in length and emits flashes at the rate of just over one per second. In the days before batteries, villagers used to put the fireflies in bottles to serve as torches. Because they stick to the same trees – which are chosen because they are always free of keringga weaving ants (see below) – local fishermen are said to use them as navigational beacons. Only the males are synchronous flashers, and scientists have yet to come up with an explanation for their behaviour. The females, which are the first to settle in the trees, shortly after sunset, emit a dimmer light, and the males, which fly around the water level as it gets dark, join the females which respond to their flashes. The light is produced by cells on the firefly's lower abdomen.

20cm. The male cicada is the noisiest jungle resident. The incredible droning and whining noises are created by the vibration of membranes in the body, the sound of which is amplified in the body cavity.

One of the most famous insects is the praying mantis. In *Malayan animal life*, MWF Tweedie writes: "They owe their name to the deceptively devotional appearance of their characteristic pose, with the fore legs held up as if in prayer. In reality the mantis is, of course, waiting for some unwary insect to stray within reach; if it does, the deadly spined fore limbs will strike and grasp and the mantis will eat its victim alive, daintily, as a lady eats a sandwich." There are several other species of mantis, and the most intriguing is the flower mantis (*Hymenopus coronatus*) which is bright pink and can twist and extend itself to resemble a four-petalled flower, a camouflage which protects it from predators, while attracting meals such as bees.

Of the less attractive insect life, it is advisable to be wary of certain species of wasps and hornets. The most dangerous is the slender banded hornet (*Polistes sagittarius*) which is big (3cm long) and has a black and orange striped abdomen. Its nests are paper-like, and hang from trees and the eaves of houses by a short stalk. They are extremely aggressive and do not need to be provoked before they attack. The golden wasp (*Vespa auraria*) is found in montane jungle – notably the Cameron Highlands, and, like the hornet above, will attack anything coming near its nest. The wasp is a honey-gold colour, it nests in trees and shrubs and its sting is vicious. There are several other wasp species which attack ferociously, and stings can be extremely painful. One of the worst is the night wasp (*Provespa anomala*), which is an orangy-brick colour and commonly flies into houses at night, attracted by lights. Bee stings can also be very serious, and none more so than that of the giant honey bee, which builds pendulous combs on overhanging eaves and trees. It is black with a yellow mark at the front end of the abdomen; multiple stings can be fatal.

Another insect species to be particularly wary of is the fire ant (*Tetraponera rufonigra*). It has a red body and a big black head; it will enthusiastically sting anything it comes into contact with, and the pain is acute. Weaver ants (*Oecophylla smaragdina*) are common but do not sting. Instead, their powerful jaws can be used as jungle sutures to stitch up open wounds. The bites alone are very painful, and the ant (which is also known as the *kerengga*) adds insult to injury by spitting an acidic fluid on the

Environment – mud-slinging in the greenhouse

Malaysia is spending US$10m a year on a slick public relations counter offensive to the anti-tropical timber lobby in the West. That's a lot of money, until compared with the US$4.5bn it earns every year from its trees. For the past decade, Malaysia has been the world's biggest exporter of tropical timber.

But the bald figures disguise the fact that the export of raw logs has been reduced by about half in recent years, in line with Malaysia's policy of sustainable forestry management. In 1991 a government minister defended Malaysia's logging policy by saying that "it's not our responsibility to supply the West with oxygen." But things have changed since then and the government has gone green. While continuing to expose Western hypocrisy in environmental matters, Malaysia has done much to clean up its own back yard. Most importantly, it has undertaken to reduce log production to sustainable levels, following apocalyptic warnings of what might happen if it didn't.

Malaysia now claims to be practising selective logging techniques (see page 384), felling a maximum of seven to 12 trees per hectare. Critics have long alleged, however, that Malaysia's forestry laws are being flouted by illegal loggers and corrupt timber concessionaires. The government's answer to these allegations was the introduction in 1993 of tough new laws involving heavy fines and lengthy custodial sentences for poachers and illegal loggers. Concessionaires, whose ranks include sultans and senior politicians, are now liable for the same fines and sentences. Forest rangers will be empowered to arrest and will have the back-up of the police and the army.

The government insists that its stricter policies were not motivated by pressure

from the West. It simply says that it would not be so stupid or greedy as to kill the goose that lays the golden egg and it maintains that sustained-yield harvesting means its forests will be there in perpetuity.

The government has long railed against Western nations for their double standards over the environment. Its line is that because industrialized countries have already cleared their forests in the name of development, why shouldn't Malaysia be free to do the same? At the Earth Summit in Rio de Janeiro in June 1992, the Prime Minister, Dr Mahathir Mohamad, noted that poor countries have been told to preserve their forests and other genetic resources for research purposes. He said: "This is the same as telling these countries that they must continue to be poor because their forests and other resources are more precious than the people themselves". In the wake of Rio, hopes that a new global environment fund would help cover the costs of enforcing environmental protection, have been dashed. Dr Mahathir says Western countries have reneged on their undertaking.

There are still holes in Malaysia's forestry policies; adequately policing large tracts of forest against illegal loggers is impossible. Local environmental groups continue to call for greater accountability and a crackdown on corruption. A small élite of extremely wealthy, corrupt and powerful men still control much of the timber trade. But even the government's critics concede that great strides have been made in environmental protection. Until the rest of the world recognizes this, the government has sworn to keep making its point: that the people who created the greenhouse effect should not be throwing stones.

Background

bite. It is difficult to extract the pincers from the skin, and once attached, the ant will not let go. The biggest of all ants, the giant ant (*Camponotus gigas*), can be nearly 3cm in length; (it is also variously known as the elephant ant and the 'big-bum ant'). They are largely nocturnal, however, so tend to cause less trouble in the jungle.

Peninsular Malaysia is malaria-free, although the Aedes, tiger mosquito, is a daytime mosquito that carries dengue fever

Other jungle residents worth avoiding are the huge, black, hairy *Mygalomorph* spiders, whose bodies can be about 5 cm long. Their painful bites cause localized swelling. Scorpions are dangerous but not fatal. The biggest scorpion, the wood scorpion (*Hormurus australasiae*) can grow to about 16cm long; it is black, lives under old logs and is mainly nocturnal. In rural areas, the particularly paranoid might shake their shoes for the spotted house-scorpion (*Isometrus maculatus*), which is quite common. Centipedes (*Chilopoda*) have a poisonous bite and can grow up to about 25cm in length.

The environmental costs of growth

As Malaysia has become more wealthy, and the middle class has burgeoned, so environmental concerns have gained greater prominence. In 1993 the Department of the Environment released figures revealing that of Peninsular Malaysia's 116 major rivers, 85 were either 'biologically dead' or 'dying'. Air quality is also a source of concern, especially in the Klang Valley, an agglomeration of industrial activity around Kuala Lumpur. Environmental Impact Assessments (EIAs) are now, in theory, compulsory for every development project, but most companies undertake to do them only grudgingly, if at all. The claim that, as a developing country, Malaysia can ill-afford the 'luxury' of such things is wearing very thin as wealth spreads with each year of eight percent growth. The government recognizes that the environment is fast becoming a political issue, and like any good political party is trying to climb aboard the bandwagon.

Most accounts of Malaysia's environmental problems – some would characterize it as a 'crisis' – concentrate on the East Malaysian states of Sarawak and Sabah. In a sense the peninsula is a lost cause: deforestation has been so extensive that the only large areas remaining are already gazetted as national parks. In East Malaysia, though, there is a sense that if only logging could be better controlled then the natural wealth of Malaysian Borneo could be preserved.

The haze

The Air Pollution Index reached 851 on September 24, 1997; a figure of 300 is considered 'hazardous'

For years now, Malaysia (and Singapore) has had to deal with what is locally called 'the haze': a choking fog that reduces visibility to no more than a few metres and causes severe health problems. The source of the haze is the fires that seasonally devastate huge areas of Sumatra and Indonesian Borneo. These were most serious in 1997, but have returned, at varying levels of seriousness, almost every year since.

In 1997 the government seriously contemplated evacuating the entire population of the East Malaysian state of Sarawak – more than two million people – but wondered where to put them. The airport in Kuching was closed and residents rushed to stockpile water and basic necessities. Schools, factories and government offices stayed shut as the smog became a threat to health. Fishermen did not venture out on the seas. Visibility became so bad that people stopped using their vehicles. A state of emergency was declared and people advised to stay indoors.

The source of the fires is Indonesia where loggers, estate managers and shifting cultivators use burning to clear land for cultivation. Though this is now illegal the Indonesian government lacks the resources to police. The failure to introduce a coherent zoning policy or to control car emissions has been attacked. There is little doubt that the pollution from cars and industry has combined with the smoke from the fires to produce a particularly unpleasant concoction leading to eye irritation, asthma attacks, headaches and breathing difficulties. In 1994 the Malaysian cabinet was presented with a Clean Air Action Plan but it was rejected because of fears that it might undermine the country's industrialization efforts. During the fires of 2000 Malaysian Environment Minister, Datuk Law Hieng Ding, asked the local media not to dwell upon the air-quality index because it might keep tourists away. While the Malaysian government may have been in denial, many residents were dusting off their face masks and visibility in the Straits of Melaka was so poor that the Malaysian marine police put out navigation warnings.

Background

What may be remarkable to many westerners was the time it took before the politics of blame took hold. Former President Suharto of Indonesia apologized to his fellow Asean nations at an environment conference in September 1997, but criticism from Malaysia and Singapore, the two countries most affected after Indonesia, was astonishingly muted. It was the media in the two countries, chivvied on by an irate public making their feelings known through newspaper letter columns and radio talk shows, that encouraged the governments of Malaysia and Singapore to take a more forthright stance.

Nothing much changes, it seems, when it comes to the haze. In July 2001 the haze was back – albeit not as seriously as during 1997 – and new Forestry Minister Marzuki Usman was saying much the same as his predecessors: Indonesia doesn't have the money, the personnel or the plans to deal with the fires. The inaction and the lack of accountability is beginning to get to Indonesia's neighbours. On July 15, 2001 Singapore's *Straits Times* demanded 'firm action', 'collection action' and a 'regional solution'. The newspaper even suggested that the United Nations might take a role.

Books

Malaysia

Burgess, Anthony: Burgess lived in Malaysia between 1954 and 1957, learnt Malay, and mixed with the locals to a far greater extent than Maugham or Conrad, and this is reflected in a much more nuanced understanding of the Malay character. After leaving Malaya in 1957, he taught in Brunei until 1960. Among his books are Time for a Tiger (1956), *The Enemy in the Blanket* (1958) and *Beds in the East* (1959) which were later published together by Penguin as *Malayan Trilogy*.

Novels

    Conrad, Joseph: Perhaps the finest novelist of the Malay archipelago, books include Lord Jim, the tale of Jim, who abandons his ship and seeks refuge from his guilt in Malaya, earning in the process the sobriquet Lord, and *Victory*, arguably Conrad's finest novel, based in the Malay Archipelago. Both are widely available in paperback editions from most bookshops. Also worth reading is *The Rescue*, Penguin: London. Set in the Malay Archipelago in the 1860s; the hero, Captain Lingard, is forced to choose between his Southeast Asian friend and his countrymen.

    Keith, Agnes *Land below the Wind* (1969) Ulverscroft: Leicester. Perhaps the best-known English language book on Sabah.

    Maniam, KS *The Return* (1983) Skoob Books: London. The novel, by a Indian Malaysian, is about the difficulties a Hindu has in finding a home in Malaysia, especially since the Indian in question is educated at a British colonial school.

    Maugham, William *Somerset Maugham's Malaysian Stories* (1969) Heinemann: London and Singapore. Another English novelist who wrote extensively on Malaysia. These stories are best for the insight they provide of colonial life, not of the Malay or Malay life.

    Theroux, Paul *The Consul's File* (1979) Penguin. A selection of short stories based on Malaysia.

Bird, Isabella *The Golden Chersonese* (1883 and reprinted 1983) Murray: London, reprinted by Century paperback. The account of a late 19th century female visitor to the region who shows her gumption facing everything from natives to crocs.

Travel

    Bock, Carl *The Headhunters of Borneo* (1985, first published 1881) OUP: Singapore. Bock was a Norwegian naturalist and explorer and was commissioned by the Dutch to make a scientific survey of southeastern Borneo. His account, though, makes much of the dangers and adventures that he faced, and some of his 'scientific' observations are, in retrospect, clearly highly faulty. Nonetheless, this is an entertaining account.

Background

Charles, Hose *The Field Book of a Jungle Wallah* (1985, first published 1929) OUP: Singapore. Hose was an official in Sarawak and became an acknowledged expert on the material and non-material culture of the tribes of Sarawak. He was one of that band of highly informed, perceptive and generally benevolent colonial administrators.

King, Victor T (edit) *The Best of Borneo Travel* (1992) OUP: Oxford. A compilation of travel accounts from the early 19th century through to the late 20th. An excellent companion to take while exploring the island. Published in portable paperback.

Mjoberg, Eric *Forest Life and Adventures in the Malay Archipelago*, OUP: Singapore.

O'Hanlon, Redmond *Into the Heart of Borneo* (1984) Salamander Press: Edinburgh. One of the best recent travel books on Borneo. This highly amusing and perceptive romp through Borneo in the company of poet and foreign correspondent James Fenton, includes an ascent of the Rejang River and does much to counter the more romanticized images of Bornean life.

History Harrisson, Tom *World Within* (1959) Hutchinson: London. During the Second World War, explorer, naturalist and ethnologist Tom Harrisson was parachuted into Borneo to help organize Dayak resistance against the occupying Japanese forces. This is his extraordinary account.

Barber, Noel *The War of the Running Dogs: Malaya 1948-1960* (1971) Arrow Books. This is one of numerous accounts of the Malayan Emergency and the successful British efforts to defeat the Communist Party of Malaya.

Turnbull, Mary C *A History of Malaysia, Singapore and Brunei* (1989) Allen and Unwin. A very orthodox history of Malaysia, Singapore and Brunei, clearly written for a largely academic/student audience.

Chapman, F Spencer *The Jungle is Neutral*. An account of a British guerrilla force fighting the Japanese in Borneo – not as enthralling as Tom Harrisson's book, but still worth reading.

Payne, Robert *The White Rajahs of Sarawak*. Readable account of the extraordinary history of this East Malaysian state.

Natural history Briggs, John *Mountains of Malaysia: a Practical Guide and Manual* (1988) Longman: London. Briggs has also written Parks of Malaysia, useful for anyone intending to especially visit the country's protected areas (Longman: Kuala Lumpur).

Cranbrook *Earl of Riches of the Wild: Land Mammals of South-East Asia* (1987) Oxford University Press.

Cubitt, Gerald and Payne Junaidi *Wild Malaysia* (1990) London: New Holland. Large format, coffee table book, lots of wonderful colour photos, reasonable text, short background piece on each national park.

Hanbury-Tenison, Robin *Mulu, the Rain Forest* (1980) Arrow/Weidenfeld. This is the product of a Royal Geographical Society trip to Mulu in the late 1970s; semi-scholarly and useful.

Payne, Junaidi et al *Pocket Guide to Birds of Borneo*, World Wildlife Fund/Sabah Society.

Payne, Junaidi et al *A Field Guide to the Mammals of Borneo*, World Wildlife Fund/Sabah Society. Good illustrations, reasonable text, but very dry.

Tweedie, MWF and Harrison, JL *Malayan Animal Life* (1954 with new editions) Longman.

Wallace, Alfred Russel *The Malay Archipelago* (1869). A classic of Victorian travel writing by one of the finest naturalists of the period. Wallace travelled through all of island Southeast Asia over a period of some years. The original is now re-printed.

Other books Leee, Kit *Adoi* (1989) Times Books: Singapore. An amusing book of Malaysian attitudes to most things.

Craig, Jo Ann *Culture Shock Malaysia*. One in a series of Culture Shock books, this examines and assesses the do's and don'ts of Malaysian and Singapore society. Useful for those going to live or spend an extended period in the region.

Lat: Lat is Malaysia's foremost cartoonist. His images of the effects of social and economic change on a simple kampung boy are amusing and highly perceptive. His cartoons are compiled in numerous books including *Kampung boy* and *Town boy*, published by Straits Times Publishing.

Books on Malaysia and the wider Southeast Asian region

Buruma, Ian *God's Dust*, (1989), Jonathan Cape: London. Enjoyable journey through Burma, Thailand, Malaysia and Singapore along with the Philippines, Taiwan, South Korea and Japan; journalist Buruma questions how far culture in this region has survived the intrusion of the West.

Caufield, C *In the Rainforest*, (1985) Heinemann: London. This readable and well-researched analysis of rainforest ecology and the pressures on tropical forests is part-based in the region.

Dingwall, Alastair *Traveller's Literary Companion to South-east Asia*, (1994) In Print: Brighton. Experts on Southeast Asian language and literature select extracts from novels and other books by Western and regional writers. The extracts are annoyingly brief, but it gives a good overview of what is available.

Fraser-Lu, Sylvia *Handwoven Textiles of South-East Asia*, (1988), OUP: Singapore. Well-illustrated, large-format book with informative text.

King, Ben F and Dickinson, EC *A Field Guide to the Birds of South-East Asia*, Collins: London. (1975). Best regional guide to the birdlife of the region.

Osborne, Milton *Southeast Asia: an Introductory History*, (1979), Allen & Unwin: Sydney. Good introductory history, clearly written, published in a portable paperback edition and recently revised and reprinted.

Reid, Anthony *Southeast Asia in the Age of Commerce 1450-1680*, Yale University Press: New Haven. (1988 and 1993). Perhaps the best history of everyday life in Southeast Asia, looking at such themes as physical well-being, material culture and social organization; meticulously researched.

Sesser, Stan *The Lands of Charm and Cruelty: Travels in Southeast Asia*, Picador: Basingstoke. (1993). A series of collected narratives first published in the *New Yorker* including essays on Singapore, Laos, Cambodia, Burma and Borneo. Finely observed and thoughtful, the book is an excellent travel companion.

Young, Gavin *In Search of Conrad*, Hutchinson: London. (1991). This well-known travel writer retraces the steps of Conrad; part travel-book, part fantasy, it is worth reading but not up to the standard of his other books.

Pentes, Tina and Truelove, Adrienne (1984) *Travelling with Children to Indonesia and South-East Asia*, Hale & Iremonger: Sydney. Wheeler, Maureen *Travel with Children*, Lonely Planet: Hawthorne, Australia.

Further information

A decent map is an indispensable aid to travelling. Although maps are usually available locally, it is sometimes useful to buy a map prior to departure to plan routes and itineraries.

Maps & guides

Regional maps Bartholomew Southeast Asia (1:5,800,000); Nelles Southeast Asia (1:4,000,000); Hildebrand Thailand, Burma, Malaysia and Singapore (1:2,800,000); ITM (International Travel Map) Southeast Asia.

Country maps Bartholomew Singapore and Malaysia (1:150,000); Nelles Malaysia (1:1,500,000); Nelles West Malaysia (1:650,000); Nelles Singapore (1:22,500); Nelles Indonesia (1:4,000,000).

City maps Nelles Singapore; Bartholomew Singapore.

Background

Other maps   Tactical Pilotage Charts (TPC, US Airforce) (1:500,000); Operational Navigational Charts (ONC, US Airforce) (1:500,000). Both of these are particularly good at showing relief features (useful for planning treks); less good on roads, towns and facilities.

Locally available maps   Maps are widely available in Malaysia and Singapore. Both the Singapore and Malaysian tourist boards produce good maps of their respective capital cities and in the case of Malaysia a series of state maps, rather poorer in quality. The Sabah and Sarawak tourist boards also publish reasonable maps.

Map shops   In London, the best selection is available from Stanfords, 12-14 Long Acre, London WC2E 9LP, T020-78361321; also recommended is McCarta, 15 Highbury Place, London N15 1QP, T020-73541616.

Malaysia Nelles Map; Shell Map of Malaysia (available from Shell stations in Malaysia). Concertina Road Maps – Peninsular Malaysia and Sabah, Sarawak and Brunei, published by Falcon Press.

Singapore

10

Singapore

*To some, it has all the ambience of a supermarket
checkout lane. It has even been described as a
Californian resort-town run by Mormons. It has
frequently been dubbed sterile and dull - a report in* The
Economist *judged Singapore to be the most boring city
in the world and for those who fail to venture beyond the
plazas that line Orchard Road, or spend their 3½ days
on coach-trips to the ersatz cultural extravaganzas, this
is not surprising. But there is a cultural and architectural
heritage in Singapore beyond the one which the
government tries so hard to manufacture. Despite its
brash consumerism and toytown mentality, Singapore is
certainly not without its charm.*

*Singapore is difficult to fathom, especially from afar.
Beneath its slick veneer of westernized modernity, many
argue that Singapore's heart and soul are Asian. Behind
the computers, hi-tech industries, marble, steel and
smoked-glass tower blocks, highways and shopping
centres is a society ingrained with conservative
Confucian values.*

*For those stopping over in Singapore for just a few days
– en route, as most of the island's tourists are, to
somewhere else – there are several key sights that should
not be missed. Many who visit, however, consider that it
is far more important to enjoy the food. The island has
an unparalleled variety of restaurants to suit every
palate and wallet. Hawker centres in particular are a
highly recommended part of the Singapore epicurean
experience – they are inexpensive, and many are open
into the early hours.*

Essentials

Planning your trip

Where to go
*For those planning
on staying more than
a few days Footprint's
Singapore Handbook
offers comprehensive
coverage*

Singapore is a city state with a land area of just under 650 sq km. Moreover, public transport in the city is impeccably quick and efficient, so nowhere is exactly 'off the beaten track'. It is possible to get a good feel for the place and to enjoy many of Singapore's places of interest on a week-long stay. That said, if you stop over for just a weekend, expect to leave wondering why you didn't plan to remain a little longer. Singapore is also a nifty jumping off point for exploring neighbouring Malaysia and Indonesia. Indeed, parts of Peninsular Malaysia, including the historic city of Melaka and the Indonesian islands of the Riau archipelago, are accessible on a day trip. Below is a slightly contrived – and by no means exhaustive – attempt to pigeonhole and categorize Singapore's attractions.

The popular image of Singapore as a city state is that it is so well managed that it has lost its charm and erased its history. This is not true and there is a great deal here to interest those with a historic bent. The best **historic sights** in the central colonial core include the Asian Civilisations Museum, the Singapore History Museum and the Battle Box in Fort Canning Park. Slightly further afield are Fort Siloso, Images of Singapore and Surrender Chambers, which are all on Sentosa Island. Changi Prison and the Kranji War Memorial and Cemetery are also worth visiting.

In the 1960s and 1970s, as its leaders tried to create a new modern post-colonial Singapore, a large slice of the republic's colonial heritage was bulldozed to make way for apartment blocks and the other accoutrements of modernity. Fortunately, and not a demolition ball's swing too soon, the government realized that in cleaning up the city it was also in danger of erasing its heart. Singapore's diverse **architectural styles** are reflected in everything from the grandeur of the colonial core to skyscrapers towering over the shophouses of Chinatown, as well as individual buildings like the golden-domed Sultan Mosque and the impressively garish Kong Meng San Phor Kark (see page 631).

Singapore is a great place to bring young **children**. It is clean, safe and efficient, there are good hospitals, you can drink the water, drivers take notice of pedestrian crossings – all in all it is a child-friendly and parent soothing place to visit. There are also a multitude of places to see, including the Singapore Philatelic Museum, the Children's Discovery Centre of the Singapore History Museum, Sentosa, Haw Par Villa, Jurong Bird Park, Science Centre, Singapore Discovery Centre, East Coast Park, Singapore Zoological Gardens and the Night Safari.

Singaporeans have taken **shopping** to their hearts and to new heights. While the city is not the bargain basement place it was – don't come with empty suitcases waiting to be filled with goodies – it is still a great place to browse and buy with care. The advent of the air-conditioned shopping plaza means there is no need to work up a sweat while losing your wealth.

The tigers have gone and the largest creature left alive, aside from *Homo sapiens*, is the wild pig, hanging on by its trotters on some outlying islands. But there are **parks**, **gardens** and a great **zoo**; the Botanic Gardens and National Orchid Garden, Underwater World, Sentosa, Jurong Bird Park, the Chinese and Japanese Gardens, Singapore Zoological Gardens, Sungei Buloh Nature Reserve, Bukit Timah Nature Reserve and Pulau Ubin.

While most people leave Singapore with some unnecessary plastic object to be quickly discarded, the memory that often lingers the longest is of the **gastronomic delights** the place has to offer. With such a medley of people – Chinese, Malay, Indian and European – considerable victual buying power, and a seemingly unquenchable desire to snack and binge, Singapore must have one of the greatest concentrations of eateries on the planet. Not only is cleanliness a by-word in Singapore (the Delhi quick-step doesn't make it here), but it is also possible to get a great meal for just a few dollars (or a few hundred). Come with a willingness to give your taste buds a good gallop.

There is no best season to visit Singapore and it is hot throughout the year. It gets even stickier before the monsoon breaks in November, while the hottest months are July and August. The wettest months are November, December and January, during the period of the north-east monsoon, when it is also coolest – but even 'cool' days are hot by most temperate people's standards. As one would expect, the hottest time of day is early afternoon when the average temperature is around 30°C, but even during the coolest time of the day, just before dawn, the temperature is still nearly 24°C.

When to go
For daily weather reports, T5427788 and www.gov.sg/metsin/ forecast.html

The Singapore Tourism Board is a useful place to contact. They produce a good free official guide called *New Asia-Singapore*, as well as pamphlets detailing hotels, restaurants and so on. Their website has regularly updated information on hotels, festivals and other tourist-related information – www.newasia-singapore.com

Finding out more

Useful websites Websites offer a whole range of information on a vast variety of topics. Below is only a selection. Note that websites in Asia are multiplying like rabbits and this makes searching a sometimes frustrating business.

www.technofind.com.sg The largest search engine for Singapore websites, updated daily. It covers just about every topic including tourism and is a good place to start hunting.

www.sg The Singapore Infomap site which has website directories covering everything from leisure and entertainment to the economy, and from the National Heritage Board to Singapore's limitless choice of cuisine.

www.asiatravel.com/singapore.html Asia Travel's website is useful for hotel reservations, weather reports, the very latest travel information and exchange rates, and also has a map detailing some places of interest.

asnic.utexas.edu/ asnic.htm The website for the Asian Studies Network Information Center at the University of Texas has information on the history and politics of Singapore.

www.A20.com.sg A relatively new site, with information on Singapore's past; maps, photographs, building plans, government speeches, files and documents.

www.singnet.com.sg/~leeahkee/ Good links to government, educational, travel, employment, leisure and food sites.

singaporeeverything.com/ A good general Singapore site covering most things – shopping, entertainment, jobs and more.

www.yahoo.com/Regional Countries/[name of country] Insert country name to access information, including material from other travel guides.

www.city.net/regions/asia Pointer to information on Asian countries.

www.branch.com:80/silkroute/ Information on hotels, travel, news and business in Asia.

www.agora.stm.it/politic Information on political parties and organizations; good links, by country or by region.

www.aseansec.org Home page of the Asean Secretariat, the Southeast Asian regional organization of which Singapore is a founder member. Lots of government statistics, acronyms etc.

www.ste.com.sg Provides a bulletin board for businesses to post notices and advertisements and market their products; also a directory of licensed travel agents in Singapore.

Singapore

www.singstat.gov.sg/ For the truly pedantic – a site devoted to statistics regarding Singapore.

www.cia.gov/cia/publications/factbook/geos/sn.html The CIA's factbook on Singapore. Good source of general background information and statistics.

Disabled travellers

Singapore is the most wheel-chair friendly city in Southeast Asia

The Singapore Council of Social Services publishes *Access Singapore*, a guidebook especially for physically impaired visitors, Copies can be picked up from the SCSS offices at 11 Penang Lane, T3361544, or by post from *National Council for Social Service*, Disabled Service Department, 11 Penang Lane, Singapore 238485. Their offices are open 0900-1300, 1400-1800 Mon-Fri. Additional information can be found at the Global Access-Disabled Travel Network Site, www.geocities.com/Paris/1502

Gay & lesbian travellers

Singapore is a pretty straight place. There are two clauses in Singapore's penal code that deal with homosexual sex, namely: Section 377: 'Whosoever voluntarily has carnal intercourse against the order of nature with any man, woman or animal, shall be punished with imprisonment for life, or with imprisonment for a term which may extend to 10 years, and shall also be liable to a fine'; and Section 377(a): 'Any male person who, in public or private, commits or abets the commission of or procures the commission by any male person of, any act of gross indecency with another male person, shall be punished with imprisonment for a term which may extend to two years'. However, it is not illegal to be gay. The law only criminalizes the homosexual act, not the homosexual person. Notwithstanding these two clauses in the penal code, there are a good number of handy websites for gay and lesbian visitors and a fairly active gay scene. Check out the following: www.plu-singapore.com (a site with lots of background information on homosexuality in Singapore, but not much on the gay scene); and www.utopia-asia.com/tipssing.htm (the best site giving details on what's happening, where and when).

Student travellers

Student travellers will find Singapore a generally expensive place and not one where being a student will lead to great savings on entrance fees or public transport.

Travelling with children

Singapore is one of the most child-friendly cities in Asia. Not only is it safe and clean, with world-class medical facilities, but there are also lots of things for children to do. With stacks of places to eat, drink and snack, a very efficient transport system and lots of air-conditioned refuges to cool off, you shouldn't be put off bringing little people to the miniscule republic. Just bear in mind that if children are not used to the tropical heat it can be exhausting – so don't expect them to keep going for a full day, and make sure they are regularly topped up with fluids and coated in sun protection.

The attractions that children are likely to find most enthralling (tested by Joshua and Ella, aged seven and five) are: the Singapore Philatelic Museum (for stamp-mad youngsters); Sentosa (especially Underwater World and Fantasy Island); the Haw Par Villa (gruesome and weirdly entertaining for quirkier children); the Jurong Bird Park (excellent); the Science Centre (lots of hands-on exhibits and a great movie theatre); the Singapore Discovery Centre (not bad, especially for boys who like martial toys); and the superb Singapore Zoological Gardens and Night Safari. The Singapore Infomap for Kids at www.sg/kids/link.htm lists child-oriented attractions, and also has good entertainment and educational resources. Another good site is *Travel for Kids* at www.travelforkids.com/Funtodo/Singapore/singapore.htm A useful book is *Singapore for Kids: A Parent's Guide*, by Supka, Nicola (S$14.95, ISBN 9812321276).

Women travellers

Singapore is safe and it is rare for women to be harassed. Unlike some neighbouring countries, it is not considered peculiar for young women to travel alone. There is no need for any special precautions.

Before you travel

Visitors must possess a passport valid for at least six months, a confirmed onward/return ticket, sufficient funds to support themselves in Singapore and, where applicable, a visa.

Visas & immigration
For Singapore embassies worldwide, see page 657.
For the latest visa information, check www.mha.gov.sg/sir

No visa is required for citizens of the Commonwealth, USA or Western Europe. On arrival in Singapore by air, citizens of these countries are granted a one-month visitor's permit. Tourists entering Singapore via the causeway from Johor Bahru in Malaysia or by sea are allowed to stay for 14 days. Nationals of most other countries (except India, China and the Commonwealth of Independent States) with confirmed onward reservations may stop over in Singapore for up to 14 days without a visa. It is necessary to keep the stub of your immigration card until you leave.

Nationals of the following countries require visas before entering Singapore: Afghanistan, Algeria, Armenia, Azerbaijan, Bangladesh, Belarus, Burma, Cambodia, China, Estonia, Georgia, Hong Kong, India, Iraq, Jordan, Kazakhstan, Kyrgyzstan, Lao PDR, Latvia, Lebanon, Libya, Lithuania, Russia, Syria, Tajikistan, Tukmenistan, Tunisia, Ukraine, Uzbekistan, Vietnam and Yemen.

Visas can be extended for up to three months at the Singapore Immigration Head Office, Singapore Immigration Building, 10 Kallang Road, Singapore 208718, T1800-3916400 (toll free information line) . Applicants need to supply: 1) A completed Form 14, Form V3a and Data Amendment Card, all obtainable from the Visit and Visa Section of the Immigration Head Office. 2) A completed form V75 if the application is being made on medical grounds. 3) An onward/return ticket. Processing the application takes a minimum of one day. Alternatively, it can be just as easy to nip across the causeway to Johor Bahru (in Malaysia) and then re-enter Singapore on a two-week permit.

Immigration Department Singapore Immigration Head Office, Singapore Immigration Building, 10 Kallang Road, Singapore 208718, T3916100.

Duty-free allowance One litre of liquor, one litre of wine or port, one litre of beer or stout. Note that because of the government's strict anti-smoking policy, there is no duty free allowance for tobacco.

Customs
Singapore is a duty-free port

Currency There is no limit to the amount of Singapore and foreign currency or travellers' cheques you can bring in or take out.

Export restrictions There is no export duty, but export permits are required for arms, ammunition, explosives, animals, gold, platinum, precious stones and jewellery, poisons and drugs. No permit is needed for the export of antiques.

Narcotics are strictly forbidden in Singapore and, as in neighbouring Malaysia, trafficking is a capital offence which is rigorously enforced. Dawn hangings at Changi prison are regularly reported and Singapore has the highest execution rate per head of population in the world. Trafficking in more than 30 g of morphine or cocaine, 15 g of heroin, 500 g of cannabis or 200 g of cannabis resin and 1.2 kg of opium is punishable by death. In 1998 ecstasy was also added to the list of drugs that carry the mandatory death penalty. Those convicted of lesser drug-related offences face 20-30 years in Changi prison and 15 strokes of the rotan, a punishment devised by the British colonial administration. Passengers arriving from Malaysia by rail may have to march, single-file, past sniffer dogs.

Prohibited items

In 1992, the Singapore government banned the importation and sale of chewing gum, after the MRT Corporation claimed the substance threatened the efficient running of its underground trains. Chewing tobacco, toy currency, pornographic material and seditious literature are also prohibited items.

Singapore

Vaccinations Certificates of vaccination against cholera and yellow fever are necessary for those coming from endemic areas within the previous six days. Otherwise, no certificates are required for Singapore. There is no longer any malarial risk on the island, although sometimes there are outbreaks of dengue fever. Vaccination services are available at the Tan Tock Seng Hospital, Moulmein Road, T3595958 or 3595929 (telephone beforehand).

What to take It is not necessary to arrive in Singapore laden down with products that you think will be unavailable. With one or two exceptions, like chewing gum and toy guns, everything is easily purchased in Singapore and, more often than not, more cheaply than at home. Treat travelling to Singapore as you would travelling to Munich, Manchester, Minneapolis or Melbourne. Bring what you seriously shouldn't leave behind, but don't consider bringing the kitchen sink let alone a six-month supply of dental floss.

Money

Currency
For exchange rates, see inside the front cover or any major newspaper or www.oanda.com/ converter/classic

Local currency is dollars and cents. Bank notes are available in denominations of S$2, 5, 10, 20, 50, 100, 500, 1,000 and 10,000. Coins are in 1, 5, 10, 20 and 50 cent and 1 dollar denominations. In March 2002, the Singapore dollar was valued at S$1.82 to US$1. Brunei currency is interchangeable with Singapore currency; the Malaysian Ringgit is not.

It is possible to change money at banks, licensed money changers and hotels – although a service charge may be added. Licensed money changers often give better rates than banks. Singapore is one of the most plastic-friendly countries in the region and there are ATMs (cashpoint machines), seemingly, on every street corner. Cash can be withdrawn using a credit card or Cirrus card providing you have a PIN. Singapore is a major regional banking centre, so it is relatively easy to get money wired from home. Bank opening hours: 0930-1500 Mon-Fri, 0930-1130 Sat. There is no black market.

Credit cards Most of Singapore's hotels, shops, restaurants and banks accept the major international credit cards, and many cash machines allow you to draw cash on *Visa* or *MasterCard*. After bargaining, expect to pay at least 3% for credit card transactions; most shops insist on this surcharge although you do not have to pay it. **Notification of credit card loss** *American Express*, T2998133; *Diners Card*, T2944222; *MasterCard*, T5332888; *Visa Card*, T1-800-3451345.

Tax Visitors can claim back their 3% Goods and Services Tax from shops displaying the 'Tax Free for Tourists' sign when they spend S$300 or more. A claim form is issued and this is then presented at customs on leaving the country, when visitors are reimbursed. It is also possible to claim by post; the refund is paid either by bank cheque or to a credit card account. The Singapore Tourism Board publishes a brochure, *Tax refund for visitors to Singapore*.

Getting there

Air
For airport information see page 582

If you want to work out connections with specific cities, the Changi website has a useful flight planning facility. Type in your city of origin and – wham! – it will show the flights, airlines and routes available: www.changi.airport.com.sg/flight_schedules/flisch_ctnt.htm

Changi Airport is the region's busiest and best connected and most major airlines fly here. Around 60 airlines service Singapore, flying to and from 149 destinations. These include from North America: *American Airlines, Continental, Northwest Airlines* and *United*. From Europe: *Air France, British Airways, Finnair, KLM, Lufthansa, SAS*, and *THY Turkish Airlines*. From Australia and New Zealand: *Air New Zealand, Ansett Australia* and *Qantas*. From the Middle East and South Asia: *Air India,*

Air Madagascar, Air Mauritius, Biman Bangladesh, Egypt Air, Emirates, Gulf Air, Indian Airlines, PIA, Royal Nepal Airlines, Saudi Arabian Airlines and *Sri Lankan Airlines*. From East Asia: *Air China, All Nippon Airways, Asiana Airlines, Cathay Pacific, China Airlines, China Eastern, China Southern, China Southwest, China Yunnan, EVA, JAL* and *Korean Airways*.

From Southeast Asia As an international crossroads, Singapore is within easy reach of all key points in the region and there are flights to Changi Airport from destinations throughout Southeast Asia. Regional airlines that serve Changi, by country, are: Brunei, *Royal Brunei Airlines*; Cambodia, *Royal Air Cambodge*; Indonesia, *Bouraq* and *Garuda*; Malaysia, *MAS*; Myanmar, *Myanmar Airways International*; Philippines, *Philippine Airlines*; Singapore, *SIA* and *Silk Air*; Thailand, *Bangkok Airways, PB Air* and *Thai*; Vietnam, *Vietnam Airlines*.

Tickets to Southeast Asian destinations are subject to minimum selling price restrictions imposed by a cartel of regional airlines. It is still possible to get special deals to selected destinations from discount travel agents and Singapore's *Yellow Pages*, but tickets bought in Bangkok and Penang are generally cheaper. The Singapore-Kuala Lumpur air shuttle (operated jointly by *SIA* and *MAS*) runs every hour from Changi Terminal 2. Singapore-KL shuttle tickets can be bought on a first-come-first-served basis at Changi Airport, and are only available on standby; arrive 1½-2 hours beforehand, S\$130. For return flights to Kuala Lumpur, just buy a single ticket as it is cheaper to purchase tickets in Malaysia.

If you can afford the time, then it is usually cheaper to take a bus or train to Kuala Lumpur in Malaysia and buy long-haul flights there. It is also much cheaper when flying between Singapore and other points in Malaysia to use Johor Bahru's airport across the causeway. Johor Bahru is well connected to the Malaysian domestic network. Chartered express coaches ply between Singapore and JB airport; they leave Singapore from the *Novotel Orchid Inn* on Dunearn Road, but are reserved for MAS passengers only, S\$12 (adult), S\$10 (children). The courier ensures express clearance of Malaysian customs and immigration. Details from *MAS* office in Singapore: 190 Clemenceau Avenue, T3366777. Likewise, for those wishing to fly to destinations in Indonesia, it is cheaper to take the ferry to the Indonesian island of Batam (see page 580) and then catch a domestic flight from there. However, for most people the saving in fares will probably not outweigh the additional hassle.

From Malaysia Bus There are bus services to Singapore from a number of towns in **Road** Malaysia. These include: Kuala Lumpur (S\$17), Melaka (S\$11), Butterworth (S\$30), Mersing (S\$11), Kota Bahru (S\$30), Kuantan (S\$17), Ipoh (S\$27) and Penang (S\$30). (The fares quoted here are from Singapore – tickets bought in Malaysia are cheaper.) Most long-distance buses arrive at the Lavender Street Terminal at the junction of Lavender Street and Kallang Bahru. However, the Singapore-KL Express arrives at the Ban San Terminal on Queen Street. From Johor Bahru's Larkin Bus Terminal and from the train station, express bus 170 offers a quick and efficient service to Singapore. Buses leave every 6-10 minutes or so (more frequently during peak hours), but note that boarding in JB is only permitted at Larkin and the train station. The service crosses the Tuas Causeway, pauses at the Woodlands immigration point for customs formalities, stops at Singapore's Ban San Terminal at the northern end of Queen Street (at the junction with Arab Street; see map, page 620), and then runs along Rochor Road and Bukit Timah Road to Woodlands Road. The journey from JB takes about an hour (and costs S\$2.40), including customs and immigration formalities at the border. There is also the rather more luxurious JB-Singapore Express, which departs from the Larkin Bus Terminal for the Ban San Terminal every 10 minutes.

If leaving Singapore for destinations in Malaysia then note that buses to more distant destinations like Butterworth, Kota Bahru and Ipoh tend to leave in the late afternoon. It is best to book tickets a few days ahead of departure, especially if intending to travel over a holiday period. The Singapore-KL Express from the Ban San Terminal on Queen Street leaves at 0900, 1300, 1700 and 2200 (S$25). Again, it is best to book a couple of days ahead.

Long-distance bus companies are: *Singapore-Johor Bahru Express*, T2928149; *Kuala Lumpur-Singapore Express*, T2928254; *Malacca-Singapore Express*, T2935915.

Taxis Rather than taking a bus, it is possible to catch a long-distance taxi from Malaysia to Singapore. However, this usually requires a change of vehicle in Johor Bahru. (In other words, it is necessary to take a taxi from, say, Melaka, Kuantan, KL or Butterworth to JB, and then another taxi on to Singapore.) From JB there are scores of taxis to the Rochor Road terminus (S$6 per person, but if you need a full cab, S$24).

From Thailand As well as buses from destinations in Malaysia, there are also long-distance services from Bangkok and Hat Yai in Thailand. These obviously route their journeys through Malaysia. Services from Thailand arrive at the Golden Mile Complex on Beach Road and fares from Singapore are S$35 to Hat Yai (S$45 for VIP coach) and S$70 to Bangkok. There are several agents selling tickets close to the station. Note that if you are leaving Singapore for Thailand, then it is cheaper to book a ticket to Hat Yai and then pay for the rest of the journey in Thai baht; or even cheaper still to catch a bus to JB, one from JB to Hat Yai, and then a third from Hat Yai to Bangkok.

Sea A small fraction of Singapore's visitors arrive in the world's busiest port by ship, although cruising has become fashionable again and sea arrivals are growing by nearly 50% a year. Passenger lines serve Singapore from Australia, Europe, USA, India and Hong Kong. Ships either dock at the World Trade Centre or anchor in the main harbour with a launch service to shore. Entry requirements are the same as those described on page 577. *Star Cruises*, T7336988, F7333622, are one of the biggest companies operating in the region. *Orient Lines*, *Pearl Cruises*, *Seabourn Cruise Lines*, *Silversea Cruises* and *Seven Seas Cruise Lines* also dock at Singapore. A timetable of all shipping arrivals and departures is published daily in the *Shipping Times* (a section of the *Business Times*). According to some travellers, freighter operators are reasonably amenable to marine hitchers who want lifts to Vietnam (although it is difficult to enter Vietnam by sea), the Philippines or Indonesia.

From Indonesia and Malaysia There are regular high-speed ferry connections between **Singapore** and **Indonesia's Riau islands** of Batam (Sekupang and Batu Ampar) and Bintan (Tanjung Pinang and Loban). Return fares to Batam vary from S$20 to S$28 (45 minutes journey time), ferries leave from the World Trade Centre, south of town. Ferries to Bintan leave from Tanah Merah ferry terminal (East Coast), and cost S$42 return (1½ hours). From the Riau islands it is possible to travel by boat to Sumatra or by air to many other destinations in Indonesia (cheaper than flying direct from Singapore). It is also possible to take a high-speed catamaran from Tanah Merah to Pulau Tioman, off the east coast of Peninsular Malaysia, 4½ hours (S$90 one-way, S$148-168 return), but Penguin ferries do not operate during the rainy season between October and March. Ferry operators have their offices in the Singapore Cruise Centre, on the second level of the World Trade Centre, and include *Auto Batam*, World Trade Centre, T5427105; *Dino Shipping*, T2760668; *Penguin Ferries*, T5427105; and *Widi Express*, T2727540. Auto Batam and Penguin are the two companies that operate ferries to Bintan and Pulau Tioman (Malaysia). Intending passengers should arrive at the terminal one hour before departure if they do not already have a booked ticket.

Singapore

There is also a ferry from Changi Ferry Terminal to Tanjung Belungkor, east of Johor Bahru in Malaysia. Most people use this service to get to the beach resort of Desaru. Passengers S$19 (S$26 return); cars S$20; journey time 45 minutes. Ferry times 0815, 1115, 1415 and 1715, Singapore to Tanjung Belungkur; 0945, 1245, 1545 and 1845, Tanjung Belungkor to Singapore. Contact **Ferrylink Pte**, T5453600 or 7336744 for reservations. To get to the terminal, take bus 2 to Changi Village and then a taxi.

If travelling from Tanjung Belungkur to Singapore, fares are considerably cheaper (payable in Ringgit)

It is possible to enter Singapore from Malaysia by bumboat from Johor Bahru (S$5), Tanjung Pengileh or Tanjung Surat (S$6) in southern Johor to Changi Point, on the northeast tip of Singapore – a good way of beating the bottleneck at the causeway. First boat 0700, last at 1600. Boats depart as soon as they have a full complement of 12 passengers.

The Tanjong Pagar Railway Station is on Keppel Road, T2273800, to the south of the city centre. Singapore is the last port of call for the Malaysian railway system (Keretapi Tanah Melayu – KTM). The domed station – apparently inspired by Helsinki's – opened in 1932 and was renovated in 1990, though you wouldn't know it. The design, with its rubber-covered walls and their images of rubber tappers, tin miners and other Malay scenes, was heralded when it opened. Also notable are the four fine Art Deco images on the front of the station depicting commerce, agriculture, industry and shipping – suitably industrious for the new, as well as the old, Singapore. The station is notable in another respect too: the building and the land are Malaysian, not Singaporean. This was contrived as part of the deal when Singapore left the Malaysian Federation in 1965 and Malaysia ended up controlling the KTM. The two countries have been wondering how to handle this oddity of history ever since. In August 1998, Singapore moved its immigration officials from the Tanjong Pagar station to new purpose-built facilities at Woodlands, near the causeway on the Straits of Johor. But Malaysia refused to do the same. This means that visitors have to clear Singaporean immigration at the Woodlands and then continue for another 30 minutes, before clearing Malaysian immigration and customs at Tanjong Pagar. They are still trying to sort out their differences.

Train

There are two main lines connecting Singapore and Malaysia: one up the west coast to KL and Butterworth and on to Thailand, and another line which goes through the centre of Peninsular Malaysia and on to Kota Bahru on the northeast coast. Three fully air-conditioned express trains make the trip daily between Singapore and Kuala Lumpur, 6½ hours (S$34-68, S$40 for second class sleeper, and S$19 for third class seat), departing at 0800, 1445 and 2210. The overnight sleeper arrives in Kuala Lumpur at 0635. There is also a daily train from Singapore to Butterworth, opposite Penang, 0810, arriving 2200. For a connection to Bangkok, passengers stay a night in Butterworth and then leave at 1400, arriving in Bangkok the following day at 1138. It is possible to take a train (for S$2.90) to Johor Bahru – just across the border in Malaysia – and then catch a (much cheaper) connection further north, but it requires a wait. Trains are clean and efficient and overnight trains have cabins in first class, sleeping berths in second class, and restaurants.

Transport to town From the station, bus 10 travels up Robinson Road, past Collyer Quay to Empress Place and the Nicoll Highway; bus 100 goes up Robinson, Fullerton and Beach roads; bus 30 travels west; bus 84 goes to the World Trade Centre; and buses 97 and 131 travel through the centre of town and then up Serangoon Road and through Little India.

Singapore

Touching down

Airport information
Flight information, T5424422 (give flight number). Changi airport's website is www.changi.airport. com.sg/

Almost all visitors arrive at Singapore's **Changi Airport** – regularly voted the world's leading or favourite airport. In 2000 the airport bagged no less than 16 best airport awards. The old British military base at Seletar is used for small plane arrivals and departures, notably flights from/to Pulau Tioman, off the east coast of Malaysia (see below for details).

Changi airport is at the extreme eastern tip of the island, about 20 km from town. There are two terminals, divided between airlines (all clearly indicated). A third terminal is currently under construction, but will not be completed until early 2006 The airport's stress-free terminals belie its status as one of the world's most hectic transit hubs. It processes around 26,000,000 passengers a year – around seven times more than the population of Singapore. About 80% of Singapore's tourists arrive by air and it takes only 20 minutes from touchdown to baggage claim – characteristically called 'accelerated passenger through flow'.

Changi's facilities are excellent and include banks, hotel reservations and Singapore Tourist Board desks, a medical centre, business centre, children's discovery corner, internet centre, day rooms, restaurants, left-luggage facilities, mail and telecommunications desks, shopping arcades, supermarkets, sports facilities (health centre and swimming pool), hairdresser and accommodation. Apart from the internet centre, which is 24 hours, all open from 0700 to 2300. Everything is clearly signposted in English and the two terminals are connected by a monorail. There is an excellent canteen/food centre in Terminal 2, reached via the multi-deck car park. A tourist information pack is available just after Immigration, near the Customs Hall.

Airport tax Payable on departure – S$15 for all flights to all countries. A PSC (Passenger Service Charge) coupon can be purchased at most hotels, travel agencies and airline offices in town before departure, which saves time at the airport.

Sleeping at Changi AL *Le Meridien Changi*, 1 Netheravon Rd, T5427700, F5425295, www.meridien- changi.com Very well run, first class hotel, situated on Changi Beach, just north of the airport. Recommended for efficiency. **A** *Transit Hotel 1*, Level 3 Changi Airport Terminal 1, T5430911, F5458365, www.changi.airport.com.sg Short-term rate quoted (6 hrs). A good place to take a break if you are stuck at Changi for an extended period. **B** *Transit Hotel 2*, departure/transit lounge south, Terminal 2, T5428122, F5426122, www.changi.airport.com.sg Excellent hotel on the airport property, with short stay facility (price quoted is for six hours). Booking is recommended. They also provide a 'freshen up' service including up-service of showers, sauna and gym from S$5.

Transport to town Hotels will only meet guests with a previous arrangement; some charge, but others offer the service free. The car pick-up area is outside the arrivals halls of both terminals.

A number of buses run between the airport and nearby bus interchanges. **Bus 16** runs to Raffles City and then down Orchard Road, takes less than an hour and costs S$1.20 (non-air conditioned) or S$1.50 (air conditioned). It is easy to catch from Orchard Road. **Bus 36**, which also runs along Orchard Road to Raffles City, is faster but only operates in the morning between 0600 and 0900, when the service operates from the city to airport, and from 1700 and 2000 in the evening, when it plys between the airport and city. Exact fare needed.

Airport shuttle: between 0600 and midnight, every 15 minutes (1800 to midnight) and every 30 minutes (0600-1800), adults S$7, children S$5, booking counters in arrivals halls. These minibuses will drop off at any destination within the CBD. Note that if you are a in a group of three or four, it is probably cheaper to take a taxi (see below).

Touching down

Electricity: 220-240 volts, 50 cycle AC; most hotels can supply adapters.

Emergencies: Police: T999. Ambulance/Fire brigade: T995.

Singapore Tourist Board Tourist Hotline: T1800-736 2000 (toll free).

Business hours: Normal banking hours are 0930-1500 Monday-Friday, 0930-1130 Saturday. Some do not offer foreign exchange dealings on Saturday, although money changers operate throughout the week and for longer hours. Most shops in the tourist belt open around 1030 and close at 2100. Sunday is a normal working day around Orchard and Scotts roads.

Time: Eight hours ahead of GMT.

Weights and measures: Metric.

IDD code for Singapore: 65.

Directory enquiries: T103.

An **MRT** line is currently under construction from the city out to Changi. It is scheduled for completion in 2002 and will provide quick and easy access by train.

Car hire Avis and Hertz desks are in the arrivals hall (close 1800). *Avis*, T7371668; *Hertz*, T18007344646; *Budget*, T7420119.

Taxis queue up outside the arrival halls. They are metered but there is an airport surcharge of S$3, which increases to S$5 on Fri, Sat and Sun and after 1700. A trip to the centre of town should cost about S$20. Most taxi companies operate a limousine service (London cab or Mercedes) with a flat rate of S$37, or a six-seater for S$42. To book limousine service from your hotel, call *City Cab*, T5522222, *Comfort*, T293554, or *TIBS*, T4823888.

This is a military airport, but is also used for connections with Pulau Tioman off Malaysia's east coast and for some charter flights. Although the authorities do not allow photographs on the tarmac, checking-in is all very relaxed and informal – very different from the rather brusque efficiency of Changi. There are no public buses to Seletar, most people take taxis, and as at Changi there is a S$3 surcharge. When a scheduled flight is arriving from Tioman the airline usually calls so that the required number of taxis are waiting. **Seletar Airport**

Singapore Tourism Board, Tourism Court, 1 Orchard Spring Lane, Singapore 247729, T1800-7362000, www.stb.com.sg The office is open 0830-1700 Mon to Fri, 0830-1300 Sat. Other offices at: 3 Temasek Boulevard, Suntec City Mall, T1800-3325066, open 0800-1830 daily; Level 1, Liang Court Shopping Centre, 177 River Valley Road, T3362888, open 1030-2130 daily; 160 Orchard Road, Orchard Point@H20 Zone T1800-7388169, open 1100-2230 daily. All are good sources of brochures and maps. Complaints can also be registered at these offices. There is a 24-hour Touristline which gives automated information in English, Mandarin, Japanese and German, T1800-8313311 (toll free). Indonesian Tourist Board, T7377422. Malaysian Tourist Board, Ocean Building, 11 Collyer Quay, T5326351. **Tourist information**

American Express/Singapore Tourist Board Map of Singapore and *The Map of Singapore*, endorsed by the Singapore Hotel Association, are both available free from STB offices and many hotels. The best street map to Singapore is the Periplus Map, available at bookshops. Other useful maps are the *Secret Map of Singapore*; *Secret Food Map of Singapore*; *Singapore Street Directory*. The Singapore Tourism Board (STB) produces a profusion of guides to the city (13 at last count), including the general official guide which is updated each month. It is worth making a visit to one of the STB offices (see above) or pick up brochures and maps on arrival at Changi Airport. Other free maps are available and can be picked up from hotels and tourist offices. The best is *The Map of Singapore*, published by *Miller Freeman Pte* Ltd. **Maps & guides**

Singapore

Invaluable for making the most of Singapore's incomparable public transportation is the annual *TransitLink Guide*, which lists all bus and MRT routes and stops. A snip at S$1.50 for 413 pocket-sized pages.

Local customs & laws

Clothing Singapore dress is smart but casual. It is rare to find places insisting on jacket and tie, although jeans and T-shirts are taboo at some nightclubs. Flip-flops, sleeveless T-shirts and denim cut-offs look out of place in Singapore.

Conduct in private homes Most Singaporeans remove their shoes at the door – more out of a keen sense of cleanliness than any deep religious conviction. No host would insist on visitors doing so, but it is the polite way to enter a home.

Eating Chinese meals are eaten with chopsticks and Malays and Indians traditionally eat with their right hands. It is just as acceptable, however, to eat with spoons and forks. In Malay and Indian company, do not use the left hand for eating.

Tipping Tipping is unusual in Singapore. In cheaper restaurants it is not expected, although in more upmarket places when a service charge is not automatically added to the bill, a tip is usual. Most international hotels and restaurants, however, add 10% service charge and 4% government tax to bills. In general, only tip for special personal services.

Prohibitions There are several rules and regulations visitors should note: smoking is discouraged and prohibited by law in many public places, such as buses, taxis, lifts, government offices, cinemas, theatres, libraries and department stores and shopping centres – and all air-conditioned restaurants. First offenders can be fined up to S$1,000 for lighting up in prohibited places. Many hotels now provide non-smoking floors. Littering may incur a fine of up to S$1,000 for first time offenders and up to S$2,000 for repeat offenders, with the added prospect of corrective work of some kind. Although jaywalking is less rigorously enforced than it used to be, crossing the road within 50 m of a pedestrian crossing, bridge or underpass could cost you S$500.

Safety Singapore is probably the safest big city in Southeast Asia. Women travelling alone need have few worries. It is wise, however, to take the normal precautions and not wander into lonely places after dark.

Where to stay

For a full listing area by area, see page 635

In April 2001, Singapore had 186 hotels listed on their website with more than 30,000 rooms. There are many others at the bottom of the price range that are not listed. Many of the excellent international class hotels are concentrated in the main shopping and business areas, including Orchard and Scotts roads, and near Raffles City and the Marina complexes. They are all run to a very high standard and room rates range between S$250 and S$650, although discounts are almost always on offer and few people pay the full rate. Enquire at the airport hotel desk on arrival whether there are any special offers. After a room glut in the early 1980s, Singapore's hotel industry is now suffering a room shortage and when a large convention or two hits town, rooms can be hard to find.

Singapore offers an excellent choice of hotels in our upper categories, from luxury to tourist class. Though rooms may be more expensive than equivalent classes of hotels elsewhere in the region, they try to make up for this in terms of service. It is rare to stay in a hotel that does not offer attentive and professional care. Budget hotels are thin on the ground and hardly what most backpackers would describe as 'budget'.

Hotel price codes and facilities

LL (S$400+) and **L** (S$300-400)
Singapore has some of the very best hotels in the world. These offer unrivalled personal service, sumptuous extras, luxury rooms and bathrooms, and just about every amenity that you can think of. Most of the top hotels now provide two in-room phone lines (for modems and calls), 24-hour business facilities, several pools, jacuzzis, health spas, tennis courts, numerous restaurants, and much else besides.

AL (S$200-300)   Most of the middle to upper range hotels in this category will provide a business centre (although it is worth checking whether these operate around the clock). Coupled with this, there will be an executive floor or two, with a lounge for private breakfast and evening cocktails, or for entertaining clients. Most of these hotels will also provide a personal safe in each room. There will be a fitness centre and swimming pool, and they may have a health centre as well as several restaurants.

A (S$150-200) and **B** (S$100-150)   Hotels in this category will range from very comfortable to functional. Rooms in the 'A' category will have most extras – like a minibar, TV and tea and coffee-making

facilities. They may also have a swimming pool, but it is likely to be small. They will have a coffee shop and perhaps a restaurant. Rooms in the 'B' category may be lacking some, or most, of these amenities, but should still be clean, comfortable and serviceable.

C (S$50-100)   There are not many hotels in this category in Singapore. Rooms may be air-conditioned with a hot water shower attached; there might also be a coffee shop. These are no-frills, functional affairs. There are some bargains to be had, but there are also hotels in this category which are pretty sordid.

D (S$25-50) and **E** (less than S$25)   Hotels and guesthouses in these two categories (and there aren't many) are basic places, with shared bathroom facilities and box-like rooms. There are a few that are clean and perfectly adequate and these are the registered establishments; others are squalid. The places on third or fourth floors of apartment buildings usually have no licence, and they are often the dirtiest and least well run. Most of these places provide a basic breakfast.

However, there are a few cheaper places to stay and dorm beds can be had for S$10 or so (see box opposite).

Taxes of 10% (government) plus 3% (goods) plus 1% (services) are added to bills in all but the cheapest of hotels.

Getting around

In an attempt to discourage Singaporeans from clogging the roads with private cars, the island's public transport system was designed to be cheap and painless. Buses go almost everywhere, and the Mass Rapid Transit (MRT) underground railway provides an extremely efficient subterranean back-up. A useful guide to Singapore's transport system is the annual pocket-sized and pocket-priced (S$1.50) *TransitLink Guide*, listing all bus and MRT routes and stops, available at news outlets, bookshops and MRT stations, as well as at many hotels.

Bus

For anyone visiting Singapore for more than a couple of days, the bus must be the best way of getting around. SBS (***Singapore Bus Service***) and TIBS (***Trans-Island Bus Services***) are efficient, convenient and cheap. Routes for all the buses are listed (with a special section on buses to tourist spots) in the aforementioned *Transit Link Guide*. If you intend to do much bus travel, then this guide is well worth buying. The Singapore Tourism Board's *Official Guide* (free from STB offices) also carries a tourist-friendly synopsis of the service.

All buses are operated by a driver only, so it is necessary to have the exact fare to hand. Fares range from 60¢ (non a/c) to S$1.50 and buses run from 0600 to 2400 Monday to Sunday. For those intending to use the bus system extensively, it is well worth considering purchasing a Singapore Explorer ticket – S$7 for one day, unlimited travel on both SBS and TIBS. Tickets are available from TransitLink offices at Raffles Place, City Hall, Bugis, Dhoby Ghaut, Somerset, Orchard and Newton MRT stations and at many hotels. The sightseeing Singapore Trolley travels between Orchard Road, the river, Chinatown, *Raffles Hotel*, Boat Quay, Clarke Quay, Suntec City all day. S$9 for adults, S$7 for children, provides you with unlimited rides throughout the day. For more information call **Singapore Explorer**, T3389205/3396833.

Car hire This is one of the most expensive ways to get around. It is not worth it unless you are travelling to Malaysia as parking is expensive in Singapore (parking coupons can be bought in shops and daily licence booths). If travelling to Malaysia, it is cheaper, in any case, to hire a car in Johor Bahru, Malaysia. Rental agencies require a licence, passport and for the driver to be over 20. Car rental cost is anything from S$60 to S$350 per day, depending on size and comfort, plus mileage. Vans and pick-ups are much cheaper as they are classified as commercial vehicles and are taxed at a lower rate.

Driving is on the left, the speed limit 50 km per hour (80 km per hour on expressways) and wearing a seat belt is compulsory. Avoid bus lanes (indicated by an unbroken yellow line) during rush hour. Remember that to drive into the restricted zone a licence must be purchased (S$3). In addition to car hire counters at the airport and booking offices in some top hotels, the *Yellow Pages* lists scores of local firms under 'Motorcar Renting and Leasing'. **Avis**, T7371668; **Hertz**, T1800-7344646; **Budget**, T7420119.

Cycling This is not a bicycle-friendly city. Bicycles are available for hire at a number of public parks and other quieter spots on the island, including East Coast Parkway, Sentosa, Pasar Ris, Bishan and Pulau Ubin. Expect to pay S$3-8 per hour or around S$20 per day; some outfits also ask for a deposit. **East Coast Bicycle Centre**, East Coast Parkway, bikes for rent including tandems (S$3 per hour), open 0800-1830. **Sentosa Island Bicycle Station**, near Ferry Terminal, S$3 per hour, Monday-Friday 0900-1800, Saturday and Sunday 0900-1900.

Mass Rapid Transit (MRT)
See the MRT map at the end of the book. For more information, call T1800-779 9366 (toll free, Singapore only), or see www.smrt.com.sg

Since November 1987, Singapore has had one of the most technologically advanced, user-friendly light railway systems in the world – about a third of the system is underground. The designer-stations of marble, glass and chrome are cool, spotless and suicide-free, thanks to the sealed-in, air-conditioned platforms. Nine of the underground stations serve as self-sufficient, blast-proof emergency bunkers for Singaporeans, should they ever need them. Smoking is strictly banned on all public transport – transgression is punishable by a large fine. (*Big Macs* and durians are also not allowed on the MRT.)

The US$5 bn MRT is indeed a rapid way of transiting – it is electrically driven and trains reach 80 km per hour. Within minutes of leaving the bustle of Orchard Road, passengers hear the honey-toned welcome to the Raffles City interchange. The MRT's 66 fully automated trains operate every 2½-8 minutes, depending on the time of day, between 0530 and 0030. There is a north-south loop and an east-west line with interchanges at Raffles City/City Hall and Jurong East. The lines cover the main tourist belt.

Fare stages are posted in station concourses, and tickets dispensed, with change, from the vending machines. Fares range from 70¢ to S$1.60. Stored value TransitLink cards for the MRT and buses are priced from S$12 to S$50 (including a S$2 refundable deposit), available from TransitLink ticket booths at MRT stations. Buses have 'validator machines'. (There are note changing machines which will change S$2 notes into coins.) There is even a S$7 tourist souvenir ticket. Children pay the same price as adults.

Singapore

The Northeast Line is due to open in late 2002. A new line is currently under construction from the city out to Changi Airport and is scheduled for completion in 2002. A new line, the Circle Line, is planned. The first part, the Marina Line, is due to open around mid-2006 and the next one is scheduled for late 2006, although a final completion date is yet to be confirmed.

There are more than 15,000 taxis, all of them metered and air-conditioned, which ply the island's roads. Taxis cannot be hailed anywhere; it's best to go to a taxi stand or about 50 m from traffic lights. The taxis' bells are an alarm warning cabbies once they're over the 80 km per hour expressway speed limit. Fares start at S$2.40 for the first 1 km, and rise 10¢ for every subsequent 240 m up to 10 km, after which they rise by 10¢ every 225 m. 10¢ is also added for every 30 seconds waiting time. There is a peak period surcharge of S$1 for trips commencing between 0730 and 0930 Monday-Saturday, between 1630 and 1900 Mon-Fri, and from 1130 to 1400 on Sat. These surcharges do not apply on public holidays. A surcharge of S$1.50 is levied on all trips beginning from the Central Business District (CBD) between 1630 and 1900 on weekdays, and between 1130 and 1400 on Saturday (except on public holidays). If this surcharge is levied then the peak period surcharge does not apply. If there are more than two passengers there is a 50¢ surcharge; luggage costs S$1 extra and there's a 50% 'midnight charge' from 2400 to 0600. There is also a S$3 surcharge for journeys starting from (but not going to) Changi International Airport or Seletar Airport, and a S$3.20 flat fee for calling a radio taxi, which rises to S$5.20 if booked more than 30 minutes in advance. Trips paid for with credit cards enjoy a 10% surcharge on top of the fare, and taxis hired between 1800 on the evening before a public holiday and 2400 on the day of the public holiday also get hit with a S$1 surcharge. TIBS taxis now has a fleet of London cabs which may be hired by the hour, and have the advantage of accommodating five passengers. There's a surcharge here too though, of S$1. Even with this veritable extravaganza of surcharges, Singapore's taxis are still excellent value for money and are certainly worth considering if in a group of three or four. Not only do they provide a view of Singapore which is absent from the MRT (at least in the city centre), but taxi drivers, like their brothers (and a few sisters) in most cities, are a great source of information, from political opinion to tourist practicalities. Unlike most of the rest of Asia, language is not a barrier to communication.

The CBD area scheme restricts all cars and taxis from entering the area 0730-1900 Monday-Friday, 0730-1015 Saturday, unless they purchase an area licence (S$3 cars, $1 for motorbikes). Passengers entering the restricted zone are liable unless the taxi is already displaying a licence. Taxis displaying red destination labels on their dashboards are going home and are only required to take passengers in the direction they are going. Taxis are usually plentiful; there are stands outside most main shopping centres and hotels. Smoking is illegal in taxis. For taxi services ring: *Comfort CabLink*, T5521111; *Premier Cabs*, T5522828; *City Cab*, T5522222; *TIBS*, T4811211.

Descendants of the rickshaw, trishaws have all but left the Singapore street scene. A few genuine articles can still be found in the depths of Geylang or Chinatown, but the biggest population of trishaws is to be found off New Bugis Street, by the Albert Centre (see the Little India map, page 617); they cater for tourists only these days and charge accordingly, making trishaws the most expensive form of public transport in town. As ever, agree a price before climbing in and expect to pay about S$30 for a 45-minute ride. Top hotels offer top-dollar trishaw tours. Off-duty trishaw drivers hang out in a large pack at the bottom of Bras Basah Road, near the Singapore Art Museum. The eponymous *Trishaw Tours Pte*, T5456311/8283133, also offers trishaw tours.

Taxis
Taxis are the fastest and easiest way to get around in comfort

Trishaws

Singapore

Hitchhiking The idea is an anathema to most Singaporeans and those trying are unlikely to have much success.

Boat Ferries to the southern islands – Sentosa, Kusu, St John's etc – leave from the World Trade Centre or it is possible to hire a sampan from Jardine Steps on Keppel Road or Clifford Pier. Boats for the northern islands go from Changi Point or Ponggol Point.

Keeping in touch

Communica-tions **Internet** Singapore is one of the most wired and internet savvy places in the world, so there are loads of internet cafés. More to the point, hotels, government agencies like the Singapore Tourism Board and more have excellent websites. Websites and email addresses are listed where appropriate in this guide; see in particular those under Finding out more, page 575.

Internet cafés include: *T2*, Changi International Airport (Level 3). *Cybernet Café*, 57 Tanjong Pagar Road. *Café@Boat Quay*, 82 Boat Quay, T230014. *Eden*, Level 2, Wheelock Place, Orchard Road, T8870178. *Cyberstar ComCentre*, 19 Stamford Road, open 24 hours. *Cyber Arena*, Stamford Road (just along from ComCentre), open 0900-2345. *Internet Café*, Liang Seah Street. *Flyingcows.net*, next to Bencoolen Hotel, Bencoolen St. *Cyberheart Café*, Orchard Road, T7343877.

Post The main post office is in Crosby House, Robinson Road, and offers a basic service round the clock. There are 1,300 other postal outlets. Post Office opening hours are 0830-1700 Monday-Friday, 0830-1300 Saturday. Changi Airport, 0800-2000 Monday-Sunday. Local **postal charges** start at 22¢ (20 g). International postal charges are 50¢ (postcard), 50¢ (aerogramme), S$1 (letter, 20 g). For the latest charges see www.singpost.com.sg/rt01menu.htm The Singapore Post Office provides four sizes of sturdy carton, called Postpacs, for sending parcels abroad. These can be bought cheaply at all post offices. **Poste Restante**: Singapore Post, Robinson Road Branch, 71 Robinson Road #01-00, Singapore. Open Monday-Friday 0830-1800, Saturday 0830-1400. Closed on Sunday and public holidays. Correspondents should write the family name in capital letters and underline it to avoid confusion.

Fax and telex All post offices and almost all hotels have facilities for outgoing messages.

Telephone In public **payphones** the minimum charge is 10¢ for three minutes. Card phones are quite widespread – cards can be bought in all post offices as well as in supermarkets and newsagents, and come in units of S$2, S$5, S$10, S$20 and S$50.

Singapore has three **mobile phone** networks (*CDMA*, *GSM900* and *GSM1800*), and three mobile phone providers (*SingTel*, *M1* and *Starhub*). Access codes are: SingTel, 001; for M1, 002; and Starhub, 008.

Singapore's IDD code is 65. For details on country codes, dial 162. **International calls** can be made from public phones with the red 'Worldphone' sign; these phones take 50¢ and S$1 coins or phonecards. International Phone Home Cards are available at all post offices and come in units of S$10 and S$20. Credit card phones are also available. IDD calls made from hotels are free of any surcharge.

Media **Newspapers and magazines** The press is privately owned and legally free, but is carefully monitored and strictly controlled. It runs on Confucianist principles – respect for one's elders – which translates as unwavering support of the government. In the past, papers that were judged to have overstepped their mark, such as the former *Singapore Herald*, have been shut down. The *Straits Times* has been likened to Beijing's *People's Daily* for the degree to which it is a mouthpiece of the government.

The English language dailies are the *Straits Times* (and the *Sunday Times*), which runs better foreign news pages than any other regional newspaper (available on the internet at http://straitstimes.asia1.com.sg/home); the *Business Times* (http://business-times.asia1.com.sg/home); and the *New Paper*, Singapore's very own tabloid. A more recent addition is the *Asian Times*, printed in Singapore, Bangkok and Hong Kong.

Radio   English language radio stations are Gold (90.5FM), Class (95FM), Perfect Ten (98.7FM), NewsRadio (93.8FM) and Symphony (92.4FM). It is also possible to pick up stations beamed across from Batam in Indonesia to the south and from Malaysia to the north. The *BBC World Service* broadcasts 24 hours a day on 88.9FM thanks to an old British forces transmitter. The 'London Calling' programme guide is available from bookshops. In addition to English language stations, there are also local Chinese, Indian and Malay language stations. These are listed on www.mediacorpradio.com/

Television   Channels 5, 8 and 12 show English, Chinese, Malay and Tamil programmes; most sets also receive Malaysian channels. Many large hotel TV sets receive satellite channels and are also linked with the teletext system, which has information on entertainment, sports, finance, aircraft arrivals and departures and special events from 0700 to 2400. Programmes for all channels are listed in the daily newspapers.

Food and drink

Eating is the national pastime in Singapore and has acquired the status of a refined art. The island is a tropical paradise for epicureans of every persuasion and budget. While every country in the region boasts national dishes, none offers such a delectably wide variety as Singapore. Fish-head curry must surely qualify as the national dish, but you can sample 10 Chinese cuisines, North and South Indian, Malay and Nonya (Straits Chinese) food, plus Indonesian, Vietnamese, Thai, Japanese, Korean, French, Italian (and other European), Russian, Mexican, Polynesian and Scottish. There's a very respectable selection of Western food at the top end of the market, a few good places in the middle bracket, and swelling ranks of cheaper fast food restaurants like *Kentucky Fried Chicken* and *McDonald's* and an explosion of pizza outlets. For young, trendy Singaporeans, coffee culture has replaced food court fare, and the favoured spots are places like *Delifrance*, *Spinelli's* and *Starbuck's*, which are giving a buzz to thousands.

Do not be put off by characterless, brightly lit restaurants in Singapore; the food can be superb. Eating spots range from high-rise revolving restaurants to neon-lit pavement seafood extravaganzas. A delicious dinner can cost as little as S$3 or more than S$100, and the two may be just yards away from each other. For example, it is possible to have a small beer in one of the bars of the Raffles Hotel for S$8, or more, and then stagger 10 m across the road and indulge in a huge plate of curry and rice for S$2. For a listing of over 100 more pricey restaurants, *Singapore's Best Restaurants* is worth purchasing; it gives a description of the food and a price guideline and is available from most bookstores for $10.30. It is updated annually. *The Secret Food Map*, available at most bookstores for S$5, is also a good buy. Another book worth getting is *Good Food, 500 Great Eating Places Near the MRT Station*, produced by the MRT and MPH Publishers. For short descriptions of Singapore's varied cuisines see the Food and drink entry of the Malaysia Essentials section, page 51.

The government might have cleared hawkers off the streets, but there are plenty of hawker centres in modern Singapore. Food courts are the modern, air conditioned, sanitized version of hawker centres. They provide the local equivalent of café culture and the human equivalent of grazing. Large numbers of stalls are packed together under one roof. Hawker centres are found beneath HDB blocks and in some specially

Hawker centres & food courts

Singapore

allocated areas in the city; while food courts are usually in the basement of shopping plazas. The seats and tableware may be basic, but the food is always fresh and diners are spoilt for choice. Customers claim themselves a table, then graze their way down the rows of Chinese, Malay and Indian stalls. It is not necessary to eat from the stall you are sitting next to. Vendors will deliver to your table when the food is ready and payment is on receipt. The food is cheap and prices are non-negotiable.

Coffee shops Mainly family concerns, traditional Singaporean coffee shops or *kopi tiam* are located in the older part of the city, usually in old Chinese shophouses. They serve breakfast, lunch and dinner, as well as beer, at prices only marginally higher than those at hawker centres.

Fast food cafés Despite Singapore's gourmet delights, fast food outlets do a roaring trade in Singapore. As well as the standard names in fast food fare, there are now chains of more sophisticated 'cafés', selling a wider range of European food. In particular, there is *Spinelli's*, who provide a very good range of fresh coffees (ground or beans), and *Delifrance*, known for its freshly-baked croissants, danish pastries and filled baguettes. Ask whether the pastries are freshly baked, as they weren't on an occasion we sampled their food. Check the *Yellow Pages* for branch addresses of the various fast food restaurants. They include: *A&W* (which in 1968 became the first fast-feeder in town), *Burger King*, *Denny's*, *KFC*, *McDonald's*, *Milano Pizza*, *Orange Julius*, *Pizza Hut*, *Shakey's Pizza* and one called *Fat Mama*. *Delifrance* has probably expanded fastest with restaurants at Clifford Centre, Marina Square, The Dynasty, Wisma Atria, The Promenade, Holland Village and Changi Airport. They also run several bistros at Holland Village and Tanglin Mall.

Drink Every hawker centre has at least a couple of stalls selling fresh fruit juice, a more wholesome alternative to the ubiquitous bottles of fizzy drink. A big pineapple or papaya juice costs S$2. You can choose any combination of fruits to go in your fruit punch. Freshly squeezed fruit juices are widely available at stalls and in restaurants. Fresh lime juice is served in most restaurants, and is a perfect complement to the banana-leaf curry, tandoori and dosai. Carbonated soft drinks, cartons of fruit juice and air-flown fresh milk can be found in supermarkets. For local flavour, the Malay favourite is *bandung* (a sickly sweet, bright pink concoction of rose essence and condensed milk), found in most hawker centres, as well as the Chinese thirst quenchers, soya bean milk or chrysanthemum tea. *Red Bull* (*Krating Daeng*), the Thai energy tonic, is also widely available and is the toast of Singapore's army of Thai building site labourers.

Tiger and Anchor beers are the local brews and Tsingtao, the Chinese nectar, is also available. Tiger Beer was first brewed at the Malayan Breweries with imported Dutch hops and yeast on Alexandra Road in 1932, and was the product of a joint venture between Singapore's *Fraser & Neave* and *Heineken*. Recently, *Tiger Beer* has produced two new brews: *Tiger Classic* is a strong bottled beer and *Tiger Light*, which is now available on draught in some bars. *Anchor* was the result of German brewers *Beck*'s setting up the rival *Archipelago* Brewery. Because of its German roots, Archipelago was bought out by *Malayan Breweries* in 1941 and is today part of the same empire. Some bars (such as *Charlie's* at Changi) specialize in imported beers, but even local beer is expensive (around S$6 a bottle in hawker centres and S$8 a glass in bars and pubs). There is an international selection of drinks at top bars, but they're often pricey. Coffee houses, hawker centres and small bars or coffee shops around Serangoon Road, Jalan Besar and Chinatown have the cheapest beer. Expect to pay around S$8-10 for a half pint of beer in most smart bars. Most bars do have a happy hour (or hours) though, where bargains can be had.

There is no shortage of wine available in Singapore, but it is expensive; Australian wines are generally a better deal than imported European ones. Supermarkets all have good wines and spirits sections.

The Singapore Sling is the island's best known cocktail. It was invented in the Raffles Hotel in 1915 and contains a blend of gin, cherry brandy, sugar, lemon juice and angostura bitters.

Shopping

Singapore is a shopper's paradise. There is an endless variety of consumer goods and gimmicks, with no import duty or sales tax on most items. The choice seems almost unlimited. But don't be deluded that there are bargains galore with rock-bottom prices to match the variety. Prices are, in fact, much the same as, say, those in Europe or the US. High wages, soaring rents and a strong dollar have all eaten into the country's price advantage. Singapore's retailers have had to weather several years of stagnant demand. Local shoppers seem to be spending their disposable income in other ways (or themselves go shopping abroad) and tourists no longer come with empty suitcases to stuff them full of goodies. Even the people who used to come here from places like Manila, Bangkok and Jakarta can buy just about everything at home. That said, there are some good buys and sales can throw up the odd bargain.

Probably the best area for window shopping is around Scotts and Orchard roads, where many of the big complexes and department stores are located (see page 608). This area comes alive after dark and most shops stay open late. The towering *Raffles City Complex*, *Parco* at Bugis Junction and Marina Square are the other main shopping centres. The East Coast shopping centres are not frequented by tourists. Serangoon Road (or Little India), Arab Street and Chinatown offer a more exotic shopping experience with a range of 'ethnic' merchandise.

Best buys Singapore has all the latest electronic gadgetry and probably as wide a choice as you will find anywhere. It also has a big selection of antiques (although they tend to be overpriced), arts and crafts, jewellery, silks and batiks. For branded goods, Singapore is still marginally cheaper than most other places, but for Asian-produced products it is no longer the cheapest place in the region.

Holidays and festivals

Singapore's cultural diversity gives Singaporeans the excuse to celebrate plenty of festivals, most of which visitors can attend. The Singapore Tourist Board produces a brochure every year on festivals, with their precise dates, or check the STBs website (www.newasia-singapore.com/).

January *New Year's Day* (1st January – public holiday).

February
The most important event in the entire Chinese calendar

Chinese New Year (movable – public holiday,). This five-day lunar festival is celebrated in January or February. Each new year is given the name of an animal in 12-year rotation and each has a special significance. The seasonal Mandarin catchphrase is *Gong Xi Fa Chai* (Happy New Year).

Thaipusam (movable – in the Hindu month of Thai, usually February). In honour of the Hindu deity Lord Subramaniam, or Murgham, the son of Lord Siva. Held during the full moon in the month of Thai, it is a festival of penance and thanksgiving with a procession from the Chettiars' Temple on Tank Road to the Vinayagar Temple on Keong Saik Road. The highlight of Thaipusam is the second day, when devotees assemble in their thousands at the Sri Perumal Temple on Serangoon Road. Devotees pay homage to Lord Subramaniam by piercing their bodies, cheeks and tongues with sharp skewers (*vel*) and hooks, weighted with oranges and carrying steel structures bearing the image of Lord Subramaniam.

592 HOLIDAYS & FESTIVALS

Hari Raya Haji (movable – public holiday, falls on the 10th day of Zulhijjah, the 12th month of the Muslim calendar). This festival honours Moslems who have made the pilgrimage to Mecca. The feast day is marked by prayers at mosques and the sacrificial slaughter of goats and buffalo for distribution to the poor as a sign of gratitude to Allah.

Jade Emperor's Birthday (movable) Crowds converge on the Giok Hong Tian Temple on Havelock Road to celebrate the Jade Emperor's birthday. A Chinese opera is performed in the courtyard of the temple and lanterns are lit in the doorways of houses.

T'se Tien Tai Seng's (the Monkey God's) Birthday (movable – but celebrated twice a year, in Feb and Oct) Participants go into a trance and pierce their cheeks and tongues with skewers before handing out paper charms. Celebrated at the Monkey God Temple, Eng Hoon Street, near Seng Poh market, Tiong Bahru Road, South Chinatown.

March-April *Kwan Yin's Birthday* (movable) Chinese visit temples dedicated to the goddess of Mercy (like the one on Waterloo Road). Childless couples come to pray for fertility.

Qing Ming (movable – early April) A Chinese ancestor-worship extravaganza in which family graves are spruced up and offerings of food and wine placed on tombs to appease their forebears' spirits.

Tamil New Year (movable April/May) Begins at the start of the Hindu month of Chithirai. Pujas are held at Singapore's main temples to honour Surya, the sun god. An almanac containing the Hindu horoscope is published at this time.

Easter (movable – Good Friday is a public holiday) Services are held in the island's churches. There is a candlelit procession in the grounds of St Joseph's Catholic Church, Victoria Street.

May-June *Labour Day* (1 May, public holiday)

Vesak Day (movable – public holiday, usually in May, on the full moon of the fifth lunar month) Commemorates the Buddha's birth, death and enlightenment and is celebrated in Buddhist temples everywhere. Kong Meng San Phor Kark See Temple in Bright Hill Drive and the Temple of a Thousand Lights in Race Course Road are particularly lively. In Singapore celebrations begin before dawn, monks chant sutras (prayers) and lanterns and candles are lit to symbolize the Buddha's enlightenment.

August-September *National Day* (9 August: public holiday) To celebrate the Republic's independence in 1965. The highlight of the day is the military parade, air force fly-past and carnival procession on and around the Padang and National Stadium.

Festival of the Hungry Ghosts (*Yu Lan Jie*) (movable – runs for 30 days after the last day of the sixth moon) Banquets are given by stallholders, lavish feasts are laid out on the streets and there are roving bands of Chinese street opera singers, puppet shows and lotteries. Then there is the ritual burning of huge incense sticks and paper 'hell money' to appease the spirits, who are believed to wander around on earth for a month after the annual opening of the gates of hell.

Mooncake or Lantern Festival (movable – mid-way through the Chinese eighth moon) This Chinese festival commemorates the overthrow of the Mongul Dynasty in China. Children parade with elaborate candlelit lanterns and eat mooncakes filled with lotus seed paste. According to Chinese legend, secret messages of revolt were carried inside these cakes and led to the uprising which caused the overthrow of their oppressors. A gentler interpretation is that the round cakes represent the full moon, the end of the farming year and an abundant harvest – a bucolic symbolism that must be lost on most city-born Singaporeans.

Navarathri Festival (movable) Nine days of prayer (*navarathiri* means 'nine lights'), temple music and classical dance honour the consorts of Siva, Vishnu and Brahma (the Hindu trinity of Gods). Music and dance performances can be viewed at all Hindu temples from around 1930-2200 each night of the festival. The festival is celebrated notably at the Chettiar Temple on Tank Road, ending with a procession on the 10th day along River Valley Road, Killiney Road, Orchard Road, Clemenceau Avenue and returning to the temple.

Deepavali (movable – public holiday, usually in October or November in the Hindu month of Aipasi). The Hindu festival of lights commemorates the victory of Lord Krishna over the demon king Narakasura, symbolizing the victory of light over darkness and good over evil. Every Hindu home is brightly lit and decorated for the occasion. Shrines are swamped with offerings and altars piled high with flowers. Row upon row of little earthen oil lamps are lit to guide the souls of departed relatives in their journey back to the next world, after their brief annual visit to earth during Deepavali.

October-November

Thimithi Festival (movable, in the Hindu month of Aipasi). This Hindu festival, in honour of the goddess Draupadi, often draws a big crowd to watch devotees fulfil their vows by walking over a 3 m long pit of burning coals in the courtyard of the Sri Mariamman Temple on South Bridge Road. Fire walking starts at around 1600 on the arrival of the procession from Perumal Temple on Serangoon Road.

Hari Raya Puasa or Aidil Fitri (movable – public holiday). Marks the end of Ramadan, the month of fasting for Muslims and is a day of celebration. Once the Muftis have confirmed the new moon of Syawal, the 10th Islamic month, Muslims don traditional clothing and spend the day praying in the mosques and visiting friends and family. During Ramadan, Muslims gather to eat at stalls after dark; Geyland Serai and Bussorah Street (near Arab Street) are favourite makan stops, see page 619.

December
Christmas here is a spectacle of dazzling lights, the best along Orchard Rd, where trees are bejewelled with fairy lights

Christmas Day (**25 December**: public holiday) Shopping centres and hotels compete to have the year's most extravagant or creative display. These seasonal exhibitions are often conveniently designed to last through to Chinese New Year. It would not be untypical, for example, to find Santa riding on a man-eater in the year of the tiger. In shopping arcades, sweating tropical Santa Clauses dash through the fake snow. Choirs from Singapore's many churches line the sidewalks and Singaporeans go shopping.

Health

The **water** in Singapore, most of which is pumped across the causeway from Johor, Malaysia, and treated in Singapore, is clean and safe to drink straight from the tap.

Medical facilities Singapore's medical facilities are amongst the best in the world. See the *Yellow Pages* for listing of public and private hospitals. Medical insurance is recommended. Gleneagles, at the western end of Orchard Road, is probably the best place to go in an emergency. As well as a large A & E department, it has a 24-hour medical clinic, with a price list provided, for longer care. Mount Elizabeth Hospital also has a very good reputation. Most big hotels have their own doctor on 24-hour call. Other doctors are listed under 'Medical Practitioners' in the *Yellow Pages*. Pharmaceuticals are readily available over the counter and registered pharmacists work 0900-1800. The Traveller's Health and Vaccination Clinic at the Tan Tock Seng Hospital (Level B2, 11 Jalan Tan Tock Seng, T3572222/3525650, www.ttsh.gov.sg/MMD/medical/cdc/clinic.html) provides specialist advice and treatment for travel-related illnesses and a vaccination service.

Singapore

Sights

Colonial core

Use City Hall MRT for the Padang and Raffles City. For the Singapore Art Museum, History Museum or Fort Canning Park, use Dhoby Ghaut MRT

Situated to the north of the Singapore River, the colonial core is bordered to the northeast by Rochor Road and Rochor Canal Road, to the northwest by Selegie Road and Canning Hill, and to the southeast by the sea. The area is small enough to walk around – just. To walk from the Singapore Art Museum in the far northwest corner of this area to the mouth of the Singapore River shouldn't take more than 30 minutes. You may want to take a cab to get over to Fort Canning Park if it is a particularly hot and humid day.

The Padang

The Padang ('playing field' in Malay), the site of most big sporting and other events in Singapore – including the National Day parades – is at the centre of the colonial area. Many of the great events in Singapore's short history have been played out within sight or sound of the Padang. It was close to here that Stamford Raffles first set foot on the island on the morning of 28 January 1819, where the Japanese surrendered to Lord Louis Mountbatten on 12 September 1945, and where Lee Kuan Yew, the first Prime Minister of the city state, declared the country independent in 1959.

The Padang originally fronted on to the sea, but due to land reclamation now stands a kilometre inland. After the founding of Singapore in 1819, English and Indian troops were quartered here and the area was known as 'The Plain'. The name was only later changed to Padang. In 1942, when Singapore fell to the invading Japanese, all the European population of the colony were massed on the Padang before the troops were marched away to prisoner-of-war camps, some to camps in Malaya and Siam (where they helped to build the infamous Bridge over the River Kwai), others to Changi (see page 630). The **Cricket Club**, at the end of the Padang, was the focus of British activity. A sports pavilion was first constructed in 1850 and a larger Victorian clubhouse was built in 1884 with two levels, the upper level being the ladies viewing gallery. The **Singapore Recreation Club** (the SRC) building, at the northern end of the Padang, has been built on the site of a former club built in 1883 by the Eurasian community, who were excluded from the Cricket Club. The newish building is a modern, green-glass affair with polished brown columns: a nouveau antidote to the venerable Cricket Club at the other end of the Padang. In 1963 the club lifted its membership restrictions and allowed anyone to join, and today fewer than a fifth of the members are Eurasian.

Flanking the Padang are the houses of justice and government: the domed **Supreme Court** (formerly the *Hotel de l'Europe*) and the City Hall. The neo-classical **City Hall** was built with Indian convict labour for a trifling S$2 mn and was finished in 1929. The Japanese surrendered here to Lord Louis Mountbatten and on the same spot, Lee Kuan Yew declared Singapore's independence. Today it contains law courts – the overflow from the Supreme Court next door. To get in, enter via the lower entrance at the front. Hearings usually start at 1000 and the public are allowed to sit at the back and hear cases in session.

On the seaward side of the Padang from the City Hall is **Tan Kim Seng's Fountain**. Along the base the following words are inscribed: "This fountain is erected by the municipal commissioners in commemoration of Mr Tan Kim Seng's donation towards the cost of the Singapore Water Works". This tells only part of the story for the fountain is a remnant of pristine Singapore's

Singapore

filthy past. Mr Tan, a prosperous Straits Chinese, made a gift of S$13,000 in 1857 to finance the island's first municipal water works on the condition that the water be available to all, free of charge. At the time it was just beginning to be recognized that Singapore's appallingly high mortality rate – which was higher than the island's birth rate (only immigration kept the population growing) – was linked to dirty water. Unfortunately, the terms of Mr Tan's gift were not adhered to; indeed, some people question whether the money ever went on improving Singapore's water supply at all and instead suggest that it was, so to speak, syphoned off for some other nefarious purpose. Certainly, it was not for another 60 years that mortality rates declined significantly, especially among Singapore's Chinese, Indian and Malay communities. Perhaps the city fathers erected this fountain when their guilt got the better of them.

Under construction and stretching right along the seafront is the Esplanade: theatres on the Bay. This will become the centre of Singapore's performing arts when it is completed in 2002. There will be a concert hall, lyric theatre, three smaller studios, and an outdoor performing space. It will all contribute to Singapore's medium-term plan to become the arts centre of the region.

Esplanade & the river

For a detailed map of the Esplanade and river, see page 604

Between the High Street and Singapore River there are a number of architectural legacies of the colonial period: **Old Parliament House**, the **Victoria Memorial Hall** and **Victoria Theatre**, and **Empress Place**. It was in this area that the Temenggongs, the former Malay rulers of Singapore, built their kampung; the royal family was later persuaded to move out to Telok Blangah. The **Victoria Theatre** was originally built as the Town Hall in 1856, but was later adapted by Swan and Maclaren to celebrate Queen Victoria's jubilee, integrating a new hall (the Memorial Hall) and linking the two with a central clock tower. (During the Japanese Occupation the clock, like those in other occupied countries, was set to Tokyo time, which seems a strange thing to do even during a world war.) The buildings are still venues for Singapore's multi-cultural dance, drama and musical extravaganzas. The Victoria Concert Hall (the right-hand section of the building) is the home base of the Singapore Symphony Orchestra.

In front of the theatre is the original **bronze statue of Sir Thomas Stamford Raffles**, sculpted in bronze by Thomas Woolner in 1887. There is a story that the statue was saved from destruction at the hands of the invading Japanese by a cunning curator, who hid it away. It seems, however, that the truth is rather more banal: the colonnade previously surrounding the statue was destroyed during the fall of Singapore and the statue was removed to the National Museum for the duration of the Occupation. When Lee Kuan Yew first came to power in 1965, his Dutch economic adviser Dr Albert Winsemius told him to get rid of the Communists but to "let Raffles stand where he is today. Say publicly that you accept the heavy ties with the West because you will very much need them in your economic programme".

Old Parliament House, built in 1827, is the oldest government building in Singapore. Designed by George Coleman, it was originally intended as a residence for the wealthy Javanese merchant John Maxwell, who was appointed by his friend Raffles as one of Singapore's first three magistrates. He never lived here, however, because of a dispute over the legal rights to the land, and he later leased it out to the government as a Court House. With the construction of a Supreme Court in St Andrews Road in 1939, the building stood empty for a decade, before becoming the Assembly Rooms in the 1950s and later Parliament House. Just to the north of Parliament House is a small bronze statue of an **elephant** – a gift from Siam's (Thailand's) King

Singapore general

Singapore

Singapore

Chulalongkorn, Rama V, who visited Singapore in 1871. (At the time, King Chulalongkorn was itching to get to Europe, but he had to make do with checking out Singapore and one or two other colonial possessions in Asia. He had to wait a few years before he got to the real centre of *siwilai* – civilization.)

Old Parliament House became too small to accommodate the expanding body of MPs and a new S$80 mn Parliament House has been built next to the old building. Parliamentary debate in Singapore is modelled on the Westminster system and, as in the Old Parliament, there is a Strangers' Gallery where the public – and visitors – can witness Singapore's democracy in action. The public entrance is on Parliament Place, opposite the Supreme Court. In an attempt to educate Singapore's youth about their parliamentary system, there is a sound-proofed gallery where a commentary is provided, a Moot Parliament where schoolchildren can sharpen their debating skills and a History Corner with interactive computer programs.

Empress Place, on the river and near to the Old Parliament, was one of Singapore's first conservation projects. Built as the East India Company courthouse in 1865 and named after Queen Victoria, Empress of the Empire, it later housed the legislative assembly and then became, in turn, part of the immigration department, the offices of other assorted government agencies, and a museum. Now this thoroughly confused building is undergoing yet another reincarnation as the second wing of the Asian Civilisations Museum, which is due to open in 2002. This will house a full display of the museum's collection (see page 599). In front of Empress Place stands the **Dalhousie Memorial**, an obelisk erected in honour of Lord James Dalhousie, Governor-General of India, who visited Singapore for three days in 1850. He is credited on the plaque as having emphatically recognized the wisdom of liberating commerce from all restraints.

Raffles Hotel
Just about anyone who's anyone visiting Singapore still makes a pilgrimage to this hotel

The revamped Raffles Hotel – with its 875 designer-uniformed staff (a ratio of two staff to every guest) and 104 suites (each fitted with Persian carpets), eight restaurants (and a Culinary Academy) and five bars, playhouse and custom-built, leather-upholstered cabs, is the jewel in the crown of Singapore's tourist industry. In true Singapore-style, it manages to boast a 5,000 sq m shopping arcade and there's even a museum of Rafflesian memorabilia on the third floor. ■ *1000-2100 Mon-Sun, free*. Next to the museum is the **Jubilee Hall Theatre**, which is named after the old Jubilee Theatre that was demolished to make way for the Raffles extension (see below).

Raffles Hotel's original (but restored) billiard table still stands in the Billiard Room. Palm Court is still there and so is the Tiffin Room, which still serves tiffin. Teams of restoration consultants undertook painstaking research into the original colours of paint, ornate plasterwork and fittings. A replica of the cast-iron portico, known as 'cad's alley', was built to the original 19th-century specifications of a Glasgow foundry.

There has been a vigorous debate over whether or not in the process of its lavish restoration Raffles has lost some of its atmosphere and appeal. (The same complaint has been levelled at the renovated *Railway Hotel* in Hua Hin, Thailand and the *Strand Hotel* in Rangoon, Burma.) There is no doubt that it has been done well – architecturally it can hardly be faulted, and the lawns and courtyards are lush with foliage. There is also no doubt that it is an immensely comfortable and well-run hotel. But critics say they've tried a little too hard. The month after it reopened (on former Prime Minister Lee Kuan Yew's birthday, 16 September 1991), *Newsweek* said that in trying to roll a luxury hotel, a shopping mall and a national tourist attraction into one, "The result is synergy run amok ... great if you need a Hermes scarf, sad if you'd like to imagine a tiger beneath the billiard table."

South of Raffles lies **St Andrew's Cathedral**, designed by Colonel Ronald MacPherson and built in the 1850s by Indian (Tamil) convict labourers in early neo-gothic style. Its interior walls are coated with a plaster called *Madras chunam*, a decorative innovation devised by the Indian labourers to conceal the deficiencies of the building materials. The recipe for *Madras chunam* was egg white, egg shell, lime and a coarse sugar (called jaggery), mixed with coconut husks and water into a paste. Once the paste had hardened, it was polished to give a smooth surface, and moulded to give many of the buildings their ornate façades. Note the window commemorating Raffles as the founder of modern Singapore. The cathedral is often packed – 13% of Singapore's population are Christian – and there are several services a day in different languages (see the notice board in the northwest corner of the plot for times of service).

(margin: Cathedrals & churches)

Built in 1835 (the spire was added in 1850), the **Armenian Church of St Gregory** the Illuminator (the first monk of the Armenian church) on Hill Street is the island's oldest church and was designed by Irish architect George Coleman. This diminutive church seats 50 people at a squeeze. The design is said to have been influenced by London's St Martin-in-the-Fields and Cambridge's Round Church. The construction of the church was largely funded by Singapore's small Armenian community, although a number of non-Christian Asians also contributed. Agnes Joaquim is buried here – she discovered what is now the national flower of Singapore, the Vanda Miss Joaquim orchid. On the other side of the road from the church is a strange pagoda-roofed block – the **Singapore Chinese Chamber of Commerce & Industry** building. This rather unhappy edifice was erected in 1964. Two stone lions imported from mainland China guard the entrance and the murals on either side of the gate are copies of similar murals in Beijing.

One of George Coleman's pupils, Denis McSwiney, designed the **Roman Catholic Cathedral of the Good Shepherd**, on the junction of Queen Street and Bras Basah Road. It was used as an emergency hospital during the Second World War. The building has been gazetted as a national monument, but even so looks as though it could do with a lick of paint. **CHIJMES** or the **Convent of Holy Infant Jesus**, opposite the Cathedral on Victoria Street, is a complex consisting of the convent, chapel and **Caldwell House** (designed by George Coleman). It has been redeveloped by a French architect into a sophisticated courtyard of handicraft shops – selling goods from Indonesia, Thailand, the Philippines, the Peranakan region, Mexico and Turkey! – as well as bars and restaurants. Originally, the convent was run by four French Catholic nuns, opening its doors to 14 fee paying pupils, nine boarders and 16 orphans in 1854. As well as being an orphanage and school for older girls, the convent became a home for abandoned babies, who were often left at the gates of the convent at the point of death. The gothic-style church, designed by French Jesuit priest Father Beurel, was added at the turn of the century. The church is now used for concerts and wedding ceremonies (and photo opportunities). Even the stained glass was painstakingly dismantled and renovated to a high standard.

Also on Armenian Street, close to Stamford Road, is a restored school. Tao Nan School was built in 1910 and became one of the first Chinese schools in Singapore. It has been taken over by the Singapore Museums Department and in 1997 opened as the Asian Civilisations Museum, which is well worth a visit. As its name suggests, the focus of the museum is Asian culture and

(margin: Asian Civilisations Museum to Coleman Street)

*(margin, vertical: Singapore)*

civilization – 5,000 years of it. Although the museum is fairly new, with the opening of Empress Place (see page 598) scheduled for 2002, so its remit is changing. It now considers itself a 'boutique museum' and will concentrate on displaying the Chinese collections: the 'Chinese Scholar Tradition' or 'Connoisseurship'. The museum is set on three floors. On the first floor is an outstanding collection of Peranakan pieces, displaying the exquisite level of workmanship in jewellery, beadwork and ceramics achieved by Singapore's original 'Baba' Chinese. Some of the pieces are on loan, while the museum gradually builds up its own collection. On the floor above is a display of calligraphy and its accoutrements. Along with the permanent collection, the

Colonial core

0 metres 100
0 yards 100

■ **Sleeping**
1 Conrad
2 Fullerton
3 Grand Plaza
4 Peninsula Excelsior

5 Raffles
6 Ritz Carlton
7 Westin Plaza
8 Westin Stamford

● **Eating**
1 Hill Street Food
Centre

Singapore

museum displays travelling exhibitions, which are often excellent. ■ *0900-1800 Tue-Sun (0900-2100 on Wed, free from 1800 to 2100 on this day). S\$3 adults, S\$1.50 children. Free guided tours in English, Tue-Fri 1100 and 1400, and additional 1530 tour at the weekends. For information on out-reach programmes, nhb_acm@nhb.gov.sg www.nhb.gov.sg*

Almost next door to the museum is **The Substation** at 45 Armenian Street is an offbeat cinema that also mounts small art exhibitions.

Nearby at 23B Coleman Street is the **Singapore Philatelic Museum**. It is a small but extremely well run museum and is not just of interest to philatophiles. Children especially will find it a wonderful place to follow up on

Route of Thaipusam procession

their stamp collections. Its aim is to educate the general public on the history of Singapore's – and, more widely, the world's – postal system. Children (or adults for that matter) can design their own stamps and print them out, use touch screen computers to test their knowledge of philately, tackle puzzles, or just admire the collection of stamps and envelopes. There is a good 'History Thru Stamps' Gallery, which uses stamps to recount aspects of Singapore's history. Children and adults can become members of the SPM and there is also a good resource centre where visitors can access the museum's book collection and database. ■ *0900-1730 daily, S$2 (S$1 for children). A 5-min walk from the City Hall MRT station.*

Singapore Art Museum

To wander through the wondrously cool galleries is a welcome break from the heat

Bras Basah Road was so-called because wet rice – *bras basah* in Malay – was dried here on the banks of the Sungai Bras Basah (now Stamford Canal). The former Catholic boys school **St Joseph's Institution**, opposite the RC Cathedral at 71 Bras Basah Road, is another good example of colonial religious architecture. Built in 1867, it is now home to the **Singapore Art Museum**, where there are travelling exhibitions every month or so, both modern and classical. The Singapore Art Museum's own collection is modest and, understandably, predominantly features Singaporean and Malaysian artists' work. There are always pieces from the collection on show providing an interesting insight into how Singaporean and Malaysian artists have selectively absorbed Western and Eastern influences. While St Joseph's was being renovated, a feature wall was discovered behind a row of built-in cupboards. Two supporting columns bear an entablature emblazoned with the words *Santa Joseph Ora Pro Nobis* (Saint Joseph pray for us) and it is presumed that the school chapel was located here. ■ *0900-1800 Tue-Sun (0900-2100 on Wed, when admission is free), S$3 adults, S$1.50 children and senior citizens. Free guided tours at 1100 and 1400 Tue-Fri (1030 in Japanese) and an additional tour at 1530 on Sat and Sun.*

Singapore History Museum

Across the green on Stamford Road is this museum, which, until a few years ago, was the only national museum in Singapore. However, now that the contemporary fine art collection has been shifted across the square to the Singapore Art Museum (see above) and the collection of Asian art has moved to the Asian Civilisations Museum (see page 599) on Armenian Street, the gallery has been left with the task of exhibiting on and educating about Singapore's history. The idea of setting up a museum was first mooted by Stamford Raffles in 1823; it was finally built in 1887 and named the Raffles Museum. It was most recently renovated in 1991, after which it was renamed. As a whole, the museum is rather disappointing given the quality of Singapore's other attractions. There is little coherence between its varied exhibits and little sense of narrative. Nor are the pieces displayed terribly interesting or beautiful. Only the 20 dioramas on the left of the main entrance, the Rumah Baba Peranakan collection on the second floor, the Jade Collection and a collection of William Farquhar's natural history drawings are permanent. The diorama scenes visually recount 20 important episodes in the history of Singapore, from Raffles' first landing on a jungled island inhabited by fisherfolk through to Independence. They are interesting enough – especially for children – and provide an easy-to-digest, staccato view of Singapore over the last two centuries or so. The interior of a Peranakan home provides detailed information on the contents of each room. The latest exhibit is 'The Singapore Story – overcoming the odds': A 3-D experience said to be the only high definition 3-D show in town. The attached **Children's Gallery** has changing exhibits, full of hands-on activities, every six months. During the week it is closed for two

Singapore

hours every morning and afternoon for school groups. There is plenty of hands-on activity for children. ■ *0900-1800 Tue-Thu and Sun, 0900-2100 Wed (when admission is free), S\$3, children S\$1.50 (50c extra to view the dioramas and S\$1 extra for the 3-D show). Free guided tours from the information counter at 1100 and 1400 Tue-Fri, with additional tours at 1530 at the weekend (1030 in Japanese). Slide shows through the day in the AV Theatre, T8379940 for latest exhibit information.*

Behind the Singapore History Museum is Fort Canning Park. The British called it Singapore Hill, but its history stretches back centuries earlier. It is known as Bukit Larangan, or Forbidden Hill, by the Malays, as this was the site of the ancient fortress of the Malay kings and reputedly contains the tomb of the last Malay ruler of the kingdom of Singapura, Sultan Iskandar Shah. Archaeological excavations in the area have uncovered remains from the days of the Majapahit Empire. It is thought that the palace was built in the early 14th century and then abandoned in 1396 in the wake of Siamese (Thai) and Majapahit (Javanese) attacks. Furthermore, when Raffles and his companions landed in 1819, it is said that Malay oral history still recalled the former 14th-century palace and its sultans and would not accompany the British up the hill for fear of the spirits. In a letter written to Sir William Marsden at the time of his first landing on Singapore, Raffles mentions the ruins of the Malay fortress. The name Canning Hill was given to this slight geological protuberance in the 1860s in honour of the first Viceroy of India, Viscount George Canning.

Fort Canning Park
The Amazon Basin this may not be, but the park does make a welcome distraction from the more urban delights of Singapore City

Over the last few years Canning Hill has evolved into something a little more ambitious than just a park. The **Battle Box**, opened in 1997, is a museum contained within the bunker where General Percival directed the unsuccessful campaign against the invading Japanese in 1942. Visitors are first shown a 15-minute video recounting the events that led up to the capture of Singapore. They are then led into the Malaya Command headquarters – the Battle Box – where the events of the final historic day, 15 February 1942, are re-enacted. Visitors are given earphones and are then taken from the radio room, to the cipher rooms and on to the command room, before arriving at the bunker where Percival gathered his senior commanders for their final, fateful, meeting. It is very well done with a good commentary, figures and film. The bunker is also air conditioned, a big plus after the hot walk up. During the Second World War, though, it was stiflingly hot – air was inefficiently re-circulated in case of gas attack. There is also a small traditional museum and a souvenir shop. ■ *1000-1800 Tue-Sun, last admission 1700, S\$8 (S\$5 children). Dhoby Ghaut is the nearest MRT.*

Above the Battle Box are the **ruins of Fort Canning** – the Gothic gateway, derelict guardhouse and earthworks are all that remain of a fort which once covered 3 ha. There are now some 40 modern sculptures here. Below the sculpture garden to the southeast is the renovated **Fort Canning Centre** (built 1926), which is the home venue of Theatre Works and the Singapore Dance Theatre. In front of Fort Canning Centre is an old Christian cemetery – **Fort Green** – where the first settlers, including the architect George Coleman, are buried. The graves of these early settlers have been exhumed but the gravestones remain, embedded in the boundary wall. Along with George Coleman, there is a Russian and, unusually, a Chinese – for this was a Christian burial ground – and it may indicate an early convert to Christianity. While Sir Stamford Raffles may have lived here, he did not die here. He fell out with the East India Company, and died of a presumed brain tumour the day before his 45th birthday. His funeral in North London went unnoticed by London society, and it was only later that he was reburied in Westminster Abbey.

Chettiar Temple

Below Canning Hill, on Tank Road, is the Hindu **Chettiar Temple**, also known as the **Sri Thandayuthapani Temple**. The original temple on this site was built in the 19th century by wealthy Chettiar Indians (money lending caste). It has been superseded by a modern version, finished in 1984, and is dedicated to Lord Subramaniam (also known as Lord Muruga). The ceiling has 48 painted glass panels, angled to reflect sunset and sunrise. Its *gopuram*, the five-tiered entrance, aisles, columns and hall all sport rich sculptures depicting Hindu deities, carved by sculptors trained in Madras. This Hindu temple is the richest in Singapore – some argue, in all of Southeast Asia. It is here that the spectacular Kavadi procession of the Thaipusam festival culminates (see page 54). ■ *Many Hindu temples close in the heat of the day, so are best seen before 1100 and after 1500.*

Singapore River and the City

Merlion

'Ulysses by the Merlion'

...this lion of the sea
Salt-maned, scaly,
wondrous of tail,
Touched with power,
insistent on this brief
promontory...
Puzzles.
Edwin Thumboo

Standing guard at the mouth of the **Singapore River** – though rather dwarfed now by a new bridge – is the mythical **Merlion**, half-lion, half-fish, the grotesque saturnine symbol of Singapore. The statue was sculpted by local artist Lim Nang Seng in 1972 and stands in the miniscule **Merlion Park**, an unaccountably popular stop for tour groups, where there is a souvenir shop which is sometimes rather ambitiously billed a museum. The Merlion is best viewed from the Padang side of the river. It is inspired by the two ancient (Sanskrit) names for the island: *Singa Pura* meaning 'lion city', and *Temasek* meaning 'sea-town'. The confused creature is emblazoned on many a trinket and T-shirt.

Singapore River and the city

Related maps
A Colonial core,
page 600
B Chinatown,
page 613

Directly behind the Merlion stands the imposing, recently converted, **Fullerton Hotel** (see page 636), in prime position, overlooking the mouth of the river, formerly the General Post Office. Until 1873 this site was occupied by Fullerton Fort, built to defend the Singapore River from seaborne attack. Fullerton Building was erected in 1925-28 by a firm of Shanghai-based architects. The heavy, almost Scottish, design seems a little out of place in tropical Singapore and, perhaps appropriately, the firm left the colony in the early 1930s after they had been struck off the architect's register for professional misconduct.

Cavenagh Bridge, erected in 1869 by convict labourers (the last big project undertaken by convicts here), was originally called Edinburgh Bridge to commemorate the visit of the Duke of Edinburgh. It was later renamed Cavenagh in honour of Governor WO Cavenagh, the last India-appointed governor of Singapore. The bridge was constructed from steel shipped out from Glasgow (supplied by the same company that furnished the Telok Ayer Market), and was built to provide a link between the government offices on the north side of the river and Commercial Square to the south. However, it was apparently built without a great deal of thought to the tides: *tongkangs*, the lighters that transferred cargo from ships to the godowns (warehouses) at Boat Quay, and vice versa, could not pass under the bridge at high tide and would have to wait for the water level to drop. It became a footbridge in 1909 when the Anderson Bridge superseded it, but it still bears its old sign that forbids bullock carts, horses and heavy vehicles from crossing.

One of the more striking buildings on the river, for its sheer size, is the headquarters of the **United Overseas Bank** (UOB) backing onto Chulia Street, which towers to the maximum permissible height of 280 m (to avoid collision with low-flying aircraft). The octagonal tower is said to represent a pile of coins, although this seems simply too crass to believe. Below, in the open under-court area, is a large bronze statue by **Salvador Dali** entitled *Homage to Newton*, cast in 1985. A bronze statue of a squat bird, by **Fernando Botero**, sits on the waterfront, while behind the UOB, on Chulia Street and next to the OCBC Centre, is a giant reclining figure by Henry Moore.

Along the south bank of the river, facing Empress Place, is Boat Quay – commercially speaking, one of the most successful restoration projects of the Urban Redevelopment Authority (URA). In the early 19th century this part of the river was swamp and the original roomah (*rumah* means house) *rakits* were rickety, stilted affairs, built over the mud. However, by the mid-1850s Boat Quay had emerged as the centre of Singapore River's commercial life, with three-quarters of the colony's trade being transferred through the godowns here. The opening of the Suez Canal in 1869 increased trade still further, but the development of the steamship around the same time threatened the commercial vitality of the area: vessels became too large to dock here. Merchants, worried that shipping companies would move their business to the new port of Tanjong Pagar which opened in 1852, began to use lighters, or *tongkangs*, to load and unload ships moored outside the river. *Tongkangs*, (lighters), barges and sampans once littered the river, but they were cleared out to Marina Bay, or destroyed and scuttled, as part of the government's river-cleaning programme over a period of 10 years during the 1990s. Singapore River is now said to be 'pollution-free' (although it only takes a quick glance to see that this is blatant rubbish), but what it gained in cleanliness it has lost – some would argue – in aesthetics.

Boat Quay

Boat Quay has become, for tourists, one of the most popular places to eat or drink in Singapore

Singapore

With technological advances threatening to undermine Boat Quay's vitality, it is perplexing that the area's merchants didn't sell up and move on. One popular explanation is that the curve of the river made it look like the belly of a carp – a sure indicator of commercial success according to chinese folk wisdom. The wealthier the merchant the higher their godowns were constructed, giving the frontage an attractively uneven appearance. By the time the Urban Redevelopment Authority (URA) announced its conservation plans in 1986, Boat Quay had fallen on hard times. The original inhabitants were encouraged to leave, the shophouses and godowns were restored and renovated, and a new set of owners moved in. The strip now provides a great choice of drinking holes and restaurants for Singapore's upwardly mobile young, expats and tourists alike.

Elgin Bridge marks the upriver end of Boat Quay. The bridge was built in 1929 to link the community of Chinese merchants settled on the south side of the river with the Indian traders of the High Street on the north side, and was named after Lord Elgin, Governor-General of India. It is, in fact, the fifth bridge to be built on this site. The first was constructed in 1819 and was the only bridge across the river at that time. Note the roundels depicting the Singapore lion, which are under a palm tree on the bases of each cast-iron lamp at either end of the bridge. They were designed by Cavalieri Rodolofo Nolli.

Clarke Quay Further upriver, Clarke Quay has also been renovated and redeveloped. This was once godown country – in colonial days, the streets around the warehouses would have been bustling with coolies. It is now a pleasant pedestrian area, with 150-odd shops, restaurants and bars. Clarke Quay has a slightly different feel to Boat Quay; while the latter consists of individual enterprises, the former is controlled by a single company that keeps close tabs on which shops and food outlets open. The atmosphere is more contrived, more managed and controlled and less vivacious. Unsurprisingly, this is more of a family place, while young, single people tend to congregate downriver at Boat Quay. In the pedestrian lanes, overpriced hawker stalls and touristy knick-knack carts set up from lunchtime onwards, selling all manner of goods that people could do without. Despite this, it is still a lot of fun, especially at night, and unlike Boat Quay it is possible to snack from stalls while wandering the alleys of the area. On Sundays there is a flea market here during daylight hours.

A good way of seeing the sights along Singapore River is on a **bumboat cruise**, which can be taken from Clarke Quay or Boat Quay. A rather banal recorded commentary points out the godowns, shophouses, government buildings and skyscrapers lining the river bank. ■ *Bumboats operate 0900-2300, S$10 (S$5 for children). A river taxi also operates from here, S$1 (morning) and S$3 (afternoon).*

On the waterfront, a makeshift theatre provides **wayang performances**. Wayang was traditionally performed in tents by travelling artists who would move from town to town, performing for special occasions. The *tongkangs* moored alongside the quay are now used as floating restaurants. Traditionally they were used as lighters, to transport cargo from larger ships. The eyes were painted on them so that they could see where they were going. ■ *Every Wed and Fri at 1945-2030. The performers prepare themselves from 1800 onwards and onlookers are welcome to watch the making-up process.*

Riverside Point Spanning the river at Clarke Quay is a pedestrian bridge, **Read Bridge**, erected in the 1880s and named after a famous businessman of the day. The antique lamps have been recently added to a structure which, when it was built, looked more modern than it does now. Read Bridge leads to **Riverside**

Singapore

Point, an arcade of upmarket shops and restaurants. Across Merchant Road via an aerial walkway is yet another shopping centre-cum-restaurant complex – **Riverside Village** – with its component parts, **Merchant Square** and **Central Mall**. This was reputedly once a centre of prostitution and racketeering, which is hard to believe now that fornication and fraud have given way to fusion cuisine and fashion. At the northwest corner of the complex is the attractive **Tan Si Chong Su Temple**, which has successfully resisted attempts at modernization. The temple was built in 1876 as an ancestral temple and assembly hall of the Hokkien Tan clan. The money was donated by Tan Kim Cheng (1829-92) and Tan Beng Swee (1828-84), sons of the wealthy philanthropist Tan Tock Seng. The temple faces the Singapore River – as *feng shui* (geomancy) dictates – and it is particularly rich in carvings and other decoration. The series of two courtyards and two altar halls symbolizes *li*, the admired characteristic of humbling oneself in deference to others. The dragon-entwined columns, round windows and granite panels are comparatively unusual. Above the main altar table are four Chinese characters that translate as 'Help the world and the people'.

A little further south is **Clifford Pier**, which was built in the 1930s. It is possible to hire rather expensive boats here to cruise up and down the river and around Marina Bay. Bumboats and junks also take visitors on longer watery tours to Pulau Kusu and the islands of the south (see page 634). It is possible to hire a bumboat yourself, but expect to pay around S$60 per hour.

From Change Alley it is a short walk to the heart of Singapore's financial district. **Shenton Way** (Singapore's equivalent of Wall Street), **Raffles Place**, **Robinson Road** and **Cecil Street**, all packed tight with skyscrapers, form the financial heart of modern Singapore. These streets contain most of the buildings that give the city its distinctive skyline, and it is best seen from the **Benjamin Sheares Bridge** or from the boat coming back from Batam Island. The first foreign institutions to arrive on the island still occupy the prime sites: the Hong Kong and Shanghai Banking Corporation and Standard Chartered Bank. A short walk away down Philip Street is the small **Wak Hai Cheng Bio Temple**, built in 1826, looking particularly diminutive against the buildings around it. The name means 'Guangdong [Canton] Province Calm Sea Temple' and the purpose is pretty clear: to ensure that Chinese immigrants making the voyage through the dangerous South China Seas arrived safely. The two key gods depicted here are Xuan Tien Shang Di (the Heavenly Father) in the right-hand hall and Tien Hou (the Heavenly Mother) in the left. Tien Hou is a particular favourite of sailors. The figures on the roof are extremely vivid and so is some of the carving inside.

Another piece of old Singapore amidst the new is the **Lau Pa Sat Festival Market**, once known as Telok Ayer, between Robinson Road and Raffles Quay. This was the first municipal market in Singapore. The first market here was commissioned by Stamford Raffles in 1822, but the present structure was designed by James MacRitchie and built in cast-iron shipped out from a foundry in Glasgow in 1894. (A little piece of irrelevance: the same foundry cast the iron for Cavenagh Bridge.) It is said to be the last remaining Victorian cast-iron structure in Southeast Asia and was declared a national monument in 1973, but was dismantled in 1985 to make way for the MRT, before being rebuilt. It is now a thriving food centre.

East of the city proper, Marina South is a vast expanse of land, reclaimed from the sea in the 1970s and 1980s as an overspill area for the envisaged spread of

Financial centre
See the Chinatown map, page 612

Singapore

Marina South

Singapore's financial district. **Marina Village** was built, complete with restaurants, bars, concert venues, discos, a night bazaar and a 24-hour bowling alley. Initially, the enterprise didn't take off and the ebullient Moroccan businessman who financed the venture fled the country. However, it has gradually gained in popularity and the restaurants and bars are relatively well patronized.

Transport Raffles Place **MRT** station is in the heart of the financial district, just south of the Singapore River. **Buses** 124, 174 and 190 run direct from Orchard Road. For Marina South, take the MRT to Marina Bay and then the shuttle bus to Marina South. Tanjong Pagar is the nearest MRT stop to the Tanjong Pagar container terminal. It is best to explore this from Cavenagh Bridge near the mouth of the Singapore River to Clarke Quay takes about 20 minutes. **Bumboat** tours of the river leave from Clarke Quay and Raffles Landing, while a handful of boats offering an assortment of short **cruises** to the southern islands depart from Clifford Pier.

Orchard Road

Emerald Hill This area was laid out by 30 different owners between 1901 and 1925; conforming to the established theme was considered good manners, which has resulted in a charming street of Peranakan (Straits Chinese) shophouses. These have been carefully restored to their original condition and combine European and Chinese architectural elements.

Orchard Road

■ Sleeping	9 Regalis Court *C5*
1 Four Seasons *B2*	10 Regent *C1*
2 Goodwood Park *A3*	11 Shangri-La *A1*
3 Grand Hyatt *B3*	12 Sheraton Towers *A3*
4 Hilton *B2*	13 Singapore Marriott *B3*
5 Le Meridien *B5*	14 Traders *C1*
6 Lloyd's Inn *C5*	15 YMCA International
7 Meritus Negara *B2*	House *B6*
8 Orchard *B2*	16 YWCA *C6*

● Eating
1 Cuppage Thai Food *B5*
2 Esmirada's *B5*
3 Grill on Devonshire *C4*
4 Hard Rock Café *B2*
5 Korean (in Specialists' Centre) *B5*
6 Orchard Maharajah *B5*
7 Planet Hollywood *B2*

Related maps
A Little India,
page 617
B Colonial core,
page 600

0 metres 200
0 yards 200

At the end of Orchard Road is Dhoby Ghaut, which got its name from the Bengali and Madrasi *dhobis* who used to wash the clothes of local residents in the stream which ran down the side of Orchard Road and dry them on the land now occupied by the *YMCA*. *Ghaut* is a Hindi word meaning landing place or path down to a river, while *dhoby* is from the Sanskrit word *dhona*, meaning to wash. The *dhobis* would walk from house to house collecting their clients' washing, noting each piece down in a little book using a series of marks (they were illiterate). In 2001, a large chunk of Dhoby Ghaut was being redeveloped as part of the extension programme of the MRT. It will become an interchange linking the northeast with City Hall. The plans are to make this an extensive entertainment and retail area, though it is not expected to be completed until 2002.

Dhoby Ghaut

At the western end of Orchard Road are the Botanic Gardens, on Cluny Road, not far from Tanglin. The gardens contain almost 500,000 species of plants and trees from around the world in its 47 ha of landscaped parkland, primary jungle, lawns and lakes. In 1963 former Prime Minister Lee Kuan Yew launched the successful Garden City campaign and most of the trees lining Singapore's highways were supplied by the Botanic Gardens. The gardens now cater for the recreational needs of modern Singapore. Every morning and evening, the park fills with joggers and Tai Chi fanatics. During the day, wedding parties pose for pictures among the foliage. The bandstand in the centre of the gardens is used for live music performances at the weekends.

Botanic Gardens
The gardens are beautifully laid out and well worth a visit

Singapore

Pubs & bars	3 Far East Plaza *B3*	11 Orchard Towers *B2*	20 Wheelock Place *B3*
8 Ice Cold Bar *B4*	4 Hilton Shopping	12 Paragon *B4*	21 Wisma Atria *B3*
9 No 5 Emerald Hill *B4*	Plaza *B2*	13 Plaza Singapura *B6*	
10 Number 5 Bar *B4*	5 HPL House *B2*	14 Scotts *B3*	
11 Que Pasa Bar *B4*	6 Lucky Plaza *B3*	15 Shaw Centre *B3*	
	7 Ngee Ann City *B3*	16 Specialists' Centre *B5*	
Shopping	8 Orchard Emerald *B4*	17 Tanglin *B2*	
1 Centrepoint *B5*	9 Orchard Plaza *B5*	18 Tanglin Mall *C1*	
2 Far East Centre *B2*	10 Orchard Point *B5*	19 Tanglin Place *C1*	

The Botanic Gardens were founded by an agri-horticultural society in 1859. In the early years they played an important role in fostering agricultural development in Singapore and Malaya, as successive directors collected, propagated and distributed plants with economic potential, the most famous of which was rubber. Henry Ridley, director of the gardens from 1888 to 1912, pioneered the planting of the Brazilian para rubber tree (*Hevea brasiliensis*). In 1877, 11 seedlings brought from Kew Gardens in London were planted in the Singapore gardens. An immediate descendant of one of the 11 originals is still alive in the Botanic Gardens today, near the main entrance. By the lake at the junction of Tyersall and Cluny roads, there is a memorial to Ridley on the site where the original trees were planted. Ridley was known as 'Mad Ridley' because of the proselytizing zeal with which he lobbied Malaya's former coffee planters to take up rubber instead. ■ *0500-2400 Mon-Sun, T4709900. A map can be acquired from the Ranger's office, 5 mins' walk into the garden.*

The Botanic Gardens also house the **National Orchid Garden**, where 700 species and 2,100 hybrids of Singapore's favourite flower are lovingly cultivated. It is billed as the 'Largest Orchid Showcase in the World'. The gardens began to breed orchids back in 1928 and those on show include Singapore's national flower, Miss Agnes Joaquim's orchid, discovered in the late-19th century by the eponymous Miss Joaquim in her garden. The Mist House contains a collection of rare orchids, whilst the Yuen-Peng McNeice Bromeliad Collection houses 300 species and 500 hybrids from Central and South America. ■ *0830-1900, last ticket sales at 1800, admission S$2, S$1 children. The closest entrance to the Botanic Gardens for the Orchid Garden is on Tyersall Ave. Lots of buses run past the Botanic Gardens including nos 7, 77, 105, 106, 123 and 174, alighting at the junction of Cluny and Napier roads, next to Gleneagles Hospital. Suitable for wheelchairs. T4719955 for further information.*

Transport There are 3 **MRT** stations on, or close to, Orchard Rd. Dhoby Ghaut MRT station lies at the eastern end of Orchard Rd, close to the northwest corner of the colonial core. The Somerset MRT stop is on Somerset Rd, which runs parallel to Orchard Rd. The Orchard MRT station is at the intersection of Orchard Rd and Scotts Rd, towards the western end of the strip and close to the main concentration of hotels. A profusion of **bus** services run eastwards along Orchard Rd – at last count, some 20 in all. For routes west, walk 1 block south of Orchard Rd.

To walk Orchard Road from end to end is quite a slog – from Dhoby Ghaut to the north-western end of Orchard Road past Scotts Road is around 2½ km. This is fine if you're taking it slowly, stopping off for brief respites in one of the many air-conditioned shopping arcades. Otherwise, consider hopping on a bus or taking the MRT.

Chinatown

The area known as **Kreta Ayer** encompasses **Smith**, **Temple**, **Pagoda**, **Trengganu** and **Sago streets**. This was the area that Raffles marked out for the Chinese kampong and it became the hub of the Chinese community, deriving its name from the ox-drawn carts that carried water to the area. Renovation by the URA has meant that these streets still retain their characteristic baroque-style shophouses, with weathered shutters and ornamentation.

After Raffles' initial foray to Singapore in 1819, he left the fledgling colony in the hands of Major Farquhar with instructions on how it should be developed. When Raffles returned for a shufti in October 1822, he was horrified to find his instructions being ignored and the city expanding in an alarmingly haphazard fashion. He promptly countermanded Farquhar's plans and orders and established a committee with even more explicit instructions. The committee allocated an area to each ethnic group and the Chinese were awarded this slice of land, southwest of the river.

Immigrants from China settled in Singapore in the latter half of the 19th century and recreated much of what they had left behind. Clan groups began migrating from the southern provinces of China to the *Nang Yang* or 'Southern Seas' in successive waves from the 17th century. By 1849 the Chinese population had reached 28,000, but the area they inhabited was largely confined to a settlement between Telok Ayer and Amoy streets. The greatest numbers migrated in the 40 years after 1870, mostly coming from the southeastern coastal provinces, with the Hokkiens forming the majority. Each dialect group established their own temple. The Hokkiens founded **Thian Hock Keng** in 1821, the Cantonese established **Fu Tak Chi** on Telok Ayer Street around the same time, as did the Teochews who built **Wak Hai Cheng Bio** on Philip Street. Streets, too, were occupied by different Chinese groups, with clubs and clan houses – or *kongsi* – aiding family or regional ties. The *kongsi* were often affiliated with secret societies, or *tongs*, which controlled the gambling and prostitution industries and the drug trade.

Expansion of the financial district meant that Chinatown was being demolished so rapidly that by the time the authorities realized that tourists actually wanted to see its crumbling buildings, many of the streets had already been destroyed. In any case, Chinatown had become a slum, with overcrowding and poor sanitation being very real problems. A clean-up campaign was undertaken; its markets were cleared out, shops and stalls relocated, shophouses refurbished and the smells and noises of Chinatown banished to a world that only a few confused grandparents care to remember. Many residents have moved out to new, modern flats in HDB (Housing Development Board) estates scattered around the island. To preserve what was left of the city's architectural history, the Urban Redevelopment Authority (URA) was established in the 1970s to list old buildings and provide a framework for restoration and conservation.

The typical Straits Chinese house accommodated the family business on the ground floor, leaving the second and third floors as family living quarters – sometimes accommodating two families (and in later years, as Chinatown became desperately overcrowded, up to five families). A few wealthy Chinese merchants – or *towkays* – built their houses according to traditional Chinese architectural conventions, but almost all of these have long since been demolished. One which has survived is **Tan Yeok Nee's mansion** on Tank Road, at the eastern end of Orchard Road (see page 608). Another is the **Thong Chai Medical Institute** on Eu Tong Sen Street, at the corner of Merchant Road. It was built in southern Chinese palace style with three halls, two inner courts and ornamental gables, and was completed in 1892. By the late-19th century it had become a centre for traditional medicine, offering its services free to the poor; *thong chai* means 'benefit to all'. In 1911, during a malaria outbreak, it distributed free quinine. The building also became a focal point for the Chinese community, being the headquarters for the Chinese guilds. The Chinese Chamber of Commerce began life here (its headquarters are now on Hill Street, see page 599). The building was made a national monument in 1973 and has recently been expertly renovated.

History
There's no MRT here yet; a new NE line is under construction. Nearest MRT stations: Raffles Place, in the Financial District to the east, and Outram Park, to the west

Chinatown architecture

Singapore

Chinatown

Singapore

Related map
A Singapore
River and the
city, page 604
B Colonial
Core, page 600

N

0 metres   100
0 yards   100

■ **Sleeping**
1 Amara *F2*
2 Damenlou & Swee
   Kee Restaurant *D3*
3 Duxton *E2*
4 Inn at Temple St *C2*

5 Keong Saik *D1*
6 Royal Peacock *D1*

● **Eating**
1 L'Angelos *D3*
2 Blue Ginger *E2*

3 Café Gypsy *C3*
4 Da Paolo's *C3, E2*
5 Efferus *C3*
6 Futoshi *D3*
7 Gaetano *C3*
8 Indochine *C3*

9 Mama Africa *C4*
10 Pasta Brava *E2*
11 Senso *C3*
12 Shidong *C4*
13 Tea Chapter *D2*
14 Tiong Shiang *C2*

B

Singapore River

Raffles Landing Site
Raffles Statue
Empress Place

Anderson Bridge
Merlion

Bird Sculpture

Cavenagh Bridge

Collyer Quay

Marina Bay

Chulia St
Market St

UOB Building & Dali's Homage to Newton
Battery St
Henry Moore Sculpture
Raffles Place

Fulleton Rd

Clifford Pier

Raffles Place
Raffles Place (Interchange) M

Collyer Quay

Change Alley

Square Court

Raffles Quay

Lau Pa Sat Festival Market M

To Marina South

Spanish Consulate
Bookstore

East Coast Parkway

Marina Wharf

⑤   ⑥

15 La Voix *C4*

● **Pubs & bars**
16 Beaujolais Winebar *D3*
17 JJ Mahoney's *E2*

Singapore

In **Sago Street** (or 'death house alley' as it was known in Cantonese, after its hospices for the dying), **Temple Street** and **Smith Street**, there are shops making paper houses and cars, designed to improve the quality of the after-life for dead relatives (by burning the models after the funeral, it is believed that one's worldly wealth hurries after you into the next world). Also on these streets, shops sell all the accoutrements needed for a visit to a Chinese temple. At Number 36 Smith Street there is a three-storey building that was originally home to a famous Cantonese opera theatre – Lai Chun Yen – and formerly Smith Street was also known as 'Hei Yuen Kai', or Theatre Street. The English probably gave Sago Street its name in the early 19th century, as Singapore became a centre of high-quality sago (a muti-purpose palm yielding starch) production for export to India and Europe. By 1849, there were 15 Chinese and two European sago factories here.

Perhaps because death and health go hand-in-glove, there are also a number of **Chinese medicine shops** in this area – for example, *Kwang Onn Herbal* at 14 Trengganu Street and others on Sago Street. Chinese traditional medicine halls still do a roaring trade, despite the advantages of Medisave schemes and 21st-century pharmaceuticals. On show are antlers and horns, dried frogs and flying lizards, trays of mushrooms and fungi, baskets of dried seahorses (S$10 each) and octopus, sharks' fins and ginseng. Presumably rarer, and because they are illegal, body parts like tiger penis and ground rhino horn are kept out of sight. Looking at this cornucopia of the dried and the pickled, it is easy to wonder how the Chinese ever discovered that flying lizard seeped in tea is good for athlete's foot. It shows enormous dedication. The **Hong Lim Complex** on **Upper Cross Street** has several more such medicine halls. There are also a few skilled Chinese calligraphers still working from shops around Upper Cross Street.

For anyone looking for a full range of Chinese products, one of their best bets is to visit the **Yue Hwa Chinese Emporium** on the corner of Eu Tong Sen and Upper Cross streets. *Yue Hwa* is an Aladdin's Cave of Chinese goodies, from silk camisoles, to herbal medicines, to beaded bags and Chinese tea. Just north of here, between Upper Pickering Street and North Canal Road, is a small area of green called **Hong Lim Park**.

Sri Mariamman Temple As if to illustrate Singapore's reputation as a racial and religious melting-pot, the Hindu Sri Mariamman Temple is situated nearby at 244 South Bridge Road. There was a temple on this site as early as 1827, making it Singapore's oldest Hindu place of worship. Stamford Raffles is said to have granted the land to Narian Pillai, a Tamil who accompanied Raffles to Singapore during his second visit on board the *Indiana*, and set up Singapore's first brickworks. The basic layout of the present, gaudy Dravidian (South Indian) structure dates from 1843, although it has been much renovated and extended over the years. The temple shop is piled high with books on Hindu philosophy and cosmology and, unsurprisingly, is run by a Chinese family. The building is dedicated to Sri Mariamman, a manifestation of Siva's wife Parvati. (She is believed to be particularly good at curing epidemics and other major health scares, which at that time in Singapore were the norm rather than the exception.) The *gopuram*, or tower, here is particularly exuberant and the sacred cows seated along the top of the boundary wall add a rather pleasing bucolic touch to the affair. The temple is the site of the annual Thimithi festival, which takes place at the end of October or the beginning of November. Devotees cleanse their spirits by fasting beforehand and then show their purity of heart by walking over hot coals (see page 593). To the north of the temple, also on South Bridge Road, is the **Jamae Mosque**, built in 1826 by the Chulias from southern India. It harnesses an eclectic mix of Anglo-Indian, Chinese and Malay architecture.

Chinese temple-carvers still live on **Club Street**, which also has a number of *kongsi* along it. Many of the buildings along **Mosque Street** were originally stables. It was also home to Hakkas, who traded in second-hand paper and scrap metal – today it is better known for its Chinese restaurants. Number 37 Pagoda Street was one of the many coolie quarters in the area – home to Chinese immigrants, who lived in cramped conditions, sleeping in bunk spaces.

Telok Ayer Street This street is full of shophouses and fascinating temples of different religions and was once one of the most important in Singapore. The city's oldest Chinese temple, the Taoist **Thian Hock Keng** Temple, or Temple of Heavenly Happiness, is a gem (notwithstanding the naff fibreglass wishing well in one corner). The temple is also very popular; the coaches lined up outside give the game away – but don't let this put you off. Telok Ayer Street was the perfect place for merchants and traders to establish themselves, as it was right on the seafront. (It also became notorious for its slave trade in the 1850s.) The temple was funded by a wealthy merchant of the same name and building commenced in 1839. Skilled craftsmen and materials were all imported from China, the cast-iron railings came from Glasgow and the decorative tiles from Holland. The building was modelled on 19th-century southern Chinese architectural traditions, with a grouping of pavilions around open courtyards, designed to comply with the dictates of geomancy (*feng shui*).

Singapore

The main deity of the temple is Tien Hou, the Goddess of Seafarers, and she is worshipped in the central hall. The image here was imported from China in the 1840s and the temple soon became a focal point for newly arrived Hokkien immigrants who would gather to thank Tien Hou for granting them a safe journey. In the left-hand hall there is an image of the Lord of Laws (Fa Zhu Gong), while in the right, is the Prince of Prominence, Zai Si Xian He. The ubiquitous Kuan Yin, the Goddess of Mercy, also makes an appearance. The temple's position on the waterfront quickly came to an end, in the 1880s, when one of Singapore's first land reclamation projects moved the shore several blocks east. Well worth a visit.

A little way north of Thian Hock Keng is another much smaller Chinese temple, the Fuk Tak Chai temple. This is situated in an area that has been recently gentrified and is now known as **Far East Square**. Within the square is a jumble of renovated shophouses, with bars and bistros and a handful of shops. The two buildings of interest here are the **Chui Eng Free School**, 131 Amoy Street, one of the first free schools in Singapore – although sadly only the façade remains – and the **Fuk Tak Chai Temple**, now a museum, at 76 Telok Ayer Street, one of the oldest of Singapore's temples, restored in 1998. Coolies arriving in Singapore made this their first stop, giving thanks for safe arrival. This modest but elegantly proportioned temple, with just one court and shrine room, was built in 1824 by the Hakkas and Cantonese. *Telok Ayer* means water bay in Malay; before land reclamation, this temple stood on the waterfront and was constantly under attack from processes of coastal erosion. It's a little oasis of calm amidst the frenetic life of the city and holds a limited display of exhibits, including some Peranakan jewellery, Chinese stone inscriptions, a pair of porcelain pillows, a model of a Chinese junk and an excellent 'diorama' of Telok Ayer Street, as it must have been in the mid-1850s. ■ *Daily 1000-2200, free*. **The Pavilion**, also within the square, is on the site where Chinese opera was once performed and is now used as a centre for the performing arts.

The Al-Abrar Mosque, also on Telok Ayer Street, was built between 1850 and 1855 by Indian Muslims, who were also responsible for the fancy turrets of the **Nagore Durgha Shrine** – a little further up the street – which was built in 1829. Designated a national monument, the shrine is a blend of architectural styles – Palladian doors and Doric columns combined with more traditional Indian-Islamic touches like the perforated roof grilles...and then there are the fairy lights. An intriguing architectural sight is the **Telok Ayer Chinese Methodist Church**, 235 Telok Ayer Street. The church was built in 1924 and combines a mixture of Eastern and Western influences. There is a flat roof with a Chinese pavilion and a colonnaded ground floor. It is all rather odd. During the Second World War it was used as a refugee camp.

One of Chinatown's more interesting places to visit is the Tea Chapter, at 9 Neil Road, where visitors are introduced to the intricacies of tea-tasting in elegant surroundings. Visitors are invited to remove their shoes (sometimes an aromatic experience in itself) and can choose either to sit in one of their special rooms or upstairs on the floor. Relaxing Chinese plink-plink music, muffled feet, a tiny cup of delicious Supreme Grade Dragon Well, Scarlet Robe or Green Iron Goddess of Mercy at your lips and the cool atmosphere (it's air conditioned upstairs) all contribute towards a soothing experience. As the brochure rather extravagantly puts it: "It is a mythical dream come true for those seeking solace from a harsh and unfeeling existence". This is a popular place for young Singaporeans to visit on a Sunday afternoon. There is also a range of teas available to buy in the shop. ■ *1100-2300 Mon-Sun*.

Tea Chapter

Singapore

Jinriksha station The white building on the corner of Tanjong Pagar and Neil Road was the Jinriksha Station, built in 1903, and now the *Dragontown Seafood Restaurant*. It served as the administration centre for the jinriksha pullers. Jinrikshas arrived from Japan via Shanghai in the 1880s and soon became the most popular way to travel. By 1888 there were 1,800 in use, pulled by immigrants who lived in Sago and Banda streets. At the turn of the century, the fare for a 30-minute trip would have been 3 cents, 20 cents for an hour.

Bird singing On Sunday mornings, bird lovers gather at the corner of **Tiong Bahru** and Seng Poh roads for traditional bird singing competitions, where row upon row of thrushes, merboks and sharmas sing their hearts out, in antique bamboo cages with ivory and porcelain fittings, hung from lines. The birds are fed on a carefully controlled diet to ensure the quality of their song. Owners place their younger birds next to more experienced songsters, to try to improve their voices and pick up new tunes. Birds start twittering at 0730 and are spent by 1000. On the opposite side of the road, there's a shop selling everything you need for your pet bird – including porcelain cage accoutrements. Come here early and combine a visit to hear the birds with breakfast in one of the traditional coffee shops nearby: fresh baked *roti* washed down with sweet black or milky coffee. If you walk on down Seng Poh Road you will come to a fabulous **wet market**; every conceivable vegetable, fruit, fish, meat, beancurd you could ever want to purchase is available here. ■ *MRT to Tiong Bahru or Outram Park, or the bus stops right opposite this spot – bus nos 16, 33 and 36.*

Transport There is currently no **MRT** station within Chinatown, but a new north-east line is under construction (and causes considerable disruption down the main artery of the area, Eu Tong Sen and South Bridge roads). The closest stations at present are Raffles Place, within the financial district, a short walk from the eastern edge of Chinatown, or Outram Park, at the western edge. Many **bus** services run through this area – nos 124, 143, 174 and 190 operate direct from Orchard Rd.

Little India

Serangoon Road
If Little India is the heartland of Indian Singapore, then Serangoon Rd is its soul

Serangoon Road was named after the Rongong stork which used to inhabit swampland in the area. By 1828, Serangoon Road was established as 'the road leading across the island', but the surrounding area remained swampland until the 1920s when its brick kilns and lime pits attracted Indian (mainly Tamil) labourers to the area. In 1840 the race course was completed, which drew Europeans to settle here. (The road names Cuff, Dickson and Clive would have been private lanes to the European residences.)

Wet markets The lively **Zhujiao** (previously **Kandang Kerbau** or **KK) Market**, on the corner of Buffalo and Serangoon roads, is an entertaining spot to wander. Spices can be ground to your own requirements. Upstairs there is a maze of shops and stalls; the wet market is beyond the hawker centre, travelling west along Buffalo Road. New legislation introduced in 1993, which ruled that no animals could be slaughtered on wet market premises, saw the end of the chicken-plucking machine. It used to do the job in 12.4 seconds.

Kandang Kerbau – Malay for corral – was the centre of Singapore's cattle-rearing area in the 1870s. The cattle trade was dominated by Indians and among them was IR Belilios, a Venetian Jew from Calcutta who gave his name to a road nearby. The roads around KK have names connected to the trade: Lembu (cow) Road and Buffalo Road. With the boom in the cattle trade,

Little India

To Sri Vadapathira
Kaliamman Temple
Shophouses
Petain Rd
To Lavender Food Square
To Wooden
Handicrafts

Jalan Besar
Stadium

To Sakayamuni Buddha Gaya
Temple (150m) & Leong San
See Temple (150m)
Sri Perumal Temple
Shophouses
King Georges Av
To Leong San See
Temple
Antique Shop
Farrer Park
Rangoon Rd
Kitchener Rd
Owen Rd
Serangoon
Plaza
Burmah Rd
Sam Leong Rd
Jalan Besar
Plaza
Maude Rd
Tyrwhitt Rd
Birch Rd
Mustafa
Centre
Syed Alwi Rd
Anguillia
Mosque
Roberts La
Desker Rd
Kinta Rd
Rowell Rd
Foochow
Methodist
Rotan
La
Race Course La
Hindoo Rd
Kapor Rd
Kelantan La
Kelantan Rd
Khang La
Norris Rd
Jalan Besar
Veerasamy Rd
Sri Veeramaka-
liamman Temple
Chitty Rd
Pitt St
Belilios Rd
Cuff Rd
Upper Weld Rd
Weld Rd
Arab St
Spice
Mill
Perak Rd
Upper Dickson Rd
Kerbau Rd
Jewellery
shops
Church of True Light
Sim Lim
Tower
Little India
Buffalo Rd
Kuna's
Handicrafts
Dunlop St
Abdul Gaffoor
Mosque
Rochor Canal Rd
Zhujiao
Campbell La
Little India Arcade
Mayo St
Bukit Timah Rd
Hastings Rd
Rochor Canal
Sungei Rd
Madras St
Ophir Rd
Bukit Timah Rd
Rochor Canal Rd
Sim Lim
Square
Rochor Rd
MacKenzie Rd
Albert St
Albert
Complex
Fu Lu Shou
Complex
Niven Rd
Short St
Burlington
Square
The Bencoolen
New Bugis St
Rickshaw
Centre
Selegie Rd
Prinsep St
Kuan Yin Thong
Hod Cho Temple
Albert Centre
Chinese Pharmacy
Nanyang Academy
of Fine Arts
Tamil
Methodist
Sri Krishnan Temple
Stamford
Arts Centre
Selegie Centre
Bencoolen Link
Fortune
Centre
Wilkie Rd
Middle Rd
Bencoolen St
Waterloo St
Queen St
Sculpture Square
Sophia Rd
Prinsep
Link
Bencoolen
Mosque
Paradiz Centre
Church of St
Peter & St Paul
Victoria St
Maghain Aboth Synagogue
Singapore Art
Museum
Bras Basah Rd

⟹ Route of Thaipusam
procession

N
0 metres 100
0 yards 100

Singapore

Sleeping
1 Albert Court &
restaurants *D2*

2 Bencoolen *E2*
3 City Bayview *E3*
4 Dickson Court *C3*
5 Goh's Homestay *C2*
6 Kerbau *C1*
7 Little India
Guesthouse *B2*
8 Perak Lodge *C2*
9 Sun Sun *D2*

● **Eating**
1 Ananda Bhavan *C2*
2 Andhra Curry *C1*
3 Banana Leaf Apolo *C1*
4 D'Deli *C1*
5 Delhi *B1*
6 Indochine & Action
Theatre *E3*
7 Kamal's Vegetarian *C2*

8 Komala's Fast Food *C2*
9 Komala Vilas *C1, C2*
10 La Fête du Cuisinier *E3*
11 Muthu's Curry *B1*
12 Our Makan Shop *B1*
13 Soya Bean *D2*
14 Woodlands *C2*

Related maps
A Arab Street,
page 620

B Colonial core,
page 600

C Orchard Road,
page 608

related activities established themselves in the area; the cattle provided power for wheat-grinding, pineapple preserving and so on.

Opposite the market on Serangoon Road is the **Little India Arcade**, another Urban Redevelopment Authority (URA) project. This collection of handicraft shops is a great place to pick up Indian knick-knacks: leather sandals and bags, spices and curry powders, incense, saris and other printed textiles. There is also a food court here. On the north side of Campbell Road, facing onto the Little India Arcade, is *Kuna's* – an excellent little handicraft shop – and *Jothi's Flower Shop*, where garlands of jasmine flowers are strung for Hindu devotees to take to the temple. Hindu holy days are Tuesday and Friday, when business is particularly brisk. Down Dunlop Road – named after Mr AE Dunlop, the Inspector General of Police whose private road this was – is the **Abdul Gaffoor Mosque**. A mosque was first built on this site in 1859 by Sheikh Abdul Gaffoor bin Shaikh Hyder, although the current brick structure was erected in 1910. It is hardly a splendid building, but nonetheless has been gazetted as one of Singapore's 32 national monuments. Avoid visiting the mosque during Friday prayer day and in the evenings. Just off Dunlop Road, on Perak Road, is another architecturally unremarkable building, the **Church of True Light**, which was erected in 1850 to serve Little India's Anglican community of Hock Chew and Hinghwa descent. ■ *0900-1300 Sat-Sun; if you pass by at this time it's worth a quick look.*

Walking up Serangoon Road, take a right at Cuff Road to see Little India's last **spice mill** at work in a blue and mustard yellow shophouse, owned by P Govindasamai Pillai. It's hard to miss the chugging of the mill, let alone the rich smells of the spices. Here spices are ground for use on the day of cooking. ■ *Closed 1300-1400.*

The **Sri Veeramaka-liamman Temple** on Serangoon Road was built for the Bengali community by indentured Bengali labourers in 1881 and is dedicated to Kali, the ferocious incarnation of Siva's wife. The name of the temple means 'Kali the courageous'. It is similar in composition to most other temples of its kind and has three main elements: a shrine for the gods, a hall for worship and a *goporum* (or tower), built so that pilgrims can identify the temple from afar. The goporum of this temple – with its cascade of gaudy, polychromed gods, goddesses, demons and mythological beasts – is the most recent addition and was only completed in 1987. Worshippers and visitors should walk clockwise around the temple hall and, for good luck, an odd number of times. The principal black image of Kali in the temple hall (clasping her club of destruction – not a woman to get on the wrong side of) is flanked by her sons, Ganesha and Murugan. ■ *Closed 1230-1600 Mon-Sun.*

Further up Serangoon Road is another Indian temple, **Sri Perumal**, with its high goporum sculptured with five manifestations of Vishnu. The temple was founded in 1855, but much of the decoration is more recent. This carving was finished in 1979 and was paid for by local philanthropist P Govindasamy Pillai, better known as PGP, who made his fortune selling saris. Like other Hindu temples, there is greatest activity on the holy days of Tuesdays and Fridays. For the best experience of all, come here and to the Sri Veeramakaliamman and Hindu Chettiars (see page 618) temples during the two-day festival of **Thaipusam** – generally held in January (see page 54) – which celebrates the birthday of Murugan, one of Kali's sons. ■ *0630-1200 and 1800-2100 Mon-Sun.*

Further north at 366 Race Course Road (parallel to Serangoon Road) is the Buddhist Sakayamuni Buddha Gaya Temple – or Temple of One Thousand Lights – dominated by a 15 m-high, 300 tonne, rather crude, statue of the Buddha surrounded by 987 lights (the lights are turned on if you make a donation). The image is represented in the attitude of subduing Mara – the right hand touches the ground, calling the Earth Goddess to witness the historic Buddha's resistance of the attempts by Mara to tempt him with her naked dancing daughters. At the back of the principal image is a smaller reclining Buddha. Devotees come here to worship the branch of the sacred Bodhi tree – under which the Buddha gained enlightenment – and a replica mother-of-pearl footprint of the Buddha showing the 108 auspicious signs of the Enlightened One. ■ *0730-1645 Mon-Sun, remove shoes before entering.* Across the road is the Chinese Mahayana Buddhist **Leong San See Temple** – or Dragon Mountain Temple – with its carved entrance (where you don't have to remove your shoes). It is dedicated to Kuan Yin (the goddess of mercy) who had 18 hands, which are said to symbolize her boundless mercy and compassion. The principal image on the altar shows her modelled, as usual, in white, surrounded by a mixed bag of Chinese Mahayana folk gods and Theravada images of the Buddha.

Sakayamuni Buddha Gaya Temple

Numerous **buses** run up Serangoon Rd, including nos 64, 65, 106, 111 and 139 direct from Orchard Rd. Bugis is the most convenient **MRT** stop for Little India, although a 10-min walk is required to get into the heart of the area. A new MRT line currently under construction will run along Race Course Rd, which runs parallel to Serangoon Rd.

Transport

Arab Street

Originally this area was a thriving Arab village known as Kampong Glam (Glam Village). There is some disagreement over the origins of this name. Some commentators have attributed it to the Gelam tribe of sea-gypsies who once lived in the area. More likely, it refers to the glam tree from which Bugis seafarers extracted resin to caulk their ships.

Singapore's Arabs were among the area's earliest settlers, the first being a wealthy merchant called Syed Mohammad bin Harum Al-Junied who arrived in 1819, a couple of months after Stamford Raffles. The Alkaffs were another important local Arab family, who built their ostentatious mansion on Mount Faber. Arab merchants began settling in the area around Arab Street in the mid-19th century.

History
Bugis MRT station, near SW edge of Arab St and Lavender MRT, in NE. No 7 is the only bus direct from Orchard Rd

The **Sultan Mosque** with its golden domes, on North Bridge Road, attracts thousands of the faithful every Friday. Completed in 1928 and designed by colonial architect Denis Santry of Swan & Maclaren, it is an eclectic mixture of Classical, Moorish and Persian. The original building, constructed in the 1820s, was part of a deal between the Temenggong of Johor and the East India Company, in which the company donated S$3,000 towards its construction and the Temenggong leased the land to the trustees of the mosque. ■ *0900-1300, 1400-1600.* **NB** *Visitors in shorts, short skirts or sleeveless T-shirts will not be permitted to enter.* Next door is the old **Kampong Glam Istana**, built in the early 1840s as the Temenggong Ali Iskander Shah's palace.

Mosques
The focal point of the Arab quarter is Singapore's largest mosque, the Sultan Mosque

In the maze of side streets around the Sultan Mosque, there is a colourful jumble of Malay, Indonesian and Middle Eastern merchandise. Excellent selections of batik (which is sold in sarong lengths of just over 2 m) jostle for space

Stalls & shops

Singapore

with silk and Indian textiles (especially along Arab Street), wickerware, jewellery, perfumes and religious paraphernalia. In the weeks before Hari Raya Puasa, which marks the end of the fasting month of Ramadan (see page 57), Bussorah Street is lined with stalls selling all kinds of traditional muslim and malay foods – after dark it is a favourite haunt of famished Muslims. Bussorah Street has been gentrified as part of the URA's redevelopment efforts: it is now a pedestrianized, tree-lined street of elegant shophouses. Tombstone-makers are based along Pahang Street.

Bugis Street Bugis Street is southwest of Arab Street, right across the road from the Bugis Street MRT station. It is packed with stalls selling cheap T-shirts, copy watches and handicrafts – like a street market you might see in Thailand or Malaysia, but something that seems rather out of place in modern day Singapore. For those who like to see Singapore not just as a giant shopping plaza but also as a real life experiment in ersatz existence, then Bugis Street offers more than keyrings and Oriental flim-flam. The whole street has been re-created from a road that was demolished to make way for the MRT in the mid-1980s. Some people maintain that the reason it was demolished, and then brought back from the dead, sums up Singapore's approach to life. On the opposite side of Victoria Street is the new Parco Bugis Centre, a high-tech shopping plaza (in reconstructed air-conditioned shophouses) bustling with life, and containing restaurants, shopping malls and yet another of Singapore's fabulous fountains.

Arab Street

Related maps
A Little India,
page 617
B Colonial core,
page 600

0 metres 100
0 yards 100

■ **Sleeping**
1 Golden Landmark
2 Intercontinental
3 Shang Onn
4 Waffles Homestay
5 Willy's Guesthouse

● **Eating**
1 Bibik's Place
2 La Smorfia
3 Pivdofr
4 Rumah Makan
Minang

Waterloo Street, much of which has been pedestrianized, cuts across New Bugis Street and is also worth a modest detour. The **Sri Krishnan Temple** at 152 Waterloo Street dates back to the 1870s, when a simple attap hut protected two Hindu images (Krishna didn't arrive until the 1880s). Over the years it has been expanded and refined as the Hindu population of the surrounding area has prospered. Almost next door is a large, modern Mahayana pagoda, dedicated to **Kuan Yin** – the **Kuan Yin Thong Hod Cho Temple**. This temple is particularly popular – try visiting around lunchtime (1200-1300) when scores of worshippers come here to pray for good fortune. The central image is of multi-limbed Kuan Yin (see page), while on either side are Ta Ma Tan Shith and Hua Tua. The latter was an important Han Dynasty figure (third century BC) who is now the patron saint of Chinese medics. Perhaps not coincidentally, on the other side of the street in Cheng Yan Court is a collection of **traditional Chinese pharmacies**, selling the usual range of dried fungi, antlers, bones, herbs, roots like ginseng, dessicated sea horses and other unidentified body parts.

Temples

Sentosa

To the west of Tanjong Pagar port (see page 605), on Keppel Road, is the World Trade Centre. Most people visit the centre either to get to Sentosa, to take the boat to Batam and Bintan islands in Indonesia's Riau Archipelago (see page 580), or to use the cable car which connects Sentosa with Mount Faber. Also here is the **Singapore Maritime Showcase**. This is a museum devoted to Singapore's role as one of the world's largest and most efficient ports. A 12-minute 'Maritime Odyssey' transports you rather jerkily in a container through past, present and future Singapore. An extensive model of the port gives some idea of its size, a video wall describes the process of loading and unloading, there are banks of computers providing touch screens for maritime information and a game, and some basic Lego to construct your own port. Neptune Topaz provides a bridge and control panels for potential naval recruits and a short unexciting film about key ports of the world. The wooden models of ships are more fun. A cheap way to spend a rainy afternoon with bored children, but not worth a special visit. ■ *1030-1830 Tue-Fri, 1030-2030 Sat and Sun. Free except for the Maritime Odyssey, which costs S$2, S$1 children. Bus or taxi is the most convenient way to get here; numerous buses stop at the World Trade Centre, including nos 10, 30, 61, 84, 93, 97, 100, 131, 143, 145 and 166. Buses 65 and 143 run direct from Orchard Rd. A new MRT line currently under construction will terminate here.*

World Trade Centre
Tanjong Pagar MRT, then bus to World Trade Centre and on to Sentosa, or Tiong Bahru MRT and bus to ferry terminal

Opposite the exhibition halls of the World Trade Centre lies the **Telok Blangah Johor State Mosque**, dating from the 1840s. It was the focal point of the pre-Raffles Malay royalty in Singapore. Nearby is the tomb of the Temenggong Abdul Rahman (the *Tanah Kubor Rajah* or *Tanah Kubor Temenggong*), who was partly responsible for negotiating Singapore's status as a trading post with Stamford Raffles. The Johor royal family lived at Telok Blangah until 1855, when the town of Iskandar Putri was founded on the other side of the straits; it was renamed Johor Bahru in 1866.

Singapore

Other attractions on Sentosa

Sentosa is open 0730-2300 Mon-Thu, 0730-2400 Fri-Sun and public holidays. Some attractions close before 2300 – many at 1900

Apart from battling with the hordes of people, another downside to Sentosa is that a day here tends to be an expensive, as well as an entertaining, experience. A family of four can easily get through S$200. Basic admission is S$5 (S$3 for children), but there is a charge for each attraction. There are various combination tickets that include admission to Sentosa and to selected attractions. It is slightly cheaper to buy tickets this way at the World Trade Centre or on Mount Faber at the cable car entrance, rather than purchasing tickets at individual attractions after arrival (see each entry for admission charges). The disadvantage of purchasing tickets in this way is that it commits you before seeing what is on offer. Some combination tickets also tie you in to a tour.

Travelling anti-clockwise around the island, the first attraction of interest is the **Underwater World**, the largest walk-through oceanarium in Asia. It is highly recommended and is the highlight of any visit to Sentosa. A 100 m tunnel, with a moving conveyor, allows a glimpse of some of its 350 underwater species and 5,000 specimens. Giant rays glide overhead, while thick-lipped garoupa and spooky moray eels hide in caves and crevices. The 'creatures of the deep' tank, with giant octopus and spider crabs, is impressive. Other smaller tanks house cuttlefish, turtles, reef fish, sawfish, corals, sea urchins and other marine creatures. ■ *0900-2100, feeding times are well worth arriving for: 1130, 1430, 1600 and 1630, S$17 (S$11 children). Monorail station 2, bus nos 2 and A.*

Sentosa Island

Related map
A Singapore general,
page 596

0 metres 500
0 yards 500

Sleeping
1 Beaufort
2 Shangri-La Rasa Sentosa
3 Sijori Resort

Eating
1 Sentosa Food Centre
2 Sir Basil's Café & Bar

━━━ Monorail
----- Cable car

Singapore

Just before the Underwater World is the **Asian Village** – a short walk from the ferry terminal, but not worth much of a mention. The idea was to construct three theme villages for East Asia, South Asia and Southeast Asia. They're pretty dismal, although some quality souvenirs are for sale. 'Adventure Asia' is a rather half-hearted attempt at an all-Asian kiddies' funfair. ■ *1000-1900, rides are individually priced (S\$2-S\$3); S\$5 for the paddle boats.* An all-Asian restaurant and a village theatre, built up a hillside and capable of seating up to 800 people, are other attractions. This is Singapore's attempt at virtual reality: rather than having to travel to these places, the sights are all conveniently brought together on a single site. ■ *Free, but the various shows have an entrance charge, 1000-2100. Monorail station 1, bus nos 2 and C.*

Fort Siloso, on the westernmost point, is Singapore's only preserved coastal fort, built in the 1880s to guard the narrow western entrance to Keppel Harbour. It provides an informative visit, especially if you are interested in the fall of Singapore. It is possible to explore the underground tunnels, artillery nests and bunkers, experience a mock firing of a seven-inch gun, run riot over the assault course and play various interactive computer games with a martial tinge. The fort was built to guard against a seaward attack, but, as every amateur student of Singapore's wartime history knows, the Japanese assault was from the north. The guns of Fort Siloso were turned landwards, but could do little to thwart the Japanese advance. When news of the surrender came through, the soldiers of the Royal Artillery (many from the Indian subcontinent) sabotaged the guns to prevent them falling into enemy hands.

The **Butterfly Park and Insect Kingdom Museum** is a 1-ha park containing 2,500 butterflies at all stages in their life cycle. Also here is a rather antiseptic museum of dead butterflies and insects. ■ *0900-1830, S\$6 (S\$3 children). Monorail station 4, bus nos 2 and A.*

The **Sijori WonderGolf** course is fun: 45 mini-holes each, with some novel obstruction to surmount. ■ *0900-2100, S\$8-10 (S\$4-6 children).*

The **Musical fountain** is a disco-lit fountain which gyrates, together – with a rather unorchestrated laser light show – to everything from Joan Jett and the Blackhearts to the *1812 Overture*. Shows lasting 30 minutes are at 1700, 1730, 1930, 2030 and 2130. The later three shows have additional laser effects emitted from the 37 m, 12 storey-tall **Merlion**. This stupendous, laser-emitting symbol of Singapore joins with the fountains to create the 'Musical Fountain and Rise of the Merlion Show'. At other times of day, the Merlion can be climbed either up to its mouth or its crown for views over Sentosa, the city and port. There is a shop here – since nothing can be built on Sentosa without some merchandising outlet – that is themed as a Bugis shipwreck. The Bugis were the feared Malay seafarers who sailed from Sulawesi and controlled the seas of the Malay archipelago before the European period. They have often been likened to the Vikings and, like the Vikings, they were famed for their fearlessness and for their seafaring skills – and for the terror they instilled in the hearts of coastal communities. (The word bogey is said to be derived from bugis, and was first used in 1836 as another term for the devil. Thackeray wrote: "The people are all naughty and bogey carries them off". In 1865 the word was bastardized once more into bugbear, a hobgoblin reputed to devour naughty children.) ■ *Merlion open 0900-2200, last admission 2130, S\$3 (S\$2 children). Monorail station 1 and 4, bus nos 2, A, C.*

Singapore

Images of Singapore, **Pioneers of Singapore** and the **Surrender Chambers** offer a well-displayed history of Singapore, focusing on key figures from the origins of the city state as an entrepôt through to the modern period, and also telling the traumatic Second World War story. The wax models are not up to Madame Tussaud's standard, but the history is well told for those interested in such things. ■ *0900-2100, S$5-8 (S$3-5 children). Monorail station 4, bus nos 2 and A.*

The southwest 'coast' of the island has been redeveloped, with tens of thousands of cubic metres of golden sand shipped in, along with 300 mature coconut palms and over 100 ornamental shrubs and flowering trees. Three **beaches** have been created here: Central, Siloso and Tanjong. ■ *Monorail station 5 for Tanjong and Central and station 2 for Siloso, bus nos 2, A and M or the Beach Train, which runs from Fort Siloso to Tanjong Beach.* The **Dolphin Lagoon**, near Tanjong Beach, provides 'Meet the Dolphin' sessions at 1100, 1530 and 1730 (plus 1330 on weekends and public and school holidays). ■ *1100-1800, S$13 (S$7 children). Monorail 5.*

Volcanoland, a 'multimedia entertainment park', is another of the newer attractions: it takes you on a subterranean journey into the earth and is supposed to trace the evolution of life – although your children will pass no exams with this rubbish. The main show is entertaining enough, but the rest of the complex is rather disappointing and, as with so much on Sentosa, the visitor exits from the multimedia extravaganza – no doubt filled with grand, but erroneous, thoughts about the origins of life – straight into a shop. There are also occasional Mayan dances, although these are in no sense authentic; time your visit to coincide with these shows if desired. ■ *1000-1900, volcano erupts every 30 mins from 1030, S$12 (S$6 children). Bus nos A and C.*

The **Sentosa Orchid Gardens**, very close to the ferry terminal, have 10,000 plants and over 200 species of orchid. Within the gardens is a restaurant, a fish pond with koi carp, a Japanese tea room and various other gazebos, boulders and associated paraphernalia, and – yes, you've guessed it – a souvenir shop. ■ *0930-1830, S$3.50 (children S$2). Monorail stations 1 and 7, bus nos 2, A, C and E.*

Fantasy Island, advertised as the 'ultimate water adventure', is a must for children: white water river rapids, play areas in the water and aquatic slides are fun and well-designed. The various slides and chutes are graded from 1 to 4 and there is an area reserved purely for smaller children with lifeguards keeping a wary eye out. Public lockers and changing rooms, but no towels provided. Various snack bars on site. A sunny day here can turn a pallid European into a lobster in less time than it takes to say thermador. At weekends it is packed. ■ *1030-1900, S$16 (S$10 children). Monorail stations 1 and 7; bus nos 2, A, C, E and M.*

Close to Fantasy Island is **Cinemania**, a high-tech movie extravaganza. Combining high definition film with state-of-the-art sound and seats, raised on hydraulic jacks, it creates what is rather ambitiously called hyper reality. The blurb warns that you should give this a miss if you have back, neck or heart problems, are pregnant, suffer from epileptic fits or have a surname beginning with B. ■ *Show every 30 mins, 1100-2000, S$10 (S$6 children). Monorail stations 1 and 7, bus nos 2, A, C, E and M.*

The **Maritime Museum** is housed in a building in the shape of a boat, and traces the development of marine vessels from the earliest fishing boats through to the modern day. It also tells the history of Singapore as a port. ■ *1000-1800, free, closed Mon and Tue. Monorail station 7, bus nos A, C, E and M.*

Sentosa Island Tour S$28 from the following hotels: *Sheraton Towers, Mandarin, Boulevard, Shangri-La, Orchard* and *Hilton International.*

Golf on one of two courses – Serapong or Tanjong, contact Sentosa Golf Club, T2750022, 0700-1900. **Horse riding** near *Sijori Resort.* **Watersports** at *Sports Entertainment Club,* on southwest coast.

Transport

Bicycles Tandems and trishaws for hire from the ferry terminal and near Central Beach, open 1000-1800. For cycling enthusiasts, there is a 6 km cycle track around the island.

 Bus Service 'A' operates from the World Trade Centre bus terminal to Sentosa from 0700-2000 Mon-Thu, 0700-2300 Fri-Sun. To get to the World Trade Centre take buses 65, 167 or 143 from Orchard Rd; 61, 84, 143, 145, 166 and 167 from Chinatown (the nearest MRT station is at Tanjong Pagar, from which buses 10, 97, 100 and 125 go to the World Trade Centre). Bus 'C' leaves from the Tiong Bahru MRT station for the ferry terminal and Musical Fountain, and operates 0700-2200 Mon-Thu, 0700-2300 Fri-Sun. Service 'E' plies Orchard Rd, Bras Basah Rd and Marina Square, stopping at Lucky Plaza, *Mandarin Hotel*, Peranakan Pl, *Meridien Hotel*, Plaza Singapura, Bencoolen St, POSB Headquarters, Raffles City and *Pan Pacific Hotel*, 1000-2000. Bus services 'A' and 'C' cost S$6 (S$4 for children). Bus service 'E' is S$7 (S$5 for children). These are return fares and include entrance to Sentosa (normally priced at S$5).

 On Sentosa, **free buses** (operating every 10 mins, 0900-2230 Mon-Sun) link the ferry terminal, Underwater World, Fort Siloso and Images of Singapore. The free night bus (1930-2230 Mon-Sun) runs between the *Beaufort* and *NTUC* hotels, and the Musical Fountain and ferry terminal. The **monorail**, also free, links all the island's attractions and runs at 10-min intervals (0900-2200 Mon-Sun).

 Cable car Operates 0830-2100 Mon-Sun. An alternative way to reach Sentosa is via the cable car. There are 3 stops: Mount Faber (the highest point in Singapore, with scenic views and seafood restaurants – worthwhile), the Cable Car Tower adjacent to the World Trade Centre and the Cable Car Plaza on Sentosa. Fares are S$5.90 one way, S$6.90 return. Admission to Sentosa is in addition to these fares. **Ferry** The ferry from the World Trade Centre leaves every 20 mins from 0930 to 2100, every 15 mins 0830-2100 Sat and Sun. Fare USS$1.30 return (with entrance to Sentosa, USS$6.30). **MRT** A new MRT line is under construction, which will terminate at the World Trade Centre. **Taxis** Taxis are charged a toll of S$3 and can only drop off/pick up at the hotels on Sentosa.

Singapore West

Haw Par Villa (formerly **Tiger Balm Gardens**) is at 262 Pasir Panjang Road, on the way out to Jurong. Built by Aw Boon Haw and Aw Boon Par, brothers of Tiger Balm fame, it was their family home until they opened it to the public. The delightful estate was finally sequestrated by the Singapore government in 1985 and turned into a theme park. Boon Haw originally designed the gardens for his family's enjoyment. But his gory sculptures have instilled a sense of traditional morality in generations of Singaporeans. Sequences depict wrongdoers being punished in creative ways, most notably in the Ten Courts of Hell (which is reached along the Alley of the Ten Shops of Tack): one is having his tongue cut out, another is galled by a spear, others are

Haw Par Villa
The MRT West line runs via 9 stops from the city to Boon Lay. Some sights are far from a station, so take a bus or taxi. Jurong East Interchange links the MRT West line with the MRT North line

variously impaled on spikes, gnawed by dogs, boiled in oil, bitten by snakes, sliced in two, drowned in the Filthy Blood Pond or ground into paste by enormous millstones. Some of the allegories and stories are obscure to say the least: a pig dressed in what appears to be a forerunner to the 'Y' front; acrobatic mermaids; and tangoing fowl. Though doubtless highly significant to the cognoscenti of Chinese mythology, many of the stories will be lost on the uninitiated.

The island's most revolting theme park, a gaudy adventureland of Chinese folklore and the biggest Chinese mythological theme park in the world

Its 9-ha site is five times the size of the original villa and its grounds. There is a large section on ancient China, with pagoda-roofed buildings, arts and crafts shops and restaurants serving authentic cuisine, as well as traditional theatre – in which lion dances and wayangs are performed. The 'Creation of the World Theatre' tells classic tales from the Qin Dynasty; in the 'Legends and Heroes Theatre', a life-like robot is programmed to relate stories; and a video in the 'Spirit of the Orient Theatre' explains Chinese folklore, customs, traditions and festivals. At the beginning of 1998 the threat of closure hung over these venerable gardens. The number of employees has been slashed and some attractions have been closed to save money. *0900-1800 Mon-Sun, S$5 (S$2.50 children).* **NB** *Do not even think about visiting Haw Par Villa over Chinese New Year – each year about 12,000 people saunter around it in the space of about 4 days. MRT westbound to Buona Vista, then bus 200; or to Clementi and then bus 10. Direct buses to the Haw Par Villas are 10, 30, 51, 143 (runs from Orchard Rd) and 200.*

Holland Village

This is especially worth visiting at the weekend. This is really a residential area – and was once the home to the British forces barracked in Singapore – but it also developed into one of the trendier parts of suburban Singapore. There are restaurants and bars, small craft and antique shops, and a good wet market – Pasar Holland. The Holland Village Shopping Centre, on the first floor of Holland Avenue, is a good stop for Asian arts and crafts and there are ample

Singapore West

*Related map
A Singapore general,
page 596*

places to eat (see page 651) and relax while exploring the area. ■ *Take the MRT to Buona Vista and then walk up Commonwealth Ave to Holland Ave (about 15 mins), or take buses 106 or 200.*

Situated on Jalan Ahmad Ibrahim, Jurong Bird Park is a beautifully kept 20-ha haven for more than 8,000 birds of 600 species from all over the world, including a large collection of Southeast Asian birds. As it is now difficult to see most of these birds in the wild in Southeast Asia, a trip here is well worthwhile. Highlights include the world's largest collection of Southeast Asian hornbills and South American toucans and an entertaining air-conditioned penguin corner, complete with snow. Another main attraction is one of the largest walk-in aviaries in the world, with a 30 m-high man-made waterfall and 1,500 birds. There is also an interesting nocturnal house, with owls, herons, frogmouths and kiwis and bird shows throughout the day (the birds of prey show – at 1000 and 1600 – is particularly good). There is a monorail service round the park for those who find the heat too much (S$2.50, S$1 for children). ■ *0900-1800 Mon-Fri, 0800-1800 weekends and public holidays, T2650022. Bird shows at 1000, 1100, 1500 and 1600 daily, S$12 (S$5 children under 12), family tickets S$20. MRT westbound to Boon Lay then SBS bus 194 or 251 from Boon Lay MRT interchange.*

Jurong Bird Park

On Yuan Ching Road are these gardens, which extend over 13 ha on two islands in Jurong Lake. The Chinese garden – or Yu-Hwa Yuan – is said to be modelled on an imperial Sung Dynasty garden and specifically on the classical style of Beijing's Summer Palace. There are artfully scattered boulders, Chinese pavilions and a brace-and-a-half of pagodas to give it that Oriental flavour, but it is hard to believe that the Sung emperors would have been happy with this. Rather more refined is the Penjing Garden (Yun Xiu Yuan – or Garden of Beauty), a walled bonsai garden, which reputedly cost S$6 mn to develop. The garden contains 3,000 miniature potted penjing (bonsai) trees, sourced from all over Asia. The two outside the entrance are said to come from Sichuan and to be over 280 years old. They symbolize male and female lions guarding the entrance, but just in case these arboreal defenders should fail, there is also a pair of stone lions to act as back-up. Close to the main entrance is a large statue of the sage Confucious (551-479 BC), looking suitably studious and wise, and a stone boat craftily concealing a food outlet. On a small rise in the middle of the Chinese garden is the main pagoda, which towers up through six levels. It is possible to sweat your way to the top for a great view of HDB blocks. ■ *0900-1800 daily, S$4.50 (S$2 children), T2643455. MRT to Chinese Gardens (W10) and then walk the 200 m across the open-grassed*

Chinese & Japanese Gardens

Singapore

area to the east gate. Alternatively, take bus nos 335 or 180 which also run to the MRT stop and the east gate, or 154 which runs past the main west gate.

The Science Centre
This centre, on Science Centre Road, might be aimed more at children than adults – it is usually packed with schoolchildren enjoying a few hours away from cramming – but there is plenty of fun for grown-ups too. The central hub of the museum has a figure of Einstein talking in a rather forced German accent, hatching chicks and various other exhibits, including a computer screen where it is possible to conduct plastic surgery on your face. From this hub radiates the Hall of Life Sciences, a Virtual Science Centre, the Aviation Centre, a children's Discovery Centre and a Physical Science Hall. In the Aviation Centre, where Changi Airport makes a predictably significant appearance, visitors are guided around the wonders of flight by Archie the Archaeopteryx – a sort of avine dinosauric maître d'. For an extra S\$3 (S\$2 children) it is possible to fly a simulator. The Hall of Life Science's theme is humanity's impact on the earth and here there are some live animals along with a few talking dummies, including a dinosaur (spouting surprisingly unscientific rubbish) and Charles Darwin (far too thin) talking with an American-accented gorilla. Disney's *Jungle Book* has a lot to answer for. Overall, the centre succeeds in its mission to make science come alive, with plenty of gadgets and hands-on exhibits. It makes most sense to come here with children who will be able to spend several hours having fun and maybe even learn something. ■ *1000-1800 Tue-Sun, S\$3 (S\$1.50 children). To get there, take SBS 66 or 335 from Jurong East MRT.*

In the **Omni-theatre** next door, the marvels of science, technology and the universe can be viewed in a 284-seat amphitheatre, with a huge hemispherical (3-D) screen and a 20,000 watt sound system. Take a seat-of-your-pants thrill ride while learning about the science of roller coasters, climb Everest or experience an exploding volcano (films change periodically). Excellent films and very popular. ■ *1000-2100 Tue-Sun, S\$10 (S\$4 children) for Omninax movies (screened hourly 1000-2000 Tue-Sun); S\$6 (S\$3 children) for Planetarium show at 1000 and 1100, T5603316/5641432; T5689100 for film schedules. Take the MRT to Jurong East, and walk the last 300 m through the HDB block and across Townhall Rd to the museum. Bus nos 66, 198, 335 and TIBS bus no 178 run direct to the museum. Alternatively, get bus nos 51, 78, 97 or 147 to the Jurong East Interchange and then change to a 335 or walk the last 10 mins.*

Ming Village
This is one of the last factories in the world that faithfully reproduces Chinese porcelain antiques using traditional methods – from mould-making to hand-throwing – dating from Sung, Yuan, Ming and Qin dynasties. All the pieces are painted by hand and the factory blurb maintains that traditional methods of craftsmanship are scrupulously followed. It is possible to take a guided tour around the factory premises, at 32 Pandan Road, and seeing the work that goes into the pots certainly helps explain why the prices are so high in the showroom. The shop has an export department which will pack items for shipment. The village also runs traditional pottery and painting classes for long-stay and short-stay group visitors. The **Pewter Museum**, which has moved to the Ming Village, has daily demonstrations of traditional pewter-making processes. ■ *0900-1730 daily, free admission and guided tour, T2657711. MRT to Clementi, then bus 78. Or take the free Trolley Ming Village Shuttle Service which picks up at Orchard Hotel at 0920 and 1045, at Mandarin Hotel (South Wing) 0925 and 1050, Raffles Hotel 0935 and 1100 and Pan Pacific Hotel 0940 and 1105.*

Located at the western end of the island, the Singapore Discovery Centre is really a glorified S$70 mn PR exercise for Singapore Inc, concocted by the Singapore Defence Forces. A fair number of the attractions are military, like the shooting gallery, military tactics gallery and an array of military equipment from aircraft to night vision goggles – you can even make a simulated parachute jump, manoeuvring to your landing spot. There is also a children's adventure playground, a re-creation of significant events from Singapore's history with a walk-through gallery of shophouses and early HDB flats, and a stomach-churningly realistic motion simulator where, for example, you can follow a missile in flight. It is, as one might expect, well done with lots of hands-on interactive computer exhibits. It is also fascinating as an illustration of nation-building. The two main lessons to be learned here are that Singapore is dedicated to world peace and constructive engagement and that if you mess with Singapore you'll be in for a shock. There is also, of course, a food court and retail outlet for those who are empty of stomach or would like to be of pocket. ■ *0900-1900 (last admission 1800) Tue-Sun, S$9 (S$5 children), extra charge for motion simulator (S$4) and shooting gallery (S$3). Westbound MRT to Boon Lay (W12) and then connecting SBS bus nos 192 and 193 from the Boon Lay interchange, or direct on SBS bus nos 192 and 193. See also www.asianconnect.com/sdc*

Singapore Discovery Centre

East Coast

Katong is an enclave of Peranakan architecture and there are still streets of well-preserved shophouses and terraced houses in their original condition. Restaurants in Katong serve some of the best Peranakan food in Singapore, including delicious pastries and sweets**Joo Chiat Road**, which runs south down to the sea, is interesting for its unchanged early 20th-century shophouse fronts. The extravagant façades, found both here and on Koon Seng Road, are an excellent example of the Singapore Eclectic Style which evolved in the 1920s and 1930s. This whole area was originally a coconut plantation owned by a family of Arab descent – the Alsagoffs. A portion was purchased by a wealthy Chinese, Chew Joo Chiat, after whom a number of the roads are named (not just Joo Chiat Road; also Joo Chiat Lane, Joo Chiat Terrace and Joo Chiat Place). While most of the traditional businesses here have closed down or moved out, there are still some candlemakers struggling to make a living and a few other craftspeople. ■ *For Katong, take bus 14 or 16 from Orchard Rd; for Joo Chiat Road take the MRT to Paya Lebar.* ■ *Bus no 16 from Orchard Rd runs down Joo Chiat Rd, as does no 33.* **Peter Wee's Katong Antique House**, at 208 East Coast Road, is well worth a visit if you are in the area, with its unsurpassed collection of Peranakan antiques and an owner who is probably the most knowledgeable person in Singapore on the Peranakan culture.

Katong & Geylang Serai
The MRT East line runs all the way to Pasir Ris. For the coast it is best to take a bus (No 16 from Orchard and Bras Basah rds) or taxi

Singapore

This popular recreation area has beaches and gardens, as well as a tennis centre, driving range, sailing centre, the **Big Splash** and a food centre. In fact, there are assorted sports and entertainment facilities strung out over several kilometres – although they are largely patronized by locals rather than foreign visitors. The sand along these beaches was imported from nearby Indonesian islands. The **East Coast Recreation Centre**, in East Coast Park, has the usual array of crazy golf, foodstalls, cycling, canoes and fun rides. A good half-day excursion, especially if you are with children, is to hire bicycles and ride along the track that winds its way up the East Coast. There are no hills and lots of

East Coast Park

food and drink stops. It's more fun than battling with the crowds and cars, and also comparatively quiet during the week. ■ *1200-1745 Mon-Fri and 0900-1745 Sat and Sun, S\$3, S\$2 for children (baby seats, though not up to European standards, are available). Getting to the East Coast Park is a little tricky by public transport during the week as there is no direct bus. Either take bus 16 from Orchard Rd (the airport bus) and get off at Marine Parade, or bus 197 which runs down North Bridge Rd and South Bridge Rd. From Marine Parade, walk towards the park and the sea, crossing the expressway. On weekends and public holidays, bus 401 runs from the Bedok MRT station to the East Coast Park, passing many of the attractions, using the service road.*

The **Crocodilarium**, 730 East Coast Parkway, has over 1,200 inmates, bred in pens. Note that it is a commercial operation, not a zoological centre, and the animals here will end up as shoes and handbags. The best time to visit is at feeding times (1100 Tuesday, Thursday and Saturday). The Crocodilarium also stages crocodile-wrestling bouts; ring for times. Crocodile-skin goods are for sale. ■ *0900-1700 Mon-Sun, S\$2 (S\$1 children), T4473722. No direct buses; take the MRT to Paya Lebar or Eunos and then take a taxi.*

The **Singapore Crocodile Farm** at 790 Upper Serangoon Road is, like the Crocodilarium on the East Coast, a commercial set-up. Here, visitors can learn about skinning techniques and various other methods of transforming scary reptiles into quiescent handbags and shoes. This farm, with its population of about 800 crocodiles, has been on the same site since 1945, importing crocodiles from rivers in Sarawak. ■ *0830-1730 Mon-Sun. Buses 81, 84, 97, 111 and 153 all run along Upper Serangoon Rd and stop opposite the farm.*

Changi Prison

James Clavell's novel King Rat is more enlightening than a visit to Changi

Changi Prison is on Upper Changi Road. The prison, as featured on the 'Go to Jail' square in the Singapore version of Monopoly, is where Singapore's hangman dispenses with drug traffickers – with gruesome regularity. It was originally built to house 600 prisoners, but during the war more than 3,500 civilians were incarcerated here. In 1944, POWs were moved into the prison, and 12,000 American, Australian and British servicemen were interned in and

East Coast

0 metres 500
0 yards 500

■ **Sleeping**
1 Chancellor
2 Hotel 81-Opera
3 Malacca
4 Sea View

● **Eating**
1 House of Sundanese Food & Peranakan Inn

Singapore

around it. It is mostly visited by Second World War veterans – there is a small museum with reproductions of WRM Haxworth's paintings and the then 17-year-old trooper George Aspinall's photographs, which record the misery of internment. A replica of the atap-roofed Changi Prison chapel stands in the prison yard. The memorial chapel's original altar cross, whose base was made from a Howitzer shell casing, was returned to the chapel in 1992. The Chapel holds a service on Sunday evening at 1730, T5451411. The Prison Museum has an interesting display. For more information, T7366622. ■ *MRT to Tanah Merah and then bus 2, or bus 2 direct from Orchard Rd.*

North of the island

This temple at 184 Jalan Toa Payoh lies due north of the city, within the modern suburb of Toa Payoh. This Fujian temple's full name is Lian Shan, Shuang Lin – which means Lotus Hill, Twin Groves – referring to the *sal* grove in Kunisnara, near Patna, where the Buddha attained enlightenment. It is the largest Buddhist temple in Singapore and was originally built between 1898 and 1905. However, since then Singapore's urban expansion has enveloped it. Chunks of its original 4 ha area have been chipped away for housing development and, perhaps to atone for the effrontery, the Singapore Tourist Board gave the temple its own Suzhou-style rock garden. Despite the redevelopments, the temple retains its excellent wood carvings and some fine Thai images of the Buddha. There is also a statue of Kuan Yin and a corpulent image of the Maitreya Buddha. ■ *Take the MRT to Toa Payoh. Then take bus 8 or 26, getting off at HDB block 195, one stop past the Toa Payoh stadium.*

Siong Lim Temple
The MRT North line loops right around this part of the island and has 23 stops. TIBS buses – the Trans-Island Bus Service – are also useful

This Chinese Temple Complex (Bright Hill Drive) has, since its construction in 1989, grown into a sprawling, million dollar religious centre whose golden roofs spread over 7½ ha. Fed up with tastefully mouldering 19th-century Chinese temples? Then this is the place for you. This is Chinese temple garishness on a truly gargantuan scale; restrained was clearly not a word in the architect's vocabulary. From the main entrance on Sin Ming Avenue, pilgrims climb up through a series of halls with images of the historic Buddha and various other gods and goddesses from Chinese Mahayana Buddhism's extensive repertoire. There are halls for prayer and meditation, a pool containing thousands of turtles, a Buddhist library, an old people's home (and, appropriately, a crematorium), as well as a 9 m-high marble statue of Kuan Yin, the 15-headed goddess of mercy, carved by Italian sculptors. At the top of the complex is a regular office block surmounted by a large gold *stupa*. The walkways are crowded with hawkers selling jade bangles, Buddhist icons and dubious medicinal remedies. Resident geriatrics in the old people's home spend their last days making paper cars and other worldly symbols, which are torched after their deaths and, they hope, follow them into the next world. ■ *Take bus 130 from Raffles City or Clifford Pier; alight at the Sin Ming Drive stop which stops opposite the crematorium, then walk on to the T-junction and turn left down Sin Ming Ave to the main entrance. Alternatively, take the MRT to Ang Mo Kio, cross the road to the Ang Mo Kio bus interchange and board bus 130. The golden stupa of the temple can be seen from some way off.*

Kong Meng San Phor Kark
This complex has been the backdrop for many kung-fu movies and is one of the largest such complexes in Southeast Asia

Singapore

These zoological gardens, at 80 Mandai Lake Road, have one of the world's few open zoos – with moats replacing bars – making it also one of the most attractive zoos, with animals in environments vaguely reminiscent of their habitats. In its promotional brochure, the 20-ha zoo claims that its

Singapore Zoological Gardens

open-design concept has paid off: 'Our reward is happy animals. The proof lies in the zoo's good breeding record: unhappy animals do not make love!'. Only the polar bears and the tigers seemed unhappy in their surroundings. It contains over 170 species of animals (about 2,000 actual animals), some of them rare – like the dinosauric Komodo dragons and the golden lion tamarin – as well as many endangered species from Asia, such as the Sumatran tiger and the clouded leopard. The pygmy hippos are relatively recent newcomers; they live in glass-fronted enclosures (as do the polar bears), so visitors can watch their underwater exploits. Animals are sponsored by companies; Tiger Beer, for example, sponsors the tigers and Qantas the kangaroos.

There are animal shows throughout the day carrying a strong ecological message: primates and reptiles (at 1030 and 1430), and elephants and sealions (at 1130 and 1530). Animal feeding times are provided upon arrival. The latest addition to the zoo is a Treetops Trail, where visitors can view primates, crocodiles, squirrels and pheasants from a 6 m-high boardwalk. There is a children's area too, with farm animals, a miniature train and play equipment. There are tram tours for those too weary to walk (S$2.50 and S$1), with recorded commentaries, and several restaurants. Elephant, camel and pony rides are on offer at various times each afternoon. A shop sells environmentally sound T-shirts and cuddly toy animals. Overall, it is a well-managed and informative zoo; it's well worth the trip out there. Video cameras can be hired (S$10 per hour). ■ *S$12, S$5 for children, 0830-1800 Mon-Sun, T2693411, www.asianconnect.com/zoo/ MRT to Ang Mo Kio, SBS 138 from the Ang Mo*

North of the Island

Related map
A Singapore general,
page 596

Kio interchange or MRT to Choa Chu Kang, TIBS 927. Alternatively, take bus 171 to Mandai Rd and then cross the road to board the SBS 138 to the zoo. On Sun and public holidays Trans-island bus service (TIBS) 926 runs from the Woodlands bus interchange, direct to the zoo. Taxis cost about S$10 to the zoo from the Orchard Rd area. A bus service runs every 30 mins from 0730 until 2300 from Orchard and Scott Rds (ask at your hotel), S$5 one way. Another option is to book a ticket on the a/c Zoo Express, which provides guided tours on demand (contact Elpin, T7322133).

The unique Night Safari is situated adjacent to the zoo, covering 40 ha of secondary growth tropical forest. The area has been cunningly converted into a series of habitats, populated with wildlife from the Indo-Malayan, Indian, Himalayan and African zoogeographical regions. The park supports 1,200 animals belonging to 110 species, including the tiger, Indian lion, great Indian rhinoceros, fishing cat, Malayan tapir, Asian elephant, bongo, striped hyaena, Cape buffalo and giraffe. Visitors can either hop on a tram to be taken on a 40-minute guided safari through the jungle, lit by moonglow lighting and informed by a rather earnest commentary, or they can walk along three short trails at their own pace – or they can do both. The whole affair is extremely well conceived and managed, and the experience is rewardingly authentic – possibly because the night-time ambience hides the seams that are usually so evident in orthodox zoos. Children love the safari experience, believing that they truly are chancing upon animals in the jungle. At the entrance 'lodge' there is a good noodle bar, as well as a *Burger King*. There is also another small café at the East Lodge. ■ *1830-2400, S$15.45, children S$10.30. Safaris start at 1930 but restaurants are open from 1630. The last tram leaves at 2315. NB No flash cameras permitted. Take the trans-island bus (TIBS) 171 (it stops at Orchard Blvd and Scotts Rd) to Mandai Rd and then cross the road and board the SBS 138, which goes direct to the Night Safari. By MRT, either get off at Ang Mo Kio and then board the SBS 138, or alight at Choa Chu Kang and board the TIBS 927. A taxi from the city will cost around S$12 and takes 30 mins.*

Night Safari

The **Kranji War Memorial and Cemetery**, Woodlands Road, on a gentle hillside overlooking the Straits of Johor, is where Allied soldiers killed in Singapore in the Second World War are buried. In the heart of the cemetery is the war memorial, bearing the names of 24,346 Allied servicemen who died in the Asia-Pacific region during the war. The design of the memorial is symbolic, representing the three arms of the services – the army, navy and airforce. The upright section represents a conning-tower, the lateral elements are wings, and the walls symbolize army lines. Flowers are not allowed to be placed on graves, in case tiger mosquitoes breed in the jars. ■ *Bus 170 goes direct from Rochor Rd; alight opposite the entrance to the cemetery. On weekends, bus 181 also stops here.*

The Kranji War Memorial & Cemetery

Sungei Buloh Nature Park, Neo Tiew Crescent, is Singapore's first designated wetland nature reserve. It is an important stopover point for birds migrating along the East Asian Flyway. Carefully constructed hides throughout 87 ha provide excellent observation points for visitors, to view birds like sea eagles, kites and blue herons. There is also a mangrove swamp to walk through. ■ *0730-1900 Mon-Fri, 0700-1900 weekends and public holidays. S$1, children S$0.50, T6690377. Binoculars for hire. Audiovisual show 0900, 1100, 1300, 1500 and 1700 Mon-Sat, every hour between 0900 and 1700 on Sat and Sun. Take MRT to Kranji or Woodlands stations. Alternatively, take TIBS bus 170 from*

Nature reserves
The best time to visit this park is in Nov

Singapore

Queen's St to the Woodlands interchange. At Kranji or Woodlands, board TIBS bus 925 to Kranji Reservoir. On weekends, bus 925 runs all the way to the park entrance, but on weekdays it is a further 20-min walk to the park.

A wonderful contrast to the bustle of modern Singapore

Bukit Timah Nature Reserve, on Hindhede Drive off Upper Bukit Timah Road, nestles in the centre of the island and has a resident population of wild monkeys, pythons and scorpions. It was one of the first Forest Reserves, established in 1883 for the purposes of protecting the native flora and fauna. The naturalist Alfred Russel Wallace collected beetles at Bukit Timah in 1854. Jungle trails go through the forested terrain (130 million-year-old tropical rainforest) that once covered the whole island. The artificial lakes supply the city with much of its water. Clearly marked paths (one of them metalled) in the 81-ha reserve lead to Singapore's highest point (164 m) for scenic views. A visitors' centre includes an informative exhibition on natural history ■ *0830-1830. The nature reserve is at its quietest and best in the early mornings. Though the visitors' centre isn't open until 0830, it is possible to enter the reserve earlier. Entrance to the reserve is free and is on Upper Bukit Timah Rd, opposite Courst furniture store, down Hindhede Drive, T4709900. Take the SBS buses 5, 67,75, 170, 171, 172, 173, 182, 852 to Upper Bukit Timah Rd.*

Singapore's Islands

Pulau Ubin

Ferries for Pulau Kusu and St John's leave from the World Trade Centre; for Pulau Ubin, bumboats go from Changi Point; private hire boats for Sisters Island leave Jardine Steps or Clifford Pier

The source of granite for the causeway and Singapore's earlier buildings and skyscrapers, the name Pulau Ubin derives from the Javanese word for 'squared stone'. Ubin village affords a taste of Singapore in bygone days, with dilapidated wooden shophouses, coffee-shops and community spirit. The island, with its beaten-up cars and old taxis, quarry pits, jungle tracks, hills, beaches and challenging trails, is a mountain-biker's paradise and has become a popular destination for that reason, as the trails are quite challenging; it is possible to hire bicycles in the village. There is also an outward bound centre on the island and students come here to experience outdoor living. For details, T5461197. Wildlife on the island includes the red jungle-fowl (from which domesticated chickens are descended), straw-headed bulbul, Brahminy kites, white-bellied fish eagles, mangrove pitta, flying fox bats, fruit bats and tomb bats, the Oriental whip snake (an unmissable bright yellow colour), long-tailed macaques, house musang, civet and wild pigs. The hill in the centre of the island provides great views over to Singapore. There are some sandy beaches on the north shore – though they can be dirty at low tide.

This vision of Pulau Ubin might be about to change as the island's first holiday resort has now opened (see Sleeping, page 635). The Urban Redevelopment Authority (URA) has also published plans to reclaim an additional 2,694 ha on Pulau Ubin and Pulau Tekong (the majority on Tekong). For more information on the island, T5424108/5424842.

Canoes, kayaks and mountain bikes are all available for hire on the island. Mountain bikes can also be hired from Changi Village – S$20 per day (S$10 returnable deposit). ■ *From Changi Point it costs S$1.50 to go to Pulau Ubin; bumboats go when they're full – very frequently at the weekends – and operate between 0600 and 2300. It is possible to charter the whole vessel if you want to be alone, or are bored waiting for the boat to fill up. (For transport to and from Changi Village, see page 630.)*

Essentials

Sleeping

LL *Conrad*, 2 Temasek Blvd, Marina Bay, T3348888, F3339166, www. conradinternational.com.sg Close to Suntec City, and good for the business traveller. A total of 509 beautifully designed contemporary-style rooms, with lots of space, big windows and a large desk. Superb service, excellent meeting rooms and an impressive mezzanine level for functions. US$1.3 mn has been invested in almost 3,000 artworks throughout the hotel. Decent sized pool for lengths and adequate fitness centre. Recommended. **LL** *Raffles*, 1 Beach Rd, T3371886, F3397650, www.raffles.com Much has been said about *Raffles* and, despite criticisms, it is still a great place to stay – if you can afford it. There are 9 restaurants and a Culinary Academy, 5 bars (see separate entries under Eating and drinking, page 641) and is surrounded by 70 shops. The 104 suites have been immaculately refurbished, with wooden floors, high ceilings, stylish colonial furniture and plenty of space. Bathrooms are the ultimate in luxury and the other facilities are excellent – a peaceful rooftop pool with jacuzzis, state of the art fitness centre, both 24 hr. About half Raffles' guests are business visitors; corporate rates available. Very exclusive and highly recommended. **LL** *Ritz Carlton*, 7 Raffles Ave, Marina Bay, T3378888, F3380001, www. ritzcarlton.com Both this hotel and the *Conrad* were designed by US Hirsch Bedner. Very contemporary furnishings; considerable investment in artworks (notably the Frank Stella and the Dele Chihuly glass balls below the lobby area); rooms are very attractive, with wooden floors and big bathrooms that provide stunning views of the harbour and river. Large pool area with jacuzzi in well landscaped grounds, huge fitness centre. Good business facilities. Recommended.

L *Intercontinental*, 80 Middle Rd, Bugis Junction, T3387600, F3387366, www. internconti.com This beautifully designed hotel is one of the best in Singapore. It is situated at the edge of the colonial core in the Arab St area, in an attractively renovated and extended block of Art Deco shophouses, with a high rise block behind. It has over 400 good sized rooms with spacious bathrooms and every luxury provided, attractive rooftop pool with jacuzzi and well-equipped fitness centre. Business centre with small meeting room. The *Shophouse Room* is the hotel's showpiece and costs an extra S$60 – for which you get original colonial furniture and parquet flooring.

L *Westin Stamford and Westin Plaza*, 2 Stamford Rd, T3388585, F3382862, www. westin.com.sg Listed in the *Guinness Book of Records* as the tallest hotel in the world, this 2-tower complex was designed by Chinese architect IM Pei, who also designed the futuristic Bank of China building in Hong Kong. Haze permitting, the *Compass Rose Restaurant* on the top floor can provide stunning views over 3 countries – Singapore, Malaysia and Indonesia. There are 13 restaurants, an attractive triple circular pool (great for children) and a high-tech fitness centre. But with over 2,000 rooms and a vast echoing lobby, it is all a little overwhelming – and too large for that personal touch. However, it has a good reputation in the business world. **L-AL** *Grand Plaza*, 10 Coleman St, T3363456, F3399311, www.parkroyal.com. au Although the outside of this building is pretty hideous, with its marble cladding, the interior is not so ostentatious and despite its size (340 rooms), it feels quite intimate. There are 2 restaurants, an attractive but smallish pool and jacuzzi, gym and health spa, all on the third floor. It also has a large ballroom and 2 smaller meeting rooms, business centre. Recommended.

AL *Peninsula Excelsior*, 5 Coleman St, T3372200, F3393847, pen_exc@ytchotels. com.sg On our last visit, this was still (just) operating as 2 separate hotels, but changes were afoot. A communal lobby on the sixth floor will be open by the time this book goes to press. The addition of a pool, gym and spa (all on the sixth floor) will greatly enhance the facilities of what was 2 neighbouring, rather unimpressive hotels. Once

Colonial core
■ on map, page 600
Most accommodation is well placed for exploring the sights of the colonial city on foot, as well as the restaurants and bars of Clarke and Boat quays

Singapore

Dorm beds

Singapore is not the cheapest of places to stay, but there are a number of budget hotels and guesthouses which offer dorm beds, usually with lockers for safe keeping, for around S$8-16 per night for fan-cooled dorm rooms and S$25 for more salubrious air-conditioned dorms. For the further information on each hotel or guesthouse see relevant entry below.

Orchard Road

YMCA International House, *1 Orchard Road, T3366000, F3373140, hostel@YMCA.org.sg a/c dorms.*
YWCA, *Fort Canning Road, T3384222, F3374222, www.ywcafclodge.org.sg/ main.htm a/c dorms.*

Little India

Goh's Homestay, *40-43 Upper Weld Road, T3396561, gohshomestay.tripod.com*
Hawaii Hostel, *2nd Floor, 171B Bencoolen St, T3384187.*
Lee Boarding House, *7th Floor, 52 Peony Mansion, 46-52 Bencoolen St, T3383149, F3365409.*

Arab Street

Season Homestay, *26A I iang Seah Street, T3372400.*
Shang Onn, *Purvis Street, T3384153.*
Willy's Homestay, Cosy Corner and **Waffles Homestay**, *2/F, 490 North Bridge Road, T3370916 (Willy's and Cosy Corner), T3388826 (Waffles).*

---

the first phase has opened, work will commence on upgrading the rooms, and it may end up being a decent place to stay. For now, it's pretty average. **C** *Metropole*, 41 Seah St, T3363611, F3393610, www.metro-hotel.com A smallish business hotel with 54 rooms and no frills, good location for the price.

Singapore River & the City
■ *on map, page 604*
Price codes:
see inside front cover

AL-L *Grand Copthorne Waterfront*, 392 Havelock Rd, T7330800, F7378880, grandcopthorne@cdlhotels.com.sg This rather overblown monster has a rambling, disjointed lobby, a good gym, 2 tennis courts and a small but attractive pool (all on the 6th floor), extensive business services, a sushi bar and a fusion restaurant (*Brio's*). With 537 rooms, there's no sense of intimacy here, but it seems to be doing a roaring trade, so they must have got something right. **AL** *Fullerton*, 1 Fullerton Square, T7338388, F7358388, www.fullertonhotel. com Great position at the head of the Singapore River, this is Singapore's 5-star newcomer (it opened in early 2001). It has 399 rooms in Phillipe Stark style, very functional and well equipped, but slightly on the small side compared (say) with the Ritz Carlton. The restaurants are excellent: the Chinese *Jade*; French *Lighthouse* (very expensive); international *Town Club*; and seafood *Post Bar*. However, service can be poor and recent visitors have reported teething problems. On the plus side, the swimming pool is stunning with views directly over the Singapore River, with the high-rise CBD on one side and Boat Quay on the other.

AL *Merchant Court*, 20 Merchant Rd, T3379993, F3369993, www.raffles-intl.com This 500-room hotel, owned by the *Raffles* group, is a welcome addition to the mid-range bracket of hotels, many of which are looking rather tired. Attractive free-form pool in rooftop garden setting with slides and a separate jacuzzi overlooking the river. Excellent fitness centre managed by *Lifestyles*. Great location makes it an appealing choice.

AL-A *G@llery Evason*, 76 Robertson Quay, T8498686, F8366666, www.six-senses.com/gallery Marketed as the 'First hip hotel in Singapore', this Philip Stark-styled hotel provides 223 minimalist rooms, divided between 3 ultra-modern blocks. Brightly coloured cushions provide some light relief from the austerity in the standard rooms; showers only in these rooms. The 'Ladies Floor' has a pleasant sitting area with books and magazines provided. The hotel plans to be a completely non-smoking hotel. The fifth floor pool is certainly different, with glass on all sides; it

Singapore

must be an unnerving experience swimming here. At present the restaurant provides fusion cuisine and Imac computers for anyone's use to surf the internet. Artwork by local students adorn the public spaces as part of a scheme named 'art in alternative spaces'. A totally original hotel. Recommended.

LL *Four Seasons*, 190 Orchard Blvd, T8317300, F7330669, www.fshr.com Hard to beat, this intimate hotel of 250 rooms (and 400 staff) provides exceptional personal service; there's no check-in desk and all guests are greeted by name. Rooms are elegantly decorated in traditional European style, with feather pillows, writing desk, multi-disc player, and spacious bathrooms. The hotel has a unique Asian art collection, with attractive artwork in all the rooms. There are 2 pools – one is for lengths – and the hotel boasts the only a/c tennis courts in Singapore, a golf simulator and a well-equipped health and fitness centre, with attendants on hand all day. Restaurants include Cantonese and contemporary American cuisine, with lunchtime buffet. Although, primarily a business hotel, children are well catered for. Recommended.

LL *Goodwood Park*, 22 Scotts Rd, T7377411, F7328558, www.goodwoodparkhotel. com.sg Apart from *Raffles*, this is the only other colonial hotel in Singapore. It has had a chequered history, beginning life in 1856 as the German Recreation Club, the Teutonia. During the First World War it was declared enemy property and was seized by the government. In 1929 it was converted into a hotel, but then during the Second World War it was occupied by the Japanese. After the war it became a War Crimes Trial Court and did not resume functioning as a hotel until 1947. The exterior is looking a little scruffy and the lobby area isn't very encouraging, but the rooms are exceptional. Of the 235 rooms, there is a choice of colonial or modern style. The former have ceiling fans and windows that can be opened, with very stylish minimalist decor and lots of space. The modern rooms are slightly smaller, but they overlook the Mayfair pool and some rooms on the ground level lead straight out poolside. All rooms are fitted with the latest electronic equipment. There is a lovely pool area, set in a garden with pagodas, and another larger pool for lengths. It has several restaurants (see Eating, page 641). Recommended.

LL *Grand Hyatt*, 10-12 Scotts Rd, T7381234, F7321696, www.singapore.hyatt. com Owned by the Sultan of Brunei, this hotel has an unusual lobby area with bird prints on the walls, a bustling atmosphere, stunning flower arrangements, larger than average rooms – all with an alcove sitting area (some with poolside view) – and separate showers. Its selling point must be its garden and fitness facilities. There is a spectacular large fifth floor garden, with a roaring waterfall and very attractive pool area, poolside bar and restaurant. The executive class rooms have their own private Balinese garden (good for families), while those on the fifth floor open out onto a large terrace area. There are also squash courts, 2 tennis courts, huge fitness centre with aerobics classes, fabulous jacuzzi and sauna. In the basement is a very popular bar, *Brannigans*, while on the mezzanine level is a good restaurant, *Mezza9*. This is mainly a hotel for corporate clients, but good discounts available. Recommended.

L *Hilton*, 581 Orchard Rd, T7372233, F7322917, www.hilton.com The first international hotel in Singapore. Its 434 average-sized rooms were recently renovated and despite its age it maintains a good reputation. Particularly popular with business people (with its function rooms constantly in demand) and with Japanese tour groups. *Tradewinds* restaurant serves local and North Indian food in alfresco atmosphere at the poolside, the *Inn of Happiness* serves Chinese food, *Harbour Grill* for French cuisine (different French chefs visit every month), the *Checkers Deli* on the ground floor sells chocolates and desserts and has a reputation for its Philadelphia cheesecake. The *Kaspia Bar* has the largest range of vodkas in Singapore and live jazz. Small, rather dated pool, good fitness centre. **L** *Le Meridien*, 100 Orchard Rd, T7338855, F7327886, meridiensales@pacific.net.sg Open-plan lobby, with 4 terraces of rooms and garlands of orchids. Good sized rooms (corner rooms are larger) with queen sized beds and

Orchard Road

■ *on map, page 608*
Price codes:
see inside front cover

There is little to differentiate between the numerous 4- and 5-star hotels strung out along the road, concentrated towards the western end

Singapore

attractive decor; ask for a room overlooking the pool, as these have a balcony. Good pool for lengths, but barren seating area. Fitness centre.

L *Meritus Negara*, 10 Claymore Rd, T7370811, F7379075, http://singaporehotels. net/meritus_negara/index.php3 This 200-room hotel slightly off Orchard Rd, quieter and away from the crowds, prides itself on an intimate atmosphere. It pampers business visitors with a personalized service (no reception counters here) and a very high standard throughout. There are no 'club' floors; but rooms are unusual and larger than average. Bathrooms are spacious and there are separate showers. There is a large pool (but rather exposed sitting area), a very sophisticated fitness centre and jacuzzi. Recommended. **L** *Orchard*, 442 Orchard Rd, T7347766, F7335482, orcharde@ singnet.com.sg Rooms here have been recently renovated – they are decent sized and the bathrooms have separate showers; a luxury in Singapore. Large pool but no shade, excellent fitness centre and sauna. Its claim to fame is its magnificent ballroom, which seats 1,000 for dinner and 1,500 for conferences.

L *Regent*, 1 Cuscaden Rd, T7338888, F7328838, www.regenthotels.com.sg Huge ostentatious lobby with bubble lifts and a rather sterile atmosphere, reminiscent of tenement blocks. Situated in a quiet location at western end of Orchard Rd, this hotel is notable for its excellent service and attention to detail. Gloomy corridors and 440 large but quite plain rooms. There is an excellent fitness centre, but a boring circular pool and barren sunbathing area. **L** *Shangri-La*, 22 Orange Grove Rd, T7373644, F7373370, www.shangri-la.com/ eng/hotel/ This is one of Singapore's finest hotels, set in a beautifully maintained, spacious landscaped garden. There are 300 plus rooms, recently very stylishly refurbished; those in the refined and relaxed Valley Wing are superior and the service is exceptional. The excellent leisure facilities include a spacious pool area surrounded by greenery and waterfalls, jacuzzi, indoor pool, good fitness centre, squash and tennis courts, and a 3-hole pitch and putt golf 'course'. Possibly the best conference facilities in town. There are 3 good restaurants: *Shang Palace* for *dim sum*, the Japanese *Nadamon* and the outstanding *Blue*, a Californian restaurant on the top floor. Winner of Singapore Tourism Board's award for best hotel year after year. Recommended. **L** *Sheraton Towers*, 39 Scotts Rd, T7376888, F7371072, www.sheraton.com Quietly sophisticated lobby, with waterfalls and beautiful flowers everywhere, 400 rooms with bare corridors but good rooms. The more expensive rooms provide an exceptional service, with lots of extras thrown in. The *Cabana* rooms on the rooftop overlook the pool. Attractive pool area with bar. Popular with US visitors and 80% business guests. Italian restaurant open evenings only and exclusive Chinese restaurant. The hotel has won the Singapore Tourist Board service award for 6 years.

AL *Singapore Marriott*, 320 Orchard Rd, T7355800, F7359800, marriot@singnet. com.sg Another 350-room monster, which was once the *Dynasty*. Its distinguishing feature is its rather ridiculous pagoda 'hat' at the top of the tower block. Unusual lobby, with 10 m-high palm trees and the usual array of facilities. Good fitness centre, large swimming pool with separate whirlpool and *Garden Terrace Café*. Extensive business services, efficient but unwelcoming, very central. **AL** *Traders*, 1A Cuscaden Rd, T7382222, F8314314, www.shangri-la.com Lavish pots of orchids at the entrance makes it feel special, but there isn't much to mark this hotel apart from the competition. It has 547 rooms and about three-quarters of its guests are business people. The rooms are average, but there is an attractive pool area with a large pool. It has a fitness centre, a business centre and 3 restaurants. No frills.

A *VIP*, 5 Balmoral Crescent, T2354277, F2352824. Situated in quiet area of the city close to *Garden Hotel* and west of the Newton MRT station. A/c, restaurant, pool, good rooms with TV, minibar etc. **B** *Lloyd's Inn*, 2 Lloyd Rd, T7377309, F7377847, www.lloydinn.com A/c, restaurant, scrupulously clean, well-appointed rooms – if a little cramped – quiet location in suburban road near River Valley Rd/Somerset MRT, off Killiney Rd. **B** *Regalis Court*, 64 Lloyd Rd, T7347117, F7361651, www.somerset.com.sg

Attractive, renovated colonial-style boutique hotel, originally a school. It provides 43 beautifully appointed rooms, decked out with Indonesian furniture and decor and wooden floorboards. The standard rooms have no windows, but they are well lit. The price is so reasonable because there is no pool or fitness centre. *Peranakan* restaurant on the ground floor and self-service breakfast. Set in a quiet street behind Orchard Rd, it's hard to beat at the price. Highly recommended. **B** *YWCA*, Fort Canning Rd, T3384222, F3374222, www.YWCAfclodge.org.sg Large new building with 200 plus rooms, pool, tennis courts, ballroom, exhibition hall. It is not clear why it's called a *YWCA* – it is not your average youth hostel. Dorms **B**.

C *Metropolitan YMCA*, 60 Stevens Rd, T7377755, F2355528. All rooms are a/c, a newly renovated no frills place, providing efficient service and clean serviceable rooms. The added bonus is a large swimming pool. Very good value. Recommended. **C** *YMCA International House*, 1 Orchard Rd, T3366000, F3373140, hostel@YMCA.org.sg The old *YMCA* which stood on Stamford Rd was used by the Japanese during the war as their dreaded interrogation and torture centre. Facilities are well above the usual *YMCA* standards, a/c, restaurant, rooftop pool, squash courts, badminton, billiards and fitness centre. Grotty from the outside, but it is very clean and efficient. Good value for this location, S$25 for 4 bed a/c dorm. Recommended.

L *Duxton*, 83 Duxton Rd, T2277678, F2271232, www.duxtonhotels.com.sg Intimate, stylish 50-room hotel in row of refurbished shophouses. Deluxe rooms are split level, but even these are small at this price. Guests have use of the large pool at the *Amara Hotel*. Restaurant (*L'Aigle d'Or*, page 647). Mainly frequented by business people as it's convenient for the financial district. Its ambience and size make it stand out among Singapore's other luxury hotels. Overpriced on the published rate, but good discounts available either from hotel or from travel agents. Recommended. **AL** *Amara*, 165 Tanjong Pagar Rd, T2244488, F2243910, reserv@amara.com.sg Well maintained, with 338 average-sized rooms and good extras such as self-service launderette. Several restaurants (with one of the best Thai restaurants in town – *Thanying*, see page 647) and a coffee shop serving a good buffet spread (mid-range), decent sized pool, with café area for steamboat and barbecues. Four tennis courts, jogging track and a gym. Business centre. Good location to explore Chinatown or for business visitors.

AL *Copthorne Harbour View*, 81 Anson Rd, T2241133, F2220749, www.harbourviewhotel.com.sg/ Good Japanese restaurant, average sized pool and over 400 large but basic rooms in this high-rise block. Request a harbour view as the view of Tanjong Pagar container port is worth an hour's quiet attention. Good location for business district and access to Chinatown. Health centre but no gym, personal safes in more expensive rooms. Business centre with limited secretarial assistance. Meeting room available. Popular with Japanese clients. **AL** *Furama*, 60 Eu Tong Sen St, T5333888, F5341489, www. furama-hotels.com Grand lobby belies rather scruffy featureless rooms; it needs a facelift. Restaurant and very basic gym. The building itself stands out from the crowd for its unusual but rather ugly and dated design.

A *The Inn at Temple Street*, 36 Temple St, T2215333, F2255391, www.theinn. com.sg Billing itself as a boutique hotel, the 42 rooms here do have a certain charm, being well appointed with safes, TVs, Peranakan-style furniture (made in Indonesia) and attached shower (in the standard rooms) or bath (in the deluxe rooms). On the downside, the rooms are very small; not even the deluxe rooms have space for a desk (except in the few single rooms), which will put off business travellers. **B** *Damenlou*, 12 Ann Siang Rd, T2211900, F2228926, yokewong12@hotmail. com Despite the rather seedy entrance, this remains a great little place. A/c, attached bathroom, TV, minibar; cheaper rooms are very small but neat and clean, and well presented. Very friendly management and located in an attractive street of shophouses, 1st floor Cantonese restaurant. Recommended. **B** *Keong Saik*, 69 Keong Saik Rd, T2230660, F2250660,

Chinatown
■ *on map, page 613*
Chinatown accommodation has more individuality, but can be on the small side

Singapore

keongsaik@pacific.net.sg An intimate little 'business' hotel in a sensitively restored shophouse, with 25 a/c immaculately presented rooms containing attractive all-wood furniture. It is let down by small room size, with little space for anything other than the bed. Standard rooms have no windows or skylights (attic rooms). **B** *Royal Peacock*, 55 Keong Saik Rd, T2233522, F2211770, rpeacock@ cyberway.com.sg A total of 79 rooms spread along 10 shophouses, similar standard to *Keong Saik*, rooms marginally larger, but again standard rooms have no natural light and showers only. A/c, charming little restaurant, *Butterfly Pub* (with karaoke); price includes continental breakfast. Avoid rooms over the pub. Recommended for general feel of the hotel, but not for room size,

Little India
■ *on map, page 617*
Price codes:
see inside front cover

A *Albert Court*, 180 Albert St, T3393939, F3393252, sales.mktg@albertcourt.com.sg An unusually designed hotel (a mixture of Western and Peranakan), lying behind a courtyard of renovated shophouses. This is an intimate place built to high specifications, with attractive extras. Ask for a room with big windows. Restaurant but no other facilities. Right next to a good range of restaurants in Albert Court. Recommended. **A** *City Bayview*, 30 Bencoolen St, T3372882, F3382880, bayviews@mbox4.singnet. com.sg A/c, restaurant, leafy rooftop pool. Neat little hotel block with business facilities, personal safes in rooms, attentive and friendly service, popular with tour groups. The rooms are smallish, but the hotel is competitively priced and well run.

B-C *Bencoolen*, 47 Bencoolen St, T3360822, F3362250, bencolen@pacific.net.sg This new hotel is basic and uninspired, but rooms are clean and the bathrooms are larger than average for this price range. There's a tiny plunge pool and sunbathing area on the second floor. Complimentary continental breakfast at the café on the street. **B-C** *Perak Lodge*, 12 Perak Rd, T2997733, F3920919, www.peraklodge.net A small boutique hotel, with just 34 rooms in a restored and protected building. We haven't been here to check it out, but are told that it is 'decorated in an ethnic style to enhance a cosy ambience'. Rooms come with a/c, TV, attached shower, safe and complimentary tea and coffee-making gear.

C *Dickson Court*, 3 Upper Dickson Rd, at Jl Besar end, T2977811, F2977833, dickson @magix.com.sg A surprising little enclave in this bustling street. New, smart, clean and simple, with friendly management. Good value. Price includes simple buffet breakfast. **C** *Kerbau*, 54/63 Kerbau Rd, T2976668, F2976669. A/c, small hotel in modernized shophouse on this quiet street. The rooms are nothing special, but clean with attached showers, and if you get one looking out onto Kerbau Rd it is possible to open the shutters in the evening and watch Indian life from above. Good value. **D** *Goh's Homestay*, 40-43 Upper Weld Rd, T3396561, F3398606, gohshomestay.tripod.com/ Dorm beds **E**, small and basic but very clean rooms with cold water showers, separate hot showers available. Breakfast in a small yard at the back, emai. A popular guesthouse, Goh understands the needs of the backpacker.

Most budget
accommodation (such
as it is) is to be found
in the Little India and
Arab St areas to the
north of town

D *Little India Guesthouse*, 3 Veerasamy Rd, T2942866, F2984866. Some a/c, no private bathrooms, but spotless male/female shower areas and immaculate rooms. No food served here, but plenty on the street. Good location in the heart of Little India and all in an attractive salmon-pink shophouse. Recommended. **D** *Sun Sun*, 260A-262A&B Middle Rd, T3384911, F4686624 (for attention of Madame Ong). This is a great little hotel of only 17 rooms, up a flight of stairs at the southern edge of Little India, run by a Chinese couple. All rooms have communal facilities, but the showers and toilets are very clean. The rooms are large but plain, with a sink in one corner, and an extra few Singapore dollars buys you a/c. Sadly under threat of closure. Recommended.

Arab Street
■ *on map, page 620*

AL *Golden Landmark*, 390 Victoria St, T2972828, F2982038. This 400-room tower block (with Arabic overtones) is looking older than its 1980s birthdate would indicate. It has an Indonesian restaurant, a big pool, corporate floors and a business centre. It caters mainly for tours and corporate clients – not many Europeans stay here.

B-C *Park View*, 81 Beach Rd, T3388558, F3348558, www.parkview.com.sg A/c, medium-sized hotel. No pool or gym, but the well-appointed rooms – the deluxe rooms are a good size and better value than the cramped standard (no windows) and superior rooms.

D *Shang Onn*, Purvis St, T3384153. Ten rooms in another ugly apartment block, no breakfast, but efficient service and rooms are adequate (fan only), no dorms, long-term visitors encouraged, not very friendly but recommended. **D-E** *Cosy Corner, Waffles Homestay and Willy's Homestay*, 2/F, 490 North Bridge Rd, T3370916 for Cosy Corner and Willy's, T3388826 for Waffles. All 3 of these establishments are in a row, on the first floor, above a series of Muslim and Indian restaurants on North Bridge Rd, just south of Liang Seah St. Under one management, they are all of a similar price and there's not much to choose between them; some a/c and shared bathrooms only. Dorm beds available, **E**. City backpacking establishments are rarely desirable places and these say it all. Willy's does have a roof top though, which provides a little light relief.

In Arab St, budget accomodation is centred on, or close to, Liang Seah St, a narrow street of shophouses that are gradually being gentrified

L-LL *Beaufort*, Bukit Manis Rd, T2750331, F2750228, beaufort@singnet.com.sg A/c, restaurants, large (33 m) pool, gym, tennis courts, archery, volley ball court, squash courts, access to the 18-hole Tanjong golf course, and 27 acres of grounds. The most refined of the hotels on Sentosa, smaller, quieter and more elegant than the *Rasa Sentosa*, with excellent service. **AL** *Shangri-La Rasa Sentosa*, 101 Silosa Rd, T2750100, F2751055, www.shangri-la.com At the southern tip of the island, facing the beach, a/c, restaurant, free-form pool, sports facilities, creche, clean beach (sterilized sand imported from Indonesia) with water OK for swimming. Built in a curve, behind Fort Siloso, this hotel has first-class facilities and an unsurpassed view of the oil refinery just across the water, competitive weekend package deals available – though it can get very busy then. **A** *Sijori Resort*, 23 Beach View, T2712002, F2752002, situated close to the action by the 37 m-high Merlion. This hotel/resort opened in early 1997 and is clearly positioned to tempt those people who wish to make full use of Sentosa's attractions.

Sentosa
■ on map, page 622
Staying in these three hotels, as Stan Sesser put it in his New Yorker piece on Singapore, is rather like being a prisoner in a theme park

A *Sea View*, 26 Amber Close, T3452222, F3451741, www.seaview.com.sg Ugly big block and not particularly friendly. Note that this place is considerably cheaper if booked from the airport hotel desk. **C** *Chancellor*, 181 Joo Chiat Rd, T7422222, F3488677, www.asiabiz.com/chancellor Smallish rooms in shophouses, but nice showers and clean and efficient. Pastel shades and a huge TV in each room. Good value, but 10 mins' walk from the MRT. **C** *Hotel 81-Opera*, 305 Joo Chiat Rd, T3448181, F3420991, www.hotel81.com.sg Good value place to stay for business visitors on a budget. An attractive shophouse hotel with reasonable rooms. **C** *Malacca*, 97-99 Still Rd, T3457411, F4405121. Another good value business hotel in this area of town, 20 mins' walk from nearest MRT station (Eunos). Rooms are very well appointed at the price, with a/c, TV, and attached bathrooms; payment in cash only. **C-D** *Guillemard*, 50 Geylang Rd (Lorong 18), T8417577, F8417511, guillemard. com.sg/ Modern corner block, with weekly and monthly room rates. Convenient for business visitors needing somewhere cheaper and out of town centre. Small rooms though.

East Coast
■ on map, page 630

Singapore

Eating

Expensive *Annalakshmi*, 02-10 *Excelsior Hotel* and Shopping Centre, 5 Coleman St, T3399993. North and South **Indian** vegetarian cuisine; Samy's banana-leaf and fish-head curries are unrivalled. Run on the same basis as Kuala Lumpur's *Annapoorna* – staffed by unpaid housewives, with profits going to the Kalamandhir Indian cultural group. The health drinks are excellent – especially *Mango Tharang* (mango juice, honey and ginger) and *Annalakshmi Special* (fruit juices, yoghurt, honey and ginger). The restaurant, which sprawls out onto the verandah overlooking the tennis courts,

Colonial core
● on map, page 600
Price categories:
see inside front cover

closes at 2130. Recommended. *Bobby Rubinos*, Fountain Court, CHIJMES, 30 Victoria St, T3375477.

International; good menu of ribs, burgers and chicken. Booking recommended. *Compass Rose*, *Westin Stamford Hotel*, 2 Stamford Rd, T4316156. Great venue for a romantic dinner or business lunch atop Singapore's tallest hotel building. Serves buffet lunch and afternoon tea. *Doc Cheng's*, *Raffles Shopping Arcade*, Seah St. **New Asian**, unusual combinations of flavours, but the rather irritating blurb on the menu may put some off. Even so, the food can be excellent.

Gatsby, Fountain Court, CHIJMES. Extensive menu of **international** seafood, meat dishes and salad, and a choice for children too. *Grappas*, CHIJMES, Gallery Floor, 30 Victoria St, T3349928. Large **Italian** restaurant in this trendy courtyard. Extensive menu, with mostly pasta and risotto dishes as well as some meat entrees; booking advisable. Recommended. *Hai Tien Lo*, *Pan Pacific Hotel*, 37th Floor, Marina Square, T4348338. **Cantonese** restaurant in elegant surroundings, with stunning views of the city. Sharks' fins, steamed lobster and Kobe beef are specialities. *Dim sum* lunches on Sun. *Inagiku*, 3rd Floor, *Westin Stamford and Westin Plaza*, 2 Stamford Rd, T4315305. The Raffles City corporate dinner brigade eat at this pricey **Japanese** restaurant, which is divided into sections, providing different food in each. Booking advisable. *Lei Gardens*, Gallery Floor, CHIJMES, 30 Victoria St, T3393822, F3342648. A menu which is said to comprise 2,000 dishes. Outstanding **Cantonese** food: silver codfish, emperor's chicken and such regulars as *dim sum* and Peking duck. Dignatories, royalty and film stars dine here. Tasteful décor and a 2-tier aquarium displaying the day's offerings. Despite seating for 250, you need to book in advance. Worth every penny. Recommended.

Maison de Fontaine, Gallery Floor, CHIJMES, 30 Victoria St, T3347663. Excellent, sophisticated **French** restaurant in an attractive setting. *Raffles Grill*, *Raffles Hotel*, 1 Beach Rd (main building, 1st floor), T3311611. Excellent **French** cuisine in elegant colonial surroundings, with silver plate settings, chandeliers and reproduction Chippendale furniture and windows opening onto Palm Court. Serves breakfast, lunch and dinner. *Ristorante Bologna*, *Marina Mandarin Hotel*, 6 Raffles Blvd, Marina Square, T3318470. Award-winning **Italian** restaurant, house specialities include *spaghetti alla marinara* and baked pigeon. Diners lounge amidst sophisticated décor whilst wandering minstrels strum. *Shrooms*, CHIJMES, Victoria St, T3362268. **Western** food in a stylish restaurant. Selection of champagnes and liqueurs on offer too. *Tatsu Sushi*, Gallery Floor, CHIJMES, 30 Victoria St, T3325868. **Sushi** bar.

Mid-range *Empire Café*, Ground Floor, *Raffles Hotel*, 1 Beach Rd, **International** food served; not bad for pork chops and oxtail stew, prepared by Chinese cooks and served on marble-topped tables. Also serves chicken rice, burgers and ice creams. Open 24 hrs. *Ah Teng's Bakery* adjoins, selling pricey pastries, pies and biscuits – mostly local favourites. *House of Sundanese Food*, several outlets spread around town, eg, Suntec City Marina Square, T5343775. Typical **Sundanese** dishes from West Java, with a real home-cooked taste including spicy salad (*keredok*), charcoal-grilled seafood (*ikan Sunda* and *ikan mas*) and curries. Simply decorated non-a/c restaurant. *Imperial Herbal*, Hotel, 3rd Floor, 41 Seah St, T3370491. Unusual, delicately flavoured **Chinese** food. A resident in-house herbalist takes your pulse (for a fee) and recommends a meal with the appropriate rejuvenating ingredients to balance your *yin* and *yang*. Booking recommended for dinner.

La Cave, B1-10 Fountain Court, CHIJMES, 30 Victoria St, T3379717. **Fusion** cuisine with good servings and a lovely ambience. The chef, Daniel, trained in Lyon and worked for a time at *Raffles*. Good value and excellent service. There is also a bar here, open 1700-2300, with food served from 1900. *Ocho Tapas Bar*, Gallery Floor, CHIJMES, 30 Victoria St. **Spanish** tapas. *Pennsylvania Country Oven*, Ground Floor, Stamford House, Stamford Rd. For Americans craving **New England** cooking, with kitsch interior to boot. *Ramayana*, 6 Raffles Blvd, Marina Square, T3363317. **Indonesian** restaurant, big on seafood and an extensive range of milk shakes. *Roweal's*, Gallery Floor, CHIJMES, 30 Victoria St. 'Country' **international** food: beef casserole, chicken dishes, nachos, potato wedges. *Sanur*, 3rd Floor, 133 New Bridge Rd. Cramped **Malay/Indo-nesian** restaurant ideally placed for shoppers, specialities include fish-head curries and spicy grilled chicken or fish.

Cheap *Komala's Fast Food*, Peninsula Plaza, Coleman St. One of Komala's fast food outlets, serving good **South Indian** delicacies including *thalis, masala dosas* and *idlis*, served at competitive prices; a/c. Next door is the more upmarket *Ganges Restaurant*, which lays on a good lunchtime **Indian vegetarian** buffet spread.

Hawker centres and food courts Cheap *Fountain Terrace*, Suntec City, Marina Square. Trendy food court situated under the enormous fountain. *Water Court*, basement of Raffles City. Sophisticated food court, mostly frequented by business people with a penchant for extravagant sandwiches and patisseries – no chicken rice or mutton biryani here.

Seriously cheap *Funan Centre*, South Bridge Rd. This big shopping plaza contains one of the better food courts in Singapore in its basement, with a huge range of foods to choose from; in particular, an excellent Indian stall. *Hill Street Food Centre,* west side of Hill St. 3 floors of hawker stalls, lots of Muslim food and plenty of everything else, very popular and great value.

Tiffin Expensive *Tiffin Room, Raffles Hotel,* 1 Beach Rd (main building, ground floor). Tiffin curry buffet (plus à la carte menu) in pristine white, overlit ersatz Victorian grandeur. The food is good, but at S$35 for the buffet, you're paying a lot more for the surroundings than for the curry. Reservation recommended, no sleeveless T-shirts or shorts.

Cafés Mid-range *Café Aria*, Young Musicians' Society Arts Centre, Waterloo St. Popular for a coffee stop. *Dôme*, next door to the Singapore Art Museum on Bras Basah Rd. Delicious focaccia sandwiches, patisseries and some of the best coffee in town, good café atmosphere and a pleasant stop for a mid-morning break. *Fat Frog*, The Substation, Armenian St. Attractive leafy courtyard, serving **wholefood** snacks, sandwiches, soups and some Asian dishes.

Tea, cakes and coffee Mid-range *Ah Teng's Bakery*, Raffles Arcade. Pricey, but it has all the goodies you dream about at the end of a long trip away from home. Complimentary second cup of coffee. *Compass Rose Lounge*, Westin Stamford Hotel, 2 Stamford Rd. Best views in Singapore, strict dress code, expect to queue. *Seah Street Deli*, Ground Floor, *Raffles Hotel*, North Bridge Rd. New York-style deli, serving everything from corned beef and smoked salmon to cheesecakes and Turkish pastries.

Expensive *Bangkok Garden*, Keck Seng Tower, 133 Cecil St (financial district), T2207310. Almost anything **Thai** is available, even if it's not on the menu; speciality fruit juices and crab dishes are very popular. *Bastiani's*, one of the best places to eat on Clarke Quay, situated on the waterfront, near to *Hooters* (close to the footbridge), T4330156. Large bar on the ground floor with dining room upstairs. An interesting and varied menu (but pricey) of **Mediterranean** food. Separate smokers' area, airy spacious dining room overlooking the river, frequented by local expat community who enthusiastically endorse the restaurant. *Brewerkz*, Riverside Point, opposite Clarke Quay, T4387438. This very popular **American-style** restaurant and bar provides most of its seating under awnings by the riverfront. Great place for lunch, with a menu of satay, buffalo wings, nachos, burgers, steaks and pizza. Also has a children's menu. *Bua Thai,*

Singapore River & the City
● *on map, page 604*
Price categories:
see inside front cover

Singapore

Robertson Quay. Extensive choice of **Thai** cuisine in this new development. *Café Iguana*, Riverside Point, opposite Clarke Quay. Classic choice of **Mexican** dishes. *Diandin Leluk*, Riverside Point, opposite Clarke Quay, T4382890. A **Thai** restaurant that doesn't seem as popular as the immensely successful *Brewerkz* next door. *Hot Stones Steak and Seafood*, 53 Boat Quay, T5355188. Serving **International** fare, this restaurant's speciality is cooking steaks, chicken or seafood on sizzling-hot Serpentine rock at your table.

Kinara, 57 Boat Quay, distinctive wooden doors at the entrance. North **Indian** frontier cuisine, good choice of tandoori-baked meat or vegetarian alternatives. *Moomba*, behind *Penny Black*, on Circular Rd. **Australian** food and a good selection of wine (to take out); also sells wine fridges – a must for anyone residing here! *O'Brien's Irish Sandwich Bar*, UOB Building, on the waterfront (just east of Boat Quay). A very popular lunch spot for business people, serving **International** food. *Pasta Fresca da Salvatore*, 30 Boat Quay. This 24-hr **Italian** serves fresh, tasty pizzas and a good range of pasta dishes. *Sukhothai*, 47 Boat Quay, T5382422. Extensive **Thai** menu, but the food can be a little hit and miss; booking recommended.

Mid-range *Blaze Café*, Ground Floor, The Cannery, Clarke Quay. **International** food served, including pizza, pasta, hotdogs, fish and chips, burgers – a good place to bring the children. *Chilis*, 75 Boat Quay. A good menu with **American** fare – burgers, grills, sandwiches – and reasonably priced for this prime location. *Riverside Indonesian Restaurant*, Riverside Point, opposite Clarke Quay, T5350383. Bright functional interior, with some alfresco dining overlooking the river, serving **Indonesian** food: baked pomfret, chilli crabs, grilled chicken. An attractive location. *Sushi Dokoro Yoshida*, 58 Boat Quay, T5341401. Another river front restaurant specializing in **Japanese** *izakaya* (barbecued fish). Designed around a sushi bar, also a branch in Lucky Plaza, Orchard Rd.

Cheap *House of Sundanese Food*, 55 Boat Quay. Typical **Sundanese** dishes, with a real home-cooked taste from West Java including spicy salad (*keredok*), charcoal-grilled seafood (*ikan Sunda* and *ikan mas*) and curries. Simply decorated non-a/c restaurant. *Nonya and Baba*, 262/264 River Valley Rd, T7341382. Simple place serving excellent **Peranakan** food, which blends Chinese and Malay cuisine in a unique fusion. Lots of coconut milk and seafood, with dishes such as *otak otak* (spicy pressed fish in coconut milk). The owner is an Elvis fan. The *Next Page Pub*, in a refurbished shophouse, is nearby (see Bars below).

Hawker centres and food courts Cheap *Lau Pa Sat Festival Market* (formerly the Telok Ayer Food Centre), at the Raffles Quay end of Shenton Way in the old Victorian market (see page 607). Good range of food on offer: Chinese, Indian, Nonya, Korean, Penang, ice creams, fruit drinks – it's well worth a browse. *Satay Club*, evening stalls in the pedestrian streets of Clarke Quay. The food is good but, being a tourist trap, it's almost double the price of other food courts. **Seriously cheap** *Food Court*, Basement of Liang Court, next door to Clarke Quay. Good choice of Asian stalls, *Burger King* and a play area for children.

Cafés Mid-range *Bar Gelateria Bellavista*, Clarke Quay. Delicious Italian ice cream, indoor and outdoor seating. *Dome*, in the UOB Building, to the east of Boat Quay. *Japanese Book Cafe*, Mohammed Sultan Rd. A novel concept; very simple menu and plenty of books to browse through. *Polar Café*, B1-04 OUB Centre, Raffles Place (also branch in Lucky Plaza, Orchard Rd). The original home of the curry puff, first created at its former premises on Hill St in 1926.

Orchard Road
● *on map, page 608*
Price categories:
see inside front cover

Expensive *Au Jardin*, EJH Corner House, Singapore Botanic Gardens Visitors' Centre, 1 Cluny Rd, T4668812. Situated in the former garden director's black and white bungalow, with only 12 tables, this **French** restaurant is elegant and sophisticated, with a menu which is changed weekly. Booking essential.

Blu, *Shangri-La Hotel*, 22 Orange Grove Rd, T7302598. Situated on the 24th floor, Blu provides stunning views, great service and excellent **Californian** food. Recommended. *Bombay Woodlands*, 19 Tanglin Rd, Tanglin Shopping Centre, Orchard Rd, T2352712. Very reasonably priced for the area, **Indian vegetarian** food.

Bumbu, Orchard Shopping Centre, Orchard Rd. Trendy spot offering **Indonesian** cuisine. *Chico's N Charlie's*, 05-01 Liat Towers, 541 Orchard Rd, T7341753. An expat **Mexican** hangout; good atmosphere, plenty of choice of hacienda food, excellent Margaritas and good value. *Esmirada's*, corner of Peranakan Place and Orchard Rd, T7353476. **Mediterranean** food in Spanish-style taverna, good salads, paella, couscous. Always packed, reservations recommended. *Gordon Grill*, Lobby, *Goodwood Park Hotel*, 22 Scotts Rd, T7301744. One of the last grills in town, Singapore's only **Scottish** restaurant with haggis on the menu – at 24 hrs advance notice. Plenty of choice cuts of meat to choose from. Superb desserts. *Grill on Devonshire*, 6 Devonshire Rd, off Orchard Blvd, T7339400. Attractive setting, with indoor or leafy garden setting, trendy place serving 'modern **international**' cuisine, which probably means lots of torn basil and balsamic vinegar.

Harbour Grill and Oyster Bar, *Hilton Hotel*, 581 Orchard Rd, T7303393. Contemporary surroundings with nautical theme, serving **international** food. Delicacies include caviar and smoked salmon; monthly guest chef. Impeccable service. *Kintamani*, *Novotel Apollo*, 405 Havelock Rd, T7332081. **Balinese**-style interior, extensive buffet spread available at lunch and dinner. *Korean Restaurant*, Specialists' Centre, Orchard Rd, T2350018. This imaginatively named **Korean** restaurant is well known for its *bulgogi* meat barbecues. *Les Amis*, Shaw Centre, 1 Scotts Rd, T7332225. Great **French** food, excellent service and extensive wine list. Closes at 2200.

Maxim's de Paris, *The Regent*, 1 Cuscaden Rd, T7393091. **French** extravaganza in an art deco setting, booking recommended, excellent food and the most extensive wine list in Singapore. Pay through the nose for this spot of sophistication. *Mezza9*, *Grand Hyatt Hotel*, 10-12 Scotts Rd, T7307189. Incorporates **Western Grill, Japanese food, Chinese**, a salad bar and a patisserie. A la carte during the week and a set-price buffet brunch on Sun 1100-1500. *Min Jiang*, *Goodwood Park Hotel*, 22 Scotts Rd, T7375337. Large, noisy room, expansive **Szechuan** menu, with excellent reputation – delicious hot and sour soup, and good choice of seafood, 7 private rooms as well, booking recommended.

Pasta Fresca da Salvatore, Shaw Centre (convenient for movies upstairs at Shaw Lido Complex), **Italian**. Fresh, tasty pizzas and a good range of pasta, open 24 hrs. *Pete's Place*, *Grand Hyatt*, Scott's Rd, basement, T7381234. One of the oldest **Italian** restaurants in Singapore, huge helpings, popular set price Sun brunch. *Saigon*, Cairnhill Pl, 15 Cairnhill Rd, off Orchard Rd, T2350626. Spacious and relaxed surroundings, superb **Vietnamese** food, with very helpful waiters to give advice, pan-fried beef recommended, and innovative and tasty dishes such as crab in beer. *Seasons*, *Four Seasons Hotel*, 190 Orchard Blvd, T7341110. Sophisticated surroundings and unusual **international** food combinations make this a relaxed and pleasurable gastronomic experience. At weekends they cater for children. *Shahi Maharani*, 25 Scotts Rd, T2358840. **North Indian** tandoor – especially good seafood dishes. Live performances during dinner; a cosy place. *Suntory*, 06-01 Delfi Orchard, 402 Orchard Rd, T7325111. A **Japanese** restaurant for sushi, tempura, teppanyaki and shabu-shabu-lovers with a serious yen (or two).

Mid-range *Cuppage Thai Food*, 49 Cuppage Terr, T7341116. Popular **Thai** restaurant with outside tables and photographs of the food to aid decision making, makes for a good evening if combined with a visit to one of the bars in the area. Recommended. *Hard Rock Café*, 02-01 HPL House, 50 Cuscaden Rd. One of the best bets for **international** food: a decent steak, buffalo wings or a bacon cheeseburger, open until 0200. *Lei Gardens*, Orchard Shopping Centre, 321 Orchard Rd, T7343988, and Orchard Plaza, 150 Orchard Rd, T7382448. Menu which is said to comprise 2,000 dishes. Dignatories, royalty and film stars dine here. Tasteful décor and a 2-tier aquarium displaying the day's offerings. Worth every penny. Book in advance. Recommended. *Maharani*, 05-36 Far East Plaza, Scotts Rd, T2358840. Rated as one of the best for **North Indian** cuisine – tandoori chicken and kormas are specialities.

Olio Dome, Wheelock Pl, 501 Orchard Rd, T7377044. Great place for lunch when resting from the retail therapy, with a choice of sandwiches and salads from the blackboard; **Mediterranean** food. *Orchard Maharajah*, 25 Cuppage Terr, T7326331. Excellent **North Indian** food – tandoori and Kashmiri – 7 different types of bread to choose from. Conveniently located in a converted shophouse close to some good bars. *Papa Joe's*, Peranakan Pl, Orchard Rd, T7327012. Under the same ownership as *Esmirada's* (see above). Serves **Caribbean** food at lunch and from 1800 to 2230 in the evenings, but is better known for its disco.

Planet Hollywood, Liat Towers, 541 Orchard Rd, T7327827. Opened to much showbiz fanfare in 1997, but it isn't up to much. There's a limited menu of **international** food: pizza, pasta and burgers. Young trendies come for the surroundings (leopard and zebra skin walls and carpets) and the merchandise, not for the food. No booking available. *Sanur*, 17/18, 4th Floor, Centrepoint, 176 Orchard Rd, T7342192. Cramped **Malay/Indonesian** restaurant ideally placed for shoppers, specialities including fish-head curries and spicy grilled chicken or fish.

Singapore Polo Club, 80 Mount Pleasant Rd (just off Thomson Rd). If you're not put off by the polo set or visiting sultans, the Polo Club is a great place to dine (or drink Pimms) on the verandah – especially on match days (Tue, Thu and Sat) when there's plenty to look at. There is a snack menu (steak sandwich, fish and chips etc) for the verandah overlooking the turf and a smarter restaurant inside. **International** food served. *Sushi Tei*, Paragon, 290 Orchard Rd. **Japanese**; great conveyor-belt sushi.

Tambuah Mas, 4th Floor, Tanglin Shopping Centre, T7332220 (another branch at Level 5, Shaw Centre). Very popular and cramped a/c **Indonesian** restaurant. What it lacks in ambience, it more than makes up for with the food; specialities include *ayam goreng istimewa* (marinated fried chicken). Recommended. *Tony Romas'*, Orchard Rd Shopping Centre, Orchard Rd. Good **international** rib joint. *Yushiada Ya*, basement of Lucky Plaza, Orchard Rd. **Japanese** restaurant serving excellent sushi.

Cheap *Bintang Timur*, Far East Plaza, 14 Scotts Rd, T2354539. Excellent **Malay** satays and curries, the ambience allows you to forget that you're in a shopping centre.

Hawker centres and food courts *Newton Circus*, Scotts Rd, north of Orchard Rd. Despite threats of closure by the government, this huge food centre of over 100 stalls is still surviving and dishing up some of the best food of its kind. **Seriously cheap** *Taman Serasi,* Cluny Rd, opposite entrance to Botanic Gardens, small centre but well known for roti John and superb satay; mainly Malay stalls, excellent fruit juice. Many of the plazas along Orchard Rd provide foodcourts in their basements. Convenient and cheap.

Cafés *Bar Gelateria Bellavista*, Clarke Quay. Delicious Italian ice cream, indoor and outdoor seating. **Mid-range** *Checkers Deli*, *Hilton Hotel*, Orchard Rd, for a fabulous selection of cheesecakes, cakes and pastries. *Dôme*, Lane Crawford House, Orchard Rd and The Promenade on Orchard Rd. Delicious focaccia sandwiches, patisseries and some of the best coffee in town, good café atmosphere and a pleasant stop for a mid-morning break. *Goodwood Park Hotel*, Scotts Rd. Sophisticated buffet tea, served on the lawn by the pool. *Rose Veranda*, *Shangri-La Hotel*, 22 Orange Grove Rd, said to offer the best tea in town. Recommended. **Cheap** *Cyberheart Café*, basement of Orchard Shopping Centre, Orchard Rd. Pizzas, pasta and sandwiches and lots of fun with the net.

The last couple of years has seen a burgeoning of restaurants along Club St. All are top-end eateries, catering for city business people, and all seem to be vying to create the most ostentatious menu (foie gras, venison and seafood are standard fare). Having said this, the standard of cuisine is extremely high.

Chinatown
● on map, page 613
Price categories:
see inside front cover

Expensive *L'Aigle d'Or*, *Duxton Hotel*, 83 Duxton Rd, T2277678. A few Oriental touches and a good vegetarian selection, extensive, expensive **French** menu with wine list to match, sophisticated atmosphere, popular as a business venue at lunchtime, booking recommended. *L'Angelos*, Club St. Another contender for the 'richest menu on Club Street' contest, with foie gras, duck, pork tripe and veal – classic **French** food, run by a Frenchman. *Blue Ginger*, 97 Tanjong Pagar Rd, T2223928. In restored shophouse, good home-cooked **Nonya** (Peranakan) food and relaxed atmosphere. *Da Paolo's*, 66 Tanjong Pagar Rd, T2247081, and Club St (see map, page 613, for location). There are 3 *Da Paolo's* in Singapore, of which 2 are in Chinatown, in restored shophouses decorated in contemporary fashion. Popular with expats, **Italian** homemade pasta, but overpriced. *Efferus*, 47 Club St, T3246769, efferus@pacific.net.sg 'Contemporary Moorish or **Mediterranean** cooking with Middle Eastern and North African edge'; menu of foie-gras, octopus, veal and crispy duck, attractive, rather quirky little place.

Futoshi, 7 Ann Siang Rd, T2271396. Provincial **Japanese** food, tempura, teppanyaki, sushi, sashimi; intimate little place. *Gaetano*, 36 Club St, T3253360, gaetano@singapore.com Large **Italian** restaurant, with a wide range of pasta dishes and a good choice of fish. Large number of covers and a little cramped for the price. *Indochine*, 49 Club St, T3230145. **Indochinese food**; plenty of fish on the menu here, from squid to mussels to tiger prawns, the ground floor is the *Sa Vanh Bar*, ethnically decorated with a laidback feel, whilst dining is on the upper floor. Running water on both levels adds to the serene atmosphere, but they have undermined this a tad by arranging the tables too close together for comfort. The bar is open 1700-0300.

Mama Africa, 88 Telok Ayer St, T5329339, on the eastern edge of Far East Square. A diverse and quirky menu; oysters or standloper snoekfish, ostrich or venison. Surround yourself in **African** memorabilia and transport yourself from Asia to the dark continent, if only for an hour or two. *Matsu*, *Copthorne Harbour View Hotel*, 81 Anson Rd, T4216242. Excellent **Japanese** restaurant. *Orchard Garden*, 4th Floor, Lucky Chinatown Shopping Centre, New Bridge Rd. **Chinese** restaurant; *dim sum* at lunchtime. *Senso*, 21 Club St, T2243534. An all-**Italian** experience, with 'neo-classical Italian cooking'. Superb cuisine, great atmosphere, sophisticated London-style joint.

Shidong, 2 Club St. East-west **international** menu, simply designed interior and contrasting food on the menu, from laksa to nonya chicken curry to New Zealand lamb, but disappointing desserts. *Streeters*, Keong Saik Rd. Great **Spanish** tapas bar with paella that enthusiasts of the place say is worth killing for. *Thanying*, *Amara Hotel*, T2224688. Provides the best **Thai** food in town, extensive menu and superb food (the 15 female chefs are all said to have trained in the royal household in Bangkok). Specialities include deep fried garoupa, *yam som-o* (spicy pomelo salad), *khao niaw durian* (durian served on a bed of sticky rice – available from May-Aug), as well as such classics as *tom yam kung* (spicy prawn soup with lemongrass); booking necessary.

Singapore

Recommended. *La Voix* 1 Club St, T2206586. Fabulous **French** menu (good choice of fish), extensive wine list and exquisitely designed dining cubicles gives this place a great sense of intimacy; very stylish.

Mid-range *Café Gypsy*, 92 Club St. **Spanish** tapas bar. *Pasta Brava*, 11 Craig Rd, Tanjong Pagar. Tastiest **Italian** in town in an equally tasty shophouse conversion; fairly expensive, but good choice of genuine Italian fare. Recommended. *Sanur*, 3rd Floor, 133 New Bridge Rd. **Malay/Indonesian** restaurant, one of a chain, specialities include fish-head curry and spicy grilled chicken.

Swee Kee, 12 Ann Siang Rd, T2228926. This first-floor **Chinese** restaurant has acquired some degree of local renown due to the owner Tang Kwong Swee – known to his friends as 'Fish-head' – having run the same place for 60 years (although the location has changed). Recommended are the deep fried chicken, Hainanese style, fish-head noodle soup and prawns in magi sauce; very popular.

Cheap *Fratini*, 1 Neil Rd, T3238088. Cheap and cheerful **Italian** pasta joint in a restored shophouse. *Hillman*, 1st Floor, Block 1 Cantonment Rd, (southern end of Chinatown). Popular, good value, wholesome **Cantonese** stews served out of earthenware pots. *New Nam Thong*, 8 Smith St. **Cantonese**, including *dim sum*, from 0400 and a lunchtime menu. *Tai Tong Hoi Kee*, 2 Mosque St. **Cantonese**, *dim sum* from 0400. *Tiong Shiang*, corner of Keong Saik and New Bridge roads. Very popular **Hainanese** corner café, with tables spilling out onto the street.

Hawker centres and food courts Seriously cheap *Tanjong Pagar Plaza Food Centre*, Tanjong Pagar Rd, southern end. *Murray Terrace Food Alley*, for a strip of cheap Chinese and Malay restaurants. *Amoy Street Food Centre*, just south of Al-Abrar Mosque at southern end of Amoy St. Excellent little centre, worth a graze. *Chinatown Complex Hawker Centre*, Block 335, 1st Floor, Smith St. Recommended stall: *Ming Shan* (No 179), for its *kambing* (mutton) soup; famed for decades, though a pretty scruffy food centre.

Tea, cakes and coffee shops *Tea Chapter*, 9A-11A Neil Rd, Chinatown, T2261175. An excellent little place on 3 floors with a choice of seating (on the floor or at tables), a peaceful atmosphere, plenty of choice of teas as well as sweet and savoury snacks, games for those who want to tarry, and the director, Lee Peng Shu, and his wife enthusiastically talk you through the tea tasting ceremony (if you wish). Recommended.

Little India
● *on map, page 617*
Price categories:
see inside front cover

Restaurants here range from sophisticated a/c places to the simplest of banana plate eateries. For North Indian cuisine, the best option is to trot down to the southern end of Race Course Rd, where there are 6 good restaurants in a row, all competing for business, including the *Banana Leaf Apolo*, *Delhi* and, most famous of all, *Muthu's*. Some of the best vegetarian restaurants – South Indian particularly – are found on the other side of Serangoon Rd, along Upper Dickson Rd.

Expensive *La Fête du Cuisinier*, 161 Middle Rd, T3330917, on the corner of Waterloo St and Middle Rd. A surprising location for one of the more sophisticated restaurants in town. Exquisite **French Creole** cuisine – a lavish menu of foie gras, oysters and crab (and that's only the starters). Attractive setting, elaborate French décor in Marie Antoinette style. *Indochine*, 42 Waterloo St. Indoor or outdoor seating, a sister restaurant to the better known outlet on Club St (in Chinatown). Range of **Indochinese** cuisine.

Mid-range *Andhra Curry*, 41 Kerbau Rd. **South Indian** cuisine, popular place in the heart of things. *Banana Leaf Apolo*, 56-58 Race Course Rd, T2938682. **North Indian**

Singapore

food, another popular fish-head curry spot, a/c and more sophisticated than the name might imply – although the food is still served on banana leaves to justify the name. Recommended. *D' Deli*, 60 Race Course Rd. **North Indian, Mughlai and Kashmiri**, under same management as *Delhi* just up the road, with a similar good reputation.

Delhi, Race Course Rd. **North Indian** food including chicken tikka, various tandooris, as well as creamy Kashmiri concoctions. Popular and award-winning restaurant. *Jaggi's*, 34 Race Course Rd. **North Indian** cuisine, immaculately clean and extremely popular. *Komala Vilas*, 76-78 Serangoon Rd, T2936980, and 12 Buffalo Rd. **South Indian** thalis and masala dosas, bustling café, with a little more room upstairs. Recommended. *Muthu's Curry*, corner of Rotan Lane and Race Course Rd, T2937029. **North Indian** food, reckoned by connoisseurs to be among the best banana leaf restaurants in town; *Muthu's* fish-heads are famous. Recommended. *Our Makan Shop*, Race Course Rd. Sparse looking place, but extremely popular – so they must be doing something right; another excellent **Indian** joint.

Cheap *Kamal's Vegetarian*, Cuff Rd. **Vegetarian** restaurant; excellent paper and masala dosas. *Komala's Fast Food*, Upper Dickson Rd. This is the fast food end of the Komala empire – **South Indian** delicacies including *thalis*, *masala dosas* and *idlis* are served in an a/c restaurant. Very popular and recommended. *New Delhi*, Broadway Hotel, 195 Serangoon Rd. Good, cheap vegetarian and non-vegetarian **North Indian** food, specialities are chicken and almond, and seafood curries.

Ponthuk Bawean Restaurant, Dunlop Rd (at Jln Besar end). Simple, open-air **Malay** restaurant in a wonderfully gaudy shophouse, serving such dishes as beef *rendang*, chilli eggs and spicy beans. *Soya Bean*, corner of Middle Rd and Short St. Popular noodle joint. *Woodlands*, 12 Upper Dickson Rd (off Serangoon Rd), T2971594. Thalis, masala dosa and **vegetarian** curries, good and cheap. Recommended.

Hawker centres and food courts Seriously cheap *Albert Centre*, between Waterloo and Queen streets. There's a huge area of hawker stalls here. *Lavender Food Square*, Lavender Rd, north of Little India. Is one of the best hawker centres in town. *Paradiz Centre Basement Food Centre*, 1 Selegie Rd, recommended stall: *Mr Boo's Teochew Mushroom Minced Meat Mee* (No 34). *Zhujiao or Kandang Kerbau (KK) Food Centre*, on the corner of Buffalo and Serangoon roads. Wide range of dishes, and the best place for Indian Muslim food: curries, *rotis*, *dosai* and *murtabak* are hard to beat (beer can be bought from the Chinese stalls on the other side).

Cafés Mid-range *Café Oriel*, Ground Floor of Selegie Arts Centre, off Prinsep St. Popular for its pizzas.

Tea, cakes and coffee shops *Zhong Guo Hua Tuo Guan*, 52 Queen St (name above the tea house is in Chinese characters), just by the Albert and Waterloo streets roadside market. This traditional Chinese tea house has quite a few outlets, including this atmospheric one. It sells Hua Tuo's ancient recipes, helpful for 'relieving of heatiness' and 'inhibiting the growth of tumor cells,' amongst other things. Very friendly proprietress will introduce you to wild ginseng and showfrog or longan (a fruit like a lychee) herbal jelly, and tell you why you will feel better (that's if you can get any of the concoctions down!).

Arab St is the best area for Muslim food of all descriptions – Malay, Indonesian, Indian or Arabic. There are some good restaurants around the Sultan Mosque and many more on noisy North Bridge Rd. Try the Parco Bugis Shopping Centre for non-Muslim restaurants including good Italian ones, and New Bugis St for simple open-air fare and jugs of cold beer.

Arab Street
● *on map, page 620*
Price categories:
see inside front cover

Expensive *Masakatsu*, Ground Floor, Parco Bugis Shopping Centre, 80 Middle Rd, T3348233. **Japanese**. Known for its hotpot. Book at weekends. *Olive Tree Restaurant* and Café, *Intercontinental Hotel*, 80 Middle Rd, T4311061. The café is situated in the Parco Bugis shopping mall, whilst the restaurant is cosier and separate from all those frantic shoppers. Both serve the same good **Mediterranean** food – there's a good buffet. *Pasta Fresca da Salvatore*, Shaw Centre. Fresh **Italian** food; tasty pizzas and a good range of pasta dishes, open 24 hrs. *Pimai Thai*, *Intercontinental Hotel*, 80 Middle Rd, T4311064. Excellent **Thai** menu with unusually extensive dessert buffet. *La Smorfia*, 36 Purvis St, T3384322. **Italian** food made by an Italian chef (originally from Al Forno); lots of pasta, some pizza and seafood, and authentic Italian desserts.

Mid-range *Bibik's Place*, Pahang St. Upmarket little place in a renovated shophouse, excellent **Nonya** dishes. *Pivdofr*, 1 Llang Seah St, T3362995. A shophouse café serving classic **International** fare such as pizza, macaroni cheese or pork chops. Good service. *Sketches*, Parco Bugis Shopping Centre, 80 Middle Rd, T3398386. A novel approach to ordering **Italian**, with boxes to tick for 9 types of pasta, 8 sauces and some garnishes. Quick and fairly basic food. *Sushi Sagano,* Parco Bugis Shopping Centre, Victoria St, T3376766. **Japanese**; the set menu is affordable, seafood is good as is the sashimi. *Wholmeals*, Parco Bugis Shopping Centre, 200 Victoria St, T3379257. All food is low fat and low salt. Good set lunch with choice of four main courses. Fab juice drinks too.
Cheap *Rumah Makan Minang*, Kandahar St (facing onto the Istana Kampong Glam). Small restaurant serving cheap **Padang** (West Sumatran) dishes, including beef *rendang* (dry beef curry), spicy grilled fish and *kangkung*. *Zam Zam Restaurant*, junction of Arab St and North Bridge Rd. **Muslim Malay-Indian** dishes served in busy and chaotic coffee shop. Very popular and recommended for a taste of the other Singapore – spicy meats, chargrilled seafood, creamy curries.

Sentosa
Price categories: see inside front cover

Around the World Trade Centre Expensive *Alkaff Mansion*, Mount Faber Ridge, 10 Telok Blangah Green, T2786979. Built in the 1920s, this huge house has undergone a S$3 mn refurbishment and makes a magnificent restaurant surrounded by parkland. Go here for the atmosphere, not the food, which is very average. If you do eat, the **continental** cuisine is better than the **Indonesian**. *Long Beach Seafood*, 31 Marina Park, Marina South, T3232222. One of the island's most famous **seafood** restaurants, specializing in pepper and chilli-crabs, drunken prawns and baby squid cooked in honey. *Prima Tower Revolving Restaurant*, 201 Keppel Rd, T2728822. Revolving restaurant atop a huge silo looks out over the harbour and city, established 20 years ago with the same chef still working here. **Beijing** cuisine, particularly good Peking duck, book in advance.

Cheap *Han's*, 8 branches around the city including Harbour Promenade World Trade Centre (WTC). This chain of restaurants is Singapore's answer to the Greasy Spoon – cafes without the acute accent on the 'e', single dish **Chinese** meals, simple (largely fried) breakfasts, some **European** food including such things as steaks, burgers and fries, all served in large helpings at very competitive prices.

Seriously cheap *Dotty Café*, Bukit Chermin Rd, off Keppel Marina, T2708575, and Telok Blangah Rd, just west of where the cable car goes over the road. Call Dorothy before you go and plan your **seafood** menu to get the best catch of the day. Eat under fairy lights, right on the sea, and admire yachts moored next door, very quiet and peaceful.

Sentosa There are fast food outlets and restaurants dotted around the island. The *Sentosa Food Centre*, close to the ferry terminal, is a squeaky-clean hawker centre, serving Malay, Chinese, Peranakan, Indian and Western cuisine. The dishes are pricier than elsewhere in Singapore and the food is sometimes disappointing; open 1100-2200.

Other restaurants at the ferry terminal include the *Singapore Riverboat* (a paddle wheel steamer) and the *Camellia Restaurant*. Beside the Merlion is *Sir Basil's Café and Bar*, and there are also several burger outlets and snack bars at Siloso, Central and Tanjong beaches, as well as those associated with many of the individual attractions. In short, visitors will not starve during their visit. There are more elegant restaurants at the hotels, of which the best is *Siggi's* at the *Beaufort*, T2750331. It's worth splashing out on the **New Asia** buffet while sitting on the terrace alfresco.

Singapore West

Price categories: see inside front cover

Expensive *Au Petit Salut*, Jl Merah Saga, Holland Village, T4751976. **French** patisserie-style restaurant. Some main course dishes, but come here for the pastries and cakes.

Brazil Churrascaria, 14-16 Sixth Ave, T4631923. If carnivore-style is your thing, this **Brazilian** restaurant – with its huge skewers of barbecued (*churrascaria* is Portuguese for barbecue) meat – is for you; as much meat as you can eat. *Cha Cha Cha*, 32 Lorong Mambong, Holland Village, T4621650. Small and informal **Mexican** restaurant, with some outdoor seating and an extensive menu. *Da Paolo*, Jl Merah Saga, Holland Village, T4761332. **Italian** restaurant with indoor or terrace dining. The most sophisticated restaurant on this strip, with food to match. *Lucerne*, Pasir Panjang Village, T7761221. Sophisticated **Swiss** restaurant.

Michelangelo's, Jl Merah Saga, Holland Village, T4759069. Under same management as *Sistina* and *Original Sin*, **Italian**, range of pasta dishes and other specialities. Pleasant surroundings (both indoor or terrace seating), fairly average food for the price. Booking recommended, especially at the weekend. *Original Sin,* Jl Merah Saga, Holland Village, T4755605. Under same management as *Michelangelo's* and *Sistina*. **Mediterranean vegetarian** restaurant, with some really intriguing dishes. Indoor or terrace dining. Booking recommended, especially at the weekend. Recommended. *Shayray*, Lorong Mambong, Holland Village. **North Indian**, tandoori. Recommended.

Sistina, Jl Merah Saga, Holland Village, T4767782. Under same management as *Michelangelo's* and *Original Sin*, this place is primarily a **pizza** joint. Attractive location, with indoor or outdoor dining. Booking recommended, especially at the weekend. *Sukhothai*, Lorong Mambong, Holland Village. **Thai**, authentic and recommended. *Sushi Tei*, 20 Lorong Mambong, Holland Village. **Japanese** sushi bar, where you grab food from a conveyor belt as it glides by.

Wala-Wala, 31 Lorong Mambong, Holland Village, T4624288. Buzzy atmosphere and pretty tiles on the tables in this **Mexican** restaurant; good, honest, no pretentions. *Westlake Eating House*, Empress Dr, off Farrer Rd, 1st flr of an HDB block. Big indoor and outdoor restaurant serving **Singapore-Chinese** food. Extensive menu, including delicious black-peppered prawns and baby kailan; great value for money.

Mid-range *African Heartbeat*, The Aquarius, 21 Science Park Rd, T7757988, situated in Science Park 2 (and not very easy to locate). Fun décor (jungle foliage, water features and flaming torches) and genuine **African** cuisine. *Baden-Baden*, 42 Lorong Mambong, Holland Village, T4685585. **German** fare such as smoked pork loin, mashed potatoes and sauerkraut at very reasonable prices. *NYDC*, 30 Lorong Mambong, Holland Village, T4692998. Stands for New York Dessert Café, this is the place to come for your sugar fix, with cheesecake to die for. Also serves savoury food. *Qhue*, 242 Pasir Panjang Rd, T4716501. **Fusion** cuisine with indoor or outdoor seating. Excellent choice of food and good atmosphere. *Samy's Curry Restaurant*, Civil Service Club, Dempsey Rd. A wonderful **Indian** establishment where food is served at your table on a banana leaf – you pay for what you take – great value and very atmospheric. Recommended.

Singapore

East coast

● on map, page 630
Price categories:
see inside front cover

The east coast is a particularly good place to experience **seafood** in one of the large casual-style restaurants, where customers pick their own fish from tanks and then choose how they'd like it cooked.

Expensive *Al Forno East Coast*, 400 East Coast Rd, T3488781. Authentic **Italian** cuisine with fine, but pricey Italian wine to match. *Casa Bom Vento*, 467 Joo Chiat Rd, T3487786. **Eurasian and Peranakan** cuisine. Famous for its Katong jelly drink – unique to this restaurant. *Chao Phaya Thai Seafood*, Block 730, 2nd flr, Ang Mo Kio Ave 6, T4560118. Enormous informal restaurant with huge choice of authentic **Thai** dishes, including chilli crab, *tom yam kung* and green, yellow or red curried fish. *Granita's*, 17 Crescendo Building, Upper East Coast Rd, T2421353. **Californian-Mediterranean** cuisine in intimate restaurant. *The Olea*, 158 Upper East Coast Rd, T4493880. Authentic **Greek** cuisine, classics such as tzatziki and souvlaki lamb. Also has a deli which sells range of olives, taramasalata, etc.

Mid-range *AJ's Tandoori*, 328 Joo Chiat Rd, opposite *Hotel 81*, T4401257. Typical **North Indian** menu; Kashmiri chicken is good. *Bernie's*, 961A Upper Changi Rd, T5422232. **American** fare in a laid-back setting, with friendly staff and big American-style helpings. *Harry Ramsden's*, 210 Stadium Rd, T4473333. A branch of the famous northern **English** chain of fish and chip restaurants. Even serves mushy peas and pots of tea. *Kim's Seafood Restaurant*, 477 Changi Rd, T7421119. Claypot pepper crabs are the speciality in Mr Tan's cheap and informal **seafood** restaurant, open to 0130 weekdays and 0230 on Sat. *Palm Beach Seafood Restaurant*, Kallang Leisure Park, 1st and 2nd floors, 5 Stadium Walk, T3443088. Located near the International Building and the National Stadium, spread over 4 a/c flrs, basic decor; tiled flooring and melamine crockery, good shellfish at a fair price – the chilli crab is a speciality.

Peranakan Inn, 210 East Coast Rd. Prompt service in this popular restaurant, selling classic **Peranakan** food such as *galangal, ayam buah keluak, chap chye* and *itek tim*. *UDMC Seafood Centre*, 1000 East Coast Parkway. There are 10 outlets here and they're all good. In particular: *Gold Coast Live Seafood*, T4482020, and *Jumbo Seafood*, East Coast Parkway, T4423435. Serving Singapore specialities like chilli crabs and black pepper crayfish. *International Seafood Centre*, East Coast Parkway, provides trolleys to choose your fish pre-cooked. Not for the squeamish. Recommended.

Cheap *Charlie's*, Block 2, 01-08, Changi Village, T5420867. Charlie's folks, who were first generation immigrants from China, set up the *Changi Milk Bar* in the 1940s, then *Charlie's Corner* became the favoured watering hole and makan stop for sailors and riggers for decades. His mum still fries up the chips that gave them the reputation as the best chippies east of London's Isle of Dogs, excellent chilli-dogs, spicy chicken wings and other **international** food, as well as 70 beers to choose from, closed weekends. Recommended. Bus to Changi Point from Tampines MRT. *House of Sundanese Food*, 218 East Coast Rd, T3455020. Typical **Sundanese** dishes from West Java include spicy salad (*keredok*), charcoal-grilled seafood (*ikan sunda, ikanemes*) and curries, a/c restaurant with real home-cooked food, small portions.

Singapore's islands

Mid-range *Pulau Ubin Seafood*, T5458202 (ask for Liang), is on the northeast shore of Pulau Ubin, at the end of a jungly track. Recently reopened, the **seafood** served here seems to have deteriorated in quality. Reports of second rate cuisine at sky-high prices.

Entertainment and nightlife

Bars

Bar and Billiard Room, *Raffles Hotel*, Beach Rd. Relocated from its original position, the bar is lavishly furnished with teak tables, oriental carpets and two original billiard tables. *China Jump*, Fountain Court, CHIJMES, Victoria St. This bar and restaurant has outdoor seating and some booths inside. The menu is hardly revolutionary and the name should really be USA Jump, since it serves the usual American bistro-style food of burgers, salads, generic Mexican and a few adapted Asian dishes to give it a drizzle of local ambience. Food is good despite the lack of culinary inspiration. Cocktails and beer. *Compass Rose*, atop *Westin Stamford Hotel*, the cocktail lounge is situated in the Stamford Tower and provides a good choice of bevvies. *Father Flannagan's Irish Pub*, CHIJMES, Fountain Court, 30 Victoria St. Ersatz Irish pub with Irish beer on tap and a high density of local business people. Some Irish food (stews etc) also available.

Hu'u, Singapore Art Museum, 71 Bras Basah Rd. *Lock, Stock and Barrel Pub*, 29 Seah St. This dark bar/pub with juke box is popular with expats on a budget and backpackers. Extended happy hour from 1600 to 2000. *The Long Bar*, Raffles Hotel, 1-3 Beach Rd. The home of the Singapore Sling, originally concocted by bartender Ngiam Tong Boon in 1915 (see page 591), now on 2 levels and extremely popular with tourists and locals alike, gratuitous tiny dancing mechanical punkah-wallahs sway out of sync to the cover band. *Paulaner Brauhaus*, Millenia Walk. Micro brewery serving pricey beer to business folk. German sausage and other Teutonic delicacies also served. *Somerset's*, *Westin Stamford*, Raffles City. Large and pleasant bar, with frieze of the Padang in the days before Raffles City, live jazz music. *Writers' Bar*, *Raffles Hotel*, 1 Beach Rd (just off the main lobby). In honour of the likes of Somerset Maugham, Rudyard Kipling, Joseph Conrad, Noel Coward and Herman Hesse, who were said either to have wined, dined or stayed at the hotel. Bar research indicates that other literary luminaries from James A Michener to Noel Barber and the great Arthur Hailey are said to have sipped Tigers at the bar – as the bookcases and momentoes suggest.

Colonial core

There are lots of bars on Boat and Clarke quays; those at the former are wilder and less packaged, although the last few years has seen a slight deterioration in quality as locals have moved on and tourists have become the dominant clientele. One of the more dramatic changes over the past couple of years is the development along the riverfront westwards. Both Robertson's Walk and The Quayside are gradually filling up with shops and restaurants, and the nearby Mohammed Sultan Rd has become an extremely popular watering hole; the entire street is lined with bars and clubs. The west side is a row of restored shophouses, whilst the east is a modern high-rise block. There are 15 or so to choose from; this list is not comprehensive.

Singapore River & the City

Amoeba, 207 River Valley Rd (north of Mohammed Sultan Rd). Specializes in champagne. *Brewerkz*, Riverside Point. One of the micro breweries which are all the rage in Asia. Good beer, but pricey. *Crazy Elephant*, Clarke Quay, T3371190. Live music (house band), popular place for a drink following a meal. *Escobar*, 36 Boat Quay. A Latin American bar with salsa and cocktails to match. *Espana*, 45 Boat Quay. Margueritas, daiquiris and jugs of Heineken, accompanied by Latin music. *Front Page*, 18 Mohammed Sultan Rd. Also serves seafood.

Harry's Bar, 28 Boat Quay. Large bar with seating outside overlooking the river, popular with City boys, serves pricey food on the 1st floor, jazz band. *Molly Malone's*, 42 Circular Rd (behind Boat Quay). Irish pub, complete with stout and Irish folk music (also serves food). *Newsroom Bar*, 11 Unity Rd (but actually on Mohammed Sultan Rd).

Singapore

Spacious bar with Chinoserie charm (replicas of terracotta soldiers and earthenware vases from the T'ang dynasty adorn the place). Happy hour from 1700 to 2100 daily, open till midnight. *Penny Black*, 26 Boat Quay. A stylized English Victorian London pub, with some classic English food. *Riverbank Bar*, 68 Boat Quay. Live music.

Siam Supperclub, Mohammed Sultan Rd. A tastefully decorated place (with a reputed 56 Buddha images on display), spirit mixes such as 'Buddha jumps over the wall' available. *Sugar*, 13 Mohammed Sultan Rd. Cushioned walls and deeply cool. *Tivoli Bar*, just to the north of *Newsroom Bar*, to south of Unity St. *Trader Vics*, 5th Floor, *New Otani Hotel*, River Valley Rd. Hawaii 5-0 décor and Chin-Ho's favourite cocktails – try a few goblets of Tikki Puka Puka for something violently different. *Wong San's*, Mohammed Sultan Rd. One on both sides of the street, the Eastside version is also a sushi bar. *The Yard*, 294 River Valley Rd. The Singaporean version of a London pub, complete with darts, dominos, fish 'n' chips and Newcastle Brown Ale.

Orchard Road *Bar None*, *Marriott Hotel*, Orchard Rd. Live music. *Brannigan's* (basement of *Grand Hyatt*), 10/12 Scotts Rd. Open until 0100, 0200 on Fri and Sat, American style, touristy bar with loud live music and video screens, haunt of the infamous SPG (Singapore Party Girl), very popular. *Hard Rock Café*, HPL House, 50 Cuscaden Rd, west end of Orchard Rd. Complete with limo in suspended animation and queues to enter. *Ice Cold*, 9 Emerald Hill. If you like a slightly anarchic feel to your bars, with loud music and darts, then this is a good place. In an old shophouse at the top of the pedestrianized section of Emerald Hill, good place for a drink away from Orchard Rd, popular with locals, 35 beers to choose from, Happy Hours 1700-2100.

Kaspia Bar, Hilton Hotel, Orchard Rd. For the widest selection of vodkas in Singapore and live jazz. *Mezza9*, *Grand Hyatt Hotel*, Orchard Rd, provides a selection of 30 Martinis. *Muddy Murphy's*, Orchard Hotel Shopping Arcade, Irish pub. *Number 5*, 5 Emerald Hill. Happy hours 1200-2100 Mon-Sat, 1700-2100 Sun, at the top of the pedestrianized section of Emerald Hill, retro-chic restored shophouse bar and restaurant (upstairs), popular with young expats and Chuppies (Chinese yuppies), great music. Recommended. *Observation Lounge*, *Mandarin Hotel*, 333 Orchard Rd. Circular cocktail bar on the 38th floor. *Que Pasa*, 7 Emerald Hill. This is a wine bar in a converted shophouse, with a small snack menu of tapas, oysters and olives and an extensive wine menu. It is near the top of the pleasant pedestrianized section of Emerald Hill and next door to the slightly wilder *Ice Cold Bar*. *Woodstock*, Rooftop, Far East Plaza, 14 Scotts Rd. Take the bullet lift up the outside of the building, expect to hear hard rock, open until 0200.

Chinatown There are several quiet bars on Duxton Hill, Chinatown, in a pleasant area of restored shophouses – a retreat from the hustle and bustle of Boat Quay or the city. Duxton Road and Tanjong Pagar Road also provide a dozen or so bars in restored shophouses.

Beaujolais Winebar, 1 Ann Siang Hill, T2242227. Very pleasant wine bar in restored shophouse, serves reasonably priced wine, candles in wine bottles on the window-sills, atmospheric, good cheese and charcuterie platters. Recommended. *Carnegie's*, Far East Square, Pekin St, has 366 shooters to choose from. *Elvis Pub*, 1A Duxton Hill, T2201268. The name says it all: nothing but Elvis played all night, Fri is particularly lively. *Fluid*, 11 Purvis St, has 100 shooters and a range of vodkas available. *JJ Mahoney's*, 55 Duxton Rd, T2256225, is not quite the Irish bar the name might suggest; beer and karaoke.

Sentosa *Alkaff Mansion*, Mount Faber Ridge, 10 Telok Blangah Green. Perfect for sundowner 'stengahs' on the terrace, with an excellent view of the harbour.

Singapore

There are a number of pubs and bars in a row of restored shophouses in Pasir Panjang Village, along what is known as *The Pub Row*

Changi Sailing Club, Changi Village, pleasant and, surprisingly, one of the cheapest places for a quiet beer, overlooking the Strait of Johor. *Charlie's*, Block 2, 01-08, Changi Village. Charlie Han describes his bar as 'the pulse of the point', tucked away behind the local hawker centre, he is a teetotaller but serves 70 brands of beer from all over the world, which you can sip as you watch the red-eyes touchdown on runway one; *Charlie's* is best known for its fish and chips; see above. Closed weekends. Recommended.

Entertainment

Colonial core *Somerset's*, *Westin Stamford Hotel*, Raffles City. Large and pleasant bar with frieze of the Padang in the days before Raffles City, with live jazz music.

   Singapore River and the City *Crazy Elephant*, Clarke Quay, T3371190. House band, mostly covers. *Harry's Quayside*, 28 Boat Quay. Jazz Wed-Sat, blues on Sun. *Molly Malone's*, 42 Circular Rd (behind Boat Quay). Irish folk. *Riverbank Bar*, 68 Boat Quay. House band.

   Orchard Road *Bar None*, *Marriott Hotel*, Orchard Rd, live music. *Brannigan's*, Basement, *Hyatt Regency Hotel*, 10/12 Scotts Rd. Popular American-style, touristy bar with loud live music and video screens. Open until 0100, 0200 on Fri and Sat. *Fabrice's World Music Bar*, Basement, *Singapore Marriott Hotel*, 320 Orchard Rd. Good bands from around the world. *Hard Rock Café*, HPL House, 50 Cuscaden Rd: AOR covers (Boston, Chicago and the like); forget conversation. Queues to get in. *Kaspia Bar*, *Hilton Hotel*, Orchard Rd. Jazz. *Studebakers*, Penthouse of Pacific Plaza, Orchard Rd. Live performances and dancing. *Top Ten Club*, Orchard Towers, 400 Orchard Rd. Good black American or Philippine disco funk bands, some soul as well.

Most classical music performances are held at The *Singapore Cultural Theatre* and the *Victoria Hall* – the Singapore Symphony Orchestra gives regular performances and there are often visiting orchestras, quartets and choirs. The Singapore Symphony Orchestra also performs in many free open-air shows in the Botanic Gardens. The National Theatre Trust promotes cultural dance performances and local theatre as well as inviting international dance and theatre groups to Singapore. *Kala Mandhir*, Temple of Fine Arts, 1st Flr, Excelsior Hotel Shopping Centre, T3390492. Classes available in dance, instrumental music, percussion and singing. Fabulous array of Indian instruments. It might be possible to take a one-week course here, although most are longer.

   Chinese Street Opera (Wayang) Traditional Chinese street operas (*wayang*) mostly take place during the 7th lunar month, following the Festival of the Hungry Ghosts (see page 606). They are regularly staged on makeshift wooden platforms which are erected in vacant lots all over the city. To the sound of clashing cymbals and drums, the wayang actors – adorned in ornate costumes and with faces painted – act out the roles of gods, goddesses, heroes, heroines, sages and villains from Chinese folklore.

   Clarke Quay now has a permanent (though it looks deliberately temporary) stage, where there are short performances every Wed and Fri at 1945-2030 (see page 606). The audience is encouraged to watch the artists apply their make-up backstage from 1815 and the performance starts at 1930. Subtitles are projected onto a screen.

Colonial core *Rascals*, *Pan Pacific Hotel*, Marina Square, 6 Raffles Blvd. Open 1800-0300, extended happy hour, Sun is gay night. *Reading Room*, *Marina Mandarin Hotel*, Marina Square, is a smart, expensive and pretentious disco which attracts a younger crowd. *Scandals*, *Westin Plaza Hotel*, *Raffles City Complex*, popular hotel disco.

Singapore River and the City *Dbl O* (pronounced 'Double O'), Robertson Walk, 11 Unity St. New posh dance club, with a spacious dance floor and 10 m-high ceilings. Open 2000 to 0300; happy hour 2000-2200. *Hard Landers*, 231 River Valley Rd, on the eastern corner of Mohammed Sultan Rd. Fashioned after a Chinese Huay Quan or clan house. Open 1700-0300, with happy hour from 1700-2100 daily. *Liquid Room*, Gallery Ev@son, 76 Robertson Quay. Hi-tech disco. On two floors, with different music on each, the Sound Bar is open from 1900-0300 daily, whilst the Liquid Room is open from 2230-0300. Happy hour is from 1900-2100.

For a useful listing of bars and clubs around Singapore, see www.metroage. com/

Lox, Boat Quay, Blk 3C River Valley Rd. A soul and hip hop club situated on the 1st floor, open 1900-0300, happy hour 1900-2200. Cover charge on weekends. *Rootz*, 20 Upper Circular Rd, behind Boat Quay. Soul and groove music. Open 1800-0300, happy hour 1800-2200. *Tajie*, 27 Mohammed Sultan Rd. Varied music and popular with the younger crowd. Open 1800-0300, happy hour Mon-Thu 1800-2130. *Velvet Underground*, 17 Jiak Kim St (off Kim Seng Rd), next door to *Zouk's* (see below) and under the same management. Small nightclub, open until 2100-0300 Tue-Sat, cover S$25, free for women on Wed nights. Recommended. *Zouk's*, 17-21 Jiak Kim St, T7382988. Possibly the hippest club-bar in town with great music, open 1900-0300 Wed-Sat.

Orchard Road *Ridleys*, *ANA Hotel*, Nassim Hill. Another good club, open 1800-0300, 1930-0300 weekends, happy hour 1800-2200. *Roar*, 15 Cairnhill Rd. A new dance club with lots of space – 7,000 sq ft – 2 bars and a dance floor. Open 1800-0300 weekdays and 2000-0300 Sat. Happy hour 1800-2100. *Sparks*, Level 7, Ngee Ann City, Orchard Rd. The biggest disco in all of Asia, very glitzy with KTV rooms and jazz bar, packed at weekends, open 1900-0300, happy hour 1900-2100 daily. Cover: S$15 Mon-Thu, S$20 Fri-Sun. *Top Ten Club*, Orchard Towers, 400 Orchard Rd. Huge converted cinema, often has live black-American or Filipino disco bands. Recommended. *Venom*, Pacific Plaza, Scott's Rd, a recent addition to the scene, glamorous and exclusive. *Woodstock*, Rooftop, Far East Plaza, 14 Scotts Rd. More a bar, but open until 0200. Bullet lift up the outside of the building, expect long-haired clientele and hard rock.

Chinatown *Boom Boom Boom*, Far East Square, 130 Amoy St. Open until 0200.

Theatre, dance & comedy
Most theatrical and dance performances are held at the Victoria Hall

Action Theatre, Waterloo St, next to the Synagogue. Provides small scale productions either on an outdoor stage or in a small auditorium. *Boom Boom Room*, 3 New Bugis St, T3398187. Cabaret and stand-up comedy shows. Popular with locals; tame by international standards. Cabaret Tue-Thu 2230-0100 and until 0200 on the other nights. No happy hour. *The Esplanade: theatres on the Bay* is under construction next to the Padang (see page 595) and is due for completion in 2002. There will be a concert hall, lyric theatre, three smaller studios and an outdoor performing space.

Raffles Jubilee Hall, 328 North Bridge Rd, T3311732, holds occasional theatrical performances. *The Substation*, 45 Armenian St, set up in a former power station, T3377800. The latest offering on the thespian and artistic scene, this venue has an intimate small theatre where it stages plays and shows avant garde films. It also holds drama workshops. *Sculpture Square*, 155 Middle Rd. Open 1100-1800 Mon-Fri and 1200-1800 weekends. Housed in Middle Rd church, which has been converted to a light and airy exhibition space, this is a centre for 3D work, with changing exhibitions. *Stamford Arts Centre*, 155 Waterloo St. A centre for the performing arts, with Chinese opera, Nrityalaya performances, and traditional Indian dance and drama.

Cinema
The Straits Times Life section publishes listings daily ,or visit www.metroage.com/

With more than 50 cinemas, Singapore gets most of the blockbusters soon after their release in the US. Tickets cost about S$7 and shows continue throughout the day, with late night viewing at weekends. Censors have loosened up slightly in recent years; there's a new RA category for those over 21 years old, which means a little more sex and violence hits the screens. When the *Cathay*, at the southeastern end of Orchard

Road, opened in 1939 and became the first a/c public building in Singapore, local celebrities turned up in fur coats. It has sadly recently stopped screening films.

The new cinema experience can be had at *GV Grand*, top floor of Great World City, Zion Rd, T7358484, booking recommended. For S$25 you can relax in an easy chair and eat a meal at the same time. There are several other multiplex cinemas, including: *Parco Bugis Junction* on Victoria St, opposite Bugis MRT, the *Lido Cineplex* at the Shaw Centre, *Orchard Rd* and *Suntec City*, Marina Square.

Directory

Australia High Commission, 17 Forster Crescent, Yarralumla, Canberra ACT 2600, T001 61 2 273 3944. **Austria Consulate**, Raiffeisen Zentral Bank, Osterreich AG, Am Stadtpark 9, 1030 Vienna, T001 43 (1) 71707 1250. **Belgium**, 198 Avenue Franklin Roosevelt, 1050 **Brussels**, T001 32 (2) 660-2979. **Canada**, 1305-999 West Hastings Street, **Vancouver**, T001 1(604) 669 5115. **Denmark**, Snorresgade 20, DK02300, **Copenhagen**, T001 45 (32) 548360. France, 12 Square de l'Ave Foch, 75116 Paris, T001 33 (1) 4500 3361. **Germany**, Friedrichstrasse 200, 10117 Berlin, T001 49 (30) 22634318. **Hong Kong**, Units 901-2, Admiralty Centre Tower 1, 9th Flr, 18 Harcourt Rd, **Hong Kong**, T527 2212. **Indonesia**, Block X/4 KAV No 2, Jl HR Rasuna Said, Kuningan, **Jakarta**, 12950, T001 62 (21) 520 1489. **Japan**, 15-12-3 Roppongi, Minato-ku, Tokyo, T001 81 (3) 35869111. **Malaysia**, 209 Jln Tun Razak, Kuala Lumpur 50400, T02 (03) 2161 6277. **Netherlands**, Westerlaan 10, 3016 CK Rotterdam, Rotterdam, T001 31(10) 4642888. **New Zealand**, 17 Kabul St, Khandallah, Wellington, T001-64-4-479 2076. **Norway**, Veritasveien 1, Hovik, T001 47 6757 9760. **Portugal**, Lusograin, Rua dos Franqueiros 135-1, 1100 Lisbon, T001 351 1 885 4170. **Spain**, Rosellon, 257, 4B, 08008 Barcelona, T001 34 93 237 8401. **Sweden**, Storgatan 42, Stockholm 11455 T001 46 8 660 0135. **Thailand**, 129 South Sathorn Rd, Bangkok, T001 66 2 286 2111. **UK**, 9 Wilton Cres, London SW1X 8SP, T001 44 20 7235 8315. **USA**, 3501 International Pl, NW, Washington DC 20008, T001 1 202 537 3100.

Embassies & consulates

Hospitals and emergency services **Alexandra**, 378 Alexandra Rd, T4755222. **East Shore**, 321 Joo Chiat Pl, T3447588. **Gleneagles**, 6A Napier Rd, T4737222. **Mount Alvernia**, 820 Thomson Rd, T2534818. **Mount Elizabeth**, 3 Mount Elizabeth, T7372666. **National University**, 5 Lower Kent Ridge Rd, T7795555. **Singapore General**, Outram Rd, T2223322. *Traveller's Health and Vaccination Clinic*, Tan Tock Seng Hospital Medical Centre, Level B2, 11 Jalan Tan Tock Seng, T3572222 or 3525650, F3525661, www.ttsh.gov.sg/MMD/medical/cdc/clinic.html For a full listing of medical facilities in Singapore, see www.gov.sg/moh/mohiss/hospsvcs/main.html In case of emergency, dial **T995** for an ambulance.

Medical facilities

Singapore

658

Singapore

Footnotes

11

660

Footnotes

Malaysian words and phrases

Basic phrases

Yes/No ia/tidak
Thank you Terimah kasih
You're welcome Sama-sama
Good morning/Good afternoon (early) Selamat pagi/Selamat tengahari
Good afternoon (late)/Good evening/night Selamatpetang/Selam at malam
Welcome Selamat datang
Goodbye (said by the person leaving) Selamat tinggal
Goodbye (said by the person staying) Selamat jalan
Excuse me/sorry Ma'af saya
Where's the...? Dimana...
How much is this...? Ini berapa?
I [don't] understand Saya [tidak] mengerti
I want... Saya mahu
I don't want Saya tak mahu
My name is... Nama saya...
What is your name? Apa nama anda?

Sleeping

How much is a room? Bilik berapa?
Does the room have air-conditioning? Ada bilik yang ada air-con-kah?
I want to see the room first please Saya mahu lihat bilik dulu
Does the room have hot water? Ada bilik yang ada air panas?
Does the room have a bathroom? Ada bilik yang ada mandi-kah?

Travel

Where is the railway station? Stesen keretapi dimana?
Where is the bus station? Stesen bas dimana?
How much to go to...? Berapa harga ke...?
I want to buy a ticket to... Saya mahu beli tiket ke...
How do I get there? Bagaimanakah saya
Is it far? Ada jauh?
Turn left / turn right Belok kiri /belok kanan
Go straight on! Turus turus!

Time and days

Monday Hari Isnin (Hari Satu)
Tuesday Hari Selasa (Hari Dua)
Wednesday Hari Rabu (Hari Tiga)
Thursday Hari Khamis (Hari Empat)
Friday Hari Jumaat (Hari Lima)
Saturday Hari Sabtu (Hari Enam)
Sunday Hari Minggu (Hari Ahad)
Today Hari ini
Tomorrow Esok
Week Minggu**Month** Bulan
Year Tahun

Numbers

1 satu
2 dua
3 tiga
4 empat
5 lima
6 enam
7 tujuh
8 lapan
9 sembilan
10 sepuluh
11 se-belas
12 dua-belas...etc
20 dua puluh
21 dua puluh satu...etc
30 tiga puluh
100 se-ratus
101 se-ratus satu
150 se-ratus limah puluh
200 dua ratus...etc
1,000 se-ribu
2,000 dua ribu...
100,000 se-ratus ribu
1,000,000 se-juta

Basic vocabulary

a little sedikit
a lot banyak
all right/good baik
and dan
bank bank
bathroom bilek mandi
beach pantai
beautiful cantik
bed sheet cadar

bus station setsen bas
buy beli
can boleh
cannot tak boleh
cheap murah
chemist rumah ubat
cigarette rokok
clean bersih
closed tutup
coffee kopi
cold sejuk
crazy gila
day hari
delicious sedap
dentist doktor gigi
dirty kotor
doctor doktor
drink minum
eat makan
excellent bagus
expensive mahal
fruit buah
he/she dia
hospital rumah sakit
hot (temperature) panas
hot (chilli) pedas
I/me saya
ice air batuais
island pulau
male lelaki
man laki
market pasar
medicine ubat ubatan
milk susu
more lagi/lebeh
open masuk
please sila
police polis
police station pejabat polis
post office pejabat pos
railway station stesen keretapi/tren
restaurant restoran/kedai makanan
room bilik
sea laut
ship kapal
shop kedai
sick sakit
small kecil
stand berdiri
stop berhenti
sugar gula
taxi teksi
tea teh

they mereka
that itu
ticket tiket
toilet (female) tandas perempuan
toilet (male) tandas lelaki
town bandar
trishaw beca
very sangat
wait tunggu
water air
we kami
what apa
when bila
woman perempuan
you awak/anda

A practical alternative

Malaysian English, which has been dubbed 'Manglish', as opposed to Singaporean English ('Singlish'), has evolved its own usages, abbreviations and expressions. Its very distinctive pronunciation can be almost unintelligible to visitors when they first arrive. The first thing many visitors notice is the use of the suffix *lah* which is attached to just about anything and means absolutely nothing. English has been spoken in the Malay world since the late 18th century, but over time, it has been mixed with local terms. The converse has also happened: English has corrupted Malay to such a degree that it is now quite common to hear the likes of 'you pergi-mana?' for 'where are you going?' In abbreviated Malaysian- Chinese English, can is a key word. 'Can-ah?' (inflection) means 'may I?'; can-lah means yes; cannot means no way; also can means 'yes, but I'd prefer you not to' and how can? is an expression of disbelief.

The man who first applied the term Manglish to mangled Malaysian English was Chinese-Malaysian satirist Kit Leee, in his book Adoi (which means ouch). It gives an uncannily accurate and very humorous pseudo-anthropological rundown on Malaysia's inhabitants. His section on Manglish, which should be pronounced exactly as it is written, is introduced: Aitelyu-ah, nemmain wat debladigarmen say, mose Malaysians tok Manglish... Donkair you Malay or Chinese or Indian or everyting miksup... we Malaysians orways tok like dis wan-kain oni. Below are extracts from his glossary of common Manglish words and phrases (which will help decipher the above).

atoyu (wat) gentle expression of triumph: 'What did I tell you?'
baiwanfriwan ploy used mainly by shop assistants to promote sales: 'If you buy one you'll get one free'.
betayudon mild warning, as in 'You'd better not do that'.
debladigarmen contraction of 'the bloody government'; widely used scapegoat; for all of life's disappointments, delays, denials, and prohibitions.
hauken another flexible expression applicable in almost any situation, eg 'That's not right!', 'Impossible!' or 'Don't tell me!'.
izzenit from 'isn't it?' but applied very loosely at the end of any particular statement to elicit an immediate response, eg Yused you will spen me a beer, izzenit?
kennonot request or enquiry, contraction of 'can or not': 'May I?' or 'Will you?' or 'Is it possible?'
nola a dilute negative, used as a device to interrupt, deny or cancel someone else's statement.
oridi contraction of already.
sohau polite interrogative, usually used as a greeting, as in 'Well, how are things with you?'
tingwat highly adaptable expression stemming from 'What do you think?'
wan-kain adjective denoting uniqueness; contraction of 'one of a kind'. Sometimes rendered as wan-kain oni ('only').
watudu rhetorical question: 'But what can we do?'
yala non-committal agreement, liberally used when confronted with a bore.
yusobadwan expression of mild reproach: 'That's not very nice!'

With thanks to Kit Leee and his co-etymologists: Rafique Rashid, Julian Mokhtar and Jeanne MC Donven. Leee, Kit (1989) Adoi, Times Books International: Singapore)

Glossary

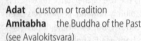

A

Adat custom or tradition
Amitabha the Buddha of the Past
(see Avalokitsvara)
Atap thatch
Avalokitsvara also known as
Amitabha and Lokeshvara, the name
literally means 'World Lord'; he is the
compassionate male Bodhisattva, the
saviour of Mahayana Buddhism and
represents the central force of creation
in the universe; usually portrayed with a
lotus and water flask

B

Bahasa language, as in Bahasa Malaysia
Barisan Nasional National Front,
Malaysia's ruling coalition comprising
UMNO, MCA and MIC along with seven
other parties
Batik a form of resist dyeing common
in Malay areas
Becak three-wheeled bicycle rickshaw
Bodhi the tree under which the
Buddha achieved enlightenment
(Ficus religiosa)
Bodhisattva a future Buddha. In
Mahayana Buddhism, someone who has
attained enlightenment, but who
postpones nirvana in order to help
others reach the same state
Brahma the Creator, one of the gods
of the Hindu trinity, usually represented
with four faces, and often mounted on
a hamsa
Brahmin a Hindu priest
Budaya cultural (as in Muzium Budaya)
Bumboat small wooden lighters, now
used for ferrying tourists in Singapore
Bumiputra literally, 'sons of the soil';
Malays as opposed to other races in
Malaysia

C

Cap batik stamp
Chedi from the Sanskrit cetiya (Pali,
caitya) meaning memorial. Usually a
religious monument (often
bell-shaped) containing relics of the
Buddha or other holy remains. Used
interchangeably with stupa
Cutch see Gambier

D

Dalang wayang puppet master
DAP Democratic Action Party,
Malaysia's predominantly Chinese
opposition party
Dayak/Dyak collective term for the
tribal peoples of Borneo
Dharma the Buddhist law
Dipterocarp family of trees
(Dipterocarpaceae) characteristic of
Southeast Asia's forests
Durga the female goddess who slays
the demon Mahisa, from an Indian epic
story

E

Epiphyte plant which grows on
another plant (but usually not parasitic)

F

Feng shui the Chinese art of geomancy

G

Gambier also known as cutch, a dye
derived from the bark of the bakau
mangrove and used in leather tanning
Gamelan Malay orchestra of
percussion instruments
Ganesh elephant-headed son of Siva
Garuda mythical divine bird, with
predatory beak and claws, and human
body; the king of birds, enemy of naga
and mount of Vishnu
Gautama the historic Buddha
Geomancy or feng shui, the Chinese
art and science of proper placement

Godown   Asian warehouse

Goporum   tower in a Hindu temple

Gunung   mountain

H

Hamsa   sacred goose, Brahma's mount; in Buddhism it represents the flight of the doctrine

Hinayana   'Lesser Vehicle', major Buddhist sect in Southeast Asia, usually termed Theravada Buddhism

I

Ikat   tie-dyeing method of patterning cloth

Indra   the Vedic god of the heavens, weather and war; usually mounted on a three headed elephant

J

Jataka(s)   birth stories of the Buddha, of which there are 547; the last 10 are the most important

K

Kajang   thatch

Kala (makara)   literally, 'death' or 'black'; a demon ordered to consume itself; often sculpted over entranceways to act as a door guardian, also known as kirtamukha

Kampung   or *Kampong*, village

Kerangas   from an Iban word meaning 'land on which rice will not grow'

Keraton   see kraton

Kinaree   half-human, half-bird, usually depicted as a heavenly musician

Kongsi   Chinese clan house

Kris   traditional Malay sword

Krishna   an incarnation of Vishnu

Kuti   living quarters of Buddhist monks

L

Laterite   bright red tropical soil/stone sometimes used as a building material

Linga   phallic symbol and one of the forms of Siva. Embedded in a pedestal shaped to allow drainage of lustral water poured over it, the linga typically has a

succession of cross sections: from square at the base through octagonal to round. These symbolize, in order, the trinity of Brahma, Vishnu and Siva

Lintel   a load-bearing stone spanning a doorway; often heavily carved

Lokeshvara   see Avalokitsvara

Lunggyi   Indian sarong

M

Mahabharata   a Hindu epic text written about 2,000 years ago

Mahayana   'Greater Vehicle', major Buddhist sect

Mandi   Malay bathroom with water tub and dipper

Maitreya   the future Buddha

Makara   a mythological aquatic reptile, somewhat like a crocodile and sometimes with an elephant's trunk; often found, along with the kala, framing doorways

Mandala   a focus for meditation; a representation of the cosmos

MCA   Malaysian Chinese Association

Meru   the mountain residence of the gods; the centre of the universe, the cosmic mountain

MIC   Malaysian Indian Congress

Mudra   symbolic gesture of the hands of the Buddha

N

Naga   benevolent mythical water serpent, enemy of Garuda

Naga makara   fusion of naga and makara

Nalagiri   the elephant let loose to attack the Buddha, who calmed him

Nandi/Nandin   bull, mount of Siva

NDP   New Development Policy

Negara   kingdom and capital, from the Sanskrit

Negeri   also negri, state

NEP   New Economic Policy

Nirvana   'enlightenment', the Buddhist ideal

O

Orang Asli   indigenous people of Malaysia

P

Paddy/padi   unhulled rice
Pantai   beach
Pasar   market, from the Arabic 'bazaar'
Pasar malam   night market
Perahu/prau   boat
Peranakan   'half caste', usually applied to part Chinese and part Malay people
Pradaksina   pilgrims' clockwise circumambulation of a holy structure
Prang   form of stupa built in the Khmer style, shaped rather like a corncob
Prasat   residence of a king or of the gods (sanctuary tower), from the Indian prasada
Pribumi   indigenous (as opposed to Chinese) businessmen
Pulau   island
Pusaka   heirloom

R

Raja/rajah   ruler
Raksasa   temple guardian statues
Ramayana   the Indian epic tale
Ruai   common gallery of an Iban longhouse, Sarawak
Rumah adat   customary or traditional house

S

Sago   multi-purpose palm
Sal   the Indian sal tree (Shorea robusta), under which the historic Buddha was born
Sakyamuni   the historic Buddha
Silat   or bersilat, traditional Malay martial art
Singha   mythical guardian lion
Siva   one of the Hindu triumvirate, the god of destruction and rebirth
Songket   Malay textile interwoven with supplementary gold and silver yarn
Sravasti   the miracle at Sravasti where the Buddha subdues the heretics in front of a mango tree

Sri Laksmi   the goddess of good fortune and Vishnu's wife
Stele   inscribed stone panel or slab
Stucco   plaster, often heavily moulded
Stupa   see chedi
Sungai   river

T

Tamu   weekly open-air market
Tanju   open gallery of an Iban longhouse, Sarawak
Tara   also known as Cunda; the four-armed consort of the Bodhisattva Avalokitsvara
Tavatimsa   heaven of the 33 gods at the summit of Mount Meru
Theravada   'Way of the Elders'; major Buddhism sect also known as Hinayana Buddhism ('Lesser Vehicle')
Tiffin   afternoon meal – a word that was absorbed from the British Raj
Timang   Iban sacred chants, Sarawak
Tong   or towkay, a Chinese merchant
Totok   'full blooded'; usually applied to Chinese of pure blood
Towkay   Chinese merchant
Triads   Chinese mafia associations
Tunku   also Tuanku and Tengku, prince

U

Ulama   Muslim priest
Ulu   jungle
UMNO   United Malays National Organization
Urna   the dot or curl on the Buddha's forehead, one of the distinctive physical marks of the Enlightened One
Usnisa   the Buddha's top knot or 'wisdom bump', one of the physical marks of the Enlightened One

V

Vishnu   the Protector, one of the gods of the Hindu trinity, generally with four arms holding the disc, the conch shell, the ball and the club

W

Waringin   banyan tree
Wayang   traditional Malay shadow plays

Footnotes

Malay food glossary

For more information on the varied national menu, please see page 49 in the Essentials chapter.

assam sour
ayam chicken
babi pork
belacan hot fermented prawn paste
daging meat
garam salt
gula sugar
ikan fish
ikan bakar grilled fish
ikan bilis anchovies
ikan panggang spicy barbecued fish
kambing mutton
kerupak prawn crackers
ketupat cold, compressed rice
kueh cakes
lemang glutinous rice in bamboo
limau lime
makan food
manis sweet
mee noodles
minum drink
nasi rice
roti canai pancakes served with lentils and curry
roti john baguette filled with sardine/egg mixture
roti kosong plain pancake
sambal spicy paste of pounded chillis, onion and tamarind
sayur vegetables
sayur manis sweet vegetables
sayur masak lemak deep fried marinated prawns
sejuk crab
soto ayam spicy chicken soup
sotong squid
tahu beancurd
telur egg
udang prawn

Singapore food glossary

Chinese and local food

Bak chang   local rice dumpling filled with savoury or sweet meat and wrapped in leaves

Bak choy   Chinese cabbage

Bak kut the   local pork rib soup, with garlic and Chinese five spice

Belachan   fermented prawn paste

Bird's nest   edible nest of the swiftlet, made from glutinous secretions of their salivary glands

Char kway teow   broad rice noodles fried with sweet sauce and additions of cockels, Chinese sausage, bean sprouts or fish cake

Char siew   Chinese sweet barbecued pork slices

Chendol   a dessert: a cone of ice shavings topped with coloured syrups, brown syrup, coconut milk, red beans, attap seeds and jelly

Cheng ting   a Chinese dessert of a bowl of syrup with herbal jelly, barley and dates

Chicken rice   rice boiled in chicken stock and ginger, served with steamed chicken slices

Chilli padi   an extremely hot variety of chilli

Choi sum   Chinese vegetable served steamed with oyster sauce

Claypot rice   rice cooked in a clay casserole with pieces of chicken, Chinese mushroom, Chinese sausage and soy sauce

Congee   Chinese porridge

Dian sin/dim sum   Chinese sweet and savoury dumplings served at breakfast and lunch

Dow see   Chinese fermented salted black beans

Fish sauce   known as *nampla* in Thai, a brown sauce made from salted dried fish, used as a salt seasoning

Garoupa   white fish popular in Asia

Gula malacca   coarse palm sugar sold in lumps, from the sap of the Palmyra palm

Hainanese chicken rice   chicken served with spring onions and ginger dressing, soup and rice boiled in chicken stock or coconut milk

Hoisin sauce   Chinese thick seasoning with a sweet-spicy flavour

Hokkien mee   yellow noodles fried with sliced meat, squid, prawns and garnished with strips of fried egg

Kang kong   a Chinese vegetable – water convolvulus

Kway teow   broad rice noodles

Laksa   spicy coconut soup of thin white noodles garnished with bean sprouts, quail's eggs, prawns, shredded chicken and dried bean curd

Lor mee   a dish of noodles served with slices of meat, eggs and a dash of vinegar in a dark brown sauce

Rojak   salad of cucumber, pineapple, turnip, fried beancurd tossed in a prawn paste with peanuts, tamarind and a sugary sauce

Tau hui   a dessert made from a by-produt of soya bean, served with syrup

Teh tarek   tea made with evaporated milk

Yu char kway   deep-fried Chinese breadsticks

Indian

Aloo gobi potato and cauliflower dish
Bhindi okra or lady's fingers
Biryani North Indian dish of basmati rice and meat, seafood and vegetables
Brinjal aubergine or eggplant
Dhal pureed lentils
Dhosas large crispy pancakes served with potatoes, onions and spices
Gulab jumun fried milk balls in syrup
Idli steamed rice cake
Keema spicy minced meat
Kofta minced meat or vegetable ball
Korma mild curry with a yoghurt sauce
Lassi yoghurt based drink
Murgh chicken
Murtabak roti (bread) which has been filled with pieces of mutton, chicken or vegetables
Pakora vegetable fritter
Pilau rice fried in ghee and mixed with nuts, then cooked in stock
Pudina mint sauce
Raita side dish of cucumber, yoghurt and mint
Rogan josh spicy lamb curry with yoghurt
Roti prata flat round pancake-like bread
Saag spinach
Sambar fiery mixture of vegetables, lentils and split peas
Tandoori style of cooking: meat is marinated in spicy yoghurt and then baked in a clay oven
Tikka small pieces of meat or fish served off the bone, marinated in yoghurt and baked
Vindaloo very hot curry Malay/Indonesian
Assam sour
Ayam chicken
Babi pork
Daging meat
Es avocado chilled avocado shake
Es delima dessert of water chestnut in sago and coconut milk
Gado-gado cold dish of bean sprouts, potatoes, long beans, tempeh, bean curd, rice cakes and prawn crackers, topped with a spicy peanut sauce
Garam salt
Gula sugar
Ice kachang similar to *chendol* (see Chinese food) but with evaporated milk instead of coconut milk
Ikan fish
Ikan bakar grilled fish
Kambing mutton
Kepala ikan fish head, usually in a curry or grilled
Kerupak prawn crackers
Ketupat cold, compressed rice
Kueh cakes
Lemang glutinous rice in bamboo
Limau lime

Lontong rice cakes in a spicy coconut-milk topped with grated coconut and sometimes bean curd and egg

Makan food

Manis sweet

Mee noodles

Mee rebus yellow noodles served in a thick sweet sauce made from sweet potatoes. Garnished with sliced hard-boiled eggs and green chillies

Mee siam white thin noodles in a sweet and sour gravy made with tamarind

Nasi biryani saffron rice flavoured with spices and garnished with cashew nuts, almonds and raisins

Nasi lemak rice boiled in coconut milk

Rijsttafel Indonesian meal consisting of a selection of rice dishes, to which are added small pieces of meat, fish, fruit and pickles

Roti canai pancakes served with lentils and curry

Roti john baguette filled with sardine/egg mixture

Roti kosong plain pancake

Sambal   spicy paste of pounded chillis, onion and tamarind

Satay pieces of chicken, beef or mutton skewered onto sticks and grilled

Sayur vegetables

Sayur masak lemak deep fried marinated prawns

sejuk crab

Soto ayam chicken soup

Sotong squid

Tahu beancurd

Telur egg

Tempeh   preserved deep fried soya bean

Udang prawn

Thai

Gai haw bai toey fried chicken in pandanus leaves

Gai tom kla chicken and coconut soup

Kaeng jud soup

Kaeng paad curry

Kaeng phet kai hot chicken curry

Kai tom kha lemon grass chicken soup with coconut milk

Khao rice

Larb minced chicken or pork flavoured with spices, herbs and lime

Mi krob crisp thin noodles with shrimp, egg and sweet and sour sauce

Pak krasan a cabbage-like vegetable

Phrik chillies

Pla thot sam rot fried garoupa with sweet and sour sauce

Poo paad gari curried crab

Tom kam kung   hot and sour spiced seafood soup

Yam salad

Index

Note: grid references to the colour maps are shown in italics after place names.
So Alor Star *M1A2* will be found on map 1, grid A2.

Footnotes

Shorts

0011548

0683356

-610

during my stay in the event that the
the full amount due.

D VACATION GETAWAY

Centre

104

Footnotes

Map index

Advert index

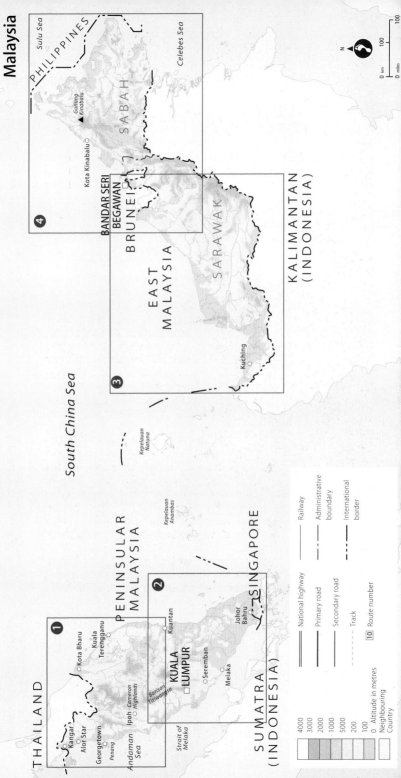

Malaysia

Sulu Sea

PHILIPPINES

SABAH

▲ Gunung Kinabalu

Celebes Sea

○ Kota Kinabalu

④

BANDAR SERI
BEGAWAN

BRUNEI

EAST
MALAYSIA

SARAWAK

○ Kuching

③

KALIMANTAN
(INDONESIA)

South China Sea

Kepelauan
Natuna

PENINSULAR
MALAYSIA

Kepelauan
Anambas

① THAILAND

○ Kota Bharu

Kangar ○
Alor Star ○
Georgetown ○
Penang ○

○ Kuala
Terengganu

Ipoh ○ Cameron
Highlands ○

Andaman
Sea

Barisan
Titiwangsa

② KUALA
LUMPUR

○ Kuantan

○ Seremban

Melaka ○

Johor
Bahru ○

SINGAPORE

SUMATRA
(INDONESIA)

Strait of
Melaka

N

0 km   100
0 miles   100

	National highway
	Primary road
	Secondary road
	Track
10	Route number

	Railway
	Administrative boundary
	International border

4000
3000
2000
1000
500
200
100
0 Altitude in metres
    Neighbouring
    Country

Map 2

Kuala Lipis

Sungai Jelai

Tembeling

Tapah Road

Jerantut

8

Teluk Intan

Fraser's Hill

Sungai Jerok

Gunung Benom (2,107m)

PAHANG

Sungai Pahang

Barisan Titiwangsa

Sungai Bernam

Tanjung Malim

Kuala Kubu Bahru

Mentakab

Temerloh

SELANGOR

1

Genting Highlinds

2

9

Triang

Kuala Selangor

Sungai Selangor

Batang Berjuntai

Kanching Falls

68

10

Kuala Selangor National Park

5

54

Rawang

Templer Park

Kemayan

Jeram

Batu Caves

Jinjang

Gombak

NEGERI

Tas Be

Kapar

Meru

KUALA LUMPUR

Ampang

SEMBILAN

Subang

Petaling Jaya

Ulu Langat

Pulau Ketam

Pulau Klang

Klang

Shah Alam

Cheras

Tasek Damp

Port Klang

Serdang Bahru

Kajang-Sungai Chua

Pulau Lumut

Jenjarom

Telok Datok

Kampong Dengkil

Semenyih

Bangi

Bahau

Ladang Geddes

Merib

Banting

Salak

52

Sungai Langat

Seremban

Kuala Pilah

5

Sri Menanti

Gemas

Bt En

Rembau

B

Port Dickson

Tampin

North-South Highway

Cape Rachado

Simpang Empat

Gunung Lede (Mt Ophi 1,276m)

Tanjung Bidara

Ayer Keroh

Tangkal

Tanjung Kling

MELAKA

Melaka

5

Pulau Besar

Muar

Strait of Melaka

C

SUMATRA (INDONESIA)

1

2

3

Map 3

South China Sea

Map 4

A

N

0 km   30
0 miles   30

South China Sea

Tempasuk
(Bird Sanctuary)

Kota Belud

Surusup

Tuaran

*Gunung
Kinabalu
National
Park*

Mengkabong

Tamparuli

*Tunku Abdul Rahman
National Park*

Telipok

*Gunung
Kinabalu
(4,101m)*

Pulau Gaya

Kota Kinabalu

Tanjung Aru

Kundasang

Putatan

Penampang

*Rafflesia
Forest Reserve*

*Pulau Tiga
National Park*

Kinarut

*Gunung Alab
(1,964m)*

*Mawar
Waterfall*

Papar

Manggis

Patau

Tambunan

Kuala
Penyuh

*Sungai
Papar*

*Gunung
Trusmadi
(2,642m)*

L A B U A N

*Crocker Range
National Park*

*Pulau
Labuan*

Menumbok

Beaufort

Keningau

B

Telok Brunei

Melalap

Tenom

*Agricultural
Research Station,
Orchid Centre*

**BANDAR SERI
BEGAWAN**

Muara

Sipitang

Sindumin

BRUNEI & MUARA

Brunei

Merapok

Lawas

Tutong

Labu

Tomani

Lumut

Limbang

Bangar

*Gunung
Lumaku
(1,966m)*

Kuala
Belait

Seria

TUTONG

Kampong
Batong
Duri

Sapulut

Lutong

BRUNEI

TEMBURONG

Partit
Baru
Amo

Miri

Kuala
Baram

Labi

Ladan Hills

Baram

Teraja

BELAIT

Sungai Limbang

Sungai Trusan

Long
Semado

*Lambir Hills
National Park*

Marudi

*Gunung Mulu
(2,376m)*

Sungai Beliat

Map 3

*Gunung Mulu
National Park*

C

*Niah
National
Park*

Long
Terawan

Sungai Tutoh

Long
Seridan

*Gunung Murudi
(2,423m)*

**KALIMANTAN
(INDONESIA)**

*Loagan Bunut
National Park*

*Bukit Batu Bali
(2,082m)*

Sungai Baram

Kelabit Highlands

Bario

Sungai Patah

Sungai Tinjar

S A R A W A K

*Gunung
Skalap*

Long
Peran

Sungai Belepeh

Long Muma

1

2

3

Kuala Lumpur Rail Transit System

MRT System

Singapore Strait

Legend:
- North - South MRT line
- East - West MRT line
- Lines not completed
- LRT

E3 Kallang · E2 Lavender · E1 Bugis · Boulevard · Nicoll Highway · Millenia · Convention Centre · C2 City Hall · C1 Raffles Place · M1 Marina Bay · Museum · Farrer Park · Little India · N4 Newton · N3 Orchard · N2 Somerset · N1 Dhoby Ghaut · Clarke Quay · W3 Tiong Bahru · Chinatown · W2 Outram Park · W1 Tanjong Pagar

East-West / stations:
Changi Airport · E12 Pasir Ris · E11 Tampines · Expo · E10 Simei · E9 Tanah Merah · E8 Bedok · E7 Kembangan · E6 Eunos · E5 Paya Lebar · E4 Aljunied · East Coast Parkway · Boon Keng · Harbour Front

North-South and branches:
Punggol · Punggol LRT · Sengkang · Sengkang LRT · Buangkok · Hougang · Kovan · Serangoon · Woodleigh · Sennett · Tampines Expressway · Central Expressway

N14 Sembawang · N12 Yishun · N11 Khatib · N15 Admiralty · N16 Woodlands · N17 Marsiling · N18 Kranji · N20 Yew Tree · N21 Choa Chu Kang · N22 Bukit Gombak · N23 Bukit Batok · Bukit Panjan · Seletar Expressway · Bukit Timah Expressway

N10 Yio Chu Kang · N9 Ang Mo Kio · N8 Bishan · N7 Braddell · N6 Toa Payoh · N5 Novena · Pan-Island Expressway

W10 Chinese Garden · W11 Lakeside · W12 Boon Lay · W9 Jurong East · W8 Clementi · W7 Buona Vista · W6 Commonwealth · W5 Queenstown · W4 Redhill · Ayer Rajah Expressway · Kranji Expressway

N · 0 km 2 · 0 miles 2

Will you help us?

We try as hard as we can to make each Footprint Handbook as up-to-date and accurate as possible but, of course, things always change. Many people email or write to us – with corrections, new information, or simply comments. If you want to let us know about your experiences and adventures – be they good, bad or ugly – then don't delay; we're dying to hear from you. And please try to include all the relevant details. Your help will be greatly appreciated, especially by other travellers. In return we will send you details about our special guidebook offer.

email Footprint at:
mas3_online@footprintbooks.com

or write to:

Elizabeth Taylor
Footprint Handbooks
6 Riverside Court
Lower Bristol Road
Bath
BA2 3DZ
UK

Footprint travel list

Footprint publish travel guides to over 120 countries worldwide. Each guide is packed with practical, concise and colourful information for everybody from first-time travellers to travel aficionados . The list is growing fast and current titles are noted below. For further information check out the website **www.footprintbooks.com**

Andalucía Handbook
Argentina Handbook
Bali & the Eastern Isles Hbk
Bangkok & the Beaches Hbk
Barcelona Handbook
Bolivia Handbook
Brazil Handbook
Cambodia Handbook
Caribbean Islands Handbook
Central America & Mexico Hbk
Chile Handbook
Colombia Handbook
Costa Rica Handbook
Cuba Handbook
Cusco & the Sacred Valley Hbk
Dominican Republic Handbook
Dublin Handbook
East Africa Handbook
Ecuador & Galápagos Handbook
Edinburgh Handbook
Egypt Handbook
Goa Handbook
Guatemala Handbook
India Handbook
Indian Himalaya Handbook
Indonesia Handbook
Ireland Handbook
Israel Handbook
Jordan Handbook
Laos Handbook
Libya Handbook
London Handbook
Malaysia Handbook
Marrakech & the High Atlas Hbk
Myanmar Handbook
Mexico Handbook
Morocco Handbook

Namibia Handbook
Nepal Handbook
New Zealand Handbook
Nicaragua Handbook
Pakistan Handbook
Peru Handbook
Rajasthan & Gujarat Handbook
Rio de Janeiro Handbook
Scotland Handbook
Scotland Highlands & Islands Hbk
Singapore Handbook
South Africa Handbook
South American Handbook
South India Handbook
Sri Lanka Handbook
Sumatra Handbook
Syria & Lebanon Handbook
Thailand Handbook
Tibet Handbook
Tunisia Handbook
Turkey Handbook
Venezuela Handbook
Vietnam Handbook

Also available from Footprint
Traveller's Handbook
Traveller's Healthbook
Traveller's Internet Guide

Available at all good bookshops

www.footprintbooks.com
A new place to visit

Acknowledgements

Kimmy Nalo, Malaysia; Fiona Boulton, UK; Richard van der Vliel, Holland; Katherine Dickens and Denis Gailleton, UK; Paul and Carline Andrews; Karin de Wit, Holland; Virginia and David Bush; Mark Huijben, Holland; Steven Watson; Sophia Hill, UK; Sabina and Peter Sahni Davison, Singapore; Paul Provoost, Holland; Mairead Kennedy; Liz Bridges and Tim White, UK; Annuar Yusoff; Eric Abelen, Holland; Phoebe Bruce; Alison Smith; Sarah Sorensen; Ralph Arnoldussen, Holland; Piergiorgio Pescali, Italy; Alexander Yee, Malaysia; Marcelo Pozzo, Argentina; Ida Aan Tan, Singapore.

Special thanks to Kim Jane Saunders.

Joshua Eliot and Jane Bickersteth

Joshua Eliot first visited Malaysia as a teenager. Since then he has taken a degree in Asian Studies at London's School of Oriental and African Studies, written children's books and academic papers, lectured on cruise liners, familiarised businessmen working in the country, advised military personnel, and given radio broadcasts. He travels regularly to Malaysia and Singapore to keep tabs on developments.

Jane Bickersteth first visited Malaysia in the early '80's when she accompanied an intrepid band of mothers and children on a journey upriver into the interior. Since then she has returned on several occasions. She also knows Singapore well, and is the co-author of Footprint's Singapore Handbook.